# Handbook of Research in Trans-Atlantic Antitrust

*Edited by*
Philip Marsden

*Director, Competition Law Forum and Senior Research Fellow,*
*British Institute of International and Comparative Law, UK*

**Edward Elgar**
Cheltenham, UK • Northampton, MA, USA

Published by
Edward Elgar Publishing Limited
Glensanda House
Montpellier Parade
Cheltenham
Glos GL50 1UA
UK

Edward Elgar Publishing, Inc.
William Pratt House
9 Dewey Court
Northampton
Massachusetts 01060
USA

A catalogue record for this book
is available from the British Library

**Library of Congress Cataloguing in Publication Data**

Handbook of research in trans-Atlantic antitrust / edited by Philip Marsden.
   p. cm.—(Elgar original reference)
   Includes bibliographical references and index.
   1. Antitrust law (International law). 2. Consolidation and merger of corporations—Law and legislation. 3. Conflict of laws—Antitrust law. 4. Intellectual property (International law) 5. Consumer protection. I. Marsden, Philip, 1965– II. Series.
   K3850.H36   2007
   343′.0721—dc22

                                                          2006013786

ISBN 978 1 84542 181 6 (cased)

Printed and bound in Great Britain by MPG Books Ltd, Bodmin, Cornwall

# Contents

# Contributors

**Alden F. Abbott**, Associate Director, Bureau of Competition, Federal Trade Commission.

**Christian Ahlborn**, Partner, Linklaters.

**Steven D. Anderman**, Professor, University of Essex.

**David Bailey**, Solicitor, Linklaters and King's College London.

**Donald I. Baker**, Partner, Baker and Miller LLP.

**Daniel Calleja**, Director of Air Transport at the European Commission.

**Neil Campbell**, Partner, Competition Group, McMillan Binch Mendelsohn LLP, Toronto.

**Ariel Ezrachi**, Slaughter and May Lecturer in Competition Law, University of Oxford, and Director, Oxford Centre for Competition Law & Policy.

**Albert A. Foer**, President, American Antitrust Institute.

**Thomas Fujiwara**, Department of Economics, University of British Columbia.

**Mark Furse,** Senior Lecturer in Commercial Law, University of Glasgow.

**Kevin E. Grady**, Alston & Bird, LLP.

**Casey Halladay**, Member of the Competition Group, Cleary Gottlieb, London.

**David W. Hull**, Partner, Covington & Burling LLP.

**Armando Irizarry**, Counsel for Intellectual Property, Office of Policy and Coordination, Bureau of Competition, Federal Trade Commission.

**Alison Jones**, Reader in Law, King's College London and Solicitor, Freshfields Bruckhaus Deringer.

**Julian M. Joshua**, Partner, Howrey, LLP, Brussels.

**William E. Kovacic**, Commissioner, US Federal Trade Commission.

**David Lawsky**, Reuters.

**Philip Marsden**, Director, The Competition Law Forum and Senior Research Fellow, British Institute of International and Comparative Law.

**Suzanne Michel**, Deputy Assistant Director, Office of Policy and Coordination, Bureau of Competition, Federal Trade Commission.

**Gunnar Niels**, Director, Oxera.

**Okeoghene Odudu**, Herchel Smith Lecturer and Fellow in Law, Emmanuel College, Cambridge and Deputy Director, Centre for European Legal Studies, Faculty of Law, University of Cambridge.

**Gesner Oliveira**, Fundação Getúlio Vargas.

**Dieter Paemen**, Clifford Chance LLP.

**Anestis Papadopoulos**, Researcher, London School of Economics.

**Julián Peña**, Allende & Brea, and ForoCompetencia.

**Russell Pittman**, Director of Economic Research and Director of International Technical Assistance, Economic Analysis Group, Antitrust Division, US Department of Justice.

**Juan Antonio Rivière y Martí**, Consumer Liaison Officer, Directorate General for Competition, European Commission.

**Margaret Sanderson**, Vice President, CRA International Limited.

**Andrew Scott**, Law Department, London School of Economics and Political Science.

**J. Gregory Sidak**, Visiting Professor of Law, Georgetown University Law Center.

**Hal J. Singer**, President, Criterion Economics, LLC.

**Adriaan ten Kate**, Head of Economics Department, Federal Competition Commission.

**Maria Tineo**, Counsel for International Affairs, International Anitrust Division, Federal Trade Commission.

**Karel van Miert**, European Commissioner for Transposrt (1989–92) and Competition (1993–99).

**Thomas Vinje**, Clifford Chance LLP, Brussels.

**Omar Wakil**, Partner, Competition Group, McMillan Binch Mendelsohn LLP.

**Jeremy Weinberg**, University of Virginia School of Law, 2006.

**Gregory J. Werden**, Senior Economic Counsel, Antitrust Division, US Department of Justice.

**Tony Woodgate**, Partner, Simmons and Simmons.

# Preface

When Edward Elgar invited me to put together a research handbook on trans-Atlantic antitrust issues, I saw it as an opportunity to do something different. Many comparative antitrust books focus predominantly on the positions in America and Europe. This is natural, but we can always benefit from other perspectives and experiences. I wanted to add some extra voices to the discussion to make it a more truly trans-Atlantic offering. I invited authors from a range of jurisdictions and asked if they would address particular pressing issues. I was pleased that so many responded positively: we have papers by well-established and leading experts in the field, including former and senior officials. I also wanted to include some 'up and comers', as well as practitioners who usually do not get an opportunity to reflect on systemic issues amid a busy practice.

Some books are put together after a conference. In our case, we decided to meet part-way through. Most of the authors assembled in London in May 2005, at the British Institute of International and Comparative Law, to present and discuss their working drafts. This was an excellent opportunity to exchange views, and also to reflect on current and pending developments.

This is not a textbook, and does not attempt to describe every aspect of antitrust. The issues selected and the views expressed are important and challenging ones and I thank the contributors for their time and hard work. Thanks also to my research fellow at the British Institute, Peter Whelan, who helped enormously with the editing. This law is stated as at March 2006.

I hope that you find the arguments and ideas expressed in this handbook to be stimulating and I encourage you to respond with your own thoughts and publications, and thereby contribute to the growing international understanding on antitrust issues.

Dr Philip Marsden
British Institute of International and Comparative Law, London,
March 2006

# 1 Unilateral effects from mergers: the *Oracle* case

*Gregory J. Werden*[1]

At the end of 2004, Oracle Corp. announced the completion of an acquisition begun over 18 months earlier with its tender offer jfor the shares of PeopleSoft, Inc. The acquisition had been challenged by the US Government and several states primarily on the grounds that it would have significant unilateral (non-coordinated) anticompetitive effects.[2] On 9 September 2004, following a 19-day trial and extensive briefing, Judge Vaughn Walker held that the government failed to establish that the acquisition would violate US antitrust law, and the government did not appeal his decision.

The *Oracle* decision[3] was the first to provide an extensive discussion of unilateral effects, and it is highly significant that Judge Walker was receptive to unilateral effects theories and to the use of economic theory in analyzing and quantifying unilateral effects. But these positive aspects of his decision could be overshadowed by shortcomings in its articulation of the relevant economic analysis. Judge Walker inaccurately stated the conditions under which a differentiated products merger gives rise to significant unilateral effects, and he took an overly narrow view of the range of valid unilateral effects theories.

The discussion below first briefly summarizes the US Government's view of competition between Oracle and PeopleSoft and its unilateral effects theory. That summary serves as a foundation for an assessment of Judge Walker's treatment of unilateral effects, which curiously never addressed the specific theory the government actually presented. Concluding comments highlight his important insights on the advantages of greater reliance on economic models in the assessment of unilateral effects from differentiated products mergers.

## The US Government's theory of the *Oracle* case[4]

Oracle and PeopleSoft competed in the sale of Enterprise Resource Planning (ERP) software, which provides tools for efficiently automating essential operating functions within large organizations. The US Government's complaint focused specifically on Human Relations Management (HRM) software, which deals with pay, benefit and other employee matters, and Financial Management Systems (FMS), which deal with receipts, accounts receivable and the like.

HRM and FMS software products have widely varying degrees of functionality in terms of the number of transactions and users supported, and in terms of the ability to accommodate various complexities and adapt to users' particular and changing needs. Some organizations require, and acquire, products with much greater functionality than others. The procurement of the HRM and FMS software products with the greatest functionality entails a six to 18 month process in which customers work with (generally two) vendors to determine what HRM or FMS software to use and negotiate a price for it. A period similar in length is then required for the customer and vendor to implement the software.

The complaint focused on the particular HRM and FMS software products dubbed 'high-function',[5] and the complaint alleged there were just three vendors of high-function HRM and FMS software – Oracle, PeopleSoft, and the German company SAP AG. The US Government argued that Oracle's acquisition of PeopleSoft would result in substantial increases in the amount paid to license HRM or FMS software by many customers, specifically those for which the high-function products of Oracle and PeopleSoft provided the two most attractive options.

A fundamental aspect of the US Government's unilateral effects theory was that each procurement of high-function HRM and FMS software constituted an entirely separate competition, so the price charged by a vendor in any one of these competitions was set independently of its prices in other competitions. High-function HRM and FMS software products are customized; their use entails an ongoing relationship with the vendor; and they are licensed on terms that preclude sublicensing. Consequently these products cannot be arbitraged, and economic forces do not operate to eliminate or limit price differences across customers. There was also considerable evidence that vendors offered different customers significantly different discounts off list prices.

The US Government's theory analogized the procurement process to an auction and maintained that the acquisition would eliminate People-Soft as a bidder. In many auctions the absence of PeopleSoft would allow Oracle to win with a higher bid than it or PeopleSoft otherwise would have made. The government also identified customers that recently had procured high-function HRM or FMS software for which the absence of PeopleSoft would have been highly significant. But customers differed in complicated ways, so the government could not point to particular characteristics of organizations that universally caused them to require high-function HRM or FMS software or necessarily caused them to find the products of Oracle and PeopleSoft more attractive than those of SAP.

**Judge Walker's treatise on unilateral merger effects in differentiated products industries**

Oracle was not the first US merger case litigated on a unilateral effects theory. In *Staples*[6] and *Swedish Match*[7] proposed mergers were enjoined on the basis of such theories. In *Gillette*,[8] *Kraft* (1995)[9] and *Long Island Jewish Medical Center*[10] courts found that there was insufficient evidence to sustain challenges to mergers based on such theories. But none of these decisions discussed unilateral effects theories at great length or articulated particular elements of proof. Judge Walker therefore sought guidance from economic and legal literature rather than precedent, and he provided other judges with a treatise on unilateral effects.

Judge Walker's treatise focused on the only theory he deemed relevant in *Oracle*. Under that theory the merging firms sell competing differentiated products that are the first and second choices for a significant number of customers. His presentation of that theory began badly by citing the wrong economic model as its basis. Economists rely extensively on the Bertrand model in analyzing the unilateral effects of mergers involving differentiated consumer products. Theoretical analyses include Shapiro,[11] Werden,[12] and Werden and Froeb,[13] and analyses of particular mergers include Hausman, Leonard and Zona,[14] Hausman and Leonard,[15] Nevo,[16] and Werden.[17] Judge Walker cited instead the model of 'monopolistic competition'.[18]

The Bertrand model was introduced by Joseph Louis François Bertrand.[19] From the game theory perspective through which economists now view competitive interaction, it is a model of a 'simultaneous-move' 'one-shot' game, which means competitors interact just once and all decide at the same time what actions to take. To determine which actions competitors take, economists apply the concept of 'Nash non-cooperative equilibrium', developed by John F. Nash, Jr,[20] which defines an equilibrium as a set of actions by competitors such that none has an incentive to alter its action in light of the actions being taken by its rivals. The Bertrand model posits that the actions of competitors are the prices they charge, so the Bertrand–Nash equilibrium is a set of prices such that each competitor is happy with its price, given its rivals' prices.

In the Bertrand model, a merger combining two differentiated products, and not reducing costs, leads to price increases,[21] if only very small price increases. The merged firm finds it in its unilateral self-interest to raise the prices of both products because raising the price of either causes an increase in sales and profits for the other. Shapiro usefully develops this intuition and discusses factors affecting the magnitudes of the price increases.[22] Werden and Froeb survey literature on the analysis of differentiated products mergers using the Bertrand model.[23]

The model of monopolistic competition was introduced by Edward Chamberlin[24] and Joan Robinson,[25] who pioneered the analysis of differentiated products. The model of monopolistic competition assumes that entry into an industry is entirely free and mainly has been used to compare the entry that occurs with socially optimal entry.[26] Economists have not used the model to analyze differentiated products mergers.

Far more important than Judge Walker's citation to the wrong economic model was his misleading characterization of the conditions necessary for significant unilateral effects from mergers involving differentiated products. He appears to have imposed conditions more stringent than economic theory supports and more stringent than the US enforcement agencies had applied.

The Horizontal Merger Guidelines (HMGs) promulgated by the US Department of Justice and Federal Trade Commission state:

> Substantial unilateral price elevation in a market for differentiated products requires that there be a significant share of sales in the market accounted for by consumers who regard the products of the merging firms as their first and second choices . . . The price rise will be greater the closer substitutes are the products of the merging firms, i.e., the more the buyers of one product consider the other product to be their next choice.[27]

Judge Walker insisted that 'the factors described' by the HMGs 'are not sufficient' because the HMGs' discussion 'emphasizes only the relative closeness of a buyer's first and second choices' while 'the relative closeness of the buyer's other choices must also be considered in analyzing the potential for price increases'.[28] To make out a unilateral effects case, Judge Walker opined that 'a plaintiff must prove not only that the merging firms produce close substitutes but also that other options available to the buyer are so different that the merging firms likely will not be constrained from acting anticompetitively'.[29]

Unilateral merger effects are significant only if customers would not readily substitute away from the merging products in the event their prices rose slightly, but that does not imply that unilateral merger effects are insignificant unless non-merging products are substantially different from the merging products. Differentiated products arise primarily in consumer goods industries in which brands are important, and what determines the unilateral effects of the merger of sellers of differentiated consumer products are consumer preferences among brands. Consumers may have strong preferences, and products strongly preferred by many consumers have considerable market power. When two strong brands merge, the prices of both may increase significantly. The most important factor in determining the magnitude of the unilateral price increases following the merger is the proportion of the sales lost by each merging product that is recaptured by the other when the price of the first product is increased slightly. Shapiro dubbed these proportions 'diversion ratios'.[30]

Judge Walker may have misunderstood the central role played by consumer preferences and diversion ratios. He made much of the fact that many customers prefer FMS and HRM software from SAP over that from Oracle or PeopleSoft, but the existence of many such consumers does not negate the existence of many customers having Oracle and PeopleSoft products as their first and second choices.[31] He also asserted that 'the issue is not what solutions the customers would *like* or *prefer* for their data processing needs; the issue is what they *could* do in the event of an anticompetitive price increase by a post-merger Oracle'.[32] The most natural reading of this dictum, however, is totally at variance with the economic theory. Consumers 'could' do anything, but what matters is what they would do, which is what they 'prefer' to do.[33]

Most importantly Judge Walker appears to have mistakenly declared that a differentiated products merger can produce significant anticompetitive effects only if the merged firm would occupy a near-monopoly position. In explaining the basic theory, he adopted the terminology of one of the defence experts, who used the word 'node' to describe a narrow region of a 'product space' that 'is defined by characteristics of the product'.[34] Judge Walker explained: 'The unilateral effects theory is concerned about there being only one vendor operating inside the node, thereby being able to increase price unilaterally.'[35] Thus he held that, when 'a plaintiff is attempting to prove that the merging parties could unilaterally increase prices', the 'plaintiff must demonstrate that, the merging parties would enjoy a post-merger monopoly or dominant position, at least in a "localized competition" space'.[36] Judge Walker indicated that his notion of dominance was 'essentially a monopoly . . . position'.[37]

Consequently Judge Walker held that the 'presumption of anticompetitive effects' in the HMGs[38] was 'unwarranted'.[39] That presumption arises under certain circumstances if the merging firms' combined market share is at least 35 per cent. In assessing the evidence presented at trial, Judge Walker also framed the central question as whether 'PeopleSoft and Oracle are engaged in localized competition to which SAP is not a party',[40] and he rejected the challenge to the proposed acquisition because the evidence failed to demonstrate that.[41]

Judge Walker's unilateral effects treatise is mistaken if read to say that a differentiated products merger can produce significant unilateral anticompetitive effects only if the merged firm would approach monopoly status. This is easily seen in the special case in which the merging firms are identical and consumer demand is linear. Under these conditions Shapiro[42] shows that the proportionate increase in price from a merger is given by the expression $md/2(1-d)$, in which $m$ is the pre-merger price-cost margin for both merging products (price minus marginal cost, all divided by price) and $d$ is the diversion ratio from either merging product to the other.

Suppose the diversion ratios between two merging products are both one-third, so when the price of either is increased slightly the substitution to the other amounts to one-third of the decrease in sales of the first merging product. Suppose also that both merging products have pre-merger price-cost margins of 40 per cent, which is in the range commonly observed. Simple arithmetic reveals that the merger leads to 10 per cent increases in the prices of both merging brands. This is a significant unilateral effect, yet non-merging products account for two-thirds of the diversion away from either merging product as its price is increased and easily could have a collective market share even greater than two-thirds.

Another useful demonstration can be made using the 'logit' model of consumer demand, variations on which are commonly used by economists in the analysis of differentiated products.[43] In this model each consumer makes a choice from a set of alternatives. The utility associated with an alternative is modelled as the sum of two components – one common to all consumers and one that is customer-specific. The latter component is treated as random because it is not observable, and a convenient assumption as to its statistical distribution leads to the logit model.

Consumer preferences in the logit model have a property simplifying the assessment of the unilateral merger effects: When the price of one alternative is increased slightly, the substitution away from it is distributed over the others in proportion to their shares as first choices. The simplest version of the logit model specifies the common component of demand as $\alpha-\beta p$, in which $p$ is the price of a choice, $\alpha$ is a constant indicating a choice's average preference and $\beta$ is a constant determining the degree of substitutability among alternatives.

Consider the merger of any two brands in a six-brand market with logit demand, and assume that all brands have the same sales, so the merging brands are neither dominant nor isolated from other brands. The 40 per cent margins in the prior example can be replicated by assuming all brands are priced before the merger at £1, the pre-merger demand elasticity at the market level is 0.5 and $\beta$ is 2.9. These assumptions produce diversion ratios almost exactly half as large as before (0.16). In this case there is no simple formula for the price increases resulting from a merger, but they work out to be 5.7 per cent for the two merging brands,[44] and competition authorities are likely to view such price increases as significant.

Contrary to what readers are apt to take away from Judge Walker's decision, the Bertrand model is generally used to analyze differentiated products mergers, and it indicates that mergers can cause significant price increases even if the merging firms face substantial competition. For a merger to produce significant price increases, the merging brands must be next-closest substitutes from the perspective of a significant number of individual customers. But when viewed from the overall perspective of all customers collectively, the merging brands need not be especially close substitutes.[45]

### Judge Walker's treatise on unilateral effects omitted important theories, including the US Government's theory

Judge Walker began his treatise on unilateral effects by asserting that they come in just two strains – the one considered in the previous section and one in which the merged firm is dominant because of a cost advantage over smaller rivals.[46] This taxonomy appears to exclude some unilateral effects theories well accepted by economists, notably those based on auction models.[47] This is curious because Judge Walker described the use of an auction model by one of the expert witnesses to predict the effects of Oracle's proposed acquisition.[48] Either Judge Walker did not appreciate that the unilateral effects of mergers in an auction model may differ from those in the Bertrand model, or he ignored the differences. Either way, a striking fact about his decision is that Judge Walker never acknowledged that the government was arguing that the acquisition would have significantly differing effects on different customers, which is characteristic of many auction models but not a Bertrand model.

There are many types of auctions associated with many economic models.[49] The most familiar type of auction, and the type in which it is simplest to analyze a merger's unilateral effects, is the English auction. When the auctioneer sells items to bidders in an English auction, the level of bids ascends and bidding is open: bidders shout out their bids or communicate them in any number of other ways that are observed by the other bidders. The auction continues as long as the bidding is advanced, and the selling price is the final bid. English auctions are commonly used to sell art, antiques and collectibles.

Consider an auction in which the four bidders value a Victorian Wedgwood jardinière at £100, £110, £120 and £200. As the bidding progresses the first bidder drops out at £100, the second at £110, and the auction ends when the third bidder drops out at £120. The winning bidder pays £120 or a small increment more, which in this example is far less than he is willing to pay. If the two bidders willing to pay the most were to merge (perhaps by getting married), the winning bid would fall to the third-highest value, £110. If the auctioneer procures an item from the bidders rather than sells to them, the level of bids descends. The winner is the bidder able to provide the good or service at the lowest cost, and the winning bid is the second-lowest cost of any bidder.

In an English auction the winning bid is affected by a merger only if the merging bidders have the two highest values (when they buy) or two lowest costs (when they sell). Consequently a merger may affect the winning bid in relatively few individual auctions. Even if infrequent, these effects can be substantial if the third-highest value or third-lowest cost differs significantly from the second-highest value or second-lowest cost.

In the Bertrand model generally applied to differentiated products, the merging firms cannot raise prices just to those customers having the merging products as their first and second choices. Price increases are moderated, often greatly, by the fact that a price increase for one of the merging products would cause some customers to switch products of non-merging firms. The extent of this moderating effect is determined mainly by diversion ratios, which can be low and cause the unilateral effect of mergers to be insignificant. In an English auction there is no switching to products of non-merging firms because bidding to one customer is independent of bidding to another.

Judge Walker explained that Oracle contended that an auction model was 'wholly inappropriate' because the customers were 'extremely powerful at bargaining' and software vendors did 'not simply "bid" for business' but rather engaged in 'extensive and prolonged' negotiations 'with the purchaser having complete control over information disclosure'.[50] But this sort of power and control by customers characterizes a procurement auction, and the negotiations that follow the bids may only turn what is essentially a sealed-bid auction into what is essentially an English auction.[51]

Judge Walker did not endorse any of Oracle's objections to the use of an auction model. Rather he rejected the specific application of an auction model by the government's expert on the sole grounds that the winning bid shares used to calibrate the model were 'unreliable data' because a far greater range of products should have been included.[52] Judge Walker never attempted to explain why an auction-like analysis, with a separate competition for each customer, was not the right analysis in the case.[53]

Judge Walker found the US Government's evidence unpersuasive in part because 'drawing generalized conclusions about an extremely heterogeneous customer market based upon testimony from a small sample is not only unreliable, it is nearly impossible'.[54] But he failed to notice, or preferred to ignore, that no generalization was required given the government's contention that Oracle would raise price to just selected customers. Judge Walker also found the government's evidence wanting because it did not include econometric estimates of diversion ratios.[55] But he failed to realize, or declined to acknowledge, that diversion ratios are irrelevant in the

English auction model the government used to analyze the merger. Diversion ratios are critical in the Bertrand model, because manufacturers cannot raise prices to just selected customers, and the effects of mergers depend critically on the proportion of the sales lost by raising prices to all customers that is recaptured when some switch to products combined by the merger. But there are no lost sales in an English auction model.

The US Government's theory of the *Oracle* case relied heavily on the notion that high-function HRM and FMS software was sold through a procurement process resembling an English auction and having a separate competition, with separate prices, for each customer.[56] Judge Walker neither acknowledged that this was the government's theory nor recognized that auction models provided an important class of unilateral effects theories distinct from those based on the Bertrand model.

**Conclusions**
Judge Walker followed the traditional structural approach to merger analysis, so his critical holdings were that the relevant markets were not limited to high-function HRM and FMS software and that the competitors in the relevant markets were not limited to Oracle, PeopleSoft and SAP.[57] Nevertheless the most interesting aspect of his decision may be its stress on the limitations of the structural approach and its suggestion of an alternative that economists have advocated.

Judge Walker discussed at some length the 'difficulties in defining the relevant market in differentiated product unilateral effects cases',[58] which long have been noted by economists.[59] He also explained that market shares may not be good predictors of unilateral competitive effects with differentiated products.[60] Werden and Froeb[61] demonstrate this systematically by evaluating mergers in randomly generated industries. Most interestingly, Judge Walker declared:

> Despite the problems with qualitative analyses, modern econometric methods hold promise in analyzing differentiated products unilateral effects cases. Merger simulation models may allow more precise estimations of likely competitive effects and eliminate the need to, or lessen the impact of, the arbitrariness inherent in defining the relevant market. For example, some merger simulation methods compensate for potential errors in market definition.[62]

Merger simulation generates quantitative predictions of unilateral merger effects using oligopoly models such as the Bertrand model or an auction model, after first calibrating the models to match critical features of the industries. Economists have advocated and employed merger simulation in cases involving differentiated consumer products, e.g. Hausman and Leonard,[63] Werden and Froeb,[64] Werden.[65] It may be hoped that the lasting impact of Judge Walker's decision will come, not from the shortcomings of his unilateral effects analysis, but rather from his positive comments on the use of modern economic analysis.

Despite the fact that the European Commission came to some different conclusions, the case exposed no apparent methodological or policy differences. Rather the European Commission benefited from Judge Walker's decision and took a somewhat different view of complex facts. Hence another positive feature of *Oracle* may be progress toward convergence between US and European competition policies.

**Notes**

1. Senior Economic Counsel, Antitrust Division, US Department of Justice. The views expressed herein are not purported to represent those of the US Department of Justice. Tom Barnett and Craig Conrath provided helpful comments.
2. The 26 February 2004 complaint is available on the Justice Department's website at http://www.usdoj.gov/atr/cases/f202500/202587.pdf.
3. *United States* v. *Oracle, Inc.*, 331 F. Supp. 2d 1098 (N.D. Cal. 2004). Hereafter referenced as *Oracle*.
4. The facts of the case are presented here in a highly simplified form and largely from the US Government's point of view. The concise views of the litigants on the facts and the law can be found in their post-trial briefs. Plaintiffs' Post-Trial Brief (Redacted Public Version), available at: http://www.usdoj.gov/atr/cases/f204500/204591.pdf; Oracle Corporation's Corrected Post-Trial Brief (Public Version), available at http://www.oracle.com/peoplesoft/OraclePostTrialBrief.pdf. Judge Walker's lengthy decision provides far greater detail on the facts, and readers also may consult the US Government's even longer Proposed Findings of Fact (Public Version), available at http://www.usdoj.gov/atr/cases/f204500/204565.pdf.
5. The government's post-trial brief explained that high-function software 'tracks thousands of transactions and supports thousands of concurrent users', allows a user to 'mold the software to meet its business needs without expensive and inefficient software customization', can 'perform multiple related transactions seamlessly . . . and with a high degree of ease and sophistication', is capable 'of handling international aspects of a business, such as multiple currencies, multiple languages, and multiple legal regimes', can 'accommodate rapid growth, acquisitions, and reorganizations', and is able 'to reflect actual units of business, rather than a pre-set business organization, and usefully link the data from those units'.
6. *FTC* v. *Staples, Inc.*, 970 F. Supp. 1066 (D.D.C. 1997).
7. *FTC* v. *Swedish Match*, 131 F. Supp. 2d 151 (D.D.C. 2000).
8. *United States* v. *Gillette Co.*, 828 F. Supp. 78 (D.D.C. 1993).
9. *New York* v. *Kraft General Foods, Inc.*, 926 F. Supp. 321 (S.D.N.Y. 1995).
10. *United States* v. *Long Island Jewish Medical Center*, 983 F. Supp. 121 (E.D.N.Y. 1997).
11. Shapiro, Carl (1996), 'Mergers with differentiated products', *Antitrust*, **10**(2), 23–30.
12. Werden, Gregory J. (1996), 'A robust test for consumer welfare enhancing mergers among sellers of differentiated products', *Journal of Industrial Economics*, **44**, 409–13.
13. Werden, Gregory J. and Luke M. Froeb (1994), 'The effects of mergers in differentiated products industries: logit demand and merger policy', *Journal of Law, Economics, & Organization*, **10**, 407–26.
14. Hausman, Jerry, Gregory Leonard and J. Douglas Zona (1994), 'Competitive analysis with differentiated products', *Annales d'Economie et Statistique*, **34**, 159–80.
15. Hausman, Jerry A. and Gregory K. Leonard (1997), 'Economic analysis of differentiated products mergers using real world data', *George Mason Law Review*, **5**, 321–46.

16. Nevo, Aviv (2000), 'Mergers with differentiated products: The case of the ready-to-eat cereal industry', *RAND Journal of Economics*, **31**, 395–421.
17. Werden, Gregory J. (2000), 'Expert report in *United States* v. *Interstate Bakeries Corp. and Continental Baking Co.*', *International Journal of the Economics of Business*, **7**, 139–48.
18. *Oracle*, p. 1113.
19. Bertrand, Joseph L.F. (1883), 'Review of "Théorie Mathématique de la Richesse Sociale", and "Recherches sur les Principes Mathématiques de la Théorie de Richesse"', *Journal des Savants*, **67**, 499–508. A modern translation by James Friedman appears in Andrew F. Daughety (ed.), *Cournot Oligopoly*, Cambridge: Cambridge University Press, pp. 73–81, 1988.
20. Nash, John (1951), 'Non-cooperative games', *Annals of Mathematics*, **54**, 286–95, reprinted in Andrew F. Daughety (ed.), *Cournot Oligopoly*, Cambridge: Cambridge University Press, pp. 82–93, 1988.
21. Deneckere, Raymond and Carl Davidson (1985), 'Incentives to form coalitions with Bertrand competition', *RAND Journal of Economics*, **16**, 473–86.
22. Shapiro, note 11.
23. Werden, Gregory J. and Luke M. Froeb (2007), 'Unilateral competitive effects of horizontal mergers', in Paolo Buccirossi (ed.), *Advances in the Economics of Competition Law*, Cambridge, Mass.: MIT Press.
24. Chamberlin, Edward H. (1933), *The Theory of Monopolistic Competition*, Cambridge, Mass.: Harvard University Press, 8th edn 1962, ch. 4.
25. Robinson, Joan (1933), *The Economics of Imperfect Competition*, London: Macmillan, 2nd edn 1969.
26. Archibald, G.C. (1987), 'Monopolistic competition', in John Eatwell et al. (eds), *The New Palgrave: A Dictionary of Economics*, vol. 3, London: Macmillan, pp. 531–5.
27. US Department of Justice and Federal Trade Commission (1992), Horizontal Merger Guidelines, at § 2.2. Similarly, ¶ 28 of the European Commission's 2004 Guidelines on the assessment of horizontal mergers under the Council Regulation on the control of concentrations between undertakings (O.J. C 31/03) state:

> The higher the degree of substitutability between the merging firms' products, the more likely it is that the merging firms will raise prices significantly. For example, a merger between two producers offering products which a substantial number of customers regard as their first and second choices could generate a significant price increase. Thus, the fact that rivalry between the parties has been an important source of competition on the market may be a central factor in the analysis.

28. *Oracle*, p. 1117. Judge Walker also asserted that the HMGs 'later acknowledge as much in section 2.212'. But that section addresses only the scenario in which buyers 'limit the total number of sellers they consider' and 'either of the merging firms would be replaced in such buyer's consideration by an equally competitive seller not formerly considered', Horizontal Merger Guidelines at § 2.212.
29. Ibid. As explained infra, Judge Walker would have been correct if he had been discussing the US government's unilateral effects theory based on an English auction model, but he was not discussing such a model.
30. Shapiro, note 11.
31. *Oracle*, pp. 1167–8.
32. *Oracle*, p. 1131.
33. Judge Walker may have understood this but chose his words unwisely in attempting to say that a slight preference for a product would not prevent switching to alternatives in the event of a small price increase.
34. *Oracle*, pp. 1170–71.
35. *Oracle*, p. 1118.
36. *Oracle*, p. 1123.
37. Ibid.
38. Horizontal Merger Guidelines at § 2.211.

39.  *Oracle*, p. 1123.
40.  *Oracle*, p. 1168.
41.  *Oracle*, pp. 1166–9, 1172. It is possible to understand Judge Walker to have held only that the US Government did not prove what it set out to prove. This interpretation is suggested by the way in which he began (p. 1166) his discussion of the government's evidence:

> Plaintiffs rest their theory of anticompetitive effects on an attempt to prove that Oracle and PeopleSoft are in a 'localized' competition sphere (a 'node') within the high function FMS and HRM market. This sphere does not include SAP or any other vendors, and a merger of Oracle and PeopleSoft would, therefore, adversely affect competition in this localized market.

It is also possible to understand Judge Walker to have found facts sufficient to decide the case against the government under a correct view of unilateral effects. This interpretation is suggested by the way in which (p. 1172) he began his findings of fact on unilateral effects:

> The court finds that the plaintiffs have wholly failed to prove the fundamental aspect of a unilateral effects case – they have failed to show a 'node' or an area of localized competition between Oracle and PeopleSoft. In other words, plaintiffs have failed to prove that there are a significant number of customers (the 'node') who regard Oracle and PeopleSoft as their first and second choices.

This passage refers to a 'node' within a space of consumer preferences, although Judge Walker defined a 'node' as a region in a space of product characteristics. The passage also indicates not just that SAP competed with Oracle and PeopleSoft but also that few customers found the Oracle and PeopleSoft products to be their first and second choices.
42.  Shapiro, note 11.
43.  See Werden, Gregory J. and Luke M. Froeb (2002), 'The antitrust logit model for predicting unilateral competitive effects', *Antitrust Law Journal*, **70**, 257–60; Werden, Gregory J., Luke M. Froeb and Timothy J. Tardiff (1996), 'The use of the logit model in applied industrial organization', *International Journal of the Economics of Business*, **3**, 83–105.
44.  The only additional assumption necessary for these calculations is that the marginal cost of each of the brands does not vary with the quantity produced.
45.  The logit model makes this clear because all brands are, by definition, equally close. The substitution pattern described above causes the cross-elasticity of demand for each brand to be the same with respect to the price of any given brand, which makes brands equally close substitutes by one reasonable measure.
46.  *Oracle*, p. 1113. The HMGs (§ 2.2) identified two classes of unilateral effects. In one the product is homogeneous and firms are distinguished primarily by their production capacities. The EC's guidelines (¶¶ 32–5) also mention that scenario. The court's dominance theory falls within this class, as does a theory based on the Cournot model.
47.  Within the class of unilateral effects involving differentiated products, the HMGs (§ 2.21, n.21) specifically mention an auction model, and the EC's guidelines (¶ 29) refer to 'bidding markets'. For analyses of mergers in the context of auction models, see Dalkir, Serdar, John Logan and Robert T. Masson (2000), 'Mergers in symmetric and asymmetric noncooperative auction markets: the effects on prices and efficiency', *International Journal of Industrial Organization*, **18**, 383–413; Froeb, Luke and Steven Tschantz (2002), 'Mergers among bidders with correlated values', in Daniel J. Slottje (ed.), *Measuring Market Power*, Amsterdam: Elsevier, pp. 31–45; Tschantz, Steven, Philip Crooke and Luke Froeb (2000), 'Mergers in sealed versus oral auctions', *International Journal of the Economics of Business*, **7**, 201–12; and Waehrer, Keith and Martin K. Perry (2003), 'The effects of mergers in open-auction markets', *RAND*

*Journal of Economics*, **38**, 287–304. Werden and Froeb, note 23, present insights from both this literature and unpublished work.

48. *Oracle*, pp. 1169–70. Acting for the US Government, R. Preston McAfee modeled competition as an English procurement auction (the meaning of which is explained presently). His model predicted price increases of 5–11 per cent for high-function FMS software and 13–30 per cent for high-function HRM software.
49. Klemperer, Paul (2004), *Auctions: Theory and Practice*, Princeton: Princeton University Press, ch. 1.
50. *Oracle*, p. 1172.
51. Analysis of the merger at the European Commission used a model of a sealed-bid auction largely on theory that vendors would not believe what Oracle told them about competing offers: Bengtsson, Claes (2005), 'Simulating the effect of Oracle's takeover of PeopleSoft', in Peter A.G. van Bergeijk and Erik Kloosterhuis (eds), *Modelling European Mergers: Theory, Competition Policy and Cases*, Cheltenham, UK and Northampton, MA, USA: Edward Elgar, pp. 133–49. Oracle argued somewhat differently that the procurement process would not reveal enough to vendors to cause them to bid differently to different customers.
52. *Oracle*, pp. 1158–61, 1170.
53. Near the end of his decision Judge Walker (pp. 1172–3) indirectly addressed the evidence on whether prices differed significantly across customers. He rejected an analysis of Oracle's pricing to 222 customers because it was not a 'formal stud[y] of price discrimination' and did not consider the pricing of PeopleSoft or SAP. But Judge Walker was addressing, not the merits of the government's unilateral effects theory in general, but rather only one expert's justification for having presented no econometric evidence.
54. *Oracle*, p. 1167.
55. *Oracle*, p. 1172.
56. Having a separate competition for each customer means that nothing ties the effects of the merger on US customers to the effects of the merger on non-US customers. That, in turn, explains the government's argument that geographic scope of the markets was just the US.
57. *Oracle*, pp. 1132, 1158–6. The US Government relied heavily on the testimony of customer witnesses (pp. 1125–30), but Judge Walker questioned (pp. 1130–31) the 'grounds on which these witnesses offered their opinions', faulting their testimony for failing 'to present the cost/benefit analyses that surely they employ' in making procurement decisions. Although he acknowledged the 'preferences of these customer witnesses for the functional features of PeopleSoft or Oracle products', he found (p. 1131) that 'the issue is not what solutions the customers would *like* or *prefer* for their data processing needs; the issue is what they *could* do in the event of an anticompetitive price increase by a post-merger Oracle'. In addition, Judge Walker identified (pp. 1136, 1138–9, 1141) what he saw as significant gaps in the knowledge of several of the government's other industry witnesses.
58. *Oracle*, pp. 1120–23.
59. Werden, Gregory J. and George Rozanski (1994), 'The application of section 7 to differentiated products industries: the market delineation dilemma', *Antitrust*, **8**(3), 40–43.
60. *Oracle*, pp. 1121–2.
61. Werden, Gregory J. and Luke M. Froeb (1996), 'Simulation as an alternative to structural merger policy in differentiated products industries', in Malcolm Coate and Andrew Kleit (eds), *The Economics of the Antitrust Process*, Boston: Kluwer Academic Publishers, pp. 65–88.
62. *Oracle*, p. 1122.
63. Hausman, Jerry A. and Gregory K. Leonard (1997), 'Economic analysis of differentiated products mergers using real world data', *George Mason Law Review*, **5**, 321–46.
64. Werden, Gregory J. and Luke M. Froeb (2002), 'Calibrated economic models add focus, accuracy, and persuasiveness to merger analysis', in Swedish Competition Authority (ed.), *The Pros and Cons of Merger Control*, pp. 63–82, at 70–78.

65.   Werden, Gregory J. (1997), 'Simulating the effects of differentiated products mergers: a practical alternative to structural merger policy', *George Mason Law Review*, **5**, 363–86.

## References

Archibald, G.C. (1987), 'Monopolistic competition', in John Eatwell et al. (eds), *The New Palgrave: A Dictionary of Economics*, vol. 3, London: Macmillan, pp. 531–5.

Bengtsson, Claes (2005), 'Simulating the effect of Oracle's takeover of PeopleSoft', in Peter A.G. van Bergeijk and Erik Kloosterhuis (eds), *Modelling European Mergers: Theory, Competition Policy and Cases*, Cheltenham, UK and Northampton, MA, USA: Edward Elgar, pp. 133–49.

Bertrand, Joseph L.F. (1883), 'Review of "Théorie Mathématique de la Richesse Sociale", and "Recherches sur les Principes Mathématiques de la Théorie de Richesse" ', *Journal des Savants*, **67**, 499–508; a modern translation by James Friedman appears in Andrew F. Daughety (ed.), *Cournot Oligopoly*, Cambridge: Cambridge University Press, pp. 73–81, 1988.

Chamberlin, Edward H. (1933), *The Theory of Monopolistic Competition*, Cambridge, Mass.: Harvard University Press, 8th edn 1962.

Dalkir, Serdar, John Logan and Robert T. Masson (2000), 'Mergers in symmetric and asymmetric noncooperative auction markets: the effects on prices and efficiency', *International Journal of Industrial Organization*, **18**, 383–413.

Deneckere, Raymond and Carl Davidson (1985), 'Incentives to form coalitions with Bertrand competition', *RAND Journal of Economics*, **16**, 473–86.

European Commission (2004), 'Guidelines on the assessment of horizontal mergers under the Council Regulation on the control of concentrations between undertakings', O.J. C 31/03.

Froeb, Luke and Steven Tschantz (2002), 'Mergers among bidders with correlated values', in Daniel J. Slottje (ed.), *Measuring Market Power*, Amsterdam: Elsevier, pp. 31–45.

Hausman, Jerry A. and Gregory K. Leonard (1997), 'Economic analysis of differentiated products mergers using real world data', *George Mason Law Review*, **5**, 321–46.

Hausman, Jerry, Gregory Leonard and J. Douglas Zona (1994), 'Competitive analysis with differentiated products', *Annales d'Economie et Statistique*, **34**, 159–80.

Klemperer, Paul (2004), *Auctions: Theory and Practice*, Princeton: Princeton University Press.

Nash, John (1951), 'Non-cooperative games', *Annals of Mathematics*, **54**, 286–95; reprinted in Andrew F. Daughety (ed.), *Cournot Oligopoly*, Cambridge: Cambridge University Press, pp. 82–93, 1988.

Nevo, Aviv (2000), 'Mergers with differentiated products: the case of the ready-to-eat cereal industry', *RAND Journal of Economics*, **31**, 395–421.

Robinson, Joan (1933), *The Economics of Imperfect Competition*, London: Macmillan, 2nd edn 1969.

Shapiro, Carl (1996), 'Mergers with differentiated products', *Antitrust*, **10**(2), 23–30.

Tschantz, Steven, Philip Crooke and Luke Froeb (2000), 'Mergers in sealed versus oral auctions', *International Journal of the Economics of Business*, **7**, 201–12.

US Department of Justice and Federal Trade Commission (1992), *Horizontal Merger Guidelines*.

Vickrey, William (1961), 'Counterspeculation, auctions, and competitive sealed tenders', *Journal of Finance*, **16**, 8–37.

Waehrer, Keith and Martin K. Perry (2003), 'The effects of mergers in open-auction markets', *RAND Journal of Economics*, **38**, 287–304.

Werden, Gregory J. (1996), 'A robust test for consumer welfare-enhancing mergers among sellers of differentiated products', *Journal of Industrial Economics*, **44**, 409–13.

Werden, Gregory J. (1997), 'Simulating the effects of differentiated products mergers: a practical alternative to structural merger policy', *George Mason Law Review*, **5**, 363–86.

Werden, Gregory J. (2000), 'Expert report in *United States* v. *Interstate Bakeries Corp. and Continental Baking Co.*', *International Journal of the Economics of Business*, **7**, 139–48.

Werden, Gregory J. and Luke M. Froeb (1994), 'The effects of mergers in differentiated products industries: logit demand and merger policy', *Journal of Law, Economics, & Organization*, **10**, 407–26.

Werden, Gregory J. and Luke M. Froeb (1996), 'Simulation as an alternative to structural merger policy in differentiated products industries', in Malcolm Coate and Andrew Kleit (eds), *The Economics of the Antitrust Process*, Boston: Kluwer Academic Publishers, pp. 65–88.

Werden, Gregory J. and Luke M. Froeb (2002), 'Calibrated economic models add focus, accuracy, and persuasiveness to merger analysis', in Swedish Competition Authority (ed.), *The Pros and Cons of Merger Control*, Stockholm: Swedish Competition Authority, pp. 63–82.

Werden, Gregory J. and Luke M. Froeb (2002), 'The antitrust logit model for predicting unilateral competitive effects', *Antitrust Law Journal*, **70**, 257–60.

Werden, Gregory J. and Luke M. Froeb (2007), 'Unilateral competitive effects of horizontal mergers', in Paolo Buccirossi (ed.), *Advances in the Economics of Competition Law*, Cambridge, Mass.: MIT Press.

Werden, Gregory J. and George Rozanski (1994), 'The application of section 7 to differentiated products industries: the market delineation dilemma', *Antitrust*, **8**(3), 40–43.

Werden, Gregory J., Luke M. Froeb and Timothy J. Tardiff (1996), 'The use of the logit model in applied industrial organization', *International Journal of the Economics of Business*, **3**, 83–105.

## Cases

*FTC* v. *Staples, Inc.*, 970 F. Supp. 1066 (D.D.C. 1997).

*FTC* v. *Swedish Match*, 131 F. Supp. 2d 151 (D.D.C. 2000).

*New York* v. *Kraft General Foods, Inc.*, 926 F. Supp. 321 (S.D.N.Y. 1995).

*United States* v. *Gillette Co.*, 828 F. Supp. 78 (D.D.C. 1993).

*United States* v. *Long Island Jewish Medical Center*, 983 F. Supp. 121 (E.D.N.Y. 1997).

*United States* v. *Oracle, Inc.*, 331 F. Supp. 2d 1098 (N.D. Cal. 2004).

# 2 Transatlantic issues in the European merger review of *Oracle/PeopleSoft*: harmonious dissonance

## *Thomas Vinje and Dieter Paemen*[1]

### Introduction

On 1 May 2004, a new Regulation[2] replacing the previous regulation on merger control[3] came into force, one of the primary features of which was the introduction of new wording against which concentrations would be appraised. Previously, the EC Merger Regulation (ECMR) required that mergers be reviewed with regard to whether they created or strengthened a dominant position as a result of which effective competition would be significantly impeded in the common market or a substantial part of it.[4] Under the new ECMR, transactions are to be blocked if they would 'significantly impede effective competition, in the common market or in a substantial part of it, in particular as a result of the creation or strengthening of a dominant position' (known for short as the 'SIEC test').

Views differ on the extent to which Regulation 139/2004 introduced new law. Considerable debate has surrounded the adoption of the SIEC test in relation to whether the new wording presented a confirmation of existing practice supported by the existing law or the introduction of a new standard.[5] Less dissent exists with regards to the intention behind the change in wording of the substantive test: to recognize explicitly the power of the European Commission ('the Commission') to examine mergers that lead to so-called 'unilateral' or 'non-coordinated effects' under the traditional single dominance threshold and thereby address the existing or perceived 'enforcement gap' of the Commission to review transactions that do not lead to a dominant market position.[6] One of the intended effects of the change was to align the letter of the law if not also the practice of EC merger control more closely to the law and practice of other jurisdictions where antitrust regulators examine unilateral effects of mergers below the threshold of dominance, most prominently the United States. This would enhance the ability of the reviewing agencies in the EU and the US to coordinate their activities and achieve greater transatlantic consistency in merger control.

This goal has been sought by both companies and their lawyers in the hope that it will lead to greater efficiency and predictability of the merger review process. However, as shown by the experience of the *Oracle/PeopleSoft* case, where the transaction was examined under a unilateral effects theory of harm (even though the old ECMR still applied), in what was described as 'close coordination' with the antitrust division of the US Department of Justice (DOJ),[7] the application of similar broad theories of competitive harm and consultation between the enforcement authorities across the Atlantic does not preclude very significant differences in the ways they assess a particular transaction.[8]

In particular, the *Oracle/PeopleSoft* case highlighted that the investigation of a transaction under the same nominal theory of unilateral or 'noncoordinated' effects does not mean that the theory will be applied in the same manner as in the US and EU: the US and the EU agencies are subjected to different evidentiary standards. Even if similar substantive tests are applied, differences in the procedural rules under which the agencies operate and political pressures to conduct independent review processes and reach independent conclusions also create significant hurdles to transatlantic coordination and consistency. As discussed below, while the same decision to clear the Oracle/PeopleSoft merger was reached in the EU and US on the basis of similar considerations, these broad similarities obscure the differences between the Commission's approach and that of the DOJ and the District Court.

### The review of *Oracle/PeopleSoft*

Oracle's takeover bid for PeopleSoft was in many ways an exemplary candidate to benefit from more coordination and more consistent review by the EU and US agencies. Oracle and PeopleSoft were both California-based companies which sold their software globally. Moreover, Oracle's offer for PeopleSoft was hostile and the animosity between the parties was extremely high,[9] with the target using the antitrust process as its main defence mechanism to ward off the merger. A rapid and consistent resolution was the most desirable outcome for all involved, including customers who faced uncertainty over the fate of the significant investments they had made or were about to make in the parties' products.

*The transaction*

The transaction concerned particular kinds of enterprise applications software (EAS), which is software automating business processes of organizations (including businesses, governmental and educational institutions). Enterprise applications are different from infrastructure software such as operating systems and databases. In the industry, three broad categories or 'pillars' of enterprise applications software are distinguished: enterprise resource planning (ERP) software, which automates common back office functions of an organization including accounting and HR management, customer relationship management (CRM) software, which automates the sales, marketing and customer support functions of an organization, and supply chain management (SCM) software, which relates to software supporting the purchasing function of an organization.

Typically costing tens to hundreds of thousands or even millions of Euros, EAS is not bought in a shrink-wrapped box at the local computer shop, but is typically sold as part of a negotiation process in which the customer weighs the different suppliers' product feature sets and prices against its own needs and options. EAS software is highly differentiated, with products of the different suppliers supporting a large number of different features in different ways. The purchase process generally involves several stages: an initial stage in which a number of suppliers are invited to pitch their software as a solution for the customer's automation need, one or more further evaluation rounds in which a more limited number of suppliers' products are tested and evaluated in light of the customer's needs and then a comparison with the automation functionality already offered by the customer's incumbent EAS. More often than not, no more than two of the vendors involved in the evaluation round are then retained for the final round of negotiation about the terms of the transaction. These negotiations take place bilaterally; vendors do not know directly what their competitor has proposed for the final deal, although customers may or may not tell them what the competing vendor's best deal was (or what the customers contend it was) in order to play the final round competitors off against each other.

Oracle and PeopleSoft offered a range of ERP software as well as CRM, but primarily had overlapping strengths in two subcategories or 'subpillars' of ERP software, namely financial management software (FMS) and human resource management software (HR or HRM software). Oracle was one of the pioneers in the financial management automation arena, while PeopleSoft was founded as a provider of and had become a leader in HR software.

Independent analyst data published periodically in the ordinary course of business suggested that the EAS business, as well as the ERP pillar and the FMS and HR subcategories thereof, would remain highly fragmented after completion of the transaction. Despite being the world's second-largest software provider overall after Microsoft, Oracle's traditional strength is in databases, and it lags far behind the industry leader, Germany-based SAP, in EAS. The analyst reports suggested that the highest market share the parties would have post-merger would still be well below the 25 per cent threshold advanced by the EU's guidelines on horizontal mergers as a safe harbour.

The largest provider of EAS was (and still is) SAP, which in many ways invented EAS as a software category. Indeed, the main rationale behind the transaction was to put Oracle in a better position to challenge the market leader SAP. Other vendors in the business included companies such as Lawson, IFS and Microsoft. Microsoft had recently entered the market through acquisitions, and planned on leveraging its strong position in client PC software to access the EAS functionality to grow its market share. In addition, customers were increasingly opting to purchase the functionality of enterprise software, including HR and FMS software, as a service over the Internet, without having the need to run software on their own server hardware. The installation and maintenance of such software is outsourced to a third party. It is part of a larger, recently initiated but rapidly growing trend towards the deployment of software as a service (SaaS) under a subscription model, which enables customers to obtain software functionality with limited up-front costs and to add additional functionality incrementally.

In addition to these commercial vendors, some customers consider their automation needs to be unique and develop custom-built software, often with the help of IT consultants such as IBM Global Services. A significant portion of the market relied on these 'custom built' solutions, which, having declined in popularity in the wake of cheaper and more powerful pre-built solutions, are regaining interest with the advent of low-cost open source software and development resources.

*The agencies' pas de deux on the road to EU clearance*
Following Oracle's announcement of the hostile tender offer on 6 June 2003, Oracle's antitrust advisers quickly contacted the European and US antitrust authorities. On 12 June, Oracle submitted its Hart Scott Rodino filing to the US DOJ. The DOJ issued a Second Request[10] on 30 June 2003. Under the old ECMR, Oracle was under a one-week deadline to file the Form CO.[11] However, that rule had already become a dead letter by the time Oracle announced its takeover bid and the amending regulation was soon to abolish the rule. While Oracle's US advisers worked on achieving compliance with a very substantial request for additional information, in Europe, Oracle kept in touch with the EU, filing a briefing paper about the transaction and providing a draft of its Form CO. The case team at the European Commission did not indicate a particular desire to proceed quickly with the review of the transaction, and did not enforce the one-week filing rule, which would have triggered deadlines for a decision to clear or open an in-depth Phase II investigation under the ECMR. It appeared at that point that the Commission case team shared Oracle's desire to coordinate the timing of its procedure with that of the US. Instead of pressing

for an early notification, it held several meetings with Oracle's advisers and, in addition to surveying the customers and competitors, issued a first request for information before Oracle filed its Form CO.

In October, the Commission case team requested that a Form CO be filed, perhaps under pressure from PeopleSoft, which had argued that Oracle had launched the takeover bid in an attempt to spread uncertainty among current and potential PeopleSoft customers and thereby to weaken the company without actually intending to pursue the bid. Oracle then filed its Form CO on 14 October 2003, as a consequence of which a Phase I Decision on whether to investigate the transaction in detail was required to be taken within a month.

By that stage, it was clear that substantial compliance with the DOJ's second request in the US would not be certified before the expiry of the one month Phase I review period in Europe, and that a Commission Decision on whether to initiate a Phase II review (lasting up to an additional four months) would occur before the DOJ had come to a conclusion about the transaction. On 17 November 2004, the Commission issued a decision to the effect that it had serious doubts about the transaction, thus kicking off the four-month Phase II investigation.[12]

Just before Christmas, the Commission issued a third, very substantial, request for information (a second request for information requesting sales opportunity data had been issued in October 2003). The request imposed a two-week deadline, expiring just after the New Year. Oracle was unable to meet the deadline, and the Commission stopped the clock (that is, suspended the running of Phase II) for a first time in January 2004, until Oracle was able to comply fully with the EU's request in early February. By having suspended Phase II, the Commission avoided running out of time and being required to issue a Statement of Objections opposing the transaction before the Assistant Attorney General in charge of the DOJ's antitrust division had decided on whether to bring an injunction suit in a Federal District Court against Oracle to try and block the merger, or let the transaction proceed. Thus, by stopping the clock, the Commission avoided prejudging the Assistant Attorney General's position on what was ultimately a transaction involving two US-based companies.

Meanwhile, in the United States, Oracle was certified to have complied with the DOJ's Second Request in January 2004. On 26 February, the DOJ's Assistant Attorney-General for antitrust decided to oppose the merger in court. Soon after, and once the clock was running again in the EU proceedings, the Commission issued a Statement of Objections also opposing the deal.[13]

The DOJ's decision to sue returned the onus to the Commission, which faced the expiry of its four-month period for its running Phase II investigation in a matter of weeks, whereas the injunction proceeding in the US was almost guaranteed to take longer. The Commission may have considered that it had solid objections on the basis of which to oppose the deal, and perhaps even that a prohibition decision following a DOJ decision to oppose the deal was consistent with a transatlantic coordination objective. It vigorously defended its objections at the Oral Hearing that took place in Brussels following the Statement of Objections. However, the Oral Hearing was in many ways a turning point in the procedure. At the hearing, Oracle was able for the first time to make its objections to other Commission services and to representatives of the Member States' competition authorities, and directly confront the arguments of the Commission and PeopleSoft.[14]

To its credit, the Commission recognized it needed more evidence to reach a definitive conclusion about the transaction and issued a fourth (and ultimately final) request for information in early April 2004. This request asked for a truly massive amount of detailed quantitative information about virtually every aspect on every sales opportunity to which Oracle had been a party over the previous years around the world, and sought to address the evidentiary gaps that Oracle had laid bare at the Oral Hearing. The request again asked for information that Oracle did not retain in the ordinary course of business, this time with regard to hundreds of sales opportunities, and required Oracle to query all of the enterprise applications sales staff at each of its regional business units who had been involved in the sales opportunities individually, a highly time-consuming process. The request again provided a two-week deadline to respond, which was impossible for Oracle to meet and led to a second suspension of the Phase II proceedings. This time the suspension lasted several months, with Oracle providing the sales opportunity information it had collected to the Commission on a rolling basis as it became available.

In the US, Judge Vernon Walker of the Federal District Court for the Northern District of California, a highly respected judge with a background as an experienced private antitrust practitioner, was designated to preside over the trial. The trial did not commence in earnest until early June, and lasted for almost two months, with closing arguments being presented on 20 July. At trial, the DOJ presented various customer witnesses and executives of PeopleSoft, Microsoft and Bearing Point in support of its case, as well as testimony from economic experts. Oracle also presented customer witnesses and economic experts, including witnesses from competitors (such as Lawson and ADP) and systems integrators, amongst others. Both parties extensively cross-examined the witnesses, and cited generously from internal documents collected during discovery and from depositions of individuals taken in preparation of trial. On 9 September 2004, Judge Walker ruled in favour of Oracle.[15]

Victory for Oracle in the US court did not mean the Commission ceased its investigation. The day after the US judgment, the Commission sent Oracle a letter stating it had not yet provided all the information requested by the Commission in its fourth information request and insisted that Oracle provide the (relatively small amount of) information that was still outstanding and issued another request for additional information about competing vendors. Oracle provided this information at the end of September and the beginning of October. On 26 October 2004, the Commission announced its Decision to clear the transaction, on the basis that the transaction did not 'strengthen or create a dominant position as a result of which effective competition would be significantly impeded in the common market or in a substantial part of it'.[16] The Commission's review proved to be the longest in its merger review history, lasting a total of 16 months from the announcement of the deal to final clearance. It was also one of only a few transactions that were cleared unconditionally after a Phase II investigation.[17]

*Transatlantic harmony*
Commission statements following the clearance decision suggest that the Commission case team coordinated closely with their counterparts at the DOJ throughout the proceeding,[18] and one might take away from the above description of the process that there was significant consistency in the development of the two review processes across the Atlantic. It might be inferred from the unusual timing of the procedure, influenced by a very long pre-notification process and two clock-stopping events, that the Commission sought to align the timing of its procedure with that of the US, and recognized that the US authorities should take the lead in a transaction involving two US companies. The main steps in the Commission's procedure (the Decision to open Phase II proceedings, the issuance of a Statement of Objections, and the issuance of a final clearance Decision) broadly followed the major milestones in the US clearance process (the issuance of a second request, the decision to request an injunction in court, and the order of the District Court). The Commission's Decision ultimately came to the same resolution of its investigation as the outcome of the US process, that is to say, a finding that the transaction should not be opposed. And the Commission's decision takes into account and repeatedly cites the evidence presented at the US trial, mainly by the DOJ.

Furthermore, the substantive conduct of the proceedings on both sides of the Atlantic and their ultimate outcome suggest a significant degree of concurrence between the Commission and the DOJ (and ultimately between the Commission and the US court). Like the DOJ, the Commission's review ultimately focused on the likelihood of competitive

harm following from unilateral effects of the transaction.[19] Both the DOJ
and the Commission (and, it would appear, ultimately Judge Walker)
appear to have taken the view that unilateral effects resulting from the closeness of competition between the merging parties should be reviewed under
the criterion of whether the parties were each other's 'closest' competitors
for a substantial number of customers, with other competitors unable to
counter the competitive harm.[20] Both the DOJ and the Commission based
their objections on the view that the relevant market was for high function
EAS, in which only Oracle, PeopleSoft and SAP competed, and which did
not include other players such as best-of-breed providers and outsourcers.[21]
The Commission, like the DOJ and the US court, did not give much cre-
dence to Oracle's efficiency claims.[22] Like the DOJ, the Commission
throughout most of the procedure took the view that the transaction would
lead to a reduction of players on the market from three to two, and that this
reduction would harm consumers.[23] In order to support their objections,
both the Commission and the DOJ relied on, amongst other things, statements from customers and competitors, discount regressions and merger
simulation models.[24]

*Transatlantic dissonance*
However the aforementioned elements of correspondence between the
Commission and US review processes suggest a greater degree of congru-
ence than was in fact present during the months between the announcement
of the transaction and the clearance by the Commission. The views and
actions of the Commission and the DOJ and indeed Judge Walker diverged
significantly on a number of issues, including market definition, market
players, the theory of competitive harm, the application of the unilateral
effects theory, and evidentiary matters. While the Commission's approach
to its review of Oracle/PeopleSoft indicates a willingness to take into
account and show deference to the review conducted by the US authorities,
it also emphasizes that coordination and cooperation with the US does not
mean that the Commission will not conduct its own investigation and reach
independent conclusions.

*Market definition*
PRODUCT MARKET DEFINITION   Both the Commission and the
DOJ hypothesized early on in the proceedings that there was a separate
market to be defined comprising HR and FMS applications for the high
end, that is to say the largest corporations and government organizations.[25]
However the two authorities defined their relevant high end market quite
differently. The Commission defined a separate relevant market for 'high-
function EAS purchased by large enterprises with complex needs'.[26] 'Large

and complex enterprises' were defined as organizations with over 10 000 employees and/or with revenues of at least €1 billion, whereas 'high function' related to the capabilities of the product. It was assumed that such high-function software was typically sold to customers with complex needs in the context of large deals, and thus the Commission adopted a proxy for deals in the relevant market, namely those involving at least 1 million Euro in net new licence revenue.

The DOJ similarly identified a market for 'high-function FMS and HRM software' purchased by 'large complex enterprises (LCEs) with high-level functional needs'.[27] However, the DOJ added a number of additional product, customer and software performance characteristics to its product market definition, such as the ability to integrate with other enterprise software from the same vendor in suites.

The DOJ also used very different proxies to identify sales opportunities involving high function FMS and HR software. The DOJ did not attempt to define proxies for the high-definition markets by reference to customer revenue or employee numbers. Rather, high-function deals were considered to be those HR and FMS deals worth over 500 000 USD (rather than 1 million Euro as the Commission had hypothesized).

Oracle heavily criticized both the Commission and the DOJ for defining their own high-function market even though the concept of 'high function' was completely foreign to the industry and appeared to be designed to draw a circle around only Oracle, PeopleSoft and SAP. While it is not uncommon for vendors and industry analysts to identify within EAS and its 'pillars' a high end, a mid-market and a low end, these concepts generally correspond to the customer's size, not to the value of their purchases or the complexity of their needs. Whereas small customers generally buy different HR and FMS software to mid-sized or large customers, the software sold to mid-sized customers and large customers tends to be the same. Moreover, criteria to distinguish these segments varied very significantly from vendor to vendor and from analyst to analyst, as the US court's judgment highlighted. As testimony to this, both the DOJ and the EU struggled to find cognizable and identifiable real-world criteria to identify a separate set of high-function customers, and ultimately each adopted different criteria to define the 'high-function' market. Moreover, neither agency was able to establish on the basis of their proxies that there was evidence of price discrimination between high-function and non-high-function customers unrelated to common volume discounts.

The US court found that no market for high-function software sold by Oracle, PeopleSoft and SAP was proved. The court noted that even the DOJ's own expert testimony admitted that 'plaintiff's product market has no quantitative metric that could be used to determine the distinction between a high function and a mid-market product'[28] and concluded that 'the court cannot delineate product boundaries in multi billion dollar merger suits based upon the mere notion that there is "something different" about the merging products and all others'.[29]

The US court found that the products of providers of outsourced software (a form of software as a service), other vendors such as Lawson and Microsoft characterized as mid-market vendors by the DOJ, and so-called 'best of breed' providers who specialize in selling a narrow solution rather than a broad suite of different HR or FMS software, were all in the 'high function' market. With regard to the latter, Judge Walker noted that vendors with a broad enterprise software offering like SAP and Oracle sold bundles of software and offered discounts on the entire bundle in order to ensure that the customer purchases the components of the bundle from a vendor such as Oracle rather than from a best-of-breed vendor.

The US court did agree with the DOJ that so-called 'incumbent solutions', that is to say the software already installed at the customer, were not proved to be a competitive constraint. The court's opinion was silent on whether solutions developed in-house by the customer could constrain a combined *Oracle/PeopleSoft* merger. All things considered, however, Judge Walker's opinion reads as a scathing rejection of the DOJ's contended 'high-function' HR and FMS software suites market.

By contrast, the Commission explicitly upheld its definition of a high-function market for FMS and HR in its final decision. It did so even though it too failed to present viable and credible demarcation criteria for the supposed high-function market, and the proxies it offered had been undermined by the finding by the US court that views differed widely as to what these proxies might be.[30]

In contrast to the US court's conclusions, the Commission rejected the notion that the products of outsourced software providers or best-of-breed vendors were part of the market. Unlike the US court's judgment, which only addresses incumbent solutions, the Commission's Decision also explicitly excludes 'custom-built' solutions from the market.[31] The Commission did not consider that best-of-breed providers or outsourcers would provide credible supply-side substitution by repositioning post-merger. While the Commission agreed that the high-function market was not limited to SAP, Oracle and PeopleSoft, but also included other vendors of packaged software such as Lawson and Microsoft, it identified additional companies as credible suppliers to high-end customers, including QAD and IFS.

In upholding its high-function market definition, the Commission, while clearly differing from the US court, arguably upheld at least in general terms the position the DOJ defended at trial. However it has been argued by some defending the DOJ's position that Judge Walker misunderstood the market definition the DOJ advanced, which was supposedly that *each* sales opportunity for high-function HR and FMS represents a separate market. This, however, was not a position presented or defended by the DOJ at trial,[32] and certainly was not alleged by the Commission during its investigation of the merger. In any event, if this is indeed the approach to market definition the DOJ intended to convey, even the superficial consistency between the Commission and the DOJ appears to have been minimal.

It is worthy of note that, although both agencies struggled with the definition of the relevant market, neither argued forcefully that it was in fact not an essential step in the analysis of the unilateral effects theory of competitive harm that ultimately took centre stage to both procedures, as has been argued in the economic literature. As is discussed below, non-coordinated (or unilateral) effects are said to arise where a merger eliminates an important competitive constraint on one or more firms, who consequently have increased market power, without having engaged in coordinated behaviour.[33] A proper analysis of unilateral effects looks at how the removal of a competitive constraint influences the parameters of competition among the remaining players on the market post-merger. Such an analysis presupposes that all possible constraints existing post-transaction on the merged entity are considered. A limitation of the constraining alternatives through a narrow definition of the market potentially preempts and interferes with an unbiased unilateral effects analysis: it may exclude *a priori* from the analysis alternatives that in fact present important competitive constraints post-merger. If anything, a definition of the relevant market is likely to flow from the unilateral effects analysis in the form of the identification of those players' products that do present an important competitive constraint.

At the same time, an analysis of unilateral effects is only workable if alternative products and services that clearly do not constrain the pricing of the overlapping products are discarded from the analysis. Arguably the soundest analytical approach is thus to assume a fairly broad definition of the market that includes the product overlaps of the parties generously defined to include all credible alternatives, which is then subjected to economic analyses to assess their impact on the products and services of the merging parties. This approach could arguably have been followed by the Commission and the DOJ in *Oracle/PeopleSoft* and might have eliminated some of the problems they faced in their analysis of the transaction (as well as some of the bias inherent in using narrow starting hypotheses for the definition of the relevant market.)

Ultimately, however, it appears that, for each its own reasons, neither agency could have wholly ignored the task of defining a relevant market on which the merging parties' products overlap. In his decision, Judge Walker emphasized the central role of market definition in horizontal merger analysis under US law, suggesting that, had the DOJ taken the approach of identifying unilateral effects without defining a market, it would not have been more successful than it ultimately proved to be with a market definition based on thin evidence.

For its part, the Commission works under the established practice that market definition is the first step in any competitive effects analysis; failing to define a relevant market would have been a significant departure from previous practice and perhaps exposed its Decision to reversal by the Court of First Instance. Thus in both the US and the EU, market definition remains a necessary step in the analysis of competitive effects. Moreover the Commission had to define a relevant market in which only Oracle, PeopleSoft and SAP were present in order to support its allegation that the merger would lead to coordination between the merged entity and SAP. Absent such a narrow market, no market structure could be claimed to satisfy the required conditions for a finding of coordinated effects. In addition, no non-coordinated effects could be alleged without such a narrow market definition because the parties' shares on a broader market would likely remain below the 25 per cent market share safe harbour provided for in the Commission's Guidelines on Horizontal Mergers,[34] on the basis of the market shares in the EAS market and HR and FMS segments as reported by all major analysts.

The Commission initially hypothesized that only SAP, Oracle and PeopleSoft participated in the high-function HR and FMS markets. In its Decision to initiate a Phase II investigation, it calculated market shares for the high-end market it was then considering based on these companies' licence revenues in relation to customers with revenues in excess of 1 billion Euro and/or more than 10 000 employees; it did not take into account other vendors' sales that met these criteria that the Decision subsequently found to have supplied this market. On the basis of this initial calculation, the Commission found that the combined entity would have a 30% market share in FMS compared to 70% for SAP, and a 57% market share in HR compared to 43% for SAP. These figures were not based on a market definition commonly used in the industry. On the contrary, it contrasted starkly with the far lower figures for Oracle, PeopleSoft and SAP reported periodically by market analysts, which did not suggest that the combined entity would exceed a 25% market share, or overtake SAP as market leader. In its final Decision, the Commission did not include market shares for its high-function markets as such, although it did provide share data based on revenue figures reported by one market analyst firm for the broader HR and FMS markets, from which it excluded most of the other vendors for which analysts provide share data (which for the Commission did not fall within its market definition).

The significant discrepancy between the market shares reported periodically by reputable market share analysts and the shares the Commission initially calculated for its narrowly defined high-function markets did not deter it from vigorously pursuing a unilateral effects theory, even though it was far from clear that the merged entity would exceed the 25% market share safe harbour post-transaction. This raises the question as to the practical application of the safe harbour. The 25% safe harbour is designed to award assurance to companies who believe they have a market share under the 25% threshold based upon analyst data commonly used in the course of their business. However, as the *Oracle/PeopleSoft* decision highlights, the utility of the 25% safe harbour can be questioned if the Commission defines the market in a way that does not allow market shares to be assessed with readily available share data, or in a way that is so narrow that it guarantees that the parties' combined share will exceed the threshold. The Commission often appears to define markets very narrowly, perhaps in an attempt to assess a worst-case scenario, and while parties to merger review proceedings can anticipate a variety of possible narrow segmentations, which segmentation the Commission ultimately upholds may be difficult to predict.

GEOGRAPHIC MARKET DEFINITION   Even more starkly contrasting were the Commission's and DOJ's approaches to geographic market definition. In what seemed like an attempt to diminish the significance of overall EAS market leader SAP, which is based in Germany and is traditionally stronger in Europe than in the US, the DOJ defended a US-only market definition, on the basis of the contention (controverted at trial) that European and US prices did not constrain each other and that the sales process involved extensive local contact by local sales offices with the customer. Oracle fiercely contested that the market was limited to the US, an argument the court eventually upheld.

Similarly, in Europe, Oracle had argued in its notification, consistently with the sole existing Commission merger decision in the EAS sector, that the relevant geographic market was 'at least EEA wide'. The Commission, although in its Decision mischaracterizing Oracle's position as having defended a market limited to the EEA, consistently upheld a worldwide market definition. The Commission's and DOJ's views on geographic market definition could thus hardly have been more diametrically opposed.

*Theory of competitive harm*   Further divergence between the US and EU approaches was reflected in the theories of competitive harm the

Commission and the DOJ pursued as the grounds for raising concerns about the transaction. The DOJ fairly quickly honed in on the potential unilateral effects caused by an Oracle-PeopleSoft combination, and argued at trial that these effects would reduce competition in the high-function EAS markets. It did not pursue other theories, except for a brief attempt to formulate a coordinated effects theory in its post-trial brief and, even in that context, the DOJ's theory of customer allocation by industry type did not focus on the same coordinated effects as alleged by the Commission, which instead emphasized customer allocation on the basis of the installed base of Oracle and SAP.

In contrast, the Commission's decision in November to initiate a second phase in-depth investigation was based almost exclusively on the allegation that, in the alleged high-function market, SAP and Oracle as the only remaining players would tacitly conspire to allocate customers, raise prices or slow down innovation under a theory of coordinated effects. This was a surprising contention to anyone familiar with the industry, especially in view of market characteristics which were not in the slightest conductive to coordinated effects (based on criteria identified by the Commission's and Court of First Instance's coordinated effects cases) and of the bitter rivalry between SAP and Oracle that has only grown since the merger was consummated. Nevertheless, the Commission's concern that Oracle and SAP would collude remained the central concern throughout most of its investigation. In its decision to initiate Phase II, the Commission also raised concerns about vertical leveraging of Oracle's database position into the market for applications and vice versa, and it maintained those concerns in its March 2003 Statement of Objections although, absent real cause for concern, it did not vigorously pursue them. In short, unilateral effects were not raised at all by the Commission until a few days before the issuance of the Statement of Objections, when for the first time it communicated concerns about non-coordinated effects.

Even as the Commission switched theories to focus on a unilateral effects theory of harm, significant divergences already existed between the Commission and the DOJ in the way this theory was applied.

*Application of the unilateral effects theory*
DIFFERENT APPROACHES    The unilateral effects theory presented by the Commission in its Statement of Objections was based on the view that the merger would limit the choices of (i) customers who, for reasons related to the product and vendor characteristics, viewed Oracle and PeopleSoft as 'closest' competitors and believed they could only choose Oracle or PeopleSoft software; (ii) customers who wanted to source HR and FMS software from different suppliers; and (iii) customers who did not want

database software from Oracle (a prerequisite for running Oracle applications, which only run on Oracle databases), or at least wanted to source applications and database software from different suppliers.

Because the Commission hypothesized that the market was limited to Oracle, PeopleSoft and SAP, the elimination of PeopleSoft as an option would mean these categories of customers would face a reduced choice (in the case of customers who wanted HR and FMS software from different suppliers and customers who did not want database software from Oracle or from different suppliers) of only one alternative (SAP), or (in the case of customers who saw their only alternatives as Oracle and PeopleSoft) even no alternative to Oracle. In the latter case, there would be no remaining price constraints on Oracle. In the former, the competition with SAP 'would be insufficient to shield consumers from significant harm'.[35] This was said to have significant adverse effects on customers in terms of price, product variety, product quality and innovation.[36]

The Commission defended its use of a unilateral effects theory under the old regulation in the Statement of Objectives with reference to the European Court's case law[37] and the recitals of the (old) ECMR,[38] which it interpreted to support a broad reading of dominance that included situations in which an oligopoly or collective dominant position would be created in which the oligopolists would have market power without coordination.[39] It argued that 'post transaction, both the merged entity and SAP would be in a position to exercise market power'. However, in the Decision, the Commission declares, without qualifying the validity of its non-coordinated effects theory, that 'on the basis of new evidence collected after the Oral Hearing, it has been concluded that no such anticompetitive effects are likely to result from the merger'.[40] As noted above, this evidence led the Commission to conclude that the relevant market was not limited to three players pre-merger, and therefore would not lead to a reduction of choices to Oracle and SAP post-merger.

The DOJ was more generic in its unilateral effects argument. It did not raise the choice of database as a constraint on customer's choice. Instead it focused on Oracle and PeopleSoft as closest competitors and argued that the elimination of competition from PeopleSoft would lead to higher prices and reduced innovation, and that SAP would not be able to reposition itself to replace lost competition. It based its analysis on customer and competitor testimony, anecdotal discount analysis, a discount regression analysis and an econometric model.

The US court ultimately found that, in order to find a reduction of competition post-merger, it is necessary to show that there are a significant number of customers who regard Oracle and PeopleSoft as their first and second choices. The court characterized this customer group as a 'node' over which the merged entity could exercise monopoly power absent repositioning by other suppliers such as SAP. It concluded that the DOJ had failed to make such a showing, noting that the DOJ had failed to present econometric analyses such as diversion ratios or cross-price elasticities. The DOJ had argued it was unable to present the court with econometric data because price discrimination (which it viewed as pervasive on the high-function EAS markets) rendered these data unreliable, but the court instead found the DOJ had failed to prove that price discrimination was pervasive in any verifiable way.

Thus the DOJ pleaded a significantly narrower theory than the Commission defended in its Statement of Objections, namely one limited to product closeness. In addition, the court's judgment in relation to unilateral effects based on closeness of substitution of the merging parties appears significantly narrower than the Commission's theory.[41] The court's notion that a node must be established in which the merging parties would enjoy a post-merger monopoly or dominant position is not, however, reflected in the Commission's Statement of Objections or in the Decision. Moreover the court found that it is not sufficient 'that the merging parties produce close substitutes' but that it must also be shown 'that the other options available to the buyer are so different that the merging firms likely will not be constrained from acting anticompetitively',[42] which the Commission did not attempt to do. Under the court's theory, it is not sufficient to show that the parties are each other's most important competitors if in fact one or more other rivals is close behind.[43]

Worthy of note in this context is the reference the Commission makes to other factors justifying its finding that no unilateral effects were likely, which were not explicitly identified in the US court's decision. The Commission came to its conclusion that non-coordinated effects are unlikely, *inter alia*, based on its finding that the quantitative analysis of the sales opportunity data (including in particular the substantial amount of data collected after the Oral Hearing during the final months leading up to the Decision) did not provide proof that the number or identity of bidders had an appreciable effect on prices offered.

However, paragraph 205 of the Commission's Decision notes that its conclusion regarding non-coordinated effects was also based on the finding that a number of characteristics of the EAS market rendered these effects unlikely: *first*, the customers involved in the relevant market are sophisticated buyers who can structure the bidding process to exert pressure on the bidders, including reinviting previously excluded bidders, and who control the information flow about who else is bidding and, *second*, the market would still contain more bidders than buyers usually invited in the final round, including a very strong player in the form of SAP.

This finding is perhaps unsurprising in light of the finding that the analysis of the sales opportunity data could not be relied upon. Without evidence that the removal of PeopleSoft as a competitive constraint would have an effect on pricing, the Commission did not have a basis to maintain its non-coordinated effects objections to the merger. The above noted market characteristics further support the Commission's clearance Decision. Had the Commission found that the customers were much less in control of the purchasing process, or that no additional bidders would remain over and above the number usually invited to participate in a sales opportunity, those factors in and of themselves would not have justified a prohibition, because they would not have provided proof of a price effect. As these factors were not central to the finding of whether unilateral effects were likely to occur or not, it was not surprising that the US court did not address them at any length in its decision. It is nevertheless interesting to observe the kinds of non-quantitative evidence related to market characteristics the Commission will take into account in evaluating the likelihood that non-coordinated effects will follow from a merger, as they are not described in detail in the Horizontal Merger Guidelines.

*Evidentiary matters*   A final example of significant substantive transatlantic divergence between the agencies in the *Oracle/PeopleSoft* case can be found in the manner in which they treated the burden of proving the concerns they alleged, and in the way in which they collected and analysed supporting evidence.

GENERAL   The Commission initially relied on information gathered through information requests to Oracle and its customers and competitors, as well as data supplied by PeopleSoft. It also conducted a discount regression analysis and applied a merger simulation model. As noted above, as part of its information requests, it collected (an ultimately very significant amount of) sales opportunity data. The analysis of this data ultimately showed that the number or identity of competitors involved in an opportunity did not influence the discounts awarded by Oracle.[44]

The DOJ based its decision to request an injunction on the internal documents gathered from Oracle and on information gathered from customers, PeopleSoft and other competitors. The sources of information available to each agency were therefore very similar. However, unlike the Commission, the DOJ was required to prove its assertions to a court, but this also meant it had the advantage of obtaining evidence from Oracle, PeopleSoft and other market participants through discovery. The DOJ also relied on information provided by PeopleSoft, statements by market participants, and presented discount regressions and a merger simulation. Perhaps because of the nature of a US court proceeding, the DOJ at trial relied heavily on oral witness testimony, which generally does not play a role in proceedings before the Commission.[45]

SALES OPPORTUNITY DATA    Unlike the Commission, the DOJ did not collect sales opportunity data and, consequently, it could not provide a detailed analysis of these data at trial.[46] This is surprising in view of the fact that the Commission did conduct a sales opportunity data analysis and had collected the relevant data, and that Oracle had provided both agencies with a waiver of confidentiality, which would have allowed the DOJ to analyse at least the data provided by Oracle. In view of the different types of data which Commission and the DOJ may have access to during their review processes, the degree of cooperation between the two agencies and the increasing importance of economic analysis of data in the review of mergers, the role of waivers provided by the parties is potentially very significant. In principle, a waiver is a concession made by the notifying party or parties to assist the agencies by allowing them to exchange information, and not a right on which the agencies can insist. In practice, however, notifying parties are all too keen to retain good relations with the agencies reviewing their transaction, and refusals to grant an agency a waiver are viewed as potentially damaging to the constructive relationship with the agency. This psychological advantage that the agencies have, particularly at the initiation of an investigation, gives them significant leverage to exact broad waivers that allow fairly extensive exchange of information between them.

In theory, these waivers should allow both agencies to circumvent the drawbacks of their respective evidence-gathering procedures. However, much depends on the frequency of communications between the agencies and the resources available to deal with this 'foreign' evidence. Current merger practice would seem to suggest there is no systematic and institutionalized mode, regularity or intensity of contact between them. In addition, they often lack the resources or the time to consider fully the evidence that could be generated through the use of waivers.

DISCOVERY EVIDENCE    Neither the Commission nor the DOJ had the ability to gather the extensive internal documentation and testimony from the parties and third parties that Judge Walker had access to at trial following an extensive process of discovery. However, as the result of the suspension of Phase II proceedings following its final request for information, the Commission could (and, much to its credit, did) ultimately take advantage of the evidence revealed at the US trial. Among the more interesting pieces of information for purposes of the Commission's investigation that became available at trial was information obtained from competitors about their sales and sales plans, which provided further evidence suppliers other than Oracle, PeopleSoft and SAP were present in the high-function HRM and FMS markets. Without the trial, the Commission could not have had access to this information, which highlights the evidentiary limitations to which the Commission is subject compared to a full US proceeding.

MERGER SIMULATION MODELS   Both the DOJ and the Commission made use of merger simulation models to predict the effects of the merger. Referring to such models as 'evidence' is perhaps inappropriate, insofar as econometric models are economists' creations and do not provide proof (but merely an indication) of the potential effects of the merger on the basis of the economists' hypotheses.

Because a merger simulation model is invariably prepared by economists on behalf of the agency or the parties (that is to say, not in an impartial manner), and often depends on controverted hypotheses about the definition or structure of the market and the factors influencing competition on the market, the results of these models unfortunately tend not to be very surprising. Depending on whether the model is presented to support objections to the transaction or the absence thereof, the model will tend to show or not to show a significant price increase as a result of the merger. For this reason, it has been suggested that agencies should seek to employ models that are actually used in business by business people, although it is not clear that many businesses actually apply such models in practice. Another concern with models is that they try to distil into a limited number of variables what is usually too complex to be captured in a formula, as a result of which these models are often accused of presenting oversimplifications (for example, the potential for repositioning, the significance of buyer power and so on). Apart from potentially reflecting a distorted view of the actual effect of the merger, this tendency towards simplification renders these models subject to attack by opposing economists, leading to a debate between economists about the model and distracting attention away from the effects of the transaction itself (a 'battle of the models').

In defence of merger simulations, it has been pointed out that no methodology reliably predicts the effects of mergers, and that the virtue of simulation is focusing the investigation on facts and assumptions that are most pertinent. However, one of the advantages of the use of merger simulation models is also its greatest potential pitfall: attempts to focus on the most relevant facts can also lead to ignoring other relevant factors.

The Commission and the DOJ each took a different view of which type of econometric model was most appropriate to estimate the effects of the Oracle/PeopleSoft merger. In its model first presented in the Statement of Objections, the Commission's economists assimilated the EAS sales process to a sealed bid auction. In a sealed bid auction, bidders simultaneously submit bids so that no bidder knows the bid of any other participant. The highest bidder pays the price they submitted. By contrast, the DOJ took the view that a simpler model, the English auction or oral ascending auction model, best fitted the facts of the relevant market. Unlike a sealed bid auction, in an oral auction analysis, participants bid openly against one another, with each bid being higher than the previous bid. The auction ends when no participant is willing to bid further, or when a predetermined 'buy-out' price is reached, at which point the highest bidder pays the price. Put simplistically, the DOJ's model assumed the vendors knew the prices offered by their competitors, while, in the Commission's model, it was assumed that only the customer knew the terms offered by each vendor.[47]

Both models were designed on the assumption that there was a high-function market on which there were only three bidders, SAP, Oracle and PeopleSoft, in which contracts were awarded to the best bidder on the basis of an auction. These assumptions appeared to be contradicted by the realities of the EAS business, to which a high-function market definition concept was foreign and in which the process of selling EAS was more akin to a complex negotiation than the straightforward auction suggested by either model. Ultimately both the US court and the Commission concluded that the respective simulation models led to unreliable predictions of competitive harm because both relied on incorrect assumptions. The US court found that the model presented by the DOJ's economic expert relied on unreliable estimates of market shares, while the Commission found that its own model did not yield useful results as it assumed fewer market participants than the Commission ultimately acknowledged that participated in the high function market.

However, where the model is carefully designed to reflect as many factors as possible that influence the competitive process, where it relies on assumptions about the market that are agreed to be accurate and reliable, and where it is calibrated and applied to take into account the different views about the key issues involved in the transaction in order to allow an objective testing of these diverging views and the price effects, merger simulation models may still indeed provide a useful complement to empirical evidence and other forms of economic analysis. Neither the US court nor the Commission rejected the potential value of econometric models generally. Indeed the Commission explicitly stated that merger simulation models could be a useful tool to assist the Commission in undertaking an economic assessment of the likely impact of a merger.

In sum, the *Oracle/PeopleSoft* case reflects less coherence between the review processes of the authorities than one might conclude from the similar outcome of both procedures. At the same time, the case also shows the Commission's willingness to take into account evidence from the US proceedings, which contributed to the Commission's ultimate decision to clear the transaction.[48]

**Conclusion**

What does the *Oracle/PeopleSoft* review on both sides of the Atlantic tell us about how mergers raising potential unilateral effects issues are likely to be dealt with and whether cooperation between the Commission and the DOJ will lead to a consistent review of mergers?

As regards the treatment of unilateral effects, although the *Oracle/PeopleSoft* transaction was reviewed under the EMCR before its substantive test was amended, the Commission's decision to clear with regard to its unilateral effects concerns was not based explicitly or solely on a finding that it did not have the power to apply unilateral effects analysis below the dominance threshold, and it fully pursued this analysis in its Decision in order to reach its conclusion. The case could have thus provided a source of information as to how unilateral effects will be analysed by the Commission. However, by basing its clearance decision on a finding that there were additional players on the high function market, the Commission did not answer many questions raised by a unilateral effects analysis. For example, when will the Commission employ a traditional market structure analysis and when will it apply a direct measurement of anticompetitive effects through use of econometric techniques? If the Commission applies econometric techniques, which ones will it use? What percentage price increase must be predicted to result from a merger in order to lead to its prohibition on the basis of unilateral effects? These questions remain unanswered even after the issuance of the new ECMR and the Horizontal Merger Guidelines, and will need to be addressed in the Commission's decision practice under the new ECMR in future cases.

With respect to coordination between the agencies in such cases, *Oracle/PeopleSoft* suggests that the close cooperation between the agencies led to some degree of deference by the Commission to the DOJ's views, and high-level consistency between the views of the agencies. Further coordination on a uniform approach to the hypotheses underlying the investigation, *e.g.*, market definition, the types of evidence relied on, or the standards applicable to the theories of harm investigated could have proved fruitful to the agencies. However, the *Oracle/PeopleSoft* case also highlights that the two agencies face different constraints, and that coordination and consistency do not necessarily imply uniformity of approach, as the Commission will conduct an independent analysis of the transaction and reach its own conclusions, from the perspective of EC law and within the procedural framework imposed on it. In the *Oracle/PeopleSoft* case, the Commission ultimately conducted the most rigorous analysis on the basis of the broadest evidentiary basis available.

## Notes

1. Clifford Chance LLP, Brussels. Both authors represented Oracle Corporation throughout the European Commission's review of its acquisition of PeopleSoft Inc., as well as in connection with Oracle's subsequent acquisition of Siebel Systems Inc., also referred to in this text. The authors are grateful to their colleagues Frances Dethmers, Anna Morfey and Alexis Gerratt for their insightful comments on an earlier draft of this chapter.
2. Council of Ministers of the European Union (2004), Council Regulation (EC) No 139/2004 of 20 January 2004 on the control of concentrations between undertakings [2004] OJ L 24/1.
3. Council of Ministers of the European Union (1989), Council Regulation (EEC) No 4064/89 of 21 December 1989 on the control of concentrations between undertakings [1989] OJ L 395/1 as amended by Council Regulation (EC) No 1310/97 of 30 June 1997 [1997] OJ L 180/1.
4. Ibid., Article 2(2) and (3). In this text, where relevant, Council Regulation (EC) No 139/2004 will be referred to as 'Regulation 139/2004' or the 'new ECMR' and Council Regulation (EEC) No 4064/89 as the 'old ECMR'.
5. See Baxter, S. and F. Dethmers (2005), 'Unilateral effects under the European Merger Regulation: how big is the gap?', [2005] *ECLR*, 380; Gonzales-Diaz, F. (2004), 'The reform of European merger control: Quid novi sub sole?', *World Competition*, **27**(2), 177–99: 'However, it is submitted that the reality is that the substantive threshold of intervention under the new test remains unchanged [. . .]. There is no reason thus why the elimination of the dominance criterion as the only assessment criterion should lead to a lowering of the intervention threshold.'
6. See generally Baxter, S. and F. Dethmers (2005), 'Unilateral effects under the European Merger Regulation: how big is the gap?', [2005] *ECLR*, 380. Below, the terms 'unilateral effects' (the term commonly applied in US merger review practice) and 'non-coordinated effects' (the term adhered to by the European Commission) are generally used as shorthand to refer to the review of the likelihood of competitive harm on the basis of the theory of unilateral effects under the single dominance threshold, to distinguish the unilateral effects theory of harm from the theory of single dominance.
7. European Commission (2004), Press Release on the *Oracle/PeopleSoft* clearance decision, IP/04/1312, 26 October.
8. Case COMP/M.3216, *Oracle/PeopleSoft*, C(2004) 4217 final, Commission Decision of 26 October 2004 ('Decision'), unpublished. A non-confidential version of this Decision is available at http://europa.eu.int/comm/competition/mergers/cases/decisions/m3216_en.pdf. A non-confidential summary of the Commission's Decision ('Summary') is contained in [2005] OJ L 218/6. References to the Decision in this text relate to the full version of the Decision. Where statements included in the Decision and referred to in this text are reflected in the Summary, references to the paragraph numbers in the Summary are provided. The full order of Judge Vaughn Walker of the Federal District Court for the Northern District of California, which led to clearance of the merger in the US, can be found at 331 F.Supp.2d 1098.
9. PeopleSoft strongly resisted the takeover, and the companies fought each other in the courts and in advertisements.
10. Second requests are requests issued by the reviewing agency (the DOJ or the Federal Trade Commission) in the context of a merger review of a transaction for 'additional information and documentary material relevant to the proposed acquisition'. A Second Request combines a burdensome set of interrogatories with what is usually a very extensive document request. After an initial Hart–Scott–Rodino Act (HSR) filing is made,

a waiting period, typically 30 days, must be observed prior to closing. If substantive antitrust issues cannot be resolved during that period, the agency will issue a Second Request to each party to the transaction. Issuance of a Second Request extends the HSR waiting period, typically until 30 days after certification of 'substantial compliance' with the Second Request. See 15 U.S.C. §18a. Productions of 1000 or more boxes of documents in response to a Second Request have become commonplace in US merger review proceedings. See Cook, Robert N., 'The paperless Second Request', available at http://www.ftc.gov/bc/bestpractices/robertcook.pdf.

11.  Council Regulation (EEC) No 4064/89, Article 4(1).
12.  Article 6(1)(c) Decision in Case No COMP/M.3216, *Oracle/PeopleSoft*, 17 November 2003, SG (2003) D/232949, unpublished, referenced at the following website: http://europa.eu.int/comm/competition/mergers/cases/index/by_dec_type_art_6_1_c.html.
13.  Statement of Objections in Case No COMP/M.3216, *Oracle/PeopleSoft*, SG-Greffe (2004) D/200967, not published.
14.  Along with other cases such as *Sony/Bertelsmann*, the *Oracle/PeopleSoft* case suggests that the emphasis of the Courts and the Commission on the need to support prohibition decisions with solid economic evidence has increased the importance of the Oral Hearing, which can serve as a forum for confrontation and explanation of the different pieces of economic evidence against and in support of the transaction.
15.  *Oracle/PeopleSoft*, 331 F.Supp.2d 1098 (ND. Cal. 2004).
16.  Decision, paragraph 219. As discussed below, the Commission interpreted dominance to cover single dominance, coordinated effects as well as unilateral effects below the dominance threshold.
17.  See also Reeves, T. (April 2005), 'Some reflections on significant recent cases', Advanced EC Competition Law Conference, IBC, London.
18.  Commission press release regarding the initiation of Phase II, IP/03/1556, 17 November 2003; Commission press release regarding its decision to clear the transaction, IP/04/1312; Loughran, M. and J. Gatti (Spring 2005), 'Merger control: main developments between 1 September and 31 December 2004', *Competition Policy Newsletter*, 73 at page 75.
19.  See *Oracle/PeopleSoft*, 331 F.Supp.2d 1098 (ND. Cal. 2004) at 1165 and Decision, paragraphs 187–205, and Statement of Objections in Case No COMP/M.3216, *Oracle/PeopleSoft*, SG-Greffe (2004) D/200967, not published, paragraphs 224–64. It is, however, unclear whether the authorities argued in favour of the same substantive standard to assess closeness of substitution. The Commission appears to have argued that the standard should be 'close competitors for a substantial number of customers'. The DOJ by contrast appears to have argued that Oracle and PeopleSoft were each other's closest competitors without qualification (i.e., for a majority of customers). See DOJ Post Trial Brief, filed 13 July 2004, 31:8 and Statement of Objections in Case No COMP/M.3216, *Oracle/PeopleSoft*, SG-Greffe (2004) D/200967, not published, paragraph 245.
20.  See DOJ Post Trial Brief, filed 13 July 2004, 31:8 and Statement of Objections in Case No COMP/M.3216, *Oracle/PeopleSoft*, SG-Greffe (2004) D/200967, not published, paragraph 245.
21.  See DOJ Post Trial Brief, filed 13 July 2004, 14:23–20:12; Decision, paragraphs 88–115.
22.  See DOJ Post Trial Brief, filed 13 July 2004, 46:18; *Oracle/PeopleSoft*, 331 F.Supp.2d 1098 (ND. Cal. 2004) at 1175.
23.  Sees DOJ Post Trial Brief, filed 13 July 2004, 2:2; Statement of Objections in Case No COMP/M.3216, *Oracle/PeopleSoft*, SG-Greffe (2004) D/200967, not published, paragraph 224.
24.  See generally: *Oracle/PeopleSoft*, 331 F.Supp.2d 1098 (ND. Cal. 2004) and the Decision.
25.  The European Commission and the DOJ used different acronyms to refer to the same type of software. The European Commission referred to 'HR' and 'FMS' software whereas the DOJ referred to 'HRM' and 'FMS' software.
26.  See Decision, paragraph 116.

27. See *Oracle/PeopleSoft*, 331 F.Supp.2d 1098 (ND. Cal. 2004) at 1123–4.
28. *Oracle/PeopleSoft*, 331 F.Supp.2d 1098 (ND. Cal. 2004) at 1158.
29. Ibid.
30. The Commission's proxies for the high-function market were initially designed on the basis of the hypothesis adopted early in Phase I of its procedure that the relevant market was 'the market for core HR and FMS software for large enterprises'. See Article 6(1)(c) Decision in Case No COMP/M.3216, *Oracle/PeopleSoft*, 17 November 2003, SG (2003) D/232949, paragraphs 8–35, not published.
31. It did so in spite of evidence that custom-built solutions are very prevalent in the EAS industry and continue to be a viable option for customers. Indeed studies predict the popularity of custom-built solutions will increase with the increased use of open source software and Web services. However, the Commission has traditionally excluded in-house solutions from the market and continues to do so, most recently in its definition of the market in the *Oracle/Siebel* case, which also involved EAS software. See Case COMP No M/3978, *Oracle/Siebel* (not yet published).
32. The DOJ does hint at this view in its post-trial brief, but it was never argued by the DOJ's trial attorneys.
33. See the Commission's Guidelines on the assessment of horizontal mergers under the Council Regulation on the control of concentrations between undertakings [2004] OJ C31/5, paragraphs 22 and 24.
34. Guidelines on the assessment of horizontal mergers under the Council Regulation on the control of concentrations between undertakings [2004] OJ C31/5.
35. Statement of Objections, paragraph 260.
36. Statement of Objections, paragraph 224.
37. Case T-102/96 *Gencor* v. *Commission* [1999] ECR II-753 and *Kali and Salz* [1998] ECR I-1375.
38. In particular, Recital 14. However the Commission's justification of non-coordinated effects as a category of collective dominance would appear to find no support either in the case law of the European Court on collective dominance or in the Commission's Horizontal Merger Guidelines.
39. Statement of Objections, paragraphs 219–23.
40. Decision, paragraph 187.
41. Judge Walker's view on the requirements for a finding of unilateral effects is also narrower than the view taken by the DOJ, with respect to the need to show that the merged entity would be able to exercise monopoly power within the 'node'.
42. 34:23–6.
43. 143:24–144:8.
44. It appears to be becoming increasingly common for the Commission to request very significant amounts of data from merging parties as well as third parties, in large measure as the result of the increased role of economic analysis in the Commission's review of mergers. Often companies will not have maintained the information requested by the Commission, and its collection will be time-consuming, which may be a problem in view of the deadlines the Commission's review is subjected to under the ECMR. Merging parties who do not collect relevant data early in preparation of the Commission's review may be faced with delays in the review process as a result of suspensions of the ECMR time periods following a failure to respond to the Commission's information requests in a timely manner. Merging parties are therefore often well served by collecting data early. As third parties may also be faced with a request for data, which they are obliged to provide under penalty of fines, one could ask whether companies who have not retained data such as information on sales opportunities should consider doing so for purposes of their ability to dispense quickly with an increasing number of Commission requests for data.
45. The DOJ was criticized by the Court and by commentators for relying heavily on anecdotal customer predictions of harm, which the customers did not substantiate. The Commission did not rely on witness testimony, but does rely on individual customer statements in its Statement of Objections and its Decision to substantiate a number of its findings.

46. The DOJ limited itself to collecting discount approval forms, documents retained by Oracle on the basis of which sales people requested authorization from their managers to grant discounts to win a sales opportunity, which contained a fairly limited amount of information, and the fairly limited amount of information Oracle kept on sales opportunities in electronic form, which was not very reliable and also incomplete.
47. While the Commission's approach seems closer to approximate reality insofar as it reflects a limited amount of transparency in the market, it also seemed somewhat at odds with the Commission's allegation, retained in its Statement of Objections, in which the model was also presented, that coordinated effects would occur on the basis of, among other factors, market transparency.
48. To a much more limited extent, some evidence collected by the Commission was also evaluated by the Court. Thus the responses of a systems integrator to the Commission's request for information were disclosed in the context of third-party discovery, and the responses of that systems integrator, notably in connection with its views about the likelihood of entry, were debated at trial.

## References

Baxter, S. and F. Dethmers (2005), 'Unilateral effects under the European Merger Regulation: how big is the gap?', *ECLR*, 380.

Cook, Robert N., 'The paperless Second Request', available online at the following website: http://www.ftc.gov/bc/bestpractices/robertcook.pdf.

Council of Ministers of the European Union (1989), Council Regulation (EEC) No 4064/89 of 21 December 1989 on the control of concentrations between undertakings [1989] OJ L 395/1 as amended by Council Regulation (EC) No 1310/97 of 30 June 1997 [1997] OJ L 180/1.

Council of Ministers of the European Union (2004), Council Regulation (EC) No 139/2004 of 20 January 2004 on the control of concentrations between undertakings [2004] OJ L 24/1.

European Commission (2004), Press Release on the *Oracle/PeopleSoft* clearance decision, IP/04/1312, 26 October.

Gonzales-Diaz, F. (2004), 'The reform of European merger control: quid novi sub sole?', *World Competition*, **27**(2), 177–99.

Loughran, M. and J. Gatti (Spring 2005), 'Merger control: main developments between 1 September and 31 December 2004', *Competition Policy Newsletter*, 73.

Reeves, T. (April 2005), 'Some reflections on significant recent cases', Advanced EC Competition Law Conference, IBC, London.

## Cases

*Gencor v. Commission* [1999] ECR II-753.

*Kali and Salz* [1998] ECR I-1375.

*Oracle/PeopleSoft*, Case COMP/M.3216, C(2004) 4217 final, Commission Decision of 26 October 2004 ('Decision'), unpublished. (A non-confidential version of this Decision is available at: http://europa.eu.int/comm/competition/mergers/cases/decisions/m3216_en.pdf. A non-confidential summary of the Commission's Decision ('Summary') is contained in [2005] OJ L 218/6.)

# 3 Merger to monopsony in Canada, Europe and the United States: a selected international comparison
## Margaret Sanderson[1]

## Introduction

In this chapter, I discuss how competition agencies in Canada, Europe and the United States have dealt with mergers that give rise to monopsony (or oligopsony) power concerns.[2] In Canada, several recent mergers involving purchasers of agricultural products and natural resources have raised concerns about excessive buyer power, notwithstanding a finding that downstream markets are competitive.[3] Mergers of processors of agricultural inputs have raised similar concerns in the United States, where some commentators have advocated that different review standards be adopted to deal with monopsony concerns in these marketplaces.[4] In Europe, monopsony concerns have been raised one step higher in the chain of distribution in mergers of large supermarket chains.

While the merger guidelines across Canada, Europe and the United States are clear in stating the analytical issues involved in assessing whether a merger results in market power to a single buyer (or set of coordinating buyers) are no different than if the market power were to arise on the selling side, a review of the cases refutes this claim. Differences exist across the jurisdictions in terms of when buyer power concerns in mergers will raise competition agency scrutiny. In Europe, the Commission's guidelines indicate it will only seek to remedy mergers raising buyer power issues when final consumers are likely to be affected negatively. As a result, it is not sufficient to have market power only in upstream purchasing markets to raise concerns in Europe; upstream and downstream market power have been the concern instead. In Canada and the United States, remedial action has been sought when mergers give rise to monopsony concern notwithstanding competitive downstream markets. As a result, final consumers do not need to be negatively affected.

In the United States, the federal antitrust agencies have sought remedies when the merger is likely to affect economic efficiency negatively. Cases involving a strict transfer of rents from one producer to another by virtue of changed bargaining positions following the merger but which do not have a negative impact on overall efficiency have not been pursued. In

Canada, the record is more mixed. In some merger cases where the Competition Bureau has successfully obtained divestitures based on monopsony concerns, it is not clear in fact that there will be efficiency losses. Instead, some of the Canadian merger remedies appear to be aimed at fixing the distribution of rents between the merging parties and upstream suppliers at pre-merger levels. Distribution concerns are also evident in some of the EU decisions, notwithstanding the guidelines.

There is little doubt that public policy in respect of mergers is often concerned with distributional effects. However this is a much stronger case in instances where consumer welfare is deemed paramount, and hence a consumer welfare standard is the stated policy goal. Among Canada, Europe and the United States, only the European Commission is consistent in adhering to a consumer welfare standard for mergers involving either seller or buyer power. Interestingly the United States, as a strong supporter of consumer welfare when considering mergers involving market power, takes more of a total surplus approach when dealing with mergers involving monopsony power. The Canadian policy is unclear. While until recently Canadian merger policy had a total surplus orientation, this changed with the *Superior Propane* case.[5] Current jurisprudence in Canada requires considering the 'adverse social effects' of wealth transfers from consumers to producers as part of any trade-off analysis between merger efficiencies and anticompetitive effects. Thus far, the Canadian Competition Tribunal has only considered transfers from low-income individuals to the merging firms as adverse social effects. Transfers between firms have not been considered socially adverse. Given this standard, Canadian competition authorities should be closer to the US treatment of mergers involving monopsony issues, and hence intervening only when there are likely to be negative efficiency effects. Redistributing upstream rents between suppliers and merging parties should not be cause for concern.

In the next section, I review the economics of monopsony power. This is followed by discussion of illustrative cases in Canada, the United States and the European Union. Some concluding remarks close the chapter.

### The economics of monopsony power

Monopsony or oligopsony reflect market power on the buying side of the market, as opposed to the more usual competition framework involving market power on the selling side (that is, monopoly or oligopoly power). In the textbook case of monopsony, the sole purchaser chooses the input quantity to purchase in order to maximize the value received from using the input less the total expenditure. When the input is homogeneous, price discrimination is not possible and an upward-sloping supply curve for the input exists,[6] the monopsonist lowers the input price by lowering its input purchases below competitive levels. It is only by reducing its purchases that the monopsonist is able to reduce the input purchase price because lowering the price of one unit also serves to lower the price paid for all other units.[7]

The source of inefficiency is the reduced input purchase quantities: the below-competitive input purchase level is associated with an allocative inefficiency (or 'deadweight loss') caused by the monopsonist's decision not to purchase additional units for which the marginal value exceeds the marginal cost of the input supply. This is analogous to the familiar deadweight loss or allocative inefficiency associated with the exercise of market power when considering monopoly.[8]

Economists' concern with monopsony stems from the efficiency loss associated with fewer inputs being purchased relative to a competitive market. As a result, it is important to distinguish monopsony from arguments over the split of upstream profits among possible suppliers. It is possible the merger may change the bargaining position of purchasers in their dealings with suppliers, thereby shifting the terms of trade between purchasers and suppliers, but this need not alter the quantity of input purchases.[9]

Alternatively the structure of pricing may be non-linear, having two-part tariffs (i.e., a fixed fee plus a payment based on volume purchased), or quantity discounts, which may allow the merged firm to reduce the total payment made to suppliers without reducing the quantity of inputs purchased from those suppliers. In such circumstances, there is no monopsony efficiency loss, although to the extent that returns to input suppliers are reduced over the longer term we might expect reduced entry or possible exit in the production of inputs, which in turn should raise returns to input suppliers again. If, instead, a reduction in the economic return to suppliers reduces their output over the longer term owing to barriers to entry in input supply markets, there is an efficiency loss. The theoretical case used to illustrate this type of monopsony power in economic textbooks is the small, isolated town with one mill as employer that seeks to lower wage rates. A single buyer of labour exists – the mill. It faces numerous individual labourers without any offsetting bargaining power. The monopsony mill sells its output in a competitive downstream market. A South African case involving a gold mine's acquisition of services provides one of the few real examples where the textbook monopsony case was argued to exist.[10]

Note that monopsony power can exist even when output markets are competitive, as ultimately what matters are the alternatives available to input suppliers. An efficiency loss is still evident even with competitive downstream markets, since input suppliers that would have produced the relevant input at the competitive marginal cost of doing so do not supply it owing to the distorted input prices. As a result, there is a clear economic case to be made for blocking mergers that are likely to lead to substantial monopsony power, even if output markets are competitive. There is an even stronger case to be made for blocking mergers that enhance market power on the buying and selling sides of the market as the efficiency losses associated with monopsony are enhanced when market power in output markets exists.[11]

At the same time, competitive output markets may act to attenuate monopsony concerns in the following manner. When the merging firms compete in competitive output markets and when inputs are combined in fixed proportions to yield final output, any reduction of input purchases necessarily reduces the merged firm's outputs. By reducing input purchases, the monopsonist cedes market share in the output market.[12] As a result, while input costs may decline owing to lower input prices and lower input purchases, these potential cost savings may be offset by the reduction in margin earned on the forgone output.

The ability of the input purchaser to force a price and input purchase reduction below competitive levels depends critically on the alternatives that are available to suppliers. If suppliers have numerous ready alternatives, then supply is highly elastic. At high firm supply elasticities, any attempt to lower input prices will require a considerable reduction in input purchases. As a result, the input purchaser will have little ability to suppress price below the competitive level, implying little loss in efficiency.

Something similar can occur when the value to the purchaser of the marginal input purchased increases rapidly for slightly lower purchase levels. For instance, it might be the case that at the typical level of purchases one additional unit of input more or less makes little difference, but for somewhat lower input purchases an additional input is extremely valuable because it allows the monopsonist to produce at lower cost. In this case too, the monopsonist would have a very limited incentive to reduce input prices by cutting back on its purchases.

With this economic framework in mind, what have competition agencies been doing?

**Canada**
The Competition Bureau has examined monopsony issues in several recent mergers. Monopsony has been most extensively examined in beef packing and forestry mergers, where upward-sloping supply curves are possible.[13] These cases provide interesting contrasts, as the Bureau has made the most information and the more comprehensive economic analysis available in the matters it decided not to challenge. Where the Bureau has succeeded in obtaining the merging parties' consent to divestiture remedies based on

monopsony concerns the public record of analysis is minimal. These cases appear not to meet the economic conditions associated with efficiency loss, putting the need for remedies in doubt.

Monopsony issues remain an active area of examination in Canada, as the recent filing by the Bureau challenging a proposed grain-handling joint venture attests. On 10 November 2005, the Bureau filed an application before the Competition Tribunal challenging a grain handling joint venture between the Saskatchewan Wheat Pool and James Richardson International Limited at the Port of Vancouver. While framed as a situation of reduced competition for the marketing of grain-handling services to third party grain companies, mergers involving grain elevators may be viewed as monopsony cases.[14]

*Cargill Limited/Better Beef Group of Companies*
The last Canadian merger that raised potential monopsony concerns involved Cargill Limited's ('Cargill') acquisition of the Better Beef Group of Companies ('Better Beef'). Cargill is one of Canada's largest agricultural merchandisers and processors operating in a wide range of businesses, including integrated beef packing, with significant packing facilities based in Western Canada. Better Beef operates the largest integrated beef-packing facility in Eastern Canada, the main product of which is boxed beef. The Bureau examined the competitive effects of the transaction in four areas: (i) cattle procurement; (ii) production and disposition of hides and rendering source products; (iii) production, distribution and sale of boxed beef; and (iv) production, distribution and sale of case-ready beef. In addition to Better Beef and Cargill, there are two other large packers with operations in Western Canada and two packers with smaller facilities in Ontario. Concentration among Canadian firms is high as a result.

Shortly before dealing with the Cargill/Better Beef merger, the Bureau had completed a broader investigation of monopsony allegations made against Canadian packers following the US and other countries' ban on imports of Canadian beef with the discovery of bovine spongiform encephalopathy ('BSE') in Canada in May 2003.[15] With the closure of the US border, prices for Canadian cattle plummeted, yet beef prices remained at historical levels, yielding substantial profits for packers. As a result, packers were accused of coordinating the prices paid to ranchers for cattle contrary to the conspiracy provisions of the Competition Act, and also of engaging in anti-competitive practices contrary to the abuse of dominance provisions of the Competition Act, notably refusal to deal, using captive supply to drive down cattle prices and margin squeezing. There were also allegations of strategic bidding among packers to depress cattle prices, black listing or boycotting of auction houses, cattle producers or feedlots attempting to sell cattle, and reducing prices offered for cattle by an amount equivalent to government aid. In late April 2005, the Bureau reported the results of its investigation, finding no evidence of conduct contrary to the Competition Act.[16]

As part of its investigation, the Bureau commissioned three expert studies: one industry study,[17] which analysed the cattle and beef markets prior to and after the BSE discovery; and two economic studies, which employed advanced empirical techniques, to study the impact of the BSE discovery on Canadian cattle prices.[18] Prior to the BSE discovery Canada and the United States comprised one North American market for cattle and beef pricing: about 23 per cent of Canadian cattle destined for slaughter were exported to United States packers prior to the BSE discovery,[19] and an even greater percentage of Canadian beef was exported to the United States – over 70%.[20] Canadian cattle prices are found to move together with US cattle price series in the long run.[21] With the closure of the border, a substantial volume of Canadian cattle and beef supply needed to find alternative buyers, resulting in an acute over-supply situation.[22] Cattle cannot be stored indefinitely; past a certain age, the value embodied in a head of cattle declines.[23] With fewer export options and insufficient Canadian slaughter capacity to accommodate all of the formerly exported cattle, Canadian cattle inventories grew.[24] The border closing represented a significant negative demand shock that had the effect of lowering prices for cattle as Canadian slaughterhouses were operating in an environment with limited excess capacity and substantial oversupply of cattle. Such economic circumstances would naturally lead to lower prices paid to ranchers for cattle. These conditions may also have led to increased monopsony power on the part of Canadian packers, given the reduced number of purchasers available to ranchers.

To disentangle these potential effects, the Bureau relied on economic modelling employing new empirical industrial organization techniques.[25] A structural economic model of the industry was developed that allows for market power of retailers and packers at both the input procurement and output stages. The model accounts for the major parties involved in the beef sector, namely fed/cull cattle suppliers, packers, retailers and consumers. Various assumptions are employed in respect of how prices are determined at the different stages of interaction along the distribution chain.[26] The model is used to develop profit maximization conditions that are then estimated empirically using publicly available monthly price data from January 1997 to September 2004. Parameters to measure market and monopsony power are part of this estimation. To exercise monopsony power, input purchases are reduced, thereby lowering the overall input purchase price below competitive levels. Within the model, monopsony power is possible at the retailer/wholesaler level against beef packers, and also at the packer level against cattle producers – either for fed or cull cattle.[27]

The data used for estimation are at the national level, with the exception of the prices for cattle (fed, feeder, heifer) that are based on Alberta prices. As a result, the 'relevant markets' are implicitly national. This is clearly too broad for some areas, like estimating the potential market power at the retailer level, because retailer markets are local. Indeed it may even be too broad for purposes of estimating monopsony power at the packer level, as the Bureau's examination of the merger involving Cargill and Better Beef found that Better Beef's Ontario facility did not compete to a material degree with Cargill's Alberta facility in cattle procurement. In other areas, a 'national' market may be too narrow, given the extent of trade between Canada and the United States when the border is open.

Making use of national data nonetheless, no appreciable monopsony power of beef packers is found in fed cattle markets, but significant monopsony power is found in cull cattle markets, and this power increased with the border closing.[28] The difference between fed and cull cattle is not surprising given that the US border reopened to boneless beef from cattle under 30 months in age (i.e., fed cattle) shortly after the BSE finding (in September 2003 after the initial border closing in May 2003), and hence there was a far less severe shock affecting the products derived from fed cattle than for cull cattle. As well the results suggest increased monopoly power by packers against wholesalers/retailers with the border closing, which acts to compound the effects on prices for live cattle since increased monopoly power of packers would reduce beef output, and packers' demand for live cattle.[29] Simulations are used in an attempt to distinguish the importance of the market power and monopsony effects.

It is useful to bear in mind the scale of effects that the border closing entailed, particularly for cull cattle and the products derived therefrom. About 31 per cent of the Canadian cull slaughter is exported, and hence the border closing represents a reduction in demand of nearly one-third.[30] The pre-BSE event estimate of monopsony power in cull cattle is 0.198, rising to 0.585 with the border closure (full monopsony power would yield an estimate equal to 1). Given that the estimates of monopsony and market power are well below levels that would indicate collusion, and with no evidence of communication between packers and presumably no evidence of common or joint practices among the packers that might be pursued under joint abuse of dominance, the Bureau closed its investigation.[31]

The fact that some monopsony (or oligopsony) power was found to exist but the estimated magnitude of such power was small is consistent with US studies that have sought to measure oligopsony price distortions in fed and beef cattle markets. In a survey of the various empirical studies that have been undertaken, Ward (2002) concludes that price distortions of 3 per cent or less were found in most studies of monopsony power in meat packing.[32]

The Bureau's empirical findings in the cattle and beef pricing investigation did not lead it to challenge the subsequent merger of Cargill and Better Beef. Instead the Bureau determined there was little direct competitive overlap between the merging parties in the areas over which they procured fed cattle.[33] In contrast to the cattle and beef pricing investigation that used national data, the Bureau's examination of the Cargill/Better Beef merger concluded that there are two relevant geographic markets for cattle procurement: Western Canada (including Manitoba) plus certain US northern plains states, and Eastern Canada plus certain northeastern US states.[34] The distance from Better Beef's facility to cattle producers in Manitoba and other western provinces was the key to this finding. With each firm in a separate geographic market for cattle procurement, the merger was not likely to increase monopsony power.

On the output side, the merging firms were found to operate in a broader North American market in boxed beef, hides and rendering source products. While the Bureau found the geographic market was more limited in respect of case-ready beef,[35] and the merging firms would have a large post-merger share, the Bureau concluded the threat of entry and countervailing power on the part of retail grocery firms made it unlikely that the merger would result in a substantial prevention or lessening of competition. While the empirical study found no evidence of monopsony power at the retailer level, this was based on national data, which is too broad given the Bureau's defined relevant market for case-ready beef. In addition, the Bureau noted that Cargill's two case-ready plants in eastern Canada are dedicated to one large grocery retailer under long-term contract. Market contacts with grocery retailers also unveiled a lack of concern about the merger's impact on prices for case-ready beef to retailers.

There have been three forestry mergers within the British Columbia interior since 2004 that have caused the Competition Bureau to launch extensive investigations related to potential monopsony power. In two of these acquisitions, divestitures of sawmills and associated rights to timber (known as 'tenure') have been consented to by the merging parties in order to complete the acquisitions. The three transactions are: (i) Canfor Corporation's acquisition of Slocan Forest Products Ltd., where one sawmill in northern British Columbia was divested; (ii) West Fraser Timber Co. Ltd.'s acquisition of Weldwood of Canada Ltd., which resulted in a consent agreement to divest two sawmills in the British Columbia interior, and (iii) Tolko Industries Ltd.'s acquisition of Riverside Forest Products Ltd., which resulted in an initial hold separate agreement that has since expired without additional remedies being sought to date.[36]

There is very little public information available from the Competition Bureau on any of these transactions. No competitive impact statements have been filed with the consent agreements before the Competition Tribunal, and no technical backgrounders have been issued on any transaction.

In the Canfor/Slocan merger, the Bureau filed a consent agreement with the Competition Tribunal in late March 2004 requiring Canfor to divest its sawmill in Fort St James following the Slocan acquisition. In the short press release announcing the divestiture, the Bureau indicates the merger would have resulted in 'less choice' for log sellers, wood remanufacturers and wood-chip sellers. The divestiture is noted as preserving competition in the 'Prince George area' of British Columbia for log buying, lumber supply to remanufacturers and the sale and supply of wood chips.

In December 2004, the Bureau filed a consent agreement with the Tribunal requiring West Fraser to divest certain assets following its merger with Weldwood. The Bureau's news release notes the transaction 'could result in a substantial lessening of competition in two local markets', neither of which is defined in the release. The consent agreement requires that West Fraser and Weldwood sell their sawmill interests in Babine Forest Products Limited, in Burns Lake and Decker Lake, along with the mills' associated tenures. West Fraser also agreed to surrender certain timber-harvesting rights in the Williams Lake and 100 Mile House forest districts.[37] The Bureau concluded that these measures would remove significant barriers to competition and permit a new player to enter the market or an existing competitor to expand its capacity.

From the minimal information on the public record, it is impossible to piece together the Bureau's rationale for divestitures in these two transactions. The most basic information such as relevant markets and shares is not disclosed, let alone the theory of competitive harm. As a result, it is impossible to determine whether the Bureau has properly applied the economic theory of monopsony to these cases. Making use of other publicly available information, however, suggests the Bureau's monopsony concerns are unlikely to be ones of economic inefficiency but may instead relate to altered bargaining positions between log suppliers and mills.

As these three forestry mergers (and others that have not been challenged by the Bureau)[38] indicate, the softwood lumber industry in British

Columbia is undergoing consolidation. With each transaction, the merging firms forecast significant efficiencies from larger-scale operations, integrated use of tenure harvests, and optimized mill production.[39] Canadian forestry companies are striving to lower costs in the face of imposition of duties on softwood lumber and the rising value of the Canadian dollar against the US dollar.

Given the lack of information from the Bureau, the following stylized argument is used to illustrate the potential that sawmill mergers have to raise monopsony concerns. Imagine there are numerous log sellers operating in a particular area, some of whom may be quite small (e.g., individuals with private land that harvest timber to supply to nearby mills, or log suppliers who bid on harvest rights under the British Columbia Timber Sales (BCTS) auction programme). The costs involved in shipping logs long distances mean that the number of mills that are willing to compete for a given harvest from a particular area is limited, and as a result geographic markets are circumscribed by transportation costs (although the size of these local markets would be a critical matter of dispute). Thus the markets for the purchase of logs are spatially differentiated. As a result, a merger that reduces the number of potential purchasers for a given set of log suppliers might result in decreased competition for log harvests and lower prices being paid to local suppliers.

Where a single price is paid for logs at the mill (to which transportation costs are added) log supply would be an increasing function of the mill's purchase price. In such circumstances, to lower the price paid for logs, the merged firm would have to reduce its log purchases, which in turn reduces its lumber output, causing it to cede share to rivals in competitive downstream markets. Reduced log purchases also mean lower capacity utilization which lowers mill efficiency. Reducing log purchases to lower log input prices need not improve overall profitability once the impacts on mill efficiency and reduced output are taken into account.

To the extent that the mergers have been driven by a desire to rationalize production by closing smaller, less efficient facilities there may be increased throughput at remaining facilities. But with larger mills the merged firms need greater log volumes to operate efficiently. Not only does this drive demand at the merged firms' mills, but it may also drive demand at neighbouring mills as they respond to the mergers by seeking to improve efficiency at their own facilities.

Consider, for example, the Prince George area where the Bureau required Canfor to divest its Fort St James' mill. Maps of BC sawmill locations available from the US Department of Agriculture Forest Service show a tight clustering of numerous mills surrounding the Canfor and Slocan mills in the Prince George, Fort St James and neighbouring

Vanderhoof forest districts.[40] Within this area, Canfor operated six mills
and Slocan had one mill in 2005. Significant capacity increases are evident
at several mills; for example, the former Slocan mill at Vanderhoof has
capacity to process 1.3 million cubic metres in 2005, up 36 per cent from
2004 and Canfor's two Prince George mills have 2005, capacity at nearly
1.7 million cubic metres, up 30% from 2003 capacity levels. With increasing capacity, the merged firm will be demanding greater volumes of logs,
which is not conducive to exercising monopsony power.[41] Nearby rival
mills have also increased capacity; for example, The Pas Lumber
Company has increased its Prince George mill capacity by 27% from 2004
levels, to 826 000 cubic metres. Another rival, West Fraser, operates a similarly large mill in the vicinity.

With increasing capacity and a densely distributed system of mills, economic theory predicts strong incentives to compete intensively with other
mills for log supply in order to keep the sawmills operating at high capacity, which in turn counteracts any monopsonistic pressure that may come
from increased shares of local mill capacity.[42] Using US data for the
period 1958 to 1988, Murray (1995) estimates these effects for sawmills
and pulpmills. His results are more suggestive of competition than
monopsony overall. In respect of sawlogs, he finds less monopsony power
on average than for pulpmills with time trends showing a steady decline
in monopsony power in sawlog markets.[43] Even where monopsony power
is found to exist in his study (for pulpwood supplies) the estimated distortion is just under 2% of private pulpwood supplies in the 1983–88
period, which he considers small relative to other factors that have
reduced the forest land base.[44]

A second important characteristic of log supply markets that acts
against mergers reducing efficiency through monopsony is price discrimination. Sawmills tend to negotiate log purchases on a seller-by-seller
basis, meaning that the price paid to one supplier need not have any
bearing on what is paid to another. As a consequence, even if a merger
leads to an increase in buyer concentration and this increase in concentration results in an ability to insist on lower log prices from nearby suppliers, a reduction in overall purchases is not necessary to effectuate the
decrease in price.[45] Without a reduction in input purchases, there is no
efficiency loss. Furthermore it is well established in the economics literature that price discrimination can lead to lower average prices and higher
output than would prevail if firms were restricted to a single price.[46] As
well, price discrimination can act to intensify competitive rivalry. In
forestry markets, with firms spatially differentiated, mills will have
differing valuations for log supply, depending on location. Because mills
are typically distributed with a reasonable degree of proximity to each

other, and large mills need greater log supply than the immediately adjacent area can supply to operate efficiently, mills will compete more intensely at the margins of their territory for logs. The margin of one mill's territory may be another mill's inframarginal log supply, however. In such circumstances, the ability to price discriminate is likely to force firms to compete more intensely.[47]

Finally industry characteristics make it unlikely that mills are able implicitly to coordinate their behaviour in a manner that effectively leads to below-competitive input purchases and below-competitive input prices. To coordinate input purchasing effectively would require agreement among a large and diverse set of mills. Mills are not likely to have similar cost structures, giving them differing incentives in respect of log purchases, making it difficult to reach profitable terms of agreement and also making it difficult to monitor adherence to any agreed-upon terms. Monitoring is further complicated by the lack of transparency in setting price terms. Terms are negotiated timber stand by timber stand and involve personal valuations of numerous factors, making it difficult for mills to monitor the terms offered to log suppliers by competing mills.[48] Effective coordination seems highly unlikely pre-merger, and a merger would do little to change this situation.

The foregoing implies that, at worst, a sawmill merger could lead to a shift in bargaining power such that rents are transferred from log suppliers to the merged mills. As this is just a shift in wealth involving no change in the degree of economic efficiency, the inquiry into the effects of the merger should arguably end there.

Nonetheless it might be argued that transfers are a relevant concern for competition policy even when efficiency effects are absent. After all, transfers from consumers to producers are an important consideration in any jurisdiction where merger review seeks to maximize consumer surplus. In my view, however, transfers should not be an important merger policy consideration in monopsony cases. Why should transfers matter in one case but not in the other? The difference stems from the legislative intent. While it might be argued that merger laws should be enforced with a view to maximizing consumer surplus, as opposed to total surplus, there is nothing in the policy and legislative debates to suggest that merger law should be enforced to maximize *some* producers' surplus but not other producers' surplus when total surplus is unchanged and consumers are not negatively affected.

In the case of BC forestry mergers, for example, the source of the transfer will either be log suppliers or the provincial government, as the ultimate owner of much of the timber, given the scale of Crown timber holdings in Canada. Log suppliers using the provincial government timber auction program will be able to pass through much, if not all, of any expected reduction in the price for delivered logs paid by mills, should one exist. Should a merger reduce the localized supply options dramatically, so that the most accessible mills in a particular area will pay less than previously, suppliers will rationally reduce the bids they submit in timber auctions for the right to harvest timber in the affected areas. Competitive suppliers can be expected to pass through the entire amount of the expected price decrease to the province, leaving supplier margins unchanged at the competitive level, and stumpage prices lower post-merger than pre-merger if in fact mills were to seek to reduce input purchase prices. Suppliers of privately-owned wood may not have the ability to pass a price decrease through, and may therefore bear the transfer themselves.

Whether any transfer is borne by the province or by individual suppliers, it is doubtful that merger policy is the appropriate means to remedy any inequities. The province has multiple means to counterbalance any reduction in stumpage revenue should it occur, notably taxation; and if the merger results in higher profits earned by the merged entity, some of this reduction in stumpage revenue will be automatically offset by higher corporate tax revenue. Finally, even in circumstances where one might wish to consider the socially adverse component of transfers, notably those from lower-income entities to higher-income entities, as 'unfair' or in need of remedy, the number of relatively low-income individuals affected by a wealth transfer involving lower prices paid to private timber holders by larger mills are likely to represent a very small fraction of log supply. As a result, any such transfers should be easily counterbalanced by even modest efficiency gains resulting from the mergers.

## United States

Compared to Canada, the US federal antitrust authorities appear to follow more closely an economic framework when assessing monopsony merger cases. These principles are clearly enunciated by the Federal Trade Commission in its statement related to Caremark's acquisition of Advance:

> A buyer has monopsony power – or a group of buyers has oligopsony power – when it can profitably reduce prices in a market below competitive levels by curtailing purchases of the relevant product or service. The exercise of this power causes competitive harm because the monopsonist or the group will shift some purchases to a less efficient source, supply too little output in the downstream market, or do both.
>
> In the present case, there is no reason to expect a monopsony or oligopsony outcome – *i.e.*, one in which overall purchases from pharmacies are reduced –

even if the acquisition enables the merged PBM [prescription benefit management] (or PBMs as a group) to reduce the dispensing fees they pay to retail pharmacies.

. . .

At most, the acquisition is likely to increase the bargaining power of the merged PBM and to increase its shares (and correspondingly reduce the pharmacies' shares) of the gains flowing from contracts between the PBM and the pharmacies.[49]

Caremark Rx is a pharmaceutical services company while Advance PCS is a provider of health improvement services. The merged firm is expected to negotiate the dispensing fees paid to retail pharmacies on a firm by firm basis, and hence there would be no reduction in input purchases following the merger even if the total price paid by the merged Caremark/Advance to retail pharmacies were to decline owing to a change in bargaining power.

While reaching a different conclusion, similar reasoning was applied by the Department of Justice's Antitrust Division in its assessments of Aetna Inc.'s acquisition of the Prudential Insurance Company of America,[50] and Cargill, Incorporated's acquisition of Continental Grain Company. In both Justice Department cases, the mergers proceeded following divestitures.

The Aetna/Prudential merger was alleged to have negative upstream and downstream effects. The monopsony allegations related to the purchase of physician services in Houston and Dallas, Texas. As well, the merger was alleged to end the head-to-head competition between Aetna and Prudential in the sale of health maintenance organization (HMO) and HMO-based point-of-service (HMO-POS) health plans in Houston and Dallas. While specific buying side shares were not given, the merger was alleged to give Aetna output shares of 63% in Houston and 42% in Dallas.[51] In assessing the merged entity's leverage over Houston and Dallas physicians, the Justice Department examined Aetna's aggregate share of all patients in a locality and Aetna's share of individual physicians' businesses. The nature of the relationship between physicians and insurers was such that, as the number of Aetna patients increased for a particular physician, that physician faced increasing costs of replacing Aetna patients should he/she reject Aetna's contract terms.[52] Aetna also had an 'all products clause' in its agreements that required a physician to participate in all of Aetna's health plans if the physician participated in any plan. This clause acts to increase the potential lost income to a physician who rejects the rates or other terms of any one Aetna plan, thereby increasing physician switching costs.

Like the *Caremark* case, Aetna's contracting for physician services was physician (or practice) specific, and hence the standard single price monopsony theory did not apply. Price discrimination existed, but, unlike *Caremark*, the Justice Department expected the Aetna/Prudential merger to lead to inefficient input levels. How so? Lower prices paid to physicians by Aetna were expected to cause some physicians to drop out of the market, to curtail their hours or to spend less time with each Aetna HMO patient, thereby lowering the supply of physician service inputs and driving the expected efficiency loss.[53] It is this context that the Department alleged the merger provided 'Aetna the ability to unduly depress physician reimbursement rates in Houston and Dallas, likely leading to a reduction in quantity or degradation in the quality of physicians' services'.[54] The remedy had Aetna divest its interests in the Houston operations of NYLCare-Gulf Coast and the Dallas operations of NYLCare-Southwest, an earlier acquisition of Aetna's.

In the Cargill/Continental merger, the Justice Department agreed that final output markets were competitive given worldwide markets for grain and oilseed products.[55] As well, the transaction was expected to generate considerable synergies overall as Cargill closed some duplicative facilities and reduced Continental's headquarters staff.[56] Unlike the insurer cases just cited, in this case there is a single input price rather than supplier-specific pricing. The monopsony concerns were twofold. First, post-merger Cargill was alleged to have monopsony power over the purchase of corn, soybeans and wheat from farmers within nine local or regional markets. As the cost of transporting grain is high relative to the value of the product, farmers generally sell their grain within a limited geographic area surrounding their farms.[57] In these areas, farmers were found to depend on competition among Cargill, Continental and only a few other grain companies to obtain a competitive price for their grain,[58] leading to substantial increases in concentration should the merger proceed.[59] While entry into the operation of country elevators is easy and hence no country elevators were required to be divested, this is not the case for port elevators which are larger, more expensive structures, and good deepwater loading sites without environmental risks are limited.[60] Within any port, entry of a new facility would substantially increase port capacity, pressuring prices downward and making entry risky.[61] The Justice Department claimed that many farmers 'located within overlapping Cargill/Continental elevator draw areas depend solely on competition among Cargill, Continental and perhaps a small number of other nearby grain companies to obtain a competitive price for their products'.[62] In order to preserve competition in these localized areas, the merged firm agreed to divest either a Cargill or a Continental elevator in eight (or nine) locations, including four river elevators, two rail elevators and two (or three) port elevators in the US Midwest and West.[63]

The second monopsony concern was that, following the merger, Cargill and one other company would account for approximately 80 per cent of the authorized delivery capacity for settlement of Chicago Board of Trade corn and soybean futures contracts, which would increase the risk of price manipulation. To address this concern, the parties agreed to divest Continental's port elevator in Chicago.[64]

In articulating its theory of competitive harm from the transaction, the Justice Department noted the potential efficiency distortions. On the monopsony issue related to corn, soybean and wheat purchases, the Justice Department expected farmers to respond to lower input prices by growing different crops or changing the location where crops are sold towards more distant locations.[65] In either case, input quantities would be reduced to the merged entity and hence efficiency losses would result. Efficiency losses also occur even if local farmers divert their purchases to more distant elevators as transportation costs rise above otherwise efficient levels. While the direction of the expected effect was first to have the merger reduce prices paid to farmers rather than reduce its input purchases, the Justice Department expected efficiency losses in the form of reduced input purchases and unnecessarily higher costs to farmers for transportation had the divestitures not been agreed to. According to the US Department of Agriculture, the Justice Department estimates were that cash prices to farmers would likely fall by only 1 to 3 per cent, but given the narrow producer profit margins small price reductions would lead to noticeable declines in farmer incomes thereby driving the noted efficiency losses.[66]

Some US commentators argue for a stricter antitrust analysis of mergers involving buyer power issues, and hence mergers involving monopsony allegations should be challenged at lower concentrative thresholds than those involving power in output markets.[67] In making these arguments, Carstensen argues that buyers have different incentives than sellers, most noticeably in respect of the notion of 'cheating' in that, for sellers, while all jointly benefit from higher output prices the incentive for a single seller to expand output at the higher price and hence disrupt coordinated conduct (either implicit or explicit) does not exist on the buying side. In Carstensen's view, all buyers have an interest in keeping input prices low and hence 'cheating' by increasing input prices is less likely. However, this ignores the fact that any seller operating in a competitive output market wants to maximize profits and often the means to do this is through increasing sales. To increase output sales requires greater input purchases, but to increase input purchases more attractive input prices must be offered, and hence the analogous 'incentive to cheat' exists equally on the buying side of the market as it does on the selling side.

Carstensen is also concerned that firms as large buyers in particular product lines have increased incentive to manipulate the public prices for the input. As the prices for many agricultural commodities rely on prices posted on public trading markets, any manipulation of these trading markets has widespread consequences. Such concerns are shared by antitrust authorities, as the Justice Department's actions in respect of the Cargill/Continental merger indicate. Mergers raising monopsony issues are also claimed to increase the potential for price discrimination and may allow firms to dictate terms that transfer risk without appropriate compensation to upstream producers.

In respect of price discrimination, Carstensen notes that in beef cattle preferential contractual terms may be granted to certain producers that are better than the cash market (i.e., spot) terms available to other producers. But, as noted above, price discrimination need not be welfare reducing and may act to increase the rivalry between firms. As well, differential terms need not be true price discrimination in that the product at issue may include different service or volume commitments by the producer that make the bundled offering through the contract more valuable to the buyer than purchases of the product alone (without certain service or quality commitments) on the spot market.

In respect of the transference of inappropriate levels of risk, Carstensen's concern is that the monopsonist processor transfers inordinate risk back to producers, perhaps owing to pressures the processor faces from powerful retailers, which consumes the producers' capital invested in the production of the input, given the sunk and large switching costs faced by producers – that is, they have few alternatives in the short run for their capital investments. Carstensen notes that this concern is more than one of a simple wealth transfer, since the attractiveness of entry and innovation at the producer level is reduced and government subsidies may increase to prop up producers. Yet, in the longer run, as exit of producers occurs the returns to producers should rise and hence the market would be expected to readjust of its own accord, albeit government intervention may preclude efficient restructuring.

In response to these claims, Marius Schwartz replied that there is no economic reason to have different standards or treatment of buyer power relative to selling power.[68] The economics is clear that customers in downstream markets do not have to be negatively affected to justify taking a monopsony merger case. Where there is an efficiency distortion in respect of input markets, as Schwartz believes existed in respect of the Cargill/Continental transaction, antitrust action is warranted. On the question of whether an input reduction is needed to justify action or transfers alone are enough, Schwarz appears agnostic. He notes that, even in instances where wealth transfers are the only potential merger impacts either in the short or long run, there may be policy reasons to oppose a merger with distributional impacts.[69]

**Europe**

The analytical framework used by the European Commission's Competition Directorate-General ('DG Comp') to assess mergers creating or strengthening buyer power is found at paragraphs 61–3 of its Horizontal Merger Guidelines. At paragraph 61, DG Comp makes the link between reduced input purchases leading to lower input prices the relevant concern:

> The Commission may also analyse to what extent a merged entity will increase its buyer power in upstream markets. On the one hand, a merger that creates or strengthens the market power of a buyer may significantly impede effective competition, in particular by creating or strengthening a dominant position. The merged firm may be in a position to obtain lower prices by reducing its purchase of inputs.[70]

Unlike Canada or the United States, DG Comp goes on to link these upstream effects with consumer impacts in downstream markets, noting that the reduced input purchases 'may, in turn, lead [the merged firm] also to lower its level of output in the final product market, and thus harm consumer welfare'. The focus on consumer welfare is emphasized again at paragraphs 62–3 of the Guidelines, which note:

> increased buyer power may be beneficial for competition. If increased buyer power lowers input costs without restricting downstream competition or total output, then a proportion of these cost reductions is likely to be passed on to consumers in the form of lower prices.
>   In order to assess whether a merger would significantly impede effective competition by creating or strengthening buyer power, an analysis of the competitive conditions in upstream markets and an evaluation of the possible positive and negative effects described above are therefore required.

With such an approach in place, there should be fewer mergers challenged on the basis of monopsony concerns in Europe since the Guidelines indicate both upstream and downstream output effects are required. As a result, unlike the case of North America, where mergers among processors of agricultural or natural resource products have raised monopsony issues, no similar concerns have been expressed by DG Comp, presumably because downstream agricultural markets (e.g., wheat) or natural resource products (e.g., lumber) are typically broadly defined and hence frequently competitive. Instead the cases raising substantial monopsony concerns for DG Comp have been in respect of supermarket mergers as these involved substantial increases in downstream concentration levels as well. Supermarket mergers have also raised competition issues in some EU countries.[71]

Buyer power and its impact on competition in food retailing was the subject of a detailed study commissioned by DG Comp in 1999.[72] As part of this study, the food retailing sectors in France, Germany, Spain and the United Kingdom were examined with attention paid to the impacts on three product groups: washing powders and detergents, coffee, and butter and margarine. While the food distribution sectors in each country had become more concentrated over time, since many grocery products will not have upward sloping supply curves[73] or have relatively few producers,[74] there are likely to be few mergers that cause efficiency losses due to monopsony. Indeed, while some supermarket chain mergers have raised competition concerns, many more have occurred without incident.[75] The study's authors recommend adoption of an analytical framework for the analysis of buyer power that poses the following questions: (i) is there significant buyer power?; (ii) is the buying power against relatively powerless suppliers?; (iii) does the buyer have significant selling power?; (iv) are there significant productive efficiency gains associated with buyer power?; and (v) does the buyer attempt to constrain its suppliers' other actions or deliberately create a 'dependency relationship'?[76] Where buyer power is found to exist following a merger, action is only recommended when such power is exercised against relatively powerless suppliers, the buyer has significant selling power and no productive efficiency gains exist from the exercise of the buying power. The Dobson study's framework has not been applied in all cases, as noted below. In particular, there is little in some of the European case decisions to indicate application of the economic theory of monopsony; instead some mergers have raised concerns owing to the prospect of a change in bargaining positions between suppliers and supermarkets post-merger.

In one of its early decisions in this area, DG Comp declared the Kesko/Tuko merger to be incompatible with the common market in 1996. The case is not strictly one of monopsony, as the Commission found the merged entity would be dominant in respect of output markets. The relevant market having been defined as limited to supermarkets and no broader than Finland,[77] the merger would have led to substantial concentration. Post-merger, nationally Kesko's share would have been at least 55% of the Finnish market.[78] In different local markets, Kesko's post-merger share varied between 40% and 90%.[79] Additional considerations were found to augment Kesko's dominance beyond market share such as Kesko's control over large retail outlets, sites suited for retail outlets in Finland, customer loyalty schemes and private label products, and their buying position.[80] In respect of its buying power, Kesko's dominant position in output markets was found to provide it with substantial bargaining power over suppliers. This gate-keeper position in combination with Kesko's and Tuko's private label products that compete with suppliers' products would have allowed the merged firm to extract concessions from suppliers in respect of prices and marketing support with the outcome that effective competition would be significantly impeded. In such circumstances it is easy to see that the merged firm could have reduced its input purchases from suppliers, substituting its private label products, in order to lower prices from suppliers.

In 1999, the Commission dealt with the Rewe/Meinl supermarket merger in Austria, ultimately approving the transaction following significant restructuring of the transaction. Given the Commission's concerns that the originally proposed acquisition would provide the merged Rewe/Billa/ Meinl with a dominant position in eastern Austria, particularly in Vienna where it would hold a 65–70% market share, rising to over 80% in eight of Vienna's 23 districts,[81] Rewe agreed to only acquire the Meinl outlets outside Eastern Austria (i.e. Vienna, Lower Austria and Northern Burgenland) and an additional number of Meinl outlets throughout Austria that would be converted into drugstores.[82] In addition to its large share position, the Commission noted that, compared to competitors, Rewe/Billa and Meinl have a particularly well-developed network of highly productive, large stores,[83] with especially favourable locations,[84] an efficient centrally managed chain-store system,[85] and following the transaction a dominant position in respect of procurement.[86] The result was a conclusion that the originally structured transaction would place Rewe/Billa/Meinl in a dominant position in the food retailing market in Austria.[87]

The Commission's decision includes a lengthy discussion of its analysis in respect of monopsony power. The Commission takes pains to emphasize that obtaining more favourable purchase prices is not considered to be per se detrimental. It is only if the 'powerful buyer' also occupies a strong position in the selling market, which following the merger is no longer 'kept sufficiently in check by the competition' that any savings derived from monopsony power would not be expected to be passed on to customers.[88] Efficiency losses are possible as the dominant position in the buying and selling markets means that products not distributed by the dominant supermarket are not likely to have an alternative means of reaching final consumers.[89] As well, the dominant buyer has the ability to determine the success of product innovations.[90]

Because the relevant issue is one of available options to suppliers, the relevant market in monopsony cases is properly defined by DG Comp around the set of suppliers and their alternative distribution options. In the case of supermarkets, DG Comp draws distinctions by product category, considering 'meat and sausages' separate from 'poultry and eggs', 'dairy products' and so forth.[91] Within these categories, differences exist between suppliers. Thus, while there are typically many, small, fragmented suppliers of fresh products, like meat and sausages, dairy products, bread and pastries, in the non-food area suppliers are large multinational firms.

Nonetheless, a common feature across these categories is the prominence of Austrian goods over other products, even for international brands. Austrian consumers were found to have strong preferences for Austrian goods, which led the Austrian food-retailing trade to buy predominantly from Austrian suppliers.[92]

Having defined the procurement markets in this manner, the Commission found the merger would create or strengthen a dominant position for Rewe/Billa/Meinl in nine Austrian procurement markets.[93] Across these categories, the Commission found the producers were much less concentrated than food retailers,[94] the food-retailing trade is the most important sales channel,[95] even prior to the merger Rewe/Billa had the highest share in these procurement markets,[96] and the characteristics that provide the merged Rewe/Billa/Meinl with dominance in downstream markets augment its strength in procurement,[97] particularly when it can make use of private brands strategically to reduce its dependence on suppliers.[98] The case (at least in the merger's original form) is very much like that of Kesko/Turo, leading the Commission to have significant concerns in respect of downstream (and upstream) market power prior to the transaction being restructured.

In 2000, having been notified by the merging parties Carrefour and Promodès of their intention to merge, the Commission referred the downstream analysis of the merger analysis back to the individual country authorities in France and Spain, having received requests from the French and Spanish competition authorities to allow them to assess local downstream market effects.[99] Following this referral, the Conseil de la Concurrence found the Carrefour/Promodès merger was likely to impair competition in 27 of the 99 local downstream markets affected by the transaction.[100] With the local authorities assessing downstream effects, the Commission focused its analysis on the potential upstream market effects in respect of procurement. While the earlier supermarket mergers that raised upstream (and downstream) market power issues would have created firms with very high market shares post-merger, the Carrefour/Promodès transaction would have combined the third and fourth largest supermarket chains measured by square footage.[101] Combined, the merged firm would have held less than 30% of the national market, measured by surface area or number of stores.[102] Post-merger market shares less than 35% do not typically raise concerns in respect of unilateral market power when considering the selling side of markets. There is no reason to believe a share under this would be a problem on the buying side of the market.

Nonetheless the Commission was worried that the new entity might be in a position eventually to acquire a dominant position in the upstream procurement market through a 'spiral effect', whereby the merged firm might be able to obtain more favourable terms in its relations with suppliers in turn disadvantaging its downstream rivals, with any improvement in its downstream position feeding back into improved terms with suppliers and so forth.[103] In essence, as the buyer acquires a larger size, the fear is that it is able to negotiate more favourable purchasing conditions and, hence, increase its downstream market share. A higher downstream share reinforces the upstream effects. While consumers might benefit from the firm's improved terms with suppliers in the short run, downstream competition would suffer in the long run as the theory hypothesizes the merged entity would increase its market position.[104] While postulated as a theory, the Commission's decision does not indicate how this 'spiral effect' would occur. Indeed, as noted above, the Commission did not even consider downstream local market effects since these were dealt with by the national competition authorities. Presumably any downstream remedy would 'break the spiral', resolving any possible upstream effects (assuming these even exist) at the same time it resolved downstream effects.

Notwithstanding the prior released Dobson report analysis that included the food retailing sector in France and found it unlikely that supermarket mergers would cause efficiency losses due to monopsony, in the Carrefour/Promodès merger assessment the Commission identified a threat point ('taux de menace') whereby, once a supplier relied on a single distributor for 22% of its sales, the distributor's interactions with the supplier could threaten that supplier's financial survival.[105] The 22% figure was arrived at following a survey of suppliers. In the case of Carrefour/Promodès, the merged firm would have exceeded the 22% threat point in respect of four product groups, none of which meets or is likely to have upward sloping supply.[106] The 'threat point' should not be confused with monopsony as a result. There is little prospect of a reduction in input purchases of these products. Indeed, given the low national shares of a merged Carrefour/Promodès even were it to attempt to reduce its own purchases of these goods in order to lower its input prices, suppliers have ample alternatives available. As a result, the merger was highly unlikely to reduce efficiency in upstream markets. The identified buyer power issues appear to be entirely driven by concern over the distribution of upstream profits among suppliers and supermarkets, rather than economic efficiency.

Notwithstanding the lack of merit in these economic arguments, the Commission succeeded in obtaining behavioural undertakings[107] from Carrefour and a divestment of Carrefour's 42% interest in the société GMB, which controlled Cora, a competing supermarket chain.[108] In addition to being a competitor to Carrefour, Cora had created a buying group, called Opera, with another supermarket competitor, Casino, that was seen as a counterweight to the Carrefour/Promodès group.

Apart from retail supermarket mergers, the other noteworthy European case raising buying power issues was Boeing's acquisition of MDC.[109] The Boeing decision differs from the supermarket merger cases in that the improved bargaining position of Boeing vis-à-vis its suppliers was deemed to put its European competitor Airbus at a disadvantage. Thus the focus was much more on the financial consequences for competitors from failing to have comparable positions vis-à-vis suppliers than for consumer impacts. The remedy provided that Boeing would not exert or attempt to exert undue or improper influence on its suppliers.

**Conclusions**

While the analysis of mergers involving market power on the buying side is regarded as being no different from the analysis of market power on the selling side of the market, competition authorities in Canada, the European Union and the United States have tended to approach monopsony power in mergers differently. Not only have these agencies taken different approaches from each other but, in the case of Canada and the United States, the policy approach differs from that taken to mergers addressing market power on the selling side. As happens when trade-offs exist, the thorny issue of how best to handle transfers between firms has arisen in these cases. The European Commission's guidelines suggest the transfer issue has been resolved by focusing on final consumers. In practice, this approach is borne out in some but not all decisions. In the Carrefour/Promodès decision and the Boeing/MDC cases, the concerns have been squarely in respect of upstream transfers and not about efficiency losses due to monopsony. In Canada and the United States, there is not a final consumer-oriented focus in monopsony mergers. In keeping with economic theory, mergers that give rise to monopsony power concerns but which have no negative consequences on final output markets may be subject to challenge. In the United States, the Federal Trade Commission has clearly stated that its policy approach is one of maximizing total surplus, hence mergers that simply change bargaining positions between upstream market participants are not subject to challenge. The Justice Department's record is consistent with the FTC's policy statement, despite not making definitive policy statements. In Canada, it is unclear what the policy approach is, given the limited publicly available information. Thus it is not clear whether transfers alone are sufficient to challenge a merger.

Challenging mergers raising monopsony concerns on the basis of transfers is not good public policy. The difficulty for policy makers, in these circumstances, is deciding a priori which set of producers is more deserving of potential transfers. Moreover, even if the distributional effects of mergers are deemed to be an important policy consideration, Canada's experience in trying to administer such a system by considering only the 'socially adverse' wealth effects of mergers to weigh against expected cost savings from the merger (which all of the monopsony cases noted herein have involved) demonstrates this is extremely complicated. In fact, it is so complicated that, in cases of seller market power, jurisdictions like the United States have opted for the simpler price standard or consumer surplus standard. But no equivalent simple test exists for monopsony. Is the owner of the natural resource (whether this is a wealthy private landowner, government or a farmer) always more deserving of the transfer than the shareholders of the intermediate processing firm or the shareholders of the wholesaler/distributor or retailer or the final consumer? Finally, if policy choices are made that certain transfers, as for example to farmers, are important, merger policy is a very indirect way to achieve such objectives. Tax transfers or even marketing boards are much more direct. Of course, marketing boards transfer wealth from consumers to farmers, which is contrary to maximizing consumer surplus. Given these complications, merger policy in respect of monopsony is likely to be most effective when the economics is paramount. Hence only those transactions that result in economic efficiency losses should be challenged.

**Notes**

1. Vice President, CRA International Limited, Toronto Canada. I would like to thank Matthew Smith for research assistance, Penelope Papandropoulos for her insights on the European Commission decision in respect of the Carrefour/Promodès merger and Andrew Tepperman for many valuable discussions on the economic issues presented in this chapter. I also owe many thanks to Philip Marsden for his tremendous patience. All errors and omissions are solely my responsibility.
2. Throughout this chapter, 'oligopsony' may be substituted for 'monopsony' in the discussion. For simplicity I use 'monopsony' to denote market power in purchasing.
3. These mergers have involved cattle procurement and purchases of logs by sawmills. Monopsony issues have also been considered in a merger between motion picture exhibitors.
4. See, for example, Carstensen, Peter C. (17 February 2004), 'Buyer power and merger analysis – the need for different metrics', statement prepared for the Workshop on Merger Enforcement held by the Antitrust Division and the Federal Trade Commission, Washington DC, wherein he notes at 1, 'My interest in the problems that buyer power poses for antitrust analysis comes out of my study of the problems farmers and ranchers face in the marketing of their products.'
5. *Canada (Commissioner of Competition)* v. *Superior Propane Inc.* [2002] C.C.T.D. No. 10. For a discussion of the case, see Sanderson, Margaret (2002), 'Competition Tribunal's redetermination decision in *Superior Propane*: continued lessons on the value of the total surplus standard', *Canadian Competition Record*, Spring/Summer.
6. If the supply of the input was flat, the monopsonist could not change the price of the input by lowering its purchases. Not all industries will have upward-sloping supply curves. In a study of 26 US manufacturing industries, for example, 16 industries were found to have upward-sloping supply functions, while seven had flat supply functions and three had downward-sloping supply functions (see Shea, J. (1993), 'Do supply curves slope up?', *Quarterly Journal of Economics*, **108**, 1–32). Outside of manufacturing, the supply curves for many agricultural products generally slope upward (see Dobson

Consulting (1999), *Buyer Power and its Impact on Competition in the Food Retail Distribution Sector of the European Union*, Study prepared for the European Commission – DGIV, at 13.

7. See Trebilcock, Michael, Ralph Winter, Paul Collins and Edward Iacobucci (2002), *The Law and Economics of Canadian Competition Policy*, Toronto: University of Toronto Press, p. 69: 'The distortion in the monopsony purchase arises because, at any output, the marginal expenditure exceeds the supply price of the product. The marginal expenditure is higher than the supply price because to elicit an additional unit of supply the monopsonist must raise the price paid on all units, not just on the marginal unit'.

8. 'The analysis of the monopsonist reminds us that inefficiencies associated with market power arise from insufficient quantities, not excessive prices' (Trebilcock et al., *The Law and Economics of Canadian Competition Policy*, p. 70).

9. The division of the gains from trade between two bargaining firms depends on the profits each firm would lose in the event that no trade occurs. In the context of a manufacturer negotiating with a distributor, if the manufacturer has many attractive distribution channels available to it and the manufacturer's product is highly desirable so that the distributor would lose considerable sales if it failed to stock the manufacturer's product, the split of rents between the manufacturer and distributor will be more heavily weighted to the manufacturer. A merger that reduces the number of distributors may change this dynamic, allowing the merged distributor to capture a larger share of the gains from trade than was the case pre-merger. There is no change in the quantity of product bought by the distributor, however, and hence no change in input purchases.

10. The merger involved the hostile takeover by Harmony Gold Mining Company Limited of Gold Fields Limited. The merger raised no concerns in output markets because the market for gold is global. In contesting the merger, Gold Fields argued the merger would likely lead to a substantial lessening of competition in the purchasing of inputs as the merged firm could force down prices and lower output. Gold Fields also argued the merger would have negative dynamic consequences as there would be less investment in new products by suppliers. The South African Competition Tribunal did not accept Gold Fields' claims as suppliers' reports suggested otherwise. The merger was found not to lessen substantially competition in purchasing markets. See South African Competition Tribunal's decision and order *In the large merger between: Harmony Gold Mining Company Limited and Gold Fields Limited*, Case 93/LM/NOV04, 18 May 2005, available online at the following website: http://www.comptrib.co.za/decidedcases/pdf/93LMNov04reasons.pdf.

11. Of course, should the merger substantially lessen competition in output markets, it may be challenged whatever the buying power effects.

12. This may cause an additional distortion if the reduced output by the monopsonist is replaced by less efficient firms, thereby raising overall industry costs.

13. The Competition Bureau has also considered potential upstream market power issues in other transactions, such as the mergers involving the large format book retailers Chapters and Indigo and the motion picture exhibitor chains Cineplex Galaxy and Famous Players of Canada. These cases also raised downstream issues in certain local areas, with divestitures agreed to as a means of remedying the Bureau's concerns. In the Cineplex Galaxy/Famous Players transaction, the Bureau did not find the merged entity was likely to impact negatively the terms agreed to with Hollywood distributors. See Competition Bureau Backgrounder, 'Acquisition of Famous Players by Cineplex Galaxy', 28 July 2005, available at: http://www.competitionbureau.gc.ca/internet/index.cfm?itemID=1921&lg=e. With Indigo/Chapters, the parties agreed to adhere to a particular code of conduct for dealing with publishers. The Bureau's concerns were that the merged firm would have the ability to negatively affect the terms of trade with smaller Canadian publishers thereby potentially affecting the selection of books published. See Competition Bureau News Release, 'Competition Bureau Reaches Agreement with Trilogy, Chapters and Indigo', 5 April 2001, (available at: http://www.competitionbureau.gc.ca/internet/index.cfm?itemID=492&lg=e).

14.  The same situation arose in the Competition Tribunal's review of the merger of two meat-rendering businesses, Rothsay and the Ontario Rendering Company Limited in *Canada (Director of Investigation and Research)* v. *Hillsdown Holdings Canada*, 41 C.P.R. (3d) 44, (1992), where the Tribunal noted that, if the product at issue is thought as renderable material, then the competition analysis focuses on the possible monopsony power of the renderers as buyers of the raw materials. Alternatively, if the product is thought of as rendering services provided by renderers to slaughterhouses, meat-processing plants and so on, the analysis focuses on the possible market power of the renderers as sellers of the rendering service.
15.  The US border was reopened in September 2003 to Canadian boneless beef from cattle aged less than 30 months.
16.  Competition Bureau Backgrounder on the Competition Bureau's Examination into Cattle and Beef Pricing (available at http://www.competitionbureau.gc.ca/internet/index.cfm?itemID-1311&lg=e).
17.  Grier, Kevin (February 2005), 'Analysis of the Cattle and Beef Markets Pre and Post BSE' (available at http://www.competitionbureau.gc.ca/PDFs/Cattle%20and%20Beef%20Markets_Industry%20Report.pdf) [hereafter referred to as the 'Kevin Grier study'].
18.  Bessler, David (February 2005), *A Time Series Analysis of Canadian Cattle and Beef Prices and Quantities Prior To and Following the May 2003 Discovery of BSE in the Canadian Cattle Herd* (available upon request to the Competition Bureau Information Centre) [hereafter referred to as the 'David Bessler study']; and Love, Alan (4 March 2005), *An Investigation of the Effects of BSE on the Canadian Cattle and Beef Markets* (available upon request to the Competition Bureau Information Centre) [hereafter referred to as the 'Alan Love study']. Summaries of the economic studies are available on the Bureau website at http://www.competitionbureau.gc.ca/PDFs/Cattle%20and%20Beef%20Markets_Economic%20Report.pdf.
19.  Kevin Grier study, p. 3.
20.  Kevin Grier study, p. 4.
21.  Professor Bessler uses an Error Correction Model to model interactions between various Canadian and US prices series for cattle and beef. Monthly data over the period January 1990 to May 2004 are studied, with the model running through May 2003 when the border closed.
22.  Kevin Grier study, p. 6.
23.  Kevin Grier study, p. 5.
24.  Kevin Grier study, p. 39.
25.  Alan Love study.
26.  Consumers take prices as given, and have retail demand for beef that depends on beef, chicken, and pork prices and total expenditures on meat. All other participants are modelled as explicitly solving a maximization problem given the estimated consumer demand relationship. Retailers buy beef from domestic packers or they may import beef. Retailers are treated as price takers for imports but the model allows for retailers to have market power for domestic purchases and sales. Packers buy cattle and produce beef for domestic and (potentially) export markets. They are price takers for export markets but the model allows packers to have potential market power domestically. Finally cattle producers sell feed and cull cattle on domestic markets and for export, and may retain an inventory of fed cattle. Cattle producers are price takers for both input purchases and sales. Cattle supply will depend on output prices (domestic and export), feed prices and the costs of keeping cattle as inventory.
27.  Fed cattle are steers and heifers from feedlots that have reached optimum slaughter weight. Cull cattle are older animals (usually over 30 months) that are culled each year from beef or dairy herds to reduce the size of the herd. The meat from cull cattle is typically ground or used for further processed products such as corned beef and other processed products. Culls represent about 17 per cent of Canadian slaughter and 24 per cent of total exports. See Kevin Grier study.
28.  Alan Love report, p. 100.
29.  Alan Love report, p. 97.

30. Kevin Grier study, p. 3.
31. As the Bureau indicates, 'the size of a business, even one that dominates a particular market, does not in itself raise an issue under the Act unless the business engages in conduct to restrict competition'. See Competition Bureau Backgrounder on The Competition Bureau's Examination into Cattle and Beef Pricing (available at http://www.competitionbureau.gc.ca/internet/index.cfm?itemID=1311&lg=e).
32. Ward, Clement E. (2002), 'A review of causes for and consequences of economic concentration in the U.S. meatpacking industry', *Agriculture, Food & Resource Issues, A Journal of the Canadian Agricultural Economics Society*, **3**, 1–28.
33. The Bureau defined the relevant upstream product market as the procurement of fed cattle, or slaughter cattle under 30 months of age. Fed cattle are steers and heifers that have reached an optimum slaughter weight of 1200 to 1400 pounds. See Competition Bureau Backgrounder on the Acquisition of Better Beef by Cargill Limited (available online at the following website: http://www.competitionbureau.gc.ca/internet/index. cfm?itemID=1941&lg=e).
34. The Bureau's analysis also established that, during the period when the border with the United States was closed to all cattle trade, the two relevant geographic markets were (1) Western Canada (including Manitoba) and (2) Eastern Canada. When the border was closed, even at the peak of Better Beef's purchases of fed cattle in Western Canada, the volume Better Beef procured in Western Canada was modest in proportion to Better Beef's internal requirements, the total volume of fed cattle in the entire Western Canada herd, and even in proportion to the size of the Manitoba herd. For example, in 2004, Better Beef's purchases of fed cattle in Alberta were negligible and its purchases in Manitoba were less than 10 per cent of Manitoba's total fed cattle inventory. Finally claims that Better Beef had a disproportionately large effect on price determination, both in Manitoba, and perhaps as far west as Alberta, were not supported by the Bureau's empirical examination, although this examination is not publicly available. As a result, the Bureau concluded that, even if the Canada/US border were to close again to fed cattle, the effects of the merger would not be significant enough to result in a substantial prevention or lessening of competition in the procurement of fed cattle. See Competition Bureau Backgrounder on the Acquisition of Better Beef by Cargill Limited.
35. Case-ready beef is boxed beef that has been further cut, fabricated and packaged into servings suitable for display and sale in retail stores. The Bureau concluded the geographic market for case-ready beef is limited owing to shelf life and transportation costs. The Bureau found that the broadest definition of the relevant market for case-ready beef is the provinces of Ontario and Quebec, where both Cargill and Better Beef operate plants. See Competition Bureau Backgrounder on the Acquisition of Better Beef by Cargill Limited.
36. The author is an expert retained by Tolko in respect of its acquisition of Riverside.
37. http://www.competitionbureau.gc.ca/internet/index.cfm?itemID=238&lg=e.
38. In March 2004, Riverside Forest Products Ltd. acquired the assets of Lignum Ltd., notably involving mill facilities in the Williams Lake area where Riverside already had a sawmill facility (see http://www.riverside.bc.ca/about/news-lignum.htm).
39. Canfor expected CDN$60 million in annual synergies at the time it announced the transaction, for example (see http://www.canfor.com/_resources/news/n031125_Canfor_ Slocan_combine.pdf). West Fraser expected annual synergies of CDN$80 million at the time of its announcement (see http://www.cnw.ca/fr/releases/archive/July2004/21/ c4901.html).
40. Spelter, Henry and Matthew Alderman, United States Department of Agriculture Forest Service, 'Profile 2005: softwood sawmills in the United States and Canada', Research Paper FPL-RP-630 [hereafter referred to as '2005 Sawmill Profile'].
41. It is possible that some of the capacity increase is driven by the increased log supply available owing to increased timber rights related to the effects of the Asian Mountain Pine beetle, which has caused the BC Government to increase its annual allowable cut in the northern parts of the province. Nonetheless there will be pressure to deploy any increased capacity efficiently whatever the reason behind the expansion.

42. Murray, Brian C. (1995), 'Measuring oligopsony power with shadow prices: U.S. markets for pulpwood and sawlogs', *Review of Economics and Statistics*, **77**(3), 489.
43. Ibid., 495.
44. Ibid., 496.
45. In the classic treatment of monopsony, a reduction in price to one seller implies an identical reduction in price to other sellers; so when supply is elastic the only way to impose a price reduction overall is to cut back on purchases.
46. As indicated in the Competition Bureau's *Enforcement Guidelines for Illegal Trade Practices: Unreasonably Low Pricing Policies*, 2002, p. 15: 'It is not unusual for the same products to be simultaneously sold at different prices in different geographic markets. Prices can be influenced by variations in costs, market demand or the intensity of local competition. Requiring a firm to charge the same prices in all of the markets in which it operates risks inhibiting legitimate price competition. For example, a firm may decide to forego competitive price incentives in one local market if it is required to similarly reduce its prices in all of its markets.'
47. Cooper, James C., Luke Froeb, Daniel P. O'Brien and Steven Tschantz, (2005), 'Does price discrimination intensify competition? Implications for antitrust', *Antitrust Law Journal*, **72**, 2005, 327–73; Corts, Kenneth S. (1998), 'Third-degree price discrimination in oligopoly: all-out competition and strategic commitment', *RAND Journal of Economics*, **29**, 306–23.
48. The physical characteristics of various timber stands are also expected to differ across areas as well.
49. Statement of the Federal Trade Commission, *In the Matter of Caremark Rx, Inc./ AdvancePCS*, FTC File No. 031 0239, pp. 2–3 (available at http://www.ftc.gov/os/ caselist).
50. *United States, et al.* v. *Aetna, Inc., et al.*, No. 3-99CB1398-H (N.D. Tex.) (Complaint filed 21 June 1999); available at http://www.usdoj.gov/atr [hereafter referred to as *Aetna Complaint*].
51. *Aetna Complaint*, para. 33.
52. Schwartz, Marius (1999), 'Buyer power concerns and the *Aetna–Prudential* merger', Address to the fifth Annual Health Care Antitrust Forum, Northwestern University School of Law, Chicago Illinois, 20 October, text released 30 November 1999.
53. Ibid.
54. *Aetna Complaint*, para. 33.
55. MacDonald, James, Economic Research Service, US Department of Agriculture (1999), 'Cargill's Acquisition of Continental Grain: Anatomy of a Merger', *Agricultural Outlook*, September, p. 22.
56. Ibid., p. 21.
57. *United States of America* v. *Cargill, Incorporated, and Continental Grain Company*, Case Number 1:99CV01875 (GK), Competitive Impact Statement [hereafter referred to as '*Cargill Competitive Impact Statement*'], at 4, available at: http://www.usdoj.gov/atr/ cases/f2500/2584.html.
58. *United States of America* v. *Cargill, Incorporated, and Continental Grain Company*, Civil Action No. 99-1875 (GK), United States Response to Public Comments, 11 February 2000 [hereafter referred to as '*Cargill Response to Public Comments*'].
59. *United States of America* v. *Cargill, Incorporated, and Continental Grain Company*, Civil No. 1:99CV01875, Complaint, filed 8 July 1999 [hereafter referred to as '*Cargill Complaint*'], paras 30–33.
60. MacDonald (1999), pp. 23–4.
61. Ibid.
62. *Cargill Competitive Impact Statement*, at 4.
63. The divested elevators were (1) Continental's river elevator at Lockport Illinois; (2) Continental's river elevator at Caruthersville Missouri; (3) Cargill's river elevator at East Dubuque Iowa; (4) Cargill's river elevator at Morris Illinois; (5) Continental's rail elevator at Salina Kansas; (6) Continental's rail elevator at Troy Ohio; (7) Continental's port elevator at Stockton California, (8) Continental's port elevator at Beaumont Texas; and (9) Cargill's port elevator at Seattle Washington if Cargill

acquires the Continental port elevator at Tacoma. See *Cargill Response to Public Comments*.
64. The Chicago port elevator divestiture was also regarded as resolving competition issues for local grain farmers in the area. As well, Cargill's divestiture of its Morris river elevator was regarded by the Justice Department as of assistance in resolving Chicago Board of Trade concentration issues. See *Cargill Response to Public Comments*.
65. Schwartz, Marius (1999), 'Buyer power concerns and the *Aetna–Prudential* merger', Address to the fifth Annual Health Care Antitrust Forum, Northwestern University School of Law, Chicago Illinois, 20 October, text released 30 November 1999, at footnote 5.
66. MacDonald (1999), p. 24.
67. See, for example, Carstensen, Peter C. (2004), 'Buyer power and merger analysis – the need for different metrics', statement prepared for the Workshop on Merger Enforcement held by the Antitrust Division and the Federal Trade Commission, Washington, DC, 17 February. Carstensen argues that mergers below six buyers are problematic, and national market shares for retailers of 20 per cent designate monopsony power.
68. Schwartz, Marius (2004), 'Should antitrust assess buyer market power differently than seller market power?', comments prepared for the DOJ/FTC Workshop on Merger Enforcement, Washington, DC, 17 Feburary.
69. Ibid., p. 4.
70. European Commission (2004), 'Guidelines on the assessment of horizontal mergers under the Council Regulation on the control of concentrations between undertakings', *Official Journal of the European Union*, 2004/C, 31/03.
71. For example, the UK Competition Commission expressed concern over the possible acquisition of Safeway plc by Morrison, Sainsbury, Tesco and Wal-mart (Asda).
72. Dobson Consulting (1999), *Buyer Power and Its Impact on Competition in the Food Retail Distribution Sector of the European Union*, Prepared for the European Commission – DGIV, May ('Dobson study').
73. Ibid., p. 151.
74. In some circumstances, a limited number of buyers negotiates with a limited number of suppliers (i.e., there is 'bilateral bargaining'). See Dobson study, p. 144.
75. Appendix I of the Dobson study provides a list of the retail mergers over 1990–98. Of 55 mergers, only two have raised objections by Comp DG.
76. Dobson study, p. 21.
77. The Commission noted the catchment area for a supermarket is local, but overlapping catchment areas together with population distribution lead the competitive interactions between geographically proximate supermarkets to have 'chain-reaction' effects on more distant supermarkets and hence relevant geographic markets may be expanded beyond very local areas.
78. Commission Decision, Case No IV/M.784 – Kesko/Tuko, Council Regulation (EEC) N/4064/89 at paragraph 93.
79. Kesko/Tuko Decision, para. 99.
80. Kesko/Tuko Decision, para. 106.
81. Commission Decision, Council Regulation (EEC) No 4064/89, Case No IV/M.1221 – Rewe/Meinl, para. 34.
82. http://europa.eu.int/rapid/pressReleasesAction.do?reference=IP/99/83.
83. Rewe/Meinl Decision, para. 37.
84. Rewe/Meinl Decision, para. 42.
85. Rewe/Meinl Decision, para. 49.
86. Rewe/Meinl Decision, para. 54.
87. Rewe/Meinl Decision, para. 70.
88. Rewe/Meinl Decision, para. 71.
89. Rewe/Meinl Decision, para. 74.
90. Ibid.
91. Rewe/Meinl Decision, para. 77.
92. Rewe/Meinl Decision, para. 83.

93. Rewe/Meinl Decision, para. 88. The nine procurement markets are dairy products; bread and pastries; soft drinks; hot beverages; basic foodstuffs; baby foods; pet foods; detergents, polishes and cleaning products; and body-care products and cosmetics. See listing, para. 94.
94. Rewe/Meinl Decision, para. 89.
95. Rewe/Meinl Decision, para. 94.
96. Rewe/Meinl Decision, para. 98.
97. Rewe/Meinl Decision, paras 107–10, 115.
98. Rewe/Meinl Decision, para. 111.
99. Commission Européenne, Décision de la Commission du 25.01.2000 renvoyant en partie l'affaire n°COMP/M.1684-CARREFOUR/PROMODES and DECISION DE LA COMISIÓN reenviando parcialmente el caso n° IV/M.1684. CARREFOUR/ PROMODES a las autoridades nacionales del Reino de España sobre la base del artículo 9 del Reglamento del Consejo n° 4064/89, 25.01.2000.
100. Conseil de la Concurrence, avis n° 00-A-06 du 3 mai 2000 relatif à l'acquisition par la société Carrefour de la société Promodès.
101. Commission des Communautés Européennes, Procedure Concentrations Décision Article 6(1)(b), Affaire n°COMP/M.1684-Carrefour/Promodès [hereafter referred to as EU Carrefour/Promodès Decision], at para. 39.
102. EU Carrefour/Promodès Decision, para. 36. Even if the market is limited to the format 'hypermarché', the merged firm would have held 25–35% of the national market, facing equivalent-sized competitors in Leclerc and Auchan at 20–30% and 15–20%, respectively (see para. 43).
103. EU Carrefour/Promodès Decision, para. 45.
104. EU Carrefour/Promodès Decision, para. 46.
105. EU Carrefour/Promodès Decision, para. 52.
106. EU Carrefour/Promodès Decision, para. 53 for the four product groups.
107. Broadly speaking, the undertakings involved a commitment, for a period of three years, not to modify Carrefour's and Promodès' existing contracts with suppliers (whose turnover is below 1.5 bn Euros), in respect of volumes, price, delivery and some other conditions, as well as a commitment to continue purchasing from suppliers whose turnover represented at least 25 per cent sales to Carrefour/Promodès.
108. EU Carrefour/Promodès Decision, para. 92 and Annexe 1.
109. See http://europa.eu.int/comm/competition/mergers/cases/decisions/m877_19970730_600_en.pdf.

## References

Bessler, David (2005), 'A time series analysis of Canadian cattle and beef prices and quantities prior to and following the May 2003 discovery of BSE in the Canadian cattle herd', February, available upon request to the Competition Bureau Information Centre.
Canadian Competition Bureau (2001), 'Competition bureau reaches agreement with trilogy, chapters and Indigo', 5 April, available online at the following website: http://www.competitionbureau.gc.ca/internet/index.cfm?itemID=492&lg=e.
Canadian Competition Bureau (2002), *Enforcement Guidelines for Illegal Trade Practices: Unreasonably Low Pricing Policies.*
Canadian Competition Bureau (2005), 'Acquisition of famous players by Cineplex Galaxy', Competition Bureau Backgrounder, 28 July, available online at the following website: http://www.competitionbureau.gc.ca/internet/index.cfm?itemID=1921&lg=e.
Carstensen, Peter C. (2004), 'Buyer power and merger analysis – the need for different metrics', statement prepared for the Workshop on Merger Enforcement held by the Antitrust Division and the Federal Trade Commission, Washington, DC, 17 February.
Cooper, James C., Luke Froeb, Daniel P. O'Brien and Steven Tschantz (2005), 'Does price discrimination intensify competition? Implications for antitrust', *Antitrust Law Journal*, **72**, 327–73.
Corts, Kenneth S. (1998), 'Third-degree price discrimination in oligopoly: all-out competition and strategic commitment', *RAND Journal of Economics*, **29**, 306–23.

Dobson Consulting (1999), 'Buyer power and its impact on competition in the food retail distribution sector of the European Union', study prepared for the European Commission – DGIV.

European Commission (2004), 'Guidelines on the assessment of horizontal mergers under the Council Regulation on the control of concentrations between undertakings', *Official Journal of the European Union*, 2004/C, 31/03.

Grier, Kevin (2005), 'Analysis of the cattle and beef markets pre and post BSE', available at http://www.competitionbureau.gc.ca/PDFs/Cattle%20and%20Beef%20Markets_Industry %20Report.pdf, February.

Love, Alan (2005), '*An investigation of the effects of BSE on the Canadian cattle and beef markets*', 4 March, available upon request to the Competition Bureau Information Centre.

MacDonald, James (1999), 'Cargill's acquisition of Continental Grain: anatomy of a merger', *Agricultural Outlook*, September.

Murray, Brian C. (1995), 'Measuring oligopsony power with shadow prices: U.S. markets for pulpwood and sawlogs', *Review of Economics and Statistics*, **77**(3).

Sanderson, Margaret (2002), 'Competition tribunal's redetermination decision in *Superior Propane*: continued lessons on the value of the total surplus standard', *Canadian Competition Record*, Spring/Summer.

Schwartz, Marius (2004), 'Should antitrust assess buyer market power differently than seller market power?', Comments prepared for the DOJ/FTC Workshop on Merger Enforcement, 17 February, Washington, DC.

Schwartz, Marius (1999), 'Buyer power concerns and the *Aetna–Prudential* merger', Address to the Fifth Annual Health Care Antitrust Forum, Northwestern University School of Law, Chicago Illinois, 20 October; text released 30 November.

Shea, J. (1993), 'Do supply curves slope up?', *Quarterly Journal of Economics*, **108**, 1–32.

Spelter, Henry and Matthew Alderman (2005), 'Profile 2005: softwood sawmills in the United States and Canada', United States Department of Agriculture Forest Service, research paper FPL-RP-630.

Trebilcock, Michael, Ralph Winter, Paul Collins and Edward Iacobucci (2002), *The Law and Economics of Canadian Competition Policy*, Toronto: University of Toronto Press.

Ward, Clement E. (2002), 'A review of causes for and consequences of economic concentration in the U.S. meatpacking industry', *Agriculture, Food & Resource Issues, A Journal of the Canadian Agricultural Economics Society*, **3**, 1–28.

*Cases*

*Canada (Commissioner of Competition)* v. *Superior Propane Inc.* [2002] C.C.T.D. No. 10.

*Canada (Director of Investigation and Research)* v. *Hillsdown Holdings Canada*, 41 C.P.R. (3d) 44, (1992).

*In the large merger between: Harmony Gold Mining Company Limited and Gold Fields Limited*, Case 93/LM/NOV04, 18 May 2005, at http://www.comptrib.co.za/decidedcases/pdf/ 93LMNov04reasons.pdf.

*In the Matter of Caremark Rx, Inc./AdvancePCS*, FTC File No. 031 0239, pp. 2–3, available at http://www.ftc.gov/os/caselist.

*United States, et al.* v. *Aetna, Inc., et al.*, No. 3-99CB1398-H (N.D. Tex.) (Complaint filed 21 June, 1999), available at http://www.usdoj.gov/atr.

*United States of America* v. *Cargill, Incorporated, and Continental Grain Company*, Civil No. 1:99CV01875, Complaint, filed 8 July 1999.

*United States of America* v. *Cargill, Incorporated, and Continental Grain Company*, Case Number 1:99CV01875 (GK), Competitive Impact Statement, available at http://www.usdoj.gov/atr/cases/f2500/2584.html.

*United States of America* v. *Cargill, Incorporated, and Continental Grain Company*, Civil Action No. 99-1875 (GK), United States Response to Public Comments, 11 February 2000.

# 4 Tweedledum and Tweedledee? Regime dynamics in US and EC merger control

*Andrew Scott*[1]

In recent years, a number of dichotomous decisions of the US and EC merger authorities have given commentators pause to consider continuing discrepancies between the two jurisdictions. The latest contribution to these dramas – the decision of the Court of First instance (CFI) in the *GE/Honeywell* case – was delivered in December 2005.[2] In some quarters, these experiences have prompted the drawing of disparaging inferences regarding the architecture and approach of the EC system. Dissatisfaction at outcomes in particular cases has fomented rhetorical denunciation of the underpinning structure of European merger control. On a dispassionate analysis, however, this critique may prove to be both uninformed and unwarranted. Indeed many of the supposed differences between the merger control regimes of the US and the EC may be more apparent than real. The aim of this chapter, therefore, is not to investigate the degree of convergence or continuing discrepancy between the substantive US and EC merger laws as evident in their application in recent cases.[3] Rather it is to consider a number of facets of the institutional structures and processes by which merger control is conducted in the respective jurisdictions. By teasing out differences and identifying similarities between the two regimes, the intention is to highlight the peculiar features of each.

The starting point for the following discussion is the appreciation that, at least at first glance, the two regimes are demonstrably similar in structure. Both require prior notification of 'large' mergers; both sieve out a large proportion of notified cases in a short first-stage review and concentrate in more depth only on identifiably worrisome cases, and both see a very small minority of cases proceeding on for consideration before a court. Moreover both regimes operate in a context of multilayered merger control in which the interaction with (Member) State-level authorities must be taken into account; in both there is some measure of insulation of the antitrust authorities from political influence, and both have become much more sophisticated in evaluating the likely competitive effects of mergers.

In the first two sections of the chapter, the respective systems are introduced, and comment on the evolution of merger control in each jurisdiction is offered. In the United States, this evolution has involved a shift away from a court-centred model to an essentially administrative scheme. In the EC, the proper role of the Community courts in supervising administrative merger review has become a focus of attention following a recent, interventionist juridical turn. The second section concludes with two general reflections based on the comparative exercise: the first notes the persistent structural differences between the merger regimes of the EC and US, while the second confronts the sceptical contention that either or both merger regimes can be too easily subverted by political influence.

The final two sections focus on two areas in which the architects of the US regime may learn from the EC experience. The third section considers whether the noted emergence of an administrative scheme in the US has yet been accompanied by the introduction of such procedural safeguards as one might expect of a sound bureaucratic system. The final section considers the multilayered dimension of merger control in the two jurisdictions, and suggests that the US regime may benefit from a greater degree of certainty as to the respective roles of state and federal level actors.

## US merger control: the administrative character of an ostensibly juridical regime

It is still possible to describe the basic features of the US model of merger control by reference to legal rules and court decisions. For practical purposes, however, this notionally juridical model has metamorphosed over the past three decades. It is now more accurate to consider the regime as bureaucratic, with the judicial aspect being invoked only in the hardest of cases. The following paragraphs trace and explain this development.

### The juridical façade of US merger control

Merger control has been an element in US antitrust since its inception in the late nineteenth century. A number of federal statutes now regulate the competition aspects of company mergers, acquisitions and joint ventures.[4] The pre-eminent legal test against which such transactions are assessed is stated in section 7 of the Clayton Act.[5] This prohibits the acquisition of voting securities or assets in another company where 'in any line of commerce or in any activity affecting commerce in any section of the country, the effect of such acquisition may be substantially to lessen competition, or to tend to create a monopoly'. In addition, sections 1 and 2 of the Sherman Act,[6] and section 5 of the Federal Trade Commission Act,[7] can each be used to found a challenge to a merger.[8]

Three categories of potential plaintiff are envisaged under the US regime. The first consists of two national government authorities: the Antitrust Division of the US Department of Justice (DoJ), and the Federal Trade Commission (FTC). The DoJ is the law enforcement arm of the executive branch of the federal government.[9] Antitrust enforcement was specifically funded from 1903, while the first dedicated Assistant Attorney General was appointed in 1933 to head an Antitrust Division. The FTC is an independent regulatory administrative body operating at arm's length from executive influence.[10] It was established under the Federal Trade Commission Act of 1914 to work in conjunction with – but not to supersede – the DoJ as the federal antitrust enforcer. It is headed by five Commissioners, each of whom is appointed by the President for a seven-year term.

Section 7 also allows mergers to be challenged under federal law by state Attorneys General. This is an instance of the states' *parens patriae* capacities. A number of individual states have also introduced their own merger laws.[11] The result is that, in a given case, a number of state Attorneys General may assert jurisdiction, perhaps alongside one of the national authorities. Such cases may involve the mutual application of section 7, or a combination of both state and federal laws.

The final category of potential plaintiff, private individuals or companies, will generally have most difficulty in bringing a suit. They must be able to satisfy stringent antitrust standing rules which have been constrained by tight judicial interpretation of the Clayton Act.[12] Moreover private plaintiffs will only rarely be able to develop a sufficiently sophisticated case to mount a serious challenge.

The ostensible forum for the determination of the legality of merger transactions under section 7 is the federal district court.[13] Generally the determinative stage in a merger suit will be that focused on the award of interim relief. A preliminary injunction is formally designed only to prevent the completion of the merger prior to a full judicial hearing and decision on the award of a permanent injunction securing prohibition. A full trial, however, would normally be expected to run for a number of years. Subjected to this delay, the business case for a merger will often dissolve, causing the parties to forgo their plans. Similarly plaintiffs tend not to continue with litigation if the request for a preliminary injunction is denied. For both sides, the sheer cost of pursuing an action to its definitive conclusion will bear heavily on willingness to proceed. Thus, whatever the outcome, the decision on interim relief generally marks the end of a merger case. One caveat to this position is that the losing party may appeal against the grant or refusal of a preliminary injunction by the district court to the US Court of Appeals.[14] The appeals court will normally expedite any such hearing. Appellate decisions are subject to further review at the discretion of the US Supreme Court, but few cases ever reach this stage. Indeed, in the past three decades, there have been none.[15]

This focus on the role of court proceedings and ultimately on formal legal decisions, however, does not reflect a true picture of contemporary

US merger control. Indeed any representation that emphasizes the role of the court borders on the misleading. Only a very small proportion of mergers are ever considered by the courts. A bureaucratic dimension to merger control has evolved around the process by which the FTC and DoJ determine whether to file complaints with the district court. It is 10 years since this movement of 'the primary locus of merger law from the courts to the enforcement agencies' was identified and considered by commentators.[16] The transition to this more administrative and regulatory system, however, was initiated much earlier by the passage of the Antitrust Improvements Act (the Hart–Scott–Rodino Act) in 1976. It accelerated with the growth in sophistication of the use of economic analyses and the increased recourse to the negotiation of remedial consent decrees. The result is that there is now 'a generation of antitrust lawyers and business people [who] have no memory of merger law as jurisprudence – a body of case law created by the interaction of advocates before neutral arbiters – as opposed to regulation'.[17] This change has been lamented by some.[18]

### The bureaucratic heart of US merger control
The Hart–Scott–Rodino Act was introduced in order to allow the authorities an opportunity to review mergers before they had been consummated. It was a response to the long-recognized and inordinate difficulty in unravelling transactions after integration of the parties, and the attendant limitation of the ability to restore pre-merger competitive conditions. The regime has, to all intents and purposes, 'eliminated indefinite jeopardy'.[19] The Act was updated with effect from 2001.

The administrative process prescribed by the Act is broadly equivalent to the two-phase assessment conducted under the ECMR. The Act requires each party to any merger or acquisition that meets given jurisdictional thresholds to notify the DoJ and the FTC before completing the deal in question.[20] Notification involves the completion of an HSR Premerger Notification and Report Form. The parties must provide basic information on themselves, their ownership interests, the transaction, the affected industries and, critically, all preparatory materials (electronic or hard copy) generated in the evaluation and analysis of the acquisition. The preparation of this filing is generally considered to be 'relatively simple, and fairly low cost' so that 'it could even be called rudimentary'.[21] Information provided to the DoJ or FTC, including the fact that a filing has occurred, remains confidential unless the parties consent to waive this right.[22] In the fiscal year 2004, 1454 transactions were notified.[23]

One notable corollary of notification is the payment of a filing fee. The HSR regime requires the acquiring party to pay a filing fee the size of which is dependent on the scale of the transaction.[24] It has been observed that the United States 'relies heavily [upon pre-merger notification filing] fees to pay for the operation of its federal antitrust agencies'.[25] Indeed it has been questioned 'whether the fundraising aspect of . . . merger control . . . distorts its legitimate objectives' by introducing an incentive to expand the class of transactions that must be notified.[26]

The agencies monitor compliance with the HSR requirements by reviewing newspapers and industry publications for announcements of transactions that have not been reported, and through information received from competitors, customers, suppliers and interested members of the public.[27] Failure to notify a transaction that meets the jurisdictional thresholds is punishable by a fine of $11 000 per day of the violation.[28] To 'jump the gun' by integrating the businesses in some manner is also unlawful, and is punishable by the same level of fine.[29] Thus there is an incentive to notify as soon as is practicable. Where a transaction does not exceed the notification thresholds, it remains open to the DoJ or FTC to investigate and seek to prevent the consummation of the merger. Particularly in these circumstances, the authorities may still move to unwind a completed merger.[30]

The parties to the merger must not consummate their transaction until the expiry of a waiting period of 30 calendar days after filing.[31] This initial waiting period offers the US authorities an equivalent timescale to that enjoyed by the European Commission in undertaking its Phase I assessment. If, at first glance, the notified transaction appears likely to warrant closer scrutiny, one or both of the two authorities will seek 'clearance' to conduct an initial inquiry from the other. Traditionally the FTC has been cleared to investigate mergers in chemicals, oil and gas pipelines, food and food distribution, cable television, pharmaceuticals, retailing and textiles. The DoJ generally leads on telecommunications, banking and finance, steel, electric power, air transport, beer and newspapers.[32]

Occasionally clearance discussions between the authorities become contentious: 'in cases involving multiple product lines or new industries where there is no history of involvement on the part of either agency, the DoJ and the FTC engage in what is sometimes a protracted "turf war"'.[33] In 1948, a first attempt was made to overcome the inevitable friction that the concurrent jurisdiction of the DoJ and FTC engenders.[34] This agreement provided for a clearance procedure, under which each prospective investigation is allocated to the agency with the greater expertise in the relevant markets. The liaison agreement was updated with new inter-agency procedures introduced in 1993 and 1995, with the result that clearance will be resolved within nine business days of the notification of a transaction. More recently the two authorities revisited the matter of clearance disputes and elaborated a definite and comprehensive scheme of allocation of all cases on the basis of industry.[35] This agreement was rescinded, however, after political pressure from Congress was brought to bear.[36]

The DoJ and FTC can waive the prohibition on consummation of the transaction during the initial waiting period where they perceive no competition problems. Such early termination is the most common outcome following notification, and may occur from as few as three days into the waiting period. In 2004, early termination was requested in 85 per cent of cases notified (1241), with 76 per cent (943) of such requests being granted.[37]

Should either authority consider it necessary to conduct a fuller analysis of the transaction, or be unable to conclude that there is no potential competition problem within the available time, it will make a request for additional information. This is commonly known as the issuance of a 'second request'. Before taking this step, the authority concerned will usually allow the parties and others (for example, competitors or customers) additional opportunities to explain why the transaction should or should not be investigated further. Where a second request seems likely, the parties will sometimes withdraw their original notification and resubmit without the need to pay a further fee.[38] By doing so they allow the authorities more time to undertake their preliminary assessment in the hope that the provision of fuller information at this stage will pre-empt the need for any second request. Only a small proportion of cases involve a second request following the preliminary review. In 2004, only 35 (2.5 per cent) of the 1454 notified transactions were subject to a second request.[39]

A second request entails the extension of the waiting period for a further 30 days following full compliance with the request for information.[40] The initiation of the second waiting period is often suspended for some time while full compliance with information requests is awaited. These information requests can be extremely broad, and coupled with many highly detailed interrogatories. The collation of the material required by the authority, and the conduct of the legal and economic analysis necessary to comply with a second request, place an onerous burden upon the resources of the parties.[41] One estimate is that 'full compliance with a second request can often require five or six months of work and cost the parties several million dollars each'.[42] Primarily for this reason, the injunction to avoid a second request wherever possible has been installed as one of the 'ten commandments' for counsel advising on US mergers.[43] The authorities also enjoy broad powers that can be invoked to obtain documents and other testimony from third parties. The authorities' assessment of mergers is generally undertaken in accordance with the analytical framework set out in the *Horizontal Merger Guidelines* (the Guidelines), adopted jointly by the DoJ and FTC in 1992.

These Guidelines were revised in 1997.[44] Parties will often agree to delay closing their transaction to allow the authority involved to complete its assessment.

At the culmination of the second waiting period, the DoJ or FTC determines whether to file a complaint with a federal district court. Alternatively the authority concerned may clear the merger at any point having quelled any incipient concerns, or negotiate remedies with the parties that will become the subject of a consent decree. Parties frequently seek to negotiate a settlement with the investigating agency if faced with the prospect of litigation. Their alternative courses are to abandon the transaction – and 'practicality dictates that most deals win agency approval or vanish in a puff of smoke' – or decide to proceed notwithstanding the position adopted by the authority in question.[45]

Strictly speaking, a merger is never 'cleared' by the DoJ or FTC. Where no preliminary injunction is sought, or even where early termination of the first 30-day waiting period has been allowed, the authorities can later decide to request further information and conduct further analysis if it is considered that the merger does in fact threaten to harm competition.[46] There is no limitation period for Clayton Act violations.[47]

If the merging parties choose to negotiate a settlement with a plaintiff authority, collective efforts will be directed towards identifying appropriate behavioural or structural remedies.[48] Should agreement be reached, the agency involved will normally still proceed by way of lodging a complaint with the court but will ally this with a request for a consent decree. If the court's judgment confirms the consent decree, the parties must comply with the conditions it states within the outlined timeframe.

Should the DoJ or FTC decide to challenge a merger transaction it may seek a temporary restraining order, a preliminary injunction to prevent closure of the merger transaction or a permanent injunction. If the district court awards a preliminary injunction, the DoJ as plaintiff can seek a permanent injunction from the court should the case not be otherwise resolved. In contrast the FTC as plaintiff would generally revert to internal administrative procedures at this point.[49]

In 2004, the FTC challenged 15 transactions. These resulted in ten consent orders, one administrative complaint, one unsuccessfully litigated case, and three abandoned transactions. Meanwhile the DoJ brought nine challenges, resulting in five consent decrees, two abandoned transactions, one unsuccessfully litigated case, and one other transaction that was restructured so as to alleviate the identified antitrust concerns.[50] Interestingly, the litigative record of the authorities has deteriorated markedly. In the mid-1960s, it could be said that 'the sole consistency . . . is that under section 7 the Government always wins'.[51] During the Clinton and first George W. Bush administrations, however, the DoJ and FTC won only ten of 22 cases that were litigated to a decision.[52]

**EC merger control: the juridical turn of an ostensibly administrative regime**
After a long period in which the inadequacy of the general competition provisions of the EC Treaty in dealing with mergers became increasingly evident,[53] a dedicated EC control regime was instituted in 1990.[54] This regime has since been enhanced periodically on the strength of deepening experience of its use. These reforms have been designed primarily to respond to two main drivers of change: the need to optimize the allocation of cases between the national and supranational tiers of governance, and the desire to improve the procedural guarantees offered by the system. As regards the most recent revisions, further impetus was provided by the perceived need to revise the substantive test for merger analysis. Article 2 ECMR now prescribes a 'significant impediment to effective competition' test, which is analogous to the substantial lessening of competition standard.

Alongside these legislative revisions, the Community courts have recently sought to impose a discipline on the operation of the merger system by insisting that the Commission offer strong proof of any facts and assumptions on which it bases its decisions. The courts have been less willing simply to accept at face value the Commission's explanations. This juridical turn may have significant ramifications for the willingness of the Commission to press forward with innovative analyses in future cases.

*Fine-tuning of an administrative regime*
Experience of the operation of the EC merger regime has occasioned periodic incremental development of the basic scheme introduced in 1990. The first significant revision took place in 1997, when a new jurisdictional threshold was introduced in an attempt to lift the burden of duplicative merger assessments at the national level.[55] Further substantial amendment and consolidation, sufficient in scope to warrant an entire recasting of the regulation, came into effect in May 2004.[56] To accompany the recast Merger Regulation, the Commission passed a new implementing regulation,[57] published a Notice on the appraisal of horizontal mergers,[58] elaborated a set of best practice guidelines for the conduct of merger investigations,[59] and instigated a range of internal reforms designed to improve the management of the merger regime.[60]

Under the EC regime, the Directorate-General for Competition (DG Comp) is responsible for each of the three main components of merger control: the decision on whether to open a full investigation (Phase I), the full investigation and the determination of suitable remedies. The second and third elements comprise the subject matter of Phase II proceedings. Moreover the same team within DG Comp carries any given notification through Phases I and II. Decisions at the end of Phase I are taken by the Commissioner responsible for competition policy (currently Neelie Kroes) using powers delegated to her by the full Commission. Decisions concluding Phase II investigations are taken by the full College of Commissioners. They are then published in the 'L'-series of the *Official Journal*, subject to appropriate excisions reflecting the legitimate commercial sensitivities of the undertakings concerned.

The scope of the EC merger control regime extends only to 'concentrations with a Community dimension'. Within this range, however, the competence of the EC authorities is exclusive: Article 21 ECMR is explicit in confirming the 'sole jurisdiction' of the Commission, subject only to review by the Court of Justice, and in precluding the application of national legislation to concentrations with a Community dimension. The concept of a 'Community dimension' is developed by reference to alternative turnover thresholds stipulated in Article 1 ECMR;[61] the definition of a 'concentration' is elaborated in Article 3 ECMR.[62] Undoubtedly the quantitative nature of these tests allows some mergers that are of Community interest to remain within the jurisdiction of national authorities. This is a necessary concession to the need for a bright-line determinant of jurisdictional competence in a context where speed of assessment is imperative in sustaining business opportunities and confidence.

The procedural aspects of the EC merger regime are prescribed by the recast Merger Regulation and the associated new implementing legislation. These legal bases were revised in 2004 in large part in response to perceived limitations of the existing procedures, which had been highlighted by judicial criticism.[63] What the amendments did not comprise was any revision of the basic characteristics of the EC merger control regime. This remains a bipartite system of time-constrained ex ante control, wherein qualifying mergers must be notified in advance and progress towards their completion is normally suspended pending clearance. The main changes relate to the time period for investigation. As regards the more complex cases, the reforms were designed to allow sufficient time for all parties concerned to contribute appropriately without loss of the efficiency-inducing tightness of deadlines. Further reforms saw parties' procedural guarantees and the Commission's investigative powers enhanced.

Where parties intend to proceed with a concentration that possesses a Community dimension, (normally) the acquiring party is obliged by Article 4 ECMR to notify its intentions to the Commission in advance; prior notification is mandatory. Failure to inform the Commission, or implementation of a transaction without notification, can leave parties liable to fines of up to 10 per cent of the aggregate turnover of the undertakings concerned in each case.[64] Notification is made using Form CO, of which there is a 'short form' version for use in connection with a 'simplified procedure'.[65] Completion of Form CO is a significant task. Indeed one estimate has suggested that 'possibly ten times as much data is required for an ECMR filing compared to an HSR filing'.[66] The closer parallel may be that every notification 'is like doing an initial in-depth review [preparing a response to a second request] in the United States'.[67] Clearly these comparisons do not apply so strongly to transactions notified under the simplified procedure.[68]

Notification has a number of consequences, most notably the automatic suspension of further progress prior to clearance.[69] This suspension will last until a substantive decision is made, or the relevant time limits for a decision expire. It will also cause basic details of the transactions concerned to be published in the *Official Journal*.[70] In 2004, there were 249 such notifications.[71] This figure pales into insignificance against the number of transactions notified under the Hart–Scott–Rodino thresholds: 'the European system . . . catches only the big or really big transactions'.[72]

At Phase I, having confirmed that the transaction lies within the scope of the Merger Regulation, the Commission must either clear the transaction,[73] agree modifications to it with the parties,[74] or determine that the preliminary examination 'raises serious doubts as to its compatibility with the common market'.[75] In each case, the Commission must publish reasons for its conclusions. The assessment is based on information gleaned from Form CO. In addition, the Commission enjoys strengthened investigatory powers under Article 13 ECMR, and can seek further information from government, national authorities or private undertakings under Article 11 ECMR. In the case of 'serious doubts', the Commission must instigate Phase II proceedings. Remedial commitments can be agreed at Phase I only 'where the competition problem is readily identifiable and can be easily remedied'. The time limits for Phase I proceedings are outlined in Article 10(1) ECMR. The basic rule is that a decision must be taken within 25 working days following notification. The deadline can be extended to 35 working days where the Commission has received a request for referral to a national authority, or where it is seeking to agree remedial commitments with the parties. This is a very tight schedule. In 2004, 220 transactions were cleared unconditionally at Phase I, and a further 12 were cleared with conditions attached.

Where Phase II proceedings have been initiated and the Commission takes the preliminary view that the transaction poses competition problems, it will deliver a formal 'statement of objections' to the undertakings concerned.[76] This is normally achieved by 35 working days into the assessment process. Ultimately the Commission can 'base its decision only on objections on which the parties have been able to submit their observations'.[77] There is no provision for a second request filing in the EC. All information is provided 'up-front' in Form CO, although as noted above the Commission can seek additional information in the later stages of the review by negotiation with the parties, or by using powers under Articles 11 and 13 ECMR.

The time limits under Phase II are tight given the depth of the investigation. The recent revisions of the Merger Regulation, however, have been designed so as to introduce a measure of flexibility into the proceedings. Decisions under Article 8 ECMR must normally be taken within 90 working days of the initiation of Phase II.[78] The parties can make one request for an extension to this period of a maximum of 20 working days. The Commission, with the consent of the parties, can also extend the timetable to an extent, and can suspend the timetable where it finds it necessary to request further information from the parties. The 90 working-day period can be extended to 105 working days should the parties offer remedial commitments designed to resolve the perceived impediment to competition. Should the Commission fail to reach a decision within the prescribed time limits, the concentration is deemed to be compatible with the common market.[79]

At the end of Phase II, the Commission can clear or prohibit the transaction.[80] Clearance can be either conditional or unconditional. In 2004, seven decisions (3 per cent) were taken at the culmination of Phase II. Of these, two were unconditional clearances, four were conditional clearances, and there was one prohibition. This total is similar to those of the two previous years, although from 1999 to 2001 the annual total was around 20. Since the inception of the merger regime in 1990, there have been 28 full clearances, 74 clearances with remedies and 19 prohibitions in total at Phase II. Decisions at Phase II are taken by the full College of Commissioners, and regardless of the type of decision involved are subsequently published in the *Official Journal* subject to appropriate excisions with respect to commercially sensitive information. This publication in itself instils a certain discipline as it ensures that the Commission's reasoning can be subject to critical scrutiny by the undertakings concerned and the wider epistemological community. Moreover, Commission decisions are subject to the supervision of the Community courts.

A number of procedural guarantees serve to protect the interests of a range of parties during the investigative process. The main parties are allowed full opportunity to familiarize themselves with the perceived competition concerns: 'rights of the defence [are to] be fully respected in the proceedings'.[81] They receive a Statement of Objections from the

Commission, and from this point are allowed access to the Commission file subject to the protection of legitimate business secrets.[82] They can make such response as they deem appropriate to the Commission, perhaps submitting further evidence or suggesting third parties who may be able to corroborate facts. Formal oral hearings must be held where requested by the notifying parties. These proceedings are conducted by a Hearing Officer in private.

Third parties to the concentration also have the opportunity to submit comments on the proposal during Phase I in response to the Commission's publication of details in the *Official Journal*. The Merger Regulation provides further opportunity for their involvement during Phase II. First, they may be asked to submit information under an Article 11 ECMR request. Secondly, and more proactively, third parties may seek a hearing with the Commission under Article 18(4) ECMR. The Commission has the discretion to grant such a hearing, except where the third party can show that it holds a 'sufficient interest' in the outcome of the investigation. Where such a hearing is to take place, the Commission provides the third parties concerned with a note of the main issues that the concentration raises, and will allow a set period of time for the submission of written observations. The Commission may then invite participation in a formal hearing.

Having spent some time at DG Competition, one commentator – Jonathan Baker, formerly of both the DoJ and the FTC – suggested that DG Competition may benefit from developing more full analyses not only of the potential harm that a given transaction may cause (as was the observed tendency), but also of the benefits that it may bring. He thought it necessary for case workers to appreciate not only the 'bad guy story' of why the transaction might harm competition, but also the 'good guy story' as to how it might enhance competition or create efficiencies.[83] This impression coalesced in a perceived need for the Commission better to develop and test evidence. He considered that much evidence was drawn too uncritically straight from written responses to questionnaires sent to merging firms, rivals and customers,[84] and concluded that this may be achieved by the introduction of a greater measure of adversarial process into the Phase II analysis. It may be that the relative freedom from contentious testing of hypotheses in court has contributed to this perceived one-sidedness of Commission investigations.

*The juridical turn in EC merger control*
Article 21(2) ECMR provides for the review of Commission decisions under the Merger Regulation by the Community courts. In the normal case, challenges are brought before the Court of First Instance, and appealed as necessary on points of law only to the Court of Justice. The exception arises

where a matter is brought by a Member State under Article 230 EC. In such a case, the complaint is heard by the Court of Justice at first instance. Such challenges have been relatively rare. Since 2002, however, the Commission has seen a number of its decisions overturned by the Court of First Instance.[85] It may be that legal complaints will in future be brought more readily. Certainly, one of the main barriers to legal action, the time delay before delivery of the judgment, has been mitigated by the introduction of a 'fast-track' procedure in 2001. Nevertheless it is noticeable that, whereas court proceedings on preliminary injunctions in the US are almost invariably completed within six months, the EC procedure can still take in excess of a year.[86]

The issue of the requisite standard of proof which the Commission must achieve in order to prohibit a concentration is a somewhat vexed question.[87] By virtue of the ex ante nature of the exercise, the difficulty faced by the Commission is that it must always enter the realms of conjecture to some degree. There will always be scope for different decision makers to come to alternative conclusions as to likely future outcomes. Article 230 EC allows the court jurisdiction over acts of Community institutions on grounds, inter alia, of the 'infringement of [the] Treaty or of any rule of law relating to its application'. Article 21(2) ECMR refers to the 'review' of Commission decisions by the Community courts. There is no straightforward means to determine the appropriate level of this juridical intervention. It must be remembered, however, that what is proposed under the Merger Regulation is the interference with the basic right to enjoy property without interference. Thus the burden falling on the Commission to justify intervention must be high. In its *Kali und Salz* judgment, the Court of Justice was emphatic that 'evidence of the lack of effective competition . . . must be very strong'.[88]

The requisite legal standard of proof has been the font of much deliberation in a series of recent court decisions. In the *Airtours* case, the Court of First Instance appeared to consider, sometimes explicitly and certainly impliedly, that the onus on the Commission was to 'prove conclusively' its findings.[89] It did allow, however, that a 'discretionary margin' must be afforded the primary decision taker.[90] Nonetheless it set about a 'forensic demolition' of the Commission's findings,[91] pronouncing that, far from being based on 'cogent evidence', they had been 'vitiated by a series of errors of assessment'.[92] Few commentators would dispute that 'the *Airtours* judgment is of particular importance for the strict standard of substantiation and evidence laid down by the CFI'.[93] This standard was wielded again in *Tetra Laval* v. *Commission* and *Schneider Electric* v. *Commission*.[94] Each case saw the Court of First Instance complain that errors in the Commission's reasoning, and the paucity of some substantiating evidence, deprived the respective decisions of probative value. The validity of approach of the CFI in *Tetra* has subsequently been confirmed by the Court of Justice: the existence of the Commission's margin of discretion 'does not mean that the Community courts must refrain from reviewing the Commission's interpretation of information of an economic nature'.[95] Arguably these cases mark a new juridical turn for the Community courts in their approach to EC merger law. They seem less willing to withdraw exclusively to the role of an administrative court when faced with sophisticated economic arguments,[96] and more ready to interrogate the premises on which the Commission acts.

This shift may have a bearing on perceived differences in culture that some commentators have identified when comparing the US and EC regimes. For example, it has been suggested that 'the threshold for government intervention is different, and connotes a different balance of risk-taking and risk-aversion of future market harm'.[97] As regards Europe, the perception is that there is 'a greater willingness to take a stab at a longer-term prediction about competitive consequences . . . people may be more willing to accept preventative regulatory measures, even if it isn't clear to everyone that a problem is going to materialise'.[98] In contrast, the purported default position of the US regime is to worry 'about regulation that stops too many mergers . . . [and] count the costs of error . . . in prohibiting or conditioning mergers that are not price-raising';[99] 'the idea [in the US] . . . is that it is better to make a mistake and allow something through (in which case the market may yet correct the error) than it is to make a mistake and block a potentially beneficial transaction (in which case consumers will never see the benefits)'.[100]

Such a difference in bureaucratic cultures may exist, but to the extent that it has done so this is probably a result of attitudes expressed by the courts in the respective jurisdictions. The insistence on proof of anti-competitive effects that has been a feature of court decisions in the US since the 1980s has conditioned the attitudes of those preparing complaints.[101] Such an insistence is only now becoming evident in the EC. If the juridical turn in EC merger jurisprudence prompts Commission staff to become less willing to prohibit mergers without incontrovertible proof of likely competitive harm, the perceived cultural differences may soon dissolve.

### *Non-identical twins? Persistent structural differences between the EC and US*

While there are notable similarities between the two systems, it is important also to recognize the important differences that affect the size and timing of burdens placed on merging parties. On one hand, the respective jurisdictional thresholds are such that the US authorities review a very much larger number of transactions each year than their European counterparts; 'even after the amendments to Hart–Scott–Rodino, the US demands pre-merger filings from a far greater universe of companies than Europe does'.[102] The result is that more cases enter the system in the US and suffer time delays, financial costs and administrative burdens as a result. This discrepancy may be overplayed however. Insofar as the point is a comparative one, it is important to recognize also the number of transactions in Europe that do not possess a Community dimension but which remain subject to review by one or more national-level competition authorities.

On the other hand, the EC requires significantly more information to be provided from the outset by parties that propose a notifiable transaction. Form CO involves the completion of 'an elaborate initial filing . . . in every case within the jurisdictional threshold, and then the Commission [can] obtain additional information and hold an oral hearing, if the review [is] carried forward'.[103] Therefore the financial and administrative burdens associated with notification fall on all notifying companies. In contrast, in the US, this burden falls only on the very much smaller number of companies that propose transactions that invoke second requests.

These differences can be attributed to choices made as to the form of the respective merger regimes. It is notable, however, that the two systems tend to produce similar results in terms of the numbers of transactions that are prohibited or made subject to remedies, and that they achieve this by undertaking similar reviews of transactions against comparable benchmarks. While they may look a little different, the two systems are clearly cut from the same oak.

*Susceptibility to political influence*
One criticism that has been levelled at the EC merger regime in particular is that it is too susceptible to the play of political influence: that it allows scope for special pleadings to upset the pure competition assessment. Perhaps unsurprisingly, such assertions are made most often in response to particular decisions that have gone against the interests of the commentator.

It is certainly true that decisions at the culmination of Phase II proceedings in the EC regime are taken, not within DG Competition, but rather by the full College of Commissioners. That is, decisions are confirmed after cogitation by a cadre of individuals charged collectively with pursuing a broad range of policy objectives, some aligned with but others tangential to the aims of competition policy. Such decisions, however, must be taken against the criteria stipulated in Article 2 ECMR, and must be justified by a detailed statement of reasons that is made publicly available. Moreover this reasoning is subject to the supervisory jurisdiction of Community courts charged with assessing the logic of decisions, and in particular with uncovering any abuse of process. While wider political sensibilities may conceivably influence merger decisions, they can do so only where they can be expressed in argument pertinent to the competition assessment. This is likely to be possible only where the wider concerns in question in fact have a direct bearing on the competition question. Tellingly, in a seminal article on the evolution of US merger policy, Thomas Leary acknowledged that, during the first part of his tenure at the FTC, there were four cases in which the Commissioners did split along party lines (albeit only four cases among over 7000 notifications and 84 second requests).[104]

It is also worthy of note that no competition regime will ever be entirely insulated from political influence. At the very least, it is open to politicians to influence decisions in individual cases indirectly by the design of and strategic direction given to the merger regime: 'antitrust decision-making on a merger does not . . . take place in a political vacuum'.[105] Redolent of this fact was a recent exchange between two esteemed commentators on US antitrust over the impact that the election of Presidential candidate John Kerry would have had on US antitrust policy in general.[106] As a general proposition, therefore, it seems fair to assert that the EC merger regime is neither more nor less susceptible to political influence than any of its major comparators.

### Procedural limitations in the emergent US enforcement model

Given the movement of the US merger regime from a court-centred to a more regulatory model, a question arises as to whether adequate procedural safeguards have also been introduced. The subtle and unanticipated character of the shift gives reason to be sceptical. Certainly, by comparison with the EC regime, at least two key, problematic areas can be highlighted: the relative lack of transparency regarding the authorities' actions and the absence of judicial oversight of either the administrative process or the bulk of decision-making.

*Transparency in merger enforcement*

The move away from the formal court decision as the endpoint for US merger cases has left practitioners in general with less – or at least more fragmented – public source material on which to base their counsel.[107] Judicial decisions are published and can be scrutinized for insight into how the decision-makers will analyse particular situations. In the absence of some equivalent form of access to past administrative decision making, those considering prospective mergers lose a degree of certainty as to how regulators will approach their case. There is a concomitant increase in the associated business risk, and some meritorious transactions will be forgone

to the detriment of the instant parties and the wider society. This concern
has been ably summarized:

> the agencies' review process . . . is based on a law enforcement model in which
> the agencies assemble and evaluate information unilaterally and confidentially.
> This is the norm for statutory mechanisms under which the truth is hammered
> out through the adversarial process in the courtroom, after the government has
> made a decision to prosecute. The process has fundamental infirmities, however,
> when carried into traditional regulation because it lacks important procedural
> safeguards . . . thus, where administrative agencies sit with a regulatory role, they
> typically go about their activities with a greater degree of openness and
> balance.[108]

The question is whether the US merger authorities yet operate with the requisite degree of transparency.[109]

Insofar as merger decisions are still the product of legal enforcement,
there is little problem regarding transparency. On filing a complaint with
the district court, the DoJ or FTC must present a detailed statement of
their case. Subsequently this viewpoint will be tested before the court, and
the judge will offer a reasoned conclusion affirming or rejecting the agency's
contentions. Similarly the authorities' tendency to have negotiated settlements confirmed by way of consent decrees results in the publication of
competitive impact statements from which lessons for future scenarios can
be drawn.

There is less reason to be sanguine where the DoJ or FTC decides to clear
a transaction without seeking remedies. This category comprises around
98 per cent of all notified cases each year. Of particular note, however, are
those cases that are cleared having undergone a second request review.
These are cases in which the authority concerned will have identified a
prima facie competition problem during the first waiting period, but
regarding which concerns will have somehow been assuaged. The absence
of any legal obligation on the authorities to explain the reasons underpinning any decision not to file a complaint in such a case has been described
as a 'fundamental defect'.[110] Certainly, it is markedly different from the
position under the EC merger regime. There the obligation to take a reasoned decision one way or the other ensures that the parties always receive
a formal explanation from the agency, irrespective of whether the case is
decided at Phase I or Phase II. Moreover a version with commercially sensitive information redacted is also made available to the general public. One
suggestion has been that the US authorities should publish an analysis of
all cases regarding which they issue a second request. This would entail an
additional requirement only in respect of the small number of cases that
are cleared after a second request. Cases that are settled and those against

which a suit is brought are already reported publicly in some depth.[111] This would involve only a handful of cases each year, and while 'the burden of such a requirement would be relatively limited . . . the benefits . . . would be considerable'.[112]

Of course the authorities must balance the advantage to be gained from full publication against the costs of doing so. Clearly any requirement for merger authorities to prepare and publish substantive decision documents would have resource implications. The merger authorities may also wish to reserve comment on the basis that any inadvertent admissions may be used against them in future cases before the district court. It is ironic that this 'administrative defect is the result of a law enforcement vestige that remains in the US system'.[113]

While the DoJ and FTC have not yet conceded the need to publish reasoned decisions on cases where no complaint is to be filed, they have moved to redress the transparency problem in a number of ways. First, they have published guidance on a number of core issues.[114] Such material offers general prescriptions that companies can expect – all other things being equal – to apply in the case of their own prospective transactions. Secondly, the two authorities have published aggregate figures relating to the cases they investigated between 1996 and 2003.[115] Thirdly, the FTC has in fact begun to offer some measure of explanation of some cases.[116] In the instances in which this has happened – often those cases regarding which there has been media attention or disagreement among the Commissioners – the detail offered has ranged from two or three pages only to (in one case) around 50 pages. Fourthly, the many speeches made by the DoJ and FTC officials at public gatherings can also explicate given areas of interest. Moreover, there will always be some measure of judicial direction on offer, albeit most often from the lower courts only.[117] Even collectively, however, such measures are arguably insufficient. While indubitably helpful, officials' speeches generally disclaim any association with the 'agency view', and the guidelines are in some respects over-general and even obsolete.[118] The case summaries that have been published to date have been insufficiently thorough, inconsistent in coverage, and published on a too selective basis.[119] At the same time, the tailored presentation of cases by agency lawyers before a court may sometimes obscure the approaches adopted in practice within the authorities.[120]

Importantly, however, the FTC has indicated that it will soon publish further, more detailed commentaries on the *Merger Guidelines* – guides to the guidelines – that are informed by recent experience. The intention is to bring greater transparency to the agencies' merger analysis, and therefore greater certainty to businesses and merger practitioners.[121] It can be hoped that this initiative will go some way to overcoming the jurisprudential vacuum left by the move from the court. It may also mitigate the agencies' unwillingness to publish full discussions of the assessment of individual decisions.

*The effective absence of judicial supervision*

An adjunct to the matter of transparency is the absence of judicial supervision of the administrative process. Where transparency allows a public assessment of the merger review process and substantive decision, legal review secures a route to redress for disgruntled (third) parties. In Europe, the Community courts will endeavour to verify the facts on which the Commission has relied and to assess whether all proper procedural steps have been satisfied. In the US, 'the de facto administrative model . . . never provides this kind of judicial review of the internal processes of the agency (except sometimes decisions related to consent decrees)'.[122] The purported absence of any formal decision where cases are cleared is the camouflage that disguises the real administrative choices that are being made. The absence of any significant judicial oversight, 'despite the substantial power that the agencies exercise over the merging parties and at times over third parties with legitimate interests',[123] is a real defect of the administrative system as it actually exists.

**Managing multilayered merger enforcement**

A key dynamic underpinning the incremental reforms of the EC merger regime since its inception in 1990 has been the desire to perfect the mechanisms for the allocation of cases between the national and supranational tiers of governance. These are intended to secure a process of merger assessment for each individual case that is as streamlined as possible. In contrast, in the US there is scope for multiple authorities to seek to review the same transaction, albeit that these reviews are often coordinated. Identifiable weaknesses arising from this system of dual review leave the status quo vulnerable to revision. The proposal for reform most often aired is the preclusion of state-level enforcement. An alternative may be to institute a more formal division of exclusive responsibilities between the state Attorneys General on one hand and the FTC and DoJ on the other, mirroring the European model.

*The EC approach: a managed system of exclusive competences*

In Europe, where a merger satisfies one or other of the jurisdictional tests within the EC merger control regime (and thereby possesses a 'Community dimension') it must be notified to the European Commission and not any national authority.[124] In such circumstances, national jurisdiction is explicitly excluded by Article 21(3) ECMR. Conversely, where the jurisdictional tests are not met, the European Commission has no competence to review a merger. Thus the system is one of exclusive competence: as a general rule, a transaction can be reviewed either by one or more national authorities or by the European Commission, and not by both.

The relative crudity of the determinants of EC jurisdiction is mitigated to some degree by mechanisms included in the Merger Regulation that allow for the referral of notified mergers between the respective tiers of governance. The two aims of the system are to ensure that cases are allocated to the most appropriate competition authority, and to reduce where possible the need for firms to notify transactions in numerous disparate jurisdictions (the 'one-stop shop principle'). This need for a degree of flexibility in the system for case allocation was recognized from the outset, although originally it was expected that case referrals would be resorted to only in exceptional circumstances. Originally the 'Dutch clause' (Article 22(4) ECMR) and the 'German clause' (Article 9 ECMR) were considered little more than tokens to salve the sensibilities of national legislatures.[125]

After the introduction of the original Merger Regulation, the view quickly gained currency that the case allocation mechanisms included were inadequate to the task. Indeed the first revision of the Merger Regulation in 1997 involved the introduction of what were intended to be more sensitive threshold criteria to ensure that all significant transactions with a cross-border effect were considered at the supranational level.[126] This addition was largely ineffectual. Industry representatives continued to bemoan the 'huge inefficiency for business' caused by the need to make multiple filings of mergers across various Member States.[127]

The further refinement of the system of reattribution of cases was one of the primary aspirations underpinning the revision of the Merger Regulation that culminated in its recasting in 2004.[128] Recital 11 of the new Merger Regulation explains that the system 'should operate as an effective corrective mechanism in the light of the principle of subsidiarity . . . tak[ing] due account of legal certainty and the "one-stop shop" principle'. This refinement involved no change to the turnover threshold criteria, but rather the enhancement of the existing mechanisms for referral to and from the European Commission and the introduction of the possibility of pre-notification referral. The Commission has published a *Notice* on how it expects the new system to operate.[129] The ultimate aim is to ensure that the authority in the best position to deal with each given case actually does so. The general understanding, however, is that 'referrals remain a derogation from the general rules which determine jurisdiction based upon objectively-determinable turnover thresholds';[130] 'they should normally only be made when there is a compelling reason for departing from "original jurisdiction" over the case in question'.[131]

The broad intention that national authorities should be able to request the referral back of mergers that will have an impact on competition in a distinct market within the given Member State is noted in Recital 15 to the recast Merger Regulation. The referral mechanism is designed to allow proper scrutiny of cases which, although seemingly innocuous from the Community perspective, may have a significant impact within individual Member States. The detail of the mechanism is set out in Article 9 ECMR. The provision is now generally recognized as an important element in the overall scheme of case allocation. It was revised slightly with the introduction of the new Merger Regulation in order to facilitate referral back. The Article 9 ECMR process is subject to explicit time limits.[132] As of November 2005, 67 requests had been made under the Article 9 ECMR, of which only three had been refused.

Recital 12 of the Merger Regulation recognizes the heavy regulatory burden that can fall on parties to transactions that do not possess a Community dimension, but which qualify for examination under a number of national merger control regimes. It explains that 'multiple notification of the same transaction increases legal uncertainty, effort and cost for undertakings and may lead to conflicting assessments'. Recital 15 builds upon this recognition to suggest that Member States, either individually or in concert, should be enabled to refer to the European Commission transactions that do not possess a Community dimension to ensure that they receive appropriate assessment. This aspiration is catered for by Article 22 ECMR.

Article 22 ECMR was originally designed to alleviate potential difficulties posed by the absence of a regime of merger control in the Netherlands (hence the 'Dutch clause'). Its primary function now relates to the functioning of the 'one-stop shop' principle. A staging post on this transition was reached in 1997 when the provision was amended to allow two or more Member States to refer a transaction to the Commission where they felt that it was better placed to act.[133] As it stood, the measure was widely thought to be procedurally uncertain and difficult to use.[134] The recast Merger Regulation has introduced deadlines for Member States to make or join referral requests, alongside other revisions designed to improve efficiency. The joint use of the new provision by Member States should serve to preclude the duplication of investigations in a number of jurisdictions.

As of November 2005, the Article 22(4) ECMR procedure had been utilized on only 11 occasions. It might be expected that the greater emphasis on the one-stop shop principle following the recasting of the Merger Regulation will see more cases being referred jointly by Member States under Article 22 ECMR in future. There is some evidence of such a shift to date, with five requests having been made since the revision of the regulation.

A key innovation in the revised Merger Regulation was the introduction of the possibility for the notifying parties to have arranged in advance which competition authority would review their proposal. The inability to do so had been considered a central weakness of the existing system owing to the delay, increased cost and administrative inefficiency with which it burdened firms. The European Commission has noted, however, that 'pre-filing referrals should in principle be confined to those cases where it is relatively straightforward to establish, from the outset, the scope of the geographic market and/or the existence of a possible competitive impact'.[135]

Pre-notification referrals can be made in either direction: from the European Commission to a national competition authority where the transaction evinces a Community dimension but may significantly affect competition in some distinct, national market or markets (Article 4(4) ECMR), or from a Member State to the Commission should the transaction be reviewable under the merger regimes of at least three Member States (Article 4(5) ECMR). In the latter circumstance, the merger is then treated as though it possessed a Community dimension, so that it falls within the exclusive competence of DG Competition. Requests can be made by the parties for either full or partial referral. As of November 2005, ten referrals had been made to Member States under Article 4(4), while 37 referrals had been made under Article 4(5) ECMR.

Where an investigation remains at the supranational level, the Commission will work 'in close and constant liaison' with national competition authorities, and will copy all important documents, including details of proposed commitments, to them.[136] National authorities have the right to make representations on any given case at every stage of the assessment process, and to that end have access to the file.[137] Moreover, as a group, representatives of the national authorities contribute to deliberations by means of their membership of the Advisory Committee on Concentrations.[138] In particular, this Committee will consider a preliminary draft of the Commission's decision and offer its opinion. The Commission must 'take the utmost account' of this submission, but is not bound by it.[139]

*The US approach: concurrent jurisdictions of state and federal actors*
In any given case, a number of state Attorneys General may assert jurisdiction, perhaps alongside one of the national authorities. Such cases may involve the mutual application of section 7, or a combination of both state and federal laws. In such circumstances, there is routine effort to identify a

single state or small group of states to take the lead in analysing a merger,[140] and to liaise with the national antitrust agency concerned.[141] This effort proceeds along lines prescribed in a 1998 protocol agreed between the two federal antitrust enforcers and state Attorneys General.[142] In terms of their substantive assessments, many states will act in accord with a set of guidelines agreed in 1993 by the National Association of Attorneys General (NAAG).[143]

This existing scheme is open to a range of criticisms. First, review by both state and federal-level actors can introduce additional delay and cost for the merging parties. This may arise from the receipt of differing information requests from the separate agencies, difficulty in coordinating multiple party meetings, or even the mundane costs of travel to various sites. Secondly, dual review imposes additional cooperation costs on the agencies involved. It has been suggested that 'duplication and second-guess [become] virtually inevitable . . . [while] resources expended on coordination could be better applied to analysis and enforcement'.[144] Thirdly, there is a suspicion that state-level actors can be more susceptible to the influence of local interest constituencies,[145] although it is difficult to proffer empirical evidence to shore up such concerns.[146] A fourth concern is the obvious risk of 'divergence in enforcement approaches or remedies'.[147]

*A more formal system of case allocation?*
There is a standard proposal for reform of the current system. Having considered the persistent possibility of dual state and federal review, the International Competition Policy Advisory Committee concluded that 'a more rational or sensible approach would be to give exclusive federal jurisdiction to determine competition policy and the competitive consequences of mergers in federally regulated industries to the DOJ and FTC'.[148] Other commentators agree that for the majority of cases the national-level authorities 'enjoy boundless advantages'.[149]

As it is, Congress has legislated neither to preclude the role of the states nor to prescribe a uniform merger review standard or process. Whether any effort to legislate so as to preclude state-level actors from engaging in federal merger enforcement would be constitutional is a moot point.[150] In any event, a legislative proposal to this effect would have to survive what could be expected to be a highly politically charged legislative arena, and foreseeable legal challenge. Interestingly, however, the Antitrust Modernization Commission, established under Act of Congress in 2002 to review the state of US Antitrust laws,[151] has recently sought views on the role to be played by state Attorneys General in merger enforcement, whether merger enforcement should be limited to the federal level, and what lessons can be learned from the European referral system.[152] This suggests that the possibility of reform is at least hypothetically open.

An alternative might be to foment a consensus on a model of exclusive enforcement that respects the interests of state level actors. It is noticeable that, while there exists an apparent orthodoxy that merger control is generally best left to the national-level authorities, as regards mergers that primarily affect local markets state Attorneys General are widely acknowledged as enjoying the comparative advantage of familiarity.[153] In this context, the model provided by the EC system might offer substantial guidance. Of course, the major constraint in devising any such more formal system allotting specific responsibilities to the two levels of governance is that not all states possess merger laws or developed enforcement mechanisms.[154]

### Conclusion

The central aim of this survey has been to tease out the differences and identify the similarities between the US and EC merger control regimes, and by doing so to highlight the peculiar features of each. A further aim has been to point up a small number of areas in which mutual learning is both feasible and to be recommended. Most particularly, the abiding lesson of any review of the US and EC merger regimes must be that both currently place heavy burdens on the parties to very significant numbers of transactions that are ultimately proved to be unproblematic from a competition perspective. Surprisingly this truism has as yet engendered little energy geared towards reform. Ultimately, however, there can be little argument that both 'the world's principal merger review models deserve a second look'.[155]

### Notes

1. Law Department, London School of Economics and Political Science. I would like to thank Morten Hviid for helpful comments, to enter the usual disclaimer regarding remaining errors, and gratefully to acknowledge the support of the Economic and Social Research Council.
2. Cases T-209/01 and T-210/01, *Honeywell* v. *Commission*; *General Electric* v. *Commission*.
3. Whether convergence in the respective substantive standards has occurred remains a topic of vigorous debate. For some time, EC policy-makers in particular have been keen to stress the convergence of understandings as applied to individual cases by US and EC officials (see, for example, Monti, M. (14 November 2001), 'Antitrust in the US and Europe: a history of convergence', speech delivered to ABA Roundtable, Washington; Monti, M. (28 February 2004), 'Convergence in EU–US Antitrust Policy Regarding Mergers and Acquisitions: An EU Perspective', speech delivered to UCLA conference, Los Angeles). At least formally, this convergence was indeed signalled by the move to a 'significant impediment to effective competition' test in the recast Merger Regulation (Regulation 139/2004/EC (2004) OJ L24/1 – the 'ECMR'). Commentators have noted that recently issued merger guidelines provide further reason to expect similar outcomes, at least for horizontal mergers (see Facey, B. and H. Huser (2004), 'Convergence in international merger control: a comparison of horizontal merger guidelines in Canada, the European Union, and the United States', **19**, *Antitrust*, 43). Other commentators maintain, however, that 'the disparity between the antitrust regimes of the

United States and the European Union is [still] most acute in the area of merger control', and that use of the same rhetoric (for example, in talk of 'consumer welfare') can and does mask a variety of different policy choices. They propose that the 'real policy differences be openly acknowledged, rather than obscured with ambiguous verbiage': see Gifford, D. and R. Kudrle (2005), 'Rhetoric and reality in the merger standards of the United States, Canada, and the European Union', **72**, *Antitrust Law Journal*, 423, 425, 468–9.

4.   For an excellent overview of US antitrust law, see Broder, D. (2005), *A Guide to US Antitrust Law*, London: Sweet & Maxwell; on mergers, see especially chs 5 and 6. For more detailed reviews of US merger law and procedure, see ABA Section of Antitrust Law (2004), *Mergers and Acquisitions: Understanding the Antitrust Issues*, 2nd edn, Chicago: ABA Publishing and ABA Section of Antitrust Law (2001), *The Merger Review Process: A Step-by-Step Guide to Federal Merger Review*, 2nd edn, Chicago: ABA Publishing. For an interesting review of the development of US merger policy, see Leary, T. (2002), 'The essential stability of merger policy in the United States', **70**, *Antitrust Law Journal*, 105.

5.   15 U.S.C. §18. As originally drafted, section 7 was limited in scope and was generally considered a 'dead letter' (see *US* v. *Philadelphia National Bank* 374 U.S. 321 (1963), 339–40). It was amended and clarified in 1950 (by the Celler-Kefauver Antimerger Act), and again in 1980.

6.   15 U.S.C. §§1–2. Section 1 prohibits contracts, combinations or conspiracies in restraint of trade, while section 2 prohibits monopolization, attempts to monopolize, and conspiracies to monopolize. Notably, these sections require proof of existing harm to competition, whereas section 7 is designed to arrest in its incipiency any substantial lessening of competition which seems reasonably likely to result from a merger. Moreover the amendments to section 7 have left the Sherman Act provisions virtually obsolete as tools of merger control.

7.   15 U.S.C. §45. This power, which is intended to prevent any unfair method of competition or unfair and deceptive act or practice, is available only to the Federal Trade Commission, and is usually based upon a section 7 claim.

8.   Other relevant statutes which apply in specific contexts include the National Cooperative Research and Production Act of 2003 (15 U.S.C. §4301 *et seq.* – research and development and production joint ventures); the Bank Merger Act (12 U.S.C. §1828); the Natural Gas Act (15 U.S.C. §717(c)); the Federal Power Act (16 U.S.C. §824b), and the Telecommunications Act of 1996 (Pub. L. No.104, 110 Stat. 56).

9.   For further information, see http://www.usdoj.gov/atr.

10.   For further information, see http://www.ftc.gov.

11.   While every state has introduced some form of antitrust statute, only 14 deal explicitly with mergers. Of these, eight contain provisions that are broadly equivalent to section 7: see ABA Section of Antitrust Law (2004), above, note 3, 10–12.

12.   See *Brunswick Corp* v. *Pueblo Bowl-O-Mat Inc* (1977) 429 US 477; *Cargill Inc* v. *Monfort of Colorado Inc* (1986) 479 US 104. The ABA Section of Antitrust Law recently identified only 65 decisions in the past 20 years that involved private merger enforcement actions. It described this number as 'a minute proportion of the entire merger activity, especially when one considers the enormous merger activity of the 1990s': see ABA Section of Antitrust Law (2005), 'Government enforcement institutions: the Enforcement roles of states with respect to federal antitrust laws in merger cases', available at http://www.abanet.org/antitrust/comments/2005/10–05/gov-enforc.html, 12.

13.   There are 94 district courts, organized into 12 geographic circuits.

14.   Appeals from decisions of the district courts go to one of 13 circuit courts of appeal: the DC Circuit Court of Appeals, the First to Eleventh Circuit Courts of Appeals, and the Court of Appeals for the Federal Circuit (whose jurisdiction is subject matter-based).

15.   This is due in no small part to the shift in enforcement model that accompanied the introduction of the Hart–Scott–Rodino Act in 1976; see Baker, D. (2005), 'Making the best of a legal lemon', **8**, *Global Competition Review*, 17, 18. The last such case was *US* v. *General Dynamics*, 415 U.S. 486 (1974).

16. Blumenthal, W. (1997), 'Symposium: twenty years of Hart–Scott–Rodino merger enforcement – introductory note', **65**, *Antitrust Law Journal*, 813, 815. See, for example, Steuer, R. (1995), 'Counseling without case law', **63**, *Antitrust Law Journal*, 823; Weiner, M. (1995), 'Antitrust and the rise of the regulatory consent decree', **10**, Fall, *Antitrust*, 4; First, H. (1995), 'Is antitrust "law"?', **10**, Fall, *Antitrust*, 9 (at 9: 'there is a strong sense today that we are seeing something new in antitrust enforcement, a shift on the policy continuum toward bureaucratic regulation'); Melamed, A.D. (1995), 'Antitrust: the new regulation', **10**, Fall, *Antitrust*, 13 (at 13: 'antitrust has evolved in recent years, subtly and almost imperceptibly, toward a new form of regulation').

17. Sims, J. and D. Herman (1997), 'The effect of twenty years of Hart–Scott–Rodino on merger practice: a case study in the law of unintended consequences applied to antitrust legislation', **65**, *Antitrust Law Journal*, 865, 865.

18. See, for example, Melamed, above, note 16, 14 ('there is an externality and resulting market failure in the consent decree process. An individual defendant's private calculus of the costs and benefits . . . does not take into account the effects of the decree on third parties – on their expectations about law enforcement and the corresponding adjustments to their conduct'); First, above, note 16, 9.

19. Bittlingmayer, G. (2002), 'The antitrust emperor's clothes', *Regulation*, 46, 48.

20. 15 U.S.C. §18a. The HSR notification process is elaborated further in the Premerger Notification Rules (16 C.F.R. §§801–3), and is administered primarily by the FTC. The thresholds are that either (i) the acquiring party will hold voting securities or assets in the acquired firm of more than $212.3 million, or (ii) the acquiring party will hold voting securities or assets in the acquired firm of between $53.1 million and $212.3 million; one party has at least $106.2 million in total worldwide assets or annual net sales, and the other party has at least $10.7 million in total worldwide assets or annual net sales. These thresholds are now adjusted annually to take account of inflation; see Pfunder, M. (2005), 'Indexing comes to the HSR Act', *Antitrust Source*. The lower threshold was raised from $15 million to $50 million effective from 1 February 2001, with the result that notification fell from a peak of just less than 5000 in the fiscal year 2000 to a current rate of less than 1500 per annum. The acquisition of certain types of securities or assets is exempt from notification, for example the acquisition of foreign assets or convertible non-voting securities: 15 U.S.C. §18a(c).

21. *Per* Janet McDavid, cited in Samuels, D. (2005), 'Merger control in the rear-view Mirror', **8**, *Global Competition Review*, 29, 33.

22. Broder, above, note 4, paras 6.26–6.30.

23. FTC/DoJ (2005), *Annual Report to Congress: Fiscal Year 2004*, Washington: FTC/DoJ, 1. This represented an increase of 43 per cent from the 1014 transactions reported in fiscal year 2003. However, in the last full fiscal year prior to the revision of the merger thresholds (2000), 4926 transactions had been reported. The total dollar value of reported transactions was around $630 billion. This figure had reached a high point of $3 trillion in 2000 during the last major merger wave and before change was made to the notification thresholds.

24. The fee is currently $45 000 for transactions valued at $106.2 million or less, $125 000 for transactions valued between $106.2 million and $530.7 million, and $280 000 for transactions valued at more than $530.7 million. Again, these thresholds are adjusted annually to take account of inflation.

25. Kovacic, W. (1998), 'Merger enforcement in transition: antitrust controls on acquisitions in emerging economies', **66**, *University of Cincinnati Law Review*, 1075, 1085.

26. *Per* William Baer, cited in Samuels, above, note 21, 33.

27. DoJ/FTC (2005), above, note 23, 6.

28. 15 U.S.C. §18a(g).

29. Such violations have been described as 'a priority for the antitrust division' (see Pate, R. Hewitt, 2002), 'Antitrust enforcement at the DOJ: issues in merger investigations and litigation', speech delivered to NY Bar Association, New York, 10 December), and have been pursued with alacrity. For example, in *US* v. *Gemstar TV Guide International Inc* (2003) unreported, Civil Action No. 03 0198 (D.D.C), the DoJ agreed a settlement which saw a

merged company pay a fine of $5.676 million on account of its price fixing and allocation of customers in violation of the pre-merger waiting period requirements prior to its merger in July 2000. This reflected the maximum penalty under the $11 000 per day per pre-merger party rule. See generally, Krauss, J. (October 2002), ' "Gun-jumping": what are the standards governing pre-consummation activities?', *Global Competition Review*, 48.

30.  Following the upward revisions of the jurisdictional thresholds in 2001, this possibility has been highlighted by the authorities. Cases have been brought on a number of subsequent occasions: for example, *In re MSC Software*, FTC Docket No. 9299 (final consent, 1 November 2002); *In re Aspen Tech Inc*, FTC Docket No. 9310 (admin complaint, 6 August 2003) – see generally, Sher, S. (2004), 'Closed but not forgotten: government review of consummated mergers under section 7 of the Clayton Act', **45**, *Santa Clara Law Review*, 41.

31.  15 U.S.C. §18a(b). The waiting period is 15 days for a cash tender offer or an acquisition in bankruptcy. Any waiting period begins only on submission of a complete filing and payment of the requisite fee.

32.  ABA Section of Antitrust Law (2004), above, note 4, 12–16.

33.  Koberstein, N. and J. Hegarty (2003), 'US antitrust law: enforcement of laws governing mergers and acquisitions', *Competition Law Journal*, **361**, 366.

34.  *Liaison Agreement of the FTC and the Antitrust Division (1948)*, available at http://www.usdoj.gov/atr/foia/divisionmanual/ch7.pdf.

35.  DoJ/FTC (2002), *Memorandum of Agreement Between the Federal Trade Commission and the Antitrust Division of the US Department of Justice Concerning Clearance Procedures for Investigations*, available at http://www.ftc.gov/opa/2002/02/clearance/ftcdojagree.pdf. See also Majoras, D. (17 April 2002), 'We have a competition problem: how can we remedy it?', speech delivered to Houston Bar Association, Houston.

36.  Kolasky, W. (2005), 'US merger review: a "Goldilocksian" perspective', **8**, *Global Competition Review*, 14, 16.

37.  DoJ/FTC (2005), above, note 23, 5 and Appendix A. The equivalent figures for 2003 were 69 per cent (700) and 86.6 per cent (606). Arguably, therefore, it remains the case that, even after the 2001 revisions of the jurisdictional thresholds, there is a significant number of 'competitively innocuous transactions that constitute the vast bulk of Hart–Scott–Rodino filings that are needlessly burdened': see Blumenthal, above, note 16, 819.

38.  Resubmission is free only if made within two business days of the withdrawal, and if there is no substantial difference in the proposed transaction. It can be done only once.

39.  DoJ/FTC (2005), above, note 23, 4. Of these, 20 were issued by the FTC and 15 by the DoJ. The same number of second requests was made in 2003, although this represented 3.6 per cent of notified cases.

40.  This period is limited to ten days in cases of cash tender offers or certain bankruptcy transactions.

41.  Congress has moved to enhance the opportunity for parties to seek relief from requests on the grounds that they are unreasonably cumulative, unduly burdensome, or duplicative, or that they have already been substantially complied with. These changes are now reflected in internal procedures: see DoJ (2001), *Second Request Internal Appeal Procedure*, available online at the following website: http://www.usdoj.gov/atr/public/8430.htm. Moreover, since her appointment as Chairman of the FTC, Deborah Majoras has established a task force charged with streamlining and otherwise improving the merger review process: see Ewing, K. and J.-R. Gonzalez-Magaz (2005), 'Higher thresholds and new rules for unincorporated entities', *The Antitrust Review of the Americas 2006*, London: Global Competition Review, pp. 24, 25.

42.  Kolasky, above, note 36, 15.

43.  Newborn, S. and V. Snider (2005), 'The Ten Commandments of getting your deal through', *The Antitrust Review of the Americas 2006*, London: Global Competition Review, p. 13.

44.  On the history of revisions to and influence of the US Merger Guidelines since their original introduction in 1968, see ABA Section of Antitrust Law (2004), above, note 4, 16–26.

45.  Steuer, above, note 16, 845.

46.  This possibility should not be overplayed: while 'the theoretical possibility of a later suit for divestiture still exists . . . it is hard . . . to imagine such a lawsuit in the absence of some failure to disclose the circumstances of the transaction honestly': see Wood, D. (2003), 'A comparison of merger review and remedy procedures in the United States and European Union', in Lévêque and Shelanski (eds), *Merger Remedies in American and European Union Competition Law*, Cheltenham, UK and Northampton, MA, USA: Edward Elgar, p. 69.

47.  In *US* v. *E.I. du Pont de Nemours & Co*, 353 U.S. 586 (1957), a transaction was challenged 30 years after it had been consummated.

48.  See generally, DoJ (2004), *Antitrust Division Policy Guide to Merger Remedies*, Washington: DoJ; available at: http://www.usdoj.gov/atr/public/guidelines/205108.htm; Baer, W. and R. Redcay (2003), 'Solving Competition problems in Merger Control: The Requirements of an Effective Divestiture Remedy', in Lévêque and Shelanski (eds), *Merger Remedies in American and European Union Competition Law*, Cheltenham: Edward Elgar, ch. 3.

49.  Broder, above, note 3, paras 8–19 and 8–28; ABA Section of Antitrust Law (2004), above, note 4, 31.

50.  FTC/DoJ (2005), above, note 23, 2. The rate of challenge has been fairly consistent over time: see Leary, above, note 4.

51.  *US* v. *Von's Grocery Co.*, 384 U.S. 270, 301 (1966).

52.  Kolasky, above, note 36, 15.

53.  That Article 82EC can apply to mergers was first confirmed by the Court of Justice in 1973; see Case 6/72 *Europemballage Corporation and Continental Can Co. Inc.* v. *Commission* [1973] ECR 215. However the provision could be used only where a merger could be classed as an abuse of an already existing dominant position; it could not encompass the scenario where a merger itself created dominance. Moreover it could not be deployed to pre-empt a problematic merger, and allowed only the draconian, and hence underemployed, remedy of ex post divestiture. The Commission's long-held view regarding the applicability of Article 81EC was that it could not apply to the total or partial acquisition of ownership of enterprises, but rather was limited to agreements and concerted practices between undertakings that remained independent; see European Commission (1966), *Memorandum on the Concentration of Enterprises in the Common Market*.

54.  Council Regulation (EEC) No 4064/89 on the control of concentrations between undertakings [1989] OJ L395/1; corrected version [1990] OJ L257/13. On the EC merger regime generally, see Navarro et al. (2005), *Merger Control in the European Union: Law, Economics and Practice*, 2nd edn, Oxford: OUP.

55.  Council of Ministers of the EU (1997), *Council Regulation (EC) 1310/97 amending Regulation (EEC) No 4064/89 on the control of concentrations between undertakings* [1997] OJ L180/1. See, generally, Turner, V. and C. Ahlborn (1998), 'Expanding success? Reform of the EC Merger Regulation', **19**, *European Competition Law Review*, 249.

56.  Council of Ministers of the EU (2004), *Council Regulation (EC) No 139/2004 on the control of concentrations between undertakings* (2004) OJ L24/1 (hereinafter 'ECMR' or 'Merger Regulation').

57.  European Commission (2004b), *Commission Regulation (EC) No 802/2004 of 7 April 2004 implementing Council Regulation (EC) No 139/2004 on the control of concentrations between undertakings* (2004) OJ L133/1 (Regulation 802/2004).

58.  European Commission (2004a), *Commission Notice on the Assessment of Horizontal Mergers Under the Council Regulation on the Control of Concentrations Between Undertakings*, [2004] OJ C31/3.

59.  Available online at http://www.europa.eu.int/comm/competition/mergers/legislation/regulation/best_practices.pdf.

60.  This included the establishment of the new office of Chief Economist in DG Competition. It has been suggested, however, that 'the Chief Economist's team will probably need to triple in size before it can systematically play a role comparable to what agency economics groups do in the United States'; see Baker, J. (3 September 2005), 'My summer vacation at the European Commission', *Antitrust Source*.

61.  Paragraph 2 states that a concentration has a Community dimension where (a) the combined aggregate worldwide turnover of all the undertakings concerned is more than €5000 million; and (b) the aggregate Community-wide turnover of each of at least two of the undertakings concerned is more than €250 million, unless each of the undertakings concerned achieves more than two-thirds of its aggregate Community-wide turnover within one and the same Member State. It is noticeable that the threshold levels have remained unchanged since their introduction in 1990. In effect, given the impact of inflation, this amounts to a gradual diminution of around 25%.
     Paragraph 3 offers an alternative test: a concentration . . . has a Community dimension where (a) the combined aggregate worldwide turnover of all the undertakings concerned is more than €2500 million; (b) in each of at least three Member States, the combined aggregate turnover of all the undertakings concerned is more than €100 million; (c) in each of at least three Member States included for the purpose of point (b), the aggregate turnover of each of at least two of the undertakings concerned is more than €25 million; and (d) the aggregate Community-wide turnover of each of at least two of the undertakings concerned is more than €100 million, unless each of the undertakings concerned achieves more than two-thirds of its aggregate Community-wide turnover within one and the same Member State.
62.  Recital 20 explains that the focus is on transactions that 'bring about a lasting change in the structure of the undertakings concerned'. This implies a degree of permanence in the change of structure. The basic legal definition of a concentration is set out in the five paragraphs of Article 3 ECMR.
63.  Cases T-310/01 and T-77/02, *Schneider Electric SA* v. *Commission* [2002] ECR II-4071; Ragolle (2003), '*Schneider Electric* v. *Commission*: the CFI's Response to the Green Paper on Merger Review', *European Competition Law Review*, 176. More generally, see Hofmann, H. (2003), 'Good governance in European merger control: due process and checks and balances under review', *European Competition Law Review*, 114.
64.  Article 14 (1) and (2) ECMR. See further, Modrall, J. and S. Ciullo (2003), 'Gun-jumping and EU merger control', **24**, *European Competition Law Review*, 424.
65.  A simplified procedure for notifying concentrations that do not raise significant competition concerns was introduced by the Commission effective from September 2000 (see European Commission, 2000a, *Commission Notice on a Simplified Procedure for Treatment of Certain Concentrations under Council Regulation 4064/89* [2000] OJ C217/32). This extended the limited waivers already available under Section C of Form CO for a joint venture with little likelihood of any impact on competition within the EEA. This applies to three categories of concentration: (a) concentrative joint ventures which have only negligible actual or potential activities in the European Economic Area; (b) concentrations where none of the parties operates either in the same product and geographic markets, or in product market that are upstream or downstream of each other; (c) concentrations where the combined market share is less than 15% where there is horizontal competition, and 25% in markets where the relationship is vertical. A request for dispensation from the full notification requirements must be included with the notification; the Commission reserves the right to refuse such a request. Moreover it can revert to the normal procedure if this is deemed appropriate. The decision on a case notified in this way will be delivered in 'short-form'.
66.  *Per* Malcolm Nicholson, cited in Samuels, above, note 21, 35.
67.  *Per* Janet McDavid, cited in Samuels, ibid. 33.
68.  Notably, 57% of cases decided in 2004 had been notified under the procedure; see European Commission (2005b), *Report on Competition Policy 2004*, SEC(2005) 805 final, para.142.
69.  Article 7 ECMR.
70.  Article 4(3) ECMR.
71.  This total has fallen off slightly from a peak of 345 notifications in 2000. Up-to-date statistics on EC merger control are available at http://www.europa.eu.int/comm/competition/mergers/cases/stats.html.
72.  *Per* Janet McDavid, cited in Samuels, above, note 21, 33.

73. Article 6(1)(b) ECMR.
74. Article 6(2) ECMR.
75. Article 6(1)(c) ECMR.
76. Article 12(1), Regulation 802/2004.
77. Article 18(3) ECMR.
78. Article 10(3) ECMR.
79. Article 10(6) ECMR.
80. Clearance decisions are made under Article 8(2) ECMR; prohibition decisions under Article 8(3) ECMR.
81. Article 18(3) ECMR.
82. Article 18(3) ECMR; Article 17(3), Regulation 802/2004. Such access is intended to enable firms to acquaint themselves with the evidence, so that they can express their views effectively on the conclusions reached by the Commission in its statement of objections. An infringement of the rights of the defence occurs where the non-disclosure of the documents in question might have influenced the course of the procedure and the content of the decision to the applicant's detriment (Case T-221/95, *Endemol v. Commission* [1999] ECR II-1299, para. 87).
83. Baker, J. *op. cit.* note 60, 3.
84. Ibid., 5.
85. Case T-342/99 *Airtours* v. *Commission* [2002] ECR II-2585; Case T-5/02 *Tetra Laval BV* v. *Commission* [2002] ECR II-4519; Cases T-310/01 and T-77/02 *Schneider Electric SA* v. *Commission* [2002] ECR II-4071; Case T-114/02 *Babyliss SA* v. *Commission* (unreported).
86. A standard explanation is the delay caused by translation needs. Notably, however, in Case T-87/05 *EDP-Energias de Portugal* v. *Commission* (21 September 2005, not yet reported) the time taken to decide the case was only seven months.
87. For further discussion, see Nicholson, M., S. Cardell and B. McKenna (2005), 'The scope of review of merger decisions under Community law', 1, *European Competition Journal*, 123; Bright, C. (19 January 2005), 'Going beyond the new orthodoxy: reflections on the state of merger control', speech delivered at UEA CCP, Norwich; Vesterdorf, B. (2005), 'Standard of proof in merger cases: reflections in the light of recent case law of the Community Courts', 1, *European Competition Journal*, 3; Bay, M., J. Calzado and A. Weitbrecht (2005), 'Judicial review of mergers in the EU and the fast-track procedure', *European Antitrust Review 2006*, 38; Swift, J. (21 September 2004), 'Judicial control of competition decisions in the UK and EU', speech delivered to Competition Commission, London; Bailey, D. (2003), 'Standard of proof in EC merger proceedings: a common law perspective', **40**, *Common Market Law Review*, 845.
88. Case COMP/M1016, *Price Waterhouse/Coopers & Lybrand* [1999] OJ L50/27, para. 105.
89. Case T-342/99 *Airtours* v. *Commission* [2002] ECR II-2585, para. 210.
90. Ibid., paras 64–5.
91. Overd, A. (2002), 'After the Airtours appeal', *European Competition Law Review*, 375.
92. Case T-342/99 *Airtours* v. *Commission* [2002] E.C.R. II-2585, [2002] 5 C.M.L.R. 7, para. 294. Perhaps the most incontrovertible instances were the Commission's misinterpretation and reliance on a single page extract of an undated report, and its reference to an internal econometric study. The first report the Commission had never seen in its full form, the second it never produced before the court (paras. 128 and 132). Interestingly, the Commission considered that its economic analysis in the *Airtours* case 'was probably more refined than in earlier cases': see Christensen and Rabassa (2001), 'The *Airtours* decision: is there a new Commission approach to collective dominance', *European Competition Law Review*, 227.
93. Haupt, H. (2002), 'Collective dominance under Article 82 and EC merger control in the light of the *Airtours* judgment', *European Competition Law Review*, 434, 443.
94. Case T-5/02, *Tetra Laval BV* v. *Commission* [2002] ECR II-4519; Cases T-310/01 and T-77/02, *Schneider Electric SA* v. *Commission* [2002] ECR II-4071.
95. Case T-114/02, *Babyliss SA* v. *Commission* Reported in: [2003] ECR-II 1279, *EDP-Energias Portugal* v. *Commission* is still unreported.

96. Gerber, D. (1994), 'The transformation of European Community competition law?', **35**, *Harvard International Law Journal*, 97.
97. Fox, E. (2002), 'United States and European merger policy: fault lines and bridges for mergers that create incentives for exclusionary practices', **10**, *George Mason Law Review*, 471, 474–5.
98. Wood, above, note 46, 73.
99. Fox, above, note 97, 475.
100. Wood, above, note 46, 73.
101. The recognized watershed decision, although not itself a merger case, was *Continental T.V., Inc.* v. *GTE Sylvania Inc.*, 433 U.S. 36 (1977).
102. Wood, above, note 46, 72.
103. Baker, D. (2005), 'Making the best of a legal lemon', **8**, *Global Competition Review*, 17, 18.
104. Leary, above, note 4, 132.
105. Baker, D., above, note 103, 17.
106. Kolasky, W. (September 2004), 'What would a Kerry Administration antitrust program look like?', *Antitrust Source*; Kovacic, W. (September 2004), 'The future of US competition policy', *Antitrust Source*.
107. Steuer, above, note 16.
108. Blumenthal, above, note 16, 821.
109. For further discussion on this point, see Gelfand, D. and J. Calsyn (January 2005), 'Transparency in antitrust merger review: a modest proposal for more', *Antitrust Source*; Grimes, W. (2003), 'Transparency in federal antitrust enforcement', **51**, *Buffalo Law Review*, 937 (and subsequent comments in that journal issue).
110. Baker, D., above, note 103, 19.
111. Gelfand and Calsyn, above, note 109, 6–7.
112. Ibid., 7.
113. Baker, D., above, note 103, 19.
114. See DoJ/FTC (1997), *Horizontal Merger Guidelines*, rev. edn, Washington: DOJ/FTC; DoJ/FTC (2000), *Antitrust Guidelines for Collaborations Among Competitors*, Washington: DoJ/FTC; DoJ, above, note 48. Each of these documents is available online at the following website: http://www.usdoj.gov/atr/public/guidelines/guidelin.htm.
115. FTC (2004), *Horizontal Merger Investigation Data, Fiscal Years 1996–2003*, available at http://www.ftc.gov/opa/2004/02/horizmerger.htm.
116. Gelfand and Calsyn, above, note 109, 3–6.
117. The district court has recently offered guidance on both unilateral effects and coordinated effects: see *Federal Trade Commission* v. *Arch Coal Inc* 329 F. Supp. 2d 109 (D.D.C. 2004) and *US* v. *Oracle Corp.* 331 F. Supp. 2d 1098 (N.D. Cal. 2004).
118. Gelfand and Calsyn, above, note 109, 2.
119. Ibid., 6.
120. Baker, D., above, note 103, 18 ('[FTC and DoJ] lawyers almost seem to forget their recent pre-complaint dialogue with the parties . . . [and] will try . . . to revert to the vintage populism from the pre-1974 Supreme Court merger decisions').
121. Majoras, D. (18 November 2004), 'Looking forward: merger and other policy initiatives at the FTC', speech delivered to ABA Antitrust Section Fall Forum, Washington.
122. Baker, D., above, note 103, 19.
123. Ibid.
124. See above, note 61.
125. Article 9 in particular was a controversial inclusion in the original Merger Regulation, and was the last clause to be agreed in the legislative process; see Brittan, L. (1990), 'The law and policy of merger control in the EEC', *European Law Review*, 351, 355.
126. This comprised the insertion of Article 1(3) ECMR (see above, note 61), by Council Regulation (EC) 1310/97 amending Regulation (EEC) No 4064/89 on the control of concentrations between undertakings [1997] OJ L180/1.
127. *Per* Rufus Ogilvie Smals, cited in Select Committee on the European Union (2001–2002), *Thirty-second Report: the Review of the EC Merger Regulation*, HL 165, London: Stationery Office, para. 31.

128. A review of the 'Community dimension' criteria and of the rules on the referral of cases to Member State authorities was required under Articles 1(4) and 9(10) of the original Merger Regulation. This was delivered to the Council of Ministers in June 2000 (European Commission, 2000b, *Report to the Council on the Application of the Merger Regulation Thresholds*, COM(2000) 399 final). For comment on the referral procedures, see Dominguez Perez, D. and R. Burnley (2003), 'The article 9 referral back procedure: a solution to the jurisdictional dilemma of the European Merger regulation?', *European Competition Law Review*, 364; Sinclair, D. (2002), 'Reflections on the European Commission's proposals to amend the jurisdictional test in the Merger Regulation: a hall of mirrors?', *European Competition Law Review*, 326.

129. European Commission (2005a), *Commission Notice on case referral in respect of concentrations*, [2005] OJ C56/2.

130. Ibid., para. 7.

131. Ibid., para. 13.

132. To instigate a referral, the national authority must detail its concerns within 15 working days of its receipt of a copy of the notification from the European Commission. It is open to the Commission to invite a request: Article 9(2) ECMR.

133. Council Regulation (EC) 1310/97 amending Regulation (EEC) No. 4064/89 on the control of concentrations between undertakings [1997] OJ L180/1.

134. Prior to the revision of the Merger Regulation, Article 22 ECMR was used jointly by Member States on only three occasions: Case COMP/M.2698, *Promatech/Sulzer* (2002); Case COMP/M.2738 *GEES / Unison* (2002) and Case COMP/M.3136 *GE/AGFA NDT* (2003).

135. European Commission (2005a), *Commission Notice on case referral in respect of concentrations*, [2005] OJ C56/2, para. 14.

136. Article 19(1) and Recital 20 ECMR.

137. Article 19(2) ECMR.

138. Article 19(3)–(7) ECMR.

139. Article 19(6) ECMR. A disagreement occurred between the Commission and the Advisory Committee in Case IV/M043, *Magneti Marelli / CEAc* [1992] 4 CMLR M61.

140. Flexner, D. and M. Racanelli (1994), 'State and federal antitrust enforcement in the United States: collision or harmony?', **9**, *Connecticut Journal of International Law*, 501, 509–10.

141. Hawk, B. and L. Laudati (1996), 'Antitrust federalism in the United States and decentralization of competition law enforcement in the European Union: a comparison', **20**, *Fordham International Law Journal*, 18, 30. See also Calvani, T. (2003), 'Devolution and convergence in competition enforcement', **24**, *European Competition Law Review*, 415, 416–17.

142. DoJ/FTC (1998), *Protocol for Coordination in Merger Investigations Between the Federal Enforcement Agencies and State Attorneys General*, available online at the following website: http://www.usdoj.gov/atr/public/guidelines/1773.htm.

143. NAAG (1993), *Horizontal Merger Guidelines*, reprinted in **4**, *Trade Regulation. Reports*.

144. Wise, M. (1999), 'Review of United States Competition Law and Policy', **1**, *OECD Journal of Competition Law and Policy*, 9, 60–61.

145. Rose, J. (1994), 'State Antitrust Enforcement, Mergers and Politics', **41**, *Wayne Law Review*, 71, 117–21.

146. ABA Section of Antitrust Law (2005), above, note 12, 8.

147. Ibid., 9.

148. ICPAC (2000), *Final Report to the Attorney General and Assistant Attorney General for Antitrust*, Washington: DoJ, 144. See also Calvani, T. (2003), 'Devolution and convergence in competition enforcement', **24**, *European Competition Law Review*, 415, 416–17.

149. Calkins, S. (2003), 'Perspectives on state and federal antitrust enforcement', **53**, *Duke Law Journal*, 673, 696.

150. Ginsburg, D. and S. Angstreich (2000), 'Multinational merger review: lessons from our federalism', **68**, *Antitrust Law Journal*, 219, n. 32.

151. See further http://www.amc.gov/index.html.
152. AMC (2005), *Request for Public Comment: Enforcement Institutions*, 70 Fed. Reg. 28902–28907, 19 May, Part C.
153. See First, H. (2001), 'Delivering remedies: the role of the states in merger enforcement', **69**, *George Washington Law Review*, 1004, 1036–9; Calkins, S. (2003), 'Perspectives on state and federal antitrust enforcement', **53**, *Duke Law Journal*, 673, 680; ABA Section of Antitrust Law (2005), above, note 12, 6.
154. Indeed to date only 14 states have introduced antitrust statutes that deal explicitly with mergers, although this figure does not reflect those that rely solely on federal laws.
155. *Per* William Rowley, cited in Samuels, above, note 21, 33.

## References

ABA Section of Antitrust Law (2001), *The Merger Review Process: A Step-by-Step Guide to Federal Merger Review*, 2nd edn, Chicago: ABA Publishing.
ABA Section of Antitrust Law (2004), *Mergers and Acquisitions: Understanding the Antitrust Issues*, 2nd edn, Chicago: ABA Publishing.
ABA Section of Antitrust Law (2005), *Government Enforcement Institutions: The Enforcement Roles of States with Respect to Federal Antitrust Laws in Merger Cases*, available at http://www.abanet.org/antitrust/comments/2005/10–05/gov-enforc.html.
AMC (2005), *Request for Public Comment: Enforcement Institutions*, 70 Fed. Reg. 28902–28907, 19 May, Part C.
Baer, W. and R. Redcay (2003), 'Solving competition problems in merger control: the requirements of an effective divestiture remedy', in F. Lévêque and H. Shelanski (eds), *Merger Remedies in American and European Union Competition Law*, Cheltenham, UK and Northampton, MA, USA: Edward Elgar, ch. 3.
Bailey, D. (2003), 'Standard of proof in EC merger proceedings: a common law perspective', **40**, *Common Market Law Review*, 845.
Baker, D. (2005), 'Making the best of a legal lemon', **8**, *Global Competition Review*, 17.
Baker, J. (2005), 'My summer vacation at the European Commission', *Antitrust Source*, 3 September.
Bay, M., J. Calzado and A. Weitbrecht (2005), 'Judicial review of mergers in the EU and the fast-track procedure', *European Antitrust Review 2006*, 38.
Bittlingmayer, G. (2002), 'The antitrust Emperor's Clothes', *Regulation*, Fall, 46.
Blumenthal, W. (1997), 'Symposium: twenty years of Hart–Scott–Rodino merger enforcement – Introductory Note', **65**, *Antitrust Law Journal*, 813.
Bright, C. (2005), 'Going Beyond the New Orthodoxy: Reflections on the State of Merger Control', speech delivered at UEA CCP, Norwich, 19 January.
Brittan, L. (1990), 'The law and policy of merger control in the EEC', *European Law Review*, 351.
Broder, D. (2005), *A Guide to US Antitrust Law*, London: Sweet & Maxwell.
Calkins, S. (2003), 'Perspectives on state and federal antitrust enforcement', **53**, *Duke Law Journal*, 673.
Calvani, T. (2003), 'Devolution and convergence in competition enforcement', **24**, *European Competition Law Review*, 415.
Christensen, P. and V. Rabassa (2001), 'The *Airtours* decision: is there a new Commission approach to collective Dominance?', *European Competition Law Review*, 227.
Council of Ministers of the EU (1997), *Council Regulation (EC) 1310/97 amending Regulation (EEC) No 4064/89 on the control of concentrations between undertakings* [1997] OJ L180/1.
Council of Ministers of the EU (2004), *Council Regulation (EC) No 139/2004 on the control of concentrations between undertakings* (2004) OJ L24/1.
DoJ (2001), *Second Request Internal Appeal Procedure*, available online at the following website: http://www.usdoj.gov/atr/public/8430.htm.
DoJ (2004), *Antitrust Division Policy Guide to Merger Remedies*, Washington: DoJ, available at: http://www.usdoj.gov/atr/public/guidelines/205108.htm.

DoJ/FTC (1997), *Horizontal Merger Guidelines*, rev. edn, Washington: DoJ/FTC.
DoJ/FTC (1998), *Protocol for Coordination in Merger Investigations Between the Federal Enforcement Agencies and State Attorneys General*, available online at the following website: http://www.usdoj.gov/atr/public/guidelines/1773.htm.
DoJ/FTC (2000), *Antitrust Guidelines for Collaborations Among Competitors*, Washington: DoJ/FTC.
DoJ/FTC (2002), *Memorandum of Agreement Between the Federal Trade Commission and the Antitrust Division of the US Department of Justice Concerning Clearance Procedures for Investigations*, available at: http://www.ftc.gov/opa/2002/02/clearance/ftcdojagree.pdf.
DoJ/FTC (2005), *Annual Report to Congress: Fiscal Year 2004*, Washington: FTC/DoJ.
Dominguez Perez, D. and R. Burnley (2003), 'The Article 9 Referral Back Procedure: a Solution to the Jurisdictional Dilemma of the European Merger Regulation?', *European Competition Law Review*, 364.
European Commission (1966), *Memorandum on the Concentration of Enterprises in the Common Market*, EEC Competition Series Study Series (Number 3).
European Commission (2000a), *Commission Notice on a Simplified Procedure for Treatment of Certain Concentrations under Council Regulation 4064/89* [2000] OJ C217/32.
European Commission (2000b), *Report to the Council on the Application of the Merger Regulation Thresholds* COM(2000) 399 final.
European Commission (2004a), *Commission Notice on the Assessment of Horizontal Mergers Under the Council Regulation on the Control of Concentrations Between Undertakings*, [2004] OJ C31/3.
European Commission (2004b), *Commission Regulation (EC) No 802/2004 of 7 April 2004 implementing Council Regulation (EC) No 139/2004 on the control of concentrations between undertakings* (2004) OJ L133/1 (Regulation 802/2004).
European Commission (2005a), *Commission Notice on case referral in respect of concentrations*, [2005] OJ C56/2.
European Commission (2005b), *Report on Competition Policy 2004*, SEC(2005) 805 final.
Ewing, K. and J.-R. Gonzalez-Magaz (2005), 'Higher thresholds and new rules for unincorporated entities', *The Antitrust Review of the Americas 2006*, London: Global Competition Review, p. 24.
Facey, B. and H. Huser (2004), 'Convergence in international merger control: a comparison of horizontal merger guidelines in Canada, the European Union, and the United States', **19**, *Antitrust*, 43.
First, H. (1995), 'Is antitrust "law"?', **10**, Fall, *Antitrust*, 9.
First, H. (2001), 'Delivering remedies: the role of the states in merger enforcement', **69**, *George Washington Law Review*, 1004.
Flexner, D. and M. Racanelli (1994), 'State and federal antitrust enforcement in the United States: collision or harmony?', **9**, *Connecticut Journal of International Law*, 501.
Fox, E. (2002), 'United States and European merger policy: fault lines and bridges for mergers that create incentives for exclusionary practices', **10**, *George Mason Law Review*, 471.
FTC (2004), 'Horizontal merger investigation data, fiscal years 1996–2003', available at http://www.ftc.gov/opa/2004/02/horizmerger.htm.
Gelfand, D. and J. Calsyn (2005), 'Transparency in antitrust merger review: a modest proposal for more', *Antitrust Source*, January.
Gerber, D. (1994), 'The transformation of European Community competition law?', **35**, *Harvard International Law Journal*, 97.
Gifford, D. and R. Kudrle (2005), 'Rhetoric and reality in the merger standards of the United States, Canada, and the European Union', **72**, *Antitrust Law Journal*, 423.
Ginsburg, D. and S. Angstreich (2000), 'Multinational merger review: lessons from our federalism', **68**, *Antitrust Law Journal*, 219.
Grimes, W. (2003), 'Transparency in federal antitrust enforcement', **51**, *Buffalo Law Review*, 937.
Haupt, H. (2002), 'Collective dominance under article 82 and EC merger control in the light of the *Airtours* judgment', *European Competition Law Review*, 434.

Hawk, B. and L. Laudati (1996), 'Antitrust federalism in the United States and decentraliza-tion of competition law enforcement in the European Union: a comparison', **20**, *Fordham International Law Journal*, 18.
Hofmann, H. (2003), 'Good governance in European merger control: due process and checks and balances under review', *European Competition Law Review*, 114.
ICPAC (2000), *Final Report to the Attorney General and Assistant Attorney General for Antitrust*, Washington: DoJ.
Koberstein, N. and J. Hegarty (2003), 'US antitrust law: enforcement of laws governing mergers and acquisitions', *Competition Law Journal*, 361.
Kolasky, W. (2004), 'What would a Kerry Administration antitrust program look like?', *Antitrust Source*, September.
Kolasky, W. (2005), 'US merger review: a "Goldilocksian" perspective', **8**, *Global Competition Review*, 14.
Kovacic, W. (1998), 'Merger enforcement in transition: antitrust controls on acquisitions in emerging economies', **66**, *University of Cincinnati Law Review*, 1075.
Kovacic, W. (2004), 'The future of US competition policy', *Antitrust Source*, September.
Krauss, J. (2002), ' "Gun-jumping": what are the standards governing pre-consummation activities?', *Global Competition Review*, 48, October.
Leary, T. (2002), 'The essential stability of merger policy in the United States', **70**, *Antitrust Law Journal*, 105.
Majoras, D. (2002), 'We have a competition problem: how can we remedy it?', speech deliv-ered to Houston Bar Association, Houston, 17 April.
Majoras, D. (2004), 'Looking forward: merger and other policy initiatives at the FTC', speech delivered to ABA Antitrust Section Fall Forum, Washington, 18 November.
Melamed, A.D. (1995), 'Antitrust: the new regulation', **10**, Fall, *Antitrust*, 13.
Modrall, J. and S. Ciullo (2003) 'Gun-jumping and EU merger control', **24**, *European Competition Law Review*, 424.
Monti, M. (2001), 'Antitrust in the US and Europe: a history of convergence', speech deliv-ered to ABA Roundtable, Washington, 14 November.
Monti, M. (2004), 'Convergence in EU–US antitrust policy regarding mergers and acquisi-tions: an EU perspective', speech delivered to UCLA conference, Los Angeles, 28 February.
NAAG (1993), *Horizontal Merger Guidelines*, reprinted in **4**, *Trade Regulation Reports*.
Navarro et al. (2005), *Merger Control in the European Union: Law, Economics and Practice*, 2nd edn, Oxford: OUP.
Newborn, S. and V. Snider (2005), 'The Ten Commandments of getting your deal through', *The Antitrust Review of the Americas 2006*, London: Global Competition Review, p. 13.
Nicholson, M., S. Cardell and B. McKenna (2005), 'The scope of review of merger decisions under Community law', **1**, *European Competition Journal*, 123.
Overd, A. (2002), 'After the *Airtours* appeal', *European Competition Law Review*, 375.
Pate, R. Hewitt (2002), 'Antitrust Enforcement at the DOJ: issues in merger investigations and litigation', speech delivered to NY Bar Association, New York, 10 December.
Pfunder, M. (2005), 'Indexing comes to the HSR Act', *Antitrust Source*, January, 1–8.
Ragolle (2003), '*Schneider Electric* v. *Commission*: the CFI's response to the green paper on merger review', *European Competition Law Review*, 176.
Rose, J. (1994), 'State antitrust enforcement, mergers and politics', **41**, *Wayne Law Review*, 71, 117–21.
Samuels, D. (2005), 'Merger control in the rear-view mirror', **8**, *Global Competition Review*, 29.
Select Committee on the European Union (2001–2), *Thirty-second Report: the Review of the EC Merger Regulation*, HL 165, London: Stationery Office.
Sher, S. (2004), 'Closed but not forgotten: government review of consummated mergers under section 7 of the Clayton Act', **45**, *Santa Clara Law Review*, 41.
Sims, J. and D. Herman (1997), 'The effect of twenty years of Hart–Scott–Rodino on merger practice: a case study in the law of unintended consequences applied to antitrust legisla-tion', **65**, *Antitrust Law Journal*, 865.
Sinclair, D. (2002), 'Reflections on the European Commission's proposals to amend the juris-

dictional test in the merger regulation: a hall of mirrors?', *European Competition Law Review*, 326.
Steuer, R. (1995), 'Counseling without case law', **63**, *Antitrust Law Journal*, 823.
Swift, J. (2004), 'Judicial control of competition decisions in the UK and EU', speech delivered to Competition Commission, London, 21 September.
Turner, V. and C. Ahlborn (1998), 'Expanding success? Reform of the EC merger regulation', **19**, *European Competition Law Review*, 249.
Vesterdorf, B. (2005), 'Standard of proof in merger cases: reflections in the light of recent case law of the Community courts', **1**, *European Competition Journal*, 3.
Weiner, M. (1995), 'Antitrust and the rise of the regulatory consent decree', **10**, Fall, *Antitrust*, 4.
Wise, M. (1999), 'Review of United States competition law and policy', **1**, *OECD Journal of Competition Law and Policy*, 9.
Wood, D. (2003), 'A comparison of merger review and remedy procedures in the United States and European Union', in Lévêque and Shelanski (eds), *Merger Remedies in American and European Union Competition Law*, Cheltenham, UK and Northampton, MA, USA: Edward Elgar, p. 69.

*Cases*
*Airtours* v. *Commission*, [2002] ECR II-2585.
*Brunswick Corp* v. *Pueblo Bowl-O-Mat Inc* (1977) 429 US 477.
*Cargill Inc* v. *Monfort of Colorado Inc* (1986) 479 US 104.
*Endemol* v. *Commission*, [1999] ECR II-1299.
*Europemballage Corporation and Continental Can Co. Inc.* v. *Commission*, [1973] ECR 215.
*Federal Trade Commission* v. *Arch Coal Inc* 329 F. Supp. 2d 109 (D.D.C. 2004) *General Electric* v. *Commission*, [2005] Case T-210/01.
*Honeywell* v. *Commission*, [2005] Case T-209/01.
*Magneti Marelli / CEAc*, [1992] 4 CMLR M61.
*Price Waterhouse/Coopers & Lybrand*, [1999] OJ L50/27.
*Schneider Electric SA* v. *Commission*, [2002] ECR II-4071.
*Tetra Laval BV* v. *Commission*, [2002] ECR II-4519.
*US* v. *E.I. du Pont de Nemours & Co*, 353 U.S. 586 (1957).
*US* v. *Oracle Corp.* 331 F. Supp. 2d 1098 (N.D. Cal. 2004).
*US* v. *Philadelphia National Bank* 374 U.S. 321 (1963).
*US* v. *Von's Grocery Co.*, 384 U.S. 270, 301 (1966).

# 5 A transatlantic assessment of the evolving use of behavioural merger remedies

*Neil Campbell, Casey Halladay and Omar Wakil**

## Introduction

Competition law enforcement authorities have a well-known predisposition for 'structural' rather than 'behavioural' remedies to resolve concerns in merger transactions.[1] This is evident from the published guidelines of the US Federal Trade Commission (the FTC),[2] the US Department of Justice (the DOJ) and the European Commission (the Commission),[3] as well as in public statements by senior officials in Canada's Competition Bureau (the Bureau)[4] and its recent draft information bulletin on the subject.[5]

Despite being the typical remedy in non-merger cases, behavioural merger remedies are often dismissed in merger cases as complicated, difficult to implement and in need of ongoing monitoring. The US Supreme Court commented nearly half a century ago that divestiture is the preferred remedy for anticompetitive mergers as it is 'simple, relatively easy to administer, and sure', while behavioural remedies can be 'cumbersome and time-consuming'.[6] More recently, an International Competition Network report observed:

> Behavioural remedies cover a wide range of potential applications but require a substantial amount of monitoring and enforcement. Moreover [. . .] behavioural remedies have significant disadvantages in terms of cost, effectiveness and risk of market distortion.[7]

We believe that the criticisms of behavioural remedies in merger cases are overstated. While monitoring and enforceability issues require careful attention, they are increasingly manageable through private contracts, arbitration mechanisms and other techniques that may be combined with court orders by or undertakings provided to competition authorities. Moreover it cannot be assumed that the public and private costs associated with behavioural remedies are always higher than for structural remedies, nor is there any a priori basis for expecting that behavioural remedies will necessarily be less effective or result in market distortion.

We begin by outlining an analytical framework that can be used to assess behavioural remedies not only on their own merits but relative to the alternative of divestiture (which carries an assortment of effectiveness, monitoring, enforceability and cost issues as well). We then examine the existing legal frameworks and leading cases involving behavioural resolutions in Canada, the EU and US.[8] This survey demonstrates the considerable frequency and range of circumstances in which such remedies have been used in the EU and Canada, and occasionally in the US, notwithstanding the stated policies favouring divestiture. The lesson from this historical review is that a behavioural remedy is a viable and effective option in a wide variety of situations. We conclude that a 'divestiture-first' mentality is not warranted and that enforcement agencies should be open to the use of carefully designed behavioural remedies.

**A suggested analytical framework**
We start from two simple general principles that should not be controversial in jurisdictions with well-established merger control regimes such as the EU, US and Canada: (a) mergers should not be interfered with unless the relevant decision maker determines that the substantive threshold of anticompetitive effects is likely to be exceeded; and (b) if the merging parties propose a remedy that eliminates the likely anticompetitive effects (or reduces them below the statutory standard), the basis for intervention disappears. These principles provide a solid basis for examining the use of behavioural remedies as an alternative to divestitures from the perspective of both public law enforcement and private commercial interests.

*The public interest in effective remedies*
The primary public benefit of merger regulation is to prevent (or, in the less common post-closing context, remove) anticompetitive effects. Achieving this objective is a necessary condition for a remedy to be regarded as effective. The ability to monitor and enforce any remedy is also a relevant consideration, as are the costs associated with doing so and the risk that the remedy may fail to operate effectively.

However competition authorities do not (and should not) conduct a detailed cost/benefit analysis on each potential remedy. Merging parties are better placed to identify remedy options and to assess the private benefits and costs of such options. Agencies should then focus on evaluating whether a proposed remedy is likely to address effectively the public interest in maintaining and/or restoring competition. While this could include consideration of any enforceability, monitoring, cost or other concerns that are sufficiently serious to reject a remedy proposal, this is quite different from a quantitative or comparative analysis relative to other potentially available remedial options.

We are not aware of any jurisdiction in which agencies or courts are given a specific mandate to rank remedies and micro-manage the selection of the one which is optimal or which is regarded as preferable. In a contested case, an agency will be entitled to obtain a remedy that reduces the expected anti-competitive effects below the statutory intervention threshold (an 'effective remedy').[9] There is no reason to apply a different standard to negotiated resolutions.

This principle is well established in the divestiture context. For example, if merging parties are prepared to eliminate a problematic competitive overlap by divesting one party's entire business, it should matter little whether they choose to retain the acquiror's or the acquiree's business. Similarly it is not the role of an agency to select which prospective purchaser it would prefer to acquire divested assets as long as the purchaser can demonstrate that it will provide adequate competition to the merged entity.

The same principle should apply when considering a behavioural remedy as an alternative to a divestiture, or indeed in looking at multiple behavioural alternatives. The agency has a legitimate interest in obtaining an effective remedy, but if the merging parties can propose a behavioural solution that meets the effectiveness standard (including addressing any monitoring, enforceability or cost issues that would significantly undermine effectiveness), there is no legitimate basis for agency objection.

*Private benefits and costs*
From a systemic perspective, the private benefits to and costs borne by the merging parties and any third parties affected by the merger remedy are relevant to an overall assessment. In theory, an agency discharging a mandate to protect the public interest in competition should consider such benefits and costs. However the agency does not directly receive the benefits or incur the costs, and hence may tend to undervalue them.[10]

Merging parties are well positioned to develop and implement remedies that minimize the erosion of merger efficiencies and that reflect practical marketplace realities. In some situations, they will prefer focused behavioural remedies instead of divesting businesses/assets that may have played an important role in the decision to initiate a transaction and may be expected to generate significant synergies or efficiencies. Behavioural commitments allow for remedies to be tailored closely to competition concerns whereas structural remedies have an inherent lack of flexibility given their broad scope and permanent effects. They may be particularly appropriate for complex sectors such as financial services, high technology or network industries.[11] Similarly, behavioural solutions could provide an efficient alternative to prohibition of entire transactions, for instance by controlling costs or requiring supply or access in vertical mergers that would otherwise allow an integrated firm to deny or to raise the cost of inputs to its rivals or to deny or to limit access by rivals to downstream customers.[12]

There is a well-known moral hazard inherent in allowing merging parties to propose remedies. They have incentives to minimize the scope of remedies and may deliberately or unintentionally propose remedies that may be less than fully effective. But this risk is as applicable to divestitures as it is to behavioural remedies. In the divestiture context it has led to increasing agency vigilance in areas such as formation of viable divestiture packages, auction/trustee processes and confirmation of the likely competitive effectiveness of purchasers.[13] In addition, where agencies are concerned about the effective implementation of a behavioural order, it can be backed up with a more intrusive 'crown jewel' divestiture as a fallback provision.[14] The more varied forms of behavioural remedies add challenges for agencies that are attempting to assess the effectiveness of remedy proposals on a case-by-case basis. However, as greater experience is attained, such assessments will become easier; indeed standards and precedents for various common types of behavioural commitments are already developing, as can be seen from the cases reviewed below.

### Relative strengths and weaknesses of divestiture remedies

Divestiture reduces the likelihood that competition would otherwise be lessened in two ways: by reducing the size and market power of the merged firm; and by establishing a sufficiently strong competing firm. However divestiture orders often are not as simple as they appear nor can it be assumed that they will automatically be successful. Experience in the US, Canada and Europe indicates that there are significant challenges to implementing divestiture remedies effectively. These include the following:[15]

1. Creating a viable asset package: if a divestiture is to achieve the goal of remedying anticompetitive effects, it must offer an asset package with the 'critical mass' and resources necessary to allow the buyer to compete effectively with the merged firm. Where the business and assets which are sold do not meet this threshold, the effectiveness of divestiture as a remedy may be jeopardized: finding a buyer will be difficult, since potential buyers are usually industry participants who are able to recognize a flawed asset package. Moreover, even if a buyer is found, it will have difficulty competing effectively if the asset package is insufficient.[16]

2. Finding a suitable buyer: the primary pool of potential buyers will often be drawn from competitors in the seller's industry or in nearby product or geographic markets. Finding a single suitable buyer may be difficult

where the industry has few remaining competitors,[17] buyers lack either the interest or the financial resources to purchase the assets, or there are regulatory constraints that limit the available buyers. Similarly, it is not always easy to determine whether a buyer is committed to competing in the business for the long term. There is always a risk that the buyer may decide at some future point to redeploy or liquidate the assets, potentially eliminating the value of the divestiture remedy.[18]

In addition, divestiture processes normally involve at least two elements of behavioural remedies:

1.  Hold separate arrangements: except in the rare situations where a divestiture is negotiated and completed to a 'buyer up front' prior to or simultaneously with the consummation of the main merger, comprehensive 'hold separate' provisions are a core component of divestiture remedies. Depending on the time allowed for the merging parties to complete a divestiture and the possible supplementary period for a trustee to do so, the 'hold separate' arrangements may last for as long as a year or two.[19] During this period, the merging parties will be subject to extensive behavioural commitments regarding the independent and competitive operation of the business to be divested, maintenance of assets, prohibitions on exchanges of competitively sensitive information, and so on. The monitoring, enforceability and cost objections which are often raised for behavioural remedies are not regarded as impediments to the regular and successful use of hold separate arrangements.
2.  Monitoring the divestiture process: during potentially lengthy pre-divestiture periods, the merged firm may be required to submit regular and detailed reports to the competition agency regarding the progress of the divestiture and compliance with the hold separate commitments.[20] This is often accompanied by the appointment of a monitor/trustee who is responsible for verifying that such commitments are fulfilled. Once a potential buyer has been found, the competition agency may also be actively involved in evaluating and approving or rejecting the buyer. In addition to overseeing the sale process, the agency will usually pay some attention to post-closing developments to ensure that the remedy has been effective.[21] Given the extensive monitoring that may be involved in divestiture cases, behavioural remedies should not be dismissed simply because they too require monitoring.

In our view, behavioural remedy proposals should be regarded as acceptable where (a) the commitments are likely to reduce the anticompetitive effects of the merger below the statutory competitive effects threshold; and

(b) monitoring and enforcement can be achieved in a reasonable manner and without excessive costs to the competition agency or third parties. The case for using behavioural remedies is particularly strong where they can preserve merger efficiency gains that would otherwise be undermined by a divestiture or prohibition order.

## Behavioural remedies in Canada
*Legal framework*
The statutory basis for behavioural remedies is found primarily in the consent agreement (formerly consent order) provisions in sections 92(1)(e)(iii) and (f)(iii) of the Competition Act.[22] In addition, the Competition Tribunal has powers to include behavioural elements where they are ancillary to 'structural' dissolution, divestiture or prohibition orders.[23] However, as a practical matter in most cases, the merging parties negotiate behavioural remedies with the Commissioner. Indeed, in the *Air Canada* (*'Gemini II'*) case,[24] Mr Justice Hugessen of Canada's Federal Court of Appeal described the Competition Tribunal's ability to order the dissolution of a merger or the divestiture of assets as 'important and even *drastic* powers' that '*constitute a rather blunt instrument* for the implementation of Canada's competition policy'.[25] As a result, he observed that the option of behavioural remedies encourages parties to 'engage in constructive negotiations and to agree upon an order which may contain a vast range and number of fine-tuned provisions designed to satisfy the requirements both of public interest and commercial reality'.[26]

A merger remedy (either behavioural or structural) must eliminate the substantial lessening or prevention of competition caused by the merger (which does not necessarily imply reverting to the pre-merger situation). In *Southam*,[27] the first contested merger proceeding[28] to deal with the issue of remedies in a significant way,[29] the Supreme Court of Canada stated:

> The evil to which the drafters of the Competition Act addressed themselves is substantial lessening of competition. It hardly needs arguing that the appropriate remedy for a substantial lessening of competition is to restore competition to the point at which it can no longer be said to be substantially less than it was before the merger.[30]

The Tribunal has, however, clearly indicated a preference for structural rather than behavioural remedies on several occasions. For instance, in the *Ridge Landfill* case it said:

> once there has been a finding that a merger is likely to substantially prevent or lessen competition, a remedy that permanently constrains that market power should be preferred over behavioural remedies that last over a limited period of

time and require continuous monitoring of performance. This is not to say that, in cases where both the respondents and the Commissioner consent, behavioural remedies cannot be effective. However, the Tribunal notes that enforcing the remedy proposed by the respondents would have the potential of being cumbersome and time-consuming and that monitoring such order would involve the Commissioner in commercial conduct more than would the administration of the divestiture order.[31]

It is noteworthy that the behavioural remedy proposed by the respondents was one which the Commissioner's economic expert considered insufficient to alleviate the substantial lessening and prevention of competition, likely to lead to collusion, and unlikely to create more than a 'trivial non-competitive fringe' of third party competitors. There were, in short, very serious concerns with the effectiveness of that particular remedy, over and above any principled preference for divestiture remedies.[32] Moreover the Tribunal's concern that the Commissioner would need to be involved in the on going monitoring of the parties' commercial conduct would not necessarily be valid in other situations since many behavioural remedies can be designed without ongoing monitoring by a competition enforcer.

*Enforcement agency practice*
The Competition Bureau has expressed a clear preference for structural remedies, which it believes 'are usually necessary to eliminate the substantial lessening or prevention of competition arising from a completed or proposed merger'.[33] In 2004 it acknowledged that 'In a small number of cases, a behavioural remedy has been selected as a complement to a structural remedy and in a very small number of cases as the best option because of the unique facts of the case.'[34] More recently, in an October 2005 draft *Information Bulletin on Merger Remedies*, it took the position that 'Stand-alone behavioural remedies are rarely accepted by the Bureau' primarily because 'It is difficult to design a behavioural remedy that will adequately replicate the outcomes of a competitive market'.[35] However, the Bureau went on to create a third category of 'quasi-structural' remedies which it described as 'certain actions' that allow the merged entity to retain ownership of the assets or businesses acquired in the merger but have 'structural implications for the marketplace'.[36] It identified a number of 'actions' that most observers would regard as behavioural including 'those that reduce barriers to entry, provide access to necessary infrastructure or key technology, or otherwise facilitate entry or expansion'.[37]

*Leading cases*
Semantics aside, behavioural remedies have played a significant role in many cases and no significant failures have been identified. The following

cases have been resolved using behavioural remedies in consent orders/ agreements, or in undertakings from merging parties:[38]

*Asea Brown Boveri/Westinghouse* (1989)[39]   In this early case, the Bureau determined that the proposed merger was likely to result in a substantial lessening of competition in the market for certain large power transformers, where the merged entity would have a market share of approximately 75%. The consent order ultimately issued by the Tribunal required ABB to petition the federal Department of Finance for tariff reductions and remissions (suspension of tariff duties for a specified period). These requirements were intended to lower the entry barriers to the Canadian market and allow foreign manufacturers to compete with ABB in Canada. In separate undertakings (curiously, not part of the consent order), ABB also agreed not to bring any anti-dumping complaints against US manufacturers of transformers for five years.[40]

*Molson/Elders (Carling O'Keefe)* (1989)[41]   The merger of Molson and Elders (the parent of Carling Breweries) combined two of Canada's three largest breweries. Despite the resulting duopoly (with a fringe of import and micro-brewery suppliers), the Bureau permitted the merger to proceed for various reasons including the substantial efficiency gains expected and an anticipated reduction in regulatory barriers to interprovincial trade. However, in the Quebec market where Molson would have a particularly strong position, it was required to guarantee access to its distribution system for local and potential foreign competitors (excluding the other large competitor, Labatts) on a non-profit, fee-for-service basis.

*Air Canada* (1989)[42]   The '*Gemini I*' case involved a consent order application arising out of the proposed combination of the computer reservation systems ('CRS') of Air Canada and Canadian Airlines to create the Gemini CRS which would have roughly an 80% share of the CRS market in Canada. Given the overwhelming importance of Air Canada and Canadian Airlines in the domestic air travel market, the Bureau concluded that any other competing CRS would require access to the Air Canada and Canadian flight information in the Gemini system in order to survive and that behavioural commitments could effectively guarantee such access. The undertakings therefore included a requirement that Air Canada and Canadian Airlines provide all other CRS's operating in Canada with a direct link to their internal reservation systems, if the competitor airlines offered Gemini reciprocal access to their reservation systems.[43] The remedy also included firewalls prohibiting Air Canada and Canadian Airlines employees from sharing 'commercially sensitive information' between the two airlines in order to prevent the use of Gemini as a vehicle for coordinated behaviour.

*CAPAC/PROCAN* (1990)[44]   This case involved the proposed merger of two of only three organizations in Canada that collected performing rights fees for the public use of music. As both societies employed long-term (five-year) contracts with their members, barriers to entry for new societies were considered to be high. The Competition Bureau allowed the merger to proceed on the strength of an undertaking from the parties to amend the terms of member contracts to reduce the term from five years to three years, along with a member option to terminate the contract with notice after the second year. This is a simple illustration of how unilateral contract changes can sometimes provide a very simple remedy.

*Imperial Oil/Texaco* (1990)[45]   The proposed merger of two of Canada's largest integrated oil companies raised concerns in several product and geographic markets. After extensive negotiations between the parties and the Bureau as well as two hearings before the Tribunal, a consent order was issued which included various divestitures plus a requirement that Imperial guarantee unbranded gasoline supply to independent dealers in Ontario and Quebec for a seven-year period. The independent dealers sourced from the vertically integrated merging parties but also competed with their refineries and terminal operations. The supply guarantee provisions dealt in detail with the volumes and prices of the product to be made available to the independents in order to protect their effectiveness as competitors in the downstream markets.[46]

*Canada Post Corporation/Purolator* (1993)[47]   The Bureau chose not to challenge Canada Post Corporation's ('CPC') acquisition of 75% of Canada's largest courier company, Purolator, which was a direct competitor of Canada Post's 'Priority Courier' business. Crucial to this decision were CPC's commitments to refrain from subsidising Purolator with revenues from its 'exclusive privilege in letter mail'; to maintain Purolator as a separate corporate entity with a separate board of directors; and to conduct any dealings between Purolator and CPC on an 'arm's length commercial basis'. While aspects of this remedy were similar to traditional 'hold separate' arrangements, the prohibition of cross-subsidisation is a very sophisticated form of behavioural remedy.

*Lafarge Canada/Holnam* (1998)[48]   The transaction resulted in Lafarge Canada's acquisition of a cement distribution terminal in New Westminster, British Columbia that raised competition concerns. Lafarge Canada agreed to divest the New Westminster facility and also entered into behavioural undertakings requiring it to waive non-competition provisions in the asset purchase agreement. Such a waiver would allow Holnam to supply cement into the BC interior from facilities in Washington and Montana that were not part of the transaction.[49] These behavioural undertakings were not ancillary to the divestiture: they provided the full remedy in a specific market where competition would otherwise have been prevented by a covenant in the contract governing the transaction.

*Air Canada/Canadian Airlines* (1999)[50]   This merger yielded extensive undertakings governing Air Canada's future conduct in the Canadian airline industry. The undertakings were aimed at reducing entry barriers to Canadian air travel markets in the hope of inducing new entrants. The undertakings included requirements that Air Canada surrender to other Canadian carriers up to 28 arrival/departure slots at Toronto's capacity-constrained Pearson Airport during peak hours and that it permit 'eligible' Canadian carriers to participate in Air Canada's frequent flyer programme on commercially reasonable terms, on a non-exclusive basis, for five years.[51] A structural undertaking to divest, on a 'best efforts' basis, the Canadian Regional Airlines Ltd. subsidiary proved to be a failure and the behavioural provisions ended up being the operative remedies.

*Chapters/Indigo* (2001)[52]    The Competition Bureau concluded that the merger of Canada's two largest booksellers would lessen competition substantially in both the downstream (retail) and upstream (publishing) book markets. The parties and the Bureau eventually negotiated a draft consent order that contemplated significant divestitures as well as substantial behavioural remedies. The behavioural provisions included a detailed five-year Code of Conduct governing terms of trade with publishers. Such suppliers were protected by limits on Chapters/Indigo's ability to demand discounts from them, the establishment of minimum payment deadlines, and constraints on the timing and volume of book returns to publishers. Other behavioural terms prohibited the parties from acquiring or opening any new stores for two years or enforcing restrictive covenants against the opening of other book stores in any of their shopping centre leases.[53] While the Bureau had predicted that the divestitures would 'encourage expansion or new entry by other booksellers, thereby maintaining choices for consumers and competition in the book industry',[54] they failed to do so. When neither the parties nor a trustee could identify a buyer for the divestiture assets, the stores ultimately reverted to Chapters/Indigo ownership. The behavioural remedies provided the only protection against Chapters/Indigo exercising the market power resulting from the merger.

*Avis/Budget Rent-a-Car* (2002)[55]    The Bureau allowed the merger of two of the largest car and truck rental businesses in Canada after accepting behavioural undertakings that included a Code of Conduct governing Avis's interaction with the Budget licensees/franchisees. In addition, the merged firm was required to implement (and provide certified annual reports to the Bureau regarding) a compliance program to educate employees about the relevant provisions of the Competition Act as well as the 'special obligations' imposed under the Code of Conduct.[56]

*Astral/Télémédia* (2002)[57]    The Bureau was concerned that the proposed acquisition of French-language radio stations would result in a substantial lessening of competition in French-language radio advertising in six local markets. In addition to the divestiture of six AM radio stations (to be sold as a network), the consent order contained significant behavioural remedies, including a Code of Conduct to protect advertisers. It prohibited Astral from using exclusive or long-term (i.e. over 12 months) advertising contracts or 'meet-or-release' or 'most-favoured-nation' clauses within such contracts. Astral was also required to place the Télémédia FM radio stations in four of the six local markets under the control of a trustee, to be operated as competitors to the Astral stations in those markets until the earlier of (i) six months after the opening of a new FM station in that market; or (ii) 42 months. In addition, Astral agreed not to acquire or seek to acquire new French-language radio stations in the six local markets for a period of three years.

*Canadian National Railway/BC Rail* (2004)[58]    The Bureau determined that this proposed transaction raised serious competition issues in two markets: rail interline transportation of commodities (such as lumber) between the BC Rail territory and elsewhere in North America, and rail transportation of grain from the Peace River area. These concerns were addressed with highly complex behavioural remedies. Those relating to rail interline transportation included the regulation of rates to be charged by CN to connecting rail carriers and the setting of performance benchmarks for transit times, non-discrimination protections for shippers and other protections against rate increases or service reductions.[59] CN was also prevented from materially increasing rates or curtailing service levels in the transportation of grain.[60] Under the consent agreement, the Commissioner can also appoint a monitor with the authority to obtain records from CN and interview CN officials, and designate an auditor to examine CN records to ensure compliance. Although the Bureau subsequently stated that as a matter of policy it 'will not agree to remedies where there is a need for continuing monitoring of key aspects of an agreement such as pricing',[61] the *CN Rail* agreement attempts to avoid the need for 'continual monitoring' through the use of arbitration if disputes arise.

*Quebecor/Sogides* (2005)[62]    The Competition Bureau determined that there were insufficient grounds to challenge Quebecor Media's acquisition of publishing and distribution group Sogides after the parties agreed to enter into a Consent Agreement with the Commissioner. The agreement was designed to eliminate the possibility of information exchanges between Sogides' president, who would be a Quebecor employee post-merger, and a competitor of Quebecor's bookstores, in which Sogides' president had a significant interest. The agreement included a requirement that the president resign from the board of directors of the competitor. While the context was different from many firewall remedies, the implementation was straightforward.

### Behavioural remedies in Europe

*Legal framework*

In the groundbreaking *Gencor/Lonrho*[63] case, the European Commission refused to accept undertakings that it considered to be 'behavioural in nature' because it did not think that it had authority to do so under the Merger Regulation.[64] On appeal, the Court of First Instance held that the Commission has the power to accept any commitments that are capable of rendering a notified transaction compatible with the common market and 'the categorisation of a proposed commitment as behavioural or structural is therefore immaterial'.[65]

In *Tetra Laval/Sidel*, the Court of First Instance ruled that the Commission has an obligation to take commitments offered regarding future conduct into account in assessing whether it was likely that the merged entity would act in a manner that could result in the creation of a dominant position.[66] The Court of Justice subsequently upheld the lower court's findings.[67]

*Enforcement agency practice*

'The starting point for designing an appropriate remedy' according to the Commission, 'is the competition concern resulting from the structural change brought about by a concentration, which is normally best addressed by a structural remedy.'[68] The Commission's December 2000 *Notice on Remedies* indicates, however, that the Commission will consider behavioural solutions. It specifically identifies two circumstances where behavioural remedies may be appropriate, namely where (a) a divestiture of a business is impossible (e.g., because there is unlikely to be a buyer for the business to be divested); and (b) competition problems result from 'specific features', such as the existence of exclusive agreements, the combination of networks or the combination of key patents.[69]

The Commission has also acknowledged that combinations of structural and behavioural remedies may be warranted in complex cases:

> More complex situations call for more sophisticated solutions. In cases where a horizontal overlap is accompanied by vertical integration and ensuing risks of foreclosure, the most appropriate solution may consist in a remedy package combining a divestiture with obligations to grant access rights or to provide an open interface to connect third party products to the parties' equipment.[70]

It is unclear whether this approach will change in light of the Commission's October 2005 *Merger Remedies Study* (the 'EC Study'),[71] which analysed the design, implementation and effectiveness of remedies imposed in cases under the EC Merger Regulation. The EC Study reviewed 40 decisions that adopted 96 different remedies, accounting for 42% of the 227 remedies adopted by the Commission between 1996 and 2000. Interviews with market participants, such as sellers, buyers, licensors, licensees, grantors, grantees and trustees, were conducted to obtain information about how remedies had operated. The EC Study does not categorise cases as 'structural' or 'behavioural' but instead distinguishes between (i) commitments to transfer market position (e.g., divestiture of a controlling stake, a business unit, or a package of assets), (ii) commitments to exit from a joint venture, (iii) commitments to grant access (e.g., access to infrastructure or technology) and (iv) other commitments (e.g., withdrawal of a brand from a market).[72] The study is somewhat critical about both the implementation and the effectiveness of 'access commitments' and concluded that they were not a particularly effective remedy, primarily because of difficulties in establishing access terms and monitoring access.[73]

However, the EC Study sample included only ten remedies where access commitments were the primary remedial measure imposed to resolve the competition concerns identified (i.e., they were not simply supplementary measures to a divestiture remedy).[74] The EC Study itself acknowledges that it 'provides only limited generalised findings on access commitments' because 'the sample of analysed cases was very small' and in five of them later market developments suggested that the remedies were unnecessary, making it difficult or impossible to judge effectiveness in these cases.[75]

It was also noted that 'in reviewing access commitments, the Study faced the problem of identifying the appropriate companies to interview. Unlike the situation in divestiture commitments where the identity of the purchaser is known, access commitments often do not have an obvious beneficiary, being offered unilaterally to the world at large or to an open ended category of beneficiaries that are not always known to the Commission'.[76] Thus, while the EC Study identifies some potential concerns with this type of behavioural remedy and constructively develops a number of conditions that appear to be important in designing workable access remedies,[77] its criticisms on behavioural remedies should be treated cautiously and suggest that more empirical work would be helpful.

*Leading cases*
A review of recent cases in Europe suggests that the Commission is in fact very willing to accept behavioural solutions in appropriate circumstances:[78]

*Boeing/McDonnell Douglas* (1997)[79]   The Commission found that the proposed merger of two of the three players in the worldwide market for large commercial jet aircraft would lead to a significant strengthening of Boeing's dominant position. Contrary to the approach of the US Federal Trade Commission,[80] the Commission considered that a strengthening of a dominant position would arise from McDonnell Douglas' competitive potential in large commercial jet aircraft, along with the enhanced opportunity for Boeing to enter into long-term exclusive supply deals with airlines, and from the acquisition of McDonnell Douglas' defence and space activities (which confer advantages in the commercial aircraft sector through 'spill-over' effects in the form of R&D benefits and technology transfer). For present purposes the high-profile divergence between the US FTC and Commission substantive assessment is of less interest than the fact that the Commission accepted behavioural commitments to resolve its concerns, including the cessation of existing and future exclusive supply agreements; the 'ring-fencing' of McDonnell Douglas' commercial aircraft activities; the licensing of certain key patents to other jet aircraft manufacturers; commitments not to abuse relationships with customers and suppliers; and a commitment to report annually to the Commission on military and civil aeronautics R&D projects benefiting from public funding.

*Astra/Zeneca* (1999)[81]   In order to remove concerns identified by the Commission, the merging parties agreed, inter alia, to 'grant viable and independent third party exclusive distribution rights' for a pain betablocker called Tenormin in Sweden and Norway for a period of at least ten years. The parties also undertook to 'divest' Astra's entire interest in dual combination beta-blockers throughout the EEA to a viable and independent third party. As AstraZeneca would retain rights to these products outside the EEA, the 'divestiture' was to be effected by the grant of an indefinite and exclusive trademark licence, granting of the necessary patent rights and a supply agreement. An independent trustee was appointed to report to the Commission on the price arrangements to be adopted in the distribution agreement and on the identity and characteristics of the potential distributors and purchasers identified by AstraZeneca.

*Vivendi/Canal+/Seagram* (2000)[82]   The Commission was concerned that the proposed merger would have strengthened and/or created a dominant position for pay-television in certain member states. The parties provided substantial undertakings to address the competition problems including to divest a stake in pay-TV operator BSkyB and to give rival pay-TV operators access to Vivendi films. In particular, the parties undertook not to grant to Canal+ 'first-window' rights covering more than 50% of Universal's production and co-production.[83] By adding Universal's music content to Vivendi's multi-access portal, Vizzavi, the transaction also raised serious doubts as to the creation of a dominant position on the emerging pan-European market for portals and on the emerging market for online music. In order to remove these concerns, Vivendi offered to give rival portals access to Universal's online music content for five years. Disputes were to be resolved by a detailed arbitration mechanism.

*Shell/BASF (Project Nicole)* (2001)[84]   The Commission cleared the proposed joint venture of the parties worldwide polypropylene and polyethylene interests subject to a number of structural and behavioural commitments. The parties agreed to divest plants with polypropylene resin and polypropylene compound production capacity as well as BASF's Novolen technology business. In addition, the joint venture company was to license its metallocene patent rights to any interested third parties or not assert its patent rights against them if they licensed technology from elsewhere. Disagreements with third parties about the licensing and non-assertion obligations were subject to what they termed 'pendulum arbitration' pursuant to which an arbitrator would select between the positions presented without fashioning a compromise. The Commission subsequently reported that the divestiture buyer of the Novolen business lodged a complaint with the Commission that BASF was not complying with its licensing obligations. It alleged BASF was not transferring all of the 'know-how' available to the licensor. The commitments given by the merging parties did not specify 'know-how' and the Commission has suggested that this could have undermined the effectiveness of the remedy.[85]

*EdF/EnBW* (2001)[86]   This merger involved the acquisition of joint control of German electricity company Energie Baden-Württemberg AG (EnBW) by Electricité de France (EDF) and Zweckverband Oberschwäbische Elektrizitätswerke (OEW), an association of nine southwest German districts. The Commission concluded that it would have led to the strengthening of EDF's dominant position on the market for eligible customers (i.e., large customers able to chose their electricity supplier) in France. In order to eliminate these competition concerns, EDF agreed to make 6000 Megawatts of generation capacity located in France (a quantity equal to 30 per cent of the eligible market) available to competitors annually for five years in order to allow alternative supply sources to develop.[87] At the end of that period the Commission was to decide whether the market had developed sufficiently and either terminate or prolong EDF's obligation to grant access to generation capacities. In a separate undertaking, EDF also undertook not to exercise its voting rights in French electricity generator Compagnie Nationale du Rhône (CNR) and to withdraw its representative from the CNR board of directors. This commitment was intended to help CNR become an active competitor.[88]

*DaimlerChrysler/Deutsche Telekom* (2002)[89]   The proposed transaction involved a joint venture for the collection of tolls from heavy vehicles on German motorways. However onboard units to be installed in trucks for the purpose of the toll collection could also be used to offer value-added services for telematics[90] applications: without any further technical adaptations, the onboard units could be used to provide localisation and text services, whereby written information could be exchanged between the haulage companies and the trucks. As the units would be distributed without charge, the Commission thought it highly likely that truck fleet owners would use this box to source value-added services and would not install a second telematics unit in each truck. DaimlerChrysler could thus control the access of third party telematics services providers to the onboard units. To ensure non-discriminatory access to the telematics gateway, the Commission accepted the formation of an independent telematics gateway company, not controlled by the parties, that operated a central interface through which telematics services could be fed into the 'Toll Collect' system and provided to all trucks equipped with an onboard unit.

*SEB/Moulinex* (2002)[91]   The Commission approved the combination of SEB and Moulinex, two France-based manufacturers of small electrical household appliances, subject to conditions. SEB agreed to grant exclusive licences to third parties to use the Moulinex brand for a period of five years for the sale of small electric household appliances in certain countries. SEB also agreed that it would not reintroduce the Moulinex brand for a further period of three years from the expiry of the exclusive licence, so as to allow the licensee time for the gradual introduction of a brand name of its own. Disputes were to be resolved by arbitration.

*Siemens/Drägewerk* (2003)[92]   This proposed JV combined the two leading European players in medical ventilators and anaesthesia delivery systems. The Commission was concerned lest the joint venture result in preferences to Siemens' patient monitors by withholding the interface information necessary for competitors' monitors to be able to interface with the ventilators and other relevant equipment sold by the joint venture. In addition to divesting its Life Support Systems unit, which includes the company's worldwide anaesthesia delivery and ventilation business, Siemens undertook to provide interface information to connect its equipment to third party monitors, which cured the Commission's concerns.[93]

*Newscorp/Telepiù* (2003)[94]   The merger of Telepiù with Newscorp's Stream subsidiary would have resulted in a near-monopoly in the Italian pay-TV market. The Commission concluded that authorising the merger with behavioural remedies was more beneficial to consumers than the disruption that would have been caused by the likely closure of Stream.[95] In the Commission's view, the challenge was to impose conditions that would ensure that the market remained open long enough for competitive constraints to develop from Digital Terrestrial Transmission broadcasters, new satellite TV channels and others. The Commission ultimately accepted a complex remedy package containing both structural and behavioural undertakings. The behavioural conditions included the following:

1. Access to content: to ensure the availability of movies and sports matches, Newscorp agreed to waive exclusive rights to such content for non-satellite transmission. Non-satellite competitors would also be able to buy premium content from Newscorp on specified conditions. For potential satellite competitors, access to content was facilitated by allowing rights owners to terminate unilaterally without penalty their contracts with Stream/Telepiù and by limiting the duration of future contracts.[96]
2. Access to satellite platform: in order to give competitors the option of broadcasting by satellite without setting up their own platform, Newscorp agreed to grant satellite competitors access to its own platform and to offer all related services under fair and reasonable conditions. Newscorp also agreed to grant licences for certain of its proprietary technology to all applicants on a fair and non-discriminatory basis.

*Alcan/Pechiney* (2003)[97]   The Commission's review of the proposed merger between vertically integrated Canadian and French aluminium companies identified concerns in a number of markets, but Alcan was able to address the Commission's concerns by offering divestments and other conditions. The investigation identified, inter alia, three technology markets where the transaction would combine the two leading active licensors in the aluminium metal production chain: alumina refining technology, smelter cell technology and anode baking furnace technology. Alcan undertook to continue offering licences for the technologies referred to above at terms and conditions comparable to those applied prior to the transaction (and divest Alcan's anode baking furnace technology altogether). Alcan's commitments to the Commission provided in part that, if 'Alcan and the third party are unable to reach agreement on the terms of a Licence, either party may submit the matter to arbitration'.[98]

*Piaggio/Aprilia* (2004)[99]   The Commission found that the merger between two scooter and motorbike producers would likely impede effective competition in Italy through control of a considerable number of well-known brands and models including those equipped with a state of the art 50cc 4-stroke engine produced by Piaggio. However, the parties were able to address the Commission's concerns by undertaking to supply Piaggio's 50cc 4-stroke engine on commercial terms to other producers that wished to equip their models with such an engine.

*AREVA/Urenco* (2004)[100]   The parties proposed to acquire joint control over Enrichment Technology Company ('ETC'), which is active in the development and manufacturing of centrifuges for uranium enrichment. ETC would supply its parents and also third parties, but AREVA and Urenco were to remain competitors on the downstream market for enriched uranium. The Commission was concerned that the venture could lead to the creation of a joint dominant position in relation to the provision of enriched uranium in the European Union, in particular by the joint control over enrichment capacity increases. The Commission was also concerned that the joint control of ETC could also be used to coordinate the provision of enriched uranium. In order to eliminate the Commission's concerns, AREVA and Urenco each agreed to remove their respective veto rights in relation to any future capacity expansions. Second, the flow of commercially sensitive information between ETC and its parents would be prevented by a series of measures that would be closely monitored. Third, the parties committed themselves to supply the European Supply Agency ('ESA') with additional information which would enable ESA to monitor the provision and pricing of enriched uranium and respond, if necessary.

*TUI/CP Ships* (2005)[101]   The transaction combined CP Ships and Hapag-Lloyd (the subsidiary of acquiror TUI) to create the world's fourth-largest operator in container liner shipping. The Commission had particular concerns with the post-merger concentration levels and potential for anticompetitive coordination in the Europe–North America shipping lanes, and conditioned clearance of the merger on Hapag-Lloyd's commitment to withdraw from two shipping conferences operating on those lanes.

*Amer Group/Salomon* (2005)[102]   Amer Group of Finland agreed to acquire the Salomon business of Adidas-Salomon AG. The transaction combined two of the leading players in the market for 'winter sport hard goods' such as alpine and cross-country skis and related equipment, and triggered filing requirements in Member States Austria, Germany, Italy, Poland, Spain and the UK. All Member States agreed to refer the case to the Commission, which determined that the proposed transaction could significantly impede effective competition in the markets for cross-country skis (especially in Germany, Austria and France). Of particular concern was a cooperation agreement between Salomon and Fischer GmbH, the global leader in cross-country ski manufacturing. The Commission considered that the agreement 'gave rise to the risk of [a] coordinated market conduct' among the leading players in the industry, by adding Amer and its subsidiary Atomic Austria GmbH (Fischer's main rival) to the Fischer/Salomon mix. To address these concerns, the Commission required Salomon to undertake a 'significant reduction of the scope of the cooperation agreement', with particular focus on 'the elements of the agreement which facilitate the coordination of the commercial strategies of the parties'. Clauses 'limiting the independent market conduct of Fischer' were also to be removed from the agreement.

### Behavioural remedies in the US
*Legal framework*
The Antitrust Division of the US Department of Justice, pursuant to its mandate in Section 15 of the Clayton Act,[103] and the Federal Trade Commission, under the authority of Section 13(b) of the Federal Trade Commission Act,[104] may bring suit under Section 7 of the Clayton Act to prevent and restrain proposed mergers that are likely to 'substantially lessen competition, or tend to create a monopoly'.[105] Where one of the agencies

concludes that a merger is likely to lessen competition substantially, it may (1) seek an injunction in federal district court preventing the parties from completing the transaction; (2) seek a divestiture order in respect of a completed transaction; (3) negotiate a settlement; or (4) accept a 'fix-it-first' remedy that allows the merger to proceed after modifications that address the competition concerns.[106]

On the whole, American courts tend to favour structural remedies over behavioural or 'conduct' remedies. This view dates from at least as early as the Supreme Court's 1961 landmark decision in the *DuPont* case,[107] in which a majority of the Court recognised divestiture to be the 'most drastic' but also the 'most effective' of merger remedies.[108] The majority remarked that divestiture should 'always be in the forefront of a court's mind when a violation of section 7 [of the Clayton Act] has been found'.[109]

Under US law, mergers may also be challenged by private litigants who have suffered an antitrust injury (and by state Attorneys-General representing the interests of their citizens). In this context, the Supreme Court has indicated that a private divestiture remedy is consistent with the Act's 'clear intent to encourage vigorous private litigation against anticompetitive mergers'.[110]

*Enforcement agency practice*
The US enforcement agencies have adopted a similar approach. In April 2003, the FTC issued a statement regarding merger remedies[111] and the DOJ issued similar guidelines in October 2004.[112] Despite some differences in detail, both articulate a clear preference for structural over 'conduct' remedies. Indeed the FTC statement does not discuss behavioural remedies, other than as an adjunct to certain structural solutions. The DOJ guidelines indicate limited circumstances where behavioural remedies may be appropriate (e.g. to facilitate or support structural solutions, when outright prohibition or a structural remedy would sacrifice significant efficiencies, or when a structural solution is infeasible).

The DOJ guidelines identify four main concerns about more widespread use of conduct remedies:[113]

1. the direct costs associated with monitoring the merged firm's activities and ensuring adherence to the decree;
2. the indirect costs associated with efforts by the merged firm to evade the 'spirit' (if not the explicit terms) of the remedy (e.g., a commitment not to raise price may result in the merged firm reducing quality instead);
3. the potential to restrain pro-competitive behaviour (e.g., a requirement not to discriminate against rivals in the provision of a necessary input

can raise difficult questions of whether cost-based differences justify differential treatment and thus are not truly discriminatory);

4. impeding the merged firm from responding efficiently to changing market conditions.

*Leading cases*
Consistent with the antipathy the US agencies – particularly the DOJ – appear to have towards behavioural remedies, they employ such solutions less frequently than authorities in either Canada or Europe. Nevertheless there are some notable – and indeed quite high-profile – recent examples of sophisticated conduct remedies:

*AOL/Time Warner* (2000)[114]   The FTC was concerned that the proposed trans-action would lessen competition in the residential broadband Internet access market, undermine AOL's incentives to promote digital subscriber line ('DSL') broadband Internet service as an emerging alternative to cable broadband and restrain competition in the market for interactive television ('ITV'). The FTC ultimately accepted a complex five-year consent order under which AOL Time Warner was (a) required to open its cable system to competitor Internet Service Providers ('ISPs'), (b) prohibited from interfering with content passed along the bandwidth contracted for by non-affiliated ISPs and from interfering with the ability of non-affiliated providers of interactive TV services to interact with interactive signals, triggers or content that AOL Time Warner had agreed to carry, (c) prevented from discriminating on the basis of affiliation in the trans-mission of content, or from entering into exclusive arrangements with other cable companies with respect to ISP services or interactive TV services; and (d) required to market and offer AOL's digital subscriber line ('DSL') services to subscribers in Time Warner cable areas where affiliated cable broadband service is available in the same manner and at the same retail pricing as they do in those areas where affiliated cable broadband ISP service is not available. Notably the order also contained an arbitration process for resolving disputes as to what rates non-affiliated ISPs should pay to gain access. A 'Monitor Trustee' was appointed 'to monitor Respondents' compliance with the terms of this Order'.[115]

*AT&T/MediaOne* (2000)[116]   The DOJ determined that the combination of AT&T and MediaOne's interests in a joint venture called 'Road Runner', the second-largest provider of broadband Internet access in the US, would sub-stantially lessen competition in the aggregation, promotion and distribution of broadband content. Under the terms of the consent decree, AT&T was required to exit the Road Runner joint venture. In addition, AT&T was required to obtain prior approval from the DOJ before entering into certain types of agreements with Time Warner, one of the Road Runner investors, or with AOL, which then had a pending merger agreement with Time Warner. That requirement, which was to remain in place for two years after AT&T exited Road Runner, would apply to any agreement that jointly proposed to provide a residential broadband service, or any agreement that would prevent either party from offering a resi-dential broadband service to customers in any geographic region. It was also to apply to agreements that would prevent the inclusion of any content in a cable modem service offered by either party, or that would prevent either party from providing preferential treatment to content provided by others.

*Boeing/Hughes* (2000)[117]   The FTC determined that Boeing's acquisition of Hughes Space and Communications from General Motors would reduce or eliminate competition in three key areas: potentially disadvantaging or raising the costs of other competitors for a certain classified programme for which Boeing is the sole supplier of systems engineering and technical assistance ('SETA') services and Hughes was one of two competing contractors; gaining access to competitively sensitive non-public information concerning satellite and launch vehicle suppliers which could reduce competition, as well as innovation and quality, for satellites and launch vehicles; and, as a supplier of both satellites and launch vehicles, having the ability to disadvantage or raise the costs of competing launch vehicle suppliers by withholding satellite information necessary to make a satellite compatible with a launch vehicle. Behavioural remedies were used to resolve each of these concerns. Boeing was prohibited from providing SETA services to the US Department of Defense for the problem classified programme. A firewall was established to prevent Boeing's launch vehicle division from gaining access to non-public information that its satellite division receives from competing suppliers that launch Boeing satellites. Similarly its satellite division was prohibited from gaining access to non-public information that its launch vehicle business receives from competing satellite suppliers. In addition Boeing was required to provide all necessary satellite interface information (which is used to make satellites compatible with launch vehicles) to all other launch vehicle suppliers.

*Conoco/Phillips* (2002)[118]   The FTC was concerned that the proposed merger would substantially lessen competition in a number of markets, including the fractionation of natural gas 'raw mix' into specification products, such as butane and ethane, in Texas. Phillips was a 30% owner of a company that owned interests in two of the four fractionators in this region and Conoco had an interest in one of the others. The FTC alleged that the combined firm would have access to competitively sensitive information of fractionators accounting for more than 70% of the market capacity and would have veto rights over significant expansion decisions. While the focus of the consent order was the divestiture of several refineries and terminals, there was a behavioural component which required the companies to create firewalls to prevent the transfer of competitively sensitive information among the three partially owned fractionators.

*Nestlé/Ralston* (2002)[119]   In connection with a divestiture remedy, the FTC required Nestlé to supply product and technical assistance to the divestiture buyer for up to two years in order to allow the buyer time to implement its own plans to manufacture the products or to enter into a co-packing agreement with a third party. The consent order also provided for the appointment of a monitor to ensure that Nestlé provided the transitional supply as required, provided the necessary technical assistance and administrative services and maintained a 'firewall' between its employees that receive the buyer's confidential information and Nestlé employees operating the competing Nestlé businesses.

*Nestlé/Dreyer's* (2003)[120]    Nestlé and Dreyer's Grand Ice Cream agreed to divest three of Dreyer's brands and Nestlé's distribution assets to settle FTC concerns that their merger would lessen competition in the market for the sale of super-premium ice cream to the retail channel. The proposed order also contained significant behavioural terms: it required Dreyer's to make non-exclusive its licence to manufacture, distribute and sell Starbucks super-premium ice cream; and it allowed Mars and Ben & Jerry's to terminate their relationships with Dreyer's. In addition, the settlement contained a number of behavioural commitments to ensure that a proposed purchaser of the divested assets could operate profitably and provide viable competition. These provisions required, among other things, that Nestlé and Dreyer's distribute the divested brands for the buyer for one year, provide technical assistance and administrative services for one year and supply additional premium ice cream or novelty products to the buyer for distribution for up to five years to enable it to operate profitably while it developed additional distribution arrangements.[121]

*Aloha Petroleum/Trustreet Properties* (2005)[122]    Aloha Petroleum proposed to acquire the half interest in an import-capable terminal at Barbers Point that it did not already own, along with retail gasoline assets of Trustreet Properties on the island of Oahu, Hawaii. The proposed transaction would have reduced the number of gasoline marketers with ownership of, or guaranteed access to, a refinery or an import-capable terminal from five to four. It would have also reduced from three to two the number of bulk suppliers willing to sell to unintegrated retailers. The FTC thus maintained that the acquisition would be likely to result in higher prices for bulk supply of gasoline and sought an injunction to block the acquisition. It subsequently filed a motion seeking dismissal after the merging parties announced a 20-year throughput agreement giving Mid Pac Petroleum, which owned and operated several retail gasoline stations in Hawaii and also supplied gasoline to several other stations owned and operated by third parties, substantial rights to use the Barbers Point terminal. The FTC considered that the throughput agreement would essentially substitute Mid Pac for Trustreet as a bulk supply gasoline marketer in Hawaii.[123]

### Lessons from Canada, Europe and the US
*When are behavioural remedies appropriate?*
It is often not clear from the record whether behavioural remedies were selected because divestiture or prohibition orders would be infeasible or inefficient, or simply because the merging parties proposed a behavioural approach that was considered by the agency to be effective. In some cases there may have been a desire to avoid a drastic structural remedy in multi-jurisdictional cases where other agencies were not taking remedial action, the Commission's approach in *Boeing/McDonnell Douglas* being a potential example. In any event, it is clear that behavioural solutions ranging from modest contractual adjustments to complex regulatory arrangements have been accepted in a wide range of circumstances.

Our survey of recent cases suggests that the types of behavioural remedies accepted by Canadian, European and, occasionally, American agencies seek to achieve three main objectives:[124]

1.  Lowering entry barriers, facilitating access to critical inputs (e.g., airport landing slots,[125] computer reservation systems,[126] distribution networks,[127] frequent flyer programmes,[128] interface information,[129] satellite platforms[130]), lifting of contractual restrictions,[131] lower tariffs[132] and other techniques.[133]
2.  Protecting vulnerable customers and suppliers, through the modification of contracts,[134] access/supply commitments,[135] the implementation of codes of conduct[136] and price caps.[137]
3.  Preventing coordinated behaviour, using firewalls to limit exchanges of competitively sensitive information between competitors that have ownership or joint venture linkages.[138]

Alistair Lindsay has attempted to identify those circumstances in which behavioural remedies may be appropriate to resolve competition concerns by dividing problem merger cases into four categories.[139] He observes that structural remedies are properly used in the first of his four categories,[140] but that the general preference for structural solutions does not hold in his categories 2, 3 and 4, where behavioural remedies should be the norm:

1.  'Category 1' cases involve mergers where the parties will either individually or collectively with competitors have a clear ability to raise prices or reduce service standards. 'This covers cases of unilateral dominance and cases where the prediction of collective dominance is robust and does not depend on the fine-tuning of the economic model.'
2.  In 'Category 2' cases, the merged group may have the ability to raise prices or reduce service standards, but whether they can depends on the way in which the participants interact in the market. 'This covers cases of collective dominance where the concerns are real but the predictive models offer no certainty about whether a competitive or a non-competitive oligopoly will result.'
3.  'Category 3' cases are those where the merged entity will or may have the ability and incentive to act in specific ways that would or might have exclusionary consequences in the market but which are not themselves unlawful. 'This covers "indirect effects" of conglomerate mergers, many of the concerns traditionally voiced in vertical mergers and occasionally arises in horizontal mergers where the market has specific features which would give the merged group an incentive to follow a particular course of conduct.'

4. In 'Category 4' cases, the merged group will or may have the ability and incentive to act in specific ways that are themselves unlawful. 'This covers, for example, cases where the market structure will facilitate predatory pricing or the formation of a cartel.'

One difficulty with Lindsay's model is that the classification of particular cases will not always be clear because there is some subjectivity in the category definitions. Also the model does not link specific types of behavioural commitments to each of the general categories. Nevertheless it is a very useful contribution to the growing appreciation of the range of situations where behavioural remedies may be useful.

*Enforceability is not necessarily a problem*
While behavioural remedies often take longer to complete than divestitures, ensuring effective results over an extended time period is a challenge in either case. The critical dimensions of enforceability are the formal powers of the agency or court, formulation of enforceable commitments and incentives to comply.

1. Formal powers: the starting point for enforceability is that the relevant agency must have powers available to ensure that commitments are implemented. While the mechanisms vary depending on the procedural characteristics of each system, the European Commission, the Competition Bureau and the US federal agencies all have the ability to obtain enforceable commitments through orders, agreements or undertakings in contested and consent proceedings.
2. Formulating enforceable commitments: an agency should be able to structure a meaningful remedy if it has acquired a good understanding of the marketplace dynamics and the substantive competition concerns. In a divestiture context, there will often be non-trivial scope issues related to the product, geographic and other characteristics of the business and assets to be divested. To the extent that a behavioural remedy involves more complex elements, the agency may need to undertake a particularly careful assessment in order to confirm that commitments will be enforceable in a practical sense. In either case, supplementary inputs from other market participants may be of assistance and agencies already solicit such views in many cases. Once the concept is developed, reducing it to a written form is analogous to drafting a good 'contract' between the merging parties and the agency (which in effect is a representative for the customers, suppliers and/or competitors who are akin to 'third party beneficiaries'). Here again, divestiture remedies tend to be easier because precedents are well

developed, although it will still be necessary to take care with critical elements such as the definition of the divestiture package. Although behavioural commitments may be more complex, there are now an increasing number of precedents that provide guidance on how diverse types of remedies can also be codified successfully.

3. Incentives to comply: most companies make good faith efforts to comply with court or tribunal orders and formal undertakings or commitments given to competition authorities. Designing a remedy in which the merging parties have built-in incentives to comply can further reduce the likelihood that an agency will have to resort to formal powers to enforce a remedy. One of the most powerful techniques is the inclusion of 'crown jewel' fallback provisions if the primary remedy is not implemented as required. As noted above, this approach can be used with behavioural as well as divestiture remedies. Other more specific substantive and procedural incentives may also be employed, depending on the circumstances of a particular case.

*Monitoring can often be privatised*
One of the most important advances in remedy implementation over the past decade is a growing realisation that both the monitoring of a merged firm for non-compliance and enforcement action (actual or threatened) in response thereto can often be spearheaded by other market participants.

Customers or suppliers (or competitors, in cases where remedies are directly relevant to them) are often able to observe whether the merged firm is failing to comply with public commitments (e.g. a code of conduct or supply obligation), or appears to be acting anticompetitively (e.g. unexplained price increases or changes to non-price dimensions of competitive behaviour such as service reductions). Where they can detect such behaviour, they will usually have ample ability and incentive to act as reliable private monitors. This can reduce or in some cases eliminate the need for detailed and bureaucratic reporting by the merging firm to the applicable enforcement agency. While this is less certain to occur in consumer product markets, it will often be a very useful approach in other contexts.

*Enforcement can often be privatised*
Contracts can sometimes make private enforcement feasible. For example, the *Gemini I* consent order required that other CRSs seeking links to the Air Canada and Canadian Airlines reservation systems not only had to offer reciprocal access, but also had to enter into a contract incorporating a common set of CRS rules. In this way a level playing field would be created. The Tribunal noted that such contracts would allow 'parties to the link contracts enforcing these obligations by suing for injunctive relief or for damages'.[141]

While the reciprocal linking mechanism was highly customized for the CRS industry and the competition concerns in the *Gemini I* case, the concept of reducing enforceability and monitoring issues through contracts has considerable potential application to other situations. For example, supply commitments can readily be dealt with through contracts, or at least minimum conditions that must be incorporated in contracts, between the merged firm and the affected customers. This has been done in various cases in Canada, Europe and in the United States.[142] Further use of such mechanisms should be encouraged, which will lead to gradual fine-tuning of timing and procedural design issues that should enhance such processes.

Alternatively arbitration can be used to allow for private enforcement by the beneficiaries of behavioural remedies. The European Commission has adopted arbitration mechanisms as a support for behavioural remedies in at least 30 cases,[143] including the *Vivendi Canal+ Seagram*, *Shell/BASF*, *SEB/Moulinex* and *Alcan/Pechiney* cases referred to above.[144]

The Competition Bureau is the second major agency in the world to experiment with this approach.[145] For example, it has used codes of conduct to set post-merger boundaries that Indigo must respect in its dealings with publishers, governing Astral's relationship with advertisers, regulating Cendant's conduct towards Budget licensees and, most recently, CN's rate levels, performance times and other conduct-related obligations.[146] In each of these cases, the codes of conduct contained arbitration clauses that permitted publishers, advertisers, licensees or shippers to initiate private arbitration proceedings to enforce the protections provided by the code.[147]

Arbitration regimes have the potential to reduce monitoring and enforceability issues in a number of ways:

1. The customers or suppliers (or occasionally competitors, when necessary to preserve competition) who are the intended beneficiaries of a behavioural remedy will normally be well placed to identify any contravention or circumvention of the merged firm's commitments.
2. The merged firm need not produce extensive periodic reports on the firm's activities in the affected marketplace.
3. Agency resources need not be applied to review such reports.
4. A well-designed arbitration mechanism may rarely need to be invoked, because its mere existence will provide an incentive for the merged firm to comply with commitments.[148]

There are a host of procedural issues involved in designing an arbitration mechanism. In the commercial context, these may be customised in the contract between the parties,[149] or the standard rules of various arbitral organisations may be used. For purposes of competition law remedies, the enforcement agency will normally be negotiating an arbitration regime on behalf of the customers, suppliers or competitors that may later need to use it, and the agency may wish to retain some rights to monitor and/or intervene in the process. Ensuring timely and cost-effective dispute resolution will also be important. We expect that the models used by agencies will continue to evolve as they gain experience and receive feedback from private sector participants.[150]

*Non-merger cases corroborate the feasibility of behavioural remedies*
The feasibility of behavioural remedies is abundantly demonstrated in non-merger cases. Prohibition and mandatory behavioural orders are common remedies in monopolisation or abuse of dominance cases in the US,[151] EU[152] and Canada.[153] A few of the numerous recent examples are summarised below:

1.  The US Department of Justice prosecuted a monopolization case that focused on exclusionary rules relating to competing payment cards such as AMEX, as well as reduction of rivalry resulting from the substantial commonality of bank membership in the VISA and MasterCard networks.[154] The court ordered the exclusionary rules revoked and permanently enjoined the defendants from promulgating similar rules in the future.
2.  Complaints in Europe by the Sabre CRS regarding discriminatory practices by Air France, which had an ownership interest in the competing CRS Amadeus, were resolved after Air France agreed to comply with a code of good behaviour guaranteeing other competing CRS's equivalent terms to Amadeus.[155]
3.  In the *INTERAC* case, the Canadian Competition Tribunal issued a consent order requiring the monopoly network joint venture in the debit card and related electronic financial services markets to make access available to competitors that had not participated in the formation of the system.[156]

In the highest profile monopolisation and abuse cases ever pursued by the DOJ and the Commission, the concept of a structural remedy was rejected in favour of exceptionally detailed and sophisticated behavioural remedies that will govern Microsoft's future conduct in various markets.[157] Disclosure of essential interface information was the remedy in the US case and on the interoperability portion of the EU case, while unbundling was the principal remedy on the media player portion of the EU decision.

Interestingly, concerns about monitoring did not appear to be paramount in either case. The DOJ, for instance, announced without fanfare that 'The Division's attorneys and economists will continue to monitor closely Microsoft's compliance with the settlement'.[158] Similarly, the European Commission noted that it would appoint a monitoring trustee, 'To ensure effective and timely compliance with this decision [. . .] which will, inter alia, oversee that Microsoft's interface disclosures are complete and accurate, and that the two [bundled and unbundled] versions of Windows are equivalent in terms of performance'.[159]

## Conclusions

The common stated concerns about behavioural merger remedies appear to be overstated. A review of cases indicates that the European Commission, the Competition Bureau and even the US Federal agencies have, despite their stated scepticism as a matter of policy, employed diverse and innovative behavioural remedies in many merger cases in addition to their routine use in non-merger cases. Proponents of the divestiture remedy preference in merger cases have failed to articulate a compelling reason why behavioural remedies should not be considered with an open mind when merging parties provide proposals that remedy competition concerns in a manner that is enforceable and operational without undue monitoring difficulties.

## Notes

\*   Neil Campbell and Omar Wakil are partners in the Competition Group at McMillan Binch Mendelsohn LLP in Toronto. Casey Halladay is a member of the Competition Group at Cleary Gottlieb, based in the London office. The Canadian portions of this chapter draw upon Campbell, Neil and Omar Wakil (2005), 'Merger Law Developments: the Quiet But Effective Use of Behavioural Remedies in Canadian Merger Control', Langdon Hall Competition Law Invitational Forum, Cambridge, 4–6 May 2005; and Campbell, Neil and Casey Halladay (2002), 'The Use of Behavioural Remedies in Canadian Merger Law', Canadian Bar Association Annual Fall Conference on Competition Law, Ottawa, 3 October 2002. The authors would like to thank Nadia Colangelo and Tushara Weerasooriya for research assistance.

1.   There is some ambiguity about the scope of the terms 'structural' and 'behavioural'. For example, the US Department of Justice has observed that although structural remedies generally involve the sale of physical assets, '[i]n some instances, market structure can also be changed by requiring, for example, that the merged firm create new competitors through the sale or licensing of intellectual property rights': see US Department of Justice – Antitrust Division (October 2004), *Policy Guide to Merger Remedies*, online: http://www.usdoj.gov/atr/public/guidelines/205108.pdf [DOJ Guide] at 7. To avoid confusion, we will focus on divestiture remedies, which are the most common form of structural remedy, and use the term 'behavioural remedies' to describe any form of ongoing regulation of a firm's post-merger behaviour including licensing (but with recognition that the behavioural category encompasses many different forms of remedy).

2.   Federal Trade Commission (2 April 2003), *Statement of the Federal Trade Commission's Bureau of Competition on Negotiating Merger Remedies*, online: http://www.ftc.gov/bc/bestpractices/bestpractices030401.htm [*FTC Statement*].

3. European Commission (2001), *Commission Notice on Merger Remedies*, OJ [2001] C 68/3, online: http://europa.eu.int/eur-lex/pri/en/oj/dat/2001/c_068/c_06820010302en00030011. pdf [*Commission Notice*].
4. See, e.g., Jorré, G. (3 October 2002), 'CBA Competition Law Section Annual Fall Conference: Remedies Panel', paper presented to the Canadian Bar Association 2002 Annual Fall Conference on Competition Law at 1, 'structural remedies are the norm'; Letter from Konrad von Finckenstein QC to Messrs Cleghorn and Barrett, 11 December 1998, at 41, online: http://strategis.ic.gc.ca/pics/ct/rbceng.pdf [*RBC/BMO Letter*], 'the most effective structural remedy is the divestiture of assets away from the merged company to others that will provide effective and sustainable competition'.
5. Canadian Competition Bureau (October 2005), *Information Bulletin on Merger Remedies in Canada* (draft) at 14 [*Information Bulletin on Merger Remedies*].
6. See *United States v. E.I. duPont de Nemours & Co.*, 366 U.S. 316 at 331 (1961). The majority also stated that 'the public interest should not in this case be required to depend on the often cumbersome and time-consuming injunctive [i.e. behavioural] remedy. Should a violation of one of the prohibitions be thought to occur, the Government would have the burden of initiating contempt proceedings and of proving by a preponderance of the evidence that such a violation had indeed been committed': ibid. at 333–4.
7. See International Competition Network, ICN Merger Working Group: Analytical Framework Subgroup (June 2005), *Merger Remedies Review Project: Report for the fourth ICN annual conference*, online: htpp://www.internationalcompetitionnetwork. org/ICN_Remedies_StudyFINAL5-10.pdf at 11 [*Merger Remedies Review*]. The report does acknowledge that 'Nonetheless, some jurisdictions use behavioural remedies, where, typically, structural alternatives may not be viable or in multi-jurisdictional transactions where a behavioural remedy could be more easily tailored to the identified competitive harm'.
8. Our survey of European and US cases focuses on the past five years. In Canada, where the case flow is lower, we also cover several older cases that have played an important role in the development of current practices.
9. See, e.g., *Canada (Director of Investigation and Research) v. Southam Inc.* (1992), 47 C.P.R. (3d) 240; Case T-102/96 *Gencor v. Commission* [1999] ECR II-753, at paragraph 316; *Ford Motor Co. v. United States*, 405 U.S. 562 at 573 (1972): 'The relief in an antitrust case must be 'effective to redress the violations' and 'to restore competition'. See OECD (2004), *Merger Remedies*, DAF / COMP (2004) 21 at 238, (the 'United States' section), online: http://www.oecd.org/dataoecd/61/45/34305995.pdf; 'The goal is neither to "improve" deals that do not rise to the level of a violation, nor to make the competitive landscape better than the state of the world before the transaction. In each case, the remedy is tied to the anticompetitive effects likely to result from the merger. This law enforcement model thus implies a limited but important role for public enforcers in crafting merger remedies: to preserve competition in the market, or to restore it to its pre-merger state.'
10. In practice, the merging parties can be relied upon to assess the efficiencies and the costs related to alternative remedy proposals. However the agency would need to be attentive to proposals that generate significant costs for third parties.
11. A leading member of the US antitrust community has made similar observations. See Steptoe, Mary Lou (Acting Director, Bureau of Competition), Federal Trade Commission (14 March 1995), 'The FTC's merger program: new remedies and increased enforcement', available on Westlaw at 1995 WL 130674 F.T.C.: 'up until this decade divestiture of a plant or facility was the nearly exclusive remedy used to address section 7 violations [. . .] However in the past few years I think we have become more sophisticated in our analysis. Part of this change is due to the fact that increasingly mergers are *technology driven*, rather than facility driven' (emphasis added).
12. On vertical mergers generally, see Sunshine, Steven C. (11 May 1995), 'Vertical merger enforcement policy', address at the American Bar Association Section of Antitrust Law Spring Meeting, Washington DC, 5 April 1995; online: http://www.usdoj.gov/atr/public/speeches/2215.htm.

13.   The FTC has been the leading and most demanding agency in these areas: see *FTC Statement*, above, note 2.
14.   This approach has been used in several Canadian cases to ensure compliance with the behavioural orders: see, e.g., *Asea Brown Boveri/Westinghouse*, *infra*, note 39; *Imperial Oil/Texaco*, below, note 45; and *Ultramar/Coastal*, below, note 46.
15.   See *FTC Statement*, above, note 2; *DOJ Guide*, above, note 1 and *Commission Notice*, above, note 3. See also Federal Trade Commission, *Divestiture Study*, online: http://www.ftc.gov/opa/1999/08/divestreport.htm; and Sanderson, M. and A. Wallwork (1993), 'Divestiture relief in merger cases: an assessment of the Canadian experience' (1993), **38**, *McGill L.J.* 757 [*Sanderson & Wallwork*]. Sanderson & Wallwork set out a three-part test for effectiveness at para. 18: (1) a viable asset package; (2) an independent purchaser; and (3) timely divestiture.
16.   These issues are well illustrated by the Canadian *Chapters/Indigo* case, below, note 19. The fact that no willing buyers were found was likely attributable to an insufficient asset package. If a buyer had emerged, it is also questionable whether the acquisition would have yielded an effective competitor. Intervenors had warned the Tribunal that 'a prospective purchaser does require a critical mass of stores to achieve the economies of scale necessary to compete against the new *Chapters/Indigo* entity' and that 'the assets designated for divestiture under the DCO are "unlikely to be sufficiently profitable to be attractive to a purchaser"'. Curiously the Bureau agreed to a divestiture of only 13 book superstores in the consent order despite arguing in its 'Statement of Grounds and Material Facts' that a 'minimum critical mass' of 24 superstores would be needed to 'support the corporate overhead associated with a national chain'. Another example of a failed divestiture occurred in the *Agricore/UCG* case, where the sale period for the divestiture of a grain elevator was extended ten times before the merged entity filed an application before the Competition Tribunal arguing they should not have to sell the terminal at all because conditions had changed. For a summary of the case, see: Jorré, Gaston (3 November 2003), 'Current Competition Issues Relating to Port Terminal Grain Handling Services: Remarks to the Standing Committee on Agriculture and Agri-Food', online: http://www.competitionbureau.gc.ca/internet/index.cfm?itemID= 2004&lg=e.
17.   For example, in *Asea Brown Boveri/Westinghouse*, below, note 39, at paras. 19 and 22, only one Canadian competitor remained in the market for 'large' power transformers post-merger, and there were no remaining Canadian competitors in the market for 'very large' transformers.
18.   In *Imperial I*, below, note 45, at page 8, the Tribunal required that the prospective purchaser be someone 'who will maintain the viability of the divested assets'. In the absence of such a buyer, the Tribunal was willing to order a 'crown jewels' divestiture of all of the Texaco assets in Atlantic Canada rather than only the Eastern Passage Refinery and certain retail service stations and terminals. As events unfolded, this concern was prescient. Ultramar acquired the refinery pursuant to a seven-year undertaking to operate the facility, subject to a 'no material adverse change' clause. Three years later, Ultramar sought to close the refinery in reliance on the adverse change clause. The Bureau reviewed the matter in detail but decided there was no basis for taking any further enforcement action under the Act.
19.   See, e.g., *Chapters/Indigo*, below, note 52. See also *Sanderson & Wallwork*, above, note 15 at paras 36–7.
20.   See *Sanderson/Wallwork*, above, note 15 at 772.
21.   In *Asea Brown Boveri/Westinghouse*, below, note 39, for instance, the Bureau monitored conditions in the power transformer market for over four years. Similarly, when Ultramar proposed to acquire Texaco's Atlantic Canadian assets following the *Imperial II* divestiture, the total period of monitoring extended more than five years, beginning with Ultramar's undertakings in connection with the acquisition in September 1990 and then revised undertakings given in 1993. See *Imperial II*, below, note 45.
22.   *Competition Act*, R.S.C. 1985, c.C-34, ss.92(1)(e)(iii) and (f)(iii). See also s.105, which provides for the registration and enforceability of consent agreements. These

provisions, which became part of the Act during the 1986 amendments, reflected the proposal in Economic Council of Canada (1969), *Interim Report on Competition Policy*, Ottawa: Queen's Printer at 144, which recommended that, in addition to blocking a merger, the Competitive Practices Tribunal (a conceptual predecessor to the current Competition Tribunal) should have the power to allow the merger 'to proceed in altered form, or subject to other conditions designed to ensure that potential disadvantages were reduced to the point where they were outweighed by potential good effects'.

23. The Tribunal has discussed these provisions in *Southam*, below, note 27 at 250–51; *Commissioner of Competition* v. *Canadian Waste Services Inc.*, [2001] C.C.T.D. No. 32 (QL) at para. 47 [*Ridge Landfill*].

24. *Canada (Director of Investigation and Research)* v. *Air Canada* (1993), 49 C.P.R. (3d) 417 (F.C.A.), rev'g 49 C.P.R. (3d) 7 (Comp. Trib.) [*Gemini II*]. (This case involved an application to vary the original consent order granted in the *Gemini I* proceedings, discussed further below, note 42.)

25. Ibid. at 430 (emphasis added).

26. Ibid. He further observed (at 433) that the rationale behind the 'blunt instrument' of divestiture/dissolution is that these tools are 'designed to lead to the sophisticated solutions of s.92(1)(e)(iii)'.

27. *Canada (Director of Investigation and Research)* v. *Southam Inc*, (1992), 47 C.P.R. (3d) 240. (This citation refers to the Tribunal's remedies decision; for the Tribunal's decision on the merits, see (1992), 43 C.P.R. (3d) 161.)

28. The Tribunal has specifically declined to adopt a more demanding test for the approval of non-structural consent orders. Faced with the argument from American Airlines, a competitor which has obtained intervenor status in a merger consent order proceeding, that 'because there are significant regulatory [i.e. behavioural] aspects to the order, the Tribunal should adopt a different test' by asking 'whether or not there are changes to the consent order which could be made to significantly improve its effectiveness', the Tribunal required only that the proposed remedy remove the substantial lessening of competition: see *Gemini I*, below, note 42.

29. In its first contested merger case, *Canada (Director of Investigation and Research)* v. *Hillsdown Holdings (Canada) Ltd.* (1992), 41 C.P.R. (3d) 289 at 345, the Tribunal dealt with remedies in very brief fashion, rejecting the Director's request for a divestiture order as the transaction was not found to lessen competition substantially. See also the discussions in Director of Investigation and Research (1992), *Annual Report, 1992*, Ottawa: Supply and Services Canada at 12 and Goldman, C.S. and J.D. Bodrug (1993), 'The *Hillsdown* and *Southam* decisions: the first round of contested mergers under the Competition Act' (1993) **38**, *McGill L.J.*, 724.

30. *Canada (Director of Investigation and Research)* v. *Southam Inc.* (1997), 71 C.P.R. (3d) 417 at 445 (S.C.C.). Thus, as Iacobucci J noted at 444, '*some* lessening of competition following a merger is tolerated, because the Act proscribes only a *substantial* lessening of competition'. This standard was initially suggested by the Tribunal in the *Palm Dairies* consent proceedings at 548, where remedies were required to have a 'critical threshold of effectiveness', namely, that of eliminating the likely prevention or lessening substantially of competition'. The proposed order in that case was held not to meet the test: *Director of Investigation and Research* v. *Palm Dairies Limited*, [1986] C.C.T.D., consent order online: http://www.ct-tc.gc.ca/CMFiles/CT-1986-001_0044_38KPL-4192004-8637.pdf? windowSize=popup, and reasons and order, online http://www.ct-tc.gc.ca/CMFiles/CT-1986-001_0050_38KQB-4192004-8781.pdf?windowSize=popup.

31. *Canada (Commissioner of Competition)* v. *Canadian Waste Services Holdings Inc.* (2001), 11 C.P.R. (4th) 425 (Comp. Trib) at para. 110. The Tribunal also noted that:

In *United States* v. *E.I. Du Pont de Nemours et al.*, 366 U.S. 316 (1961), the court rejected Du Pont's proposed behavioural remedy under which Du Pont would retain the shares whose purchase gave rise to the violation, but would 'pass through' the voting rights to Du Pont shareholders. The Supreme Court held, at page 6 (QL) para. 24, that divestiture is the appropriate remedy for mergers that violate the Clayton Act (15 U.S.C.): Divestiture or dissolution has traditionally been the remedy for Sherman Act violations whose heart is intercorporate combination and control [. . .]. Divestiture has been called the most important of antitrust remedies. It is simple, relatively easy to administer, and sure. It should always be in the forefront of a court's mind when a violation of [s.] 7 has been found. Similarly, in *Community Publishers Inc. et al.* v. *NAT et al.*, 892 F. Supp. 1146 at 1176 (West. Dist. Ark., 1995) at 36 (QL), the United States District Court rejected a form of permanent hold separate order proposed by NAT.

32.  The same can be said of the Tribunal's rejection of proposed behavioural remedies in *Palm Davies* (see above, note 30, and *Southam* (see above, note 27).
33.  See OECD (2004), *Merger Remedies.* DAF / COMP (2004) 21 at 128 (the 'Canada' section), online: OECD http://www.oecd.org/dataoecd/61/45/34305995.pdf [*OECD, Merger Remedies,* 'Canada'].
34.  Ibid., at 125.
35.  *Information Bulletin on Merger Remedies,* above, note 5, at 14.
36.  Ibid., at 12–13.
37.  Ibid., at 12.
38.  There is no specific statutory basis for undertakings in the Competition Act. While undertakings arguably are enforceable in the ordinary courts as a legal contract, in practice the Bureau has addressed the enforceability issue by requiring the merging party(ies) to consent in advance to an application at any time to the Tribunal for a consent order on the same terms as the undertakings. For further discussion, see Campbell, A.N. (1997), *Merger Law and Practice: The Regulation of Mergers Under the Competition Act,* Toronto: Carswell, pp. 279ff.
39.  *Canada (Director of Investigation and Research)* v. *Asea Brown Boveri Inc.,* [1989] C.C.T.D. No. 35 (QL) (Comp. Trib.) [*ABB*]. See also *Consumers Packaging/Domglas* (1989) summarized in Industry Canada (25 April 1989), News Release and accompanying Backgrounder, 'DIR decision on the acquisition of the assets of Domglas Inc. by Consumers Packaging Inc'; and Director of Investigation and Research (1990), *Annual Report for the Year Ended March 31, 1990,* Ottawa: Supply and Services Canada, p. 12 [*Annual Report 1990*]. The proposed acquisition of Domglas by Consumers Packaging raised concerns in various inelastic segments of the 'rigid-wall packaging materials' market (both companies produced glass containers for a wide range of applications). However the Bureau allowed the merger to proceed on the basis of the merged entity's undertaking to obtain tariff reductions under the Canada–US Free Trade Agreement, which would lower entry barriers for American firms. Consumers Packaging also undertook to guarantee adequate long-term supply to vulnerable customers on 'equitable terms and conditions' (a much simpler supply commitment than was subsequently employed in *Imperial Oil/Texaco,* below, note 45.
40.  In the event that ABB was unable to achieve the tariff reductions and remissions by the deadlines specified in the order, certain assets were designated for divestiture. Failure to divest those assets within a 120-day period would trigger a second, larger divestiture requirement. The divestiture condition accompanied a 'hold separate' provision in the consent order which required ABB to maintain the Westinghouse assets as an independent, financially viable package 'until either the more permanent remedies come into effect or it becomes apparent that they will not be achieved'.
41.  Industry Canada, News Release and accompanying Backgrounder (6 July 1989), 'Proposed merger of the brewing operations of Molson and Carling O'Keefe'. See also the comments in *Annual Report 1990,* above, note 39 at 14–15.
42.  *Canada (Director of Investigation & Research)* v. *Air Canada* (1989), 27 C.P.R. (3d) 476 at 513 (Comp. Trib.) [*Gemini I*].
43.  With respect to Air Canada and Canadian, the provisions also included an obligation to participate in all other CRS's operating in Canada on commercially reasonable terms; a requirement to provide complete, timely and accurate information concerning their

respective schedules, fares and seat availability to all CRS's operating in Canada on the same timing and basis as such information is provided to Gemini and a prohibition against pressuring travel agents, through the use of commission incentives or service levels, to book tickets through Gemini instead of other CRS's. A similarly detailed set of behavioural restrictions applied to the operations of the Gemini system. The sophistication and precision of the order is also evident in a provision designed to provide a ' "level playing field" within the industry'. It required any CRS requesting direct links to the Air Canada or Canadian reservation systems to enter into a contract incorporating all of the restrictions in the consent order relating to the daily operation of Gemini. In this way, other airlines could not gain an advantage over Air Canada and Canadian by virtue of the constraints imposed on them by the consent order.

44. For a summary of the case, see *Annual Report 1990*, above, note 39 at 11–12.
45. For the initial reasons of 10 November 1989, see *Canada (Director of Investigation and Research)* v. *Imperial Oil Ltd.* (1989), 45 B.L.R. 1 at 7 (Comp. Trib.) [*Imperial I*]. The Tribunal released its final decision on the merits on 26 January 1990, see *Canada (Director of Investigation and Research)* v. *Imperial Oil Ltd.*, [1990] C.C.T.D. No. 1 (QL) [*Imperial II*], and issued the consent order on 6 February 1990, see *Canada (Director of Investigation and Research)* v. *Imperial Oil Ltd.*, [1990] C.C.T.D. No. 3 (QL) [*Imperial III*], aff'd (1992), 41 C.P.R. (3d) 493 (F.C.A.).
46. A similar remedy was attempted in *Canada (Commissioner of Competition)* v. *Ultramar/Coastal Ltd.*, [2000] C.C.T.D. No. 4 (QL) (Comp. Trib.). In *Ultramar*, the Commissioner negotiated a detailed behavioural remedy to address a mixture of vertical and horizontal concerns related to Ultramar's acquisition of the main oil terminal supplying independent gasoline marketers in the Ottawa area in conjunction with Ultramar's plans to restart its own dormant terminal. The Tribunal refused to issue the consent order after concluding that Ultramar's proposed offer to supply independent marketers at 'wholesale prices to be negotiated' was insufficient because it did not require that 'reasonable commercial terms' be provided.
47. Industry Canada (26 November 1993), News Release and accompanying Backgrounder, 'DIR will not oppose Canada Post's acquisition of Purolator'.
48. See Competition Bureau (16 October 1998), Information Notice, 'British Columbia Portland Cement merger settled' online: Competition Bureau http://www.competitionbureau.gc.ca/internet/index.cfm?itemID=778&lg=e and Competition Bureau (9 March 1999), Information Notice, 'Lafarge completes divestiture of Portland Cement terminal', Competition Bureau, available online at the following website: http://www.competitionbureau.gc.ca/internet/index.cfm?itemID=721&lg=e. See also *Annual Report 1990*, above, note 39 at 16–17.
49. The Bureau took a similar approach to a non-competition clause in an agreement between Petro-Canada and North Atlantic Refining regarding the latter's purchase of a refinery in Come By Chance, Newfoundland: see Competition Bureau (3 January 2001), News Release, 'Competition concerns resolved – restrictions attached to Newfoundland Refinery lifted', available online at the following website: http://www.competitionbureau.gc.ca/internet/index.cfm?itemID=478&lg=e<http://strategis.ic.gc.ca.
50. See Competition Bureau (21 December 1999), Information Notice and accompanying Backgrounder and Undertakings, 'Competition bureau announces it will not oppose acquisition of Canadian Airlines' online: http://www.competitionbureau.gc.ca/internet/index.cfm?itemID=619&lg=e. See also: *Ottawa, Annual Report 1990*, above, note 39 at 14–15.
51. Other undertakings required Air Canada to enter into interlining and joint fare agreements upon request of any other Canadian carrier; give Canadian air carriers a right of first refusal to purchase surplus Air Canada airplanes, for a three-year period; assign, at the option of any new discount carrier, Air Canada's facilities at Hamilton airport at cost, and refrain from establishing a discount carrier service in Eastern Canada until September 2001; change its travel agent commission incentive programme to focus only on international flights, and to eliminate market share sales targets; and divest positions

at the 20 airports in which it held more than 60% of ticket counters, as well as certain gates and loading bridges at Pearson airport and Dorval airport in Montreal.

52.   See *Canada (Commissioner of Competition)* v. *Trilogy Retail Enterprises L.P.*, [2001] C.C.T.D. No. 29 (QL) (Comp. Trib.) (Reasons Regarding Consent Order), Competition Tribunal online: http://www.ct-tc.gc.ca/CMFiles/CT-2001-003_0033_38OYT-4232004-2298.pdf?windowSize=popup>?; and *Canada (Commissioner of Competition)* v. *Trilogy Retail Enterprises L.P.*, [2001] C.C.T.D. No. 20 (QL) (Comp. Trib.) (Consent Order), Competition Tribunal online: http://www.ct-tc.gc.ca/CMFiles/CT-2001-003_0031b_49IAL-992004-7584.pdf?windowSize=popup.

53.   Similar commitments not to enforce lease clauses as entry barriers were obtained from a merger involving two of Chapters' predecessor entities in the mid-1990s. See Industry Canada (21 March 1995), News Release and accompanying backgrounder, 'DIR will not challenge Smithbooks' acquisition of Coles Book Stores Limited' where the merging parties also agreed not to seek restrictive covenants in any future leases and to inform their landlords that they 'will not take action to block access to retail sites by competing book stores'. Similarly the Bureau decided not to challenge a merger between two retail chains which sold women's clothing after accepting binding undertakings not to enforce restrictive clauses in more than a hundred leases and not to enter into new leases for a three-year period that contained restrictions on entry by competitors. See Competition Bureau (5 June 2002), News Release, 'Exclusive landlord deals eliminated in bureau review of Reitmans-Shirmax merger', available online at: http://www.competitionbureau.gc.ca/internet/index.cfm?itemID=410&lg=e.

54.   See Competition Bureau (5 April 2001), News Release, 'Competition bureau reaches agreement with Trilogy, Chapters and Indigo', online: www.competitionbureau.gc.ca/internet/index.cfm?itemID=492&lg=e.

55.   See Competition Bureau (27 November 2002), Information Notice, 'Competition bureau obtains undertakings to resolve concerns in Cendant acquisition of Budget Rent a Car', online: http://www.competitionbureau.gc.ca/internet/index.cfm?itemID= 421& lg=e. The undertakings were not publicized on its website, but can be obtained by contacting the Bureau.

56.   The 'special obligations' included undertakings not to 'exert control over the competitive aspects of the operations of the Budget Licensee's car rental business'; to implement a firewall to prevent the sharing of information (other than details concerning fleet size and gross revenues) between the Budget licensees and Avis's parent; and to operate the assets of Budget 'in a manner that is consistent with the promotion and growth of the Budget brand'. These undertakings appear to be an effort on the Bureau's part to preserve the competitive relationship that existed between Avis and Budget in Canada premerger as well as the independence of Budget's local licensees.

57.   *Commissioner of Competition* v. *Astral Media Inc., Telemedia Radio Inc., Radiomedia Inc.*, [2002] C.C.T.D. No. 24b (Comp. Trib.) (registered consent agreement), online: http://www.ct-tc.gc.ca/CMFiles/CT-2001-010_0024b_38JVR-472004-7594.pdf?windowSize=popup; and *Commissioner of Competition* v. *Astral Media Inc., Telemedia Radio Inc., Radiomedia Inc.*, [2003] C.C.T.D. No. 30b (Comp. Trib.) (amended consent agreement), online: http://www.ct-tc.gc.ca/CMFiles/CT-2001-010_0030b_38JPD-472004-8330.pdf? windowSize=popup.

58.   *The Commissioner of Competition* v. *British Columbia Railway Company and Canadian National Railway Company* [2004] C.C.T.D. 1b (Comp. Trib.) (registered consent agreement), online: http://www.ct-tc.gc.ca/CMFiles/CT-2001-010_0030b_38JPD-472004-8330.pdf?windowSize=popup. See also Competition Bureau (2 July 2004), News Release, 'Competition bureau obtains remedies in BC Rail merger', online: http://www.competitionbureau.gc.ca/internet/index.cfm?itemID=256&lg=e.

59.   CN's rate commitments are intended to ensure that shippers will continue to have direct access to competing carriers for haulage of traffic between BC Rail points and Vancouver, where those competing carriers pick up the railcars for transportation to their final destination. The 'Open Gateway Tariffs' set specific rates in five geographic areas for four different weight load categories, each of which are to be adjusted annually

according to an index to account for productivity gains. Disputes are, in the first instance, to be 'escalated' by written notice to the attention of CN's Marketing Director for Forest Products for resolution and, ultimately, to be resolved by arbitration. CN's performance on transit times are to be measured against historical average times from each of the five zones identified in the Open Gateway Tariffs. Monitoring is to be done by CN itself and regular performance reports submitted to the Canada Transportation Agency. CN is subject to financial penalties if it fails to meet the agreed-upon benchmarks, with any penalties to be paid into a trust fund and used towards upgrades of the BC Rail line. Disputes about the penalties are to be settled by arbitration. Several provisions are included to ensure that shippers are not discriminated against through unfavourable car supply conditions for choosing competing carriers over CN for long haul transportation. Disputes relating to the fair allocation of cars under the 'Open Gateway Tariffs' are, ultimately, to be resolved by arbitration. In assessing whether discrimination had occurred, the agreement stipulates that a variety of factors be taken into consideration, such as 'the commercial policies and operational practices prevalent throughout CN's Canadian rail network'. Shippers are also allowed to order additional cars through CN in times of shortage and to lease additional cars as required.

60. Specific provisions included an undertaking to link pricing levels of 'Single Car Rates' on export grain movements from the Peace River area to Vancouver and Prince Rupert, as well as multi-car rebates, to price levels in 'competitive zones'. Other provisions mirrored the remedies agreed to on the rail-interlining portion of the case, such as the setting of transit time benchmarks and safeguards relating to the non-discrimination in the supply of railcars. Similarly, arbitration is available as a dispute-resolution mechanism.

61. See *OECD, Merger Remedies*, 'Canada', above, note 33 at 130.

62. See Competition Bureau (13 December 2005), News Release, 'Bureau resolves competition concerns over Quebecor/Sogides merger', online: http://www.competitionbureau. gc.ca/internet/index.cfm?itemID=2014&lg=e. See also *Canada (Commissioner of Competition)* v. *Quebecor Media Inc., 127901 Canada Inc. and Pierre Lespérance*, [2005] C.C.T.D. 1c (Comp. Trib.) (registered consent agreement), online: http://www.ct-tc. gc.ca/CMFiles/CT-2005-010_0001c_38MZD-12192005-4503.pdf?windowSize=popup.

63. Case M.619, *Gencor/Lonrho*, OJ [1997] L 11/30.

64. Council of Ministers of the European Union (2004), Council Regulation (EC) No 139/2004 of 20 January 2004 on the control of concentrations between undertakings (the EC Merger Regulation), replacing Council Regulation (EC) No 4064/89, OJ [2004] L 24/1.

65. Case T-102/96, *Gencor Ltd.* v. *Commission*, [1999] ECR II – 753.

66. Case T-5/02 *Tetra Laval* v. *Commission*, [2002] ECR II – 4381.

67. Case C-13/03 *Commission of the European Communities* v. *Tetra Laval BV*, [2005] ECR I – 987.

68. See OECD, *Merger Remedies*, DAF / COMP (2004) 21 at 255 (the 'European Union' section), online: http://www.oecd.org/dataoecd/61/45/34305995.pdf.

69. Commission Notice on Merger Remedies, OJ [2001] C 68/3.

70. Ibid.

71. See European Commission (October 2005), *Merger Remedies Study*, online: http://www.europa.eu.int/comm/competition/mergers/others/remedies_study.pdf.

72. There is no clear split between structural and behavioural remedies within these four categories; although 'commitments to grant access' are clearly behavioural, other categories, for instance, 'commitments to transfer a market position', contain remedies that some would consider behavioural, such as long-term exclusive licences.

73. Above, note 71, at p. 165.

74. Within this group of ten primary access remedies, four commitments dealt with granting access to infrastructure, five concerned access to technology or IPRs, and one concerned the termination of an exclusive agreement. The Study distinguished such 'stand-alone and on-going' access commitments from transitional arrangements ancillary to a divestiture, such as temporary supply arrangements designed to give the purchaser of the acquired business certain limited start-up assistance. Ibid., at p. 114.

75. Ibid.

76. Ibid.
77. These are: '(1) non-exclusive licences granting access to critical assets, such as IPRs, should be offered and granted to a sufficient number of potential users; (2) licences should clearly spell out the field of use, the correct territorial dimension, a sufficient period of time to make access to the assets worthwhile, and should be granted under terms that make access commercially feasible (in particular, the costs of the licence must not be too high); (3) such commitments should not contain clauses that could adversely affect the competitive outcome, by for example, conveying competitive advantages to the licensors (such as information on the sales volumes and/or values of the licensees); (4) licences should not facilitate co-ordination of the competitive behaviour of the grantor and its beneficiaries; and (5) interviewed parties consistently pointed out the need for review clauses in commitments involving the grant of access. By providing for a response to unexpected market developments, a review clause can ensure that the impact of the Commission's intervention on the parties in such cases is limited' (Ibid. at p. 165).
78. Case M.986, *Agfa-Gevaert/DuPont*, OJ [1998] L 211. See also Blessing, M. (4 October 2002), 'EC merger regulation: arbitration as a means of policing commitments', paper presented at the International Arbitration Institute Conference in Paris, 4 October 2002 and Blessing, M. (2003), *Arbitrating Antitrust and Merger Control Issues*, Zurich: Helbing & Lichtenhahn. [*Blessing*].
79. *Boeing/McDonnell Douglas*, Case No IV/M.877, OJ [1997] L 336/16, online: http://europa.eu.int/comm/competition/mergers/cases/decisions/m877_19970730_600_en.pdf. See also European Commission (1997), Press Release, 'The Commission clears the merger between Boeing and McDonnell Douglas under conditions and obligations' (IP/97/729), online: http://lists.essential.org/1997/antitrust/msg00042.html.
80. See Federal Trade Commission (1 July 1997), News Release, 'FTC allows merger of the Boeing Company and McDonnell Douglas Corporation', online: http://www.ftc.gov/opa/1997/07/boeing.htm.
81. Case M.1806, *Astra/Zeneca*, OJ [2000] C 53/14.
82. Case M.2050, *Vivendi/Canal+/Seagram*, OJ [2000] C 311/3.
83. Films shown on pay-TV shortly after cinema exhibition and video rental are said to be released on 'first window'; that is before they are available more widely on television.
84. Case M.1751, *Shell/BASF*, OJ [2000] C052.
85. *Merger Remedies Review*, above, note 7, at 27–9.
86. Commission clears purchase by EdF of a stake in German electricity firm EnBW subject to conditions. While the principal competition remedies were behavioural, the parties also committed themselves to address separate issues in Switzerland by divesting EnBW's shareholding in a Swiss electricity company called WATT AG.
87. 5000 MW would be supplied in the form of virtual power plants and 1000 MW in the form of back-to-back agreements to existing co-generation power purchase agreements. Access to this capacity was to be granted via auctions prepared and operated by EDF under the supervision of a trustee.
88. A similar case is Case M.2947, *Verbund/EnergieAllianz*, OJ [2003] C 15/05. There the Austrian power company Österreichische Elektrizitätswirtschafts-AG (Verbund) proposed to merge with five Austrian regional power suppliers grouped together as EnergieAllianz. The Commission determined that the merger would have created or strengthened a dominant position in markets for the supply of electricity to certain customers and distributors. To resolve these concerns, the parties agreed to divest Verbund's controlling stake in APC, its distributor for large customers, together with a number of behavioural commitments. In connection with the divestiture, the parties entered into a three-year power supply contract that would cover the bulk of APC's electricity requirements, and large customers of the parties were also granted the unilateral right to cancel their contracts. The Commission also required that a volume of electricity totalling 450 gigawatt-hours be auctioned each year until July 2008. This is intended to increase liquidity, so as to encourage entry to and expansion on the Austrian small customers market and to improve the range of sources open to small distributors. In addition, the

parties also submitted a package of commitments that set a price cap for a transitional period in order to encourage the mutual integration of markets in balancing energy in Austria and the neighbouring countries.
89. Case M.2903, *DaimlerChrysler/Deutsche Telkom*, OJ [2003] C 288-02.
90. 'Telematics' is the combination of telecommunication with informatics (e.g., the passing of information from one computer to another via a telephone line or other electronic link, in this case the integration of wireless communications, vehicle monitoring systems and location devices).
91. Case M.2621, *SEB/Moulinex*, OJ [2003] C 88-06.
92. Case M.2861, *Siemens/Drägerwerk*, OJ [2002] C 311-05. See also European Commission (30 April 2003), Press Release, 'Commission clears *Siemens/Drägerwerk* hospital equipment venture subject to divestitures' (IP/03/602), online: http://europa.eu.int/rapid/ pressReleasesAction.do?reference=IP/03/602.
93. A similar example is Case M.3083, *GE/Instrumentarium*, OJ [2004] L 109/1. The parties were two of the four leading manufacturers of patient monitors in Europe. As in *Siemens/Dräger*, above, note 92, the Commission was concerned that GE could favour its own patient monitors by withholding the interface information necessary to connect third party monitors to GE's anaesthesia delivery systems and ventilators. GE undertook to divest Spacelab, including its worldwide patient monitoring business, and also gave the Commission a commitment to provide interface information to connect its equipment to third party monitors.
94. Case M.2876, *Newscorp/Telepiu*, OJ [2002] C 255/07. See also European Commission (4 February 2003), Press Release, 'Commission clears merger between Stream and Telepiù subject to conditions' (IP/03/478), online: http://europa.eu.int/rapid/ pressReleasesAction.do?reference=IP/03/478.
95. The Commission considered but ultimately rejected the parties' assertion of a 'failing firm defence'.
96. Newscorp also undertook not to 'black-out' so-called 'second window' movie rights. These are rights relating to the delayed and cheaper release of blockbuster movies on pay-TV. In the absence of these conditions, Newscorp would have been able to decide to buy only 'first window' rights while at the same time preventing potential competitors from buying second window rights. This additional undertaking further lowered barriers to entry.
97. Case M.3225, *Alcan/Pechiney (II)*, OJ [2003] C 204/04.
98. Ibid. As in the *Shell/BASF*, above, note 84, the arbitration mechanism provided that 'each party shall submit a single proposal for the terms of the Licence to the arbitration panel. The arbitration panel must select, within [. . .] of the arbitration hearing and by majority decision, one of the two submitted proposals in its entirety'.
99. Case M.3570, *Piaggio/Aprilia*, OJ [2004] 252/02.
100. Case M.3099, *AREVA/Urenco*, [2004] C 141/06. See also European Commission (10 June 2004), Press Release, 'Commission clears uranium enrichment equipment joint venture between AREVA and Urenco' (IP/04/1189), online: http://europa.eu.int/rapid/ pressReleasesAction.do?reference=IP/04/1189.
101. Case M.3863, *TUI / CP Ships*. See also European Commission (12 October 2005), Press Release, 'Commission clears the planned acquisition of CP Ships by TUI, subject to conditions', online: http://europa.eu.int/rapid/pressReleasesAction.do?reference=IP/05/ 1265&format=HTML&aged=0&language=EN&guiLanguage=en.
102. Case M.3765, *Amer Group/Salomon*. See also European Commission (13 October 2005), Press Release, 'Commission clears planned acquisition of Salomon by Amer Group, subject to conditions', online: http://europa.eu.int/rapid/pressReleasesAction.do? reference=IP/05/1267&format=HTML&aged=0&language=EN&guiLanguage=en.
103. 15 U.S.C. §25 (1914). See *FTC Statement*, above, note 2.
104. 15 U.S.C. §53(b) (1914). See *DOJ Guide*, above, note 1.
105. Ibid., §18. See also *International Shoe Co.* v. *Federal Trade Comm.*, 280 U.S. 291 (1930).
106. See generally Areeda, P.E. and H. Hovenkamp (1998), *Antitrust Law*, vol. IVA, New York: Aspen, rev. edn, at 105.

107. Above, note 6. The case involved a DOJ challenge to DuPont's 23% holding in General Motors, which allegedly provided it with an unfair advantage over its competitors in selling automotive fabrics and paint finishes to GM. A 4–3 majority of the Court ultimately rejected DuPont's proposed remedy of a 'pass-through' divestiture of its voting rights in GM to the individual DuPont shareholders, instead requiring full divestiture of DuPont's 63 million shares in GM over a ten-year period.
108. Ibid. at 326.
109. Ibid. at 331. The Court stated (at 329–30) that divestiture 'has traditionally been the remedy for Sherman Act violations whose heart is intercorporate combination and control' and that 'it is reasonable to think immediately of the same remedy when section 7 of the Clayton Act, which particularizes the Sherman Act standard of illegality, is involved'.
110. *California* v. *American Stores Co.*, 495 U.S. 271 (1990) at 284.
111. *FTC Statement*, above, note 2.
112. *DOJ Guide*, above, note 1.
113. Ibid. at 8–9.
114. *America Online, Inc. and Time Warner Inc.*, File No. 001 0105, Docket No. C-3989, online: http://www.ftc.gov/os/2000/12/aoldando.pdf.
115. Ibid. at 13.
116. *United States of America* v. *AT&T and Media One*, online: http://www.usdoj.gov/atr/cases/f6600/6622.pdf. See also US Department of Justice (25 May 2000), News Release, 'Justice Department requires AT&T to divest Mediaone's interest in road runner broadband internet access service', online: http://www.usdoj.gov/atr/public/press_releases/2000/4829.htm.
117. *The Boeing Company*, File No. 001 0092, Docket No. C-3992, available online: http://www.ftc.gov/os/2000/09/boeingdo.htm. See also Federal Trade Commission (27 September 2000), Press Release, 'Federal Trade Commission clears Boeing Co.'s acquisition of Hughes Space and Communications', online: http://www.ftc.gov/opa/2000/09/ boeing.htm.
118. *Conoco Inc. and Phillips Petroleum Company*, File No. 021 0040, Docket No. C-4058, online: http://www.ftc.gov/os/2002/08/conocophillipsdo.pdf.
119. *Nestlé Holding and Ralston Purina Company*, File No. 011 0083, Docket No. C-4028, online: http://www.ftc.gov/os/2002/02/nestledo.pdf. See also Federal Trade Commission (11 December 2001), Press Release, 'FTC reaches consent agreement that imposes conditions on the purchase of Ralston Purina, Co. by Nestlé S.A.', online: http://www.ftc.gov/opa/2001/12/nestleralston.htm. Other examples of supply agreements connection with divestiture remedies include *Alcoa/Reynolds* (2000): see US Department of Justice (6 June 2000), Press Release, online: http://www.usdoj.gov/atr/cases/f4600/4661.pdf and Competitive Impact statement, online: http://www.usdoj.gov/atr/cases/f4900/4922.pdf; *Georgia Pacific/Fort St. James* (2000), see US Department of Justice, Press Release, online: http://www.usdoj.gov/atr/public/press_releases/2000/7024.pdf and Competitive Impact Statement (01/25/2001), online: http://www.usdoj.gov/atr/cases/f7300/7364.pdf; *Dow/Union Carbide* (2001), File No. 991 0301, Docket No. C-3999, online: http://www.ftc.gov/os/2001/02/dowuniondo.pdf; and *Philip Morris/Nabisco* (2001), File No. 001 0215, Docket No. C-3987, online: http://www.ftc.gov/os/2000/12/philmorrisagree.pdf.
120. *Nestlé Holdings, Inc.; Dreyer's Grand Ice Cream Holdings, Inc.; and Dreyer's Grand Ice Cream, Inc.*, File No. 021 0174, Docket No. C-4082, http://www.ftc.gov/os/caselist/0210174.htm. See also Federal Trade Commission (25 June 2003), Press Release, 'Nestlé-Dryer's settle FTC charges', online : http://www.ftc.gov/opa/2003/06/nestle.htm.
121. In her concurring statement, Commissioner Anthony said that, while she voted to accept the proposal, she had 'concerns' that the distribution volume commitments made by the merging parties were 'a more regulatory form of relief than I ordinarily like to see, in large part because they effectively will require the Commission to supervise the super-premium ice cream marketplace for the next five years'. Anthony also noted that there was no guarantee that the divestiture buyer's distribution system would

be profitable once the volume commitments end, and that 'All the risk of failure is borne by [the buyer] and ultimately, consumers – not the parties'.

122.  FTC File No. 151 0131. See also Federal Trade Commission (6 September 2005), Press Release, 'FTC resolves Aloha Petroleum litigation, online: http://www.ftc.gov/opa/2005/09/alohapetrol.htm.
123.  This case has various similarities to *Ultramar / Coastal*, above, note 46.
124.  Marleen Van Kerckhove, Donna Patterson and Julie Goshorn have, similarly, reviewed a series of European and US cases and concluded that behavioural remedies could be acceptable alternatives to structural remedies in a number of situations, notably to address concerns about foreclosure, access to networks or technology and potential coordinated behaviour. See Van Kerckhove, Marleen, Donna Patterson and Julie Goshorn (2006), 'Are conduct remedies workable in merger control? U.S. and EU practices compared.' [Publication pending.]
125.  See, e.g., in Canada, *Air Canada / Canadian*, above, note 50.
126.  See, e.g., in Canada, *Air Canada (Gemini I)*, above, note 42.
127.  See, e.g., in Canada, *Molson / Elders*, above, note 41.
128.  See, e.g., in Canada, *Air Canada / Canadian*, above, note 50.
129.  See, e.g., in the US, *Boeing / General Motors (Hughes)*, above, note 117.
130.  See, e.g., in Europe, *Newscorp / Telepiu*, above, note 94.
131.  See, e.g., in Canada, *CAPAC / PROCAN*, above, note 44.
132.  See, e.g., in Canada, *ABB*, above, note 39.
133.  E.g., in Europe, *Newscorp/Telepiu*, above, note 94; *Daimler Chrysler/DeutscheTelekom*, above, note 89; and *GE/Instrumentarium*, above, note 93.
134.  E.g., in Europe, *Astra/Zenca*, above, note 81; *AGFA Gevaert/DuPont*, above, note 78 ; *Boeing/McDonnell Douglas*, above, note 79; in Canada, *Lafarge/Holnam*, above, note 48; *Chapters/Indigo*, above, note 52; *Avis/Budget*, above, note 55; *CNR/BC Rail*, above, note 58; and *Smith Books/Coles*, see Industry Canada, Press Release, 'Competition Bureau files application with Cónsent of Indigo and Chapters', online: http://www.ic.gc.ca/cmb/welcomeic.nsf/0/85256a220056c2a485256a3200779267?OpenDocument.
135.  E.g., in Canada, *Imperial Oil/Texaco*, above, note 45.
136.  See *Gemini I*, above, note 42; *Chapters/Indigo*, above, note 52; and *Astral/Télémédia*, above, note 57.
137.  E.g., *Piaggio/Aprilia*, above, note 99; *Verbund/Energie Allianz*, above, note 88.
138.  E.g., in Europe, *AREVA / Urenco*, above, note 100; in Canada, *Air Canada (Gemini I)*, above, note 42, *Canada Post/Purolator*, above, note 47; and in the US, *Boeing/General Motors (Hughes)*, above, note 117 and *Conoco/Phillips*, above, note 118.
139.  Lindsay, A. (October/November 2001), 'Behavioural remedies revisited: GE/Honeywell', *Global Competition Review*, at 24 [*Lindsay*].
140.  Although he says that, even in these cases, in exceptional circumstances, behavioural remedies may be appropriate.
141.  *Gemini I*, above, note 42, at 488.
142.  See, e.g., in Canada, *Imperial Oil/Texaco*, above, note 45; in Europe, *Piaggio/Aprilia*, above, note 99; and in the US, *Nestlé/Dreyer's*, above, note 120.
143.  See *Blessing*, above, note 78. See also Blanke, Gordon (2006), 'The use and utility of international arbitration in EC Commission merger remedies', Groningen: Europa Law Publishing.
144.  See *Vivendi/Canal+/Seagram*, above, note 82, *Shell/BASF*, above, note 84, *SEB/Moulinex*, above, note 91 and *Alcan/Pechiney*, above, note 97. See also the commentaries on *Indigo/Chapters*, above, note 52; *Astral/Télémédia*, above, note 57; *Avis/Budget*, above, note 55; and *CN/BC Rail*, above, note 58.
145.  See generally Rowley, J.W. and A.N. Campbell (March 2005), 'Arbitration in support of behavioural competition law remedies', IBC UK Conference on International Dispute Resolution and Competition – The Interface Between ADR and Competition Law, March 2005; and Thomson, K.E., C. Margison and C. Whittome (September 2003), 'Arbitration in a Canadian antitrust setting', IBA Annual Conference, San Francisco.

146. See the commentaries on *Indigo/Chapters*, above, note 52; *Astral/Télémédia*, above, note 57; *Avis/Budget*, above, note 55; and *CN/BC Rail*, above, note 58.
147. Arbitration clauses have been used to similar effect in the undertakings given in the *Air Canada/Canadian Airlines* case, above, note 50 at 14ff. Other examples of arbitration provisions in remedial orders and agreements may be found in the consent agreement in *Commissioner of Competition* v. *United Grain Growers Limited*, available online: http://www.ct-tc.gc.ca/CMFiles/CT-2002-001_0105a_38MWW-8162005-8722. pdf?windowSize=popup, where disputes about prices and other terms in connection with interim supply arrangements pending a divestiture were to be settled by arbitration. See also Competition Bureau (17 October 2002), Press Release, 'Grain case settled: Agricore United agrees to divest port terminal', online: http://www.competitionbureau. gc.ca/internet/index.cfm?itemID=459&lg=e; the consent order in *Canada (Director of Investigation and Research)* v. *Canadian Waste Services Inc.*, [1998] C.C.T.D. No. 10 (QL) at no. 15ff (Comp. Trib.), where a divestiture was accompanied by an agreement to offer cost-based access to landfill and disputes arising under the access agreement were to be resolved by arbitration; and *Canada (Director of Investigation and Research)* v. *ADM Agri-Industries, Ltd.*, [1997] C.C.T.D. No. 25 (QL) at no. 16ff (Comp. Trib.), where the divestiture of a mill was accompanied by a supply agreement which provided that disputes were to be resolved by arbitration.
148. Experience to date in Canada and Europe appears to corroborate this point – so far as is publicly known, there have been very few arbitration proceedings commenced under the regimes established in numerous merger remedy cases.
149. See generally Rowley, J.W., QC (February 2005), 'The agreement to arbitrate: getting it right', *Chambers Client Report*.
150. See, e.g., the proposals for a standard EU merger arbitration framework in Blessing, above, note 78.
151. Professors Areeda and Hovenkamp have noted that, while structural remedies may be considered by courts in §2 monopolization cases, 'dissolving monopoly power to the maximum possible degree does not necessarily dictate divestiture of assets, or divestiture to the maximum extent consistent with economies of scale', and that 'where *less drastic remedies* hold promise of being adequate within a reasonable period of time, it may be wise in some situations to give them a chance, *reserving divestiture as a last resort*': Areeda, P.E. and H. Hovenkamp (1998), *Antitrust law*, New York: Aspen (emphasis added).
152. See Whish, R. (2004), *Competition Law*, 5th edn, London: Butterworths, at 209, where he notes that a structural remedy may be ordered under Article 82 'provided there is no equally effective behavioural remedy'.
153. Abuse of dominance and other reviewable distribution practices in Part VIII of the Competition Act provide for prohibition or other remedial orders to restore competition.
154. *United States* v. *Visa USA., Inc.*, 163 F. Supp. 2d 322, 2001 US Dist. LEXIS 16156, 2001-2 Trade Cas. (CCH) P73440 (S.D.N.Y. 2001), aff'd 344 F.3d 229, 2003 US App. LEXIS 19281, 2003-2 Trade Cas. (CCH) P74151 (2d Cir. N.Y. 2003).
155. European Commission (15 March 1999), Press Release, 'Commission opens procedure against Air France for favouring Amadeus reservation system', IP/99/171, available online at the following website: http://europa.eu.int/rapid/pressReleasesAction.do?reference=IP/99/171&format=HTML&aged=1&language=EN&guiLanguage=en. See also European Commission (1 December 2000), 'International cooperation – SABRE/Amadeus' *European Commission Bulletin*, available online at the following website: http://europa.eu.int/abc/doc/off/bull/en/200007/p 103052.htm. The case bears some similarity to the *Gemini I* proceeding which led to standard rules for CRSs operating in Canada: see above, note 42.
156. *Canada (Director of Investigation and Research)* v. *Bank of Montreal et al.* (1996), 68 C.P.R. (3d) 527 (Comp. Trib.).
157. See *Commission Decision relating to a proceeding under Article 82 of the EC Treaty against Microsoft Corporation* (Case No. 37.792) COM (2004) 900 final (24 March 2004) (The Decision is under appeal to Court of First Instance); and *United States* v. *Microsoft*

*Corporation*, Final Judgment of 12 November 2002, United States District Court for the District of Columbia, No. 98-1232, online: http://www.usdoj.gov/atr/cases/f200400/ 200457.htm. For a commentary on the effects of the EU remedy, see Mensching, Jürgen (22 October 2004), 'The Microsoft decision – promoting innovation', Sweet & Maxwell, 4th Annual Competition Law Review Conference, 22 October 2004, online at: http://europa.eu.int/comm/competition/speeches/text/sp 2004_017_en.pdf. For a commentary on the virtues of the complex US remedy, see Majoras, Deborah Platt (4 October 2002), 'Antitrust remedies in the United States: adhering to sound principles in a multi-faceted scheme', Canadian Bar Association National Competition Law Section Annual Fall Conference, 4 October 2002, online: http://www.usdoj.gov/atr/ public/ speeches/200354.pdf.

158.   See the US DOJ (30 June 2004), 'Statement by Assistant Attorney General R. Hewitt Pate regarding Microsoft settlement', online: http://www.usdoj.gov/atr/public/press_ releases/2004/204452.htm.

159.   European Commission (24 March 2004), Press Release, 'Commission concludes on Microsoft investigation, imposes conduct remedies and a fine', IP/04/382, online: http://europa.eu.int/rapid/pressReleasesAction.do?reference=IP/04/382&format=HT ML&aged=0&language=EN&guiLanguage=en. The Monitor Trustee was subsequently appointed and has advised the Commission that Microsoft's proposed disclosures on the interoperability side of the case are inadequate. See European Commission (22 December 2005), Press release, 'Commission appoints Trustee to advise on Microsoft's compliance with 2004 Decision', IP/05/1215, available online at the following website: http://europa.eu.int/rapid/pressReleasesAction.do?reference=IP/05/ 1215&format=HTML&aged=1&language=EN&guiLanguage=en and European Commission (22 December 2005), Press release, 'Commission warns Microsoft of daily penalty for failure to comply with 2004 decision', IP/05/1695, online: http:// europa. eu.int/rapid/pressReleasesAction.do?reference=IP/05/1695&format=HTML&aged=0 &language=EN&guiLanguage=en.

## References

Areeda, P.E. and H. Hovenkamp (1998), *Antitrust Law*, rev. edn, vol. IVA, New York: Aspen.

Blanke, Gordon (2006), 'The use and utility of international arbitration in EC Commission merger remedies', Groningen: Europa Law Publishing.

Campbell, A.N. (1997), *Merger Law and Practice: The Regulation of Mergers Under the Competition Act*, Toronto: Carswell.

Campbell, Neil and Casey Halladay (2002), 'The use of behavioural remedies in Canadian merger law', Canadian Bar Association Annual Fall Conference on Competition Law, Ottawa, 3 October.

Campbell, Neil and Omar Wakil (2005), 'Merger law developments: the quiet but effective use of behavioural remedies in Canadian merger control', Langdon Hall Competition Law Invitational Forum, Cambridge, 4–6 May.

Canadian Competition Bureau (October 2005), *Information Bulletin on Merger Remedies in Canada* (Draft).

Competition Bureau (16 October 1998), Information Notice, 'British Columbia Portland Cement merger settled', online: Competition Bureau, available online at the following website: http://www.competitionbureau.gc.ca/internet/index.cfm?itemID=778&lg=e.

Competition Bureau (9 March 1999), Information Notice, 'Lafarge completes divestiture of Portland Cement terminal', Competition Bureau, available online at the following website: http://www.competitionbureau.gc.ca/internet/index.cfm?itemID=721&lg=e.

Competition Bureau (21 December 1999), Information Notice and accompanying Backgrounder and Undertakings, 'Competition bureau announces it will not oppose acquisition of Canadian Airlines', available online at the following website: http://www. competitionbureau.gc.ca/internet/index.cfm?itemID=619&lg=e.

Competition Bureau (3 January 2001), News release, 'Competition concerns resolved – restrictions attached to Newfoundland refinery lifted', available online at the following website:    http://www.competitionbureau.gc.ca/internet/index.cfm?itemID=478&lg=e <http://strategis.ic.gc.ca.

Competition Bureau (5 April 2001), News release, 'Competition Bureau reaches agreement with Trilogy, Chapters and Indigo', available online at the following website: www. competitionbureau.gc.ca/internet/index.cfm?itemID=492&lg=e.

Competition Bureau (5 June 2002), News release, 'Exclusive landlord deals eliminated in Bureau review of Reitmans–Shirmax Merger', available online at: http://www. competitionbureau.gc.ca/internet/index.cfm?itemID=410&lg=e.

Competition Bureau (17 October 2002), Press release, 'Grain case settled: Agricore United agrees to divest port terminal', online: http//www.competitionbureau.gc.ca/ internet/index.cfm?itemID=459&lg=e.

Competition Bureau (27 November 2002), Information Notice, 'Competition Bureau obtains undertakings to resolve concerns in Cendant acquisition of Budget Rent a Car', online: http://www.competitionbureau.gc.ca/internet/index.cfm?itemID=421&lg=e.

Competition Bureau (2 July 2004), News release, 'Competition Bureau obtains remedies in BC Rail merger', online: http://www.competitionbureau.gc.ca/internet/index.cfm?itemID= 256&lg=e.

Competition Bureau (13 December 2005), News release, 'Bureau resolves competition concerns over quebecor/Sogides merger', available online at the following website: http://www. competitionbureau.gc.ca/internet/index.cfm?itemID=2014&lg=e.

Council of Ministers of the European Union (2004), Council Regulation (EC) No 139/2004 of 20 January 2004 on the control of concentrations between undertakings (the EC Merger Regulation), replacing Council Regulation (EC) No 4064/89, OJ [2004] L 24/1.

Economic Council of Canada (1969), *Interim Report on Competition Policy*, Ottawa: Queen's Printer.

European Commission (1997), Press release, 'The Commission clears the merger between Boeing and McDonnell Douglas under conditions and obligations' (IP/97/729), online: http://lists.essential.org/1997/antitrust/msg00042.html.

European Commission (15 March 1999), Press release, 'Commission opens procedure against Air France for favouring Amadeus reservation system', IP/99/171, available online at the following website: http://europa.eu.int/rapid/pressReleasesAction.do?reference=IP/99/ 171&format=HTML&aged=1&language=EN&guiLanguage=en.

European Commission (1 December 2000), 'International cooperation – SABRE/Amadeus', *European Commission Bulletin*, available online at the following website: http://europa. eu.int/abc/doc/off/bull/en/200007/p103052.htm.

European Commission (2001), *Commission Notice on Merger Remedies*, OJ [2001] C68/3, online: http://europa.eu.int/eur-lex/pri/en/oj/dat/2001/c_068/c_06820010302en00030011.pdf.

European Commission (4 February 2003), Press release, 'Commission clears merger between Stream and Telepiù subject to conditions' (IP/03/478), available online at the following webiste: http://europa.eu.int/rapid/pressReleasesAction.do?reference=IP/03/478.

European Commission (30 April 2003), Press release, 'Commission clears Siemens/ Drägerwerk hospital equipment venture subject to divestitures' (IP/03/602), online: http://europa.eu.int/rapid/pressReleasesAction.do?reference=IP/03/602.

European Commission (24 March 2004), Press release, 'Commission concludes on Microsoft investigation, imposes conduct remedies and a fine', IP/04/382, online: http://europa.eu.int/ rapid/pressReleasesAction.do?reference=IP/04/382&format=HTML&aged=0&language= EN&guiLanguage=en.

European Commission (10 June 2004), Press release, 'Commission clears uranium enrichment equipment joint venture between AREVA and Urenco' (IP/04/1189), online: http://europa.eu.int/rapid/pressReleasesAction.do?reference=IP/04/1189.

European Commission (12 October 2005), Press release, 'Commission clears the planned acquisition of CP Ships by TUI, subject to conditions', online: http://europa.eu.int/rapid/ pressReleasesAction.do?reference=IP/05/12652format=HTML&aged=0&language= EN&guiLanguage=en.

European Commission (13 October 2005), Press release, 'Commission clears planned acquisition of Salomon by Amer Group, subject to conditions', online: http://europa.eu.int/

rapid/pressReleasesAction.do?reference=IP/05/1267&format=HTML&aged=0&language=EN&guiLanguage=en.

European Commission (October 2005), *Merger Remedies Study*, online: http://www.europa.eu.int/comm/competition/mergers/others/remedies_study.pdf.

European Commission (22 December 2005a), Press release, 'Commission appoints Trustee to advise on Microsoft's compliance with 2004 Decision', IP/05/1215, available online at http://europa.eu.int/rapid/pressReleasesAction.do?reference=IP/05/1215&format=HTML&aged=1&language=EN&guiLanguage=en.

European Commission (22 December 2005b), Press release, 'Commission warns Microsoft of daily penalty for failure to comply with 2004 decision', IP/05/1695, online: http://europa.eu.int/rapid/pressReleasesAction.do?reference=IP/05/1695&format=HTML&aged=0&language=EN&guiLanguage=en.

Federal Trade Commission (1 July 1997), News release, 'FTC allows merger of the Boeing Company and McDonnell Douglas Corporation', online: http://www.ftc.gov/opa/1997/07/boeing.htm.

Federal Trade Commission (1999), *Divestiture Study*, available online at: http://www.ftc.gov/opa/1999/08/divestreport.htm.

Federal Trade Commission (27 September 2000), Press release, 'Federal Trade Commission clears Boeing Co.'s acquisition of Hughes Space and Communications', online: http://www.ftc.gov/opa/2000/09/boeing.htm.

Federal Trade Commission (11 December 2001), Press release, 'FTC reaches consent agreement that imposes conditions on the purchase of Ralston Purina, Co. by Nestlé S.A.', online: http://www.ftc.gov/opa/2001/12/nestleralston.htm.

Federal Trade Commission (2 April 2003), *Statement of the Federal Trade Commission's Bureau of Competition on Negotiating Merger Remedies*, available online at http://www.ftc.gov/bc/bestpractices/bestpractices030401.htm.

Federal Trade Commission (25 June 2003), Press release, 'Nestlé-Dryer's settle FTC charges', online: http://www.ftc.gov/opa/2003/06/nestle.htm.

Federal Trade Commission (6 September 2005), Press release, 'FTC resolves Aloha Petroleum litigation', online: http://www.ftc.gov/opa/2005/09/alohapetrol.htm.

Goldman, C.S. and J.D. Bodrug (1993), 'The *Hillsdown* and *Southam* decisions: the first round of contested mergers under the Competition Act' (1993), **38**, *McGill L.J.*, 724.

Industry Canada, Press release, 'Competition Bureau files application with consent of Indigo and Chapters', available online at the following website: http://www.ic.gc.ca/cmb/welcomeic.nsf/0/85256a220056c2a485256a3200779267?OpenDocument.

Industry Canada (25 April 1989), News Release and accompanying Backgrounder, 'DIR decision on the acquisition of the assets of Domglas Inc. by Consumers Packaging Inc'.

Industry Canada (6 July 1989), News Release and accompanying Backgrounder, 'Proposed merger of the brewing operations of Molson and Carling O'Keefe'.

Industry Canada (26 November 1993), News Release and accompanying Backgrounder, 'DIR will not oppose Canada Post's acquisition of Purolator'.

Industry Canada (21 March 1995), News Release and accompanying backgrounder, 'DIR will not challenge Smithbooks' acquisition of Coles Book Stores Limited'.

International Competition Network, ICN Merger Working Group: Analytical Framework Subgroup (June 2005), 'Merger remedies review project: report for the fourth ICN annual conference', online: http://www.internationalcompetitionnetwork.org/ICN_Remedies_StudyFINAL5-10.pdf.

Jorré, Gaston (3 October 2002), 'CBA Competition Law Section Annual Fall Conference: Remedies Panel', paper presented to the Canadian Bar Association, 2002 Annual Fall Conference on Competition Law.

Jorré, Gaston (3 November 2003), 'Current competition issues relating to port terminal grain handling services: remarks to the Standing Committee on Agriculture and Agri-Food', online: http://www.competitionbureau.gc.ca/internet/index.cfm?itemID=2004&lg=e.

Lindsay, A. (October/November 2001), 'Behavioural remedies revisited: GE/Honeywell', *Global Competition Review*.

Majoras, Deborah Platt (4 October 2002), 'Antitrust remedies in the United States: adhering to sound principles in a multi-faceted scheme', Canadian Bar Association National Competition Law Section Annual Fall Conference, 4 October 2002, online: http://www. usdoj.gov/atr/public/speeches/200354.pdf.

Mensching, Jürgen (22 October 2004), 'The Microsoft decision – promoting innovation', Sweet and Maxwell 4th Annual Competition Law Review Conference, online at http://europa.eu.int/comm/competition/speeches/text/sp 2004_017_en.pdf.

OECD (2004), *Merger Remedies*, DAF/COMP 21, online: http://www.oecd.org/dataoecd/61/45/34305995.pdf.

Rowley, J.W., QC (February 2005), 'The agreement to arbitrate: getting it right', *Chambers Client Report*.

Rowley, J.W. and A.N. Campbell (March 2005), 'Arbitration in support of behavioural competition law remedies', IBC UK Conference on International Dispute Resolution and Competition – The Interface Between ADR and Competition Law.

Sanderson, M. and A. Wallwork (1993), 'Divestiture relief in merger cases: an assessment of the Canadian experience' (1993), **38**, *McGill L.J.*, 757.

Steptoe, Mary Lou, Federal Trade Commission (14 March 1995), 'The FTC's merger program: new remedies and increased enforcement', available on Westlaw at 1995 WL 130674 F.T.C.

Sunshine, Steven C. (11 May 1995), 'Vertical merger enforcement policy', Address at the American Bar Association Section of Antitrust Law Spring Meeting, Washington, DC, online: http://www.usdoj.gov/atr/public/speeches/2215.htm.

Thomson, K.E., C. Margison and C. Whittome (September 2003), 'Arbitration in a Canadian antitrust setting', IBA Annual Conference, San Francisco.

US Department of Justice (25 May 2000), News release, 'Justice Department requires AT&T to divest Mediaone's interest in road runner broadband internet access service', online: http://www.usdoj.gov/atr/public/press_releases/2000/4829.htm.

US Department of Justice (6 June 2000), Press release, online: http://www.usdoj.gov/atr/cases/f4600/4661.pdf.

US Department of Justice (30 June 2004), 'Statement by Assistant Attorney General R. Hewitt Pate regarding Microsoft settlement', available online at the following website: http://www.usdoj.gov/atr/public/press_releases/2004/204452.htm.

US Department of Justice – Antitrust Division (October 2004), *Policy Guide to Merger Remedies*, online: http://www.usdoj.gov /atr/public/guidelines/205108.pdf.

Whish, R. (2004), *Competition Law*, 5th edn, London: Butterworths.

*Cases*

*Agfa-Gevaert/DuPont*, OJ [1998] L 211.

*Alcan/Pechiney (II)*, OJ [2003] C 204/04.

*America Online, Inc. and Time Warner Inc.*, File No. 001 0105, Docket No. C-3989, online: http://www.ftc.gov/os/2000/12/aoldando.pdf.

*AREVA/Urenco*, [2004] C 141/06.

*Astra/Zeneca*, OJ [2000] C 53/14.

*Boeing/McDonnell Douglas*, Case No IV/M.877, OJ [1997] L 336/16, online: http://europa.eu.int/comm/competition/mergers/cases/decisions/m877_19970730_600_en.pdf.

*California* v. *American Stores Co.*, 495 U.S. 271 (1990).

*Canada (Commissioner of Competition)* v. *Canadian Waste Services Holdings Inc.* (2001), 11 C.P.R. (4th) 425 (Comp. Trib.).

*Canada (Commissioner of Competition)* v. *Quebecor Media Inc., 127901 Canada Inc. and Pierre Lespérance*, [2005] C.C.T.D. 1c (Comp. Trib.) (registered consent agreement), online: http://www.ct-tc.gc.ca/CMFiles/CT-2005-010_0001c_38MZD-12192005-4503.pdf?windowSize=popup.

*Canada (Commissioner of Competition)* v. *Trilogy Retail Enterprises L.P.*, [2001] C.C.T.D. No. 20 (QL) (Comp. Trib.) (Consent Order), Competition Tribunal online: http://www.ct-tc.gc.ca/CMFiles/CT-2001-003_0031b_49IAL-992004-7584.pdf?windowSize=popup.

*Canada (Commissioner of Competition)* v. *Trilogy Retail Enterprises L. P.*, [2001] C.C.T.D. No. 29 (QL) (Comp. Trib.) (Reasons Regarding Consent Order), Competition Tribunal online: http://www.ct-tc.gc.ca/CMFiles/CT-2001-003_0033_38OYT-4232004-2298.pdf? windowSize=popup>?
*Canada (Commissioner of Competition)* v. *Ultramar Ltd.*, [2000] C.C.T.D. No. 4 (QL) (Comp. Trib.).
*Canada (Director of Investigation and Research)* v. *ADM Agri-Industries, Ltd.*, [1997] C.C.T.D. No. 25 (QL).
*Canada (Director of Investigation and Research)* v. *Air Canada* (1993), 49 C.P.R. (3d) 417 (F.C.A.), rev'g 49 C.P.R. (3d) 7 (Comp. Trib.).
*Canada (Director of Investigation and Research)* v. *Asea Brown Boveri Inc.*, [1989] C.C.T.D. No. 35 (QL) (Comp. Trib.).
*Canada (Director of Investigation and Research)* v. *Bank of Montreal et al.* (1996), 68 C.P.R. (3d) 527 (Comp. Trib.).
*Canada (Director of Investigation and Research)* v. *Hillsdown Holdings (Canada) Ltd.* (1992), 41 C.P.R. (3d) 289.
*Canada (Director of Investigation and Research)* v. *Imperial Oil Ltd.* (1989), 45 B.L.R. 1 at 7 (Comp. Trib.).
*Canada (Director of Investigation and Research)* v. *Imperial Oil Ltd.*, [1990] C.C.T.D. No. 1 (QL).
*Canada (Director of Investigation and Research)* v. *Imperial Oil Ltd.*, [1990] C.C.T.D. No. 3 (QL).
*Canada (Director of Investigation and Research)* v. *Southam Inc.* (1992), 47 C.P.R. (3d) 240.
*Commissioner of Competition* v. *Astral Media Inc., Telemedia Radio Inc., Radiomedia Inc.* [2002] C.C.T.D. No. 24b (Comp. Trib.) (registered consent agreement), online: http://www.ct-tc.gc.ca/CMFiles/CT-2001-010_0024b_38JVR-472004-7594.pdf? windowSize=popup.
*Commissioner of Competition* v. *Astral Media Inc., Telemedia Radio Inc., Radiomedia Inc.* [2003] C.C.T.D. No. 30b (Comp. Trib.) (amended consent agreement), online: http://www.ct-tc.gc.ca/CMFiles/CT-2001-010_0030b_38JPD-472004-8330.pdf?windowSize=popup.
*Commissioner of Competition* v. *Canadian Waste Services Inc.*, [2001] C.C.T.D. No. 32 (QL).
*Commission of the European Communities* v. *Tetra Laval BV*, [2005] ECR I – 987.
*Community Publishers Inc. et al.* v. *NAT et al.*, 892 F. Supp. 1146 at 1176 (West. Dist. Ark., 1995).
*Conoco Inc. and Phillips Petroleum Company*, File No. 021 0040, Docket No. C-4058, online: http://www.ftc.gov/os/2002/08/conocophillipsdo.pdf.
*DaimlerChrysler/Deutsche Telkom*, OJ [2003] C 288-02.
*Director of Investigation and Research* v. *Palm Dairies Limited*, [1986] C.C.T.D., consent order online: http://www.ct-tc.gc.ca/CMFiles/CT-1986-001_0044_38KPL-4192004-8637.pdf? windowSize=popup, and reasons and order, online: http://www.ct-tc.gc.ca/CMFiles/CT-1986-001_0050_38KQB-4192004-8781.pdf?windowSize=popup.
*Ford Motor Co.* v. *United States*, 405 U.S. 562 (1972).
*GE/Instrumentarium*, OJ [2004] L 109/1.
*Gencor/Lonrho*, OJ [1997] L 11/30.
*Gencor* v. *Commission* [1999] ECR II-753.
*International Shoe Co.* v. *Federal Trade Comm.*, 280 U.S. 291 (1930).
*Nestlé Holdings and Ralston Purina Company*, File No. 011 0083, Docket No. C-4028, online: http://www.ftc.gov/os/2002/02/nestledo.pdf.
*Newscorp/Telepiu*, OJ [2002] C 255/07.
*Piaggio/Aprilia*, OJ [2004] C 252/02.
*SEB/Moulinex*, OJ [2003] C 88-06.
*Shell/BASF*, OJ [2000] C 052.
*Siemens/Drägerwerk*, OJ [2002] C 311-05.
*Tetra Laval* v. *Commission*, [2002] ECR II – 4381.
*The Boeing Company*, File No. 001 0092, Docket No. C-3992, available online: http://www.ftc.gov/os/2000/09/boeingdo.htm.
*The Commissioner of Competition* v. *British Columbia Railway Company and Canadian National Railway Company*, [2004] C.C.T.D. 1b (Comp. Trib.) (registered consent

agreement), online: http://www.ct-tc.gc.ca/CMFiles/CT-2001-010_0030b_38JPD-472004-8330. pdf?windowSize=popup.

*United States* v. *E.I. duPont de Nemours & Co.*, 366 U.S. 316 at 331 (1961).

*United States* v. *Visa USA., Inc.*, 163 F. Supp. 2d 322, 2001 US Dist. LEXIS 16156, 2001-2 Trade Cas. (CCH) P73440 (S.D.N.Y. 2001), aff'd 344 F.3d 229, 2003 US App. LEXIS 19281, 2003-2 Trade Cas. (CCH) P74151 (2d Cir. N.Y. 2003).

*United States of America* v. *AT&T and Media One*, online: http://www.usdoj.gov/atr/cases/f6600/6622.pdf.

*Verbund/EnergieAllianz*, OJ [2003] C 15/05.

*Vivendi/Canal+/Seagram*, OJ [2000] C 311/3.

# 6 Judicial review of mergers in Europe: *Tetra Laval, GE/Honeywell* and the convergence toward US standards

*Jeremy Weinberg*[1]

## Introduction

More than sixteen years after the European Commission issued its first formal regulation on merger control, its decisions are now confirmed to be subject to rigorous and meaningful standards of proof and judicial review. With its February 2005 final judgment in *Commission* v. *Tetra Laval*,[2] the European Court of Justice has clarified muddy precedents and laid out a strict, clear evidentiary test the Commission and other litigants must meet in seeking to block or support a merger of two corporate enterprises. More fundamentally, the judgment marks another shot across the bow of the European Commission, whose competition regulators were forced to adopt a more exacting posture after three of their merger decisions were overturned by the Court of First Instance in 2002.[3] In *Tetra Laval*, the admonition comes from the Community's highest judicial body, fortifying the swing away from the Court of First Instance's laxer policing in the early years of the European single market. In the subsequent *GE/Honeywell* judgment,[4] laced throughout with references to *Tetra Laval*, the Court of First Instance has further driven home the message. Although ultimately upholding the Commission's decision to block the merger, the Court's opinion is again critical of much of the Commission's economic reasoning and factual analysis. Regulators, as well as litigants, have been duly notified: where the judiciary once was the dog that never barked, its review now has serious bite.

Section 1 of this chapter explains the constitutional and statutory basis – more precisely, the jurisdiction granted by treaty and regulation – for European Community judicial review of merger cases, and recaps how Community courts exercised this authority up through the tide-turning trio of 2002 judgments. Next, the related but distinct issues of standard of proof and standard of judicial review that were at the heart of the *Tetra Laval* case are considered. Section 2 first examines the new three-part evidentiary standard enunciated in the judgment, finding it a reasonable expression of the degree to which a party must prove its case in the regulatory portion of merger review. It then assesses the level of judicial deference to the

Commission's administrative decisions. The conclusion, based on the limited case law to date, is that, although the Community courts appear now to be more active in exercising their duty of judicial review, they refrain from substituting their judgment for that of administrative experts, as the Commission had contended in *Tetra Laval*. The section ends with a look at how the Court of First Instance interpreted, applied, reinforced and refined the *Tetra Laval* standards in its evaluation of the landmark *GE/Honeywell* case. The Court's opinion clarifies that a strict standard of review applies to facts, an intermediate standard to economic reasoning, and an extra-strict standard to prospective analysis. Finally, section 3 notes parallels and differences between the EC's jurisprudence and standards prevailing in America. Accounting for the different structural posture of judicial merger challenges in the US and Europe (a preliminary injunction under the adversarial process versus review of an administrative determination) helps explain why the Community courts seem to have adopted the demanding US evidentiary standards rather than simply deferring to agency expertise. And in both jurisdictions, courts are clearly setting a high bar for enforcers' more innovative theories of competitive harm. Throughout the chapter, the arguments and holdings in the *Tetra Laval* final judgment are the vehicle for much of the discussion, but the *GE/Honeywell* ruling and other precedents and practice are also considered.

### Section 1    The sources and exercise of merger review authority
*The treaties and early cases*
The 1957 Treaty of Rome creating the European Community (EC) provided four bases for the European Court of Justice (ECJ) to invalidate an act of one of the Community's institutions. 'Annulment', in EC parlance, can be justified on the grounds of lack of jurisdiction, procedural error, error of law, or misuse of power.[5] The EC treaties[6] have long been viewed as the 'constitutional' documents of the European Community; provision for judicial review on treaty matters is thus built into the EC's founding charter, unlike the United States where the practice awaited Chief Justice John Marshall's decision in *Marbury* v. *Madison*.[7] Over decades of caselaw, Community judges have added to these four elements other grounds for review: 'error of fact, error of appreciation . . . and absence of reasoning'.[8] These factors can be especially crucial in merger cases because of their dependence on complex economic analysis.

The EC Treaty designates the European Commission as the institution responsible for competition policy. The Commission's mandate has grown considerably in scope and importance since 1957, particularly since the single-market initiative began in 1986 and took effect in 1992. However the actual relevant provisions on competition,[9] Articles 81 and 82, do not by their terms give the Commission power to bar anticompetitive behaviour by two firms in the process of combining.[10] The Commission sought to plug this gap in its powers in a 1973 test case, *Continental Can*,[11] through a broad interpretation of Article 82. Although it lost on the facts, it won on the principle that Article 82's aim of curbing corporate dominance had to be interpreted in the light of other Community interests. Thus, the ECJ held, the Commission enjoyed the implied authority to enjoin a merger that would increase a dominant actor's capability of altering market structure to the detriment of consumers.[12] It was a broad, indeed bold, reading of the Treaty, surprising many observers but of course pleasing the Commission.[13] Nevertheless, given that the treaty language applied only to mergers involving an already dominant firm – not to a pairing of two medium-size actors who together would be dominant – the Commission sought to codify and extend its authority by pursuing a formal merger regulation in 1973. The EC's Member State governments, however, refused to approve the draft proposed by the Commission, perhaps because its scope was too sweeping.[14] Not until the successive terms of Peter Sutherland and Sir Leon Brittan as Commissioner for Competition in the mid-to late-1980s was the Brussels bureaucracy able to generate enough political will among Member States to enact a formal regulation allowing it to review mergers in the Community.[15]

This 1989 governing EC Merger Regulation was revised in 1997 and again in 2004,[16] but the brief article on judicial review has remained the same: 'Subject to review by the Court of Justice, the Commission shall have sole jurisdiction to take the decisions provided for in this Regulation.'[17] Lest that provision lead the sometimes molasses-like European Court of Justice to face a docket full of competition cases, the Court of First Instance (CFI) also was established in 1989, with jurisdiction over appeals of competition cases decided by the European Commission.[18] In addition to relieving caseload pressure on the ECJ, the CFI was charged with 'the task of scrutinizing the Commission's fact-finding more closely'.[19] Subsequent case law has established that the CFI has 'exclusive jurisdiction, first, to establish the facts . . . and second, to assess those facts'.[20] By contrast, the ECJ can hear appeals only on matters of law. Thus, while the ECJ was and remains the final voice on standards of judicial review in merger cases, as underscored recently in *Tetra Laval*, as a practical matter for parties and the Commission, most legal decisions and all factual evaluation are resolved at the level of the CFI.[21] This is similar to practice in the United States, where district courts and appeals courts, not the Supreme Court, handle the vast bulk of contested antitrust cases.[22]

The first challenges to Commission decisions under the Merger Regulation that reached the Court of First Instance in the early 1990s were raised by third parties: competitors, employees and minority shareholders. Actual parties to the few contentious denials or modifications of mergers elected not to appeal, owing to the time-consuming and uncertain path of litigation through Community courts.[23] Even when a third party was able to establish a legitimate basis for a complaint, it had to persuade the judges that the Commission had made a 'manifest error' in fact or law, and the early challenges were unsuccessful. As one Brussels-based lawyer observed in 1994:

> The early signs are that the Court will not attempt to substitute its own view of the effectiveness of competition in relevant markets. Only the Commission has the necessary expertise and fact-finding powers to carry out such a factual analysis. The future role of judicial review by the Community courts is likely to be limited to ruling on important issues of law or procedure and ensuring that the Commission does not make manifest errors in applying the law to the facts.[24]

Whether it was the choices of parties not to appeal, the tentative jurisprudence of the tenderfoot CFI, or a genuine absence of Commission errors in the specific cases that arose, the bottom line for most of the first decade of the EC Merger Regulation was clear: the Commission called the shots and EC courts – and firms – stayed out of its way. By one count, of more than two thousand merger notifications between 1990 and 2002, Commission decisions were reversed by the judiciary only a handful of times.[25] Even today, only about 30 cases under the Merger Regulation have reached the Community courts,[26] so conclusions about the scope of EC judicial review have inherently been somewhat limited.[27] The importance of the *Tetra Laval* judgment in February 2005 is that it is one of the few cases in that group – and the only one since the watershed reversals of the Commission in 2002 – to have advanced up to and been ruled upon by the European Court of Justice. Conclusions today can thus rest on greater authority.

*2002: the Commission's annus horribilis*
The Court of First Instance, hitherto something of a wallflower, began to signal a shift in direction with its 1998 judgment in *Kali & Salz*, the first major substantive appeal under the EC Merger Regulation.[28] The Commission had ordered two merging German potash producers to sever one company's links with a French potash producer on the grounds that otherwise the combined firm would be too dominant in the European market. Ruling on an appeal by the French Government and a French competitor, the CFI found that the structural links between the French and German entities were insufficient to influence competitive conduct.[29] The French companies in this case appealed to the Court of Justice, which acknowledged that 'review by the Community judicature . . . must take

account of the discretionary margin' to which the Commission was entitled in economic analysis. Nevertheless, the Court held, Commission decisions still must rest on a 'sufficiently cogent and consistent body of evidence'.[30] After examining the Commission's reasoning and factual analysis in detail, the Court found such evidence in this case to be lacking, and struck the Commission's entire decision attaching conditions to the merger.[31]

Whether *Kali & Salz* marked an exception or a rule would not become clear until 2002. Between June and October that year, the CFI overturned three Commission decisions blocking or limiting planned mergers of British travel operators, French power equipment makers, and French drinks packagers.[32] While each case presented different issues – collective dominance, market definition, and conglomerate effects, respectively – the common theme was that the Court no longer was accepting the Commission's case at face value. Together, the judgments amounted to 'the Commission's *annus horribilis* as far as merger decisions go,' the president of the Court of First Instance would write later.[33] The harshest language appeared in the first announced decision, *Airtours*. Representative excerpts are enough to make almost any competition regulator blush in sympathy:

> The Commission's findings are based on an incomplete and incorrect assessment of the data submitted to it during the administrative procedure. . . . It is apparent from a cursory examination of [a holiday market demand forecast] . . . that the Commission construed that document without having regard to its actual wording and overall purpose, even though it decided to include it as a document crucial to its finding.
>
> . . .
>
> The Commission's approach to volatility . . . amounts to acting in the way that it criticises
>
> . . .
>
> The Commission's examination of competition obtaining between the main tour operators at the time of the notification was inadequate.[34]

The upshot was that the Commission had prohibited the merger of two British travel operators on the basis of dubious claims about the potential for remaining players to collaborate in a highly fluid market operating with much imperfect information. '[F]ar from basing its prospective analysis on cogent evidence,' the Court held, the Commission's decision 'is vitiated by a series of errors of assessment as to factors fundamental to any assessment of whether a collective dominant position might be created'.[35]

The CFI's message in the other two cases was similar. In *Tetra Laval*, handed down in October 2002, the world leader in carton packaging (Tetra

Laval, known best for its TetraPak cardboard juice and milk boxes) sought to acquire a leading player in plastic bottling (Sidel). The European Commission, fearing the combined company would use its leverage to discourage or to gouge beverage makers who might seek to switch their packaging from carton to plastic, blocked the combination, despite behavioural and structural remedies promised by the companies.[36] But in manifold respects, the Court said, the Commission made 'manifest errors of assessment'.[37] One chief flaw lay in the regulators' reliance on poorly supported forecasts of demand growth for plastic bottling; another was the refusal to pay any heed to the merged undertaking's assurances that it would not engage in anticompetitive behaviour. These weaknesses were fatal especially given the prospective nature of the analysis in this 'conglomerate effects' case, since the 'leveraging' feared by the Commission was only a future risk, not a current reality.

In *Schneider*, issued the same week as *Tetra Laval*, the Commission had ordered two merging French utilities to sell a subsidiary. But the Court rapped the regulators twice over, on substance for 'errors, omissions and inconsistencies' in their assessments of national electrical equipment markets,[38] and on procedure for not notifying the merging parties 'with sufficient precision' in the initial Statement of Objections of what would prove to be the ultimate ground for insisting on the divestiture.[39] The parties thus had no opportunity to propose appropriate remedies. The Court overturned the Commission's order.

Any one of these Court of First Instance decisions would have been bound to reverberate deeply through the halls of DG COMP (the Commission's Directorate-General Competition) in Brussels. Taken together, they exerted irresistible pressure on the EC merger regulators to mend their ways. Just two weeks after *Tetra Laval* came down, Competition Commissioner Mario Monti announced a comprehensive draft four-part reform package, consisting of a revised Merger Regulation,[40] guidelines for assessing dominance in horizontal mergers,[41] best practices on handling merger investigations,[42] and, most immediately and arguably most significantly, staffing and resource changes, including the appointment of a new Chief Economist in DG COMP to oversee economic analysis in merger cases.[43] Although the reforms – all subsequently enacted, with some modifications – built on proposals already in the works before *Airtours*, Monti conceded that the outcomes of the three cases created 'an opportunity for even deeper reform than originally envisaged'.[44] While Monti and others at the Commission put a brave face on the judicial 'setbacks,' insisting they would not severely deter merger regulators from pursuing anti-competitive combinations,[45] at the same time he acknowledged:

there are no doubt lessons to be drawn from the judgments: in particular, it is clear that the CFI is now holding us to a very high standard of proof, and this has clear implications for the way in which we conduct our investigations and draft our decisions. We have taken very seriously into account the shortcomings in our process highlighted in the judgments by strengthening our reforms even further.[46]

Certainly the clear lesson for the staff in the competition directorate, if they had ever thought otherwise, was that judicial review was not just a platitude of the EC Treaty. The bureaucrats in Brussels would henceforth conduct their merger review analysis knowing that the judges in Luxembourg would not shrink from looking over their shoulders.

## Section 2    Substantive standards of review after *Tetra Laval*

The Commission did not resist the Court of First Instance judgments in *Airtours, Schneider* and *Tetra Laval*, and soon issued decisions approving all three mergers. Nevertheless, it felt stung and confused by the standards of review the CFI now was applying. 'The CFI has imposed a disproportionate standard of proof for merger prohibition decisions,' upsetting the balance of interests between merging parties and consumer protection, the Commission declared in late 2002.[47] It added that the CFI 'has also exceeded its role, which is to review the administrative decision of the Commission for clear errors of fact or reasoning, and not to substitute its view of the case for that of the Commission'.[48] Seeking clarification of the legal standards to apply in future cases, the Commission in January 2003 filed an appeal of the *Tetra Laval* decision with the European Court of Justice. The Court heard oral argument in January 2004,[49] its Advocate General issued an advisory opinion largely in support of the CFI in May 2004, and the Court issued its final judgment upholding the CFI decision in February 2005.[50]

The present section examines in depth the standards announced and analysis used in the ECJ's *Tetra Laval* final judgment, in the context of the prior EC merger jurisprudence already discussed. Five points are worth emphasizing at the outset. First, although the case's key articulations are fuller, fresher and generally clearer than the precedents, *Tetra Laval* represents continuity with, not a departure from, the legal standards used hitherto. Second, although the case concerned the original 1989 EC Merger Regulation, the relevant holdings apply equally under the new Merger Regulation that went into effect in May 2004. Third, what the case held is to a large extent secondary to who held it: just as the US Supreme Court exerts far more authority than a circuit court ever can, a decision from the European Court of Justice, the EC's highest and oldest judicial body, carries weight that the younger, junior CFI cannot. Fourth, institutionally speaking, the outcome of the appeal is unsurprising: had the ECJ reversed the CFI, it would have essentially cut the legs out from under its subordinate institution, crippling its authority on merger decisions (and perhaps its wider jurisprudence) and implying to litigants that they might always get a better hearing before the high court.[51]

Fifth and finally, the EC judiciary in no case has set an unreasonable bar for the Commission to meet. As one seasoned antitrust attorney commented about the 2002 decisions, the CFI judgments do 'no more and no less than require the Commission to prove its case' and go 'no further than the [c]ourt has gone in general competition cases'.[52] The ECJ's judgment in the *Tetra Laval* appeal is consistent with this characterization, while also going further to set out a new three-part evidentiary test and to offer authoritative guidance on the scope of EC judicial review in merger cases.

As Bo Vesterdorf, the President of the Court of First Instance, has observed, there are in fact two distinct but related 'standards' at issue in these cases: the standard of proof and the standard of judicial review.[53] The first is the standard that the Commission must adhere to in evaluating the facts and party submissions before it. The second – also known as 'scope of review', in American legal parlance – is the standard that the Courts must adhere to in evaluating the legality of a Commission decision to enjoin a merger.[54] While in principle a legislature may define what standards are to be used, the EC powers-that-be have been silent on these questions in merger cases, leaving the matter for judicial interpretation. Inasmuch as the two standards are separable (they are blended in the Commission's ground of appeal and the ECJ's judgment) this section examines each standard in turn.

*Standard of proof*
The Commission's appeal raised two pertinent arguments on the standard of proof.[55] One of these the Court either ignored or folded opaquely into its analysis of the other, and can be disposed of quickly. This argument maintained that the CFI's demanding standard of proof amounted to a de facto presumption of legality of mergers and thus was inconsistent with a 'symmetrical double obligation' implied by Article 2 of the Merger Regulation.[56] Article 2 requires the Commission to prohibit a concentration that creates or strengthens a dominant position but approve a concentration that does not. The supposed rationale was the Community legislature's wish to 'protect equally' the private business interests of the merging parties and the public interest in effective competition consumer protection'.[57] This obligation correspondingly called for a 'symmetrical test' to govern the standard of proof required of the Commission, since the Commission 'must prove the merits of its assessment equally' whether

enjoining or approving a merger.[58] In effect, it seems, the Commission argued that the proper standard of proof is a 50–50 balancing act. When the evidence is 51% in the Commission's favour, it wins.

Although exhibiting a certain ingenuity in theory, this symmetry argument is unworkable in practice. Evidentiary determinations, by regulators or by judges, are far too subjective to be reduced to such a finely calibrated balance of probabilities, even if a symmetrical test were normatively desired. The ECJ's apparent choice to ignore this argument (after its summation it is not addressed head-on anywhere in the judgment) perhaps reflects a commendable unwillingness to define crucial standards of review in the terminology of mathematics as opposed to law.[59]

The Commission's stronger and more fundamental objection was that the standard of 'convincing evidence,' which the CFI had articulated in *Airtours*[60] and applied in its *Tetra Laval* judgment to find the Commission's packaging forecasts wanting, was an unjustified departure from a less demanding 'cogent and consistent' standard the ECJ had set forth in *Kali & Salz*. The *Kali & Salz* formulation, the Commission said, obliged it to examine the relevant market closely, weigh all relevant factors, use consistent reasoning, and base its assessment on evidence that is factually accurate, not insignificant, and capable of substantiating the conclusions drawn. But unlike 'convincing evidence', the regulators argued, the *Kali & Salz* standard still left room for the Court and Commission to reach different interpretations on the same evidence – and for the Commission's interpretation to prevail. As long as the Commission followed the above practices, its decisions could be overturned only if 'manifestly wrong'.[61]

Tetra Laval, the nominal opposing litigant in what at this stage was really a tussle between the CFI and the Commission, contended that the Commission's objection was merely 'semantic', that it was unavailing since there existed 'no consistent terminology with regard to the requisite standard of proof' and that in any case the *Kali & Salz* formulation did not preclude the courts from conducting their own detailed examination of the facts upon which the Commission relied.[62]

In this difference of opinion, the ECJ forthrightly and unsurprisingly stood shoulder to shoulder with its junior court. 'The Court of First Instance correctly set out the tests . . . laid down in the judgment in *Kali & Salz*,' the ECJ held, adding that use of the term 'convincing evidence . . . by no means added a condition relating to the requisite standard of proof but merely drew attention to the essential function of evidence, which is to establish convincingly the merits of an argument or, as in the present case, of a decision on a merger'.[63] Nevertheless, presumably with the aim of avoiding future battles of linguistic interpretation and giving guidance to judges, regulators, and litigants, the justices in paragraph 39 of the ruling laid out a new, three-part formulation:

> Not only must the Community Courts, *inter alia*, establish whether the evidence relied on is [1] factually accurate, reliable and consistent but also [2] whether that evidence contains all the information which must be taken into account in order to assess a complex situation and [3] whether it is capable of substantiating the conclusions drawn from it.[64] [Numerical brackets added]

The evidence, in other words, must be valid, sufficiently complete and properly used in drawing conclusions. Put simply, it must be enough to prove the case in the eyes of a reasonable judge.

Although this test basically sews together various strands of prior Community Court judgments rather than marking a change of course, it brings useful clarity to a muddled issue.[65] In particular, it fleshes out what had hitherto been mere labels attached to the evidentiary standard (convincing, sufficient, cogent, etc.) by attaching the three clear and distinct meanings: integrity of fact, sufficiency of record and capability of substantiation. Additionally the Court of Justice here wisely avoids the Court of First Instance's term 'convincing', which has more of a connotation of standard of review than standard of proof (although the term returns in *GE/Honeywell*, and is convenient shorthand). Here, instead of begging the question 'convincing to whom?' the Court hints at a strict standard of review in which the role of the judiciary is to 'establish' whether the Commission met its burden of proof. Unlike assessments about which reasonable people may disagree, a fact is either established or it is not: clearly the role of the courts shall be to ensure that the facts rest on solid ground.

Applying this standard of proof to the instant case, the ECJ in *Tetra Laval* agreed, in stinging language, with the CFI's method of determining the faults in the Commission's enjoinment analysis; '[t]he Court of First Instance carried out its review in the manner required of it. It explained and set out the reasons why the Commission's conclusions seemed to it to be inaccurate in that they were based on insufficient, incomplete, insignificant and inconsistent evidence'.[66] Although the result is unmistakably an indictment of the Commission's analysis, the regulators nevertheless can be satisfied that the broader purpose of their appeal was served: they now have a much better picture of the evidentiary yardsticks a court will use in evaluating their attempt to enjoin a merger.

With the formulation of the test clear, the question is how the EC courts will apply it: the question of the standard of judicial review, suggested by the word 'establish' and discussed in the section below. A final important point bearing on the standard of proof, however, is *Tetra Laval*'s nature as a 'conglomerate effects' case. The Commission's theory was that the Tetra Laval/Sidel combination would leverage Tetra's existing dominance in the carton packaging market to achieve a similarly dominant position in plastic bottling. Proving this theory was contingent on showing that the plastic bottling market several years out would grow by a sufficient amount, and that the new Tetra Laval would be able to capture a high proportion of that growth. The Commission argued that 'a margin of discretion is inherent in any [such] prospective analysis' and that the CFI's high standard of proof was effectively demanding 'virtually unequivocal evidence' that was impossible to deliver in a market forecast.[67] The ECJ, however, chose to emphasize the flip side of this argument: that precisely because the conglomerate effects analysis was predictive (and therefore subject to greater uncertainty), the quality of evidence had to be higher than in an ordinary case.[68] Review under *Tetra Laval*'s new paragraph 39 test is 'all the more necessary in the case of a prospective analysis,' the Court said, adding that in conglomerate concentrations, where there is no history of leveraging on which to base projections, 'the quality of the evidence produced by the Commission . . . is particularly important, since that evidence must support the Commission's conclusion that, if such a decision were not adopted, the economic development envisaged by it would be plausible'.[69] As interpreted by Wilmer Hale attorneys, the language of the judgment 'does not preclude prohibition of conglomerate mergers under the Merger Regulation, [but] it imposes stringent legal and practical constraints on the Commission's ability to challenge such mergers on the basis of "leveraging"-type theories of competitive harm'.[70] The extent of these constraints would become even more apparent when the *GE/Honeywell* case was decided (see below, section 2, under 'Applying and refining the standards in *GE/Honeywell*').

### Standard of judicial review

The ECJ's disposition of the standard of proof issue in *Tetra Laval* is a useful and clear resolution of an important question: how well must merger regulators prove their case. And yet it is still somewhat akin to the inquiry of how many angels can dance on the head of a pin, or, in a criminal and civil law context, what are the precise delineations between the standards 'beyond a reasonable doubt', 'clear and convincing evidence' and 'preponderance of the evidence'. For the underlying question an appellate judge must answer, in a merger case or any other, is not simply whether the finder of fact met his burden. It is also *how closely should the judge look* in determining whether or not the burden was met. This is the question of the standard of judicial review.

Although standards of judicial review and proof are inevitably intertwined, the issues are distinct. The standard of proof is foremost an 'evidentiary' question; judicial review incorporates this evidentiary analysis, but goes beyond it to include a 'checks and balances' element involving questions of institutional prerogative and priority, in particular vis-à-vis the administrative interpreter of a statute or regulation. This, at bottom, is what the *Airtours*, *Schneider* and *Tetra Laval* cases are all about. How much power will EC judges exercise? How closely will the judicial branch review administrative decisions? How deferential will it be, and will the level of deference depend on the type of assertions made? In a technical sense, it is uncontested that the European Court of Justice, as the ultimate arbiter of Community law, has the final word. In a practical sense, the European Commission's word is usually the only one that counts, since most of its decisions are uncontested and it might have an impregnable defence in at least some of those that are. But the dispute here is neither technical nor practical; it is fundamentally political: who makes the call in the close-call cases? On the one hand, economic expertise resides with the merger regulators. On the other, judges, not bureaucrats, are the ones ultimately charged with upholding Community law and ensuring that the actions of EC bodies do not exceed the bounds of reasonableness.

The Court, happily for itself, is both a party to this dispute and the judge of it. Unsurprisingly, given its institutional incentives, its history of assertiveness,[71] and, indeed, the authority granted to it under the Community's founding treaties,[72] it resolved the issue in favour of the judiciary, not the Commission.

*'Manifest error' and the Commission's 'margin of discretion'*    The starting point for considering the standard of judicial review is again the ECJ's much-cited final judgment in *Kali & Salz*. The 1998 potash producers case held that the basic provisions of the EC Merger Regulation:

> confer on the Commission a certain discretion, especially with respect to assessments of an economic nature . . . Consequently, review by the Community judicature of the exercise of that discretion, which is essential for defining the rules on concentrations, must take account of the discretionary margin implicit in the provisions of an economic nature which form part of the rules on concentrations.[73]

Subsequent jurisprudence and commentary have yielded further interpretations and elaborations of this standard. As the Court of First Instance ruled in the 2003 *Petrolessence* case, permissible judicial review 'must be limited to ensuring compliance with the rules of procedure and the statement of reasons, as well as the substantive accuracy of the facts, the absence of manifest errors of assessment and of any misuse of power'.[74] Judge Vesterdorf and Advocate General Tizzano emphasize, however, that this 'discretionary' standard does not give the Commission licence to cut corners, for it still must meet the appropriate standard of proof, i.e., conduct a rigorous investigation, base conclusions on well-supported facts, etc. 'Where the evidence, which the CFI must scrutinise closely, does not reasonably support the conclusions drawn from it, the CFI must find that the Commission has committed a manifest error of appreciation,' Judge Vesterdorf writes in his personal commentary.[75] The operative term in this judicial review standard is 'manifest error,' which the Court of First Instance president argues 'allows for certain flexibility in the Courts' control'.[76] Indeed, what errors may be 'manifest' will vary with the specifics of every case (if not the temper of every judge).

Invoking the *Kali & Salz* standard of judicial review in its *Tetra Laval* appeal, the Commission argued that the Court of First Instance 'fail[ed] to take account of the discretion conferred on the Commission with regard to complex factual and economic matters', thereby infringing the grounds for review it was authorized to invoke under Article 230 of the EC Treaty.[77] Specifically the Commission contested the CFI's finding that it committed manifest errors of assessment in its analysis, most importantly in considering the trend toward plastic bottling for liquid dairy products and for fruit juices.[78] Not only was its analysis unassailable (or at least shielded by the Commission's margin of discretion), but in fact the CFI was essentially guilty of the same methodological flaws it ascribed to the Commission.[79]

In a brief, two-paragraph discussion, the ECJ settled this score in favour of the Court of First Instance. The outcome is again unsurprising, but the language used is notably lukewarm.[80] The Court basically restated the CFI's main points in a favourable light, holding that 'it is not apparent from the example given by the Commission [on dairy/juice plastic-bottle growth forecasts] that the Court of First Instance exceeded the limits applicable to the review of an administrative decision by the Community Courts'.[81] Other Commission objections it dismissed as pertaining to findings of fact, not law, making them ineligible for review by the ECJ, thereby in effect endorsing the lower court's close review of the facts. 'It is therefore unnecessary to give a ruling on the merits of those findings . . . it need be stated only that the Court of First Instance was able to base those findings on various items in the contested decision.'[82] The overall impression is not that the ECJ ringingly endorses the CFI's analysis and Commission's failings, but that it finds the CFI's criticisms plausible and within the appropriate margin for the exercise of *judicial* discretion. Whether the Commission's errors were so manifest that the ECJ would have overturned the denial of merger approval on a *de novo* review is far from clear. But, the ECJ confirms, neither it nor the Commission is ultimately the finder of fact: that duty is for the Court of First Instance, and will not be inquired into on appeal.

The ECJ thus concluded that, while 'the Commission has a margin of discretion with regard to economic matters, that does not mean that the Community Courts must refrain from reviewing the Commission's interpretation of information of an economic nature'.[83] In other words, the Commission's margin for discretion amounted to a rebuttable presumption in favour of its economic analysis, but was not a licence to reach incorrect or far-fetched conclusions.[84]

*A case of judicial activism?*   The Commission's complaint with the Court of First Instance was of course broader than just the differing interpretations of the 2005 milk-market numbers. It was the very principle of the judiciary overturning what the competition regulators thought was a well-settled and reasonable administrative determination (well within its margin of discretion) that the Tetra Laval/Sidel combination created a dangerous risk of dominance in the drinks packaging market. In a variation on the 'judicial activism' criticism sometimes levelled at US judges, the Commission's first ground of appeal complained that the CFI had changed the very nature of EC judicial review of mergers. The use of a 'convincing evidence' standard of proof, which the Commission saw as tougher than 'cogent and consistent evidence', had the effect of 'transform[ing] the role of the Community Courts into that of a different body which is competent to rule on the matter in all its complexity and which is entitled to *substitute its views* for those of the Commission,' the merger regulators complained (emphasis added).[85] The third ground of the Commission's appeal echoed this criticism. It challenged a specific CFI product-market definition on bottling-machine manufacturing equipment, claiming that the Court 'failed to observe the limits of its power of judicial review, distorted the contested decision and *substituted its own assessment* for that of the Commission, without even explaining the reasons for the rejection of the latter's analysis' (emphasis added).[86]

There is perhaps no better way to raise judges' hackles than to accuse them of basing their rulings on personal interpretations or preferences rather than points of law. Judge Vesterdorf, as would be expected given his role in crafting the Court of First Instance's *Tetra Laval* judgment and sitting in other cases, resists this charge. He argues that the CFI's increasing willingness to reverse Commission merger determinations showed that the Court 'has simply been more exacting latterly than it arguably was previously when applying the well-established [*Kali & Salz*] principles'.[87] While the EC courts are obliged by the terms of their creation to police strictly both facts and matters of law, 'judicial control of complex economic assessments by the Community is, and ought to be, restrained'.[88] The 'manifest error' standard succeeds in doing so, he maintains.

With respect to the *Tetra Laval* case, however, Advocate General Tizzano, while agreeing with the standard to be used, differs with its application and with Judge Vesterdorf's potentially self-serving spin. Discussing the Commission's objection to the CFI's finding that use of plastic bottling would not increase for long-life milk, Tizzano writes that 'I agree with the Commission that with that terse statement . . . the Court of First Instance incorrectly *substituted its own point of view* for the Commission's, formulating its own autonomous prediction of future developments in the market' (emphasis added).[89]

The aim here is not to assess who is right and who is wrong, nor to referee allegations of judicial activism. Certainly compared with its judgments in earlier years, the CFI in 2002 took a more robust approach to its review, and in doing so found the Commission's denials of merger approval in *Airtours*, *Schneider* and *Tetra Laval* to be insufficiently supported. The critical language the Court used and the cumulative effect of the three judgments made their impact more powerful than a single, more neutral-sounding case such as *Kali & Salz*. On the other hand, it is quite possible that by 2002 the Commission simply had grown careless and/or overconfident in its merger review and, in at least these three cases, merited judicial rebuke and reversal. The Competition Directorate's internal overhaul and intensified focus on sophisticated economic analysis in the wake of the decisions implies at least a modicum of fault. Judicial review may well have been performing exactly the function for which it was intended.

Ultimately the only view that really matters on this question is that of the European Court of Justice (barring an unlikely treaty or statutory override of judicial authority in this realm by Member-State governments). The ECJ's strong position upholding the Court of First Instance on all grounds of appeal, leaving little daylight between the two judgments, is a firm endorsement of the CFI's newly rigorous approach to judicial review. As Wilmer Hale's Brussels-based lawyers commented after the final judgment in *Tetra Laval*, the 'ECJ has signaled that it will generally not entertain appeals asserting that the CFI engaged in excessive scrutiny of the Commission's assessment and therefore overstepped the permissible boundaries of judicial review'.[90]

Although the Commission's charge of judicial activism via substituted assessments met with little acceptance, a related and more legitimate criticism could be that the Community courts' standard of judicial review sacrifices predictability for flexibility. Indeed Judge Vesterdorf's commentary repeatedly emphasizes the courts' need for a 'flexible standard' given the wide variety of merger cases the CFI confronts.[91] 'The intensity of judicial control, even under a classic judicial review standard,' he writes, 'will fluctuate depending on the underlying standard of proof/legal test that ought to be met by the administrative body having taken the decision on the merits, the context of the case, the complexity of the issues raised and so on.'[92] Most potential litigants are unlikely to find such a sliding scale of judicial scrutiny attractive, as it makes calculating the outcome of their case far more difficult. On the other hand, as merger caselaw continues to build up, the level of judicial scrutiny attaching to different situations should become clearer. Moreover predictability matters much more at the Commission's administrative stage of review, where the vast majority of cases are handled and settled. Preserving room for manoeuvre in the cases that are appealed simply allows the EC courts to properly check and balance the Commission's decisions if and when dubious outcomes or reasoning so impel.

*Applying and refining the standards in* GE/Honeywell

The Court of First Instance's first opportunity to put the *Tetra Laval* standards into practice came in the appeal of what is perhaps the most hotly debated and contested case in EC merger history: the Commission's refusal in 2001 to approve the proposed worldwide combination of US multinational behemoths General Electric and Honeywell. (The Commission's decision,[93] which sparked a trans-Atlantic furore over seemingly divergent substantive standards of merger review, derailed the merger; legal responsibility for break-up fees may have been the impetus behind the appeal, whose outcome was hardly timely.) As if to underscore the absence of predictability on the subject of judicial review, the eagerly anticipated result, handed down on 14 December 2005, confounded most observers' expectations that the CFI, as it had in *Tetra Laval, Airtours* and *Schneider*, would overturn the decision. The Court agreed with the Commission's findings that the horizontal overlaps between GE's and Honeywell's jet engine and small marine gas turbine businesses would have harmed competition in Europe, and found this pillar of the Commission's decision sufficient to block the merger. This outcome spared the Commission what would have been an embarrassing coda to the high-profile case. But the bulk of the 100-plus page opinion, which included 15 citations to the Court of Justice's judgment in *Tetra Laval*, and another 21 citations to the CFI's judgment in that case, was spent identifying evidentiary shortcomings and deficient reasoning in the Commission's conglomerate effects analysis. 'Far from vindicating the Commission,' one top law firm opined after the ruling, 'the Court rejected most of the rationale for its decision.'[94] While the regulators had won the GE/Honeywell battle, the CFI made clear that they had lost the wider war for freedom to employ novel theories of anticompetitive effects.

The Court spent considerable time near the beginning of the opinion recapitulating and elaborating upon the standards set forth in *Tetra Laval*, in a section captioned 'The standard of proof and the scope of the Community judicature's power of review'.[95] Citing *Kali & Salz* and *Tetra Laval*, the Court observed at the outset that 'the Community judicature's power of review is restricted to verifying that the facts relied on are accurate and that there has been no manifest error of assessment'.[96] It added that the EC Merger Regulation 'does not establish a presumption' one way or the other about the compatibility of a proposed transaction with the common market.[97] Whether this is meant to level the playing field of judicial review by signalling to the Commission that anticompetitive effect must be shown and not presumed, or is simply an attempt to clarify a confusing passage in the Court of First Instance's *Tetra Laval* judgment, is not entirely clear; comments in future jurisprudence about the presumption (or lack thereof) bear watching.[98]

Next, perhaps aiming to further clarify the framework for judicial review, the Court specifically 'dr[e]w attention to the essential difference between factual matters and findings, on the one hand, which may be found to be inaccurate by the Court in the light of the arguments and evidence before it, and, on the other hand, appraisals of an economic nature'.[99] Factual matters are subject to *Tetra Laval*'s three-part standard of proof evidentiary test (which the CFI cites directly, and subsequently equates with its shorthand label used in *Tetra Laval*, 'convincing evidence'). This yields a binary determination to be established by the Court: either the factual findings are accurate, in which case they will be upheld, or they are inaccurate, in which case they will be struck down. Economic appraisals, meanwhile, are entitled to a 'margin of assessment' in the course of judicial review. By implication, the Court's inquiry here is not binary: although the opinion is not explicit about how the margin is to be determined (thus leaving plenty of useful room for manoeuvre for judges), a discussion later in the text suggests that the Court requires that the Commission appraisal be 'plausible'.[100] Per *Tetra Laval*, of course, it is already settled that the Court cannot 'substitute' its own judgment for that of the Commission.

No explanation is offered for the use of the term 'margin of assessment', a subtle departure from the phrase 'margin of discretion' used in EC precedents (including by the Court of Justice in its *Tetra Laval* decision). In context, the meaning appears the same. Nevertheless the rephrasing is helpful, as it clarifies where the 'margin of assessment' fits into the framework of judicial review: an economic 'appraisal' is more clearly an 'assessment' than it is an act of 'discretion', and reasoning that falls outside the 'margin of assessment' is, intuitively, a 'manifest error of assessment'.

Alternatively, or additionally, the Court's diction could be construed as a subtle signal to the Commission that it must focus on its analytical task at hand, not on the amount of freedom/discretion it has in reaching decisions.

The Court draws one further, related distinction regarding the type of assertion made by the Commission. In addition to facts, whose accuracy must be provable, and appraisals, whose reasoning must be plausible, there are scenarios. (I use 'scenarios' for simplicity; the Court's term is 'prospective analysis,' which includes, but is not necessarily limited to, conglomerate effects cases, e.g., *GE/Honeywell* and *Tetra Laval*, where the Commission asserts that the merged entity will bundle and leverage its offerings in anticompetitive fashion.) In these forward-looking claims, the CFI notes, 'the chains of cause and effect following a merger may be dimly discernible, uncertain and difficult to establish'.[101] Accordingly, 'effective judicial review is all the more necessary'.[102] The Commission's prospective analysis must provide 'convincing evidence' that conglomerate effects would 'in all likelihood' create or strengthen a firm's market dominance; its methodology must include 'envisag[ing] various chains of cause and effect with a view to ascertaining which of them are the most likely'.[103]

Last but not least in its preliminary discussion of applicable standards, the Court also re-emphasized *Tetra Laval*'s admonition that the Commission's analysis must 'take into account' the prospect that future anticompetitive behaviour by a merged entity would be deterred by the threat of prosecution under Article 82 for abuses of market power.[104] In doing so, the Commission need not exhaustively examine and apply the relevant legal standards to show that it could win such a case (doing so would be 'too speculative'), but it must identify what conduct might be unlawful, gauge the likelihood of detection and prosecution, and factor that into its appraisals.[105]

Taken together, the Court's discussion and treatment of these concepts in the introductory section and throughout the exhaustive opinion bring the standard of proof/standard of review framework into sharper relief, and make clear that different standards apply to different types of evidentiary matter that the Commission seeks to assert. The Court's clearest statement, late in the opinion, notes that, in economic appraisals, given the Commission's margin of assessment, 'the Court's role is confined to a review of whether that appraisal is free of manifest errors. By contrast, the Commission has no margin of assessment in relation to questions of fact'.[106] Indeed the Court's exhaustively close examination of the evidence underscores that factual review is not for mere 'manifest error', but rather for genuine accuracy.

The bottom line that emerges is that in merger cases the EC judiciary will apply a strict standard of review on economic facts, a deferential review on economic appraisals (although, given that the appraisals must rest on a

*Table 6.1   EC Merger judicial review standards after* Tetra Laval *and*
GE/Honeywell

| Standard/type of evidence asserted | Standard of proof: Commission's evidence must be . . . | Standard of review: Court's scrutiny will be . . . |
|---|---|---|
| Economic facts | *'convincing'* (3 elements: demonstrating integrity of fact, sufficiency of record, capability of substantiation) | *strict* (establishing accuracy of factual evidence) |
| Economic appraisals (e.g., existence or not of market dominance) | within a *'broad margin of assessment'* (requiring a 'plausible' cause–effect chain and account of deterrence factors from threat of future prosecution for anticompetitive conduct; predicated on convincing evidence) | *intermediate* (reviewing assessment only for 'manifest error' and declining to substitute the Court's appraisal makes it nominally deferential, but reviewing the underlying factual evidence enables strictness) |
| Economic scenarios (e.g., likelihood of bundling/ conglomerate effects) | *'convincing'-plus* (demonstrating 3 elements above and account of deterrence factors, plus demonstrating that scenario is 'most likely' of various possible cause–effect chains) | *strict* (demanding 'most likely' outcome) |

strictly reviewed factual basis, the notion of deference here should not be overstated) and an even stricter standard of review over conglomerate effects theories of harm. Table 6.1, drawing from the *Tetra Laval* and *GE/Honeywell* final judgments, summarizes my reading of the present standards. In practice, of course, the dividing lines between the boxes can be arbitrary or blurry: what the Commission might believe is 'economic appraisal' could be deemed a 'factual finding' by the Court, in circumstances where it wished to take advantage of a strict standard of review.

Applying these various principles in the body of the opinion, the Court upheld the Commission's findings that General Electric had a dominant position in large commercial jet aircraft engines before the merger, and that the combination with Honeywell would strengthen this position as well as create new dominance in regional jet engines and small marine gas turbines. The Commission had extensive documentation to support these claims; even though they were disputable, these were essentially economic appraisals that fell within the regulators' 'margin of assessment'. But around these sections, each with its own lengthy analysis of the evidence, the Court took the Commission to task for its conclusions on vertical overlap and conglomerate effects. The basic problems in the Commission's case, cited again and again, were failure to marshal sufficient evidence for its claims and gaps in its causal chains of reasoning. For example, in considering the market for standard supplier-furnished equipment, the Court focused on the 'absence of any economic studies' that might have established the likelihood the merged entity would have engaged in abusive market practices.[107] On bundling of avionics and non-avionics equipment, the Court noted that GE's small market share in one segment meant that in most there would have been 'no causal link' between the merger and potential bundled offers.[108] Typical of the Court's objections to the Commission's approach was its discussion of technical bundling (emphasis added):

> *The lack of any detailed analysis* of the technical integration which might be achieved as between engines, on the one hand, and avionics and non-avionics products, on the other, and of the likely influence of such integration on the way the different markets concerned might evolve, also *makes the Commission's case less credible. It is not enough for the Commission to put forward a series of logical but hypothetical developments* which, were they to materialise, it fears would have harmful effects for competition on a number of different markets.[109]

Rather, the Court said, the onus was on the Commission to 'carry out a specific analysis of the likely evolution of each market' where it asserted the merger would create a dominant position, and 'to produce convincing evidence to bear out that conclusion'.[110] Its failure to do so amounted to yet another 'manifest error of assessment' that the Court could not accept.

With salvos such as that, and a rigorous look at the economic evidence throughout, the Commission might count itself lucky that the Court of First Instance did not overturn the entire decision.[111] Refraining from doing so could be construed as an institutional signal that the Court was hesitant to rub regulators' noses in their past errors, particularly given the Commission's internal improvements to its merger review regime in the intervening years (see notes 39–45 and accompanying text). On a purely legal interpretation the *GE/Honeywell* ruling, like *Tetra Laval* before it, serves notice that the EC judiciary is deeply reluctant to embrace novel theories of competitive harm. This reluctance forces the Commission to establish a convincing case against a merger on more traditional grounds (e.g., horizontal overlap), or else to let it proceed unmolested. The Court's opinion 'drives a stake through the heart of the conglomerate effects theory,' said one Brussels-based lawyer and ex-Commission staffer.[112] Even a lawyer who had represented General Electric seemed pleased overall with the ruling, pronouncing it the 'final nail in the coffin' of overly aggressive merger reviews by the Commission.[113]

## Section 3   Comparing trans-Atlantic models of judicial review

While *Tetra Laval, Airtours, Schneider* and *GE/Honeywell* have left Europe's competition police with much egg on their face, going to Court has not been all smooth sailing of late for their US counterparts either. Two recent high-profile challenges – *FTC* v. *Arch Coal*[114] and *United States* v. *Oracle*[115] – foundered for reasons similar to the cases in Europe: the Court was not persuaded by the government's evidence and reliance on novel theories of anticompetitive harm. While myriad differences between the United States and Europe competition regimes make close comparisons something of an apples-to-oranges exercise, this section seeks to identify and explain common elements in the judicial approach. First, it describes important structural and procedural differences in US and Community merger enforcement. Second, it lays out the classic, deferential US standard for judicial review of administrative agency action by which the European Commission wished to be measured, explaining that such an approach would be unsuitable in the absence of an adversary system of inquiry. Third, it sets forth the actual operative standards in most US merger situations, highlighting the conclusions from the *Arch Coal* and *Oracle* decisions, whose echoes of the rigorous regime at which the Community courts have now arrived are obvious. Finally, it offers some additional potential reasons behind the apparent trans-Atlantic convergence.

*Structural differences in merger enforcement*
The most obvious difference between merger enforcement in the European Community and the United States is also, for present purposes, one of the least important. The EC, like almost every country in the world that regulates competition, has a single enforcement body, the Commission, not the dual US structure in which the Federal Trade Commission and Department of Justice (DoJ) Antitrust Division have largely overlapping authority. (I leave aside the roles of American state and European Member-State regulators, which are generally subordinate in major merger cases. I also leave aside enforcement by private parties, which plays a key role in the US but, to date, has been of minimal importance in the EC.[116]) As an independent administrative agency rather than a purely prosecutorial unit, the FTC is more analogous to the European Commission/DG Comp than is the Antitrust Division; hence most of the discussion below focuses on FTC challenges. It is worth remembering, however, that from a US court's point

of view, there is not (usually) a significant difference which federal entity is attempting to block the combination,[117] despite a perception among practitioners that judges often defer more to the FTC than to the Antitrust Division.[118]

Related to a more unified prosecutorial structure is Europe's more centralized and coherent judiciary. In the United States, merger cases and appeals are heard by disparate district and circuit courts across the country, with the Supreme Court maintaining a decades-long silence on merger standards since the *General Dynamics* decision in 1974.[119] In Europe, the Court of First Instance acts as a single specialist competition court, helping keep standards consistent; the Court of Justice is ready to step in, as *Kali & Salz* and *Tetra Laval* showed, to enunciate standards when necessary. In practice, this difference matters less than one might think, as US judges manage to avoid circuit splits on key questions (reflecting the relatively settled nature of most aspects of competition doctrine), and merger cases are in any event primarily fact-intensive. Still the decentralized nature of US courts means that one should take the generalizations about their approach in this chapter with a grain or two of salt.

The most important structural differences between the US and EC regimes revolve around the timing, posture and manner in which courts enter the process. In the US, the FTC typically acts to block a proposed merger by filing a complaint and then getting court approval for a preliminary injunction to bar the merger from proceeding.[120] In theory, the purpose of the preliminary injunction is simply to allow time (before the merger closes and unscrambling becomes impossible) for a full-scale agency adjudication. Under FTC procedures, the adjudication would include a trial before an administrative law judge, and potentially an appeal to the five Federal Trade Commissioners, to establish whether or not a proposed merger does in fact substantially diminish competition in a given product or geographic market or markets. As all parties recognize, however, a court's issuance of a preliminary injunction for all intents and purposes kills the deal permanently, and so the FTC never issues its own final adjudicative ruling.[121] In the EC, by contrast, the Commission can and does issue a binding negative determination on its own authority, obliging the parties who wish to contest it to take the affirmative step of lodging a challenge in the Court of First Instance, then spending years in litigation in Luxembourg before an outcome is settled. (And not until 2002 was there much of a sign that such a challenge could be successful.) Case captions are simple illustrations of the different posture of review: in US district court, it is *FTC* v. *Company*; in the Court of First Instance, it is *Company* v. *Commission*. But the key point is that, in an injunctive proceeding, there is no 'final administrative determination' for a court to review, only a preliminary judgment to make: hence the standards for judicial decision are different (see below, 'The rigorous approach').

Finally there is the role of the political branches in defining parameters for courts to follow. In the United States, Congress has codified the 'substantial evidence' criterion and preliminary injunction standards in the enforcement provisions of the Clayton Act, Federal Trade Commission Act and the Administrative Procedure Act.[122] In Europe, on the other hand, writes the Court of First Instance's Judge Vesterdorf, '[o]nly one thing is entirely clear in the standard of review debate: that neither the Merger Regulation nor the Treaty contains any direct or indirect reference as to the appropriate standard of proof or standard of judicial review in the field of merger control'.[123] Thus EC courts have been left to chart an appropriate level of administrative oversight *sua sponte*, without the assistance – or, one might say, the interference – of Member State political masters.

*The unsuitability of deference*
One model the EC judiciary might have adopted is the classic 'substantial evidence' standard of US administrative law, used in judicial review of Federal Trade Commission rulings and all manner of other administrative agency adjudications. As a standard of proof, the most common formulation describes substantial evidence as 'such relevant evidence as a reasonable mind might accept as adequate to support a conclusion'; it must be 'more than a scintilla'.[124] As a standard of review, *Black's Law Dictionary* defines the substantial evidence rule as the 'principle that a reviewing court should uphold an administrative body's ruling if it is supported by evidence on which the administrative body could reasonably base its decision'.[125] Although the standard is malleable enough that it can mean different things to different courts,[126] the unmistakable gist is deference, on the rationale that courts lack agencies' economic expertise. Judge Richard Posner (whose own expertise is the exception that proves the rule) captures, colourfully as usual, the essence of judges' role in applying the standard: 'Our only function is to determine whether the [FTC's] analysis of the probable effects . . . is so implausible, so feebly supported by the record, that it flunks even the deferential test of substantial evidence.'[127]

Under the Clayton Act and Federal Trade Commission Act, the existence of substantial evidence binds a reviewing court to accept the agency's findings of fact, although not necessarily its resulting economic analysis.[128] Practically speaking, however, Judge Posner discerns from an evaluation of caselaw that courts do then use the same test to evaluate the FTC's economic conclusion that a merger would substantially lessen competition and must be enjoined. 'The substantial evidence rule (like the clearly erroneous rule) applies to ultimate as well as underlying facts, including economic judgments,' Judge Posner writes. 'This is implicit in the many cases that hold that the ultimate question under the Clayton Act – whether the challenged transaction may substantially lessen competition – is governed by the substantial evidence rule.'[129] In other words, courts typically uphold FTC decisions unless they are quite clearly off base. As one important early precedent put it, the codification of the 'substantial evidence' standard forbade a court 'mak[ing] its own appraisal of the testimony, picking and choosing for itself among uncertain and conflicting inferences'.[130]

Such deferential interpretations of the judicial role would have been music to the ears of the European Commission, whose appeal in *Tetra Laval*[131] can be seen essentially as an argument that its conclusions, too, should be evaluated under an equivalent of the 'substantial evidence' standard.[132] The 'convincing evidence' test[133] is indeed more demanding than 'substantial evidence'. In formulation as a standard of proof, the key difference appears to be the quantum of evidence required: while the US standard requires only 'more than a *scintilla*', the EC standard (per *Tetra Laval*'s paragraph 39 test) requires '*all the information* which must be taken into account in order to assess a complex situation' (emphasis added).[134] This corresponds to the Court of First Instance's frequent objections in *Tetra Laval* and *GE/Honeywell* that the Commission failed to muster sufficient economic studies to support its arguments. In application as a standard of review, the difference is seen in the meticulous scrutiny of the evidentiary record by the Court of First Instance (supported by the Court of Justice) in the two cases, compared with the deferential approach of US courts. Indeed the analysis can be as simple as comparing the words used: 'convincing' clearly suggests a higher burden than 'substantial'. It is true that, on economic appraisals, the CFI grants a 'margin of assessment' (formerly the 'margin of discretion') looser than the strictures of the convincing evidence test, and correspondent with what Judge Posner described as the substantial evidence test's deferential embrace of economic judgments. However the margin of assessment is a second-level inquiry that comes into play only when the economic appraisals have been found to rest upon convincing evidence. In other words, the strict scrutiny at the fact-finding level, not the more relaxed evaluation of the Commission's economic analysis, does the work for the Court.

Notwithstanding the Commission's objections, a more demanding test and standard of review than 'substantial evidence' is in fact appropriate in European merger determinations, for otherwise, DG Comp decision making would be all but devoid of the key element on which US merger challenges are resolved: the adversary system. Usually the adversary element arises in litigation over preliminary injunctions, proceedings which are increasingly indistinguishable from full trials.[135] In *FTC v. Arch Coal*, for example, the district court conducted a two-week trial involving more than 20 witnesses and hundreds of exhibits, followed by 700 pages of post-trial proposed findings of fact and briefs and an 89-page opinion[136] (ultimately denying the relief sought by the government). Because almost all cases are resolved at the preliminary injunction stage, there is virtually never a final administrative action determination comparable to that assembled by the European Commission for a court to review. Rather a judge evaluates the evidence presented, as framed by the adversarial arguments and the FTC's complaint. The rare exception is when the FTC chooses to file a post-merger administrative complaint, relying on its authority to proceed with its own adjudicative process despite losing (or not bringing) a preliminary injunction.[137] Only in such cases, and only if the losing party seeks judicial review of the adjudicated outcome, does the 'substantial evidence' criterion apply in a US merger determination. Even then, since the FTC's adjudicative process revolves around a full trial before an administrative law judge, including cross-examination, the adversary element is strongly incorporated. Although this happens at the administrative level rather than during judicial review, agency conclusions that have already been through an internal process wringer have less need of going through another one in court.

In carrying out a non-deferential review of the facts,[138] and enjoying the benefit of briefing, exhibits and oral argument from the aggrieved merger party or parties, the Court of First Instance is ensuring that the adversary element is a factor in merger review in Europe, just as in the US. Although the CFI can only review a tiny fraction of cases – fewer, it seems, than US courts do at the preliminary injunction stage[139] – its approach forces the Commission to internalize a strict standard of proof ('convincing evidence'), through the implied threat of a strict standard of review. Because the Commission is not a precise counterpart of the FTC or other US administrative agency, and because its review procedures are not inherently adversarial, the EC judiciary has taken a sensible approach in determining that its conclusions do not merit an equivalent of deferential 'substantial evidence' review.

*The rigorous approach*

What standards, then, do US courts use when a merger challenge must be resolved by litigation? As with 'substantial evidence,' the relevant criterion in an FTC case is defined by statute. Section 13(b) of the Federal Trade Commission Act 'provides for the grant of a preliminary injunction where such action would be in the public interest – as determined by a weighing of the equities and a consideration of the Commission's likelihood of success on the merits'.[140] In practice, courts tend to emphasize the 'likelihood of success' prong of the two-part test, and, to the extent equities are considered, to give greater weight to public equities than to the private side.[141] The statutory test deliberately omits the 'irreparable harm' element that is traditionally considered in preliminary injunction situations, and so which, in theory, would apply in Department of Justice merger challenges. As in FTC cases, however, as a practical matter, courts simply focus on the 'likelihood of success' aspect.[142]

Fleshing out 'likelihood of success' has led courts to various, similar formulations for what the FTC must show (which are helpfully recapped near the beginning of the *Arch Coal* opinion[143]): a 'reasonable probability' that the proposed transaction would substantially lessen future competition;[144] an 'appreciable danger' of future coordinated interaction based on a 'predictive judgment';[145] 'questions going to the merits so serious, substantial, difficult and doubtful as to make them fair ground for thorough investigation, study, deliberation and determination by the FTC in the first instance and ultimately by the Court of Appeals'.[146] So, while actual proof of anticompetitive harms is not required (the action is technically only 'preliminary'), it is clear that the balance and the probability of the evidence must weigh in the FTC's favour.

Once the agency (or the Department of Justice) produces prima facie evidence that a merger will produce a firm controlling an undue share of a relevant market and increasing concentration of that market, the government wins a rebuttable presumption of illegality and the burden shifts to the corporate defendant. The ultimate burden of proof always lies with the government, however. In any event, the vitality of this presumption has ebbed continually over the four-plus decades since it was laid down by the Supreme Court in *United States* v. *Philadelphia National Bank*,[147] as courts have employed an analysis of the government's evidence bearing similar depth to that conducted by the EC's Court of First Instance in *Tetra Laval* and *GE/Honeywell*.

In *United States* v. *General Dynamics*,[148] for instance, the Supreme Court upheld a district court finding that the statistical evidence the government relied on in arguing to block a merger involving Midwestern coal producers was insufficient. Although the increase in industry concentration illustrated by the statistics was enough to make out a prima facie case based on *current* market shares, the government's numbers did not account for long-term industry supply contracts, one company's evaporating coal reserves, and declining national and regional consumption of coal, all of which sharply reduced the prospect of *future* market dominance by the combined firm. 'Because of these fundamental changes in the structure of the market for coal, the District Court was justified in viewing the statistics relied on by the Government as insufficient to sustain its case,' Justice Stewart held for a 5–4 majority.[149]

While *General Dynamics*, somewhat curiously, has proved to be the Supreme Court's last word on merger standards, lower courts have continued to chip away at the presumption, instead putting stock in the quality of the government's evidence. In *United States* v. *Baker Hughes*, the lumpiness of unit sales statistics the government marshalled to block the combination of two oil-rig equipment makers fatally undermined its argument, the D.C. Circuit Court of Appeals held.[150] The influential opinion was authored by future Supreme Court justice Clarence Thomas and joined by his once and future colleague Ruth Bader Ginsburg. More recent merger challenges by the FTC further illustrate the exacting eye that district courts have long brought to merger challenges, sometimes agreeing with the government (accepting the FTC's bids to block the *Staples/Office Depot* combination and *Swedish Match*'s acquisition of a competing tobacco business[151]) and sometimes not (barring on appeal the FTC's attempt to enjoin the *Tenet Healthcare* Missouri hospital merger[152]).

Parallels between the US and EC judicial approaches are perhaps most striking in a pair of high-profile government losses in 2004: *Arch Coal*, a coordinated effects case which permitted an acquisition of coal mines in Wyoming, and *Oracle*, a unilateral effects case which permitted the enterprise software giant's acquisition of rival PeopleSoft. Perhaps the most crucial connection is their reliance on relatively novel and untested theories of competitive harm, just as the European Commission sought to prove its cases based on a conglomerate effects hypothesis. Although treatment of the myriad evidentiary issues in these complex cases is beyond the scope of this chapter, one commentator's well-argued view highlights key similarities between these decisions and *Tetra Laval* and *GE/Honeywell*: 'The conclusion to be drawn, at least from *Arch Coal*, is that a fact-intensive review of objective market realities is more likely to persuade a court that the consumers' subjective fears and the agencies' economic theories truly point to likely anticompetitive effects,' writes James Keyte, an antitrust partner at Skadden, Arps, in an American Bar Association-published article entitled 'Arch Coal and Oracle put the agencies on the ropes in proving anti-competitive effects'.[153] Among Keyte's other conclusions (emphasis added) are that '*agencies' burden of proof* on demonstrating likely anticompetitive effects *is, in practice, growing more stringent*. . . . coordinated effects – at least where the agencies' structural case is weak – requires *convincing evidence* that collusion is likely, not just feasible. . . . Reliable expert economic evidence remains critical, but elusive, in unilateral effects cases'.[154] Overall, Keyte believes that:

[a]lthough both decisions cover a variety of complex Section 7 issues, on the question of plaintiff's burden of proof the cases are uniform: where the

structural case is relatively weak, Section 7 plaintiffs will be required to demonstrate that tangible anticompetitive effects are in fact probable; merely offering theories and opinion testimony (even from customers) concerning likely anticompetitive effects will not suffice. *It is not so much the particular phrasing of the legal standard as its application* – at least for these courts – that reflects the practical adoption of an unusually rigorous probability standard for assessing competitive effects. Indeed, separate and apart from any particular holding, *these decisions must be understood and considered for their systematic and exacting application of a probability standard to every theory and piece of evidence the agencies had to offer.*[155]

Like their EC counterparts in *Tetra Laval* and especially *GE/Honeywell* (see above, section 2, 'Applying and refining the standards in *GE/Honeywell*'), the emphasis of these judges is on the enforcement agency's factual evidence, not its reasoning, and the ultimate probability, not mere plausibility, of its analysis. Although it is by no means clear that every court deciding a preliminary injunction motion would apply the same level of scrutiny (and the same skill), the carefully crafted *Arch Coal* and *Oracle* opinions are bound to be highly influential, among federal judges and federal enforcers alike. Keyte surmises that the 'one-two punch' from these cases will make both the FTC and the Department of Justice hesitant 'to jump back into the judicial ring', at least without a stronger evidentiary record.[156]

Overall, then, how differently do US and EC courts approach review of agency merger challenges? The short answer is that they seem much closer than before – closer than in the 1990s days when EC judicial review was often nonexistent or a rubber stamp but it is too soon to tell just how close. The European Commission has conducted routine review of mergers for only the last decade and a half, and the key jurisprudence in this area (*Kali & Salz, Airtours, Schneider, Tetra Laval, GE/Honeywell*) is but a few years old or less. Moreover both *Tetra Laval* and *GE/Honeywell* have been conglomerate effects cases, not challenges under more conventional theories, so the extent to which the EC courts will demand strong evidence in routine cases remains uncertain. It seems at least fair to say that the recent evolution toward a tougher approach to EC review has given litigants challenging the Commission a substantive fighting chance in EC courts that it was not clear they enjoyed before. Going to court to challenge an outcome felt to be unjustified – a reflex consideration, at least stereotypically, among many in the American antitrust bar and boardrooms, but much less so in Europe – is thus an increasingly viable and worthwhile potential strategy for aggrieved parties in the EC, at least on substantive grounds. Procedurally, however, the delays and other hurdles that continue to beset the EC process still pose considerable obstacles, frequently rendering merger challenges commercially moot as their resolution would take longer than the parties to a proposed combination could afford to wait.[157]

If the growing alignment of standards between EC and US courts is still somewhat tentative, what already is apparent is a growing similarity in judicial assertiveness and institutional role. The seemingly cautious approach of the Court of First Instance's first decade is receding rapidly into the rearview mirror. A report by the global law firm Freshfields Bruckhaus Deringer after *Tetra Laval* was handed down in February 2005 sounded a theme common to much of the post-judgment commentary: the outcome of the case 'provides an important illustration of the "checks and balances" that exist in EU merger control. It confirms that, nowadays, judicial review is an integral part of the EU merger review process'.[158] The same commentary about an American court decision might now seem so banal as to be absurd: of course checks and balances and judicial review are integral features of the American system, in merger cases and virtually all else besides. It was not ever thus, however: US courts in the early postwar era tended to accept the arguments of government antitrust regulators even when the anticompetitive effects were, by today's standards, laughable.[159] Only after *General Dynamics* in 1974, when increasingly sophisticated economic analysis made it more possible for litigants to challenge successfully the government's statistical evidence, did the government regularly start losing cases. *Tetra Laval* might ultimately prove to be the EC's version of the *General Dynamics* case. If so, it would show both how far apart the two continents' judiciaries have been, and how much closer they are now becoming.

*Further accounting for convergence*

Assuming that the *Tetra Laval* standards, the demonstrated scrutiny of evidence in US merger cases, and the institutional assertiveness exemplified by the 2002 CFI judgments and *GE/Honeywell* do represent at least something of a convergence between EC and US judicial standards,[160] what then accounts for such a trend? As already outlined, the dominant factors would seem to be the Community courts' move to assume an adversarial rather than deferential posture toward the Commission's competition regulators, perhaps because their conclusions were becoming careless (see above, section 1, '2000: the Commission's *annus horribilis*', and section 3, 'Structural differences in merger enforcement'); and enforcers' increasing tendency to rely on envelope-pushing theories of competitive harm. This section briefly advances three further potential explanations: first, the evolution of economic theory, global markets and judicial understanding thereof; second, that growing transnational legal networks and increased efforts at international harmonization in competition law may be exerting some influence on

EC judges; and third, that the growth of the EC administrative state inherently invites more judicial review. Each is examined in turn.

First, prevailing economic understandings on both sides of the Atlantic are far different today than decades ago, when US antitrust policy was animated by a small-business mentality (see *Brown Shoe*) and Europe was little more than a customs union lacking common competition rules. In the US, the Chicago School's efficiency and consumer welfare-oriented antitrust analysis has gone mainstream, while the European Commission has preached a not altogether dissimilar liberalizing approach. Meanwhile globalization has reshaped the markets in which corporations seek to combine, fostering similarities and reducing differences. Converging judicial standards thus reflect converging economics, as well as a more sophisticated approach to the field by judges and regulators. Indeed part of the raison d'être of the Court of First Instance was to create a judicial body with more specialized economic understanding.

Second, recent years have seen an upswing in international cooperation and awareness in competition law and law more generally – operation of the 'transnational networks' identified by Anne-Marie Slaughter as key drivers of trends toward globalization.[161] Two formal EU–US agreements on cooperation by their competition regulators testify to this,[162] as do the principles of international comity expressed by the US Supreme Court in the 2004 *Empagran* case.[163] Harmonization efforts through the International Competition Network, the World Trade Organization and the Organization for Economic Cooperation and Development, even if resulting in few concrete achievements, and even though typically involving regulators and practitioners more than judges, are bound to have something of a spillover effect on judicial approaches to antitrust.[164] At the very least, litigants are well aware of both the evidence and the arguments that have been presented in different trans-Atlantic forums, and their success or failure: think of GE-Honeywell and Boeing-McDonnell Douglas. Additionally, beyond competition law, exchanges and visits by senior judges to colleagues in other nations, citations by US Supreme Court justices to opinions of the European Court of Human Rights, use of the Internet and the increased internationalization of the practice of law likely contribute, albeit indirectly, to a tendency toward common judicial approaches to common situations such as merger review.

Third, the EC's *acquis communautaire* (body of laws and regulations) is famously some 200 000 pages long and growing more as the membership and powers of the European Union continue to expand. Administrative regulation has been heavy since the Treaty of Rome, but especially since the EC's 1986–92 single market initiative and the obligations for continuing regulatory oversight that the programme brought upon the European Commission.

Such a growing corpus of law almost by definition mandates a greater judicial role in policing it. When the modern US administrative state was born under President Franklin Roosevelt, the Supreme Court at first famously resisted the encroachment of the federal government into new areas of regulation. Although Justice Roberts's 'switch in time that saved the nine' ultimately allowed the New Deal measures to move forward, courts relaxed only their tendency to object, never their right to review. Perhaps reflecting institutional or political biases in favour of European integration, EC courts have come from the opposite angle, tending at first to side with the central authority, not against it. In the beginning, this might well have disguised the courts' exercise of their review prerogative. But the assertive judgments in *Tetra Laval* and the 2002 trio, and the many criticisms in *GE/Honeywell*, represent a more established EC judiciary exercising oversight of a European Commission that is likewise far more active than it was previously. The courts' confidence and willingness to take responsibility for upholding EC law on mergers has grown in tandem with the Commission's administrative duties in the field.

**Conclusion**

This chapter has argued that the final judgments by the European Court of Justice in *Tetra Laval* and by the Court of First Instance in *GE/Honeywell* represent a growing, organic convergence in the standards that courts in the European Community and the United States employ in reviewing merger cases. After a cautious first decade, the EC judiciary is now exercising vigorous but not unreasonable oversight of the European Commission's competition regulators. It will presumably continue to play such a role, but the necessity of action may diminish: the strong message sounded by *Tetra Laval* and the other 2002 cases has already triggered useful reforms in the Commission's internal processes that should make evidentiary shortcomings less likely in future cases. The next priority is to continue to pursue institutional reforms in the Community judiciary itself, particularly with regard to docket management, so that the Court of First Instance one day will be able to hear and decide an appeal of a merger decision before it becomes as moot as *GE/Honeywell*.

*Tetra Laval* and *GE/Honeywell* largely settle the law with regard to standards of proof and judicial review in cases brought by the Commission. The effect, appropriately, should be to focus the Commission and prospective merging parties, not on the degree of rigour of after-the-fact judicial oversight, but rather on the quality of the evidence in their specific situation. If the Commission's new proposal to augment private enforcement of competition law[165] takes wing, the next challenge for Community courts may be to decide what evidentiary standards apply in private suits. Continued strict application of 'convincing evidence' may be all they need to do.

## Notes

1. J.D., University of Virginia School of Law, 2006, M.Sc. London School of Economics, 1994. My appreciation to Larry Fullerton and to Glen Robinson for their comments. Errors remain mine.
2. *Commission* v. *Tetra Laval*, Case C-12/03 [2005], E.C.R. I-987 [hereinafter *Tetra Laval*]. References in the text to *Tetra Laval* shall be to this European Court of Justice judgment unless it is clear from context that it refers to the Court of First Instance judgment or the advisory opinion in the case by the Advocate General of the Court of Justice. A brief companion case, C-13/03, challenging the Commission's divestiture order, was filed, argued and decided alongside the main case. Tetra Laval prevailed on similar grounds.
3. *Airtours* v. *Commission*, Case T-342/99 [2002] E.C.R. II-2585 [hereinafter *Airtours*]; *Schneider Electric* v. *Commission*, Case T-310/2001 [2002] E.C.R. II-4071 [hereinafter *Schneider*]; *Tetra Laval* v. *Commission*, Case T-5/2002 [2002] E.C.R. II-4381 [hereinafter *Tetra Laval Court of First Instance Judgment*].
4. *General Electric Co.* v. *Commission*, Case T-210/01 [2005], E.C.R. (not yet reported) [hereinafter *GE/Honeywell*]. The companion case, *Honeywell International* v. *Commission*, T-209/01 [2005], E.C.R. (not yet reported), was decided on largely similar grounds.
5. As phrased by Bellamy, Sir Christopher, (1999), 'Anti-trust and the courts roundtable', *Fordham Ann. Antitrust Conf.* 369, 389, cited by Clough, Mark (2004), 'The role of judicial review in merger control', **24**, *N. W. J. Int'l L. & Bus.*, 729, 730 (symposium issue on European competition law). The somewhat more cumbersome Treaty language allows invalidation of an act of a Community institution for 'lack of competence, infringement of an essential procedural requirement, infringement of this Treaty or of any rule of law relating to its application, or misuse of its powers': Treaty Establishing the European Community, 24 Dec. 2002, O.J. (C 325) 33 (2002) [hereinafter EC Treaty], Art. 230. Articles in the current version of the treaty have been renumbered in amendments since the original Treaty of Rome.
6. The European Community shortened its moniker from the original 'European Economic Community' under the 1991 Maastricht Treaty. This chapter uses the abbreviation EC to refer to the European Community, not to the European Commission, the powerful executive and administrative secretariat whose responsibilities include the creation and oversight of competition policy. The European Union (EU), a term today often used interchangeably with European Community, is formally a distinct legal entity. This chapter uses the label EC or European Community, since 'Community law' is the proper term and prevailing legal regime in the merger review context. The proposed Treaty Establishing a Constitution for Europe, defeated in national referendums in France and the Netherlands in spring 2005, would have unified the legal entities and done away with the Community–Union distinction.
7. *Marbury* v. *Madison*, 1 Cranch 137 (1803).
8. Bellamy, above, note 5, at 389. Bellamy sat as the United Kingdom judge on the Court of First Instance, 1992–99.
9. 'Competition', of course, is the more common internationally used term for antitrust.
10. See Goyder, D.G. (2003), *EC Competition Law*, 337 ('Neither the actual wording of the Article [81] nor the evidence of those who participated in the negotiations leading up to the Treaty or in its early administration support any contrary argument.').
11. *Europemballage and Continental Can* v. *Commission*, Case 6/72 [1973] E.C.R. 215.
12. Ibid.
13. See Goyder, above, note 10, at 337.
14. Ibid., at 338.
15. Sutherland and Brittan were aided by an ECJ decision in *BAT and R.J. Reynolds* v. *Commission and Philip Morris*, Cases 142/84 and 156/84 [1987] E.C.R. 4487, which invoked Article 81 in allowing the Commission to block a merger; because the Treaty article clearly lacked the specificity to provide sufficient guidance to the Commission or EC courts in crafting merger policy, the national governments stepped in to write their

own regulation in order to avoid leaving *Philip Morris* as the key precedent. See Goyder, above, note 10, at 339.

16. Council of Ministers of the European Union (2004), Council Regulation (EC) 139/2004 of 20 January 2004 on Control of Concentrations Between Undertakings [hereinafter the EC Merger Regulation], 2004 O.J. (L 024) 1 (superseding (EEC) 4064/89 of 21 December 1989, as amended by (EC) 1310/97 of 30 June 1997).

17. EC Merger Regulation, Art. 21(2).

18. The CFI is now composed of 25 judges, one from each EU Member State, appointed for a renewable term of six years by consensus of Member State governments. They generally hear cases in chambers of three or five judges.

19. Ritter, Lennart and W. David Braun (2004), *European Competition Law: A Practitioner's Guide*, citing Council Decision 88/591 of 24 October 1988 (1988 O.J. L 319/1), recitals 4 and 6 (establishing the CFI and assigning it judicial review from the ECJ).

20. See *Commission* v. *Tetra Laval*, Opinion of Advocate General Tizzano, Case C-12/03 P (2004) [hereinafter *Tetra Laval Advisory Opinion*] (citing cases).

21. National court review in merger cases is limited by the EC Merger Regulation to cases without a 'Community dimension', defined in terms of market share and revenue in two or more EU Member States. This chapter ignores national court review because the ECJ/CFI have jurisdiction in all economically significant cross-border cases.

22. Likewise, in both jurisdictions, the vast bulk of merger cases are uncontested after administrative review and negotiations with the parties.

23. Brown, Adrian (1994), 'Judicial review of Commission decisions under the Merger Regulation: the first cases', **15**, *Eur. Competition L. Rev.*, 296, 305 ('It is not usually commercially viable for [parties directly involved in a concentration] to wait for two years or more to find out whether the proposed merger will be allowed to proceed.').

24. Ibid.

25. Guerrero, Kevin (2003), Note, 'A new "convincing evidence" standard in European Merger review', **72**, U. *Cin. L. Rev.*, 249, 281–2. See also: Vesterdorf, Bo (2005), 'Standard of proof in merger cases', **1**, *European Competition Journal*, **3**, 27 (noting that, in a decade of merger control, the CFI annulled four clearance decisions and four prohibition decisions, and issued two additional divestiture orders in prohibition cases).

26. Vesterdorf, above, note 25, at 26.

27. Departing from legal analysis into the realm of politics and ideology, one can speculate that the Community courts were inclined to give the Commission much latitude in the early years of the Merger Regulation as a way of reinforcing the Commission's authority as the ultimate guardian of the EC's 1992 single-market initiative. Commission scrutiny of mergers served to extend the boundaries at least of EC administrative law, an interest that some in the EC judiciary might sympathize with and in fact rank as more important, at least at that time, than sharply defining the intra-EC boundaries of authority. This suggestion is premised on the notion that judges – and indeed Commissioners and their staff – tend to be 'pro-European' rather than 'Eurosceptic,' i.e., generally to favour more power for the EC's supranational institutions at the expense of Member-State national governments.

28. *France and Others* v. *Commission*, Joined Cases C-68/94 and 30/95 [1998] E.C.R. I-1375 [hereinafter *Kali & Salz*]. See Goyder, above, note 10, at 366 (summarizing case).

29. Although one might speculate that the Court's decision was influenced by the hot breath of the French Government, cases in Community courts invariably pit one nation's interests against another's, so any judge aiming to please national masters will probably find it a fool's errand. The CFI had ruled against French interests in two earlier appeals where Air France contested an acquisition made by British Airways. See Brown, above, note 23, at 297–302 (citing cases where Air France cleared procedural hurdles but lost on substance).

30. *Kali & Salz*, paras 224, 228.

31. The Commission eventually issued a new decision approving the concentration, although too late to matter commercially to the parties in interest. See Goyder, above, note 10, at 392.

32. *Airtours, Schneider* and *Tetra Laval* cases.
33. Vesterdorf, above, note 25, at 31. Vesterdorf was the judge–rapporteur in the CFI's *Tetra Laval* judgment and a member of the judges' chamber in the *Schneider* case. Vesterdorf, above, note 10, at 22.
34. *Airtours*, paras 127, 130, 145, 181.
35. Ibid., para. 294.
36. Commission Decision COMP/M. 2416 – *Tetra Laval/Sidel* (30 October 2001), 2004 O.J. L 43, 13.
37. *Tetra Laval Court of First Instance Judgment*, para. 132 and *passim*.
38. *Schneider*, para. 404.
39. Ibid., para. 422.
40. Council of Ministers of the European Union (2004), Council Regulation (EC) 139/2004, above, note 16, (final version), available at http://europa.eu.int/eur-lex/pri/en/oj/dat/2004/l_024/l_02420040129en00010022.pdf.
41. European Commission (2004), Guidelines on the Assessment of Horizontal Mergers under the Council Regulation on the Control of Concentrations Between Undertakings, 5 February 2004, 2004/C 31/03, O.J. (C 31) 5, available at http://europa.eu.int/eur-lex/pri/en/oj/dat/2004/c_031/c_03120040205en00050018.pdf (final version). These are akin to the better-known Horizontal Merger Guidelines issued by the US Department of Justice and Federal Trade Commission.
42. European Commission, DG Competition Best Practices on the Conduct of EC Merger Proceedings, available at: http://www.europa.eu.int/comm/competition/mergers/legislation/regulation/best_practices.pdf (final version).
43. See Monti, Mario (2002), 'Merger Control in the European Union: A Radical Reform', Address to the European Commission/IBA Conference on EU Merger Control (7 November 2002), available at: http://europa.eu.int/comm/competition/speeches/index_2002.html.
44. Ibid.
45. See Guerrero, above, note 25, at 280.
46. Monti, above, note 43.
47. European Commission (2002), Press Release, 'Commission appeals CFI ruling on *Tetra Laval/Sidel* to the European Court of Justice', IP/02/1952 (20 December 2002).
48. Ibid.
49. The written and oral proceedings were all conducted in English. The Court dismissed a Tetra Laval motion for the Commission's appeal to be translated into French. See *Tetra Laval Advisory Opinion*, para. 55.
50. The Commission raised five grounds of appeal. This chapter concentrates almost exclusively on the first one, questioning the CFI's scope of judicial review and the standard of proof it demanded, as this was the primary challenge and sufficient to decide the case in favour of Tetra Laval. The Commission lost on the other four challenges as well. On the second ground, the Court agreed with the CFI that the Commission had been wrong not to dismiss out of hand the behavioural commitments not to engage in anti-competitive behaviour that the merging parties made during the course of negotiations with the Commission – an interesting topic for further study. The Court dismissed the remaining three grounds of appeal, regarding product market definition and two assessments of product market dominance, as raising questions of fact, not law. The third ground does implicate questions of judicial review that shall be considered herein, but overall these challenges raised case-specific issues as opposed to the more broadly applicable holdings on judicial review/standards and behavioural commitments. See *Tetra Laval*, para. 17 and *passim*.
51. See Wilmer Hale and Dorr, Tetra Laval – A Landmark Judgment on EC Merger Control (11 March 2005), at 1, available at http://www.wilmerhale.com/publications/ [hereinafter Wilmer Hale Report] ('Had the ECJ upheld the arguments raised by the Commission, this may well have had a chilling effect on the CFI's willingness to subject the Commission's merger decisions to strict scrutiny. This in turn would have severely limited the effectiveness of judicial review.').

52. Clough, above, note 5, at 746.
53. Judge Vesterdorf defines 'the standard of proof [a]s the threshold that must be met before an adjudicator decides that a point is proven in law,' while '[s]tandard of review is the standard that a reviewing tribunal or appellate court applies when reviewing the legality of a decision of an administrative body or lower tribunal'. Another term for 'standard of review' is 'judicial control'. See Vesterdorf, above, note 25, at 5–6, 7.
54. Appeals of course also can challenge the Commission's clearance of a merger, but these would be brought by third parties (e.g., competitors, governments, employees, or minority shareholders), not the merging parties themselves. Third parties typically have a higher burden in pursuing an appeal because to establish standing they first must prove they face a 'direct and individual' consequence from the merger setting them apart from other claimants. See *Plaumann* v. *Commission*, Case 25/62 [1963] E.C.R. 95.
55. The first ground of appeal also raised a third key challenge, regarding the proper 'margin of discretion' the Commission should enjoy in a prospective analysis, which is considered below, in Section 2, under 'Standard of poof'.
56. *Tetra Laval*, para. 29.
57. Ibid.
58. Ibid.
59. Advocate General Tizzano's advisory opinion considered and rejected this argument of the Commission, concluding that (1) other Merger Regulation language allowing a combination to go ahead if the Commission did not act within the specified deadline suggested a presumption of authorization, and (2) a presumption in favour was preferable to the opposite since resultant ill-effects still could be addressed ex post under the Commission's Treaty authority to police anti-competitive behaviour (*Tetra Laval Advisory Opinion*, paras 79 and 81).
    According to CFI President Bo Vesterdorf, this appeal was the first time the question had been considered in EC case law. Wilmer Hale lawyers observed that the ECJ apparently elected to leave the Advocate General's opinion to stand as 'persuasive authority for future "grey zone" evidentiary cases' (Wilmer Hale Report, above, note 51, at 4). Judge Vesterdorf argues in his law journal commentary – not the CFI judgment – in favour of a 'flexible' standard, given the impossibility of applying a purely symmetrical standard to cases that are 'close calls' (Vesterdorf, above, note 25, at 25, 29–31).
60. *Airtours*, para. 63; see generally Guerrero, note 25.
61. *Tetra Laval*, paras 26–7.
62. Ibid., paras 32–3. Both parties can claim to be justified in finding the standard of proof language to be inconsistent. Matters certainly might have been clearer had the CFI not departed in *Airtours* from the *Kali & Salz* language. On the other hand, civil-law systems place less weight on precedent than does the common-law tradition.
63. *Tetra Laval*, paras 38, 41.
64. Ibid., para. 39.
65. 'Cogent and consistent' and 'convincing evidence' were not even the only two formulations the CFI has used. The *Tetra Laval Court of First Instance Judgment* also urged the Commission to base its conclusions on '*prudent analysis*' of the independent studies or on a *solid, coherent body of evidence*' (para. 212) (emphasis added). Three subsequent cases in 2003 muddied the waters further, with references to 'precise and coherent evidence', evidence 'sufficient to rule out clearly any serious doubt,' and refusal to accept a Commission allegation 'not founded on any evidence capable of proving it to the required legal standard'. See Vesterdorf, above, note 25, at 20. The CFI president, writing before the ECJ judgment was handed down, acknowledges that the various formulations 'do not reveal a clear standard of proof' and expressed hope that the ECJ would 'shed more light into this rather obscure issue' (ibid., at 26–7).
66. *Tetra Laval*, para. 48.
67. Ibid., para. 28.
68. Ibid., para. 42.
69. Ibid., paras 39, 44.

70. Wilmer Hale Report, above, note 51, at 1.
71. In the 1960s the Court promulgated the doctrines of 'direct effect' and 'supremacy,' making EC law self-executing, binding and preemptive of the national law of Member States. See *Costa* v. *Enel*, Case 6/64, [1964] E.C.R. 585 (direct effect), *Van Gend & Loos* v. *Netherlands*, Case 26/62 [1963] E.C.R. 1 (supremacy).
72. EC Treaty, Art. 220.
73. *Kali & Salz*, paras 223–4. The judgment imported into the merger arena what already was a staple principle of ECJ jurisprudence, what antitrust solicitors at Slaughter & May have called the 'reluctance of the European Court to second-guess the exercise by the European Commission of its discretion in economic matters'. See Nicholson, Malcolm, Sarah Cardell and Bronagh McKenna (2005), 'The scope of review of merger decisions under Community law', 1, *Eur. Competition J.*, 123. The principle was articulated first in the 1966 case *Consten and Grundig*, which held that 'the exercise of the Commission's powers necessarily implies complex evaluations on economic matters. A judicial review of these evaluations must take account of their nature by confining itself to an examination of the relevance of the facts and the legal consequences which the Commission deduces therefrom'. *Etablissements Consten SARL and Grundig-Verkaufs-GmbH* v. *Commission*, Joined Cases 56 and 58/64, [1966] E.C.R. 299, 347, cited by Nicholson et al. at 123.
74. *Petrolessence and SG2R* v. *Commission*, Case T-342/00 [2003] E.C.R. II-1161, para. 101.
75. See also Advocate General Tizzano's *Tetra Laval Advisory Opinion*, para. 88 (arguing that the *Kali & Salz* test 'make[s] it possible for the Community judicature to exercise an adequate review' without having to reconsider the merits of the Commission's assessments).
76. Vesterdorf, above, note 25, at 18.
77. *Tetra Laval*, para. 19. The four Treaty grounds for review are lack of jurisdiction, procedural error, error of law and misuse of power, see above, note 4.
78. In *Tetra Laval Court of First Instance Judgment*, paras 210–13, the CFI zeroed in on what it saw as several chinks in the Commission's case: a concession at oral argument that significant growth could not be expected in the market for long-life milk, which accounted for half of total liquid dairy product sales; conflicting independent studies on market growth that the Commission had relied on; and failure to consider that an alternative plastic technology might capture growth the Commission expected to accrue to the Tetra Laval/Sidel product. Additionally, and crucially, the CFI also found that the Commission had neglected to analyze the market for packaging juices in glass bottles, a key substitute product for both carton and plastic.
79. The ECJ characterized the Commission's complaint thusly: 'that the Court of First Instance failed to demonstrate that the Commission's estimates of the growth in use of PET [plastic bottling] were based, first, on factual errors, secondly, on findings of fact which were not established or on conclusions drawn from manifestly insignificant evidence, thirdly, on inconsistencies or errors in reasoning or, fourthly, on the omission of relevant factors' (*Tetra Laval*, para. 31).
80. It is not the aim of this chapter to judge whether the CFI or the Commission had the better of the econometric and methodological debate. Readers with a yen for picking apart economic analysis may compare and contrast the Commission's decision. It is, however, notable that Advocate General Tizzano's advisory opinion, while supporting the CFI's position in the other four grounds of appeal, agreed with the Commission's objections to the CFI's milk-market analysis. The CFI's conclusion on growth estimates, Tizzano wrote, 'is invalidated by an incomplete or inaccurate assessment of the relevant factors and is not, in any case, supported by adequate reasoning'. Overall he deemed the Commission's first ground of appeal 'in part well founded' – he agreed with the CFI that the Commission had insufficiently analyzed the glass-bottle market – and thought this element of the original Commission decision 'must be upheld' (*Tetra Laval Advisory Opinion*, paras 96, 112). Tizzano's view, of course, was not binding; though, and ultimately the ECJ saw things differently.
81. *Tetra Laval*, para. 46.

82. Ibid., para. 47.
83. Ibid., para. 39.
84. It is to be noted that this evidentiary presumption is distinct from the question of presumption of legality of a merger, discussed above, notes 56–9 and accompanying text.
85. *Tetra Laval Final Judgment*, para. 27.
86. Ibid., para. 96.
87. Vesterdorf, above, note 25, at 22. He concedes that the *Petrolessence* judgment, above, note 74, is a possible exception.
88. Vesterdorf, above, note 25, at 17.
89. *Tetra Laval Advisory Opinion*, para. 94.
90. Wilmer Hale Report, above, note 51, at 1.
91. Vesterdorf, above, note 25, at 29.
92. Ibid., at 31–2. While in some sense this may sound like a licence for judicial activism, Judge Vesterdorf cites in support settled English case law to the effect that 'the actual application of the orthodox principles of judicial review will of course vary according to the subject matter of the case' and 'in law context is everything'. See ibid., at n.31 (citing the judgment of the Competition Appeals Tribunal in Case 1023/4/1/03, *IBA Health Ltd*. v. *OFT*, para. 219) (citations omitted).
93. Decision 2004/134/EC (Case No COMP/M.2220 – *General Electric/Honeywell*) (OJ [2004] L 48.).
94. EU Bulletin, Hogan & Hartson, 15 December, 2005. Available at http://www.hhlaw.com/newsStand/pubDetail.aspx?publication=2050.
95. *GE/Honeywell*, paras 57–76.
96. Ibid., para. 60.
97. Ibid., para. 61.
98. After stating that no presumption applies, Para. 61 goes on to reference Para. 120 of *Tetra Laval* v. *Commission*.
99. Ibid., para. 62.
100. Ibid., para. 351.
101. Ibid., para. 66.
102. Ibid., para. 64.
103. Ibid.
104. Ibid., para. 73.
105. Ibid., paras 73–4.
106. Ibid., paras 489–90.
107. Ibid., para. 339.
108. Ibid., para. 402.
109. Ibid., para. 429.
110. Ibid.
111. 'One gets a funny feeling reading the judgments that the result was a close run thing and it could easily have turned out differently' was the early reaction at EU Law Blog, http://eulaw.typepad.com/eulawblog/2005/12/general_electri.html.
112. David Wood of Gibson, Dunn & Crutcher, quoted in Meller, Paul (2005) 'European Court upholds veto of G.E.–Honeywell deal', *New York Times*, p. C7, 15 December.
113. Chris Bright of Shearman & Sterling, quoted in Matlack, Carol (2005), 'Are Euro regulators losing power?', *Business Week Online*, 14 December.
114. *FTC* v. *Arch Coal*, 329 F.Supp. 2d 109 (D.D.C. 2004).
115. *United States* v. *Oracle Corp*., 331 F. Supp. 2d 1098 (N.D. Cal. 2004).
116. The role of private enforcement in Europe could be set to grow significantly in coming years. In a green paper published on 19 December 2005, the Commission sought feedback on options for encouraging private actions for damages. The aim is to strengthen the overall enforcement regime, potentially by making 'double damages' available for cartel abuses, without encouraging spurious litigation – a fine line to walk, as US experience shows. Still, if the proposal goes forward, it would mark another important convergence in the US and European enforcement regimes. As the *Financial Times* pointed out in an editorial, '[I]f Brussels can be surer of catching actual anti-

competitive conduct after it happens – through better focused prosecutions and wider, partly-privatised enforcement – then it has less need to worry about, and perhaps exaggerate, potential anti-competitive effects in its merger rulings'. (*Financial Times*, leader, 'Privatising antitrust: EU wants more companies to sue for competition damages', 21 December 2005). The Commission proposal notes that the burden of proof in such cases might need to be lowered in order to help claimants, given that information asymmetry and disclosure rules currently favour defendants. The green paper [COM(2005) 672] and related background materials are available at http://www.europa.eu.int/comm/competition/ antitrust/others/actions_for_damages/index_en.html.

117. Testimony of William Blumenthal, FTC General Counsel, before Antitrust Modernization Commission, 3 November 2005, at 3 ('The Commission asks whether the standard DOJ must meet to obtain a preliminary injunction to block a merger differs, as a practical matter, from that the FTC must meet. The answer is no.') The testimony of Blumenthal and other experts is available at http://www.amc.gov/commission_hearings.htm.
118. Testimony of Michael N. Sohn, chairman of the law firm Arnold & Porter, before the Antitrust Modernization Commission, 3 November 2005, at 10.
119. *United States* v. *General Dynamics*, 415 U.S. 486 (1974).
120. For the Department of Justice, since it does not conduct internal adjudications, the preliminary injunction is a tool to stop the merger while both sides prepare for a full trial.
121. 'For all practical purposes to merging parties, after losing in a preliminary injunction proceeding brought by the FTC, "preliminary" relief means *final*' (Sohn testimony, note 118, at 12).
122. 'The findings of the commission, board, or Secretary as to the facts, if supported by substantial evidence, shall be conclusive,' states the Clayton Act's enforcement provision with regard to mergers, codified at 15 U.S.C.A. 21(c). The equivalent provision in §5 of the FTC Act, codified at 15 U.S.C.A. §45(c), although omitting the word 'substantial', has been construed identically by the courts. The Administrative Procedure Act, applying to agency adjudications in general and not just the FTC, specifies that 'The reviewing court shall . . . hold unlawful and set aside agency action, findings, and conclusions found to be . . . unsupported by substantial evidence.' Codified at 15 U.S.C.A. §706.
123. Vesterdorf, above, note 25, at 11.
124. See *Consolidated Edison* v. *NLRB*, 305 US 197, 229 (1938) and *FTC* v. *Indiana Fed'n. of Dentists*, 476 U.S. 447, 454 (1986). See also *Beneficial Corp.* v. *FTC*, 542 F.2d 611, 616 (3rd Cir. 1976), *cert. denied*, 430 U.S. 983 (1977). Alternatively, and similarly, 'substantial evidence' has been explained as evidence that would justify a judge's refusal to direct a verdict were a case before a jury. See *Harbor Banana Distributors, Inc.* v. *FTC*, 499 F.2d 395 (5th Cir., 1974).
125. *Black's Law Dictionary*, 8th edn (2004).
126. Louis Jaffe, one of the deans of administrative law scholarship, says the substantial evidence approach allows a reviewing court to examine the fairness of the entire fact-finding process; other observers maintain that a reviewing court's posture toward an agency should resemble that of an appeals court to a trial court, i.e., it should apply a 'reasonableness' or 'clearly erroneous' standard. Quoted in Aman, Alfred C. and William T. Mayton (2001), *Administrative Law*, p. 457. Note that, even under Jaffe's broad formulation, scrutinizing the *fairness* of the fact-finding *process* is not the same as scrutinizing every fact itself.
127. *Hospital Corporation of America* v. *FTC*, 807 F.2d 1381, 1385 (7th Cir. 1986).
128. 'The findings of the commission, board, or Secretary as to the facts, if supported by substantial evidence, shall be conclusive,' states the Clayton Act's enforcement provision with regard to mergers, codified at 15 U.S.C.A. 21(c). The equivalent provision in §5 of the FTC Act, codified at 15 U.S.C.A. §45(c), although omitting the word 'substantial', has been construed identically by the courts.
129. *Hospital Corp. of America* v. *FTC*, 807 F.2d at 1385, citing Section 7 cases *Yamaha Motor Co., Ltd.*, v. *FTC*, 657 F.2d 971, 977 and n.7 (8th Cir. 1981); *Fruehauf Corp.* v.

FTC, 603 F.2d 345, 351 (2d Cir. 1979); *RSR Corp.* v. *FTC*, 602 F.2d. 1317, 1320, 1325 (9th Cir. 1979); *Ash Grove Cement Co.* v. *FTC*, 577 F.2d 1368, 1377–79 (9th Cir. 1978).

130. *FTC* v. *Algoma Lumber Co.*, 291 U.S. 67, 73 (1934).

131. *Tetra Laval*, paras 25–36.

132. 'The Commission takes the view, first of all, that the standard of "convincing evidence" differs substantially, in degree and in nature, both from the obligation to produce "cogent and consistent" evidence, established in *Kali & Salz*, and from the principle that the Commission's assessment must be accepted unless it is shown to be manifestly wrong. The standard is different in degree because, unlike the standard of "convincing evidence", that of cogent and consistent evidence does not rule out the possibility that another body might reach a difference conclusion if it were competent to give a decision on the matter. The standard required is likewise different in nature inasmuch as it transforms the role of the Community Courts into that of a different body which is competent to rule on the matter in all its complexity and which is entitled to substitute its views for those of the Commission. The Court of First Instance was inconsistent in that it referred to the test of manifest error of assessment yet applied a very different test' (*Tetra Laval*, para. 27). See generally *Tetra Laval*, paras 25–36, 96–7.

133. Again, although the ECJ did not use the term 'convincing evidence' in its opinion, it defended the CFI's use of it, and the CFI returned to the phrase in *GE/Honeywell*.

134. In other respects, the two tests seem similar: the EC's third element, 'capable of substantiating the conclusions drawn from it', is simply another way of saying, as US courts do, that evidence must be such that 'a reasonable mind might accept as adequate to support a conclusion'. The first element, that evidence must be 'factually accurate, reliable and consistent', seems embraced by the third, since inaccurate, unreliable and inconsistent evidence would not reasonably support an agency factual determination.

135. Indeed, in merger challenges brought by the Department of Justice Antitrust Division, the preliminary injunction proceeding is often consolidated with the trial over a permanent injunction.

136. See testimony of William Blumenthal, FTC General Counsel, before the Antitrust Modernization Commission, 3 November 2005, at 7.

137. See, e.g., *Hospital Corporation of America* v. *FTC*, 807 F.2d 1381; *FTC* v. *Butterworth Health Corp.*, 946 F.Supp. 1285 (W.D. Mich. 1996).

138. See above, note 105.

139. In both the US and the Community, of course, the vast bulk of prospective mergers are resolved at the enforcement agency level, without litigation.

140. *FTC* v. *H.J. Heinz Co.*, 246 F.3d 708, 714 (D.C. Cir. 2001); see §13(b) of the Federal Trade Commission Act, as amended in 1973, codified at 15 U.S.C. §53(b).

141. See Sohn testimony, note 118, at 8–9.

142. Ibid., at 10.

143. *Arch Coal*, 329 F.Supp. 2d, 115–17.

144. *FTC* v. *Staples, Inc.*, 970 F. Supp. 1066, 1072 (D.D.C. 1997).

145. *Heinz*, 246 F.3d at 719 (quoting *Hospital Corporation of America* v. *FTC*, 807 F.2d at 1389).

146. *FTC* v. *University Health*, 938 F.2d 1206, 1218 (11th Cir. 1991).

147. *United States* v. *Philadelphia National Bank*, 374 U.S. 321, 363 (1963) (blocking a combination of two major Philadelphia banks seeking to expand in the suburbs).

148. *United States* v. *General Dynamics*, 415 U.S. 486 (1974).

149. Ibid., at 501.

150. *United States* v. *Baker-Hughes*, 908 F.2d 981, 991 (D.C. Cir. 1990) ('In the aftermath of *General Dynamics* and its progeny, a defendant seeking to rebut a presumption of anticompetitive effect must show that the prima facie case inaccurately predicts the relevant transaction's probable effect on future competition').

151. *FTC* v. *Swedish Match*, 131 F. Supp. 2d 151 (D.D.C. 2000).

152. *FTC* v. *Tenet Health Care Corp.*, 186 F.3d 1045 (8th Cir. 1999).

153. Keyte, James (2004), 'Arch Coal and Oracle put the agencies on the ropes in proving anticompetitive effects', **19**, *Antitrust* 79.

154. Ibid., at 79.
155. Ibid., at 79–80.
156. Ibid., at 79.
157. Even after the introduction of expedited review procedures in 2001 and 2002 by both the Court of First Instance and the European Commission, the administrative and judicial review process still usually takes ten months even in the best of circumstances, considerably longer than in the United States and too long for most parties to endure.
      Detailed consideration of the procedures involved in EC judicial review of mergers is beyond the scope of this chapter. For a useful discussion of the procedural aspects see Ritter and Braun, *European Competition Law: A Practitioner's Guide*, pp. 1147–70.
158. Freshfields Bruckhaus Deringer, 'The Tetra Laval Case' (February 2005) at 2, available at http://www.freshfields.com/practice/comptrade/publications/pdf/10831.pdf ('The ECJ's judgment in Tetra Laval provides an important illustration of the "checks and balances" that exist in EU merger control. It confirms that, nowadays, judicial review is an integral part of the EU merger review process.').
159. See, e.g., *Brown Shoe Co., Inc.* v. *United States*, 370 U.S. 294 (1962) (forbidding merger between a shoe retailer and shoe wholesaler that would have given the combined company a market share of around 5 per cent).
160. 'Convergence', in this discussion, is a one-way street: EC courts seem to be moving in the US direction, not vice versa.
161. Slaughter, Anne-Marie (2004), *A New World Order*.
162. See Agreement between the Government of the United States of America and the Commission of the European Communities Regarding the Application of Their Competition Laws, 23 September 1991, 30 I.L.M. 1491, reprinted in **4**, Trade Reg. Rep. (CCH) PARA 13,504, available at http://www.usdoj.gov/atr/public/international/docs/ec.htm; and Agreement Between The Government of the United States of America and the European Communities on the Application of Positive Comity Principles in the Enforcement of Their Competition Laws, 4 June 1998, 37 I.L.M. 1070, reprinted in **4**, Trade Reg. Rep. (CCH) PARA 13,504A, available at http://www.usdoj.gov/atr/public/international/docs/1781.htm.
163. Above, note 122.
164. And judges participate in transnational forums too. Judge Vesterdorf's commentary cited in this chapter originated as a speech before the Third Annual Merger Control Conference organized by the British Institute of International and Comparative Law, held in December 2004 (Vesterdorf, above, note 25, p. 3).
165. Above, note 115.

### References

Aman, Alfred C. and William T. Mayton (2001), *Administrative Law*.
Bellamy, Sir Christopher (1999), 'Anti-Trust and the Courts Roundtable', *Fordham Ann. Antitrust Conf.*, 369.
Brown, Adrian (1994), 'Judicial review of commission decisions under the Merger Regulation: the first cases', **15**, *Eur. Competition L. Rev.*, 296.
Clough, Mark (2004), 'The role of judicial review in Merger Control', **24**, *N.W. J. Int'l L. & Bus.*, 729.
Council of Ministers of the European Union (2004), Council Regulation (EC) 139/2004 of 20 January 2004 on Control of Concentrations Between Undertakings, 2004 O.J. (L 024) 1.
European Commission, 'DG competition best practices on the conduct of EC merger proceedings', available at http://www.europa.eu.int/comm/competition/mergers/legislation/regulation/best_practices.pdf.
European Commission (2002), Press Release, Commission Appeals CFI Ruling on *Tetra Laval/Sidel* to the European Court of Justice, IP/02/1952 (20 December 2002).
European Commission (2004), 'Guidelines on the assessment of horizontal mergers under the Council regulation on the control of concentrations between undertakings', 5 February

2004, 2004/C 31/03, O.J. (C 31) 5, available at http://europa.eu.int/eur-lex/pri/en/oj/dat/
2004/c_031/c_03120040205en00050018.pdf.
Freshfields Bruckhaus Deringer, 'The Tetra Laval Case' (February 2005) at 2, available at
http://www.freshfields.com/practice/comptrade/publications/pdf/10831.pdf.
Goyder, D.G. (2003), *EC Competition Law*, Oxford: Oxford University Press.
Guerrero, Kevin (2003), Note, 'A New "Convincing Evidence" standard in European Merger
review', **72**, *U. Cin. L. Rev.*, 249.
Keyte, James (2004), 'Arch Coal and Oracle put the agencies on the ropes in proving anti-
competitive effects', **19**, *Antitrust*, 79.
Matlack, Carol (2005), 'Are Euro regulators losing Power?', *BusinessWeek Online*, 14
December 2005.
Meller, Paul (2005), 'European court upholds veto of G.E.–Honeywell Deal', *New York
Times*, p.C7, 15 December.
Monti, Mario (2002), 'Merger control in the European Union: a radical reform', Address to
the European Commission/IBA Conference on EU Merger Control (7 November 2002),
available at http://europa.eu.int/comm/competition/speeches/index_2002.html.
Nicholson, Malcolm, Sarah Cardell and Bronagh McKenna (2005), 'The scope of review of
merger decisions under Community law', **1**, *Eur. Competition J.*, 123.
Ritter, Lennart and W. David Braun (2004), *European Competition Law: A Practitioner's
Guide*, Kluwer Law International.
Slaughter, Anne-Marie (2004), *A New World Order*, Princeton: Princeton University Press.
Vesterdorf, Bo (2005), 'Standard of proof in merger cases', **1**, *European Competition Journal* 3.

## Cases
*Airtours* v. *Commission*, Case T-342/99, [2002] E.C.R. II-2585.
*Ash Grove Cement Co.* v. *FTC*, 577 F.2d 1368 (9th Cir. 1978).
*BAT and R.J. Reynolds* v. *Commission and Philip Morris*, Cases 142/84 and 156/84, [1987]
E.C.R. 4487.
*Beneficial Corp.* v. *FTC*, 542 F.2d 611 (3rd Cir. 1976), *cert. denied*, 430 U.S. 983 (1977).
*Brown Shoe Co., Inc.* v. *United States*, 370 U.S. 294 (1962).
*Commission* v. *Tetra Laval*, Case C-12/03, [2005] E.C.R. I-987.
*Consolidated Edison* v. *NLRB*, 305 US 197 (1938).
*Costa* v. *Enel*, Case 6/64, [1964] E.C.R. 585.
*Etablissements Consten SARL and Grundig-Verkaufs-GmbH* v. *Commission*, Joined Cases 56
and 58/64, [1966] E.C.R. 299.
*Europemballage and Continental Can* v. *Commission*, Case 6/72, [1973] E.C.R. 215.
*France and Others* v. *Commission*, Joined Cases C-68/94 and 30/95, [1998] E.C.R. I-1375.
*Fruehauf Corp.* v. *FTC*, 603 F.2d 345 (2d Cir. 1979).
*FTC* v. *Algoma Lumber Co.*, 291 U.S. 67 (1934).
*FTC* v. *Arch Coal*, 329 F.Supp. 2d 109 (D.D.C. 2004).
*FTC* v. *Butterworth Health Corp.*, 946 F.Supp. 1285 (W.D. Mich. 1996).
*FTC* v. *H.J. Heinz Co.*, 246 F.3d 708 (D.C. Cir. 2001).
*FTC* v. *Indiana Fed'n. of Dentists*, 476 U.S. 447, 454 (1986).
*FTC* v. *Staples, Inc.*, 970 F. Supp. 1066 (D.D.C. 1997).
*FTC* v. *Swedish Match*, 131 F. Supp. 2d 151 (D.D.C. 2000).
*FTC* v. *Tenet Health Care Corp.*, 186 F.3d 1045 (8th Cir. 1999).
*FTC* v. *University Health*, 938 F.2d 1206 (11th Cir. 1991).
*General Electric Co.* v. *Commission*, Case T-210/01, [2005], E.C.R.
*Harbor Banana Distributors, Inc.* v. *FTC*, 499 F.2d 395 (5th Cir., 1974).
*Honeywell International* v. *Commission*, T-209/01, [2005], E.C.R.
*Hospital Corporation of America* v. *FTC*, 807 F.2d 1381 (7th Cir. 1986).
*Marbury* v. *Madison*, 1 Cranch 137 (1803).
*Petrolessence and SG2R* v. *Commission*, Case T-342/00, [2003] E.C.R. II-1161.
*Plaumann* v. *Commission*, Case 25/62, [1963] E.C.R. 95.
*RSR Corp.* v. *FTC*, 602 F.2d. 1317 (9th Cir. 1979).

*Schneider Electric* v. *Commission*, Case T-310/2001 [2002] E.C.R. II-4071.
*Tetra Laval* v. *Commission*, Case T-5/2002, [2002] E.C.R. II-4381.
*United States* v. *Baker-Hughes*, 908 F.2d 981 (D.C. Cir. 1990).
*United States* v. *General Dynamics*, 415 U.S. 486 (1974).
*United States* v. *Oracle Corp.*, 331 F. Supp. 2d 1098 (N.D. Cal. 2004).
*United States* v. *Philadelphia National Bank*, 374 U.S. 321 (1963).
*Van Gend & Loos* v. *Netherlands*, Case 26/62, [1963] E.C.R. 1.
*Yamaha Motor Co., Ltd.*, v. *FTC*, 657 F.2d 971, 977 and n.7 (8th Cir. 1981).

# 7 Discounts, rebates and selective pricing by dominant firms: a trans-Atlantic comparison

*Christian Ahlborn and David Bailey*

## A. Introduction

The antitrust control of discounts and selective pricing by dominant firms is commanding a lot of attention in Europe and elsewhere at the moment. On both sides of the Atlantic there has been high-profile enforcement activity. Two cases decided in 2003 (*Michelin* v. *Commission* and *British Airways* v. *Commission*) are among the most prominent and controversial in the EU. Separately in the US private actions in particular have challenged the discounting practices of dominant companies, notably in *Virgin* v. *British Airways*[1] and *3M* v. *LePage's*,[2] respectively. Action by the Canadian Commissioner of Competition in *Canada Pipe*[3] provides yet another example of recent intervention.

The high level of enforcement activity has exposed fundamental differences in analytical approach between Europe, on the one hand, and North America, on the other. In the EU, *Michelin II* and *Virgin/British Airways* involved loyalty-inducing schemes which were deemed by the European Commission and the Court of First Instance (CFI) to have an exclusionary structure and were prohibited per se. They are symptomatic of a broader trend in the application of EC law to unilateral conduct, which has long been insufficiently based on economic analysis. In contrast, the authorities and courts in the US and Canada have generally adopted a less interventionist approach towards rebates and discounts, preferring to focus on whether anticompetitive effects are realistic or not.

At the same time it is possible to discern a number of similarities between the enforcement of the laws on discounts in the US, the EU and Canada. For one thing, controversy has arisen on both sides of the Atlantic regarding the approach taken and the conclusions reached in cases, most notably in *Michelin II*[4] and *LePage's*. Secondly, and this point in many ways relates to the first, certain aspects of the law in this area are far from settled. Former Attorney-General Pate has noted that:

> the bundling and fidelity rebate areas are among the murkiest regarding single firm conduct. Clarity will come, here as it has in other areas, from courts'

continued learning from economics as well as from the ongoing conversation between jurisdictions.[5]

At the time of writing British Airways is testing the CFI's assessment of the exclusionary character of its reward scheme before the European Court of Justice (ECJ).[6] Against this background of controversy and uncertainty, the European Commission has recognized the need to reconsider the law and policy under Article 82 and consequently its Directorate-General for Competition published a Discussion Paper on exclusionary abuses on 19 December 2005.[7] It held a public meeting to discuss further the most important topics raised by the submissions made in connection with the Discussion Paper on 14 June 2006. Beyond that date, the future course of the Commission's Article 82 review is uncertain. Meanwhile in the US, the US Department of Justice (DoJ) and Federal Trade Commission (FTC) are holding joint public hearings on 'Competition Policy Related to Single-Firm Conduct' in Summer 2006.[8]

The uncertain legal position and the need for further reflection by enforcement agencies reflects the state of flux of economic theory and a limited degree of empirical analysis. Thus in *LePage's* the US enforcement agencies jointly recommended to the Supreme Court that 'it would be preferable to allow the case law and economic analysis to develop further and to await a case with a record better adapted to development of an appropriate standard'.[9] In particular the agencies observed that: 'Although there are references to bundled rebates in the scholarly literature, the theoretical and empirical analysis of that practice as a potentially exclusionary mechanism is relatively recent and sparse'.

It concluded that 'the Court would be well served to await further development of the case law and further insights from academic commentary, before attempting to devise a standard to govern [this] important business practice of currently uncertain exclusionary effect'.[10] All in all, it is clear that discounting practices of dominant firms are subject to much scrutiny and there is continuing debate on both sides of the Atlantic about the appropriate analytical framework used to evaluate exclusionary conduct in general and discounts in particular.

This chapter provides an overview of the economic literature of various forms of discounts and selective pricing, as well as a short summary of case law on discounts and selective pricing under the control of dominance/monopoly provisions on both sides of the Atlantic. Section B sets out the various forms of non-uniform pricing and suggests three main categories for the assessment of discounts and selective pricing according to the type of alleged competitive harm. Section C gives a short overview of the economic literature, followed by a section (Section D) which sets out the analytic framework and the implications which flow from the economic literature. Section E sets out the law on discounts and selective pricing in the EU, US and Canada, while Section F draws conclusions.

## B. Discounts and selective pricing
### 1 Different types of uniform pricing
Discounts, rebates and selective price cuts are all types of non-uniform prices. They can be classified in numerous ways. One key distinction is between non-linear pricing, e.g. where the unit price decreases with the number of units purchased but where all customers are offered the same price schedule (economists refer to this as 'second degree' price discrimination), and linear pricing, i.e. where the unit price does not depend on the number of units purchased, but where different groups of customers are offered different prices (so-called 'third degree' price discrimination).

The distinction between second degree and third degree price discrimination is mirrored in the Commission's Discussion Paper which talks about 'conditional rebates', i.e. 'rebates' which are 'granted to customers to reward a certain (purchasing) behaviour of these customers' and 'unconditional rebates' which are 'granted to certain customers and not to others and which are independent of customers' purchasing behaviour'.

Conditional discounts and rebates (or non-linear pricing) can be further classified, according to the following:

a.   the type of threshold of trigger: which may be defined by a fixed number of units (quantity discounts/rebates) by a share of the purchasers' requirement ('market share' discounts/rebates) or by other obligations, such as exclusivity (exclusive discounts/rebates);
b.   the scope of application, whether they are forward-looking, i.e. applicable only to incremental purchases above the threshold ('prospective' discounts/rebates) or backward-looking, i.e. applicable to all sales once the threshold has been exceeded ('retroactive' discounts/rebates); and
c.   the scope of products, i.e. whether they apply to the units purchased of a single type of product ('single item' discount/rebate) or aggregate purchases across a range of products (bundled discounts).

Discounts, rebates and selective pricing are at the interface of three types of exclusionary antitrust concerns: non-uniform pricing can have effects similar to exclusive dealing arrangements (loyalty or quasi-exclusive discounts); non-uniform pricing can have effects similar to tying arrangements (bundling or quasi-tying discounts); and finally non-uniform pricing can have an effect similar to predatory pricing strategies.

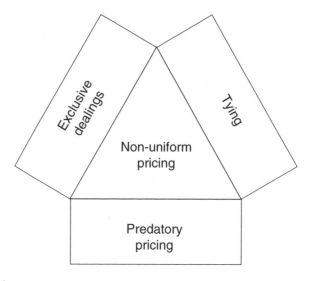

*Figure 7.1*

## 2   Loyalty/target discounts: the exclusivity analogy

Loyalty or target discounts are discounts that are conditional on the customer purchasing all (or almost all) of its requirements from the supplier in question. Loyalty or target discounts may take a number of different forms (see Figure 7.1). They can be explicitly conditional on an exclusive purchasing requirement or a high share of the customer's total requirements. They may also be conditional on growing sales year on year. And they can take the form of quantity discounts with customer-specific thresholds where the threshold is set close to the customer's total purchasing requirements. General quantity discounts, by contrast, can only exceptionally amount to a loyalty or target discount, namely where the group of customers is fairly homogeneous in terms of requirements and where the quantity threshold is equivalent to that requirement.

While the similarities between loyalty discounts and exclusive dealing are obvious, it is worth noting that loyalty discounts are generally less restrictive than exclusive dealing, in terms of both scope of foreclosure and impact: first, the discount scheme may exclude less than the exclusive dealing contract insofar as the volume target may allow the buyer to purchase from alternative sources (e.g. a market share discount of 80% or a quantity discount in a growing market).

Furthermore, as Hovenkamp pointed out:

> most discount programs lack the 'lock in' feature that characterizes unlawful exclusive dealing. In a case of unlawful exclusive dealing the defendant seller enters into a contract for a specified period requiring the purchaser to take all of

its product from that seller. By contrast, the typical discount contract is typically conditional: if you want to obtain a 20% discount, then you must purchase all (or a specified percentage) of your goods from the contracting seller. The penalty for not taking the specified percentage is not a breach of contract suit or termination of a franchise. Rather, it is simply the loss of the discount. But the loss of discount is not a penalty at all if a rival is willing to match the discounted price.[11]

Only in extremes does the foreclosure effect of loyalty discounts equal that of an exclusive dealing arrangement, namely (a) where it is conditional on exclusive purchasing and (b) where the discount is of such magnitude that other suppliers are not willing or able to match it.

### 3   Bundled discounts: the tying analogy

Bundled discounts, by contrast, have obvious similarities to tying.[12] Tying occurs when the purchase of one good (the tying good) is made conditional on the purchase of another good (the tied good). Tying generally has two explicit or implicit conditions. First, that the tie occurs between 'separate products'; secondly, tying has implied a degree of coercion, namely '[preventing] goods from competing directly for consumers' choice on their merits, i.e. being selected as a result of 'buyer's independent judgement'.[13]

As with loyalty discounts and exclusive dealings, bundled discounts are generally less restrictive than tying: first, when products are 'tied together' customers face an explicit contractual condition (in the case of contractual tying) or an implicit contractual conditional (e.g. in the case of technological tying which makes the purchase of the tied product dependent on the purchase of the tying product). For bundling discounts this link is far less absolute. The customer merely forgoes the discount which, again, is not a penalty if a competitor is willing to match the discounted price.

Secondly, and related to the first point, bundled discounts do not necessarily imply an element of coercion. Such coercion would only be given if the discount were of such magnitude that it would be impossible for rivals to match the dominant firm's discounted prices. Only in an extreme form may bundled rebates have a similar effect to that of tying; they are generally less restrictive.

One final point: the tying analysis refers to a scenario where a firm active in the tying and the tied market faces competition in the tied market. By contrast, where competition takes place among bundles, one generally reaches the view that the components of that bundle are not 'separate products' and that consequently no 'tying' occurs. A similar logic applies to bundled discounts: where firms compete in bundles, the components of the bundle should be regarded as 'single items' discount, not as a bundled discount.

*4   Other discounts and selective pricing: the predation analogy*

Discounts (both single-item discounts and bundled discounts) may also raise antitrust concerns which are similar to predatory pricing in the sense that, hypothetically, 'equally efficient competitors' may be forced out of the market as a result of below-cost pricing.

As with predatory pricing, concerns about discounts with a viable quasi-predatory effect are based on strong asymmetry between the dominant firm on the one hand and its actual or potential competitors, for example with regard to size (where there are significant economies of scale), access to capital markets or reputation of brands. Despite general similarities, however, there are important differences between general predation and quasi-predatory discounts.

First, with general predation, sacrifices and predation occurs sequentially: the incumbent incurs losses in a particular market and recoups these losses at a later stage once existing competitors have been driven out of the market. This involves relatively high 'up-front' costs as well as a significant degree of uncertainty (i.e. whether exit will occur). With discounts with quasi-predatory effect by contrast, sacrifice and recoupment tend to occur simultaneously: for single-item discounts, losses are incurred at the marginal sales while recoupment takes pace at the infra-marginal sales; for bundled discounts, the losses are incurred with the products which are subject to intense competition and recouped with the products which are not subject to (intense) competition. As a result, quasi-predatory discounts are more likely to be sustainable given that recoupment takes place simultaneously and is not subject to the same degree of uncertainty.

The second difference relates to the plausibility of below-cost pricing. While (contrary to assumptions of many authorities) uniform below-cost pricing can have a certain benign explanation, e.g. in the context of multi-sided markets (not every discothèque which grants women free entrance, nor any newspaper which is fully financed by advertising, displays predatory intent), such explanations are not numerous. The situation is different for discounts: the fact that discounts lead to prices below costs (where discounts are attributed to certain types of products or certain marginal sales) may have many pro-competitive reasons. This means that 'below cost' discounts will occur much more frequently, but that in most cases there may be a pro-competitive explanation.

**C. Economic analysis**

*1   Overview*

The economic theory regarding discounts and selective pricing is in a state of flux. It is generally recognized that discounts are pervasive in many industry sectors, including sectors in which there are no dominant firms and where therefore discounts cannot be driven by anticompetitive considerations: 'nobody would claim that the coffee shop on the street corner offering a free expresso for every ten euro of sales is doing so with sinister exclusionary motives.'[14]

Indeed, most discounting practices have pro-competitive motives, ranging from economies of scale or scope to customer bargaining power and to the alignment of interests between manufacturers and distributors.

At the same time, there have been an increasing number of economic models showing that certain types of discounts can be anticompetitive. As Hovenkamp put it:

> in recent years, discounting practices have provided fertile soil for economic theory and the development and strategic rationales for discounting. The rationales are complex, however, and are often beyond the capability of a court to manage. In this respect the theory of anti-competitive discounting is in much the same position as the theory of predatory pricing was in the 1970s: no shortage of theories, but a frightening inability of courts to assess them.[15]

The remainder of this section explores the procompetitive and anti-competitive rationales for each of the three categories of discounts and selective pricing, namely (i) loyalty discounts, (ii) bundled discounts, and (iii) other types of discounts and selective pricing.

### 2   Loyalty (quasi-exclusivity) discounts
*(a) Pro-competitive rationales for loyalty (quasi-exclusivity) discounts*[16]
Loyalty discounts are vertical in nature and many of the pro-competitive rationales for exclusive dealings are equally applicable:

- *Aligning the interests of manufacturers and distributors:* the diverging interests of manufacturers and distributors may lead to problems, particularly where monitoring is difficult and costly. Loyalty discounts may be an efficient way to address this problem. For example, a manufacturer may need to provide costly training to a retailer (e.g. to enable them to offer a complementary service), but he may be reluctant to invest in such training unless he can ensure that it will benefit exclusively or predominantly his products. Loyalty discounts may be particularly important where monitoring is costly.
- *Risk allocation and solution to hold-up problems:* where suppliers require significant customer-specific investment (e.g. on-site plants of industrial minerals specifically dedicated to a paper mill), loyalty discounts (whether as exclusive discounts or as steep quantity discounts) provide a way to allocate risk between the supplier and

customer and to prevent hold-up problems, and may be an alternative to a take-or-pay obligation.

- *Increasing price competition at the downstream level:* fidelity discounts may increase price competition at the downstream level where customers (or retailers) are of different sizes. Market share discounts enable firms to provide similar discounts to buyers of different size which, assuming a competitive downstream market, would be passed on to the end-customer. They allow the manufacturers to lower prices at the margin while earning higher prices on 'infra-marginal' sales.
- *Customer bargaining power:* finally, what may look like a fidelity discount could actually be a buyer exercising his bargaining power, e.g. through an auction process whereby the lowest bidder wins all of the customer's business for a specified period.

*(b) Anti-competitive rationales for quasi-exclusivity discounts*   The economic literature has shown that in certain circumstances loyalty discounts may be an efficient way to exclude rivals.[17]

Loyalty discounts as exclusionary practice are based on the assumptions of (i) asymmetry between the firms, e.g. where one firm (the dominant firm) has an 'assured base' of sales and where competition is limited to the remainder of the market; and (ii) rival firms facing significant fixed costs. The dominant firm's assured base may be the result of a 'must-have' brand, other forms of strong product differentiation, capacity constraints of the dominant firm's rivals or switching costs.

In these circumstances, reducing demand through loyalty discounts may deprive the rivals of the dominant firm of the minimum viable scale and trigger exit or deter entry. As regards loyalty discounts as a means to entry deterrence, Spector presents two models where loyalty discounts may lead to entry deterrence where (i) the firms face many small customers which are unable to coordinate their behaviour and (ii) the firms are in a market with few bigger customers.

In the first model, the dominant firm simply offers each of the customers an exclusive contract in return for a small discount. Each of the customers then faces a prisoner's dilemma: if they could coordinate, they would all agree not to enter into an exclusive contract with the dominant firm and to benefit from lower prices as a result of the entry of a new firm. In the absence of coordination, each customer risks being worse off by not signing (and hence not benefiting from the loyalty discount), while a sufficient number of customers may sign up for exclusivity, such that entry by another firm would not be possible. This may lead to the situation of all customers signing up and the entrant being foreclosed.

In the second model, foreclosure arises by 'bribing' a sufficient number of the large customers (by offering them discounted price in return for exclusivity which is slightly more preferential than the price which would prevail after entry) such that the entrant is deprived of the minimum efficient scale, while charging the other customers the monopoly price.

A third model concerns loyalty discounts as a means of eviction. In the two previous models, the success of the loyalty discounts is dependent on the threat that an entrant would not be able to make a sufficient return to cover its fixed costs. However, where a rival is not a potential entrant but an actual competitor, it is likely to have already sunk its fixed costs, in which case the exclusionary strategy will not succeed in evicting him. In this case, there is only a role for loyalty discounts as an anticompetitive tool to the extent that there are recurrent fixed costs (new production facilities, advertising or R&D).

Pricing is a contractual mechanism and does not offer the same degree of commitments as other exclusionary measures. While there are ways to address this credibility problem at least partially (for example by building a reputation for aggressive responses), this nevertheless limits the effectiveness of discounts as an exclusionary tool.

### 3   Bundled (quasi-tying) discounts

*(a)   Pro-competitive rationales for bundled (quasi-tying) discounts*   As other forms of non-uniform pricing, bundled discounts are ubiquitous or, in the words of US DoJ and FTC, 'a common business practice'.[18] Bundling discounts serves a number of pro-competitive and welfare-enhancing purposes,[19] ranging from transaction and distribution cost savings to quality improvements, increased consumer convenience, increase in demand and price discrimination.

Costs savings in production and distribution are a key driver for many bundled discounts. Evans and Salinger give the example of cold remedies where customers have the choice between separate packages of pain relievers and decongestants and a cheaper integrated product:

> A customer who buys separate packages of pain relievers and decongestants pays $6.48 ($3.49 for the [pain relievers] and $2.99 for the decongestant) for a package of 24 CVS private label tablets. A customer pays $3.99 for a package of 24 CVS private label tablets that have the same dosage as the two separate packages. Therefore CVS charges 38 per cent less for the combination product than it does for the two separate products.[20]

According to Evans and Salinger, 'Given the high degree of competition, the CVS-branded price must reflect packaging, distribution and store-related fixed costs'.[21] The authors point in particular to the economies of packaging and the economies of combining drugs into a single tablet as an explanation for the discount.

Price discrimination is another benign explanation. As George Stigler observed in his Note on Block-booking,[22] where customers have different reservation prices for individual goods (e.g. one group valuing product A highly and product B lowly, and vice versa for a second group), bundling the two products averages different demand elasticities and allows the seller to capture a larger share of the consumer surplus.

An example may illustrate this point. Suppose there are two cinema goers. Customer 1 is willing to pay €10 to see 'The Chainsaw Massacre' and €2 for 'Sissy', while Customer 2 prefers romance and is willing to pay €4 to see 'The Chainsaw Massacre' and €11 for 'Sissy'. The marginal cost of showing each film is zero. Without bundling, the price for the films are €10 and €11, respectively, with Customer 1 watching 'The Chainsaw Massacre' and Customer 2 watching 'Sissy'. When the cinema introduces a double feature for €14, both customers buy the bundle. Customer 2 gets a surplus of €1 and the cinema's profit increases from €21 to €28.

*(b) Anti-competitive rationales for bundled (quasi-tying) discounts*
Recently the economic literature has come up with alternative, anticompetitive explanations for bundled discounts by dominant firms.[23] Two explanations, in particular, mirror the antitrust concerns raised by tying more general.

First, bundled discounts could create an equivalent effect to contractual tying. According to Rubinfeld, '[t]he "contractual tying" scenario is one in which a firm with monopoly power raises the standalone price of its monopoly product – presumably to some above-monopoly level – and then introduces a bundled rebate program offering a "sham" discount.'[24]

Rubinfeld uses the following example to illustrate the point:

> Suppose that a firm is selling its monopoly product A at a price of $100 and its non-monopoly product B at a price of $50. The firm then raises the standalone prices of products A and B by 10 per cent to $110 and $55, respectively. At the same time, the firm offers a 10 per cent rebate to all customers that buy the bundle of A and B. For those buying the bundle, the combined price remains $150. However, there is now an incentive for customers that bought A from the monopolist and B from a competitor to buy the bundle.[25]

Thus bundled discounts, in the same way as contractual tying, could be a mechanism for a dominant firm to extend its monopoly power into related markets and to foreclose competitors in those markets.

According to Rubinfeld, bundled discounts could be used as a means to create or raise barriers to entry, in particular where such discounts force rivals to offer each of the products to which the bundled discounts apply.

## 4 Other quasi-predatory discounts and selective pricing

### (a) Pro-competitive rationales for other discounts and selective pricing

Many of the pro-competitive rationales outlined for quasi-exclusivity and quasi-tying discounts are also applicable, in particular price discrimination, customer bargaining power and the alignment of manufacturers' and distributors' interest.

With *discrimination*, the existence of an assured base and a share of the market open to competition means that there are customers in the different price elasticises or that customers have different parts of their demand. The dominant firm would want to charge a higher price with respect to sales to the assured base (where customers are locked in, have a strong preference or no alternative) than to the share of the market open to competition (where customers are willing and able to switch to rival suppliers).

As mentioned in relation to fidelity discussions, non-linear and elective pricing will frequently be the result of customer bargaining power rather than an element in unilateral strategy. As such, discounts and rebate are a standard force of price competition.

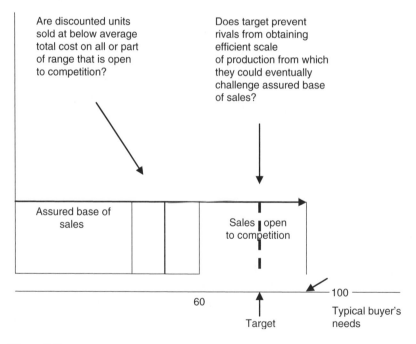

*Figure 7.2*

*(b) Anti-competitive rationales for other (quasi-predatory) discounts and selective pricing*   The potential anti-competitive rationale for quasi-predatory discounts mirror those quasi-exclusive discounts. The rationale is again based on the assumption that the dominant firm has an assured base of sales and that only part of the market is open to competition, i.e. is accessible to the dominant firm's rivals. Further assumptions are significant economies of scale, sale, network effects and/or first mover advantages.

In this scenario, discounts which would result in effective prices below cost if attributed solely to the share of the market which is open to competition could prevent entry (and/or induce exit) and could thereby allow the dominant firm to protect its assured base of sales. In this way the sacrifices incurred in the competitive part of the market would be recouped by the protected monopoly profits from the assured base.

As with the anticompetitive rationales for the other two types of discounts, the story of competitive harm also relies on very specific assumptions and equally faces a credibility problem (see Figure 7.2).

## 5   Conclusion
A number of general conclusions can be drawn from the economic analysis. First, loyalty discounts, bundled discounts and other forms of discounts are ubiquitous even in sectors where there are no dominant firms. There are numerous benign (i.e. welfare-enhancing) reasons for their existence, including cost savings, increased demand, customer convenience, price discrimination and solutions to principal–agency problems, which apply in a wide range of circumstances. In other words, discounts frequently lead to lower price, higher quality and expanding output, outcomes which competition is supposed to achieve.

Secondly, under certain conditions, all three types of discounts may have anticompetitive effects. Contrary to the efficiency-enhancing effects of discounts, the anticompetitive effects frequently rely on restrictive assumptions. Finally, there does not exist a simple set of criteria which clearly distinguish between benign and harmful discounts; in other words, there is a significant likelihood of enforcement errors.

## D.   Analytical framework
### 1   Analytical framework
This section considers how the economic analysis translates into legal rules for discounts and other forces of non-uniform pricing. Two aspects need particular consideration: (i) what is the optimal antitrust rule for discounts in light of the procompetitive and anticompetitive effects of discounts in isolation is; and (ii) how these rules relate to the rules on comparable non-price behaviour (such as exclusionary dealings or tying).

*(a) Error costs and direct enforcement cost*   It is increasingly recognized that some form of economic welfare[26] should be the benchmark for antitrust policy. In the context of discounting, this means that any legal rule should forbid discounting if, and only if, it lowers consumer welfare (or alternatively, total welfare). Or, put differently, any legal rule should minimize its enforcement costs and remedy its error costs and its administrative costs.

Any legal rule, and in particular any antitrust rule regarding discounts will be subject to two types of errors, namely 'false positives' (discounts which violate the legal rule even though it is benign) and 'false negatives' (discounts which do not violate the legal rule even though they are harmful). The administrative costs concern the costs of the agencies, the courts, the parties, etc. in dealing with the legal rule. In designing a policy with respect to discounts, policy makers face two fundamental trade-offs.

The first is the trade-off between false positives and false negatives. By making it harder (easier) to establish that discounts are illegal, authorities can reduce (increase) the risk of false positives in return for an increased (reduced) risk of false negatives.

The second trade-off is between error costs on the one hand and administrative costs on the other hand. Authorities are able, to some extent, to reduce both types of error by conducting a more detailed investigation (i.e. by considering more factors and reviewing more data). This means the authorities face a trade-off between error costs on the one hand and enforcement costs on the other.

Enforcement of antitrust works at two levels: first, at a direct level in the case under investigation. Antitrust, however, is also designed to have a deterrent effect through administrative fines, damages or loss of reputation (i.e. it is aimed at having an indirect effect on firms which are not currently subject to an investigation). Errors occur at both levels of enforcement. Given that the decision-making process is different at both levels (agencies and courts take decisions on the basis of significant information at the direct level, whereas firms unilaterally determine strategy and behaviour on the basis of their own know-how and market intelligence at the indirect level). The optimal trade-off between the various courts may also be different.

Key factors in deciding the optimal legal rule with respect to a particular behaviour are (i) the relative frequency of harmful effect to benign effect of niche behaviour (in our context, the frequency of pro-competitive discussions relate to anti-competitive discounts); (ii) the frequency of false positives and false negatives (i.e. how often a pro-competitive discount is to be regarded as anticompetitive and viceversa; and (iii) the cost of each type of error (in other words, how costly it is to prohibit procompetitive discounts and to allow anticompetitive discounts).

The greater the frequency of procompetitive relative to anticompetitive discounts, the greater the relative frequency of the false positives and the greater the cost of false positives, the more permissible should be the legal rule.

*(b) Consistency requirement*  Finally, it is also important to ensure that the legal rule in question does not distort business behaviour as a result of inconsistent treatment. For example, if the rules governing pricing abuses were more severe than those governing non-price abuses, there is little risk that prices would shift from one type of abuse to another merely for circumvention. The same consistency also has to be ensured in dealing with different forms of non-linear pricing.

*2  Implications from the analytical framework*
*(a) General aspects*  The conclusions from the economic analysis allows us to draw some general conclusions regarding the optimal legal rule for non-uniform pricing of dominant firms.

First and foremost, given that discounts (and indeed each type of discounts) are generally procompetitive and only sometimes anticompetitive, rebates should not be subject to a 'per se' prohibition; an effects-based analysis is called for.

Secondly, the widespread use of discounts and the risk of potentially stifling effects of an enforcement against a practice which generally leads to lower prices and increased output suggests the use of a 'safe harbour' as guidance for firms. For these safe harbours to be workable, they need to be based on information available to the dominant firm at the time of the pricing decision.

Thirdly, the appropriate legal rule needs to properly evaluate the likely harm to competition and ascertain the extent to which it might be compensated for by the reality or prospect of efficiencies. A 'structured' rule of reason approach may be appropriate in this regard.

Fourthly, as mentioned above, fidelity discounts should not be treated more harshly than exclusive dealings (in most cases more leniently as it is generally less restrictive). The same holds for bundled discounts and tying.

Finally certain forms of below-cost discounts should be prohibited to ensure consistency with predatory pricing.

It is useful to take a closer look at two of these conclusions, namely: (i) the issue of appropriate safe harbours; and (ii) the relevant factor for an effects-based analysis.

*(b) Relevant factors for the analysis*  Advocates of an effects-based approach towards tying have suggested a number of sectors to determine harm to competition and efficiencies.[27]

(i) HARM TO COMPETITION    Factors to determine competitive harm include, for example:

- *a plausible theory of competitive harm*: as a first step, the relevant antitrust authorities should be able to set out a plausible 'story' how a particular discount could lead to competitive harm, be it through quasi-tying, quasi-exclusivity or quasi-predation;
- *confirmation of the underlying assumptions*: the assumptions on which the theory is based (for example significant economies of scale) must be confirmed by the facts;
- *potential harm*: the authorities must demonstrate a possibility of harm, e.g. the possibility of excluding an equally efficient competitor (in the context of discounts, this may take the form of price/costs tests – see further below);
- *absence of alternative ways to compete*: it should also be shown that rivals of the dominant firm do not have alternative routes to the market which would allow them to become viable competitors, nor alternative ways to compete (e.g. through product differentiations);
- *actual or likely impact*: it should be demonstrated that discounts have an actual or likely impact in the market; where it cannot be shown that a decline in rivals' market shares has occurred (or is likely to occur), an impact should not be presumed.

(ii) EFFICIENCIES    Factors which would demonstrate efficiencies are as follows:

- *plausible story of efficiencies*: as has been explained, in general it will not be too difficult to establish a plausible story explaining why discounts lead to efficiencies; and
- *behaviour of non-dominant firms*: the use of similar discounts by non-dominant firms in the same market is a strong indicator for efficiencies.

*(c) Standard and burden of proof: balancing harm and efficiencies*    A policy of a per se prohibition towards discounts, and even potentially anti-competitive discounts, is clearly inappropriate. This still leaves a wide range of possible 'effects-based' approaches, with different evidential requirements for harm to competition and balancing mechanisms. For example, a policy with a high evidential requirement for efficiency, a low evidential requirement for competitive harm and a balancing mechanism tilted towards prohibition (for example by shifting the burden of proof of a net benefit to the dominant firm), is in practice very similar to a policy of per se prohibition.

- Conduct permissible as long as plausible efficiency explanation

- Conduct permissible as long as likely efficiency explanation

- Burden of balancing likely harm and efficiencies on Commission

- Structured rule of reason

- Burden of balancing likely harm and efficiencies on dominant firm

- Conduct prohibited as long as harm is likely

- Conduct prohibited as long as harm is plausible

*Figure 7.3*

Given that quasi-exclusive, quasi-tying and quasi-predatory discounts and rebates are ubiquitous, even among non-dominant firms, that discounts are likely to be anticompetitive only in limited circumstances and that the costs of false positives are relatively high (i.e., namely a shifting of price competition), the error cost analysis strongly suggests a policy which is closer to a per se permission rather than a per se prohibition (see Figure 7.3).

*One final point*: antitrust in general, and antitrust policy with respect to discounts in particular, lacks the precision to operate an unstructured rule of reason (which would quantify competitive harm and efficiencies and truly balance the two effects). A structured rule of reason (which develops certain screens which in turn lead to certain presumptions and where balancing only occurs in a very limited number of cases) may be more realistic.

*(d) Safe harbours*    One way to define a safe harbour in relation to pricing by dominant firms is by way of the 'equally efficient competitor' test, according to which conduct is regarded as exclusionary (and hence potentially problematic) if it is 'likely in the circumstances to exclude from the defendant's market an equally or more efficient competitor'.[28] This test is based on the idea that firms should not be punished for being more efficient (i.e. having lower costs than their competitors), and this has been widely used in US predatory pricing cases. Applying the 'equally efficient com-

petitor' test to discounts and selective pricing would lead to the safe harbour for single item discounts, independently of whether the discount or selective pricing is 'quasi-exclusivity' or 'quasi-predatory': it would be regarded as lawful as long as the net price (i.e. the price after all discounts are considered) exceeds the dominant firm's relevant cost threshold (generally marginal costs or average variable costs (AVC)).

For bundled (or quasi-tying) discounts, the 'equally efficient competitor' test leads to a different result, as the requirement of net price above the appropriate level of costs does not necessarily ensure the survival of an equally efficient competitor. Here a discount or selective pricing would be regarded as lawful, as long as the net price of the allegedly 'tied product' in the bundle is above the dominant firm's relevant cost threshold (marginal cost or average variable cost), where the 'net price' is the competitive price of the tied product minus the entire discount on all products in the relevant bundle.

The 'equally efficient competitor' test provides a clear safe haven based on information available to the firms in question at the time of their pricing decision. Furthermore the approach is consistent (at least in the US). The advantage of a clear and clearly administrable safe haven comes at the price of some under-deterrence, in other words at the price of certain false negatives. Examples have been listed in Section C above and relate to scenarios (i) where entrants are originally less efficient but could be expected to become equally efficient over time (e.g. through growth or increased learning) or (ii) where entry even by a permanently less efficient competitor may increase consumer welfare. There are alternative approaches, which protect some form of 'managed entry' (e.g. by distinguishing between an assured base and a contestable part of the market or by taking account of the difference in size between the dominant incumbent and the new entrant). However, these alternative approaches do not draw a clear line between lawful and unlawful behaviour, and induce firms to use antitrust as a protection against price competition.

As Hovenkamp pointed out, the issue is similar to the question of 'whether "above cost" prices could ever be found predatory under the antitrust laws'.

> Briefly the answer was (1) yes, it is possible to model situations in which above cost prices can be exclusionary and certainly in the situation where the dominant firm had attained scale economies that lower output rivals could not; but (2) the antitrust laws should not be used to attack above cost predatory pricing because (a) once the courts permit above cost prices to be condemned as predatory there will be no shortage of rivals who wish to attack them; and (b) antitrust is a blunt instrument for dealing with pricing claims, producing far too many false positives; so (c) a rule condemning above cost pricing as predatory would chill far too much behaviour that is entirely pro-competitive.[29]

### E. The law on rebates and selective discounts: general issues

*1   Overview*

The North American competition authorities and courts have tended to adopt a much more pragmatic approach towards rebates and discounts: whilst discounts that are explicitly conditioned on outright exclusivity may be condemned, less aggressive discounting structures are analysed on their merits and are only likely to be condemned where a real adverse effect on competition has arisen. By contrast, the European institutions, especially the European Commission, have tended to be much more doctrinaire in their approach, appearing to analyse discounts by reference to their structure rather than to their effects: the tendency is to say a discount has this structure, therefore it is exclusionary – even if there is manifest evidence that this is not the case. Whereas certain 'features' of a discount system may be determinative in condemning a discount scheme in the EC, US and Canadian antitrust law is much more concerned with establishing an actual adverse effect on competition arising from such a scheme.[30] Thus there appears to be a marked difference in analytical approach between the respective jurisdictions.[31]

*2   Legal standards and institutional structures*

Although US anti-trust law is *potentially broader in scope* than EC law insofar as it expressly prohibits the holding of a monopoly as well as the abuse of a monopoly, the way in which the US courts have interpreted §2 is *much narrower in practice*[32] than EC law as it has been applied to firms only with much higher market shares and the scope of the offence of 'monopolization' is substantially narrower than that of Article 82. The narrow interpretation of §2 can, in part, be explained by the difficulties encountered in attempting to distinguish procompetitive and anticompetitive use of discounts and the need to minimize the resultant risk of error costs, and in part by the prominent role played by private enforcement in the US.

Competition laws around the world combine in various ways and involve administrative and/or judicial systems of enforcement to different extents: in the US and Canada they are enforced primarily through a judicial system,[33] in the EC primarily through an administrative system.[34] A former official of the US Department of Justice has noted that its actions must always face

> the crucible of cross-examination before an independent fact-finder [whereas] in Europe, the Commission is sometimes said to act as investigator, prosecutor, judge, and jury as judicial review is slow and highly deferential to the Commission's factual determinations.[35]

In the EC the Commission (and after 1 May 2004 the competition authorities of the Member States) is the 'gatekeeper' of enforcement; as such, it is largely responsible for the selection of cases under Article 82 and, in the first instance, developing substantive criteria and imposing remedies. Whereas, in the US, the courts actually take the decision to enjoin and sanction conduct, in the EC the current system of judicial review of Article 82 decisions is generally considered to be unsatisfactory and ineffective.[36]

While public enforcement bodies on both sides of the Atlantic have become increasingly skilled in deploying economic analysis and using consumer welfare as their criteria for bringing or not bringing cases, plaintiffs are not motivated by such considerations and are driven by the prospect of adequate compensation. In the US the high level of private enforcement is driven mainly by the prospect of treble damages. Consequently the interpretation of US law has been highly influenced by 'indirect effects' of private litigation such as stifling pro-consumer forms of price competition.[37] The need for similar caution in the application of EC law has not yet presented itself: compensatory damages are not trebled and private enforcement remains largely underdeveloped.[38]

### 3  The degree of market power and abuse

The degree of market power required for the control of unilateral conduct and the consequences of such a finding differ across the Atlantic. As regards the degree of market power, although similar methods of analysis are used in both the US and the EC,[39] the US standard has generally been applied at a significantly higher share of a defined market.[40] A separate point is that a finding of market power, or rather dominance, in the EC means such firms have a 'special responsibility' not to allow their conduct to impair genuine undistorted competition[41] on account of the perceived prejudice that their activities may cause to the interests of competitors, customers or consumers.

Once sufficient market power has been established in Europe and North America, the extent of a firm's market power vis-à-vis its competitors should inform and influence the subsequent analysis of allegedly exclusionary behaviour.[42] In the US the standards of monopolization tend to be calibrated against their effects on the market, so that conduct of a firm with a particularly strong market position is more likely (but not necessarily) to have an appreciable impact on the market.[43] In the EC, however, the Commission and the Courts perceive there to be a set of 'per se' rules against discounts in particular – under which anticompetitive object equals anticompetitive effect[44] – with the consequence that every dominant firm (irrespective of the extent of their economic strength) is subject to the same set of rules. This is noticeably at odds with the idea that the 'special responsibility' of dominant companies should be considered in the light of the specific circumstances of each case.[45]

### F. US law on discounts and selective price cuts

*1   Description*

*(a) Overview*   'Under the best of circumstances, applying the requirements of §2 can be difficult because the means of illicit exclusion, like the means of legitimate competition are myriad.'[46] Added to this difficulty, when hearing actions challenging the conduct of monopolists, US courts are very concerned about the risks of undue regulatory intervention and unjustified private litigation deterring beneficial price competition.[47] Consequently US antitrust law is unwilling to presume that discounts are anticompetitive. Instead a case-by-case approach has been developed, concentrating very much on the effect that a pricing practice has, rather than its form.

When attempting to distinguish between procompetitive and anticompetitive discounts, US law has so far drawn a useful distinction between discounts offered on single products (whether they are quasi-exclusivity discounts or other forms of discounts), on the one hand, and discounts offered on multiple products (commonly referred to as 'bundled discounts'), on the other. As we shall see, the standard applying to single-products discounts is relatively clear, whereas the correct analysis of bundled discounts continues to be subject to much debate.

*(b) Quasi-exclusivity/loyalty discounts*   The US courts have refused to condemn discounts allegedly designed to induce loyalty, by, for example, calculating the discount by reference to the amount by which customers' purchases exceed their purchases in the previous year.[48]

Loyalty discounts are typically assessed under the conventional price/cost tests established by the Supreme Court in *Brooke Group*, requiring proof that the dominant firm priced below an 'appropriate' measure of cost and that the firm had a reasonable prospect of recouping its investment in below-cost prices.[49] Alternatively loyalty discounts may fall within the mischief of §2 insofar as they actually result in the same effect as an unlawful exclusive dealing agreement. The *Concord Boat*[50] aptly demonstrates the approach adopted by the US courts.[51] The Eighth Circuit Court of Appeals gave judgment in favour of Brunswick, the dominant stern drive engine manufacturer, because there was insufficient factual and expert evidence to support the finding that its discounts had monopolized the market.[52] Significantly the Court perceived that the Supreme Court judgment in *Brooke Group* had drawn a bright line in favour of vigorous price competition, even by firms with market power, and that therefore courts should be sceptical of antitrust claims based on discounting. It stated that 'If a firm has discounted prices to a level that remains above the firm's average variable cost, the plaintiff must overcome a strong presumption of legality by showing other factors indicating that the price charged is anti-competitive.'[53]

The judgment in *Concord Boat* accurately reflects the belief, widely held in the US, that loyalty discounts and other discounts having similar effects to exclusive dealing have procompetitive effects and that any anticompetitive effects will depend upon the particular circumstances of the schemes and the relative market power of the firm in question.

*(c) Quasi-tying/bundled discounts*  While single item discounts have been assessed under a generally accepted standard, the legal position is more complicated in the case of multi-product discounts.[54] A prominent case in point is the controversial ruling of the Third Circuit Court of Appeals in *3M v. LePage's*.[55]

On the facts of this case,[56] 3M conceded that it had a monopoly in the transparent tape market; the key question was whether 3M had wilfully acquired or maintained its monopoly. The jury returned a verdict for LePage's on the §2 claims, awarding damages of more than $22 million (before trebling) on each claim. A divided panel of the Court of Appeals reversed the district court's denial of 3M's motion for judgment as a matter of law in relation to the maintenance of monopoly claim. Subsequently a divided en banc Court of Appeals affirmed the monopoly maintenance judgment.[57]

Although 3M's bundled discount scheme did not amount to predatory pricing under the rule in *Brooke Group*,[58] 3M's strategy resulted in de facto exclusive dealing contrary to §2. The case is controversial for many reasons, not least because it suggests that a monopolist in one product may not use bundled discounts. However it is also not entirely clear on what basis the Third Circuit found 3M liable.[59] In the Court of Appeals' view, the anticompetitive effects of bundled discounts were 'best compared with tying', where the vice is coercion of customers[60] and the foreclosure of the market to any competitor who does not manufacture an equally diverse group of products. It is open to question whether there was sufficient evidence for the jury to find that LePage's was as efficient as 3M or that it could not have made comparable offers. Moreover the judgment sparked further controversy by narrowly confining the possible valid business justifications in this field. The Supreme Court denied permission to appeal.[61]

*(d) Other (single item) discounts*  In addition to loyalty discounts, dominant firms may engage in a wide variety of (single item) discounting practices. Frequently firms may offer standardized volume discounts and quantity discounts with a view to stealing a march on its competitors and winning new customers. To decide whether such run-of-the-mill discounts are exclusionary, US law seeks to determine whether such price cuts make consumers worse off by unsustainably reducing the price below an

appropriate measure of cost. In other words, a predation standard is applied to determine whether the price cut should be treated as impermissibly exclusionary and thus unlawful. The judgment of the First Circuit Court of Appeals in *Barry Wright* v. *ITT Grinnell*[62] provides a good illustration of the US approach to such run-of-the-mill discounts. The case concerned the lawfulness of discounts granted by Pacific, a manufacturer of 'snubbers' which are used in pipe systems for nuclear power plants, to secure the loyalty of Grinell, a customer accounting for about 50% of snubber purchases in the US.[63] Both the district court and the court of appeals rejected a claim of a violation of §2 because the discount offered was not predatory.[64] The theoretical possibility that Pacific's discounted prices could harm competition did not justify the risk of deterring procompetitive price cutting by entertaining that possibility in litigation. Accordingly Judge Breyer (as he then was) stated that:

> above-cost price cuts are typically sustainable; that they are normally desirable (particularly in concentrated industries); that the 'disciplinary cut' is difficult to distinguish in practice; that it, in any event, primarily injures only higher cost competitors; that its presence may well be 'wrongly' asserted in a host of cases involving legitimate competition; and that to allow its assertion threatens to 'chill' highly desirable pro-competitive price cutting.[65]

*(e) Assessment of the US case law*    For a long time, there was no settled view within the US as to the terms upon which the monopolization standard should be applied to pricing practices.[66] However it is now clear that the conventional price/cost tests for predatory pricing established in *Brooke Group* apply to single-product discounts.[67] The test is supported by mainstream economic analysis, consistent with the law on exclusive dealing and predation, and helps secure legal certainty. It also makes clear that the US antitrust law's goal is efficiency-maximization. Contemporary §2 jurisprudence does not seek to protect those smaller competitors who are less efficient than the dominant firm, thereby offering an appropriate safe harbour by applying an 'equally efficient competitor' test.[68] US law, it seems, is more willing to accept the risk of false negatives given (i) the inherent difficulties of trying to distinguish legitimate and illegitimate price competition and (ii) the concerns about undue regulatory intervention and unjustified private litigation chilling beneficial price competition.

At the time of writing, the standard applied to bundled discounts is much less clear. A debate has arisen as to whether and to what extent the grant of such discounts should be controlled. The judgment in *LePage's* indicates that the US courts have not yet developed a workable and economically robust standard for assessing such behaviour, bearing in mind the need to avoid the application of §2 chilling the competitive dynamism and efficiency-enhancing behaviour of dominant firms. As former Assistant Attorney-General Pate has stated:

> In general, we in the United States are certainly open to the possible procompetitive effects of bundled rebates, bundled pricing, fidelity discounts, whichever term you would like to use, and certainly not in favour of using per se rules to address this sort of conduct.[69]

It is likely to be for this reason in *LePage's* (quite apart from the evidential difficulties in that case) that the US enforcement agencies submitted to the Supreme Court that 'at this juncture, it would be preferable to allow the case law and economic analysis to develop further and to await a case with a record better adapted to development of an appropriate standard'.[70]

## G. EU law on discounts and selective price cuts
### 1 Description
*(a) Overview* Article 82 does not specifically state that offering discounts and rebates to customers is abusive: however, case law of the European Court of Justice (ECJ) and the Court of First Instance (CFI) has established that discounts and rebates may constitute an abuse. There is no comprehensive, clear and unambiguous statement on the interests protected by Article 82 in the case law on Article 82. Rather the practices condemned, the interests protected and the objectives pursued by the Commission in enforcing that provision, as well as the Court's interpretation thereof, reflected a patchwork quilt of rules that have tended to be ad hoc assessments rather than parts of a coherent analytical framework. Historically there is much to be said for the rather circular view that Article 82 simply prohibits the practices which the Commission deems to be incompatible with the common market, subject, of course, to judicial review.

*(b) Quasi-exclusivity/loyalty discounts* The ECJ has held that Article 82 prohibits dominant firms from lawfully entering into exclusive dealing agreements with a customer.[71] That being so, the Commission and the Community Courts applied Article 82 to loyalty discounts having an equivalent effect to exclusive dealing.[72] Thus, EC law on discounts has emerged from the prohibition on exclusive dealing and thus, unlike US law, cost concepts have not been deployed and the predatory pricing rule in *AKZO* v. *Commission* has not been applied.

Loyalty discounts were famously condemned by the ECJ in its seminal judgment in *Hoffmann-La Roche* v. *Commission*.[73] That case was primarily concerned with 'loyalty' discounts offered by Roche to customers who agreed to take all or substantially all of their vitamin requirements from Roche. The ECJ held that, where a dominant firm offers discounts to a customer in return for the latter's loyalty, this can amount to an abuse of a dominant position.[74] The underlying competition concern was one of anti-competitive exclusion, i.e. that such pricing practices limit a customer's choice of supplier and make access to the market more difficult for competitors.[75] The principle enunciated in *Hoffman-La Roche* has recently been affirmed and applied by the CFI in the well-known and controversial case: *British Airways* v. *Commission*.[76]

In *Virgin/British Airways*, the Commission,[77] upheld by the Court, found that British Airways (BA) had abused its dominant position by offering fidelity-building payments to travel agents, over and above their basic commission on selling BA tickets, as a reward for increasing marketing and ticket sales. Seemingly, the primary problem with the incentive scheme lay in the

> progressive nature [of the performance reward scheme] with a very noticeable effect at the margin, the increased commission rates were capable of rising exponentially from one reference period to another, as the number of BA tickets sold by agents during successive reference periods progressed.[78]

As a result, the Court held that this structure created a powerful and unlawful pull in favour of BA,[79] and found that BA's schemes were likely to have a restrictive and concrete effect on the UK markets for air travel agency services and air transport.[80] The Court's assessment of abuse was not affected by the fact that BA's share of the market fell consistently during the operation of the scheme and, by 1999, stood at less than 40% of the relevant market.[81] British Airway's loss of market share could not evidence a lack of competitive impact because, in the Court's view, competitors could have gained an even greater proportion of the market in the absence of the scheme. Finally BA was unable to substantiate any cost justification for its performance reward schemes with the required degree of precision. Consequently, the Court held the schemes had an exclusionary effect and thus fell within the mischief under Article 82 EC.[82]

The Commission has also extended the application of Article 82 to situations in which the dominant firm did not actually make the discount conditional on exclusivity, but rather set a volume target individually for each customer which could be met, in practice, only if the customer acted as if the discount were conditional upon him acquiring the whole of his requirements from the dominant firm.[83] These considerations have been applied, by analogy, to discounts aggregated on overall purchases of different products. Discounts granted on a customer's marginal requirements are yet another variant of discounts which are likely to be impermissible under Article 82.[84]

*(c) Quasi-tying/bundled discounts*   A system of discounts on overall purchases of different products may give rise to concerns under Community

competition law, although such schemes have received comparatively less attention (and enforcement scrutiny) to date. However bundled discounts are likely to give rise to two broad concerns under EU law:

- dissuading customers from acquiring products from, and thus fore-closing, competing suppliers; and/or
- being the functional equivalent of tying arrangements, where the objection is primarily directed to its effect on competition in the market for the tied product.

In *Hoffmann-La Roche* v. *Commission*[85] the ECJ upheld the Commission's decision objecting to discounts offered by Hoffmann-La Roche to those customers who acquired a portfolio of its vitamin products. The Court found that the discount scheme was exclusionary insofar as it discouraged customers from purchasing an individual vitamin from Roche's competitors and that bundled pricing was the functional equivalent of tying and thus contrary to Article 82(d).

Bundled discounts have mainly been addressed in cases which have raised other competition concerns. Among the interesting practices considered in *Hilti*,[86] for example, the Commission (and the Court) found that reduced discounts on nail gun cartridge-only orders constituted an abuse of a dominant position, since the avowed purpose of such a pricing policy was to make the sale of cartridge strips conditional upon purchasing a corresponding amount of nails.[87] Such a bundled pricing policy was found to have the object or effect of excluding competing nail makers.

A more recent example of the Commission's enforcement activity against bundled discounts is provided by its recent investigation into the pricing practices of Coca-Cola and its bottlers in the supply of carbonated soft drinks to supermarkets and the HORECA sector. Of particular interest for these purposes are the concerns the Commission expressed in relation to the 'range provisions' which Coca-Cola used to offer significant discounts to customers who purchased an entire range of drinks cabinets for different products and distribution channels.[88]

Notwithstanding these concerns, however, on 22 June 2005 the Commission closed its five-year investigation and accepted a commitment from Coca-Cola to exclude purchases of non-cola flavoured drinks in the discount calculation for cola-flavoured drinks. It is important to note that this decision is without prejudice to whether the bundled pricing practices at issue actually constituted an infringement of Article 82.[89] Together with the publication of the Commission Discussion Paper, discussed below, and the strong possibility of a more refined approach to the assessment of discounts, the *Coca-Cola* commitments decision indicates that enforcement activity towards bundled discounts is likely to continue to evolve.

*(d) Other discounts/selective price-cutting*   Other types of discounts and selective price cuts have also been subject to scrutiny under Community competition law. It had been thought (following the ruling in *Hoffmann-La Roche*) that unconditional discounts (i.e. quantity discounts exclusively linked with the volume of purchases from the producer concerned) were lawful 'per se' under Article 82. However the CFI's judgment in *Michelin II* condemned a discount scheme expressed purely in volume terms and which did not discriminate between customers with identical volumes. *Michelin II* tends to confirm the tendency of the Community judicature to treat certain types of conduct as exclusionary by virtue of their structure. The ECJ's judgment in *Compagnie Maritime Belge Transport*[90] is also significant for the treatment of selective price cuts, although not involving net losses, under EC law. Both cases will be discussed below.

The judgment in *Michelin II* makes clear that the ECJ in *Hoffmann-La Roche* did not exhaustively define the categories of abusive loyalty discounts. In *Michelin II* the CFI upheld a Commission decision imposing a fine of €19.76 million on la Manufacture Française de Pneumatiques Michelin for having abused its dominant position in replacement tyres for heavy vehicles in France. In particular the Commission objected to the offer of 'a complex system of rebates, discounts and/or various financial benefits whose main objective was to tie resellers to it and to maintain its market shares'.[91] The CFI held that 'the mere fact of characterising a discount system as quantity rebates does not mean that the grant of such discounts is compatible with Article 82 EC',[92] hence the particular circumstances in which a discount is granted must be carefully investigated. The Court applied the following test to determine the lawfulness of the discounts:

> according to settled case-law, a discount system which seeks to tie dealers to an undertaking in a dominant position by granting advantages which are not based on a countervailing economic advantage and to prevent those dealers from obtaining their supplies from the undertaking's competitors infringes Article 82 EC.[93]

Perhaps most strikingly in the case of Michelin's standardized quantity discounts, the CFI noted that the discounts were calculated on the dealer's entire turnover over a one-year period and that there was a noticeable effect at the margin (reaching each sales target meant extra commission on all, not just incremental, sales). This being so, the CFI held that the discounts 'built', or rather induced, the loyalty of its dealers to sell more and more Michelin tyres from one year to the next.[94]

A further case of importance for EC law on above-cost selective price cuts is *Compagnie Maritime Belge Transports* v. *Commission*.[95] One of the most contentious issues in the case concerned the pricing practices adopted by the members of a shipping liner conference, Cewal, to drive out its principal competitor on routes between Europe and West and Central Africa. In contrast to the below-cost selling at issue in *AKZO* v. *Commission*,[96] the practice known as 'fighting ships' applied by Cewal was above cost but was specifically aimed at sailings of its competitor and involved a decrease in earnings for the members of Cewal. In the Commission's view, as upheld by the Community Courts, the selective price cuts employed by Cewal members, although they did not involve net losses, still constituted an abuse contrary to Article 82. The discounts did not constitute a proportionate reaction by a dominant undertaking to competition presented by the entry onto its market of a new competitor. As has been examined elsewhere,[97] *Compagnie Maritime Belge* was in many ways an exceptional case, but it reiterates a point of general significance in contemporary EC law: that costs are not (yet) the decisive criterion for determining whether price cuts by a dominant undertaking are abusive.[98] Self-evidently the judgment of the Court in *AKZO* v. *Commission* does not preclude the application of Article 82 to cases where a dominant firm engages in selective price cutting even though its prices remain above its costs.

## 2   Assessment of the EC case law

It is important to note that EC law on discounts grew out of the ruling in *Hoffmann-La Roche* that it is unlawful for a dominant firm to enter into an exclusive dealing agreement with a customer.[99] An assumption is generally made that the buyer is committed to buying the quantity that is necessary to receive the rebate. However, unlike exclusive dealing, the competitors of a dominant company always have the possibility of matching (or, indeed, improving upon) the discounts offered by a dominant undertaking. Whether they are in fact able to do so mostly depends, of course, upon their relative efficiency, and the relationship between the discount and the costs of the dominant company and its competitors.[100] Moreover, the analogy to exclusive dealing overlooks the fact that discounts are a form of price competition and should, in principle, be analysed like other pricing practices. A further source of criticism has been the tendency on the part of the Commission and the Community Courts to treat quasi-exclusivity discounts as unlawful 'per se'.[101] By upholding the decisions of the Commission in *Michelin II* and *British Airways* the CFI has given the Commission great control over the discounting policies of dominant companies. While this may be understandable in light of the pre-existing case law of the ECJ on loyalty discounts, as has been pointed out by other commentators, it creates a serious disincentive for dominant firms to engage in procompetitive pricing.[102]

As regards both loyalty discounts and bundled discounts, there appears to be an inconsistency between the rules on bundled discounts, on the one hand, and tying, on the other; it is important for future EC practice to acknowledge that, in most cases, loyalty discounts and bundled discounts are less restrictive than tying.

The case law and decisional practice on all types of discounts has also been criticized for adopting an unduly restrictive approach to efficiencies. In the past, rebates were permissible only if they were restricted to passing on cost savings to the buyer, otherwise they were deemed to unlawfully limit the advantage for the buyer in choosing another supplier's product. However, there are signs in the Commission's Discussion Paper, discussed below, that the EC may be becoming more receptive to an efficiency defence on the part of the dominant firm.

Finally it should be acknowledged that there is no per se prohibition of non-discriminatory prices which does not entail below-cost sales. It is clear from cases such as *Hilti* and *Compagnie Maritime Belge* that there is not (yet) a clear safe harbour for above-cost selective price-cutting creating a risk of overenforcement and the potential chilling of beneficial price competition.[103]

## H. The Commission Discussion Paper[104]

### 1   Description

*(a) Overview*   The European Commission has recognized the need to review the law and policy under Article 82, launching an internal review in 2003 which resulted in the publication of a Directorate-General Competition Discussion Paper in December 2005. The Discussion Paper should precipitate a period of extensive public consultation, which is likely to result in further reflection by the Commission. At the time of writing, there is no official guarantee that the Paper will result in the adoption of official Guidelines on the application of Article 82 or that the principles contained therein will necessarily alter the Commission's enforcement priorities in the future.[105] Rather it appears to be the first step in a process of piecemeal reform of the law and policy under Article 82.

*(b) 'Consumer welfare' should be the primary objective of Article 82*   It is often suggested that the Commission and the Court have applied and interpreted Article 82 with a view to protect competitors rather than the competitive process, thereby seeming to suggest that the Community's competition policy vis-à-vis dominant firms is necessarily different in purpose and scope from other systems of antitrust law. Contrary to that view, the Discussion Paper clearly indicates that:

● Article 82 (at least as far as exclusionary abuses are concerned) shares the same aim of most systems of competition law, namely the protection of consumer welfare by promoting the activities of efficient firms, whether or not they hold a dominant position.[106]

- A dominant firm is entitled to 'compete on the merits'[107] which, in relation to pricing abuses, means a dominant firm is entitled to out-perform less efficient competitors.[108, 109]

*(d) Proposed assessment of quasi-exclusivity discounts*   Most pricing abuses concern themselves, to a greater or lesser extent, with a cost–price analysis. Whereas the case law on rebates is derived from the prohibition on exclusive dealing, the Discussion Paper takes a welcome step forward insofar as it introduces price–cost standards for the analysis of both rebates which are conditional upon a customer's buying behaviour and those that are unconditional.[110] In this section, we intend to focus on conditional discounts on all of a customer's purchases, or in other words, 'retrospective or quasi-exclusivity discounts', since these continue to be subject to the closest scrutiny under the standard set forth in the Discussion Paper.[111]

*(e) DG Competition's Approach*   The Discussion Paper begins by rehearsing some of the factors which have characterized the strict scrutiny of rebates to date.[112] DG Competition then purports to break away from the earlier jurisprudence by introducing an economic model that seeks to assess the foreclosing effect of the rebate on commercially viable amounts supplied by competitors as efficient as the dominant company. DG Competition is concerned about those rebates which enable a dominant undertaking to use the non-contestable portion of demand of each customer (the amount which would supposedly be purchased from the dominant company in any event) as leverage to abusively discount the price for the proportion of demand open to competition (i.e. the 'contestable' portion of demand), resulting in possible foreclosure.[113] In this regard, it is not the last unit before the rebate is triggered that is relevant to this assessment but rather commercially viable amounts supplied by efficient competitors and entrants.

The touchstone of the proposed assessment of the rebate is the 'effective price' offered by the dominant company, which is calculated by allocating the whole discount to the contested portion of demand. Where the effective price is below the average total cost of the dominant company, the Discussion Paper considers it may be difficult for competitors as efficient as the dominant company to compete for the contestable portion of demand.

*The 'required share' v. the 'commercially viable share'*   However the contestable proportion of demand is often difficult to calculate in practice. That being so, the Discussion Paper seeks to calculate what the contested portion would be if the effective price were equal to the dominant firm's average total costs, termed the 'required share'. The Paper then compares the required share with the commercially viable share per customer, that is, the share of the market that an entrant can reasonably be expected to capture.[114] Where the required share is larger than the commercially viable share, the rebate scheme is presumed to have a foreclosure effect.

Where the required share exceeds the commercially viable share per customer, paragraph 162 of the Discussion Paper establishes a rebuttable presumption of an abuse if: the rebate threshold is an individualized volume or percentage target; the rebate scheme affects a substantial part of demand in the market; and there is no clear indication of a lack of foreclosure effect.[115] The evidential burden then shifts on to the dominant company to show that there is no evidence of possible foreclosure or there is a justification or efficiency defence in favour of the impugned rebate scheme.

In cases where it is not possible to calculate the 'required share' or 'commercially viable share', DG Competition appears to revert to a qualitative (and wholly subjective) assessment of whether 'the rebate system hinders expansion or entry by competitors'.[116]

In exceptional circumstances, in cases where the rebated price is above average total cost, DG Competition reserves the right to take enforcement action where it is concerned that there might nonetheless be a market-distorting foreclosure effect. In particular, DG Competition may depart from the price–cost standard where it appears that entrants may not be as efficient as a dominant company due to certain scale or learning disadvantages which may only be overcome with time.[117]

### 2   Preliminary Assessment of the Discussion Paper

The Discussion Paper should be welcomed in taking a step away from the overly formalistic case law and decisional practice and positively introduce economic analysis, and in particular cost concepts, into the assessment of rebates. The Discussion Paper explicitly shifts the analysis beyond form and away from treating all conditional rebates as the functional equivalent of exclusive dealing. A very good illustration of the shift is the relevance of the reference period for calculating rebates. Whereas the CFI held in *Michelin II* that 'the longer the reference period, the more loyalty-inducing the quantity rebate system',[118] the Discussion Paper correctly states that 'in most cases the length of the reference period has no bearing on the loyalty enhancing effect'.[119] In our view, however, while the analysis has moved in the right direction, it has not yet moved far enough.

As a general observation, and contrary to the insights of the analytical framework above, the Discussion Paper appears to adopt an unduly strict treatment of conditional rebates on all purchases which may have unintended adverse consequences for consumer welfare.[120] As noted above, rebates are ubiquitous and are generally procompetitive. Furthermore there are numerous efficiency-enhancing reasons for the grant of rebates by dominant companies which should not be dismissed or disregarded out of hand. That being so, it is vital that the Commission's future approach to rebates should not overestimate the risks of anticompetitive outcomes and should avoid an overinclusive application of Article 82 which chills the efficiency-enhancing behaviour of dominant firms.

Despite the absence of a perfect touchstone, DG Competition correctly looks to the relation of the discounted price to a measure of costs as a way of segregating rebates that are abusive from those that are not. DG Competition has chosen ATC as the relevant cost benchmark for determining whether the discounted price for contestable sales is abusive. The reason given for using this benchmark is that rebates can be exclusionary for a long time without a profit sacrifice on the part of the dominant company.[121] It is submitted that the average total costs standard is inappropriate and unduly restrictive.

A rebate that leaves prices above average avoidable costs (AAC) is moving prices in the right direction (in the absence of any plan to eliminate a competitor[122]) and should not be presumed to exclude equally efficient competitors. Moreover the below AAC test is a useful way of separating economically harmful price cutting from the more frequent price cutting which benefits consumers.[123] That being so, the appropriate price–cost benchmark should be average avoidable cost.[124] One can understand the intuitive idea behind this benchmark since it is also consistent with the 'as efficient competitor' standard proposed by the Discussion Paper for assessing pricing abuses.[125] That standard clearly implies that competition law should not seek to protect those, (smaller), competitors who are less efficient than the dominant firm.[126] That standard also has the merit of encouraging (rather than deterring) price competition and minimizes the incidence of false positives that might otherwise occur.[127]

DG Competition's treatment of conditional rebates on all purchases in particular appears to be overly focused on the ability of a new entrant to enter the market, saying at one point that it 'will be attentive that the rebate system does not foreclose potential competitors'.[128] While entry is of course a relevant consideration, the competitive responses of existing competitors are also important. Indeed the fact that the dominant firm's rivals have successfully managed to establish themselves on the market and despite the existence of the rebate scheme may be capable of further expansion is strongly probative of no anticompetitive effect.[129]

Of further importance is the fact that the Discussion Paper is not sufficiently receptive to a meaningful efficiency defence on the part of the dominant firm. As noted above, there is a panoply of strong economic reasons for offering discounts. By contrast, the Discussion Paper adopts an unduly narrow view of the possible justifications for discounting by dominant firms. For example, in line with the Commission's past practice, the rebate scheme must be 'indispensable' to obtain cost advantages, that is to say, limited to the cost savings properly attributable to the scheme.[130] This approach is inconsistent with the economic reality that rebates by any firm (whether dominant or not) generate efficiencies which are no less valid even though they may not be 'indispensable' in the eyes of the Commission.[131]

Of equal concern to the foregoing conceptual problems are various practical difficulties which the Discussion Paper gives rise to. In particular the Discussion Paper fails to provide sufficient certainty in relation to what a dominant firm is lawfully entitled to do. Although the Paper correctly proposes to frame the abuse standard in terms of the 'equally efficient competitor' test, as explained above, it fails to apply that test properly to rebates. In so doing the Paper does not establish an adequate safe haven in relation to pricing by dominant firms. To be workable in practice and consistent with economic theory, the Commission should propound a safe haven which regards discounts and selective price cutting as lawful as long as the rebated price exceeds the dominant firm's average avoidable cost. In any event, further practical difficulties may be encountered in attempting to determine, or rather estimate, accurately the effective share and the commercially viable share.

### Conclusion

In our view, former Assistant Attorney-General Pate cogently observed that

> The bundling and fidelity rebate areas are among the murkiest regarding single firm conduct. Clarity will come, here as it has in other areas, from courts' continued learning from economics as well as from the ongoing conversation between jurisdictions.[132]

There have been cases on both sides of the Atlantic, notably the judgments in *Michelin II* and *LePage's*, which have both sparked controversy and signalled the need to rethink the rules of law in this area. The key challenge for the future remains the development of rules which clearly and sensibly distinguish between dominant firms' rebates which are likely to have a material adverse effect on competition from those where they are in fact a normal part of the competitive process. We believe that both economic analysis and cost-error analysis have a key role to play in that regard; in particular the law on rebates should concern itself more with the question of whether the grant of rebates results in a dominant firm selling at less than cost.

In that spirit, the US Department of Justice and Federal Trade

Commission public hearings on 'Competition Policy Related to Single-Firm Conduct' in Spring 2006[133] and the European Commission's Discussion Paper of December 2005 should be welcomed in attempting to rethink the approach to rebates and move the law in the right direction. Henceforth, on both sides of the Atlantic, exclusionary conduct should be proved by reference to its actual or likely anticompetitive effects. That said, the Discussion Paper's proposed approach still appears to be unduly restrictive and in particular presumes quasi-exclusivity discounts are abusive even though they (i) can be economically rational for a dominant firm to grant, (ii) may increase price competition, and (iii) are demanded by customers.

It is to be hoped that the authorities on both sides of the Atlantic will develop an analysis of rebates of any form based upon a realistic assessment of the likely harm to competition, on the one hand, and the benefits of regulatory intervention, on the other; ultimately this analysis should be guided by the insights of economic analysis and the analytical framework described above.

### Notes

1. *Virgin Atlantic Airways Ltd.* v. *British Airways plc* 257 F.3d 256 (2d Cir. 2001).
2. *LePage's Inc.* v. *3M*, 324. F.3d 141 (3d Cir. 2003); *cert.* denied, 124 S. Ct. 2932 (2004). The Department of Justice has also taken action against exclusive dealing, where appropriate, see e.g. *United States* v. *Dentsply International, Inc*, 399 F.3d 181 (3d Cir. 2005); see also McDonald (31 March 2005), Deputy Assistant Attorney General Antitrust Division, U.S. Department of Justice, 'Hot Topics in Monopolization Law and Policy', 31 March 2005.
3. *Canada (Director of Investigation and Research)* v. *Laidlaw Waste Systems Ltd* (1995) 64 C.P.R. (3d) 216.
4. See e.g. the element of 'surprise' at the CFI's judgment in *Michelin II* expressed by the Director-General for Directorate-General of Competition, Philip Lowe at the Fordham conference in 2003.
5. R.H. Pate (23 October 2003), 'The common law approach and improving standards for analysing single firm conduct', Thirtieth Annual Conference on International Antitrust Law and Policy, Fordham Corporate Law Institute, available at http://www.usdoj.gov/atr/public/speeches/202724.htm.
6. Case C-95/04 P *British Airways* v. *Commission* (appeal pending before the ECJ).
7. See section F.6.
8. See Department of Justice Press Release, 28 November 2005 and Press Release, 5 June 2006, available at http://www.usdoj.gov/atr/.
9. See Brief for the United States as Amicus Curiae, available at http://www.usdoj.gov/atr/cases/f203900/203900.htm.
10. Ibid.
11. Hovenkamp, Herbert (August 2005), 'Discounts and exclusions', University of Iowa Legal Studies Research Paper No.05-18, page 8, available at: http://papers.ssrn.com/sol3/papers.cfm?abstract_id=785966#PaperDownload.
12. They may also have aspects similar to predatory pricing. These similarities are considered in subsection 4, below.
13. US Court of Appeals for the District Court of Columbia in *Microsoft III*, 253 F3d 34, 346 U.S. ADP D.C. 330.
14. Spector, David (2005), 'Loyalty rebates: an assessment of competition concerns and a proposed structured rule of reason', *Competition Policy International*, **1**(2), Autumn, 92, available at http://www.cepremap.ens.fr/depot/docweb/docweb0514.pdf.

15. Hovenkamp, *supra* n.11.
16. For more details, see RBB Economics (2005), 'Selective price cuts and fidelity rebates', OFT 804, available at: http://www.oft.gov.uk/NR/ rdonlyres/DB851D94-1FBE-46EA-85A4-53E4DA0BB0F8/0/oft804.pdf.
17. For more details, see Spector, *supra* n.14. See also Tom, W.K., D.A. Balto and N.W. Averitt (2000), 'Anticompetitive aspects of market share discounts', 67 *Antitrust Law Journal*, 615.
18. Brief for the United States as *amicus curiae*, *3M* v. *LePage's Inc*. No 02-1865, 19 (S Ct filed 28 May 2004), available at http://www.usdoj.gov/osg/briefs/2003/2pet/6invit/2002-1865.pet.ami.inv.pdf.
19. For a detailed description of underlying reasons for bundling and tying, see Evans, David S. and Michael Salinger (2005), 'Why do firms bundle and tie? Evidence from competitive markets and implications for tying law', *Yale Journal on Regulation* 37, available at: http://papers.ssrn.com/sol3/papers.cfm?abstract_ id=550884#PaperDownload.
20. Ibid., 40.
21. Ibid., 42.
22. See Stigler, George (1964), '*United States* v. *Lowe's Inc*.: a note on block-booking', 1363 *Supreme Court Review*, 152 University of Chicago Press.
23. David Rubinfeld provides a list of anticompetitive explanations of bundled rebates in his article '3M's bundled rebates: an economic perspective', **72**, *U. Chi. L. Rev*, 243 (2005).
24. Ibid., 252.
25. Ibid.
26. Either consumer surplus or alternatively, total welfare, i.e. consumer surplus plus profits.
27. Spector, *supra* n.14. For more details, see RBB Economics, *supra* n.16.
28. Posner, Richard A. (2001), *Antitrust Law*, 2nd edn. University of Chicago Press, pp. 194–5.
29. See Hovenkamp, *supra* n.11, 10.
30. See e.g. *Virgin Atlantic* v. *British Airways*, *supra* n.1.
31. Significantly, there has also been a marked difference in approach within each jurisdiction too: there is now a consensus in the US that contemporary interpretation of §2 has correctly moved away from the expansionist approach articulated in earlier cases such as *US* v. *Aluminum Co. of America (ALCOA)*, 148 F.2d 416 (2d Cir 1945). Equally the Commission's Discussion Paper indicates a possible evolution in law and policy under Article 82 EC.
32. *United States* v. *Grinnell Corp*., 384 U.S. 563, 570–71 (1966).
33. In the US the Antitrust Division of the Department of Justice is the responsible agency empowered to bring both civil and criminal proceedings under §2. Separately and significantly it is well known that there is a high level of private enforcement of US antitrust law, including §2.
34. Under Council (EC) Regulation 1/2003 OJ [2004] L 1/1, there is an administrative procedure before the Commission, whose decisions are subject to judicial review by the European Court of First Instance. For more detail on the EC system, see the OECD Peer Review Report on the Competition Law and Policy in the European Union, 6 January 2006, available at http://www.oecd.org/dataoecd/7/41/35908641.pdf.
35. See Kolasky (9 November 2001), 'Conglomerate mergers and range effects: it's a long walk from Chicago to Brussels', George Mason University Symposium, page 26. A former Deputy Attorney-General, D. Majoras, now Chairman of the Federal Trade of Commission, has also stated that 'it cannot be overstated how much knowing we may have to prove our case to an independent fact-finder disciplines our decision making at the Antitrust Division'.
36. Unlike the development in credible judicial review under the EC Merger Regulation, see e.g. Bailey (2003), 'Standard of proof in EC merger proceedings: a common law perspective', *CMLRev*, 845–88.
37. See e.g. *Verizon Communications Inc*. v. *Law Offices of Curtis V. Trinko, LLP*, 540 U.S. 398, at 407 (2004).
38. It will be interesting to see how private enforcement may change in the US (whether the

American Modernization Commission may propose the de-trebling of damages: http://www.amc.gov/index.html) and in the EC (whether the Commission may propose new legislation on private enforcement following the responses to its Green Paper on the subject) and how this may affect the sum of direct costs and error costs and thereby affect the future direction of the law on abusive discounts and other exclusionary practices; available at DG Competition's website: http://europa.eu.int/comm/competition/antitrust/others/actions_for_damages/index_en.html.

39. Case 85/76 *Hoffman-La Roche* v. *Commission*, [1979] ECR 461.
40. In the EC there is a risk that an undertaking may be found dominant in the whole or a substantial part of the single market if its market share exceeds 40% and its share is considerably greater than that of its competitors. That said, the difference between the concepts of monopoly power in the US and dominance in the EC is mostly a question of degree; after all 'competition law is not an area of law in which there is much scope for absolute concepts or sharp edges'. (Case No: 1041/2/1/04 *The British Horseracing Board* v. *Office of Fair Trading*, judgment of 2 August 2005, at para. 167.
41. Case 322/81 *Michelin* v. *Commission*, [1983] ECR 3461, para. 57: the concept of special responsibility deprives dominant firms of the right to behave in certain ways which would be unobjectionable if adopted by a non-dominant firm.
42. This was argued persuasively, by RBB Economics *supra* n.16, paras 1.27 and 4.157.
43. *Aspen Skiing Co.* v. *Aspen Highlands Skiing Corp.*, 472 U.S. 585, 605 (1985) (quoting Bork, Robert H. (1978), *The Antitrust Paradox*, 138).
44. See Case T-203/01, *Manufacture Française des Pneumatiques Michelin* v. *Commission*, [2003] ECR II-4071, para. 241.
45. See, most recently, Case T-210/01, *General Electric* v. *Commission*, judgment of 14 December 2005, para. 550. See also Case C-396/96, *Compagnie Maritime Belge* v. *Commission*, [2000] ECR I-1365, at para. 114. See also Case No. 1001/1/1/01, *Napp Pharmaceutical Holdings Limited and Subsidiaries* v. *Director General of Fair Trading*, at para. 219 and 337.
46. *United States* v. *Microsoft Corp.*, 253 F. 3d 34, 58 (D.C. Cir. 2001) (en banc) (per curiam).
47. See e.g. *Matsushita Elec. Industrial Co.* v. *Zenith Radio Corp.*, 475 U. S. 574, 594 (1986).
48. In its submissions to the OECD the US Department of Justice has observed that 'The few American antitrust decisions that have dealt with simple discounts or rebates illustrate both the importance of factual evidence of an anticompetitive effect (rather than simply of an effect on a competitor) and the substantial judicial concern about deterring beneficial price cuts. Courts are generally unwilling to assume these discounts are anticompetitive, even if the discounter has market power; they are reluctant to force monopolists to charge high prices.' See OECD (29 May 2002), 'OECD roundtable on loyalty or fidelity discounts and rebates', page 2, available at http://www.ftc.gov/bc/international/docs/compcomm/2002-Rdtable%20on%20Loyalty%20or%20Fidelity.pdf.
49. *Brooke Group Ltd* v. *Brown & Williamson Tobacco Corp.* 509 US 209 (1993).
50. *Concord Boat Corp.* v. *Brunswick Corp.* 207 F.3d 1039 (8th Cir. 2000), available at http://www.ca8.uscourts.gov/opndir/00/03/983732P.pdf.
51. The case concerned a private action challenging inter alia the grant of discounts conditional upon customers acquiring a substantial proportion of their requirements from Brunswick. The key features of Brunswick's rebate scheme were as follows: offering 1% off in exchange for 60% of requirements, offering a 2% discount for 70% of requirements and 3% off in exchange for 80% of purchases; offering additional discounts based on % of purchases for a multi-year 'market share' period; and offering additional discounts based simply on absolute volumes purchased.
52. The Court held that the boat builders failed to produce sufficient evidence to demonstrate that Brunswick had foreclosed a substantial share of the stern drive engine market through anticompetitive conduct.
53. *Concord Boat*, *supra* n.50.
54. In *Ortho Diagnostics* v. *Abbott Laboratories* 920 F Supp 455 (S.D.N.Y 1996) the Southern District Court of New York held that a competitor can complain of a bundle price if: (i) it is predatory by the usual tests; or (ii) the competitor can show that he is at

least as efficient as the supplier of the bundle whose pricing makes it unprofitable for the competitor to continue to produce.

55.  *Supra*, n.2. A similar pricing scheme was condemned in an earlier case: *SmithKline Corp. v. Eli Lilly & Co.* 575 F.2d 1056 (3d Cir. 1978). Cf. *Virgin Atlantic Airways Ld* v. *British Airways plc* 257 F.3d 256 (2d Cir. 2001) rejecting as 'theoretical' the allegation that BA used incentive agreements to bundle routes where BA had a monopoly with routes where it faced competition.

56.  The defendant company, Minnesota Mining & Manufacturing Co, better known as 3M, manufactured Scotch-brand transparent tape, which until the early 1990s had more than 90% of the market for brand-name transparent tape. LePage's, an office supply manufacturer, decided in 1980 to start selling 'second-brand' and 'private-label' transparent tape, which is sold under the retailer's name. By 1992, LePage's had 88 per cent of the private-label tape market. During the early 1990s 3M decided to enter the private-label market. LePage's attacked 3M's use of 'bundled rebates' through which customers such as Kmart, Staples and Office Depot could earn cash back from 3M in exchange for purchasing certain quantities of 3M products, including tape. In response 3M introduced a bundled discount programme which was, allegedly, structured in such a way that LePage's customers had incentives to stop purchasing from LePage's and purchase exclusively from 3M to obtain the maximum discount.

57.  The Court of Appeal (quoting Areeda & Hovenkamp (1995), *Antitrust Law: An Analysis of Antitrust Principles and their Application*, 749, at 83–4 (Supp. 2002)) stated that: 'depending on the number of products that are aggregated [in the bundle on which rebates are offered] and the customer's relative purchases of each, even an equally efficient rival may find it impossible to compensate for lost discounts on products that it does not produce'.

58.  *Supra*, n.40.

59.  *LePage's Inc.* v. *3M* Brief for the United States as Amicus Curiae, at p. 16: discussing how the Court: (1) referred to the potential of the bundled rebates to exclude an equally efficient competitor, but did not point to any evidence supporting that conclusion in the 3M case; (2) discussed the ability of LePage's to match 3M's discounts but only in the abstract; (3) rejected 3M's business justification but, again, without explaining how the evidence supported that conclusion.

60.  Glazer & Henry (Fall 2003), 'Coercive vs. incentivising conduct: a way out of the Section 2 impasse?', **18**, *Antitrust*, 45.

61.  124 S. Ct. 2932 (2004).

62.  *Barry Wright Corp.* v. *ITT Grinnell Corp.*, 724 F.2d 227 (1st Cir. 1983).

63.  In response to Barry Wright attempting to supply snubbers to Grinnell, Pacific had offered Grinnell a large discount on its total snubber purchases if it would promise to buy large quantities of snubbers from Pacific. When Grinnell agreed, Barry Wright sued, alleging a violation of §2.

64.  'The competitive marketplace that the antitrust laws encourage and protect is characterized by firms willing and able to cut prices in order to take customers from their rivals. . . . Here we have a price that exceeds both "average cost" and "incremental cost" – that exceeds cost however plausibly measured.' And, as to those prices, 'virtually every court and commentator agrees' that they are lawful, 'perhaps conclusively, but at least presumptively': 724 F.2d 227 at p 231 (1st Cir. 1983).

65.  Ibid., at p. 235.

66.  See Hovenkamp, *supra*, n.11.

67.  *Barry Wright Corp.* v. *ITT Grinnell Corp.*, 724 F.2d 227 (1st Cir. 1983).

68.  Posner (2001), *Antitrust Law*, *supra*, n.62.

69.  Pate *supra*, n.5.

70.  See Brief for the United States as Amicus Curiae, available at http://www.usdoj.gov/atr/cases/f203900/203900.htm.

71.  Case 85/76 *Hoffmann-La Roche* v. *Commission*, [1979] ECR 461.

72.  The case law has not made use of the cost-related analysis applied in the context of predation claims.

73. *Supra*, n.71.
74. Joined Cases 40/73 etc *Suiker Unie* v. *Commission*, [1975] ECR 1663; Case C-85/76 *Hoffmann-La Roche* v. *Commission*, [1979] ECR 461; Case T-65/89 *BPB and British Gypsum* v. *Commission*, [1993] ECR II-389.
75. However the case law has also been concerned with a discount's discriminatory qualities, see e.g. Case T-219/99 *British Airways* v. *Commission* judgment of 17 December 2003.
76. *Michelin II, supra* n.44; *British Airways* v. *Commission*, ibid.
77. See Case COMP/34.780, OJ, [2000] L 30/1. The Commission defined a relevant market consisting of the sale of scheduled air transport through travel agents in the United Kingdom. Notwithstanding BA's declining fortunes, the Commission objected to various incentives schemes it had used to encourage travel agents to market and sell its tickets in preference to other airlines. In particular the Commission condemned various marketing agreements, which enabled travel agents to receive a performance reward based on the volume of sectors flown on BA. The Commission also took issue with BA's system of performance rewards, which entitled travel agents to an extra commission of up to 3% for international tickets and up to 1% for domestic tickets. Under the system of performance rewards, every percentage point of growth in sales over a minimum of 95% earned the travel agent an additional 0.1% by way of extra commission on the sale of international tickets.
78. See Case T-219/99 *British Airways* v. *Commission*, [2003] ECR II-5917, para. 272.
79. Ibid.
80. Paragraph 294.
81. BA held a share of almost 48% at the beginning of the 1990s.
82. In particular, the CFI held, at para. 288: 'BA can have had no interest in applying its reward schemes other than ousting rival airlines and thereby hindering maintenance of the existing level of competition or the development of that competition on the United Kingdom market for air travel agency services.'
83. See *Michelin II, supra* n.44.
84. *ICI – Solvay* OJ, [1991] L 152/40.
85. Case 85/76 [1979] ECR 461, at paras 110–11.
86. *Eurofix-Bauco* v. *Hilti* OJ, [1988] L 65/19, upheld on appeal in Case T-30/89 *Hilti AG* v. *Commission*, [1991] ECR II-1439, upheld on appeal in Case C-53/92 P *Hilti AG* v. *Commission*, [1994] ECR I-667.
87. Recital 75.
88. The Commission took the preliminary view that such bundled pricing had 'the effect of making sales space in outlets harder to obtain for rival suppliers and of raising sales space prices for those suppliers. The likely effect of this is reduced variety of choice and reduced downward pressure on prices to the detriment of the consumer'. See the non-confidential version of the Commission Decision of 22 June 2005, *Coca Cola*, paragraph 35, available online at the following website: http://europa.eu.int/comm/competition/antitrust/cases/decisions/39116/commitments_fr.pdf.
89. Nevertheless the Commission accepted the following commitment: 'No Combined Payments. The Companies will not condition any payment or other advantage granted with respect to any TCCC-Branded Cola [carbonated soft drinks] or TCCC-Branded Orange [carbonated soft drinks] upon a customer's stocking one or more additional TCCC-Branded beverages'. (Ibid., p. 22).
90. *Cewal* OJ, [1993] L 34/20, upheld on appeal to the CFI in Joined Cases T-24/93 to T-26/93 and T-28/93 *Compagnie Maritime Belge Transports* v. *Commission*, [1996] ECR II-1201, upheld on appeal by the ECJ in Joined Cases C-395/96 P and C-396/96 P *Compagnie Maritime Belge Transports* v. *Commission*, [2000] ECR I-1365.
91. OJ, [2002] L 143/1 recital 213.
92. *Michelin II, supra* n.44, at para. 62.
93. Ibid., para. 74.
94. Ibid., para. 95, 'a quantity rebate system in which there is a significant variation in the discount rates between the lower and higher steps, which has a reference period of one year and in which the discount is fixed on the basis of total turnover achieved during

the reference period, has the characteristics of an [unlawful] loyalty-inducing discount system'.
95.   *Supra*, n.90.
96.   Case C-62/86 *AKZO* v. *Commission*, [1991] ECR I-3359.
97.   Whish (2003), *Competition Law*, LexisNexis, ch. 18.
98.   Another case of interest on the abusive nature of selective price cutting (at least in certain circumstances) is Case T-228/97, *Irish Sugar* v. *Commission*, [1999] ECR II-2969.
99.   So, for example, an agreement to pay a 25% discount to a customer who agrees to buy all of his requirements from the dominant firm is treated as analytically equivalent to an agreement on that customer's part to buy all of his requirements from the dominant firm.
100.   The Commission Discussion Paper, as explained below in section G.6, introduces the cost–price relationship into the analysis of discounts which has been palpably absent from the EC approach to fidelity discounts to date. It is submitted that future practice should focus more on the question of whether the grant of discounts results in a dominant firm selling at less than an appropriate measure of cost.
101.   I.e., that there is no need to demonstrate, in a particular case, that there would be an anticompetitive effect, as the anticompetitive effect is presumed from the very fact of the practice.
102.   That being so, BA is keen to test the CFI's assessment of the exclusionary character of BA's commissions under Article 82, and has therefore appealed against the CFI judgment to the ECJ (Case C-94/04 P *British Airways* v. *Commission* (judgment pending)). Very interestingly, in its appeal to the ECJ, BA has argued that 'competition law requires the Court to examine the actual or likely effects of allegedly abusive conduct' (OJ, [2004] 106/22), which is exactly the same analytical framework being put forward by the Commission in its Discussion Paper (para. 4).
103.   *CEWAL II*, *supra* n.90, para. 132 of Advocate General Fennelly's Opinion.
104.   DG Competition discussion paper on the application of Article 82 of the Treaty to exclusionary abuses, December 2005, available at http://europa.eu.int/comm/competition/ antitrust/others/article_82_review.html.
105.   See Commission Press Release IP/05/1626, 19 December 2005.
106.   This is consistent with the judgment of ECJ: *AKZO supra*, n.96, para. 70.
107.   The precise meaning of this frequently used but rather amorphous statement is not altogether clear, but, if it were to mean anything, it should underline the fact that competition authorities and plaintiffs cannot have recourse to Article 82 for protection against exclusion resulting from superior economic performance, but only from exclusion resulting from abuse of market power. It has also been the subject of a recent OECD Roundtable 'Competition on the Merits', 22 December 2005, available at http://www.oecd.org.
108.   Discussion Paper, para. 63.
109.   For example, while the benchmark for 'as efficient' would normally be the costs of the dominant company, the Commission considers that it may depart from this standard when certain competitors are placed at a disadvantage for non-cost-related reasons such as the strategic 'first-mover advantage' of the dominant firm (para. 67).
110.   The distinction between conditional and unconditional rebates was discussed above and moves the law away from the old distinction between 'fidelity' and 'quantitative' discounts. Quasi-tying rebates are addressed by the Discussion Paper under the proposed analytical framework for tying and consequently lie beyond the scope of this section.
111.   Footnote 96 warns that the combination of conditional and unconditional rebate schemes would be assessed both individually on their own merits and collectively. The Discussion Paper does not elaborate on whether further adjustments would be made to the analytical framework when analysing the collective effect of rebates.
112.   For example, in considering the strength of the inducement, the Discussion Paper considers whether the threshold is set significantly above the level that customers would expect to purchase from the dominant firm in any event (para. 152) as well as the level

of the rebate percentage and the level of the threshold at which the rebate is applicable (para. 153).

113. Discussion Paper, paras 153–4. In this regard, it is not the last unit before the rebate is triggered that is relevant to this assessment but rather commercially viable amounts supplied by efficient competitors and entrants.
114. Discussion Paper, para. 156. For the most part the Discussion Paper focuses on the share to be captured by new entrants (see in particular para. 157) but the Commission also refers to whether the effective share is larger than the shares of customer requirements actually purchased from efficient competitors; existing competitors are at the very least equally important to the overall analysis.
115. As would be the case where there was evidence of aggressive and significant entry/expansion and/or switching of customers.
116. Discussion Paper, para. 164.
117. Such disadvantages may derive from the need to enter below the minimum efficient scale or from learning costs which only allow suppliers to reduce costs with experience over a period of time; see Discussion Paper, para. 67.
118. Case T-203/01 *Manufacture Française des Pneumatiques Michelin* v. *Commission*, [2003] ECR II-4071, para. 88.
119. Discussion Paper, para. 161.
120. Consumer welfare is recognized by the Commission as the objective of Article 82 as regards exclusionary abuses; see Discussion Paper, para. 4.
121. Discussion Paper, para. 154 (i.e. recoupment is possible immediately).
122. If exclusionary intent is to be considered, the structure of the scheme is, in and of itself, sufficient proof of such intent in most cases.
123. Other commentators have suggested a test based on average variable cost; see, e.g., O'Donoghue (June 2003), 'Over-regulating lower prices: time for a rethink on pricing abuses under Article 82 EC', Eighth Annual EU Competition Law and Policy Workshop.
124. Of course there may be certain exceptional cases, such as a firm approaching quasi-monopoly, where the effective discounted price falls below ATC and does have an exclusionary effect and therefore should be subject to antitrust assessment.
125. Discussion Paper, para. 63.
126. Discussion Paper, para. 67 suggests that the standard may not apply where the competitor is less efficient today than the dominant firm but would become as efficient if it attained the dominant firm's scale. Although there may be cases where above-average avoidable cost discounts by a dominant firm reduce allocative efficiency yet improve productive efficiency, as discussed in section D above, the optimal legal rule is one which minimizes both substantive error and enforcement costs.
127. At the very least there would need to be strong grounds for intervention where the discounted price exceeded a dominant firm's average avoidable cost, such as evidence of the rebate's adverse effect on entry and expansion by competitors.
128. Discussion Paper, para. 157.
129. The suggested analysis can be contrasted with the approach in the *British Airways* case: while the contested reward scheme was in operation, British Airway's share of the market fell consistently, so that, in the year before the decision was taken, it had less than 39% of the relevant market. The Commission and the CFI held that British Airway's loss of market share could not evidence a lack of competitive impact because, in the absence of the contested scheme, it was perfectly possible that British Airways would have lost an even greater proportion of the market. See Case T-219/99 *British Airways* v. *Commission*, [2003] ECR II-5917, para. 298.
130. Discussion Paper, para. 173.
131. See section C above.
132. Pate (23 October 2003), 'The common law approach and improving standards for analyzing single firm conduct', Thirtieth Annual Conference on International Antitrust Law and Policy, Fordham Corporate Law Institute.
133. See Department of Justice (28 November 2005), Press release available online at the following website: http://www.usdoj.gov/atr/public/press_releases/2005/213369.pdf.

## References

Areeda & Hovenkamp (1995), *Antitrust Law: An Analysis of Antitrust Principles and their Application*.
Bailey, D. (2003), 'Standard of proof in EC merger proceedings: a common law perspective', *CMLRev*, 845–88.
Bork, Robert H. (1978), *The Antitrust Paradox*.
Department of Justice (28 November 2005), Press release, available at http://www.usdoj.gov/atr/public/press_releases/2005/213369.pdf.
Evans, David S. and Michael Salinger (2005), 'Why do firms bundle and tie? Evidence from competitive markets and implications for tying law', *Yale Journal on Regulation*, 37, available at http://papers.ssrn.com/sol3/papers.cfm?abstract_id=550884#PaperDownload.
Glazer & Henry (Fall 2003), 'Coercive vs. incentivising conduct: a way out of the Section 2 impasse?', **18**, *Antitrust*, 45.
Hovenkamp, Herbert (August 2005), 'Discounts and exclusions', University of Iowa Legal Studies Research Paper No.05-18, page 8, available online at the following website: http://papers.ssrn.com/sol3/papers.cfm?abstract_id=785966#PaperDownload.
Kolasky, W. (9 November 2001), 'Conglomerate mergers and range effects: it's a long walk from Chicago to Brussels', George Mason University Symposium.
McDonald, B. (31 March 2005), 'Hot topics in monopolization law and policy', presentation given at US Department of Justice.
OECD (29 May 2002), 'OECD Roundtable on loyalty or fidelity discounts and rebates', at http://www.ftc.gov/bc/international/docs/compcomm/2002Rdtable%20on%20Loyalty%20or%20Fidelity.pdf, at 2.
Pate, H. (23 October 2003), 'The common law approach and improving standards for analysing single firm conduct', Thirtieth Annual Conference on International Antitrust Law and Policy, Fordham Corporate Law Institute, available at http://www.usdoj.gov/atr/public/speeches/202724.htm.
Posner, Richard A. (2001), *Antitrust Law*, 2nd edn, Chicago.
RBB Economics (2005), 'Selective price cuts and fidelity rebates', OFT 804, available online at the following website: http://www.oft.gov.uk/NR/rdonlyres/DB851D94-1FBE-46EA-85A4-53E4DA0BB0F8/0/oft804.pdf.
Spector, David (2005), 'Loyalty rebates: an assessment of competition concerns and a proposed structured rule of reason', *Competition Policy International*, **1**(2), Autumn, 92, available online at the following website: http://www.cepremap.ens.fr/depot/docweb/docweb0514.pdf.
Stigler, George (1963), '*United States* v. *Lowe's Inc.*: a Note on Block-Booking', *Supreme Court Review*, University of Chicago Press.
Whish (2003), *Competition Law*, LexisNexis.
Willard, K., David A. Balto and Neil W. Averitt (2000), 'Anticompetitive aspects of market share discounts', *Antitrust Law Journal*, 615.

## Cases

*AKZO* v. *Commission*, Case C-62/86 [1991] ECR I-3359.
*Aspen Skiing Co.* v. *Aspen Highlands Skiing Corp.*, 472 U.S. 585, 605 (1985).
*Barry Wright Corp.* v. *ITT Grinnell Corp.*, 724 F.2d 227 (1st Cir. 1983).
*BPB and British Gypsum* v. *Commission*, Case T-65/89, [1993] ECR II-389.
*British Airways* v. *Commission*, Case C-95/04 P (appeal pending).
*Brooke Group Ltd* v. *Brown & Williamson Tobacco Corp.* 509 US 209 (1993).
*Canada (Director of Investigation and Research)* v. *Laidlaw Waste Systems Ltd* (1995) 64 C.P.R. (3d) 216.
*Cewal* OJ, [1993] L 34/20, upheld on appeal to the CFI in Joined Cases T-24/93 to T-26/93 and T-28/93 *Compagnie Maritime Belge Transports* v. *Commission*, [1996] ECR II-1201, upheld on appeal by the ECJ in Joined Cases C-395/96 P and C-396/96 P *Compagnie Maritime Belge Transports* v. *Commission*, [2000] ECR I-1365.
*Compagnie Maritime Belge* v. *Commission*, Case C-396/96, [2000] ECR I-1365.

*Concord Boat Corp.* v. *Brunswick Corp.* 207 F.3d 1039 (8th Cir. 2000), available at http://www.ca8.uscourts.gov/opndir/00/03/983732P.pdf.

*Eurofix-Bauco* v. *Hilti* OJ, [1988] L 65/19, upheld on appeal in Case T-30/89 *Hilti AG* v. *Commission*, [1991] ECR II-1439, upheld on appeal in Case C-53/92 P *Hilti AG* v. *Commission*, [1994] ECR I-667.

*General Electric* v. *Commission*, Case T-210/01, judgment of 14 December 2005.

*Hoffmann-La Roche* v. *Commission*, Case 85/76, [1979] ECR 461.

*ICI – Solvay* OJ, [1991] L 152/40.

*Irish Sugar* v. *Commission*, Case T-228/97, [1999] ECR II-2969.

*LePage's Inc.* v. *3M*, 324. F.3d 141 (3d Cir. 2003); *cert.* denied, 124 S. Ct. 2932 (2004).

*Manufacture française des pneumatiques Michelin* v. *Commission*, Case T-203/01, [2003] ECR II-4071.

*Matsushita Elec. Industrial Co.* v. *Zenith Radio Corp.*, 475 U. S. 574, 594 (1986).

*Michelin* v. *Commission*, Case 322/81, [1983] ECR 3461.

*Napp Pharmaceutical Holdings Limited and Subsidiaries* v. *Director General of Fair Trading*, Case No. 1001/1/1/01.

*Ortho Diagnostics* v. *Abbott Laboratories* 920 F Supp 455 (S.D.N.Y 1996).

*SmithKline Corp.* v. *Eli Lilly & Co.* 575 F.2d 1056 (3d Cir. 1978).

*The British Horseracing Board* v. *Office of Fair Trading*, Case No: 1041/2/1/04, judgment of 2 August 2005.

*United States* v. *Aluminum Co. of America (ALCOA)*, 148 F.2d 416 (2d Cir 1945).

*United States* v. *Dentsply International, Inc*, 399 F.3d 181 (3d Cir. 2005).

*United States* v. *Grinnell Corp.*, 384 U.S. 563, 570–71 (1966).

*United States* v. *Microsoft Corp.*, 253 F. 3d 34, 58 (D.C. Cir. 2001) (en banc) (per curiam).

*Verizon Communications Inc.* v. *Law Offices of Curtis* v. *Trinko, LLP*, 540 U.S. 398, at 407 (2004).

*Virgin Atlantic Airways Ltd.* v. *British Airways plc* 257 F.3d 256 (2d Cir. 2001).

# 8 A dominant firm's duty to deal: EC and US antitrust law compared

*Alison Jones*[1]

## Introduction

In recent years, the US and EC antitrust authorities have achieved greater convergence in their approaches to agreements and mergers, respectively. In particular, the modernization of Article 81 of the EC Treaty and the EC Merger Regulation, characterized by a shift from a formalistic to a more economic approach, has helped to achieve that convergence.[2] The approaches of the US and EC antitrust authorities to firms with monopoly power or a dominant position are, however, still much further apart. Many commentators in the EC have been calling for a more economic approach to be adopted in the application of Article 82 which might, at the same time, have the effect of bringing the approach more closely in tune with that adopted in the US. In 2003, the European Commission announced that it would review its approach to Article 82 and in December 2005 it published a Discussion Paper setting out possible principles for its future application of Article 82 to exclusionary abuses.[3]

The objective of this chapter is not to deal with the Discussion Paper and the reform of Article 82 generally. Rather its intention is to explore the case law dealing with refusal to supply under Article 82 EC against its backdrop and to compare and contrast EC law with that adopted in the US. By way of introduction, section 1 of the chapter sets out the main elements and objectives of both Article 82 and section 2 of the US Sherman Act of 1890. Section 2 then discusses the process of review currently occurring in Europe and the difficulty involved in constructing a set of coherent yet predictable and workable rules which can be used to identify anticompetitive conduct of dominant firms. Section 3 then looks closely at the EC and US cases on refusal to deal. Section 4 summarizes the conditions of liability set out in the EC and US cases whilst, in conclusion, section 5 of the paper reflects on the similarities and differences evident in the two sets of case law and whether, and if so how far, they do in fact diverge. It also considers whether either provides a satisfactory analytical framework for distinguishing between lawful and unlawful refusals to deal or whether some refinements in approach are necessary.

**Section 1 Article 82 and section 2: elements and objectives**

Article 82 does not prohibit the holding of a dominant position per se, but only the *abuse* of it. It is well known that its two key substantive elements require an undertaking (or undertakings)[4] (1) to hold a dominant position and (2) to have committed an abuse of that dominant position.[5] In addition, the ECJ has held that conduct prima facie contrary to Article 82 can be objectively justified, for example, where the dominant firm was acting proportionately to protect its own legitimate commercial interests[6] or to ensure safety.[7] A question which is currently unclear is whether the concept of objective justification can be used as a mechanism for raising procompetitive or efficiency justifications which can then be weighed against any abusive effects of the conduct identified. In his opinion in *Syfait* v. *Glaxosmithkline AEVE*,[8] Advocate General Jacob stated his belief that the distinction between an abuse and its objective justification was rather artificial. Unlike Article 81, Article 82 does not contain any specific exception for conduct otherwise falling within it and the very fact that the conduct is characterized as an 'abuse' suggests that a negative conclusion has already been reached (in contrast with the more neutral terminology used in Article 81(1)). He thus concluded that 'it is more accurate to say that certain types of conduct on the part of a dominant undertaking do not fall within the category of abuse at all. However, given that the Commission has, in the light of some previous Community case-law, developed its submissions in terms of objective justification, it may be convenient for present purposes to assume that structure'.[9] In its Discussion Paper, the Commission suggests that exclusionary conduct should be able to escape the prohibition of Article 82 where the dominant firm either can provide an objective justification for its behaviour[10] or can demonstrate that its conduct produces efficiencies which outweigh the negative effect on competition.[11] It thus appears to envisage both an objective justification and a separate efficiency defence.[12]

Article 82 may, at first sight, be equated with section 2 of the Sherman Act of 1890 which prohibits monopolization and attempts to monopolize.[13] As with Article 82, proof of monopoly power is not sufficient to establish a section 2 claim. Rather section 2 only prohibits the conduct of a single firm when it actually monopolizes or dangerously threatens to monopolize a market.[14] The key offence of monopolization 'has two elements: the possession of monopoly power in the relevant market, and . . . the wilful acquisition or maintenance of that power as distinguished from growth or development as a consequence of a superior product, business acumen, or historical accident'.[15]

There are, however, critical differences between Article 82 and section 2.[16] In one sense at least, section 2 is broader as it prohibits conduct by a firm which does not have monopoly power but which threatens to acquire it. Article 82 does not prohibit attempts to obtain a dominant position but applies only once the threshold of dominance has been reached.[17]

In many ways, though, section 2 has been interpreted to have a much narrower reach than Article 82 and to impose fewer restrictions on the behaviour of individual firms. First, the US courts have demanded that a higher threshold be met for a finding of monopoly power than the ECJ has required for a finding of dominance.[18] Not only do market shares have to be significantly higher, but US courts are now less willing to use market shares as a proxy for monopoly power.[19] Rather they view them simply as the starting point in the assessment of whether a firm possesses monopoly power.[20] The courts accept that a whole range of factors is relevant to the determination, adopting a more effects- than form-based approach. A high market share, even one as high as 100%, will be treated as irrelevant, where there is ease of entry.[21] This position is in contrast to that which exists in the EC where a finding of dominance has been made against a firm with a market share of only 39.7%,[22] where a 50% market share triggers a presumption of dominance,[23] and where analysis of the impact of other factors relevant to a finding of dominance has, in early cases at least, been weak and unconvincing.[24]

Secondly, the offence of monopolization requires a causal link between the conduct and the monopoly power. The second limb of the offence, 'the wilful acquisition of maintenance of that power',[25] requires that the anticompetitive conduct must *cause* the acquisition, maintenance or extension of the monopoly power.[26] In contrast, Article 82 requires only an *abuse* of a dominant position. A quick glance at the list of potentially abusive conduct immediately reveals that that conduct does not necessarily have to maintain or strengthen that dominant position. It clearly condemns *exploitative* abuses, such as monopoly pricing (for example, Article 82(a) condemns the imposition of unfair selling prices),[27] as well as anticompetitive or exclusionary abuses. In the US, the exercise of legitimately obtained monopoly power through the charging of monopoly prices is not condemned. On the contrary, it is seen as a *reward* for innovation and the lawful winning of the competitive battle.[28] In *Verizon Communications* v. *Law Offices of Curtis V Trinko LLP*, Justice Scalia stated:

> The mere possession of monopoly power, and the concomitant charging of monopoly prices, is not only not unlawful; it is an important element of the free-market system. The opportunity to charge monopoly prices – at least for a short period – is what attracts 'business acumen' in the first place; it induces risk taking that produces innovation and economic growth. To safeguard the incentive to innovate, the possession of monopoly power will not be found unlawful unless it is accompanied by an element of anticompetitive conduct.[29]

Thirdly, as a consensus has emerged that the paramount, but perhaps not the sole, goal of the Sherman Act is now consumer welfare and efficiency,[30] the US courts have adopted an economic approach to the requirement that there should be wilful acquisition or maintenance of monopoly power.[31] Although this recognition still leaves ideological differences as to how best to achieve that objective[32] and the conundrum of how to distinguish competitive from exclusionary conduct which look alike,[33] it is clear that the mere fact that the conduct injures or excludes a competitor is not sufficient to establish a monopolization claim (producing a better product at a lower price will of course drive an inferior producer from the market). Rather the prohibition of 'exclusionary' or 'predatory' conduct requires proof of anticompetitive effects.[34] In applying section 2, however, the Supreme Court has stressed the need for caution. It has become fearful of wrongly condemning legitimate competition and so chilling aggressive competition, the very conduct the antitrust laws are designed to protect.[35] Indeed in *Trinko* the Supreme Court stated that false positives counselled against an undue expansion of section 2 liability.[36] It will be seen that this view has profoundly affected the development of the case law on refusal to deal.

In the EC, the fact that Article 82 forms part of the EC Treaty means that it has been construed teleologically in the light of the Treaty's aims and objectives, particularly the goal of single market integration and open market access.[37] Not only do the structure of Article 82 and the case law interpreting it indicate a concern with conduct that has anticompetitive effects to the prejudice of consumers,[38] therefore, but it indicates concern with conduct which manipulates or prevents the flow of goods between the Member States.[39] Further, and in accordance with the ordoliberal school of thought, conduct which precludes access to market and sourcing of products from other suppliers has sometimes been condemned.[40] In early cases at least, conduct damaging smaller firms perceived to be in need of protection from the power of a more dominant firm has been found to infringe Article 82.[41] Even in more recent cases there is no consistent requirement that anticompetitive effects in an economic sense must be proved.[42] Rather some of the decisional practice and case law continues to reflect a concern that small and medium-sized firms should have free and open access to a market without obstacles created by a dominant firm.[43] This has led to allegations that Article 82 has been applied to protect competitors and not just the competitive process.[44]

The language used by the ECJ in the cases adopts somewhat ambiguous terminology which may support a wide reading of Article 82. It has been held that conduct of a dominant firm that distorts competition on the market and inhibits the fragile competition that already exists on the market in consequence of the very existence of the dominant firm may constitute an abuse.[45]

> The concept of abuse is an objective concept relating to the behaviour of an undertaking in a dominant position which is such as to influence the structure of the market where, as a result of the very presence of the undertaking in question, the degree of competition is weakened and which, through recourse to methods different from those which condition normal competition in products or services on the basis of commercial operators, has the effect of hindering the maintenance of the degree of competition still existing on the market or the growth of that competition.[46]

In addition, the ECJ has held that, although holding a dominant position is not itself a 'recrimination', a dominant firm has a 'special responsibility' towards the competitive process 'not to allow its conduct to impair genuine undistorted competition on the common market'[47] (and it seems this responsibility may grow with the degree of dominance).[48] The focus has therefore arguably been on the protection of the structure within the market. The notion that a dominant firm has a special responsibility towards the competitive process has no equivalent in US law[49] and may account for some of the stricter, more formalistic and more interventionist decisions and judgments adopted in the EC. Indeed both the Commission and Court have, in some situations, come close to laying down per se prohibitions of particular conduct by dominant firms.[50]

**Section 2    Review and modernization: economics and the search for a unifying principle**

In the last ten years the European Commission has reviewed and overhauled the working and application of both Article 81 and the EC Merger Regulation.[51] The failure to introduce any substantive change in approach to Article 82 has, therefore, been conspicuous in its absence. Commentators have complained that it is wrong that the influence that economic thinking has had on the Community rules applicable to agreements and mergers had not been felt to the same extent within the sphere of Article 82.[52] Partly in response to this kind of criticism, the Commission announced that it would review its approach to Article 82 and, possibly, draft guidance on its application.[53] Although the Commission must obviously respect the law set out by the Community courts, the Commission has played, and continues to play, a central role in the enforcement of the EC competition rules which is unmatched by its US counterparts.[54] It thus retains an influential role in the development of competition policy.

Since the announcement of this review, many papers, presentations and conferences have been dedicated to the question of how Article 82 can and should be reformed and, in particular, whether there is a need to move from the current, rather form-based approach to a more economics-based assessment. Many commentators, including the Commission's own economic advisory group on competition policy ('EAGCP', reporting in the context of DGCOMP's internal review[55]), have argued that the Commission should, as in the US and as it now does in the context of Article 81, pursue a main goal of the protection of competition on the market as a means of enhancing consumer welfare and efficiency.[56] The EAGCP thus urged the Commission to abandon its formalistic approach focusing on the form of the conduct involved, and to adopt an effects-based one requiring the identification of anticompetitive effects generated by the business behaviour. Formalistic tests may dictate different results for conduct with similar or identical effects. In contrast, an economic approach requires an examination of 'the actual working of competition in the particular market without prejudice and to explain the harm for consumers from the practice in question. Without the discipline provided by this routine, the authority may be tempted to identify the "protection of competition" with the preservation of a particular market structure e.g., one that involves actual competition by a given company'.[57]

It has also been argued that a more economic approach would lead to greater consistency in treatment of Article 82 cases, ensure that anticompetitive behaviour does not outwit legal provisions through careful use of commercial practices, whilst at the same time ensuring that procompetitive strategies are not wrongly thwarted and that competitors are not protected at the expense of competition. Further, greater clarification of the framework underpinning the application of Article 82 would provide greater predictability and legal certainty.[58] The need for clarity and certainty is critical for the provision of advice to businesses, is essential to ensure that procompetitive business practices are not 'chilled'[59] and of particular importance where a multiplicity of bodies (in Europe the Commission, the national competition authorities and national courts[60]) have jurisdiction to enforce the rules.

In its Discussion Paper the Commission has responded to the fairly widespread, but certainly not unanimous,[61] call for it to expressly state its objectives in the enforcement and application of Article 82 and also to adopt an economic approach focused on the effects and not the form of the conduct.[62] In paragraph 4 it states that, in the context of exclusionary abuses, 'the objective of Article 82 is the protection of competition on the market as a means of enhancing consumer welfare and of ensuring an efficient allocation of resources'.[63] The Commission thus agrees that Article 82 is designed to protect 'competition, and not competitors as such', and that its central concern is exclusionary conduct of a dominant firm which hinders competition and thereby harms consumers.[64]

Even if this goal is accepted, the difficult question remains as to how such exclusionary conduct can be identified. Can all the cases and decisions adopted in the context of exclusionary abuses be explained by reference to one underlying principle? The identification of such a principle would prevent Article 82 from becoming a 'series of ad hoc and unpredictable rules that are consistent neither with each other nor with the policy goals of the law'.[65] As in the US, various tests have been proffered in the search for a coherent, predictable and workable mechanism for determining whether the conduct will lead to the exclusion of a competitor in a way which will adversely affect consumer welfare (i.e. is it on balance anti- or pro-competitive), for example:[66]

- the profit sacrifice test: does the conduct reduce the dominant firms' profits in order to impair the ability of rivals to compete and to earn monopoly profits in the longer term?;[67]
- the no economic sense test: 'the conduct is not exclusionary or predatory *unless* it would make no economic sense for the defendant but for its tendency to eliminate or lessen competition';[68]
- the equally efficient competitor test: conduct is impermissible if it is likely to exclude from the market an equally or more efficient competitor;[69]
- the limiting production test (grounded in the wording of Article 82(b)): conduct that limits either the dominant firm's or its competitors' production to the prejudice of consumers;[70] and
- the consumer welfare effects test: the conduct has or will have the effect of allowing the dominant firm to maintain prices and reduce output or adversely affect quality or innovation in a relevant market. The application of this test would seem to demand a rule of reason analysis, similar to that which has been adopted by some US courts,[71] requiring proof of anticompetitive effects which must then be weighed against any legitimate (and not pretextual) procompetitive justifications proffered by the defendant.[72] Although intuitively attractive as it uses consumer welfare effects rather than indirect factors as its benchmark, this test demands difficult and complex analysis which may in reality be impossible to apply accurately and consistently.[73]

Although theoretically desirable, the truth seems to be that none of these tests individually can provide a correct answer in all cases. Indeed, Hewitt Pate, former Assistant Attorney General at the US Department of Justice, has commented that 'the perfect test in theory would of course be one that consistently and accurately condemned *all*, but *only*, that conduct which leads to a net decrease in economic welfare. No such test exists in the real world'.[74] In selecting a test or a method for making this analysis, therefore, it may be necessary to take into account the need to set out rules that are sufficiently certain and not too difficult to apply but which do not create too high a risk of false positives.[75] In the US, for example, it seems that the DOJ would prefer to apply a more transparent but underinclusive test[76] than one, such as the consumer welfare effects test, which may create too high a risk of false positives.[77]

The Commission, in its Discussion Paper, endorses the use of an economic approach and does not therefore support per se rules in the application of Article 82 to exclusionary abuses.[78] It does not, however, having set out a consumer welfare objective, advocate that a full rule of reason analysis is appropriate in all cases. Rather it proposes a general framework for analysis together with specific guidance on how that framework is applied to certain types of behaviour (predatory pricing, single branding and rebates, tying and bundling, and refusal to supply).[79] The Commission states that, since the central concern is foreclosure, i.e. conduct which limits competitive constraints on the dominant company and so harms consumers, the determination should focus on (i) whether the conduct in question is capable of foreclosing efficient competition from the market and (ii) whether, in the specific market context, a market-foreclosing effect is likely. 'Article 82 prohibits exclusionary conduct which produces actual or likely anticompetitive effects in the market and which can harm consumers in a direct or indirect way.'[80] Where exclusionary conduct is demonstrated the Commission accepts that the Article 82 prohibition will be avoided if the dominant undertaking can either provide an objective justification for its behaviour or if it can demonstrate that its conduct produces efficiencies which outweigh the negative effect on competition.[81]

In the sections dealing with specific conduct, it sets out situations in which presumptions of exclusionary conduct can be made (for example, predation can be assumed if the dominant firm prices below a certain cost benchmark) and states that, in the assessment of alleged price-based exclusionary conduct, the principles are based on the premise that 'in general only conduct which would exclude a hypothetical "as efficient" competitor is abusive'.[82] The approach proposed by the Commission thus generally advocates a 'structured' rule of reason which differs for each category of abuse but which is based on the same underlying principle. In this way the Commission has sought to achieve a balance between precision and predictability and to set out transparent and workable proxies as rules for when conduct is illegal.[83]

It should be remembered, however, that this was simply intended to be a 'discussion' paper on exclusionary abuses, designed to provoke debate in this complex area. Further it is not an exhaustive examination of Article 82 (which also deals with exploitative abuses and price discrimination). It remains to be seen whether exploitative and discriminatory abuses will be included in any guidelines that might be published in 2006 or 2007.

It must also not be forgotten that it is the ECJ which is charged with responsibility for interpreting the provisions of the Treaty. Arguably its case law, and the wording of Article 82 itself, do not support the view that a sole consumer welfare and efficiency goal should be pursued in the enforcement and application of Article 82.[84] In this regard, the Commissioner for Competition, Neelie Kroes, stated:

> I am aware that it is often suggested that – unlike section 2 of the Sherman Act – Article 82 is intrinsically concerned with 'fairness' and therefore not focussed primarily on consumer welfare. As far as I am concerned, I think that competition policy evolves as our understanding of economics evolves. In days gone by, 'fairness' played a prominent role in section 2 enforcement in a way that is no longer the case. I don't see why a similar development could not take place in Europe.[85]

So far, this evolution has not been made explicit in the case law under Article 82. Although the Commission may set its own enforcement priorities, policies and rules which conflict with those set out by the Court will obviously lead to difficulties and confusion for national courts. A clear statement on the current objectives of Article 82 and the burden and standard of proof in these cases by the Court would thus be extremely welcome. Indeed the pending appeal of *British Airways* v. *Commission*[86] may provide the ECJ with the opportunity to provide some guidance on these issues. The grounds of appeal contend, amongst other things, that the CFI erred in law by failing to consider the actual and likely effects of the allegedly abusive conduct and by failing to consider whether the conduct in question harmed consumers.

A further problem is that it is not entirely clear that the structure of Article 82 lends itself to the two-stage approach weighing exclusionary conduct against demonstrable efficiencies. Unlike Article 81, Article 82 is not explicitly divided into two separate parts and it is not certain that the concept either of abuse or of objective justification provides, as developed by the Court, a forum for balancing the anticompetitive and procompetitive benefits identified.[87] Further in no case has a separate efficiency defence modelled on Article 81(3) been accepted by the ECJ.

It should also be mentioned that many of the issues being considered in the context of the European review are also being discussed in the US before the Antitrust Modernization Commission ('AMC') and in DOJ/FTC joint hearings on single-firm conduct. The AMC was created in 2002[88] and charged with an obligation to (1) examine whether the need exists to modernize the antitrust laws and to identify and study related issues; (2) to solicit views of all parties concerned with the operation of the antitrust laws; (3) to evaluate the advisability of proposals and current arrangements with respect to any issues so identified; and (4) to prepare and submit to Congress and the President a report.[89] The report is to 'contain a detailed statement of the findings and conclusions of the Commission, together with recommendation for legislative or administrative action the Commission considers to be appropriate'.[90] The objective of the DOJ/FTC joint hearings on single-firm conduct is to seek insight and information in this difficult area and to aid the agencies when determining whether single-firm conduct may violate Section 2. It is unclear whether or not any report or guidelines will follow.

As part of the AMC's extremely broad review (which is also examining enforcement institutions, merger enforcement, remedies, new economy issues, the Robinson–Patman Act, immunity and exemptions, regulated industries, criminal and international issues), it is considering the rules on Exclusionary Conduct and whether the substantive standards for determining whether conduct is exclusionary or anticompetitive under section 1 or section 2 should be revisited.[91] In the context of section 2, one criticism made of the case law is that, as in Europe, there has been a tendency to group or 'pigeon-hole' allegations of dominant firms' conduct into discrete categories of improper acts, developing category-specific liability standards and diverting attention away from central analytical concepts.[92] The question of whether there is a perfect monopolization test for distinguishing exclusionary conduct from competition on the merits is thus being debated. Further the Exclusionary Conduct Study Group has submitted questions for public comment on when a refusal to deal with a rival in adjacent market violates section 2 whether the Supreme Court in *Trinko* states an appropriate legal standard, whether the essential facilities doctrine constitutes an independent basis of liability for single firm conduct under section 2, and, if these standards are not appropriate, how the standards for exclusionary or anticompetitive conduct should be determined (e.g. through legislation, judicial development, *amicus* efforts by DOJ and FTC).[93]

The application of both Article 82 and section 2 raises many complex issues. The way that these are addressed and resolved within the context of the EC review will no doubt affect the way the rules governing refusal to deal develop in the future. The sections below look closely at the current rules on refusal to supply prior to considering the conditions for liability and whether any change in approach may be desirable.

### Section 3   Cases on unilateral refusal to deal

*3.1   Introduction*

A refusal to deal is not per se illegal under either EC or US antitrust law. There is therefore no unconditional duty to deal so that a monopolist or dominant firm will not necessarily act unlawfully by refusing to supply a customer or competitor.[94] In both jurisdictions, however, there are cases establishing that Article 82 or section 2 might, in certain circumstances, impose an obligation to deal. The cases have dealt with both refusal to supply a customer who is not an actual or potential competitor of the dominant firm (with the object of harming a competitor on the dominated market) and refusal to deal with a competitor who operates, or wishes to operate, in competition with the dominant firm on the dominated market or a market downstream to the dominated market. In each case, the potential competition concern arises from the exclusion of a competitor in either the dominated or downstream market, respectively.

The exact circumstances in which an obligation to deal may, or should, be imposed is uncertain, however, and has provoked widespread debate. There are a number of factors which make this area especially controversial.

First, an obligation to deal interferes with a firm's freedom of contract and right to dispose freely of its property. This concern has been voiced in both the US and the EC. In the US in 1919, Justice McReynolds stated in *United States* v. *Colgate & Co* that '[i]n the absence of any purpose to create or maintain a monopoly, the [Sherman] act does not restrict the long-recognized right of trader or manufacturer engaged in an entirely private business, freely to exercise his own independent discretion as to parties with whom he will deal'.[95] Similarly, in *Oscar Bronner* v. *Mediaprint Zeitungs-und Zeitschriftenverlag GmbH & Co. KG*, Jacobs AG stated that 'the right to choose one's trading partners and freely to dispose of one's property . . . [are]. . . generally recognised principles in the law of the Member States, in some cases with constitutional status'.[96]

Further, in cases involving a refusal to deal with a competitor there is a concern that it may be difficult to identify conduct which has an anticompetitive effect[97] and, in particular, that the imposition of an obligation to deal may: (1) discourage innovation both by (a) the dominant firm (if it thinks it will be forced to share its innovations) and (b) its competitors (by removing the incentive to develop their own inputs). This leads to a tension between static and dynamic efficiencies since consumer welfare may be increased not only by price competition in the form of lower prices on a downstream market but also through dynamic efficiencies resulting from innovation and the creation of new products. The acceptance of market power may therefore be the best way to promote investment and innovation incentives and dynamic efficiency. The tension between forced sharing and incentives to invest have been noted both by the Supreme Court in *Trinko* and by Advocate General Jacobs in *Oscar Bronner*.[98] This tension is especially acute in the sphere of intellectual property, where the intellectual property right is specifically granted to investors as a reward for effort; and (2) not be effective. Enforcement may be difficult and costly and the competition authority or court may have to consider what terms of dealing it is reasonable to impose, a task it is not ideally suited to perform. In *Trinko*, for example, Justice Scalia stated that an obligation to deal also required the courts to act as central planners, identifying the proper price, quantity and other terms of dealing, a task to which they were ill-suited.[99]

### 3.2   Refusal to supply a customer

*3.2.1   EC law*   In both the US and EC cases can be found that may be explained on the grounds that the refusal to supply a customer was motivated by a desire to exclude competition in the dominated market. In these cases the refusal to supply operates in a similar way to an 'exclusive dealing' provision. A dominant firm may, for example, make supply conditional upon a customer discontinuing a course of dealing with a competitor. The purpose is thus to forestall the competitor's access to customers.[100]

In *United Brands* v. *Commission*,[101] United Brands refused to continue supply of its Chiquita bananas to a Danish ripener/distributor who had engaged in an advertising and promotion campaign for a rival with the net result that it sold fewer of United Brands' Chiquita bananas. The ECJ upheld the Commission's finding of abuse, stating that the 'refusal to sell would limit markets to the prejudice of consumers' and would 'discourage its other ripener/distributors from supporting the advertising of other brand names and that the deterrent effect of the sanction imposed upon one of them would make its position of strength on the relevant market that much more effective'.[102]

Although the judgment clearly displays concern about the adverse effect of the conduct on competition on the relevant market, it does not analyse in any detail what those effects will be.[103] Further, statements of the Court indicate a broader desire to ensure that the conduct of dominant firms should not hurt customers abiding by regular commercial practice. The ECJ stated that a dominant firm could not stop supplying a long-standing customer who abides by regular commercial practice and that any such refusal to supply would amount to discrimination with might in the end eliminate a trading party from the relevant market.[104] The Court did recognize, however, that even a dominant undertaking must have the right to take steps to protect its commercial interest, so long as its behaviour is proportionate to the threat and is not aimed at strengthening or abusing its dominant position.[105]

*3.2.2   US law*   In *United States* v. *Colgate & Co* the Supreme Court indicated that a refusal to deal could infringe the Sherman Act where there was a 'purpose to create or maintain a monopoly'. Subsequently the Court has found violations of section 2 where there has been clear intent or purpose to monopolize a market through a refusal to deal.[106]

In *Lorain Journal Co.* v. *United States*,[107] the Supreme Court found, in an attempted monopolization case, that Lorain Journal had engaged in wrongful exclusionary behaviour by refusing to accept advertisements from firms that also advertised with a competing radio station. The background to this case was that Lorain Journal had for a long period enjoyed a substantial monopoly in Lorain of the mass dissemination of news and advertising, both of a local and a national character. That position was threatened, however, when a radio station opened in the Lorain area. Lorain Journal then commenced its policy of refusing to accept local advertisements from any local advertiser who advertised, or who Lorain Journal believed was about to advertise, with the radio station.[108] The District Court 'found expressly that the purpose and intent of this procedure was to destroy the broadcasting company'.[109] The Supreme Court accepted this and that, were Lorain Journal to succeed in its destruction and elimination, it would have restored its substantial monopoly of the mass dissemination of all news and advertising, inter-state and national, as well as local, and would deprive the Community of a radio station. The Supreme Court thus held that, although a business did generally have the right to select its customers and to refuse to accept advertisements from whomever it pleases, that right was neither absolute nor exempt from regulation. 'Its exercise as a purposeful means of monopolizing interstate commerce is prohibited by the Sherman Act.'[110]

### 3.3   Refusal to supply a competitor

*3.3.1   EC law*   A majority of refusals to supply cases in the EC have involved a situation where the refusal has affected competition not in the dominated market but between the dominant firm and a competitor in a downstream or ancillary market.

COMMERCIAL SOLVENTS   The starting point of this line of case law is *Commercial Solvents Corp* v. *Commission*.[111] In this case Commercial Solvents, a US multinational company, had stopped supply of a raw material, aminobutanol, to a small Italian pharmaceuticals company, Zoja. Zoja used the material to produce an ethambutol-based anti-TB drug. Commercial Solvents' decision to refuse supply was principally motivated by the fact that it had decided to manufacture ethambutol itself. The ECJ upheld the Commission's finding of an abuse, stating that a dominant producer of a raw material, able to control the supply to manufacturers of derivatives, could not, just because it decided to start manufacturing these derivatives in competition with its former customers, 'act in such a way as to eliminate their competition which . . . would amount to eliminating one of the principal manufacturers of ethambutol in the Common Market'.[112] It thus stated that:

> an undertaking which has a dominant position in the market in raw materials and which, with the object of reserving such raw material for manufacturing its own derivatives, refuses to supply a customer, which is itself a manufacturer of these derivatives, and therefore risks eliminating all competition on the part of this customer, is abusing its dominant position.[113]

Although this case may now be seen as an example of leveraging by a dominant firm of its market power into a downstream market, the criticism following this case focused on the failure of either the Commission or the ECJ to address the anticompetitive harm that was likely to be caused by the refusal to supply and/or the possible efficiencies or benefits which might have resulted from Commercial Solvents' decision to integrate vertically.[114] Although the judgment did not impose an absolute prohibition on a refusal to supply by a dominant firm, it did suggest a broad basis for the doctrine in EC competition law and a particular concern with fairness in treatment of customers.

*Commercial Solvents* involved a refusal to supply a product to an existing customer.[115] Subsequent decisions and cases have considered extension of the principle to cases dealing with new customers, physical infrastructure, intellectual property rights and other resources.

DEVELOPMENT OF THE SO-CALLED ESSENTIAL FACILITIES DOCTRINE *Commercial Solvents* has been relied and expanded upon by the Commission to develop an essential facilities doctrine in a line of cases dealing with access to airline computer reservation services,[116] interlining arrangements[117] and port facilities.[118] It was only in a case involving access to port facilities, however, that the Commission first used the term 'essential facilities', making it clear that both a refusal to grant access to an essential facility and/or a grant of access on unfavourable terms might be contrary to Article 82. In *Sealink/B&I Holyhead: Interim Measures*.[119] The Commission stated:

> A dominant undertaking which both owns or controls and itself uses an essential facility, i.e., a facility or infrastructure without access to which competitors cannot provide services to their customers, and which refuses its competitors access to that facility or grants access to competitors only on terms less favourable than those which it gives its own services, thereby placing the competitors at a competitive disadvantage, infringes Article [82], if the other conditions of that Article are met.

APPLICATION TO CASES INVOLVING INTELLECTUAL PROPERTY RIGHTS Debate over the circumstances where there may be an obligation to deal and the existence[120] and the extent of the essential facilities doctrine has become intertwined with the debate over whether it can constitute an abuse to refuse to license another (or others) to use an intellectual property right.

Although in *Volvo AB* v. *Veng*[121] the ECJ indicated that a refusal to license registered designs to manufacture replacement car panels could not in itself constitute an abuse,[122] it is well known that the ECJ in *RTE & ITP* v. *Commission (Magill)*[123] upheld a Commission decision finding that a copyright holder with a dominant position had committed an abuse of that position by refusing to license its rights to others. The controversy that surrounded the judgment[124] were somewhat tempered by the relatively narrow terms of the judgment and by subsequent cases which have reiterated that it will only be in exceptional circumstances that a refusal to license will constitute an abuse.

The *Magill* case involved a refusal by TV broadcasters to grant a licence to copy TV listings protected by copyright conferred by national legislation. The refusal prevented Magill from using the information to publish a weekly TV guide containing comprehensive listings for the week ahead which would have competed with the guides which each broadcaster published to its own programmes. The Commission held that this behaviour constituted an abuse of a dominant position and this decision was upheld by the CFI and ECJ. On appeal the ECJ held, as it had done in *Volvo* v. *Veng*, that since the exclusive right of reproduction formed part of an author's copyright, a refusal to grant a licence by an undertaking holding a dominant position would not *in itself* constitute an abuse. It could, however, do so in 'exceptional circumstances'. On the facts, the Court found such circumstances to exist.[125]

First, the information on programme scheduling was an indispensable raw material for the compilation of a TV guide. The refusal to provide that information, relying on copyrights, prevented the appearance of a *new* product – a comprehensive TV guide – which the appellants did not offer and for which there was a potential consumer demand and constituted a breach under Article 82(b).

Secondly, there was no justification for the refusal. Neither the activity of television broadcasting nor of publishing TV magazines provided a justification for such a refusal. Thirdly, the broadcasters, contrary to the principle set out in *Commercial Solvents*,[126] had, by refusing to provide information, 'reserved to themselves the secondary market of weekly television guides by excluding all competition on that market . . . since they denied access to the basic information which is the raw material indispensable for the compilation of such a guide'.

The narrow terms of the judgment, which stressed the exceptional circumstances of the case, did not therefore suggest that the general right to exercise copyright, or other intellectual property rights, would be undermined. Rather the unusual nature of the Irish and UK copyright, which were not works of creative or intellectual endeavour but compilations of information, may suggest that the authorities were not so wary of protecting the innovation and investment of the dominant firm.[127]

THE JUDGMENTS IN LADBROKE, OSCAR BRONNER AND IMS
Three subsequent judgments[128] of the CFI and ECJ have dealt with the question of when a refusal to license or refusal to supply may constitute an abuse of a dominant position. All three of these more recent cases suggest that an obligation will be imposed only in a relatively narrow range of circumstances.

In *Tiercé Ladbroke SA* v. *Commission*[129] the CFI indicated that, following *Magill* and *Commercial Solvents*,[130] a refusal by French race course societies to license televised broadcasts of horse races to Ladbroke's betting outlets in Belgium was not abusive: in this case the societies were not present on the betting market (on which the product was offered);[131] the televised broadcasting of races was not 'indispensable' to the bookmaker's main activity (the taking of bets);[132] and the refusal to license did not prevent the emergence of a new product.[133]

In *Oscar Bronner* v. *Mediaprint*,[134] a regional newspaper sought access to the home distribution system of a larger national newspaper group which held a substantial share of the daily newspaper market. The ECJ held, relying on its previous judgments in *Commercial Solvents* and CBEM v. CLT and IPB (Telemarketing),[135] that, to constitute an abuse, the refusal to supply a rival would have to relate to indispensable goods or services and would have to be likely to eliminate all competition in the downstream market from the person requesting access. Further it held that, even if the principles set out in *Magill*[136] applied in cases involving property and not intellectual property, the refusal to supply would (i) still have to be likely to eliminate all competition in the daily newspaper market on the part of the person seeking access, (ii) be incapable of objective justification; and (iii) the access would have to be indispensable to the carrying on of the other person's business, there being no actual or potential substitute for it.[137] The ECJ stressed that to be indispensable it would not be enough for the person seeking supply to argue that it would not be economically viable for it to create the facility. Rather it would, at the very least, have to be shown that it was not economically viable for an undertaking in a similar position of the dominant firm to create the facility.[138] In *Oscar Bronner* these circumstances were clearly not met.[139] The ECJ thus seemed to heed the opinion of its Advocate General that generally firms should have the right to choose trading partners and freely to dispose of property,[140] and that incentives for dominant undertakings (and competitors) to invest in efficient facilities should not be undermined by freely allowing competitors, upon request, to share the benefits.[141]

Returning to the question of when a refusal to grant a copyright licence might constitute an abuse (in this case over an '1860 brick structure', a system for representing regional pharmaceutical sales data in Germany),[142] the ECJ in *IMS Health GmbH & Co OHG* v. *NDC Health GmbH & Co KG*[143] held, following *Magill*, that it would be sufficient for three cumulative conditions to be satisfied:[144] (1) the refusal prevents the emergence of a new product not offered by the dominant firm for which there is potential consumer demand;[145] (2) that it is unjustified; and (3) the refusal excludes any or all[146] competition on a secondary market (because access to the material is indispensable). The ECJ did find that a secondary market existed in this case as it held that it was sufficient that a 'potential' or 'hypothetical' market were identified upstream (i.e. there were two stages of production). 'Such is the case where the products or services are indispensable in order to carry on a particular business and where there is an actual demand for them on the part of undertakings which seek to carry on the business for which they are indispensable.'[147] Although the ECJ set out a clear presumption against the licence, it nonetheless envisaged that it should be available if these stringent conditions were met.

THE MICROSOFT CASE   In *Microsoft* the Commission held that Microsoft had abused its dominant position in the PC operating system market by refusing to share interoperability information with competitors who needed the information to compete in the work group server market.[148] The consequence of this was to stifle innovation in the affected market and to diminish consumers' choices by locking them into a homogenous Microsoft solution. The Commission rejected the major objective justification put forward by Microsoft relating to its intellectual property rights, concluding that, 'on balance, the possible negative impact of an order to supply on Microsoft's incentives to innovate is outweighed by its positive impact on the level of innovation of the whole industry'.[149] Although it could be argued that the intellectual property rights in both *Magill* (copyright over TV listings) and *IMS* (copyright over a brick structure, essentially a grid superimposed on a map of Germany) were weak, so that the competition authorities did not have to be so wary of protecting and undermining the creative or intellectual endeavour in these cases,[150] the remedy of interoperability in *Microsoft* arguably did require compulsory licensing of a more substantive intellectual property right. The decision is, however, currently on appeal to the CFI. In proceedings for interim relief before the CFI,[151] the question of whether the value of IP rights should be taken into account was raised before, but not decided by, the President of the CFI. The CFI concluded that a prima-facie case had been made out. 'In substance, it must be ascertained whether the circumstances taken into account by the Commission are correct in fact and capable in law of founding the conclusion that there are exceptional circumstances which justify ordering the applicant to disclose valuable information protected by intellectual property rights.'[152]

### 3.3.2 US law

ASPEN SKIING, KODAK AND TRINKO    Subsequent to its opinion in *United States* v. *Colgate & Co*, the Supreme Court upheld some allegations of monopolization where a firm with monopoly power had refused to supply with the purpose of monopolizing a downstream market.[153] In *Aspen Skiing Co* v. *Aspen Highlands Skiing Corp*,[154] however, the Supreme Court held that a monopolist's refusal to continue in a commercial marketing arrangement with its only competitor on the monopolized market constituted unlawful monopolization.

In *Aspen* the Supreme Court affirmed an award of treble-damages to Aspen Highlands Co ('Highlands') on the grounds that Aspen Skiing Co ('Ski Co') had monopolized the market for downhill skiing services in Aspen, Colorado.[155] The facts of the case were that for quite some time Ski Co (which owned three mountains) and Highlands (which owned one) had operated an interchangeable multi-area ticket programme allowing skiers to ski on all four mountains. Following numerous disputes in which Ski Co demanded a greater allocation of revenues from the scheme, Ski Co withdrew from the joint marketing programme. It also took steps to thwart Highland's attempts to offer its own all-area package, even refusing to accept vouchers from Highlands to pay the retail prices of its lift tickets. Before the Supreme Court, Ski Co denied that it had a duty to cooperate with a competitor.[156] A violation of section 2 could not be established without evidence of substantial exclusionary conduct.[157]

The Supreme Court stressed that the absence of a duty to transact business with another firm did not mean that the right was unqualified.[158] Rather *Lorain Journal* had established that a refusal to deal in an effort to destroy a small competitor and to regain its monopoly violated section 2. In its assessment the Supreme Court took account of the fact that Ski Co made a significant change to its pattern of distribution (and had not just simply rejected a novel offer to cooperate). In determining whether the conduct could properly be categorized as exclusionary, the Court did not, however, simply consider its effect on Highlands.

> In addition, it is relevant to consider its impact on consumers and whether it has impaired competition in an unnecessarily restrictive way. If a firm has been 'attempting to exclude rivals on some basis other than efficiency', it is fair to characterize its behavior as predatory. It is, accordingly, appropriate to examine the effect of the challenged pattern of conduct on consumers, on Ski Co.'s smaller rival, and on Ski Co. itself.[159]

Applying this test the Supreme Court found that Ski Co had engaged in exclusionary behaviour: skiers preferred the multi-area pass and were adversely affected by its elimination; Highlands was significantly injured by it and was steadily losing market share; and critically Ski Co had no business justification for its conduct which led to its forgoing daily tickets sales.[160] It thus concluded

> Although Ski Co.'s pattern of conduct may not have been as 'bold, relentless, and predatory' as the publisher's actions in Lorain Journal, the record in this case comfortably supports an inference that the monopolist made a deliberate effort to discourage its customers from doing business with its smaller rival . . . Thus the evidence supports an inference that Ski Co. was not motivated by efficiency concerns and that it was willing to sacrifice short-run benefits and consumer goodwill in exchange for a perceived long-run impact on its smaller rival.[161]

This judgment imposing liability where the defendant was attempting to exclude rivals on some basis other than efficiency[162] was controversial. Although some feared that it would discourage beneficial collaboration if a subsequent decision to abandon it was subject to challenge, later cases indicated that the reach of the case was relatively narrow and that the plaintiff's success was perhaps partly attributable to the defendant's decision not to challenge the finding of monopoly power and its lack of any well conceived efficiency justification.[163] In cases where a convincing business justification, or compensating efficiencies, has been raised, the monopolization claim has ordinarily be rejected.[164] In *Olympia Equipment Leasing Co v. Western Union Telegraph Co*,[165] for example, the Seventh Circuit[166] held that Western Union did not act anticompetitively when it withdrew sales agent services, which it had provided for its competitor. It had a legitimate business justification for its decision (the desire to liquidate its stocks) and Olympia could have employed its own sales force if it wanted to remain in business.[167]

In *Eastman Kodak Co v. Image Technical Services Inc.*,[168] the Supreme Court stressed that any business justification raised should be tested to ensure that it was not pretextual. Indeed the Court held, relying on *Aspen*, that the reason for the refusal was critical. 'It is true that, as a general matter, a firm can refuse to deal with its competitors. But such a right is not absolute; it exists only if there are legitimate competitive reasons for the refusal.'[169]

In an attempt to constrain the ambit of section 2 in this sphere the government urged the Supreme Court in *Trinko* to adopt a narrow view of it, maintaining that a refusal to cooperate with a competitor should not constitute unlawful monopolization '*unless* it would make no economic sense for the defendant but for its tendency to eliminate or lessen competition'.[170] Although the Supreme Court did not adopt this position,[171] and even though the nature of the facts of the case could arguably be said to constrain the reach of the opinion, the opinion represents a clear retreat from *Aspen*, adopting a sceptical stance 'toward the benefits of judicial policing of refusals to deal'.[172]

The fact that makes *Trinko* a slightly different case is that a statutory scheme, the Telecommunications Act of 1996, already mandated the defendant (a local telephone service provider) to share its network with its rivals on just, reasonable and non-discriminatory terms. One of those rivals (AT&T) provided telephone services to the plaintiff. Although complaints about the service Verizon had provided to competing providers had been settled with regulators,[173] the plaintiff claimed that the defendant's conduct also violated section 2. The District Court dismissed the action but the Second Circuit reversed, suggesting that the allegations could establish a monopolization claim under either the essential facilities doctrine or the monopoly leveraging doctrine.[174]

Justice Scalia gave the opinion on behalf of six members of the Supreme Court.[175] The Court first clarified that the Telecommunications Act did not exclude the operation of the antitrust rules[176] before considering whether the refusal to share its network could violate section 2. In considering section 2, the Supreme Court stressed the tension that resulted from compelling firms to share an advantage with the underlying purpose of the antitrust law, since it might lessen the incentive for the monopolist, the rival or both to invest in economically beneficial facilities.[177] Further it noted that forced sharing required the courts to act as central planners (for which they were ill-suited) and might facilitate the supreme evil of antitrust, collusion.[178] Its starting point was as follows:

> Thus, as a general matter, the Sherman Act 'does not restrict the long recognized right of [a] trader or manufacturer engaged in an entirely private business, freely to exercise his own independent discretion as to parties with whom he will deal'. (*United States* v. *Colgate & Co.*, 250 U.S. 300, 307 (1919)).[179]

After referring to *Aspen* and noting that the right to refuse to deal with other firms was not unqualified, it was stressed that the Court had been 'cautious' in recognizing such exceptions, 'because of the uncertain virtue of forced sharing and the difficulty of identifying and remedying anticompetitive conduct by a single firm'.[180]

It then went on to hold that this case did *not* fit within existing exceptions or provide a basis for recognizing a new one.[181] It did not fall within the limited exception recognized in *Aspen*, which it stated was 'at or near the outer boundary of section 2 liability'.[182] In *Aspen* (1) the defendant had itself decided to cease participation in the cooperative venture, (2) the uni-lateral termination of the voluntary, and presumably profitable, course of dealing suggested a willingness to forsake short-term profits to achieve an anticompetitive end and the defendant's unwillingness to cooperate even if compensated at retail price revealed a distinctly anticompetitive bent;[183] and (3) the products sought were already available to customers. In con-trast, in *Trinko* (1) there had been no voluntary course of dealing or sug-gestion that there would have been one, absent the statutory scheme so that prior conduct shed no light upon the motivation of the refusal to deal, (2) there was a critical difference in pricing behaviour as 'Verizon's reluc-tance to interconnect at the cost-based rate of compensation available under §251(c)(3) tells us nothing about dreams of monopoly'[184] and (3) the services required in this case were not otherwise available to the public but were only shared in consequence of the statutory right to access (which thus created something brand new, the wholesale market for leasing network elements).[185]

The Supreme Court also considered that the case did not justify adding to existing exceptions from the proposition that there is no duty to aid com-petitors. It emphasized the importance of the existence of a regulatory structure designed to deter and remedy anticompetitive harm. The regime diminished the likelihood of major antitrust harm and indicated that the benefits to competition provided by antitrust would be small. It had also been an effective steward of the antitrust function. The slight benefits of intervention were, therefore outweighed by its costs and risks.[186]

Although, therefore, the effective and expert statutory regime providing for access was central to the conclusion in *Trinko* that it was unnecessary to force access under section 2,[187] (see also the discussion of the essential facilities doctrine below) the tone of this case is unwelcoming to refusal to deal cases.[188]

THE ESSENTIAL FACILITIES DOCTRINE    A possible separate cate-gory (or sub-category) of refusal to deal cases involves the essential facili-ties doctrine. Under this doctrine it appears that a firm which controls an essential facility, which cannot be duplicated by competitors, may have an obligation to allow others access to it on reasonable terms. The doctrine has been developed in the lower courts.[189] A widely cited case applying it, and setting out its critical elements, is *MCI Communications Corporation* v. *AT&T*,[190] a decision of the Seventh Circuit.[191] The court held that a monopolist which controls an essential facility (or 'bottleneck') can 'extend monopoly power from one stage of production to another, and from one market into another. Thus, the antitrust laws have imposed on firms con-trolling an essential facility the obligation to make the facility available on nondiscriminatory terms'.[192] The court set out four conditions[193] which would need to be proved by the plaintiff before the doctrine could be applied: (1) control of an essential facility by a monopolist, (2) a competitor's inability practically or reasonably to duplicate the essential facility, (3) the denial of use of the facility to a competitor, (4) the feasibility of providing the facility.[194]

Because of the stringency of the conditions set out, there have been relatively few successful essential facility cases. Nonetheless the doctrine is controversial and contested[195] and the Supreme Court has never affirmed its existence. In particular, concern has been expressed that some courts have treated the doctrine as a stand-alone antitrust violation, divorced from traditional antitrust requirements, including proof of exclusionary conduct. Without this, 'the essential facility doctrine loses its mooring in §2 of the Sherman Act. It begins to operate as a "fair access" statute that forces one set of private firms to accommodate another set even when competition is not improved. As a result the doctrine is either superfluous[196] or else inconsistent with basic antitrust principles'.[197]

In *Trinko* the Supreme Court expressed distaste for the essential facilities doctrine. It cited approvingly articles attacking the doctrine[198] and set out policy reasons against it but did not go so far as to deny its existence. It ruled that its conclusion in that case would remain unchanged 'even if we considered to be established law the "essential facilities" doctrine . . . We have never recognized such a doctrine . . . and we find no need either to recognize it or to repudiate it here'. Rather the Court stressed that it would be indispensable to any essential facility claim that access to the facility be unavailable. As access existed in *Trinko*, the doctrine was on the facts otiose.[199] It thus dismissed the argument based on essential facilities to the extent that it was distinct from the general refusal to deal argument. Since then lower courts have been swift to throw out essential facilities claims where a federal agency is authorized to compel access to a competitor's infrastructure.[200]

REFUSAL TO LICENSE   Whether or not an intellectual property right holder should be required, under antitrust rules, to license use of its rights to others has also been a hotly debated issue in US antitrust law. As with regard to essential facilities, the Supreme Court has not ruled on this important issue and different views have been reflected in the circuits.

In *Data General Corp v. Grumman Systems Support Corp*,[201] a manufacturer refused to continue licensing arrangements in respect of its copyrighted diagnostic program (MD/ADEX) to a computer service provider (which competed in the service market). The crux of the service provider's case was that only the manufacturer could develop the diagnostic tool, which was an essential device in the repair of computers. After reviewing *Aspen* and *Kodak*, the First Circuit[202] concluded that a monopolist's unilateral refusal to deal might constitute prima-facie evidence of exclusionary conduct which could be rebutted by proof of a valid business justification, i.e. proof of countervailing benefits to the competitive process. The court recognized, however, that the involvement of intellectual property rights (copyright) meant that the case raised different and sensitive issues and required harmonization, as best could be done, of the federal antitrust and copyright rules. Its solution was to hold that, while exclusionary conduct can include a monopolist's refusal to license a copyright, an author's desire to exclude others from use of its copyrighted work was a 'presumptively valid business justification'.[203] *Data General* thus put in place a clear presumption of legality in case of refusal to license copyright.[204]

In *Image Technical Services* v. *Eastman Kodak*,[205] however, the Ninth Circuit adopted a modified approach. This case concerned an allegation by independent service operators (ISOs) that Kodak had used its monopoly in the market for replacement parts for its photocopiers to create a monopoly in the service market. The Supreme Court had remanded the case after it set aside the district court's award of summary judgment to Kodak.[206] On remand, the jury gave a verdict for the ISOs.[207] The Ninth Circuit, having concluded that Kodak did have monopoly power in the replacement parts market, held that its refusal to deal in order to create or maintain a monopoly would be prohibited unless it had a legitimate business justification.[208] Kodak stated that the existence of its patents and copyrighted parts provided a valid business justification. The Court accepted that 'while exclusionary conduct can include a monopolist's unilateral refusal to license a [patent] or copyright' or to sell its patented or copyrighted work, a monopolist's 'desire to exclude others from its [protected] work is a presumptively valid business justification for any immediate harm to consumers',[209] and that the district court had not given adequate weight to Kodak's intellectual property rights. Nonetheless it affirmed the jury's finding, concluding that it was more probable than not that the jury would have found the presumptively valid business justification rebutted on the grounds of 'pretext'.[210] The Court was therefore willing to go behind the exercise of intellectual property rights and to examine the intent or motivation of the firm when refusing to sell or license.

The federal court of appeals, which has particular expertise in patent and copyright cases,[211] however, declined to follow this approach in *CSU, LLC* v. *Xerox Corp.*[212] This case also concerned the decision of a photocopy supplier not to sell parts to ISOs. The Federal Circuit considered that, since in a patent infringement suit (which is not objectively baseless), an antitrust defendant's subjective motivation is immaterial, the intent of Xerox in refusing to sell or license its patented works should also be irrelevant.

> In the absence of any indication of illegal tying, fraud in the Patent and Trademark Office, or sham litigation, the patent holder may enforce the statutory right to exclude others from making, using or selling the claimed invention free from liability under the antitrust laws. We therefore will not inquire into his subjective motivation for exerting his statutory rights, even though his refusal to sell or license his patented invention may have an anticompetitive effect, so long as that anticompetitive effect is not illegally extended beyond the statutory patent granted.[213]

The Federal Circuit thus rejected the Ninth Circuit's view that the presumption that a copyright holder had a valid business justification for any unilateral refusal to license could be rebutted by evidence that the defence was pretextual to mask anticompetitive conduct. It considered that this was a central departure from the First Circuit's view in *Data General*, which it preferred, that rebutting the presumption would be an uphill battle and appropriate only in the rare cases in which imposing antitrust liability is unlikely to frustrate the Copyright Act objectives.[214]

### Section 4   Conditions for liability
#### 4.1   EC law
The cases considered establish that the following practices may, subject to the existence of an objective justification for the conduct, constitute an abuse: a refusal to supply an existing customer where it is designed to disrupt competition between the dominant firm and its actual or potential competitors on the market of supply (e.g. where the refusal to supply a customer is aimed to discourage a customer from handling a competitor's products), and a refusal to supply or a refusal to license an existing customer/competitor or a third party/potential competitor where the refusal will disrupt competition between the dominant undertaking and the customer in a downstream market.

The *United Brand* case suggests a broad basis for liability where there is a refusal to deal with a customer. In this case the ECJ did not explicitly consider what anticompetitive harm would follow from dissuading distributors to advertise competitors' products and displayed concern about access to market for competitors and non-discriminatory and fair treatment of customers.

The longer line of cases dealing with refusal to supply or license a competitor or potential competitor in a downstream market, however, makes it easier to derive conditions for liability and, arguably, reflect a more progressive approach.

First, the cases seem to demand the existence of a primary and a secondary market, i.e. that the dominant firm leverages its dominant position from the dominated market into the secondary market. Although not all commentators agree that the Commission and ECJ correctly found two separate markets in *IMS*, the ECJ was nonetheless clear that the refusal to supply should eliminate any or all competition on a secondary market.[215]

Secondly, the cases demand that access to the product, service or facility should be 'indispensable' for the competitor to compete on the market (otherwise the refusal would not eliminate all, any or some[216] competition on the secondary market). Although the Court has not clarified exactly what it means by 'indispensable', the ECJ in *Bronner* stated that there should be no actual or potential substitutes for it and it was not sufficient that it was not economically viable for the person seeking supply (although it did not rule out the fact that a product or service would be indispensable if its creation would be economically unfeasible).

Thirdly, in the context of refusal to license an intellectual property right at least, it seems that it may be a requirement that the party seeking the licence should wish to offer a new product, not duplicating that offered by the dominant firm, for which there is a consumer demand.[217] The suggestion is that a refusal to license should not prevent the development of the secondary market to the detriment of consumers. Although it is unclear what constitutes a 'new' product,[218] the requirement could just simply be seen as setting out one mechanism for establishing how, in the context of refusal to license, the refusal has an adverse impact on consumer welfare.[219]

Fourthly, the refusal to supply or license will not be abusive if it is objectively justified (or it will only be abusive if unjustified).[220] There is little case law on the question of what may constitute an objective justification but factors such as the absence of capacity, fear of quality degradation, security, the deterrence of free-riding or the lack of creditworthiness should constitute legitimate justifications. In the United Kingdom, the competition authorities have found justifications such as intention to exit the market and illegality to be relevant to the appraisal.[221]

Another important issue is whether a different obligation exists where there is a termination of an existing relationship (rather than a refusal to supply). In some of the cases, there is undoubtedly an undercurrent theme that the dominant firm should treat existing customers fairly (Article 82 itself explicitly addresses discriminatory treatment of trading partners).[222] It would therefore seem possible to read *Commercial Solvents* as placing a more onerous burden on the dominant firm where the refusal to supply is of an existing customer. However, an alternative, and perhaps better, view is that, in subsequent cases, which have relied upon *Commercial Solvents*, the ECJ has in fact refined the principle over time, adopting a more economically rigorous approach, and, further, that it may simply be that it is easier to establish a breach where there has been a previous course of dealing with the customer requesting supply, or indeed another customer.[223] In such cases the decision to cease supply or to refuse supply to an additional customer may provide evidence of the unreasonableness of the decision, of a decision to sacrifice profits with the objective of excluding a competitor,[224] of an anticompetitive objective and/or that the decision has led to a decrease in consumer welfare.[225]

### 4.2 US law

US cases also establish that the following practices may constitute unlawful monopolization:[226] a refusal to supply a customer aimed at preventing it from handling a competitor's products, and a refusal to supply or a refusal to license an existing customer/competitor or a third party/potential competitor where the refusal will disrupt competition between the dominant undertaking and the customer in a downstream market. It has also been accepted that a refusal to deal with a competitor on the monopolized market may constitute unlawful monopolization. The conditions for liability in the US are, however, markedly different to those in the EC.

In *Lorain Journal* the Supreme Court was, in contrast to the ECJ in *United Brands*, focused on the competitive harm that resulted from Lorain Journal's conduct (the elimination of its only competitor). Although the case has been criticized for giving insufficient thought to the significance of the impact on competition,[227] the conduct adopted affected, at little or no cost to Lorain Journal, the radio station's access to key customers, making it impossible to obtain advertising revenues and to survive on the market. This would restore Lorain Journal's monopoly power. As the defendant could not provide any legitimate procompetitive justification for the policy pursued (other than its desire to maintain market power),[228] the section 2 claim succeeded.[229]

The Supreme Court's opinion in *Aspen* clearly set out an economic approach to section 2, focusing on both the adverse impact of the refusal to deal on the competitive process and any redeeming efficiencies which might exist. Although the Court did rely on the profits Ski Co sacrificed in furtherance of its policy, the range of factors considered arguably supports the view that the opinion required a rule of reason 'balancing approach that compares the adverse impact of the refusal to deal on the competitive process with any efficiency effect that may simultaneously arise, taking into account the possibility of less restrictive alternatives that might produce comparable efficiencies'.[230]

*Trinko* has, however, significantly altered the position. Although the opinion was given in the context of a regulated industry, it is undoubtedly of general importance to refusal to deal cases. Instead of demanding a rigorous weighing of adverse effects and efficiencies the case imposes a strong assumption that refusals to deal are not anticompetitive. It adopts a restrictive interpretation of *Colgate* stressing the right of a firm, even one with monopoly power, to choose the parties with whom it will deal,[231] it reverses, without referring to it, the burden of proof set out in *Eastman Kodak*[232] and reconceives *Aspen* as a case at the boundary of section 2 and an exception to a strong freedom-not-to-deal principle.[233]

It promotes a cautious approach to section 2, stating that exceptions to the freedom-not-to-deal principle should be limited because of the dangers involved in falsely condemning efficient conduct;[234] the difficulty involved in identifying anticompetitive conduct; the difficulties presented to courts in remedying unlawful refusals to deal; and the danger of undermining incentives to invest. The opinion comes down firmly in favour of 'business freedom'.[235]

When trying to derive conditions that will support liability for refusal to deal in the future, however, a difficulty is that the opinion states a lot about what does *not* constitute unlawful monopolization and says little about what *does*. The sceptical view of refusal to deal claims indicates that it will now only be in a narrow set of circumstances that a refusal to aid a competitor will constitute unlawful monopolization in US law. Indeed the indication is that lower courts appear to be reading *Trinko* as requiring profit sacrifice, a willingness to forsake profits with the expectation of recoupment after elimination of competition.[236] The cases signify that cutting off a prior (presumably profitable) course of dealing without other apparent explanation may support an inference of profit sacrifice with anticompetitive motivation,[237] which shifts the burden of proof to the defendant to establish an alternative and legitimate justification for the cut-off. The trouble with this position is that these factors do not present a coherent mechanism for distinguishing anticompetitive from legitimate business behaviour since they are not determinative of the question of whether the conduct has harmed consumer welfare.[238]

The sceptical view of section 2 set out in *Trinko*, and the Court's fear of condemning efficient conduct, also cast doubt upon the existence of a free-standing essential facility doctrine. It may also provide indirect support for the stance adopted by the Federal Circuit which, in the context of refusals to license, has acted to protect intellectual property rights and to diminish the role of the antitrust rules. It may support its message that the simple grant of an intellectual property right reflects the view that consumer welfare will be best promoted by encouraging investment.[239]

**Section 5   Conclusions**

The discussion above indicates that the EC and US approaches to refusal to deal are really quite disparate. Whilst the EC authorities have adopted a fairly broad view of circumstances in which an obligation to supply may be imposed, the US authorities and courts have narrowed the scope of section 2 in this sphere, preferring to accept false negatives rather than false positives which may chill procompetitive conduct.

Although there has been an evolution in Europe and later cases show greater readiness to adopt a more economic approach when considering the question of abuse, there is still little transparency, no clear indication of the objectives pursued and a willingness to intervene in refusal to supply and refusal to license cases. If the goal is a consumer welfare one, it would seem necessary that the refusal to deal should both exclude a competitor *and* do so in a significant way (in a way that harms consumers). An approach more closely aligned with ordoliberal thinking would, however, be more concerned with the exclusionary impact of the refusal to deal and with the availability of access to the market to the competitor or potential competitor, than its significance from a consumer welfare perspective. In the line of cases dealing with intellectual property rights, it seems that the Court has been concerned with both the fact and the significance of the exclusion: that it should prevent the emergence a new product (and the development of the secondary market) and exclude any competition on the secondary market. In the general refusal to supply cases, however, the judgements *could* perhaps be interpreted as displaying greater concern with open market access. Although they have been concerned about exclusionary impact of a refusal to deal on competition in the downstream market, they have not spelt out what the competitive significance of such exclusion should be.

In addition, it would seem critical, were an economic approach being adopted, that both the short-term impact of an obligation to supply and its long-term effect on investment or innovation should be considered. The source of the bottleneck should therefore be of relevance: whether it derives from an intellectual property right, significant investment and innovation or whether it derives from historical legacy, economies of scale or scope or network externalities. Although the Advocate General in *Oscar Bronner* stressed the importance of balancing these factors, this point has not been specifically addressed by the ECJ.

In conclusion, although later EC cases do support a more nuanced approach to Article 82, the judgments do not make it clear that the focus of the search is on exclusionary conduct with anticompetitive effects and/or how such effects are to be identified. An explicit recognition of a consumer welfare and efficiency objective is necessary to dispel fears that the rules may be used to condemn conduct which forecloses access without adverse effects and which unduly protects competitors on the market. Identification of the objectives of Article 82 is fundamental to a sound understanding of the applicable rules and the principles underlying them.

The Commission seeks to address these types of criticism in its Discussion Paper. Although the guidelines seek to clarify that with regard to exclusionary abuses, the objective of Article 82 is the protection of competition on the market as a means of enhancing consumer welfare and of ensuring an efficient allocation of resources, it is not at all clear that the structure proposed in relation to refusals to supply will achieve this objective. The Commission proposes different approaches depending upon whether the situation involves a termination of an existing supply relationship; a refusal to start supplying an input, including an IPR; or a refusal to start supplying an input which is information necessary for interoperability. The conditions imposed in each case do not, however, give faith that an abuse will only be found where refusal to deal is likely to have a negative effect on competition. On the contrary, the distinctions drawn between the different scenarios are hard to justify in economic terms[240] and presumptions of abuse are too readily applied. For example, in cases of termination of an existing supply relationship, the Commission states that a negative effect on competition in the downstream market will normally be presumed if the input owner is itself active in the downstream market and terminates supplies to one of its few competitors.[241] Under the structure set out this will mean that the burden will too easily shift to dominant firms to defend the behaviour on the basis of objective justifications or efficiencies. The suggested framework in refusal to supply cases does not, therefore, arguably do enought to advance or improve the position set out in the case-law.

The courts in the US do, in applying section 2, pursue a consumer welfare and efficiency objective. The cases on refusal to deal, however, disagree as to how best to achieve that goal. The opinion in *Apsen* indicated that a fuller rule of reason-type analysis should be conducted to determine whether legitimate justifications outweigh the anticompetitive impact of a refusal to deal. In *Trinko*, however, the Supreme Court suggests that, since the cost of condemning efficient conduct is great and it is hard to identify and remedy exclusionary conduct,[242] a cautious approach to section 2 should be adopted. It now seems unlikely that a plaintiff will be able to make a refusal to deal (or essential facilities) case in the absence of profit sacrifice,[243] and it is almost impossible for a plaintiff to establish that a refusal to license constitutes unlawful monopolization. The sweeping presumptions set out in these cases may, however, mean that the true impact of the refusal to deal or refusal to license on consumer welfare and efficiency will be obscured.[244]

# Notes

1. BA BCL Reader in Law, King's College London, solicitor, Freshfields Bruckhaus Deringer. The author wishes to thank Deirdre Trapp, Margaret Bloom, Robert Skitol and Brenda Sufrin for their helpful comments when reviewing this chapter.
2. See section 2. But see e.g. Jones, A., 'Analysis of agreements under US and EC antitrust law – Convergence or divergence?', 51 *Antitrust Bull.* (forthcoming, 2006).
3. European Commission (December 2005), 'DG Competition discussion paper on the application of Article 82 of the Treaty to exclusionary abuses', available at http://europa.eu.int/comm/competition/antitrust/others/discpaper 2005.pdf. ('Discussion Paper'). The paper, drafted in the style of guidelines, is intended to provoke debate as to how European markets are best protected from dominant companies' exclusionary conduct. The Commission has said that the purpose of the review is not to achieve convergence with other jurisdictions (although this might be a positive side-benefit of it), see frequently asked questions (MEMO/05/486). Following receipt of comments on the consultation on the dicussion paper, the most important topics raised were discussed in a public hearing in June 2006, see http://ec.europa.eu/comm/competition/antitrust/others/ article_82_review.html.
4. The concept of an undertaking has been broadly defined to include all entities engaged in economic activity, Case C-41/90 *Höfner and Elser* v. *Macroton* [1991] ECR I-1979, [1993] 4 CMLR 306. It is also possible for the purposes of Article 82 for two or more independent undertakings to be found to be collectively dominant on a market, see e.g. Cases C-395 and 396/96P, *Compagnie Maritime Belge Transports SA* v. *Commission* [2000] ECR I-1365, [2000] 4 CMLR 1076. See Discussion Paper, paras 43–50.
5. It provides that any abuse by one or more undertakings of a dominant position within the common market or in a substantial part of it is prohibited insofar as it affects trade between Member States. The prohibition thus applies only where five essential elements are established: (1) one or more undertakings, (2) a dominant position, (3) the dominant position is held within the common market or a substantial part of it, (4) an abuse, and (5) an effect on inter-state trade. It sets out an illustrative but non-exhaustive list (Case 6/72, *Europemballage Corporation and Continental Can Co Inc* v. *Commission* [1973] ECR 215, [1973] CMLR 199) of the type of conduct which may constitute an abuse.
6. See e.g. Case C-27/76, *United Brands* v. *Commission* [1978] ECR 207, [1978] 1 CMLR 429, paras 189–90.
7. Case C-53/92P *Hilti AG* v. *Commission* [1994] ECR I-666, [1994] 1 CMLR 590.
8. Case C-53/03 28 October 2004. The ECJ subsequently declined jurisdiction in this case; see judgment of 31 May 2005.
9. Case C-53/03 28 October 2004, para. 72.
10. The conduct is either objectively necessary or indispensable because of, for example, reasons of safety or health (so that without the conduct the products cannot or will not be produced or distributed in the market) or the conduct is a loss-minimizing reaction to competition from others (a meeting competition defence).
11. Discussion Paper, paras 77–92.
12. The Commission states that for the efficiency defence to apply the dominant firm must demonstrate that (i) efficiencies are realized or likely to be realized a result of the conduct concerned; (ii) the conduct concerned is indispensable to realize these efficiencies; (iii) the efficiencies benefit consumers; and (iv) competition in respect of a substantial part of the products concerned is not eliminated (Discussion Paper, paras 84–92). For a critique of this structure see, e.g. Fox, E., 'Comments on the Discussion Paper of DG Competition on the Application of Article 82 of the Treaty to Exclusionary Acts', available at http://ec.europa.eu/comm/competition/antitrust/others/article_82_review.html. Many of the commentators at the public hearing criticized this proposed approach to efficiencies (see above n 3).
13. 'Every person who shall monopolize, or attempt to monopolize, or combine or conspire with any other person or persons, to monopolize any part of the trade or commerce

among the several States, or with foreign nations, shall be deemed guilty of a felony.' In addition to prohibition of monopolization and attempts to monopolize, it thus also prohibits conspiracies to monopolize. The requirement of a conspiracy means, however, that such cases often overlap with section 1 Sherman Act cases. Ordinarily an unlawful conspiracy is easier to establish under section 1 than under section 2.

14.   *Spectrum Sport Inc* v. *McQuillan* 506 US 447, 459 (1993).

15.   *United States* v. *Grinnel Corp.* 384 US 563, 571–572 (1966). In *Spectrum Sport Inc* v. *McQuillan* 506 US 447, 459 (1993) it was established that in an attempted monopolization case it is necessary for the plaintiff to prove that (1) the defendant has engaged in predatory or anticompetitive conduct with (2) a specific intent to monopolize and (3) a dangerous probability of achieving monopoly power.

16.   Article 82, like Article 66 ECSC, was not modelled on section 2 of the Sherman Act but was arguably more significantly influenced by German competition law; see e.g. Gerber, D. (1998), *Law and Competition in Twentieth Century Europe: Protecting Prometheus*, Clarendon Press and below, n 40.

17.   As the EC threshold of dominance is much lower, this may not be such a significant difference as it at first appears; see n 24 below. Indeed, the absence of such a power in the EC could be one reason why the threshold is so much lower, see e.g. Calvani, T. and J. Fingleton, 'Dominance: a comparative economic and legal analysis'.

18.   Arguably, if an effects-based approach is adopted when determining whether an abuse or the wilful acquisition of maintenance of monopoly power has occurred, that in itself will provide evidence of dominance. Thus an effects-based approach requires less weight be to put on a separate verification of dominance; see e.g. EAGCP (July 2005), 'An economic approach to Article 82', available at http://europa.eu.int/comm/competition/publications/studies/eagcp_july_21_05.pdf. The retention of a dominance test may, however, provide an important screen and act as an important limit on excess intervention especially in the EC where the concept of an abuse is currently drafted broadly. Indeed a higher threshold of dominance would arguably helpfully limit the scope of Article 82.

19.   In the 1970s, US courts placed much greater emphasis on market share 'that it was common for counsel for companies enjoying a substantial market share to advise against the collection of market share data lest it be used in an antitrust proceeding as proof of market power' (Calvani, T. and J. Fingleton, 'Dominance: a comparative economic and legal analysis', in *ABA Issues in Competition Law and Policy*, (forthcoming), chapter 39).

20.   In the US, a 'market share in excess of 70 percent establishes a prima facie case of monopoly power, at least with evidence of substantial barriers to entry and evidence that existing competitors could not expand output. In contrast, courts virtually never find monopoly power when market share is less than about 50 percent. The greatest uncertainty exists when market shares are between 50 percent and 70 percent' (ABA (2002), *Antitrust Law Developments*, 5th edn, 235–6). (The offence of attempted monopolization may occur, however, where the market shares are significantly below this threshold. Cases are likely to be taken very seriously where the defendant's market share is about 50 per cent, and although the offence is extremely unlikely to be committed by a firm with less than 30 per cent, attempted monopolization cases have succeeded where the defendant's market share has been between 30 and 50 per cent (ABA (2002), *Antitrust Law Developments*, 5th edn, 304–5).

21.   For example, in *US* v. *Syufy* 903 F.2d 659 (9th Cir. 1990) the Ninth Circuit rejected a finding of monopoly power where the defendant had at times had a market share of 100 per cent on the Las Vegas Movie Market. Evidence indicated that new entrants could, and did, penetrate the market. 'A high market share, though it may ordinarily raise an inference of monopoly power, will not do so in a market with low entry barriers or other evidence of a defendant's inability to control prices or exclude competitors' (903 F.2d 659, 664 Judge Kozinski).

22.   In Case T-219/99 *British Airways* v. *Commission* [2003] II ECR 5917, [2004] 4 CMLR 1008, appeal before the ECJ pending Case C-95/04 P, the CFI upheld the Commission's finding of dominance based on a market share of 39.7%. Controversially, the Commission states in its Discussion Paper that a finding of single-firm dominance

cannot be ruled out where a firm has a market share greater than 25%; see Discussion Paper, para. 31.

23. In Case C-62/86 *AKZO Chemie BV* v. *Commission* [1991] ECR I-3359, [1993] 5 CMLR 215, para. 60 the ECJ stated: 'With regard to market shares the Court has held that very large shares are in themselves, and save in exceptional circumstances, evidence of the existence of a dominant position (judgment in Case 85/76 *Hoffmann-La Roche* v. *Commission* [1979] ECR 461, para. 41). That is the situation where there is a market share of 50% such as that found to exist in this case.'

24. Many of the factors relied upon as other factors indicating dominance in the cases are ambiguous and could provide evidence of either barriers to entry *or* efficiencies, see e.g. Case 27/76 *United Brands* v. *Commission* [1978] ECR 207, [1978] 1 CMLR 429, Case 85/76 *Hoffmann-La Roche* v. *Commission* [1979] ECR 461, [1979] 3 CMLR 211 and Case 322/81 *Michelin* v. *Commission* [1983] ECR 3461, [1985] 1 CMLR 282. In its Discussion Paper, the Commission concedes that 'Market share is only a proxy for market power, which is the decisive factor. It is therefore necessary to extend the dominance analysis beyond market shares' (Discussion Paper, para. 32). It thus recognizes that factors such as product differentiation, and the degree of competitive restraint exerted by competitors will be relevant as well as the market position of buyers and the existence of barriers to entry and expansion. If the barriers to expansion faced by rivals and to entry faced by potential rivals are low, the fact that one undertaking has a high market share may not be indicative of dominance: see paras 32–42.

25. As distinguished from growth or development as a consequence of a superior product, business acumen or historic accident, *United States* v. *Grinnell Corp* 384 US 563, 570–71.

26. In attempted monopolization cases it must threaten to do so, see above, n 15 and e.g. ABA (2002), *Antitrust Law Developments*, 5th edn, 229.

27. See e.g. Case C-27/76 *United Brands* v. *Commission* [1978] ECR 207, [1978] 1 CMLR 429, para. 225. See also Article 82(c) which condemns price discrimination causing secondary line injury. There are few EC cases dealing with exploitative abuses. Rather the decisional practice and case law focuses on anticompetitive abuses.

28. Far from maintaining or strengthening a dominant position, the charging of monopoly prices may be the signal for new entry and actually attract new entrants and competitors into the market. Although the monopoly pricing may therefore harm consumers in the short run in the long run it may make the market more competitive. For this reason it could be argued that a policy of intervention should not be adopted: both because the competition authority is not qualified to determine what price is appropriate and because the policy would reduce, and possibly forgo, the chance to protect consumers in the future by competition rather than policy intervention; see e.g. EAGCP (July 2005), 'An economic approach to Article 82', at 11.

29. *Verizon Communications* v. *Law Offices of Curtis V Trinko LLP* 540 US 398 (2004). In the US, industry-specific regulations are used to control the exercise of monopoly power through charging monopoly prices.

30. 'On the contrary, [debate suggests] that Congress designed the Sherman Act as a "consumer welfare prescription" (Bork, R. (1978), *The Antitrust Paradox*, 66)', *Reiter* v. *Sonotone Corp.* 442 US 330, 343 (1979), reaffirmed in *NCAA* v. *Board of Regents of University of Oklahoma*, 468 U.S. 85, 107–8 (1984). In Bork's view, the maximization of consumer welfare, equated with allocative efficiency, would be a state of affairs in which consumer welfare cannot be increased by moving to an alternative state of affairs through judicial decree: Bork, R. (1978), *The Antitrust Paradox*, 58–66. The Supreme Court did not elaborate on this point, however. Many commentators take the view that consumer not total welfare is more consistent with original Sherman Act goals (the maximization of welfare must not be to the detriment of consumers; see e.g. Sullivan, L.A. and W.S. Grimes (2000), *The Law of Antitrust: An Integrated Handbook*, West, 12–13 and Motta, M. (2005), *Competition Policy: Theory and Practice*, Cambridge University Press, 18–22. See also the view set out by the Commission in its Discussion Paper, below n 63 and accompanying text.

31. It seems that the requirement of wilfulness does not require a subjective intent to monop-

olize a market. It is the effect of the conduct rather than the intent of the monopolist that is important, the assumption being that no monopolist monopolizes, unconscious of what he is doing, see *Aspen Skiing Co* v. *Aspen Highlands Co* 472 US 585, 612 and footnote 44 (1985) set out in n 157 below.

32.   How best to protect the market and consumers, see Fox, E. (2003), 'We protect competition, you protect competitors', **26**, *World Competition*, 149; and Fox, E. (2005), 'Is there life in *Aspen* after *Trinko*? The Silent Revolution of Section 2 of the Sherman Act', **73**, *Antitrust Law Journal*, 153.

33.   'Aggressive, competitive conduct by any firm, even one with market power, is beneficial to consumers. Courts should prize and encourage it. Aggressive, exclusionary conduct is deleterious to consumers, and courts should condemn it. The big problem lies in this: competitive and exclusionary conduct look alike'; see Easterbrook (2003), 'When is it worthwhile to use courts to search for Exclusionary conduct?', *Comb Bus L Rev*, 345, 346.

34.   'The question whether [the defendant's] conduct may properly be characterized as exclusionary cannot be answered by simply considering its effect on [the plaintiff]. In addition, it is relevant to consider its impact on consumers and whether it has impaired competition in an unnecessarily restrictive way. If a firm has been "attempting to exclude rivals on some basis other than efficiency," it is fair to characterize its behaviour as predatory.' See *Aspen Skiing Co* v. *Aspen Highlands Skiing Corp.* 472 US 585, 605 (1985), discussed below, n 159 and accompanying text. Between 1945 and the late 1970s (before the Chicago School began to ascend) a broader range of conduct was deemed improper as the courts held the view that one of the purposes of the Sherman Act was to protect smaller individuals and businesses from the might and power of larger firms. The preservation of a more atomized industry was considered desirable, bigness was treated suspiciously and the view was taken that ease of entry for small businesses should be facilitated. The early cases suggested that, if the firm's deliberate conduct conferred, protected or extended the monopoly rather than it being thrust upon the defendant, an offence would be committed; see e.g. *US* v. *Aluminium Co of America* 148 F.2d 416 (2nd Cir, 1945), *US* v. *Griffith* 334 US 100 (1948). At the end of the 1970s the ideology changed, however; see above, n 30.

35.   *Matsushita Elec Industrial Co* v. *Zenith Radio* 475 US 574, 594 (1986).

36.   *Verizon Communications* v. *Law Offices of Curtis V Trinko LLP* 540 US 398, 414 (2004), Justice Scalia. The Supreme Court in *Trinko* adopted a cautious approach to section 2 which was arguably designed to minimize error and direct costs in its enforcement. It appears to recognize that 'cost–benefit' analysis should be applicable in section 2 cases.

37.   Case 6/72 *Europemballage Corporation and Continental Can Co Inc* v. *Commission* [1973] ECR 215, [1973] CMLR 199.

38.   Article 82 is 'aimed at practices which may cause damage to consumers directly, but also to practices that are detrimental to consumers through impact on an effective competitive structure'; Case 6/72 *Europemballage Corporation and Continental Can Co Inc* v. *Commission* [1973] ECR 215, [1973] CMLR 199, para. 26.

39.   Case C-27/76 *United Brands* v. *Commission* [1978] ECR 207, [1978] 1 CMLR 429.

40.   The 'ordoliberal' school of thought was arguably influential at the time of drafting the EC competition law provisions and in the first applications of Article 82. The ordoliberals considered it critical to limit and control private power and to protect individuals' freedom of action in the interests of a free and fair political and social order. Ease of access to the markets for firms was a central part of their desire to keep markets open and so to achieve efficiencies. The leading ordoliberal theorists were the economists Walter Eucken and the lawyers Franz Böhm and Hanns Grossmann-Doerth; see e.g. Gerber, D. (1994), 'Constitutionalizing the economy: German neo-liberalism, competition law and the "New Europe"', **42**, *American Journal of Comparative Law*, 25.

41.   See in particular Cases 6 and 7/73 *Istituto Chemioterapico Italiano Spa and Commercial Solvents Corp* v. *Commission* [1974] ECR 223, [1974] 1 CMLR 309 discussed below. This view seems to be rooted in the 'ordoliberal' school of thought.

42.   Although the Commissioner for Competition stated in 2005 that the objective of

Article 82 should be the enhancement of consumer welfare and efficient allocation of resources, see below, n 63 and accompanying text.

43. See especially, e.g., Case T-219/99 *British Airways* v. *Commission* [2003] II ECR 5917, [2004] 4 CMLR 1008 appeal pending Case C-95/04 P and Case T-203/01 *Michelin* v. *Commission (Michelin II)* [2003] II ECR 4071.

44. The approach focuses on the presence of a number of competitors on the market rather than the question of whether the exclusion of a competitor will have an impact on consumer welfare. The difficulty with this view is that more competitors on the market will not necessarily bring about greater efficiencies if the policy protects less efficient competitors in a market.

45. 'Since the course of conduct under consideration is that of an undertaking occupying a dominant position on a market where for this reason the structure of competition has already been weakened, within the field of application of article [82] any further weakening of the structure of competition may constitute an abuse of a dominant position.' (Case C-85/76 *Hoffmann-La Roche* v. *Commission* [1979] ECR 461, para. 91).

46. Case C-85/76 *Hoffmann-La Roche* v. *Commission* [1979] ECR 461, para. 9. But see below, section 2.

47. Case 322/81 *Michelin* v. *Commission* [1983] ECR 3461, para. 57.

48. Case C-333/94P *Tetra Pak II* [1996] ECR I-5951, para. 24, Cass C-395-296/96 P *Compagnie Maritime Belge Transports SA* v. *Commission* [2000] ECR I-1364, opinion of Fennelly AG, para. 1137, paras 112–19 (ECJ).

49. On the contrary the philosophy does not condemn monopoly power that is gained unexpectedly or unavoidably, rather, having been urged to compete, a successful competitor should not be turned upon when he wins, *United States* v. *ALCOA* 148 F.2d 416, 430 (2d Cir 1945) (Judge Hand).

50. For example, in the area of exclusive dealing and loyalty rebates, see e.g. Case C-85/76 *Hoffmann-La Roche* v. *Commission* [1979] ECR 461 and Case T-203/01 *Michelin* v. *Commission (Michelin II)*, [2003] II ECR 4071; also, e.g., Waelbroeck, D. (2005), 'Michelin II: a per se rule against rebates by dominant companies?', *Journal of Competition Law and Economics*, **1**(1), 149.

51. The Commission responded to the stream of criticism about its formalistic approach to vertical agreements by adopting (following a Green Paper on vertical restraints in competition policy, COM(96) 721) a new Block Exemption for Vertical agreements [1999] OJ L336/21, [2000] 4 CMLR 398 and comprehensive guidelines explaining both the operation of the block exemption, and analysis of vertical restraints that do not fall within it, [2000] OJ C291/1, [2000] 5 CMLR 1074. The Guidelines heralded a more 'economic approach in the application of Article 81 to vertical restraints'. Modernization of the regime governing horizontal cooperation agreements followed (see Regulation 2658/2000 [2000] OJ L304/3 and Regulation 2659/2000 [2000] OJ L304/7 and the Commission's Guidelines on the applicability of Article 81 to horizontal cooperation agreement [2001] OJ C3/2). On 1 May 2004 changes to the regime governing technology transfer agreements were introduced (Commission Regulation 772/2004 [2004] OJ L123/11 and Guidelines on the application of Article 81 of the EC Treaty to technology transfer agreements OJ [2004] C 101/2) along with procedural changes aimed at ensuring more effective enforcement of Article 81 (Regulation 1/2003 [2003] OJ L1/1). On 1 May 2004 a new EC Merger Regulation also introduced significant jurisdictional, procedural and substantive changes to the merger rules (Regulation 139/2004 [2004] L 24/1).

52. Instead, individual cases had been decided on an ad hoc basis without any clear general analytical or intellectual framework and without dealing with a number of important issues not directly raised in the cases; see e.g. Temple Lang, J. and R. O'Donoghue (2002), 'Defining legitimate competition: how to clarify pricing abuses under Article 82 EC', **26**, *Fordham Int'l LF*, **83**, 83–4.

53. It was announced by the then Commissioner for Competition, Mario Monti, at the 8th EC Competition law and policy workshop in Fiesole, Florence, June 2003.

54. In the US the Antitrust Division of the Department of Justice ('DOJ') and the Federal Trade Commission ('FTC') have had a less central role in the shaping of the antitrust rules.

Although both agencies issue Guidelines on the application of the antitrust rules to specific business practices (designed to lower the costs to business of complying with the law by reducing uncertainty and providing critical guidance on moulding practices to comply with the antitrust rules) and publish speeches which shed light on enforcement priorities and policies, 90–95% of antitrust cases are brought by private litigants. In addition, when the Department of Justice or State Attorneys intervene in an antitrust case they have to defend their position before a federal court judge unless the case is settled (for example through use of a consent decree). The US process is therefore centred on litigation.

55.  See Report by the EAGCP (July 2005), 'An economic approach to Article 82'. The EAGCP is an association of academic economists, appointed by the Commissioner for Competition, to advise DG COMP and the Commission on competition policy.

56.  European Commission (2004), 'Guidelines on the application of Article 81(3)', [2004] OJ C 101/97, para. 13. In Case 6/72 *Europemballage Corporation and Continental Can Co Inc* v. *Commission* [1973] ECR 215, [1973] CMLR 199, para. 25 the ECJ held that the purpose of Article 81 and 82 should be consistent.

57.  'Its policy of intervention may then merely have the effect of protecting the other companies in the market from competition. This would enable them to maintain their presence in the market even though their offerings do not provide consumers with the best choices in terms of prices, quality or variety.' See EAGCP (July 2005), 'An economic approach to Article 82', 8–9.

58.  Uncertainty may prevent undertakings from engaging in business practices (e.g. pricing schemes), which increase competition on the market and are beneficial for the consumers.

59.  This is a particular concern in the US where treble damages are available in case of breach.

60.  The national authorities may, and in some circumstances must, apply Article 82 when applying national competition law (Regulation 1/2003, art 3 [2003] OJ L 1/1).

61.  See e.g. Eilmansberger, T. (2005), 'How to distinguish good from bad competition under Article 82 EC: in search of clearer and more coherent standards for anti-competitive abuses', **42**, *CMLR*, 129.

62.  See e.g. EAGCP (July 2005), 'An economic approach to Article 82'.

63.  'Effective competition brings benefits to consumers, such as low prices high quality products, a wide selection of goods and services, and innovation. Competition and market integration serve these ends since the creation and preservation of an open single market promotes an efficient allocation of resources throughout the Community for the benefit of consumers' (Discussion Paper, para. 4). Prior to its publication the Competition Commissioner Neelie Kroes stated that the Commission would develop and explain theories of harm on the basis of sound economic policy and that it would focus enforcement on behaviour that has actual or likely restrictive effects on the market which harm consumers. 'In our view, the objective of Article 82 is the *protection of competition* on the market as a means of enhancing consumer welfare and ensuring an efficient allocation of resources.' See Kroes, N. (23 September 2005), 'Preliminary thoughts on policy review of Article 82', speech at the Fordham Corporate Law Institute New York. She was thus clear about her own philosophy: it is competition, and not competitors, that is to be protected.

64.  It considers this interpretation to be consistent with the ECJ's definition of abuse in Case C-85/76 *Hoffmann-La Roche* v. *Commission* [1979] ECR 461, para. 9 set out above (see n 46 and accompanying text); see Discussion Paper, paras 57–60. This view is widely supported by the comments received in response to the Discussion Paper, available at http://ec.europa.eu/comm/competition/antitrust/others/article_82_review.html.

65.  Vickers, J. (3 September 2004), 'Abuse of market power', speech to the 31st annual conference for the European Association of Research in Industrial Economics, Berlin, available at www.oft.gov.uk.

66.  See e.g. Vickers, J. (3 September 2004), 'Abuse of market power', speech to the 31st annual conference for the European Association of Research in Industrial Economics, Berlin, available at www.oft.gov.uk; Temple Lang, J. and R. O'Donoghue (June 2005),

'The concept of an exclusionary abuse under Article 82', Research Paper for Global Competition Law Centre Conference; and Fletcher, A. (15 March 2005), 'The reform of Article 82: recommendations on key policy objectives', speech at the Competition Law Forum in Brussels, available at www.oft.gov.uk.

67. The profit sacrifice test has received significant support since the Supreme Court's judgment in *Verizon Communications* v. *Law Offices of Curtis V Trinko LLP* 540 US 398 (2004); see especially n 236 and accompanying text. Because, however, profit sacrifice is used as a proxy for anticompetitive effects, there is a concern that the test can be both underinclusive (leading to false negatives) and overinclusive (leading to false positives); see e.g Vickers, J. (3 September 2004), 'Abuse of market power', speech to the 31st annual conference for the European Association of Research in Industrial Economics, Berlin, available at www.oft.gov.uk; Elhauge, E. (2003), 'Defining better monopolization standards', **56**, *Stan L Rev*, 253, 255; and Salop, S. (2006), 'Exclusionary conduct, effect on consumers and the flawed profit-sacrifice standard', **73**, *Antitrust Law Journal*, 311 (arguing that both the profit sacrifice and no economic sense tests are flawed standards which will lead to errors because they are short-cuts and not tied directly to the anticompetitive effects of the conduct).

68. Brief for the United States and the Federal Trade Commission as Amici Curiae supporting petitioner in *Verizon Communications* v. *Law Offices of Curtis V Trinko LLP* 540 US 398 (2004). Normally (but not necessarily) there will be a sacrifice of short-term profits or goodwill in order to maintain or obtain long-term monopoly power. This is the test that the current Antitrust Division of the DOJ has distilled from the Supreme Court's section 2 case law in an attempt to articulate and defend an objective, transparent and economically based framework for assessing single-firm conduct; see, e.g., H. Pate, testimony before Antitrust Modernization Commission, 29 September 2005. See also Werden, G. (2006), 'Identifying exclusionary conduct under section 2: the "no economic sense" Test', **73**, *Antitrust Law Journal*, 413.

69. See, e.g., Posner, R. (2001), *Antitrust Law*, 2nd edn, 193–256. The defendant can rebut by proving that the conduct is on balance efficient. The test is likely to be underinclusive as less efficient firms may exercise competitive constraints over their competitors and it may allow the elimination of new firms that are currently less efficient but would be likely to become more or equally efficient in the long term.

70. See Temple Lang, J. (2003), 'Anticompetitive non-pricing abuses under European and national law', in B. Hawk (ed.), *Fordham Corporate Law Institute*, 235; and, e.g., Temple Lang, J. and R. O'Donoghue (2005), 'The concept of an exclusionary abuse under Article 82', Research Paper for Global Competition Law Centre Conference, June.

71. The rule of reason standard was first set out in *Standard Oil Co of NJ* v. *United States* 221 US 1 (1911) which was, in fact, principally a monopolization case. Although conducting a balancing approach that compares adverse effects against efficiencies and considers the possibility of less restrictive alternatives is uncertain and unpredictable, it has the advantage, compared with profit sacrifice and the no economic sense test of taking all relevant factors into account.

72. In *United States* v. *Microsoft Corp* 253 F.3d 34, 58–9 (DCCir), *en banc, cert denied* 534 US 952 (2001) the DC Circuit found that for a monopolist's act to be condemned as exclusionary an approach consistent with a rule of reason should be adopted: (1) the act must harm the competitive process and thereby harm consumers (harm to one or more competitors will not suffice); (2) the plaintiff must demonstrate that the conduct has the requisite anticompetitive effect; (3) the monopolist can proffer a procompetitive justification for its conduct (conduct is a form of competition on the merits because it involves greater efficiency or enhanced consumer appeal); (4) if the pro-competitive justification is unrebutted, the plaintiff must demonstrate the anticompetitive harm outweighs the procompetitive benefit; and (5) the focus should be on the effect and not the intent of the conduct.

73. 'Although one can command a judge or jury to consider all relevant circumstances and decide whether the pro-competitive aspects of certain conduct outweigh the anticompetitive aspects of that conduct, this does not mean that the judge or jury can do so

accurately. In fact, there is no guarantee that people who do this sort of thing for a living can do so accurately' (H. Pate testimony before Antitrust Modernization Commission, 29 September 2005, 8–9). See also Werden, G. (2006), 'Identifying exclusionary conduct under section 2: the "no economic sense" Test', **73**, *Antitrust Law Journal*, 413.

74. H. Pate testimony before Antitrust Modernization Commission, 29 September 2005, 8–9.
75. In the UK, for example, in endeavouring to distinguish between anti- and pro-competitive behaviour, the OFT has found it useful to consider the consumer-welfare, profit sacrifice and the 'as efficient' competitor tests.
76. The DOJ supports the use of the no economic sense test; see above, n 68. There is also support for the view that the Supreme Court's opinion in *Trinko* demands, as in a predation case, a profit sacrifice, a willingness to forsake profits with the expectation of recoupment; see below, n 236 and accompanying text.
77. 'The traditional criticisms of the consumer welfare effects liability standard are correct. The test is too difficult for businesses to apply, it gives rise to too much uncertainty, it creates too high a risk of "false positives", and it leads to costly, lengthy litigation in which judge and jury are left with too little guidance'. (H. Pate testimony before Antitrust Modernization Commission, 29 September 2005, 12).
78. Rather it envisages that all exclusionary conduct may escape the prohibition of Article 82 where that conduct can be objectively justified or where it can be demonstrated that it produces efficiencies which outweigh the negative effects on competition. See n 11 and accompanying text.
79. Discussion Paper, section 5.9.
80. Discussion Paper, para. 55.
81. See above, n 12 and and accompanying text.
82. Discussion Paper, section 6 and paras 61–8. Foreclosure of an 'as efficient' competitor can in general only result if the dominant undertaking prices below its own costs. This decision is likely to provoke controversy and considerable discussion, both because of the problems involved in its application and because of its potential to be insufficiently precise (and to lead to false negatives. For example, the behaviour of a dominant firm may be constrained by the existence of a less efficient competitor). In a speech at the CLA and BIICL Conference on Article 82 on 22 November 2005, the Commission's Chief Economist, Lars-Hendrik Röller, accepted that a number of problems were involved in the application of this test.
83. It seems likely, however, that some of the proposals at least will not be workable. See also discussion below section 5.
84. See above, section 1 and, e.g., Case T-219/99 *British Airways* v. *Commission* [2003] II ECR 5917, [2004] 4 CMLR 1008 where the CFI at least appears to have ruled out the need for a detailed enquiry into the actual or likely effects of the conduct on competition; but see the pending appeal before the Case C-95/04 P. The grounds of appeal are set out at [2004] OJ C 106/22; see below, n 86 and accompanying text.
85. Kroes, Neelie (23 September 2005), 'Preliminary thoughts on policy review of Article 82', speech at the Fordham Corporate Law Institute New York. She also gave a speech at the UK Presidency's 'European Consumer and Competition Day' in London on 15 September 2005 in which she linked competition policy to the attainment of the goals of the EU's 'Lisbon Strategy' and expressed its objective to be the benefit of consumers.
86. Case C-95/04 P appeal pending from the judgment of the CFI in Case T-219/99 *British Airways* v. *Commission* [2003] II ECR 5917, [2004] 4 CMLR 1008. The grounds of appeal are set out at [2004] OJ C 106/22. The Advocate General in this case has stated that the purpose of Article 82 is to protect the structure of the market and to protect competition in the internal market from distortions, see paras 67–69. In Case T-168/01 *GlaxoSmithKline Unlimited* v. *Commission*, 27 September 2006, however, the CFI held at para. 118 that 'the objective assigned to Article 81(1), which constitutes a fundamental provision indispensable for the achievement of the missions entrusted to the Community, in particular for the functioning of the internal market . . . is to prevent

undertakings, by restricting competition between themselves or with third parties, from reducing the welfare of the final consumer of the products in question . . .'.

87.  The concept of objective justification is not developed and does not contain an explicit balancing role or consumer benefit test. Arguably the concept of abuse itself contains the forum see nn 8–10 and accompanying text.

88.  It was created by statute, Antitrust Modernization Commission Act of 2002, Pub. L. No. 107-273, ss.11051-60, 116 Stat. 1856. For details of the DOJ/FTC hearings see the DOJ website: www.usdoj.gov/atr/public/hearings/single_firm/sfchearing.html. The goal of the hearing is to promote dialogue, learning and consensus building among interested parties.

89.  Ibid., s. 11053.

90.  Ibid., s. 11058.

91.  See, generally, www.amc.gov/index.html.

92.  '[S]uch as presenting a hypothesis of how the conduct will produce an anticompetitive effect and evaluating efficiency justifications – that ought to govern the evaluation of all acts of alleged exclusion. Courts faced with novel theories of improper exclusion often struggle to fit a new theory into the existing classification scheme rather than address the theory on its own terms. These concerns have inspired many observers to seek a new unified analytical framework that would replace the traditional classification scheme' (Gavil, A.I., W.E. Kovacic, J.B. Baker (2002), *Antitrust Law in Perspective: Cases, Concepts and Problems in Competition Policy*, Thomson West, 665–71.

93.  Although the AMC is holding hearings (and is generating many interesting papers) and it will eventually issue a final report, it is unlikely to generate significant change, especially in the context of section 2. The law in this sphere will therefore continue to be driven by what happens in the courts. The DOJ/FTC joint hearing on refusals to deal was held on 18 July 2006, see www.usdoj.gov/atr/public/hearings/single_firm/sfchearing.html.

94.  In some situations, however, a regulatory agency may impose a duty to deal; see e.g. the discussion of *Verizon Communications* v. *Law Offices of Curtis V Trinko LLP* 540 US 398 (2004) below.

95.  250 U.S. 300, 307 (1919).

96.  Case 7/97 *Oscar Bronner* v. *Mediaprint Zeitungs- und Zeitschriftenverlag GmbH & Co. KG* [1998] ECR I-7791, [1999] 4 CMLR 112, para. 56.

97.  The single monopoly profit theory ('SMP') suggests that a refusal to deal is efficient if the firm could already extract monopoly profits in the dominated market so that the refusal to deal does not increase monopoly power. However there are situations were refusal to deal can have an anticompetitive effect on consumers and enable the firm to raise prices on the dominated or downstream market.

98.  In *Verizon Communications* v. *Law Offices of Curtis V Trinko LLP* 540 US 398, 407–408 (2004) Justice Scalia noted that forced sharing was in tension with the purpose of the antitrust laws since it might lessen the incentive for the monopolist, the rival or both to invest in economically beneficial facilities (below, n177). See also the opinion of Jacobs AG in Case C-7/97 *Oscar Bronner* v. *Mediaprint Zeitungs- und Zeitschriftenverlag GmbH & Co. KG* [1998] ECR I-7791, [1999] 4 CMLR 112, especially paras 56–8 (Jacobs AG) below, n 141.

99.  540 US 398, 408 (2004), see below, n 178. The EAGCP warns in its paper, 'An economic approach to Article 82', July 2005, 46, that intervention is likely to be difficult and costly and 'the competition authority is likely to be drawn into the process of determining the *terms* on which dealing must take place, i.e. prices, conditions and technical specifications. The authority is not really qualified to set such terms, so its intervention may cause substantial inefficiencies. Thus, the competition authority should be aware of the harm that it may cause, and intervene cautiously, refraining from active involvement in the dealing terms.' In the UK, the Competition Appeal Tribunal in 1016/1/1/03 *Genzyme Limited* v. *OFT* [2004] CAT 4 held that a firm that had abused its dominant position through the operation of an unlawful margin squeeze was primarily responsible for bringing the abuse to an end and that a direction should be necessary only if it was unwilling or unable to find a solution. The judgment thus initially gave the parties

a period to negotiate a remedy. Since, however, the conduct of the dominant firm essentially precluded a negotiated settlement, the CAT in the end imposed directions, erring in favour of an approach which would be more likely to stimulate than mute competition [2005] CAT 32.

100. In its Discussion Paper the Commission does not deal with this type of behaviour in the section dealing with refusal to supply. It considers that halting supplies to punish buyers for dealing with competitors (or refusing to supply buyers that do not agree to exclusive dealing or tying arrangements) is best viewed as an instrument to achieve another purpose, i.e. exclusive dealing or tying and should be analysed as such. Such practices are normally aimed at excluding the competitor of the dominant company, not the buyer. In its section on refusal to supply it thus concentrates on the situation where a dominant company denies a buyer access to an input in order to exclude that buyer from participating in an economic activity (vertical rather than horizontal foreclosure).

101. Case C-27/76 *United Brands* v. *Commission* [1978] ECR 207, [1978] 1 CMLR 429.

102. Case C-27/76 *United Brands* v. *Commission* [1978] ECR 207, [1978] 1 CMLR 429, paras 183 and 192.

103. There did not seem to be any intention to prevent the distributors from handling competing goods, only to prevent them from actively engaging in advertising campaigns. The analysis should, therefore, arguably have focused upon the question of whether the conduct raised its rivals' costs or reduced their access to the market sufficiently to allow United Brands to exercise its market power through raising of prices, see e.g. Krattenmaker, T. and S. Salop (1986), 'Anticompetitive exclusion: raising rivals' costs to achieve power over price', **96**, *Yale LJ*, 209.

104. Ibid., paras 182–3.

105. See also *BBI/Boosey & Hawkes: Interim Measures* [1987] OJ L286/36, [1988] 4 CMLR 67 where the Commission, relying on Case C-27/76 *United Brands* v. *Commission* [1978] ECR 207, [1978] 1 CMLR 429, held that a refusal to supply a customer that wished to set up in competition with the dominant firm constituted an unlawful abuse.

106. Sometimes referred to as 'Colgate intent' cases. For the relevance of the 'intent' of the monopolist in monopolization cases, see above, n 31 and below, n 157.

107. 342 US 243 (1951).

108. Lorain Journal monitored the radio station to identify those that did advertise with the station. Contracts were then terminated and not renewed until after those using the station's facilities had ceased to do so. The plan was effective, causing many merchants to cease or abandon plans to advertise with the radio station.

109. 342 U.S. 143, 148–149 (1951).

110. 342 U.S. 143, 155 (1951). 'While the Supreme Court never used the term "exclusive dealing" in the *Lorain Journal* case, the practice condemned under §2 was in fact exclusive dealing' (Hovenkamp, H. (1999), *Federal Antitrust Policy: The law of competition and its practice*, 2nd edn West, 303).

111. Cases 6 and 7/73 *Istituto Chemioterapico Italiano Spa and Commercial Solvents Corp* v. *Commission* [1974] ECR 223, [1974] 1 CMLR 309.

112. Cases 6 and 7/73 [1974] ECR 223, [1974] 1 CMLR 309, para. 25.

113. Cases 6 and 7/73 [1974] ECR 223, [1974] 1 CMLR 309, para. 25.

114. Shortly after the *Commercial Solvents* judgment, Judge Pescatore, at that time President of the ECJ, stated that the judgment was intended to protect a small firm for the benefit of consumers; see Korah, V., 'The interface between intellectual property rights and antitrust: the European experience', **69**, *Antitrust Law Journal* (2002), 801, 808.

115. See also *BP* v. *Commission* [1997] OJ L117/1 and Case 311/84 *CBEM* v. *CLT and IPB* ('*Telemarketing*') [1985] ECR 3261.

116. *London-European Sabena* [1988] OJ L317/47, [1989] 4 CMLR 662.

117. *British Midland/Aer Lingus* [1992] OJ L96/34, [1993] 4 CMLR 596.

118. See e.g. *Sealink/B&I Holyhead: Interim Measures* [1992] 5 CMLR 255, *Sea Containers Ltd. Stena Sealink* [1994] OJ L15/8, [1995] 4 CMLR 84 and *Port of Rødby* [1994] OJ L /52. In *GVG/FS* [2004] OJ L 11/17 the Commission concluded simply that restricting access to the railway network (an essential facility) constituted an abuse of a dominant

position if it excluded a potential competitor from the market. The Commission also relied on it in its *IMS* and *Microsoft* decisions; see below, nn 143 and 148.

119. [1992] 5 CMLR 255.

120. The ECJ has never acknowledged the existence of an essential facilities doctrine separate from the principle of refusal to supply set out in Cases 6 and 7/73 *Istituto Chemioterapico Italiano Spa and Commercial Solvents Corp* v. *Commission* [1974] ECR 223, [1974] 1 CMLR 309.

121. Case C-238/87 [1988] ECR 6211.

122. It did hold, however, that the exercise of the exclusive right might amount to an abuse if, for example, the dominant firm were arbitrarily to refuse to supply spare parts to independent repairers, to fix prices for spare parts at an unfair level, and/or to decide no longer to produce spare parts for a car which was still in widespread circulation, Case C-238/87 [1988] ECR 6211, paras 8–9.

123. Cases C-241&2/91P *RTE & ITP* v. *Commission* [1995] ECR 1-743, [1995] 4 CMLR 586.

124. The judgment appeared to prohibit the simple exercise of copyright, the exclusive right to reproduce the work and to refuse licences. It thus led to concern amongst rights holders that the case would set a precedent and would provide a springboard for a wholesale attack on the exercise of intellectual property rights more generally, and would allow third parties to free-ride on the innovation of an intellectual property holder and deter firms from innovation and investment.

125. It therefore upheld the Commission's order under Article 3 of Regulation 17 requiring the appellants to provide the information. The imposition of that obligation, along with the possibility of making authorization of publication dependent on conditions, including payment of royalties, was the only way of bringing the infringement to an end.

126. Cases 6 and 7/73 *Istituto Chemioterapico Italiano Spa and Commercial Solvents Corp* v. *Commission* [1974] ECR 223, [1974] 1 CMLR 309.

127. In Case 7/97 *Oscar Bronner* v. *Mediaprint Zeitungs- und Zeitschriftenverlag GmbH & Co. KG* [1998] ECR I-7791, [1999] 4 CMLR 112, para. 63, Jacobs AG stressed that one of the special circumstances in *Magill* (Cases C-241&2/91P *RTE and ITP* v. *Commission* [1995] ECR I-743, [1995] 4 CMLR 586) that swung the balance in favour of the obligation to license was that 'the provision of copyright protection for programme listings was difficult to justify in terms of rewarding or providing an incentive for creative effort'. Further the copyright seemed to be being exploited to gain a benefit as a by-product of the defendants' function as TV broadcasters.

128. In Case T-65/98 *Van den Bergh Foods* v. *Commission* [2004] 4 CMLR 14, paras 145–63 the CFI rejected the parties' argument that the Commission had failed to establish an abuse of a dominant position by providing retail outlets with freezers exclusively for the provision of its ice cream. One of the arguments raised by the parties was that the ice cream cabinets were not an essential facility, since there was no material constraint preventing competitors from installing cabinets in retail outlets wishing to stock alternative brands of impulse ice cream. The CFI rejected this argument as irrelevant as the Commission had not claimed that the freezers were an essential facility. The abuse was upheld broadly on the grounds that the dominant firm had created outlet exclusivity in 40% of retail outlets.

129. Case T-504/93 [1997] ECR II-923, [1997] 5 CMLR 309.

130. It also stressed that the refusal to license was not discriminatory. The societies had not granted *any* licence in Belgium so the refusal to supply did not discriminate between operators on the Belgian market, Case T-504/93 [1997] ECR II-923, [1997] 5 CMLR 309, para. 124. This indicates that the outcome of the case might have been different if the societies had licensed to some but not all betting shops in Belgium.

131. It had not reserved to itself an ancillary activity which might be carried out by another as part of its activities on a neighbouring but separate market; Case T-504/93 [1997] ECR II-923, [1997] 5 CMLR 309, para. 133.

132. On the contrary, Ladbroke was not only present on the betting market in Belgium but in fact occupied a significant position as regards bets on French races and had the largest share of the main betting market, Case T-504/93 [1997] ECR II-923, [1997] 5 CMLR 309, paras 130 and 132.

133. The refusal to supply could not fall within Article 82 'unless it concerned a product or service which was either essential for the exercise of the activity in question, in that there was no real or potential substitute, or was a new product whose introduction might be prevented, despite specific, constant and regular potential demand on the part of consumers'; Case T-504/93 [1997] ECR II-923, [1997] 5 CMLR 309, para. 131.

134. Case 7/97 *Oscar Bronner* v. *Mediaprint Zeitungs- und Zeitschriftenverlag GmbH & Co. KG* [1998] ECR I-7791, [1999] 4 CMLR 112.

135. Cases 6 and 7/73 *Istituto Chemioterapico Italiano Spa and Commercial Solvents Corp* v. *Commission* [1974] ECR 223, [1974] 1 CMLR 309, Case 311/84 *CBEM* v. *CLT and IPB* ('*Telemarketing*') [1985] ECR 3261.

136. In Case 7/97 *Oscar Bronner* v. *Mediaprint Zeitungs- und Zeitschriftenverlag GmbH & Co. KG* [1998] ECR I-7791, [1999] 4 CMLR 112, para. 40 the ECJ stated: 'In *Magill*, the Court found such exceptional circumstances in the fact that the refusal in question concerned a product (information on the weekly schedules of certain television channels) the supply of which was indispensable for carrying on the business in question (the publishing of a general television guide), in that, without that information, the person wishing to produce such a guide would find it impossible to publish it and offer it for sale (paragraph 53), the fact that such refusal prevented the appearance of a new product for which there was a potential consumer demand (paragraph 54), the fact that it was not justified by objective considerations (paragraph 55), and that it was likely to exclude all competition in the secondary market of television guides (paragraph 56).' In *Bronner* itself, however, the Court required only that the refusal eliminate all competition in the daily newspaper market on the part of a person requesting the service.

137. Case C-7/97 [1998] ECR I-7791, [1999] 4 CMLR 112, para. 41.

138. Case C-7/97 [1998] ECR I-7791, [1999] 4 CMLR 112, paras 45–6.

139. There were other methods of delivering newspapers and there were no technical, legal or economic obstacles making it impossible, or unreasonably difficult, to establish another nationwide home delivery scheme; Case C-7/97 [1998] ECR I-7791, [1999] 4 CMLR 112, paras 43–4.

140. See above, n 96.

141. There would be no incentive for a competitor to develop competing facilities if access were freely available. Although competition might be increased in the short term it could, therefore, be reduced in the long-run (see above, n 98). These conflicting interests should be carefully balanced when determining whether to interfere with a dominant undertaking's freedom to contract; Case C-7/97 [1998] ECR I-7791, [1999] 4 CMLR 112 especially paras 56–8 (Jacobs AG).

142. For the danger of relying on the extent to which the right 'deserves' intellectual property right protection, see e.g. Geradin, D. (2004), 'Limiting the scope of Article 82 EC: what can the EU learn from the US Supreme Court's judgment in *Trinko* in the wake of *Microsoft, IMS*, and *Deutsche Telekom*?', *CMLRev*, 1519.

143. Case C-418/01 *IMS Health GmbH & Co OHG* v. *NDC Health GmbH & Co KG* [2004] 1 ECR 5039, [2004] 4 CMLR 1543. The proceedings in this case were complex. Not only did the Commission originally take interim measures imposing an obligation to license *NDC Health/IMS: Interim Measures* [2002] OJ L59/18, [2002] 4 CMLR 111 (which were suspended by the CFI, Case T-184/01 [2001] ECR II-3193, [2002] 4 CMLR 46 upheld by the ECJ, Case C-481/01 [2002] ECR I-3401, [2002] 5 CMLR 44) but separate litigation took place before the German courts. This case followed from a preliminary reference under Article 234 EC from the Landgericht Frankfurt am Main and did not follow on from the Commission's proceedings. In fact, in the light of changes in circumstance, the Commission interim decision was ultimately withdrawn; see Commission Decision 2003/741/EC [2003] OJ L268/69, IP/03/1159.

144. Case C-418/01 [2004] 1 ECR 5039, [2004] 4 CMLR 1543, paras 38 and 52. It left it to the national court to determine whether these conditions had in fact been satisfied. In particular, it was uncertain whether NDC wanted to offer a new product.

145. In its interim decision, the Commission had stated that the judgment in *Ladbroke* had clarified that 'there is no requirement for a refusal to supply to prevent the emergence

of a new product in order to be abusive', *NDC Health/IMS: Interim Measures* [2002] OJ L59/18, [2002] 4 CMLR 111, para. 180.

146. The CFI used the word 'any' in para. 38 and 'all' in para. 52.

147. Case C-418/01 [2004] 1 ECR 5039, [2004] 4 CMLR 1543 paras 44–5. In its Discussion Paper, the Commission relying on this statement declares that even if there is not an existing market for the input, as it is used only by the owner in a captive market, it is sufficient a potential or even a hypothetical market, to be identified. 'Such is the case where there is actual demand for the input on the part of undertakings seeking to carry out the activity for which the input is indispensable' (Discussion Paper, para. 227).

148. 24 March 2004. The Commission applied the refusal to supply principles and relied in particular on the ECJ's ruling in *Magill*. For a thorough examination of this case, see, e.g., Geradin, D. (2004), 'Limiting the scope of Article 82 EC: what can the EU learn from the US Supreme Court's judgment in *Trinko* in the wake of *Microsoft, IMS*, and *Deutsche Telekom*?', *CMLRev*, 1519.

149. 24 March 2004, para. 783.

150. In its decision the Commission indicates that IMS had essentially hijacked the industry standard. The weak nature of the right is not, however, evident from the CFI's judgment; see Jones, A. and B. Sufrin (2004), *EC Competition Law: Text, Cases, and Materials*, 2nd edn, OUP 509–10. But see also above, n 127 and accompanying text.

151. Case T-201/04 R *Microsoft* v. *Commission* 22 December 2004.

152. Case T-201/04 R *Microsoft* v. *Commission* 22 December 2004, para. 207.

153. See e.g. *Eastman Kodak Co* v. *Southern Photo Materials Co* 273 US 359 (1927) where Kodak, desiring to integrate forward into retail distribution of photographic supplies, refused to sell at wholesale prices to a retailer that had refused to be bought by it. The Supreme Court found that the refusal to deal was 'in pursuance of a purpose to monopolize', at 375.

154. 472 US 585 (1985).

155. A destination ski resort with 'super powder', 'a wide range of ski runs', 'an active night life' and 'some of the best restaurants in North America'. The Court of Appeals affirmed both on the basis that the multi-day, multi-area ticket could be characterized as an essential facility which Ski Co had a duty to market jointly with Highlands and on the basis that evidence supported a finding that Ski Co's intent in refusing to market the ticket was to create or maintain a monopoly, 738 F.2d 1509 (CA10, 1984).

156. The question of whether Ski Co had monopoly power was vigorously disputed at trial and in the Court of Appeals but was not challenged before the Supreme Court; see 472 US 585, 596 and footnote 20 (1985). In the lower courts, Ski Co had argued that, on the contrary, it was required to refuse to participate in such an agreement with a competitor and to act independently.

157. Ski Co also argued that the Court of Appeals had incorrectly relied on the essential facilities doctrine and that an anticompetitive intent did not transform non-exclusionary conduct into monopolization. The Supreme Court dealt with these arguments in footnote 44: 'Given our conclusion that the evidence amply supports the verdict under the instructions as given by the trial court, we find it unnecessary to consider the possible relevance of the "essential facilities" doctrine, or the somewhat hypothetical question whether nonexclusionary conduct could ever constitute an abuse of monopoly power if motivated by an anticompetitive purpose. If, as we have assumed, no monopolist monopolizes unconscious of what he is doing, that case is unlikely to arise.'

158. 'The absence of an unqualified duty to cooperate does not mean that every time a firm declines to participate in a particular cooperative venture, that decision may not have evidentiary significance, or that it may not give rise to liability in certain circumstances. The absence of a duty to transact business with another firm is, in some respects, merely the counterpart of the independent businessman's cherished right to elect his customers and his associates. The high value that we have placed on the right to refuse to deal with other firms does not mean that the right is unqualified', 472 US 585, 601 (1985).

159. 472 US 585, 605 (1985). In this passage in footnotes 32 and 33 the Supreme Court relied on both Areeda and Turner and Bork for its conclusions, 'Thus, "exclusionary" compre-

hends at the most behavior that not only (1) tends to impair the opportunities of rivals, but also (2) either does not further competition on the merits or does so in an unnecessarily restrictive way' (Areeda, P. and D. Turner (1978), *Antitrust Law*, 78; Bork, B.H. (1978), *The Antitrust Paradox: A Policy at War with Itself*, New York: Basic Books, 138).

160.    'The jury may well have concluded that Ski Co. elected to forgo these short-run benefits because it was more interested in reducing competition in the Aspen market over the long run by harming its smaller competitor. That conclusion is strongly supported by Ski Co.'s failure to offer any efficiency justification whatever for its pattern of conduct', 472 US 585, 608 (1985). It rejected the argument that the usuage could not be properly monitored or that the conduct was motivated by a desire to disassociate itself from the inferior skiing services offered by Highland.

161.    472 U.S. 585, 610–611 (1985).

162.    472 U.S. 585, 605 (1985).

163.    'Even before *Trinko*, some lower courts had sought confine *Aspen's* reach by depicting its outcome as the product of unusual facts (i.e. gerrymandered market definition and a frail defense by the monopolist)', Gellhorn, E., W.E. Kovacic and S. Calkins (2004), *Antitrust Law and Economics*, 5th edn, Thomson West, 176–7.

164.    See, e.g., *Olympia Leasing Co* v. *Western Union Tel Co* 797 F.2d 370 (7th Cir. 1986), cert denied 480 US 934 (1987) (discussed below) and *Paschall* v. *Kansas City Star Co*, 727 F 2d 441 (8st Cir 1980) *en banc, cert denied* 469 US 872 (1984) where the Eighth Circuit found that a firm with 100% of the Kansas newspaper market had not unlawfully monopolized the market by refusing to deal with independent carriers and decided to distribute its papers itself. The Court concluded that the decision did not facilitate price discrimination, increase barriers to entry into the primary market or enable a rate-regulated monopoly to evade the regulated price.

165.    797 F2d 370 (7th Cir 1986) *cert denied* 480 US 934 (1987). The defendant Western Union had a monopoly in telex services. Originally it had, in addition to the provision of telex services, leased terminal equipment to its customers. When it decided to withdraw from this market it provided customers with a list of independent suppliers from whom they could obtain the equipment. Later it found that it was shifting its stocks too slowly and it ceased referring customers to alternative suppliers. The plaintiff's sales dropped dramatically in consequence and it brought proceedings. A jury found Western guilty of monopolization, but the Seventh Circuit reversed this.

166.    Either party may appeal all or part of the judgment of a district court to one of the 13 courts of appeals. Essentially, 12 of these circuit courts preside over district courts according to area. The First Circuit to the Eleventh Circuit and the DC Circuit handle appeals from cases brought in district courts in different states within their circuit. The Court of Appeals for the federal circuit, however, has nationwide jurisdiction to hear all cases involving specialized issues, in particular patent cases. It thus has special expertise in these spheres. Opinions of the court of appeals are binding on all district courts within its circuit but not on district courts in other circuits (although they may carry advisory weight there). The inevitable consequence of this system is that 'splits' in circuits may arise. These splits may encourage the Supreme Court to hear an appeal and to resolve the conflicting precedent.

167.    It thus distinguished the facts of this case from *Aspen*, 797 F2d 370, 379 (7th Cir 1986) *cert denied* 480 US 934 (1987).

168.    504 US 451, 485–6 (1982). The Supreme Court was in this case simply determining whether the District Court had been right to grant summary judgment of the case to Kodak. Controversially the Supreme Court considered that the plaintiff's claim that Kodak had monopoly power in the market for its own spare parts and that it had consequently monopolized the market and market for services by limiting the availability of spare parts to independent service organizations ('ISOs') was not unreasonable.

169.    504 US 451, footnote 32 (1982), relying on *Aspen Skiing Co* v. *Aspen Highlands Skiing Co.*, 472 U.S., at 602–5. On remand the justification raised was found to be pretextual; see below, n205 and accompanying text.

170.    Brief for the United States and the Federal Trade Commission as Amici Curiae sup-

porting petitioner in *Verizon Communications* v. *Law Offices of Curtis V Trinko LLP* 540 US 398 (2004).

171. Arguably it did affirm the narrower profit sacrifice test (so merging the predation and non-price predation standards under section 2); see below, n 236 and accompanying text.

172. H. Pate, testimony before Antitrust Modernization Commission, 29 September 2005.

173. The New York Public Service Commission and the Federal Communications Commission.

174. The Supreme Court made it clear that, in a monopoly leveraging case, it was a requirement that there be a 'dangerous probability of success' in monopolizing a second market; see below, n 188.

175. The other three Justices considered that the plaintiff in this case did not have standing to sue.

176. Section 60(1)(b) provides that 'nothing in this Act or the amendments made by this Act shall be construed to modify, impair or supersede the applicability of any of the antitrust laws' and thus prevented the shielding of the regulated entities from antitrust scrutiny.

177. 540 US 398, 407–408 (2004), see above, n 98.

178. 540 US 398, 408 (2004), see above, n 99.

179. 540 US 398, 408 (2004). Note that the Court here omits the first part of the sentence quoted from *Colgate*, that the right was in the absence of any purpose to create or maintain a monopoly which was stressed in both *Aspen* and *Lorain Journal*, see above n 95 and accompanying text.

180. 540 US 398, 408 (2004).

181. For the view that 'the *Trinko* facts fit the *Aspen* principle better than do the *Aspen* facts', see Fox, E. (2005), 'Is there life in *Aspen* after *Trinko*? The silent revolution of section 2 of the Sherman Act', **73**, *Antitrust Law Journal*, 153.

182. 540 US 398, 409 (2004).

183. 540 US 398, 409 (2004). The accepted view is, however, that it is the objective effect of the conduct, not the subjective intent or motivation behind it, which is relevant. Intent is relevant to the extent it helps to understand the likely effect of the conduct, see *United States* v. *Microsoft Corp* 253 F.3d 34, 59 (DCCir), *en banc, cert denied* 534 US 952 (2001).

184. 540 US 398, 409 (2004). In contrast Aspen's behaviour suggested it considered that its future monopoly retail price would be higher than its own retail price which the plaintiff had offered to pay.

185. The unbundled elements existed only deep within the bowels of Verizon and were brought out on compulsion to rivals at considerable expense and effort, 540 US 398, 409 (2004). This was not the case in *Aspen* or *Otter Tail Power Co* v. *United States* 410 US 366 (1973) where the defendant had already provided services to some customers (the transmission of power over its network) while refusing it to others, below, n 191.

186. For a contrasting view in Europe, see the Commission's *Deutsche Telekom* decision [2003] OJ L 263/9. For a discussion of the different facts and factors influencing the decision, see Geradin, D. (2004), 'Limiting the scope of Article 82 EC: what can the EU learn from the US Supreme Court's judgment in *Trinko* in the wake of *Microsoft, IMS*, and *Deutsche Telekom*?', *CMLRev*, 1519, 1545–52.

187. Antitrust analysis had to be attuned to the structure and circumstances of the industry at issue; see 540 US 398, 411 (2004).

188. The Supreme Court also held that the conduct could not constitute unlawful monopolization through leveraging on the grounds that it presupposed anticompetitive conduct, which in that case could only be the refusal to deal case it had rejected. 'The Court of Appeals also thought that respondent's complaint might state a claim under a "monopoly leveraging" theory (a theory barely discussed by respondent, see Brief for Respondent 24, n 10). We disagree. To the extent the Court of Appeals dispensed with a requirement that there be a "dangerous probability of success" in monopolizing a second market, it erred, *Spectrum Sports, Inc.* v. *McQuillan*, 506 U.S. 447, 459 (1993). In any event, leveraging presupposes anticompetitive conduct, which in this case could only be the refusal-to-deal claim we have rejected' (*Verizon Communications* v. *Law Offices of Curtis V Trinko LLP* 540 US 398, footnote 4 (2004)).

189.  See, e.g., *Hecht* v. *Pro-Football Inc* 570 F2d 982, 993 (DC Cir 1977) *cert denied* 436 US 956 (1978).
190.  *MCI Communications Corp* v. *AT&T Co* 708 F.2d 1081, 1132–1133 (7th Cir 1983).
191.  It concerned AT&T's refusal to allow MCI to connect is telephone lines with AT&T's nationwide telephone network, thus preventing it from providing long-distance telephone services. The court found that AT&T's refusal to provide the interconnections, which were technically and economically feasible, constituted an act of monopolization. The Court relied on *Otter Tail Power Co* v. *United States* 410 US 366 (1973), a case in which Otter Tail, an electric utility company, had, amongst other things, refused to sell power at the wholesale level or to 'wheel' power from other wholesale energy supplies (to transfer the electric power through its transmission lines) in order to prevent competition at the retail level. The Supreme Court found that the Federal Power Act had not impliedly repealed the antitrust laws and that the antitrust decree of the District Court (requiring Otter Tail to sell electric power and to wheel power over its transmission lines at compensatory rates and under terms and conditions filed and subject to approval by the regulator, Federal Power Commission (FPC)) would not interfere with the functions of the FPC. The Supreme Court held that the defendant had used its monopoly power to foreclose competition into the retail level in violation of section 2 and that an order to supply would not threaten its capacity to serve the public and to render adequate service to its customers. In this case the Court was able to make an order to deal without having the burden of itself dealing with the detail because the FPC could regulate prices and scrutinize the terms of the contracts.
192.  708 F2d 1081, 1132 (7th Cir) *cert denied* 464 US 891 (1993).
193.  708 F2d 1081, 1132–1133 (7th Cir) *cert denied* 464 US 891 (1993). See also the formulation set out in *Hecht* v. *Pro-Football Inc* 570 F2d 982, 993 (DC Cir 1977) *cert denied* 436 US 956 (1978).
194.  It may also be the case that (5) a defendant that has legitimate business justification for the refusal to grant access may defeat the claim. See the discussion of *Aspen Skiing*, above.
195.  'The so-called "essential facility" doctrine is one of the most troublesome, incoherent and unmanageable of bases of Sherman §2 liability. The antitrust would almost certainly be a better place if it were jettisoned, with a little fine tuning of the general doctrine of the monopolist's refusal to deal to fill in the resulting gaps.' See Hovenkamp, H. (1999), *Federal Antitrust Policy: The law of competition and its practice*, 2nd edn West, 305. See also, e.g., Areeda, P. (1989), 'Essential facilities: an epithet in need of limiting principles', **58**, *Antitrust LJ*, 841; Areeda, P. and H. Hovenkamp, *Antitrust Law*, paras 771–2; Pitofsky, R. (2002), 'The essential facilities doctrine Under US antitrust law', **70**, *Antitrust LJ*, 443, Brief for the United States and the Federal Trade Commission as Amici Curiae supporting petitioner, section II B in *Verizon Communications* v. *Law Offices of Curtis V Trinko LLP* 540 US 398 (2004).
196.  If proof of anticompetitive effects is required the doctrine is unnecessary since liability could be established under the general cases dealing with refusal to deal under section 2.
197.  Hovenkamp, H. (1999), *Federal Antitrust Policy: The law of competition and its practice*, 2nd edn, West, 310.
198.  540 US 398, 410–11 (2004), referring to Areeda, P. (1989), 'Essential facilities: an epithet in need of limiting principles', **58**, *Antitrust L. J.*, 841.
199.  540 US 398, 411 (2004), relying on Areeda, P. and H. Hovenkamp, *Antitrust Law*, 150,; 773e (2003 Supp.) where it is stated that 'essential facility claims should . . . be denied where a state or federal agency has effective power to compel sharing and to regulate its scope and terms'.
200.  See, e.g, *Covad Communications Co* v. *BellSouth Corp* 374 F.3d 1044 (11th Cir 2004), *MetroNet Services Corp* v. *Quest Corp* 383 F.3d 1124 (9th Cir 2004), *New York Mercantile Exchange, Inc.* v. *Intercontinental Exchange, Inc.* 323 F.Supp. 2d 559 (SDNY 2004). But in *Nobody in Particular Presents, Inc* v. *Clear Channel Communications, Inc.* 311 F.Supp.2d 1048 (D.Colo 2004) the court declined to grant summary judgment against a plaintiff that alleged the defendant's rock radio stations constituted an essential facility for advertising and promoting rock concerts.

201. 36 F.3d 1147 (1st Cir 1994).
202. An essential facilities claim was pursued before, but rejected by, the District Court and not pursued before the First Circuit.
203. 36 F.3d 1147, 1187 (1st Cir 1994). It noted that the copyright monopoly is based on Congress's empirical assumption that the right to 'exclude others from using their works creates a system of incentive that promotes consumer welfare in the long term by encouraging investment in the creation of desirable artistic and functional works of expression. It would not require the defendant to prove and reprove the merits of this legislative assumption in every case where a refusal to license a copyrighted work came under attack. The desire to exclude others appears therefore to provide both the anti-competitive effects and justification for it'; see Gellhorn, E., W.E. Kovacic and S. Calkins (2004), *Antitrust Law and Economics*, 5th edn, Thomson West, 500–501.
204. 36 F.3d 1147, 1187 n 44 (1st Cir 1994). On the facts, it found that Grumman had raised no triable issue. Wary of the policy behind the Sherman Act, however, the Court stressed that it was not holding that an antitrust plaintiff could never rebut a presumption. Rather there might be rare cases in which the imposition of antitrust liability would be unlikely to frustrate the objective of the Copyright Act.
205. 135 F.3d 1195 (9th Cir 1997).
206. See above, n 168 and accompanying text.
207. The Divisional Court entered a permanent injunction requiring Kodak to sell all of its parts to the ISOs.
208. In *Eastman Kodak Co* v. *Image Technical Services Inc* 504 US 451, 480 footnote 29 the Supreme Court held that power gained through, e.g., a patent, could give rise to liability if a seller exploits his dominant position in one market to expand his empire into another.
209. 135 F3d 1195, 1218 (9th Cir 1997). It thus adopted a modified *Data General* presumption. It considered this presumption harmonized the goals for the relevant statutes, took into account the long-term effects of regulation and would focus the mind of the factfinder on the primary interest of both intellectual property and antitrust laws.
210. Of the thousands of parts needed, only 65 were patented and evidence established that protection of intellectual property played no part in the decision. The parts manager testified that patents did not cross his mind at the time Kodak began its policy and no distinction was made between proprietary parts covered by tooling or engineering clauses and patented or copyrighted products.
211. The Supreme Court denied certiorari in *Xerox* despite the split in circuits; see above, n 166.
212. 203 F.3d 1322 (Fed Cir 2000), *cert denied* 531 US 1143 (2001). As the refusal to sell patented parts clearly involved its exclusive jurisdiction it applied Federal Circuit law and not that of the Tenth Circuit (the regional circuit in which the District Court had sat). See also *Intergraph Corp* v. *Intel Corp* 195 F.3d 1346 (Fed Cir 1999).
213. 203 F.3d 1322, 1327 (Fed Cir 2000), *cert denied* 531 US 1143 (2001).
214. In one sense the judgment in *Trinko* supports this conclusion, since it stresses the importance of investment incentives in refusal to deal cases. On the other hand, the focus on anticompetitive motive lends support to the view of the Ninth Circuit; see Skitol, R. (May 2004) 'Correct answers to large questions about *Verizon* v. *Trinko*', theantitrustsource.
215. It seems unlikely that this will ever operate as a constraint in a case involving IP; see above, n 147. But see the differing view set out in *Trinko* above, n 185 and accompanying text.
216. See the differing wording used in the cases above.
217. See above, n 145.
218. See, e.g., Geradin, D. (2004), 'Limiting the scope of Article 82 EC: what can the EU learn from the US Supreme Court's judgment in *Trinko* in the wake of *Microsoft, IMS*, and *Deutsche Telekom*?', *CMLRev*, 1519.
219. Arguably, when balancing the interest in protection of copyright and the economic freedom of its owner against the interest in protection of free competition, it should be taken into account whether the refusal to grant a licence prevents the development of

the secondary market to the detriment of consumers, Case C-418/01 [2004] 1 ECR 5039, para. 48, AG Tizano, point 62.

220. See above, n 8 and accompanying text.

221. OFT rejection of a complaint *EI du Pont (Holographic System)*, 22 September 2003 and OFCOM rejection of a complaint, *Re-investigation of a complaint from Floe Telecom Limited against Vodafone Limited*, 30 June 2005.

222. See discussion of the *United Brands* and *Commercial Solvents* cases and Article 82(c) above.

223. In *Magill*, for example, the broadcasters had happily licensed the listings to daily and weekend newspapers free on a short-term basis, Cases C-241&2/91P *RTE and ITP* v. *Commission* [1995] ECR I-743, [1995] 4 CMLR 586, para. 9.

224. See e.g. *Aspen Skiing Co* v. *Aspen Highlands Skiing Corp*, 472 U.S. 585 (1985). There may, however, be a distinction between cases involving exhaustible finite resources where an obligation to supply may not be feasible and, e.g., intellectual property licences which may not be physically exhaustible in the same way.

225. In the Discussion Paper, para. 217, the Commission states that the fact that the dominant company has supplied an input to one or more customers in the past shows that it at a certain point in time considered it efficient to engage in supply relationships. 'This and the fact that its customers are likely to have made investments connected to these supply relationships creates a rebuttable presumption that continuing these relationships is pro-competitive.'

226. Or an unlawful attempt to monopolize.

227. 'The Supreme Court never considered what percentage of the market was foreclosed by Lorain Journal's practices – an essential requirement in exclusive dealing cases.' See Hovenkamp, H. (1999), *Federal Antitrust Policy: The law of competition and its practice*, 2nd edn, West, 303.

228. 342 U.S. 143, footnote 8 (1951).

229. It is thus widely perceived to be a case where no efficiency justification was presented; see, e.g, Bork, R.H. (1978), *The Antitrust Paradox: A Policy at War with Itself*, Basic Books, reprinted with a new Introduction and Epilogue, 1993, 345.

230. Pitofsky, R. (29 September 2005), 'Standards for exclusionary behavior under section 2 of the Sherman Act', Comments to the Antitrust Modernization Commission. A case-by-case approach, focusing or exclusionary or predatory conduct without a valid business justification, is also supported by the Supreme Court in *Eastman Kodak* where it stated: 'Legal presumptions that rest on formalistic distinctions rather than actual market realities are generally disfavoured in antitrust law. This Court has preferred to resolve antitrust claims on a case-by-case basis, focusing on the "particular facts disclosed by the record" ', 504 US 451, 466 (1992).

231. Remember that in quoting *Colgate* the court did not repeat the first part of the sentence that the right was in the absence of any purpose to create or maintain a monopoly, see above, n179 and accompanying text. Rather the Court considered that, although the Sherman Act is the 'Magna Carta' of free enterprise, 'it does not give judges *carte blanche* to insist that a monopolist alter its way of doing business whenever some other approach might yield greater competition': 540 US 398, 415–16 (2004).

232. See above n 168 and accompanying text (Justice Scalia dissented in *Kodak*).

233. In post-*Trinko* refusal to deal cases, lower courts now typically recite the catechism that plaintiffs state a cause of action only if the facts fall within *Aspen's* narrow exception from the no-duty-to-deal principles, or within a nearly-obliterated essential facilities doctrine.' See Fox, E. (2005), 'Is there life in *Aspen* after *Trinko*? The silent revolution of section 2 of the Sherman Act', **73**, *Antitrust Law Journal*, 153. The author relies on, e.g., *Covad Communications Co.* v. *BellSouth Corp.*, 374 F.3d 1044, 1049 (11th Cir. 2004) ('*Trinko* now effectively makes the unilateral termination of a voluntary course of dealing a requirement for a valid refusal-to-deal claim under *Aspen*.'); see also *Covad Communications Co.* v. *Bell Atl. Corp.*, 02 Civ. 7057 (DG), 2005 U.S. App. LEXIS 3418, at 14–15, 23–5 (11th Cir. 1 March 2005); *New York Mercantile Exch., Inc.* v. *Intercontinental Exch., Inc.*, 323 F. Supp. 2d 559, 571 (S.D.N.Y. 2004).

234.   Chilling pro-competitive conduct such as capital investment in critical business infra-
       structure or research and development on innovative products.
235.   Preferring it to competition and competitive opportunity, see Fox, E. (2004), 'The
       Trouble with Trinko' 52nd Annual Antitrust Spring Meeting, ABA; and Fox, E. (2005),
       'Is there life in *Aspen* after *Trinko*? The silent revolution of section 2 of the Sherman
       Act', **73**, *Antitrust Law Journal*, 153.
236.   If the profit sacrifice test is put in place as an overarching test for section 2 liability there
       is a danger of error as is may be both under- and overinclusive as a test (much procom-
       petitive conduct entails the sacrifice of current profit in the pursuit of greater profit over
       the longer term); see Werden, G. (2006), 'Identifying exclusionary conduct under section
       2: the "no economic sense" Test' **73**, *Antitrust Law Journal*, 413. H. Pate takes it as an
       endorsement of the DOJ's no economic sense test; see H. Pate, testimony before Antitrust
       Modernization Commission, 29 September 2005, 8. See, e.g., *Nobody in Particular
       Presents, Inc* v. *Clear Channel Communications, Inc*. 311 F.Supp.2d 1048 (D.Colo 2004).
237.   Arguably, by distinguishing *Aspen*, where the defendant refused to provide a product
       that it already sold at retail, from Trinko, where the service were not otherwise mar-
       keted, the Court 'put to rest any claim that the a monopolist must make available to
       would-be competitor . . . "intermediate goods" i.e. goods which are not part of a seller's
       final product already made available for purchase by others': H. Pate, Testimony before
       Antitrust Modernization Commission, 29 September 2005, 6. Contrast the view of the
       ECJ in *IMS* set out above. See also, e.g., *Covad Communications Co* v. *Bell Atlantic* (DC
       Cir 2005), *Covad Communications Co* v. *BellSouth Corp* 374 F.3d 1044 (11th Cir 2004),
       *MetroNet Services Corp* v. *Quest Corp* 383 F.3d 1124 (9th Cir 2004), *American Central
       Eastern Texas Gas Co* v. *Union Pacific Resources Group Inc* (unpublished) (5th Cir
       2004), *New York Mercantile Exchange, Inc.* v. *Intercontinental Exchange, Inc*. 323
       F.Supp. 2d 559 (SDNY 2004). The Supreme Court has only recognised a unilateral duty
       to deal where the firm was previously engaged in voluntarily providing the product
       service (whether to the plaintiff or another), see *Eastman Kodak Co* v. *Image Technical
       Services Inc* 504 US 451 (1992), *Aspen Skiing*, 472 US 585, *Otter Tail Power Co* v. *US*
       410 US 366 (1973), *Lorain Journal Co* v. *US* 342 US 143 (1951), *Eastman Kodak Co* v.
       *Southern Photo Materials Co* 273 US 359 (1927).
238.   Fox, E. (2005), 'Is there life in *Aspen* after *Trinko*? The silent revolution of section 2 of
       the Sherman Act', **73**, *Antitrust Law Journal*, 153. relying on, e.g., *Covad
       Communications Co* v. *Bell Atlantic* (DC Cir 2005 (Section 2 claim dismissed where
       defendant had no previous course of dealing with plaintiff/competitor); *New York
       Mercantile Exch., Inc.*, 323 F. Supp. 2d at 571–72 (Section 2 claim dismissed where defen-
       dant 'proffered a legitimate business reason for its refusal to deal with' plaintiff); *A.I.B.
       Express, Inc.* v. *FEDEX Corp.*, 358 F. Supp. 2d 239, 250 (S.D.N.Y. 2004) (because the
       defendant sacrificed profits and offered the same service to consumers for a lower price
       than it offered to competitors, 'the decision to terminate revealed an anticompetitive
       bent'). See *Covad*, 2005 U.S. App. LEXIS 3418, at 23–4 (motion to dismiss one section
       2 claim denied where plaintiff sufficiently alleged sacrifice of opportunity to make prof-
       itable sale); *Metronet Servs. Corp.* v. *Qwest Corp.*, 383 F.3d 1124, 1132 (9th Cir. 2004)
       (defendant's termination of a voluntary course of dealing was not a section 2 violation
       where defendant intended to increase short-term profits). But see, e.g., *Creative Copier
       Services* v. *Xerox Corp.*, 344 F. Supp. 2d 858, 866 (D. Conn. 2004) (rejecting defendant's
       argument that 'Trinko established a new rule in refusal to deal cases, namely, that a com-
       plaint is deficient unless the plaintiff has specifically alleged that the defendant could not
       possibly make a short-term profit from the challenged conduct').
239.   See above, nn 203 and 214.
240.   It is, for example, hard to see why a termination of an existing supply relationship
       requires appraisal under a different standard to a refusal to start supplying an input,
       see above nn 222, 223 and accompanying text. The Discussion Paper demands in the
       latter, but not the former case, that the input is indispensable to carry on normal eco-
       nomic activity in the downstream market. This indicates a too interventionist stance in
       termination cases, see Discussion Paper, section 9, especially 9.2.1–9.2.2.

241. Discussion Paper, para. 222.
242. Which may, in any event, eventually be rectified through the workings of the market.
243. It has preferred instead to support the right of a firm to choose its trading partners unless there is clear evidence of anticompetitive harm and no off-setting business justification.
244. See, e.g. Fox, E. (2005), 'Is there life in *Aspen* after *Trinko*? The silent revolution of section 2 of the Sherman Act', **73**, *Antitrust Law Journal*, 153, and Pitofsky, R. (2001), 'Challenges of the new economy: issues at the intersection of antitrust and intellectual property', **68**, *Antitrust LJ*, 913 (setting out the view that in cases at the intersection between intellectual property and antitrust there should be an analysis to consider the effect of the refusal to deal on competition and the importance of the refusal to deal for the protection of incentives to innovate). See also 'Symposium: the federal circuit and antitrust', **69**, *Antitrust Law Journal*, 627 (2002).

## References

American Bar Association Antitrust Section (2002), *Antitrust Law Developments*, 5th edn, ABA.
Areeda, P. (1989), 'Essential facilities: an Epithet in need of limiting principles', **58**, *Antitrust LJ*, 841.
Areeda, P. and H. Hovenkamp, *Antitrust Law*.
Areeda, P. and D. Turner (1978), *Antitrust Law*, 78.
Bork, R.H. (1978), *The Antitrust Paradox: A Policy at War with Itself*, New York: Basic Books.
Calvani, T. and J. Fingleton 'Dominance: a comparative economic and legal analysis'. in (ABA, forthcoming), *Issues in Competition Law and Policy*, Chapter 39.
EAGCP, (July 2005), 'An economic approach to Article 82', available at http://europa.eu.int/comm/competition/publications/studies/eagcp_july_21_05.pdf.
Easterbrook, F.H. (2003), 'When is it worthwhile to use courts to search for exclusionary conduct?', *Comb Bus LRev*, 345.
Eilmansberger, T. (2005), 'How to distinguish good from bad competition under Article 82 EC: in search of clearer and more coherent standards for anti-competitive abuses' **42**, *CMLR*, 129.
Elhauge, E. (2003), 'Defining better monopolization standards', **56**, *Stan L Rev*, 253.
European Commission (2004), 'Guidelines on the application of Article 81(3)', [2004] OJ C 101/97.
European Commission (December 2005), 'DG Competition Discussion Paper on the application of Article 82 of the Treaty to exclusionary abuses', available at http://europa.eu.int/comm/competition/antitrust/others/discpaper 2005.pdf.
Fletcher, A. (15 March 2005), 'The reform of article 82: Recommendations on key policy objectives', speech at the Competition Law Forum in Brussels, available at www.oft.gov.uk.
Fox, E. (2003), 'We protect competition, you protect competitors', **26**, *World Competition*, 149.
Fox, E. (2004), 'The Trouble with Trinko', 52nd Annual Antitrust Spring Meeting, ABA.
Fox, E. (2005), 'Is there life in *Aspen* after *Trinko*? The Silent Revolution of Section 2 of the Sherman Act', **73**, *Antitrust Law Journal*, 153.
Gavil, A.I., W.E. Kovacic and J.B. Baker (2002), *Antitrust Law in Perspective: Cases, Concepts and Problems in Competition Policy*, Thomson West.
Gellhorn, E., W.E. Kovacic and S.Calkins (2004), *Antitrust Law and Economics*, 5th edn, Thomson West.
Geradin, D. (2004), 'Limiting the scope of Article 82 EC: what can the EU learn from the US Supreme Court's judgment in *Trinko* in the wake of *Microsoft*, *IMS*, and *Deutsche Telekom*?', *CMLRev*, 1519.
Gerber, D. (1994), 'Constitutionalizing the economy: German neo-liberalism, competition law and the "New Europe"', **42**, *American Journal of Comparative Law*, 25.
Gerber, D. (1998), *Law and Competition in Twentieth Century Europe: Protecting Prometheus*, Clarendon Press.
Hovenkamp, H. (1999), *Federal Antitrust Policy: The law of competition and its practice*, 2nd edn, West.

Jones, A. (2006), 'Analysis of agreements under U.S. and E.C. antitrust law – convergence or divergence?', 51 *Antitrust Bull* (forthcoming).

Jones, A. and B. Sufrin (2004), *EC Competition Law: Text, Cases, and Materials*, 2nd edn, OUP.

Korah, V. (2002), 'The interface between intellectual property rights and antitrust: the European experience', **69**, *Antitrust Law Journal*, 801.

Krattenmaker, T. and S. Salop (1986), 'Anticompetitive exclusion: raising rivals' costs to achieve power over price', **96**, *Yale LJ*, 209.

Kroes, Neelie (23 September 2005), 'Preliminary thoughts on policy review of Article 82', speech at the Fordham Corporate Law Institute, New York.

Motta, M. (2005), *Competition Policy: Theory and Practice*, Cambridge University Press.

Pate, H. (29 September 2005), Testimony before Antitrust Modernization Commission.

Pitofsky, R. (2001), 'Challenges of the new economy: issues at the intersection of antitrust and intellectual property', **68**, *Antitrust LJ*, 913.

Pitofsky, R. (2002), 'The essential facilities doctrine under US antitrust law', **70**, *Antitrust LJ*, 443.

Pitofsky, R. (29 September 2005), 'Standards for exclusionary behavior under Section 2 of the Sherman Act', Comments to the Antitrust Modernization Commission.

Posner, R. (2001), *Antitrust Law*, 2nd edn, Chicago Press.

Salop, S. (2006), 'Exclusionary conduct, effect on consumers and the flawed profit-sacrifice standard', **73**, *Antitrust Law Journal*, 311.

Skitol, R. (May 2004) 'Correct answers to large questions about *Verizon* v. *Trinko*', thean-titrustsource.

Sullivan, L.A. and W.S. Grimes (2000), *The Law of Antitrust: An Integrated Handbook*, West.

Temple Lang, J. (2003), 'Anticompetitive non-pricing abuses under European and national law', in B. Hawk (ed.), *Fordham Corporate Law Institute*, 235.

Temple Lang, J. and R. O'Donoghue (2002), 'Defining legitimate competition: how to clarify pricing abuses under Article 82 EC', **26**, *Fordham Int'l LF*, 83.

Temple Lang, J and R. O'Donoghue (June 2005), 'The concept of an exclusionary abuse under Article 82', Research Paper for Global Competition Law Centre Conference.

Vickers, J. (3 September 2004), 'Abuse of market power', Speech to the 31st annual conference for the European Association of Research in Industrial Economics, Berlin, available at www.oft.gov.uk.

Waelbroeck, D. (2005), 'Michelin II: a per se rule against rebates by dominant companies?', *Journal of Competition Law and Economics*, **1**(1), 149.

Werden, G. (2006), 'Identifying exclusionary conduct under section 2: the "no economic sense" Test', **73**, *Antitrust Law Journal*, 413.

*Cases*

*A.I.B. Express, Inc.* v. *FEDEX Corp.*, 358 F. Supp. 2d 239, 250 (S.D.N.Y. 2004).

*AKZO Chemie BV* v. *Commission* [1991] ECR I-3359, [1993] 5 CMLR 215.

*American Central Eastern Texas Gas Co* v. *Union Pacific Resources Group Inc* (unpublished) (5th Cir 2004).

*Aspen Skiing Co* v. *Aspen Highlands Co* 472 US 585.

*BBI/Boosey & Hawkes: Interim Measures* [1987] OJ L286/36, [1988] 4CMLR 67.

*BP* v. *Commission* [1997] OJ L117/1.

*British Airways* v. *Commission* [2003] II ECR 5917, [2004] 4 CMLR 1008.

*British Midland/Aer Lingus* [1992] OJ L96/34, [1993] 4 CMLR 596.

*CBEM* v. *CLT and IPB ('Telemarketing')* [1985] ECR 3261.

*Compagnie Maritime Belge Transports SA* v. *Commission* [2000] ECR I-1365, [2000] 4 CMLR 1076.

*Covad Communications Co* v. *BellSouth Corp* 374 F.3d 1044 (11th Cir 2004).

*Creative Copier Services* v. *Xerox Corp.*, 344 F. Supp. 2d 858, 866 (D. Conn. 2004).

*Eastman Kodak Co* v. *Southern Photo Materials Co* 273 US 359 (1927).

*Europemballage Corporation and Continental Can Co Inc* v. *Commission* [1973] ECR 215, [1973] CMLR 199.

*Genzyme Limited* v. *OFT* [2004] CAT 4.
*GVG/FS* [2004] OJ L 11/17.
*Hecht* v. *Pro-Football Inc* 570 F2d 982, 993 (DC Cir 1977) *cert denied* 436 US 956 (1978).
*Hilti AG* v. *Commission* [1994] ECR I-666, [1994] 1 CMLR 590.
*Hoffmann-La Roche* v. *Commission* [1979] ECR 461.
*Höfner and Elser* v. *Macroton* [1991] ECR I-1979, [1993] 4 CMLR 306.
*IMS Health GmbH & Co OHG* v. *NDC Health GmbH & Co KG* [2004] 1 ECR 5039, [2004] 4 CMLR 1543.
*Istituto Chemioterapico Italiano Spa and Commercial Solvents Corp* v. *Commission* [1974] ECR 223, [1974] 1 CMLR 309.
*London-European Sabena* [1988] OJ L317/47, [1989] 4 CMLR 662.
*Manufacture Française des Pneumatiques Michelin* v. *Commission* [2003] ECR II- 4071, [2004] 4 CMLR 923.
*Matsushita Elec Industrial Co* v. *Zenith Radio* 475 US 574, 594 (1986).
*MCI Communications Corp* v. *AT&T Co* 708 F.2d 1081, 1132–1133 (7th Cir 1983).
*MetroNet Services Corp* v. *Quest Corp* 383 F.3d 1124 (9th Cir 2004).
*Michelin* v. *Commission* [1983] ECR 3461, [1985] 1 CMLR 282.
*Michelin* v. *Commission ( Michelin II)*, [2003] II ECR 4071.
*Microsoft* v. *Commission*, Case T-201/04 R, 22 December 2004.
*NCAA* v. *Board of Regents of University of Oklahoma*, 468 U.S. 85, 107–108 (1984).
*NDC Health/IMS: Interim Measures* [2002] OJ L59/18, [2002] 4 CMLR 111.
*New York Mercantile Exchange, Inc.* v. *Intercontinental Exchange, Inc.* 323 F.Supp. 2d 559 (SDNY 2004).
*Nobody in Particular Presents, Inc* v. *Clear Channel Communications, Inc.* 311 F.Supp.2d 1048 (D.Colo 2004).
*Olympia Leasing Co* v. *Western Union Tel Co* 797 F.2d 370 (7th Cir. 1986), *cert denied* 480 US 934 (1987).
*Oscar Bronner* v. *Mediaprint Zeitungs- und Zeitschriftenverlag GmbH & Co. KG* [1998] ECR I-7791, [1999] 4 CMLR 112.
*Otter Tail Power Co* v. *United States* 410 US 366 (1973).
*Paschall* v. *Kansas City Star Co*, 727 F 2d 441 (8th Cir 1980) *en banc, cert denied* 469 US 872 (1984).
*Port of Rødby* [1994] OJ L /52.
*Reiter* v. *Sonotone Corp.* 442 US 330, 343 (1979).
*RTE & ITP* v. *Commission* [1995] ECR 1–743, [1995] 4 CMLR 586.
*Sea Containers Ltd. Stena Sealink* [1994] OJ L15/8, [1995] 4 CMLR 84.
*Sealink/B&I Holyhead: Interim Measures* [1992] 5 CMLR 255.
*Spectrum Sport Inc* v. *McQuillan* 506 US 447, 459 (1993).
*Standard Oil Co of NJ* v. *United States* 221 US 1 (1911).
*United Brands* v. *Commission* [1978] ECR 207, [1978] 1 CMLR 429.
*US* v. *Aluminium Co of* America 148 F.2d 416 (2nd Cir, 1945).
*US* v. *Griffith* 334 US 100 (1948).
*US* v. *Grinnel Corp.* 384 US 563, 571–572 (1966).
*United States* v. *Microsoft Corp* 253 F.3d 34, 58–59 (DCCir), *en banc, cert denied* 534 US 952 (2001).
*US* v. *Syufy* 903 F.2d 659 (9th Cir. 1990).
*Van den Bergh Foods* v. *Commission* [2004] 4 CMLR 14.
*Verizon Communications* v. *Law Offices of Curtis V Trinko LLP* 540 US 398 (2004).

# 9 Tying: a transatlantic perspective
*David W. Hull*[1]

## Introduction

At a time when the European Commission is rethinking its policy on the abuse of dominant position under Article 82, the law on tying is particularly ripe for reform. In the antitrust field, tying stands out as an area where there is a stark divergence between what the law is as set out in the case law and the general consensus in the antitrust community on what the law should be. In both the United States and the European Union, tying is generally analyzed under some form of a per se rule, while the consensus in the antitrust community is that it should be analyzed under the rule of reason, which allows for a more robust economic analysis that considers effects on the market and possible efficiencies.

In recent years, the need to bring the law on tying into line with contemporary economic thinking has generated extensive commentary among antitrust lawyers and economists. The explanation for this may be that tying is at the heart of both the US and EU versions of the recent *Microsoft* case. While any key issue in such a prominent case is likely to attract extensive comments from the antitrust community, this is particularly true with tying in this case.[2] First, the tying involved in *Microsoft* is the kind of tying that is generally recognized as generating various efficiencies, thus underscoring the shortcomings of a per se approach. Second, *Microsoft* highlights the need to find a workable approach to tying because tying is of central importance in an economy that is characterized by increasing product integration and convergence, particularly in high-tech sectors such as information technology and consumer electronics.

As discussed below, the decisions on both sides of the Atlantic in the *Microsoft* case suggest that the law in both the United States and the European Union is moving towards a rule-of-reason approach. The law remains in an unsatisfactory state, however, both because it is unclear to what extent this more flexible approach has broader application beyond the facts of *Microsoft*, and because the features of the optimal test remain unclear. Consequently the Commission's review of its approach to abuse of dominance under Article 82 with a view to issuing guidelines is a welcome exercise as guidelines could help answer these questions and bring the law more into line with current economic thinking.

This chapter has two goals. First, it summarizes how tying is treated under current economic theory and the state of the law on tying in the United States and the European Union. A comparison of the approaches to tying on both sides of the Atlantic should provide greater insights into the issues, and tying would seem to lend itself to a transatlantic comparison as both jurisdictions recently have had to deal with a similar set of facts in *Microsoft*. Second, with this background, it makes some recommendations as to the general contours of an optimal approach to tying and suggests some areas that might merit further inquiry as the Commission moves forward with its Article 82 review.

### The economics of tying

While economics has long been a mainstay of US antitrust analysis, it has only recently come to the fore in Europe. In the past few years, the EU competition rules governing restrictive agreements covered by Article 81 (e.g. vertical agreements, intellectual property licences, horizontal agreements) and mergers falling within the scope of the EU Merger Regulation have undergone major reforms in an effort to inject greater economic analysis. Article 82 seems to be on the brink of a similar sea change with the European Commission's commencement of a review of its policy under Article 82. In December 2005, the Commission issued a Discussion Paper that clearly favors an economics-based approach as opposed to a legalistic, form-based approach.[3] As part of this project, the Commission commissioned a study by a group of prominent European economists, which was released in July 2005, and which, not surprisingly, argues in favour of an effects-based approach to Article 82.[4]

Although a thorough discussion of the economics of tying is beyond the scope of this chapter, it is useful to review briefly the evolution of economic thinking on tying, and particularly the harms and benefits of tying that have been identified by economists.[5] Initially, economists were hostile to tying, viewing it as nothing more than a means for a dominant firm to extend its market power in the tying market to the tied market. Chicago School economists challenged this traditional view, arguing that tying was rarely harmful. They reasoned that a dominant firm generally could not use its dominant position in the market for the tying product to extract monopoly profits on the market for the tied product because it only had one monopoly and, if it tried to extend its monopoly, could wind up undermining it. Chicago School economists also pointed out that tying could achieve a number of efficiencies, some of which are listed below. More recently, post-Chicago School economists have challenged this view, arguing that there are circumstances in which the Chicago School's theory does not hold true, particularly when the tied market is not perfectly competitive.

While the debate on the optimal approach to tying is not yet over, there seems to be general agreement on the main benefits and harms associated with tying. The two main anticompetitive effects that have been identified are as follows:

- *Monopolizing the tied good's market*: a principle anticompetitive effect is leveraging the firm's dominance in the tying product's market to increase profits and foreclose competition in the tied product's market.
- *Protecting the monopoly in the tying good's market*: another anticompetitive effect frequently identified by economists is preservation of the firm's dominant position in the tying market. In this case, the dominant firm is concerned that a competitor will first establish its position on the tied product's market and later enter the tying product's market.

The main efficiencies generally associated with tying are as follows:

- *Lower production costs*: tying may lead to lower production costs by allowing manufacturers to achieve economies of scale.
- *Lower transaction costs*: tying reduces the transaction costs of buying the two products separately. For example, it is easier for consumers to buy software applications that are bundled rather than shopping for each separately.
- *Lower distribution costs*: tying may lead to a reduction in distribution costs in that it may be cheaper to package, ship and invoice products as one unit than separately.
- *Quality improvement*: tying may lead to an improvement in the quality of the product. For example, the success of PC manufacturers in selling a bundled product that consists of the PC, the screen, the keyboard, the mouse and other peripherals is at least partly attributable to the perception that there will be fewer glitches with hardware components designed to work together as opposed to the situation where each component is purchased separately. Such quality considerations are particularly relevant in high-tech products where technological integration is important.
- *Pricing*: tying may result in more competitive pricing for the bundled product than could be achieved if each product were sold separately. In cases where tying is used as a metering device (e.g. photocopiers and paper), it enables the seller to measure the demand for the product and tailor its pricing strategy accordingly. Economists have shown that this ability to discriminate among customers can be beneficial for some of them.

Since economists continue to debate various aspects of tying such as the precise harms and benefits associated with it, how often they arise, and how they can be measured, it may be going too far to say that they agree that tying is generally beneficial and only rarely harmful.[6] It would seem safe to say, however, that a broad consensus has emerged on at least one point: tying is not generally anticompetitive because, more often than not, it gives rise to efficiencies. Even a consensus on this limited point is useful in fashioning the best approach to tying. As discussed below, if tying is not generally anticompetitive, a per se rule – even a watered-down per se rule – would not appear to be the best approach to evaluating tying practices.

## The legal tests
*Overview*
This section reviews the legal tests for tying that have been developed in the United States and the European Union. The two jurisdictions are similar in that the prevailing test in each is a per se test, but the recent decisions on each side of the Atlantic in *Microsoft* suggest that each jurisdiction may be moving towards a rule-of-reason test. However drawing parallels between the jurisdictions based on labels assigned to the tests can be misleading. The US courts have developed a per se test that sometimes works more like a rule-of-reason test because it allows the consideration of factors that typically would only be taken into consideration under a rule-of-reason test. For its part, the European Commission has developed what it labels a rule-of-reason test, but which operates more like a version of the per se test because it places such a heavy burden of proof on the defendant.

*US law*
*(a) A peculiar per se test*    Initially, US courts were hostile to tying and applied a strict per se test under which it was sufficient to show that a tying arrangement existed and that it affected a 'not insubstantial' volume of trade. This early hostility to tying is evident in this widely-quoted passage from the US Supreme Court's judgment in *Northern Pacific Railway*:

> Among the practices which the courts have heretofore deemed to be unlawful in and of themselves are . . . tying arrangements. . . . Indeed, 'tying arrangements serve hardly any purpose beyond the suppression of competition.' . . . They are unreasonable in and of themselves whenever a party has sufficient economic power with respect to the tying product to appreciably restrain free competition in the market for the tied product and a 'not insubstantial' amount of interstate commerce is affected.[7]

While this quotation suggests that it was necessary to show market power over the tying product, in practice, this was often inferred from the existence of a tie.[8]

This approach to tying analysis was condemned by Chicago School economists. Robert Bork's *The Antitrust Paradox*, which is known for its scathing criticism of many antitrust principles that were widely accepted at the time of its publication in 1978, reserved particularly stinging remarks for the strict per se approach to tying:

> A review of the cases reveals the sterile circularity of the law's reasoning, the untenability of its premises, and the error of its most assured pronouncements. These matters have been repeatedly and conclusively demonstrated by a number of commentators, yet the law remains majestically impervious to any critical analysis.[9]

Over time, US courts have moved away from the strict per se test that was the object of Bork's criticism, watering it down to the point that it is now described as a 'highly idiosyncratic'[10] or 'modified' per se rule. Under a pure per se rule, once conduct is shown to occur, it is condemned without regard to proof of market power, effect, intention or possible justifications. For example, a naked price-fixing cartel is deemed to be anticompetitive in virtually all situations. The current per se test applied to tying does not operate like a pure per se test because it is subject to various qualifications that are not usually associated with a per se test. Perhaps the simplest explanation for the departure from a strict per se rule is that courts recognized that tying is ubiquitous and often benign. Consequently a more flexible rule was needed, and courts showed considerable creativity in achieving this flexibility while remaining, at least nominally, within the confines of a per se rule. For example, some courts found that the alleged tying and tied products constituted a single product and, thus, the arrangement was not a tie at all. Others required evidence of power in the tying product's market rather than simply inferring this from the existence of the tie. Still others allowed 'business justifications' to be pleaded as defences.

Perhaps the most prominent example of the movement away from a strict per se rule is the US Supreme Court's judgment in *Jefferson Parish*.[11] In that case, the tying involved requiring a hospital's patients to use the anaesthesiological services of a provider with which the hospital had an exclusive arrangement. The Court moved away from a strict per se test in two respects. First, in determining whether the two-products test was met, it focused on whether there was a separate demand for the tied product rather than on the functional relationship between the two products, which had been the approach in earlier cases. Second, the Court emphasized that the economic power required over the tying product was market power and not some vague notion of economic power. This insistence on proof of market power over the tying product meant that market power could no longer be inferred simply from the existence of a tie. Applying these criteria, the

Court concluded that it was inappropriate to apply the per se rule because Jefferson Parish Hospital did not have the requisite degree of power in the market for the tying product as it controlled only 30 per cent of the market for hospital services; thus the arrangement was subject to examination under a full-blown rule-of-reason analysis.

While the US courts have gradually moved away from a strict per se test, the US Supreme Court thus far has declined to abandon the per se test altogether in favour of the rule of reason, though it declined to do so by only a one-vote margin in *Jefferson Parish*. In *Jefferson Parish*, Justice O'Connor was joined by three other justices in a concurring opinion that argued for the abandonment of the per se approach in favour of the rule of reason, but the majority decided to remain with the per se rule for reasons of *stare decisis*: 'It is far too late in the history of our antitrust jurisprudence to question the proposition that certain tying arrangements pose an unacceptable risk of stifling competition and therefore are unreasonable per se.'[12] Surely, had Robert Bork written *The Antitrust Paradox* after *Jefferson Parish* was decided, he would have used this statement as an example of just the sort of majestically-impervious-to-any-critical-analysis rationale for a per se approach to tying that he condemned in the passage from his book quoted above.

As *stare decisis* is an argument of last resort, the per se rule may eventually give way to the rule of reason. Faced with lower courts that have either gone through judicial contortions to stay within a per se rule yet achieve results more consistent with a rule of reason, or that have abandoned the per se approach altogether when faced with a novel tying arrangement, as the United States Court of Appeals for the District of Columbia Circuit ('DC Circuit') did in *Microsoft*, discussed below, and with the clear weight of opinion among economists and the academic community in favour of jettisoning the per se approach in favour of a rule of reason, it would not be surprising if the US Supreme Court eventually embraces a rule-of-reason analysis.[13]

In the meantime, however, the controlling test is a per se test that comprises the following four conditions: (1) the tying and the tied products are two separate products; (2) the seller affords customers no choice but to purchase the tied product from it; (3) the seller has market power in the market for the tying product; and (4) the tying arrangement affects a not insubstantial volume of interstate commerce in the market for the tied product.[14] These conditions will be examined in greater detail below in the discussion of the features of the optimal test for tying.

*(b) A restrictive rule of reason*   Judicial dissatisfaction with the per se test is epitomized by the DC Circuit's ruling in *Microsoft* where, when faced with a novel tying claim involving the integration of new features into

platform software, the court abandoned the per se test in favour of the rule of reason under which the anticompetitive effects of the tying conduct must be weighed against the procompetitive justifications.[15] The court found that Microsoft's tying of the Internet Explorer web browser to its Windows operating system was capable of generating efficiencies for which the per se test would be unable to account. For example, tying enables independent software developers to rely on the presence of the web browser's code in the Windows operating system platform so that they do not have to go to the trouble of writing web browser code when writing applications for the platform that would use the web browser. In addition, the court found that the per se test was ill-suited to account for efficiencies generated by new and innovative product integration because the per se test was backward-looking in that it focused on historic consumer demand in determining whether separate demand for the tied product existed. Under the per se test, the first company to integrate previously distinct products would risk being condemned because, at the time of integration, there necessarily would be two distinct product markets. In contrast, a rule-of-reason analysis would give the first mover an opportunity to prove that the efficiency gain from the tie offset any harm resulting from depriving the consumer of the ability to buy the products separately.

In the short term at least, the DC Circuit's opinion is unlikely to have much formal effect on the assessment of tying claims. The court was careful to restrict its ruling to tying cases involving platform software. As a practical matter, this means that its ruling would be unlikely to apply in many cases as few companies have enough market power in platform software to be accused of tying.

In the longer term, the DC Circuit's ruling may well have an influence on the law on tying that goes beyond its narrow confines, particularly in cases involving the integration of new features into high-technology products. As one of the key rulings in the Microsoft saga and one that reflects the prevailing view that the per se test should be abandoned, it has created additional impetus for change. The court's opinion may well have an influence on the development of the law in jurisdictions other than the United States. Indeed the European Commission went out of its way to emphasize that the approach adopted in its decision in *Microsoft* was consistent with that adopted by the DC Circuit.[16] Even if the European Court of First Instance ('CFI') were to follow a different route in ruling on Microsoft's appeal against the Commission's decision, it might well take the DC Circuit's ruling into account in its deliberations and would likely give serious consideration to arguments in favour of a rule that takes into account the effects of tying in the market and the various efficiencies that it can generate.

*EU law*
*(a) A restrictive per se rule*　Prior to the European Commission's decision in *Microsoft*, which is discussed in the next section, both the Commission and the European Courts (the CFI and the European Court of Justice or 'ECJ') followed a strict per se approach in evaluating tying practices. To establish an illegal tie, it sufficed to show the following: (1) dominance in the tying product market, (2) the existence of two separate products, and (3) that the customer was coerced into purchasing the products together. As in any Article 82 case, the possibility of objective justifications for the practice was also examined, though these were typically given short shrift. There was no serious inquiry into factors that would be taken into consideration in the context of a rule-of-reason analysis such as the risk of foreclosure of competition on the tied product market or possible efficiencies generated by the tying practice.

Compared to the US case law on tying, there is scant EU case law, and the little case law that exists does not provide much guidance. The two leading cases, *Hilti*[17] and *Tetra Pak*,[18] both dealt with relatively 'easy' tying cases involving consumables. In *Hilti*, the Commission found that Hilti abused its dominant position by selling the customer cartridge strips for its nail guns only if the customer also bought its nails from Hilti. In *Tetra Pak*, the Commission found that Tetra Pak had abused its dominant position by conditioning the sale of its packaging machines on the customer's agreement to purchase the cartons used in the machines only from Tetra Pak.

Both of these cases were 'easy' in the sense that the tying and tied products were physically separate products that were not only intuitively distinct, but with respect to which it was easy to show a separate demand in the market. Thus, in both cases, the European Commission and the European Courts had no trouble rejecting arguments to the effect that the tying and tied product formed a single product. In *Hilti*, evidence that cartridge strips and nails were manufactured and sold separately by third parties was used to reject the argument that the nail guns, cartridge strips and nails formed a single powder-actuated fastening system. In *Tetra Pak*, the fact that machines and cartons were sold separately in a closely-related market involving non-aseptic packaging machines (as opposed to the aseptic packaging machines at issue in the case) was used to reject the argument that machines and cartons formed an integrated packaging system.

*Hilti* and *Tetra Pak* illustrate the per se approach to tying in that there was little attempt to analyze the effects of the practice on the market or possible efficiencies. Moreover, neither the CFI nor the ECJ articulated a coherent approach to tying cases that would provide much in the way of general guidance. The judgments were fact-driven and focused on the discrete issues presented and, because they both involved consumables, they do not address the kinds of complex issues presented in cases of technological tying, which are likely to arise with increasing frequency.

*(b) A peculiar rule of reason*   In its March 2004 decision in *Microsoft*,[19] the European Commission moved away from the strict per se approach of *Hilti* and *Tetra Pak*, towards a test that takes into consideration the effects of the tying practice in the market for the tied product and allows at least some consideration of efficiencies and procompetitive justifications. The Commission found that Microsoft's tying of its Windows Media Player to its Windows operating system constituted an illegal tie under Article 82. To reach this conclusion, the Commission applied a five-part test: (1) the tying and the tied product are two separate products; (2) the seller is dominant in the market for the tying product; (3) the seller does not give customers a choice of whether to buy the tying product without the tied product; (4) tying forecloses competition; and (5) the absence of any objective justification. While the Commission's formal statement of its test only included the first four conditions, the test actually applied by the Commission included the fifth condition, which is an element to be examined in any Article 82 case.

In its decision, the Commission had little trouble finding that Microsoft was dominant in the tying product market of operating systems and that it had given customers no choice but to take its media player with the operating system. The bulk of the Commission's analysis was focused on whether the Windows operating system and the Windows Media Player were separate products, and on whether the alleged tying arrangement foreclosed competition on the media player market. On the separate products issue, the Commission found that there was separate demand for Windows Media Player as a standalone product and, consequently, the two-products requirement was satisfied. It rejected Microsoft arguments that focused on the high degree of technological integration involved in adding Windows Media Player as a feature of Windows and the absence of demand for the Windows operating system without Windows Media Player.

On the foreclosure issue, the Commission found that, although there was currently competition in the media player market, the alleged tying arrangement had the potential to foreclose competition. In reaching this conclusion, the Commission emphasized the danger that the media player market might eventually tip towards Microsoft. The Commission also rejected the justifications put forward by Microsoft for the tie. In evaluating these justifications, the Commission placed the burden of proof on Microsoft and held it to a very high standard of proof, requiring it to show that the tying was indispensable to achieving the alleged efficiencies, i.e. that it was the only way to achieve these efficiencies.

### Comparison of the US and EU rule-of-reason tests

In considering what would be the best approach to tying under Article 82, it is useful to compare the test articulated by the European Commission in the European version of *Microsoft* with the rule-of-reason test adopted by the DC Circuit in the US version of *Microsoft*. As both cases are recent and were heavily litigated with extensive economic evidence being presented, they constitute a fruitful basis for comparison.

At the time that it issued its decision in *Microsoft*, the European Commission emphasized that it had used the same approach as the DC Circuit:

> The Commission has followed a 'rule-of-reason' approach in order to establish whether the anticompetitive effects of tying WMP outweigh any possible pro-competitive benefits. This is precisely the framework for tying cases that the US Court of Appeals laid down in 2001.[20]

While the Commission's decision clearly represents a movement away from the previous strict per se test towards a rule-of-reason approach, it differs in important respects from the US rule-of-reason approach adopted by the DC Circuit in *Microsoft*. On its face, the test articulated by the Commission in *Microsoft* bears greater similarity to the four-part per se test used by most courts in the United States than it does to the DC Circuit's rule-of-reason test. On closer analysis, however, the Commission's test represents a clear movement towards a rule of reason. First, the Commission's test leaves more room for a meaningful examination of the effects of the tying on the market for the tied product. This is because the examination of effect on trade under the US per se test is aimed at the jurisdictional requirement that the practice have the requisite effect on inter-state commerce in the tied product's market rather than the substantive question of market foreclosure. In practice, this has proved to be a fairly low hurdle rather than a rigorous inquiry into whether the anticompetitive harm is substantial enough to be of serious concern.[21] Moreover, as noted above, the test actually applied by the Commission in *Microsoft* included a fifth condition – the consideration of objective justifications and efficiencies – which is more characteristic of a rule-of-reason analysis.

While the consideration of effects and objective justifications brings the European Commission's test closer to a US rule-of-reason test, there is a critical difference: the Commission placed a much heavier burden of proof on Microsoft than would have been the case under the US rule-of-reason approach. The allocation of the burden of proof can have a decisive impact on the effect of a legal standard. In the *Microsoft* case, the burden of proof placed on the defendant was so high that, arguably, it transformed what purported to be a rule-of-reason standard into a per se test. This issue of the burden of proof is discussed in greater detail towards the end of this chapter.

**Rethinking tying under Article 82**

*A doctrine ripe for reform*

EU law on tying is in an unsatisfactory state. First, it is unclear what the prevailing rule is. While the ECJ has applied a strict per se approach in tying cases, the European Commission has recently followed a much more flexible test that it has described as a rule-of-reason test. Which test are judges and advisors to follow? Second, the case law does not articulate a coherent approach to tying, both because there are so few cases and because the two leading cases, *Hilti* and *Tetra Pak*, dealt with a narrow subset of tying cases – those where the tied product was a consumable. Third, to the extent that the current approach fails to take into account the full range of efficiencies associated with tying, either because it does not allow such efficiencies to be pleaded or because the burden of proof is allocated in a way that negates the ability of a defendant to plead them effectively, it is inconsistent with the general consensus that the optimal rule would allow for a robust consideration of efficiencies.

Given the shortcomings of the current approach, it would be a welcome development if the European Commission used the issuance of guidelines on Article 82 as an opportunity to reform the law on tying. By issuing guidelines, the Commission has an opportunity to articulate a coherent approach to tying that is more in line with contemporary economics and to inject much-needed certainty into the law. In hopes of informing the debate leading up to the adoption of any such guidelines, this section makes some recommendations as to the contours of the optimal approach to tying. It also attempts to identify areas where it might be particularly useful for the Commission to focus its inquiry.

*Per se or rule of reason?*

In considering the most appropriate approach to tying under Article 82, the threshold question is whether a per se or rule-of-reason approach should be used. The logic behind applying a per se rule to a particular practice is that, in the majority of cases, the practice is anticompetitive, so that it is not worth the time or effort to examine individual cases. As Justice O'Connor noted in her concurring opinion in *Jefferson Parish*:

> In deciding whether an economic restraint should be declared illegal per se, '[t]he probability that the anticompetitive consequences will result from a practice and the severity of those consequences [is] balanced against its procompetitive consequences. Cases that do not fit the generalization may arise, but a per se rule reflects the judgment that such cases are not sufficiently common or important to justify the time and expense necessary to identify them' . . . Only when there is very little loss to society from banning a restraint altogether is an inquiry into its costs in the individual case considered to be unnecessary.[22]

From this perspective, tying does not lend itself to a per se analysis. As discussed above, while the debate on the economics of tying continues, economists seem to be in agreement on one point: tying is not anticompetitive in the majority of cases. Judges, whether intuitively or using economic analysis, also seem to have come to this conclusion. The evolution of the case law in both the United States and the European Union reflects a recognition that tying often entails procompetitive benefits and that the legal rule must be flexible enough to take these benefits into account. In the United States, the courts have moved away from a strict per se approach to a more flexible per se approach that examines rule of reason-like criteria and, in *Microsoft*, the DC Circuit went so far as to abandon the per se approach altogether. Similarly, in the European Union, the Commission's recent decision in *Microsoft* represents a clear departure from the strict per se approach to tying applied in *Hilti* and *Tetra Pak*.

If tying is not generally anticompetitive, common sense suggests that a per se rule is inappropriate because it results in an overly-broad prohibition that catches procompetitive practices in order to prohibit those few cases where tying is anticompetitive. In recent years, the so-called 'error-cost' analytical framework has been used to articulate this common-sense proposition in a more scientific, or at least scientific-sounding, way.[23] In essence, this framework looks at the relative costs of mistakes, called 'false positives' (false convictions) and 'false negatives' (false acquittals). Thus, a per se rule for price fixing is appropriate because price fixing is almost always harmful, so it is preferable to condemn those few cases of benign price fixing in order to prevent the more numerous cases of harmful price fixing from going unpunished. By the same token, a per se rule for tying would be inappropriate because tying is generally procompetitive, so a per se rule would condemn many cases of procompetitive or benign tying in order to ensure that the rare case of harmful tying does not slip through the net.

While few would dispute that a strict per se approach is inappropriate for tying cases, some might contend that the more flexible modified per se approach currently applied in the United States, and arguably by the European Commission in its *Microsoft* decision, is preferable to the rule of reason because it allows at least partial consideration of effects and efficiencies, yet avoids some of the administrative costs associated with a full-blown rule-of-reason analysis. In her concurring opinion in *Jefferson Parish*, Justice O'Connor found that even such a modified per se approach was flawed: 'tying doctrine incurs the costs of the rule-of-reason approach without achieving its benefits: the doctrine calls for the extensive and time-consuming economic analysis characteristic of the rule of reason, but then may be interpreted to prohibit arrangements that economic analysis would show to be beneficial'.[24]

Although the modified per se test applied in tying cases may entail many of the costs associated with the rule of reason, Justice O'Connor's suggestion that it does not achieve any of the benefits would not seem to be entirely accurate. To the extent that it allows the courts to consider some of the possible justifications for the tying, such as the efficiencies for which the two-products test serves as a proxy, the modified per se test achieves at least some of the benefits of the rule of reason. Even if Justice O'Connor may have overstated the case, however, it is true that a modified per se test does not achieve all of the benefits of the rule of reason because there are some efficiencies that are not captured under a per se test, such as those identified by the DC Circuit in *Microsoft*. Perhaps even more importantly, a modified per se test does not allow for an evaluation of the effects of the tying practice on the market. Moreover, any form of per se test has the drawback that it entails different standards of proof and allocations of burdens of proof than a rule of reason, which may impede as robust an examination of efficiencies as would be possible under the rule of reason.

If the main difference between a modified per se test and a rule of reason is that the former has fewer administrative costs, but does not allow for a thorough consideration of efficiencies, the question then becomes whether it is worth the extra time and expense to go through a full-blown rule-of-reason analysis in order to minimize the risk that certain efficiencies are overlooked. One approach to this issue indicated by the DC Circuit in *Microsoft* would be to try to identify circumstances in which tying would be particularly likely to generate efficiencies that would not be captured by a per se test (in that case, tying involving platform software) and apply the rule of reason in those cases. The drawback to this approach is that it is difficult to identify in advance all of the possible circumstances in which tying would be likely to generate procompetitive effects. Another approach would be to apply the rule of reason in every case on the grounds that the extra administrative cost is a small price to pay when compared with the cost of erroneously prohibiting procompetitive tying arrangements. A compromise that is discussed in the next section would be to use a 'structured' or 'modified' rule of reason that would avoid some administrative costs, yet allow for a thorough consideration of market effects and efficiencies in those cases where such an exercise is most likely to be warranted.

*If a rule-of-reason test is appropriate, which one?*
If a rule-of-reason test is deemed to be preferable to a per se test, the question becomes whether the rule-of-reason test should be a classic rule-of-reason test or a more structured rule-of-reason test. Under the classic test, the procompetitive benefits generated by the tying practice are weighed

against the anticompetitive harms. Under a structured rule of reason, this balancing of interests only occurs if the practice meets certain screening conditions.

While a textbook rule of reason has a certain theoretical appeal, it has serious drawbacks in practice. The kind of economic analysis called for under a pure rule of reason has been likened to a 'snipe hunt' where economists, lawyers and judges embark on a futile quest for mythical creatures found only in the universe of economic theory. A prominent US judge, Frank Easterbrook, warned:

> A court could try to conduct a full inquiry into the economic costs and benefits of a particular business practice . . . [b]ut it is fantastic to suppose that judges and juries could make such an evaluation. The welfare implications of most forms of business conduct are beyond our ken. If we assembled twelve economists and gave them all the available data about a business practice, plus an unlimited computer budget, we would not get agreement about whether the practice promoted consumers' welfare or economic efficiency more broadly defined. . . . A global inquiry invites no answer; it puts too many things in issue. To get an answer to a practical problem, we must start with some assumptions and fixed points of reference.[25]

This concern over the ability of economists to arrive at an answer and of courts to understand that answer in cases that raise complex economic issues is clearly relevant to the choice of the most appropriate standard by which to judge tying practices under Article 82. With the decentralization of the power to enforce the EU competition rules that occurred with the entry into force of Regulation 1/2003 in May 2004, litigation involving Article 82 is likely to arise with increasing frequency at the national level, often in front of courts with limited experience in dealing with the kinds of difficult economic issues raised in these cases. The adoption of a rule of reason that calls for weighing complex economic evidence not only could be difficult to apply in practice, but could result in sharp divergences in the case law at the national level. Apart from the difficulty of applying a rule of reason in the context of complex litigation, it creates uncertainty for companies and their advisors, who are unlikely to stop and analyze each tying practice under a full-blown rule-of-reason analysis.

These same kinds of arguments were raised in the context of the European Commission's 'modernization' of the EU competition rules applicable to restrictive agreements pursuant to which it replaced a legalistic, rule-based approach with one grounded in modern economic theory. While the Commission gave relatively short shrift to these arguments in the debate surrounding the modernization programme, it alleviated many of the concerns by creating a series of signposts to guide companies and their advisors in the form of market-share screens, safe harbours and lists of pro-hibited 'hardcore' restrictions, all of which were spelled out in detail in a series of block exemption regulations and guidelines. These signposts enable companies to do a 'quick look' analysis of the relevant practices so that only those that clearly raise competition concerns are subject to a more detailed rule of reason-like assessment.

Out of similar concern for greater legal certainty and the need for prac-tical guidance, it would be useful if any guidelines on Article 82 incorpo-rated comparable signposts in the form of market share screens, presumptions and the like. The purpose of these screening conditions would be to eliminate cases where the risk of anticompetitive harm is sufficiently small that it is not worth carrying out a more in-depth inquiry. The following section considers possible conditions that could be applied in tying cases.

**Possible conditions**
*What order?*
In tying cases, screening conditions are either linked to the very definition of tying – i.e. the need for two distinct products and the presence of coer-cion – or they serve to filter out tying cases that do not raise competi-tion concerns under Article 82 because of lack of a dominant position on the tying product's market or foreclosure effects on the tied product's market. The screening conditions should not need to be applied in any par-ticular order. If any one of them is not met, the result should be no abuse under Article 82. Therefore, a court should be able to address the issue that seems easiest in a given case. If a case is not screened out, then the inquiry turns to whether there are objective justifications for the practice or pro-competitive efficiencies that outweigh any anticompetitive harm caused by the tying practice.

*Two products*
In determining which tying cases merit a thorough inquiry, perhaps the most obvious condition that must be met is the existence of two products because, unless there are separate products, tying is not possible. Over time, it has become clear that the two-products test also serves as a useful proxy for many of the efficiencies that can be generated by a tying arrangement. If consumers do not buy the products separately, this suggests that the benefits of the integrated product such as lower transactional costs or better technological integration outweigh any negative consequences such as reduced consumer choice. The two-products test is valuable as a screen because it is generally easier to determine whether separate products are involved than it is to prove the existence of the efficiencies for which the test

serves as a proxy. In other words, the two-products inquiry makes it possible to avoid the often difficult task of proving the underlying efficiencies.

The key challenge is formulating a workable two-products test. It is tempting to approach the separate products issue intuitively, which means that the inquiry can take on a metaphysical character. Courts using this I-know-separate-products-when-I-see-them approach may reach the same result as those using a more analytical approach grounded in economic analysis, but it is unsatisfactory in terms of achieving predictable and consistent results. In the United States, the courts have moved away from a largely intuitive approach that focuses on the functional relationship between the products to a more analytical approach that focuses on the character of consumer demand for the products. In *Jefferson Parish*, which perhaps contains the most extensive discussion of the two-products requirement, the US Supreme Court made it clear that there must be a separate consumer demand for the tied product so that it would constitute a separate product market. In that case, the Court found that hospital services and anaesthesiological services were distinct markets because the available evidence showed that patients and doctors often requested anaesthesiological services separately from hospital services.

In the European Union, the development of an analytically-sound two-products test is not helped by the language of Article 82, which prohibits 'making the conclusion of contracts subject to acceptance by the other parties of supplementary obligations which, by their nature or according to commercial usage, have no connection with the subject of such contracts'. The use of the word 'nature' invites courts to focus on the functional relationship between the products rather than on more objective criteria such as whether competitors offer the products separately. Fortunately the European Commission and the European Courts have tended to focus more on the 'commercial usage' portion of the test. For example, in *Tetra Pak*, the defendant argued that machines and cartons formed one, integrated product – a packaging system. In finding that machines and cartons were separate products, the CFI focused on commercial usage as shown through evidence from the market rather than embarking on an examination of the functional relationship. More specifically the CFI found that machines and cartons were offered separately on the closely related market for non-aseptic packaging and, thus, should be considered to be separate products on the market for aseptic packaging.

If the evidence on commercial usage shows that the products are not offered separately so that there is only one product, the matter should end there because tying is only possible if there are two distinct products. While this point seems fairly obvious, there is language in the ECJ's judgment in

*Tetra Pak* that could be read as suggesting otherwise. More specifically, the ECJ stated:

> It must . . . be stressed that the list of abusive practices set out in the second paragraph of Article [82] of the Treaty is not exhaustive. Consequently, even where tied sales of two products are in accordance with commercial usage or there is a natural link between the two products in question, such sales may still constitute abuse within the meaning of Article [82] unless they are objectively justified.[26]

This language harbours potential for confusing the analysis because it could be read as saying that, even if commercial usage shows that the products are sold together so that there is only one product, a firm may be held in violation of Article 82. This interpretation would eviscerate the two-products requirement and, indeed, would not make sense because, by definition, tying requires two products.

The confusion stems from that fact that the 'commercial usage' portion of the Article 82 test may be used in two ways in a tying case: as part of the separate products test and, in cases where separate products are shown to exist, as a justification for the tying practice not being abusive. This is precisely what happened in *Tetra Pak*. Tetra Pak first pleaded commercial usage in the aseptic packaging market to show that packaging machines and cartons were one integrated system. When the CFI rejected this argument on the grounds that commercial usage in the neighbouring non-aseptic packaging market showed that machines and cartons were sold separately, Tetra Pak then pleaded commercial usage as justifying the practice; i.e. that, since most firms did not sell the products separately, there was no abuse. The passage from the ECJ's judgment quoted above was addressing this second argument. In essence, the ECJ seemed to be saying that, even if a dominant firm were able to show that most firms did not sell the products separately, this would not necessarily mean that the tying practice was not abusive.

If the Commission issues guidelines on Article 82, it would be helpful to clarify that commercial usage is decisive on the separate products issue, even if it is not on the question of objective justifications for the tying practice. If commercial usage shows that there is no separate demand for the products, the matter should end there because tying is only possible if there are two distinct products. In other words, the passage quoted above should not be interpreted as suggesting that a firm may be held in violation of Article 82 even if there is no evidence of separate demand for the products. Rather the *Tetra Pak* language should be interpreted as only being relevant in cases where it has been established that two products exist and the argument is raised that commercial usage justifies the tying practice. Any other interpretation would risk undermining an objective, market-based test for separate products.

While past commercial usage has the advantage of providing an objective means of determining whether products are separate that avoids the vagaries inherent in the more metaphysical inquiry into the nature of the relationship between the products, it is poorly suited to the situation where a company combines two products that were previously distinct. Indeed, in their drive to achieve ever greater technological convergence, companies in high-tech markets are constantly looking for ways to combine products that were previously distinct. As the two-products test is inherently backward-looking, it is a poor proxy for efficiencies generated by new and innovative integration of previously separate products.

Although such efficiencies should be taken into account in order not to place companies engaged in innovative integration at a disadvantage, the question is at what stage in the analysis such efficiencies should be evaluated. To allow companies to plead efficiencies in connection with the two-products test would seem to undermine the value of this test as a quick-look screen. It would seem more conducive to a full evaluation of these efficiencies for them to be brought into the analysis at a later stage when efficiencies are pleaded.[27]

A final issue that the European Commission will need to consider in formulating a workable two-products test is whether the inquiry should be limited to whether separate consumer demand exists for the tied product or whether the same question should be asked with respect to the tying product. In *Microsoft*, the Commission found that separate products existed on the basis that there was separate consumer demand for media players. Microsoft argued, however, that the question should also have been whether there was a demand for operating systems without the media player, in other words, for the tying product without the tied product.

### Market power

Another obvious condition is market power. If a firm does not have power in the market for the tying product, it will not be able to force the purchaser to buy the tied product.

The use of market power as a screen has several practical advantages. First, it would not require a departure from the EU's established jurisprudence because the threshold issue in any Article 82 case is whether the defendant has a dominant position. Second, the concept of dominance is already familiar to courts and competition authorities as well as companies and their advisors. Third, although the exercise of defining the relevant market for the purpose of measuring the defendant's market share can be very difficult in some cases, in many cases, it is relatively straightforward and, thus, can provide a ready means of screening out cases where there is little risk of anticompetitive harm.

*Products are tied together*

A third possible condition that, like the two-products test, relates to the very definition of tying, would require a showing that the two products are tied together, i.e. that, as a practical matter, the customer does not have a choice of acquiring the tied product without the tying product. The two cases in which proof of such a tied sale is easiest are the classic tying case where the seller makes the sale of the tying product conditional on the purchase of the tied product, and the case of 'pure' bundling where the seller only offers the two products together, so that it is not possible to purchase either separately.

Matters become much more complicated in the case of 'mixed' bundling where the tying product and the tied product are available separately, but the seller coerces the customer into buying them together. For example, the seller may offer a package discount for the two products together that, as a practical matter, would mean that the purchase of the package is the only viable economic option. Difficult questions may arise in assessing whether the seller's strategy constitutes illegal coercion, such as what price differential is enough to support a claim of coercion and to what extent cost savings may justify charging a lower price for the bundle. In the European Union, answers to these kinds of questions are even more difficult because the law on rebate and discount schemes is in a confused state. Clearly the assessment of such schemes generally and in the specific context of tying claims is an area where Commission guidelines on Article 82 could inject much-needed clarity into the law.

Another form of tying that is likely to arise with increasing frequency in this age of technological convergence is so-called 'technological' tying where there is a technical link between the tying product and the tied product so that the tying product is designed to only work with the tied product or is designed to work better with the tied product. As discussed below in connection with efficiencies, technological tying that involves the integration of new features into high-technology products is likely to generate procompetitive efficiencies and should be judged under a deferential standard that takes full account of these efficiencies.

Many cases involving technological tying may well morph into difficult compulsory licensing cases because the only effective remedy for the alleged tie is likely to be for the dominant firm to make its interface information available to competitors so that they can make compatible products. If the interface information is already available, the alleged tie is unlikely to be effective because competitors would be free to make compatible products and there would be no appreciable foreclosure on the market for the tied product. Of course, there is the murky middle ground where some interface information has been made available, but competitors claim that they need more information to ensure that their products are not placed at a disadvantage. The EU *Microsoft* case involves just this issue: competitors on the workgroup server market claimed that they needed additional interface operation to allow their servers to work as well with the Microsoft operating system as Microsoft's own servers.

The compulsory disclosure of interface information raises a host of issues beyond the scope of this chapter and which are the subject of a heated debate in the context of the *Microsoft* appeal. For the purposes of this chapter, the key point is that, even though issues involving the disclosure of interface information may initially arise in the context of a tying allegation, the analytical framework developed for tying cases is ill-suited to deal with them; instead, they are more appropriately resolved on the basis of principles developed in the context of compulsory licensing cases.

*Foreclosure*

A fourth possible condition is that the tying practice must be shown to foreclose competition on the market for the tied product. It is the inclusion of this condition that transforms what would otherwise be some form of a per se test into a rule-of-reason test because it calls for an analysis of the economic effects of the tying practice on the tied market.

In establishing whether this condition is met, the key questions are how much foreclosure must be shown before the tying is considered significant enough to give rise to a competition concern and, relatedly, to what extent potential foreclosure must be taken into account. The answer to the first question of how much necessarily entails a degree of arbitrariness and is linked to the second question in the sense that, even if the degree of actual foreclosure is limited, if potential foreclosure is taken into account, this will affect the answer. Nevertheless, it would be helpful if the European Commission could provide some concrete guidance. At the very least, it would be helpful if there were a minimum safe harbour below which companies could be confident that foreclosure would not be considered to have a significant effect on competition.

While limiting the foreclosure inquiry to actual foreclosure would seem to be an unduly narrow approach, as plaintiffs should not have to wait until there is no more competition on the market before they can bring a successful tying claim, the difficulty is developing a workable test for potential foreclosure. *Microsoft* highlights the challenges in this regard as one of the most hotly-debated issues in that case concerned the Commission's analysis of potential foreclosure on the tied product's market. In its decision, the Commission found that Microsoft's tying of its Window Media Player to its operating system created an unacceptable risk of potential foreclosure of competition in the media player market. To reach this conclusion, the

Commission had to make a number of assumptions about the future and rely on a somewhat speculative chain of causation. It reasoned that, because Microsoft's operating system was ubiquitous, this gave Microsoft an advantage in promoting its media player, which would cause content providers to write programs only for Microsoft's Windows Media Player, which would cause the media player market to tip in Microsoft's favour.

Although a discussion of the merits of the Commission's approach in *Microsoft* is beyond the scope of this chapter, the case highlights the desirability of placing appropriate limits on what constitutes potential foreclosure because, otherwise, there is a danger that the inquiry will become too speculative and virtually impossible to apply in practice. In particular, it would be helpful if the Commission were able to provide guidance on the time period over which potential foreclosure should be measured as well as the applicable standard of proof, which is discussed below.

### Objective justifications and efficiencies

If the conditions for tying are met, the defendant may then put forward objective justifications for its practice or show that the practice generates procompetitive efficiencies that outweigh any anticompetitive harm. Thus far, defendants in EU tying cases have not been very successful in pleading objective justifications and efficiencies.

The most oft-cited example of an objective justification is where tying is necessary for reasons of health or safety. For example, in *Hilti*, the defendant argued that the tying of cartridges and nails was justified on the grounds that it was necessary to ensure that nails of the requisite quality were used with its nail guns and it even produced expert studies showing that competitors' nails were of inferior quality. The CFI rejected this line of argument on the grounds that Hilti should have complained to the appropriate authorities rather than taking the matter into its own hands. Similarly, in *Tetra Pak*, the CFI rejected the defendant's argument that the tying of machines and cartons was necessary on grounds of public health. According to the CFI, if Tetra Pak was worried about the suitability of competitors' cartons for its machines, it should have disclosed the technical specifications that cartons needed to meet to be used on its machines.

These cases suggest that defendants will rarely be successful with health and safety arguments. It almost seems that the defendant would have to show that a consumer had been injured by a competitor's inferior product after the defendant had complained to the appropriate public authority. In the context of its current review of Article 82, the Commission might well consider whether placing such a heavy burden on defendants to prove that tying lowers health and safety risks is consistent with a general analytical framework that recognizes that tying is not anticompetitive in most cases and, perhaps more importantly, whether this approach is in the best interest of consumers given the consequences if it has the effect of chilling efforts by manufacturers to make their products as safe as possible.

Efficiency arguments have not fared much better than health and safety arguments. In *Microsoft*, Microsoft argued that the integration of the Windows Media Player into the Windows operating system generated a number of procompetitive efficiencies such as lower transaction costs because consumers would not have to purchase the products separately. It also emphasized that tying produced benefits because software developers would not have to worry about writing code for the media player functionality, but could concentrate on developing new applications. The Commission rejected all of these arguments with little difficulty.

As discussed in the next section, at least part of the reason that defendants have met with so little success in justifying their tying practices is that the standard of proof and the allocation of the burden of proof work against them. As suggested below, procedural rules that place defendants at a disadvantage would seem to be at odds with the view that tying is generally benign. On the substantive side, the Commission may want to consider whether a more deferential standard for the assessment of objective justifications and efficiencies would not be more in keeping with an analysis of tying under a rule-of-reason framework.

In this regard, the kinds of efficiencies pleaded by Microsoft in the context of technological integration are at the heart of the current push towards technological convergence in the information technology and consumer electronics industries and would seem to merit more weight than they were given in the Commission's decision. These efficiencies should be judged under a deferential standard unless courts and competition authorities are prepared to start second-guessing manufacturers on product design and integration issues. In the United States, the courts have clearly applied a more deferential standard in cases involving technological tying for precisely this reason.[28]

In judging efficiencies in cases involving the integration of new features into products, the 'commercial usage' criterion of Article 82 may prove useful. As discussed above, this criterion may come into play both in determining whether there are distinct products and in evaluating possible justifications. Even if commercial usage shows that some firms offer the tied product separately so that there are separate products, if the integration of the tying and tied product is common practice in the industry, this constitutes strong evidence that the integration creates efficiencies because non-dominant firms would not have an incentive to do so otherwise.

## Standard and burden of proof
### *Importance of appropriate procedural rules*
In developing the optimal approach to tying under Article 82, one area of focus should be the correct allocation of the burden of proof and the appropriate standards of proof, both of which will play key roles in determining the actual impact of whatever substantive legal test is chosen. Unless sufficient attention is given to these procedural issues, any reform of the substantive approach to tying risks having only a limited effect in practice. The EU *Microsoft* case illustrates this risk: the European Commission announced that its decision heralded a movement away from a per se test to a rule of reason, yet the rules that it applied on the standard of proof and the burden of proof were weighted so heavily in its favour that its new rule-of-reason approach was arguably nothing but a per se approach by another name.

The procedural rules on the allocation of the burden of proof and the standard of proof should be tailored to the substantive approach to the practice at issue, which means that these rules may not necessarily be the same in all Article 82 cases. Thus, if tying is considered to be benign in most cases so that it is judged under a rule of reason, these procedural rules should reflect this presumption. As discussed below, the procedural rules currently applied in tying cases reflect the per se approach to tying in that they favour the Commission and need to be reshaped to better reflect the assumptions underlying a rule-of-reason approach.

### *Burden of proof*
In considering the most appropriate rules on the burden of proof in an Article 82 tying case, the basic steps in a rule-of-reason analysis under US law provide a useful point of comparison. In *Microsoft*, the DC Circuit set forth the basic steps in a rule-of-reason analysis in the portion of its opinion dealing with the Section 2 monopolization claim against Microsoft, and noted that the steps under a Section 1 rule-of-reason analysis were similar.[29] The steps in the rule-of-reason balancing process are as follows:

1. the plaintiff must show that the seller's conduct had an anticompetitive effect;
2. if the plaintiff establishes a prima facie case, the seller must offer pro-competitive justifications for his conduct;
3. if the seller establishes procompetitive justifications, the burden shifts back to the plaintiff to rebut the claim; and
4. if the plaintiff is unable to rebut the asserted justifications, it must show that the anticompetitive harm of the conduct outweighs the procompetitive benefit.

In the European Union, the plaintiff also has the burden of establishing the infringement. Article 2 of Regulation 1/2003[30] provides as follows:

> In any national or Community proceeding for the application of Articles 81 and 82 of the Treaty, the burden of proving an infringement of Article 81(1) or of Article 82 of the Treaty shall rest on the party or authority alleging the infringement. The undertaking or association of undertakings claiming the benefit of Article 81(3) of the Treaty shall bear the burden of proving that the conditions of that paragraph are fulfilled.

Regulation 1/2003 is unclear on the allocation of the burden of proof in establishing justifications and efficiencies in an Article 82 case. Although Article 2 explicitly places the burden of establishing procompetitive effects on the defendant in an Article 81 case, it does not specify who has the burden of proving justifications for the allegedly abusive conduct in an Article 82 case. The broad language of Recital 5 of Regulation 1/2003 suggests that this burden falls on the defendant in Article 82 as well as Article 81 cases: '[i]t should be for the undertaking or association of undertakings invoking the benefit of a defence against a finding of infringement to demonstrate to the required legal standard that the conditions for applying such defence are satisfied'. However Article 2's silence on the issue of who bears the burden of proof on efficiencies and objective justifications in an Article 82 case would seem to leave the Commission with some discretion in allocating the burden of proof on these issues.

So far the Commission has placed the burden of establishing objective justifications and efficiencies entirely on the defendant. In its *Microsoft* decision, the Commission made it clear that Microsoft bore the burden of proof on these points and that it had not discharged that burden, stating that 'Microsoft has not submitted adequate evidence to the effect that tying WMP is objectively justified by procompetitive effects which would outweigh the distortion of competition caused by it'.[31]

Thus, while the United States and European Union both place the initial burden on the plaintiff to establish the infringement in a rule-of-reason case, the two jurisdictions then appear to diverge, particularly on the question of who has the final burden of proving objective justifications and efficiencies. Under the US rule-of-reason test described above, once the defendant puts forward a plausible argument on objective justifications and efficiencies, the burden shifts back to the plaintiff to show either that these justifications are merely pretextual or that they are outweighed by the anticompetitive effects of the tying arrangement. In contrast, the EU's approach requires the defendant not only to establish the existence of efficiencies, but to show that they outweigh any anticompetitive harm.

Placing the burden on the defendant, at least in the first instance, to put forward objective justifications and efficiencies in an Article 82 case makes sense. Once the Commission has established a prima facie case under Article 82, the defendant should have the burden of explaining why its conduct is not abusive. Moreover the defendant will be in the best position to identify specific efficiencies generated by the tie and to produce evidence of those efficiencies.

Once the defendant has put forward credible evidence on efficiencies and objective justifications, however, it is questionable whether the defendant should bear the ultimate burden of proof of establishing that the efficiencies put forward outweigh any anticompetitive effects. First, who bears the burden of proof could be decisive in some cases because of the difficulty of proving efficiencies. If the basic premise is that tying is benign in the majority of cases, the burden of proof should be allocated in a way that gives the defendant the benefit of the doubt in close cases. This proposition would seem to be all the more true in cases involving technological tying because, as discussed above, there is a higher likelihood that these cases involve efficiencies and should be reviewed under a deferential standard. Second, the Commission is in a much better position than the defendant to weigh the evidence on procompetitive benefits and anticompetitive harms in these cases because it has access to much more evidence.

### Standards of proof

On the question of the relevant standards of proof in tying cases, the European Commission's current approach also appears to favour the plaintiff which, again, seems to be inconsistent with the basic premise that, if anything, the procedural rules should favour the defendant in tying cases. As discussed, in establishing the existence of an infringement in its decision in *Microsoft*, the Commission relied on a chain of causation that, at the very least, was questionable in showing that there was a risk of foreclosure on the tied product market. At least to the extent that the issue concerns predicting the future effects of a tying practice such as potential market foreclosure, it is arguable that the Commission failed to meet the standard of proof required by the ECJ's recent judgment in the *Tetra Laval*.[32] In that case, which dealt with the standard of proof to be met by the Commission in merger cases, the ECJ emphasized that it was important for the Commission to put forward convincing evidence in merger cases because the Commission is trying to predict the situation on the relevant market after the merger. On this point, the ECJ stated:

[a] prospective analysis of the kind necessary in merger control must be carried out with great care since it does not entail the examination of past

events – for which often many items of evidence are available which make it possible to understand the causes – or of current events, but rather a prediction of events which are more or less likely to occur in future if a decision prohibiting the planned concentration or laying down the conditions for it is not adopted.[33]

The ECJ then explained that it was 'particularly important' for the Commission to put forward convincing evidence in cases involving conglomerate mergers, i.e. where the parties are on neighbouring markets and there is a concern that they will be able to leverage their power in one market to increase their power in another:

> The analysis of a 'conglomerate-type' concentration is a prospective analysis in which, first, the consideration of a lengthy period of time in the future and, secondly, the leveraging necessary to give rise to a significant impediment to effective competition mean that the chains of causation and effect are dimly discernible, uncertain and difficult to establish. That being so, the quality of evidence produced by the Commission in order to establish that it is necessary to adopt a decision declaring the concentration incompatible with the common market is particularly important, since that evidence must support the Commission's conclusion that, if such a decision were not adopted, the economic development envisaged by it would be plausible.[34]

While *Tetra Laval* only dealt with the standard of proof in merger cases, the ECJ's reasoning would seem applicable to any competition case in which the Commission is required to evaluate future economic effects. The ECJ's reasoning would seem particularly relevant to the determination of the standard of proof that the Commission must meet in establishing the requisite degree of foreclosure on the tied product's market in a tying case. Establishing foreclosure not only requires the Commission to predict what will happen in the future if the tying practice continues, but requires it to establish that the dominant firm has the ability to leverage its dominant position on the tying product's market to foreclose competition on the tied product's market. Thus, the Commission must address chains of causation that are very similar to those involved in a conglomerate merger case, which, in the words of the ECJ, are 'dimly discernable, uncertain and difficult to establish'.[35] Indeed, it could be argued that the standard of proof should be even higher in the context of an Article 82 case because of the almost penal character of the high fines that can be imposed.

The issue of the appropriate standard of proof also arises in connection with the standard that the defendant must meet in establishing the existence of efficiencies and objective justifications. In *Microsoft*, the Commission required Microsoft to meet a very high standard of proof. With regard to the efficiencies flowing to independent software developers of having the Windows Media Player integrated into the Windows operating system, the Commission found that 'Microsoft has failed to supply evidence that tying of WMP is indispensable for the alleged pro-competitive effects to come into effect'.[36] Requiring the defendant not only to establish that the tying practice gives rise to procompetitive justifications, but to show also that it is indispensable for these procompetitive justifications to arise makes it virtually impossible for the defendant ever to win on the issue of efficiencies. Indeed, it is difficult to reconcile requiring the defendant to meet such a high standard of proof with any approach that purports to be a rule-of-reason approach.

The procedural rules on the allocation of the burden of proof and the standard of proof are notoriously vague. For example, until *Tetra Laval*, the European Courts typically would state that, in merger cases, the Commission was required to produce enough evidence so as to meet the 'requisite legal standard' without specifying what that standard was.[37] In the wake of *Tetra Laval*, the EU antitrust community has begun to pay more attention to the applicable procedural rules.[38] While the focus has largely been on merger cases, procedural issues merit attention in the context of Article 81 and 82 cases as well. It is to be hoped that the Commission will include procedural issues within the scope of its Article 82 review because, otherwise, any reform of the substantive rules may only have limited effect in practice.

**Conclusion**

Of the abusive practices under Article 82, tying is the poster child for the need for an approach freed from the straitjacket of a rigid legalistic approach and more in line with contemporary economic theory. While economists continue to debate various aspects of tying, a consensus seems to have emerged that, in most cases, tying is benign and should be judged under a rule-of-reason standard rather than a per se standard. Unfortunately, the prevailing substantive test for tying in the European Union is a strict per se rule that does not take into account either the effects of the tying practice on the market or all the efficiencies that it can generate. While the European Commission's recent decision in *Microsoft* suggests that the law may be moving towards a rule-of-reason approach, the procedural rules governing the allocation of the burden of proof and the standard of proof place defendants at such a disadvantage that, for all practical purposes, they may as well be operating under a per se approach.

In the context of its current review of its policy under Article 82, the question facing the European Commission is not so much whether to adopt a rule-of-reason approach to tying cases. It has already shown a willingness to do so in *Microsoft* and, more generally, a rule-of-reason approach would be consistent with its general aim of having an effects-based policy. Rather the question is, what are the optimal contours of this rule of reason? As discussed in this chapter, a structured rule of reason that includes a number of screening conditions along the lines outlined by the Commission in *Microsoft* would seem to be the best approach. It minimizes the need for the kind of open-ended inquiry called for under the classic rule of reason, where procompetitive effects are weighed against anticompetitive harm. At the same time, it allows such an inquiry in appropriate cases. Most importantly, it provides more concrete, practical guidance to companies and their advisors, as well as to competition authorities and courts, than a pure rule-of-reason approach.

The issuance of guidelines on Article 82 would allow the Commission to flesh out the screening conditions to provide as much concrete guidance as possible, in much the way it has done in the context of developing the rules and guidelines for the various categories of restrictive agreements. There are a number of questions of degree where it would be helpful to have some concrete indication of where the cut-off point is likely to be. How much foreclosure on the tied product's market is required to give rise to competition concerns? What is the relevant time period for an inquiry into potential foreclosure? How much demand must there be for the products separately for them to be considered as separate products for tying purposes? While any attempt to address these kinds of questions in the abstract is necessarily somewhat arbitrary, it may be worth sacrificing some theoretical purity for greater certainty.

In parallel with its review of the substantive rules on tying, the Commission needs to re-evaluate the procedural rules. Instead of reflecting the underlying presumption that, in most cases, tying is benign, the current rules do just the opposite. While the Commission has some constraints on what it can do in the procedural area as it must adhere to the rules set forth in Regulation 1/2003 as well as in the case law, there is still scope for recalibrating the procedural rules so that they reflect the more deferential standard that tying cases deserve.

Finally the review of its policy under Article 82 offers the Commission the opportunity to move ahead of the United States in bringing the law on tying into line with contemporary economic theory. If it does so, it may also help create more favourable conditions in Europe for the increased integration of new features into information technology and consumer electronics products and broader convergence among these sectors, which is one of the key drivers for the success of high-tech companies.

# Notes

1. Partner, Covington & Burling LLP, Brussels.
2. For an interesting debate on tying in the context of the EU *Microsoft* case, see Evans, D., J. Padilla and M. Polo (2002), 'Tying in platform software: reasons for a rule-of-reason standard in European competition law', **25**, *World Competition*, 509; Dolmans, M. and T. Graf (2004), 'Analysis of tying under Article 82 EC: the European Commission's Microsoft decision in perspective', **27**, *World Competition*, 225; Evans, D. and J. Padilla (2004), 'Tying under Article 82 EC and the Microsoft decision: a comment on Dolmans and Graf', **27**, *World Competition*, 503. For other examples of the growing literature on the EU case, see Ridyard, D. (2005), 'Tying and bundling – cause for complaint?', **6**, *European Competition Law Review*, 316; Kuhn, K-U., R. Stillman and C. Caffarra (2005), 'Economic theories of bundling and their policy implications in abuse cases: an assessment in light of the Microsoft case', *European Competition Journal*, 85; Art, J.-Y. and G. McCurdy (2004), 'The European Commission's media player remedy in its *Microsoft* decision: compulsory code removal despite the absence of tying or foreclosure', **11**, *European Competition Law Review*, 694; Furse, M. (2004), 'Article 82, Microsoft and bundling, or 'the half monti', *Competition Law*, 169.
3. An overview of the Article 82 review and links to the Discussion Paper and other documents are available at the following website: http://europa.eu/comm/competition/antitrust/others/article_82_review.html. For a series of papers discussing the application of Article 82 to a wide array of practices, see GCLC Research Papers on Article 82 EC, Global Competition Law Centre, College of Europe (2005) available at http://gclc.coleurop.be, and, in particular, Ahlborn, C., D. Bailey and H. Crossley (2005), 'An Antitrust Analysis of Tying: Position Paper', which discusses in some detail several of the themes of this chapter.
4. Report by the Economic Advisory Group for Competition Policy (2005), 'An economic approach to Article 82', online at http://europa.eu.int/comm/competition/publications/studies/eagcp_july_21_05.pdf.
5. For a more detailed summary of the evolution of economic thinking on tying, see Ahlborn, C., D. Evans and J. Padilla (2004), 'The antitrust economics of tying', **49**, *Antitrust Bulletin*, 287–341; Hylton, K. and M. Salinger (2001), 'Tying law and policy: a decision-theoretic approach', **69**, *Antitrust L. J.*, 469. For some recent articles on the economics of tying, see Tirole, J. (2005), 'The analysis of tying cases: a primer', **1**, *Comp. Policy Int'l*, 1; Carlton, D. and M. Waldman (2005), 'How economics can improve antitrust doctrine towards tie-in sales', **1**, *Comp. Policy Int'l*, 27; Nalebuff, B. (2005), 'Tied and true exclusion', **1**, *Comp. Policy Int'l*, 41; Evans, D. and M. Salinger (2005), 'Why do firms bundle and tie? Evidence from competitive markets and implications for tying law', **22**; *Yale Journal on Regulation*, 37; Kuhn, K.-U., R. Stillman and C. Caffarra (2005), 'Economic theories of bundling and their policy implications in abuse cases: an assessment in light of the Microsoft case', *European Competition Journal*, 85; Nalebuff, B. and D. Majerus (2003), 'Bundling, tying, and portfolio effects', DTI Economics Paper No. 1.
6. Debate continues over the relative frequency of beneficial and harmful ties and the implications of this for the appropriate legal standard. See Kuhn, K.-U., R. Stillman and C. Caffarra (2005), 'Economic theories of bundling and their policy implications in abuse cases: an assessment in light of the Microsoft case', *European Competition Journal*, 85; Hylton, K. and M. Salinger (2001), 'Tying law and policy: a decision-theoretic approach', **69**, *Antitrust L. J.*, 469; Grimes, W. (2002), 'The antitrust tying law schism: a critique of *Microsoft III* and a response to Hylton and Salinger', **70**, *Antitrust L. J.*, 199; Hylton, K. and M. Salinger (2002), 'Reply to Grimes: illusory distinctions and schisms in tying law', **70**, *Antitrust L. J.*, 231.
7. *Northern Pacific Ry. Co.* v. *United States*, 356 US 1, 5–6 (1958).
8. Ibid., at 7–8 ('The very existence of this host of tying arrangements is itself compelling evidence of the defendant's great power . . .').
9. Bork, R. (1978), *The Antitrust Paradox*, p. 365.

10. Areeda, P. and H. Hovenkamp (2004), *Fundamentals of Antitrust Law*, at pp. 17–75.
11. *Jefferson Parish Hospital Dist. No. 2* v. *Hyde*, 466 US 2 (1984).
12. *Jefferson Parish*, 466 US at 9.
13. The US Supreme Court may have an opportunity to revisit its approach to at least certain aspects of the approach to tying in *Independent Ink, Inc.* v. *Illinois Tool Works, Inc.*, 396 F.3d 1342 (Fed. Cir. 2005), *cert. granted*, 125 S.Ct. 2937 (2005), which is pending before it.
14. *United States* v. *Microsoft Corp.*, 253 F.3d 34, 85 (DC Cir. 2001) (*en banc*).
15. Ibid., at 84–97.
16. See text accompanying note 18 below.
17. Case T-30/89, *Hilti* v. *Commission*, [1991] ECR II-1439, confirmed on appeal in Case C-53-92 P, *Hilti* v. *Commission*, [1994] ECR I-667.
18. Case T-83-91, *Tetra Pak* v. *Commission*, [1994] ECR II-755, confirmed on appeal in Case C-333/94 P, *Tetra Pak* v. *Commission*, [1996] ECR I-5951.
19. *Microsoft*, Commission Decision of 24 March 2004 available at the following website: http://europa.eu.int/comm./competition/antitrust/cases/decisions/37792/en.pdf.
20. European Commission (24 March 2004), *Microsoft – Questions and Answers on Commission Decision*, MEMO/04/70.
21. The US Supreme Court has held that a little as $60 800 is 'not insubstantial'. *United States* v. *Loew's Inc.*, 371 US 38 (1962).
22. *Jefferson Parish*, 466 US at 33–4.
23. For a good discussion of the error-cost framework, see Hylton, K. and M. Salinger (2001), 'Tying law and policy: a decision-theoretic approach', **69**, *Antitrust L. J.*, 469.
24. *Jefferson Parish*, 466 US at 34–5.
25. Easterbrook, Frank H. (1984), 'The limits of antitrust', **63**, *Texas L. Rev.*, reprinted in **1**, *Competition Policy Int'l*, 179, at p. 188 (2005).
26. *Tetra Pak* at para. 37.
27. In its judgment in *Microsoft*, the DC Circuit recognized that efficiencies attributable to newly-integrated products were not captured by the two-products test, which is why it opted for a rule-of-reason test that would allow such efficiencies to be pleaded (p. 49).
28. For a good discussion of US and EU cases involving technological tying, see Heiner, D. (2005), 'Assessing tying claims in the context of software integration: a suggested framework for applying the rule-of-reason analysis', **72**, *Univ. of Chicago L. Rev.*, 123.
29. Ibid., at 58–9.
30. Council of Ministers of the European Union, *Council Regulation (EC) No 1/2003 of 16 December 2002 on the Implementation of the Rules on Competition Laid Down in Articles 81 and 82 of the Treaty*, OJ (2003) L1/1.
31. *Microsoft*, para. 970.
32. Case C-12/03, *Commission* v. *Tetra Laval BV*, judgment of 15 February 2005 (not yet reported).
33. Ibid., para. 42.
34. Ibid., para. 44.
35. Ibid., para. 44.
36. *Microsoft*, para. 963.
37. See, e.g.,Case T-342/99, *Airtours plc* v. *Commission*, [2002] ECR II-2585 at para. 62.
38. See, e.g., Vesterdorf, B. (March 2005), 'Standard of proof in merger cases: reflections in the light of recent case law of the Community Courts', *European Competition Journal*, 3; Reeves, T. and N. Dodoo (2005), 'Standards of proof and standards of judicial review in EC merger law', *Fordham Corporate Law Institute*.

## References

Ahlborn, C., D. Evans and J. Padilla (2004), 'The antitrust economics of tying', **49**, *Antitrust Bulletin*, 287–341.
Ahlborn, C., D. Bailey and H. Crossley (2005), 'An antitrust analysis of tying: position paper'.
Areeda, P. and H. Hovenkamp (2004), *Fundamentals of Antitrust Law*.

Art, J.-Y. and G. McCurdy (2004), 'The European Commission's media player remedy in its *Microsoft* decision: compulsory code removal despite the absence of tying or foreclosure', **11**, *European Competition Law Review*, 694.

Bork, R. (1978), *The Antitrust Paradox*, New York: Free Press.

Carlton, D. and M. Waldman (2005), 'How economics can improve antitrust doctrine towards tie-in sales', **1**, *Comp. Policy Int'l*, 27.

Council of Ministers of the European Union, *Council Regulation (EC) No 1/2003 of 16 December 2002 on the Implementation of the Rules on Competition Laid Down in Articles 81 and 82 of the Treaty*, OJ (2003) L1/1.

Dolmans, M. and T. Graf (2004), 'Analysis of tying under Article 82 EC: the European Commission's Microsoft decision in perspective', **27**, *World Competition*, 225.

Easterbrook, Frank H. (1984), 'The limits of antitrust', **63**, *Texas L. Rev.*, reprinted in **1**, *Competition Policy Int'l*, 179, at p. 188 (2005).

Economic Advisory Group for Competition Policy (2005), 'An economic approach to Article 82' available at: http://europa.eu.int/comm/competition/publications/studies/eagcp_july_21_05.pdf.

Evans, D. and J. Padilla (2004), 'Tying under Article 82 EC and the Microsoft decision: a comment on Dolmans and Graf', **27**, *World Competition*, 503.

Evans, D. and M. Salinger (2005), 'Why do firms bundle and tie? Evidence from competitive markets and implications for tying law', **22**, *Yale Journal on Regulation*, 37.

Evans, D., J. Padilla and M. Polo (2002), 'Tying in platform software: reasons for a rule-of-reason standard in European competition law', **25**, *World Competition*, 509.

Furse, M. (2004), 'Article 82, Microsoft and bundling, or "the half monti"', *Competition Law*, 169.

Grimes, W. (2002), 'The antitrust tying law schism: a critique of *Microsoft III* and a response to Hylton and Salinger', **70**, *Antitrust L. J.*, 199.

Heiner, D. (2005), 'Assessing tying claims in the context of software integration: a suggested framework for applying the rule-of-reason analysis', **72**, *Univ. of Chicago L. Rev.*, 123.

Hylton, K. and M. Salinger (2001), 'Tying law and policy: a decision-theoretic approach', **69**, *Antitrust L. J.*, 469.

Hylton, K. and M. Salinger (2002), 'Reply to Grimes: illusory distinctions and schisms in tying law', **70**, *Antitrust L. J.*, 231.

Kroes, Neelie (23 September 2005), 'Preliminary thoughts on policy review of Article 82', *Fordham Corporate Law Institute*, available online at the following website: http:// europa. eu.int/rapid/pressReleasesAction.do?reference=SPEECH/05/537&format=HTML& aged= 0&language=EN&guiLanguage=en.

Kuhn, K.-U., R. Stillman and C. Caffarra (2005), 'Economic theories of bundling and their policy implications in abuse cases: an assessment in light of the Microsoft case', *European Competition Journal*, 85.

Nalebuff, B. (2005), 'Tied and true exclusion', **1**, *Comp. Policy Int'l*, 41.

Nalebuff, B. and D. Majerus (2003), 'Bundling, tying, and portfolio effects', DTI Economics Paper No. 1.

Ridyard, D. (2005), 'Tying and bundling – cause for complaint?', **6**, *European Competition Law Review*, 316.

Reeves, T. and N. Dodoo (2005), 'Standards of proof and standards of judicial review in EC merger law', *Fordham Corporate Law Institute*.

Tirole, J. (2005), 'The analysis of tying cases: a primer', **1**, *Comp. Policy Int'l*, 1.

Vesterdorf, B. (March 2005), 'Standard of proof in merger cases: reflections in the light of recent case law of the Community Courts', *European Competition Journal*, 3.

## Cases

*Airtours plc v. Commission*, [2002] ECR II-2585.

*Commission v. Tetra Laval BV*, Judgment of 15 February 2005 (not yet reported).

*Hilti v. Commission*, [1991] ECR II-1439 (CFI).

*Hilti v. Commission*, [1994] ECR I-667 (ECJ).

*Jefferson Parish Hospital Dist. No. 2* v. *Hyde*, 466 US 2 (1984).
*Northern Pacific Ry. Co.* v. *United States*, 356 US 1, 5–6 (1958).
*Tetra Pak* v. *Commission*, [1994] ECR II-755 (CFI).
*Tetra Pak* v. *Commission*, [1996] ECR I-5951 (ECJ).
*United States* v. *Loew's Inc.*, 371 US 38 (1962).
*United States* v. *Microsoft Corp.*, 253 F.3d 34, 85 (DC Cir. 2001).

# 10 Abuse of dominance enforcement under Latin American competition laws
*Russell Pittman and Maria Tineo*[1]

The widespread adoption of competition laws in the 1990s was accompanied by controversy, especially in the US, regarding the importance and even the appropriateness of introducing such legislation early in the transition to a market economy.[2] Critics feared that active competition law enforcement would introduce too many false positive regulatory actions, becoming yet another avenue for inefficient government intervention and naïve enforcement of the law that might retard economic development by restricting productive business arrangements and otherwise reducing incentives for investment.[3] For many of these critics, one way to limit the anticipated negative effects of a competition law would be to introduce 'a competition policy system that emphasized advocacy and enforced prohibitions on naked trade restraints. [Critics] would not establish competition laws that prohibit the full range of behavior (abuse of a dominant position, mergers, vertical restraints and price discrimination) commonly subject to antitrust oversight in older Western competition systems'.[4]

No other part of a comprehensive competition law was as subject to criticism as the prohibition against abuse of dominance. It was feared that abuse provisions were particularly likely to be overenforced, thereby chilling growth-enhancing business conduct and causing considerable harm to consumers. These critics argued that the abuse of dominance provisions of new competition laws in developing countries could act as 'a Trojan Horse for the smuggling in of price controls and other dubious government harassment of successful enterprises'.[5] By limiting freedom of contract, enforcement of abuse of dominance provisions would inhibit the market economy that liberalization seeks to foster.[6]

Even proponents of the adoption of comprehensive competition laws expressed concerns about abuse of dominance provisions.[7] They questioned whether in enforcing abuse provisions new agencies would focus on 'questionable' anticompetitive practices, i.e. excessive pricing, price discrimination, or other 'exploitative' practices, as opposed to bringing actions against exclusionary practices that are generally considered more likely to be harmful to competition.[8]

This chapter explores whether fears of overenforcement of dominance provisions have been borne out in the experience of Latin America, and examines both the types of conduct ('exploitative' or exclusionary) that have been sanctioned and the particular sectors of economies where abuse enforcement has been focused. Abuse of dominance, as used in this chapter, includes, inter alia, excessive pricing, price discrimination, predatory pricing, refusals to deal/sell, exclusive contracts, tied selling or bundling, and raising rivals' costs. The principal analytical approach employed in this chapter is a comparison of abuse of dominance legal provisions and enforcement actions across eight jurisdictions, using a similar methodology to that of Pitmann (2004).

Latin America provides an interesting case study because, although the trend may now be reversing, over the past 20 years it has been a region of neoliberal, pro-market, Washington consensus reforms, and the question of whether governments that have given lip service to free markets have also refrained from large-scale economic intervention is a real one.[9] Latin America also provides a rich set of experience for examination because of its diversity, seen in the dominance provisions themselves, the institutional structure of the competition agency and the wide variety in the economic importance of each country.[10] For example, some jurisdictions prohibit practices such as excessive pricing while others do not. With respect to institutional structure and caseloads, Latin America offers a variety of experiences. Panama and Peru, for example, generally initiate fewer than 15 cases per year, while Mexico handles upwards of 200 cases each year. Similarly, in 2003, Costa Rica's agency had fewer than 20 professionals, and operated on a budget of approximately US$200 000; in the same year the Mexican agency had 120 professionals dedicated to competition, and had a budget of approximately US$15 million.

**Have fears of overenforcement of dominance provisions been borne out?**
Commentators concerned about overenforcement of the antitrust laws in Latin America have been concerned principally about the unilateral intervention of the antitrust agency in markets, in the context of broader governmental tendencies and temptations to intervene in market processes.[11] This fear is related at least in part to the particular historical relationship between business and government in Latin America, where the private sector developed not in partnership with governments (as, for example, in Asia), but rather with the 'favours' of government.[12] As far back as colonial times, when a relationship with the Spanish crown was essential for succeeding as entrepreneurs, government intervention has played a paramount role in shaping the economic institutions of the region. Government has dictated how the entrepreneurs must behave, what to produce and so

forth.[13] It is not surprising that the first opponents to the adoption of competition laws in Latin America were the business communities,[14] who feared that, in negotiating business deals, the competition law would become an additional bargaining tool for the government, rather than being used as it should, to attack government and private restrictions on competition.

Only five or ten years ago companies reached cartel agreements supervised by the government, while now governments seek to prohibit such agreements.[15] Ironically, the very fact that the forms and appearances are not much changed while the philosophy has changed – in the direction of liberalization and the support of markets – may make competition law enforcement and regulation more difficult in Latin America than in Central and Eastern Europe, where it is more obvious that nothing is as it was.

Table 10.1 presents the number of dominance, or monopolization, cases completed for 2001, 2002 and 2003, the number of anticompetitive conduct cases for the same years,[16] as well as the total number of competition cases (i.e., including mergers) for each year.

It is clear that abuse of dominance investigations do not generally account for a large share of agency caseload. For example, abuse of dominance investigations accounted for less than 2 per cent of all investigations in Brazil and Colombia, and approximately 8 per cent of all investigations in Mexico. As a proportion of all conduct investigations, dominance cases were low for in some jurisdictions (e.g., 7 per cent for Colombia), higher in others (e.g., 38 per cent in Brazil, 45 per cent in Mexico).

If attention is shifted from the number of investigations to actual enforcement actions against the alleged anticompetitive conduct by the dominant firm, it becomes clear that the number of such actions is

*Table 10.1    Number of cases completed, 2001–3*[17]

| Country | Dom. 2001 | Cond. 2001 | Total 2001 | Dom. 2002 | Cond. 2002 | Total 2002 | Dom. 2003 | Cond. 2003 | Total 2003 |
|---|---|---|---|---|---|---|---|---|---|
| Argentina | 11 | * | * | 16 | * | * | 28 | * | * |
| Brazil (CADE) | 8 | 30 | 614 | 17 | 31 | 549 | 16 | 51 | 577 |
| Colombia | 1 | 22 | 143 | 2 | 31 | 136 | 3 | 17 | 79 |
| Costa Rica | 6 | 25 | 26 | 4 | 18 | 18 | 3 | 28 | 29 |
| Mexico | 30 | 64 | 375 | 34 | 68 | 328 | 14 | 38 | 234 |
| Panama | 0 | 1 | 2 | 0 | 4 | 5 | 3 | 3 | 3 |
| Peru | 2 | 9 | 12 | 4 | 8 | 8 | 4 | 8 | 8 |
| Venezuela | 3 | 18 | 19 | 3 | 14 | 15 | 1 | 11 | 13 |

*Note:*   Dom. = dominance; Cond. = conduct.

*Table 10.2    Number of abuse findings, 2001–3*

| Country | 2001 | 2002 | 2003 |
| --- | --- | --- | --- |
| Argentina | 3 | 4 | 6 |
| Brazil | 0 | 1 | 1 |
| Colombia | 1 | 2 | 2 |
| Costa Rica | 2 | 0 | 0 |
| Mexico | 13 | 17 | 4 |
| Panama | 0 | 0 | 0 |
| Peru | 0 | 2 | 0 |
| Venezuela | 0 | 2 | 0 |
| Total | 19 | 28 | 13 |

generally low in absolute terms. Table 10.2 presents findings of abuse in each country, by year.

The number of abuse findings is minimal, and even these may reflect more the competition agencies' need to act as sectoral regulators in the absence of strong independent regulatory institutions than any tendency to intervene indiscriminately in the everyday business decisions of private firms.

A decade ago, Janusz Ordover, Russell Pittman and Paul Clyde (Ordover et al., 1994a; Ordover et al. and Pittman, 1994b) noted that many Central and Eastern European countries were setting up competition agencies but were not yet setting up agencies for regulating the behaviour of the 'natural monopoly' enterprises in sectors like energy, telecommunications and transport. They argued that, in the (perhaps temporary) absence of such regulatory agencies, the competition authorities were the only government bodies able to protect the citizenry from monopoly abuses, and that these authorities should act as 'quasi-regulators' of these 'natural monopoly' enterprises, using as their regulatory weapon the abuse-of-dominance provisions of the competition laws, until regulatory agencies were created to take their place.

Table 10.3 shows the industries that were designated as 'regulated' or 'borderline regulated' by Pittman[18] when he examined this hypothesis for the countries of Central and Eastern Europe for 1996 and 2001. He found that indeed a large percentage of abuse findings had been in these regulated sectors, where one would expect much of the enforcement energies to be devoted by traditional regulatory agencies rather than the antitrust agencies of more general jurisdiction.

Interestingly, Table 10.4 suggests that the same pattern found for the Central and Eastern European countries has held true for Latin America in the early years of the twenty-first century as well. Despite the fact that, in general, the Latin American countries have moved further than the

*Table 10.3 Regulated industries*

| Regulated sectors | Borderline regulated sectors |
|---|---|
| Postal services | Air transport |
| Electricity | Medical and health services |
| Telecommunications | Funeral, cremation, and cemetery services |
| Internet services | Waste disposal |
| Natural gas distribution | Local bus transport |
| Banking and financial services | Insurance |
| Cable television | |
| Water transport | |
| Water supply | |
| Local heating services | |

*Table 10.4 Number of abuse findings in regulated industries, 2001–3*

| Country | Abuse findings | Regulated (narrow) | Regulated (broad) |
|---|---|---|---|
| Argentina | 13 | 3 | 9 |
| Brazil | 2 | 1 | 1 |
| Colombia | 5 | 2 | 3 |
| Costa Rica | 2 | – | – |
| Mexico | 33 | 17 | 18 |
| Panama | 0 | – | – |
| Peru | 3 | 2 | 2 |
| Venezuela | 2 | – | – |
| Total | 60 | 25 (42%) | 33 (56%) |

Central and Eastern European countries in setting up independent regulatory agencies,[19] it is clear that the antitrust agencies retain a good deal of responsibility for protecting customers from abusive behaviour by these traditional 'natural monopolies': between one-quarter and one-half of the abuse findings may be characterized in this way, depending on the definition of 'regulated sectors' used.

A recent case in Brazil highlights the role the competition agency must sometimes play in these countries. The case involved charges that Matec, an affiliate of Ericsson, had unlawfully refused to sell component parts for an Ericsson MD 110 Telephone System.[20] Independent companies offering telephone system maintenance contracts claimed that they would be unable to compete effectively in the MD 110 market without access to replacement parts. In a 2003 decision, CADE found that Matec had unlawfully foreclosed competition in the market for system maintenance services, because competing companies could not operate without access to replacement parts. The foreclosure reduced consumer welfare because the affected telephone system purchasers were 'locked-in' to the MD 110 phone system by high switching costs. Competition at the point of sale for telephone systems was not adequate to forestall a market failure in the case of the federal government (which was a prime MD 110 customer) because government procurement rules prevented the government from selecting any bid but the lowest, without regard for post-purchase servicing costs.

In Mexico, the CFC has brought a series of dominance cases against Telmex, the dominant telephone services provider. One example in 2000 involved a proceeding in which the CFC found an unlawful refusal to deal. Consumers calling 800 'toll free' numbers operated by long distance companies had to purchase a Telmex pre-paid 'Ladatel' card if they wished to make the call using a Telmex public phone. Customers using public phones to call 800 numbers operated by Telmex were not subject to this expense, and Telmex refused to contract with competing operators so that they could absorb directly the cost of public phone access. The competitors, of course, could not effectively market 800 number services to companies because companies did not want callers to pay for public phone access when making a 'toll free' call. As a result of the case, callers no longer have to pay for public phone access when the 800 number is operated by a long distance provider with whom Telmex has signed an agreement.[21] If, however, Telmex does not have a signed agreement with the long distance carrier that operates an 800 number, Telmex charges $1.00 per minute.

As with the CEE countries, one may predict that in Latin America the antitrust agencies will have fewer enforcement responsibilities in the traditionally regulated sectors of the economy (hence more resources to devote to enforcement in the traditionally unregulated sectors) once the regulatory agencies become more effective.

An equally important observation is that, at least in some countries in Latin America, the competition authorities appear to be challenging some forms of government intervention in markets. For example, three of the five findings of abuse in Colombia appear to be related to government restrictions on competition. More than 20 of the 33 Mexican cases appear to involve government restrictions, with cases against Telmex, concessions in transportation, Pemex, syndicated unions, and so on. Many of the findings of abuse in non-regulated sectors likewise appear to involve other types of government restrictions. While a more detailed analysis would be necessary, it seems likely that many of the government restrictions being attacked are restrictions put in place at the request of powerful business interests with the aim of restricting competition.[22] Under those circumstances, attacking government restrictions would be an especially procompetitive use of a competition agency's scarce resources.[23]

### Design and enforcement of dominance provisions

Analysts have distinguished between two types of monopolistic practices prohibited by abuse of dominance provisions in competition laws. First, there can be prohibitions against certain practices in which the dominant firm uses its monopoly power to exploit other market participants without directly affecting the structure of the market, by, inter alia, charging high prices to customers, discriminating among customers, and paying low prices to suppliers. This conduct is sometimes referred to as 'exploitative' conduct. Second, there are prohibitions against conduct that is aimed directly at the preserving or exacerbating of anticompetitive aspects of the structure of the market: conduct that creates or maintains the monopolist's power, in which the firm tries to suppress competition by, for example, refusing to deal with a competitor, through predatory pricing, or by raising rivals' costs. Since such conduct seeks to exclude competitors and competition from the market, it is often referred to as 'exclusionary' conduct.[24]

For many scholars, the difficulty in determining what is an acceptable exercise of market power, necessary for a determination of whether an exploitative abuse has occurred, suggests that competition agencies should 'seek to minimize the extent to which they regulate prices of individual firms and focus more on seeking to prevent firms from engaging in exclusionary acts that threaten competition'.[25] Others argue that dominance provisions should prohibit *only* exclusionary conduct, not exploitative conduct. With respect to Latin America, Coate and others urged the countries adopting laws to focus on exclusionary practices.[26] In the U.S., violations of §2 of the Sherman Act generally apply only to exclusionary conduct.[27] Exploitative acts, such as charging monopolistic prices, are not attacked by enforcers because, inter alia, this type of enforcement is considered impractical and, it is feared, may discourage firms from competing as vigorously as they otherwise would.[28] Proponents of this view frown on prohibitions of excessive pricing, for example (prohibitions included in the competition laws of Brazil and some other countries), which is a purely exploitative act. Laws which prohibit practices that might be called exclusionary, such as price discrimination, but in fact are exploitative,[29] may also be deemed problematic according to this thinking. (Furthermore, while discrimination may appear 'unfair', its implications for economic welfare are generally ambiguous. Possible welfare benefits of discrimination include the supply of customers who would not pay a nondiscriminatory higher price and improving the ability of sellers to recover high levels of fixed costs.)

Certainly jurisdictions are encouraged by both commentators and fellow enforcers to bring exclusionary conduct cases as opposed to exploitative conduct cases.[30] Regardless of whether critics argue that exploitative behaviour should not be prohibited at all or in part, many agree that enforcement actions against this type of behaviour should be limited.[31]

In keeping with the European civil law tradition of spelling out in detail what is prohibited,[32] most of the Latin American competition laws have enacted dominance provisions that list a series of behaviours by a dominant firm or firms that are prohibited, and despite the widespread scepticism regarding various 'exploitative' practices, most prohibit, inter alia, price discrimination or the imposition of discriminatory conditions, and about half prohibit excessively high prices. All have restrictions on tying, which may arguably be used for either exploitation (as a pricing strategy) or exclusion (making competitive entry more difficult).[33] Table 10.5 presents the types of conduct that are most frequently specifically prohibited in the legal provisions of Latin American competition laws.

As Table 10.5 demonstrates, only a limited number of laws explicitly prohibit excessive pricing (Argentina, Brazil, Peru and Venezuela) and, as explained below, these provisions are infrequently used. All of the laws do prohibit other conduct that may be considered exploitative, such as price discrimination and tying. As the data below demonstrate, however, the inclusion of specific conduct prohibitions do not appear related to the pattern of actual enforcement actions, that is, where the defendant is found guilty. For example, 80 per cent of the enforcement actions in 2001–3 in Colombia, which prohibits fewer exploitative activities than other jurisdictions, involved exploitative conduct. On the other hand, while four jurisdictions prohibit excessive pricing, only one has actually enforced the provision in recent years.

Table 10.6 categorizes each country's enforcement actions from 2001 to 2003 where the defendant was found guilty of abuse of dominance in 'exploitative' or 'exclusionary' practices. While findings of price discrimination account for a quarter of total abuse findings from 2001 to 2003, nearly 40 per cent of enforcement actions involved either refusals to deal or exclusive dealing.

More specifically, the majority of enforcement cases (60%) during 2001–3 focused on clearly exclusionary types of abuses. Within the exclusionary cases, the greater part involved refusals to deal (34% of exclusionary cases, or 21% of total abuse findings) and exclusive dealing (26% of exclusionary cases, 16% of total cases). In Mexico, for example, 16 of the total abuse of dominance findings involved telecommunications and, of those, seven were refusals to deal, and two were exclusive dealing. In our sample there were only two findings of predatory pricing, or 3% of total

*Table 10.5  Types of abuses prohibited*

| Country | Law | Excessive pricing | Price discrimination | Predatory pricing | Refusals to deal/sell | Tied selling | Raising rivals' costs | Open-ended (catch-all) provision |
|---|---|---|---|---|---|---|---|---|
| Argentina | 2001 | yes | yes | yes | yes | yes | yes | no |
| Brazil | 1962; 1994 | yes | yes | yes | yes | yes | yes | no |
| Colombia | 1959; 1992 | no | yes | yes | yes | yes | no | no |
| Costa Rica | 1994 | no | yes | yes | yes | yes | no | yes |
| Mexico* | 1992 | no | yes | no | yes | yes | no | yes |
| Panama | 1996 | no | yes | yes | yes | yes | no | yes |
| Peru | 1991; 1996 | yes | yes | yes | yes | yes | yes | yes |
| Venezuela* | 1991 | yes | yes | no | yes | yes | yes | yes |

*Note:*  *amendments pending.

*Table 10.6   Enforcement actions by type of conduct*

| Country | Exploitative | Exclusionary |
|---|---|---|
| Argentina | 8 | 5 |
| Brazil | 1 | 2 |
| Colombia | 4 | 1 |
| Costa Rica* | 2 | 1 |
| Mexico | 7 | 26 |
| Panama | 0 | 0 |
| Peru | 0 | 2 |
| Venezuela | 2 | 0 |
| Total | 24 | 37 |

*Note:*   * The 2002 case had both exploitative and exclusionary elements.

abuse findings during that period. One of the predatory pricing cases involved telecommunications (Colombia), and the other the food industry (Mexico).

Exploitative conduct cases, which comprised 40% of the enforcement actions from 2001 to 2003, were focused on pricing practices: price discrimination accounted for 65% of the exploitative conduct cases, or 26% of total abuse findings. There was only one finding of excessive pricing, in Argentina in 2003, in the gasoline industry (retail petroleum).

While a closer examination of the cases, which is outside the scope of this chapter, is necessary for concluding definitively that these Latin American agencies are not seeking to regulate the prices or discriminatory acts of individual firms, it does appear that they are focusing more on exclusionary acts.

**Conclusion**

Enforcement actions against abuse of a dominant position appear to be of relatively low frequency in Latin America, and in many cases the competition agency appears to be compensating for ineffective institutions in regulated industries.[34] Importantly in many cases the competition agencies appear to be attacking government restrictions, far from using the 'government process to attack successful business'.[35] In Latin America, government restrictions remain a core component of restrictions on market competition, and it is a positive development if the competition agencies are seeking to dismantle them. Finally the majority of enforcement actions involve 'exclusionary' practices, suggesting that the abuse of dominance cases is not restoring price controls under the guise of antitrust, as sceptics feared.[36]

# Notes

1.  Russell Pittman is Director of Economic Research and Director of International Technical Assistance, Economic Analysis Group, Antitrust Division, US Department of Justice, and visiting professor, New Economic School, Moscow. Maria Tineo is Counsel for International Affairs at the International Antitrust Division of the Federal Trade Commission. The authors are grateful to the following colleagues for their extensive help in supplying case information and responses to questions: Patricia Agra Araújo (Conselho Administrativo de Defesa Econômica in Brazil); Marietta Arias (Comisión para la Promoción de la Competencia in Costa Rica); Humberto Guardia (Comisión Nacional de la Defensa de Competencia in Argentina); Maria Magaldi (Superintendencia para la Promoción y Protección de la Libre Competencia in Venezuela); Claudia Montoya (Superintendencia Industria y Comercio in Colombia); Carlos Noda (Indecopi in Peru); Gustavo Paredes (Comisión de Libre Competencia y Asuntos del Consumidor); and Monica Zegarra (Comisión Federal de Competencia in Mexico). They are grateful as well for helpful comments from Ignacio De Leon and Randolph W. Tritell. The views expressed herein are those of the authors and do not purport to represent the views of the United States, the Department of Justice, the Federal Trade Commission or any individual Commissioner.
2.  Pittman, Russell (2004), 'Abuse-of-dominance provisions of Central and Eastern European competition laws: have fears of over-enforcement been borne out?' (hereafter 'AODCEE'), **27**, *World Comp.*, 245 at 246. See also Boner, Roger and James Langenfeld (Spring 1992), 'Liberal trade and antitrust in developing nations', *Regulation*; Godek, Paul E. (1998), 'A Chicago School approach to antitrust for developing economies', **43**, *Antitrust Bull.*, 261; Godek, Paul E. (1992), 'One U.S. export Eastern Europe does not need', **15**, *Regulation*, 20; Rodriguez, A.E. and Mark D. Williams (1994), 'The effectiveness of proposed antitrust programs for developing economies', **19**, *N.C. J. Int'l L. & Com. Reg.*, 209; and Rodriguez, A.E. and Malcolm B. Coate (1996), 'Limits to antitrust policy for reforming economies', **18**, *Hous. J. Int'l L.*, 311.
3.  Rodriguez and Coate explain: 'by reducing the ability of firms to commit to investment contracts, active antitrust activity may result in reduced growth rates for reforming economies' (Rodriguez and Coate (1996), note 2 at 347).
4.  Kovacic, William E. (2001), 'Institutional foundations for economic legal reform in transition economies: the case of competition policy and antitrust enforcement', **77**, *Chi.-Kent L. Rev.*, 265, 290. Rodriguez and Coate clarify: 'Widespread perceptions of the virtues of antitrust policies diverge significantly from actual problems with the operational aspects of these policies. Challenging allocative distortions due to market power is an unassailable theoretical position. This premise constitutes the basis of our confidence in recommending an antimonopoly component to a liberalization program. However, in the developed world, antitrust has grown far beyond a simple attack on monopoly. While there may be some narrative linking each aspect of antitrust enforcement to the monopoly problem, the underlying assumptions of the typical enforcement program are so extreme as to render the constituent concept almost useless. *Taken as a whole, antitrust as practiced in the developed world may have adverse effects on a reform policy in the developing world, and may stunt growth'* (italics added) (Rodriguez and Coate (1996), note 2 at 358).
5.  AODCEE, note 2 at 246. Commenting on competition policies recently inaugurated in emerging market economies, the Antitrust Section of the American Bar Association noted that abuse of dominance law could, if applied unwisely, effectively restore price control under the guise of antitrust, thus taking back the freedom and rewards that the market gives. 'Introduction and recommendations of ABA Antitrust Law Section's Special Committee on International Antitrust', **62**, Antitrust & Trade Reg. Rep. (BNA) No. 1551, at 171 (6 February 1992). In Rodriguez and Coate (1996), note 1, at 338, the authors emphasize that 'Predation and dominance provisions would facilitate use of government process to attack successful business.'

6. Rodriguez and Coate offer a detailed explanation of how prohibitions against a variety of abuse of dominance conducts, including exclusive dealing, refusals to deal, price discrimination and tying, could be harmful. 'Exclusive dealing agreements may reduce the profitability of opportunism by linking more tightly the prospects of the two businesses. . . . By precluding downstream firms from signing exclusive contracts, regulators may make various business relationships untenable. . . . the antitrust regulators could attack the upstream firms for refusal to deal with various other downstream firms. . . . Such an antitrust policy creates a number of problems for a market economy . . . [a]n active refusal-to-deal policy could degenerate into price setting by the government regulators. . . . Naive enforcement of antitrust regulations against price discrimination may preclude [certain] sophisticated contract[s] by mandating a single price for each type of business relationship. Although manufacturers could claim an efficiency justification for its pricing behavior, the firm is likely to have problems proving its policy is efficient, because enforcers usually take a narrow view of efficiencies . . . Thus efficient contracting solutions are lost under active antitrust enforcement. . . . tying schemes often offer customers a low price for the purchase of a product in exchange for a commitment to buy related products from the firm at higher prices. . . . this type of tying is generally considered to be a price discrimination scheme. . . . Tying is often considered illegal per se, so no efficiency defense could be mounted. If enforcement activity prevents the partners from using tying, other less efficient contractual terms would have to be devised to make the contract self-enforcing. In some situations, no terms may exist, so the contract would not be viable' (Rodriguez and Coate (1996), note 2 at 354–7).
7. With respect to Latin America, Coate et al. recommend the following: 'For Latin American countries, prohibitions on price fixing should represent the core antitrust policy. . . . enforcement priorities should not include non-price horizontal agreements, vertical restraints, or price discrimination' (Coate, Malcolm B. et al. (1992) 'Antitrust in Latin America: regulating government and business', **24**, *U. Miami Inter-Am. L. Rev.*, 37, at 81.
8. Compared to other areas of competition law, where there is considerable convergence, if not harmonization, of enforcement practice, 'proper' enforcement of dominance provisions remains under consideration. The United States and Europe still have not yet achieved consensus on sound enforcement of abuse of dominance, or monopolization, provisions. This debate may create a degree of tension for jurisdictions in the process of adopting new competition laws, or revising their existing dominance provisions.
9. So, conversely, is the question of whether reforming governments have adequately protected their populations from the downsides of liberalization and globalization. See, for example, Chua, Amy (2002), *World on Fire: How Exporting Free Market Democracy Breeds Ethnic Hatred and Global Instability*, 1st edn, Doubleday.
10. Coate et al. highlight these differences in greater detail in Coate et al., note 6, at 50 and Table 1. See also Rodriguez and Coate (1996), note 2 at 338, where they note, for example, that 'Brazil, Mexico, Peru, and Venezuela restrict various activities of dominant firms, with some countries focusing on vertical restraints and/or price discrimination.'
11. The fears mentioned above with respect to other areas of the globe, or to a specific region other than Latin America, may have been even more valid with respect to Latin America than elsewhere. Decades of import-substituting industrialization consisting of high levels of trade protection, heavy-handed regulation and active state involvement in the productive process led industrial and labour groups to become the dominant forces in Latin American policy making. Privatization, trade liberalization and deregulation changed this pattern, and isolated politically the domestic industrial elites. This generated enormous pressures from the elites for state intervention.
12. Another fear, arguably more relevant to Central and Eastern Europe than to Latin America, was the fear of overenforcement of dominance provisions included the possibility of strategic use of these new antitrust laws by private enterprise, and in particular the possibility that a company could impose costs and restrictions on its more powerful (and perhaps simply more efficient) competitor by pursuing a complaint through the

antitrust enforcement agency. For a general discussion, see Baumol, William J. and Janusz Ordover (1985), 'Use of antitrust to subvert competition', *Journal of Law and Economics*, **28**, May, 247–66.

13. See, e.g., Veliz, C. (1980), *The Centralist Tradition of Latin America*, Princeton University Press, Princeton; De Madariaga, Salvador (1986), *El Auge y el Ocaso del Imperio Español en América*, Espasa Calpe, Madrid. See also Rodriguez, 'Government intervention in the marketplace distorts prices and resource flows from socially efficient levels. Although it is an important issue in all countries, government intrusion is particularly problematic in Latin America . . . because policy making tends to be less visible, more closed, and more centralized in these countries. Often the political process is so closed that citizens learn of new policies when they are formally announced or decreed by the political leadership. In general, policy making is dominated by high level administrators and politicians.'

14. This contrasts with Asia, where governments promoted the adoption of competition laws after the collapse of the corporate sector in order to break away from cronyism.

15. While historically in both Asia and Latin America cartels and collective market arrangements were promoted by governments, in Asia the government sanctioned the arrangement and then actively participated in it, nurturing the conglomerates to ensure their strength. In Latin America, by contrast, government tended to sanction the arrangement in a less transparent fashion, and never monitored the results.

16. Anticompetitive conduct cases include, inter alia, abuses of dominance, cartel agreements, noncartel horizontal agreements and vertical agreements.

17. Data compiled from responses to a survey conducted for a project of the International Competition Network's Competition Policy Implementation Working Group Survey are available at the following website: http://www.internationalcompetitionnetwork.org/effectivenessta.html, 'Agency Data Sheet' survey, questions 52, 53, 54, 70, 71, 72, 94, 95 and 96.

18. Pittman, Russell (2004), 'Abuse-of-dominance provisions of central and Eastern European competition laws: have fears of over-enforcement been borne out?' (hereafter 'AODCEE'), **27**, *World Comp.*, 245.

19. For example, an independent telecommunications regulator exists in seven of the eight countries examined. In only two of the countries, however, does the competition agency share jurisdiction over competition issues with the independent regulator (Brazil and Colombia); in the others it has sole jurisdiction. An independent regulatory body for energy exists in six of the eight countries examined; the competition agency has concurrent jurisdiction over competition issues in only two countries (Brazil and Panama), while in the rest the competition agency has sole jurisdiction over competition issues.

20. Inter-American Development Bank and Organization for Economic Cooperation and Development (2005), *Competition Law and Policy in Brazil: A Peer Review*, Paris, p. 25.

21. For example, during the CFC investigation, Telmex had agreements with ATT, MCI, and Sprint and others. Today, with those carriers the service is toll free for the callers. Telmex does not have agreements with many national long distance providers.

22. Robert Bork and others have argued that '[m]isuse of courts and government agencies is a particularly effective means of delaying or stifling competition': Bork (1978), *The Antitrust Paradox*, revised 1993, p. 159. Competitors may rely on government restrictions for a variety of reasons. 'Abuse of government processes presents a very different trade-off of risks and benefits than aggressive price cutting for several reasons. First, unlike predatory pricing, it frequently is likely to succeed, because the exclusionary effect often operates by force of law. Second, by comparison with predatory pricing, it may cost little to attempt. Finally, and most fundamentally, the conduct does not in any way resemble "competition on the merits". False statements to government agencies are not susceptible to any justification. They cannot be explained in terms of the defendant's effort to increase output or improve product quality, innovation or service. . . . Some staff members of the FTC have described abuse of government processes as an example of "cheap exclusion" – exclusionary conduct that is "cheap" both in the sense that it is inexpensive to attempt, and that it has little positive value to consumers because it lacks

any cognizable efficiencies'. See Roundtable on Competition on the Merits, Note by the United States, OECD (May 2005), at 4, 7; citing Creighton, Hoffman, Krattenmaker and Nagata (2005), 'Cheap exclusion', **72**, *Antitrust L. J.*, 975.

23. The Federal Trade Commission in the U.S., for example, has brought several cases in recent years that involve the alleged abuse of governmental processes to obtain market power shielded by law. See Roundtable on Competition on the Merits, Note by the United States, OECD (May 2005), at 4, 7.

24. The Supreme Court described exclusionary conduct as conduct that contributes to the acquisition or maintenance of market power by means other than competition on the merits. See *Aspen Skiing Co.* v. *Aspen Highlands Skiing Corp.*, 472 U.S. 585, 602 (1985); *Verizon Communications, Inc.* v. *Law Offices of Curtis V. Trinko, LLP*, 540 U.S. 398, 406, 408 (2004); cited in Creighton et al (2005), p. 975.

25. Organisation for Economic Cooperation and Development and The World Bank (1998), 'A framework for the design and implementation of competition law and policy', ed. R. Shyam Khemani, Washington: World Bank, p. 73.

26. With respect to Latin America, Coate et al. make the argument for focusing on exclusionary practices. See Coate et al., note 7. They suggest, 'an active predation policy must carefully focus only on exclusionary tactics of would-be monopolists, rather than on interactions associated with robust competition . . . Antitrust policy should screen cases to eliminate those where predation cannot explain the market behavior. . . .' p. 67; 'an optimal antitrust policy that considers enforcement costs and chilling effects would not focus its enforcement on vertical restraints' p. 77; 'Given the lack of experience with market economies, Latin American regulations should narrowly define price discrimination policies', at p. 79. Instead they encourage: 'Initially, Latin American governments could define a set of exclusionary practices', p. 80.

27. Unlawful monopolization requires, inter alia, proof of exclusionary conduct: 'In order to satisfy any conduct component of the monopolizing offense, the conduct in question must be capable of making a significant contribution to the creation, maintenance, or expansion of monopoly power' (Areeda and Hovenkamp (2002), **3**, *Antitrust Law*, 2nd edn, New York: Aspen, 650a).

28. Areeda and Hovenkampf (1998–2006 and supplemented May 2005: Aspen) explain, 'Many hesitate to condemn mere monopoly as such for the following reasons:

    a. Condemnation of all market power is impractical because varying degrees of power are pervasive in the economy.
    b. Condemnation of mere monopoly is unfair because the characterization of market power as monopoly is inevitably arbitrary, because bad conduct cannot be presumed, and because even equitable relief deprives the innocent monopolist of 'just' rewards.
    c. Some monopolies are economically inevitable or governmentally licensed.
    d. Condemnation of the monopolist that achieved its position solely by fair and vigorous competition could discourage others from vigorous competition that antitrust law seeks to encourage' (ibid., p. 630b).

29. There exist statements that practices such as price discrimination are exclusionary, but the authors generally agree with Posner, who argues, 'some of the practices deemed exclusionary, mainly price discrimination in its various guises (including most tie-in agreements), are monopolistic but not exclusionary. . . . They enable the monopolist to extract higher profits without preventing equally or more efficient new entrants from challenging his monopoly' (Posner, Richard A. (2001), *Antitrust Law*, 2nd edn, University of Chicago Press, pp. 41–2.

30. See Coate et al. (1992), Even exclusionary cases are subject to heated debate. See *Trinko*, 540 U.S. at 414 ('under the best of circumstances, applying the requirements of §2 "can be difficult" because "the means of illicit exclusion, like the means of legitimate competition, are myriad". . . . The cost of false positives counsels against an undue expansion of §2 liability') (quoting *United States* v. *Microsoft Corp.*, 253 F.3d 34, 58 (D.C. Cir. 2001)), cited in Creighton et al. (2005). The current debate regarding exclusionary and

other practices centres on whether the exclusionary conduct need have an exploitative effect. While in the past, and even in some cases currently, courts have been willing to find purely exclusionary conduct to be a violation, recent scholarly opinion in the U.S. has favoured requiring the plaintiff also to demonstrate the likelihood that these limitations will ultimately allow the dominant firm to exploit its position. See Pitofsky, Robert (2002), 'The essential facilities doctrine under U.S. antitrust law', **70**, *Antitrust L.J.*, 443; Facey, Brian A. and Dany H. Assaf (2002), 'Monopolization and abuse of dominance in Canada, the U.S. and the EU: a survey', **70**, *Antitrust L.J.*, 513; Muris, Timothy J. (2000b), 'The FTC and the law of monopolization', **67**, *Antitrust L.J.*, 693; Balto, David A. and Ernest A. Nagata (2000), 'Proof of anticompetitive effects in monopolization cases: a response to Professor Muris', **68**, *Antitrust L.J.*, 309; Muris, Timothy T. (2000a), 'Anticompetitive effects in monopolization cases: reply', **68**, *Antitrust L.J.*, 309. Professor Eleanor Fox has pointed out that the EC prohibits 'limiting production, markets, or technical developments' even where such limitation will not necessarily lead to exploitation. See Fox, Eleanor (2002), 'What is harm to competition? Exclusionary practices and anticompetitive effect', **70**, *Antitrust L. J.*, 371.
31. While EC law on abuse of dominant position addresses both exploitative and exclusionary types of behaviour, increasing emphasis has been placed on exclusionary behaviour. See, for example, *Hoffman-La Roche & Co.* v. *Commission of the European Communities*, (Case 85/76) [1979] ECR 461, 3 CMLR 211, ¶91 (13 February 1979).
32. See Coate, Malcolm B. et al. (1992), 'Antitrust in Latin America: regulating government and business', **24**, *U. Miami Inter-Am. L. Rev.*, 37, at 53–4. 'However, under the civil code, the law must be more specific.' Governments must write regulations to identify when a firm has a dominant position.'
33. See, for example, Pittman (1985), 'Tying without exclusive dealing', **30**, *Antitrust Bull.*, 279.
34. It is also the case that in some countries where no comprehensive antitrust law exists but sectoral laws have competition provisions, such as, Bolivia and, until recently, El Salvador, the competition provisions of the sectoral laws have inspired the development of standards for future regulation in non-regulated sectors.
35. Rodriguez and Coate (1996), note 2, p. 338. It is possible that many countries are achieving similar effects (of overregulation) through other means. Certainly the imposition of price controls in many countries, including one of the leading reformers in the 1990s, Venezuela, suggests that this is the case.
36. Introduction and Recommendations of ABA Antitrust Law Section's Special Committee on International Antitrust, **62**, *Antitrust & Trade Reg. Rep.* (BNA) No. 1551, at 171 (Feb. 6, 1992).

# References

Areeda, Philip and Herbert Hovenkamp (2002), **3**, *Antitrust Law*, 2nd edn, New York: Aspen.
Balto, David A. and Ernest A. Nagata (2000), 'Proof of anticompetitive effects in monopolization cases: a response to Professor Muris', **68**, *Antitrust L.J.* 309.
Baumol, William J. and Janusz Ordover (1985), 'Use of antitrust to subvert competition', *Journal of Law and Economics*, **28**, May, 247–66.
Boner, Roger and James Langenfeld (Spring 1992), 'Liberal trade and antitrust in developing nations', *Regulation*.
Bork, R. (1978), *The Antitrust Paradox*, revised 1993.
Chua, Amy (2002), *World on Fire: How Exporting Free Market Democracy Breeds Ethnic Hatred and Global Instability*, 1st edn, Doubleday.
Coate, Malcolm B. et al. (1992), 'Antitrust in Latin America: regulating government and business', **24**, *U. Miami Inter-Am. L. Rev.*, 37.
Creighton, Susan A. D. Bruce Hoffman, Thomas G. Krattenmaker and Ernest A. Nagata (2005), 'Cheap exclusion', **72**, *Antitrust L. J.*, 975.
De Madariaga, Salvador (1986), *El Auge y el Ocaso del Imperio Español en América*, Espasa Calpe, Madrid.

Facey, Brian A. and Dany H. Assaf (2002), 'Monopolization and abuse of dominance in Canada, the U.S. and the EU: a survey', **70**, *Antitrust L.J.*, 513.

Fox, Eleanor (2002), 'What is harm to competition? Exclusionary practices and anticompetitive effect', **70**, *Antitrust L. J.*, 371.

Godek, Paul E. (1992), 'One U.S. export Eastern Europe does not need', **15**, *Regulation*, 20.

Godek, Paul E. (1998), 'A Chicago School approach to antitrust for developing economies', **43**, *Antitrust Bull.* 261.

Inter-American Development Bank and Organization for Economic Cooperation and Development (2005), *Competition Law and Policy in Brazil: A Peer Review*, Paris.

Kovacic, William E. (2001), 'Institutional foundations for economic legal reform in transition economies: the case of competition policy and antitrust enforcement', **77**, *Chi.-Kent L. Rev.*, 265.

Muris, Timothy T. (2000a), 'Anticompetitive effects in monopolization cases: reply', **68**, *Antitrust L.J.*, 309.

Muris, Timothy J. (2000b), 'The FTC and the law of monopolization', **67**, *Antitrust L.J.*, 693.

Ordover, J.R., R. Pittman and P. Clyde (1994a), 'Competition policy for natural monopolies in a developing market economy', *Economics of Transition*, 2, 3, 317–43.

Ordover, J.R. et al. and Russell Pittman (1994b), 'Restructing the railway for competition' (co-authored with Janusz Ordover), *Przeglad Organizacji* (Warsaw), January 1994; presented at OECD/World Bank Conference on Competition Regulation in Network Infrastructure Industries (Budapest, June 1994).

Organisation for Economic Cooperation and Development and The World Bank (1998), 'A framework for the design and implementation of competition law and policy', ed. R. Shyam Khemani, Washington: World Bank.

Pittman, Russell (1985), 'Tying without exclusive dealing', **30**, *Antitrust Bull.*, 279.

Pittman, Russell (2004), 'Abuse-of-dominance provisions of Central and Eastern European competition laws: have fears of over-enforcement been borne out?', **27**, *World Comp.*, 245.

Pitofsky, Robert (2002), 'The essential facilities doctrine under U.S. antitrust law', **70**, *Antitrust L.J.*, 443.

Posner, Richard A. (2001), *Antitrust Law*, 2nd edn, University of Chicago Press.

Rodriguez, A.E. and Malcolm B. Coate (1996), 'Limits to antitrust policy for reforming economies', **18**, *Hous. J. Int'l L.*, 311.

Rodriguez, A.E. and Mark D. Williams (1994), 'The effectiveness of proposed antitrust programs for developing economies', **19**, *N.C. J. Int'l L. & Com. Reg.*, 209.

Veliz, C. (1980), *The Centralist Tradition of Latin America*, Princeton University Press.

## Cases

*Aspen Skiing Co. v. Aspen Highlands Skiing Corp.*, 472 U.S. 585.

*Hoffmann-La Roche & Co. v. Commission of the European Communities*, (Case 85/76) [1979] ECR 461, 3 CMLR 211.

*United States v. Microsoft Corp.*, 253 F.3d 34, 58 (D.C. Cir. 2001).

*Verizon Communications, Inc. v. Law Offices of Curtis V. Trinko, LLP*, 540 U.S. 398.

# 11 Substantial convergence: the US influence on the development of the regulatory framework for IP licensing in the EC

*Steven D. Anderman*[1]

## Introduction

The regulatory framework of EC competition policy for intellectual property licensing has long been influenced indirectly by developments in US antitrust policy. Prior to the first Patent Block Exemption Regulation in 1984,[2] the Commission's policy was influenced by the 'Nine No-Nos' policy of the US Department of Justice Antitrust Division in respect of patent licensing. And, throughout each stage of the era of the formalistic Block Exemption Regulations, including the unified Technology Transfer BER of 1996, the Commission's policy was partially influenced by the more economically realistic approach of US antitrust law as it responded to the pointed criticisms of the Chicago School. With the introduction of the new 'modernized' TTBER and Guidelines in 2004, however, the EC regulatory framework for IP licensing has been more substantially aligned with the Antitrust Guidelines to the Licensing of Intellectual Property produced by the US Department of Justice and the Federal Trade Commission in 1995.[3] This convergence between the USA and the EU on issues relating to the assessment of 'restrictions on competition' is immediately noticeable in the substantive rules of the TTBER and Guidelines. The adoption of different regulatory regimes for vertical and horizontal licensing agreements, in terms both of market share limits and of hard core restrictions, offers obvious evidence of a more economic approach. The degree of convergence may at first sight appear less substantial in the procedural features of the new EC regime because of the continuation of a formal BER as part of the framework of regulation. However, if one closely analyses the interrelationship between the TTBER and the framework of analysis that the Guidelines apply to agreements outside the 'safe harbour' of the TTBER and take into account the shift from notification of agreements to 'self assessment', it becomes clearer that the current mix of TTBER and Guidelines can usefully be viewed as an attempt to move towards the US policy of stand-alone Guidelines.

This high degree of convergence of the EC regulatory framework with that in the US marks quite a radical break with the previous practice of DG

Competition in dealing with the interface between Article 81 and IP licensing. The move from a legally formalistic to a more economic approach will require a substantial adjustment by legal practitioners in the field although they will be able to rely on some of the experience of US practitioners since 1995 in making that adjustment. The new approach of EC law also raises another issue for those who study the nature of the interface between competition law and IPRs: to what extent has the treatment of IP licensing under the modernized competition law taken sufficient account of the *sui generis* nature of IP licensing agreements?

The 1995 US Guidelines declared as a matter of principle that IPRs should be treated as 'essentially comparable to any other form of property' for the purposes of competition policy assessment.[4] The new TTBER and Guidelines are more cautious in their statements but they move in that direction by claiming that it is possible 'to take due account of the dynamics of technology licensing' within the rules of Article 81.[5] The purpose of this chapter is to explore this dimension of the convergence of the two regulatory frameworks. To what extent does the treatment of intellectual property rights licensing by the new EC competition rules make allowances for the exceptional features of IPRs?

**The development of EC competition policy**
EC competition policy towards technology transfers and intellectual property has evolved through three main stages: (1) before the BERs; (2) the era of the formalistic BERs, 1984–96; and (3) the modernized TTBER and guidelines introduced in 2004.

*(1) Before the BERs*
In the 1960s, intellectual property rights licensing initially enjoyed a special position under Article 81(1). The Commission accepted that exclusive patent licensing agreements, unlike exclusive distribution agreements, could be viewed as not restrictive of competition as long as the contents of the licence remained within the 'scope of the patent'. At this stage, the Commission was mainly concerned with provisions in the licensing agreement that attempted to extend the economic power of the licensor beyond its inherent scope.[6] As long as the licence conferred merely a subdivision of a licensor's rights granted by legislation, it deprived no third party of their freedom of action even if the contractual restriction conferred an exclusive right upon the licensee.[7] The implication, at this stage, was that an agreement which divided the right under a patent to manufacture, use and sell a protected product geographically came within its scope just as much as a division of technical application. Neither provision was thought to fall within the prohibition of Article 81(1).

In the early 1970s, the Commission's attitude to licensing of intellectual property rights changed dramatically owing partly to fears of the potential of intellectual property rights licences to seal off markets and limit interstate competition awakened by the *Consten/Grundig* decision.[8] A further factor was the Commission's awareness of the Nine No-Nos policy[9] developed by the Antitrust Division of the US Justice Department.[10] These restraints were viewed as per se violations and not subject to a rule of reason. At this stage, the Justice Department appeared to be unconcerned about the effects of overly strict antitrust rules upon the process of innovation.[11]

The influence of the Nine-No-Nos reached into the European Commission in the preparation of the draft block exemption. As Hartmut Johannes, the administrator within DGIV (the Competition Directorate) with responsibility for intellectual property rights, put it in 1978, 'in the art of antitrust, the Americans are the teachers and the Europeans are the pupils'. He indicated that US thinking was not accepted uncritically; in particular its per se rules and the horizontal/vertical distinction were not transferable. However he also acknowledged that, when the Commission prepared its early draft of the patent licensing block exemption, 'It knew the no nos but of course not the American critics of these no nos; the critics dated from 1981.'[12]

### (2) The era of the formalistic BERs

The first patent licensing block exemption approved by Council in 1984[13] gave recognition to the importance of the incentive to IP licensing offered by territorial exclusivity provisions.[14] The balancing test of Article 81(3) was translated into whitelists of acceptable clauses and blacklists of unacceptable clauses. The 1984 BER whitelisted contractual protection for licensees against both the active and passive sales of other licensees. This facilitative approach reflected the thaw in US policy as the analysis of the Chicago School contributed to the end of the Nine No-Nos policy.

At this stage, the block exemption was limited to pure patent licences[15] or mixed patent know-how technology licences (Article 1(1)).[16] Other intellectual property rights could be included in the licensed technology package but these had to be 'ancillary', that is, less important, than the patent. The Regulation did not apply to pure know-how licences or mixed licences once the patent had expired. By the mid-1980s, there was a clear need to complement the patent licensing BER with one for know-how licensing.[17] The Commission adopted a structure for the know-how block exemption that was similar to the patent licensing block exemption.

There were signs that the Commission was beginning to recognize the need to relax the policy of the block exemptions in certain respects, e.g. in respect of royalties, tie-ins and improvements, in the interest of encouraging investment in innovation.[18]

The renewal of the patent licensing block exemption in 1996 was taken as an occasion to reshape the Commission's policy towards block exemptions for technology licensing. The two Regulations were merged into a new, unifying TTBER (240/96) which applied to pure patent licences, pure know-how licences and mixed patent know-how licences, the most common form of technology licensing agreements. This new Regulation took its place alongside the regulatory regimes for specialization agreements; research and development agreements; franchise agreements, cooperative joint ventures, and mergers[19] which together provided a virtual 'second tier' of regulation of intellectual property licensing by competition law in addition to the underlying intellectual property legislation.

This occasion offered the Commission an opportunity to make a substantial adjustment to the regulatory regime so that it had less of an inhibiting effect upon intellectual property right licensing. It could, for example, have chosen to design the block exemption to treat vertical licensing relationships differently from horizontal relationships, but that route was not taken. It left the rules of the BER to apply to both vertical and horizontal licences with little distinction drawn between the two.[20]

The block exemption itself did not attempt a radical reform of competition policy. Instead the Commission contented itself with marginal adjustments to the existing structure.[21] At one stage, partly influenced by the economic thinking in the US Guidelines, the Commission attempted to introduce an additional market share test as a precondition to exclusive territoriality because of its concern that dominant undertakings with exclusive licences 'might prevent access to the market of the technology by third parties and eliminate competition in respect of a substantial part of the products in question'. In the final version of the TTBER 1996, however, the market share limits were taken out altogether as a precondition for exemption and instead made a basis for withdrawal, implicitly acknowledging at that stage that technology transfers had to be given special treatment by comparison with other types of commercial agreements which were all regulated by BERs with market share limits.

### (3) The TTBER in a modernized setting

By 2001, the Commission had decided that there was a clear need to change its policy towards technology transfer agreements; this was prompted partly by the change in the Commission's approach to the regulation of vertical agreements more generally under Article 81. It had begun to move away from a legalistic and form-based approach to a more economic and effects-based approach to the regulation of commercial agreements, taking into greater account the economic analysis of possible costs and benefits, or 'efficiencies', of certain restrictions and recognizing the different economic effects of vertical and horizontal agreements, respectively. This could be seen in the main characteristics of the Commission's reforms of vertical distribution agreements, such as exclusive and selective distribution and franchising (the Vertical Agreements block exemption (EC 2790/1999) and horizontal agreements, such as research and development and (EC 2659/2000) specialization agreements (EC 2658/2000)).

As part of the modernization exercise, DG Competition commissioned an Evaluation Report on the Technology Transfer Regulation[22] which stressed the need for reform of the 1996 Regulation.[23] These criticisms figured prominently in the Commission's decision to reform the regulatory framework for technology transfer. In choosing the form of a new technology transfer regulation, the Commission used the Vertical Agreements Block Exemption Regulation as a role model and gave priority to a harmonizing TTBER with its other block exemption regulations. The substantive rules in the modernization model had in turn been heavily influenced by the economic approach of US antitrust policy.

One major issue of convergence between the 2004 TTBER and Guidelines and the US Guidelines is that the accommodation with IPRs in the new TTBER and Guidelines occurs almost entirely within the logic of the doctrines of competition law. In 1995, the US Guidelines stated:

> for the purpose of antitrust analysis, the Agencies regard intellectual property as being essentially comparable to any other form of property and apply to conduct involving IP on the same basis as to conduct involving any property tangible or intangible.[24]

The US Guidelines then add:

> The Agencies apply the same general antitrust principles to conduct involving intellectual property as they apply to conduct involving any other form of tangible or intangible property. This is not to say that intellectual property is in all respects the same as any other form of property. Intellectual property has important characteristics, such as ease of misappropriation, that distinguish it from many other forms of property. These characteristics can be taken into account by standard antitrust analysis, however, and do not require the application of fundamentally different principles.[25]

The 2004 TTBER Guidelines do not state explicitly that IP protected products are treated as any other form of property rights, as did the US Guidelines in 1995, but an analysis of the new methodology makes it plain that there is relatively little special treatment for IPRs under the new analytical framework for Article 81. Most of the accommodation takes place through the incidental benefits of the logic of the ordinary interpretation of Article 81 under the modernization programme. In the Guidelines and Recitals there is evidence that the competition authorities have made a considerable effort to understand the nature of IPRs and IPR licensing. Thus they acknowledge that the creation of IPRs often entails substantial investment and that it is often a risky endeavour. They state plainly that 'in order not to reduce dynamic competition and to maintain the incentive to innovate, the innovator must not be unduly restricted in the exploitation of the IPR that turn out to be valuable'. In particular, they must be able 'to seek compensation for successful projects that is sufficient to maintain investment, taking failed projects into account'. The Commission also acknowledges that technology licensing may require the licensee to make considerable sunk investments in the licensed technology and production assets necessary to exploit it and that 'Article 81 cannot be applied without considering such ex ante investments made by the parties and the risks thereto' [para. 8]. Moreover the Guidelines have accepted that the great majority of licensing agreements are procompetitive and compatible with Article 81 [para. 9].

Nevertheless the Commission has chosen to fit the assessment of licensing agreements into the modernized framework of Article 81 and keep to the minimum any special treatment. As the Guidelines proclaim, 'in assessing licensing agreements under Article 81, the existing analytical framework is sufficiently flexible to take due account of the dynamic aspects of technology licensing'. This appears to echo the assertion of the US Guidelines that the characteristics of IPRs that make them distinct 'can be taken into account by standard antitrust analysis, however, and do not require the application of fundamentally different principles'.

The new TTBER and Guidelines have been drafted to harmonize the treatment of licensing agreements with that of other agreements under the modernized application of Article 81. In the first place, they require more of an *economic analysis* of whether licensing agreements have the object or *effect* of restricting competition. Secondly, the regulatory framework has changed procedurally to emphasize the responsibilities of the parties to make their own assessment of the competition effects of their agreements throughout their duration. There is no presumption that agreements that fall outside the safe harbour of the TTBER are caught by Article 81(1) or cannot satisfy the conditions of Article 81(3).[26] The legal status of agreements will be judged at any time on the basis of the compatibility of the agreement and its provisions with the prohibition of Article 81, in particular Article 81(3). Moreover, under Regulation 2003/1, there is no longer any need for formal application to the Commission for clearance under Article 81(1) or exemption under Article 81(3) to ensure the provisional validity of an agreement. The Commission's former monopoly over Article 81(3) has been ended and national authorities and courts now have jurisdiction, along with Article 81(1), to apply Article 81(3). The Commission's general Guidelines to the Application of Article 81(3) applies to all the modernized BERs. Thirdly, however, the new TTBER now offers only a safe harbour and not the legal certainty of exemption like the old TTBER. Previous BERs in the IP licensing field conferred an exemption on the parties without a market share test and subject only to a formal power of withdrawal by the Commission or a national competition authority.[27] The new TTBER, in keeping with the analytical approach of the modernized Article 81, takes a reduced role within the overall legal framework. Today, if an agreement is outside the scope of the safe harbour offered by the BER, the parties may nevertheless find a basis for exemption under Article 81(3) using the framework for analysis provided by the TTBER guidelines supplemented by the general Article 81(3) guidelines.

One result of the new more economic interpretation of Article 81 has been the loosening of the prescriptive legal straitjacket of the previous TTBER. Because the scope of the TTBER has been widened and the hardcore restrictions have been reduced, the new framework offers considerably greater flexibility to the parties to draft IP licensing agreements to reflect their preferred underlying commercial bargain. No longer is it necessary to twist commercial arrangements into the strictly defined categories offered by the existing BERS.[28]

However, the reduced role of the TTBER in the overall regulatory structure decreases the traditional legal certainty that EC lawyers and the parties to licensing agreements have always sought. It is now necessary to look to the framework of analysis in the Guidelines for the more complete assurance of legal enforceability. Under the new regime the TTBER's safe harbour is restricted to agreements relating to products with relatively low market shares and since the market shares of new technological products are often volatile, the parties cannot be certain that the safe harbour of the TTBER will be guaranteed. They must learn the methodology of navigating in the choppy waters of the Guidelines and that will bring them closer to the methodology used by US antitrust lawyers.

The new methodology, based on the greater economic realism of the new Regulation, starts with a division of licensing agreements into two main categories for regulatory purposes: agreements between non-competitors and agreements between competitors because of the recognition that competition concerns are considerably greater in the case of agreements between competitors. The new regime for agreements between non-competitors is deservedly more benign and consists of a reduced list of hard core restrictions, a set of severable excluded restrictions and a stipulation that the exemption will not apply where the licensed product of *one* of the parties exceeds 30 per cent of the relevant market. This reform not only applies within the confines of the safe harbour but is also integral to the analytical framework of the Guidelines.

The regulatory regime for agreements between competitors is harsher in two major respects: the exemption will not apply where the licensed product of *both* parties exceeds 20 per cent and the list of hard core restrictions is far more extensive.

The TTBER, taking a lead from the US Guidelines, gives an economically enlightened definition of vertical 'agreements', one quite close to the US test. It applies not only to the paradigm vertical case of an agreement between an inventor and a manufacturer but also to an agreement between two manufacturers as long as they are not competitors in respect of the licensed product. As the US Guidelines put it, the Agencies would only treat a licensing agreement as one between competitors if the parties would have been actual or potential competitors in a relevant market *in the absence of the licence.*[29]

Historically the BERS rather crudely distinguished between 'vertical' agreements, defined as agreements between undertakings each of which operates at a different level of the production or distribution chain, and horizontal agreements, defined as agreements between undertakings operating at the same level of the production and distribution chain. While relatively easy for lawyers to apply, this distinction meant the vertical agreements were defined narrowly and horizontal agreements too widely and, as a consequence, competition concerns were incorrectly aimed at many agreements between non-competitors.

The TTBER and the Commission's Guidelines to Technology Transfer Agreements have adopted a more economically enlightened view of the distinction between the two types of agreement. The test in TTBER, following the US model, is whether the parties would have been actual or potential competitors *in the absence of the agreement*. If, without the agreement, the parties would not have been competitors, they will be deemed to be non-competitors.[30]

Competitors are defined as 'actual' competitors, i.e. competing undertakings who in the absence of the technology transfer agreement would have been active on the relevant product and geographic markets on which the contract products are sold without infringing each other's intellectual property rights.[31] Consequently the existence of blocking patents will be important in the analysis.[32]

In product markets, 'competitors' also include 'potential' competitors, i.e., those who are realistically in a position to undertake the necessary investments and accept the switching costs of entering the same market had the price of the product been raised.[33] In 'technology markets', the definition of competitor is limited to 'actual' competitors.[34] The 2004 TTBER and Guidelines do not adopt the concept of an 'innovation market' in the same form as the US Guidelines. Instead they make reference to innovation competition in the technology market.[35] Finally, the Guidelines make special provision for 'breakthrough' products such as drastic inventions which make the competitor's technology obsolete.

Furthermore a significant departure from the US Guidelines is the Commission's decision that, if the parties are non-competitors at the time the agreement is concluded, they will continue to enjoy the more liberal regime of hard core restrictions for the duration of the agreement unless the agreement itself is materially altered.[36] This will be true even if the licensees and licensors become actual competitors at a later date because 'the licensee starts licensing out his technology or the licensor becomes an actual or potential supplier of products on the relevant market'. This was a concession made by the Commission who had originally intended a reassessment at any time that commercial conditions called for one. Outside the TTBER the position is more complex and we shall come back to it in context.[37] Once the status of the parties as contractual competitors or non-competitors is determined, and the licensing agreement is not assured of remaining in the safe harbour, the next step in the analysis of licensing agreements under Article 81(1) is to decide whether the licensing agreement as a whole or any provision within it constitutes a *'restriction on competition'* under Article 81(1).

Under the old regime, the interpretation of Article 81(1) brought many commercial agreements within its reach. The potential restrictions of competition by object were extensive because they were influenced by a theory that contractual restraints could be restrictions of competition by restricting the freedom of action of the other party or parties. In other words, if a contractual restraint restricted the rivalry between licensor and licensee or between one of them and a third party, that contractual restraint amounted to a restriction of competition under Article 81(1) of contractors and third parties associated with the contract. There was a doctrine of *appreciability* in the case of licensing agreements of small quantitative impact. And there was a doctrine of *ancillary restraints* in the case law of the ECJ in such cases as *Pronuptia, Maize Seeds, Coditel and Erauw Jacquery*, etc. However, the issue of analysing Article 81(1) closely to avoid the reach of Article 81 altogether was rarely on the practitioner's agenda since it was widely accepted that the BER was the main source of legal salvation.

Under the new regime, the economic analysis of the status of the agreement under Article 81(1) is more important to analyse because there is a greater prospect that the agreement and its provisions can be assessed as not constituting 'preventions, restrictions or distortions of competition' in the meaning of the prohibition in Article 81(1). The issue of exemptibility may never arise. The key reason for this is that, while many IP licensing agreements by their very commercial nature will contain contractual '*restrictions*' on licensors and licensees, under the new methodology fewer contractual restraints will be *restrictions on competition*.

Article 81(1) prohibits agreements which by either *object* or *effect* prevent, restrict or distort competition. Under the new methodology, the prohibition of licensing agreements with anticompetitive *objects* under Article 81(1) are still exemplified by the provisions listed as hard core restrictions in Article 4 of the TTBER. However, the concept of a hard core restriction under Article 4 has changed from that of the blacklisted provisions in the 1996 TTBER. Formerly the test whether the provision was restrictive in nature was elaborately defined and this resulted in seven black-listed restrictions. Now the test has been modified so that it also asks whether the restriction is so likely to lead to anticompetitive harm that detailed economic analysis of effects is required.[38] In consequence, the hard core restrictions are now limited to price fixing, output limitations and market allocation, and do not extend to territorial restrictions and sales restrictions. These latter provisions are now classified as exceptions to hard core restrictions in Article 4 which indicates that they are not anticompetitive in their object and are now left to be evaluated mainly on the basis of their economic effects. The beneficiaries of this analysis are agreements between non-competitors and non-reciprocal agreements between competitors.

Under the new framework, if an agreement (or a restriction within it) is not restrictive of competition by its object, there is still a need to assess whether in fact it has the *effect* of restricting competition; this assessment has more of an economic dimension and again has been influenced by US thinking.

In order to determine whether or not an agreement (or a restriction within it) has the economic *effect* of restricting competition, much will depend on whether the licensors were competitors or non-competitors before the contract was made.[39] Thus, as Guideline 12(a) asks, does the licence agreement restrict actual or potential competition that would have existed *without the contemplated agreement?* And, as Guideline 12(b) asks, does the agreement restrict actual or potential competition that would have existed *in the absence of the contractual restraint(s)?*

The test of effects will be radically different for agreements between non-competitors and those between competitors. Moreover the test of economic effect of restricting competition will apply both to competition between licensor and licensee (intertechnology competition) and competition between different licensees of the same technology in different territories (intratechnology competition).

In the case of licensing agreements between non-competitors, there is normally no intertechnological competition either actual or potential at the start of the agreement. Hence the fact of the agreement itself will not restrict competition unless the market power of the licensee threatens consumer harm through foreclosure of competition.[40] Consequently the test will concentrate on whether any provision within the licensing agreement is a *restriction of competition* by effect.

Where a licensing agreement is made between non-competitors, whether actual or potential, many restrictions on the conduct of licensor and licensee *inter se* in the licensing agreement will *not* constitute a restriction of competition under the new framework.[41] For example, many non-territorial clauses between licensors and licensees will be regarded as *ancillary restraints* and therefore 'almost always *not* restrictive of competition within the meaning of Article 81(1)'.[42]

Some examples of such restrictions are those which are indispensable to achieving the main purpose of the licensing agreement. These include (a) confidentiality obligations, (b) obligations on licensees not to sublicense, (c) obligations not to use the licensed technology after the expiry of the agreement, provided that the licensed technology remains valid and in force, (d) obligations to assist the licensor in enforcing the licensed intellectual property rights, (e) obligations to pay minimum royalties or to produce a minimum quantity of products incorporating the licensed technology, and (f) obligations to use the licensor's trade mark or indicate the name of the licensor on the product.

Moreover certain territorial restrictions *as between licensor and licensee* can be viewed as not *restrictive of competition* under Article 81(1). Where a licensor offers a sole and exclusive licence to the licensee, if the parties were not competitors before the contract was made, a pure obligation on the licensor not to appoint another licensee in the territory or not to itself exploit the licensed product in the territory might be *restrictions* but they would not be *restrictions on competition* for the purpose of Article 81(1).[43] In its new guise, the new EC framework has more fully adopted the US distinction between territorial exclusivity for production and customer sales restrictions.

A similar analysis can be performed for contractual restraints such as field of use restrictions. What is important to note here is that the new methodology recognizes that the IP owner can subdivide its powers of exploitation by contractual restriction and not be caught by Article 81(1) under the analysis of restriction on competition rather than the scope of the patent or limited licence doctrines which stem from IP law.

Consequently, in the case of agreements between non-competitors, the new methodology gives a wide scope for contractual restrictions between licensor and licensee not to be caught by Article 81(1) in the first place.

The second process of competition that is relevant for Article 81(1) is the process of intra-technology competition, normally the competition that can exist *between different licensees* producing the same product.[44]

Under EC law, since the *Consten* and *Grundig* case, there have been specific competition concerns with restrictions on intra-technology competition such as provisions placing obligations on licensees not to sell directly into the territories of other licensees. From the Commission's point of view, since such obligations are viewed as restricting the potential competition that could have existed between the licensees in different territories in the absence of such obligations, they are regarded as a restriction of competition for the purposes of Article 81(1). A more universal example of restrictions on intra-technology competition would be a price restraint placed on all licensees by a licensor.[45] In so far as a licensing agreement between non-competitors contains a restriction on intra-technology competition, it will be necessary to resort to the analysis under Article 81(3) to decide whether such restrictions of competition in the licensing agreement are acceptable under Article 81 as a whole.

For example, an obligation placed by the licensor upon the licensee not to sell directly into the territory of another licensee will be caught by Article 81(1) because it restricts intratechnological competition but will be exemptible under the TTBER in respect of *active* sales for the duration of the contract and in respect of *passive* sales for two years. This shows a particularly improved understanding of the need to encourage investment in IP licensing because every licensee gets protection against rivals' licensees and the licensor itself for a minimum of two years from the time it first markets the product in its territory. The thinking is that the licensee gets an initial period to tool up to match the efficiencies of production of its rivals. In previous BERs there was no such guarantee because the period of five years of allowed protection against passive sales in any one territory was dependent on the time left after the product was put on the market by any licensees. Hence 'second' and 'third wave' licensees could end up with less than two years' protection which might discourage investment at that stage and hence inhibit further diffusion of the technology throughout the single market.

Even if the market share of the licensee exceeds 30 per cent and the two years of the TTBER do not automatically apply, the factual analysis of the indispensability licensees need for such protection could lead to a two-year period of protection or, in the case of particularly complex and expensive technologies, possibly an even longer period of protection for licensees.

In other words, even outside the TTBER, Article 81(3) offers a relatively benign treatment of licensing agreements between non-competitors. First, it asks whether there will be any procompetitive benefits arising from the provision; whether the benefits were objectively necessary (or indispensable) to achieve those benefits and whether or not competition in the market would be eliminated – note eliminated, not merely reduced.

One feature of the new framework which needs careful attention is the assessment of competition between licensor and licensee outside the safe harbour of the TTBER. In principle, once outside the TTBER, a reassessment must be made *at that stage* of whether the agreement is one between competitors or non-competitors. The TTBER offers a special ex ante treatment of the status of the contractual relationship within the safe harbour for the purpose of applying the hard core restrictions in Article 4(3). This provision was a concession made by the Commission during the course of the final draft and it constitutes special recognition of the dynamic aspects of technology licensing.[46] To what extent does this ex ante analysis continue outside the scope of the safe harbour of the TTBER?

In the General Framework for the Application of Article 81, the Guidelines specifically mention a case where the parties become competitors subsequent to the conclusion of the agreement because the licensee develops and starts exploiting a competing technology.[47] They state that it must be taken into account that the parties were non-competitors at the time the agreement was made and that the Commission will therefore mainly focus on the impact of the agreement on the licensee's ability to exploit its own (competing) technology and the hard core restrictions will continue to apply to the parties as if they are non-competitors unless the agreement itself is materially amended after the parties have become competitors. If the reassessment is made in this way it should take sufficient account of the inherent dynamic of the licensing relationship, i.e., the fact that almost every IP licence creates potential technological competition after the licensee has mastered the technology but while the contract remains in existence.

Since the technology is inevitably transferred at the early stages of the contract, licensors view as an indispensable inducement to give an *exclusive* licence of its technology the assurance of a return for the period of the contract. That is why the licensor inserts a minimum royalties clause. Moreover that is also why it inserts a non-compete clause *in respect of the technology transferred*. The non-compete clause in respect of *intertechnological* competition between the parties at the start of the contract cannot limit the licensee's independent development of its own R&D. Some limits can be placed on its exploitation of that R&D during the period of the contract owing to the incidental effect of the minimum royalties clause.

### Licensing agreements between competitors

The treatment of licensing agreements between competitors is on the face of it much harsher than that of agreements between non-competitors. At the Article 81(1) level, there will be more restrictions by object and there will be little argument that many other territorial restrictions in the agreement can be said not to be restrictions of inter-technology competition. The longer list of hard core restrictions is accompanied by lower market share thresholds of 20 per cent. Access to the safe haven of the TTBER is clearly less open to licensing agreements between competitors.

Yet it is wrong to conclude that the competition authorities are entirely hostile to licensing agreements between competitors. The Commission has clearly felt that it had inadequate knowledge and experience of the permutations of procompetitive licensing agreements between competitors to regulate them in the TTBER with the light touch approach they used to regulate licensing agreements between non-competitors. Moreover the Commission was only too aware that this type of agreement is the source of the most serious risks of anticompetitive licensing agreements, even if that was true only in a minority of cases. As a consequence, the Commission has left the application of the full range of Article 81(3) to such agreements to the second tier of the Guidelines.

Moreover there are important concessions built into this harsher approach to licensing agreements between competitors. One is the creation of the special category of *non-reciprocal* licensing agreements between competitors.[48] Both within and outside the TTBER they are treated as honorary agreements between non-competitors.[49]

The application of Article 81(3) to licensing agreements between competitors is further ameliorated outside the TTBER and above the 20 per cent market share by a 'second safe harbour' where there are at least four other poles of independently controlled technologies and no hard core restrictions in the licensing agreement.[50] This has undoubtedly been influenced by a similar approach in the US Cooperative Agreements Act 2000.

Otherwise, under the new methodology, licensing agreements between competitors are generally more easily caught by Article 81(1) because restrictions, even ancillary restrictions, are usually *restrictions of competition* under Article 81(1) and the permitted scope for provisions is carefully regulated by Article 4(1) of TTBER.

However, even if a licensing agreement between competitors is reciprocal and its contents or market share take it outside the TTBER, the legal status of the agreement must be assessed on the issue of the balancing test of the four conditions of Article 81(3). At this point there will be a need to argue both that the provision contributes significant procompetitive benefits and that those benefits could not be obtained by a less restrictive provision, particularly one that was not restrictive by object. This indispensability test will not require a fine tooth comb and will not place the Commission in the position of pointing to less restrictive alternatives. Nevertheless, in practice, as the Commission reminds us, it is only exceptionally that the hard core restriction will fill the four conditions of Article 81(3) and in particular its indispensability condition.

Nevertheless there is a possibility for the parties to justify their licensing agreements between competitors under Article 81(3) outside the safe harbour of the TTBER. This is a change from the old legal framework and one that reflects\a roughly similar approach taken by the US Guidelines. Today, licensing agreements between competitors which fall outside the comfort zone of the BER owing to a hard core restriction in the agreement may still obtain exemption under the balancing provisions of Article 81(3) if their procompetitive effects outweigh their anticompetitive effects. The hard core restrictions, unlike the blacklists of the 1996 BER do not deliver a knock out blow to exemption. As the Commission states in its Guidelines, 'even licence agreements that do restrict competition may often give rise to pro-competitive efficiencies, which must be considered under Article 81(3) and balanced against the negative effects on competition'.[51]

Of course this exercise will be more demanding for lawyers than the application of Article 81(3) to agreements between non-competitors. The definition of the relevant market will be important. The factors mentioned in para. 132 of the Guidelines will be relevant to the analysis. Further the Commission's Notice on the Guidelines to Article 81(3) will be useful to consult to obtain a clear view of the application of Article 81(3) to IP licensing agreements. It will be necessary to understand the type of pro-competitive benefits that can be contributed by a commercial licensing agreement. It will be necessary to understand the types of competitive harms that can be caused by licensing agreements. However this extra effort may prove to be worthwhile since the framework and methodology provided by the Guidelines may prove to have a longer life as a method of regulation of technology transfers than the TTBER itself.

**Conclusions**
The new paradigm for Article 81 under modernization and its application to technology transfer agreements in the EU have produced considerable convergence with that in the USA. This is partly due to the recognition that, on the substantive issue of competition analysis of vertical agreements in general and licensing agreements in particular, the US approach offers a useful legal framework. The great gain is the achievement of separating the real 'vertical' agreements from the real 'horizontal,' agreements, providing enlightened definitions of each and providing a more lenient treatment of

the former. One side-effect of the more economic approach to regulation has been that the main form of accommodation of the licensing of IPRs has taken place within the general competition rules of Article 81. However the extent of convergence is not complete, in two important respects.

In the first place, the Commission shows a greater sensitivity to the dynamics of technology licensing by stipulating that it will offer a more careful ex ante treatment of the competitive relationship between licensor and licensee both within the TTBER and outside the safe harbour of the TTBER under the framework offered by the Guidelines. Secondly, the Commission has not moved directly to a regulatory framework of pure guidelines. Instead it has retained a TTBER and combined it with Guidelines. A careful reading of the relationship between these two tiers, however, suggests that the new EU regulatory framework may be viewed as a stepping stone towards a regulatory framework of pure guidelines at a later stage. It was probably decided that such a move would have been too drastic a step in 2004. Finally, one incidental benefit of convergence may be to cast doubt on the argument that the new type of legal framework is so IP licensing unfriendly that it discourages licensing into Europe and results in US technology owners taking decisions to transfer technology and production of new technology products elsewhere and exporting into Europe instead. Of course, such claims need to be measured empirically. As an a priori assessment of the Commission's new methodology, however, it seems undeniable that convergence should give US technology owners a degree of familiarity with the new regulatory framework within the EU and take the sting out of the loss of the guarantee offered by the previous formalistic TTBER.

## Notes

1. Professor at the University of Essex.
2. Initially, in the 1960s and early 1970s, licensing was treated leniently under EC Competition law as the Commission's Notice on Patent Licensing Agreements of 1962 (the so called 'Christmas Message') announced a policy of non-interference.
3. US Department of Justice and the Federal Trade Commission (1995), *Antitrust Guidelines to the Licensing of Intellectual Property*. The Guidelines have remained unamended even though the two agencies have been going through a thorough review of the entire issue of the interface between antitrust and intellectual property law.
4. US Guidelines, para. 2.0(a).
5. TTBER Guidelines, para. 9.
6. European Commission (1972), *First Report of Competition Policy*, pp. 65–74. Certain practices which extended the original grant of exclusivity, such as tie-ins of non-patented products with patented products; price and territorial restrictions on the sale of a patented product, post expiration royalties; licensee veto of other licensees; and territorial restrictions on a sale of unpatented products made with a patented process were viewed as a misuse of the patent and illegal per se. Other licensing practices that amounted merely to a limited licence of the powers conferred by the patent were viewed as not restrictive of competition under Article 81(1).

7. The influence of this doctrine could be seen in the Commission's Christmas Message Notice of 1962. This Notice provided that a patent licence containing only limitations as to technical applications or fields of use, quantity of products to be manufactured, or restrictions on time, or persons to carry out the licensing role would not be caught by Article 81(1). These restrictions were viewed as essentially divisions of the patentee's grant of exclusive rights. Hence it accepted that licensors involved in a single licensing relationship could give an 'exclusive' licence to a licensee for a particular territory, i.e. a licence which restricted the licensor not only from appointing any other licensee in that territory but also from making, using or selling itself in that territory, and not be caught by Article 81(1). It could also be seen in the earlier formulation of Article 4(2) of Regulation 17/62 which provided that notification was not required with respect to bilateral agreements which only imposed restrictions on the exercise of the rights of the assignee or user of intellectual property rights.

8. [1966] ECR 299.

9. The following restrictions were viewed as per se unlawful: 1. Tie-ins 2. Grant backs 3. Resale restraints 4. Tie-outs 5. Licensee vetoes 6. Mandatory package licences 7. Royalties not reasonably related to the licensees' sales of the patented product 8. Restrictions on the sale of an unpatented product manufactured with a patented process 9. Price restrictions on sales of a licensed product. See e.g. Wilson, B. (1975) Dept of Justice Luncheon Speech, 'Law on licensing practice – myth or reality straight talk from Alice in Wonderland'.

10. This was influenced by the 'patent misuse' doctrine developed by the US Supreme Court. See, for example, *Morton Salt Co* v. *G S Suppiger Co* 314 US 488 (1941); *United States* v. *United States Gypsum Co*. 333 US 364 (1947).

11. In 1967, the Assistant Attorney General announced, 'I do not believe that the impact of antitrust on patent licensing restrictions has any effect on innovative activity whatsoever . . . to me it seems probably so even if antitrust law were to go so far as to prohibit not only price fixing but also field of use restrictions, quantity restrictions, territorial restrictions, and any other restriction on the complete freedom of the licensee'. See Turner (1967), 'Antitrust and Innovation', **12**, *Antitrust Bulletin*, 277 at p. 281.

12. This was a reference to the groundswell in antitrust thinking that had been introduced by a combination of the writings of Chicago School adherents such as Bork and Posner and the experience of the administrators within the Justice Department. See Fox, E. (1981), 'The new American competition policy – from antitrust to pro-efficiency', [1981] **2**, *ECLR*, 439; see also Bork, R. (1978), *An Antitrust Paradox: A Policy at War with Itself*, 2nd edn, Basic Books; Posner, R. (1976), *Antitrust Law: An Economic Perspective*, University of Chicago Press. By 1987 the department's views had begun to change quite radically. It signalled the change by suggesting that there was a need to differentiate between horizontal and vertical restraints and to move away from a formalistic approach to an economic approach consisting of an evaluation of licensing restraints. See Lipsky, Abbot (15 November 1981), 'Current antitrust division views on patent licensing practices', *Trade Regulation Reporter*, (CCH) 55, 985.

13. Alexander (1986), 'Block exemption for patent licensing agreement EC Regulation No. 2349/84' [1986] l, *ICI*; Pichard, S. (1984), 'The Commission's patent licensing regulation – a guide', [1984] *ECLR*, 384; Korah, V. (1985), *Patent Licensing and the EEC Competition Rules – Regulation 2349/84*, Oxford: ESC Publishing.

14. 'Exclusive licensing agreements . . . are not in themselves incompatible with Article [81(1)] where they are concerned with the introduction and protection of a new technology in the licensed territory, by reason of the scale of the research which has been undertaken and the risk that is involved in manufacturing and marketing a product which is unfamiliar to users in the licensed territory at the time the agreement is made.'

15. 'Patents' were defined to include inter alia patents, European patents, patent applications, utility models, *certificats d'utilité* and *certificats d'addition* under French law.

16. 'Know-how', even if non-ancillary, could be included as long as the patent was necessary to achieve the objects of the technology and the know-how was secret and permitted a better exploitation of the licensee's patents.

17.  There was evidence that particularly US firms were hesitant to grant licences of their valuable technical information in the EC when know-how licensing agreements were of doubtful legal validity. See e.g, Hoyng, W.A. and Biesheuvel, M.B.W. (1989), 'The know-how group exemption', [1989] *CML Rev.* 219 at 220. See too Frazer, T. (1989), 'Vorsprung durch Technik: the Commission's Policy on know-how agreements', [1989] *Yearbook of Eur Law*, 1; Winn, D. (1990), 'Commission know-how Regulation 556/89: innovation and territorial exclusivity improvements and the quid pro quo', [1990] *ECLR*, 135.

18.  At this time too, the Commission began to relax its approach to the assessment of licensing in joint ventures under Art.85(1), proclaiming a policy of new realism. See European Commission (1984), *XIIIth Report on Competition Policy*. See too Anderman, S. (1997), 'Co-operation, international competitiveness and competition policy' in Deakin, S. and J. Michie (eds), *Contracts, Cooperation and Competitiveness: Studies in Economics Management and Law*, OUP.

19.  See, respectively, Reg 417/85, amended by Reg 151/93; [1993] 4 CMLR 155; Reg 418/85, as amended by Reg 151/93; [1993] 4 CMLR 163; Reg 4087/88; European Commission (1993), *Commission's Notice on Co-operative Joint Ventures OJ* [1993] C 43/2; Council of Ministers of the European Union (1989), *EC Merger Reg, Council Reg 4064/89*, OJ 1990 L257j14.

20.  On the one hand, the territorial restraints were designed as if the block exemption applied exclusively to vertical relationships. On the other hand, the block exemption treated all licensing agreements which were initially vertical as potentially horizontal so that they may not contain restraints, such as exclusive grant backs of improvements, which could prevent them blossoming into subsequent competitive relationships. Yet, by providing that its benefit could be withdrawn if technology licensing occurs in a horizontal relationship which shows signs of an anticompetitive tendency, such as cross-licensing or patent pooling, or if the parties had market shares approaching dominance, it implied that all other horizontal licensing relationships were eligible provided they otherwise qualified for the block exemption.

21.  It increased the time periods for territorial exclusivity in most cases, thus marginally increasing the incentives for investment in technology transfer. It lengthened the 'whitelist' adding to the categories of clauses which were either not caught by Article 81(1) or were exempt under Article 81(3) and it reduced the blacklist to a core of seven clauses, signalling a greater willingness to accept that vertical licensing arrangements could be procompetitive even if they contained restrictions such as tie-ins or minimum quality specifications technically necessary for the satisfactory exploitation of the technology.

22.  European Commission (2001), *Evaluation Report on the Technology Transfer Regulation* COM(2001) 786 final, 20.12.

23.  The Commission identified four types of shortcomings in the Regulation. First, because of its legal formalism and narrow definitions of scope, the Regulation was described as creating a 'legal straitjacket' in the sense that companies often had to redraft their commercial agreements to fit within its confines. Secondly, Regulation 240/96 was too narrow in scope, covering only a limited number of exclusive licensing arrangements, mainly to pure and mixed patent and know-how licences. Third, the regulatory framework lacked economic realism. The Regulation was too restrictive in the sense that the blacklist covered items such as non-compete clauses and tie-ins that were not always anticompetitive and could have efficiency-enhancing effects where the licensees were non-dominant. The Regulation made no distinction between horizontal and vertical licensing agreements despite their different legal effects. On occasion, restrictions with different legal form but with similar economic effects on markets were given different treatment. Finally, some exempted clauses raised competition concerns, particularly where licensees had strong market power.

24.  See US Guidelines, para. 2.0.

25.  US Guidelines, para. 2.1.

26.  TTBER Guidelines, paras 37, 65 and 130.

27. If there was a blacklisted provision in the agreement, the agreement was unexemptible and unenforceable.

28. The scope of the TTBER is restricted in one respect that differentiates it from the US Guidelines. Under the US Guidelines, there is no specific exclusion of any form from the antitrust 'safety zone' offered by the agencies to the parties to licensing agreements. The TTBER extends its safe harbour to a wider range of IPR licensing agreements and assignments than before. Thus, along with pure and mixed patent and know-how agreements, the list of IPRs has been expanded to include software copyright licensing agreements and design rights licensing agreements. All these IPRs are viewed as 'core' technologies in the sense that the licensing of any one (or more in combination) will constitute a transfer of technology for the purpose of the TTBER. The TTBER also allows a wider variety of IPRs to be included in the licensing package along with the core 'technology' as long as they are 'ancillary' provisions. This elaborate differentiation in the TTBER and Guidelines seems a residue of past thinking and not entirely consistent with a new, more economic approach under Article 81.

29. US Guidelines, para. 3.3.

30. Article 1(j)(ii).

31. Article 1(j)(ii); Guidelines 24 and 31.

32. If the parties own technologies that are in a one-way or two-way *blocking patent position*, the parties are considered to be non-competitors on the technology market. A one-way blocking position exists when a technology cannot be exploited without infringing upon another technology. This is for instance the case where one patent covers an improvement of a technology covered by another patent. In that case the exploitation of the improvement patent presupposes that the holder obtains a licence to the basic patent. A two-way blocking position exists where neither technology can be exploited without infringing upon the other technology and where the holders thus need to obtain a licence or a waiver from each other. In assessing whether a blocking position exists the Commission will rely on objective factors as opposed to the subjective views of the parties. Particularly convincing evidence of the existence of a blocking position is required where the parties may have a common interest in claiming the existence of a blocking position in order to be qualified as non-competitors, for instance where the claimed two-way blocking position concerns technologies that are technological substitutes. Relevant evidence includes court decisions including injunctions and opinions of independent experts. In the latter case the Commission will, in particular, closely examine how the expert has been selected. However, also other convincing evidence, including expert evidence from the parties that they have or had good and valid reasons to believe that a blocking position exists or existed, can be relevant to substantiate the existence of a blocking position (para. 32).

33. Article 1(j)(ii).

34. Article 1(j)(i).

35. TTBER Guidelines, para. 110. See too paras 142 and 208.

36. Article 4(3). In some cases it may also be possible to conclude retrospectively that, even though the licensor and the licensee produced competing products at the time the agreement was made, they are nevertheless non-competitors on the relevant product market and the relevant technology market because the licensed technology represents such *a drastic innovation* that the technology of the licensee is rendered obsolete or uncompetitive. This classification can be made at any stage when it becomes clear that the licensee's technology has become obsolete or uncompetitive on the market. (Guidelines, para. 33.)

37. See e.g. Guidelines, para. 31.

38. Guidelines to Application of Article 81(3). Cf. TTBER Guidelines para. 75: '. . . based on the nature of the restriction and experience showing that such restrictions are almost always anti-competitive'.

39. The Guidelines indicate that the agreement must affect actual and potential competition to such an extent that on the relevant market negative effects on product, innovation or variety of goods and services can be expected with a reasonable degree of probability. These effects must be *appreciable*, i.e. not *insignificant* (Guidelines to Article 81(3)

para. 24). The assessment of the effects of a licence agreement must be be made on the basis of a proper market analysis. The burden of proof that an agreement restricts competition will be on the Commission or competition authority.

40. NB. The new methodology assumes that market shares are a proxy for market power. It provides a first safe haven at 30 per cent, a second safe haven with four other poles of competition, below dominance and dominance as meaningful stages of market power for the purpose of the Guidelines.

41. However, one cannot argue that all provisions within a contract between non-competitors will not have a competitive effect. A clause in a licensee's contract that obligates him or her not to directly sell into the territory of another licensee would be one example.

42. Para. 155. Cf. Article 81(3), Guidelines para. 29. It is useful to revive the distinction between non-restrictive and exemptible clauses in licensing agreements. The white lists in previous regulations tended to combine contractual restraints not caught by Article 81(1) with those that were so caught but nevertheless exempted in a single white list of clauses. For parties engaged in self-certification today it is wise to make such distinctions clearer.

43. The Guidelines are more cautious: 'For instance, territorial restraints in an agreement between non-competitors may fall outside Article 81(1) for a certain duration, if the restraints are objectively necessary for a licensee to penetrate a new market.'

44. See in this respect e.g. judgment in *Consten and Grundig* [1966] ECR 429.

45. See TTBER Article 4(2).

46. The Commission has pointed out that Article 4(3) will apply even if the licensees and licensors become actual competitors at a later date because 'the licensee starts licensing out his technology or the licensor becomes an actual or potential supplier of products on the relevant market'.

47. See Guidelines, para. 31.

48. See definitions in TTBER Article 1(1)(c) and (d). Are the parties cross-licensing competing technologies or technologies which can be used to produce competing products? See too the special position of one-way or two-way blocking patents (Guidelines, para. 32) and 'drastic innovations' (Guidelines, para. 33).

49. A similar more lenient treatment is given to reciprocal agreements between competitors where a restriction on output is imposed only on one of the licensees. See e.g. Article 4(1)(b).

50. TTBER Guidelines, para. 131. Compare US Guidelines, para. 4.3 See too US Competitor Collaboration Guidelines 2000: innovation markets not normally contested if in total four independent technologies or comparable R&D entities exist.

51. Guidelines, para. 9.

## References

Alexander (1986), 'Block exemption for patent licensing agreement EC Regulation No. 2349/84' [1986] 1, *ICI*.

Anderman, S. (1997), 'Co-operation, international competitiveness and competition policy' in Deakin, S. and J. Michie (eds), *Contracts, Cooperation and Competitiveness: Studies in Economics Management and Law*, OUP.

Bork, R (1978), *An Antitrust Paradox: A Policy at War with Itself*, 2nd edn, New York: Basic Books.

Council of Ministers of the European Union (1989), *EC Merger Reg, Council Reg 4064/89*, OJ 1990 L257j14.

European Commission (1972), *First Report of Competition Policy*.

European Commission (1984), *XIIIth Report on Competition Policy*.

European Commission (1993), *Commission's Notice on Co-operative Joint Ventures OJ* [1993] C 43/2.

European Commission (2001), *Evaluation Report on the Technology Transfer Regulation* COM(2001) 786 final, 20.12.

Fox, E. (1981), 'The new American competition policy – from antitrust to pro-efficiency', [1981] 2, *ECLR*, 439.

Frazer, T. (1989), 'Vorsprung durch Technik: the Commission's policy on know-how agreements', [1989] *Yearbook of Eur Law*, 1.

Hoyng, W.A. and M.B.A. Biesheuvel (1989), 'The know-how group exemption', [1989] *CML Rev*, 219.

Korah, V. (1985), *Patent Licensing and the EEC Competition Rules – Regulation 2349/84*, Oxford: ESC Publishing.

Lipsky, Abbot (15 November 1981), 'Current antitrust division views on patent licensing practices', *Trade Regulation Reporter*, (CCH), 55.

Pichard, S. (1984), 'The Commission's patent licensing regulation – a guide', [1984] *ECLR*, 384.

Posner, R. (1976), *Antitrust Law: An Economic Perspective*, University of Chicago Press.

Turner (1967), 'Antitrust and Innovation', **12**, *Antitrust Bulletin*, 277.

US Department of Justice and the Federal Trade Commission (1995), *Antitrust Guidelines to the Licensing of Intellectual Property*.

Wilson, B. (1975), Dept of Justice luncheon speech, 'Law on licensing practice – myth or reality straight talk from Alice in Wonderland'.

Winn, D. (1990), 'Commission know-how Regulation 556/89: innovation and territorial exclusivity improvements and the quid pro quo', [1990] *ECLR*, 135.

*Cases*
*Consten/Grundig* [1966] ECR 429.
*Morton Salt Co.* v. *G S Suppiger Co* 314 US 488 (1941).
*United States* v. *United States Gypsum Co.* 333 US 364 (1947).

# 12 The right balance of competition policy and intellectual property law: a Federal Trade Commission perspective

*Alden F. Abbott, Suzanne Michel and Armando Irizarry*[1]

## Introduction

Historically, the policies underlying antitrust law and intellectual property ('IP') law[2] were often seen as being in conflict, with IP law being viewed as designed to 'promote' monopolies and antitrust being designed to 'combat' them.[3] More recently it has been recognized that these two legal regimes, properly understood, seek to promote innovation and the general welfare, albeit through two somewhat different mechanisms – IP law by protecting the property rights interests of (and thus financial returns to) inventors, antitrust law by combating restrictions on the competitive process that may harm consumers and slow innovation. As a 2003 United States Federal Trade Commission ('FTC') report on the interrelationship of competition and patent law explained,[4] enlightened public policy aimed at promoting innovation and welfare[5] requires that an appropriate balance be struck between these two legal regimes.

This chapter explores the appropriate balance between competition policy and IP law in the context of two contentious IP–antitrust topics. After providing a background discussion of patent law characteristics that are crucial to informed antitrust analysis, we turn specifically to (1) the treatment of ex ante price-related negotiations in standard-setting organizations, and (2) the analysis of exclusion payments made in the settlement of patent litigation. We conclude with a few general comments about the implications of our analysis for the patent–antitrust interface.

## The nature of patent law: implications for innovation and welfare

Patent law is a utilitarian set of property rules that derives legitimacy to the extent it promotes innovation and welfare.[6] Thus, the patent law system is not sacrosanct; aspects of patent law that undermine these goals are properly subject to reform. Indeed, the heavier role of government in shaping the contours of patent rules as compared to other property rules strongly suggests that patent law may be, relatively speaking, a rather socially inefficient form of property protection.[7]

Hearings on competition policy and the patent system organized by the FTC and the United States Justice Department, held in 2001 and 2002, support this implication. Evaluating the implications of those Hearings, the FTC Competition-Patent Report[8] found that 'questionable patents' (patents that are likely invalid or that contain claims that are likely overly broad) are a significant concern and can harm innovation. More precisely, the Report concluded that questionable patents (1) may directly deter third parties from undertaking innovative research because of litigation risks and costs and (2) may create licensing difficulties that substantially raise transaction costs and deter agreements that disseminate the fruits of innovation.[9] To deal with these problems, the Report urged specific patent law reforms designed to improve patent quality and minimize the anticompetitive costs of the patent system.[10]

Antitrust law is not designed to 'step in the breach' created by faulty patent rules. The fact that certain 'bad patents' exist does not mean that antitrust may be used as a sword to attack the statutorily guaranteed right to exclude that flows from legitimate patents. But the problematic nature of certain patents does suggest that antitrust analysis should not shy away from closely scrutinizing transactions involving patent questions, if those transactions hold out the possibility of extending market power beyond the legitimate scope of the property right a patent generates. The 'legitimate scope' question properly may take account of the fact that patents may be deemed 'probabilistic' property rights;[11] the complexity of patent claims often creates ambiguity as to whether particular third party activity may property be blocked by the patent, which may only be resolved by litigation.[12] As discussed below, antitrust enforcers may properly take into account these peculiar attributes of the patent system in weighing the wisdom of proposed interventions; an antitrust challenge does not undermine a patent-created property right if the patentee's claims as to the nature and breadth of the right are inaccurate.[13] In fact, according less legal respect to illegitimate invocations of patent rights may implicitly enhance the value of well-founded patent invocations, thereby actually enhancing patents' ability to drive innovation.

### Ex ante price-related negotiations by standard-setting organizations

Before we turn to the specific questions raised by potential ex ante price-related negotiations, a background discussion of standards setting, and of recent FTC cases alleging standards setting abuses, is in order.

*Background on standards*
Standards have been defined succinctly as 'any set of technical specifications that either provides or is intended to provide a common design for

a product or process'.[14] Standards have been in existence since the early days of civilization.[15] They are promulgated by governments,[16] by private groups, or arise from their spontaneous acceptance by consumers. In the United States, private standard-setting organizations ('SSOs') as we now know them began to appear in the latter part of the nineteenth century, in the midst of the industrial revolution.[17] Catastrophic events have also helped create awareness about the need for standards. For example, in 1904, a great blaze destroyed much of the city of Baltimore because the hoses brought by the fire engines that came from outside the city did not fit the city's hydrants. This led to the standardization of hydrants and hose couplings.[18] Similar circumstances led to the creation of hundreds of private SSOs that have promulgated thousands of standards that have improved our daily life, promoted efficiencies and innovation in industry and facilitated trade among nations. The adoption of standards may be particularly important in markets with 'network effects' (where the utility of the network rises as parties are added to it) and global interconnections, such as information technology and telecommunications. Thus the technological revolution that we are experiencing in these markets has benefited from, and resulted in, significant standard-setting activity.[19]

Standards are classified as de facto or de jure. A de facto standard is adopted through the self-interested actions of market participants. A classic example of a de facto standard is the Microsoft operating system, which became a standard simply because of widespread consumer demand and use, and not because it was mandated by government regulation or adopted or endorsed by a private SSO. A de jure standard may be mandated by government authority, or it may be 'highly recommended' (in the sense that it is widely adopted and used in the market, and failure of a business to adopt it will likely result in a significant competitive disadvantage).[20]

*Benefits and drawbacks of standards*
It is widely recognized that the development and adoption of standards provide valuable economic benefits. Standardization lowers the cost of products, which benefits consumers if the cost savings are passed on to them by the product manufacturer. Standardization allows much-desired interoperability among products and services in network markets.[21] For example, standardization allows users of computer technology to create their systems using products and parts from different companies, such as a Dell CPU, a Hewlett-Packard printer, and a Brother fax machine. Standardization also eliminates 'standards wars' in the market and their associated costs to both firms and consumers.[22]

There are also drawbacks associated with standards. Standards may deny consumers, to some extent, the benefits derived from competition.[23]

Competition drives competitors to innovate to make a better product or develop a better solution for the consumer's needs. The use of standards may dull this drive. Standards may also result in higher prices to consumers if the standard is encumbered with royalty-bearing patent rights. Another drawback of standards is that superior technologies may be excluded or shunned from the market because an inferior standard is mandatory or reigns as a standard owing to the 'tipping' effect or simply very strong consumer demand.[24]

*Holdups in private standards-setting: the* Rambus *case*
The problem of patent holdups is illustrated by the FTC's recent Rambus and Unocal investigations. Rambus is an example of an alleged holdup in a private SSO; Unocal illustrates an alleged holdup in a governmental regulatory standard-setting process. In both cases, it is alleged that deceptive private behaviour undermined standard-setting activities, thereby allowing market power to be exercised, to the detriment of firms using the standards and of ultimate consumers. In June 2005, the FTC and Unocal announced a proposed settlement of the *Unocal* case.[25]

In 2002, the FTC issued a complaint against Rambus, Inc. (a computer chip technology provider) charging Rambus with violating federal antitrust laws by engaging in anticompetitive acts and practices that served to deceive the JEDEC[26] Solid State Technology Association ('JEDEC'), a private SSO, into adopting a standard that JEDEC had no reason to believe was encumbered with Rambus's patents. The complaint charged that Rambus's conduct harmed competition and consumers.

According to the complaint, JEDEC develops and issues technical standards for use throughout the semiconductor industry. JEDEC endeavours to promote free competition among industry participants by not 'giving a competitive advantage to any manufacturer, [or] excluding competitors from the market'.[27] Toward this end, JEDEC seeks to ensure that, if patented technologies are incorporated into its standards, these technologies 'will be available to be licensed on royalty-free or otherwise reasonable and non-discriminatory (that is, "RAND") terms'.[28]

One of the technologies for which JEDEC developed and issued standards was a common form of computer memory chip known as SDRAM.[29] SDRAM chips are used in a wide variety of products, including computers, fax machines, printers and video game equipment. Rambus participated in JEDEC's SDRAM-related work for more than four years without ever making it known to JEDEC or its members that Rambus was actively seeking to develop patents that covered technologies proposed for – and ultimately adopted – in the SDRAM-related standards. Specifically, the complaint alleged that

> Rambus's very participation in JEDEC, coupled with its failure to make required patent related disclosures, conveyed a materially false and misleading impression – namely, that JEDEC, by incorporating into its SDRAM standards technologies openly discussed and considered during Rambus's tenure in the organization, was not at risk of adopting standards that Rambus could later claim to infringe upon its patents.[30]

The FTC alleged that Rambus's conduct caused or threatened to cause substantial harm to competition and consumers because it allowed Rambus to assert patent rights against – and to obtain substantial royalties from – memory manufacturers producing products in compliance with the relevant standards. In addition, Rambus's conduct allegedly threatened or resulted in other anticompetitive effects, including increases in the price of SDRAM chips and other products incorporating or using SDRAM technology, decreased incentives to produce the SDRAM memory chips, decreased incentives to participate in JEDEC and other SSOs, and decreased reliance or willingness to rely – both within and outside the computer memory industry – on standards set by industry SSOs.

*Holdups in a governmental setting: the* Unocal *case*
The Unocal investigation concerned conduct by the Union Oil Company of California ('Unocal') before the California Air Resources Board ('CARB'), a department of the California Environmental Protection Agency. According to the FTC's complaint,

> CARB's mission is to protect the health, welfare, and ecological resources of California through the effective and efficient reduction of air pollutants, while recognizing and considering the effects of its actions on the California economy. CARB fulfills this mandate by, among other things, setting and enforcing standards for low emissions, reformulated gasoline.[31]

The FTC complaint issued against Unocal alleges that, in the early 1990s, CARB embarked in rulemaking proceedings to promulgate specifications for low emissions, reformulated gasoline ('RFG'). CARB relied on industry, including Unocal, to provide the information it needed for these proceedings. Unocal allegedly misrepresented to CARB that certain information it provided to CARB related to RFG was non-proprietary and in the public domain, when in fact Unocal had applied for a patent that would enable Unocal to charge substantial royalties if the information was used by CARB. The complaint alleged that these statements by Unocal to CARB were materially false and misleading. CARB did use the information in its rulemaking, which resulted in standards for 'summer-time' RFG. The California refining industry spent billions of dollars to reconfigure refineries to produce RFG in compliance with the standards mandated by CARB, thus effectively locking into the production of this gasoline.

After the industry was locked in, Unocal began enforcing its patent rights through licensing and litigation.[32] Unocal prevailed in its private infringement actions and obtained judgments requiring the major refiners producing CARB to pay 5.75 cents per gallon of RFG, a not insignificant amount. Unocal's own expert estimated that approximately 90 per cent of this royalty would likely be passed to consumers through higher retail gasoline prices.

The FTC alleged that Unocal's misrepresentations harmed competition and allowed Unocal to obtain monopoly power over the technology to produce and supply RFG. Had Unocal not engaged in such conduct, the FTC contended that CARB would not have adopted RFG regulations that substantially overlapped with Unocal's patent rights, or the terms on which Unocal could enforce its patent rights would have been substantially different.

On 10 June 2005, the FTC announced two consent orders that would resolve the competitive concerns arising from the Unocal investigation and from the proposed acquisition of Unocal by Chevron Corporation. Under the terms of the orders, Chevron's acquisition was allowed to proceed, subject to the requirement that Unocal would stop enforcing its reformulated gasoline patents that were the subject of the FTC's technology market monopolization complaint. This settlement resolved the problem of competitive harm arising from Unocal's 'patent holdup'.

*Can SSO participants negotiate licensing terms and royalties ex ante?*
The SSOs' concerns that ex ante royalty negotiations may expose them to antitrust liability may have precluded SSOs from allowing such negotiations among the patent holder and SSO participants. The concern arises because participants in a standard-setting process are usually competitors, and SSOs, under whose auspices the standard-setting processes occur, may fear that ex ante negotiations will be deemed illegal price fixing or acts of 'monopsonization' (the creation of a monopsony single buyer of technology inputs).

Such concerns are ill-founded, given the state of modern antitrust analysis. A legitimate SSO (as opposed to a sham organization created to mask a cartel) is properly viewed as a welfare-enhancing joint venture aimed at jointly bringing forth an output – a standard – that yields benefits to industry and, ultimately, consumers (see previous discussion of benefits of standards). Even legitimate joint ventures, of course, may engage in collateral conduct that is anticompetitive and not reasonably related to joint venture efficiencies. Nevertheless, as explained further below, ex ante price-related negotiations by SSOs, properly analyzed, are not collateral anticompetitive conduct.

In the United States, antitrust liability and the legality of agreements among competitors are determined by analyzing the agreements under two rules: the per se rule and the rule of reason.[33] The per se rule applies to agreements that 'are so likely to harm competition and to have no significant procompetitive benefit that they do not warrant the time and expense required for particularized inquiry into their effects'.[34] Agreements that are deemed per se illegal include

> [a]greements of a type that always or almost always tends to raise price or reduce output . . . Typically these are agreements not to compete on price or output. Types of agreements that have been held per se illegal include agreements among competitors to fix prices or output, rig bids, or share or divide markets by allocating customers, suppliers, territories or lines of commerce.[35]

The only category of per se illegal conduct under which ex ante negotiations of royalties conceivably might fall is price fixing.[36] It could be said that, when a patent holder[37] and an SSO participant negotiate a royalty payment, they are fixing a price of a product component. As we will explain below, however, fixing a price in this context should not be characterized as illegal 'price fixing' as that conduct is contemplated by the antitrust laws.[38] 'As generally used in the antitrust field, "price fixing" is a shorthand way of describing certain categories of business behavior to which the per se rule has been held applicable. . . . Literalness [of the term "price fixing"] is overly simplistic and often overbroad.'[39]

Should the per se rule apply to ex ante negotiations in SSOs? It should not, for several reasons. First, the per se rule applies to agreements and practices that are 'so plainly anticompetitive . . . so often lack[ing] . . . any redeeming virtue . . . that they are conclusively presumed illegal without further examination under the rule of reason generally applied in Sherman Act cases'.[40] That is not the case with ex ante negotiations in SSOs. Those negotiations have procompetitive effects. Ex ante negotiations provide for more evenly balanced negotiating conditions than ex post negotiations, that is, negotiations that take place after adoption of the standard by the SSO. In ex post negotiations the patent holder has superior bargaining power over those who want to license the patents, because the standard covered by the patents already has been adopted and many industry members have 'locked into' the standard (absorbed standard-specific sunk costs, such as building facilities to standard). This superior bargaining power allows the patent holder to command supracompetitive royalties. With ex ante negotiations the patent holder does not have such a bargaining advantage: because the standard covered by the patent has not yet been adopted, the industry has not locked into the standard, and the SSO participants negotiating the licence with the patent holder (who ultimately determine whether the standard will be adopted) have the option of switching to another alternative if the negotiations fail because of the patent holder's unreasonable royalty demands. (In other words, ex ante negotiations facilitate competition among technologies that are inputs into future standards-based products and services; a bar on ex ante negotiations may sacrifice this competitive efficiency.) These are cognizable procompetitive effects that should suffice to preclude ex ante negotiations from being per se unlawful.

Second, the per se rule is applied after courts have had 'considerable experience' with the business relationship under scrutiny.[41] That is not the case here. The general practice of SSOs has been to discourage or prohibit ex ante negotiations for fear of antitrust liability. Antitrust enforcers and courts have seldom, if ever, had occasion to evaluate ex ante royalty negotiations. Thus there is no 'considerable experience' with ex ante negotiations.

Having disposed of the argument that ex ante price-related negotiations are per se illegal, we briefly assess them under the antitrust 'rule of reason'. The rule of reason applies to '[a]greements not challenged as per se illegal . . . to determine their overall competitive effect. These include agreements of a type that might be considered per se illegal, provided they are reasonably related to, and reasonably necessary to achieve procompetitive benefits from, an efficiency-enhancing integration of economic activity'.[42] In applying the rule of reason, we turn to the Joint Venture Guidelines jointly released by the FTC and the United States Department of Justice in 2000. According to the Guidelines, the central question in a rule of reason analysis 'is whether the relevant agreement likely harms competition by increasing the ability or incentive profitably to raise price above or reduce output, quality, service, or innovation below what likely would prevail in the absence of the relevant agreement'.[43]

There are close similarities between the benefits that the Joint Venture Guidelines recognize flow from competitor collaborations and those that flow from ex ante negotiations in SSOs. As the Guidelines state:

> The Agencies recognize that consumers may benefit from competitor collaborations in a variety of ways. For example, a competitor collaboration may enable participants to offer goods or services that are cheaper, more valuable to consumers, or brought to market faster than would be possible absent the collaboration. A collaboration may allow its participants to better use existing assets, or may provide incentives for them to make output-enhancing investments that would not occur absent the collaboration. The potential efficiencies from competitor collaborations may be achieved through a variety of contractual arrangements including joint ventures, trade or professional associations, licensing arrangements, or strategic alliances.[44]

These benefits substantially overlap the benefits, discussed above, that SSOs provide. Furthermore, note that the competitor collaborations contemplated by the guidelines include trade or professional associations, which include some SSOs. For example, the IEEE is a trade association of electrical engineers and related professions that is very active in setting standards in several industries, including information technology and communications.[45]

The Joint Venture Guidelines also contemplate that competitor collaborations may engender anticompetitive harms through a variety of mechanisms.[46]

> Among other things, agreements [among competitor collaborators] may limit independent decision making or combine the control of or financial interests in production, key assets, or decisions regarding price, output, or other competitively sensitive variables, or may otherwise reduce the participants' ability or incentive to compete independently.

> Competitor collaborations also may facilitate explicit or tacit collusion through facilitating practices such as the exchange or disclosure of competitively sensitive information or through increased market concentration. Such collusion may involve the relevant market in which the collaboration operates or another market in which the participants in the collaboration are actual or potential competitors.[47]

The narrowly circumscribed conduct of patent holders and SSO participants negotiating ex ante does not create the potential for most of these anticompetitive harms. For example, ex ante negotiations do not require that the parties combine financial interests or key assets, nor does it include decisions regarding the price at which a product or service is offered in the market. Furthermore, when parties negotiating ex ante agree to reasonable terms, their ability or incentive to compete independently should not be compromised. Ex ante negotiations could be problematic if they facilitated collusion with respect to products or services produced by SSO members, but that concern would not arise as long as the negotiations did not involve the exchange of information relating to those products or services (and legitimate negotiations over licensing terms with patentees would not require such an information exchange). In short, the Joint Venture Guidelines' analysis suggests that legitimate ex ante negotiations, properly structured, clearly would pass antitrust muster under the rule of reason.

One final potential antitrust critique of ex ante negotiations remains, namely, that joint ex ante negotiations would give an SSO collective monopsony power over patentees' technology, yielding harm to competition. Under this theory, the joint negotiations would be deemed a vehicle for monopsonization. Careful analysis, however, reveals that this antitrust concern is misplaced. Classical monopsony concerns arise when the monopsonist purchaser of a competitively supplied input pays a less than socially optimal amount for the input, leading the sellers to restrict their supply to less than the socially optimal amount. The monopsonist purchaser in turn enjoys monopoly power downstream over the final product that embodies the input, and ultimate consumers are harmed owing to an artificial restriction of final product output (which is sold at an inefficiently high price). Under this scenario, antitrust enforcers are well justified in acting to prevent the monopsony behaviour.

This 'harmful monopsony' scenario, however, is unlikely to pose a problem for ex ante price-related SSO negotiations. First, to the extent that different SSOs compete to purchase particular technology rights, any one SSO engaged in collective price negotiations cannot exercise monopsony power. Second, purveyors of technology rights that face SSOs are unlikely to be perfect competitors; they may enjoy some negotiating leverage vis-à-vis an SSO or SSOs. Third, intellectual property is not a tangible product sold in divisible units whose output can harmfully be restricted in the short run; at most, an SSO may be able to capture some rents that otherwise would have been retained by the patent holder. Although theoretically possible, it is questionable to what extent this redistribution of rents away from certain patentees (assuming it occurs) will diminish future incentives to do research that spurs innovation. Some patentees would only sacrifice 'excessive pure rents' that are above the level necessary to spur optimal innovation levels. As discussed in the FTC Competition-Patent Report, many patents make marginal contributions (at best) to innovation, some are of questionable validity, and many may be asserted in an overly broad fashion; to the extent that excessively broad assertion is curbed ex ante, companies that utilize an SSO's output (a standard) may pay lower royalties and thereby free funds for innovative research of their own.[48] Furthermore, to the extent that SSO members themselves hold patents (which is often the case), they would not have an incentive to pose onerous terms that in turn could be turned against them as patentees in future ex ante negotiating cycles. In sum, not only is a 'monopsony-induced reduction in innovation' story unlikely to arise from ex ante price negotiations, there is good reason to believe that such negotiations, by reducing costly holdups and litigation, may create a climate that is more congenial to innovation. This reinforces the notion that antitrust analysis, properly applied, should not create obstacles to SSOs' ex ante price arrangements with patent holders.

### Exclusion payments made in the settlement of patent litigation
*Overview*
The great majority of patent disputes settle before trial[49] and the great majority of those settlements are procompetitive.[50] A settlement can save public and private resources that would otherwise be consumed by litigation, and it can provide certainty that will encourage business investment.[51]

Many settlements contribute to marketplace competition because they result in a licence or cross-licence that allows the accused infringer to market or continue marketing its product.[52] Moreover a cross-licence may provide a procompetitive benefit by eliminating the problem of 'blocking patents' that potentially could prevent both parties from bringing their products to market.[53]

Courts generally favour settlements as an efficient means to avoid litigation,[54] but these public policy considerations do not mean that all settlements are presumptively efficient regardless of the cost. Because the patentee and accused infringer may be horizontal competitors or potential competitors when they enter the settlement agreement, the agreement may attract antitrust scrutiny if, for instance, the parties agree to allocate markets or fix prices as apart of the settlement.[55] The issue of the proper role of antitrust in evaluating patent settlement agreements has come to the forefront of US law with the recent challenges, brought by the FTC, the attorneys general of the individual states and private litigants, to patent settlements in the pharmaceutical arena. The exact terms of the settlement agreements at issue in these cases vary, but they have the common feature of requiring a payment from a brand-name drug manufacturer (the patentee) to a generic drug manufacturer (the accused infringer) in exchange for a promise by the generic company to refrain from marketing its product for some time. We will term the payment from the brand-name company to the generic an 'exclusion payment'.

The courts that have undertaken an antitrust analysis of these agreements have varied in their approach and conclusions. One court of appeals found an interim settlement agreement that included an exclusion payment to constitute a per se antitrust violation.[56] Another court, overturning an FTC decision, found an agreement between Schering-Plough and Upsher-Smith to be legal, in part because the exclusion payment fell within the exclusionary power of Schering's patent.[57] Commentators also have varied in their analysis.[58] In this section, we set forth our thoughts on how to approach the antitrust analysis of these agreements in a manner that considers the nature of the patent property right and the exclusionary power of the patent at issue in the dispute. Our prior comments about the probabilistic nature of patent rights will help inform our application of antitrust analysis to this area.

Settlement agreements including exclusion payments are horizontal restraints that violate the antitrust laws if they 'unreasonably' limit competition.[59] To assess the reasonableness of a horizontal restraint, courts begin by asking whether the conduct appears to be a practice that would 'always or almost always tend to restrict competition and decrease output', or instead is 'designed to increase economic efficiency and render markets more, rather than less, competitive'.[60] Horizontal restraints are evaluated along an analytical continuum in which a challenged practice is examined in the detail necessary to understand its competitive effect.[61] Although it is true that 'when there is an agreement not to compete in terms of price or output, no elaborate industry analysis is required to demonstrate the anti-competitive character of such an agreement',[62] it remains necessary to consider whether the parties offer plausible and cognizable efficiency justi-fications for the agreement in determining the extent of the inquiry required.[63] A horizontal restraint may have legitimate procompetitive efficiencies when it creates a new product or improves the operation of the market, for example.[64] In evaluating whether a settlement including an exclusion payment is anticompetitive because it 'tends to restrict competi-tion and decrease output', we consider the likely effects of the agreement and any plausible, cognizable efficiency justifications.

*Assessing uncertain litigation outcomes*
The analysis of the competitive effects of a settlement including an exclu-sion payment must view the agreement from the point-in-time in which the parties entered the agreement.[65] At that point-in-time, the outcome of the patent litigation is uncertain. Indeed, the very purpose of the settlement is to eliminate that uncertainty. The payment from a branded drug manufac-turer to a potential generic entrant in exchange for ending the litigation and setting generic entry for a future date can be characterized as the brand's payment to eliminate the chance that the generic company will win the liti-gation or otherwise market its product at an earlier date.[66] There is no dispute among the courts and commentators who have examined these agreements that this is a fair characterization of the exclusion payment. The disputes centre on whether such agreements are anticompetitive or whether they are within the scope of the patentee's exclusionary right.[67]

It is incorrect to begin an examination of the likely affect of an agree-ment (including an exclusion payment) from the premise that the patentee could exclude all competitors for the term of the patent. There is no cer-tainty that a court will find that an accused product actually infringes, a matter on which the patentee has the burden of proof.[68] In fact, accused infringers frequently win litigation by demonstrating that they do not infringe the asserted patent. In 2003, of 339 written judicial decisions addressing infringement, courts found the patent not infringed 75 per cent of the time.[69] A more optimistic study still shows patentees losing litigation 42 per cent of the time.[70]

Moreover, the fact that a patent has been issued by the Patent and Trademark Office ('PTO') is no guarantee that the courts will uphold its validity, despite the statutory presumption of validity.[71] 'The validity of a patent is always subject to plenary challenge on its merits. A court may invalidate a patent on any substantive ground, whether or not that ground was considered by the patent examiner.'[72] Empirical studies have demonstrated that courts invalidate nearly half of all issued patents litigated to judgment on validity issues. A study examining nearly all written, final validity decisions by either the district courts or the United States Court of Appeal for the Federal Circuit during the eight-year period 1989 to 1996 found that 46 per cent of patents challenged in litigation were found to be invalid.[73] A more recent survey found that, in 2003, of 201 judicial decisions addressing validity, 58 per cent found the patent invalid.[74] The presumption of validity is simply a procedural device for allocating the burden of proof to an accused infringer who seeks to demonstrate a patent's invalidity in patent litigation.[75] 'The presumption has no separate evidentiary value.'[76] It should not be understood to alter antitrust law's approach to the uncertain outcome of the litigation at the time of the settlement agreement.

The FTC's survey of patent litigation in the pharmaceutical industry between brand-name drug manufacturers, as patentees, and generic drug manufacturers, as accused infringers, parallels these trends. Of 30 cases resolving patent litigation between a brand-name drug manufacturer and the first generic company to file an application with the Food and Drug Administration ('FDA') to sell a generic version of the drug at issue between 1992 and 2002, the generic applicant prevailed by proving either the invalidity of the patent or noninfringement 73 per cent of the time.[77]

The exclusion payments themselves demonstrate the uncertainty of the litigation. One commentator has noted that the willingness of the brand company patentee to make the very large payments at issue in most of these cases indicates significant doubts about the validity of the patent or the strength of the infringement claim. 'A firm willing to pay roughly $75 million per year to keep an alleged infringer out of the market when a successful preliminary injunction would have done the same thing for the cost of obtaining the injunction indicates that the prospects for a preliminary injunction were very poor.'[78] Others have recognized that the size of an exclusion payment is proportional to the strength of a generic applicant's case.[79] In other words, 'the less likely the patentee is to win, the more it is willing to pay a generic to stay out of the market'.[80] According to one model, if the patentee has a 25 per cent chance of losing, it will be willing to pay up to 25 per cent of the value of its monopoly to exclude its competitors without a trial.[81] The accuracy of the model's numbers is not important, but this feature of exclusion payments nicely illustrates their nature as the purchase of 'insurance' against potential competition.[82] The greater the risk of competition, the higher the premium paid to avoid the risk.

*A payment to eliminate uncertain competition can be anticompetitive*

The market structure in which generic entry occurs and the uncertainties inherent in patent litigation demonstrate that the purpose and effect of an agreement between brand and generic pharmaceutical companies containing an exclusion payment may be to delay potential, albeit uncertain, competition. An agreement that purchases 'insurance' that eliminates the risk of potential competition is likely to harm competition, absent any countervailing, procompetitive efficiencies. As the Supreme Court has said, '[t]he anti-trust laws are as much violated by the prevention of competition as by its destruction'.[83] The fact that the potential competitor's status is uncertain in no way changes the analysis, for antitrust law condemns agreements to prevent competition even when a potential entrant's prospects for successful entry are not assured.[84] A leading antitrust treatise succinctly articulates the principle: 'the law does not condone the purchase of protection from uncertain competition any more than it condones the elimination of actual competition'.[85]

As a matter of economics, agreements to prevent uncertain competition clearly are anticompetitive and harm consumers, absent significant efficiencies. Preventing potential competition causes harm to consumers in a manner similar to that caused by destroying existing competition, though discounted by the probability of entry. Consumers are always better off with the possibility of competitive entry and lower prices than they are with the certainty of no entry. Reflecting this economic reality, the courts have long recognized that even agreements to delay uncertain competition have anticompetitive effects. Since *Chicago Bd. of Trade* v. *United States*,[86] the rule of reason inquiry has focused on the restraint's 'effect, actual or probable'.

Because the reduction in uncertain competition itself is sufficient to demonstrate an anticompetitive effect, proving what would have happened absent the restraint is not an element of an antitrust action.[87] Even if subsequent events meant the likely effects of the agreement would not have materialized – for example, because the potential entrant's plant had burned down, it failed to obtain necessary regulatory approvals, or for some other reason – that would not alter the conclusion that, when the agreement was entered into, it was likely to cause substantial competitive harm.[88]

The D.C. Circuit's opinion in *United States* v. *Microsoft Corp.*[89] illustrates the importance of this policy for antitrust law. Applying the rule of reason under Section 2 of the Sherman Act, the D.C. Circuit confirmed that impeding 'nascent' rather than actual competition is a fully cognizable anticompetitive effect. Rejecting Microsoft's argument that the government did not establish a causal link between Microsoft's foreclosure of

Netscape's and Java's distribution channels and the maintenance of Microsoft's monopoly, the court held that it could infer causation even when the exclusionary conduct is aimed at nascent competitive technologies. 'Admittedly, in the former case there is added uncertainty, inasmuch as nascent threats are merely *potential* substitutes. But the underlying proof problem is the same – neither plaintiffs nor the court can confidently reconstruct a product's hypothetical technological development in a world absent the defendant's exclusionary conduct.'[90] It was not the government's burden to establish a 'but for' world: to show that Java or Netscape would have become viable substitutes for Microsoft's operating system. Rather, the central question was whether 'as a general matter the exclusion of nascent threats is the type of conduct that is reasonably capable of contributing significantly to a defendant's continued monopoly power' and whether the potential entrants constituted nascent threats at the time the conduct was undertaken. As the court recognized, 'it would be inimical to the purpose of the Sherman Act to allow monopolists free rein to squash nascent, albeit unproven, competitors at will'.[91]

*Exclusion payments made in the settlement of pharmaceutical patent litigation can harm competition*
Applying these principles to exclusion payments made in the settlement of pharmaceutical patent litigation demonstrates that such agreements can be anticompetitive. A settlement of pharmaceutical patent litigation containing an exclusion payment is effectively a temporal market allocation arrangement, under which the brand company retains it sales for several years and shares its profit with the potential generic entrant, which, in return, refrains from selling its competing product. Here, just as in *Microsoft*, a potential generic entrant clearly constitutes a threat to a brand company.[92]

The uncertainty about whether the generic ultimately would have prevailed in the patent case does not undermine the likely anticompetitive effects of the settlements including exclusion payments. It clearly would be anticompetitive for an incumbent to pay a potential generic rival to defer entry until a specific date in the future, even if the generic's ability to obtain FDA approval was uncertain. From an economic point of view, there is no reason to treat uncertainty due to patent litigation any differently. Although some patents that are litigated through trial will be found valid and infringed, the anticompetitive harm stems from the settlement's elimination of any chance that the market will be competitive before the agreed-to generic entry date.[93] As one commentator has explained, '[t]he very fact of that uncertainty [that the patentee may win the patent litigation] suggests that exclusion payments are anticompetitive – that on average such agreements exclude at least some generics that in fact had a legal right to compete'.[94]

There is no basis for the assertion that, to demonstrate the anticompetitive effect of agreements containing exclusion payments, it is necessary to show that other factors, including the loss of the patent litigation, would not have prevented generic entry in any event. Just as Microsoft's exclusionary conduct provided less competition in an expected sense, so too can agreements containing exclusion payments. Given the obvious effect that large payments to stay off the market have on a generic firm's decision about when to enter, the challenged agreements are 'likely enough to disrupt the proper functioning of the price-setting mechanism of the market', that they may be deemed anticompetitive even without proof that they actually 'resulted in higher prices . . . than would occur in [the conduct's] absence',[95] based on proof that the generic would have entered the market earlier absent the payment. Indeed, as the Court of Appeals observed in *Microsoft*, to rest antitrust liability on a requirement that plaintiffs 'reconstruct the hypothetical marketplace' absent the challenged conduct would merely encourage 'more and earlier anticompetitive action'.[96]

Moreover there is no need to consider the outcome of the litigation because antitrust law distinguishes between effects achieved unilaterally and those achieved concertedly. A price-fixing agreement is unlawful even if a party could have raised prices unilaterally.[97] A patentee's proving infringement in litigation and its paying a potential entrant to withdraw its challenge are fundamentally different. Therefore, what a brand-name company might have been able to achieve unilaterally (excluding the generic by winning the patent suit) is no defence to its entering an agreement to pay its competitor not to compete.

An often-cited concurrence in *United States* v. *Singer Mfg. Co.* discusses this point. Justice White found a *separate* antitrust violation in 'the *collusive termination of a Patent Office interference proceeding* pursuant to an agreement between Singer and [its Swiss competitor]'.[98] The parties entered the agreement, wrote Justice White, 'to help one another *to secure as broad a patent monopoly as possible*, invalidity considerations notwithstanding'.[99] Justice White pointed out that 'the desire to secure broad claims in a patent may well be unexceptional – *when purely unilateral action is involved'*, but does not justify the collusive agreement to terminate a PTO interference proceeding.[100] Thus, that a branded company *might have* won its patent litigations and therefore *unilaterally* precluded the generic from entering the market does not justify paying off that competitor to *guarantee* that it remains off the market.

Of course, the antitrust analysis of these agreements must also consider whether they generate any cognizable procompetitive efficiencies. In its

*Schering* decision, the FTC acknowledged hypothetical situations in which the effect of a payment from a brand to generic company would be pro-competitive because it would hasten generic entry, such as that of the 'cash-strapped generic'.[101] However, neither the FTC nor any court that has examined these agreements has found the existence of facts sufficient to support such a situation. Moreover, unlike many patent settlements, an agreement based on an exclusion payment is typically devoid of the kind of efficiencies that can result, for example, when owners combine their conflicting intellectual property so as to produce a product that otherwise would not exist, or when a patent holder and a new entrant compromise and allow the new entrant to come to market in exchange for compensation to the patent holder.[102] For that reason, we will continue our analysis of agreements containing exclusion payments assuming that they present no cognizable procompetitive efficiencies, but recognizing that that determination is fact-specific.[103]

*The nature of a patentee's right to exclude*
In spite of the economic and antitrust analysis demonstrating that exclusion payments not having legitimate efficiency explanations can be anti-competitive because they purchase protection from potential, albeit uncertain, competition, some courts and commentators have asserted that such agreements must be allowed as falling within the patentee's right to exclude its competitors.[104] We believe this assertion misinterprets the nature of the patent right.

A patent grants a patentee a statutory right to 'exclude others from using, offering for sale, or selling the invention throughout the United States'.[105] Thus the patent system 'embodies a carefully crafted bargain for encouraging the creation and disclosure of new, useful, and nonobvious advances in technology and design in return for the exclusive right to practice the invention for a period of years'.[106] Patent policy provides relatively short-term limits on competition because of its judgment that those limits will provide greater incentives to innovate over the long run and increase social welfare by that means.[107]

*(a) The right to exclude must be exercised consistent with other laws*   The Patent Act and controlling case law has established two methods by which a patentee may exercise its right to exclude. It may seek and obtain an injunction from a court or it may persuade the accused infringer unilaterally to decide to accede to the patent.[108] Pursuant to the Patent Act, a patentee may seek, and a court may grant, 'injunctions in accordance with the principles of equity to prevent the violation of any right secured by patent, on such terms as the court deems reasonable'.[109] The justification for the

use of permanent injunctions in patent cases arises from the constitutional and statutory bases for the right to exclude, as well as a patent's status as personal property.[110] It is important to note that, before obtaining a court-awarded permanent injunction, the patentee must win its patent case by proving infringement and warding off any challenges to the validity of its patent. When a patentee exercises its right to exclude by obtaining a permanent injunction, it obtains that exclusion through the merits of its patent case and the strength of its patent – what we will call the patent's 'exclusionary power'.

If a patentee has not yet won its patent litigation, but wishes to exclude an accused infringer for the course of the litigation, the Patent Act supplies but one means for accomplishing that goal. The patentee must seek a preliminary injunction from the court, pursuant to 35 U.S.C. §283. In considering whether to award a preliminary injunction, a court considers (1) the patentee's likelihood of success on the merits; (2) irreparable harm caused to the parties by granting or denying the injunction; (3) the balance of hardships; and (4) the possible impact of an injunction on the public interest.[111] If a patentee succeeds in obtaining a preliminary injunction, it does so through the strength of its patent case and the demonstrated exclusionary power of the patent.

The Patent Act also makes clear that a patentee may exercise its right to exclude by a means other than obtaining an injunction: by unilaterally and unconditionally refusing to license its patent.[112] If a competitor chooses to exit or refrain from entering the market in the face of that refusal, it is unilaterally acceding to the strength of the patent arguments and the exclusionary power of the patent.

Thus, a patentee has the right to try to exclude allegedly infringing products by instituting a lawsuit, or even by merely threatening a lawsuit. 'The heart of [a patentee's] legal monopoly is the right *to invoke the State's power* to prevent others from utilizing his discovery without his consent.'[113] When it asserts its patent and threatens a lawsuit, the patentee can hope that the strength of its patent allegation convinces the accused infringer to accede and unilaterally decide to leave the market. Alternatively, if the accused infringer views the patent allegation as sufficiently weak to warrant continuing with the accused activity, the patentee's recourse for exercising its right to exclude is to institute litigation and invoke the State's power through a judicially granted injunction. Neither path guarantees success for the patentee. As both economists and legal scholars have remarked, 'a patent is not a right to exclude, but rather a right to *try* to exclude'.[114]

Patent law's right to exclude is not unfettered or free to be exercised by means outside this paradigm, in any manner the patentee sees fit. A patent confers a property right. 'The right to exclude recognized in a patent is but the essence of the concept of property.'[115] Indeed the Patent Act grants patents 'the attributes of personal property'.[116] The antitrust agencies also view patents as they do real property.[117] Just as the use of real property is constrained by other legal regimes, so too is a patentee's use of its intellectual property. A patentee must exercise its property right – its right to exclude – in a manner that is consistent with other laws. 'Patents are property, and entitled to the same rights and sanctions as other property.'[118] Nowhere does the Patent Act suggest otherwise. On the contrary, as the Supreme Court has explained, '[s]ince patents are privileges restrictive of a free economy, the rights which Congress has attached to them must be strictly construed so as not to derogate from the general law beyond the necessary requirements of the patent statute'.[119]

For that reason, the 'self-help' of exclusion through means that violate other laws, including the antitrust laws, cannot be justified later through a showing that the patentee could have won patent litigation (assuming such a showing were possible).[120] No one would argue that, by making an unproven accusation of patent infringement, a patentee becomes entitled to the 'self-help' remedy of confiscating the accused product in order to exclude it from the market. Confiscation violates other laws and is simply not a component of the patentee's exclusionary right, even if it does eventually prove infringement and the validity of its patent in court. The patentee obtained exclusion through the confiscation, not the exclusionary power of the patent.

Likewise the patentee's legitimate exercise of its right to exclude by either invoking state action and obtaining an injunction or obtaining the accused infringer's unilateral decision to acquiesce to the strength of the patent is entirely different from a patent holder's decision to buy off a potential challenger by an agreement to share supracompetitive returns, as occurs in the settlement of pharmaceutical patent litigation. When the patentee obtains exclusion through the 'self-help' remedy of paying an accused infringer to leave or not enter the market it obtains that exclusion through the power of the payment, not the exclusionary power of the patent. Purchasing a horizontal competitor's exclusion from the market violates the antitrust laws and nothing in the patent laws condones it. On the contrary, courts have long held that a patentee 'cannot extend his statutory [patent] grant by contract or agreement'.[121] A settlement, such as those including an exclusion payment, may be unlawful if the patent holder obtains 'protection from competition which the patent law, unaided by restrictive agreements, does not afford'.[122]

*(b)   The patent and not a payment must provide exclusion resulting from the agreement*   An attempt to justify exclusion payments entered in these

pharmaceutical patent settlement cases on the grounds that antitrust law allows other agreements that would be illegal absent the assertion of the patent misses the point that, in those cases, the source of the exclusion remains the exclusionary power of the patent rather than a payment. For example, a horizontal geographic market allocation would normally be a per se antitrust violation.[123] However, the Patent Act explicitly provides that a patentee may grant a licence to a limited territory, allowing it to establish a geographic market allocation.[124] In the face of the patentee's assertion of its patent rights, through litigation or otherwise, the licensee/accused infringer cedes territory to the patentee on the basis of its assessment of the probability that the patent might exclude it completely; that is, the patent's exclusionary power at the time of the agreement. Were the licensee to cede that territory, not because of the merits of the patentee's infringement allegations, but because the patentee offered it a payment to do so, the antitrust analysis of the agreement would change dramatically. The same principles apply to other 'market-allocations' allowed in patent licences, such as field-of-use restrictions and production limits.[125] The ability to impose such limitations is within the 'exclusionary right' of the patent owner because the patentee licenses only some portion of its bundle of property rights included within the patent grant. The licensee accepts limited competition due to the patent's strength. The antitrust analysis will differ according to whether the licensee agreed to the market allocation in recognition of the exclusionary power of the patent or, as revealed by an examination of the agreement and the market structure in which it arises, because the licensee was paid by the patentee to do so.[126]

These concepts are most easily understood in the context of a patent licensing negotiation. Those negotiations are conducted under a cloud of threatened, potential litigation. If the negotiation fails, the parties will likely become entangled in patent litigation.[127] For that reason, the terms of the licence are driven, at least in part, by the probability that the patentee could win the litigation by proving infringement and surviving a validity challenge.[128] A patentee's power to exclude accused infringers or to dictate the terms under which they may enter the market is never absolute and never described by the patentee's unilateral views of its patent coverage until it obtains a final, successful court judgment on validity and infringement. Until that time, the exclusionary power of the patent is tempered by the statistically high probability that either the patentee will fail to prove infringement or that the accused infringer will demonstrate invalidity.[129] Indeed, as explained above, generic drug manufacturers defeat charges of patent infringement 73 per cent of the time.[130] Thus, until a patentee has obtained a final, unappealable decision of validity and infringement, it is simply incorrect to accept the patentee's infringement allegations as describing the exclusionary power of its patent.[131] A brand pharmaceutical company's payment to a potential generic entrant cannot be justified by the exclusionary power of the patent simply because the brand accused the generic of patent infringement.

If the parties settle or avoid litigation by agreeing to a patent licence, the stronger the patentee's validity and infringement arguments, and the higher the probability that it will win the threatened litigation, the more advantageous the terms it can negotiate.[132] The licensee/accused infringer accepts a degree of limitation on its ability to compete freely in the market in proportion to its view of the patent merits and the probabilistic outcome of litigation. That degree of limitation reflects the exclusionary power of the patent. If the licensee/accused infringer seeks a licence of limited geographic territory, the territory might be smaller or larger, depending on the perceived strength of the patent. Analogously, the breadth of a field of use licence, the life-span of the licence and the royalty paid can all vary depending on the parties' views of the probable outcome of potential litigation. One economist has described patent rights as 'probabilistic' for this reason.[133]

An accused infringer/licensee might also agree to refrain from marketing its product for an agreed length of time in acknowledgment of the patent's exclusionary power. While such an agreement would be per se antitrust violation absent the patent dispute, antitrust allows it when the accused infringer's acquiescence and decision to refrain from competing for the agreed length of time is driven by views on the probable outcome of patent litigation, which determines the patent's exclusionary power at the time of the agreement. However, if the agreement is structured so that the patentee obtains some portion of its exclusion through a payment, even if some portion is also arguably obtained through the power of the patent, the agreement raises antitrust concerns.[134]

The FTC's consideration of the Schering/Upsher agreement illustrates this point. The FTC began its consideration of the exclusionary power of Schering's patent with the simple but fundamental principle that, short of a final court judgment on the issue, the parties' collective expectation of the outcome of their litigation – as reflected in a genuine, arm's-length settlement – represents the most accurate assessment of the subject patent's exclusionary power. The parties' litigation in this case would have fixed only the time of entry of the alleged infringers, because no money damages were at issue.[135] Therefore, *a hypothetical no-payment compromise* on the entry date would most accurately reflect their collectively expected outcome of litigation; that is, the exclusionary power of Schering's patent, and would not be illegal.[136]

Thus, any payment provision in the settlement agreements, beyond the expected savings in litigation costs,[137] will affect the compromise entry date in one direction or another: a payment from the alleged infringer to the patent holder – i.e., a royalty – would be made to gain an earlier entry than a compromise on the date alone. A payment of this kind is unremarkable and indisputably within the limits of a patent's exclusionary power. A payment in the opposite direction, however (an exclusion payment) purchases a *later* time of entry than a compromise on the date alone. A patentee would not make a substantial payment if it believed it could exclude the competition for that period solely on the basis of its patent.[138] This much more unusual form of payment raises serious antitrust concerns because its effect is to *extend* the patent holder's exclusivity beyond the exclusionary power of its patent and harm consumers by delaying the entry of low-cost generic drugs.[139]

In conclusion, as a leading article discussing pharmaceutical patent settlements explains, the right to exclude granted by a patent does not absolve exclusion payments from antitrust scrutiny:

> The legitimate exclusion value of a pharmaceutical patent is the power it actually conveys over competition, which is in turn a function of the scope of the patent and its chance of being held valid. What the pharmaceutical patentees who agree to exclusion payments seek is something more – a guaranteed insulation from competition, without the risk that the patent is held invalid. IP policy does not offer such a guarantee, and does not immunize from antitrust scrutiny those who seek it by entering into agreements that exclude potential competitors.[140]

*(c) The right to exclude is neither unbounded nor unconditional*   Patent policy does not establish the type of unbounded and unconditional right-to-exclude for patentees that those who defend exclusion payments as within the patent grant must invoke. Furthermore, the courts and Congress have incorporated strands of competition policy into patent policy and allowed antitrust concerns to limit the use of the patent right, so that patent policy extends beyond a pure incentive model to include some limitations on the right to exclude that cautions against allowing exclusion payments.[141]

For instance, the Patent Act does not establish a patentee's right to exclude even proven infringers as absolute and unyielding. The statute requires that a court consider the equities when deciding whether to grant an injunction. The equitable factors considered include: (1) whether the patentee would face irreparable injury if the injunction did not issue; (2) whether the patentee has an adequate remedy at law; (3) whether granting an injunction is in the public interest; and (4) whether the balance of hardships favours an injunction.[142] No one factor is dispositive, and a court need not give all factors equal weight.[143] The equitable factors considered in patent cases are the same as those that courts consider when deciding whether to grant an injunction in non-patent cases.[144] Although it is a 'general rule that an injunction will issue when infringement has been adjudged, absent a sound reason for denying it',[145] courts have deemed the 'principles of equity' to allow denial of a permanent injunction after a final judgment of infringement,[146] stays of an injunction pending appeal,[147] and delayed injunctions to allow time for the adoption of comparable, non-infringing devices.[148]

Moreover patent law limits a patentee's exclusionary right to the scope of the patent claims.[149] In the *Motion Picture Patents* case, the Supreme Court refused to enforce a licence in which a patentee sought to limit the use of its patented film projectors to only those non-patented films authorized by the patentee. One might argue that the patentee's statutory right to exclude gave it authority to design any condition on which it would license, but the Court rejected that view of the exclusionary right, holding that nothing in the patent law gives a patentee the right to condition the use of a patented invention with goods selected by the patentee.[150] Because that right is not within the patentee's bundle of rights, the tying condition must be judged by the general law, including the antitrust law.[151] Congress has recognized that the patent right to exclude does not allow a patentee having market power to tie sales of a commodity item to a patent licence.[152] 'Patent law creates a system of economic incentives designed to foster invention, but the incentive structure of patent law is not be augmented by leveraging the power of the patent.'[153]

Competition policy, like patent policy, also directly limits the use of patent rights. For example, some patent rights, clearly within the bundle of a patentee's property rights, are nevertheless limited by the antitrust laws in the same sense as the analogous real property rights. A patentee may assign or exclusively license its patent in the same way that an owner of real property may sell or lease its property. The patent laws expressly allow for exclusive licences and assignments of patent rights.[154] In spite of this, Section 7 of the Clayton Act[155] prohibits assignments and exclusive patent licences that harm competition by overly concentrating a market, just as it prohibits acquisitions of real property under those circumstances.[156]

In sum, exclusion payments provide 'a powerful inducement to abandon competition'.[157] By paying a generic to not enter until an agreed-upon date, a brand-name company induces the generic to accept what the force of its patent alone would not – forgoing patent challenges and staying off the market until the agreed-upon dates, several years into the future. An argument that such behaviour falls within the patentee's exclusionary right expands that right in a way that is unwarranted by either patent policy or competition policy's relationship to patents.

*Policy issues surrounding pharmaceutical patent settlements*
Some courts and commentators have argued that settlements including exclusion payments should be allowed on policy grounds, because prohibiting them would chill litigation settlements and undermine the value of a patent's incentive to innovate. As explained below, both fears are unwarranted. Rather, Hatch–Waxman's goal of encouraging generic entry and patent policy's goal of awarding an exclusionary right commensurate with the inventive contribution both caution against allowing exclusion payments.

*(a) Prohibiting exclusion payments will not chill patent settlements*   As the US antitrust enforcement agencies have recognized, the general policy of the law has been to encourage settlements.[158] Therefore some have worried that finding antitrust liability for patent settlements including exclusion payments will chill settlement activity.[159] Empirical data show this fear is unwarranted.

Preventing a brand-name drug company and its potential generic competitors from settling on terms including an exclusion payment not supported by efficiency justifications would not prevent them from using any number of other methods of reaching settlement. For example, a generic company may pay for the right to enter by taking an immediate licence, in which case it would be buying the right to compete instead of being paid not to compete, or the parties could split the patent life without a payment that purchases additional protection from competition.

To mitigate the possibility that brand-name and generic drug manufacturers might enter patent settlement agreements that could harm consumers, the FTC Generic Drug Study recommended that Congress pass legislation to require brand-name companies and generic applicants to provide copies of certain agreements to the FTC and the Department of Justice. Congress passed the Medicare Modernization Act, containing such a provision, in December 2003.[160] As a result of that legislation, during fiscal year 2004, drug manufacturers filed 14 agreements with the FTC that resolved patent infringement litigation. None of these included a payment from the brand to the generic manufacturer in exchange for the generic's agreement not to market its product.[161]

Those data indicating that 14 pharmaceutical patent litigation settlements were entered in a single year, fiscal year 2004, as compared to the 27 settlements entered between 1992 and 2002, suggest that a perceived prohibition on exclusion payments in settlements has not deterred parties from finding alternative, acceptable means to reach a settlement agreement. Moreover, of 20 final patent settlements between brand-name companies and first generic applicants identified by the FTC Generic Drug

Study, only nine included exclusion payments. Although settlements containing exclusion payments were prevalent in the pharmaceutical industry during this time, by no means were they the only mechanism used to achieve settlements.[162] Thus data from both the FTC Generic Drug Study and the agency's recent review of pharmaceutical patent litigation settlements indicate that condemnation of allegedly unjustified exclusion payments has not chilled settlement activity. The settlements filed with the FTC in 2004, after the FTC's *Schering* decision, show that legitimate patent settlements continue to take place without hindrance from the FTC decision.

*(b) Revisiting the merits of the patent litigation in the antitrust analysis would discourage settlements*    Some have argued that the exclusionary power of the patent can be properly assessed by a plenary trial on the issues of patent validity and infringement.[163] This approach views the exclusionary power of the patent in any given situation as binary rather than probabilistic: either the patent is valid and covers the accused product, or it is not. This approach presumes that, if the patent is valid and covers the accused product, patent policy allows the patentee to exclude the accused product from the market through means that would otherwise violate the antitrust laws, such as direct payment or market allocation. If the later review of the patent issues demonstrates either the patent's invalidity or non-infringement, the antitrust analysis need not consider the patent's exclusionary power and the agreement may violate the law.[164]

Such an approach disserves patentees and accused infringers equally, for they can never perform a satisfactory antitrust analysis of a settlement agreement as of the time they enter it and obtain the predictability and certainty that the settlement was meant to convey. The antitrust analysis will depend on a later court's view of the patent merits.[165] The parties have simply traded the uncertainty of the outcome of the patent litigation, based on the patent merits, for the uncertainty of the outcome of the antitrust litigation, based again on the patent merits.[166]

If the antitrust court were to find the patent valid and infringed, virtually any settlement into which the parties might enter, short of exclusion following the patent's expiration or of products falling outside the claim scope, could be deemed procompetitive compared to continuing litigation and, therefore, legal. On the other hand, if the antitrust court were to find the patent invalid or not infringed, a settlement that restrained the accused infringer in any way, as certainly most settlements would, would be deemed anticompetitive compared to continuing litigation and, therefore, illegal. The better approach, and the one that provides more respect for the patentee's exclusionary right, considers the exclusionary power of the patent, based on the parties' collective views on the probability of the outcome of the actual or anticipated patent litigation at the time of the agreement.

*(c) Prohibiting exclusion payments is consistent with patent policy* Some have worried that prohibiting exclusion payments would lessen the value of the patent and undermine the patent system's incentive to innovate.[167] This concern misunderstands that exclusion payments actually distort the patent system's incentive structure by allowing the patentee rights not granted by Congress.

Patent policy provides that the exclusionary power of the patent is proportionate to the inventor's contribution to his field. If a patented invention is truly revolutionary compared to the prior art, the patent claims are much more likely to be found novel and nonobvious over the prior art than are claims reciting only a minor distinction. Moreover, the claims protecting a pioneering invention will be interpreted broadly to cover a wide range of possibly infringing products as compared to claims protecting a minor improvement.[168] Thus, patent policy intends that claim scope and strength will be governed by the extent of the inventive contribution. That policy encourages greater leaps of technological innovation.[169] It would be contrary to that fundamental policy of patent law to allow a patentee to supplement the exclusionary power of its patent with exclusion payments. Such payments give the patentee a degree of market control that its inventive contribution could not provide and distort the patent system's incentive structure as established by Congress. By enacting the patent laws:

> Congress has implicitly balanced the trade-off between the static efficiency of competition and the low prices against the dynamic efficiency of increased incentives to seek patentable innovations. A proper economic welfare analysis of patent rights must take as given the patent rules specified by Congress with the presumption that those rules properly and correctly balance static and dynamic efficiency.[170]

A rule that allows a patentee to pay a competitor not to compete solely on the basis of an untested allegation of patent infringement reaches beyond the 'right to exclude' granted by Congress in the Patent Act and disrupts that balance.

*(d) Exclusion payments undermine the policies of the Hatch–Waxman Act* Congress intended the Hatch–Waxman Act to increase the flow of generic pharmaceuticals into the marketplace and the purpose and effect of exclusion payments is to stymie that flow. In the Hatch–Waxman Act, Congress struck a carefully considered balance between maintaining the incentives for innovation of new drug products and promoting significantly lower-priced

generic drugs.[171] Important elements in this balance were provisions that made it easier and more lucrative for generics to challenge the validity and scope of pharmaceutical patents. The brand company patentee and the generic challenger typically litigate the patent issues before a generic enters the market.[172] Most importantly, the statute provides a powerful incentive to generics to challenge weak and narrow patents in the form of a 180-day marketing exclusivity awarded to the first generic company to take on that challenge.[173] The principal goal of these provisions is to encourage generic drug manufacturers to challenge weak or narrow patents and enter the market as soon as possible.

Some have justified exclusion payments in the settlement of pharmaceutical patent litigation as 'a natural by-product of the Hatch–Waxman process'.[174] This rationale turns the Hatch–Waxman process on its head by interpreting provisions designed to *promote* patent challenges by generics to justify payments to *avoid* patent challenges.[175] Congress recognized that exclusion payments undermine the policies of the Hatch–Waxman Act when it passed the 2003 Medicare amendments to Hatch–Waxman, which require that patent litigation settlement agreements between brand and generic companies be reported to the antitrust agencies.[176] As the legislative history for that provision states:

> the industry has recently witnessed the creation of pacts between big pharmaceutical firms and makers of generic versions of brand name drugs that are intended to keep lower-cost drugs off the market. Agreeing with smaller rivals to delay or limit competition is an abuse of the Hatch–Waxman law that was intended to promote generic alternatives.[177]

Thus, properly understood, exclusion payments can undermine broad Congressional purposes, something the 2003 amendments to the Hatch–Waxman Act recognize.

*Summary*
A careful examination of some recent pharmaceutical patent litigation settlement agreements conducted within the context of the market structure in which generic entry would occur reveals that payments from the brand-name drug company to a potential generic entrant are payments made to ensure that generic entry will not occur until an agreed-upon date. By examining the Patent Act and other aspects of patent policy, we have shown that the right to 'buy-off' a potential competitor that one has only accused of infringement does not fall within a patentee's right to exclude. We have also explained how the prevention of potential, albeit uncertain, competition can be anticompetitive. Both principles are critical in the proper antitrust analysis of patent settlement agreements containing exclusion payments.

**General conclusions**
The patent–antitrust interface is and will remain one of the most complicated areas of competition policy analysis. In recent decades American antitrust policy commendably has overcome its traditional hostility to patent rights and recognized that patent law, like antitrust law, is a powerful tool for promoting welfare. Nevertheless, it would be wrong to exalt patent law over other forms of property; as is the case of other property law schemes, patent law must remain fully within the reach of antitrust law, to prevent anticompetitive restrictions that harm welfare. Indeed, because a lack of competitive vigour discourages the dynamic economic rivalry that encourages business experimentation, largely exempting patent-related arrangements from antitrust scrutiny would retard, rather than encourage, the innovation that the Patent Act seeks to achieve.

Taking into account these considerations, we have explored two contentious topics that implicate patent and competition policy: the treatment of ex ante price-related negotiations involving SSOs and patent holders, and patent litigation settlements involving 'exclusion payments' by patentees. As we have shown, allowing ex ante negotiations does not undermine patent rights holders, it merely restrains patentees from receiving excessive and economically inefficient returns due to ex post 'hold-ups'. Moreover, barring anticompetitive exclusion payments in settlement negotiations does not discourage efficient settlements; it merely prevents collusive bargains that delay entry and harm consumer welfare. In reaching these conclusions, we took due note of the peculiar characteristics of patent property rights, namely the fact that they are more 'probabilistic' in nature than other property rights.

This analysis does not derogate from the dignity of patent rights, it merely reflects the careful, issue-specific evaluation that is required to ensure that an appropriate balance is struck in jointly applying the antitrust and patent laws. In these and other areas at the patent–antitrust interface, a careful balancing of antitrust and patent considerations should yield outcomes that promote consumer welfare and innovation, consistent with the general policy goals of both legal regimes. These observations, we maintain, are general principles that apply, not just within the United States, but to the antitrust and patent systems of other nations as well.

**Notes**
1. Alden F. Abbott is Associate Director, Bureau of Competition, Federal Trade Commission, Washington, D.C. Suzanne Michel and Armando Irizarry serve respectively, as Deputy Assistant Director and Counsel for Intellectual Property within the Federal Trade Commission, Burerau of Competition, Office of Policy and Coordination. The views expressed below are their own and do not necessarily represent the views of the Federal Trade Commission or any Federal Trade Commissioner. Mr.

Abbott prepared the final version of this chapter during the spring of 2005 while on sabbatical at All Souls College, Oxford.

2. We use the terms 'antitrust law' and 'competition law' interchangeably in this chapter, although the 'competition laws' may be deemed to go beyond the antitrust laws to encompass as well all other legal rules that promote market processes. Thus 'competition policy' refers to the full panoply of legal institutions that promote reliance on markets, rather than government, to guide the use of society's resources. Although 'intellectual property law' encompasses a variety of legal schemes (including, for example, patent, trademark, copyright, and trade secret law), this chapter focuses on patent law, that branch of intellectual property law that creates general federal statutory incentives for innovation. Patent law historically has been viewed as being in great tension with competition law.

3. This stereotypical generalization was never entirely accurate; patents typically do not confer monopoly power in an economic sense, and in the past (prior to the injection of economic analysis into competition policy), antitrust law often did more to create artificial impediments to efficient business transactions than to correct 'monopolistic' interferences with efficient market transactions.

4. See Federal Trade Commission (Oct. 2003), *To Promote Innovation: The Proper Balance of Competition and Patent Law and Policy*, (hereinafter 'FTC Competition-Patent Report'), available at http://www.ftc.gov/os/2003/10/innovationrpt.pdf.

5. The term 'innovation' refers in this chapter to economic growth (encompassing both increases in the quantity and improvements in the quality of output) that is brought forth by technological change. The term 'welfare' is used herein to refer to 'total surplus' that is, the difference between the value (measured in a unit of account, such as a currency) of goods or services produced in a market and the costs of producing those goods or services. Total surplus is divided between 'consumers' surplus' (the aggregate difference between consumers' willingness to pay for the output of the market and what they are charged) and 'producers' surplus' (profits plus 'Ricardian rents,' the return to a scarce productive asset apart from profits). For a good recent summary of these concepts, see Ross, Thomas W. and Ralph A. Winter (2005), 'The efficiency defense in merger law: economic foundations and recent Canadian developments', *Antitrust L.J.*, 72, 471, at 473–4. I will not delve into the policy debate as to whether antitrust law should promote 'total surplus maximization' or 'consumer welfare maximization'; as a practical matter, under most circumstances, policies that advance total surplus maximization generally are consistent with the maximization of consumers' surplus.

6. This conclusion follows from the words of the patent and copyright clause of Article I, Section 8, Clause 8 of the United States Constitution, which seeks 'To promote the Progress of Science and useful Arts, by securing for limited Times to Authors and Inventors the exclusive Right to their respective Writings and Discoveries'. Thus property interests flowing from patent grants (arguably unlike certain other property rights) would not seem to be accorded the dignity of 'natural rights' that merit protection regardless of their utility in advancing science and technology.

7. Significantly, Landes and Posner, two leading market-oriented proponents of strong property rights, have argued that '[e]quating intellectual property rights to physical property rights overlooks the much greater governmental involvement in the former domain than in the latter . . . Government is continuously involved in the creation of intellectual property rights through the issuance of patents, copyrights and trademarks. Skeptics of government should hesitate to extend a presumption of efficiency to a process by which government grants rights to exclude competition with the holders of the rights'. See Landes, William M. and Richard A. Posner (2004), *The Political Economy of Intellectual Property Law* at 23–4, available at http://www.aei-brookings.org/admin/authorpdfs/page.php?id=985.

8. Note 4, above.

9. Licensing difficulties include 'defensive patenting' by third parties in response to questionable patents. As patents proliferate, the costly 'stacking' of royalty claims on multiple patents looms increasingly serious. The 'patent thickets' that result from such

activities raise the costs of agreements among technology developers and thereby retard contractual arrangements aimed at increasing the flow of innovation.

10. That the proliferation of patents (documented in the Report) raises concerns should not be read to suggest that 'mass patenting' by corporations has no possible efficiency explanations. One scholar, Paul J. Heald of the University of Georgia Law School, has argued that patenting may (1) reduce information costs to firms, by allowing them to assemble a portfolio of rights that signals information about themselves more cheaply than by other means; (2) prevent other firms from obtaining technological inputs necessary to the first firm's production; (3) reduce the cost of monitoring team production (patent output may be a useful, albeit imperfect, measure of the contribution of individual team members); and (4) effectively partition information assets (patent assets can readily be transferred under a liability regime that does not require the transferee to enter into costly protective agreements and that creates statutory 'gap filler' rules). See Heald, Paul J. (2005), 'A transaction costs theory of patent law', available at http://papers.ssrn.com/sol3/papers.cfm?abstract_id=385841 (posted April 2003) in **66**, *Ohio State Law Journal*, 3, 473–510. Heald's theory suggests that patent law may be seen as a cost-reducing title recording system that promotes the efficient transfer of information assets. Although this theory may be interesting, it lacks much empirical support at this time; in contrast, the FTC Competition-Patent Report refers to substantial testimony documenting the costs of patent proliferation. Future empirical work may shed light on the extent to which industry-specific patent proliferation is more beneficial than harmful.

11. This point has been made by Professor Carl Shapiro: Shapiro, Carl (2003), 'Antitrust limits to patent settlements', *Rand J. Econ.*, **34**, 391, at 407–8.

12. Obviously, the scope of property rights other than patents may be less than certain, but, in general, there is far less uncertainty about the coverage of such rights, particularly rights to tangible property. For example, the right to possess an automobile is merely a question of who holds title, and the extent of the rights covering a plot of land turns on relatively straightforward questions, such as the existence and location of an easement or a boundary line. The boundaries of a complex, patent-protected industrial process or processes may be far less clear.

13. Whether the patent was issued erroneously because it did not meet the statutory standards for patentability is a separate issue, best resolved through patent reforms that improve patent accuracy by, for example, facilitating simple post-grant appeals. As already discussed, antitrust authorities are not well-positioned to cure the problem of 'bad patents'. Of course, if a court or an administrative body strikes down a patent, property rights-based objections to antitrust enforcement are eliminated.

14. Lemley, Mark A. (2002), 'Intellectual property rights and standard-setting organizations', *Cal. L. Rev.*, **90**, 1889, at 1896.

15. Breitenberg, Maureen A. (1987), 'The ABC's of standards-related activities in the United States', *NISTIR*, 6014, at 4 (citing American Standards Association (1972), 'Through history with standards', in Rowen Glie (ed.), *Speaking of Standards*), available at: http://ts.nist.gov/ts/htdocs/210/ncsci/primer.htm (hereinafter 'Breitenberg').

16. Governments may develop their own standards or endorse and adopt private standards through the passage of laws or regulations.

17. For example, the American Society of Mechanical Engineers ('ASME') was founded in 1880; the origins of the Institute of Electrical and Electronics Engineers ('IEEE') can be traced back to 1884; the American Society for Testing and Materials ('ASTM') can be traced back to 1898.

18. Breitenberg, at 4.

19. See Mueller, Janice M. (2003), 'Symposium: patent system reform: patent misuse through the capture of industry standards', *Berkeley Tech. L.J.*, **17**, 623, at 631–2; Hansen, Marc et al. (Dec. 2003), 'Disclosure and negotiation of licensing terms prior to adoption of industry standards: preventing another patent ambush?', *Eur. Competition L. Rev.*; Skitol, Robert A. (2005), 'Concerted buying power: its potential for addressing the patent holdup problem in standard setting', *Antitrust L. J.*, **72**(2), 727, at 730 (explaining that the patent

holdup problem 'arises from the interaction of (1) proliferating patents generally and (2) proliferating needs for standards to enable interoperability among both competing and complementary products seeking to exploit new technologies').

20.  Mueller, above, note 19, at 633 (referring to highly recommended standards as 'consensual').

21.  Lemley, above, note 14, at 1896–7 (discussing network markets).

22.  For example, during the 1980s VCR war between Beta and VHS technology for the de facto standard in home videocassette recording technology, the losers of the war had to reinvest in this technology by buying a VHS player. Their Beta-formatted cassettes also lost substantial value.

23.  SSO participants will continue to compete in downstream product and service markets throughout the standard-setting process. Ideally, after development and acceptance of an efficient standard, this competition will continue, but at a reduced social cost (competitors will no longer face uncertainty about what standard to employ in production, and consumers will no longer run the risk that they are buying a product embodying a 'loser' standard that will soon be superseded). There is some risk, however, that welfare would have been greater absent an SSO-developed standard, if competition among standards had yielded a de facto standard superior (in welfare terms) to the SSO-developed standard. This is, however, basically a theoretical concern; there generally is no way to determine that the absence of an SSO standard would have yielded this superior result. Another serious competitive concern, which is beyond the scope of this chapter, is that collusion among members of an SSO may lead to development of a standard that favours their product design and excludes potentially more efficient technologies employed by firms outside the association that dominates the standard-setting body. See *Allied Tube & Conduit Corp.* v. *Indian Head*, 486 U.S. 492 (1988) (makers of steel conduit 'packed' SSO meeting with its agents and thereby obtained SSO decision disapproving plastic conduit for building construction).

24.  Lemley, above, note 14, at 1897 (discussing tipping effect).

25.  For purposes of the following discussion, the allegations set forth in the initial *Rambus* and *Unocal* administrative complaints are treated as accurate. The ultimate disposition of these allegations in the *Rambus* matter rests upon the final results of ongoing administrative litigation. For the text of the *Rambus* and *Unocal* complaints, respectively, see *In the Matter of Rambus, Inc.*, Docket No. 9302 (June 18, 2002) ('*Rambus* Complaint'), available at http://www.ftc.gov/os/2002/06/rambuscmp.htm; *In the Matter of Union Oil Company of California*, Docket No. 9305 (March 4, 2003) ('*Unocal* Complaint'), available at http://www.ftc.gov/os/2003/03/unocalcmp.htm. On 10 June 2005, the FTC announced a settlement of the *Unocal* matter in connection with the settlement of Chevron Corporation's proposed acquisition of Unocal. As noted below in the text following discussion of the Rambus matter, this settlement will prevent future competitive harm from the Unocal patent 'holdup' by precluding Unocal from enforcing the reformulated gasoline patents in question. See FTC Press Release, 'Dual consent orders resolve competitive concerns about Chevron's $18 billion purchase of Unocal, FTC's 2003 Complaint Against Unocal' (June 10, 2005), available at http://www.ftc.gov/opa/2005/06/chevronunocal.htm. See also *In the Matter of Union Oil Company of California*, Docket No. 9305 (10 June 2005) (Agreement Containing Consent Order), available at http://www.ftc.gov/os/adjpro/d9305/050610agreement9305.pdf.

26.  'JEDEC' is an acronym for Joint Electron Device Engineering Council.

27.  *Rambus* Complaint at para. 19.

28.  *Rambus* Complaint at para. 20.

29.  SDRAM is an acronym for synchronous dynamic random access memory.

30.  *Rambus* Complaint at para. 71.

31.  *Unocal* Complaint at para. 16.

32.  Unocal eventually received five patents related to RFG.

33.  Federal Trade Commission & United States Department of Justice, *Antitrust Guidelines for Collaboration Among Competitors* (2000), at §1.2 (hereinafter 'Joint Venture Guidelines'). Application of rule of reason analysis under the Guidelines to ex ante

negotiations is set forth below in the text accompanying notes 42–4 and 46–7. The antitrust analysis applied to agreements among competitors is described in somewhat more 'contemporary' language in the discussion preceding the evaluation of exclusion payments made in settlements; see notes 59–64, below. Both strands of analysis, however, embody essentially the same approach and, properly applied, should produce the same results. Given the fact that SSO price-related negotiations might at first blush (albeit incorrectly) appear to involve the traditional per se rule, I found it useful to employ the slightly more traditional analysis in discussing ex ante negotiations. In its 2003 *Polygram* opinion, the FTC eschewed the binary 'per se' and 'rule of reason' categories, in favour of a more nuanced approach in which conduct among competitors would be evaluated along a spectrum and a multi-step framework would be followed to guide analysis. Specifically, in evaluating an allegedly collusive horizontal agreement, *Polygram* indicates that an antitrust assessment should proceed as follows: (1) ask first if the agreement is 'inherently suspect' (behaviour that past judicial experience and current economic learning have shown to warrant summary condemnation) (if it is not inherently suspect, full rule of reason treatment is warranted); (2) if it is inherently suspect, then defendant can avoid summary condemnation only by articulating a legitimate justification that is cognizable (consistent with the goal of antitrust law to further competition) and plausible (cannot be rejected without extensive factual inquiry) (if defendant does not articulate such a justification, then the case is over); (3) if defendant does articulate a cognizable and plausible justification, then plaintiff must make a more detailed showing that the restraints are indeed likely, in the particular context, to harm competition; and (4) if plaintiff has not met its burden of persuasion on the first step (agreement inherently suspect) or one of the next two (either no justification or actual anticompetitive effects almost certain), then one goes to a full rule of reason test. For the FTC's *Polygram* opinion, see *In the Matter of Polygram Holding, Inc. et al.*, FTC Docket No. 9298 (24 July 2003), available at: http://www.ftc.gov/os/2003/07/polygramopinion.pdf. Although we applaud *Polygram's* enlightened and structured approach to analyzing agreements among competitors, it has not yet been formally adopted by courts or agencies other than the FTC. Accordingly, we employ the more traditional framework in assessing ex ante price-related negotiations involving SSOs. A rough and ready application of the *Polygram* framework, however, might suggest that ex ante price-related negotiations (1) are inherently suspect, but (2) have a cognizable and plausible efficiency justification, and (3) cannot be shown on detailed examination to be likely to harm competition, and (4) generally should pass muster under a full rule of reason analysis.

34. Joint Venture Guidelines at §1.2.
35. Joint Venture Guidelines at §1.2 (footnotes omitted).
36. The ex ante negotiations on which we focus are price-related negotiations (usually regarding royalties) with respect to patents that might arguably relate to the future implementation by producers of a standard under consideration by the SSO. Ex ante negotiations that are not reasonably related to the development of an SSO standard – but, instead, relate to downstream product markets that will employ the standard – are still illegal. Thus, for example, ex ante negotiations on fixing outputs or 'shar[ing] or divid[ing] markets by allocating customers, suppliers, territories or lines of commerce' for products made according to a standard would be illegal, whether conducted inside or outside an SSO.
37. It is assumed that the patent holder is also a participant in the SSO's standard-setting process. We do not address the situation where a patent holder that does not participate in the SSO's standard-setting process holds up the industry after the standard is adopted.
38. *Broadcast Music, Inc.* v. *Columbia Broadcasting System*, 441 U.S. 1, 8–9 (1979) (explaining that price fixing under the antitrust laws means something different than the literal meaning of fixing a price) (hereinafter *BMI*).
39. *BMI*, 441 U.S. at 9.
40. *BMI*, 441 U.S. at 8. Sherman Act is the name of the US antitrust law.
41. *BMI*, 441 U.S. at 9.

42. Joint Venture Guidelines at §1.2.
43. Joint Venture Guidelines at §1.2.
44. Joint Venture Guidelines at §2.1.
45. A discussion of the IEEE's standard-setting work is available at http://www.ieee.org/portal/site.
46. Joint Venture Guidelines at §2.2.
47. Joint Venture Guidelines at §2.2.
48. The concerns about patent quality, and the notion that patents are 'uncertain' or 'probabilistic' property rights, noted earlier, may serve as 'trump cards' that reinforce the inclination against antitrust challenges to legitimate ex ante negotiations.
49. Lemley, Mark A. (2001), 'Rational Ignorance at the Patent Office', *Nw. U.L. Rev.*, **95**, 1495, at 1501.
50. We refer to an agreement among competitors that furthers efficiency and enhances consumer welfare as procompetitive. We refer to an agreement that does not plausibly further efficiency and harms consumers as anticompetitive. See, for example, *Federal Trade Commission v. Indiana Federation of Dentists*, 476 U.S. 447, 459 (1986) (hereinafter *IFD*).
51. *In the Matter of Schering-Plough Corp.*, Dkt. No. 9297 (Opinion of the Commission) (Dec. 18, 2003), at 37, available at http://www.ftc.gov/os/adjpro/d9297/031218 commissionopinion.pdf (hereinafter *FTC Schering Op.*).
52. Tom, Willard K. and Joshua A. Newberg (1997), 'Antitrust and intellectual property: from separate spheres to unified field', *Antitrust L.J.*, **66**, 167, at 174–5; Federal Trade Comm'n & United States Dep't of Justice, *Antitrust Guidelines for the Licensing of Intellectual Property* at §2.3 (1995) (discussing the procompetitive benefits of licensing), available at: http://www.usdog.gov/atr/public/guidelines/ipguide. pdf (hereinafter 'IP Licensing Guidelines'); see also Hoerner, Robert J. (1998), 'Antitrust pitfalls in patent litigation settlement agreements', *Fed. Circuit B.J.*, **8**, 113, at 115 (patent settlement agreements will be analyzed similarly to patent licensing agreements).
53. IP Licensing Guidelines, above, note 52, at §5.5 ('Settlements involving the cross-licensing of intellectual property rights can be an efficient means to avoid litigation and, in general, courts favor such settlements.').
54. E.g., *Aro Corp. v. Allied Witan Co.*, 531 F.2d1368, 1372 (6th Cir. 1976) ('Public policy strongly favors settlement of disputes without litigation. Settlement is of particular value in patent litigation, the nature of which is often inordinately complex and time consuming.').
55. *United States v. Masonite Corp.*, 316 U.S. 265 (1942).
56. *In re Cardizem CD Antitrust Litig.*, 332 F.3d 896 (6th Cir. 2003).
57. *Schering-Plough Corp. v. FTC*, 2005 WL 528439 (11th Cir. 2005); see also *Valley Drug Co. v. Geneva Pharmaceuticals, Inc.*, 344 F.3d 1294 (11th Cir. 2003). In our view, jurisprudence in this area is far from settled. Accordingly, we will not delve into the details of particular cases brought by the FTC and other plaintiffs in this area but, rather, will focus on more general principles that inform the evaluation of settlement agreements including exclusion payments.
58. Contrast Hovenkamp, Herbert, Mark Lemley and Mark Janis (2003), 'Anticompetitive settlement of intellectual property disputes', *Minn. L. Rev.*, **87**, 1719, at 1759 (arguing that a payment from a patentee to an infringement defendant for the latter's exit from the market is presumptively unlawful), with Crane, Daniel A. (2002), 'Exit payments in settlement of patent infringement lawsuits: antitrust rules and economic implications', *Fla. L. Rev.*, **54**, 747 (arguing that exclusion payments should be permitted when the likelihood of success of the patentee's infringement suit is high).
59. *State Oil Co. v. Khan*, 522 U.S. 3, 10 (1997) ('Although the Sherman Act, by its terms, prohibits every agreement in "restraint of trade", this Court has long recognized that Congress intended to outlaw only unreasonable restraints.').
60. *BMI*, 441 U.S. at 19–20.
61. See *California Dental Assn'n v. FTC*, 526 U.S. 756, 781 (1999) ('What is required . . . is an enquiry meet for the case, looking to the circumstances, details, and logic of a

restraint.') (hereinafter, *CDA*); see also *In re PolyGram Holding, Inc.*, FTC Docket No. 9298 at 13–29 (discussing development of a continuum of analysis in the jurisprudence of horizontal restraints).

62. *NCAA v. Bd. Regents Okla. Univ.*, 468 U.S. 85, 109 (1984) (quoting *Nat'l Soc'y of Prof'l Eng'rs* v. *United States*, 435 U.S. 679, 692 (1978)).

63. *CDA*, 526 U.S. at 774–8; see also *In re PolyGram Holding, Inc.* FTC Docket No. 9298 at 22–4, 29–36 (discussing an analytical framework that considers whether an agreement is inherently suspect and proffered efficiency justifications before determining whether the full balancing test of the rule of reason is required).

64. *NCAA*, 468 U.S. at 101–3.

65. *Valley Drug*, 355 F.3d at 1306 (citing *SCM Corp.* v. *Xerox Corp.*, 645 F.2d 1195, 1207 (2d Cir. 1981)). Were this not the case, intervening events, such as the potential entrant's plant burning down, would absolve parties that had entered clearly anticompetitive agreements not to compete from antitrust liability. Evidence of the actual effects of an agreement may be highly probative of an agreement's likely affect on competition when entered, however. See ABA Section of Antitrust Law (2002), *Antitrust Law Developments* at 877 (collecting cases). For instance, evidence of the effect of actual generic entry on prices and market share is highly probative of the competitive conditions the parties pre-empted through an agreement to delay generic entry.

66. The market structure in which generic entry occurs creates an incentive for the parties to delay generic entry even when that entry is uncertain to occur. Because generic drugs sell for less than their branded counterparts, generic entry causes the branded company to lose more in profits than the generic company earns, with the difference accruing as consumer savings. A brand company could pay a generic to delay market entry more than the generic would earn by entering, and still be better off than if it faced competition. *FTC Schering Op.* at 21–2.

67. E.g., *Schering-Plough Corp.*, 2005 WL 528439 at 15 ('By entering into the settlement agreements, Schering realized the full potential of its infringement suit – a determination that the '743 patent was valid and that ESI and Upsher would not infringe the patent in the future'); Schildkraut, Marc (2004), 'Patent-splitting settlements and the reverse payment fallacy', *Antitrust L.J.*, **71**, 1033, at 1047–50 (acknowledging the loss of uncertain competition from settlements including exclusion payments).

68. In patent litigations, the patentee bears the burden of proving that the accused product infringes its patent by a preponderance of evidence. See *Envirotech Corp.* v. *Al George, Inc.*, 730 F.2d 753, 758 (Fed. Cir. 1984).

69. Patstats, US Patent Litigation Statistics, University of Houston Law Center, available at http://www.patstats.org/2003.html.

70. Moore, Kimberly A. (2000), 'Judges, juries, and patent cases – an empirical peek inside the black box', *Mich. L. Rev.*, **99**, 365, at 385.

71. 35 U.S.C. §282 ('A patent shall be presumed valid').

72. *Magnivision, Inc.*, v. *Bonneau Co.*, 115 F.3d 956, 960 (Fed. Cir. 1997); 35 U.S.C. §282 ('A patent shall be presumed valid', but, '[i]nvalidity of the patent' shall be a defense in any patent suit).

73. Allison, John R. and Mark A. Lemley (1998), 'Empirical evidence on the validity of litigated patents', *AIPLA Q. J.*, **26**, 185, at 205–6.

74. Patstats, US Patent Litigation Statistics, University of Houston Law Center, available at http://www.patstats.org/2003.html.

75. *Stratoflex, Inc.* v. *Aeroquip Corp.*, 713 F.2d 1530, 1534 (Fed. Cir. 1983). 'It is well-settled that an accused infringer carries the burden of providing invalidity by clear and convincing evidence', *Electromotive Div. of GMC* v. *Transp. Sys. Div. of GE*, 417 F.3d 1203, 1212, n.2 (Fed. Cir. 2005)

76. *W.L. Gore & Assocs, Inc.* v. *Garlock, Inc.*, 721 F.2d 1540, 1553 (Fed. Cir. 1983).

77. Federal Trade Commission (July 2002), *Generic Drug Entry Prior to Patent Expiration: An FTC Study*, at 15–16, available at http://www.ftc.gov/os/2002/07/genericdrugstudy.pdf (hereinafter 'FTC Generic Drug Study').

78. Hovenkamp, Herbert (2004), 'Sensible antitrust rules for pharmaceutical competition', *U.S.F. L. Rev.*, **39**, 11, at 28.

79. Cotter, Thomas F. (2003), 'Refining the "presumptive illegality" approach to settlements of patent disputes involving reverse payments', *Minn. L. Rev.*, **87**, 1789, at 1808–9; Crane, above, note 58 at 774 ('The "directional flow" of the settlement payment, therefore, will be affected by the probability of the plaintiff's lawsuit succeeding').
80. Hovenkamp et al., above, note 58, at 1758 (discussing this feature of Cotter and Crane's arguments).
81. Cotter, above, note 79, at 1806.
82. *In re Ciprofloxacin Hydrochloride Antitrust Litigation*, 2005 WL 736605 at 17 (E.D.N.Y. 2005) ('Plaintiffs' point is well-taken that the greater the chance a court would hold the patent invalid, the higher the likelihood that the patentee will seek to salvage a patent by settling with an exclusion payment'); see Priest, George L. (1977), 'Cartels and patent license arrangements', *J. L. & Econ.*, **20**, 309, at 327 (arguing that rational patentees will not reduce the royalty below zero unless they are cartelizing an industry).
83. *United States* v. *Griffith*, 334 U.S. 100 (1948), overruled on other grounds, *Copperweld Corp.* v. *Independence Tube Corp.*, 467 U.S. 752 (1984).
84. See e.g., *Blackburn* v. *Sweeney*, 53 F.3d 825 (7th Cir. 1995) (unlawful for attorneys to agree not to advertise in one another's cities); *Engine Specialties, Inc.* v. *Bombardier Ltd.*, 605 F.2d 1 (1st Cir. 1979) (unlawful for maker of snowmobiles and maker of minicycles to agree that the former would not enter the latter's market); but see, Schildkraut, above, note 67, at 1049 ('[u]ncertain competition analysis is a substantial depature from the traditional civil burdens of proof').
85. Areeda, Phillip E. and Herbert Hovenkamp (1999), *Antitrust Law* ¶2030b at 175 (hereinafter 'Areeda & Hovenkamp').
86. 246 U.S. 231, 238 (1918). Uncertainty about the time of entry may influence a plaintiff's ability to prove damages but does not alter the analysis of liability. See, e.g., *United States* v. *Microsoft Corp.*, 253 F.3d 34, 79–80 (D.C. Cir. 2001) (per curiam) (distinguishing liability and remedy); *Andrx* v. *Biovail*, 256 F.3d 799, 806, 808 (D.C. Cir. 2001) (holding plaintiff need establish only threat of injury to have standing for injunctive relief); *Microbix Biosys., Inc.* v. *BioWhittaker, Inc.*, 172 F. Supp. 2d 680, 694–5 (D. Md. 2000) (distinguishing damages inquiry from assessment of competitive effects for purposes of assessing liability under rule of reason), aff'd on other grounds, 2001 WL 603416 (4th Cir. 2001).
87. *IFD*, 476 U.S. at 461–2.
88. See, e.g., *Microbix*, 172 F. Supp. 2d at 694–5 (an exclusive supply agreement that created a barrier to competition at the time it was entered into could be condemned under the rule of reason, even though subsequent action by the FDA made it impossible for the target of the exclusionary conduct to enter the market).
89. 253 F.3d 34 (D.C. Cir. 2001) (per curiam).
90. Ibid. at 79 (emphasis in original).
91. Ibid.
92. A delay in generic entry undisputedly delays consumer access to a lower-priced drug product. An agreement to delay or prevent generic entry, if proven, provides direct evidence of anticompetitive effects that makes a conventional product market analysis unnecessary. IFD, 476 U.S. at 461 ('the finding of actual, sustained adverse effects on competition . . . is legally sufficient to support a finding that the challenged restraint was unreasonable even in the absence of elaborate market analysis') (footnotes omitted); see also Cramer, Eric L. and Daniel Berger (2004), 'The superiority of direct proof of monopoly power and anticompetitive effects in antitrust cases involving delayed entry of generic drugs', *U.S.F.L. Rev.*, **39**, 81.
93. Hovenkamp et al., above, note 58 at 1759 n.176.
94. Ibid. at 1758; Leffler, Keith and Cristofer Leffler (2004), 'Efficiency trade-offs in patent litigation settlements: analysis gone astray?', *U.S.F. L. Rev.*, **39**, 33, at 53 ('it is anticompetitive for an incumbent manufacturer to enter into an agreement to eliminate potential competition, based on the probability that the competition would in fact have occurred').
95. *IFD*, 476 U.S. at 461–2.

96. 253 F.3d at 79.
97. *Lee Moore Oil Co.* v. *Union Oil Co.*, 599 F.2d 1299, 1302 (4th Cir. 1979) ('the fact that [the defendant] might have caused the same damages' by unilateral conduct is 'irrelevant').
98. 374 U.S. 174, 197 (1963) (White J concurring) (emphasis added).
99. Ibid. (White J concurring) (emphasis added).
100. 374 U.S. at 199 (emphasis added).
101. *FTC Schering Op.* at 38–9.
102. See IP Licensing Guidelines at §3.4 (1995) ('To determine whether a particular restraint in a licensing arrangement is given per se or rule of reason treatment, the Agencies will assess whether the restraint in question can be expected to contribute to an efficiency-enhancing integration of economic activity').
103. For a response dismissing additional proposed hypothetical and generalized procompetitive justifications for settlements including exclusion payments, see Hovenkamp, Herbert, Mark D. Janis and Mark A. Lemley (2004), 'Balancing ease and accuracy in assessing pharmaceutical exclusion payments', *Minn. L. Rev.*, **88**, 712, at 714–18.
104. *Schering-Plough Corp.*, 2005 WL 528439; see also *Valley Drug Co.*, 344 F.3d 1294; Crane, above, note 58 (arguing that exclusion payments should be permitted when the likelihood of success of the patentee's infringement suit is high).
105. 35 U.S.C. §154(a)(1). The basis for that statutory right is found in Article I, Section 8, Clause 8 of the United States Constitution, which gives Congress the power '[t]o promote the Progress of Science and useful Arts, by securing for limited Times to Authors and Inventors the exclusive Right to their respective Writings and Discoveries'.
106. *Bonito Boats, Inc.*, v. *Thunder Craft Boats, Inc.*, 489 U.S. 141, 150–51 (1988).
107. See, e.g., Merges, Robert P. et al. (2003), *Intellectual Property in the New Technological Age*, at 13.
108. In addition, the patentee may license the patent and obtain compensation for the use of its property, rather than exclude all infringers. *Fromson* v. *Western Litho Plate and Supply Co.*, 853 F.2d 1568, 1576 (Fed. Cir. 1988) ('In a normal [patent licensing] negotiation, the potential licensee has three basic choices: forego all use of the invention; pay an agreed royalty; infringe the patent and risk litigation').
109. 35 U.S.C. § 283.
110. *Richardson* v. *Suzuki Motor Co.*, 868 F.2d 1226, 1247 (Fed. Cir. 1989) ('[i]nfringement having been established, it is contrary to the laws of property, of which the patent law partakes, to deny the patentee's right to exclude others from use of his property').
111. *eBay Inc.* v. *MercExchange, L.L.C.*, 126 S.Ct. 1837, 1838–39 (2006) (holding that four-factor test applies to disputes arising under the Patent Act).
112. 35 U.S.C. §271(d).
113. *Zenith Radio Corp.* v. *Hazeltine Research, Inc.*, 395 U.S. 100, 135 (1969) (emphasis added).
114. Hovenkamp et al., above, note 58, at 1761; Shapiro, above, note 11, at 395.
115. *Richardson*, 868 F.2d at 1247.
116. 35 U.S.C. §261.
117. IP Licensing Guidelines, above, note 52, at §§2.0, 2.1.
118. *Continental Paper Bag Co.* v. *Eastern Paper Bag Co.*, 210 U.S. 405, 425 (1908).
119. *Masonite Corp.*, 316 U.S. at 280.
120. Defenders of exclusion payments have not pointed to any authority holding otherwise, other than a facile reference to the patentee's statutory right to exclude at 35 U.S.C. §154.
121. *Masonite Corp.*, 316 U.S. 265; see also *Singer*, 374 U.S. at 196–7; *United States* v. *Line Material Co.*, 333 U.S. 287, 308 (1948); *Ethyl Gasoline Corp.* v. *United States*, 309 U.S. 436, 456 (1940).
122. *Masonite Corp.*, 316 U.S. at 279.
123. Areeda & Hovenkamp, note 85, at ¶2030 (noting that naked market division agreements are unlawful per se).
124. 35 U.S.C. §261.
125. *B. Braun Med.* v. *Abbott Labs.*, 124 F.3d 1419, 1429 (Fed. Cir. 1997) (discussing field-of-use restrictions); *Atari Games Corp.* v. *Nintendo of Am., Inc.*, 897 F.2d 1572, 1578 (Fed. Cir. 1990) (upholding quantity limitations in a patent licence).

126. We are not advocating an analysis based on an examination of the parties' subjective thought process. Rather, as described above, an examination of the agreement in the context of the market structure of the relevant industry should reveal the source of the exclusion, as it does in the pharmaceutical patent settlement matters. As a practical matter, there may be circumstances in which it is difficult to discern whether the source of the exclusion is the patent or a payment, but the exclusion payments made in the context of brand/generic pharmaceutical patent litigation do not appear to present that difficulty, for the reasons described above.

127. 'In a normal negotiation, the potential licensee has three basic choices: forego all use of the invention; pay an agreed royalty; infringe the patent and risk litigation.' See *Fromson* v. *Western Litho Plate and Supply Co.*, 853 F.2d 1568, 1576 (Fed. Cir. 1988) (a patent licence is a waiver by the patentee of its right to sue for infringement).

128. See, e.g., Meurer, Michael J. (1989), 'The settlement of patent litigation', *RAND Journal of Economics*, **20**, 77, at 77–9 (to avoid the threat of having its patent invalidated, a patentee will often settle a dispute by licensing the patent in exchange for royalty payments; the terms of the licence depend, in part, on the probability of the patentee prevailing in litigation). See Lanjouw, Jean O. and Josh Lerner (1997), 'The enforcement of intellectual property rights: a survey of the empirical literature', NBER Working Paper Series, Working Paper 6296, 1–4, 19, available at http://www.nber.org/papers/w6296 (the likelihood that the patentee will win the patent litigation increases the value of the patent).

129. National Academies' Board on Science, Technology and Economic Policy (2004), 'A patent system for the 21st century', available at http://www.nap.edu/html/patentsystem (discussing the patent invalidity rate and the factors affecting the issuance of invalid patents).

130. FTC Generic Drug Study, above, note 77, at 15–16.

131. Errors in granting patent rights may be expected; as previously noted, Professor Landes and Judge Posner have cautioned against an expansive view of intellectual property rights inefficiencies involved in the process of their creation. See Landes and Posner, above, note 7, at 23–4.

132. Lanjouw, Jean O. and Josh Lerner (1997), 'The enforcement of intellectual property rights: a survey of the empirical literature', NBER Working Paper Series, Working Paper 6296, 1–4, 19 (1997), available at http://www.nber.org/papers/w6296 (the likelihood that the patentee will win the patent litigation increases the value of the patent).

133. Shapiro, above, note 11, at 407–8.

134. O'Rourke and Brodley explain that a payment from the brand to the generic distorts the generic's incentives to negotiate for the earliest entry date possible. O'Rourke, Maureen A. and Joseph F. Brodley (2003), 'An incentives approach to patent settlements: a commentary on Hovenkamp, Janis and Lemley', *Minn. L. Rev.*, **87**, 1767, at 1786.

135. This is common in the context of patent litigation under the Hatch–Waxman Act because the alleged infringer there (i.e., the ANDA applicant) need not enter the market in order to challenge the referenced patent. See *Mylan Pharms., Inc.* v. *Shalala*, 81 F. Supp. 2d 30, 32 (D.D.C. 2000) (filing of ANDA with Paragraph IV Certification 'automatically creates a cause of action for patent infringement').

136. FTC Schering Op. at 25–6; see also Hovenkamp et al., above, note 58, at 1762.

137. The expected savings in the cost of litigation represent merely the transaction costs of litigation versus settlement and, therefore, do not affect the substantive merits of the dispute (i.e., the expected outcome of litigation). See Hovenkamp et al., above, note 58 at 1750–51; FTC Schering Op. at 37, n. 67.

138. Areeda, Phillip E. and Herbert Hovenkamp (2004 Supp.) *Antitrust Law*, ¶2046 at 349–50.

139. See *Andrx Pharms.*, 256 F.3d at 809 (patentee's payment to alleged infringer may strongly suggest an anticompetitive agreement). Those antitrust concerns could be addressed by legitimate efficiency explanations, such as those acknowledged by the FTC in its *Schering* opinion.

140. Hovenkamp et al., above, note 58, at 1761–2.

141. See Gifford, Daniel J. (2003), 'Antitrust's troubled relations with intellectual property', *Minn L. Rev.*, **87**, 1695, at 1705–10.
142. *eBay Inc.* v. *MercExchange, L.L.C.*, 126 S.Ct. 1837, 1838–39 (2006) (holding that four-factor test applies to disputes arising under the Patent Act).
143. *Boehringer Ingelheim Vetmedica, Inc.*v. *Schering-Plough Corp.*, 106 F. Supp. 2d 696, 701 (D.N.J. 2000).
144. See, e.g., *Weinberger* v. *Romero-Barcelo*, 456 U.S. 305, 312 (1982), cited in *eBay Inc.*, 126 S.Ct at 1839, 1841.
145. *Richardson*, 868 F.2d at 1247; see, e.g., Chisum, Donald S. et al. (2004), *Principles of Patent Law: Cases and Materials*, at 1342 ('Regardless of the justification, for more than two hundred years, the result has almost always been that, after there has been a final determination of infringement, the prevailing patent owner will be granted an injunction that permanently enjoins the adjudicated infringer from infringing the patent in suit').
146. *City of Milwaukee* v. *Activated Sludge, Inc.*, 69 F.2d 577, 593 (7th Cir. 1934) (injunction seeking to close sewage plant denied owing to public health concern); *Nerney* v. *New York, N.H. & H.R. Co.*, 83 F.2d 409, 410–11 (2d Cir. 1936) (injunction seeking to close railroad denied).
147. See, e.g., *Pall Corp.* v. *Micron Separations, Inc.*, 792 F. Supp. 1298, 1328 (D. Mass. 1992) (granting a partial stay of injunction pending appeal to ensure the availability of certain medical supplies to third parties).
148. See, e.g., *Shiley, Inc.* v. *Bentley Lab.*, 601 F. Supp. 964, 969–71 (C.D. Ca. 1985) (providing for a six-month transition period with royalties to facilitate patient care before the injunction becomes effective); *Johns Hopkins University* v. *CellPro*, 1997 U.S. Dist. Lexis 24162 (D. Del. 1997) (granting a partial stay of injunction, and certain fees during the stay, until approval of patentee's licensed medical devices by the FDA); *Moxness Products, Inc.* v. *Xomed, Inc.*, 7 U.S.P.Q.2d 1877 (M.D. Fl. 1988) (granting a stay of four months, with royalties, to allow health care providers to switch to other devices); *Schneider (Europe) AG* v. *SciMed Life Sys, Inc.*, 852 F. Supp. 813, 850–51, 861–62 (D. Mn. 1994) (providing for a one year transition period, with royalties, to allow health care providers to switch to other medical devices); *Eolas Technologies Inc.* v. *Microsoft Corp.*, 70 U.S.P.Q.2d 1939 (N.D. Ill. 2004) (allowing Microsoft a lead time of 17 weeks to develop noninfringing products; and staying the injunction pending appeal to ensure an orderly progression from the use of infringing features to noninfringing features without disruption to computer systems and capabilities that would greatly inconvenience the public).
149. See, e.g., *Mallinckrodt, Inc.* v. *Medipart, Inc.*, 976 F.2d 700 (Fed. Cir. 1992).
150. *Motion Picture Patents Co.* v. *Universal Film Mfg. Co.*, 243 U.S. 502, 518 (1917).
151. Anticompetitive tying is prohibited by section 3 of the Clayton Act, 15 U.S.C. §14. Although tying arrangements may result in anticompetitive effects that would be condemned by antitrust law, such arrangements can also result in significant efficiencies and procompetitive benefits. Carlton, Dennis W. and Jeffrey M. Perloff (2000), *Modern Industrial Organization*, at 303–4. The US antitrust agencies consider both the anticompetitive effects and the efficiencies attributable to a tying arrangement. IP Licensing Guidelines at §5.3; see also Tom and Newberg, above, note 52 at 210–15 (discussing the procompetitive benefits of tying arrangements).
152. 35 U.S.C. §271(d)(5) (A patent owner will not be guilty of patent misuse for having 'conditioned the license of any rights to the patent or the sale of the patented product on the acquisition of a license to rights in another patent or purchase of a separate product, unless, in view of the circumstances, the patent owner has market power in the relevant market for the patent or patented product on which the license or sale is conditioned').
153. Gifford, above, note 141, at 1709.
154. 35 U.S.C. §261.
155. 15 U.S.C. §18.
156. Hovenkamp et al. (2001), *IP and Antitrust: An Analysis of Antitrust Principles Applied to Intellectual Property Law*, at §14.2b1.

157. *Masonite Corp.*, 316 U.S. at 281.
158. *Standard Oil Co., (Indiana)* v. *United States*, 283 U.S. 163, 171 (1931). IP Licensing Guidelines, above, note 52, at §5.5 ('Settlements involving the cross-licensing of intellectual property rights can be an efficient means to avoid litigation and, in general, courts favor such settlements').
159. See: *Schering-Plough Corp.*, 2005 WL 528439 at 16.
160. See Section 1112 of the Medicare Prescription Drug, Improvement, and Modernization Act of 2003, Title XI, Access to Affordable Pharmaceuticals, PL 108–173, 117 Stat. 2066 (8 December 2003) (hereinafter 'Medicare Modernization Act'). For information on the types of agreements that must be filed, see 'Pharmaceutical Agreement Filing Requirements' at http://www.ftc.gov/os/2004/01/ 040106pharmrules.pdf.
161. For a summary of all agreements filed in FY 2004, see http://www.ftc.gov/os/2005/01/ 050107medicareactrpt.pdf.
162. FTC Generic Drug Study, above, note 77, at 27–35. The remaining two settlements do not fit into any of these three categories.
163. Crane, above, note 58 (arguing that exclusion payments should be permitted when the likelihood of success of the patentee's infringement suit is high).
164. See Schildkraudt, above, note 67, at 1041.
165. The later court's review of the patent merits will be undermined by the fact of the settlement, which changed the incentives of the generic from wishing to defeat the patent to supporting it in the interest of preserving the settlement (O'Rourke and Brodley, above, note 134, at 1786).
166. See *Valley Drug*, 344 F.3d at 1308 ('Patent litigation is too complex and the results too uncertain for parties to accurately forecast whether enforcing the exclusionary right through settlement will expose them to treble damages if the patent immunity were destroyed by the mere invalidity of the patent').
167. *Valley Drug Co*, 344 F.3d at 1311 n. 27.
168. *Augustine Med. Inc.* v. *Gaymar Indus. Inc.*, 181 F.3d 1291 (Fed. Cir. 1999).
169. See Kitch, Edmund W. (1977), 'The nature and function of the patent system', *J.L. & Econ.*, **20**, 265 (discussing the economic incentive for 'patent mining' provided by broad patents).
170. Leffler and Leffler, above, note 94, at 34–5.
171. See H.R. Rep. No. 98–857(I), at 14–15 (1984), reprinted in 1984 U.S.C.C.A.N. at 2647–8.
172. See: 35 U.S.C. §271(e)(2).
173. 21 U.S.C. §355(j)(5)(B)(iv); Medicare Moderinization Act, above, note 160, at §1102.
174. *Schering-Plough Corp.*, 2005 WL 528439 at 16 (quoting *In re Ciprofloxacin Hydrochloride Antitrust Litigation*, 261 F. Supp. 2d 188, 251 (E.D.N.Y. 2003)).
175. Lobanoff, Marcy (2001), Comment, 'Anticompetive agreements cloaked as "settlements" thwart the purposes of the Hatch–Waxman Act', *Emory L.J.*, **50**, 1331.
176. Medicare Modernization Act, above, note 160, at §§1111–17.
177. S. Rep. No. 107–167, at 4 (2002).

## References

ABA Section of Antitrust Law (2002), *Antitrust Law Developments*.
Allison, John R. and Mark A. Lemley (1998), 'Empirical evidence on the validity of litigated patents', *AIPLA Q. J.*, **26**, 185.
American Standards Association (1972), 'Through History with Standards', in Rowen Glie (ed.), *Speaking of Standards*.
Areeda, Phillip E. and Herbert Hovenkamp (1999), *Antitrust Law*.
Breitenberg, Maureen A. (1987), 'The ABC's of standards-related activities in the United States', *NISTIR*, 6014.
Carlton, Dennis W. and Jeffrey M. Perloff (2000), *Modern Industrial Organization*.
Chisum, Donald S. et al. (2004), *Principles of Patent Law: Cases and Materials*.
Cotter, Thomas F. (2003), 'Refining the "presumptive illegality" approach to settlements of patent disputes involving reverse payments', *Minn. L. Rev.*, **87**, 1789.

Cramer, Eric L. and Daniel Berger (2004), 'The superiority of direct proof of monopoly power and anticompetitive effects in antitrust cases involving delayed entry of generic drugs', *U.S.F.L. Rev.*, **39**, 81.

Crane, Daniel A. (2002), 'Exit payments in settlement of patent infringement lawsuits: antitrust rules and economic implications', *Fla. L. Rev.*, **54**, 747.

Federal Trade Commission (July 2002), *Generic Drug Entry Prior to Patent Expiration: An FTC Study*, at 15–16, available at http://www.ftc.gov/os/2002/07/genericdrugstudy.pdf.

Federal Trade Commission (Oct. 2003), *To Promote Innovation: The Proper Balance of Competition and Patent Law and Policy* (October), ('FTC Competition-Patent Report'), available at http://www.ftc.gov/os/2003/10/innovationrpt.pdf.

Federal Trade Commission and United States Department of Justice (2000), *Antitrust Guidelines for Collaboration Among Competitors*.

Gifford, Daniel J. (2003), 'Antitrust's troubled relations with intellectual property', *Minn L. Rev.*, **87**, 1695.

Hansen, Marc et al. (Dec. 2003), 'Disclosure and negotiation of licensing terms prior to adoption of industry standards: preventing another patent ambush?', *Eur. Competition L. Rev.*

Heald, Paul J. (2005), 'A transaction costs theory of patent law', available at http://papers.ssrn.com/sol3/papers.cfm?abstract_id=385841 (posted April 2003), in **66**, *Ohio State Law Journal*, 3, 473–510.

Hoerner, Robert J. (1998), 'Antitrust pitfalls in patent litigation settlement agreements', *Fed. Circuit B.J.*, **8**.

Hovenkamp, Herbert (2004), 'Sensible antitrust rules for pharmaceutical competition', *U.S.F. L. Rev.*, **39**, 11.

Hovenkamp, H. et al. (2001), *IP and Antitrust: An Analysis of Antitrust Principles Applied to Intellectual Property Law*, Aspen, (2001–2005 supplement).

Hovenkamp, Herbert, Mark Lemley and Mark Janis (2003), 'Anticompetitive settlement of intellectual property disputes', *Minn. L. Rev.*, **87**, 1719.

Hovenkamp, Herbert, Mark D. Janis and Mark A. Lemley (2004), 'Balancing ease and accuracy in assessing pharmaceutical exclusion payments', *Minn. L. Rev.*, **88**, 712.

Kitch, Edmund W. (1977), 'The nature and function of the patent system', *J.L. & Econ.*, **20**, 265.

Landes, William M. and Richard A. Posner (2004), *The Political Economy of Intellectual Property Law*.

Lanjouw, Jean O. and Josh Lerner (1997), 'The Enforcement of Intellectual Property Rights: A Survey of the Empirical Literature', NBER Working Paper Series, Working Paper 6296, 1–4, 19, available at http://www.nber.org/papers/w6296.

Leffler, Keith and Cristofer Leffler (2004), 'Efficiency trade-offs in patent litigation settlements: analysis gone astray?', *U.S.F. L. Rev.*, **39**, 33.

Lemley, Mark A. (2001), 'Rational ignorance at the Patent Office', *Nw. U.L. Rev.*, **95**, 1495.

Lemley, Mark A. (2002), 'Intellectual property rights and standard-setting organizations', *Cal. L. Rev.*, **90**, 1889.

Lobanoff, Marcy (2001), Comment, 'Anticompetive agreements cloaked as "settlements" thwart the purposes of the Hatch–Waxman Act', *Emory L.J.*, **50**, 1331.

Merges, Robert P. et al. (2003), *Intellectual Property in the New Technological Age*.

Meurer, Michael J. (1989), 'The settlement of patent litigation', *RAND Journal of Economics*, **20**, 77.

Moore, Kimberly A. (2000), 'Judges, juries, and patent cases – an empirical peek inside the black box', *Mich. L. Rev.*, **99**, 365.

Mueller, Janice M. (2003), 'Symposium: patent system reform: patent misuse through the capture of industry standards', *Berkeley Tech. L.J.*, **17**, 623.

National Academies' Board on Science, Technology and Economic Policy (2004), 'A patent system for the 21st century', available at http://www.nap.edu/html/patentsystem.

O'Rourke, Maureen A. and Joseph F. Brodley (2003), 'An incentives approach to patent settlements: a commentary on Hovenkamp, Janis and Lemley', *Minn. L. Rev.*, **87**, 1767.

Priest, George L. (1977), 'Cartels and patent license arrangements', *J. L. & Econ.*, **20**, 309.

Ross, Thomas W. and Ralph A. Winter (2005), 'The efficiency defense in merger law: economic foundations and recent Canadian developments', *Antitrust L.J.*, **72**, 471.

Schildkraut, Marc (2004), 'Patent-splitting settlements and the reverse payment fallacy', *Antitrust L.J.*, **71**, 1033.
Shapiro, Carl (2003), 'Antitrust limits to patent settlements', *Rand J. Econ.*, **34**, 391.
Skitol, Robert A. (2005), 'Concerted buying power: its potential for addressing the patent holdup problem in standard setting', *Antitrust L. J.*, **72**(2), 727.
Tom, Willard K. and Joshua A. Newberg (1997), 'Antitrust and intellectual property: from separate spheres to unified field', *Antitrust L.J.*, **66**, 167.

*Cases*
*Allied Tube & Conduit Corp.* v. *Indian Head*, 486 U.S. 492 (1988).
*Aro Corp.* v. *Allied Witan Co.*, 531 F.2d.1368 (6th Cir. 1976).
*Atari Games Corp.* v. *Nintendo of Am., Inc.*, 897 F.2d 1572 (Fed. Cir. 1990).
*Augustine Med. Inc.* v. *Gaymar Indus. Inc.*, 181 F.3d 1291 (Fed. Cir. 1999).
*B. Braun Med.* v. *Abbott Labs.*, 124 F.3d 1419 (Fed. Cir. 1997).
*Blackburn* v. *Sweeney*, 53 F.3d 825 (7th Cir. 1995).
*Boehringer Ingelheim Vetmedica, Inc.* v. *Schering-Plough Corp.*, 106 F. Supp. 2d 696 (D. N.J. 2000).
*Bonito Boats, Inc.*, v. *Thunder Craft Boats, Inc.*, 489 U.S. 141 (1988).
*Broadcast Music, Inc.* v. *Columbia Broadcasting System*, 441 U.S. 1 (1979).
*California Dental Assn'n* v. *FTC*, 526 U.S. 756 (1999).
*City of Milwaukee* v. *Activated Sludge, Inc.*, 69 F.2d 577 (7th Cir. 1934).
*Continental Paper Bag Co.* v. *Eastern Paper Bag Co.*, 210 U.S. 405 (1908).
*Copperweld Corp.* v. *Independence Tube Corp.*, 467 U.S. 752 (1984).
*eBay Inc.* v. *MercExchange L.L.C.*, 126 S.Ct. 1837 (2006).
*Electromotive Div. of GMC* v. *Transp. Sys. Div. of GE*, 417 F3d 1203 (Fed. Cir. 2005).
*Engine Specialties, Inc.* v. *Bombardier Ltd.*, 605 F.2d 1 (1st Cir. 1979).
*Eolas Technologies Inc.* v. *Microsoft Corp.*, 70 U.S.P.Q.2d 1939 (N.D. Ill. 2004).
*Ethyl Gasoline Corp.* v. *United States*, 309 U.S. 436 (1940).
*Federal Trade Commission* v. *Indiana Federation of Dentists*, 476 U.S. 447 (1986).
*Fromson* v. *Western Litho Plate and Supply Co.*, 853 F.2d 1568 (Fed. Cir. 1988).
*Hybritech Inc.* v. *Abbott Laboratories*, 849 F.2d 1446 (Fed. Cir. 1988).
*In re Cardizem CD Antitrust Litig.*, 332 F.3d 896 (6th Cir. 2003).
*In re Ciprofloxacin Hydrochloride Antitrust Litigation*, 2005 WL 736605.
*In the Matter of Polygram Holding, Inc. et al.*, FTC Docket No. 9298 (24 July 2003), available at http://www.ftc.gov/os/2003/07/polygramopinion.pdf.
*In the Matter of Rambus, Inc.*, Docket No. 9302 (June 18, 2002), available at http://www.ftc.gov/os/2002/06/rambuscmp.htm.
*In the Matter of Schering-Plough Corp.*, Dkt. No. 9297 (Opinion of the FTC) (Dec. 18, 2003), available at http://www.ftc.gov/os/adjpro/d9297/031218commissionopinion.pdf.
*In the Matter of Union Oil Company of California*, Docket No. 9305 (March 4, 2003), available at http://www.ftc.gov/os/2003/03/unocalcmp.htm.
*Johns Hopkins University* v. *CellPro*, 1997 U.S. Dist. Lexis 24162 (D. Del. 1997).
*Lee Moore Oil Co.* v. *Union Oil Co.*, 599 F.2d 1299, 1302 (4th Cir. 1979).
*Magnivision, Inc.*, v. *Bonneau Co.*, 115 F.3d 95 (Fed. Cir. 1997).
*Mallinckrodt, Inc.* v. *Medipart, Inc.*, 976 F.2d 700 (Fed. Cir. 1992).
*Microbix Biosys., Inc.* v. *BioWhittaker, Inc.*, 172 F. Supp. 2d 680 (2001).
*Motion Picture Patents Co.* v. *Universal Film Mfg. Co.*, 243 U.S. 502 (1917).
*Moxness Products, Inc.* v. *Xomed, Inc.*, 7 U.S.P.Q.2d 1877 (M.D. Fl. 1988).
*Mylan Pharms., Inc.* v. *Shalala*, 81 F. Supp. 2d 30 (D.D.C. 2000).
*Nat'l Soc'y of Prof'l Eng'rs* v. *United States*, 435 U.S. 679 (1978).
*NCAA* v. *Bd. Regents Okla. Univ.*, 468 U.S. 85 (1984).
*Nerney* v. *New York, N.H. & H.R. Co.*, 83 F.2d 409 (2d Cir. 1936).
*Odetics, Inc.* v. *Storage Technology Corp.*, 14 F. Supp. 2d 785 (E.D. Va. 1998).
*Pall Corp.* v. *Micron Separations, Inc.*, 792 F. Supp. 1298 (D. Mass. 1992).
*Richardson* v. *Suzuki Motor Co.*, 868 F.2d 1226, 1247 (Fed. Cir. 1989).

*Schering-Plough Corp.* v. *FTC*, 2005 WL 528439 (11th Cir. 2005).
*Schneider (Europe) AG* v. *SciMed Life Sys, Inc.*, 852 F. Supp. 813 (D. Mn. 1994).
*SCM Corp.* v. *Xerox Corp.*, 645 F.2d 1195 (2d Cir. 1981).
*Shiley, Inc.* v. *Bentley Lab.*, 601 F. Supp. 964 (C.D. Ca. 1985).
*Standard Oil Co., (Indiana)* v. *United States*, 283 U.S. 163 (1931).
*State Oil Co.* v. *Khan*, 522 U.S. 3, 10 (1997).
*Stratoflex, Inc.* v. *Aeroquip Corp.*, 713 F.2d 1530 (Fed. Cir. 1983).
*United States* v. *Griffith*, 334 U.S. 100 (1948).
*United States* v. *Line Material Co.*, 333 U.S. 287 (1948).
*United States* v. *Masonite Corp.*, 316 U.S. 265 (1942).
*United States* v. *Microsoft Corp.*, 253 F.3d 34, (D.C. Cir. 2001).
*Valley Drug Co.* v. *Geneva Pharmaceuticals, Inc.*, 344 F.3d 1294 (11th Cir. 2003).
*Weinberger* v. *Romero-Barcelo*, 456 U.S. 305 (1982).
*W.L. Gore & Assocs, Inc.* v. *Garlock, Inc.*, 721 F.2d 1540 (Fed. Cir. 1983).
*Zenith Radio Corp.* v. *Hazeltine Research, Inc.*, 395 U.S. 100 (1969).

# 13 Compulsory access as an antitrust remedy: when, why and how is it applied in EU and US law?
## Donald I. Baker and Tony Woodgate

The whole idea of compulsory antitrust access runs into a core reality of Anglo-American jurisprudence, namely, judicial reluctance to issue injunctions compelling defendants to take affirmative action that requires skill and discretion, because the task of judicially supervising a defendant's performance in an adversarial environment is so daunting.[1] Meanwhile sectoral regulators (which often have broad statutory discretion) have generally been less reluctant on this score. Regulators have simply been more willing than judges to enter contested orders for specific economic performance – in part because they often seem to have had greater confidence than judges about their capacity effectively to supervise a monopolist's performance of affirmative duties.

Modern antitrust and competition law enforcement reflects a hybrid of various policies and presumptions derived from the diverse assumptions and experiences of those who must initiate investigations and decide cases. The formal enforcement processes tend to fall in the middle of the judicial–administrative spectrum: in Europe, competition law remedies are generally framed and enforced by administrative bodies subject to judicial review, while in the US antitrust remedies tend to ordered by judges acting on the motion of a government agency or a private party.[2]

This underlying institutional difference may help explain some of the conceptual uncertainty and operational confusion that surround the 'compulsory licensing', 'essential facilities' or 'bottleneck monopoly' concepts explored in this chapter. In determining whether to invoke one of these imprecisely defined concepts, a court or administrator may be influenced, not only by the defendant's market power, motives and conduct, but also by whether the decision maker can envision a fair remedy that it could effectively enforce against a foot-dragging monopolist.

Accordingly, in this chapter we want to review carefully what decision makers have *said* in granting or denying compulsory remedies, but we also want to look equally hard at what decision makers have *actually ordered*, once having decided to impose such a remedy. As that celebrated American jurist, Oliver Wendell Holmes, Jr. has said, 'The life of the law is not in logic, but in experience.' What the decision maker has been willing to order may often be more illuminating than any accompanying explanation of the legal doctrines being ostensibly relied on in making the order. The fact that judges generally seem somewhat more cautious than administrators about the effectiveness of 'essential facilities' or 'compulsory licensing' types of orders seems to be a significant part of the complex picture.

### The underlying economic tension

The basic access issue arises when a monopolist is operating at two levels, the monopoly market ('MM') and the dependent market ('DM'), where a monopolist competes with unintegrated competitors that appear to need access to what the monopolist controls in the MM. An alternative structure is where the MM has been created by a joint venture of DM competitors that want to use the joint venture facility to exclude or handicap some or all of their DM competitors. In either structure, the alleged MM may be based on a physical network or site, or it be based on a database or technical standard, or it may rest squarely on intellectual property.

The difficult question is: when, if ever, should the party (or joint venture) controlling the MM be compelled to share the facility or rights with DM competitors? And, if so, on what terms?

This raises a fundamental long-run, short-run conflict that runs through this area. Antitrust law seeks to promote consumer welfare by maximizing a firm's incentives to innovate, invest and compete hard. This is a vital long-run goal. Meanwhile, competition policy may still sometimes be concerned that a successful monopolist can use some small but vital piece of a much bigger puzzle to prevent or foreclose competition across the board where consumers would have much to gain. This concern that encourages an 'essential facilities' doctrine tends to be driven by frustration with the current market situation, perhaps intensified by arrogance or blatant discrimination by the monopolist.

Of course, rational competition policy would not want to deter investment and innovation in something that, if successful, may become the next generation's 'essential facility'. An overly interventionist antitrust programme of requiring access would tend to deter investment and effort by a want-to-be monopolist and create a free-riding issue in favour of those who wanted to avoid the risk and cost of trying to create an alternative 'facility', even if capable of doing so.[3] As Judge Learned Hand said in his celebrated *Alcoa* monopolization opinion, 'The successful competitor, having been urged to compete, must not be turned upon when he wins.'[4]

This issue raises practical questions about what it takes to create an alleged 'essential facility' of a particular type as well as the potential benefits of opening up competition in the DM. Does the 'facility' represent a substantial investment that was risky? Or was it more or less a by-product of other activities? Is the MM large in relation to the DM? Or is the opposite true? Clearly, the consumer benefits – both short-run and long run – will be the greatest in an 'essential facilities' case where the critical bottleneck is small and does not represent a large risky investment, while the DM is large and could be highly competitive, based on investment and effort by unaffiliated competitors.

Another way to approach the same issue is to ask: 'what would an independent operator of the "essential facility" do vis-à-vis the DM competitors? How would it seek to maximize revenues?' Where the facility is characterized by strong economies of scale and/or is underutilized, the independent operator would be very likely to encourage expanded use by DM competitors and anyone else that might find it economically useful. Intellectual property fits right into this picture, but all forms of intellectual property are not necessarily equal. At one end of the IP spectrum are patent rights, which by definition are supposed to require a new invention of practical value, based on imagination, effort and investment encouraged by the exclusive legal right to collect monopoly rents if the invention proves to be novel and valuable.[5] At the other end of the IP spectrum is standardized information (e.g., on schedules or lists) that is necessarily generated in running an enterprise and yet may be eligible for copyright protection in many jurisdictions. Treating a patent as an 'essential facility' would plainly conflict with the basic 'monopoly in return for novel innovation' policy and incentives of the patent laws in a way that compelling access to a monopoly telephone company's directory information would not. Obviously there are various mid-points along the IP spectrum, depending on the amount of incremental investment, innovation and risk taking that are generally necessary to create a particular kind of intellectual property.

The long-term need to preserve the incentives to innovate, build and expand (and create alternatives) is the economic reality that constrains the use of any 'essential facilities' or compulsory licensing antitrust remedy. But the implications are somewhat different in different kinds of situations, which we shall explore in turn here.

### Basic 'essential facilities' concept

Both EU and US competition law have recognized a concept sometimes labelled the 'essential facilities' doctrine, although both the US Supreme Court and the European Court of Justice have declined recent opportunities to endorse the label. It is, in a way, just a more tailored application – often in a network context – of the rules relating to refusals to deal by a monopolist. What is clear is that the rule only applies when a firm or a group of firms competing in the DM control the MM network or other facility that all DM competitors need access to. This market structure is a necessary but not sufficient condition for the application of the doctrine. In addition, there must at least be some showing that (a) other DM competitors cannot duplicate the monopolist's facility (i.e., it is 'essential' and hence the denial of access reduces competition in the DM);[6] (b) providing access is technologically and economically feasible;[7] and (c) no valid business reason for denying access has been established (e.g., where the monopolist has been providing full access to others that do not compete in the DM).[8]

The original decision in this area dates all the way back to 1912 and is also one of the most illuminating discussions. [9] The *St. Louis Terminal Railroad* case involved a Justice Department challenge to a joint venture of 14 of the 24 railroads that exchanged traffic at this critical bridgehead on the Mississippi River. The Terminal Company controlled the ferry company and access to the two trans-Mississippi rail bridges used to reach St. Louis. The government charged a violation of Sections 1 and 2 of the Sherman Act and sought to have the Terminal Company broken up. The US Supreme Court thought otherwise. Finding that the St. Louis terrain would not permit duplication of terminal facilities, it more broadly emphasized that terminal systems, '*under proper conditions*, do not restrain, but promote commerce'. This was particularly clear in St. Louis where 24 railroads needed to be able to interchange traffic with each other – or at least each eastern railway needed to be able to interchange traffic with each western railway. Accordingly the Supreme Court, essentially at its own initiative, ordered (a) that membership in the joint venture (which was a not-for-profit entity) be opened up to all the connecting railroads 'upon such just and reasonable terms as shall place the applying company upon a plane of equality in respect of and burdens with the present' joint venture partners; and (b) that non-discriminatory service be offered to non-members on the basis of use, character and costs that were equivalent to what members were being offered. Disputes over compliance were to be submitted to the District Court and access decisions would be subject to judicial review.

Here there was a monopoly, clear network effects, and clear efficiencies, but there was clear opportunity for abuse if some DM competitors (the owner railroads) which controlled the MM (the interchange facility at St. Louis) were to exclude or substantially handicap other DM competitors which were not owners. And, of course, if this MM facility were controlled by an independent company, the latter would have been seeking to maximize the amount of transcontinental (or at least trans-Mississippi River) traffic interchanged at St. Louis, rather than at Memphis or Chicago.

The European case that may be most similar is the European Commission's ('EC') *Holyhead Harbour* decision,[10] which also involved unusual physical terrain. Here the respondent controlled the Welsh port

(Holyhead) that provided the fastest ferry connections between the UK and Ireland. Meanwhile, it offered a ferry service that competed with a second operator on the same route. Thus the port was the MM and the ferry service to Ireland was the DM. The Commission found that the respondent scheduled its arrivals and departure from Holyhead in ways designed to handicap the services of its only competitor in the DM. The EC specifically found that an independent operator of the port would not have allowed such discriminatory scheduling, because it would tend to reduce the traffic in the port. The Commission's remedy was an order requiring the respondent to modify its schedules.[11]

There are, of course, numerous cases in which the clearly monopolistic physical facility owes nothing to nature. Rather it was created by government through franchise, public funds or ratepayers' funds.[12] Or it may be clearly a natural monopoly or be characterized by such strong 'network effects' that DM competitors need access. Local telephone or electricity networks have been classic examples of natural monopolies, while a specialized trading exchange would be a clear example of network effects in operation. In fact the most frequently cited articulation of the US 'essential facilities' standard comes in a 7th Circuit Court of Appeals decision requiring the dominant US telephone company, AT&T, to open up access to its local telephone networks to its newly authorized long distance competitor, MCI.[13]

The case for imposing a duty on a monopolist to grant access to its DM competitors is probably stronger in these 'physical facilities' cases than in the other categories which we will discuss. And this is especially true where the 'facilities' monopoly is at least partially based on physical terrain or governmentally granted franchises. In these cases, it is usually difficult for the defendant to argue persuasively that the 'essential facility' is *entirely* due to its skill, foresight and investment.

### Intangible 'facilities' and statutory rights

The next variation is where the 'essential facility' is not physical at all, but rather the alleged MM is a body of information that is clearly essential to those seeing to compete in a DM which involves manipulation and distribution of such information. Lists of telephone subscribers are the classic example of information needed by the local telephone monopolist's competitors in the DM markets for 'telephone information' and 'yellow pages advertising'.[14]

Technical interface standards may constitute another, similar example: the interface information is inevitably generated by the monopolist, but is needed by the monopolist's DM competitors in order for them to design products or systems that work effectively with the MM product or system.[15] A good example would be the interface specifications for equipment designed to work on a monopoly communications network. Having an 'essential facility' based on 'deliberately withheld' information requires a finding on the monopolist's motives vis-à-vis the DM. And the problem does not exist if the needed information is generated in a competitive market. Thus the highly competitive airlines are more than willing to make flight schedules freely available to any publisher or distributor of information to potential travellers or travel agents.

This brings us to the critical *Magill* judgment of the ECJ.[16] The plaintiff wished to publish a weekly 'all channels' TV guide, while the two relevant networks (RTE and BBC) each published a weekly guide of just its own programmes. The networks claimed copyrights over their schedules and would not license Magill, although they would license daily newspapers 24 hours in advance (or 48 hours on weekends). Both the CFI and ECJ sustained the Commission's position that a copyright licence could be compelled in these circumstances. The ECJ emphasized that the information was essential to the creation of a new product in a downstream market for which there was potential demand, allowed the networks to monopolize the 'weekly guide' business, and held that there was no justification for the refusal to provide the information.

The *Magill* case seems highly special for a whole variety of reasons. First of all the IP rights were weak and involved no real incremental investment.[17] The information was simply a by-product of running a TV network. Moreover applying the 'independent operator' test is quite easy: the operator of a TV network that was not in the 'weekly guide' business would have been not only pleased but anxious to have its scheduling information in the hands of any publication that would publish it.

That many commentators have read the *Magill* judgment broadly and created alarm about IP rights in Europe is a reality. The fact that the CFI distinguished *Magill* in the *Tiercé Ladbroke* judgment,[18] and that the ECJ clarified certain aspects of the test derived from *Magill* in *IMS Health*,[19] is helpful.

The issue of an 'essential facility of deliberately withheld information' is clearly a difficult issue, particularly in the EU; and we shall discuss it more fully in due course. Where the copyright covers original or creative material, the case against compelling access is extremely strong. By contrast, where (as in *Magill*) the product is pretty much a pure by-product, created without serious risk or cost, and *is truly essential for competition in the DM*, then the *Magill* rule should govern.[20]

**Patents as essential facilities?**
Distinguishing between patents and weak copyrights (of the *Magill* type) is fundamental. At least in theory (and, hopefully, normally in practice),

a patent is awarded only after the patent applicant has established that it has created something new and useful. The patent is explicitly a reward for successful innovation and effort. Thus any programme of compulsory licensing to create competition in the DM runs right into the core policies of the patent laws, which reserve the fruits of monopoly to the successful innovator and to the potential patentee still struggling in the lab.

The US rule has been quite explicit for a long time. A patent holder has the complete right to refuse to license, as the Supreme Court held all the way back in 1908 in *Continental Paper Bag Co. v. Eastern Paper Bag Co.*, 210 US 405. This right even applies (at least in the US) where the patent holder is refusing to work the patent at all. Thus, even in circumstances where there would be no DM at all without access to the patent, the patent holder cannot be compelled to license its invention.

Similarly, in Europe, the general rule set out in *Volvo v. Veng*[21] is that, even where a patent owner enjoys a dominant market position, it is entitled to refuse to license other than in strictly limited circumstances.

The situation can be quite different analytically where patents are pooled by competitors, because this is seen as a voluntary activity going beyond just obtaining and owning a patent. There may be an antitrust inquiry into the reasons for and effects of such pooling effort under the horizontal restraint rules in Article 81 EC Treaty and Section 1 of the Sherman Act. It is one thing to say that the *individual innovator*, having been granted a patent, should have virtually total discretion to license or not, and to pick or choose among potential licensees. It is a different thing to say that *several patentees* that choose to aggregate their patents enjoy collective discretion of anything like the same degree. Two situations at least can raise significant questions. The first is where potentially 'competing' patents are included in the pool. The theory here would be that 'competing' patents may give the owners alternative, non-infringing ways of reaching the same goal, and the pool thereby eliminates potential competition in licensing.[22] Hence the pool eliminates potential competition, which, if substantial, would likely give rise to a Section 1 or Article 81 violation.

The second situation is where the pool is made up of 'essential' patents necessary to satisfy an industry standard. Here the patent pool becomes an integral part of the standards-making process. In this context, reasonable access and procedures are clearly required for the standards-setting operation; and then reasonable access would seem to be required to the pool of patents necessary to satisfy the standard. Collective exclusion from the standards-making process or flat denial of access to a pool of 'essential' patents resulting from it is likely to be treated as a serious 'boycott' issue (which would impose on the excluders a heavy burden to justify their action on efficiency, safety or other public interest grounds).

We shall return to this very difficult set of patent pooling issues in a subsequent section on the critical questions of whether and how those exercising *collective* control of a MM should (or should not) be treated differently from a *single firm* monopolist under the competition laws.

**Joint ventures v. single firm monopolies: is there a rational basis for treating joint ventures more stringently than single firm monopolies on compulsory access to facilities and/or IP rights?**

*Essential facilities generally*

The US law has proved very clear on this point. US courts and agencies have been much tougher on successful joint ventures than on successful monopolists when it comes to compelling access to facilities or rights in order to create or enhance DM competition.[23] Often this is done by ordering the joint venture to admit newcomers to membership on the same terms as existing members, but sometimes per use access is ordered. By contrast, US law gives individual firms – even those with substantial market power – very substantial latitude for whatever reason they want.[24] Patent owners have even broader discretion to refuse to deal.

By contrast, in Europe, 'essential facilities' cases are characterized by a single dominant firm rather than a joint venture as the party against which relief is being sought. The EU cases do apply both Article 81 and Article 82 to analogous cases where access to an association or standards body is essential to carrying out a commercial activity.[25] Thus the cases we have discussed, such as *Holyhead Harbour* and *Magill*, are representative of this broader reality.[26]

This broad difference in approach may become something of increasing practical importance in a world of even more global networks and systems, especially if private antitrust litigation becomes an important tool in Europe. We can anticipate that DM competitors (or others) excluded by an MM joint venture would be more likely to look at Sherman Act, section 1 remedies from the US enforcers or courts. On the other hand, DM competitors refused access by a dominant firm in the MM would be likely to look to the enforcers in Brussels or the Member States for relief under Article 82 EC Treaty or its national counterparts. (This reality has been well illustrated by the *Microsoft*[27] saga of the last few years, where Europe has been the focus of Microsoft's rivals.)

There seem a number of reasons for this significant difference in the treatment of dominant firms and joint ventures. In Europe, Article 82 EC Treaty and its progeny in the laws of the Member States clearly give the enforcement authorities broad discretion and some direction to deal with 'abuses' by 'dominant' enterprises. This invites the enforcement agencies and courts to take affirmative action to correct such conduct, including any use of monopoly power in the MM to foreclose entry or suppress competition in the DM. In addition, the European law generally allows a showing of dominance on a somewhat lesser showing of monopoly power (e.g., of market share) than modern US law seems to insist on under section 2 of the Sherman Act.

In the US, the principal focus of section 2 monopolization law has been generally focused on the MM and, more precisely, conduct designed to exclude new entrants or destroy small competitors in that market. 'Monopoly leveraging' has been hotly debated, but only rarely accepted as the basis for a section 2 violation; i.e. it is generally not a violation for a firm to use its control of the MM to gain a *competitive advantage* in the DM.[28] Rather the government or private plaintiff must show that a respondent is actively using its power in the MM to create a 'dangerous probability' of its achieving a second monopoly in the DM.

Thus, for US plaintiffs and prosecutors, section 1 of the Sherman Act is a highly preferable weapon in dealing with unjustified refusals to deal, and joint ventures are the logical target of section 1 cases. The US policy may also be implicitly influenced by Adam Smith's celebrated presumption about the collective motives and methods of competitors.[29] Stated more specifically, there may be a lesser willingness to assume that a multi-member joint venture's refusal to serve those who compete with its members is driven by procompetitive motives, efficiency goals, or need to protect goodwill, etc. It is also clearly true that the 'boycott' label regularly used in the joint venture refusal cases under section 1 has a much more pejorative flavour than any section 2 rule which might be applied, however rarely, to a quiet refusal to deal by a single firm. Finally decisions on liability may be affected by the practical reality that the court, or agency, will often find it easier to devise a workable non-discriminatory remedy in the joint venture context, based on mandating access or royalties for latecomers on the same terms as the existing partners, as opposed to having to create and dictate detailed access rules where an integrated single firm monopolist has refused to deal with DM rivals.[30]

Such a non-discrimination remedy in favour of latecomers may deny the joint venture founders an appropriate premium for their initial risk, which is clearly undesirable from a policy standpoint and may have some incrementally adverse effect on willingness of parties to create future joint ventures. The issue is probably clearest where the initial joint venture partners have succeeded over time in creating a highly successful brand (such as 'Visa' or 'Associated Press') and the late-admitted members may get a virtual free-ride vis-à-vis the brand and/or their admission may seriously dilute the differentiation that is an important part of the brand's value.[31]

*Intellectual property pools*

The antitrust analysis of access to a patent (or other intellectual property) pool generally proceeds along the lines that have developed for joint ventures. In general, the US has been more willing to exercise antitrust jurisdiction over the collective decisions of patent pools than it has over the unilateral decisions of individual owners of very critical patents, but it has not applied the *Associated Press* type of approach to patent pools by ordering a joint pool to admit additional members.[32]

The current position under EU law with regard to patent pools (or technology pools more generally) is not as developed as that in the US, in part because there have been very few decided cases. As a consequence the basic principles under EU law are set out in the EC's Guidelines on the Technology Transfer Block Exemption.[33] Under these it seems likely that a broad patent pool embodying 'essential' patents will be obliged to license these on fair, reasonable and non-discriminatory terms, and thus the EU and US results are likely to prove essentially similar. The EC's position, as set out in the Guidelines, makes two basic distinctions that have parallels in US analysis: (a) the difference between technological complements and substitutes and (b) the distinction between essential and non-essential technology. These are critical.

A pool made up of substitute technologies is of particular concern in both the US and the EU. As the EU Guidelines explain, such a pool 'restricts inter-technology competition, and amounts to collective bundling [and it will be likely that it] amounts to price fixing among competitors'.[34] Thus the creation of such a pool is likely to be illegal, especially if it generates a dominant position in the market.

The situation is entirely different, '[w]hen a pool is composed only of technologies that are essential and therefore by necessity also complements'.[35] Then the creation of the pool will be permitted, irrespective of the positions of the parties, but 'the conditions on which licences are granted may be caught by Article 81(1)',[36] as we shall discuss shortly. The EU Guidelines focus particularly on the licensing terms '[w]here the pool has a dominant position on the market'.[37] This parallels the concerns in the US jurisprudence under the 'rule of reason'.

Both the EU and US law, as it is evolving, seems to have delineated two general kinds of patent pools that are clearly permissible:

1. *A competitive pool ('Type A')*: this is essentially a joint venture which faces competition in its licensing function, and whose members lack monopoly power in the licensing market. It can include both competitive substitutes and complementary patents, without offending the EU Treaty or the Sherman Act.

2.  *A comprehensive pool ('Type B')*: this is an industry-wide pool that enables licensors to combine otherwise blocking patents and licensees to obtain largely conflict-free rights. As DOJ/FTC Guidelines explain, 'These arrangements may provided pro-competitive benefits by integrating complementary technologies, reducing transaction costs, clearing blocking positions, and avoiding costly infringement litigation.'[38]

Because Type B pools generally involve licensors with collective market power, such a pool may have some 'essential facility' characteristics. These are particularly likely to occur when the pool is implementing an industry standard that requires the use of certain patents; then antitrust rules will generally insist that the standard-making body be fairly representative and that it must assure that the pool (or individual patentees whose patents are built into the standard) provide reasonable access and licences on non-discriminatory terms. As the EU Guidelines explain, 'When participation in a standard and pool creation process is open to all interested parties representing different interests, it is more likely that technologies for inclusion in the pool are selected on the basis of price/quality considerations than when the pool is set up by a limited group of technology owners.'[39] In the US, it has come to be accepted in the last decade that a Type B pool should only cover complementary or blocking patents (i.e., what the EU calls 'essential' patents); and that it is highly desirable to have an independent expert determine the 'essentiality' question.[40]

Beneath the surface is a body of jurisprudence which essentially holds (or assumes) that a pool has less freedom to impose restraints on licensees than an individual patent owner would have if it were licensing on its own.[41] Yet neither the US nor the EU authorities have been clear when an IP pool, especially a Type B pool, can refuse to license. Thus the *US Guidelines* say, rather delphicly, 'Pooling arrangements generally need not be open to all who would like to join. However, exclusion from cross-licensing and pooling arrangements among parties that collectively possess market power may, under some circumstances, harm competition.'[42] Meanwhile the EU Guidelines are more explicit:

> Where the pool has a dominant position on the market, royalties and other licensing terms should be fair and non-discriminatory and licences should be non-exclusive. These requirements are necessary to ensure that the pool is open and does not lead to foreclosure and other anti-competitive effects on down stream markets.[43]

The net result seems to be that a Type B pool is likely to be subject to rules which begin to impose on it various forms of de facto 'common carriage' obligations. Thus a model Type B pool would probably have various antitrust safeguards designed to reduce its exposure:

1. it implements a standard created through an open process, preferably operated by traditional standards-making organizations;
2. its goal was to offer licensees a conflict-free portfolio of 'essential' patents necessary to comply with the standard;
3. its system excludes 'competing' or 'substitute' patents;
4. its determination that a patent was 'essential' rather than 'competitive' or 'substitutable' is made by an independent expert;
5. it is open to innovators of new 'essential' patents;
6. it guaranteed licensees reasonable and non-discriminatory royalties;
7. it allocated royalties based on each member's contribution to the pool's overall portfolio;[44] and
8. it permitted each patent owner to license its patents separately.[45]

The principles embodied in the EU Guidelines concerning intellectual property pools are more specific than anything the US agencies or courts have specified, and yet they seem quite consistent with US practice. The line between technological complements and substitutes is fundamental, as is the line between 'essential' and 'non-essential' in justifying a Type B pool. The fact that a pool is open to all interested parties representing different interests will make it more likely that the pool operates in a procompetitive manner. Once established, a Type B pool may only charge reasonable and non-discriminatory royalties, but would not be permitted to impose *non-compete and no challenge obligations* on licensees.

In general, the operators of joint venture Type B pools have seen the business and antitrust wisdom of providing some form of facially reasonable access; and hence we have not seen traditional 'essential facilities'-type litigation in relation to these entities.

### Conclusion

The whole idea of compelling access to something created by someone else's entrepreneurial effort and skill runs into a host of practical and psychological problems. Yet the idea that control of a relatively narrow bottleneck should allow somebody to monopolize a broad market also offends some fundamental ideas of fairness and tends to deter entry into what could be a competitive market.

Thus the task of modern competition law is to find some pragmatic resolutions that do not deter efforts by would-be monopolists or deter entry by potential competitors into the dependent markets. The access rules must be fair, foreseeable and administrable – and then applied with both regularity and realism.

The rules are probably less difficult to create and apply in the context of monopolistic physical facilities than in the context of modern information systems and networks, but this does not mean that they are without relevance in the latter. It just means that they are harder to articulate and apply rationally, which will be a challenge for policy makers, enforcement agencies and courts.

## Notes

1. This approach goes back to the famous English chancery case, *Lumley* v. *Wagner*, 42 Eng. Rep. 687 (1852), where the Lord Chancellor declined the plaintiff's request that he order the defendant to perform her contract to sing at the plaintiff's theatre. Instead the court issued a *negative injunction* that prohibited the defendant from singing anywhere else.
2. The Federal Trade Commission ('FTC') is a modest exception as an administrative agency entering orders subject to judicial review. However, in practice, the FTC has been much less involved than judges in cases where ordering compulsory licensing and 'essential facilities'-type remedies were critical – and , on a rare and relatively recent FTC foray into the area, the FTC's compulsory access order was overturned by the Court of Appeals on the ground that it had improperly applied antitrust doctrine: *Official Airline Guides* v. *FTC*, 630 F.2d 920 (2nd Cir 1980) (agency improperly imposing a duty not to discriminate on a monopolist that does not compete in the dependent market ('DM')).
3. This issue was very clearly recognized by DG Competition in its recent *Green Paper on Application of Article 82 to Exclusionary Abuses*, December 2005 ('Green Paper'): 'The main purpose of forcing [dominant] companies to supply is to improve the competitive situation in the downstream market. However investment incentives may be influenced, both negatively and positively. The knowledge that they may have a duty to supply against their will might lead companies not to invest in the first place or to invest less. Other companies may be tempted to free ride on the investment made by the dominant company instead of investing themselves' (para. 213).
4. *US* v. *Aluminium Company of America*, 148 F.2d 416 (2nd Cir. 1944).
5. Unlike the situation in the US, a European patent owner may not have unfettered discretion to charge monopoly rents under EU law. Excessive pricing may possibly constitute an abuse of discretion under Article 82, even when an IP licence is involved.
6. The *Green Paper* states: 'A facility is an indispensable input only when duplication of the existing facility is impossible or extremely difficult, either because it is physically or legally impossible to duplicate, or because a second facility is not economically viable in the sense that it would not generate enough revenue to cover its costs' (para. 229).
7. See *Green Paper*, paras 40, 234.
8. That a business justification is lacking becomes particularly clear where it can be shown that the MM facility/network is operating well below its theoretical capacity and hence an *independent, unintegrated operator* would have been likely to try to expand access for DM competitors in order to make the network/facility operate more efficiently.
9. *US* v. *Terminal RR Assn.*, 224 U.S. 383 (1912). The case is extensively discussed in Baker, D. (1993), 'Compulsory access to network joint ventures under the Sherman Act: rules or roulette?', *Utah L. Rev.* **999**, 1020–25 ('Compulsory Access').
10. *B&I Line/Sealink Harbours* [1992] 5 CMLR 255; see also *Sea Containers/Stena Sealink*, Case IV/34.689, OJ 1994 L15/8, [1995] 4 CMLR 84.
11. European Commission (1992), *Commission XXIInd Report on Competition Policy*, p. 121.
12. See *Green Paper*, para. 40.

13. *MCI Communications Corp.* v. *AT&T*, 708 F.2d 1081 (7th Cir. 1983). The Court held that the 'essential facilities' doctrine requires the plaintiff seeking access to prove '(1) control of the essential facility by a monopolist; (2) a competitor's inability practically or reasonably to duplicate the essential facility; (3) the denial of use of the facility to a competitor; and (4) the feasibility of providing the facility' (708 F.2d at 1132–3).
14. See, e.g., the EC's decision in *ITT Promedia/Belgcom* XXVIIth Report on Competition Policy (1997) p.152. In the US, the public utility regulators have generally required the local telephone companies to make this information freely available.
15. The European Commission's Green Paper on Article 82 at paras 241 and 242 singles out refusal to supply information needed for interoperability as a specific category, and states that, because of its importance, 'it may not be appropriate to supply to such refusals to supply information the same high standards for intervention' as elsewhere.
16. Joined Cases C-241/91 P and C-242/91 P, *Radio Telefis Eireann (RTE) and Independent Television Publications Ltd (ITP)* v. *EC Commission*, [1995] ECR I-743.
17. While the information did enjoy copyright protection in the UK and Ireland, it apparently would not have been eligible for such protection in many other Member States.
18. Case T-504/93 *Tiercé Ladbroke* v. *Commission* [1997] ECR II 923. The case concerned the refusal of the owner of broadcasting rights for French horse races to license these rights to the complainant's Belgian betting shops. The CFI noted that the refusal in *Magill* prevented the complainant from entering the market and creating a new product, whereas here the complainant was the leading betting shop operator in Belgium.
19. Case C-418/01 *IMS Health* v. *NDC Health* [2004] ECR 1-5039. The ECJ found that the licensing must be indispensable to produce new goods or services not offered by the owner of the IP right and for which there was demand. It was not sufficient simply to attempt to duplicate products already offered by the owner in the secondary market.
20. In addition, the European Court of Justice in *IMS Health* suggested that the undertaking requesting a licence should offer some new good or service for which there is a potential consumer demand – see also Green Paper at paras 237 to 240.
21. *Volvo* v. *Veng* (238/87) [1988] ECR 6211.
22. The same type of horizontal competition issue may arise when a corporate merger would combine key competing patents of two separate firms. Here again the proper remedy is for the government to challenge the merger, based on a 'product market' or 'innovation market' analysis and then either block the merger or require divestiture of one of the competing patents. Ordering a compulsory licence to create competition in a DM would still be a second-best regulatory solution (although it certainly is one that recurs in merger investigation settlements).
23. See *Compulsory Access*, 1076–102, discussing the practical effects of *St. Louis Terminal*, *Associated Press* v. *US*, 326 U.S. 1 (1945), and their progeny.
24. The seminal case is *US* v. *Colgate & Co.*, 250 U.S. 300 (1919), where the Supreme Court said: 'In the absence of any purpose to create or maintain a monopoly, the [Sherman] act does not restrict the long-recognized right of a trader or manufacturer engaged in a purely private business, freely to exercise his discretion as to the parties with whom he will deal.'
25. E.g. *Floral*, OJ 1980 L39/51; [1980] 2 CMLR 285, *X/Open Group*, OJ 1987 L35/36, [1988] 4 CMLR 542.
26. There have of course been some EU and Member State actions involving prominent joint ventures (such as Visa and MasterCard), but these actions have been fewer than in the US.
27. Case COMP/C-3/37.792 *Microsoft*.
28. *Berkey Photo* v. *Eastman Kodak Co.*, 603 F.2d 263 (2nd Cir. 1979) is the leading authority for the 'monopoly leveraging' theory, but it has generally been criticized and not followed in other circuits. There has also been a fair amount of academic criticism of it. All this underscores a broader American concern about excessive section 2 intervention curbing the energies and efforts of leading firms.
29. 'People of the same trade seldom meet, even merriment or diversion, but the conversation ends in a conspiracy against the public or in some contrivance to raise prices'

(Smith, A. (1776), *Wealth of Nations*, R.H. Campbell et al. (eds), Clarendon Press, 1976, at 170, as cited by a US Court of Appeals in an important joint venture access decision. *United States* v. *Realty Multi-List, Inc.*, 629 F.2d 1351, 1370 (5th Cir. 1980)).

30.  In principle the remedy is probably the same in both the joint venture and single firm cases – namely to cause those controlling the monopoly to deal with other DM competitors on the same terms as with their own DM affiliate(s). With the single firm monopolist, it is often very difficult indeed to determine *exactly what the terms of dealing are*, especially when it is an integrated enterprise in a technically sophisticated field (e.g. telecommunications). This is why regulatory powers may mandate ring-fencing or even corporate separation. By contrast, the terms of dealing between a significant joint venture and its DM members normally has to be spelled out in contracts, by-laws and operational rules.

31.  See *Compulsory Access*, at 1068–72 (discussing the post-decision impact of the *Associated Press* decision).

32.  The *Associated Press* decision ordered compulsory membership in a joint venture that created copyrighted news stories, and hence it is not totally outside of the IP realm. *Associated Press* v. *United States*, 326 U.S. 1 (1945). It thus provided compulsory on-going access to copyrighted material that the lower court had been willing to treat as important and unique.

33.  European Commission (2004), *Commission Notice – Guidelines on the application of Article 81 of the EC Treaty to technology transfer agreements* (2004/C101/02) paras 210–35 ('EU Guidelines').

34.  Ibid., para. 219

35.  Ibid. para. 220.

36.  Ibid.

37.  Ibid., para. 226

38.  DOJ/FTC (1995), *Antitrust Guidelines for the Licensing of Intellectual Property ('US Guidelines') (1995)*, para. 5.5

39.  *EU Guidelines*, para. 231.

40.  This is the teaching that flows from Section 5.5 of the *US Guidelines*, and the 26 June 1997 DOJ Business Review Letter approving the MPEG-2 pool ('MPEG BRL'). The use of 'independent experts' to determine the 'essentiality' questions in relation to a standard is also reflected in the *EU Guidelines* at para. 232.

41.  See *US Guidelines*, sections 3.4 ('framework for evaluating licensing restraints'), 5.1 ('horizontal restraints') and 5.5 ('cross-licensing and pooling arrangements'); and *EU Guidelines* paras 223–9 ('Assessment of individual restraints').

42.  *US Guidelines*, para. 5.5.

43.  *EU Guidelines*, para. 226.

44.  DOJ also has been concerned that a Type B pool could be a safety net for technological laggards; accordingly it has insisted that the cross-licensing not be royalty-free and that innovators actually receive sufficient royalties to encourage continued innovation. See Section 5.5 of the *US Guidelines*, citing earlier DOJ consent decrees.

45.  These were the type of terms blessed by DOJ on 26 June 1997, in approving a type B pool in what was recognized at the time to be a very important Business Review letter ('MPEG BRL').

## References

Baker, D. (1993), 'Compulsory access to network joint ventures under the Sherman Act: rules or roulette?', *Utah L. Rev.* **999**, 1020–25.

DOJ/FTC (1995), *Antitrust Guidelines for the Licensing of Intellectual Property ('US Guidelines') (1995)*.

European Commission (1992), *Commission XXIInd Report on Competition Policy*.

European Commission (2004), *Commission Notice – Guidelines on the application of Article 81 of the EC Treaty to technology transfer agreements* (2004/C101/02).

European Commission (December 2005), *Green Paper on Application of Article 82 to Exclusionary Abuses*.

Smith, A. (1776), *Wealth of Nations*, R.H. Campbell et al. (eds), reprinted, Clarendon Press, 1976.

## Cases
*Associated Press* v. *United States*, 326 U.S. 1 (1945).
*Berkey Photo* v. *Eastman Kodak Co.*, 603 F.2d 263 (2nd Cir. 1979).
*B&I Line/Sealink Harbours* [1992] 5 CMLR 255.
*Floral*, OJ 1980 L39/51.
*IMS Health* v. *NDC Health* [2004] ECR 1-5039.
*Lumley* v. *Wagner*, 42 Eng. Rep. 687 (1852).
*MCI Communications Corp.* v. *AT&T*, 708 F.2d 1081 (7th Cir. 1983).
*Official Airline Guides* v. *FTC*, 630 F.2d 920 (2nd Cir 1980).
*Radio Telefis Eireann (RTE) and Independent Television Publications Ltd (ITP)* v. *EC Commission*, [1995] ECR I-743.
*Sea Containers/Stena Sealink*, Case IV/34.689, OJ 1994 L15/8, [1995] 4 CMLR 84.
*Tiercé Ladbroke* v. *Commission* [1997] ECR II 923.
*United States* v. *Realty Multi-List, Inc.*, 629 F.2d 1351, 1370 (5th Cir. 1980).
*US* v. *Aluminium Company of America*, 148 F.2d 416 (2nd Cir. 1944).
*US* v. *Colgate & Co.*, 250 U.S. 300 (1919).
*US* v. *Terminal RR Assn.*, 224 U.S. 383 (1912).
*Volvo* v. *Veng* (238/87) [1988] ECR 6211.
*X/Open Group*, OJ 1987 L35/36.

# 14 Regulation in Brazil: retrospect and prospects[1]

*Gesner Oliveira[2] and Thomas Fujiwara[3]*

## 1 Introduction

The objective of this chapter is to assess the Brazilian regulatory framework and discuss the prospects for regulation in Brazil. It is impossible to overstate the importance of adequate regulation for development. GDP and productivity growth are quite sensitive to investment in infrastructure. The latter, in turn, depends on a good regulatory framework.

This study is divided into six sections. Section 2 provides a historical perspective on Brazilian economic regulation. Section 3 contains the major issues concerning the Brazilian regulatory agencies. Section 4 assesses the situation of the regulatory framework for five sectors: telecommunications, electricity, sanitation, petroleum and natural gas. Section 5 discusses financing problems with special emphasis on public–private partnerships (PPPs). A final section contains a possible agenda for regulatory policy in Brazil.

## 2 Brazilian regulation in historical perspective

The institutional aspects of the Brazilian economy during the 1980s date back to the process of industrialization of the country since the beginning of the century and more clearly after the 1930s. Under the so-called 'import substitution model', the State built up a productive structure, mainly involving infrastructure and intermediate goods and services, in order to induce industrialization. In addition to the prominent presence of the state, this model was also characterized by a closed economy producing mainly for the domestic market.

The increasing importance of the state as a regulator relative to its presence in the production of good and services is associated with three factors. First, the previous phase of privatization attracted private, national and foreign capital interested in investments in segments controlled by the state. Second, the state mechanisms of intervention had been depleted owing to the fiscal crisis and increasing distortion provoked by the usual mechanisms of intervention such as subsidies, quotas and price controls. Third, the technological development in segments previously characterized by natural monopoly extended the possibilities of the introduction of competition in those segments.

As occurred in other countries, such elements led to privatization programmes in Brazil and, as a consequence, to the necessity of regulation in segments which were under the control of state monopolies. The Brazilian programme surpassed the processes of privatization in other developing countries. It was, however, a partial process since important segments of petroleum, sanitation and banks, among others, remained in the hands of the state.

The forms and extent of privatization in Brazil have varied sharply across sectors. Telecommunications and railroads have been privatized. Partial privatization has occurred in electricity. More flexible entry permission was given to the private sector without the privatization of the state-owned company in petroleum. Concessions to private operators were provided to private operators and entry conditions were reduced to new competitors in civil aviation.

The first phase of the privatization process benefited from capital account liberalization.[4] Federal Law No. 8031/90[5] enacted the Privatization Program, which began the process of reducing direct state intervention in the Brazilian economy. Its first phase covered the 1991–94 period and focused on privatizing industrial sector enterprises such as steel, petrochemicals and fertilizers that did not require the introduction of a specific regulatory framework. Receipts from privatization totalled US$8.6 billion in this period.

The second privatization phase (1995–98) comprised the sale of state-owned companies most directly active in infrastructure sectors such as telecommunications, electricity and railroads. In all, the program represented receipts of US$86.9 billion, of which US$70.3 billion corresponded to actual revenue from sales. Table 14.1 summarizes the sectors that participated in both privatization phases in Brazil and indicates the degree of privatization (measured as private participation in production) that was observed.

In the second phase of the privatization program, given the nature of the sectors involved, specific regulatory frameworks were required. Brazil already had some government agencies with regulatory powers,[6] but they

*Table 14.1   Degree of privatization in Brazilian sectors*

| High | Medium | Low |
| --- | --- | --- |
| Petrochemical | Electricity | Financial services |
| Fertilizers | Natural gas | Petroleum |
| Steel | | Sanitation |
| Telecommunications | | |

did not have the same characteristics as the regulatory agencies created in the second half of the 1990s, as part of the process of transforming the role of the state in the economic sphere.

The new institutional environment, replacing the closed economy and its direct intervention by the open economy along with regulation, was related to private sector pressure to protect investments. Since investments involve long-term contractual commitments, the independence or autonomy of regulatory agencies provide greater certainty, making them less vulnerable to any intervention by the executive in the regulated sector.

Indeed the institutional environment in Brazil was significantly altered during the 1990s with less direct intervention in economic activity and the state taking on more of a regulatory role. The creation of regulatory agencies was one of the key features of this process of institutional change. Their format is discussed in more detail in the next section.

## 3   The Brazilian regulatory agencies

The institutional format of the regulatory agencies is new in Brazil. Table 14.2 shows, in chronological order, a subset of regulatory agencies created in Brazil in the second half of the 1990s as part of the changes associated with the privatization of infrastructure.

The following three subsections discuss the characteristics of the regulatory agencies, how the private sector evaluates two of the most important agencies (in electricity and telecommunications) and how independent the Brazilian agencies are in comparison with a sample of agencies in the world.

### 3.1   The characteristics of the Brazilian regulatory agencies

The regulatory agencies replaced the direct administration in a number of functions. Part of the decision power of the sectoral ministries was transferred to them. This requires institutional building. For the new system to work well a number of prerequisites have to be met:

1.   precise definition of the jurisdiction of each agency,
2.   coordination among the different agencies,
3.   strong technical expertise, and
4.   independence from the central administration and from any private interest.

The lack of precise definition of functions is a major problem in Brazil. There is a frequent overlapping of functions among different agencies. Take for instance the example of a merger between two companies in the distribution of natural gas. The electricity regulator, ANEEL, has jurisdiction

*Table 14.2    Brazil: regulatory agencies*

| Agency | Law | Activity | Ministry |
|--------|-----|----------|----------|
| ANEEL – Agência Nacional de Energia Elétrica | Law no. 9427, 1996 | Regulation and inspection of production, transmission, distribution and commercialization of energy | Mines and Energy |
| ANATEL – Agência Nacional de Telecomunicações | Law no. 9472, 1997 | Regulation and inspection of telecommunications | Communications |
| ANP – Agência Nacional do Petróleo | Law no. 9478, 1997 | Regulation and inspection of petroleum industry and gas | Mines and Energy |
| ANVISA – Agência Nacional de Vigilância Sanitária | Law no. 9782, 1999 | Sanitary control of the production and the commercialization of products and services, as well as the control of ports, airports and borders | Health |
| ANS – Agência Nacional de Saúde Suplementar | Law no. 9961, 2000 | Regulation and inspection of the activities that guarantee health supplemental assistance | Health |
| ANA – Agência Nacional das Águas | Law no. 9984, 2000 | Enforcement of the National Policy on Water Resources | Environment |
| ANTT – Agência Nacional de Transportes Terrestres | Law no. 10233, 2001 | Enforcement of the Conselho Nacional de Integração de Políticas de Transportes' politicies and regulation and inspection of transports' services | Transport |
| ANTAQ – Agência Nacional de Transportes Aquaviários | Law no. 10233, 2001 | | |

*Source:*    Laws cited above.

because natural gas is an input for thermoelectricity, but the regulator of natural gas is ANP. However the distribution of the product is under the responsibility of the subnational state which has a subnational regulator; finally, mergers are authorized by the competition authorities, which in the case of Brazil means three different bodies attached to two different ministries.

Lack of coordination is another great problem. It is becoming frequent to have several issues relating to shared infrastructure in electricity, telecommunications and other sectors. There is not a solid legal basis for providing a rapid and efficient decision-making process. The problem is even more serious in regard to the numerous antitrust questions which come up among regulated firms. It is far from clear which regulator has jurisdiction in many cases: the sectoral regulator or the competition authority.

The lack of adequately trained staff varies across sectors. The absence of a specific bureaucratic career for regulators within the Brazilian state remains a serious pitfall. This fact explains the relatively high rate of turnover among public officials and consequent waste of public resources in training and loss of institutional memory.

But among the desirable characteristics of the regulatory agencies, independence is the most important. Private investors need to know whether there is a regulator who will be impartial. The decision-making autonomy of these agencies is vital for the adoption of technical decisions and this is crucial for the stability and quality of the regulation, which is essential for attracting investment. We can identify eight characteristics which are associated with agencies' independence:

1. participation of Congress in the nomination of the directors of the agencies;
2. technical background for directors required by law;
3. long directors' tenure;
4. budget autonomy;
5. collective decision;
6. quarantine after completion of term;
7. appeal of decisions only to courts;
8. transparency.

The directors' tenures vary from three to five years. In five of the agencies (ANVISA, ANS, ANTT, ANTAQ and ANA) a second term is possible, as noted in Table 14.3. This can affect the agency's independence, since there might be an incentive for a director to avoid confrontation with the central administration in order to obtain another mandate.

Even when regulatory agencies enjoy functional independence, ensured by the mandate granted for their directors, there must be financial independence, otherwise regulatory agencies will inevitably be dependent upon the will of the controller of the budget. In the Brazilian case, although Congress may have some influence on the performance of the regulatory agencies through approval of the federal budget, the latter is

*Table 14.3    Agency directors*

| Agency | Designating agency directors' process | Directors' mandate | Possibility of a second term |
|---|---|---|---|
| ANEEL | Proposed by the President and appointed by the President after Senate approval | 4 years | No |
| ANATEL | Proposed by the President and appointed by the President after Senate approval | 5 years | No |
| ANP | Proposed by the President and appointed by the President after Senate approval | 4 years | No |
| ANVISA | Proposed by the President and appointed by the President after Senate approval | 3 years | One re-appointment |
| ANS | Proposed by the President and appointed by the President after Senate approval | 3 years | One re-appointment |
| ANA | Proposed by the President and appointed by the President after Senate approval | 4 years | One re-appointment |
| ANTT | Proposed by the President and appointed by the President after Senate approval | 4 years | One re-appointment |
| ANTAQ | Proposed by the President and appointed by the President after Senate approval | 4 years | One re-appointment |

*Source:*    Laws cited in Table 14.2.

strongly influenced by the executive. Thus the financial resources of the regulatory agencies must arise from the revenues with taxes for services related to the regulatory activity.

Besides agency independence from political pressures, it is crucial to insulate the decision body from the regulated companies. Thus the following characteristics of the agencies are important to prevent its capture by the private sector through lobbies and corruption: collective decision (Table 14.4), quarantine (Table 14.5), inexistence of administrative appeal within the executive and maximum transparency in its activities (Table 14.6). Tables 14.4 to 14.6 illustrate how such characteristics are present at least formally in the design of the Brazilian agencies.

*Table 14.4   Management structure of agencies*

| Agency | Board | Decisions |
|---|---|---|
| ANEEL | Collegiate regime, board composed of a Director General and four Directors<br>    There is an Attorney General as part of the organizational structure | Majority |
| ANATEL | Collegiate regime, executive board consisting of a President and four board members<br>    The organizational structure includes Consultative Council, an Attorney and an Ombudsman | Majority |
| ANP | Collegiate regime, board consisting of a Director General and four Directors<br>    There is an Attorney General as part of the organizational structure | Majority |
| ANVISA | Collegiate regime, board consisting of a President and four Directors<br>    The organizational structure comprises a Consultative Council (representatives from federal authorities, states, the Federal District, municipalities, producers, commerce, the scientific community and users), an Attorney General, an Auditor General, an Ombudsman and specialized units assigned different functions | Majority |
| ANS | Collegiate regime, board consisting of a President and four Directors<br>    The organizational structure comprises an Attorney General, an Auditor General, an Ombudsman and specialized units assigned different functions<br>There is also the Supplementary Chamber of Health, which is a standing body of an advisory character | Majority |
| ANA | Collegiate regime, board consisting of a President and four Directors | Majority |
| ANTT | Collegiate regime, board consisting of a Director General and four Directors. The organizational structure includes an Attorney, an Ombudsman and an Inspector General (whose duty is to supervise the functional activities of the agency and conduct of administrative and disciplinary proceedings) | Majority, Director General has casting vote |
| ANTAQ | Collegiate regime, board consisting of a Director General and two Directors<br>    The organizational structure includes an Attorney, an Ombudsman and an Inspector General (whose duty is to supervise the functional activities of the agency and conduct of administrative and disciplinary proceedings) | Majority, Director General has casting vote |

*Table 14.5  Quarantine arrangements for the agencies*

| Agency | Quarantine |
| --- | --- |
| ANEEL | 12 months before directly or indirectly providing services to companies under regulation of or overseen by the agency, including controlled companies, affiliates or subsidiaries, under penalty of conducting administrative advocacy<br><br>During the impediment period, a former director may continue to provide services to ANEEL or any other organ of the direct public federal administration with remuneration equivalent to that of the position previously held |
| ANATEL | For one year after leaving a position, a former board member may not represent any person or interest before the agency |
| ANP | 12 months before providing services to a company in the oil industry or distribution under penalty of committing administrative advocacy<br><br>During impediment, any former director not dismissed under the terms of Article 12 may continue to provide services to ANP or to any body of the Direct Administration, for remuneration equivalent to that of the director's position held |
| ANVISA | For one year after leaving the position, a former director is not allowed to represent any person or interest before the agency |
| ANS | For one year after leaving the position a former director of ANS may not represent any person or interest before the agency or hold an interest, position or function in an organization subject to regulation by the agency |
| ANA | There is no specific provision in this respect |
| ANTT | For one year after leaving the position a former director may not represent any person or interest before the agency |
| ANTAQ | For one year after leaving the position a former director may not represent any person or interest before the agency |

*3.2  How the Brazilian agencies are seen by the private sector*

The information of subsection 3.1 corresponds to legal definitions. In addition, it is useful to see a survey conducted by the American Chamber of Commerce in São Paulo in order to evaluate the performance of ANATEL and ANEEL. The results are based on a questionnaire, answered by regulated firms, consulting companies, associations related to the regulated sector, financial institutions and consumers. Tables 14.7 and 14.8 present the answers of some of the main questions of the survey.[9]

The survey indicates that both agencies present a reasonable level of technical expertise and transparency. However it is evaluated that

*Table 14.6   Instruments for transparency and participation in agencies*

| Agency | Organized participation of society | Transparency/accountability |
| --- | --- | --- |
| ANEEL | Any decision-making process that may affect the rights of the economic agents in the electricity sector or those of consumers, arising from administrative action of the agency or from draft legislation proposed by ANEEL, will be preceded by a public hearing | Meetings of the ANEEL board for the purpose of settling disputes among economic agents of the electricity sector or between the latter and consumers, or to rule on infractions committed against the law or regulations, may be held in public, at the board's discretion, and be electronically recorded, with the interested parties having the right to obtaining transcriptions<br><br>ANEEL management will be hired through a management contract negotiated and entered into between the management and the executive power within 90 days of the appointment of the Director General, and a copy of the instrument must be forwarded for registration at the Court of Accounts, where it will be used as reference material for operational auditing |
| ANATEL | The agency has the competence to implement, within its sphere of attributions, the nation's telecommunications policy, issue rules on the licensing, provision and usage of telecommunications services under the public regime, with prior public consultation for proposals to be submitted to the President | Deliberative board sessions for settling disputes between economic agents, or between the latter and consumers and users of telecommunications goods and services, will be held in public; sessions may be electronically recorded and interested parties have the right to obtain transcriptions |
| ANP | Initiatives concerning draft legislation or alterations of administrative rules that may affect economic agents' rights or those of consumers and users of oil industry goods and services will be preceded by a public hearing summoned and directed by ANP | Deliberative sessions of the ANP board held for the purpose of settling disputes between economic agents and between the latter and consumers and users of oil industry goods and services will be held in public |

*Table 14.6*   (continued)

| Agency | Organized participation of society | Transparency/accountability |
|---|---|---|
| | The internal regulation of ANP will rule on the procedures to be adopted to settle conflicts between economic agents and between the latter and users or consumers, with the emphasis on conciliation and arbitration | |
| ANVISA | Existence of a Consultative Council consisting of representatives of federal institutions, states, the Federal District, municipalities, producers, commerce, the scientific community and users | Management contract negotiated between its President and the Minister of Health, after prior consultation with the Ministers of Finance and Planning within a minimum (*sic*) of 120 days after the appointment of the President[7] |
| ANS | Through the Supplementary Health Chamber | The board has the function of drafting and publishing periodic reports on its activities, forwarding ANS accounting statements to the competent organs<br><br>The management of ANS is governed by a management contract negotiated between its President and the Minister of Health and approved by the Council for Supplementary Health, which sets parameters for the internal administration of ANS and indicators to assess objectively its administrative work and level of performance[8] |
| ANA | | The agency will publicize requests for the right to use water resources in the federal domain, as well as administrative actions resulting from the these requests, through publication in the official press and in at least one newspaper widely circulated in the corresponding region<br><br>The board has the competence to draw up and publish reports on the activities of the agency; forward the agency's accounting statements to the competent bodies |

*Table 14.6*    (continued)

| Agency | Organized participation of society | Transparency/accountability |
|--------|-----------------------------------|-----------------------------|
| ANTT | Draft legislation initiatives, alterations of administrative rules and the board's decisions when settling disputes that affect the rights of economic agents or users of transport services will be preceded by a public hearing<br>Any interested party is entitled to submit petition or appeal against actions of the agency, within 30 days of their becoming official | Decisions taken by the agency's board will be recorded in publicly available minutes, together with relevant documents, whenever publicity does not endanger the security of the country or violate confidentiality |
| ANTAQ | Draft legislation initiatives, alterations of administrative rules and the board's decisions when settling disputes that affect the rights of economic agents or users of transport services will be preceded by a public hearing<br>Any interested party will be entitled to submit a petition or appeal actions of the agency within 30 days of their becoming official | Decisions taken by the agency's board will be recorded in publicly available minutes, together with relevant documents, whenever publicity does not endanger the security of the country or violate confidentiality |

ANATEL has not been capable of promoting competition in the telecommunications sector. Moreover a precise definition of ANATEL's jurisdiction does not seem to be available, since the survey points to the existence of duplication of functions between the agency and the Ministry of Communications.

In regard to ANEEL, the agency is perceived as being able to promote competition. However the survey also indicates a very high level of political intervention in ANEEL's actions.

### 3.3    Brazilian regulatory agencies in comparative perspective

The previous subsection discussed agents' perception about the regulatory agencies. We now try to provide a less subjective piece of evidence. From the eight characteristics associated with independence and from the previous

*Table 14.7   Evaluation of ANATEL*

| | 2003 | | 2004 | | 2005 | |
|---|---|---|---|---|---|---|
| | Never/ Rare (%) | Often/ Always (%) | Never/ Rare (%) | Often/ Always (%) | Never/ Rare (%) | Often/ Always (%) |
| Is ANATEL's regulation process transparent and made by public consultation? | 15.8 | 84.2 | 10.0 | 90.0 | 21.2 | 78.8 |
| Does ANATEL act in a preventive way in order to promote and guarantee competition in the sector? | 86.3 | 23.7 | 71.0 | 29.0 | 77.3 | 22.7 |
| Are ANATEL personnel technically prepared?* | 60.5 | 39.5 | 34.0 | 66.0 | 35.4 | 64.6 |
| Does ANATEL act in coordination with different agencies, such as ANP, ANEEL and Cade? | 47.4 | 52.6 | 39.0 | 61.0 | 54.7 | 45.3 |
| Is there a duplication of functions between ANATEL and the Ministry of Communications? | 71.1 | 29.0 | 73.0 | 27.0 | 39.7 | 60.3 |

*Note:*   * In 2005, this question was divided into financial and technical aspects. The results above refer to the technical expertise of the agency's personnel.

*Table 14.8   Evaluation of ANEEL*

| | 2003 | | 2004 | | 2005 | |
|---|---|---|---|---|---|---|
| | Very bad/bad (%) | Regular /good /very good (%) | Very bad/bad (%) | Regular /good /very good (%) | Very bad/bad (%) | Regular /good /very good (%) |
| Do ANEEL's regulatory acts guarantee a high level of competition? | 83.45 | 16.55 | 33.33 | 66.67 | 25.00 | 75.00 |
| Do the audiences and public consultations promoted by ANEEL guarantee society's participation in the elaboration of normative instruments? | 38.73 | 61.26 | 38.89 | 61.11 | 25.90 | 74.10 |
| How do you rate the personnel's technical expertise? | 38.73 | 61.26 | 22.22 | 77.78 | 11.10 | 88.90 |
| | Very low/low % | Medium/ high/ very high % | Very low/low % | Medium/ high/ very high % | Very low/low % | Medium/ high/ very high % |
| How do you rate the level of government interference in the process of decision-making, regulation and inspection of the agency? | – | – | 16.67 | 83.33 | 0.00 | 100.00 |

description of the Brazilian agencies we can provide a general idea, at least from the formal point of view.

In order to do this, we apply an independence indicator (II) to a sample of International Competition Network (ICN) countries. The questionnaire was sent to the 86 ICN member countries, obtaining answers from 29 countries (33 per cent of the population). Further details of how the index was constructed can be found in Appendix I and in Oliveira, Machado, Novaes and Cardoso.[10]

In order to capture the independence characteristics the following measuring criterion was used: value 1 was ascribed for each of the eight elements of independence. The lack of an institutional characteristic that favours independence will be captured by the value zero. For questions with more than one item the result represents the average of values for each item. Lastly the partial points are added and II is obtained as shown in equation 14.1,

$$II = \sum_{i=1}^{8} a_i, \qquad (14.1)$$

where $i$ represents each individual question, so that $a_i \in [0; 1]$ represents the score obtained; and $0 \leq II \leq 8$. The closer the score is to eight, the higher the independence indicator is. Note that this indicator captures only formal independence. The extent to which the regulatory authority is independent in practice is not directly reflected in II.

Note also that the respondents are competition authorities. Although the answers may not be considered official and safe from error, the questions are objective and do not allow significant deviation. In any event, if there is some leeway for different interpretations of a particular question, competition authorities are presumably more capable of providing an impartial and external view.

The replies of a total of 117 regulatory agencies of various countries were analysed. Twenty-eight pertain to the telecommunications sector, 27 to the electricity sector, 25 to the fuel sector, 20 to the transportation sector and 17 to other sectors. One perceives a high concentration of agencies in four sectors, which account for 85.47 per cent of the questionnaires received. It is rather surprising that the II results do not vary in line with the development levels. One would initially think that developed countries would present a higher II than developing nations.

Table 14.9 shows the ranking of countries, obtained from the arithmetic average of the regulatory agencies of the respondent countries. It is noteworthy that the averages of II obtained by developed countries. This suggests that there is not a simple relation between the level of development and the level of independence.

*Table 14.9    Independence index (II), by country*

| Country | II average | Number of agencies |
|---|---|---|
| Serbia | 7.75 | 1 |
| France | 7.55 | 3 |
| Latvia | 7.41 | 4 |
| Italy | 7.16 | 3 |
| Portugal | 6.75 | 4 |
| Brazil | 6.66 | 4 |
| Turkey | 6.50 | 4 |
| Bulgaria | 6.44 | 3 |
| Cyprus | 5.54 | 2 |
| Hungary | 5.44 | 4 |
| Germany | 5.17 | 4 |
| Estonia | 5.12 | 5 |
| Lithuania | 5.07 | 5 |
| USA* | 4.94 | 4 |
| Spain | 4.83 | 3 |
| *Sample* | *4.60* | *117* |
| Argentina | 4.54 | 7 |
| Australia | 4.42 | 5 |
| Zambia | 4.38 | 5 |
| Pakistan | 4.03 | 5 |
| Mexico | 4.02 | 5 |
| Netherlands | 3.42 | 4 |
| Tunisia | 3.25 | 1 |
| Uzbekistan | 3.19 | 7 |
| Sweden | 3.17 | 4 |
| Ireland | 3.17 | 4 |
| Japan | 2.83 | 4 |
| Chile | 2.53 | 5 |
| Poland | 1.88 | 4 |
| Taiwan | 1.75 | 4 |

*Note:*    * The US respondents indicated that questions 4.1 and 4.2 were not applicable. In this case, we assumed those to be 0.

The Brazilian agencies are endowed with a series of formal instruments to assure its independence. Thus, Brazilian agencies present a relatively high level (sixth place) of independence within a ranking of formal independence based on a survey of 117 agencies of 29 countries, as shown in Table 14.9.

With the purpose of assessing the existence of a relationship between the level of independence and certain attributes of the regulatory agencies, equations (14.2) and (14.3) show the tested models:

*Model 1:*

$$II = \beta_0 + \beta_1.HDI + \beta_2.S\_Electr + \beta_3.S\_Telecom + \beta_4.S\_Gas + \beta_5.F\_Franc; \qquad (14.2)$$

*Model 2:*

$$II = \beta_0 + \beta_1.AGE + \beta_2.HDI + \beta_3.S\_Electr + \beta_4.S\_Telecom + \beta_5.S\_gas + \beta_6.F\_Franc \qquad (14.3)$$

where
AGE = the legal age of each regulatory agency;[11]
HDI = human development index of the country of the regulatory agency;[12]
S_Electr, S_Telecom, S_gas are vectors of dummy variables that identify the regulated sector;
F_franc is the vector of dummy variables that identifies the legal family of the country.[13]

The following hypotheses were tested: (a) the age of the agencies is associated with the independence attributes; (b) countries with a lower degree of development delegate more power to independent agencies in order to reduce a possible credibility deficit; (c) the regulated sector has a high explanatory power; and (d) legal tradition of the country matters.

The estimation for the model proposed in equation (14.2) used the series in the logarithmic form, obtained through a monotonic transformation. Additionally the observations of agencies up to one year old were eliminated. In the last decade a certain format for the regulatory agencies was established that follows a trend of more independence of the regulatory bodies.

The regression results obtained by OLS are shown in Appendix II. The dummy variables for the regulated sector and legal families appear to be significantly relevant (Tables 14A.1 and 14A.2). Note that the variable AGE, included in Model 2, is not significant.

Although preliminary, the results obtained suggest a few points. First, the existence of a negative relation between the II and the AGE of the regulatory agency shows that in the course of time the independence attribute does not become a characteristic that is present in the legal format of the regulatory agencies. Second, the existence of a negative relationship between the HDI and the II could validate the credibility hypothesis.

Developing countries lack credibility in their institutions, therefore their governments resort to a higher and not lower degree of delegation to the regulatory agencies.

The sector and the legal tradition seem to have an influence at least in terms of formal independence which is the type of independence we are being able to capture at the moment. The existence of independent regulators is crucial for attracting investment. However we note that there is not a uniform way to conceive and measure independence. Moreover we have not yet been able to capture real independence.

Our preliminary evidence suggests that there is not a positive association between development levels and independence of regulatory agencies. This could indicate that the 'credibility hypothesis' is valid. This hypothesis states that developing countries lack credibility in their institutions and therefore their governments resort to a higher and not lower degree of delegation to the regulatory agencies.

The above discussion points to the importance of formal mechanisms to guarantee agency independence. However it is also necessary to have indications of real independence. This requires an effort to go beyond the mere verification of what the law states. A possible measure is what we call 'the index of potential political influence' based on the commissioners' background. A simple form is to distinguish a 'technical background' from a 'political background'. We analysed a sample of regulators' CVs from ANATEL, ANEEL, ANP, ANVISA, ANS, ANA, ANTAQ and ANTT. If the regulator showed any technical or academic experience related to the specific sector, we consider his or her background to be technical. It was considered a 'political background' otherwise. Table 14.10 suggests that there has been an increase in the percentage of regulators with political background in 2005 compared to 2002.

In sum, Brazilian regulatory agencies represented an important institutional change. However, several improvements are still necessary:

*Table 14.10   Degree of potential political influence in the regulatory agencies*

| Year | 2002 | 2005 |
|---|---|---|
| Number of directors | 31 | 33 |
| Director without specific technical background | 2 | 4 |
| IPR | 6.5% | 12% |

*Source:*   Own elaboration; see text for the methodology.

- more coordination among the different sectoral agencies and between them and the competition authorities;
- in practice the mechanisms of financial independence do not work and agencies do not have stable and adequate human and material resources;
- *formal* independence seems to be high by international standards, but there is much to be done in terms of *real* independence;
- the degree of potential political interference seems to be high and increasing.

## 4 Regulatory frameworks in selected sectors

A single general regulatory framework is not enough. The construction of a sectoral regulatory framework constitutes a *sine qua non* condition to stimulate investment. Such a framework contains the relevant rules to participate in each segment. The following paragraphs describe the current issues in telecommunications, electricity, sanitation, petroleum and natural gas sectors. These five sectors have been chosen in a rather arbitrary way, but they are obviously important in terms of investment. They also illustrate the diversity of the regulatory situation of the Brazilian infrastructure, as Table 14.11 shows.

### 4.1 Telecommunications

Telecommunications is a success case in terms of privatization and regulation in Brazil in comparison with the other sectors. The access of the Brazilian population to fixed and mobile phones has shown a strong growth in the previous years. Since ANATEL's creation in 1997, the number of fixed telephone accesses more than doubled while the number of mobile phones in operation grew by more than 1500%.

*Table 14.11   State intervention and legal uncertainty in selected sectors*

| Sector | Degree of state intervention | | | | Level of Legal Uncertainty |
| | Generation | Transmission/ processing/ transport | Distribution | Commer- cialization | |
| --- | --- | --- | --- | --- | --- |
| Electricity | XX | XX | X | – | XX |
| Sanitation | XXX | XXX | XXX | – | XXX |
| Petroleum | XXX | XXX | XX | X | XX |
| Natural gas | XX | XXX | XX | XX | XXX |

*Note:*   X = low, XX = medium, XXX = high.

Part of the success of the telecommunications sector regulation in Brazil can be explained by the fact that, differently from what occurred in the electricity and sanitation sectors, privatization was preceded by the establishment of a regulatory framework. Thus, the General Law of Telecommunications and the creation of ANATEL in 1997 allowed and stimulated private investments after the privatization of the Telebrás system in 1998.

Besides, three aspects of the regulation in the sector contributed to its relative success: firstly, the establishment (prior to the privatization) of expansion and quality goals; secondly, the possibility of competition, with the creation of mirror-companies, competitors of the privatized regional *holdings*; and lastly, the use of mechanisms (such as price caps) of tariff correction that stimulates the productivity of the regulated firms.

However, two aspects raise concerns about regulation in telecommunications in Brazil. First, technological advance and the development of the market have made the current regulatory framework obsolete. The increasing substitution of fixed telephones by mobile phones and the creation of the so-called third-generation telecommunications, linking voice, video and data transmission in one piece, for example, imposed new challenges to the creation of a regulatory framework.

Regulation must be ruled by technological neutrality, allowing the market to select the appropriate technology. The rules of the game must adapt to the technological changes: regulation must not be divided into industries, but into services.

Second, in the last three years there have been a series of interventions by the Judiciary in the sector, altering the tariff correction index (in 2003) and forbidding the exercise of two-part tariffs in the fixed telephony and the expiration of credits in mobile 'pre-paid' telephones. In addition, it should be noted that two of the Communication Ministers have publicly manifested their opposition to the previously established contractual rules. Regardless of the merit of the question, these actions do represent breaches in contracts between ANATEL and the regulated companies, and this instability contributes negatively to investment in the sector.

*4.2   Electricity*

Privatization and regulation in electricity have failed in many aspects. The current regulation was established in the biennium of 1997–98, with the creation of ANEEL and the Wholesale Energy Market (MAE). The model divided the vertically integrated structure of the sector, attracting private ownership to the segment where there is the possibility of competition (energy generation). A price regulation scheme was established in segments characterized as natural monopolies (transmission and distribution), aiming at establishing incentives for moderate tariffs as well as for investment.

The supply crisis that culminated with the electrical energy rationing in 2001 reflects the failure of the policy adopted in the sector. However, such failure cannot be attributed only to the privatization process. By the time of the energy crisis, only 20% of the generation was privatized. Part of the problem is that the planned privatization process was not actually implemented. The lack of definition regarding crucial variables such as the price of natural gas prevented investment in thermoelectricity from increasing.

Despite the fact that the lack of energy supply was solved after the energy rationing period, the privatization process stopped and the lack of regulation promoting investments remains until today, mainly because of the instability associated with the new model for the electricity sector.

The new paradigm established by the current government assumes that a competitive model would be incapable to guarantee moderate tariffs and service continuity. Thus, the government transferred the majority of the energy production decisions to a state agency (Empresa de Pesquisa Energética), and established that the contract of forecasted energy is to be done through a minimum price auction bid.

The new model transfers the power from ANEEL to the Ministry of Mines and Energy. Thus, it centralizes the decisions in the Executive Power and does not create the stability of rules necessary to stimulate investment.

Rodrigues and Schechtman[14] point out that in a scenario where the Brazilian GDP grows at a 4 per cent annual rate, there is the possibility of a new energy rationing in 2009 or 2010, unless new investments are immediately initiated. Moreover TCI[15] estimates that the current investment gap in the sector is R$11 billion per year, assuming a 3.4 per cent annual growth over the next decade; it is estimated that the necessary average annual investments in the electricity sector is R$20.1 billion and only R$9 billion can be financed by public sources and multilateral agencies.

### 4.3 Sanitation

The major institutional problem of sanitation is the absence of a regulatory framework. Since the 1988 Constitution, four projects of sector regulation have been sent to Congress, and none of them has been approved yet.[16] However the matter is urgent. According to Census data, less than half the Brazilian urban population has access to appropriate sewage systems.

According to Turolla and Ohira,[17] the lack of consensus regarding the allocation of power between states and municipalities constitutes the main political drawback for the approval of old projects. The current structure of the sector is similar to the one established by the Planasa (National Sanitation Plan) in 1971. Nowadays, however, the public companies are not able to attend to the sector investment needs. Motta[18] points out that public companies have deficits or are dependent on subsidies and transfers from the state, being unable to promote the necessary investments in the sector, estimated at 0.5 per cent of GDP.

The lack of clear rules also avoids privatization. Only 4 per cent of the country is operated by the private sector, a figure that contrasts with neighbouring countries such as Argentina, where more than half of the municipalities make use of private sanitation services.

The regulation project recently sent by the federal government to Congress shows improvement by defining the allocation of power and seeking transparency in the taxes and cross-subsidy structures in the sector. However there are still great deficiencies in the project. Firstly, there are no instruments to encourage the efficiency of the regulated firms. In this sense, Motta and Moreira[19] point out large efficiency variations among sanitation companies, which would indicate the lack of appropriate incentives in certain locations. Moreover the study shows that the efficiency gains are not passed on to the tariffs.

Secondly, it is still possible to hire public companies without the use of competitive bids. This last point makes it possible to use political criteria when hiring companies and inhibits private participation and investment.

### 4.4   Petroleum

For over 40 years, the petroleum and natural gas sectors were dominated by Petrobras, holder of the legal monopoly over the activities of exploration, refining and transportation of petroleum derivatives. As the public monopoly was made more flexible in 1995, it became necessary to establish rules that would allow private participation in the sector, which led to the 'Petroleum Law' and the ANP (National Petroleum Agency) in 1997.

However, Petrobrás practically kept its monopoly over the refining and transportation segments, being responsible for 95 per cent of the petroleum derivatives production and controlling 90 per cent of the draining capacity of these products. Thus ANP became mostly responsible for controlling entry to the exploration sector, via auctions and resale inspection (gas stations).

Moreover, even with the end of state control over petroleum derivative prices in 2002, there is still a certain amount of government influence over Petrobrás prices. Gasoline prices in the Brazilian refineries are not in line with the international price at the moment, even with the recent rise in prices.

Petrobrás investments made possible an almost self-sufficiency in petroleum, which contrasts with the situation at the end of the 1970s, when 85 per cent of the petroleum consumed in Brazil was imported. However it is worth noting that self-sufficiency is associated with the modest growth of the economy, and consequently with the demand for fuel over recent years. Thus it is possible that, in the long run, imports and private exploration will become important to guarantee the supply of the product.

In this sense, the main challenge of the sector is to attract private investments in the exploitation and production sectors and in the import infrastructure. Indeed imports could limit somewhat Petrobrás' market power. For this it will be necessary to consider two points. First, give a guarantee of access to the transportation and distribution networks from Petrobrás, making it clear that the public company cannot discriminate in its own favour.

Second, it will be important to ensure clear rules for pricing policy, eliminating the political interference in pricing decisions. Prices below the international level make it impossible to achieve a positive return of the investments in the production and import segments, removing private participation in the sector.

*4.5   Natural gas*

Despite the fact that natural gas is responsible for only 3 per cent of the Brazilian energy matrix, the discovery of the Santos Basin reserves, which tripled the amount of reserves known in Brazil, has increased the importance of this energy source. Natural gas is also relevant as an input for the electricity sector, given that the capacity of the natural gas thermoelectrical plants' generation corresponds to almost 10 per cent of the national capacity.

The existence of recently discovered reserves increases the importance of appropriate regulation, capable of allowing investments in exploration. However, as happens with the petroleum derivatives, the current regulation does not define clear rules over access to the gas transportation and distribution structures. This matter is even more complex regarding natural gas, as both the transportation and distribution segments constitute natural monopolies.

Rodrigues and Campos Filho[20] point out the importance of the access guarantee, by third parties, to the transportation and distribution networks. This is crucial to avoid abuse of market power and to guarantee stability for exploitation investments. However the authors point out that this does not occur in practice, mentioning that market access to the Brazil–Bolivia pipelines involved long and conflicting negotiations.

Moreover the natural gas is treated by the Brazilian legislation as a petroleum derivative, subject to the determinations of the Petroleum Law. This regulatory framework ignores specific natural gas market characteristics and is not capable of setting clear rules on the sector relations. This matter is aggravated by the fact that the natural gas distribution is subject to state regulation, generating the need for a clear setting up of jurisdictions and rules for the interaction between state regulatory agencies and ANP, responsible for the regulation of exploitation and transportation links.

Therefore, as in the case of sanitation, it is necessary to create a specific regulatory framework for the natural gas sector. There is already a law project in this respect, which correctly establishes rules for competitive bids to the concession of transportation services and strengthens the role of ANP (together with another agency yet to be created) in order to establish rules and tariffs and to avoid discrimination in access to pipelines.

The above analysis suggests that there is a long way to go to complete the regulatory reform which began in the 1990s. The case of relative success of the telecommunications sectors is in clear contrast to other sectors where a regulatory framework is lacking, such as natural gas or sanitation. Competition problems are also serious when state-owned firms have retained high market power, as in the case of petroleum.

## 5    The reform in financing Brazilian infrastructure

Given the fiscal constraints of the Brazilian state, it is urgent to stimulate private investment. As the international experience suggests, the public–private partnerships (PPPs) constitute a useful instrument to spur private investments in infrastructure. The executive negotiated in Congress, in December 2004, the approval of a law which makes the implementation of projects by public and private sector partnerships possible.

After three months of postponements, the Partnership Guarantor Fund (for insolvency cases) was created and its administrator defined, as well as the assets (stockholdings) which will compose it. Despite all the initiatives taken at the federal level in relation to the PPPs, it seems very unlikely that the project contracts elected as priorities by the executive will be undertaken before 2007.

There are five projects considered priorities by the government: (1) the North–South Railway construction; (2) the recovery of the BR-116 Highway, from Rio de Janeiro to Feira de Santana (Bahia); (3) the São Paulo Railway Beltway; (4) the Railway stretch between Guarapuava and Ipiranga, in Paraná; and (5) the Rio de Janeiro city beltway. However analysts remain sceptical about the possibility of implementing such projects before 2007.

The PPPs' mechanism must not be seen as a panacea. It is a useful institutional format but it requires certain preconditions. First, it is important that the reduction of risk for the private sector is not obtained by an increase in the fiscal risk. Second, the PPP is an 'umbrella' contract, which does not replace the sector rules, but complements them. The partnership will only work if, besides the general terms of the PPP, clear rules are defined and are appropriate to each infrastructure segment.

## 6 Prospects for the future

Regulatory reform in Brazil is far from being finished. Serious difficulties and inconsistencies remain in the general regulatory framework. The regulatory agencies have to be strengthened and the sector specific rules have to be defined. With regard to the national regulatory agencies, the changes should comprise four elements:

- more coordination among the different sectoral agencies;
- permanent concern with competition matters and coordination between regulatory authorities and competition authorities;
- institutional building in order to assure that the regulatory bodies are insulated from political interference and are adequately staffed and present technical excellence;
- accountability on the part of the regulators and maximum transparency in their activities.

The ideal means to establish mechanisms aiming at these elements would be the creation of a general law of regulatory agencies. A project was sent to the Congress in April, 2004 containing part of the concerns listed here. However there is no deadline for approval and several changes would have to be made in order to ensure agencies' independence.

With respect to the sectoral regulatory framework, it is necessary to create new institutional frameworks in specific sectors (such as natural gas and sanitation), to modify rules in others (as in petroleum and electricity) and to readjust the current norms in dynamic branches such as telecommunications. Many other changes would be necessary for sectors which have not been discussed in this chapter, such as transportation and ports.

It is obvious that general macroeconomic conditions are also important to permit resumption of investment in infrastructure, especially the financing conditions and the evolution of the long-term interest rate. However the institutional and microeconomic conditions underlined in this study are equally important. Improvement of the Brazilian infrastructure hinges upon the appropriate combination of both macro and micro ingredients. And so does sustained growth.

## Notes

1. An earlier version of this chapter was presented at the international conference on 'Brazil: a sustainable economic success?' promoted by the Mercosur Chair of Sciences Po, Paris, 2005. The authors would like to thank Cinthia Konichi Paulo and Gustavo Onto for competent revision and research and their colleagues from the Study Group of Regulation, Competition and Trade (GERCC) and from Tendencias Consultoria Integrada. The usual caveats apply.

2.  Fundação Getúlio Vargas, São Paulo; email: gesner@fgvsp.br.
3.  Department of Economics, University of British Columbia; e-mail: thomasfujiwara@ yahoo.com.
4.  According to Bauman (1999), one result of capital account liberalization was that inflows of foreign portfolio investments rose from US$800 million in 1992 to US$7 billion in 1993.
5.  Published 12 April 1990.
6.  Such as the Central Bank (BACEN), created by Law No. 4595, of 31 December 1964, or the Superintendence of Private Insurance (SUSEP), created by Law No. 73, of 21 November 1966, or the Securities and Exchange Commission (CVM), created by Law No. 6385 of 7 December 1976.
7.  Under the legislation that set up ANVISA, the management contract is the instrument for evaluating the administrative performance of the agency, deciding parameters for the organization's internal administration, and indicators for periodically and objectively assessing and quantifying its performance.
8.  Under the legislation that set up ANS, the management contract will set parameters for the internal administration of the agency, as well as indicators for objectively evaluating its administrative work and level of performance.
9.  The surveys are available at www.amcham.com.br.
10. Oliveira, G., E.L. Machado, L.M. Novaes and M.R. Cardoso (2005), 'Aspects of the independence of regulatory agencies and competition advocacy', unpublished manuscript.
11. The information was obtained directly from the Internet pages of each regulatory agency.
12. The data were gathered from the World Bank for year 2004.
13. According to Djankov et al. (2003), the legal families of the countries are German, English, French, Scandinavian and Socialist.
14. Rodrigues, A.P. and R. Schechtman (26 July 2005), 'Falta agenda positiva para o setor elétrico brasileiro', *Valor Econômico*, available at www.cbie.org.br.
15. Tendências Consultoria Integrada (2005), 'Ainda sem PPP's, gastos em infra-estrutura permanecem reduzidos', *Relatório de Transporte e Logística*, Outubro.
16. PLC 199/91, PLS 266/96, PL 4147/01, PL 5296/05.
17. Turolla, F.A. and T.H. Ohira (2005), 'Saneamento básico no Brasil: evolução e desafios', mimeo.
18. Motta, Ronaldo Seroa (April 2005), 'O debate do marco regulatório de saneamento', Instituto Tendências de Direito e Economia.
19. Motta, Ronaldo Seroa and Ajax Moreira (2004), 'Efficiency and regulation in the sanitation sector in Brazil', IPEA: Texto para Discussão n. 1059.
20. Rodrigues, A.P. and L. Campos Filho (2004), 'A abertura do setor petróleo e gás natural: retrospectiva e desafios futuros', in Giambiagi, F., J.G. Reis and A. Urani (eds), *Reformas no Brasil: Balanço e Agenda*, Rio de Janeiro: Nova Fronteira, pp. 409–32.

### References

American Chamber of Commerce (August 2005), 'Relatório sobre a Agência Nacional de Energia Elétrica – ANEEL', available at http://www.amcham.com.br (accessed on 6 October 2005).
American Chamber of Commerce (September 2005), 'Relatório sobre a Agência Nacional de Telecomunicações – ANATEL', available at http://www.amcham.com.br (accessed on 6 October 2005).
Djankov, S., R. La Porta, F.E. Lopez-de-Silanez and A. Escleifer (May 2003), 'Courts', *Quarterly Journal of Economics*.
Motta, Ronaldo Seroa (April 2005), 'O debate do marco regulatório de saneamento', Instituto Tendências de Direito e Economia.
Motta, Ronaldo Seroa and Ajax Moreira (2004), 'Efficiency and regulation in the sanitation sector in Brazil', IPEA: Texto para Discussão n. 1059.
Oliveira, G., E.L. Machado, L.M. Novaes and M.R. Cardoso (2005), 'Aspects of the independence of regulatory agencies and competition advocacy', unpublished manuscript.

Pires, J.C.L. and J.G. Resi (2004), 'O setor elétrico: a reforma inacabada', in Giambiagi, F., J.G. Reis and A. Urani (eds), *Reformas no Brasil: Balanço e Agenda*, Nova Fronteira: Rio de Janeiro, 1st edn, pp. 385–408.

Rodrigues, A.P. and L. Campos Filho (2004), 'A abertura do setor petróleo e gás natural: retrospectiva e desafios futuros', in Giambiagi, F., J.G. Reis and A. Urani (eds), *Reformas no Brasil: Balanço e Agenda*, Rio de Janeiro: Nova Fronteira, pp. 409–32.

Rodrigues, A.P. and R. Schechtman (26 July 2005), 'Falta agenda positiva para o setor elétrico brasileiro', *Valor Econômico*, available at www.cbie.org.br.

Tendências Consultoria Integrada (2005), 'Ainda sem PPP's, gastos em infra-estrutura permanecem reduzidos', *Relatório de Transporte e Logística*, Outubro.

Turolla, F.A. and T.H. Ohira (2005), 'Saneamento básico no Brasil: evolução e desafios', mimeo.

**Appendix I   Independence indicator**
The objective of this section is to describe the construction of an independence indicator which reflects the different characteristics of independent regulation, mentioned in Section 3. In order to do that, we formulate a questionnaire (Table 14A.1) to different jurisdictions and regulators, contemplating the relevant topics to assess institutional independence.

The first question concerns the appointment process. The criterion used was whether the appointment occurs with participation of the

*Table 14A.1   Questionnaire on independence of regulatory agencies, international competition network*

|  |  | Electricity | Telecom | Transportation | Gas | Other |
|---|---|---|---|---|---|---|
| *8. Transparency?* |  |  |  |  |  |  |
| 8.1 Public session? | YES (1) NO (0) |  |  |  |  |  |
| 8.2 Decisions and rationales published on the internet? | YES (1) NO (0) |  |  |  |  |  |
| 8.3 Public consultation? | YES (1) NO (0) |  |  |  |  |  |
| 8.4 Public hearing? | YES (1) NO (0) |  |  |  |  |  |
| *9. Quarantine after completion of term* | YES (1) NO (0) |  |  |  |  |  |
| *10. How does the regulatory agency named in item 1 interact with your competition agency? (Mark one of the alternatives)* (a) Antitrust exemption (b) Competitive competences (c) Complementary competences (d) Antitrust regulation (e) Other (specify) |  |  |  |  |  |  |
| *11. This questionnaire was answered by?* |  |  |  |  |  |  |
| Name Email Institution |  |  |  |  |  |  |

legislature, or with the exclusive responsibility of the executive government. If the legislature participates, the agency receives 1 point; if not, it receives zero.

The second question assesses whether there is minimal technical background in the relevant area required for the executive to occupy the office. If legislation does not require academic or professional experience, it is deemed that the agency has a low technical requirement, receiving a zero grade. Otherwise the agency receives one point.

The third question attempts to measure the term of office of the main executives. The question was subdivided into three parts. The first verifies whether the term of office is fixed. If positive, the agency receives one point. The second verifies the possibility of the executive having a second term of office. If negative, the agency receives one point. The third distinguishes between long and short term of office. In this case, long term of office (of four or more years) has preference over short ones (less than four years) in terms of independence, thus receiving one point.

The fourth question assesses the budgetary autonomy of the regulatory agency. In this case it was established that 30 per cent of the agency's budget should come from own resources (fees and public services fees). For any percentage higher than this minimum, the agency receives one point.

The fifth question assesses whether or not the decisions are collective. If affirmative, the agency receives one point.

The sixth question assesses whether appeal of agency's decisions is restricted to the judiciary, excluding the possibilities of a hierarchical appeal to ministries or to other bodies of the administration. If affirmative, the agency will receive one point.

The seventh question assesses the degree of transparency of the decisions of the regulatory agency. In this case four subquestions are used. The first verifies whether or not the decision sessions are public. The second verifies whether or not the decisions are published on the Internet. The third examines whether there are public consultations. Lastly, the fourth question verifies whether public hearings exist for important cases. For each positive answer the agency receives one point. The average of the subqueries is computed as being the results for the transparency field.

The purpose of the eighth question is to verify whether the regulator is submitted to a period of quarantine upon leaving the position in the agency. One point is ascribed if there is a period of quarantine.

In order to capture the independence characteristics described previously, a second measuring criterion was used: value 1 is ascribed for each of the eight elements of independence. The lack of an institutional characteristic that favours independence will be captured by the value zero. For questions with more than one item (questions 3 and 7) the result represents the average of values for each item. Lastly, the partial points are added and II is obtained as shown in equation 14A.1,

$$II = \sum_{i=1}^{8} a_i; \qquad (14A.1)$$

where $i$ represents each individual question, so that $a_i \in [0; 1]$ represents the score obtained; and $0 \leq II \leq 8$.

The closer the score is to eight, the higher the independence indicator is. Note that this indicator captures only formal independence. The extent to which the regulatory authority is independent in practice is not directly reflected in II.

## Appendix II   Regression results of the model

*Table 14A.2   Model 1 results*

| Variable | | Coefficient | Std. Error | t-Statistic | Prob. |
|---|---|---|---|---|---|
| HDI | $\beta_1$ | −0.7817 | 0.4261 | −1.83 | 0.069 |
| S_Electr | $\beta_2$ | 0.3124 | 0.1588 | 1.97 | 0.052 |
| S_Telecom | $\beta_3$ | 0.3636 | 0.1570 | 2.32 | 0.022 |
| S_Gás | $\beta_4$ | 0.3000 | 0.1623 | 1.85 | 0.067 |
| F_Franc | $\beta_5$ | 0.2401 | 0.1204 | 1.99 | 0.049 |
| Constant | $\beta_0$ | 3.5412 | 0.3526 | 10.04 | 0.000 |
| R-squared | | 0.1057 | F-statistic | | 2.51 |
| Adjusted R-squared | | 0.0636 | Prob (F-statistic) | | 0.0346 |

*Note:*   Dependent variable: LN11; included observations: 112.

*Table 14A.3   Model 2 results*

| Variable | | Coefficient | Std. Error | t-Statistic | Prob. |
|---|---|---|---|---|---|
| AGE | $\beta_1$ | −0.1533 | 0.3280 | −0.47 | 0.642 |
| HDI | $\beta_2$ | −1.3543 | 0.7064 | −1.92 | 0.059 |
| S_Electr | $\beta_3$ | 0.2326 | 0.1995 | 1.17 | 0.247 |
| S_Telecom | $\beta_4$ | 0.3184 | 0.2015 | 1.58 | 0.118 |
| S_Gás | $\beta_5$ | 0.1980 | 0.1987 | 1.00 | 0.323 |
| F_Franc | $\beta_6$ | 0.3913 | 0.1465 | 2.67 | 0.009 |
| Constant | $\beta_0$ | 4.1139 | 0.6269 | 6.56 | 0.000 |
| R-squared | | 0.1475 | F-statistic | | 2.13 |
| Adjusted R-squared | | 0.0783 | Prob (F-statistic) | | 0.0594 |

*Note:*   Dependent variable: LN11; included observations: 81.

# 15 Regulatory and competition issues in the transatlantic air transport sector: towards a transatlantic open aviation area
*Karel van Miert and Daniel Calleja*[1]

## Introduction
The conclusion of an air transport agreement between the European Union and United States of America will be a landmark in the history of international aviation. It would represent the culmination of a process started more than 15 years ago on the European side, and should set a new template for the regulation of international aviation worldwide.

In November 2005, negotiators from the EU and US finalized the text of a comprehensive first-stage EU–US air transport agreement. As we move into 2006, we are closer than ever to an agreement that many on both sides have viewed as ultimately inevitable, but which has taken many years of work to achieve. This chapter traces the history of the negotiations.

### The development of a common air transport policy
Whereas in many sectors of the economy, the Treaty establishing the European Community gave the Commission explicit responsibility, this was not the case for the air transport sector.[2] Consequently the development of a common aviation policy at EU level, even in relation to the EU's internal market, was a long and gradual process. Prior to the development of this common policy, aviation in the European Community remained subject to national rules and bilateral agreements between pairs of Member States, following the approach of the Chicago Convention which instituted in 1944 the framework bilateral air services agreements that still governs most international aviation today.

*Internal market liberalization: the establishment of a single European aviation market*
The first steps in the development of a common air transport policy can be traced as far back as 1979, when the Commission issued a first memorandum entitled *Air Transport: A Community Approach*. This led eventually to the first legislative step in 1983 in the form of a Directive for Interregional Air Services.[3] A second, more detailed, Civil Aviation Memorandum followed in 1984, proposing rules on capacity and revenue sharing, fares and

the application of competition rules in respect of routes between Member States. Part of the rationale given by the Commission for the need to develop a common policy in the field of air transport was the success of deregulation in the United States, which had produced lower fares and greater choice for consumers.

The first political decisions to move ahead with a common aviation policy were taken in December 1987 with the adoption of what came to be known as the 'First Package'. This comprised measures that limited the right of governments to object to the introduction of new fares, and allowed some flexibility in relation to capacity and access to routes. Perhaps more important for the future was the political commitment made by the Council to continue this process towards the realization of a complete single European aviation market.

The process continued in June 1990 with the adoption of the 'Second Package'. These measures opened up the market further, allowing greater flexibility to Community carriers in relation to the setting of fares, capacity and access in relation to intra-Community routes. However it was only with the adoption of the 'Third Package', adopted in July 1992 and applied from January 1993, that the single aviation market in Europe truly became a reality. The package of three regulations, covering licensing, market access and air fares, established the concept of a Community air carrier. Any Community air carrier granted an Operating Licence in any Member State of the EU was now entitled to operate freely between any airports within the EU, although Member States retained the right to restrict access to domestic 'cabotage' routes until 1 April 1997. The 'Third Package' also replaced national restrictions on ownership and control with a requirement that Community air carriers must be majority-owned and effectively controlled by EU Member States or their nationals.

*Towards a common external policy*
Even before this final stage of liberalization of the internal market was completed in 1992, the Commission was drawing the consequences for external aviation relations. In February 1990, the Commission issued a Communication making a first proposal to the Council on aviation relations between the Community and third countries. The proposal pointed out that the gradual development of the internal market required the Community to be able to act also externally as an entity. In March 1990, Commissioner Van Miert wrote to each of the Member States pointing out that the measures already taken had established traffic rights between Member States, and that the possibility for airlines of third countries to enter the market on those routes therefore directly affected Community legislation and trade between Member States. On this basis, the Commission

stated that the grant of fifth freedom rights to third-country carriers on routes within the Community was now a matter of exclusive Community competence.

Member States were not persuaded by these arguments, and so the Commission followed its first Communication with a second, slightly modified, proposal for a decision in October 1992 arguing that action had become 'urgent and necessary'. The Commission based its arguments on Article 113 of the EC Treaty (now, after amendment, Article 133 EC), because it took the view that the conclusion of international air transport agreements fell within the sphere of the commercial policy of the Community, implying exclusive Community competence. This second proposal focused more on the practical aspects of a common external policy, recognizing that the Community should not deal with all relations at once but that a transitional period during which Member States could continue to negotiate on their own might be foreseen. However the Council continued to decline to give effect to these initiatives by the Commission and it set out its position on the subject in March 1993. The Council expressed the following position:

1. Article 84(2) [today Article 80(2)] of the Treaty constituted the proper legal basis for the development of an external policy on aviation;
2. the Member States retained their full powers in relations with third countries in the aviation sector, subject to measures already adopted or to be adopted by the Council in that domain. In this regard, it was also emphasised that, in the course of bilateral negotiations, the Member States concerned should take due account of their obligations under Community law and should keep themselves informed of the interests of the other Member States; and
3. negotiations at Community level with third countries could be conducted only if the Council deemed such an approach to be in accordance with the common interest, on the basis that they were likely to produce a better result for the Member States as a whole than the traditional system of bilateral agreements.

At around the same time, the Commission established the 'Comité des Sages' under the chairmanship of Herman De Croo to report on the future of aviation in Europe. Its report, *Expanding Horizons*, was published in January 1994. Under the heading, 'competing in a global market', the report recommended that 'a genuine Community approach to external aviation relations must be quickly established because this is vital for realising the economic potential of the Single Aviation Market'. It urged the Council to declare within six months its intention to establish a common external policy under Article 84 of the Rome Treaty within 18 months, that is, before 30 June 1995. The United States was mentioned specifically as being ready to enter into negotiations with the Community.

*Competition issues and transatlantic alliances*
Just as in other sectors, competition rules had a crucial part to play in ensuring that the benefits of the EU's internal market liberalization were passed on to consumers. However, in looking to extend the liberalization process to the transatlantic aviation market, the Commission faced the difficulty that it did not yet have the same type of investigation and enforcement powers as it had in other industries to enforce Treaty's competition rules. This became an increasingly urgent issue as the drive by EU and US airlines to forge close-knit alliances, involving the coordination of pricing, capacity and scheduling, gathered pace. The KLM/Northwest alliance had been the first at the beginning of the 1990s, but by the late 1990s most of the major US airlines either had formed or were seeking to form close alliances with European airline partners.

The Commission was able to examine these alliances only using the residual powers granted to it under Article 89 of the Treaty. Under this article the Commission made recommendations to national competition authorities which had the duty to apply the competition rules. It was intended only to be a transitional provision until the appropriate secondary legislation had been adopted by the Council. The procedures were cumbersome and inconvenient for the airlines involved, the Member States and the Commission alike. Nevertheless, with good cooperation with the respective Member States, the Commission was able to take action in respect of these alliances.

The Commission's basic approach was to accept that alliances could bring benefits to consumers and the economy as a whole, but that such benefits should not be achieved at the expense of eliminating competition in certain markets. The crucial question then became how to define the relevant market. The Commission applied the so-called 'origin/destination' approach, meaning that every combination of points of origin and destination were considered to be a separate market from the passenger's point of view. This led to some criticism that the Commission was neglecting the fact that air transport was characterised by network competition among airlines and alliances, not simply at the individual route level. The Commission refuted these criticisms by pointing out that in its examination of a number of transatlantic alliances and merger cases (Lufthansa/United/ SAS, KLM/Northwest and United/US Airways), it had accepted that certain indirect routings could be seen as suitable alternatives to non-stop services on long-haul routes. These competition cases gave the Commission a foothold in the world of external aviation policy, but it was unable to use competition policy as a tool to open international markets in the way that the United States did with its open skies policy, under which an open skies agreement was made a precondition to the grant of antitrust immunity to an alliance.

### The development of the United States 'open skies' policy

Whereas liberalization of the internal European aviation market only occurred in the late 1980s and 1990s, and followed a phased approach over a number of years, the United States acted much earlier and took a more radical approach. In October 1978, under the Carter Administration, the US Congress passed the Airline Deregulation Act, which dismantled in a single step the regulations that had previously governed market access and pricing on inter-state routes in the US domestic market. Deregulation led to an expansion in capacity and routes, entry to the market of new start-up carriers and reductions in air fares. The removal of restrictions also gave rise to the development by the major carriers of powerful hub and spoke systems, which enabled them to serve many more markets at lower unit cost than previously. It also enabled them to become stronger competitors in international markets.

US international aviation policy followed the same approach, favouring liberalization and competition, but it was not until the 1990s that this came to be formalised as what came to be known as its 'open skies' policy. Interestingly the first open skies agreement was concluded partly as a result of issues arising from an investment by a European airline in a US airline. KLM's investment in Northwest Airlines in 1989 led to a process culminating in air services negotiations between the governments of the US and the Netherlands. In September 1992, the first 'open skies' agreement was signed between the two countries, setting a new model of liberal agreement. All restrictions on the number of airlines to be designated, routes, frequency and capacity on international routes between and beyond the US and the Netherlands were removed.

However it was a further two and a half years before the Administration consolidated this policy into a new statement of international air transportation policy. In adopting the new policy in May 1995, the Department of Transportation noted that most major US airlines were planning to expand international operations. Between 1983 and 1993, the international component of US airlines' route networks measured in revenue passenger miles had grown from around 16 per cent to 27 per cent. US airline revenues from international air service had nearly tripled from $6.3 billion to $17.6 billion.

This new policy was also adopted in the wake of the report of the US National Commission to Ensure a Strong Competitive Airline Industry, which had been established by President Clinton in 1993 in response to the financial problems that were besetting the US airline industry in the early 1990s. While primarily addressing domestic issues, including modernization of the air traffic control system and reducing the tax burden on aviation, the report also recommended that the US should create a multinational system both for air services and for the ownership of air carriers. In particular the Commission recommended that the current limit on foreign ownership of voting stock of US airlines should be increased from 25 per cent to 49 per cent.

The US Department of Transport's (DOT) 1995 policy statement explicitly recognized the views not only of the National Commission, but also of the EU's Comité des Sages, that the bilateral system was limited in its ability to encompass the broad multinational market access required by the new global operating systems. The policy statement laid out a clear plan of action of which the centrepiece was an invitation to like-minded countries to enter into 'open skies' agreements. This invitation was clearly directed towards Member States of the EU. US Transportation Secretary Federico Peña had already announced on the occasion of the 50th anniversary of the Chicago Convention in November 1994 that the US would begin to explore such agreements with nine Member States of the EU.

**The Commission's 'soft rights' mandate**
Of course, for the European Commission, this new US initiative raised serious policy issues. In a letter of 17 November 1994, addressed to the Member States, the Commission drew their attention to the negative effects that such bilateral agreements could have on the Community and stated its position that an open skies agreement with the US was likely to affect internal Community legislation. It added that negotiation of such agreements could be carried out effectively, and in a legally valid manner, only at Community level.

This did not stop a number of Member States from proceeding with negotiations in 1995 and concluding open skies agreements. By May 1995, six Member States (Austria, Belgium, Denmark, Finland, Luxembourg and Sweden) had signed open skies agreements with the US and, in June 1995, the United Kingdom agreed to make a number of amendments to its agreement with the US, although not going as far as a full open skies regime.

Meanwhile other Member States were having difficulties in their relationship with the US. France had terminated its agreement with the US in May 1992, and although the UK had amended its agreement with the US in 1995, the UK–US aviation relationship was less than harmonious. There were also widespread concerns that US carriers were gaining market share at the expense of European carriers in part thanks to their lower costs.

The open skies agreements entered into by a number of Member States prompted the Commission to take more specific action. First, it tabled a Commission recommendation for a Council decision authorising negotiations with the United States and, second, it initiated the first stages of legal infringement procedures against the Member States concerned. This led to an intensification of discussions in the Council on the subject of Community negotiations with the United States, and eventually, on 17 June 1996, the Council authorised the Commission to open negotiations on behalf of the European Community with the United States.

In its decision the Council envisaged a two-stage process. In the first stage the discussions would concentrate on elements required for building a stable framework with equitable competitive conditions. If sufficient progress were made, the negotiations would be extended in the second phase to cover all subjects relevant for the establishment of a Common Aviation Area, including traffic rights. The decision to enter into the second phase would be taken on the basis of a report to be submitted by the Commission.

Thus the mandate granted to the Commission was limited, and was referred to as a 'soft rights' mandate as it explicitly excluded market access (including code sharing and leasing in so far as they related to traffic rights), capacity, carrier designation and pricing, the normal hard currency of air services negotiations. The scope of the mandate included the following matters: competition rules; ownership and control of air carriers; computer reservation systems (CRSs); code-sharing; dispute resolution; leasing; environmental clauses and transitional measures. Following a request from the United States, authorization was granted to extend the negotiations to cover state aid and other measures to avert bankruptcy of air carriers, slot allocation at airports, economic and technical fitness of air carriers, security and safety clauses, safeguard clauses and any other matter relating to the regulation of the sector.

The Council and Commission added a number of declarations to the minutes of the Council meeting at which the negotiating mandate was granted to the Commission. One of these declarations, made jointly by the two institutions, stated that, in order to ensure continuity of relations between the Member States and the US during the Community negotiations and in order to have a valid alternative in the event of the negotiations failing, the existing system of bilateral agreements would be maintained and would remain valid until a new agreement binding the Community was concluded. In a separate declaration, the Commission asserted that Community competence had now been established in respect of air traffic rights. Nevertheless the Commission suspended the legal procedure following the grant of the mandate, motivated by the reasonable prospect of re-establishing legality through a global EU agreement.

The Commission held two meetings with the US, in Washington in October 1996 and in Brussels in April 1997, and duly reported to the Transport Council in June 1997. While the US delegation had shown a real interest in the prospect of a Common Aviation Area with the EU, the US was not prepared to enter into real negotiations until all subjects related to it were on the table. In other words, the US was prepared to enter negotiations only when the Commission had a comprehensive negotiating mandate that included traffic rights. Over the following months, discussions between the Council and Commission focused on whether a pragmatic approach could be agreed whereby the Commission's mandate would be extended but Member States would be able to continue bilateral negotiations in parallel. However, by the spring of 1998, the discussions showed no sign of reaching a conclusion. The Commission concluded that the Council was unwilling to grant the Commission, within a reasonable time frame, a full mandate covering all issues, including traffic rights, which were necessary for the negotiation of a common aviation area with the US. In the meantime, several Member States were continuing to negotiate open skies agreements with the US (Germany had signed an open skies agreement in February 1996), further weakening the EU's negotiating position in possible future negotiations and constituting a further breach of EU law.

In the view of the Commission, Member States were not only failing to comply with EU law, but were also not cooperating to adopt, within a reasonable time, an EU approach making it possible to remedy the legal infringements and ensure equivalent regulatory conditions for airlines to compete on a fair and equal basis within the EU/US market.

On this basis, the Commission decided to proceed with legal action against eight Member States who had concluded aviation agreements with the United States (Austria, Belgium, Denmark, Finland, Germany, Luxembourg, Sweden and the United Kingdom). Commissioner Neil Kinnock summed up the cases:

> By unilaterally granting US carriers traffic rights to, from and within the EU while ensuring exclusively for their own air carriers the right to fly from their territory to the United States, these Member States create serious discrimination and distortions of competition, thereby rendering EU rules ineffective.

**The 'open skies' judgments of the European Court of Justice**
The European Court of Justice issued its judgments on the eight cases brought by the Commission on 5 November 2002.[4] The Court's judgments firmly establish the application of the so-called 'AETR' principle[5] in aviation by which the Community acquires an external competence by reason of the exercise of its internal competence, 'where the international commitments fall within the scope of the common rules', or 'in any event

within an area that is already covered by such rules'. The Court specified in this instance that 'whenever the Community had included in its internal legislative acts provisions relating to the treatment of nationals of non-member countries, it acquires an exclusive external competence in the spheres covered by those acts'. The Court identified three specific areas of Community exclusive competence: airport slots, computer reservation systems and intra-Community fares and rates. Even in instances where Member States had sought to take action to reflect Community law directly in the text of their bilateral agreements, the Court found that they had nonetheless failed in their obligations, because Member States no longer had competence to make undertakings of any sort on these issues.

The Court also found that the eight agreements in question contained elements which deprived Community air carriers of their rights under the Treaty, the nationality clauses in the agreements being a clear violation of the right of establishment enshrined in Article 43. Therefore, although the Court could not have invalidated the agreements under international law, they constituted an infringement of Community law for which Member States were responsible towards the beneficiaries of the right of establishment.

Like most traditional air service agreements (ASAs), the agreements that were challenged had strict clauses covering ownership and control which ensured that only airlines that are owned and controlled by nationals of the two parties to the agreement could benefit from the traffic rights granted. This meant that Community carriers majority-owned by interests from outside their home Member State were excluded from international routes to and from that country. Moreover Community carriers based in one Member State, but with an establishment in another, could not take advantage of their rights under the Treaty to fly international routes from both. These clauses therefore prevented any merger and acquisition activity involving Community carriers with international networks. They also precluded the development of Community carriers with multiple hub systems in different Member States, similar to those operated by American carriers.

Under Community law, such discrimination was now considered illegal and all Community carriers, as long as they had an establishment in a Member State, had to be able to operate international routes from there, regardless of where in the Community they had their principal place of business or of where in the Community their owners originate.

### The Commission response

The Court did not go as far as the Commission might have hoped, in that it did not rule that the grant of traffic rights on intra-Community routes to third country carriers was a matter of exclusive Community competence. But the rulings of the Court were certainly more in favour of the

Commission than those of the Member States, and were welcomed by the Commission. The Commission's Vice-President, Loyola de Palacio, responsible for transport and energy, said:

> Today's judgment is a major step towards developing a new coherent and dynamic European policy for international aviation. In most sectors of the economy, Europe speaks with one voice in international negotiations and takes a leading role in shaping events. Until now, aviation has been excluded from this approach as Member States have pursued their own individual agendas. From now on, it is clear from the Court's ruling that we will all have to work together in Europe to identify and pursue our objectives jointly. The Commission stands ready to play its part.

The Commission acted quickly after the Court judgments by issuing a Communication later the same month on the consequences of the judgments for European air transport policy.[6] It drew the inevitable and clear conclusion that the judgments had implications not only for the eight specific agreements with the United States but also for existing bilateral aviation agreements between Member States and other third countries and for any future negotiation of bilateral air services arrangements.

The Commission stressed that, in addition to the three areas of exclusive Community competence identified by the Court, there were now further issues typically addressed in bilateral air services agreements where the Community had exclusive external competence by virtue of the *acquis* having expanded considerably in the years since the agreements in question were negotiated. These additional areas included the following:

1. safety issues (covered by Regulation EC No 1593/2002 of 15 July 2002 on common rules in the field of civil aviation and establishing a European Aviation Safety Agency);
2. commercial opportunities (including groundhandling, covered by Directive 96/67 of 15 October 1996 on access to the groundhandling market at Community airports and combined transport, which gives access to the internal land transport market);
3. customs duties, taxes and (user) charges (the application of customs duties, covered by Council Directive 92/12/EEC of 25 February 1992 on the general arrangements for products subject to excise duty and the holding, movement and monitoring of such products and the exemption of aviation fuel from excise duties covered by Council Directive 92/81/EEC of 19 October 1992 on the harmonization of the structures of excise duties on mineral oils); and
4. restrictions on aircraft for environmental reasons, which is often included under the fair competition section (subject to Council

Directive 92/14 of 2 March 1992 on the limitation of the operation of aeroplanes covered by Part II, Chapter 2, Volume 1 of Annex 16 to the Convention of International Civil Aviation and Directive 2002/30/EC of the European Parliament and of the Council of 26 March 2002 on the establishment of rules and procedures with regard to the introduction of noise-related operating restrictions at Community airports).

Member States were reminded of their obligations under Article 10 of the Treaty to take all appropriate measures, whether general or particular, to ensure fulfilment of the obligations arising out of the Treaty or resulting from action taken by the institutions of the Community. Moreover the Commission emphasized the point, identified in the Court judgments, that Member States were prevented not only from contracting new international commitments but also from maintaining such commitments in force.

The Commission therefore requested the eight governments directly concerned by the judgments to activate the provisions for denunciation contained in their agreements with the United States in order to ensure at the earliest possible date compliance with the judgments of the Court of Justice. The Commission also requested the remaining seven Member States to activate the provisions for denunciation contained in their agreements with the United States in order to ensure compliance of their agreements with Community law and to avoid the necessity to pursue further infringement procedures. More generally, the Commission asked all Member States to refrain from taking international commitments of any kind in the field of aviation before having clarified their compatibility with Community law.

The judgments argued strongly in favour of the urgent development of a Community external relations policy for air transport. And finally, in order to take the first step forward in this area, the Commission urged the Council of the European Union to agree a mandate as soon as possible for negotiations to replace the existing bilaterals with the United States with an agreement at Community level.

*The US response*

The United States also acted quickly to respond to the Court judgments. Clearly the legal security of its existing bilateral agreements with Member States had been brought into serious question. The US Administration approached each of the Member States that had signed open skies agreements, proposing that they should now be amended so as to remove the incompatibility with Community law, and inviting them to a meeting in Paris to discuss the issue. (The Commission sent an uninvited representative who was, somewhat reluctantly, allowed to observe the discussions.)

The proposals included provisions under which the US would undertake to accept the designation by the Member States concerned of any carrier owned and controlled by EU nationals (instead of only nationals of that Member State), but provided the carrier was incorporated and had its principal place of business in territory of the designating Member State.

Not surprisingly, the Commission intervened immediately with the Member States formally to emphasize that the proper response to the Court judgments was to terminate their existing agreements with the US and to now grant a full negotiating mandate to the Commission. It also reminded Member States that if they were to amend their existing agreements with the US they would be infringing Community competence and that the Commission would have no alternative other than to take legal action against them. It also added that the proposals made by the US failed to recognize the fundamental rights arising from the right of establishment under the Treaty.

**A full mandate for the Commission**

Intense discussions ensued between the Council and Member States about how to give effect to the Court judgments. The terms of a comprehensive mandate for Community-level negotiations with the US formed only one part of the discussion. The most difficult discussions concerned the framework under which Member States might be able to continue negotiating bilaterally with third countries generally, given that the agreements concerned included elements of exclusive Community competence.

Agreement was reached in time for the Transport Council in June 2003, which decided finally to authorize the Commission to open negotiations with the United States with the aim of establishing an Open Aviation Area (OAA) between the EU and the US. The basic objectives of the mandate can be summarized as follows. The first objective was to remedy the elements of the existing bilateral agreements that were found to be illegal by bringing all aspects of relations under the legal umbrella of a Community-level agreement and by ensuring that there is no discrimination between Community airlines on the basis of nationality. The second was to create a single market for air transport between the EU and US in which investment can flow freely and in which European and US airlines can provide air services without any restriction, including in the domestic markets of both parties.

Achievement of the mandate in full would require significant legislative changes in the United States, in particular to remove the existing legal restrictions on foreign ownership and control of US airlines and on cabotage. It was recognized that this might take some time to achieve and the mandate therefore explicitly recognized the possibility of implementing an agreement in a staged approach.

**The 2003–2005 negotiations**

The air transport negotiations were formally launched at the EU–US Summit in Washington on 25 June 2003, only a matter of weeks after the Council had decided to grant the Commission the negotiating mandate. The joint declaration adopted by US President George Bush, European Commission President Romano Prodi and European Council President Konstandinos Simitis read as follows:

> We are pleased to announce our agreement to begin comprehensive air service negotiations between the European Union and the United States in early Autumn, following the early June decision of the Council of the European Union to approve a negotiating mandate for the Commission. This is an historic opportunity to build upon the framework of existing agreements with the goal of opening access to markets and maximising benefits for consumers, airlines, and communities on both sides of the Atlantic. The European Union and the United States will work together in a spirit of cooperation to develop a mutually beneficial approach to this crucial economic sector in a globalised economy.

The negotiations themselves started in earnest in October 2003. The first round of negotiations saw each side set out its principal negotiating objectives. While both sides had the basic aim of liberalizing the transatlantic market, it was evident from the outset that there was a difference in the level of ambition of each side.

The United States explained that its priority was to extend its 'open skies' model to the whole of the EU, so that the 10 Member States who had not yet signed 'open skies' agreements could be added to the 15 Member States that had already done so. The European Union, on the other hand, was seeking to go beyond 'open skies'. Its goal was the creation of a fully liberal market based essentially on linking together the liberalized EU market with the deregulated US market to create a single free market for aviation. This implied not only liberalization of market access beyond that covered by a traditional open skies agreement, but also a degree of convergence in regulatory matters to ensure a level playing field for the airlines of the two sides.

The negotiations focused initially on whether the legal problems identified by the European Court could be remedied through a relatively quick agreement. This gave rise to widespread concerns on the part of some, particularly among EU airlines, that the Commission was prepared to sign a so-called 'early harvest' agreement, in which the EU would make concessions to the US on market access in exchange for the US accepting a Community designation clause. In fact, this was never in the Commission's mind. In the event, it soon became apparent that the US was not prepared to accept the Community designation clause without either liberalizing market access to all Member States, or finding a way to prevent carriers from the non-open skies Member States from exercising rights to the US under other Member States' open skies agreements. Since the Commission was not prepared to pursue the first option, and since no legally acceptable solution to the second option could be found, the two sides agreed to focus attention instead on achieving a much broader, comprehensive agreement.

Given the difference in ambition between the two sides, it was recognized by the EU that its ultimate objective of an Open Aviation Area (OAA) was unlikely to be achieved in a single step. Achievement of the mandate in full would require significant legislative changes in the United States. In particular, establishing an OAA would require changing existing US laws in relation both to foreign ownership and control and to cabotage. The US made clear early in the negotiations that it would not be feasible to address these politically very sensitive issues in the run-up to the US presidential elections which would take place in November 2004.

However, shortly before the Council had granted the negotiating mandate to the Commission, in June 2003, the US Administration had already (in May) made a proposal to relax the existing restrictions on foreign investment in US airlines. Speaking at a meeting of the International Air Transportation Association (IATA) in Washington on 2 June 2003, US Secretary of Transportation Norman Mineta explained that the Administration was asking Congress to raise from 25 per cent to 49 per cent the permissible level of foreign ownership of a US airline's voting stock to give the airlines more access to foreign capital. In addition, Mineta noted that the change of law would be consistent with European Union (EU) airline ownership rules, and he expressed the hope that Congress would include this provision in the aviation reauthorization legislation on which it was working at the time.

Despite attracting the support of the US airlines, the proposal had not been acted upon by Congress by the end of 2003. Nevertheless, the EU and US negotiators took the view that a move to 49 per cent on the US side might form the basis of a first-stage EU–US air transport agreement. The two sides therefore agreed to work towards an agreement in time for the EU–US Summit in June, on the premise that the agreement would be conditional upon a change in US law to bring its limit on foreign ownership into line with that applicable in the European Union.

## June 2004

The negotiations made tremendous progress in a short time. After four further intense rounds of negotiations in the first half of 2004, the bulk of a first-stage deal had been agreed. Several important issues remained to be resolved but, with only two weeks until the EU–US Summit, the

Commission decided to seek the views of the Transport Council in June 2004. The key elements of the June 2004 draft agreement were as follows:

- acceptance by the US of the Community carrier concept by permitting Community carriers to operate to the US from any point in the Community;
- removal of all remaining restrictions on third/fourth freedom services between the EU and US;
- increase in the current level of foreign investment permitted by the US from 25 per cent of voting stock to 49 per cent, matching current EU law;
- creation of new cooperation arrangements between competition authorities;
- establishment of a joint committee to review implementation of the agreement and facilitate greater cooperation; and
- commitment to continuing negotiations on a second stage agreement, with a pre-defined set of issues.

Of the issues that remained unresolved in the draft agreement, the most important were the following:

- market access – whether or not unlimited fifth (and cargo seventh) freedom rights within and beyond the EU would be included;
- market access – whether US proposals relating to the 'indirect air carrier' concept and wet-leasing would be accepted;
- aviation security – how to deal with what the EU regarded as the extraterritorial aspects of US security measures and the need for prior consultation on new measures;
- fuel taxation – the EU demand that the agreement should allow for the possibility that fuel used by US airlines on intra-EU routes could be taxed; and
- the form of the commitment to the second stage of negotiations.

Vice President De Palacio reported to the Transport Ministers on the current state of the negotiations over lunch at the Transport Council on 11 June. The reaction of the Council was that the draft as it stood was an insufficient basis for an agreement. In particular the Commission was requested to undertake further efforts with the US, with the overall objective of improving the balance currently available. The Irish Presidency's conclusions of the discussion included specific reference to the need to focus on more balanced market access provisions and greater regulatory convergence, in particular in the fields of competition, state aids and aviation security. The basic assessment of the Ministers was that the agreement on offer would not provide EU airlines with any meaningful form of access to the domestic US market, while US airlines were already enjoying a significant degree of access to the internal EU market through fifth freedom rights. Implicit in this assessment was the view that the move on the US side from 25 per cent to 49 per cent foreign ownership would be of little or no value in commercial terms, because the existing rules on control would be unchanged. And, if an EU airline were to invest in a US carrier for strategic reasons, it would wish to exercise some degree of control over the commercial decisions of those airlines.

The Commission did not deny that the agreement on the table was unbalanced. But it was also justified in pointing out that the starting point for the negotiations was already unbalanced by virtue of the open skies agreements into which 15 Member States had already entered, and which had granted US carriers unlimited fifth freedom rights both within and beyond the EU. Vice President De Palacio's reaction to the Transport Council was to repeat her request that the Member States should terminate their agreements with the US. The Commission also opened legal procedures against the eight Member States that had been subject to the original Court judgments in 2002 for failure to have given effect to them, and commenced or reactivated legal procedures against those Member States who had agreements with the United States but had yet to come before the Court.

*November 2005*
The negotiations were put on hold pending the US Presidential elections in November 2004 and also the appointment of the new European Commission in the second half of 2004. The Commission anticipated that the negotiations would resume relatively quickly once the new US Administration was in place, but this proved not to be the case. The US had been deeply disappointed by the position taken by the Council in June 2004, and was reluctant to invest any time or energy in the resumption of negotiations unless it had a high degree of confidence that they would lead to a successful conclusion. In particular, the US negotiators stressed that unlimited fifth freedom rights both within and beyond the EU would be an essential element of any first-stage agreement.

The Commission's priority during 2005 became to secure the resumption of formal negotiations as soon as possible. Vice-President Barrot visited Washington in March 2004 to meet Secretary Mineta, and they agreed that they would continue their efforts to work towards a 'comprehensive aviation accord that will expand opportunities not only for airlines, but also for airports, tourism, business links and cargo transport'. They asked their negotiators to review further the possible elements of a US–EU air services agreement with the goal of establishing a solid basis on which formal negotiations could be resumed.

The Commission's negotiators held four technical meetings with their US counterparts, in April, May, June and September. These meetings allowed the two sides to clarify the likely scope of a first-stage agreement, taking the text of the draft agreement in June 2004 as a starting point. Discussions focused in particular on three areas of regulatory cooperation identified by the Council as areas needing improvement: competition, state aids and aviation security. The US made clear throughout that unlimited fifth freedom rights remained an essential element of a first-stage agreement. It also said that, given the political difficulty of securing changes in US law on ownership and control, this issue would now have to be uncoupled from the EU–US negotiations. If the Administration were to have any prospect of successfully changing US rules in this area, it would have to be justified on its own merits as being in the US national interest. No change would succeed if it were being made purely as a concession to Europe.

Following further contacts between Barrot and Mineta, the two sides agreed to resume the formal negotiations. Two intensive rounds were held, in Brussels in October and in Washington in November. All reports are that the negotiations were characterized by a highly constructive and business-like atmosphere. In particular there was clearly a much better spirit of cooperation between the Commission and Member States. This was partly the result of the fact that the Commission and Member States had reached in June 2005 a joint understanding on how to work together in developing the Community's external aviation policy,[7] and partly due to a thorough preparation of the EU's negotiating position during the period when formal negotiations were on hold. This helped the two sides to move quickly to find solutions to issues which in 2004 had proved insurmountable.

**The draft first-stage agreement**
On 18 November 2005, the two sides completed negotiations on the text of a first-stage EU–US air transport agreement. The EU side made clear in the record of negotiations that the Council's decision whether to proceed with the agreement would depend on an overall assessment to be made once the results of the ongoing US rule-making process on control of US carriers was known (discussed further below). The content of the first-stage agreement is comprehensive, and the principal elements may be summarized as follows.

*Market access*

- 'Community carrier' concept permitting EU airlines to operate to the US from any point in the EU (thereby remedying the legal problems identified in the 'open skies' rulings of the European Court of Justice in November 2002).

- Removal of all restrictions on international routes between the EU and US (3rd/4th freedom rights), and routes beyond the EU and US (5th freedom rights): 15 Member States already have 'open skies' with the US. This agreement extends 'open skies' to the remaining ten Member States, five of whom do not currently have an agreement with the US. At the request of Ireland, the agreement contains a transitional provision which maintains for a maximum period of three traffic seasons (18 months) a requirement that airlines operating between the US and Dublin must also operate flights to Shannon airport, and limits the number of US cities that may be served by EU airlines from Ireland.
- Removal of all restrictions on 7th freedom flights for all-cargo services operated by EU airlines but no additional 7th freedom all-cargo rights for US airlines.
- Removal of all restrictions on pricing on all routes between EU and US, but with a derogation to maintain the prohibition on price leadership by US airlines on intra-EU routes.
- Unlimited code sharing between EU, US and third country airlines.
- Creation of new opportunities for EU airlines to wet-lease aircraft to US airlines for use on international routes between the US and any third country, which was previously prohibited by the FAA.

*Regulatory cooperation*

- Security: the US has agreed on the importance of working towards compatible practices and standards and to minimize regulatory divergence in the security field. In adopting security measures for entry into its territory the US has accepted the EU demand that, where possible, it shall take account of the security measures already applied in the EU. It has also agreed to cooperate in allowing the EU to assess whether security measures at US airports meet EU requirements, with a view to facilitating the development of an approach based on 'one-stop security' in the EU. The US has also accepted an obligation to inform the responsible authorities in the EU immediately whenever it takes emergency measures.
- Safety: procedures for consultation in the event of safety concerns on either side, and recognition of the development of safety responsibilities at EU level.
- Competition: the agreement creates a new cooperation framework between the Commission and the US Department of Transportation

in the areas of competition law and policy in the field of air transport. The agreed institutional cooperation framework provides in broad terms the same areas of cooperation as the existing EU/US agreement governing the competition policy cooperation between the Commission and the US Department of Justice as well as the Federal Trade Commission. It includes notification of relevant cases, exchange of information both on general and case-related issues and regular meetings to discuss developments in the market, as well as issues of common interest. With regard to this last area of cooperation, it was agreed to set up a regular discussion forum to discuss general policy issues. The new cooperation framework between the Commission and the US DOT will facilitate the joint assessment of alliances between EU and US carriers and promote the emergence of compatible regulatory results.

- Government subsidies and support: recognition that government subsidies can distort competition, and establishment of procedures under which either side may raise concerns about measures taken by the other side. The agreement also includes an indication of the type of issues that can be raised, and requires the Joint Committee to maintain an inventory of issues raised by the two sides.
- Environment: recognition of the possibility that US airlines may be subject to taxation of aviation fuel on routes between Member States should two Member States exercise their rights under Community law to withdraw the existing tax exemption. It has also been noted explicitly by both sides that nothing in the agreement affects in any way their respective legal and policy positions on various aviation-related environmental issues, thus keeping open the EU's options in respect of future environmental measures.
- Joint Committee: establishment of a Joint Committee which will be responsible for resolving questions relating to the interpretation or application of this agreement, to review implementation of the agreement and to facilitate greater cooperation. Matters not resolved in the Joint Committee may be referred by either side to formal arbitration, the procedures for which are set out in the agreement.

*Other issues*

- Groundhandling: traditional provisions guaranteeing access to groundhandling services.
- Intermodal provisions: provisions facilitating the combination of air services with surface transportation providers in both cargo and passenger fields.

- Doing business issues: inclusion of traditional doing business provisions relating, for example, to the right to establish offices, to maintain staff and to engage sales agents in the territory of the other party.
- Computer reservation systems: the US has accepted provisions guaranteeing European CRS providers the right to operate in the US, on which the US has yet to make any commitments in the context of the GATS/WTO.

*Entry into force*

- Provisional application: it has been agreed that the agreement will be provisionally applied pending ratification. The date from which it will be provisionally applied has yet to be agreed, although it is envisaged that it will be applied from the start of the Winter 2006/2007 season (end of October 2006).
- Second stage: commitment to open negotiations on a second-stage agreement within 60 days of the date of provisional application. An agenda of priority items for the second-stage negotiations will be developed in due course.

*Ownership and control*

Given the imbalance in terms of market access arising from the existing bilateral agreements which allow US carriers extensive access to the EU internal market while EU carriers lack the possibility of operating within the US, the EU had made clear to the US that a first-stage agreement on the above basis could be acceptable to the EU only if meaningful progress were made towards relaxing restrictions on access to the US market. The creation of new opportunities for EU airlines and nationals to participate in the US domestic market through ownership and/or control of a US airline would provide a valuable alternative to direct market access through cabotage.

On 2 November 2005, the US Department of Transportation (DOT) made a formal proposal to change the way in which it would interpret US legislation governing the ownership and control of US air carriers. This was a domestic US proposal and was not linked in any way to the ongoing EU–US aviation negotiations. The proposal was made in the form of a 'Notice of Proposed Rulemaking' (NPRM), with a period of 60 days during which comments could be made by any interested party. The DOT would then proceed to make a final decision, taking into account the comments made.

The US proposal concerns the interpretation of what constitutes 'actual control' of a US air carrier. It proposes that only four areas of airline structure should remain subject to the requirement that 'actual control' is in the hands of US citizens, namely security, safety, participation in the

Department of Defense's Civil Reserve Air Fleet (CRAF) programme, and creation and amendment of corporate documentation (certificate of incorporation, by-laws etc.).

No other decisions or activities would be required to be under the actual control of US citizens. This would mean that all decisions concerning economic and commercial matters, such as choice of markets and routes, type of aircraft, pricing, could be subject to control by non-US nationals.

### Conclusions

On 5 December 2005, the EU Transport Ministers unanimously supported the results of the negotiations. The Council welcomed the 'significant' progress made in the negotiations towards an agreement which was considered 'as a matter of the highest importance for the future development of aviation worldwide'.

However the Ministers also made clear that, before proceeding with the agreement, an assessment of the reform of US control rules would be done in view of the importance for Europe to have better possibilities of access to the US market.

According to a study by the BRATTLE group,[8] undertaken in 2002, the establishment of an Open Aviation Area between the EU and the US would imply an increase in traffic of 17.7 million passengers per year, representing an increase of 9 per cent to 24 per cent in total transatlantic travel and 5 per cent to 14 per cent in intra-EU travel. Directly-related economic benefits could reach the figure of €8.1 billion a year. This figure excludes the potential impact on tourism and leisure that would be amongst the most significant beneficiaries of aviation liberalization. Moreover the effects of EU enlargement from 15 to 25 Member States were not taken into account at the time. This gives an idea of the huge importance of this agreement for transatlantic economic development.

But, more importantly, the establishment of an Open Aviation Area between the EU and US goes well beyond transatlantic relations, and could set the pattern for the future framework of international aviation relations, by eliminating restrictions on market access and introducing mechanisms leading towards increased regulatory cooperation in the aviation sector.

### Notes

1. Karel Van Miert was European Commissioner for Transport (1989–92) and Competition (1993–99). Daniel Calleja is Director of Air Transport at the European Commission. The authors want to thank David Batchelor for his valuable contribution.
2. The EC Treaty covers air transport only with one provision: Article 80(2).The ruling by the ECJ in Case 13/83, *European Parliament v. Council of the European Communities*, 1985, was a key judgment which concerned inland transport but had consequences in other modes of transport, including air transport.'

3. Council of Ministers of the European Economic Community (1983), Directive 83/416/EEC on interregional air services.
4. Court cases C-466/98, C-467/98, C-468/98, C-469/98, C-471–98, C-472/98, C-475/98, C-476/98 against the United Kingdom, Denmark, Sweden, Finland, Belgium, Luxembourg, Austria and Germany.
5. The 'AETR' principle was named after one of the parties in the following case: Judgment of the Court of Justice, AETR Cases 22/70 (31 March 1971) [1971] ECR 263.
6. European Commission (19 November 2002), 'Communication from the Commission on the consequences of the judgments for European air transport policy', COM(2002) 649.
7. Transport Council conclusions (27–8 June 2005), available online at the following website: http://europa.eu.int/comm/transport/air/international/doc/2005_06_council_conclusions_en.pdf.
8. Brattle Group (December 2002), 'The Economic impact of an EU–US Open Aviation Area. Study prepared for the European Commission, DG Energy and Transport by the Brattle Group', available online at: http://europa.eu.int/comm/transport/air/international/doc/brattle_aviation_liberalization_report.pdf.

## References

Brattle Group (December 2002), 'The Economic impact of an EU–US Open Aviation Area. Study prepared for the European Commission, DG Energy and Transport by the Brattle Group', available at http://europa.eu.int/comm/transport/air/international/doc/brattle_aviation_liberalisation_report.pdf.
Council of Ministers of the European Community (25 February 1992), Council Directive 92/12/EEC of 25 February 1992 on the general arrangements for products subject to excise duty and the holding, movement and monitoring of such products.
Council of Ministers of the European Community (2 March 1992), Council Directive 92/14 of 2 March 1992 on the limitation of the operation of aeroplanes covered by Part II, Chapter 2, Volume 1 of Annex 16 to the Convention of International Civil Aviation.
Council of Ministers of the European Community (19 October 1992), Council Directive 92/81/EEC of 19 October 1992 on the harmonisation of the structures of excise duties on mineral oils.
Council of Ministers of the European Economic Community (1983), Directive 83/416/EEC on interregional air services.
Council of Ministers of the European Union (15 October 1996), Directive 96/67 of 15 October 1996 on access to the groundhandling market at Community airports and combined transport, which gives access to the internal land transport market.
Council of Ministers of the European Union (15 July 2002), Regulation EC No 1593/2002 of 15 July 2002 on common rules in the field of civil aviation and establishing a European Aviation Safety Agency.
European Commission (19 November 2002), 'Communication from the Commission on the consequences of the judgments for European air transport policy', COM(2002) 649.
European Parliament and the Council of Ministers of the European Union (26 March 2002), Directive 2002/30/EC of the European Parliament and of the Council of 26 March 2002 on the establishment of rules and procedures with regard to the introduction of noise-related operating restrictions at Community airports.
Transport Council conclusions (27–8 June 2005), available online at the following website: http://europa.eu.int/comm/transport/air/international/doc/2005_06_council_conclusions_en.pdf.

*Cases*
Court cases C-466/98, C-467/98, C468/98, C-469/98, C-471–98, C-472/98, C-475/98, C-476/98 against the United Kingdom, Denmark, Sweden, Finland, Belgium, Luxembourg, Austria and Germany.
*European Parliament* v. *Council of the European Communities*, Case 13/83.

# 16 Issues relating to the enforcement and application of criminal laws in respect of competition
*Mark Furse*[1]

## Introduction

In an *amicus curiae* brief presented to the US Supreme Court in the case of *Empagran*[2] the UK and the Netherlands Governments accepted that '[e]ffective antitrust enforcement in an increasingly global economy depends on close governmental cooperation and coordination as well as respect for the decisions of other nations. Neither commercial transactions nor anticompetitive behaviour by private firms is constrained by national boundaries'. This case concerned the availability of treble damages and the extent of the applicability of the relevant legislation to extraterritorial claims, and is thus not directly related to the application of criminal law. It demonstrates, however, the basic fact that competition law[3] can no longer be seen (if indeed it ever was) as a matter constrained within national boundaries[4] – that the opposite is true is of course the *raison d'être* for this book. The enforcement of antitrust law by criminal procedures and penalties in the US has an impact on the enforcement of competition law by civil means in the EC, both directly and through the relationship between the US and Member States of the EC in matters such as evidence gathering and extradition. Criminal investigations in the US have uncovered cartel activity which has then been the subject of infringement decisions in the EC, and there have been coordinated investigations where the EC has acted using its civil powers and the US has acted using the full panoply of criminal powers to mutual benefit. Further there is clear evidence in the relevant EC legislation that the EC does not envisage that criminal enforcement of competition law by the Member States threatens the integrity of the EC civil regime.

However the fact that a major trading partner of the EC, which is a (if not *the*) powerhouse of competition enforcement relies in part on the vigorous application of criminal law leads to a fracture in international cooperation. EC competition law is framed exclusively in terms of administrative/civil law. Some Member States, including notably the UK, apply criminal law alongside this civil system. To a partial extent only the nature of this relationship is spelt out within the EC system itself (see below). The

US federal system relies on both civil and criminal enforcement. The ability of the US and EC to cooperate in relation to criminal enforcement is limited, as the EC can respond to any such overtures only on the basis of civil powers. The US may, however, cooperate with Member States which maintain criminal competition laws aimed at individuals. Such cooperation may, for example, result in mutual assistance during the course of investigation via the application of mutual legal assistance treaties (see below), and may lead to the extradition of those charged with offences to and from the US. It may be labouring the point to note that the resulting interrelationships between the legal systems are complex, and stating the obvious to stress that the resolution of conflicts between these systems is important to the success of global competition enforcement. Inevitably questions must be asked about the extent to which two enforcement systems, aimed at the same subject matter, but via different types of law, can peacefully and beneficially coexist.

There is a long history of the criminalization of conduct relating to competition. An edict of Diocletian (301 CE) made provision for the imposition of the death penalty in relation to, inter alia, the artificial creation of scarcity in the market for foodstuffs. Lifelong banishment from the Empire was one of the penalties facing those who breached the rules relating to what are recognizably standards laid down in relation to monopolies and cartels in the Constitution of Zeno (483 CE). Remote though this may seem, it has been argued that 'it is possible to trace from [the Constitution] . . . possibly even the Sherman Act of 1890'.[5] Legislation enacted in England in the reign of Edward VI (1547–1553) allowed for the removal of a perpetrator's ear on a third offence, and that the person 'at all times after that be taken as a man infamous'.[6] However, in the face of increasingly liberal economic philosophies in the 18th and 19th centuries such laws were, at least in the UK, abandoned and, by 7 & 8 Vict. c 24, the legislation of Edward VI was repealed. Criminal sanctions in respect of competition law did not re-enter the UK system until 2002 with the enactment of the Enterprise Act (discussed below). It was not until 1890, with the enactment of the Sherman Act in the United States, that competition law generally regained, if not a central, at least a significant, role in the regulation of economic affairs (see further below).[7]

In the US, criminal enforcement of competition law has proceeded alongside civil enforcement, albeit with fluctuations in emphasis and activity, since the inception of the regime. In the EC Member States, however, this has not generally been the case.[8] The majority of EC Member States do *not* have in place criminal laws relating to this area (and Austria, which had maintained such a law, repealed it in July 2002 as part of a process of updating its competition law[9]). The EC regime is exclusively civil, and those states which do maintain criminal sanctions have typically added them to the wider competition law regime at a later stage of its development. It may thus be expected that the relationship between civil and criminal enforcement is likely to be less certain in the EC Member States than it is in the US.

The existence of criminal law procedures in the area of competition law raises a number of issues in respect of the transatlantic competition dialogue and ongoing relationships between competition law enforcement. If the EC is taken as the operative European regime then there are only two choices: to apply civil law, or to take no action. However, where a Member State is concerned, there is the possibility, depending on the state, that criminal law may be applied. The US federal system may apply civil or criminal law, or both, to both corporations and individuals. In the EC competition law only addresses undertakings. In the Member States individuals may also be targets, subject to either civil or criminal powers. Issues arising from such a convoluted system include, but might not be limited to (1) collaboration in the process of criminal investigations; (2) the impact of criminal investigation in one state on the investigation and application of civil law in another (for example, there have been a number of significant EC Commission infringement decisions taken under art 81 EC in respect of cartel conduct which have been presaged by US criminal actions against the same actors in respect of either the same cartel, or another related cartel),[10] and in particular the impact of (3) action in one state on leniency programmes operated in another (a matter of some importance given the increasing weight placed on the efficacy of leniency programmes as a way of detecting hard-core cartels in particular); and (4) extradition from one state to another at the conclusion of a criminal investigation. As indicated, this is not an exhaustive list of all the issues that may arise (and this chapter does not offer a full overview of respective criminal laws and procedure) but these, viewed through the prism of US and UK criminal law, alongside a consideration of the wider impact on the EC civil law system, will form the focus of this contribution. We shall look first at the broad shape of the two criminal regimes of the US and the UK, and then proceed to consider further the issues set out above in relation to these.

This contribution will not consider the wider arguments made in favour of the application of criminal law procedures and sanctions in relation to competition law, although I am persuaded of the case in favour of personalizing and criminalizing hard-core breaches of competition law.[11]

### Criminal antitrust law in the federal jurisdiction of the United States

*Introduction*

Both sections 1 and 2 of the Sherman Act of 1890 incorporate within them terms making breach of the relevant standard a felony.[12] Thus in both cases it is provided that every person in breach 'shall be deemed to be guilty of a felony and, on conviction thereof, shall be punished'.[13] Peritz has noted that, in adopting this approach, the Sherman Act 'introduced uncommon-law remedies that not only recognised new harms but threatened business-men with the most coercive of sovereign powers – imprisonment and confiscation of property'.[14] By the Antitrust Procedures and Penalties Act in 1974 the offences were raised to the level of felonies, greatly increasing the level of the penalty that could be imposed. At the same time the enforce-ment budget of the Department of Justice, Antitrust Division, ('DOJ') was significantly enhanced.[15] The focus in this chapter will be on the law as it relates to cartels.[16]

### Enforcement and policy in the modern era

It will be noted that the Sherman Act does not provide any criteria for determining whether a breach of the relevant provision is to be treated as a civil or a criminal matter, and the choice of approach is left to the DOJ.[17] However, 'the [DOJ] has a long-standing policy of seeking criminal indict-ments only where it believes it can prove a clear, purposeful violation of the law'.[18] At the same time the DOJ 'has long supported the belief that the best and surest way to deter and punish cartel activity is to hold the most culpable individuals accountable by seeking jail sentences'.[19] In the Antitrust Division Manual it is stated that 'current Division policy is to proceed by criminal investigation and prosecution in cases involving hori-zontal, per se unlawful agreements, such as price fixing, bid rigging and horizontal customer and territorial allocations.'[20] Some limits have been imposed on the flexibility of the DOJ by the Supreme Court. In the case of *United States* v. *United States Gypsum Co.* the Court held that, for a crim-inal conviction to be sustained, it was necessary to prove criminal intent:

> Our question instead is whether a criminal violation of the antitrust laws requires, in addition to proof of anticompetitive effects, a demonstration that the disputed conduct was undertaken with the 'conscious object' of producing such effects, or whether it is sufficient that the conduct is shown to have been undertaken with knowledge that the proscribed effects would most likely follow. While the difference between these formulations is a narrow one . . . we conclude that action undertaken with knowledge of its probable consequences and having the requisite anticompetitive effects can be a sufficient predicate for a finding of criminal liability under the antitrust laws.[21]

Generally, however, *Gypsum* is seen as an aberrational case, and involved price verification, such that it would not be relied upon in typical per se cases involving price fixing, bid rigging or market allocation. In a typical case it is enough for the government to show in the case of a s.1 offence that the alleged perpetrator knowingly entered the conspiracy.[22] In the case of

*Andreas* it was held that an element of subjectivity was also required. Thus, for example, if a defendant merely pretended to participate in a cartel arrangement, but had every intention of cheating on that arrangement, the offence would not be proven.[23] The limitation period in respect of a prosecution being launched is five years from the commission of the offence.[24]

During the investigative stage of a criminal proceeding, the standard ingredient is the grand jury subpoena,[25] and the resources of the Federal Bureau of Investigations ('FBI') may also be called upon to assist with the maintenance of surveillance, including electronic surveillance, and the conducting of interviews of suspects. Investigations are not necessarily confined to the territory of the US, and DOJ 'attorneys have travelled abroad to interview foreign nationals and have conducted video interviews as well'.[26] Necessarily the gathering of information overseas raises difficult problems relating to jurisdiction. In *ALD* it is noted simply that the 'validity of a search or covert evidence-gathering conduct abroad depends upon the applicable foreign law'.[27] An interesting perspective on the difficulties this gives rise to is evidenced by tactics adopted during the course of the investigation run by the FBI into the lysine cartel headed by Archer Daniels Midland ('ADM'). Mark Whitacre, the informant working within ADM, invested considerable effort in persuading Japanese executives to travel to Hawaii for a meeting which was subsequently recorded and used in evidence.[28]

At the stage of the grand jury investigation 'targets' should be identified, being defined as the person 'to whom the prosecutor or the grand jury has substantial evidence linking him/her[/it] to the commission of a crime and who, in the judgment of the prosecutor, is a putative defendant'.[29] The target's counsel will be informed that the DOJ is 'seriously considering recommending indictment'[30] and will be actively 'encouraged to present all arguments as to why it would be unwise or inappropriate – for factual, legal or prosecutorial policy[31] reasons – to recommend indictment of their client.'[32] The procedures under which an indictment would be recommended within the DOJ are then set out at Chapter III.G.2.c.i of the *Antitrust Division Manual*.

Evidence of the vigour of criminal enforcement in the US is given in the DOJ workload statistics of 1994–2003[33] in Table 16.1. 1999 was an exceptional year in the history of US criminal enforcement, with over $1.1 billion in fines being secured by the DOJ,[34] and to include this figure in an averaging exercise is to distort the position somewhat. However, the trend is clear:

> in the 10 years prior to FY [fiscal year] 1997 the Division obtained, on average, $29 million in criminal fines annually. In FY 1997, the Division collected $205 million in criminal fines – which was 500 percent higher than during any previous year in the Division's history. In FY 1998, the Division obtained over $265

*Table 16.1   Grand Jury investigations*

|                        | 1994 | 1995 | 1996 | 1997 | 1998 | 1999 | 2000 | 2001 | 2002 | 2003 |
|------------------------|------|------|------|------|------|------|------|------|------|------|
| Initiated              | 28   | 30   | 27   | 28   | 30   | 19   | 26   | 26   | 26   | 48   |
| Terminated             | 62   | 45   | 32   | 20   | 16   | 30   | 35   | 19   | 17   | 19   |
| Pending                | 99   | 84   | 79   | 87   | 101  | 90   | 81   | 88   | 97   | 126  |
| *Criminal cases filed* |      |      |      |      |      |      |      |      |      |      |
| Total cases filed      | 57   | 60   | 42   | 38   | 62   | 57   | 63   | 44   | 33   | 41   |
| Individuals charged    | 50   | 32   | 22   | 29   | 52   | 46   | 60   | 39   | 32   | 28   |
| Corporations charged   | 55   | 40   | 41   | 24   | 19   | 17   | 40   | 22   | 14   | 16   |

million in criminal fines. . . . In FYs 2000–2003 fines obtained exceeded $150 million, $280 million, $75 million and $107 million, respectively.[35]

In relation to actions taken against individuals, the 'view has really begun to take hold' that 'the best and surest way to deter and punish cartel activity is to hold the most culpable individuals accountable by seeking jail sentences'.[36] Over time the length of gaol sentences imposed has increased, and the average sentence in fiscal year 2003 was 21 months.

*Territoriality*
The approach of the US courts towards territoriality has been expansive. The early case law has been largely consolidated via the Foreign Trade Antitrust Improvements Act of 1982. This provides that foreign activities are not subject to US jurisdiction unless they have a 'direct, substantial and reasonably foreseeable effect' on the US economy. The test is therefore one based on the effects doctrine, which in turn flows from the *Lotus* case.[37] The primary authority for the application of the doctrine in the context of US antitrust is that of the *ALCOA* case of 1945.[38] This position is also reflected in the relevant Antitrust Enforcement Guidelines for International Operations issued in 1995.[39] The principles of the effects doctrine have been extended to criminal enforcement and, in the case of *Nippon Paper II*,[40] the court held that a criminal prosecution could be advanced against a foreign company for activity wholly undertaken outside the US.

The extraterritorial application of US antitrust law may be limited by the principle of comity, an emerging principle of international law of particular importance in the area of competition enforcement, which has received recognition in bilateral agreements.[41] Comity was defined as early as 1895 as being the principle under which a state has regard 'within its territory to the legislative, executive, or judicial acts of another nation, having due regard both to international law and convenience, and to the rights of its own citizens'.[42] In the area of conflicting application of competition laws, comity may be the most important limiting principle. The three leading modern cases dealing with comity are *Timberlane*,[43] *Mannington Mills*,[44] and *Hartford Fire*.[45] The combined effect of these three cases is that jurisdiction may be asserted where the practice complained of has direct effect in the US, 'was meant to produce and did in fact produce some *substantial* effect'.[46]

Baker has noted that the assumption of foreign executives that they are safe from the reach of the US authorities as long as they do not stray onto US territory is a false one: 'the DOJ does not care where the meeting or communication takes place so long as it has some direct, foreseeable impact on US imports or international markets in which US enterprises and consumers make purchases'.[47] Evidence to support this view in relation to the companies themselves which are penalized is found in a DOJ table setting out Sherman Act violations yielding a fine in excess of $10 million or more.[48] As at January 2005, of the top 20 ranked in descending order of the amount of the penalty, 14 are companies outside the US and a fifteenth is the American subsidiary of a German parent. The highest of these penalties is the $500 million paid by Hoffmann-La Roche in 1999 in respect of its involvement in the international vitamins cartel, and the second-highest penalty, of $225 million, was paid by BASF AG following its engagement in the same cartel. Of the 48 instances of fines of $10 million or more being paid, only eight were levied on US companies that do not have foreign parents.[49] Foreign nationals are not immune from incarceration:

> The Division has prosecuted foreign executives from Belgium, Canada, France, Germany, Italy, Japan, Korea, Mexico, Norway, the Netherlands, South Africa, Sweden, Switzerland, and the United Kingdom for engaging in cartel activity, resulting in heavy fines and, in some cases, imprisonment. Since FY 2001, roughly one-third of the individual defendants in our cases have been foreign nationals. Foreign defendants from Canada, France, Germany, Sweden, and Switzerland have served prison sentences in U.S. jails for violating U.S. antitrust laws.[50]

The question of how citizens of the EU might be subject to the assertion of US law, via extradition and more informal procedures, is discussed below.

### Criminal competition law in the United Kingdom
*Introduction*
While the US criminal system is now well into its second century, the UK system has barely learnt to crawl, and at the time of writing no prosecutions under the relevant legislation[51] have been brought forward.[52] Section 188(1) of the Enterprise Act 2002 provides that: 'An individual is guilty of a cartel offence if he dishonestly agrees with one or more other persons to

make or implement, or to cause to be made or implemented, arrangements of the following kind relating to at least two undertakings (A and B).'

The arrangements referred to in s.188(1) are specified in s.188(2) as being the following:

> The arrangements must be ones which, if operating as the parties to the agreement intend, would–
> (a) directly or indirectly fix a price for the supply by A in the United Kingdom (otherwise than to B) of a product or service,
> (b) limit or prevent supply by A in the United Kingdom of a product or service,
> (c) limit or prevent production by A in the United Kingdom of a product,
> (d) divide between A and B the supply in the United Kingdom of a product or service to a customer or customers,
> (e) divide between A and B customers for the supply in the United Kingdom of a product or service, or
> (f) be bid-rigging arrangements.

The US experience, referred to above, clearly influenced UK policy in this respect, and during the passage of the Bill a representative of the US Attorney General was quoted as saying: 'I have had numerous lawyers pleading with me to avoid a gaol term for their client and offering to pay any sum imaginable. I have never had anyone offering to spend another week in gaol in return for a lower fine.'[53]

*Enforcement and policy*

It was anticipated in the Penrose report[54] that there might be some six to ten prosecutions a year in relation to any new offence (although this figure is likely to be an overestimate in light of the visible activity to date) and that these would 'probably be complex and the majority will be high profile'.[55] The new offence is, by design, separated from the wider body of competition law. This in part reflects an attempt to remove from the ambit of jury deliberations such issues as whether there has been a restriction of competition. However there are clear links, both functional and substantive, between the criminal and civil law regimes. In particular the same body, the Office of Fair Trading ('OFT') has the primary responsibility in relation to both the enforcement of the civil law of competition enshrined in arts 81 and 82 EC and the Competition Act 1998, and the cartel offence.

A key difference between the civil and criminal competition law in the UK[56] is that the former is addressed almost exclusively to 'undertakings' or 'associations of undertakings',[57] while the latter is addressed to individuals. This shapes the framework of the relationship between EC competition law (and its domestic reflection in the Competition Act) and the cartel offence. It is provided in EC Regulation 1/2003[58] that 'this Regulation does not apply to national laws which impose criminal sanctions on natural persons except to the extent that such sanctions are the means whereby competition rules applying to undertakings are enforced.'[59] This statement is more than merely neutral in relation to what it implies about the attitude of the EC to national criminal enforcement of competition law against individuals. The primary purpose of the Regulation is to 'ensure the effective enforcement of the Community competition rules'[60] and it would therefore appear to be accepted within the EC regime that the imposition of criminal sanctions on individuals in relation to competition law does *not* jeopardize the efficient working of the EC competition law system, notwithstanding the fact that it is clear that individuals may face criminal sanction for their participation in conduct in respect of which undertakings have been sanctioned under the civil provisions of Regulation 1/2003, and relevant domestic procedures.

*Territoriality*
The approach of the UK to the issue of territoriality follows that of the case law of the European Court of Justice ('ECJ') and Court of First Instance ('CFI') in respect of the applications of arts 81 and 82 EC, but does so via legislative, rather than judicial, language. Section 190(3) of the Act provides that 'No proceedings may be brought for an offence under section 188 in respect of an agreement outside the United Kingdom, unless it has been implemented in whole or part in the United Kingdom.' Although there is no direct interpretative link between the Enterprise Act 2002 and the operation of EC competition law, in the way that is provided in the Competition Act 1998, it is presumed that the word 'implemented' in s.190(3) will be given the meaning it has in EC cases such as *Wood Pulp*[61] and *Gencor*.[62] It is anticipated that, like the US, the UK would in appropriate circumstances seek extradition of suspects, and would contemplate the imprisonment of foreign nationals, as long as the requirements of s.188 are fulfilled.[63]

**Leniency arrangements**
Leniency programmes have been 'spectacularly successful',[64] and 'are the basis for a majority of cartel prosecutions by the United States', and 'the European Commission's experience is similar'.[65] During the passage of the Enterprise Bill through Committee the Under Secretary of State remarked on the fact that it was 'important to have a transparent leniency programme, which is an essential element in successfully cracking and prosecuting international cartels'.[66] It is increasingly the case that there have been more situations in which the relevant authorities (inter alia the DOJ, EC Commission and OFT) 'have seen more simultaneous amnesty applications, which have resulted in more opportunities for multi-jurisdictional cooperation'.[67] In both the US and the UK there are links between the

criminal and civil aspects of the leniency arrangements, and a further link exists in the UK between the domestic and EC leniency programmes. A direct analogy cannot be drawn between the UK approach, where EC law is an integral, and superior, component of its law, and the approach in relationships between the US and the EC. However, were cooperation between these two regimes to be enhanced, the UK approach provides a workable model in reconciling civil and criminal leniency programmes, and the demands of different regimes.

*Leniency in the US*
In the US, prosecutors have a clear policy:

> Individuals, but not enterprises, have the right to remain silent under the Fifth Amendment for fear of incriminating themselves. The government's response is to grant immunity for those individuals who come forward with evidence that the investigators believe will make or strengthen their cases against others. Within an enterprise, the DOJ investigators will always be interested in trying to indict the highest ranking officials who participated in, authorised, or even just condoned the conspiracy. Thus, immunity will be handed out to lower level employees and even those who participated in illegal cartel meetings in return for testimony implicating their superiors. This is definitely a 'dog eat dog' environment and the prosecutors love it.[68]

The US corporate leniency policy was reformed and clarified in August 1993,[69] and the individual leniency policy was published a year later.[70] Both policies are pertinent to criminal actions. The three conditions for the grant of individual leniency are as follows:

1. At the time the individual comes forward to report the illegal activity, the Division has not received information about the illegal activity being reported from any other source;
2. The individual reports the wrongdoing with candour and completeness and provides full continuing and complete cooperation to the Division throughout the investigation; and
3. The individual did not coerce another party to participate in the illegal activity and clearly was not the leader in, or originator of, the activity.

For corporate leniency the position is slightly more complex. Six conditions must be met for the grant of leniency in relation to a corporation reporting illegal activity before the DOJ has commenced an investigation:

1. At the time the corporation comes forward to report the illegal activity, the Division has not received information about the illegal activity being reported from any other source;

2. The corporation, upon its discovery of the illegal activity being reported, took prompt and effective action to terminate its part in the activity;
3. The corporation reports the wrongdoing with candour and completeness and provides full, continuing and complete cooperation to the Division throughout the investigation;
4. The confession of wrongdoing is truly a corporate act, as opposed to isolated confessions of individual executives or officials;
5. Where possible, the corporation makes restitution to injured parties; and
6. The corporation did not coerce another party to participate in the illegal activity and clearly was not the leader in, or originator of, the activity.

If not all of these requirements are met, leniency may still be available conditional on a seven-fold set of criteria. Conditions 3–6 match those of conditions 2–5 in the above list. The first two alternative conditions are that (1) irrespective of whether or not the DOJ has commenced investigation, the corporation is the first to seek leniency; and (2) at the time of the corporation coming forward, the DOJ does not have sufficient evidence against it for a sustainable conviction. The last condition is that 'granting leniency would not be unfair to others, considering the nature of the illegal activity, the confessing corporation's role in it, and when the corporation comes forward'. Where a corporation satisfies the initial set of leniency requirements, all corporate officers and employees who admit their involvement as part of the corporation application are also granted leniency, as long as 'they admit their wrongdoing with candour and completeness and continue to assist the [DOJ] through the investigation'. Although corporations are required to make restitution to injured parties where possible under an enhanced 'leniency plus' scheme they may now be immune from the potent threat of treble damages actions in the US, but not from actions seeking the recovery of actual damages, either in the US or, of course, in other jurisdictions where the leniency will have no force. Leniency plus should be distinguished from 'amnesty plus', which relates to arrangements whereby a defendant negotiating a plea agreement in respect of an investigation in one industry receives a sentencing reduction in respect of this cartel if they report one in another industry.

*Leniency in the UK*
Following a major overhaul of its leniency arrangements, the EC programme is now very similar to that of the US, although there are some differences in, for example, the discounts available where full leniency is not available. The UK had brought its own arrangements into much closer

alignment with the US ahead of the EC, following arguments widely made to the effect that the EC leniency arrangements as first cast were too uncertain to generate the high returns demonstrated in the US. The new EC leniency programme was set out in a notice published in 2002.[71] Necessarily this relates exclusively to the EC civil regime, and is directed to enforcement activity undertaken by the EC Commission, and not to the devolved enforcement that is a central character of the post-Regulation 1/2003 regime. The fact that the leniency available under this programme does not directly protect those who might face criminal prosecution under the laws of a Member State has invited criticism. It has thus been noted that, 'if cooperation with the EC pursuant to the 2002 Leniency Notice leads inevitably to criminal exposure for individuals under Member State laws, individuals with potential criminal exposure under Member State laws will not cooperate with leniency applications by their employers'.[72]

In the UK, which faces within its domestic system the interrelationship between civil and criminal enforcement, these concerns have been addressed. The Penrose Report identified the problem clearly:

> The difficulty faced by the OFT is how to provide sufficient comfort against criminal prosecution and the impression of custodial sentences for potential whistleblowers who inform on other cartel participants. In particular, the OFT would need a policy which would:
> – provide sufficient 'certainty' to whistleblowers that they would not personally face criminal prosecution, and
> – be consistent with the existing leniency policies operated under civil procedures in both the UK and the EC in respect of undertakings whilst
> – maintaining the integrity of the SFO [Serious Fraud Office] as the prosecuting authority and the criminal justice system in the UK as a whole.

Two separate, but related, leniency schemes are in operation. The programme operating under the civil regime of the Competition Act 1998 is set out in Part 3 of the OFT's 'Guidance as to the appropriate amount of a penalty'.[73] There are four separate elements to this programme. Under the first,[74] total immunity is available to the first undertaking coming forward before an investigation has commenced. Four conditions must be met for total immunity from financial penalties to be granted: (1) the undertaking must provide the OFT with all the information available to it; (2) it must cooperate continuously throughout the procedure; (3) it must cease its illegal activity, unless instructed otherwise by the OFT; and (4) it must not have taken steps to coerce another undertaking to join the cartel. If these four conditions are met, but an investigation has commenced, an undertaking may still benefit from a reduction in penalty where it provides the OFT with the pertinent information prior to the issuing of a statement of objections.[75] Thirdly, penalties may be reduced to those who do not meet the requirements for total immunity, as long as the first three of the above conditions are met.[76] Finally undertakings may be awarded some reduction in penalty if, in the course of an investigation into one cartel, they notify the OFT about their participation in another.[77] In this case there may be a reduction of the fine levied in respect of the first cartel as well as in relation to the second. Full, or partial, immunity has been granted in a number of cartel cases brought forward by the OFT since the commencement of enforcement activity under the Act.

In respect of the cartel offence the leniency programme is expressed somewhat differently, and takes the form of 'no-action letters'. These are explained in the following terms in the relevant guidance:

> In the context of the cartel offence, immunity from prosecution will be granted in the form of a 'no-action letter', issued by the OFT under s.190(4) of the Enterprise Act. A no-action letter will prevent a prosecution being brought against an individual in England and Wales or Northern Ireland for the cartel offence except in circumstances specified in the letter.[78]

The conditions for the grant of a no-action letter closely mirror those for the grant of civil leniency, with the initial addition of the requirement on the individual to admit participation in a criminal offence. It is, naturally, envisaged in the guidance that an approach for leniency may be made on behalf of named employees and directors (whether present or former) of undertakings seeking leniency under the civil provisions discussed above. The OFT anticipates that, where an undertaking qualifies for full leniency under the civil programme, named individuals from within that company will benefit from the grant of a no-action letter. This applies equally in the case where leniency is granted by the EC Commission directly when it is itself investigating a cartel. However the OFT has made it clear in its 'Guidance as to the appropriate amount of a penalty' that there is no direct link between its leniency programme and that in operation in other members of the European Competition Network ('ECN').[79]

It is not, at the present stage of development of the law, surprising that neither the UK nor the US recognizes in the application of their respective leniency programmes or enforcement regimes the effect of leniency granted in foreign jurisdictions. As noted above, the UK's recognition of the effect of leniency granted by the EC Commission is not to be regarded as expansive. An enhancement to the present EC–US cooperation arrangements, extended to incorporate the Member States' criminal regimes, offering mutual recognition to leniency awards, would be of clear benefit in the fight against international cartels. Substantive differences between the various leniency regimes are not substantial, and the added factor of criminal jeopardy does not appear greatly to complicate the picture, given that both the

US and the UK have been able to draw a clear link between civil and criminal leniency schemes.

## Collaboration in the course of investigations

The DOJ has stated:

> it is no longer uncommon for international antitrust authorities to discuss investigative strategies and to coordinate searches, service of subpoenas, drop-in interviews, and the timing of charges in order to avoid the premature disclosure of an investigation and the possible destruction of evidence. Such cooperation will lead to more effective antitrust enforcement in the future and the detection, prosecution, and elimination of more cartels.[80]

Within the EC competition law system a great deal of information is necessarily shared between the EC Commission and the members of the ECN relating to the civil enforcement of arts 81 and 82 EC, and there are implications for the enforcement in member states of criminal law.[81] The formal rules relating to the operation of this system were established in Regulation 1/2003, and are further clarified in a number of notices relating to various aspects of the regime. The exchange of information between the members of the ECN is governed primarily by art.12 of the Regulation. Thus art.12(1) provides that:

> *For the purpose of applying arts 81 and 82 of the Treaty* the Commission and the competition authorities of the member states shall have the power to provide one another with and use in evidence any matter of fact or of law including confidential information [emphasis added].

Information exchanged under this provision may, however, also be used in relation to the application of national competition law where it is applied 'in the same case and in parallel to' EC competition law.[82] Two provisions set out in art.12(3) relate to the use of such information in relation to the imposition of sanctions on natural persons. The first arises where the *transmitting* authority 'foresees sanctions of a similar kind in relation to an infringement of art.81 or art.82 [EC]'. It is to be expected, and hoped, that an effective operation of the ECN would mean that transmitting authorities were made aware of situations in which such information was to be used to support actions in the receiving authority, and it could be argued that the mere existence of such procedures in the receiving state should itself serve as a notice to the transmitting authorities of the likelihood of such an action.[83] Outside of the standard transmission mechanisms set out in the Regulation it would remain the case that 'additional provisions may be necessary to enable member states to exchange information for evidence . . . where the conditions of [art. 12(3)] are not met'.[84]

Referring to 'improved cooperation', the DOJ advertises the fact that this has 'provided [it] with increased access to foreign-located evidence and witnesses that has proven to be instrumental in the cracking of a number of international cartels', and at least five jurisdictions have cooperated in executing search warrants (although these are not specified).[85]

An example of increased cooperation in the sphere of competition law enforcement can be found in the revision of the UK/US Mutual Legal Assistance Treaty, which was updated on 1 May 2001. Competition law matters had previously been excluded from the scope of the Treaty, which now provides that the UK will 'offer assistance in respect of requests from the United States of America made pursuant to the Treaty for assistance in anti-trust and competition law investigations'.[86] Mutual legal assistance treaties (MLATs) generally 'require contracting parties to undertake to provide assistance in taking written testimony; conducting searches for and seizing material for use as evidence; serving summonses and tracing witnesses and suspects'.[87]

Inevitably there are differences in the rights accorded to those subject to competition law in the EC (including the UK where the rights available in civil cases are derived in part from the European Convention on Human Rights ('ECHR')[88] and the general principles of EC law) and US systems. Most glaringly, in the US system, a corporation has no privilege against self-incrimination, whereas in the EC system certain protections enshrined in the general principles of law common to the member states and in the ECHR, including the privilege against self-incrimination, extend to bodies corporate.[89] The standards of protection that apply in UK criminal proceedings are drawn from both domestic provisions, in particular the Police and Criminal Evidence Act 1994,[90] and, unless expressly provided otherwise, are not to conflict with the standards set out in the ECHR.

It would appear clear that increased coordination in investigating and taking action against hard-core anticompetitive conduct is having a positive effect on the detection, and presumably deterrence, of cartels. There appears to be no underlying tension between the fact that the investigation in one jurisdiction might be of a criminal nature, leading to individual sanctions, and that in another it might be of a civil nature and lead to sanctions only on the corporate entities involved. However even within the EC, to a substantial extent the exchange of information, and other assistance in the enforcement of criminal law, is dependent on bilateral arrangements, and is not resolved by reference to an overarching EC framework. Enhanced cooperation between the US and the EC is similarly driven by bilateral arrangements with the EC Member States, and not with the EC as a whole. This tension is unavoidable until such time as the EC itself addresses the issue of cooperation in criminal matters as they relate to competition enforcement. It remains to be seen whether the will to do this exists.

### Collaboration in enforcement and extradition

To attempt to prosecute a national of another member state is one matter, but to obtain possession of that person may be more difficult. Sir Anthony Tennant, for example, a UK national and resident, is regarded by the DOJ as an international fugitive, sought for his part in the Sotheby's/Christies cartel.[91] While he is perhaps the most high-profile 'fugitive', he is not alone.

The US has stepped up its efforts to secure custody over those charged with violations of the Sherman Act in recent years:

> In 2001, the Division adopted a policy of placing indicted fugitives on a 'Red Notice' list maintained by INTERPOL. A red notice watch is essentially an international 'wanted' notice that, in many INTERPOL member nations, serves as a request that the subject be arrested, with a view toward extradition. Multiple fugitive defendants have already been apprehended through a Division INTER-POL red notice. The Division will seek to extradite any fugitive defendant apprehended through the INTERPOL red notice watch. The Division's use of red notices clearly raises the stakes for foreign executives who hope to avoid prosecution by simply remaining outside of the United States. With the stiffening resolve that foreign governments are taking toward punishing cartel activity and their increased willingness to assist the United States in prosecuting cartel activity, the safe harbours for antitrust offenders are rapidly shrinking.[92]

However a high proportion of foreign nationals imprisoned in the US for antitrust offences have not been subject to extradition proceedings, but have voluntarily surrendered to the US authorities. While this may seem to be unusual behaviour, executives in these circumstances are offered light sentences, some opportunity to make a recommendation to the Court regarding the type and location of the prison facility to which they are sentenced and, perhaps crucially, the right to travel to the US in future so as to be able to continue with their business careers following the period of incarceration.[93]

In the UK the Enterprise Act makes express provision for extradition. Section 191 provides:

> The offences to which an Order in Council under section 2 of the Extradition Act 1870 (c. 52) (arrangements with foreign states) can apply include –
> (a) an offence under s.188,
> (b) conspiracy to commit such an offence, and
> (c) attempt to commit such an offence.

The Under Secretary of State leading the Enterprise Bill through Committee scrutiny appeared at points to be uncertain as to the prospects for UK–US extradition in respect of the extent to which the US would be able to seek extradition from the UK in respect of those indicted under ss. 1 and 2 of the Sherman Act.[94] A general principle of extradition is that of double criminality.[95] It is not immediately apparent that extradition (in either direction) will be available, given the differences between the offences as set out in the respective legislation. It was recognized by the government in Committee that:

> Automatic extradition requires both states to prosecute an offender for an identical criminal offence. There are some differences between the United Kingdom offence created under the [Act], and the United States offence brought under the Sherman Act. The US offence is not based on dishonesty, therefore a request would need to be reviewed by the UK courts to establish whether the request fulfils the criteria of it being a case where the offence applies in nature to both jurisdictions. Such a review by the courts provides an extra safeguard against automatic extradition, which is ultimately a matter for the courts to decide.[96]

It should be noted that the 2003 US/UK extradition treaty,[97] introduced substantial changes to the UK–US extradition regime, and inter alia removed the requirement for the US to present evidence of a prima facie case when making the request.

In the Summer of 2005, the ability of the US to extradite those charged with breaches of s.1 of the Sherman Act was put to the test in the UK in respect of Ian Norris. Joshua has referred to the use of extradition by the DOJ as its 'new foreign policy weapon',[98] while a Freshfields briefing report emphasized the risks UK executives now face from US prosecution following the *Norris* judgment.[99] It should be noted at the outset, however, that although Mr Norris was charged in relation to alleged cartel activity fixing the prices for carbon products between 1989 and 2000 (before the cartel offence entered into force[100]), the US prosecutors characterized the offence as being one of conspiracy to defraud and for good measure added some charges of perverting the course of justice, which are offences in the UK, and to which therefore dual criminality applied. Mr Norris's defence argued that it would be oppressive to extradite him, given his poor state of health, but the court was not persuaded, and on 1 June 2005 held that an extradition request could be considered by the Home Secretary.[101] The court in *Norris* shone important light on the approach that might be taken in relation to dual criminality issues were the US to base a request on the relationship between Sherman Act s. 1 offences and the cartel offence in the future. It held that it was not necessary for the exact elements of the two offences to coincide in every particular,[102] but rather to consider whether the conduct underpinning the offence was the same in each jurisdiction. There appears to be little doubt that this would be the case in respect of a substantial number of Sherman Act s.1 infringements and s.188 of the Enterprise Act 2002.[103] Thus, at para. 7, Evans DJ held:

> The so-called 'double-criminality rule does not require me to find a UK criminal offence to match the US offence. It requires a consideration of the defendant's conduct that has led to the foreign charge and then determine whether that conduct, had it occurred in the UK, would amount to a UK offence carrying 12 months' imprisonment or greater punishment. This approach means that whereas Mr Norris can be prosecuted in America for a cartel offence he could not, for that same conduct, be prosecuted in the UK for a cartel offence. . . . He could, however, be prosecuted for a conspiracy to defraud as the described conduct amounts to a 'dishonest cartel'. I am satisfied that all the requirements of section 137(1) and (2) [of the Extradition Act 2003] are satisfied and the cartel offence is an extradition offence.

Extradition to non-EC states by EC states remains a matter of national competence. However an agreement signed between the EU and the US in June 2003 purported to establish a basic framework for extradition arrangements and mutual legal assistance in criminal matters between the EU and the US.[104] While this would result in making some changes to existing bilateral treaties, it does not replace them, and each Member State may continue to negotiate their own bilateral extradition agreements with the US.[105] Within the EC the primary provision relating to the 'extradition' of persons from one Member State to another is the European Arrest Warrant ('EAW').[106] This replaced 'traditional cooperation relations' between Member States, based upon the 'request principle', renowned for its slowness and unpredictability, with 'a system of free movement of judicial decisions in criminal matters, covering both pre-sentence and final decisions, within an area of freedom, security and justice'.[107] This latter system is intended to result in the near-automatic acceptance of judicial decisions taken in one Member State by the appropriate authorities in the other. For an EAW to be available, art.2 of the Framework Decision requires that the criminal act must be punishable by the law of the issuing state for a maximum period of at least 12 months, or for four months, where sentence has already been passed. The maximum penalty provided under s.190 of the Enterprise Act is imprisonment for a term not exceeding five years. It is therefore clear that the UK authorities could issue an EAW in respect of a person alleged to have committed a cartel offence. However this has no impact on trans-Atlantic enforcement. An EAW cannot be issued to support extradition to a third state not part of the EC. This is to say that the US could not seek to extradite a suspect from an EC Member State which did not have a relevant extradition agreement with the US by requesting a Member State which did have such an agreement to issue an EAW. It is therefore clear that in respect of the enforcement of criminal sanctions taking the form of incarceration the legal regimes of the EC and the US offer little practical interface, whatever the position might be in respect of the alignment of enforcement priorities.

**Conclusion**

In the amicus curiae brief to the Supreme Court in *Empagran*,[108] it was recognized by the UK and the Netherlands Governments that 'enforcement systems rely on international coordination and continued respect for the values and judgments reflected in each nation's processes'. There is a clear perception held by at least some commentators in the US that vigorous US enforcement action is beneficial to the world at large. Baker suggests that 'US antitrust deterrence must be looked at globally; US fines and punishments should be set at a high enough level to get the attention of those in Zurich, Frankfurt and Osaka, even if the fine may be higher than necessary to send a message to those in New Jersey, Texas or Illinois.'[109] However it is not enough for the rest of the world to rely on the US to police global competition, and it is of clear benefit to all regimes, including the US and the EC, that cooperation in the application of competition law be as effective as possible. There is no inherent reason, as has been shown, why it is not possible successfully to coordinate criminal and civil investigations in different jurisdictions, yet some practical difficulties remain.

In essence those actions regarded as inviting criminal prosecution under s.1 of the Sherman Act align closely to a set of conduct condemned by art.81 EC, and at the substantive level it should be possible to find a way forward to enhance cooperation, while recognizing that the EC and US systems of criminal enforcement differ fundamentally. While bilateral arrangements between the US and Member States may go some way to resolve difficulties, such solutions are inherently limited in scope. One difficulty relates to the gathering of information and evidence, with the existing EC–US cooperation being substantially limited to civil investigations. This in turn means that there are limits to the sharing of information, when it would be advantageous to the enforcing authorities to be able to do so. A second difficulty relates to the operation of leniency programmes. The OFT has indicated that, where an undertaking fulfils the requirements of the EC leniency programme, it would be unlikely to prosecute officers of that company under the criminal cartel offence. No such guarantee can be made by the US authorities, and neither can the EC promise leniency to those benefiting from the US arrangements. This creates a race to leniency that may produce benefits in the uncovering of cartel conduct,[110] but which may also lead to disparate treatment of undertakings and persons in the US and EC.[111] Extradition and the enforcement of judgments and cooperation in the exercise of search warrants remain largely a matter to be determined via bilateral arrangements and is not an area in which the EC has a substantial role to play. Inevitably this creates a fracture line running between the EC and US regime, and reduces the scope for cooperation and therefore for a truly effective enforcement mechanism.

## Notes

1. Senior Lecturer in Commercial Law, University of Glasgow. I am grateful to my colleagues, in particular Ms Maria Fletcher, Professor Iain MacNeil and Jonathan Galloway of the University of Newcastle upon Tyne, who have made useful comments on drafts of this chapter. All errors and omissions are the sole responsibility of the author.
2. *F. Hoffmann-La Roche Ltd* v. *Empagran SA* 524 US (2004), judgment of 14 June, 2004.
3. The term 'competition law' will be used throughout this chapter, even when discussing the antitrust law of the United States, unless the context demands otherwise.
4. Tellingly, the US Department of Justice notes that recent 'investigations have uncovered meetings of international cartels in well over 100 cities in more than 35 countries, including . . . nearly every country in Western Europe', ('Status Report: An Overview of Recent Developments in the Antitrust Division's Criminal Enforcement Program', 1 February 2004), available at the following website: www.usdoj.gov/atr/public/guidelines/202531.htm.
5. Lord Wilberforce, Campbell and Elles (1966), *The Law of Restrictive Trade Practices and Monopolies*, 2nd edn, London: Sweet & Maxwell, chap.1, para.110.
6. 2 Edw. 6, c 15. Other European countries had also adopted severe penalties in respect of anticompetitive conduct, and in the 16th century both François I of France, and the Holy Roman Emperor Charles V enacted such laws.
7. The origins of the US law are dealt with by Thorelli (1955), *The Federal Antitrust Policy: Origins of an American Tradition*, Baltimore: Johns Hopkins Press. See also Peritz (1996), *Competition Policy in America, 1888–1992: History, Rhetoric, Law*, New York: OUP; and more generally in relation to the development of US antitrust policy, Sullivan (ed.) (1991), *The Political Economy of the Sherman Act: The First One Hundred Years*, New York: OUP. Note, however, that the Canadian competition legislation, which incorporated criminal penalties from the very beginning, was enacted the year before the Sherman Act, in 1889.
8. Canada too maintains, and enforces, criminal law in respect of certain competition offences, see s.45 of the Competition Act. For a brief overview of the Canadian approach to international cooperation, including in criminal enforcement, see Scott, ' "C" is for competition: how we get things done in a globalised business world', 17 June 2005 (www.competitionbureau.gc.ca).
9. See *ECLR* news, [2003] ECLR, N-97.
10. See, for example, Decision 2003/2/EC *Vitamins* (2003) OJ L 6/1, which was part of a chain of actions arising from the prising open of the lysine cartel by the US authorities (see *United States* v. *Andreas* 216 F.3d). It has been recognized elsewhere that:

> The explosion of international cartel prosecutions has relied heavily on the Division's ability to secure the cooperation of foreign companies and witnesses through plea agreements. Such plea agreements generate a number of complex policy issues that are not raised in domestic cases. The pleading defendant is typically a multinational corporation pleading guilty to participating in a global conspiracy, which means that: (1) it can provide the Division with access to key documents and witnesses located outside the United States; and (2) it may be the subject of criminal and/or civil investigations by foreign law enforcement authorities who have a parallel interest in investigating the cartel activity. The combination of these two factors results in a number of competing policy considerations. (Footnotes omitted) Spratling (Deputy Assistant Attorney General Antitrust Division, US Department of Justice) 4 March 1999, Speech,

'Negotiating the waters of international cartel prosecutions', available at the following website: www.usdoj.gov/atr/public/speeches/2275.htm.

11.  See in particular Elzinga and Breit (1976), *The Antitrust Penalties: A study in law and economics*, New Haven: Yale University Press (the authors argue against the imposition of custodial sanctions) and Wils (2002), *The Optimal Enforcement of EC Antitrust Law: Essays in Law and Economics*, The Hague: Kluwer Law International, and in particular Chapter 8.

12.  For a recent survey of the relevant law, see Krauze and Mulcahy (2003), 'Antitrust violations', *American Crim L Rev*, **40**, at 241–84.

13.  It should be noted that the version of the Act that was passed was radically different from that first brought forward by Senator Sherman, a Republican representing Ohio, and that he himself argued on the floor that 'All corporations can ride through it or over it without fear of punishment or detection' (*New York Times*, April 8, 1890), quoted in Peritz, 1996, n.7, p. 14.

14.  Peritz, n.7, p. 25.

15.  See generally Baker (2000–2001), 'The use of criminal law remedies to deter and punish cartels and bid-rigging', *Geo Wash L Rev*, **69**, 693.

16.  The UK, in particular, does not criminalize conduct relating to dominance, and in the US criminal enforcement activity in this area is rare. The important OECD recommendation of March 1988 (*Recommendation of the Council Concerning Effective Action Against Hard Core Cartels*, 25 March 1988, C/M(98)7/PROV) encouraged Member States to 'ensure that their competition laws effectively halt and deter hard core cartels'. In particular the law should make provision for 'effective sanctions, of a kind and at a level adequate to deter firms and individuals from participating in such cartels'. This recommendation was cited in the background materials preparatory to the bringing forward of the UK Enterprise Act. It is silent on the *nature* of these sanctions, but it could be argued that the EC, while complying with the recommendation to sanction firms, does not effectively act to deter individuals.

17.  See generally, ABA Section of Antitrust Law (2002), *Antitrust Law Developments*, 5th edn, Chicago: ABA, vol. 1, ch. 8 (hereinafter '*ALD*').

18.  *ALD*, p. 729.

19.  Hammond (Director of Criminal Enforcement, Antitrust Division, US Department of Justice); speech, 'A summary overview of the Antitrust Division's criminal enforcement programme', 23 January 2003, available at www.usdoj.gov/atr/public/speeches/200686.htm.

20.  *Antitrust Division Manual*, Chapter III.C.5, 'Standards for determining whether to proceed by civil or criminal investigation', available at www.usdoj.gov/atr/foia/division-manual/ch3.htm. These criteria closely match those set out in the UK cartel offence, s.188 Enterprise Act 2002; see below.

21.  438 US 422, 444 (1978).

22.  *United States* v. *Brown* 936 F.2d 1042, 1046 (9th Cir 1991).

23.  *United States* v. *Andreas* 216 F.3d 645 (7th Cir).

24.  18 USC s 3282 (2000).

25.  It has been argued that the 'grand jury system . . . tends to strongly favour the investigators' (Baker, 2000–2001) n.15, at p. 693.

26.  *ALD*, p. 739. See generally *Antitrust Division Manual*, above, n. 20, and the *Antitrust Division Grand Jury Practice Manual* (1991). It is noted in the *Antitrust Division Manual* that '[e]fforts to obtain evidence located outside the United States present special considerations. Staff should consult with the Foreign Commerce Section to discuss possible methods of obtaining such evidence, including alternatives to subpoenas' (Chapter III.4.a).

27.  Page 741. Issues relating to cooperation in international investigations are discussed briefly below.

28.  See Eichenwald (2000), *The Informant: A True Story*, New York: Broadway Books, p. 208, and Chapter 9. The strategy adopted by Whitacre, facing resistance from the

Japanese executives who were wary of meeting in the US, was to emphasize the attractions of Hawaii: 'In his conversations with the Japanese in recent weeks, Whitacre had been talking up Hawaii. His message was always the same: the golf, the golf, the golf. Finally, with a new sense of trust emerging among the lysine producers, the Asian companies agreed. They would meet in Hawaii and play golf' (p. 208).

29. *Antitrust Division Manual*, above, n. 26, Chapter III.G.2.c.
30. Ibid.
31. One such policy reason could be, for example, the impact of a prosecution in the US on enforcement activity in another jurisdiction, and in particular the principle of comity (discussed below).
32. Note 29.
33. Available at www.usdoj.gov/atr/public/12848.htm. More recent statistics covering the fiscal years 1995–2004 are available at www.usdoj.gov:80/atr/public/workstats.htm.
34. DoJ (1 February 2004), 'Status report: an overview of recent developments in the Antitrust Division's criminal enforcement program', available at www.usdoj.gov/atr/public/guidelines/202531.htm. A more recent status report from November 2005 is now available at www.usdoj.gov/atr/public/speeches/213247.htm.
35. Ibid.
36. Ibid.
37. *The SS Lotus (France* v. *Turkey)* (1927) PCIJ series A, no 10.
38. *United States* v. *Aluminium Company of America* 148 F.2d 416 (2d Cir, 1945).
39. Available at www.usdoj.gov/atr/public/guidelines/internat.htm. Here the following example is set out:

> SITUATION: A, B, C, and D are foreign companies that produce a product in various foreign countries. None has any US production, nor any US subsidiaries. They organise a cartel for the purpose of raising the price for the product in question. Collectively, the cartel members make substantial sales into the United States, both in absolute terms and relative to total US consumption.
> DISCUSSION: These facts present the straightforward case of cartel participants selling products directly into the United States. In this situation, the transaction is unambiguously an import into the US market, and the sale is not complete until the goods reach the United States. Thus US subject matter jurisdiction is clear under the general principles of antitrust law expressed most recently in *Hartford Fire*. The facts presented here demonstrate actual and intended participation in US commerce.

> Note that, although the effects doctrine has not yet been recognized by the judicial authorities in the application of EC competition law, the situation as presented above would also fall to be condemned under Art. 81 EC and the principle of 'implementation' (see below). A difference would arise, however, were the cartel to be *not directly* selling into the US, but accepting orders from US companies and customers in their own territories with the latter in turn importing the products into the US. It is argued that in this situation the US would still assert jurisdiction, whereas the implementation doctrine advocated by the EC would not permit the extension of Community jurisdiction to this situation, as there would have been no anticompetitive practice *implemented* in the EC.

40. *United States* v. *Nippon Paper Indus. Co, Ltd* 109 F.3d 1 (1st Cir 1997).
41. See for example the EC–US Cooperation Agreement (95/145/EC, ECSC (1995) OJ L95/45).
42. *Hilton* v. *Guyot* 159 US 113, 164 (1895).
43. *Timberlane Lumber Co* v. *Bank of America (Timberlane 1)* 549 F.2d 597 (9th Cir 1976).
44. *Mannington Mills Inc* v. *Congoleum Corp* 595 F.2d 1287 (3d Cir 1979).
45. *Hartford Fire Ins Co* v. *California* 113 S. Ct. 2891 (1993).
46. Ibid., emphasis added. For a criticism of the *Hartford Fire* judgment, see Robertson and Demetriou (1994), ' "But that was in another country": The extraterritorial application of US antitrust laws by the US Supreme Court', *ICLQ*, **43**, 417.
47. Baker, above, n. 15, at p. 712.

48.  Available at www.usdoj.gov/atr/public/criminal/207647.htm. More recent statistics show that there have now been 51 instances of total fines exceeding $10m, and that the second-highest penalty was the $300m imposed on Samsung (www.usdoj.gov/atr/public/criminal/212091.htm).

49.  The EC does not take into account in its calculation of any penalties following the finding of an infringement of Art. 81 EC, penalties paid in other jurisdictions.

50.  See n. 34.

51.  For comment on the cartel offence, see generally Furse and Nash (2004), *The Cartel Offence*, Oxford: Hart Publishing. See also Rodger (2004), 'The Competition Act and the Enterprise Act reforms: sanctions and deterrence in UK competition law', in Dannecker and Jansen (eds), *Competition Law Sanctioning in the European Union*, Kluwer, pp. 101 et seq.

52.  Although the Serious Fraud Office (SFO) has, reportedly, used powers under existing legislation to investigate an alleged cartel relating to generic drug supplies to the National Health Service. See 'Strong Medicine', *Sunday Times*, 9 November 2003, Business Section, p. 5.

53.  *Hansard*, 2 July 2002, col. 157.

54.  OFT (November 2001), *The Proposed Criminalisation of Cartels in the UK – A report prepared for the Office of Fair Trading by Sir Anthony Hammond KCB QC and Roy Penrose OBE QPM*, [2002] UKLR 97 (hereinafter the Penrose report).

55.  Penrose report, above, paras 3.6, 3.7.

56.  EC competition law may, for the present purpose, be regarded as 'law in the UK' notwithstanding its origin.

57.  The word 'undertaking' is given an expansive interpretation, and is defined as encompassing 'every entity engaged in commercial activity, regardless of the legal status of the entity, and the way in which it is financed', (case C-41/90 *Hofner and Elser* v. *Macrotron GmbH* [1993] 4 CMLR 306, at para 21).

58.  Council of Ministers of the EU, Council Regulation (EC) No 1/2003 of 16 December 2002 on the implementation of the rules on competition laid down in Articles 81 and 82 of the Treaty (2003) OJ L1/1.

59.  Recital 8.

60.  Ibid.

61.  *Re Wood Pulp Cartel: A Ahlstrom Oy* v. *Commission* joined cases C-89 etc [1988] 4 CMLR 901 at 915.

62.  *Gencor Ltd* v. *Commission* case T-102/96 [1999] ECR-II 753, [1999] 4 CMLR 971.

63.  See s.191 of the Enterprise Act, discussed below.

64.  See note 2.

65.  Ibid. Although the carrot of the EC leniency programme does not have as its counterpart stick the threat of personal liability and incarceration that is seen as one key to the success of the US system.

66.  *Hansard*, Standing Committee B, col. 173, 23 April 2002.

67.  See note 34.

68.  Note 15, at p. 708. At p. 709, Baker describes 'immunity as a vital incentive for cooperation'.

69.  The corporate leniency policy is available at the following website: www.usdoj.gov/atr/public/guidelines/0091.htm.

70.  Available at www.usdoj.gov/atr/public/guidelines/0092.htm.

71.  European Commission (2002), *Commission notice on immunity from fines and reduction of fines in cartel cases*, OJ C45/3.

72.  See Arp and Swaak, 'Immunity from fines for cartel conduct under the European Commission's new leniency notice', *Antitrust*, Summer 2002, p. 59, at p. 64. This article further provides a good comparative analysis of the US and EC leniency regimes. See also, van Barlingen, 'The European Commission's 2002 Leniency Notice after one year of operation', *Competition Policy Newsletter*, Summer 2003, 16: 'the Commission must ensure that its leniency policy is not undermined by the risk of criminal sanctions being imposed in member states on employees of companies that have received immunity from

the Commission. As neither the Commission nor member states can possibly benefit from a faltering leniency policy, they will have to resolve this issue'.

73. December 2004, at www.oft.gov.uk/Business/Legal/Competition/ca98+leniency.htm.
74. Paras 3.9–3.10 of the guidance.
75. Ibid., paras 3.11–3.12.
76. Ibid., paras 3.13–3.15.
77. Ibid., paras 3.16–3.17.
78. *The Cartel Offence: Guidance on the issue of no-action letters for individuals*, at para.3.2. Note that a modified version of this arrangement exists in Scotland.
79. At para. 3.7 of the guidance the OFT notes: 'It is in the interest of the applicant to apply for leniency to all the NCAs which have the power to apply Article 81 in the territory affected by the infringement in question'.
80. See note 34.
81. See, generally, Jansen, 'The systems of international cooperation in administrative and criminal matters in relation to Regulation EC 1/2003', in Dannecker and Jansen (eds) (2004), *Competition Law Sanctioning in the European Union*, The Hague: Kluwer, pp. 257 et seq. Jansen also comments on the ramifications of this legislation on international criminal cooperation.
82. Regulation 1/2003, art.12(2).
83. Article 22(1) of the Regulation permits an authority in one state to request another Member State's authority to 'carry out any inspection or other fact-finding measure under its national law on behalf and for the account of the competition authority of another member state', but this provision is expressly directed to the enforcement of arts 81 and 82 EC, and it would not appear that this could be used in respect of a criminal action directed against individuals *solus*.
84. See note 81. At p. 259 Jansen gives two examples:

> I. Competition authority A based in a member state where European competition law is enforced on natural persons with a criminal law system and custodial sanctions wants to use as evidence the information exchanged with the European Commission and competition authority B based in a Member State where European competition law is enforced only with an administrative law system without custodial sanctions.
> II. Competition authority A wants to use as evidence the information exchanged with competition authority B in order to enforce national competition law in another case . . .
> These additional provisions should be found in instruments of international cooperation in administrative and criminal matters.

85. See note 34.
86. *Exchange of Notes Between the Government of the United Kingdom of Great Britain and Northern Ireland and the Government of the United States of America Amending the Treaty on Mutual Legal Assistance in Criminal Matters done at Washington on 6 January 1994* (1 May 2001).
87. Furse and Nash (2004), *The Cartel Offence*, Oxford: Hart Publishing, p. 108. See generally Gilmore (ed.) (1995), *Mutual Assistance in Criminal and Business Regulatory Matters*, Cambridge: Cambridge University Press.
88. 87 UNTS 103.
89. The principle against self-incrimination flows from Article 6, ECHR, which provides, in part, that 'everyone is entitled to a fair and public hearing within a reasonable period of time'. For a discussion of this principle as applied in the context of EC civil proceedings, see Overbeek (1994), 'The right to remain silent in competition investigations', ECLR, **3**, 127.
90. Although note that the Act does not apply to Scotland, where arrest, detention, questioning and search powers are governed by a mixture of statute and common law.
91. See, for example, comments made by James Griffin of the DOJ in the BBC Channel 4 documentary, *A Crime Amongst Gentlemen*.

92. See note 34.
93. The typical language on a plea agreement with the DOJ is the following: 'The United States will not object to Defendant's request that the Court make a recommendation to the Bureau of Prisons that the Bureau of Prisons designate that Defendant be assigned to the Federal Minimum Security Camp (if possible at [CITY], [STATE]) to serve his sentence of imprisonment and that Defendant be released on his own personal recognizance following the imposition of the sentence to allow him to self-surrender to the designated institution on a specified date.' It is also rumoured, although there is no public evidence to support this, that some corporations offer substantial inducements to their employees to accept these terms. The corporation in turn may benefit from a reduction in its penalty, owing to the cooperation of itself and its staff.
94. See, for example, *Hansard*, Standing Committee B, cols 187–91 (23 April 2002). The Under-Secretary of State, Melanie Johnson, did accept, however, that 'were this Bill enacted, my understanding is that Sir Anthony Tennant probably could have been extradited' (at col. 190). Following the judgment in the case of *Norris* (see below) it is likely that an extradition request could be sustained in respect of Sir Anthony Tennant under other routes.
95. See generally Mullan (1997), 'The concept of double criminality in the context of extraterritorial crimes', [1997] *Criminal Law Review*, 17. For a wider discussion of this area, see also Snow (2002–2003), 'The investigation and prosecution of white collar crime: international challenges and the legal tools available to address them', **11**, *Wm & Mary Bill Rts J*, 9.
96. *Hansard*, Standing Committee B, cols 188–9 (23 April 2002). See also the effect of *Norris* (n. 99 below) on the importance of the 'dishonesty' standard.
97. Cm 5821.
98. Joshua (2005), 'Extradition: the DOJ's new foreign policy weapon', *Competition Law Insight*, June, p. 12.
99. *The Government of the United States of America* v. *Ian P. Norris* (Bow Street Magistrates' Court, 1 June 2005). See also Freshfields Bruckhaus Deringer, Briefing, May 2005, 'UK decision extends reach of US antitrust enforcers', www.freshfields.com.
100. In *Re Pinochet* the House of Lords held, inter alia, that for dual criminality to apply the offence had to be unlawful in the UK at the time at which it was committed in the requesting state (*R* v. *Bow Street Metropolitan Stipendiary Magistrate (No 2), Ex p Pinochet Ugarte* [2000] 1 AC 119).
101. On the basis of this judgment alone, and without considering the impact of dual criminality and its relationship to the cartel offence, *The Times* reported that 'Legal experts believe that the American prosecutors will use the precedent to begin to pursue other British-resident executives connected with past and present cartels' (1 June 2005).
102. For example, s.1, Sherman Act, does not make explicit a requirement that the conduct be 'dishonest', a key feature of s.188 of the cartel offence.
103. On 30 September 2005 the Home Secretary made a decision ordering the extradition. This is likely to be subject to further appeals (see *VBB on Competition Law*, (2005) no. 6, at pp. 20–21).
104. *Agreement on extradition between the European Union and the United States of America*, 2003/516/EC, (2003) OJ L181/25; *Mutual legal assistance agreement between the EU and the USA* (2003) OJ L181/34.
105. Article 3(1) of the agreement sets out, therefore, that 'the provisions of this Agreement are applied in relation to bilateral extradition treaties . . .'. The relationship between the EU–US agreement and existing bilateral agreements which remain in force is set out in detail at art.3. This specifies that some provisions apply in place of existing corresponding provisions, whereas others apply in the absence thereof or in addition thereto.
106. Council Framework Decision of 13 June 2002 on the European arrest warrant and the surrender procedures between Member States, 2002/584/JHA, (2002) OJ L190/1.
107. Recital 5.
108. See note 2.
109. See note 15, at p. 702.

110. Although it is also true that uncertainty is often viewed as the enemy of leniency programmes, and the existence of substantial uncertainty as to the outcome of leniency applications may dampen the number of applications made.
111. The cynic may be tempted to respond to the effect that 'they are all guilty, so what's the problem?', but, as has been recognized, certainty is important in the effective operation of leniency programmes. Those applying are faced with balancing the rewards of the illegal conduct (against the cost of punishment discounted by the risk of detection) on the one hand, with the loss of profit from the illegal activity on the other. Greater certainty as to the availability of leniency appears to be more conducive to applications.

## References

*Antitrust Division Grand Jury Practice Manual* (1991)
*Antitrust Division Manual*
Arp, D. Jarrett and Christof R.A. Swaak (2002), 'Immunity from fines for cartel conduct under the European Commission's new leniency notice', *Antitrust*, Summer.
Baker (2000–2001), 'The use of criminal law remedies to deter and punish cartels and bid-rigging', *Geo Wash L Rev*, **69**, 693.
Council of Ministers of the EU, *Council Regulation (EC) No 1/2003 of 16 December 2002 on the Implementation of the Rules on Competition Laid Down in Articles 81 and 82 of the Treaty* (2003) OJ L1/1.
DoJ (1 February 2004), 'Status report: an overview of recent developments in the Antitrust Division's criminal enforcement program', available at www.usdoj.gov/atr/public/guidelines/202531.htm.
Eichenwald (2000), *The Informant: A True Story*, New York: Broadway Books.
Elzinga and Breit (1976), *The Antitrust Penalties: a Study in Law and Economics*, New Haven: Yale University Press.
European Commission (2002), *Commission notice on immunity from fines and reduction of fines in cartel cases*, OJ C45/3.
Furse and Nash (2004), *The Cartel Offence*, Oxford: Hart Publishing.
Gilmore (ed.) (1995), *Mutual Assistance in Criminal and Business Regulatory Matters*, Cambridge: Cambridge University Press.
Hammond (23 January 2003), Speech, 'A summary overview of the Antitrust Division's criminal enforcement programme', available at www.usdoj.gov/atr/public/speeches/200686.htm.
Jansen, O. (2004), 'The systems of international cooperation in administrative and criminal matters in relation to regulation EC 1/2003', in G. Dannecker and O. Jansen (eds), *Competition Law Sanctioning in the European Union*, The Hague: Kluwer.
Joshua (2005), 'Extradition: the DOJ's new foreign policy weapon', *Competition Law Insight*, June, p. 12
Krauze and Mulcahy (2003), 'Antitrust violations', *American Crim L Rev*, **40**, at 241–84.
Mullan (1997), 'The concept of double criminality in the context of extra-territorial crimes', [1997] *Criminal Law Review*, 17.
OECD (25 March 1988), *Recommendation of the Council Concerning Effective Action Against Hard Core Cartels*, 25 March 1988, C/M(98)7/PROV).
OFT (November 2001), *The Proposed Criminalisation of Cartels in the UK – A report prepared for the Office of Fair Trading by Sir Anthony Hammond KCB QC and Roy Penrose OBE QPM*, [2002] UKLR 97.
Overbeek (1994), 'The right to remain silent in competition investigations', *ECLR*, **3**, 127.
Peritz (1996), *Competition Policy in America, 1888–1992: History, Rhetoric, Law*, New York: OUP.
Robertson and Demetriou (1994), ' "But that was in another country": the extraterritorial application of US antitrust laws by the US Supreme Court', *ICLQ*, **43**, 417.
Rodger (2004), 'The Competition Act and the Enterprise Act reforms: sanctions and deterrence in UK competition law', in Dannecker and Jansen (eds), *Competition Law Sanctioning in the European Union*, The Hague: Kluwer, pp. 101 et seq.

Scott, ' "C" is for competition: how we get things done in a globalised business world', 17 June 2005 (www.competitionbureau.gc.ca).
Snow (2002–2003), 'The investigation and prosecution of white collar crime: international challenges and the legal tools available to address them', **11**, *Wm & Mary Bill Rts J*, 9.
Spratling (4 March 1999), Speech, 'Negotiating the waters of international cartel prosecutions', available at the following website: www.usdoj.gov/atr/public/speeches/2275.htm.
Sullivan (ed.) (1991), *The Political Economy of the Sherman Act: The First One Hundred Years*, New York: OUP.
Thorelli (1955), *The Federal Antitrust Policy: Origins of an American Tradition*, Baltimore: Johns Hopkins Press.
van Barlingen, Bertus (2003), 'The European Commission's 2002 Leniency Notice after one year of operation', *Competition Policy Newsletter*, Summer, 16.
Lord Wilberforce, Campbell and Elles (1966), *The Law of Restrictive Trade Practices and Monopolies*, 2nd edn, London: Sweet & Maxwell.
Wils (2002), *The Optimal Enforcement of EC Antitrust Law: Essays in Law and Economics*, The Hague: Kluwer Law International.

## Cases
*F. Hoffmann-La Roche Ltd* v. *Empagran SA* 524 US (2004).
*Gencor Ltd* v. *Commission* case T-102/96 [1999] ECR-II 753, [1999] 4 CMLR 971.
*Hartford Fire Ins Co.* v. *California* 113 S. Ct. 2891 (1993).
*Hilton* v. *Guyot* 159 US 113, 164 (1895).
*Hofner and Elser* v. *Macrotron GmbH* [1993] 4 CMLR 306.
*Mannington Mills Inc* v. *Congoleum Corp* 595 F.2d 1287 (3d Cir 1979).
*Re Wood Pulp Cartel: A Ahlstrom Oy* v. *Commission* joined cases C-89 etc [1988] 4 CMLR 901.
*The SS Lotus (France* v. *Turkey)* (1927) PCIJ series A, no 10.
*Timberlane Lumber Co* v. *Bank of America (Timberlane 1)* 549 F.2d 597 (9th Cir 1976).
*United States* v. *Aluminium Company of America* 148 F.2d 416 (2d Cir, 1945).
*United States* v. *Andreas* 216 F.3d. (2000).
*United States* v. *United States Gypsum Co.* 438 US 422 (1978).
*United States* v. *Nippon Paper Indus. Co. Ltd* 109 F.3d 1 (1st Cir 1997).

# 17 The brave new world of extradition: a North Atlantic treaty alliance against cartels?
## Julian M. Joshua[1]

Extradition is the latest addition to the formidable arsenal deployed by the US Department of justice (DoJ) in its war on international cartels. On 30 September 2005, Ian Norris, the former CEO of the Morgan Crucible PLC made unwilling legal history as the first overseas executive whose extradition has been ordered to the US to face criminal charges under the Sherman Act, section 1. Norris, a UK resident and national, had been indicted in US District Court for allegedly running a global cartel from 1989 to 2000. The prosecution case is that he orchestrated the conspiracy from the then safe cartel haven of the UK. District Judge Nicholas Evans, sitting at Bow Street Magistrates Court in London, decided on 1 June 2005 that the alleged price-fixing conduct was an extradition offence under Britain's new Extradition Act 2003. Now the Home Secretary, Charles Clarke, has ordered Norris's extradition to the US, where he is also indicted on charges of witness tampering and destroying evidence.[2] This, with other high-profile extradition cases involving the US, has stirred a media outcry, and a lengthy battle through the appeal courts surely lies ahead. Nevertheless the DoJ is confident of the outcome, and regards the *Norris* case as a precedent for further aggressive action against fugitives who decline its generous invitation to 'have their day in court'.

Whatever the eventual outcome, the *Norris* extradition case represents the latest development in a relentless process, driven by the DoJ, that has seen a sea change in official attitudes across the world towards anti-cartel enforcement over the last decade. The UK's conversion to the cause of international cooperation to stamp out cartels is all the more remarkable given that only a quarter of a century ago it passed blocking statutes to thwart cooperation by British companies with US antitrust investigations.[3] Its Department of Trade and Industry (DTI) notoriously championed British price fixers against US efforts to enforce cartel laws even by civil-type litigation, let alone today's more robust methods.[4] American insistence on enforcing antitrust (in ways which look distinctly limp by today's standards) was viewed with patronizing incomprehension by Britain's policy mandarins. As late as 2000, before the implementation of the Competition

Act 1998, which provided for administrative fines on companies, the UK arguably still had the feeblest regime against cartels in the developed world. All this was due to change in a dramatic Pauline conversion that culminated in the UK introducing five-year jail sentences for individuals who engaged in cartel behaviour.

'Cartels are a worldwide problem which potentially affects us all', proclaimed the UK's 2001 White Paper heralding the Enterprise Bill, ironically the work of the once cartel-friendly DTI. With the implementation of section 188 of the Enterprise Act on 20 June 2003, Britain joined the US and Canada in the elite club of countries that have legislated for tough criminal penalties on hard core cartels, albeit more than a century behind its former colonies. And if domestically attitudes had undergone a sea change, on the international scene too harmony now reigns in place of strife. But if a broad consensus has emerged in the global competition law community as to the harm done by cartels, a wide gulf still separates those who see cartels as an economic phenomenon to be regulated via administrative measures and those who regard price fixing as a sophisticated form of theft. While 'Inter-Agency cooperation' is now the mantra of international antitrust enforcers across the globe, and respected bodies like the International Competition Network (ICN) operate as a forum for swapping ideas, it is the developing criminalization of covert price fixing and market sharing that has translated intentions into reality. Instruments originally devised to fight serious organized crime, the drug trade and international terrorism have been pressed into service to aid the US-led crusade against global cartels. Although no formal multilateral structure exists, the three North Atlantic antitrust enforcers – the US, UK and Canada – now form a virtual 'triple alliance' in the fight against cartels.

This chapter examines a major area in which international treaty arrangements relating to criminal law enforcement between the three jurisdictions have assumed particular significance in the field of antitrust cooperation, namely extradition.

**Extradition**
Traditionally arrangements for extradition, the process whereby one sovereign state requests another to hand over to it a person in the second state for trial on criminal charges, depend upon treaty relationships. The United States has concluded a prodigious 120 extradition treaties with other countries. (Britain and Canada were also parties to general extradition arrangements under the Commonwealth scheme and the European Convention of 1957.) Extradition arrangements invariably contained a requirement for dual criminality; i.e. the conduct had to be a crime in both jurisdictions. In each state, enabling legislation is necessary to govern the processing of

extradition requests from another. In the common law world, extradition involves a judicial and an executive stage, with the final decision lying with the Executive. These traditional arrangements, dating back to the nineteenth century, and left basically unchanged for over a hundred years, have in recent years undergone profound change.

Recent developments in extradition practice have to be seen against a broader backdrop. The events of 9/11 catapulted counter-terrorism cooperation between the US and Europe to the top of the transatlantic political agenda. As part of the operation, the treaty arrangements of EU countries with the US in this area were comprehensively reviewed.[5] If the huge shakeup of bilateral and multilateral international crime-fighting arrangements was driven initially by the need to combat global terror, a by-product of the massive and far-reaching exercise is the extension of this unprecedented level of international cooperation between justice authorities to criminal law enforcement in general and in particular 'white collar crime'.

With the globalization of business, the removal of trade barriers, instant communication and electronic fund transfers, money laundering and fraud across frontiers are facilitated and easily concealed. Financial and organized crime is an area where many states now assert extraterritorial jurisdiction, often as a result of international conventions. English law has recognized the reality of crime on a global scale and adapted accordingly to assert jurisdiction that may in an earlier age have been judged exorbitant.[6] Extradition treaties are to be interpreted in a way which does not hinder their primary purpose of 'bringing to justice those who are guilty of grave crimes committed in either of the contracting states'.[7]

Half of the extradition applications made under Britain's new legislation intended to streamline extradition procedures concern business crime. In a case that has provoked no little controversy, the Home Secretary has approved the extradition to the US of three UK bank executives indicted in Texas on Enron-linked federal fraud charges under 18 USC 1343 (wire fraud).[8]

With the *Norris* case now hitting the headlines in the UK, extradition has recently assumed an unwonted significance in antitrust enforcement as well.

### The drive against international cartels

Since 1995, the US Justice Department has waged an openly-declared war against international cartels that affect US markets. Although under section 1 of the Sherman Act conspiracy to fix prices has been a federal crime since 1890 and a felony since 1972, apart from a few sporadic bursts of desultory action, some resulting in stalemate or defeat, the Department had hitherto focused its main attentions on domestic cartels of road builders, milk producers and the like,[9] even during the 1980s and early

1990s when the EC Commission was uncovering vast Europe-wide cartels with some regularity.[10] Some self-styled experts adhered to the view that there was no such thing as an international cartel, a *Weltanschauung* from which they were jolted by the remarkable success of the Division in the ADM lysine case and the jailing of senior executives from one of America's most politically powerful corporations.[11] Since *Lysine,* and the series of other cartel investigations it generated, the US has assumed the leadership mantle in a worldwide crusade against price fixers. In fora like the OECD, perceived laggard countries, suspected of being 'soft' on cartels, are chivvied into redoubling their enforcement efforts and beefing up their legislation. The Justice Department welcomes in particular moves to make cartel behaviour a criminal offence.[12] In the US itself, some 50 federal grand juries are currently empanelled to investigate suspected cartel activity which is international if not worldwide in scope.[13]

Much of the success of the Department in uncovering secret cartels is owed to its leniency programme,[14] the deterrent effect of which is enhanced by the imposition of substantial jail sentences on those who do not seek the benefits of immunity. The highest-profile defendant to go behind bars was Alfred Taubman, the billionaire Chairman of Sotheby's, jailed for a year for masterminding the Fine Arts auction commissions conspiracy.[15] It is not only US nationals who are targets. The Sherman Act's long arm criminal jurisdiction reaches to catch activities occurring wholly abroad where they have an 'intended and substantial effect in the United States'.[16] Offenders who fix prices in America are not safe even if they take care never to set foot in the US. Following the outcry when a prominent German CEO escaped jail by agreeing a record $10 million personal fine – paid in fact by the company[17] – the Department made a point of insisting that, in every international case, at least one overseas executive serves a jail term, usually negotiated as part of a plea bargain.[18] Foreign companies have realized the advantage they might receive in the disposition of their own issues if they 'facilitate' the voluntary surrender of individual employees to US justice. But while three out of four corporate defendants were overseas companies, the proportion was reversed for individual defendants. Now the Department is aiming to redress the balance and jail more overseas executives.

But if the Antitrust Division managed to secure the presence in the US of mid-ranking executives by offering them a deal and a jail term of 'only' three or four months, its siren blandishments failed to attract the rich and powerful to the US. Sir Anthony Tennant, Taubman's well-connected British counterpart at Christie's, declined to attend trial in New York in 2001. He remains a fugitive from US justice. Because extradition under treaty depends upon the so-called 'dual criminality' principle (i.e. the underlying conduct would amount to a criminal offence had it occurred in the jurisdiction of the requested state), Justice Department officials believed they were powerless to obtain his extradition from London.[19]

## UK criminalization and transatlantic extradition

Since the above events, price fixing has indeed been made a crime in the UK. With the implementation on 20 June 2003 of the 'cartel offence' in section 188 of the Enterprise Act 2002, Britain is now ideologically much closer in antitrust matters to the United States than to its EU partners, traditionally inclined to view price fixing as a regulatory issue unsuited to the full rigours of criminal law enforcement.

Section 188 of the Enterprise Act makes it an offence, punishable by up to five years in prison, for an individual 'dishonestly' to make or implement with another individual arrangements to fix prices or share markets between undertakings operating at the same level in the supply chain. But while the new legislation may sound tough, in practice its obscure drafting, the superfluous requirement for 'dishonesty' and endless scope for turf wars and jurisdictional conflicts between the different agencies that enforce competition laws in Britain and the EC may render the convictions of high-profile defendants a distant prospect.[20] It might prove difficult in pan-European cartels to obtain evidence in usable form from other EC Member States which do not regard price fixing as a suitable target of the criminal justice system. Senior officials of the OFT have indicated that they will only pursue individuals where the core of the criminality was located in the United Kingdom or special harm was suffered by British consumers.[21] Bid rigging in the domestic construction industry is likely to prove an easier target than global cartels meeting in luxury hotels in Zurich. Whatever the chances may be of seeing CEOs of Europe's largest companies in the dock of the Old Bailey, one of the first practical manifestations of the UK's *volte-face* on the criminality of cartels was in the extradition field, though, as will be seen, it was not in fact the direct result of the passage of the Enterprise Act.

Besides criminalizing price fixing, the Enterprise Act had to make specific provision to permit the extradition of price fixers under a treaty, which basically meant extradition to the United States.[22] This provision was necessitated by the arcane system under the Extradition Act 1989, the statute consolidating earlier legislation dating from 1870 which governed Britain's extradition arrangements at the time. For extradition to be possible under bilateral treaties, as opposed to general arrangements like the European Convention on Extradition or the Commonwealth scheme, it was not enough that the conduct fulfilled a pure 'dual criminality' test. The corresponding offence in English law also had to feature on a list of specified extradition crimes (see below).[23]

The provisions of the 1989 Extradition Act have now been repealed and replaced by the UK's compendious new legislation in that area, the Extradition Act 2003. The new Act redefines what is an extradition offence in terms of pure dual criminality. This simplified definition now applies in relation to extradition to the US.[24]

### 'Extradition offences' in English law: a legislative paper chase

Under the old 1989 legislation, working out whether an offence was in fact an 'extradition crime' could be a complicated operation, especially as new criminal offences were enacted.[25] The term had a different meaning in different parts of the 1989 Act. 'Part III cases' related to requests from countries with which the UK had general extradition arrangements, basically signatories to the European Convention on Extradition and Commonwealth countries. In such cases, conduct was automatically an extradition crime which, had it occurred in the UK, would have been punishable by 12 months' imprisonment. However, for 'Schedule 1 cases', i.e. those involving extradition under a treaty, which mainly meant to the US, the law was that contained in Schedule 1 to the 1989 Act. This involved having to work back though the older extradition legislation of 1870 and the Order in Council implementing the Treaty. To cut a very long story short, the offence for which extradition was being sought had either (a) to feature on the list of generic crimes set out in Schedule 1 of the Extradition Act, 1870 as amended and updated periodically or (b) have been made 'extraditable' in terms of the Order in Council by some other means (such as that used in s.191 Enterprise Act).

The new Extradition Act of 2003 simplified the definition of what is an 'extradition offence' (as it is now called). For extradition to the US, the rigmarole of having to include the offence in the list in Schedule 1 or otherwise make it 'extraditable' was abolished. Instead, *any* offence is now extraditable if the conduct is punishable in both states by a period of at least one year's imprisonment. Basically the old 'Part III' definition is now also applied to cases where extradition is sought under a treaty. The UK's new cartel offence, with its curious emphasis on 'dishonesty', is defined differently from a Sherman Act conspiracy, but offences do not have to be described by the same terminology. So long as the conduct was punishable as a crime under the law of both jurisdictions, the new Extradition Act applies even if the offence was committed before it came into force.[26] However the dual criminality requirement itself is not satisfied retrospectively. The House of Lords held in *Re Pinochet*[27] that the conduct had to be a crime in the requested country at the time of the alleged conduct, not just at the date of the application. At first blush, British executives who violate the Sherman Act would therefore only face extradition to the US for the substantive offence if they began or continued their involvement in cartels after 20 June 2003. However, as will be seen from the *Norris* case, the ingenuity of prosecutors should not be underestimated.

**The US–UK Extradition Treaty**

Signed on 30 March 2003, the new US–UK Extradition Treaty was intended to change the present bilateral arrangements in a number of fundamental respects. The treaty has still to be ratified. It is currently before the US Senate but has encountered delays due mainly to US domestic politics.

For the time being, the 1972 treaty remains in force. The old treaty is based on a 'list' of crimes specified in a Schedule. However, under Article III (b), extradition is also available for 'any other offence' punishable by a year or more in both countries – but only if it is also (a) a felony in the US (b) an 'extraditable offence' in British law.[28]

Even if it did not suffer from the crippling handicap of a 'no own nationals' rule,[29] the treaty of 1972 had long been criticized as outmoded, the relevant provisions in Schedule I of the 1989 Act condemned as anomalous and its procedures castigated as excessively lengthy and cumbersome. One lacuna was the impossibility of extraditing to the US for conspiracy to defraud, a common law offence in English law, but one that (for whatever reason) did not feature on the 1870 list as amended. As a result, although punishable in both jurisdictions by over 12 months' jail, it was not extraditable.[30]

Under the new treaty, the dual criminality principle is retained, but the most important changes are as follows:

- Abolition of the prima facie evidence requirement in requests from the US to the UK (although, for constitutional reasons, the US will retain its requirement for 'probable cause' for requests in the opposite direction);
- Abolition of the 'list' system (which had been retained in the 1989 Act) and the need to designate specific offences as extraditable, instead making extraditable *any* offence where the conduct on which it is based is punishable under the laws of both states by at least one year's imprisonment.

If signing the treaty so quickly was driven by the common will to fight terrorist activity, its practical scope (assuming it is ratified) is likely to be much broader. It could have been tailor-made for extraditing wanted antitrust violators. There is specific provision for the tricky issues that often arise in multijurisdictional antitrust investigations.[31] Nor is a grant of amnesty by the authorities of the requested state a bar to extradition to the other.[32]

If the new US–UK treaty was negotiated by reference to the 1989 Extradition Act, which was then still applicable, most of the innovations it contained were in any case given statutory force quite independently by the new Extradition Act. The main changes to Britain's arrangements for extraditing persons to the US are thus already in force under the statute, and do not depend upon the ratification of the treaty.[33]

### The UK Extradition Act 2003

The new Extradition Act 2003 entered into force on 1 January 2004. The Act, which runs to 227 sections and four schedules, overhauled and modernized the UK's creaking extradition laws which in many respects still had a distinct Victorian flavour and had been amended only piecemeal over the years.

In addition to dispensing with much of the 'red tape' in traditional extradition arrangements, and implementing the controversial European Arrest Warrant (EAW),[34] the 2003 Act distinguishes between the following:

- 'Part 1' (or 'Category 1') territories – basically other EU Member States – for which the EAW fast-track will apply; and
- 'Part 2' territories (those with which the UK has bilateral treaty arrangements) for which the extradition procedure in the courts has been simplified but which still will require the final decision on Extradition to be made by the Home Secretary.

Although the US had pressed the British Government for its extradition requests to be equated to an EAW, the House of Lords amended Clause 1 of the Extradition Bill (now the Act) so as to bar countries which retain the death penalty for any offence from ever being designated as a 'Part 1 territory' (for which the 'political' stage is removed and the decision left entirely to the courts). This means the Home Secretary will still have the last say on all US requests, but apart from death penalty cases his role is now largely a formality and (barring appeals) the removal of the prima facie evidence requirement should considerably shorten the time it currently takes to effect extradition to the US.

While in principle the prima facie evidence test is retained for Part 2 countries, the Home Secretary may designate a state as exempted from the requirement by statutory order under s.84(7) or 86(7). The United States was designated a 'Part 2' territory by Statutory Instrument effective 1 January 2004.[35] Along with 40 other countries, including Canada, the United States has also been designated under ss.84(7) and 86(7) as a country for which the prima facie evidence rule has been dispensed with. Extradition is now available to the US simply on the basis of a statement of facts accompanying the request. Under the old legislation, evidence sufficient to amount to a prima facie case was always required in Schedule 1 cases (principally requests from the United States).[36]

However, until the new 2003 Treaty is ratified, the old treaty is still in force, although, as stated, from a US perspective anyway, the deficiencies of the old regime have all been cured by the new Extradition Act.

## The *Norris* case

The US Justice Department took the refusal of Sir Anthony Tennant to face trial by jury in the US almost as a personal affront. Until the removal in the 2003 Extradition Act of the requirement that the offence had to be either on the 1870 list or otherwise made extraditable, there was no way in which the US could secure the extradition of suspects indicted for a Sherman Act s.1 offence. Price fixing was made a statutory crime (as well as an extradition offence) in the UK from 20 June 2003, but it was generally assumed that, because of the 'dual criminality' requirement, extradition was not available for offences committed prior to its coming into force, hence the inability to obtain the extradition of Sir Anthony Tennant.

The first opportunity for the US to extradite a suspect on a Sherman Act charge was provided by the *Morgan Crucible* case. Curiously it was not Britain's criminalizing of cartel conduct that proved critical, rather the overhaul of its extradition statutes and the sea change in official attitudes towards price fixing.

This leading British PLC pleaded guilty in 2002 to two counts of interfering with justice (attempting to influence the testimony of witnesses; corruptly persuading a witness to destroy documents) and was fined the statutory maximum of $500 000 on each charge.[37] Morganite, Inc., the US subsidiary company, also pleaded guilty to the price-fixing conspiracy contrary to Sherman Act, s.1. Several named individuals, resident outside the US, were 'carved out' of the company plea agreements, leaving the way clear for them to be indicted personally. On 24 September 2003, the former CEO of Morgan Crucible, Ian Norris, and another executive were indicted by a grand jury in Philadelphia on charges of conspiracy to obstruct justice, corruptly persuading others to destroy documents to prevent their use by the grand jury, and witness tampering (Norris only).[38] Other senior executives agreed to plead guilty and serve prison terms for witness tampering or aiding and abetting the document destruction.[39] Mr Norris was also indicted on charges of conspiracy to fix prices contrary to Sherman Act, s.1 between 1989 and 2000.[40]

Like Sir Anthony Tennant, he declined the DoJ's invitation to come to the US to stand trial. At the three-day extradition hearing that began at Bow Street Magistrates' Court on 10 May, and was heard under the 'fast track' procedure established in the new Act, the Crown Prosecution Service, making the application on behalf of the US, advanced a novel argument: even if it predated the 'cartel offence' in the Enterprise Act, the underlying conduct constituting the alleged Sherman Act conspiracy in the US would have been a common law conspiracy to defraud in English law.[41] The argument could be made because, under the new Act, the 'list' was done away with and conspiracy to defraud could now be invoked as the 'British offence'. It was argued for Mr Norris that, because price fixing contrary to the Sherman Act does not require a showing of dishonesty,[42] the conduct alleged was not the same as the 'English' offence of conspiracy to defraud, which does. For the court, however, the relevant issue was not whether the offences in the US and UK are substantially similar but, more concretely, whether the conduct specified in the request constitutes an extradition offence within the definition of s.137.[43]

The District Judge at Bow Street ruled that all the charges were extradition offences. As regards the price fixing, while cartel agreements had historically not in themselves been treated as criminal or even tortious at English common law, Judge Evans held that, if the agreement involves *dishonestly doing something prejudicial to another*, it will ordinarily involve a common law conspiracy to defraud. The dishonesty need not involve deception; and as for the element of economic injury to a third party, '[i]n the case of cartel agreements, prejudice to third parties is almost bound to be present'. The Home Secretary decided on 30 September 2005 to order the extradition of Norris, but, under the new Act, his role is extremely limited: he no longer has any discretion to refuse to make an order on the ground that the extradition would be unjust or oppressive.[44]

Mr Norris's legal team is set for the long haul. His lead counsel argues that the Extradition Act 2003 is a 'Trojan Horse' for overzealous US white-collar crime prosecutors. The judge's ruling will be appealed to the High Court under s.103 of the Extradition Act 2003. The refusal of the Home Secretary to reconsider the treaty arrangements with the US on the basis that the expected reciprocity was not forthcoming is already the subject of a separate application for judicial review. The Home Secretary's order will be appealed under s.108 of the Act and fought 'all the way to the House of Lords'.[45] It could be 18 months before any final decision. Whatever the merits of this argument in relation to the making of an extradition order, it is undeniable that US prosecutors have focused on overseas executives to get across to a wider audience and in the strongest possible terms their message that there is no difference in terms of culpability between price fixing and theft. Other UK residents who have been indicted in the US on cartel charges but failed to show up for trial may now face demands for their extradition. The US even entertains hopes that the *Norris* decision may act as a precedent for extradition initiatives in other countries.

**Extradition from Canada to the US**
Given the integration of the North American market, cross-border cooperation between Canada and the US on antitrust investigations and prosecutions has been a prominent feature of the international enforcement
landscape for some years. Over the past decade, almost all international
cartels prosecuted by the Justice Department have extended to Canada, a
jurisdiction which has the distinction of having criminalized price fixing
in 1889, a year before the Sherman Act was passed. Under s.45 of the
Competition Act, conspiracy to prevent or lessen competition 'unduly' is
an indictable offence punishable by up to five years' imprisonment. Most of
the US–Canada cooperation arrangements have concerned joint investigation efforts or evidence pooling under the Mutual Legal Assistance Act
1985 and the MLAT of 1985 which are outside the scope of this chapter
(and are in any case well known to this readership).[46]

Although no one has ever been formally extradited to the US for an
antitrust crime, the US is by far Canada's principal extradition partner in
criminal matters generally, so any account of the new 'North Atlantic
Alliance' against cartels requires an explanation of Canada's arrangements
with the United States, an area which has given rise to controversy and has
frequently raised fundamental justice concerns under s.7 of the Charter of
Rights and Freedoms.[47]

Given the imperial heritage, Canadian legislative technique in the field of
extradition has been notably similar to that in the UK.[48] The Extradition
Act of 1985, like its UK equivalent of four years later, was a consolidation
of earlier legislation dating from Victorian times. It dealt however only with
extradition to and from countries (like the US) with which Canada had
treaty arrangements. The 1985 Act had not attempted to integrate into the
scheme the rendition of fugitives between Commonwealth states, which
was governed by the Fugitive Offenders Act, 1882. The new Extradition
Act of 1999 merged the two processes into a single comprehensive piece of
legislation, the declared legislative objective being to upgrade the framework to modern international standards and practices.[49]

As with the UK scheme, extradition under a treaty involved a two-stage
process with a judicial and an executive phase, and, like the UK, the old legislation had (on top of the normal 'dual criminality' requirement in the relevant
treaties) been based on the 'list' system. However the 1985 Act and its prede-
cessors defined 'extradition crime' not only by reference to the Schedule to the
Act (which comprised the list of offences) but also, in the case of a treaty, *any*
crime described in the treaty 'whether or not it is included in that Schedule'.
In addition, given that the treaties negotiated by the British Government in
Imperial times might contain provisions that might not precisely agree with
the procedure in the Canadian Act, in case of conflict between the Act and a

treaty, the treaty prevailed (s.3).[50] Canadian judges were thus spared the 'legislative paper chase' that had been imposed on their British colleagues. In fact, the treaty with the US, which as originally ratified in 1976[51] had allowed extradition only for the offences specifically listed in a Schedule to the treaty (which did not include antitrust offences), had been amended by Protocol in 1990:[52] art.2, which had incorporated the Schedule list, was deleted and replaced by a new provision requiring extradition based on pure dual criminality. By this means, price fixing was brought within the extradition framework.

Under the scheme in the 1985 Act, evidence had to be presented in the form of sworn affidavits based on first-hand knowledge of the events to meet the same evidential threshold of a prima facie case as would be sufficient under Canadian law to commit the accused for trial had the conduct taken place in Canada (s.18).

The new scheme under the 1999 Act retained the dual stage procedure but the judicial hearing is now very different from the earlier model, based as it was on the prima facie case. For present purposes, the main changes implemented in the new 1999 Act were as follows:

- Extradition to be based on dual criminality (underlying conduct and penalty) instead of a 'list', so that, subject to treaty, extradition is available for any conduct that is punishable in Canada and the requesting state by imprisonment for two years or more (s.3(1));
- Where the requesting state seeks extradition based on extraterritorial jurisdiction, a person may be extradited even if Canada would not assert extraterritorial jurisdiction in similar circumstances (s.5);
- A new procedure for setting proceedings in motion, namely the 'authority to proceed' issued by the Minister of Justice and naming the offence under Canadian law that is equivalent to the offence allegedly committed in the requesting state's jurisdiction (s.29(1));[53]
- While nominally retaining the prima facie[54] evidence test, the new Act controversially relaxed the evidentiary burden by allowing the judge to receive as evidence a 'record of the case' which summarizes the evidence but does not need to measure up to anything like Canadian evidence standards (ss.32–3).

Under s.29(1), the judge shall order the committal of the person into custody to await extradition 'if . . . there is evidence admissible under this Act of conduct that, had it occurred in Canada, would justify committal for trial. . . . on the offence set out in the authority to proceed'.[55]

The new device of the 'record of the case' has been at the centre of constitutional challenges made to the new Act.[56] Section 32 renders admissible at the extradition hearing 'evidence' that would not otherwise be admissible under Canadian law: (a) the contents of the documents contained in the record of the case . . . (b) . . . (c) evidence adduced by the person sought for extradition that is relevant to the tests set out in subsection 29(1) if the judge considers it reliable.

Under s.33, the record of the case need contain only a summary of the evidence available to the extradition partner for use in the prosecution but it may also include 'other relevant documents'. For the record of the case to be admissible in a US extradition request, the US prosecutor merely has to certify that the evidence summarized or contained in the record is available for trial and 'is sufficient under the law of the extradition partner to justify prosecution'.

Sections 32–4 determine admissibility, while the sufficiency in terms of the test in Section 29 is a matter for the judge. As Rosenberg JA pointed out however in *United States* v. *Yang*,[57] evidence is admissible at the extradition hearing which would not be admissible in a Canadian trial: second or even third-hand hearsay, non-expert opinion and prejudicial character evidence would all be permitted.

The above provisions survived constitutional challenge in *Yang*, the Court holding that, 'given the pronouncements of the Supreme Court of Canada in post-Charter extradition cases, and particularly the need to respect differences in other jurisdictions, the evidentiary provisions of the Extradition Act comply with the principles of fundamental justice'. According to Rosenberg JA, in conducting a Charter analysis, the approach of the court must necessarily be contextual. The court cited with approval the judgment of McLachlin J in *Kindler*,[58] identifying three elements that must be taken into account in the extradition context when identifying the principles of fundamental justice: reciprocity, comity and respect for differences in other jurisdictions: 'our extradition process need only meet "the basic demands of justice" '. What is required is for the fugitive to have (a) a hearing before an unbiased decision maker and to be present; (b) the right to know the case against him; and (c) the right to participate free of coercion from the requesting state. The extradition hearing is 'only a modest screening device', and the extraditee 'is not entitled to any particular form of evidence'. Nor is it the function of the extradition judge to weigh the reliability or assess the credibility of extradition evidence: this is a matter for the trial court in the requesting country.

Commentators deprecate the perceived imbalance that has developed between international comity and liberty in extradition hearings.[59] The 1999 Act has been criticized for reducing the role of extradition proceedings in Canada to a mere administrative process rather than a judicial function.[60] Whether that is so or not, Anne Warner LaForest's observation that 'Canada has gone further than virtually any other country in facilitating extradition' now needs qualification by the addition of the words 'except the UK'.[61]

Since price fixing did not feature on the Schedule to the original US–Canada treaty, it was not an extradition offence until the amendment made by the protocol in 1990.[62] Once Article 2 of the old treaty was replaced in its entirety by a new 'no list' provision allowing extradition to the US for any conduct 'which constitutes a criminal offence punishable by the laws of both contracting parties by imprisonment or other form of detention for a term exceeding one year or any greater punishment', the way was opened. Although there have been no actual extradition hearings in an antitrust case, there have been requests, and in at least one cartel investigation the suspect in Canada agreed to waive the right to a hearing and surrendered voluntarily to the ministrations of US justice. Given the express (if superfluous) provision in the 1999 Act that 'it is not relevant whether the conduct referred to in subsection (1) is named, defined or characterized by the extradition partner in the same way as it is in Canada', it might be interesting to see the fate of any dual criminality arguments based on the 'prevent or lessen competition unduly' wording of the Competition Act.

**Some reflections**
With removal to all intents and purposes of the prima facie evidence requirement in both Canadian and UK extradition practise, these two jurisdictions now practise what is close to a form of 'rendition' rather than old-fashioned extradition in their relations with the US. (The US, by contrast, requires a showing of probable cause.) The arcane legislation and old case law on whether an offence is an extradition crime has been swept away in the UK. For Human Rights lawyers, the gatekeeping role of the extradition judge in both the UK and Canada has been reduced to that of a rubber stamp. Only the most egregious prosecutorial misconduct is likely to give rise to judicial concerns about fairness or fundamental rights.

In Britain, the role of the Home Secretary at the beginning of proceedings in Category 2 cases has been limited and his discretion after the hearing to refuse extradition on grounds that it would be unjust or oppressive has been removed.

In the antitrust area, the confluence of attitudes towards enforcement in the three common law jurisdictions, and particularly the UK's newfound enthusiasm to crack down on cartels, means that the instruments available for cooperation in the criminal justice area can now be used to confront individual executives in antitrust cases. With the DoJ directing its attentions towards meting out justice (and stiffer jail terms) for all, as well as narrowing the prison time gap between American and overseas executives, the US is increasingly likely to invoke its streamlined extradition arrangements, particularly with the UK, where it considers it has unfinished business, to secure the surrender of fugitives from US justice. In the current political climate, opposition in the British media and from Human Rights groups towards assertion of US long-arm jurisdiction is likely to be dismissed by the government as the usual anti-Americanism from the chattering classes, while the lobbying by business groups against the extradition of senior executives is seen simply as the City looking after its own. The Serious Fraud Office in London, with its patchy record of securing convictions at trial in major sophisticated fraud cases, and no mechanism available to it for plea bargaining, must be looking with envy on the successes of US prosecutors in extracting guilty pleas and long prison terms from corporate perpetrators without even having to go to trial. Its chances of securing convictions under the Enterprise Act are a matter of speculation, but in the meantime the UK authorities are ready to test their 'conspiracy to defraud' theory in extradition proceedings.

With the decision of District Judge Evans in *Norris*, individuals hoping to find a safe harbour in the UK from the long reach of US justice have recently had a rude awakening. City of London executives involved in US Sherman Act investigations could find themselves on a one-way flight to the US handcuffed to a federal marshal. Nor will non-British citizens necessarily be safe even if they reside in a country where price fixing is not a crime or, if it is, which refuses to extradite its own nationals. The DoJ has announced its policy of placing wanted antitrust fugitives on Interpol Red Notices, making Heathrow a distinctly dangerous place to have one's flight diverted to.

A by-product of the move towards international criminal law cooperation could be that the EC Commission, formerly the undisputed enforcer of cartel prohibitions in Europe, and proud of its status as a partner of the DoJ, will find itself quietly sidelined by the US in favour of more committed allies, a development to which it has contributed itself by its ceding of jurisdiction to the Member States in competition cases under its Modernisation project and its powerlessness to prevent 'its' administrative enforcement system from being destabilized by piecemeal criminalization at national level. While the DoJ is keen to vaunt the virtues of cooperation, there must be limits even to its altruism, and US frustrations must be growing at the inability of the Commission to share the fruits of dawn raids conducted in tandem with US efforts.

The Commission is adumbrating the negotiation of a 'G3' cooperation agreement with the United States, but, if it is to be taken seriously by the Justice Department as an enforcement partner in the new global dispensation, a way must be found for pooling evidence. Without a treaty (as opposed to a 'soft' agreement) the legal obstacles to evidence sharing are formidable: US agencies are effectively prevented by domestic confidentiality laws from disclosing grand jury materials to their foreign counterparts. The Commission Regulation No 1/2003 prohibits any evidence sharing except inside the 'Network' of European Competition Authorities, and even there its use in serious criminal prosecutions is virtually a dead letter. An MLAT is, however, out of the question: the Commission has no criminal law powers and is not a law enforcement agency and, not being a sovereign state, the EU cannot conclude treaties. The Antitrust Mutual Assistance Agreement (AMAA) concluded by the US antitrust agencies with Australia in 1999 pursuant to the International Antitrust Enforcement Assistance Act (IAEAA) of 1994 allows some evidence pooling without need of a treaty and could be a precedent, but the basis of the agreement is reciprocity, and until some EC Member states overcome their deep-seated opposition to the use of evidence gathered in administrative proceedings for the criminal prosecution of individuals, progress on this front is likely to be slow.

## Notes

1. Partner, Howrey, LLP, Brussels, Belgium.
2. See *The Times*: 'Ex-Crucible chief to appeal against Extradition ruling', 2 June 2005; *Financial Times*, 1 October 2005, 'Clarke backs Briton's extradition to US'. The order of Judge Evans sending the case to the Secretary of State is not reported.
3. Protection of Trading Interests Act 1980. Incensed that (as they saw it) their sovereignty was being infringed by the investigations and civil suits in the Uranium saga, the UK and other jurisdictions passed blocking and claw back statutes. 'They did not regard decisions reached by British, French, Canadian, Australian and South African companies, in meetings in Paris, Johannesburg and London, as a fit subject for investigation by the United States government' (Moss, Norman (1981), *The Politics of Uranium*, André Deutsch, p.116). The Act aimed to block the jurisdiction of US courts in antitrust suits in general. Introducing the Bill, Conservative Trade Secretary John Nott did not mince his words: the purpose of the law was to 'strengthen our defences against US practices which are not only regarded as unacceptable internationally, but are having a most damaging effect on the commercial activities of British companies'. Canada passed legislation to make it an indictable offence for a Canadian citizen or resident to disclose official information to a foreign tribunal exercising jurisdiction that could significantly affect Canadian trading interests: Foreign Extraterritorial Measures Act, R.S. 1985, c. F-29.
4. See Calvani (September 2004), 'Conflict cooperation and convergence in international competition', presented at the FTC 90th Anniversary Symposium.
5. See, e.g., the EU–US agreement on extradition laying down the base line for bilateral treaties between the US and Member States. Agreement was not, however, forthcoming at EU level on two issues: non-extradition of own nationals, and the evidential rules: the US insisted on the constitutional 'probable cause' requirement for the extradition of US citizens to Europe while requiring its own requests to be assimilated to an EAW.
6. *Liansiriprasert* v . *Government of United States of America* [1991] I AC 225 (PC).
7. Per Lord Bridge in *R.* v. *Governor of Ashford Remand Centre ex parte Postlethwaite* [1998] AC 924, 947, cited with approval by Lord Slynn in *Re Al-Fawwaz* [2001] UKHL 69. The same principle underlies modern Canadian jurisprudence in this area, shaped virtually single-handedly by Gerard Vincent LaForest who, according to one critic, 'While a justice in the Supreme Court of Canada unstintingly supported the executive role over that of the judiciary – and international obligations over individual rights.'

8. Reuters, 'UK allows extradition of 3 ex-bankers for Enron', 24 May 2005. For the indictment filed on 12 September 2002 in the US District Court for the Southern District of Texas, see *US* v. *Bermingham, Darby and Mulgrew*, Cr. N: H-02-0597.
9. Statistics confirm how locally focused US enforcement efforts were. In FY 1991, only one in a hundred of the corporate defendants in cases prosecuted by the Division were foreign companies and no non-US individuals were charged. In the four-year period FY 1987–1990, not a single foreign corporation or individual was prosecuted; see ICPAC Report, February 2000, Washington DC: US Government Printing Office, footnote 16, p. 167. During the 1980s, two-thirds of the criminal cases filed by the DoJ concerned bid-rigging in the construction industry.
10. See, e.g., *Peroxide* Cartel, OJ 1985 L 35/1; *Polypropylene*, OJ 1986 L 230/1; *PVC*, OJ 1989 L 74/2; *Cartonboard*, OJ 1994 L 243/1.
11. *US* v. *Andreas and Wilson*, 216 F 3d 645 (7th Cir. 2000).
12. Hammond (10 January 2005), 'An overview of recent developments in the Antitrust Division's Criminal Enforcement Program', ABA Midwinter Leadership Meeting, Hawaii.
13. Ibid. According to Hammond, 'investigations have uncovered meetings in well over 100 cities in 35 countries, including most of the Far East and nearly every country in Western Europe'.
14. Corporate Leniency Policy, 10 August 1993, available on the following website: http://www.usdoj.gov/atr/public/guidelines/lencorp.html.
15. *US* v. *Taubman*, 297 F 3d 161 (2nd Cir. 2002).
16. *US* v. *Nippon Paper*, 109 F 2d (1st Cir. 1997).
17. *US* v. *SGL Carbon AG and Robert J. Koehler*, Koehler Plea Agreement, Criminal No. 99-244, Filed 16 June 1999, (ED, Pa.); Report in *International Herald Tribune*, 24 October 2000.
18. Hammond (8 March 2001), 'When calculating the costs and benefits of applying for corporate amnesty, how do you put a price tag on an individual's freedom?', 15th Annual National Institute on White Collar Crime.
19. Indictment, crim. N° 01 LR 429 (GBD) filed 2 May 2001 (SDNY). For the full Auction Houses saga, see Mason, *The Art of the Steal; Inside the Sotheby's–Christie's Auction House Scandal*, 2004.
20. Joshua and Harding (2002), 'Breaking up the hard core: the prospects for the proposed criminal offence', [2002] *Crim.L.R.*, 933; Joshua (2003), 'The UK's new cartel offence and its implications for EC competition law: a tangled web', **28**, *E.L.Rev.*, 620.
21. Williams, Simon (27–8 April 2005), Director Cartel Investigations OFT, 'Competition enforcement in the UK and the impact of UK criminalisation', IBC Advanced Competition Law Conference, London.
22. Enterprise Act 2002, c.40, s.191.
23. The statutory language in s.191 was laconic and oblique in the extreme and required a trawl through a whole series of legislation to work out what it was supposed to do. Section 191 provided that 'the offences to which an Order in Council under Section 2 of the Extradition Act 1870 . . . can apply include – (a) an offence under s.188; (b) conspiracy to commit such an offence . . .'. The Act of 1870 defined an 'Extradition crime' as one that, had it been committed in England or within English jurisdiction, would be one of the crimes described in Schedule 1 of that Act, a brief list of generic offences which was added to over time by later Acts. The Extradition Act 1989 repealed the Act of 1870 but preserved Schedule 1 (the list) as later amended. It also preserved 'Orders in Council' (delegated legislation) made under s.2 of the 1870 Act. These gave effect to bilateral treaties concluded with a foreign state. (In English law, treaties are not self-executing in domestic law.) The 1989 Extradition Act provided that 'extradition crime' in relation to a foreign state was to be construed by a reference to the relevant Order in Council. The US–UK treaty of 1976 was implemented and incorporated into English law by the United States of America (Extradition) Order 1976 which recited the provisions of the treaty in Schedule 1 of the Order. The treaty contains a list of specified extradition crimes but also provided in Article III (1) for extradition 'for any other offence' if

it is (a) punishable by more than 12 months' imprisonment (b) extraditable under the law of the UK and (c) a felony in US law. Whatever its obscurity (it was argued for the fugitive that '*can* apply' meant that the provision was merely an enabling measure) the statutory language as used in s.191 had been held by the House of Lords in a case concerning computer crime to make an offence 'extraditable' (and thus satisfy the conditions of the 1972 US–UK treaty and the Order in Council): *R* v. *Bow Street Metropolitan Stipendiary Magistrate, ex parte Government of the United States of America* [2000] 2 AC 21. The above is a brief and somewhat truncated summary of the scheme governing extradition to the US.

24. For category 2 countries, see s.137. Sub-sections 137(3) and (4) define extradition offences where the alleged conduct is extraterritorial. Section 191of the Enterprise Act 2003 was repealed by Section 220 of the Extradition Act 2003 since, under the pure dual criminality principle in the new extradition legislation, designating a crime as extraditable is no longer required.
25. See e.g. *R* v. *Secretary of State for Home Department, ex parte Gilmore* [1999] QB 611.
26. See e.g. *R* v. *Secretary of State for Home Department, ex parte Hill* [1999] QB 886 (under the Extradition Act 1989). Hooper J held that the wide definition of 'extradition crime' in s.2(1) of the 1989 Act could not be limited to conduct occurring after the Act came into force. Accordingly it was unnecessary to consider the government's submission that, because the 1989 Act was procedural, the presumption against retrospection did not apply.
27. *R* v. *Metropolitan Stipendiary Magistrate, ex parte Pinochet Ugarte (N° 3)* [2000] AC 147.
28. This provision was intended to allow other offences to be added as they were enacted without the need to renegotiate the treaty each time. The treaty also provided for extradition for attempt or conspiracy to commit any offence for which extradition might be granted under the laws of both parties if the offence is punishable by at least one year; and for impeding the arrest or prosecution of a person who has committed an offence for which extradition might be granted that is punishable under both laws by imprisonment for at least five years. The treaty is however 'to be read with the Act of 1870 and is not freed from it. It may limit but not extend the list under the Act of 1870': per Pill LJ in *ex parte Gilmore*, applying *re Nielsen* [1982] AC 606.
29. The 2003 Treaty also specifically provides, in Article 3, 'Extradition shall not be refused based on the nationality of the person sought'. While not refusing to extradite its own citizens, the US has a constitutional requirement for a showing of 'probable cause' in the case of its citizens. Attempts by the UK to extradite wanted suspects from the US have had a chequered history.
30. *Ex parte Gilmore*, n. 25, above. Curiously the list was amended by statute to make offences contrary to the Theft Act 1968 an extradition crime, but not conspiracy to commit such offences or conspiracy to defraud at Common Law.
31. Extraterritoriality: where the offence has been committed outside the territory of the requesting state, as often occurs in international cartels, with the conspirators believing they are safe if they meet in cartel-friendly locations, extradition will be granted 'if the laws in the Requested State provide for the punishment of such conduct committed outside of its territory in similar circumstances'. A prosecution may be brought under the Enterprise Act if the offence has been implemented in whole or in part in the United Kingdom. The formulation of the test may not be identical to the 'effects' doctrine on which the US bases its long arm jurisdiction under s.1, but in practice this may be a distinction without a difference, since the Explanatory Notes to the Bill gave as an example of implementation even a telephone call or an email sent to the UK. As it is, the US failure to ratify the treaty does not matter, since the case is covered by s.137(3) and (4) of the Extradition Act.
32. Amnesty: a grant of amnesty is no bar to an extradition request. Article 5 of the treaty provides that, while extradition shall not be granted where the person sought has been convicted or acquitted in the Requested State of the offence for which extradition is requested, it is not precluded where the competent authorities have decided not to prosecute the person for the acts for which extradition is asked. This provision assumes

particular relevance in cartel investigations now that the OFT has declared the issuance of so-called 'no action letters', a crucial arm of its prosecution policy. It will make all the more sense in future for individuals in Britain to seek leniency in both jurisdictions where there is any real risk of exposure to US prosecution.

33. Some British commentators and politicians believe that the Senate may never ratify the treaty as its members have no incentive to do so. The US has obtained all it wants by virtue of the Extradition Act 2003, while Britain's sole 'benefit', the removal of a decision on the 'political offence' exception from the judicial to the executive branch, has provoked a storm of protest from Irish-American groups and the ACLU.

34. Implemented by the Council Framework decision of 13 June 2002 (OJ 2002 L 190/1) and effective on 1 January 2004. Traditional extradition arrangements were to be replaced by a 'fast track' procedure for surrender between judicial authorities. An EAW may be issued for criminal acts punishable under the law of the issuing state by a maximum custodial sentence of at least 12 months. The key features of the scheme are the abolition of the 'no own nationals' rule and the abolition of the dual criminality requirement for a list of 32 generic offences. Oddly, despite UK criminalization, price fixing is not one of the 32 specified offences.

35. Extradition Act 2003 (Designation of Part 2 Territories) Order 2003 (S.I. 2003 N°3334). The seven EU countries which have implemented the EAW were designated 'Part 1 territories' by S.I. 2003 N° 3333.

36. Prosecution evidence fails the prima facie test if, taken at its highest, it is such that no jury properly directed could properly convict on it: *R* v. *Galbraith* [1981] 1 WLR 1039; *R* v. *Governor of Pentonville Prison, ex parte Alves* [1993] AC 284.

37. *US* v. *Morganite, Inc and The Morgan Crucible Company PLC*, Plea Agreement, Criminal No. 02-733, Filed 11 April 2002 (Eastern District Pennsylvania).

38. *US* v. *Ian P. Norris*, Indictment, Criminal N° 03-362, filed in ED Pa, 24 September 2003; Superseding Indictment, 15 October 2003. The charges are brought under 18 USC §371 and 18 USC §1512(b)(2)B.

39. *US* v. *Jacobus Kroef*, Information, Criminal N° 03-627, filed in ED Pa, 24 September 2003; Rule 11 Memorandum, filed 29 September 2003. Kroef has agreed to serve a four-month sentence, while a US executive, F. Scott Brown, will serve six months. Each will pay a $20 000 fine.

40. DoJ Press Release, 15 October 2003. A superseding indictment was returned adding the charge of price fixing. Norris could have been extradited to the US on the perverting justice charges alone, but in that case the 'Rule of Specialty' would have prevented his being tried for price fixing.

41. Common law conspiracy to defraud usually consists of an agreement by two or more persons to dishonestly deprive another of something which belongs to that person, or to which he/she would be or might be entitled, and an agreement by two or more persons to injure some proprietary rights of another, by dishonesty. The charge encompasses dishonest behaviour wider than conspiracy to commit statutory offences, such as theft and deception, and the offence may be committed even where the object of the agreement would not be an offence if conducted by one person. It is favoured by prosecutors as a fall-back or catch-all charge where bringing substantive charges might be problematic. Prosecutors are advised by the CPS to consider bringing the charge where 'the aim of the offending is to swindle a large number of people, and conspiracy to commit a substantive offence does not meet the justice of the case'. Apart from the importance for US extradition requests, the UK authorities have their own reasons to argue that cartel conduct might constitute conspiracy to defraud: the Senior Fraud Office is using this charge as the basis for investigating six generic pharmaceutical manufacturers suspected of defrauding the National Health Service by fixing prices: SFO, Press Release 10 April 2002. It was reported in *The Times* on 12 September that senior executives were likely to be charged by Christmas 2005. The application of the common law offence of conspiracy to defraud to price fixing is explored in Lever and Pike (2005), 'Cartel agreements and the statutory cartel offence – Part I', [2005] *ECLR* 90–97, cited with approval by Judge Evans.

42. See, e.g., *US* v. *United States Gypsum Co*, 438 US 422 (1978), paras 14–15 of the Court's opinion.
43. Lord Diplock in *re Nielsen*, [1984] AC 606; *US Government* v. *McCaffery*, [1984] 2 all ER 570, 572–572 in relation to the 'list' system. Canadian courts have taken the same approach: *McVey* v. *US*, [1992] 3 S.C.R. 475.
44. Under Section 93, the Home Secretary *must* order the person to be extradited unless (1) he is prohibited from doing so by any of three provisions relating to (a) the death penalty, (b) the speciality rule, (c) earlier extradition to the UK from another territory,or (2) there are competing extradition requests and the person is discharged or (3) he believes extradition would be against the interests of national security.
45. The 2003 Act simplifies the previously complex appeal process (by way of a writ of *habeas corpus*) and creates a statutory right of appeal against the District Judge's decision and the Home Secretary's decision to order or refuse extradition. The defendant cannot be extradited while the appeal is outstanding. Time limits are stipulated with a view to accelerating the procedure. There is also provision for appeal to the House of Lords with leave on a point of law of general public importance.
46. Only in force in 1990. In *Thermal Fax Paper* the US and Canada conducted joint interviews of potential witnesses and set up a common database of documents. In *Dinnerware*, simultaneous investigations were conducted in Montreal and Canada. Canada may conduct searches for the US even where there is no allegation of violation of the Competition Act.
47. See, e.g., *USA* v. *Shulman* [1998] 128 C.C.C. (3d) 475 (Ont. CA), reversed on other grounds 2001, 152 C.C.C. (3d) S.C.C.; *USA* v. *Shulman*, [2001] 1 S.C.R. 616; *USA* v. *Cobb*, [2001] S.C.R. 587; *USA* v. *Tsioubris*, [2001] S.C.R. 613. The interview by prosecutor Zubrod on CBC's Fifth Estate on 30 September 1997 is notorious as an example of threatening prosecutorial techniques to get suspects to cooperate. And a Canadian audience needs no reminder of the long-running *Peltier* controversy.
48. The Canadian Extradition Act of 1877 was closely modelled on the UK's 1870 Extradition Act: Canada could not at the time enter into treaties and these were negotiated by Great Britain.
49. According to the junior minister steering the legislation through the House of Commons, 'even with countries with a similar legal tradition such as the United States, we have heard on numerous occasions how difficult it is to obtain extradition from Canada'. One critic asserts that Canada gave in to US pressure and amended its legislation in order to comply with 'sloppy and in fact scurrilous' US extradition practice (Botting, n. 59, below).
50. As LaForest J explained, however, in *McVey*, [1992] 3 S.C.R. 475, 510, s.3 did not provide for the broad incorporation of treaty provisions into Canadian judicial proceedings, it was simply intended to avoid possible inconsistencies.
51. Treaty between the United States and Canada, signed 3 December 1971 and amended by exchange of notes on 28 June and 9 July 1974, entered into force 22 March 1976.
52. First Protocol, signed 11 January 1988.
53. The new Canadian procedure seems to have been modelled on the UK's as it then stood. Under the UK Extradition Act 1989, the Home Secretary had discretion whether or not to begin proceedings. The order to proceed had to specify the 'English offences' constituted by the foreign conduct. In practice, an order to proceed was rarely refused. Under the Extradition Act 2003, the Home Secretary's discretion on starting proceedings is removed except in cases where there are competing requests. Otherwise, where a valid request from a Category 2 country is received, he *must* issue a certificate under s.70(1), sending the proceedings to the appropriate judge. The certificate does not have to identify the 'English offence' (in contrast to the old order to proceed required under the 1989 Act and the present Canadian procedure).
54. The US–Canada Extradition Treaty was amended by the Second Protocol of 12 January 2001 (in force 30 April 2003) which formalized the 'record of the case' procedure for extradition from Canada to the US, while still requiring in the case of Canadian requests

for the documentation to be authenticated by the Canadian Department of justice and certified by the US Consulate in Canada.

55.  The 'authority to proceed' is required by s.15 to contain (inter alia) 'the name of the offence or offences under Canadian law that correspond to the alleged conduct of the person . . . as long as one of the offences would be punishable in accordance with paragraph 3(1)(b)'.
56.  See, e.g., *USA* v. *Yang*, [2001] 157 C.C.C. (3d) 225.
57.  Ibid.
58.  *Kindler* v. *Canada (Minister of Justice)*, [1991] 2 S.C.R. 779.
59.  Botting (2004), 'The confluence of extradition practice in Canada and the United States', CALT Conference, Winnipeg 31 May–2 June 2004, 'Law's Confluence'; LaForest, Anne Warner (2002), 'The balance between liberty and comity in the evidentiary requirements applicable to extradition proceedings', **28**, *Queen's LJ*, 95.
60.  Botting, n. 59, p.7.
61.  LaForest, n. 59, p.140–41.
62.  For judicial reflections on the US–Canada 'no list' treaty, see judgment of LaForest J in *McVey*, at pp. 553–4.

# References

Botting (2004), 'The confluence of extradition practice in Canada and the United States', CALT Conference, Winnipeg 31 May–2 June 2004, 'Law's Confluence'.

Calvani (September 2004), 'Conflict cooperation and convergence in international competition', presented at the FTC 90th Anniversary Symposium.

Hammond (8 March 2001), 'When calculating the costs and benefits of applying for corporate amnesty, how do you put a price Tag on an individual's freedom?', 15th Annual National Institute on White Collar Crime.

Hammond (10 January 2005), 'An Overview of Recent Developments in the Antitrust Division's Criminal Enforcement Program', ABA Midwinter Leadership Meeting, Hawaii.

International Competition Policy Advisory Committee (ICPAC) to the Attorney General and Assistant Attorney General for Antitrust (2000), *Final Report*, Washington DC: US Government Printing Office.

Joshua (2003), 'The UK's new cartel offence and its implications for EC Competition Law: a tangled Web', **28**, *E.L. Rev.*, 620.

Joshua and Harding (2002), 'Breaking up the hard core: the prospects for the proposed criminal offence', [2002] *Crim.L.R.*, 933.

LaForest, Anne Warner (2002), 'The balance between liberty and comity in the evidentiary requirements applicable to extradition proceedings', **28**, *Queen's LJ*, 95.

Mason (2004), *The Art of the Steal; Inside the Sotheby's–Christie's Auction House Scandal*.

Moss, Norman (1981), *The Politics of Uranium*, André Deutsch.

Williams, Simon (27–8 April 2005), Director Cartel Investigations OFT, 'Competition enforcement in the UK and the impact of UK criminalisation', IBC Advanced Competition Law Conference, London.

## Cases

*Cartonboard*, OJ 1994 L 243/1.

*Kindler* v.*Canada (Minister of Justice)*, [1991] 2 S.C.R. 779.

*Liansiriprasert* v. *Government of United States of America*, [1991] I AC 225 (PC).

*McVey* v. *US*, [1992] 3 *S.C.R.* 475.

*Peroxide*, OJ 1985 L 35/1.

*Polypropylene*, OJ 1986 L 230/1.

*PVC*, OJ 1989 L 74/2.

*R* v. *Bow Street Metropolitan Stipendiary Magistrate, ex parte Government of the United States of America*, [2000] 2 AC 21.

*R* v. *Galbraith*, [1981] 1 WLR 1039.

*R* v. *Governor of Ashford Remand Centre ex parte Postlethwaite*, [1998] AC 924.
*R* v. *Governor of Pentonville Prison, ex parte Alves*, [1993] AC 284.
*R* v. *Metropolitan Stipendiary Magistrate, ex parte Pinochet Ugarte (N° 3)*, [2000] AC 147.
*R* v. *Secretary of State for Home Department, ex parte Gilmore* [1999] QB 611.
*R* v. *Secretary of State for Home Department, ex parte Hill* [1999] QB 886.
*Re Al-Fawwaz*, [2001] UKHL 69.
*Re Nielsen*, [1982] AC 606.
*US* v. *Andreas and Wilson*, 216 F 3d 645 (7th Cir. 2000).
*US* v. *Bermingham, Darby and Mulgrew*, Cr. N: H-02-0597.
*US* v. *Cobb*, [2001] S.C.R. 587.
*US* v. *McCaffery*, [1984] 2 All ER 570.
*US* v. *Morganite, Inc and The Morgan Crucible Company PLC*, Plea Agreement, Criminal No. 02-733, Filed 11 April 2002 (Eastern District Pennsylvania).
*US* v. *Nippon Paper*, 109 F 2d (1st Cir. 1997).
*US* v. *SGL Carbon AG and Robert J. Koehler*, Koehler Plea Agreement, Criminal No. 99-244, Filed 16 June 1999, (ED, Pa.); Report in *International Herald Tribune*, 24 October 2000.
*US* v. *Taubman*, 297 F 3d 161 (2nd Cir. 2002).
*US* v. *Tsioubris*, [2001] S.C.R. 613.
*US* v. *United States Gypsum Co*, 438 US 422 (1978).
*US* v. *Yang*, [2001] 157 C.C.C. (3d) 225.
*USA* v. *Shulman*, [1998] 128 C.C.C. (3d) 475 (Ont. CA).
*USA* v. *Shulman*, [2001] 1 S.C.R. 616.

# 18 Lessons learned from the US experience in private enforcement of competition laws
*Kevin E. Grady*[1]

## Introduction

In writing this chapter[2] I am aware of the irony that a US antitrust practitioner should have the temerity to advise the legal community in the European Union about how to structure an effective model for private antitrust litigation. After all, a system that has two federal antitrust enforcement agencies and 50 state attorneys-general with overlapping jurisdiction to enforce antitrust laws is not an obvious role model of efficiency. Add to this legal gumbo the prospect of private antitrust litigation at both the state and federal levels, and you have the proverbial Rube Goldberg design for private antitrust litigation.

Fortunately, whether the US model is a sensible one to emulate is not the question addressed by this chapter. If it were, the answer would be a resounding 'No', and the chapter would end. Instead this chapter will address what lessons or parts of the US system would be most useful to consider as the European Union stands on the precipice of contemplating the initiation of private antitrust litigation throughout the Union.

Mario Monti, former European Commissioner for Competition Matters, obviously energized this concept of private enforcement actions in remarks he gave towards the end of his term in office in 2004. While Commissioner Monti acknowledged that private enforcement of European Commission and national competition law has been 'extremely limited to date', he went on to state that 'greater private enforcement of Community competition law would bring clear benefits for the functioning of the internal market and the competitiveness of the European economy'.[3] In a recent speech, his successor, Neelie Kroes, continued to advance this concept. She praised the idea of private antitrust enforcement as bringing 'clear benefits for the functioning of the market and the competitiveness of the economy' and for making 'the competition rules instantly relevant for citizens'.[4]

Commissioner Kroes acknowledged the 'risks' of such actions and called for a 'good dose of common sense and a rational legal framework'. The Ashurst Report[5] provided a comprehensive survey of the current state of competition law in the European Union and discussed the potential issues involved in establishing a private antitrust enforcement model. In late December 2005, the Commission issued its 'Green Paper' on damages actions for breach of Articles 81 and 82.[6] The Green Paper and the accompanying Commission Staff Working Paper raised a series of potential proposals or options to facilitate private damages actions. The Green Paper included considerations of a wide variety of options to encourage private actions as a supplement to government enforcement, including providing for the recovery of double damages for horizontal cartel cases, the potential for class actions, lessening the obligation for an unsuccessful litigant to pay costs except when the tribunal determines it acted unreasonably in asserting the claim, and suggesting changes in evidentiary rules and disclosure obligations. Many of these options are quite controversial and will obviously spark much debate and comment in the future. Candidly, however, the Green Paper may have set forth a series of options that could create a system even more burdensome and complicated than the current US system. By acknowledging the different evidentiary and procedural positions of courts in the Member States, the Green Paper seems to have acquiesced to the myriad number of jurisdictions in which private actions could be brought, raising the spectre of inconsistent judgments, forum shopping, and unnecessary complexity. Although political reality and legal precedent may have dictated this approach, such a potentially non-uniform approach to enforcing competition laws may create more problems than solutions for fostering a 'competition culture'.

In response to the speeches by Commissioners Monti and Kroes and the publication of the 'Green Paper', there has been a palpable sense of angst and concern among business leaders and members of the bar that the US private litigation phenomenon will somehow be unleashed on unsuspecting businesses in the European Union. Although I personally believe that such fears are grossly overblown and largely imaginary, I think it might be useful to understand how the US system of private enforcement has evolved over the years to its current state in order to determine what aspects, if any, the European Union may want to adopt.

In discussing the current US system, I think it is worth noting that, even as this publication goes to press, there are many voices within the antitrust community in the US seriously calling for potential reforms in the system. Indeed the current agenda of the Antitrust Modernization Commission has listed as some of its working topics the potential reforms or changes to the system of antitrust remedies and multiple private and federal and state enforcement of the US antitrust laws.[7] The Commission devoted a session, on 28 July 2005, to a discussion of the appropriate remedies and legal liabilities in private antitrust proceedings, including the subsidiary issues of treble damages, joint and several liability, prejudgment interest, attorneys' fees and injunctive relief.[8]

This chapter will provide a brief overview of the evolution and current status of antitrust private actions in the US. It will then suggest approaches that might benefit the EU in considering the appropriate role of private enforcement in a competition regime.

**Basis of private enforcement in the United States**
The US, because of its Constitution, has a federal system of governance in which both the federal government and the state governments play independent and often overlapping roles in antitrust enforcement. The basis for federal antitrust enforcement is found in ss.4 and 16 of the Clayton Act.[9] These sections permit recovery of damages and injunctive relief for any person injured in his business or property by reason of anything forbidden in the antitrust laws. The rationale for permitting private actions is that private individuals can supplement the government in serving as 'private attorneys-general' in enforcing the federal antitrust laws. Under the federal antitrust laws, there are built-in incentives to encourage such actions. The successful plaintiff can recover both treble damages and 'reasonable attorneys' fees' and costs. Under the US system, there is no provision generally for the loser to pay the opposing sides' attorneys fees or costs.[10] Consequently, unlike the system in many countries in the European Union, there is virtually no disincentive for private parties to bring antitrust private actions. Indeed, under the US system that permits contingent fee cases in which private attorneys basically fund the costs of litigation, there is no inherent way of weeding out spurious antitrust cases.[11]

**State law counterparts**
In each of the 50 states of the US, as well as the District of Columbia, Guam, Puerto Rico and the US Virgin Islands, there are counterparts to the federal antitrust laws that in many respects mirror the provisions of the federal antitrust laws, including ss. 1 and 2 of the Sherman Act,[12] ss.3 and 7 of the Clayton Act,[13] and the Robinson–Patman Act.[14] Additionally the states may have counterparts to s.5 of the FTC Act[15] that prohibits 'unfair methods of competition' and/or 'unfair or deceptive acts or practices'. While s.5 can be enforced only by the Federal Trade Commission, the state statutes often provide for actions to be filed by private parties.

Although the Supremacy Clause of the US Constitution provides that the Constitution and federal laws made pursuant to it are the 'supreme Law of the land',[16] the US Supreme Court has held that federal laws generally do not pre-empt state antitrust laws.[17] Indeed the Supreme Court has held that a state may prohibit activity that would be permitted under federal antitrust laws.[18]

Consequently, in the US, private enforcement is a reality of life, and private antitrust actions can be brought in both federal and state courts. Although there has often been much criticism of the system and periodic calls for its reformation, the likelihood of any substantial streamlining or federal pre-emption is probably remote.

### History of modern private enforcement in the US

While private litigation was available to parties during the early part of the twentieth century, most significant antitrust litigation was instituted either by the federal government or by the states. This situation seemed to change radically with the inception of the Department of Justice Antitrust Division's criminal investigations in the early 1960s into the electrical equipment industry. There were a series of highly-publicized prosecutions of business executives for antitrust violations, which in those days was merely a misdemeanour with a maximum jail term of one year and maximum fine of $50 000. After those prosecutions, there were numerous private antitrust class actions seeking to take advantage of the collateral estoppel effect of the criminal convictions.

The sudden surge of private antitrust actions was also bolstered through a series of Supreme Court decisions that very liberally applied the civil discovery rules in complex antitrust litigation and discouraged lower federal courts from granting summary judgment to defendants.[19] Consequently antitrust defendants were faced with the increasing likelihood of expensive discovery burdens and the difficulty of eliminating the private actions short of a civil trial or settlement. Given the potential recovery of treble damages and the award of attorneys fees to successful plaintiffs, there was an explosion of private antitrust litigation from the mid-1960s through the 1970s.

In the US, unlike most countries in the European Union, plaintiffs could demand jury trials in civil actions. Even though there was often criticism from the defence bar and some commentators that such cases were too complex for juries, the US system remained unchanged. Thus, antitrust plaintiffs were theoretically able to present their case to a jury of lay people who were unlikely to have any sophisticated understanding of antitrust law or economics. Additionally there were no specialized antitrust courts established, and no special group of judges who were inherently knowledgable and versed in economics and antitrust.

The US Supreme Court added additional fuel to the fire of encouraging private antitrust litigation in a series of decisions during this period. The Court took a very broad view of what constituted 'interstate commerce' in order to permit private actions to be brought in federal court under the federal antitrust laws.[20] In these cases the Court held, for example, that activities of local hospitals or sales of real estate had a sufficient impact on inter-state commerce to satisfy the jurisdictional standards of the antitrust laws. The Supreme Court held that for a claim under the Sherman Act the restraint itself did not have to be in interstate commerce so long as the activities of the parties were either 'in' or 'affecting' inter-state commerce.

In addition to providing a very broad jurisdictional base for challenging economic activity under the federal antitrust laws, the US Supreme Court also expanded the areas of the economy in which claims could be brought under federal antitrust laws. For example, the Court held that the professions were not exempt from antitrust challenge, and in one case expanded the scope of the antitrust laws to include even the legal profession.[21] Similarly the Court held that actions of a professional society of engineers in issuing its code of conduct that discouraged competitive bidding by engineers could be challenged under the federal antitrust laws.[22]

As a result of this expansion of the application of the antitrust laws to almost all areas of the economy, there was virtually an explosion of disputes that styled themselves as antitrust claims. For example, run-of-the-mill dealer termination claims and denials of medical staff privileges to doctors began to find their way into federal court as federal antitrust claims. It was not uncommon to see routine business torts take on the trappings of 'conspiracies in restraint of trade' in order to take advantage of the liberal discovery in federal courts compared to state courts, and these cases were filed by parties encouraged by the potential for recovering treble damages and reasonable attorneys' fees.

Indeed one federal appellate court, in affirming summary judgment for the defendant in an antitrust case, colourfully described the legal climate of the late 1970s by observing: 'Although this appeal presents a Brobdingnagian record which is typical of quests for the golden fleece of treble damages, this is not a typical antitrust case. Indeed this is not even an atypical antitrust case; for, despite plaintiffs' herculean efforts, we conclude that this is not an antitrust case at all.'[23]

### Supreme Court reduces incentives for plaintiffs to bring antitrust lawsuits

In a few cases beginning in the late 1970s, the Supreme Court altered the framework for analyzing antitrust claims and began slowly to whittle away at the incentives for plaintiffs to bring private antitrust claims in federal courts. In *Continental T.V., Inc.* v. *GTE Sylvania Inc.*,[24] the Court established that the rule of reason standard should govern claims challenging vertical distribution arrangements. Prior to that time, for approximately a decade, the Court had held that vertical restraints, such as territorial restrictions or exclusive dealing arrangements, should be examined under a per se standard of illegality. By analyzing a case under that stricter standard, plaintiffs were much more likely to be able to prevail because liability was automatic, and the plaintiffs only had to prove how much they had been damaged. By removing vertical restraints from the per se category, the Supreme Court substantially lessened the odds that plaintiffs would be able to reach a jury on such a claim. This single decision eliminated many of the dealer termination cases that were clogging the federal courts under the rubric of antitrust violations.

Similarly, in *Broadcast Music, Inc.* v. *Columbia Broadcasting System, Inc.*,[25] the court applied a rule of reason standard for a joint venture engaged in pricing for a new product. This decision rejected the view that all pricing agreements between competitors were necessarily per se illegal and opened the door for a more subtle approach in analyzing joint venture arrangements among competitors.

In another decision, *Illinois Brick Co.* v. *Illinois*,[26] the Court held that indirect purchaser claims could not be brought in federal court as a violation of federal antitrust laws. The Court thus denied access to federal courts for an entire category of potential plaintiffs who had not directly purchased allegedly price-fixed goods from defendants. *Illinois Brick* thus closed the federal courts to claims of alleged illegal overcharges passed down to the plaintiff purchaser through the distribution chain. Ironically, however, this decision spawned the efforts in a large number of states to permit such claims in state courts, thus leading to the reality today of multiple jurisdictions focusing on the same alleged price-fixing conspiracy, direct purchasers in federal court and indirect purchasers in state courts.

The Court also substantially altered the legal standing for per se treatment of another type of vertical restraints, illegal tying arrangements. In *Jefferson Parish Hospital District No. 2* v. *Hyde*,[27] the Court held that the per se treatment should be limited to those arrangements where the tying product has substantial market power – at least more than 30 per cent market share.

In *Northwest Wholesale Stationers, Inc.* v. *Pacific Stationery & Printing Co.*,[28] and *Federal Trade Commission* v. *Superior Court Trial Lawyers Association*,[29] the Court also limited per se treatment for claims involving group boycotts to firms that had market power or to boycotts that were designed specifically to affect price.

The Court further chopped away at the per se standard for vertical maximum price fixing. In *State Oil Co.* v. *Kahn*,[30] the court revisited its long-standing application of the per se rule to price fixing, whether maximum or minimum vertical price fixing, and held that the per se rule would not apply to maximum resale price maintenance.

In *California Dental Association* v. *Federal Trade Commission*,[31] the Court jettisoned completely the old dichotomy of analysing restraints of trade under either a per se standard of analysis or a rule of reason analysis. In noting that a professional dental association's code of conduct might have an impact on price advertising, the Court refused to apply a per se standard. Instead, the Court held that the restraint should be analyzed under a standard 'meet for the case'.

The Supreme Court also heightened the evidentiary standards for plaintiffs to prove an illegal agreement under Section 1 of the Sherman Act. In *Monsanto Co.* v. *Spray-Rite Service Corp.*,[32] the Court held that merely because a distributor plaintiff showed evidence of complaints by its competitors to a defendant manufacturer, and even if there was action taken against plaintiff by the manufacturer after receiving those complaints, this was not sufficient evidence, by itself, of an illegal 'agreement' between the defendant and the competitors. Ironically, even though the Supreme Court upheld a jury verdict for the plaintiff in that case, because it found other evidence sufficient to show an illegal agreement, the case was subsequently relied upon by federal courts for the proposition that circumstantial evidence of an illegal agreement was usually insufficient to satisfy the plaintiff's burden in an antitrust case.

This trend of scepticism towards plaintiff's antitrust claims was heightened through a trio of Supreme Court decisions in 1986. In *Matsushita Electric Industrial Co.* v. *Zenith Radio Corp.*,[33] *Anderson* v. *Liberty Lobby, Inc.*,[34] and *Celotex Corp.* v. *Catrett*,[35] the Court held that plaintiff's burden in surviving a motion for summary judgment was to eliminate the possibility that the defendant's actions were taken unilaterally, as opposed to taken pursuant to an alleged illegal agreement or conspiracy. If the defendant's actions were just as consistent with independent, lawful actions, then the plaintiff had failed to satisfy its burden, and summary judgment was appropriate for defendants. Consequently, through these decisions, the Supreme Court had substantially raised the barriers for antitrust plaintiffs to reach a jury in federal antitrust cases.

The Supreme Court not only increased the burden on plaintiffs for surviving summary judgment motions, but also emphasized certain definitional thresholds for antitrust plaintiffs to satisfy in order to proceed with an antitrust claim. As previously discussed, in *Illinois Brick Co.* v. *Illinois*,[36] the Court held that only *direct* purchasers could bring antitrust claims for illegal price fixing. In *Brunswick Corp.* v. *Pueblo Bowl-O-Mat, Inc.*,[37] the Court held that an antitrust plaintiff must have suffered 'antitrust injury', i.e., the type of injury that was contemplated to be the result of an antitrust violation. In *Cargill, Inc.* v. *Monfort of Colorado, Inc.*,[38] the Court held that a competitor who sought to enjoin an acquisition by a competitor lacked the ability to establish antitrust injury because it was complaining primarily about increased competition from the result of the acquisition, and this was not the type of 'activity forbidden by the antitrust laws'. Similarly, in *Atlantic Richfield Co. v. USA Petroleum Co.*,[39] the Court rejected a plaintiff competitor's challenge to a defendant's resale price maintenance scheme. The Court held that, even if the alleged maximum price fixing agreement was an antitrust violation, the plaintiff in this case had benefited from the alleged conspiracy rather than had been harmed, and, therefore, it was not a proper plaintiff to assert this claim.

In *Associated General Contractors of California, Inc. v. California State Council of Carpenters*,[40] the court tightened the standards for establishing 'standing' to bring private antitrust suits. In addition to the need for a plaintiff to show it suffered 'antitrust injury', the plaintiff needs to establish 'antitrust standing'. This requires the trial court to determine whether the plaintiff is the best person to assert the claim because another person may have been more directly injured. As previously discussed, the Supreme Court in *Monsanto Co. v. Spray-Rite Service Corp.* also increased the difficulty of plaintiffs using circumstantial evidence to prove an illegal 'agreement'.[41]

Following this series of Supreme Court decisions, the lower federal courts relied on those cases to rule fairly consistently against plaintiffs' claims. Consequently, by the late 1980s and early 1990s, the federal courts were viewed as increasingly hostile to the claims of federal antitrust plaintiffs.

**Impact of the Supreme Court's decisions**

Because many private plaintiffs perceived federal courts as unfriendly to antitrust plaintiffs, plaintiffs began bringing more antitrust cases in state courts. The plaintiffs' bar had several incentives to employ this strategy. First, in state courts, there was less established case law precedent dealing with antitrust issues. There, plaintiffs had more of an opportunity to write on a clean slate and avoid the kind of federal precedent that could foreclose antitrust claims from reaching a jury. In most states the trial court judge simply did not have sufficient case law and precedent to assess the merits of a claim, and thus was more inclined to permit the case to be tried to a jury.

Second, state court judges traditionally have been viewed as less likely to grant summary judgment motions in cases. State court judges generally have fewer judicial clerks and have to deal with a much wider variety of cases. Therefore those judges were unable to spend the amount of time necessary to evaluate the record and review extensive briefs that are normally filed in connection with motions to dismiss or summary judgment motions in antitrust cases. Therefore an antitrust plaintiff would perhaps feel an advantage to negotiate a favourable settlement because the odds of the case reaching a jury were much greater in state court than federal court.

Third, many federal districts have very heavy dockets, often crowded with criminal cases that receive priority over civil cases. In such districts, it may take several years before an antitrust case will be given a trial date. In contrast, many state courts have a reputation for processing cases more quickly, so plaintiffs feel they will 'have their day in court' more quickly in state court.

Finally, some state court judges developed a reputation (deserved or not) of being more favourably disposed to plaintiffs' claims. These perceptions were the motivating force behind the recent federal legislation signed into law by President Bush in 2005, called the Class Action Fairness Act.[42] The Class Action Fairness Act permits defendants to remove to federal court any state class action that satisfies the minimum diversity standard of at least one plaintiff and one defendant being from different states, provided that there is at least $5 million in controversy and there are at least 100 class members. While the Class Action Fairness Act may indeed result in more state antitrust class actions being removed to federal court, the non-class actions will not be affected. Consequently, in the US, we are likely to see competition cases continue to be brought in both state courts and federal courts.

### Particular characteristics of the United States' judicial system
One of the major motivating factors for private antitrust litigation in the US is the Constitutional right to a trial by jury in both criminal and civil cases. The Seventh Amendment to the US Constitution specifically provides for jury trials in civil cases. Consequently, unlike the European system, each antitrust case filed can ultimately come before a jury.

The standard wisdom (at least in the defence bar) is that juries often do not have the educational ability or patience to understand a complex economic case. Therefore plaintiffs are viewed as having an advantage in settlement negotiations in filing cases that may reach a jury. Unless a case is eliminated at a preliminary stage through dismissal for failure to state a claim or through summary judgment, the financial costs for the parties increase dramatically, both through expensive discovery costs, expert witnesses and then the prospect of a potentially lengthy trial with an uncertain outcome. In those circumstances, many defendants feel pressured to reach a settlement, even a costly one, rather than roll the dice and perhaps have to pay the plaintiff treble damages and reasonable attorneys' fees.

The dual judicial system at the federal and state levels creates a unique problem of simultaneous, overlapping enforcement. Such parallel actions increase the potential costs to parties defending the same basic claims in both federal and state court. For example, a corporate defendant may find itself defending antitrust claims brought by *direct* purchasers in federal court, while at the same time defending virtually the same case brought by *indirect* purchasers in state courts. The overlapping nature of these cases and the ability to have multiple cases brought in different states have led to much frustration on the part of the private defence bar.

At the federal level, if there are similar cases brought in several different federal districts, there is a federal code section, 28 U.S.C. §1407, that permits the cases to a be transferred to a single federal court to coordinate pre-trial proceedings. Unfortunately there is not a similar mechanism to coordinate multiple state court cases.

Additionally, at the federal level, because of a recent Supreme Court decision, the transferee court that handles all the pre-trial proceedings and becomes intimately familiar with the issues and facts in the case cannot retain the cases for trial. The Supreme Court in *Lexecon Inc.* v. *Milberg Weiss Bershad Hynes & Lerach*,[43] ruled that, although a district court conducting pre-trial proceedings under s. 1407(a) can handle pre-trial matters, it does not have the authority to assign a transferred case to itself for trial. Consequently the multiplicity of federal actions would remain the same after pre-trial matters had been completed, and much of the efficiency and knowledge gained in consolidating the cases is then dissipated.

Another characteristic of the US system is that there are no federal courts specifically designated to handle competition cases. Judges assigned to handle antitrust cases, therefore, may have absolutely no prior familiarity with the area of the law, either in their past legal practice or in previous cases before them. There is often a steep learning curve for judges to understand the various complexities of the antitrust laws in the US.

Another feature of the US judicial system is that expansive discovery is generally the norm under the Federal Rules of Civil Procedure. Rule 26(b)(1) provides for the discovery of any matter relevant to the claim or defence of any party, and '[r]elevant information need not be admissible at trial if the discovery appears reasonably calculated to lead to the discovery of admissible evidence'. Given the document-intensive nature of most antitrust cases, particularly after the recent explosion of electronic document discovery, the discovery aspects of antitrust cases are incredibly high. It is not unusual for complex antitrust class actions to involve the production of millions of pages of documents by defendants. The copying costs at times can exceed the costs for attorneys' fees.

Another feature of the US system is that defendants have joint and several liability for antitrust violations. There is no automatic right of contribution as there often is in connection with other torts, and therefore, there is enhanced pressure on a defendant in a multiple defendant case not to be the last one to settle for fear of having to pay the entire judgment if there is a plaintiff's verdict.

Another feature is the fact that a guilty plea or conviction in a criminal antitrust case carries the presumption of illegality in any subsequent civil antitrust suit. To the extent that the Department of Justice Antitrust Division's cartel enforcement activity has increased in recent years, the mere rumour of such investigations has usually triggered the filing of civil class actions, even before an indictment or information may be returned. The potential for civil liability flowing from the criminal investigation is obviously enhanced if there is a conviction or a guilty plea. Consequently many defendants in criminal matters are likely to plead 'nolo contendere', which does not carry the stigma or presumption of a guilty verdict or a conviction. Additionally the recent enactment of the Antitrust Criminal Penalty Enhancements and Reform Act of 2004 was aimed at encouraging leniency applications by parties involved in antitrust violations by limiting any civil recovery to 'actual damages' for cooperating leniency applicants, rather than treble damages.[44]

### The positive aspects of the civil justice system
Based on this generalized overview of the US private antitrust litigation system, one might initially throw one's hands up in horror and loudly question why any sane country would want to endure this array of private antitrust civil actions. There is a positive side to private antitrust civil actions, however, that should not be ignored. As a result of the ability of private parties to initiate antitrust actions, either in federal court or state court, the decisions rendered by the courts, particularly courts of appeal, have been the driving force in evolving and developing principles of antitrust law. Consequently US antitrust law can change and adopt new economic learning in a way that would be inconceivable in a system where only a governmental agency was permitted to bring cases, or where a governmental agency was required to give permission to private parties before they could initiate litigation.

The discretion held by the government agencies to enforce the antitrust laws is important in the US system, particularly in the criminal context, but the governmental authorities (either at the federal or the state level) do not control the ability of private parties to seek redress in the courts for perceived violations of the antitrust laws. The quality and merits of such private claims are obviously in the eye of the beholder, but one of the major reasons antitrust law has been as vibrant as it has, even during times when governmental enforcement has been less than vigorous, is the 'safety valve' of private antitrust enforcement. Private actions often can incorporate new theories that affect judicial decision making in a manner more robust than would be the case if the development of the law relied solely on government enforcement officials or legislative bodies to change the law.

Very candidly, however, because in recent years the Supreme Court has accepted very few antitrust cases to review, the national impact of private antitrust cases has not been as great as during the period before 1990. Without the Supreme Court's acceptance of antitrust cases to resolve splits within the lower federal circuits and establish national antitrust policy, the case law may evolve in one federal circuit differently than in another federal circuit. Consequently such a conflict in the circuits encourages plaintiffs to 'forum shop' with respect to the ability to pursue successfully an antitrust claim, and defendants may be advantaged or disadvantaged depending on the particular federal circuit they find themselves. Currently, for example, the Third Circuit Court of Appeals (which covers the mid-Atlantic states) is viewed by many commentators as being a more favourable forum for plaintiff antitrust cases, given recent decisions by that Circuit in antitrust litigation.[45]

### The increasing tendency to alter the imposition of treble damages through legislation

There have been attempts in recent years by certain industries or certain interest groups to alter the fundamental premise of recovering treble damages in antitrust cases. For example, beginning as early as 1984, Congress passed the National Cooperative Research Act of 1984 which would apply a rule of reason standard of analysis to research joint ventures and would limit potential liability to single damages for those research joint ventures which are reported in accord with the terms of the Act. This Act subsequently was amended and extended to production joint ventures in 1993, in the National Cooperative Research and Production Act.[46]

Most recently, Congress expanded the protection of the National Cooperative Research and Production Act of 1993 to standards development organizations in the Standards Development Organization Advancement Act of 2004.[47] This Act provides that certain standards development organizations can obtain rule of reason treatment and a cap of single damages through notification to the Department of Justice and the Federal Trade Commission.[48]

The Department of Justice Antitrust Division was instrumental in amending the legislation that created the Standard Development Organization Act of 2004 in order to add the Antitrust Criminal Penalty Enhancements and Reform Act of 2004. This Act substantially increased the statutory maximum for corporate fines from $10 million to $100 million, the statutory maximum individual fine from $350 000 to $1 million, and the maximum jail term from three years to ten years.[49] As part of the criminal penalty enhancements, the legislation also arguably increased the

inducement for corporations to use the Division's corporate leniency programme by limiting any civil recovery to 'actual damages sustained . . .
attributable to the commerce done by the [corporate leniency] applicant in
the goods and services affected by the violation'.[50] In order to qualify for
this limitation, a corporate leniency applicant must demonstrate to the
court 'satisfactory cooperation' with plaintiff's counsel in the civil case. The
ultimate decision to limit the damages to actual damages is up to the trial
court handling the subsequent civil action. Thus far, because the Act is so
new, there is little or no judicial precedent under which to evaluate the
impact of that new statute.

Finally, the current Antitrust Modernization Commission, which will
make its report to Congress in April 2007, is considering the issue of retaining or changing treble damages as part of a review of the private remedies.
It is too soon to know what recommendations, if any, the Commission may
make, but there is at least the possibility of the Commission's recommending some changes to the damage remedies for private actions in the US.[51]

**Personal recommendations for the EU to consider in order to avoid or
lessen the burdens of private enforcement of the competition laws**
It is somewhat presumptuous for a US antitrust practitioner to offer suggestions or recommendations for the European Union to consider if it were
to carry out or implement the recommendations of current Commissioner
Kroes and former Commissioner Monti, or adopt some of the options set
forth in the 'Green Paper' to increase private enforcement. Nonetheless,
at the risk of sounding preachy and with full realization that some of my
suggestions may be totally 'pie in the sky', I offer the following thoughts.

*Consider competition courts with exclusive jurisdiction over competition
claims*
There is obviously a current movement for more decentralization within the
European Union than centralization. The European Court of Justice's
decision in *Courage* v. *Crehan*,[52] which recognized that national courts had
the authority to enforce the European Union competition law, certainly is
contrary to centralization of enforcement of competition law. Indeed the
recently-released Green Paper accepted this premise in setting forth its
various 'options'. Consequently the Green Paper missed an opportunity to
standardize and facilitate meaningful private enforcement of Articles 81
and 82 by not considering the option of a court at the EC level to hear
damages actions brought by private parties for breach of EC antitrust rules.
From the standpoint of having consistent competition principles applied
across the European Union, it would be preferable to have one judicial
body applying the same laws and the same principles for competition

matters. If such a competition court were created, the European Union would gain the benefit that is sadly lacking in the US – a dedicated group of knowledgable competition judges who are familiar with competition principles, can eliminate spurious cases sooner rather than later, and are comfortable with devoting the necessary time and attention to the type of complex case that epitomizes antitrust litigation in the US. If such a judicial body were created, it would likely expedite antitrust litigation, reduce the ultimate cost of such litigation because of having more of a commitment to and knowledge of such cases, and eliminate the potential for favouritism because of a party's particular state or country.

Just as importantly, however, adopting the use of a single competition judiciary would avoid the type of enforcement bifurcation that exists in the US, where plaintiffs who carefully plead can choose either federal or state courts in which to assert antitrust claims. Thus the existence of multiple jurisdictions or court systems is most likely to lead to inconsistent results, increased costs, claims of favouritism or 'home cooking', and the European Union will have the same type of overlapping mish-mash of courts that has bedevilled US antitrust practitioners for decades.

If at all possible, the European Union should avoid the federal/state problem that is experienced in the US. Although political realities and the *Crehan* decision may be significant roadblocks to achieve this goal, the Green Paper sadly missed an opportunity to avoid the problem of multiple jurisdictions. Indeed, because the courts in the different Member States have evidentiary rules and procedures that differ even more greatly among themselves than do various state courts in the US, the Green Paper's proposals may create a worse system than currently exists in the US.

*Use fee shifting for the prevailing party under criteria that lessen the likelihood of frivolous actions*
One of the major characteristics of the US system that has led to many perceived abuses is the fact that, under the US system, a losing plaintiff seldom, if ever, pays the costs and attorney's fees of the defendant when the defendant ultimately prevails in a case. Consequently, prior to filing a case, plaintiffs or their counsel have little incentive to analyse the likelihood of prevailing on a claim.[53] In contrast, one of the hallmarks of the European system is that the prevailing party (even a defendant) can recover its costs. If the European Union were to maintain that system for all competition cases, the likelihood that the European Union would be burdened by frivolous private antitrust suits would be substantially reduced. The *in terrorem* effect of an unsuccessful plaintiff's being responsible for payment of a successful defendant's attorney's fees would be a significant factor in eliminating the almost 'risk free' nature of antitrust litigation in US courts.

In this regard, the Green Paper's proposal (Option No. 27) of requiring a claimant to pay costs only if the tribunal determines that the claimant acted in a manifestly unreasonable manner is an interesting compromise between the current US and EU approaches to the issue of which party should bear the costs of an antitrust action. Although the Green Paper's proposal would not act as much of a deterrent to spurious actions as the current system in most EU countries, it would provide more of a potential check on meritless claims than are currently found in the US courts.

*Eliminate the incentives for forum shopping among Member States*
If the European Union were to develop a single system of competition courts with exclusive jurisdiction over competition claims, the spectre of private parties seeking to gain a psychological or real advantage by filing suit in a particular state or country would be totally eliminated. There is a fear among the business community in the US, whether justified or not, that having numerous venues in which a multi-state or multi-national company can be sued works to the disadvantage of the defendant company and to the advantage of the plaintiff who may be viewed more favourably as a local citizen by a court in that jurisdiction. If there were a single competition judicial system within the European Union, any such perceived favouritism would be eliminated or substantially lessened. There would also be less likelihood that diverse theories of liability would develop within the different states within the European Union itself, thus eliminating an additional incentive for forum shopping. Currently in the US, as previously discussed, there may be different federal circuits, or different state jurisdictions, in which plaintiffs are perceived to be more favourably treated. Such perceived bias often operates to encourage more plaintiffs' antitrust cases to be brought in those jurisdictions.

*Consider transfer and trial of cases if multiple members have equal jurisdiction*
In the US, at least in the federal system, when similar, numerous cases are filed in different judicial districts, the cases may be transferred to a single federal court for purposes of discovery, but not for trial.[54] If the European Union were to forgo establishing a single competition judicial system with exclusive jurisdiction for antitrust cases, and if the individual member countries were to have their own competition systems, the European Union should at least consider a mechanism for consolidating into one court all the cases raising the same basic claims in different jurisdictions. Unlike the current US system, where the transferee court can only handle discovery matters, the transferee forum should have the ultimate responsibility for determining the liability of the parties. It is nonsensical and terribly inefficient for a transferee court that

becomes intimately familiar with the cases during the pre-trial phase of the case to have to return the case to the forwarding courts that must again begin familiarizing themselves with the issues and parties. In other words, the European Union should avoid the lack of coordination in the US that results from the US Supreme Court's decision in *Lexecon*.[55]

The Green Paper noted that, under Article 27 of Regulation 44/2001, if multiple actions are brought by the same parties in courts of different Member States, the subsequent courts must stay their proceedings until the jurisdiction of the first court is determined and must decline jurisdiction when the first court is determined to have jurisdiction. Nevertheless, the Green Paper also observed that, under Article 28, when 'related actions' are pending in more than one nation's courts, a subsequent court may decline jurisdiction, but Article 28 does not provide a jurisdictional basis for a genuine consolidation of claims. Consequently, if there is not going to be a common EC-level judiciary to handle competition cases, there should at least be a better mechanism for consolidating and resolving similar cases filed in the different Member States.

*Encourage and enhance the transparency of enforcement authorities*
I do not believe that anyone, even Commissioner Kroes and former Commissioner Monti, would argue that private antitrust litigation should ever supplant the role of the government in enforcing its laws as a matter of public policy. Indeed, in the US, parties often take advantage of the insights and policy analyses of the government enforcement officials to follow the lead of the government in seeking to enforce competition policy. The follow-on civil actions that result from government criminal investigations or indictments, for better or for worse, often rely heavily on the case and theories of the enforcement authorities.

The US enforcement agencies in recent years have benefited substantially in emulating the transparency of the European Commission in explaining the rationale for their actions (or non-actions), especially in merger cases. Private litigation in the US involving challenges to mergers, however, is very rare, although it is possible.

Another type of transparency that is beneficial to private antitrust actions, however, is the transparency that comes from speeches and policy statements by enforcement authorities, and the exchange of views in public fora with private counsel. For example, in the US, the American Bar Association's Section of Antitrust Law serves as a robust forum for the exchange of views between enforcement officials and members of the private bar on the full spectrum of antitrust issues in the various facets of the US economy. While there are currently opportunities for this type of lively exchange of views within the European Union, I believe a more formalized structure for encouraging such dialogue would benefit the appropriate development of the private antitrust actions in the European Union. Additionally such transparency and public discussion enhances both the private bar and the business community.

### Re-evaluate the significance of the attorney–client privilege

One of the cornerstones to effective antitrust compliance in the US has been the importance of attorney counselling to businesses in order to avoid antitrust liability. Indeed, I would hazard a guess that well over 99 per cent of all antitrust-related activity occurs, not inside a courtroom, but within the day-to-day advice and counselling that occur between parties and their counsel in order to avoid antitrust liability in the future. One of the great incentives to comply with the antitrust laws is to be able to avoid lengthy and expensive civil litigation. While compliance in order to avoid criminal liability is the highest priority within the US, most businesses, at least in my experience, are primarily concerned about avoiding potential civil liability because they would not even begin to think of stepping over the criminal line. In this way, the presence of private antitrust litigation in the US is a tremendous motivating factor to encourage compliance with US antitrust laws.

A crucial component in this type of compliance system is the attorney–client privilege. The privilege in the US applies both to outside counsel and to in-house company counsel. If the European Union were to adopt a form of private litigation I believe it would be crucial to have a common respect and protection for attorney–client communications. Unfortunately the decisions in the EU that have thus far addressed this issue appear to be almost openly hostile to the concept of attorney–client privilege, whether for in-house counsel or for outside counsel.[56] The recognition of a strong and vibrant privilege for attorney–client communications will be crucial to the proper functioning of any private antitrust litigation system. Unless the attorney–client privilege is recognized and respected, there will be too great a risk that advice given by counsel would potentially be disclosed in private litigation.

If the goal of the European Union is to have more compliance with or enforcement of competition rules through the mechanism of encouraging private litigation, then the concomitant attribute of this approach needs to be a stronger and broader recognition of the attorney–client privilege. The privilege is essential to the ability of companies to lessen their liability for such civil actions.

### Impose reasonable limits on the scope of discovery

I realize that for many businesses and their counsel in most of the European Union countries the entire concept of pre-trial discovery is alien.

Nonetheless, one of the fundamental foundations of civil litigation in the US is that the discovery process is important in order to determine the facts. Unfortunately, however, many times document production, depositions, interrogatory responses and other forms of discovery can be unduly burdensome and costly. Consequently, if the European Union were to establish a system of competition courts with exclusive jurisdiction and authority, inherent in this approach would be the responsibility of the judges to become actively involved in discovery and eliminate the potential for discovery abuses.

One of the failures of the current US system is that, often, the trial judge is so distracted by the many cases for which he or she is responsible that he or she is simply unable to devote the necessary time and attention at the beginning of a case in order to establish the necessary or expected boundaries for discovery. Consequently litigation costs increase because the judge is not able to prevent discovery disputes from escalating and involving increased attorney time and wasteful pleadings. Although many US courts currently impose an initial limitation on interrogatories and depositions, such arbitrary limitations seldom lend themselves to an appropriate application in a complex case. Instead, the most valuable factor in streamlining discovery to avoid abuses by either side is a seasoned jurist who knows competition law. Such a judge is in a much stronger position to ensure that the discovery process is correctly focused and appropriately balanced in providing sufficient time to conclude discovery. Through the application of such measures as sanctions or cost shifting in order to avoid discovery abuses, the judge is in the best position to ensure the parties obtain the information they need without unduly burdening their adversaries.

The Green Paper in Options Nos. 1–10 discusses various approaches that the Member States' courts might want to consider in providing a claimant with access to necessary information. These options obviously could vary substantially among courts of the different states and ultimately may be unworkable. Nevertheless the Green Paper's approach is consistent in some respects with my suggestion that the judge get actively involved early in the case to determine what documentary and testimonial evidence may be relevant and should be produced.

*Consider common economic experts as the independent arm of the court*
One of the expensive features of antitrust litigation in the US is the cost of economic experts. It is not unusual to see multiple economic experts on each side of an antitrust case dealing with such issues as defining the relevant markets, opining on the appropriateness of a class action, or testifying on issues of antitrust injury and damages. While there is much to be said for each side having its own experts, one option that might lessen the costs

to the parties would be for the competition court to designate a neutral economic expert to testify on the relevant matters.[57] Such an expert might be one retained for the case from a list either prepared by the parties jointly or developed by the judges on the competition court.

Allowing the court initially to designate its own independent expert would eliminate the potential barrier to private actions by parties who may not be as economically able to afford appropriate experts for competition cases. This feature would also be a useful screening device to discourage frivolous cases because parties would know that they may have to rely on the expert testimony of someone primarily responsible to the court, rather than to them.[58] The independence and quality of economic expert testimony would potentially improve over the current situation that occurs at trial. There would also be less tendency for expert testimony to be dismissed by the court, as often happens in the US in the wake of *Daubert* motions.[59]

In the US much time and expense is often spent battling over the respective experts of each side, and *Daubert* hearings often become the make or break issue in a case, given the necessity to support certain crucial elements through expert testimony, such as relevant markets, antitrust injury and damages. The key aspects are (1) the expert must be qualified as an expert in the field in question; (2) the data utilized must provide support for the expert's testimony and opinion; (3) the methodology used to reach those conclusions must be sufficiently reliable; and (4) the testimony must help the trier of fact to understand the evidence or to determine an issue. By potentially eliminating the battle of experts and *Daubert*-type challenges, litigation costs would be substantially reduced and the court would be reassured that it was receiving the type of information that it needed to decide the case properly. Although the logistics of selecting and determining cost sharing for experts may pose a challenge, the European Union should consider this approach to incorporating economic expert testimony into the resolution of competition cases.

Indeed, the Green Paper in Option No. 35 takes the approach of requiring the parties to agree on an expert to be appointed by the court. While such an option could be very appropriate and is consistent in part with my recommendation, it would seem to foreclose the ability of parties to hire their own experts to supplement or contest the opinions of the court-appointed expert. The option also ignores the issue of how to resolve the situation if the parties are unable to agree on an expert.

*Permit contribution for damages*
One of the other distinguishing features of US antitrust litigation is that there is no automatic right to contribution among multiple defendants when a jury awards damages.[60] Instead there is joint and several liability

among all defendants. Consequently, absent a judgment-sharing agreement reached by the defendants among themselves, the plaintiff is potentially able to pick and choose which of the parties found liable by a court is responsible for satisfying the entire judgment, regardless of the relative size of the defendants.

By permitting contribution, there would be less of an opportunity for a plaintiff to skew the liability of certain parties who may feel compelled to settle cases rather than risk the potential liability for all of the damages awarded by a jury. This is currently one of the issues being considered in the US by the Antitrust Modernization Commission. While there are clearly two sides to this issue, on balance, permitting a right of contribution would lessen the current imbalance of settlement dynamics in favour of plaintiffs in US private antitrust cases. The Green Paper in Option No. 30 suggests eliminating joint and several liability only for a leniency applicant. In my view this is much too limited a lessening of liability and would not even reach cases that do not involve hard-core, cartel behaviour.

*Allow prejudgment interest in lieu of treble damages*
Currently in the US a plaintiff cannot generally recover prejudgment interest, although a court can award simple interest for the period after service of the complaint if the Court finds the defendant acted in bad faith by asserting meritless defences or by intentionally delaying the resolution of the case.[61] On the other hand, the award of post-judgment interest is mandatory from the time the judgment is entered and appeals have been exhausted.[62] Allowing prejudgment interest, however, would likely enhance the potential for settlement of private actions. Indeed, in the ABA Section of Antitrust Law's 'Report on Remedies' the Section noted that one potential legislative model that might represent a compromise to break the current impasse over the argument about the appropriate remedies in antitrust litigation would be to permit plaintiffs to recover prejudgment interest.[63] Admittedly, allowing potential prejudgment interest may serve as an additional incentive for parties to bring antitrust actions, but such an incentive may be substantially less significant than the current US system of awarding treble damages.

As should be clear from the earlier discussion, the entire issue of treble damages is one that has created a passionate discussion between the plaintiffs and defence bars in the US for many years. Candidly, I seriously doubt that the US will ever change its current system, but this does not mean that the European Union should follow the same system. If prejudgment interest were permitted, I believe a good argument could be made that there would not be any need to allow the recovery of treble damages to serve as an incentive to encourage private actions. Instead the actual damages plus interest should be a sufficient incentive to enforce competition laws and a sufficient deterrent to those considering actions that might violate the law. Again this is an issue that the Antitrust Modernization Commission is reviewing and about which it may make recommendations to Congress. Regardless of whether or what the Modernization Commission may recommend on this point, however, I would not encourage any new model of private enforcement actions to include treble damages as a remedy, unless the European Union simply wants to become embroiled in the same controversy that has raged in the US for decades.

The Green Paper seems to have adopted a modified approach to this issue. In Option No. 16, it suggests the possibility of awarding double damages for actions against horizontal cartels. In Option No. 17 the Green Paper offers the idea of awarding prejudgment interest either from the date of the injury or from the date of the infringement. By raising the prospect of recovery of more than actual damages, the Green Paper has opened the door to the type of debate over 'over-deterrence' that has plagued the US for years. As was indicated above, if prejudgment interest were available, this alone would probably provide sufficient incentive for private actions.

*Protect the confidentiality of agency investigations*
Currently in the US, criminal federal grand jury investigations conducted by the Antitrust Division of the Department of Justice and civil investigations by the Federal Trade Commission are maintained in secrecy. The information gathered in those investigations is not voluntarily disclosed to third parties. Only upon completion of investigations, and upon appropriate application to a court, would plaintiffs in a private action be able to try to obtain documents subpoenaed by a grand jury. Even then, however, they would not have access to the work product of the government or the grand jury testimony of non-employees of a defendant corporation, and they would have to establish a compelling need for such information, such as its being otherwise unavailable through normal discovery channels.

Unfortunately the recent decision in the *VKI* v. *Commission*[64] case appears to have upheld the right of public access to documents obtained during a Commission cartel investigation. This development is not necessarily positive to the proper evolution of private antitrust litigation in the European Union. Although I recognize that the type of civil discovery in the US is not currently available in most European Union countries, I believe it is a mistake to commingle the civil and criminal antitrust discovery procedures.

This secrecy of government investigations and the general non-availability of the government's evidence to private parties means that the government is not perceived as choosing sides or aiding specific parties in private litigation. If, however, government investigations were to be viewed as 'stalking horses' for private parties in their private litigation, the impartiality of the government investigation could well be called into question. Also the work and efforts of the government attorneys may be less successful if parties that may consider cooperating with the government investigations feared that the fruits of their cooperation would ultimately redound to their detriment by being disclosed to parties in civil antitrust actions subsequently challenging their actions. Consequently, I believe it is important to maintain the privacy of government investigations as a means of fostering more cooperation with the government in its investigations, and lessening the perception of any bias of the government for or against a particular party in subsequent private antitrust litigation.

The Green Paper appears to recognize the potential problems in disclosing governmental investigative documents to private plaintiffs, but, in Option No. 28, appears to suggest that Member States limit the disclosure only of the written leniency application. The Commission Staff, in para. No. 234 of its Working Paper, seems to have recognized the value of also limiting the disclosure of documents submitted by the leniency application – at least in the form submitted by the leniency applicant.

### Conclusion
The European Union stands on the brink of a potentially exciting opportunity. The key will be to eliminate some of the negatives of private antitrust enforcement in the US and to reap the benefits of private enforcement, such as more expansive development of antitrust law and doctrine. If the European Union is successful, it will serve both its Member States and its consumer citizens in a better manner than has been the case thus far in the US. By imposing appropriate protections against the types of abuses of private litigation that the US has unfortunately experienced, the European Union will create a better private enforcement mechanism than the US model. All of those in the US antitrust bar wish the EU the very best of luck and earnestly hope that it will not make the same mistakes that the US has.

### Notes
1. Alston & Bird LLP, Atlanta, Georgia, USA.
2. I submitted this chapter prior to the European Commission's release of its Green Paper on Damages Actions on 19 December 2005. I revised the chapter in January to acknowledge the Green Paper's potential impact on the suggestions I have made in this chapter and briefly to discuss some of the Green Paper's options. In no way does this chapter purport to analyse the various options set forth in the Green Paper.
3. Mario Monti, European Commissioner for Competition Matters (17 September 2004), 'Private litigation as a key complement to public enforcement of competition rules and the first conclusions on the implementation of the new merger regulation', 8th Annual

International Bar Association Competition Conference, available online at the following website: http://europa.eu.int/rapid/pressReleasesAction.do?reference=SPEECH/04/403&format=HTML&aged=0&language=EN&guiLanguage=en.

4. Neelie Kroes, member of the European Commission in charge of Competition Policy, 'Enhancing actions for damages for breach of competition rules in Europe', dinner speech at Harvard Club (22 September 2005), available online at the following website: http://europa.eu.int/rapid/pressreleasesaction.do?reference=SPEECH/05/533&format=HTML&aged=0&language=EN&guiLanguage=en.

5. Waelbroek, Denis, Donald Slater and Gil Even-Shoshan (31 August 2004), *Study on the Conditions of Claims for Damages in Case of Infringement of EC Competition Rules* (Ashurst), http://europa.eu.int/comm/competition/antitrust/others/private_enforcement/comparative_report_clean_en.pdf.

6. European Commission (2005), 'Green Paper on damages actions for breach of the EC antitrust rules', available online at the following website: http://europa.eu.int/comm/competition/antitrust/others/actions_for_damages/index_en.html.

7. Antitrust Modernization Commission website at http://www.amc.gov.

8. See http://www.amc.gov/commission_hearings/civil_remedies_issues.htm.

9. 15 U.S.C. §§15(a), 26.

10. There are statutory exceptions to this general rule. For example, the Health Care Quality Improvement Act of 1986, 42 U.S.C. §§11101–52, provides that, in antitrust cases challenging a medical peer review action, a court has the discretion to award a prevailing defendant its attorney's fees if the plaintiff's claim was 'frivolous, unreasonable, without foundation, or in bad faith'. 42 U.S.C. §11113.

11. Under Rule 11 of the Federal Rules of Civil Procedure, however, courts do have the discretion to sanction counsel who file cases without a reasonable inquiry or asserting claims that are not warranted by existing law or by a non-frivolous argument for extending existing law or establishing new law. These types of sanctions, however, are rarely awarded in federal courts.

12. 15 U.S.C. §§1, 2.

13. 15 U.S.C. §§14, 18.

14. 15 U.S.C. §13.

15. 15 U.S.C. §45.

16. US Const. art. VI, cl.72.

17. *California* v. *ARC Am. Corp.*, 490 U.S. 93, 101 (1989).

18. *Exxon Corp.* v. *Governor of Md.*, 437 U.S. 117 (1978).

19. *Poller* v. *Columbia Broad. Sys., Inc.*, 368 U.S. 464 (1962); *Norfolk Monument Co.* v. *Woodlawn Mem'l Gardens, Inc.*, 394 U.S. 700 (1969).

20. *Hosp. Bldg. Co.* v. *Trs. of Rex Hosp.*, 425 U.S. 738 (1976); *McLain* v. *Real Estate Bd. of New Orleans, Inc.*, 444 U.S. 232 (1980).

21. *Goldfarb* v. *Va. State Bar*, 421 U.S. 773 (1975).

22. *Nat'l Soc'y of Prof'l Eng'rs* v. *United States*, 435 U.S. 679 (1978).

23. *Hayes* v. *Solomon*, 597 F.2d 958, 959 (5th Cir. 1979).

24. 433 U.S. 36 (1977).

25. 441 U.S. 1 (1979).

26. 431 U.S. 720 (1977).

27. 466 U.S. 2 (1984).

28. 472 U.S. 284 (1985).

29. 493 U.S. 411 (1990).

30. 522 U.S. 3 (1997).

31. 526 U.S. 756 (1999).

32. 465 U.S. 752 (1984).

33. 475 U.S. 574 (1986).

34. 477 U.S. 242 (1986).

35. 477 U.S. 317 (1986).

36. 431 U.S. 720 (1977).

37. 429 U.S. 477 (1977).

38.  479 U.S. 104 (1986).
39.  495 U.S. 328 (1990).
40.  459 U.S. 519 (1983).
41.  465 U.S. 752 (1984).
42.  Class Action Fairness Act of 2005, Pub. L. No. 10.9–2, 28 U.S.C. §1332(d).
43.  523 U.S. 26, 35 (1998).
44.  Standards Development Organization Advancement Act of 2004, 15 U.S.C. §4301 *et seq.*
45.  *Nelson* v. *Pilkington PLC (In re Flat Glass Antitrust Litig.)*, 385 F.3d 350 (3d Cir. 2004); *LePage's, Inc.* v. *3M (Minn. Mining & Mfg.Co.)*, 324 F.3d 141 (3d Cir. 2003); *United States* v. *Dentsply Int'l., Inc.*, 399 F.3d 181 (3d Cir. 2005).
46.  15 U.S.C. §§4301–5.
47.  15 U.S.C. §4301 *et seq.*
48.  The Act, ironically, provides protection only to the joint venture organization and not to the participating members.
49.  Standards Development Organization Advancement Act of 2004, Pub. L. No. 108–237, 118 Stat. 661.
50.  Ibid., at 666.
51.  See the issues selected for study by the Antitrust Modernization Committee at: http://www.amc.gov/pdf/meetings/study_issues.pdf.
52.  *Courage* v. *Crehan*, Case C-453/99, [2001] E.C.R. I-6297.
53.  Rule 11 of the Federal Rules of Civil Procedure requires that attorneys who sign their names to pleadings have certified that the attorney has made reasonable inquiry and that the claims or defences are warranted by existing law or a non-frivolous argument for extension or establishment for new law. If the Court determines that this Rule has been violated, it may impose sanctions on the attorneys or parties responsible, and such sanctions may include payment to the other party of reasonable attorneys' fees. Similarly, 28 U.S.C. §1927 permits a court to sanction attorneys who multiply proceedings 'unreasonably and vexatiously', including payment of attorneys' fees caused by such actions. In reality, however, federal courts very rarely impose such sanctions.
54.  *Lexecon Inc.* v. *Milberg Weiss Bershad Hynes & Lerach*, 523 U.S. 26 (1998).
55.  Ibid.
56.  Case 155/79, *AM&S Eur. Ltd.* v. *Comm'n of the European Cmtys.*, [1982] E.C.R. 1575 (holding that, with respect to EC investigations, the attorney–client privilege applies only to communication between a client and outside counsel that belongs to the bar of a Member State); Cases T-125/03 R and T-253/03 R, *Akzo Nobel Chems. Ltd.* v. *Comm'n of the European Cmtys.*, [2003] E.C.R. II-04771.
57.  In the US, Federal Rule of Evidence 706 authorizes court appointment of neutral experts, but there have been very few antitrust cases in which such neutral experts have been appointed. Nevertheless some commentators have suggested the possibility for antitrust cases. See Areeda, Phillip E. and Herbert Hovenkamp (2002), *Antitrust Law: An Analysis of Antitrust Principles and Their Application*, ¶311.
58.  Of course, if a party subsequently believed its issues were not being properly considered by the expert, then the party could have the option to employ its own expert for submission of testimony.
59.  *Daubert* v. *Merrell Dow Pharm., Inc.*, 509 U.S. 579 (1993). The *Daubert* decision by the Supreme Court held that an expert must satisfy four factors before the testimony can be admitted into evidence: (1) the proffered theory has been tested; (2) whether the theory has been subject to peer review and publication; (3) the established rate of error; and (4) whether the theory has garnered general acceptance in the field. The *Daubert* test was extended to other types of experts in *Kumho Tire Co.* v. *Carmichael*, 526 U.S. 137 (1999). Federal Rule of Evidence 702, has incorporated the provisions of *Daubert* and *Kumho Tire*.
60.  *Tex. Indus., Inc.* v. *Radcliff Materials, Inc.*, 451 U.S. 630 (1981). The Supreme Court held an antitrust defendant has no right of contribution from codefendants. The Court suggested that Congress could consider whether to allow the right of contribution, but it was not going to create such a right.

61. 15 U.S.C. §15(a). There are few cases where this type of award has been made.
62. 28 U.S.C.§1961; *DeLong Equip. Co.* v. *Washington Mills Electro Minerals Corp.*, 997 F.2d 1340, 1342 (11th Cir. 1993).
63. See: http://www.abanet.org/antitrust/comments/2004/RemediesReportCouncil.doc.
64. Case T-2/03 *Verein für Konsumenteninformation* v. *Commission*, April 13, 2005.

## References

Areeda, Phillip E. and Herbert Hovenkamp (2002), *Antitrust Law: An Analysis of Antitrust Principles and their Application*, New York: Aspen.
European Commission (2005), 'Green Paper on damages actions for breach of the EC antitrust rules': http://europa.eu.int/comm/competition/antitrust/others/actions_for_damages/index_en.html.
Kroes, Neelie (22 September 2005), 'Enhancing actions for damages for breach of competition rules in Europe', dinner speech at Harvard Club, available online at the following website: http://europa.eu.int/rapid/pressreleasesaction.do?reference=SPEECH/05/533&format=HTML&aged=0&language=EN&guiLanguage=en.
Monti, Mario (17 September 2004), 'Private litigation as a key complement to public enforcement of competition rules and the first conclusions on the implementation of the new merger regulation', 8th Annual International Bar Association Competition Conference at http://europa.eu.int/rapid/pressReleasesAction.do?reference=SPEECH/04/403&format=HTML&aged=0&language=EN&guiLanguage=en.
Waelbroek, Denis, Donald Slater and Gil Even-Shoshan (31 August 2004), *Study on the Conditions of Claims for Damages in Case of Infringement of EC Competition Rules* (Ashurst), http://europa.eu.int/comm/competition/antitrust/others/private_enforcement/comparative_report_clean_en.pdf.

## Cases

*Akzo Nobel Chems. Ltd.* v. *Comm'n of the European Cmtys.*, [2003] E.C.R. II-04771.
*AM&S Eur. Ltd.* v. *Comm'n of the European Cmtys.*, [1982] E.C.R. 1575.
*Anderson* v. *Liberty Lobby, Inc.* 477 U.S. 242 (1986).
*Associated General Contractors of California, Inc.* v. *California State Council of Carpenters* 459 U.S. 519 (1983).
*Atlantic Richfield Co.* v. *USA Petroleum Co.* 495 U.S. 328 (1990).
*Broadcast Music, Inc.* v. *Columbia Broadcasting System, Inc.* 441 U.S. 1 (1979).
*Brunswick Corp.* v. *Pueblo Bowl-O-Mat, Inc.* 429 U.S. 477 (1977).
*California* v. *ARC Am. Corp.*, 490 U.S. 93, 101 (1989).
*California Dental Association* v. *Federal Trade Commission* 526 U.S. 756 (1999).
*Cargill, Inc.* v. *Monfort of Colorado, Inc.* 479 U.S. 104 (1986).
*Celotex Corp.* v. *Catrett* 477 U.S. 317 (1986).
*Continental T.V., Inc.* v. *GTE Sylvania Inc.* 433 U.S. 36 (1977).
*Courage* v. *Crehan*, [2001] E.C.R. I-6297.
*Daubert* v. *Merrell Dow Pharm., Inc.*, 509 U.S. 579 (1993).
*DeLong Equip. Co.* v. *Washington Mills Electro Minerals Corp.*, 997 F.2d 1340, 1342 (11th Cir. 1993).
*Exxon Corp.* v. *Governor of Md.*, 437 U.S. 117 (1978).
*Federal Trade Commission* v. *Superior Court Trial Lawyers Association* 493 U.S. 411 (1990).
*Goldfarb* v. *Va. State Bar*, 421 U.S. 773 (1975).
*Hayes* v. *Solomon*, 597 F.2d 958, 959 (5th Cir. 1979).
*Hosp. Bldg. Co.* v. *Trs. of Rex Hosp.*, 425 U.S. 738 (1976).
*Illinois Brick Co.* v. *Illinois* 431 U.S. 720 (1977).
*Jefferson Parish Hospital District No. 2* v. *Hyde* 466 U.S. 2 (1984).
*Kumho Tire Co.* v. *Carmichael*, 526 U.S. 137 (1999).
*LePage's, Inc.* v. *3M (Minn. Mining & Mfg.Co.)*, 324 F.3d 141 (3d Cir. 2003).
*Lexecon Inc.* v. *Milberg Weiss Bershad Hynes & Lerach*, 523 U.S. 26 (1998).

*Matsushita Electric Industrial Co.* v. *Zenith Radio Corp.* 475 U.S. 574 (1986).
*McLain* v. *Real Estate Bd. of New Orleans, Inc.*, 444 U.S. 232 (1980).
*Monsanto Co.* v. *Spray-Rite Service Corp.* 465 U.S. 752 (1984).
*Nat'l Soc'y of Prof'l Eng'rs* v. *United States*, 435 U.S. 679 (1978).
*Nelson* v. *Pilkington PLC (In re Flat Glass Antitrust Litig.)*, 385 F.3d 350 (3d Cir. 2004).
*Norfolk Monument Co.* v. *Woodlawn Mem'l Gardens, Inc.*, 394 U.S. 700 (1969).
*Northwest Wholesale Stationers, Inc.* v. *Pacific Stationery & Printing Co.* 472 U.S. 284 (1985).
*Poller* v. *Columbia Broad. Sys., Inc.*, 368 U.S. 464 (1962).
*State Oil Co.* v. *Kahn* 522 U.S. 3 (1997).
*Tex. Indus., Inc.* v. *Radcliff Materials, Inc.*, 451 U.S. 630 (1981).
*United States* v. *Dentsply Int'l., Inc.*, 399 F.3d 181 (3d Cir. 2005).

# 19 The role of non-litigation strategies: advocacy, reports and studies as instruments of competition policy
*William E. Kovacic*[1]

## Introduction

Assessments of competition agencies tend to measure good performance by the prosecution of cases.[2] This perspective embraces an unduly narrow conception of how an agency can best promote competition. Properly understood, competition policy encompasses a large collection of policy instruments by which a country can spur business rivalry.[3] In a significant number of cases, the enforcement of prohibitions against anticompetitive practices will be a second-best alternative to the direct correction of problems rooted in the design and operation of other regulatory policies.[4] Of the full set of possible responses to competition policy problems, antitrust enforcement should not be viewed as the exclusive, or invariably superior, solution. Instead the management and staff of a competition policy agency should be aware of how tools other than litigation, or a mix of litigation and non-litigation techniques, can provide the best result.

A single-minded focus on the volume and type of cases also obscures the need for a competition agency to enhance the quality of the institutional inputs that are essential to the development of good cases and other forms of policy intervention. The observable outputs from a competition policy programme are no better than the institutions that create them,[5] and a sensible standard for evaluating a competition agency must consider whether the agency is making adequate investments to build its institutional capability.

This chapter approaches the topic in three parts. It first reviews the litigation and non-litigation tools that an agency can use to develop competition policy and discusses possible approaches for their application. The chapter then illustrates how a multidimensional strategy can promote the attainment of superior competition policy results by considering the development of competition policy for professional services. The chapter concludes by examining the types of capital investments in institutional capability that a competition policy agency must make to carry out its litigation and non-litigation programmes effectively.

**The tools of competition policy**
Good practice in formulating competition policy requires the application of a variety of policy instruments. Litigation programmes are vital ingredients of a suitable competition policy mix, yet there are many circumstances in which serious obstacles to competition are impervious to the prosecution of cases. For example, barriers to competition often take the form of government policies that enjoy immunity from antitrust statutes and can only be diminished by persuading a legislature or a government ministry to eliminate or curtail the public policy that creates the barriers. The discussion below reviews the full range of litigation and non-litigation policy instruments that a competition agency ought to have at its disposal.

*Advocacy*
One of the most important functions of a competition agency is to serve as an advocate within the government and the country at large for reliance on market processes and business rivalry to organize economy activity.[6] Government regulations that restrict entry, pricing and trade often curb new business development and distort the competitive process. Virtually every jurisdiction features such phenomena.[7] The dangers of government regulation are particularly serious in emerging markets, where public policies and cultural perceptions often reflect a basic suspicion of capitalism and a preference for statist solutions to economic problems.

In older and newer competition policy systems, the competition agency can discourage the adoption or maintenance of competition-suppressing measures by unmasking their social costs and pressing public officials to justify the restriction of business rivalry. A competition agency can supply an institutional counterweight within the government to promote liberalization measures and to resist overt or subtle efforts to sabotage market-oriented policies. Through a variety of advocacy and education activities, the competition agency can provide valuable support for policy measures, such as trade liberalization, that complement antitrust enforcement as ingredients of competition policy. Specific focal points of activity include participation in the design of privatization programs, advice to legislators on drafting economic legislation, and participation in regulatory proceedings conducted by other government institutions (such as public utility regulatory bodies) with authority to determine competition policy in specific economic sectors.

*Education and constituency development*
One important role for a competition agency is to educate business officials, consumers and government policymakers about the merits of market processes.[8] The competition policy authority can catalyse debate about the

appropriate role of government intervention in the economy and the correct choice of strategies for promoting growth. Performing the education function can help the competition agency build a political constituency for market-oriented policies. Building a political constituency for competition and other market-oriented solutions may be as vital to the competition system's effectiveness as technocratic measures (such as increasing the expertise of an agency's professional staff through training) that seek to build the system's stature.

### Research and studies

A competition agency should establish a research capability that permits it to analyse impediments to competition. The results of the competition agency's research can inform its competition advocacy activities and the selection of possible subjects for law enforcement.[9] Publication of studies also can help educate government agencies and the public generally about the appropriate paths for improving economic performance. In 2003, for example, the US Federal Trade Commission published an influential study that identified how key competition policy goals could be achieved through improvements in the US system for granting patent rights.[10]

One model for such research in transition economy environments is Hernando de Soto's formative study of the informal sector in Peru.[11] De Soto and a team of researchers examined the impact of public regulations involving housing, transportation and retailing in Lima. The study suggested how adjustments in various government regulatory policies discouraged entrepreneurs from making the type of 'sunk' investments that often are instrumental in spurring growth. De Soto and his colleagues documented how a more austere regulatory regime would reduce entry barriers and improve public administration by reducing the number of opportunities for public officials to accept bribes for giving necessary approvals. Similar work by competition authorities in other countries would provide highly informative perspectives on domestic obstacles to competition.

### Antitrust enforcement

A fourth component of competition policy is the one that appears most prominently in discussions about competition and law reform: the enforcement of prohibitions against restrictive business practices. There is considerable room for variation in determining which commands a country should adopt and deciding the sequence of efforts to apply them. A country reasonably could choose a strategy that begins with enacting basic prohibitions on hard core horizontal restraints, such as collusive tendering, and gradually adds a fuller collection of prohibitions. Alternatively a country could adopt a more elaborate set of antitrust measures, but with an express commitment to focus on simpler enforcement tasks at first and expand its operations to apply more conceptually complex and resource-intensive commands over time as the institution's capability grows.

## Competition policy and the professions

As noted above, a critical role of a competition agency is to defend reliance on competition to organize economic activity. In new and well-established market economies alike, competition agencies routinely confront pleas for exceptional treatment for important classes of suppliers of goods and services. Few industries have never sought an exemption from antitrust oversight or insisted that special circumstances called for more permissive rules. Competition officials rarely err by overestimating the intensity and durability of requests for exceptional treatment. The case for competition must be made in various settings – before legislatures, regulatory authorities and courts – every week of the year.

Arguments for exceptional treatment figure prominently in the history of efforts to apply competition law to accountants, attorneys, engineers, physicians and other providers of professional services.[12] One claim is that competition will lead service providers to injure consumers by providing inadequate levels of quality.[13] Price floors, restrictions on competitive bidding and stringent qualification standards are said to be necessary to elicit sufficient quality.

A second, closely-related claim is that consumers of professional services ordinarily cannot assess the truth of service provider assertions about the price or quality of their services. In this setting, service providers will exploit superior information to mislead consumers, to their severe detriment. Professional societies often have implemented rules that ban or severely limit advertising to address this possibility.

The professions also have argued that competition authorities and courts lack the capacity properly to diagnose commercial practices in the professions and therefore are likely to condemn behaviour that is benign or procompetitive. Even when competition agencies profess to be sensitive to purported quality justifications for certain restrictions, they are said to be unable to make well-informed, accurate distinctions.

The professions have raised substantive and institutional arguments for exceptional treatment in the courts[14] and before legislative bodies. There can be a close relationship between a successful litigation program and the intensity of demands for legislative intervention to create exemptions. A competition agency's litigation victories involving professional services can elicit determined efforts by the professions to persuade legislators to provide partial or complete dispensations from antitrust oversight.[15] An agency must be prepared to defend its jurisdiction against collateral political attacks, lest a profession immediately obtain from the legislature the immunity from antitrust oversight that it has lost in the courtroom. In such circumstances, an agency that is proficient in litigation alone is as vulnerable as a soccer team that has superior strikers but no goalkeeper. Skill in advocacy frequently is the goalkeeper of competition policy.

Regardless of the forum in which they appear and regardless of the form of their policy intervention (bringing cases or providing advice as a competition advocate), competition agencies must overcome concerns about the quality effects of competition and about their own capacity. Courts and legislatures will seek assurances that competition does not endanger quality and that the competition agencies know what they are doing.

Impediments to competition in the professions take several forms. Some behavior is purely private, such as an association's ethical code that sets price floors for services. In other cases, the obstacle is a public regulation that governs entry, pricing or advertising. The capacity to bring cases to challenge private restraints unmistakably is an important means for competition agencies to make competition policy in the professions. Many important accomplishments of competition agencies have consisted of successful lawsuits. A competition program that lacks a credible commitment to prosecute apparent misconduct is unlikely to succeed.

Litigation alone is seldom sufficient. Because legislation and administrative regulation are key sources of policy in this area, an agency must be prepared to engage in advocacy before legislatures and other government bodies with regulatory authority. Competition authorities can make useful contributions through the issuance of guidelines and advisory opinions that address issues of concern to members of the profession. The effective agency applies a multidimensional strategy that involves its skills as an enforcement body, a competition advocate and an advisor to affected business operators. Whatever the chosen policy tool, the agency will be called upon to demonstrate its knowledge and policymaking sophistication in the industry at hand.

### The importance and contributions of competition policy R&D

Whatever its chosen means, a competition agency cannot act skilfully without an adequate knowledge base. Competition policy research and development[16] supplies the knowledge base for all of the agency's policy instruments and establishes credibility in the eyes of judges, legislators, other government ministries, academics and practitioners.[17] The agency's knowledge determines its ability to comprehend accurately the competitive significance of business conduct and builds its capacity to speak persuasively to government and nongovernment audiences who may doubt its competence to treat issues of great technical complexity.

*Accumulating economic precedents*
One important variety of competition policy R&D is empirical research to test the effects of restrictions on competition. Empirical research can yield 'economic precedents' that demonstrate the validity of a hypothesis and, like legal precedents, can support specific policy interventions.[18] The agency can develop an indigenous capability to perform the relevant empirical research or contract with external bodies, such as universities, to conduct studies. The research agenda ought to include the assessment of past enforcement decisions.[19] Retrospective evaluations of enforcement choices test the wisdom of past interventions and guide future policy development.

Comparative study can inform an agency's empirical agenda. Differences in regulation among a jurisdiction's political subdivisions or across jurisdictions can permit side-by-side comparisons of the effects of different regulatory regimes. A valuable by-product of the complexity inherent in regulatory decentralization and diversity is the opportunity to perform studies that identify superior practices and facilitate a voluntary process of opting into superior approaches.

*Gathering knowledge from outsiders*
A second way to build the agency's knowledge is to conduct hearings, seminars and workshops to accumulate knowledge from informed outsiders. An agency might invite academics to present empirical or theoretical work and to inform the agency's own research agenda and to encourage academics to consider research that might assist the competition policy community. Or the agency could use hearings to obtain the current thinking of business operators within the profession about developments that bear upon the formulation of competition policy. Such proceedings also serve as a means to solicit the views of other government institutions whose decisions determine the competitive environment for the professions. The mere fact that the competition agency actively and regularly seeks to learn from external groups can help establish a reputation for openness and superior practice.

Workshops and seminars can assume special importance in an environment of policymaking fragmentation and interdependency. National competition authorities are becoming ever more aware that they do not make policy in isolation. In many sectors, competition agencies routinely discover that their decisions are only a subset of government policymaking that shapes the competitive environment.[20] With increasing frequency, competition authorities are pressed to identify relevant interdependencies, to formulate policy proposals that account for the activities of other government bodies and to build intergovernmental relationships that can facilitate competition agencies to engage in advocacy and otherwise inform government agencies about the competitive consequences of their decisions.

*Performance measurement and evaluation*

The exercises of preparing performance measures and conducting ex post evaluations of specific enforcement measures provide valuable tools for answering these critical questions about the administration of competition policy. The assessment of outcomes of substantive interventions can generate useful information about such basic matters as the choice of cases and the design of remedies. The routine evaluation of internal procedures supplies regular opportunities to determine whether the agency's organizational infrastructure and management techniques put the competition authority in the best possible position to select promising substantive initiatives and bring them to a successful close. A competition policy system is only as good as the institutions entrusted with implementation. By emphasizing internal review and improvement, a competition agency puts proper emphasis on the expansion of its knowledge base and institution building as indispensable predicates to success.

Evaluations may indicate needed adjustments in the competition agency's statutory authority. In recent decades, many competition authorities have sought and obtained important enhancements in the framework of laws, and there is every reason to believe that a key to effectiveness over time will be the installation of periodic upgrades to account for past experience and new conditions. A programme of performance measurement and evaluation could supply a better empirical foundation for designing and justifying needed changes.

Evaluation promises to play a larger role that extends well beyond a competition authority's intramural decisions about case selection and management. The legitimacy of government efforts to enforce competition policy commands depends substantially on the ability of competition policy authorities to demonstrate to a variety of external observers, such as legislators, business managers and the public at large, that chosen forms of intervention to curb restraints on business rivalry improve economic performance. Neither the intuitions of public enforcement officials nor the hypotheses of academic theorists are likely to provide a confident basis for outsiders to conclude that the government agency has selected the correct mix of policies or chosen the ideal procedures to execute programmes. Competition policy institutions face a continuing need to justify their value, and one cannot expect critical observers to accept unsubstantiated assurances of efficacy.

## Conclusion

Discussions about the optimal design of a competition policy programme need not automatically assume that a competition policy system should consist exclusively, or even chiefly, of enforcing antitrust prohibitions.

Non-litigation tools have important applications for defending the reach of antitrust jurisdiction and for extending the application of competition rules to sectors that currently enjoy exceptional treatment. Among other considerations, the design of a competition policy system should account for the tendency for the prosecution of antitrust cases to create political pressure for legislative or regulatory intervention that displaces or curtails the application of antitrust statutes in the affected sector. Competition advocacy, research and education are essential tools with which a competition agency can defend the application of competition law to such sectors. In other instances, non-litigation tools will be the best instruments for encouraging legislatures and other government bodies to dismantle regulatory barriers to competition. In these and other respects, a competition agency whose competence consists solely of prosecuting cases will be weakly equipped to repel requests for statutory or regulatory dispensations from antitrust oversight and to foster the dismantling of existing government policies that impede rivalry.

Nations can tailor competition policy systems to suit their unique needs and capabilities through their choice of tools (e.g., advocacy, education, research and law enforcement) for promoting market rivalry, the relative emphasis that competition agency gives to these tools as it begins operations and matures, and adjustments to the agency's powers over time to augment the initial portfolio of policy tools. There is considerable room to account for specific national circumstances and changing capabilities through the initial definition of responsibilities and creation of policymaking instruments, the sequencing of activities and the adjustment of powers over time.

The agency's capacity to exercise litigation and non-litigation functions effectively depends heavily on the amount and quality of its investments in competition policy research and development. In sectors such as professional services, the agency's ability to intervene wisely and to gain deference from courts, legislatures and government ministries will require a demonstration of the agency's understanding of the sectors in question. Outlays to build the competition agency's knowledge through the recruitment of skilled professionals, research, data collection, hearings and the evaluation of past interventions should be seen as indispensable ingredients of every budgetary cycle.

### Notes

1.  Commissioner, US Federal Trade Commission. The views presented here are the author's alone.
2.  See Kovacic, William E. (2004a), 'The modern evolution of US competition policy norms', **71**, *Antitrust Law Journal*, 377, 404–5, 408–10 (describing and criticizing tendency of commentators to use the prosecution of cases as main measure of competition agency quality).

3. See Khemani, R. Shyam and Mark A. Dutz (1995), 'The instruments of competition policy and their relevance for economic development', in Claudio R. Frischtak (ed.), *Regulatory Policies and Reform: A Comparative Perspective* 16 (describing policy tools by which countries can achieve competition aims).
4. See Kovacic, William E. and Andreas P. Reindl (2005), 'An interdisciplinary approach to improving competition policy and intellectual property policy', **28**, *Fordham International Law Journal*, 1062, 1064–6 (discussing how the best approach for solving competition policy problems associated with the use of intellectual property rights may reside in correcting flaws in the structure and operation of systems for granting intellectual property rights).
5. See Kovacic, William E. (2001), 'Institutional foundations for economic legal reform in transition economies: the case of competition policy and antitrust enforcement', **77**, *Chicago-Kent Law Review*, 265; Kovacic, William E. (Fall 2005), 'Achieving better practices in the design of competition policy institutions', **50**, *Antitrust Bulletin*, 511.
6. See Coate, Malcolm B. et al. (1992), 'Antitrust in Latin America: regulating government and business', **24**, *University of Miami Inter-American Law Review*, 37, 58 ('In any economy, the antitrust agency can act as a useful watchdog to protect the market economy from excessive regulation. In effect, the antitrust agency should attempt to regulate bureaucracy and minimize the burden of government on society.'); Cooper, James C. et al. (2005), 'Theory and practice of competition advocacy at the FTC', **72**, *Antitrust Law Journal*, 1091, 1092 ('[W]hen antitrust immunities are likely to render the FTC impotent to wage ex post challenges to anticompetitive conduct, advocacy may be the only tool to carry out the FTC's mission.'); Laffont, Jean-Jacques (1998), 'Competition, Information, and Development', in Boris Pleskovic and Joseph E. Stiglitz (eds), *Annual World Bank Conference on Development Economics 1998*, at 237, 245 (noting that 'a competition agency can play a valuable educational role in advocating the social benefits of fair competition.'); Jatar, Ana Julia (1998), 'Comment on "Competition, Information, and Development" by Jean-Jacques Laffont', in Boris Pleskovic and Joseph E. Stiglitz (eds), *Annual World Bank Conference on Development Economics 1998*, 258, 259 ('A competition agency should have the legal authority to challenge other government agencies' decisions that conflict with competitive principles.'); Slay, Ben (1996), 'Industrial de-monopolization and competition policy in Poland', in *De-monopolization and Competition Policy in Post-Communist Economies*, 123, 143 ('Perhaps the [Polish] Antimonopoly Office's most important (and least-discussed) function has been the advocacy of liberal, pro-competitive solutions to economic policy problems during the Polish transition.').
7. See Gavil, Andrew I. et al. (2002), *Antitrust Law in Perspective: Cases, Concepts and Problems in Competition Policy*, 990–93.
8. See Jatar, Ana Julia (January 1995), 'Competition Policy in Latin-America: The Promotion of a Social Change' (paper by the former head of Venezuela's competition authority; observing that '[c]hanges in conduct and attitudes must be considered one of the major goals in competition policy' in transition economies); Rowat, Malcolm (March 1995), 'Competition policy in Latin America: legal and institutional issues' ('Competition authorities need to make a special effort to "educate" the public about the merits of a sensible competition policy.').
9. See, e.g., Federal Trade Commission (July 2002), 'Generic drug entry prior to patent expiration: an FTC study' (empirical study of entry by generic pharmaceutical products), available at http://www.ftc.gov/os/2002/07/genericdrugstudy.pdf.
10. For the FTC's study and recommendations, see Federal Trade Commission (2003), 'To promote innovation: the proper balance of competition and patent law and policy', available at http://www.ftc.gov/os/2003/10/innovationrpt.pdf. See also Department of Justice & Federal Trade Commission (2004), 'Improving health care: a dose of competition' (study examining strategies for using competition to improve delivery of health care services), available at http://www.ftc.gov/reports/heathcare/040723healthcarerpt.pdf.
11. De Soto, Hernando (1989), *The Other Path: The Invisible Revolution in the Third World*.
12. For a discussion of these issues in the health care sector, see Kwoka, John E., Jr. (2005), 'The Federal Trade Commission and the professions: a quarter century of accomplishment and some new challenges', **72**, *Antitrust Law Journal*, 997.

13. This quality argument is not unique to the professions. Other service industries (e.g., transportation) have sought to curb or eliminate antitrust oversight by arguing that competition endangers consumers by reducing quality.
14. Examples include *California Dental Association* v. *Federal Trade Commission*, 526 US 756 (1999); *Federal Trade Commission* v. *Indiana Federation of Dentists*, 476 US 447 (1986); *National Society of Professional Engineers* v. *United States*, 435 US 679 (1978).
15. In the 1970s, the FTC sued the American Medical Association and barred the group from imposing restrictions on truthful advertising and from banning efforts by its members to solicit patients. *American Medical Association*, 94 F.T.C. 701 (1979) (finding liability), order enforced as modified, 638 F.2d 443 (2d Cir. 1980), affirmed by an equally divided Supreme Court, 455 US 676 (1982). During the appeal of the FTC's administrative decision finding liability, the US Congress seriously considered measures to withdraw the FTC's jurisdiction over any profession (including the legal and medical professions) subject to state regulation. See Kovacic, William E. (1989), 'Congress and the Federal Trade Commission', **57**, *Antitrust Law Journal*, 869, 896–7 (discussing measures to remove FTC's jurisdiction over the professions); Kovacic, William E. (1982), 'The Federal Trade Commission and Congressional oversight of antitrust enforcement', **17**, *Tulsa Law Journal*, 587, 666–77.
16. This phrase originated in Muris, Timothy J. (2003), 'Looking forward: the Federal Trade Commission and the future development of US competition policy', **2003**, *Columbia Business Law Review*, 359. See also 'More than law enforcement: the FTC's many tools – a conversation with Tim Muris and Bob Pitofsy', **72**, *Antitrust Law Journal*, 773, 826–8 (2005) (describing importance of FTC investments in competition policy research and development).
17. The discussion in this section draws in part from Kovacic, William E. (2005), 'Measuring what matters: the Federal Trade Commission and investments in competition policy research and development', **72**, *Antitrust Law Journal*, 861.
18. See Bond, Ronald S. et al. (September 1980), 'Federal Trade Commission staff report on effects of restrictions on advertising and commercial practice in the professions: the case of optometry', Bureau of Economics (presenting results of empirical study on impact of restrictions on competition in provision of optometry services); see also *PolyGram Holding, Inc.* (Federal Trade Commission, July 24, 2003) (relying, inter alia, on research concerning effects of restrictions on competition involving provision of professional services), available at http://www.ftc.gov/os/caselist/d9298htm.
19. See Kovacic, William E. (2006), 'Using ex post evaluation to improve the performance of competition policy authorities', **31**, *Journal of Corporation Law*, 503.
20. These and other interdependencies are explored in Kovacic, William E. (2004b), 'Toward a domestic competition network', in Richard A. Epstein and Michael S. Greve (eds), *Competition Laws in Conflict*, 316; Yoo, Christopher S. (2003), 'New models of regulation and interagency governance', **2003**, *Michigan State Detroit College of Law Review*, 701.

## References

Bond, Ronald S. et al. (September 1980), 'Federal Trade Commission staff report on effects of restrictions on advertising and commercial practice in the professions: the case of optometry'.
Coate, Malcolm B. et al. (1992), 'Antitrust in Latin America: regulating government and business', **24**, *University of Miami Inter-American Law Review*, 37.
Cooper, James C. et al. (2005), 'Theory and practice of competition advocacy at the FTC', **72**, *Antitrust Law Journal*, 1091.
Department of Justice & Federal Trade Commission (2004), 'Improving health care: a dose of competition', available at http://www.ftc.gov/reports/heathcare/040723healthcarerpt.pdf.
De Soto, Hernando (1989), *The Other Path: The Invisible Revolution in the Third World*.
Federal Trade Commission (July 2002), 'Generic drug entry prior to patent expiration: an FTC study', available at http://www.ftc.gov/os/2002/07/genericdrugstudy.pdf.
Federal Trade Commission (2003), 'To promote innovation: the proper balance of competition and patent law and policy', available at http://www.ftc.gov/os/2003/10/innovationrpt.pdf.

Gavil, Andrew I. et al. (2002), *Antitrust Law in Perspective: Cases, Concepts and Problems in Competition Policy*, 990–93.

Jatar, Ana Julia (January 1995), 'Competition policy in Latin-America: the promotion of a social change'.

Jatar, Ana Julia (1998), 'Comment on "Competition, Information, and Development" by Jean-Jacques Laffont', in Boris Pleskovic and Joseph E. Stiglitz (eds), *Annual World Bank Conference on Development Economics 1998*.

Khemani, R. Shyam and Mark A. Dutz (1995), 'The instruments of competition policy and their relevance for economic development', in Claudio R. Frischtak (ed.), *Regulatory Policies and Reform: A Comparative Perspective*, 16.

Kovacic, William E. (1982), 'The Federal Trade Commission and Congressional oversight of antitrust enforcement', **17**, *Tulsa Law Journal*, 587.

Kovacic, William E. (1989), 'Congress and the Federal Trade Commission', **57**, *Antitrust Law Journal*, 869.

Kovacic, William E. (2001), 'Institutional foundations for economic legal reform in transition economies: the case of competition policy and antitrust enforcement', **77**, *Chicago-Kent Law Review*, 265.

Kovacic, William E. (2004a), 'The modern evolution of US competition policy norms', **71**, *Antitrust Law Journal*, 377.

Kovacic, William E. (2004b), 'Toward a domestic competition network', in Richard A. Epstein and Michael S. Greve (eds), *Competition Laws in Conflict*, 316.

Kovacic, William E. (Fall 2005), 'Achieving better practices in the design of competition policy institutions', **50**, *Antitrust Bulletin*, 511.

Kovacic, William E. (2005), 'Measuring what matters: the Federal Trade Commission and investments in competition policy research and development', **72**, *Antitrust Law Journal*, 861.

Kovacic, William E. (2006), 'Using ex post evaluation to improve the performance of competition policy authorities', **31**, *Journal of Corporation Law*, 503.

Kovacic, William E. and Andreas P. Reindl (2005), 'An interdisciplinary approach to improving competition policy and intellectual property policy', **28**, *Fordham International Law Journal*, 1062.

Kwoka, John E., Jr. (2005), 'The Federal Trade Commission and the professions: a quarter century of accomplishment and some new challenges', **72**, *Antitrust Law Journal*, 997.

Laffont, Jean-Jacques (1998), 'Competition, information, and development', in Boris Pleskovic and Joseph E. Stiglitz (eds), *Annual World Bank Conference on Development Economics 1998*, at 237.

Muris, Timothy J. (2003), 'Looking forward: the Federal Trade Commission and the future development of US competition policy', 2003, *Columbia Business Law Review*, 359.

Rowat, Malcolm (March 1995), 'Competition policy in Latin America: legal and institutional issues'.

Slay, Ben (1996), 'Industrial de-monopolization and competition policy in Poland', in *De-monopolization and Competition Policy in Post-Communist Economies*, 123.

Yoo, Christopher S. (2003), 'New models of regulation and interagency governance', 2003, *Michigan State Detroit College of Law Review*, 701.

## Cases

*American Medical Association*, 94 F.T.C. 701 (1979) (finding liability), order enforced as modified, 638 F.2d 443 (2d Cir. 1980), affirmed by Supreme Court, 455 US 676 (1982).

*California Dental Association* v. *Federal Trade Commission*, 526 US 756 (1999).

*Federal Trade Commission* v. *Indiana Federation of Dentists*, 476 US 447 (1986).

*National Society of Professional Engineers* v. *United States*, 435 US 679 (1978).

*PolyGram Holding, Inc.* (Federal Trade Commission, July 24, 2003) available at http://www.ftc.gov/os/caselist/d9298htm.

# 20 Information please: opening antitrust to the public: why more European Union Court and Commission documents and hearings should no longer be secret
*David Lawsky*[1]

## Introduction
Antitrust agencies in the United States and Europe play peek-a-boo with the public, each showing off bits and pieces of their very different processes for making decisions. Americans have something to learn from the Europeans' carefully thought out administrative process. But Europeans also have something to learn from Americans about opening up institutions, lessons that will benefit the public and the decision-making bodies themselves: the European Commission and European Union courts.

I will argue here that when the European Commission acts against cartels or abuses of dominance the public should have access to some of the documents during the case and should be able to attend hearings now closed. Even more important, in merger cases as well as cartel and dominance cases, the European courts need to let the public see far more of what they do, including access to all filings.[2]

The European Commission has a formal timetable for each step of its administrative review of mergers and informs the public of its progress along the way. This system has been praised by lawyers for being both more organized and, crucially for our purposes, more open than the American system. For example, Warren Grimes has suggested that the American antitrust agencies should follow the European example and issue a reasoned decision in every case.[3] But once merger, cartel and monopolization (or abuse of dominance, to use the European term) cases move to the courts, the American justice system is more open in every way than its European Union counterparts in Luxembourg, the European Court of Justice and Court of First Instance.

If European Union institutions become more open, everyone will benefit, from the parties involved to the casual observer. Companies of course stand to benefit. For example, reading the Commission's briefs will provide companies with a better understanding of the Commission's legal views, and thus permit companies to follow the law more easily and less expensively.[4] In addition, more open institutions may actually improve competition law and its administration, because openness will foster better, more productive discussions among lawyers and economists from private and public institutions.

More open institutions will also improve public oversight. In a democracy reporters often stand in for the public, and journalism shines a light on government activities. Thus reporting enhances public scrutiny, which in turn serves as a check on institutions. But without adequate information, even the sharply competitive reporters in Brussels are forced to focus on leaks instead of substance, and therefore their stories are less useful to the public than they would otherwise be. And in journalism, where what happens today is the news, information delayed is often information denied. Reasoned decisions that become public six to 18 months after a decision are helpful to lawyers and academics but useless to reporters.

### A brief comparison of antitrust basics in the US and EU

United States antitrust officials must go to court and convince a judge to block mergers, punish price fixers or remedy monopolization, with the exception of a sprinkling of cases handled by Federal Trade Commission administrative law judges.[5] Most cases are resolved before a complaint is filed, typically when the agency closes its investigation or settles with the parties. Accordingly the US handles much of its work as an administrative agency, although without the clearly defined process of the European Commission. In contrast to the United States, the European Commission itself has authority to block mergers, fine cartels and punish abuse of dominance, and its decisions may be appealed to the courts.[6] The European Union and United States institutions differ in the amount and type of information they make available to the public during a case. Let us touch on differences in public disclosure between the US Federal Trade Commission (FTC), the US Department of Justice Antitrust Division, the European Commission Directorate-General Competition (DG Comp), US courts and European Union courts.

### Mergers

United States law requires Washington agencies to keep merger filings secret, while European Union law requires the exact opposite: the Commission must publish merger filings in the *European Union Official Journal*. Companies can be sure that Washington's antitrust agencies will say nothing if the FTC or Antitrust Division makes a second request for more information on a merger, because the law prohibits it. But Brussels officials issue a press release explaining their reasons when they open an in-depth second-phase investigation.

In the United States, the agency review of a non-cash tender offer is supposed to last 30 days plus 20 days for a second request, plus time needed to compile requested information. The reality is that, in cases posing what the US agencies perceive as significant concerns, negotiations can occur at several steps in the process, potentially delaying a decision for months. The European Commission process lasts 25 working days, which may be slightly extended, with the possibility of an additional in-depth review. The Commission's in-depth review has a formal timetable of steps culminating in a final deadline after 90 working days, or roughly four months, which is occasionally extended slightly.[7] During its in-depth review, the European Commission often sends companies a Statement of Objections (SO), which is a charge sheet open to rebuttal. Third parties receive redacted versions of the SO, that is, versions with commercial secrets removed. SOs are confidential but some leak to journalists. The Commission also offers parties a closed hearing to make their case before a hearing officer, who makes no decision but reports to the Competition Commissioner.[8]

Both the United States and European agencies can choose to approve a merger or require changes. US agencies file a formal complaint and settlement agreement that is public and must be approved by a federal judge. The European Commission issues a press release when it settles a case and gives its reasoned decision to the parties. Only after business secrets are removed is the reasoned decision released publicly.[9] Much later some decisions are published in translation.

The European Commission can block a deal, which at this writing it has done only 19 times in the 2838 mergers it has dealt with since 1990, and later issues a reasoned decision.[10] The FTC and Antitrust Division must convince a judge to block a deal, but the government decision to take a case to court usually convinces companies to drop their deal rather than face the time and expense of defending themselves. Court fights grow out of only a tiny sliver of the merger filings in the United States, but in the rare instance of a trial all evidence, briefs, exhibits and hearing transcripts are commonly public, except for a small amount of confidential information such as sales figures.[11] Even months or years later, any member of the public can go to a courthouse and look up the case, getting free access to a transcript if there is one, including every word spoken in court and bench conversations with the judge or meetings of the parties in the judge's office. Every file will include briefs from each side, motions, decisions and evidence.

**Cartels**
Cartel enforcement is criminal in the United States but civil in the European Union (although criminal in some Member States). In the United States, cartels often reach settlements with the agencies instead of subjecting

themselves to criminal trials, because one or more of the conspirators has turned in the others in return for immunity from fines or jail time. There are exceptions, such as the high-profile 2001 trial in New York of Alfred Taubman for fixing commissions on art with rival auction-house Christie's. Prosecutors who bring a criminal case first take it to a grand jury, which calls witnesses and hears evidence. The procedure, so secret that lawyers for witnesses are barred from the room, has been called a 'vacuum cleaner for finding government evidence.' Grand juries nearly always indict, acting on papers prepared by prosecutors.

In the European Union a civil administrative review determines whether companies violated the law and those who have can be fined up to 10 per cent of their annual worldwide turnover. In cartel cases, as in in-depth merger cases, companies have the right to a closed hearing.

**Monopolization or abuse of dominance**
One high-profile example may illustrate differences between the two systems: the *Microsoft* case,[12] the best-known antitrust case of the past 20 years. In the United States Microsoft was brought to trial by the US Justice Department. During the trial in 1998 and 1999, all testimony was public, along with thousands of pages of evidence and testimony. Motions and filings were posted on the World Wide Web by the Court, and the daily transcripts were posted by private parties. In the European case the Commission's evidence was secret and much of what the public knew was from the parallel but different US case (see note 12). The Commission conducted a hearing, but it was closed to the public. Microsoft appealed the Commission's 2004 decision to the European Courts, where one of the parties has told me that 5000 pages of arguments have been filed so far. None is public. Hearings were public, but the transcripts were not.

**Courts**
Courts in the United States are open. Long before a case goes to trial, the parties file briefs and replies, and thus arguments in the case are available to the public. A case running in parallel in both the United States and Europe (as many mergers do) can lead to the bizarre situation of having the same information secret in Brussels but available in the United States. For example, both sides filed papers in the US District Court in San Francisco when the Justice Department filed suit there to halt Oracle's hostile takeover of PeopleSoft. Meanwhile the European Commission held a closed oral hearing on the case, where both sides relied on the same arguments they had made publicly in the United States. That led to the strange situation of reporters quizzing participants in the closed hearing during

breaks to find out which of the arguments had been invoked. US court filings – or, for wire services, mere reports of those filings – provided the detail needed to understand and explain in stories what was happening behind closed doors in Brussels.

One of those involved in the case contended that the parties obtained more information through discovery in the United States than the European Commission obtained through its version of the same process, which is to send letters requesting information under Article 11 of the European Union merger regulation. In addition, US lawyers often say that the process of cross-examination of witnesses and experts by those from the other side helps as an important means of testing evidence.

When Federal District Court Judge Vaughn Walker in San Francisco decided in 2004 to permit Oracle to buy PeopleSoft, his decision came out at the same time as his judgment. The decision in Europe was accompanied by a short news release, with public release of the reasoned decision to follow later.

### Description of Commission hearings
The hearing focuses on the Commission's case so that the parties may defend themselves by raising questions about it. At the beginning of the hearing, which usually runs for one or two days, the Commission reviews the case it laid out in the SO in a presentation which usually lasts 15 to 30 minutes. The parties present the case they made in their written reply, followed by third-party presentations. After each presentation there may be brief questioning, but formal questioning takes place after all of the presentations are made. At that point the parties face questioning by the Commission, followed by representatives of the 25 Member States and third parties. After that, the parties themselves have a round of questioning to the Commission and third parties.

'The basic idea is that everyone is allowed to ask questions to everybody,' said one person who has attended many of the hearings. But the questioning does not go as far as US cross-examination, those who have attended the hearings say.[13]

### Arguments for open hearings on abuse of dominance and cartel cases
Opening up hearings on cartels and abuse of dominance would put an end to keyhole journalism, which occurs when reporters get only a narrow view from leaks. Our time and effort goes into developing sources and obtaining leaks. Even with the best intent, a leaker cannot convey to the reporter everything that happened inside, only what the leaker sees as the highlights. At other times a leaker may be self-interested and put a spin on the ball. But even if what I have is fragmentary and biased, if I know

it to be true I will report it. Competition against my journalist colleagues compels me to.

By contrast, when reporters are inside a hearing things are different. Instead of expending our energy getting crumbs to report, we take in the whole day and spend our time thinking about what we believe to be the most important points. If all the reports are the same, the public knows that something significant happened, while if everyone leads on something different, the public understands that nothing particularly outstanding took place. My experience in reporting trials is that what goes on inside the courtroom dictates the lead, not what people tell us outside. We are less easily manipulated because we have seen what happened first hand.

A London antitrust lawyer (not one acknowledged at the beginning of this chapter) told me that it would be a good idea to open up such hearings, noting: 'Even in a jury trial in Britain the public can go in and see the trial and it does not compromise whether the defendant is guilty or not guilty.'

The London lawyer was dubious about opening up the Statement of Objections and replies, expressing the view that SOs were sometimes grossly inaccurate and companies might face unfair publicity if the SOs became public, but I would disagree, on the basis of my experience in reporting cases in the United States. I do write one-sided stories when one side files papers; indeed, I often find the papers persuasive. But I write about replies too, when those are filed, and those replies can be equally persuasive. Thus over a period of time I tell both sides of the story.

If SOs remain closed a company would have a good reason to avoid an open hearing, where information about the charges against it would become public. But if the SOs and replies were open the information would already be in the public domain. While in mergers parties exercise their opportunity for a hearing only about half the time, in cartel cases hearings are the norm, because those accused of being in a cartel are watching each other closely, I am told.

Under current law and practice, the first moment we hear the voice of the parties in an official setting is when a Commission decision is appealed to court and a hearing is conducted. In the European Commission *Microsoft* case, for example, there were three years of proceedings before members of the public, including journalists, were ever able to weigh the words of the two sides. When the Commission decision was released we saw only the portions of Microsoft's written argument that the Commission chose to put in the decision, and only in the context which the Commission chose. Statements of Objection are roughly parallel to a complaint or a brief in a case in the United States. US complaints making the government's side of the case are public and are usually written to avoid confidential business information, or else a redacted version is quickly made public. Statements of Objections would give commentators a chance to assess far more clearly the arguments on both sides. Openness would also end the problem that, once information is shared with third parties, a case can become a leaky black box.

### Reasons for closed hearings before the Commission in merger cases
Merger cases differ from abuse of dominance and cartel cases. The Commission has legitimate concerns about protecting companies attempting to carry out a merger, a transaction that may be procompetitive. In addition the Commission and parties are up against the tight four-month deadline for review.

Reporters would love to see merger hearings accessible to the public. But European Commission staff and private lawyers are doubtful about opening up hearings or Statements of Objections and replies in merger cases. One outside lawyer said the limited four-month in-depth review is far too intense and pressured to add the extra layer and expense of hiring a public affairs company to deal with the press at hearings. It would be a new layer of complexity he would have to manage. Fights over which matters qualified as confidential business secrets would complicate matters further. The outside lawyer believes that the European Commission would have to take great care to make sure the press debate did not take over the process, because, he believes, some reporters are in the pocket of one party or another.

Some private lawyers and Commission staff believe the presence of even one reporter at a merger hearing would chill the relatively frank discussions that now take place. Instead of low-key hearings aimed at bringing out plain facts in a serene setting, all sides would play to the jury of public opinion, attempting to influence the general public and decision makers. Large companies could exacerbate the problem by using a public relations army to reinforce arguments and trash the other side. Even fewer merging firms might elect to have hearings, further diminishing the internal check provided by the process.

One should be careful, too, not to exaggerate the lack of openness. Even with the Commission's doors closed and its matters secret, the press gets its hands on a surprisingly substantial amount of information, these private lawyers and Commission staff argue. (This, it seems to me, is not really true because reporters get only the narrow view of those who leak to us.)

Those who are admitted to the hearing come to participate, not just to listen. Participants include customers and competitors, although some people turn down invitations out of fear of putting their heads above the parapet. However those in an industry who do attend can serve as a brake on exaggerated claims.

There is also a question about whether anyone wants more openness, other than reporters such as myself. The Commission sought public suggestions at the time it rewrote the merger and cartel regulations, and no comments from the public requested an open process. Certainly the companies involved are in no rush to have more information in the public eye or in the hands of competitors who are not in the room.

As matters stand, people involved are happy with the system. The system guarantees procedural rights and respects the rights of the parties. Opening it up could threaten the existing balanced system. For example, parties might be reluctant to exercise their right to a hearing if they had to subject themselves to open scrutiny by the press. If there is a reason to change things, it is incumbent on those who want the change to show why.

## Evaluation of arguments

Before writing this piece, I believed that all hearings should be open, in part because discrepancies between the US and European systems lead to ludicrous situations such as the one I described above involving Oracle. But the arguments of staff and private lawyers cited above persuaded me that the merger process hearings should continue to be closed to the public. I was particularly convinced by the limited period of time involved and the idea that the merger hearings are not necessarily adversarial. Similar arguments probably apply to SOs and their replies.

However, notwithstanding these arguments, Statements of Objections and the replies of parties should be open in cases involving cartels and abuse of dominance. Such openness would give the public a chance to see the views of the Commission and the parties in their own words and help observers evaluate the Commission's decision. Beyond that, the ultimate goal should be to open the hearings themselves, even if it forces a change in their nature. Open hearings would help the public better understand a case, just as it helps the Commission. Let us now look at what happens to a case when it is appealed to the courts.

## The arguments for closed briefs before the courts

Courts in the United States are open. As I have said above, those who do not attend still have an opportunity later to read transcripts (even if they do not exist, someone who wants to look at them badly enough can often pay to have them transcribed from court reporters' notes), look at the evidence and the pleadings and understand exactly what happened.

Briefs before European Union courts are closed and there is no transcript available to the public, although the court prepares a transcript for internal use and some parties employ stenographers to sit quietly in the audience and take notes for their internal use.

Those who favour the existing system have explained to me that closed briefs are a traditional and established approach common to many national legal systems of the European Union, squarely within the continental legal tradition. Such a system has been used since the inception of the European Court of Justice without difficulty. The advocates of the current system make a number of additional points.

First, as with the Commission hearings, it is important that cases are adjudicated entirely independently, without external influence by the press, third parties or others. Keeping pleadings confidential minimizes the risk of having the case judged in the press. After all, the purpose of the pleadings is to help adjudicate the matter, not to provide fodder for public comment.

Second, closed briefs help parties feel freer to produce confidential information without fearing it will be enter the public domain. Lawyers can express themselves in absolute freedom. Moreover public briefs could engender significant delays and waste limited resources, because the courts would have to filter out confidential information instead of devoting all their time to the substance of the case.

Finally, even though the briefs themselves are not public, there is still much openness. On the day a hearing occurs before the Court of First Instance, the court provides a Report for the Hearing, which includes an accurate summary of all the arguments before the court. The hearings themselves are public and the judgments are public and fully reasoned. Sometimes the judgments are longer specifically to ensure that the views of all sides are aired. The public can also request documents, but must give detailed reasons for doing so.

These arguments by advocates of the existing closed system are subject to substantial challenge both from the success of open court in the United States and on their own terms.

### Arguments for opening court briefs

Courts in the United States have tremendous authority and legitimacy because of their transparency: everyone who cares to can see exactly what went into a decision, save for a very small amount of redacted materials. Academics, researchers of all kinds and the general public examine the full, rich record days, months or years later to assess the performance of a court, witnesses or lawyers.

The question is where to strike the balance between legitimate secrecy and the right of the public to oversee its institutions. Celia Hampton, former editor of *Competition Law Insight* in London, has been seeking more openness for years. In a context of EU institutions other than courts, which are exempt from most disclosure, Hampton makes the point that

European government exists only to carry out functions on behalf of the public, including collecting and creating information that it holds for the public.

> The EU Treaty only obliges [EU institutions] to refuse public access to [information] if it consists of personal data or professional secrets. If it is held by government because it has been created or collected in the course of government work, it is public information. If not, government has no business holding it . . . The public must be able to see what the government is doing so that its propriety and efficiency can be checked.[14]

It is not enough to hear the court explain itself in a decision, even if that decision is long enough to include the parties' arguments as well as the court's conclusion. Reporters and the public we serve learn more from reading the arguments made by the parties in their own words, rather than the characterization of their arguments either in the Report for the Hearing, drained of all passion and nuance, or in decisions by the Court. We benefit from comparing both sides' arguments and making independent judgments about the Court's conclusions and reasoning. How else can a member of the public judge the courts? And whose job is it, if not the public's, to judge the courts?

Under current rules, attending a hearing at the Court of First Instance or European Court of Justice is like walking into the middle of a conversation. Before going to a competition hearing I write lead-up articles based on talks with both sides, to the extent they are willing to talk. But I have no access to the Report for the Hearing until the day of the hearing itself, and therefore I am unable to use it to prepare set-up articles or to prepare myself for the hearing. During the hearing, participants constantly refer to the briefs, down to citations to particular paragraphs, but I do not have the briefs, so I have no way of knowing what they are referring to. Similarly the court sometimes poses questions in writing to the Commission lawyers. We hear the lawyers' responses, but have no way of knowing what they are responding to.

The Report for the Hearing is offered to the public only in the language of the case, even though the court also prepares the report in its working language of French. No single reporter can know anywhere near all 21 languages used in the court – the 20 official EU languages plus Irish. A reporter assigned to spend his time at the EU courts and write about the cases there, a familiar job among journalists in the United States called the 'courthouse beat', found the job difficult, telling me: 'You go into the hearing basically blind.'

The hearing itself always has simultaneous interpretation into French, and sometimes other languages, but without knowing anything about a case it is nearly impossible to follow. This places a very high barrier in the way of reporting the court's business.

In the United States, Britain, Germany, France, Sweden, Hungary, the Czech Republic, Greece and other countries the courts are in major media centres, but Luxembourg has only the courts and some non-political institutions (and occasional European Union meetings), making it difficult for news organizations to dispatch reporters to court. The nearest centre for international media is Brussels, more than two hours away by train or car. Whether through design or insensitivity, the cumulative effect has been to discourage news organizations from doing comprehensive coverage of the courts and to prevent the public from knowing what their courts are doing.

In competition cases, at least, I have some understanding of the cases when I walk in the door. My obligation is immediately – that is, within 30 or 40 minutes after the hearing – to write a story about what happened and what it meant. People will read my story to help them understand the hearing and form their opinions. Those who were not fortunate enough to attend the hearing lack access to a transcript and have no way of knowing even what I know about the hearing.

Conferences on competition are called in part to help move the law forward, but the kinds of restrictions imposed by the European Court of Justice have inhibited exchanges of views and analysis at antitrust conferences. For example, at a November 2004 Brussels antitrust conference, Thomas Vinje, a lawyer who represented rivals of Microsoft, asked a panellist about the application of a case involving IMS Health to a pending Microsoft decision before the European Union Court of First Instance. 'I don't have the benefit of having read the papers on both sides,' replied the panellist. Later, pressed again, he said: 'Without having studied Microsoft's own arguments, the Commission is making a pretty powerful argument.' There had been a hearing that laid out the views of both sides, but the panellist, a British lawyer, had not been there and there was no official transcript.

We are also asked to believe that opinion pieces that people might write about accessible briefs would unduly influence judges. But why then is there not a similar concern about articles about the hearings? Overly influential opinion pieces about court briefs do not appear to be a problem for the United States judicial system. Are we being asked to believe that judges in European courts are much more easily influenced by outside writings?

In fact, open and available pleadings can educate lawyers and others. One British lawyer told me he looks at a United States government website to read its World Trade Organization filings, while Europeans almost never open their filings to the public.

Finally, when the opinion itself comes out, ideas are sometimes deliberately fuzzed up in order to cover splits within the panels, numerous people have told me. The court speaks with a single voice; there are no minority opinions in judgments by the Court of First Instance or European Court of Justice. Judges are appointed for only six years. The lack of dissent is supposed to protect judges from retribution at home for taking unpopular stances and to increase the legitimacy of the court by papering over splits. But the effect can be to make the reasoning of judgments even more curious and impenetrable to people who have no access to most of the basis for the opinion.[15]

Others claim that redacting confidential material from open briefs would take too much of the court's time and effort, yet US judges and lawyers manage to redact briefs quickly, efficiently and without harming the US judicial process. Why should redaction be more difficult in Luxembourg?

The European Union courts need public acceptance for their support and growth, perhaps one day beyond Luxembourg to other states. The courts should make public all non-confidential filings, as well as court transcripts and the lower courts' Reports for the Hearing, in all languages in which they are available as soon as they are available.[16] The courts exist not merely for those who appear before them but also for the broader public, which foots the bill. Only with more information can the European public give courts increased support.

## Conclusion

Warren Grimes argues in the *Buffalo Law Review* that 'transparency is a fundamental principle governing the actions of the European Commission'. As he notes, the Commission must report in detail on the reasons for its decisions in mergers while the United States agencies rarely do so. But for a reporter, the delay in making these materials accessible makes the requirements relatively meaningless. We report news, not history. And what we report largely forms the basis for current, timely public understanding of public institutions.

Checks and balances are built into democracy, but informed citizens are the ultimate check on government. And citizens cannot be fully informed without access to original source material. While a baker in Siena may or may not take much interest in the merger of a German and a French chemical company, there are people who care. More information will improve these citizens' oversight of European Union institutions. With increased openness will thus come increased public approval, which will in turn add to the strength and legitimacy of the European Commission and European Courts.

## Notes

1. News agency reporter in Brussels, specializing in coverage of competition policy at the European Union; email: pkbo@lawsky.com. I am particularly grateful to the men and

women I spoke with at the European Courts, the European Commission, the Federal Trade Commission and the Department of Justice, all of whom were very helpful. I am not identifying them by name, but I can identify some of those outside the Commission who helped. These people read the chapter or made suggestions or provided information: Don Baker, Stephen Calkins, Joe Gilchrist, Mark Clough, Celia Hampton, Clifford Jones, Sarah Lawsky and John Schmidt. I have to give special thanks to Jonathan Baker for reading this chapter and commenting at several stages. However I am responsible for all facts and opinions in this chapter.

2.　These would be in the form seen by third parties, which exclude business secrets. I am a member of the Association de la Presse Internationale (API), a group of international reporters in Brussels covering the European Union, which is in court against the Commission in an attempt to open briefs. Our lawyer, Sven Voelcker, says that courts in the United States, Canada, Sweden and Denmark all have various forms of such open filings, and that there has been no harm from them. (Court of First Instance Case T-36/04, filed on 2 February 2004.) At this writing, in October 2006, we await a hearing date.

3.　Grimes, Warren S. (2003), 'Transparency in federal antitrust enforcement', *Buff. L. Rev.*, **51**, 937–1051.

4.　This guidance would be particularly helpful because of the adoption of Council Regulation 1/2003, which requires companies to determine on their own that they are in compliance with cartel law when they make deals with each other, a change from the past practice of seeking the security blanket of advance approval from the Commission.

5.　Some believe that openness has gone too far at the Federal Trade Commission, because, under the sunshine law (the Government in the Sunshine Act: 5 U.S.C. §552b; the Commission's rule implementing the Act: Commission Rule 4.15, 1b C.F.R. §4.15), any time a majority of the five Commissioners gets together (except for certain decision-making meetings) they must hold an open meeting, notified in advance to the public.

6.　In fact, in the view of the United States Supreme Court, the Commission acts as a 'tribunal' in a judicial or quasi-judicial capacity when it makes decisions: 'We have no warrant to exclude the European Commission, to the extent that it acts as a first-instance decision maker' from being considered a tribunal, the Court said: *Intel Corporation* v. *Advanced Micro Devices*, 542 U.S. 241, 124 S. Ct. 2466, 2479 (2004).

7.　A two-week extension can take place. The clock can also be stopped while the parties supply additional information, which rarely happens. The Commission set a record for the length of a stoppage during Oracle's hostile takeover of rival software company PeopleSoft. In that instance a suspension (a second suspension, itself a rarity) lasted from April until October 2004, ending shortly after a US judge had ruled in favour of the all-American deal. The Commission decision, coming soon thereafter, followed suit.

8.　The hearing officer's mandate, available at the following website: http://eur-lex.europa.eu/ LexUriServ/site/en/oi/2001/I_162/I_16220010619en00210024.pdf, makes clear that the hearing officer has the power to ensure that procedural rules are followed, but also to go beyond that and deal with questions of substance. See Article 3, s. 3 ('The hearing officer may present observations on any matter arising out of any Commission competition proceedings to the competent member of the Commission') and Article 13, s. 2 ('In addition to the report referred to in paragraph 1 [on procedural issues] the hearing officer may make observations on the further progress of the proceedings. Such observations may relate among other things to the need for further information, the withdrawal of certain objections, or the formulation of further objections.').

9.　There is an exception to the Justice Department's silence during its review of merger cases. By law, the Department of Justice Antitrust Division publicly advises the Comptroller of the Currency on competitive effects of bank mergers during the administrative review by the comptroller. Once the comptroller acts on a bank merger, Justice has 30 days to accept that decision or challenge it in court. If not challenged within 30 days the merger becomes immune to challenge under the antitrust laws.

10.　It has taken only 225 of those cases to in-depth review, of which 78 were approved with remedies and 28 were approved unconditionally. See http://europa.eu.int/comm/ competition/mergers/cases/stats.html.

11.  Transcripts are made of major trials (sometimes daily transcripts, as in the Microsoft trial) and of trials which are appealed. Transcripts are kept on file at courthouses so that anyone may view them. When there is no transcript anyone may order one, paying by the page.
12.  *United States* v. *Microsoft Corp.*, 147 F.3d 935 (D.C. Cir 1998); *United States* v. *Microsoft Corp.*, 87 F.Supp.2d 30 (D.D.C.2000), 253 F.3d 34 (C.A. D.C. 2001) (No. 03-5030).
13.  One concern of those opposed to open hearings is that, if the public were to see the lop-sided focus on the Commission's case, it would view the Commission as the centre of criticism and form a negative view of DG Comp's arguments, with an adverse effect on the final Commission decision. However a similar negative focus on the Commission's case can also take place at public hearings before the European Union Court of First Instance when a Commission decision is challenged. No one has suggested that is a reason for closing such hearings.
14.  See ftp://ftp.cordis.lu/pub/econtent/docs/gp_comments/efj.pdf, points 1 and 2. Celia Hampton is editor of www.publicinfo.net.
15.  Majority and minority opinions not only help the public better understand the court. In other jurisdictions minority opinions have pointed the way to future decisions and given courts reasoning to use when, as occasionally happens, they alter their views.
16.  There is considerable latitude in what one means by 'public'. These days, I think it would be insufficient to put documents on public file in Luxembourg. All documents should be available in machine readable form, so that anyone can email them or post them to the web. Or the EU courts could follow the practice in some other jurisdictions, which require all filings to be made in machine readable form, such as PDF, and then post them to their own court website. Confidential materials are of course excluded.

## References

*Articles*
Grimes, Warren S. (2003), 'Transparency in federal antitrust enforcement', *Buff. L. Rev.*, **51**, 937–1051.

*Cases*
*Intel Corporation* v. *Advanced Micro Devices*, 542 U.S. 241, 124 S. Ct. 2466, 2479 (2004).
*United States* v. *Microsoft Corp.*, 147 F.3d 935 (D.C. Cir 1998).
*United States* v. *Microsoft Corp.*, 87 F.Supp.2d 30 (D.D.C.2000), 253 F.3d 34 (C.A. D.C. 2001) (No. 03-5030).

*Websites*
ftp://ftp.cordis.lu/pub/econtent/docs/gp_comments/efj.pdf.
http://europa.eu.int/comm/competition/mergers/cases/stats.html.
http://europa.eu.int/eurlex/lex/LexUriServ/LexUriServ.do?uri=CELEX:32001D0462:EN:
    HTML
www.publicinfo.net.

# 21 The goals of antitrust: thoughts on consumer welfare in the US

*Albert A. Foer*[1]

In that each nation with a formal competition policy sooner or later must attempt to define the objectives of its policy, it is useful to make several observations about the course of US antitrust that will establish the framework for this chapter.

First, there is currently no clear consensus as to whether all or some of the various goals that have been advanced for antitrust in the US are mutually compatible, whether one goal should prevail, or, if one should prevail, how it should be defined in the particulars.

Second, over time, three distinctly different types of goals for antitrust have been advanced, which I will categorize as (1) making economics work for the electorate (political goals); (2) making the most of what we have (productive efficiency) and distributing it optimally (allocative efficiency) (together, static efficiency goals); and (3) making the pie grow larger (dynamic efficiency goals).

Third, establishing a goal or the priority of multiple goals is not a once-for-all-time decision, but rather reflects a temporary consensus that is likely to morph over time to accord with changing political and economic realities, advancing knowledge and general fashions in political and economic thought. It is, in short, a product not merely of economic theorizing, but of political economy.

In the opening section of the chapter, I will comment on how the US came to the seeming anointment of one particular goal, allocative efficiency (sometimes called 'consumer welfare'), as *the* dominant or even exclusive goal of antitrust; and then I will show that the declaration of victory by the Chicago School is premature. Next I will describe the three principal categories of goals that have been advanced for antitrust, will criticize each in turn and will conclude that, despite the fact that a still-vague concept of consumer welfare dominates antitrust thinking in the US today, there is actually no consensus on the meaning of consumer welfare and no adherence to a single goal. Finally, I will address some questions presented by the absence of a single goal.

### The movement toward a single goal of antitrust
*From populism to consumer welfare*

The Chicago School, which has dominated antitrust enforcement since the election of Ronald Reagan in 1980, contends that there is now a single goal of antitrust: namely, 'consumer welfare'. The march toward the story that there is a single goal is fairly familiar,[2] but it is worth pointing to some of the key features.

From its earliest days, antitrust interpretation naturally enough concerned itself with ascertaining and executing the intent of the antitrust laws. Although Marshall's *Principles of Economics* was published in the same year that the Sherman Act passed, it is fair to say that Congress was neither steeped in economic philosophy nor greatly assisted by economists. Political sensitivities dominated the debates in 1890,[3] and again in 1912–14, as the Clayton and FTC Acts were being debated. There was great worry about the powerful new institution of trusts, about preserving the role of small producers, and about precluding transfers of wealth from consumers to monopolists.

A neopopulist attitude, defining competition largely in terms of atomized markets, dominated antitrust from the years after the end of World War II into the 1970s. What political scientist Marc Allen Eisner calls in his book of that title, 'the triumph of economics', was to a large degree a matter of occupational sociology. Antitrust enforcement had been dominated from the beginning by attorneys. Economists often played a role both in the formulation of policy and in litigation support, but they were clearly subservient to the attorneys. (People with business backgrounds or MBAs rarely played a role and still play only a very small role.) During the 1970s, the role of economists in the federal antitrust agencies underwent a dramatic growth in importance. All by itself, this portended a shift in emphasis away from matters of legislative intent and due process toward economic theories of industrial organization.

Changes were also occurring within industrial organization economics. What had been considered something of a backwater in the economics profession became a hotbed of creative thought and ideological debate as neoclassical economists imbued with price theory turned their attention to an antitrust field that had been accustomed to thinking about a structure–behaviour–performance paradigm. It is important to note that the battle within the antitrust agencies and the academic antitrust community was not merely between lawyers and economists; it was also between economists of different schools and lawyers with different political philosophies. The 'new thinking' rejected competition as something that required a particular form of industrial organization such as atomized markets in favour of a focus on the expected fruits of an efficient economy.[4]

Even before Ronald Reagan was elected President in 1980, a bipartisan movement away from neopopulism could be seen in several key appellate and Supreme Court decisions and in the beginnings of the deregulation movement. When Reagan assumed office, however, the price theorists came into executive power. The appointment as Chairman of the Federal Trade Commission of James Miller, a conservative academic economist, symbolized the ascendancy of Chicago. Reagan's first Assistant Attorney General for Antitrust, William Baxter, a law professor soaked in neoclassical economics, announced, 'The only goal of antitrust is economic efficiency.'[5]

More generally, the law-and-economics vision of leading University of Chicago professors applied neoclassical analyses to a wide swath of the law, embedding the antitrust revolution within a larger movement that had global ramifications. Deregulation, the expansion of international trade, the international application of what Joseph Stiglitz called 'the Washington consensus',[6] and the explosive growth of free markets and competition policy laws were parallel and interrelated developments.

Two names associated with the University of Chicago, Robert Bork and Richard Posner, stand out in these developments. Bork published *The Antitrust Paradox* in 1978 and it became the handbook of neoclassical antitrust. Bork compared a producer welfare goal (i.e., the producer's natural goal is to be able to charge a monopoly price) with a consumer welfare goal (the consumer would want a competitive price). He offered five reasons why the consumer welfare goal is superior.[7] 'A multiple-goal approach', he proclaimed, 'can achieve none of these things.'[8]

By these words, Bork undoubtedly dismisses the possibility that antitrust is intended to protect businesses against competition, but what does he mean by consumer welfare? His answer constitutes one of the great acts of academic legerdemain:

> Consumer welfare is greatest when society's economic resources are allocated so that consumers are able to satisfy their wants as fully as technological constraints permit. Consumer welfare, in this sense, is merely another term for the wealth of the nation.[9]

In other words, consumer welfare, to Bork, is what others call 'total welfare', not the welfare of real live consumers of the type who walk into the drugstore and make purchases.[10] By capturing the symbol of consumerism in this way, Bork pulled off a major public relations coup for laissez-faire, but he also created confusion for public discussion that still continues. We will avoid this confusion by identifying consumer welfare with policies that are of direct or indirect benefit to citizens who make purchases of the product or service in question and by identifying total welfare with policies that are intended to benefit the entire society by creating greater overall wealth.

To show that consumer welfare and total welfare are not necessarily the same, consider a merger which produces a net increase in efficiency but also leads to a significantly higher price for consumers for a significant period of time.[11] A total welfare approach would approve the merger; a consumer welfare approach might not.

In conflating consumers with the national society, Bork not only positioned neoclassical economics as proconsumer; he also avoided a more natural way of contemplating society in a democracy, namely that it is made up of citizens whose majority votes ultimately determine what is in the interest of the whole society. Instead the consumer is viewed as sovereign and his or her vote occurs in the commercial context. Politics, which is the traditional nest for the authoritative promulgation of laws, becomes separated from and in a certain respect subservient to economics.

Richard Posner was a principal developer and popularizer of the law-and-economics movement which advocates neoclassical economics as the standard for evaluating, interpreting, and ultimately passing laws. His book, *Antitrust Law: An Economic Perspective*, was first published in 1976. A second edition (now simply titled *Antitrust Law*) was published in 2001. In the more recent edition, he provides this unilateral declaration of victory for 'economic welfare' which appears to be the same as total welfare:

> Almost everyone professionally involved in antitrust today – whether as litigator, prosecutor, judge, academic, or informed observer – not only agrees that the only goal of the antitrust laws should be to promote economic welfare, but also agrees on the essential tenets of economic theory that should be used to determine the consistency of specific business practices with that goal. Agrees, that is, that economic welfare should be understood in terms of the economist's concept of efficiency; that business firms should be assumed to be rational profit maximizers, so that the issue in evaluating the antitrust significance of a particular business practice should be whether it is a means by which a rational profit maximizer can increase its profits at the expense of efficiency; and that the design of antitrust rules should take into account the costs and benefits of individualized assessment of challenged practices relative to the costs and benefits of rule-of-thumb prohibitions, notably the per se rules of antitrust illegality.[12]

*The declaration of victory is premature*

Posner's declaration of victory for Chicago is premature. While the contributions of Chicago have been persuasive in many ways, there remain other important threads in the antitrust story and proponents of alternative goals have neither surrendered nor are likely to do so. Posner himself continues to grow as an academic and as a judge, for example, by stretching out neoclassical analysis to incorporate strategic behaviour, even though he is reluctant to credit post-Chicago game theorists with much of a contribution.[13] In addition to game theory, with its emphasis on the strategic behavior of firms, what are the other threads that challenge the Chicago School?

On the far right, some in the libertarian movement reject antitrust more or less entirely, considering antitrust intervention to be a form of theft. The introduction to a recent collection of essays titled 'The Abolition of Antitrust' begins:

> Most Americans believe that the antitrust laws preserve our free market system, protect consumers from rapacious corporations, and ensure fair competition in the marketplace. However, the reverse is true. Antitrust is based on bad economics and on a false interpretation of the history of American business. It violates the sanctity of contract and abrogates a businessman's moral right to produce, trade, and profit.[14]

What drives this particular critique is an extreme individualistic perspective that finds immoral the standard used by modern antitrust. That standard was set out by University of Chicago economist Frank Knight who, in 1921, described the neoclassical assumption of perfect competition as follows: 'Under perfect competition he [the entrepreneur] would of course be completely helpless, a mere automatic registrar of the choices of consumers.'[15] To Knight and later economists, this was a model of how capitalism works. The libertarian problem with this, according to John Ridpath, is that 'Businessmen are being persecuted for not being sufficiently identityless, passive, altruistic servants of consumers . . . [This provides] the foundations for modern antitrust's assault on the most productive system man has ever known – capitalism – and on the most productive individuals in human history – the industrialists'.[16] In the battle between consumers and producers, this viewpoint sides completely with the strongest producers, recognizing no legitimate role for antitrust as a restraining factor.

A slightly less absolutist strand of libertarianism focuses not on the immorality of interfering with entrepreneurs (the 'objectivist' position quoted above) but on the inability of government to provide rules that give definitive guidance or to administer in the public interest. The influential Cato Institute, for example, says, 'Antitrust laws that allow the federal government to second-guess markets and hold up or prohibit sound business practices have no valid place in a market economy.'[17] Some who describe themselves as libertarians would continue the policy of outlawing cartels, where it is clearly understood what actions are illegal.

Congenial with a minimal intervention attitude, the public choice school carries the rational profit maximizer theorem into the realm of public institutions and concludes (with great logic but faulty premises) that since civil servants (like the economists' economic man generally) act in their own self-interest, there can be no such thing as the public interest. Therefore antitrust, controlled by the self-interest of the law enforcers, cannot serve a *public* interest.[18] This chain of thought, which is associated with the political right, is related to the 'capture theory' that government regulators are typically captured by the industry they regulate, a perspective that has proponents at both ends of the political spectrum, but has been to a large degree discredited because of its weakness as a predictor of when capture might occur.[19]

The Chicago School, which is often tinged with libertarian and public choice ideology, might be thought to find a comfortable home in the nation's business schools. After all, Chicago advocates a minimal degree of intrusion into the affairs of business based on a profound respect for the rationality of business decisions. A review of what the business schools actually teach, however, found something different in two of the three separate business school faculty groups that are concerned with the nature of competition. In the economics courses taught by economists, the instruction generally mirrored that which is taught in graduate economics departments.[20] No surprise there. However the marketing faculties and the strategic management faculties tended to work from assumptions that are significantly different from those taught by the Chicago School.[21]

Although most strategic management texts pay scant attention to antitrust,[22] many discuss the relationship of strategic management to profit maximization. The Chicago School assumption from price theory is that businesses rationally seek to maximize profits. Bork considered the profit maximization assumption 'crucial'.[23] But when Professor Norman Hawker reviewed the academic literature, this antitrust expert who teaches strategic management in a business school found only one text that specifically suggests that businesses actually seek to maximize profits, and this text acknowledged that this point of view is the subject of some dispute.[24] None of the texts denigrates the importance of profitability, but profitability is not the same as profit maximization, and the texts tend to say that there are multiple motivators at work, that it is in practice impossible to determine when firms are maximizing profit, that corporations exist to satisfy an array of stakeholders (and not merely stockholders), and that the point of strategic management is more generally presented as sustainable competitive advantage, rather than profit maximization.[25] While one might argue that nothing here is inconsistent with maximizing the discounted present value of profits in an environment of uncertainty by an institution that must overcome a range of principal–agent problems, it suggests that the Chicago School assumption needs considerable relaxation and that management has a range of discretion that is not strictly limited by the rule of profit maximization.

Similarly, whereas the Chicago School assumes that firms go about max-imizing profit in a rational way, a division exists between those that share the assumption of rational behaviour and those behaviouralist-influenced texts which assume that the behaviour of firms depends at least in part on emotional and psychological factors.[26] Behavioural economics is still in an early stage and has infrequently been applied to antitrust analysis. There is a good chance, however, that this field will grow rapidly and will contribute further to the critique of fundamental Chicago School assumptions.

When Hawker surveyed business school curricula, he found that the structure–conduct–performance concepts that long dominated antitrust analysis were still alive and well in most strategic management text books. He found 'surprising' the extent to which 'virtually all the textbooks rely on the Michael Porter model for competitive analysis'.[27] Porter, originally trained as an industrial organization economist but influenced by his exten-sive studies of corporate strategy and consulting experience, does not focus on price theory and plays down standard antitrust categories such as market definition and concentration. Instead he argues that the state of competition in an industry depends on five basic forces: the threat of new entrants into the market; bargaining power of suppliers; bargaining power of buyers; the threat of substitute products; and rivalry among existing firms.[28] The objective of strategic management becomes an effort to defend against the five forces or influence them in the firm's favour.[29]

Academic consideration of strategic behaviour has given rise to many critiques of the Chicago School. For example, the team of Patrick Bolton (a professor of finance and economics), Joseph Brodley (a professor of antitrust law), and Michael Riordan (a professor of finance and econom-ics) wrote this in their magisterial treatment of predatory pricing in 2000:

> A powerful tension has arisen between the foundations of current legal policy and modern economic theory. The courts adhere to a static, non-strategic view of predatory pricing, believing this view to be an economic consensus. This con-sensus, however, is one most economists no longer accept.[30]

The influence of Michael Porter in the business schools has been men-tioned. Porter's contribution to the debate over the goals of antitrust takes him back to a fundamental question: what is it we want from the economy? His answer is growth.[31] It is only when the economy grows that everyone can be better off. And productivity growth, he argues, 'is the missing, unstated link between competition and national standard of living. This provides the soundest explanation for why antitrust must protect competi-tion: it is the key to a nation's economic prosperity'.[32] Porter rejects the Chicago School's commitment to efficiency in favour of growth and inno-vation.[33] He advocates a hierarchy of goals with growth and inflation followed by productive (static) efficiency followed by keeping price close to costs (allocative efficiency).

Porter is heavily influenced by his own research on how competition works in many different countries.[34] International specialists such as Robert Gilpin[35] who have observed the 'Washington consensus' applied in other nations have brought a focus on the institutions that differ from nation to nation and have concluded that political economy, not neoclassical economics, is the field that best explains what is observed.[36] Some economists such as Britain's John Kay have applied this institutional insight and concluded that the neoclassical antitrust goals should be amended by inclusion of 'disciplined pluralism', which he defines as 'the process of perpetual experiment in market economies, in which most experiments fail and are terminated, but the few that succeed are quickly imitated'.[37] Like Porter, Kay gives priority to the goal of dynamic efficiency.[38]

Posner is correct to the extent that most people professionally involved with antitrust in the US today believe that antitrust ought to be disciplined by economic thinking and that it ought generally to be utilized on behalf of the largest element within the population, namely consumers. Beyond this, however, it is impossible to conclude that everyone in the antitrust community agrees on a single goal with a single meaning. The neoclassical model of economics, with its emphasis on static efficiency, is in fact under rather severe challenge from a variety of directions, including teachers of strategic management, advocates of dynamic economics focused on growth and innovation, behavioural economists, and political economists, not to mention anti-government libertarians. Posner's declaration of victory, therefore, is either premature or his definition of efficiency must be sufficiently elastic to encompass a great deal more than was originally intended by the Chicago School.

Finally, within the US, the American Antitrust Institute[39] has emerged since 1998 as a recognized organization of post-Chicago antitrust experts who are fundamentally market-oriented but nevertheless sceptical about concentrated economic power, believe that markets fail more than rarely, and that government is capable of intervening positively on behalf of, yes, the public interest, which it generally identifies with the interest of consumers. Many within the AAI believe that choice and innovation can be at least as important as price, and that distributional fairness is an appropriate goal of antitrust.

### What should be the goal of antitrust?
*A variety of goals have been advanced*
In this section, the first part sets out three categories of antitrust goals that have been advanced. The second part criticizes each of these as singular goals.

*(a)  Making economics work for the electorate*    At various times, it has
been suggested that antitrust is a fundamentally political policy and that
this should be explicitly recognized by shaping antitrust policies for politically determined ends.[40] What are these ends? Typically, they may be categorized as decentralization of economic power, freedom, fair distribution
of wealth, maintenance of a level playing field and other 'public interest'
goals.

The goal of decentralization of economic power rests on the perception
that concentrated economic power is generally accompanied by centralized
political power, which is seen as dangerous to a democratic polity. Thus
antitrust is viewed as a semi-constitutional tool for maintaining a certain
vision of democracy, akin to the fundamental political concepts of separation of powers, checks-and-balances, and federalism. Just as Americans
have traditionally feared and resisted too much political power (whether in
one person, one party, one economic class or one part of the government),
they fear that private entities with 'too much' economic power will be able
to buy their way into too much political power. Antitrust is viewed by many
as one of the few policies available for imposing a degree of popular control
over centralized economic power.

This political perception of antitrust tends to support strong policies
against unregulated monopolies or tight oligopolies. Sometimes it goes
further and advocates protection of small and medium-size businesses
without regard to their efficiency, on Jeffersonian grounds based on the
assumed moral superiority of rural life and small-scale institutions.
Stephen F. Ross has argued that an appropriate goal, which he calls
'Jacksonian', is equal economic opportunity.[41] The spirit of this latter
concept may be found in the popular phrase, 'level playing field'.[42]

Another type of political perception is that antitrust is part of the universal search for freedom,[43] so that consumers are free to make choices[44]
and producers are free to enter a market and compete without undue
restraints. Although these political goals are rarely discussed by US
enforcers or courts today, the older court opinions mentioning them, like
*Brown Shoe*,[45] have never been explicitly overruled.

Some see antitrust as a mechanism for avoiding unfair transfers of
wealth. This takes several forms. In terms of political analysis, the question
is whether antitrust should serve the interests of a particular class, which
could be consumers generally, producers generally, or some subclass of
either group such as lower-income consumers or small businesses. In terms
of political philosophy, the question might be put as to who has the primary
right to the fruits of capitalism: much of the legislative history of the
Sherman Act, for instance, suggests that Congress intended to award the
property right we call 'consumer surplus' to consumers, and that any

actions (such as a cartel's raising of prices above the competitive level) that take this property away from consumers without adequate compensation is immoral and illegal.[46] In terms of classroom economics, the argument comes down to whether antitrust should be concerned only with the dead weight loss caused by monopoly or also with the reallocation of income from consumers to monopolists (and their shareholders), made possible when monopoly rents are created.[47]

Public interest goals typically refer to policy issues raised in antitrust cases, where values other than competition may be at stake. An example would be the *National Society of Professional Engineers* case,[48] where the Society's professional ethics were called into question by the Department of Justice and a defence was offered that, in effect, if engineers do not observe 'ethical' constraints on price competition, bridges and other structures will fall down, because price competition leads to reduced professional time applied to the engineering problem. The holding, still the law, was that such public interest values as these are irrelevant in an antitrust analysis, which can only be concerned with the competitive effects. Public interest goals also often appear in the context of regulatory proceedings, where the statute requires consideration of the public interest which may be interpreted to include but not be coextensive with competition.

*(b) Making the most of what we have*  The goal of antitrust according to the Chicago School is efficiency. The idea is that society's resources are limited and therefore it is in society's interest if these limited resources are utilized in the most efficient manner. The two components of efficiency are allocational efficiency and productive efficiency.[49] By minimizing waste and maximizing productivity, there will be more for everyone. Competition is seen as the mechanism whereby the most efficient use of existing resources will be made on the basis of voluntary exchange, necessitating relatively little government involvement.

The concept of total surplus emerges as one measure of social welfare. By 'total surplus', economists mean the aggregate of consumer surplus and producer surplus created by a transaction. In the case of consumers, the surplus is the amount they would have been willing to pay for something, less what they actually had to pay in the marketplace. In general, the more competitive the market, the closer the price of a good to the producer's cost, the more consumers who desire the good will purchase it, and the greater the consumer surplus. In the case of producers, the surplus is the value of what they produced less the cost of producing it. Producer surplus is, roughly speaking, profits. From surplus must be subtracted the 'deadweight loss' caused by any prices that exceed the competitive level, since these higher prices would preclude some consumers who would have made a purchase at the competitive price. This potential output is absolutely lost to society.

A transaction that increases the total surplus is said by neoclassical economists to be efficient and therefore desirable.

It is important to distinguish between what maximizes wealth for the society and what maximizes wealth for particular members of the society. A transaction such as a merger that increases the total surplus, but does not significantly increase consumer surplus, would be considered allocatively efficient, but might not satisfy most consumers, if they find that they have to pay more as a result of the transaction.[50]

It is possible to have a compromise between total surplus and consumer surplus approaches by saying that a transaction will meet the efficiency goal of antitrust if it both creates a total surplus and achieves some economic benefits for actual consumers (i.e. people who purchase the product as opposed to 'the nation as a whole'). The fact that this somewhat sloppy and poorly defined compromise describes the way antitrust generally operates in the US today[51] merits two additional comments.

First, in the majority of instances, it is probably true that the consumer surplus standard usually correlates with the total surplus standard. That is, competition makes consumers better off and at the same time makes the society as a whole better off. While there may be occasions where this is not true, they do not seem to arise particularly often.

Second, the fact that the two standards so often work in the same direction may have interesting political consequences. Clearly there are ideological reasons available for supporting one standard or the other; that they so infrequently actually collide may reduce the play of this potentially divisive ideological factor, thereby facilitating political support for the antitrust enterprise. We will return to this toward the end of the chapter.

*(c) Making the pie larger*    The goal of efficiency, that is, of making the most of our existing limited resources, is considered a static goal, because it takes as given the resources that are already available. A different goal is dynamic efficiency,[52] which seeks to use competition as a tool for generating innovations that will expand the economic pie. It is usually understood that dynamic efficiency can have a far more dramatic effect on the economy than static efficiency, and this can be visualized by comparing the overall impact of improving the manufacturing process of a buggy whip to inventing the reciprocating engine.

Michael Porter has argued that growth of the economy should be the primary goal of antitrust.[53] 'Since the role of competition,' he says, 'is to increase a nation's standard of living and long term consumer welfare via rising productivity growth, *the new standard for antitrust should be productivity growth*, rather than price/cost margins or profitability.'[54] Porter continues: 'All combinations or practices scrutinized in antitrust should be subjected to the following question: how will they affect productivity growth?'[55]

Porter does not deny a place for additional goals, but rather posits a hierarchy in which productivity growth comes first, with technical (static) efficiency the second most important goal, interpreted in a more subtle way to incorporate improvements in product quality, features and services, as well as product or service value measured by price. For Porter, the third goal in importance would be limiting short-term price/cost margins or profitability. But he considers this (today's predominant goal in the US) a dubious goal for antitrust because it fails to measure true consumer welfare by ignoring product value and because we care much more about the long-term trajectory of value, prices and costs than we do about consumer welfare in the short run.[56]

Note that Porter has turned the current priorities of antitrust on their head: the traditional view (to the extent that a traditional view exists) ranks goals in the order of profitability/price–cost margins (i.e., allocative efficiency), followed by cost (static efficiency), followed by innovation (dynamic efficiency). Porter's alternative approach ranks innovation (dynamic efficiency) highest, followed by value improvement (static productivity), followed by profitability/price–cost margins (allocative efficiency).

If Porter's hierarchy were to replace current priorities, large elements of accepted antitrust analysis would have to be supplemented or replaced. Porter himself advocates not worrying about market definition, but rather utilizing what he calls the 'five forces framework' and the 'diamond framework'.[57] Applying his priorities to merger analysis, he doubts that mergers will be efficient and profitable just because companies propose it, and advocates a much more restrictive enforcement policy for mergers of leading firms.[58]

To recapitulate, there are three types of antitrust goals that have often been advocated. None of these stands unchallenged in today's thinking. In the next section, we present the major criticisms of each goal.

### *Each of these goals has rightly been criticized*
*(a) Political goals* Explicitly attributing political goals to everyday antitrust decisions may have a number of drawbacks. Political goals tend to be subjective rather than objective. As such, they may invite law enforcers and judges to reach personal decisions of great economic importance. In addition to making prediction difficult, this opens the door to abuse, ranging from partisan decisions to outright bribery. It may enhance the ability of some industries with political power to 'capture' antitrust

enforcement. Maintaining a professional objectivity within the antitrust enforcement agencies needs to be a high priority, because the financial stakes in policy decisions are sufficiently high to make corruption a distinct possibility. (One of the great and unremarked achievements of American antitrust is that it has been tainted by so little evidence of corruption over its long history.[59])

Political goals do not offer clear direction. From where would the direction arise? The public is not at all well educated on antitrust issues and is almost never offered options on antitrust during elections.[60] At best, presidential elections provide some direction along the lines of 'more regulation or less governmental regulation' of the economy. At this level of generality, there is no popular guidance to a decision-maker.

Moreover what is popular enough at one time to be considered a majority view may be a minority view after the next election. There is a danger in having economic policies, including antitrust, swing wildly from administration to administration, with reversals taking a toll in the inability of businesses to plan for the future. While change of direction as a result of election politics is legitimate, it is arguably better for the antitrust system if change takes place more incrementally.

Let us take a specific example of the difficulty in operationalizing a political goal. A case can be made that freedom is the basis of overall antitrust policy, as Commissioner Thomas Leary of the FTC has argued.[61] Freedom might imply, among other things, that consumers should have a range of choices when they go into the market place. But how many choices? If a merger in a five-company industry is about to leave four companies standing, how do we know if this will allow consumers an appropriate range of choices? And what does freedom mean if we are offered the choice of a small company having the freedom to compete on the merits or a large company having the freedom to drive the smaller one out of business by extreme aggressive tactics? If two successive administrations could each formally adopt an abstraction such as freedom as the goal of antitrust, but reach very different decisions when faced with real cases, then freedom may be a background value, but is too abstract to serve as a directive-giving goal. (I would not expect Commissioner Leary to disagree.)

There is today (and indeed, there probably always has been) general agreement that antitrust policy should, to at least some important degree, be about the efficient operation of markets. Political goals may import considerations such as environmental policy or health policy that have little to do with the functioning of markets. If we import these kinds of goals that do not relate to competition into antitrust, such a mismatch would make antitrust decisions much more difficult to predict. All things being equal, predictability is a desirable feature because of its impact on investment decisions. Arguably if non-economic goals play a significant role in antitrust decisions, the economy will become less and less efficient, which in the end will be harmful to consumers. Such an outcome might benefit certain limited interests, but it would not benefit the overall interest of the community.

It is also argued that many of the political goals of antitrust can in theory be accomplished by other policies. For example, wealth distribution can be accomplished by tax policy; environmental protection by environment laws; encouragement of small businesses by special subsidies; honest governance by the securities laws, and so on. The argument is that day-to-day antitrust should be founded on objective, staple criteria and that political goals should be left to other venues. Part of the influence of this argument rests on an assessment of the likelihood that alternative solutions will be produced by the political system in a timely and case-appropriate way; and part rests on the assumption that the economic efficiency alternative is scientific and objective. Commenting on the former condition is beyond the scope of this chapter.

*(b)  Static efficiency goals*   The leading candidate for an objective, logical – indeed, scientific – alternative to political goals is neoclassical economic analysis. Yet adoption of neoclassical economics as the sole determinant of antitrust policy is itself a political decision, if only because it displaces decisions made over a long period of time by the Congress and the courts.

A quick overview of neoclassical economics is in order. The underlying value is voluntary exchange in a market place where the interplay of supply and demand sets the price of a transaction. A system is considered optimal when no further exchanges can be made that will make a person better off without harming another. In the strong form of Pareto optimality, a commercial transaction should be allowed if someone benefits and no one is harmed. This makes intuitive sense. It helps us define efficiency as that state of affairs where no further exchanges will make the society better off.

Lurking in this concept, however, are the questions that Harold Lasswell long ago used to define the nature of politics: who gets what, when, how?[62] Somewhere along the line, neoclassical economists recognized that it is too difficult to find real-life Pareto optimal situations, because in real life people are always getting harmed without compensation as a result of apparently voluntary exchanges. Consequently a weaker, more easily identifiable version of Pareto optimality (potential Pareto) became accepted by many economists, including the Chicago contingent. In this weaker version, it is not necessary that no one actually be harmed; it is only necessary that *in theory* no one would be harmed.[63]

For example, suppose a merger in which the merging parties will become more efficient such that they would have the ability to reduce both their costs and their prices. If the reduced prices were to be passed on to consumers, no one would be injured, thus it is theoretically possible to achieve strong Pareto optimality. But what if the merged company, now facing reduced competition, actually raises its prices and passes on the increased profits to its shareholders in the form of dividends rather than to consumers in the form of lower prices? Consumers could have been made better off (so the weakened version of optimality would be satisfied) but they were not in fact made better off. Indeed, if prices are increased, they are made worse off. On the other hand, if the increased profits are passed on to shareholders and shareholders spend more money in the economy and invest in enterprises that create new jobs, there will presumably be an eventual trickle-down benefit to the general population, including the class of consumers. (We will not discuss what discount rate should be applied when the quantity and timing of 'trickle down' is so thoroughly unpredictable.)

The switch to a weaker version of optimality means that the consumers who are injured by the merger may not be the same ones who will presumably benefit at a later date from the trickle-down benefits to the whole society. The point is that the objective aspect of Pareto optimality, upon which the neoclassical efficiency goal rests, has been undermined by a problem of fairness, which means that political considerations have been admitted into the game in a fundamental way. Let us be blunt: the innocuous little shift by certain economists from strong Pareto to potential Pareto optimality amounts to a political decision that current stockholders should be allowed to benefit from a merger at the expense of the class of consumers who will purchase the merged firm's products.

Several other questions arise from the neoclassical assumptions about what constitutes efficiency. First, although strong Pareto optimality makes intuitive sense with respect to the participants in the exchange, what about others who are affected by the exchange but are not themselves participants? A voluntary exchange that benefits both the parties may be harmful to those who are not parties unless such externalities are made part of the consideration. For example, a merger that enhances the efficiency of the surviving company and does not raise prices for the company's products may also result in the closing down of a corporate headquarters, costing the headquarters' city a loss of tax revenues, jobs and philanthropy; these externalities are not currently taken into account. There thus seems to be something extraordinarily arbitrary about concluding that a transaction is efficient even though all the costs are not taken into account.[64]

Also questioned is why competition policy should focus exclusively on prices. The microeconomic focus on price is the result of a definition of efficiency that is based on exchange, in that exchange is carried out by a universal medium of value, i.e. monetary price. Price is the one value that can easily be quantified, hence made susceptible to scientific measurement and manipulation. When you ask consumers why they want competition to play a large role in the economy, it is true that they will likely point to competitive prices as being advantageous. (It is also possible that they will say that competition is desirable because it drives out waste.) But, if they take a moment to think about it, they will likely mention other effects that they desire from competition: a reasonably wide range of products and services to choose from (and the empowerment of leverage that this suggests) and the progressivity and growth of a system that encourages improvements and innovations. Competition that brings low prices will often also engender the other desiderata of variety and innovation. But not always. If a competitive system that delivers only competitive prices is not likely to be entirely satisfactory, why should we accept price as if it were a proxy for all the desiderata?

Is there not a confusion of goal and by-product? A telling criticism of the efficiency standard, therefore, is that efficiency should not be conceived as the primary goal of antitrust so much as an important desired output of a competitive system. The system itself might better be conceived as the goal.

Static efficiency as a goal has the benefit of sounding scientific and quantifiable. We should in theory be able to place a dollar value on efficiency gains. Assuming we can, however, antitrust inevitably places us in the situation of having to weigh putative efficiency gains against putative competition losses. While some of the gains and some of the losses may be measured in terms of prices, this precision is lost if what is perceived to be at stake includes more than prices (e.g., a reduction in the number of competitors, reduction in choices, reduction in future innovations). These incommensurables undermine the claims of objective science put forward by overemphasis on microeconomic price theory.

Perhaps the largest problem is that a static efficiency gain must sometimes be compared to a dynamic efficiency loss. If, as I pronounced earlier but will not document here, dynamic efficiencies are often far more important than allocative efficiency gains, it would seem that static efficiency should not always be the singular or even the highest-ranking goal of antitrust.

*(c) Dynamic efficiency*    If political goals are too subjective and too changeable and static efficiency goals are too narrow, can dynamic goals provide the direction that antitrust needs? There are several drawbacks to this idea, as well.

First, there are many antitrust situations in which dynamic efficiency is not particularly relevant. As a recent book on dynamic competition concluded: 'Dynamic analysis would probably do little to alter antitrust decisions in markets that already appear competitive in a traditional, static sense, because the structure of such markets – the presence of numerous actual competitors or low barriers to entry – already makes antitrust action unlikely to improve consumer welfare.'[65] Porter may handle this by saying there is a hierarchy of goals: if innovation is irrelevant, then we should turn to the static efficiency price/cost goals. What is unclear, however, is how to weigh the goals against each other when two or all three are relevant and they do not point in the same direction.[66]

Second, while we can agree on the importance of growth, we have a limited understanding of how to generate innovation. In particular, we can only be very vague about what types of market structure or incentives are most likely to lead to innovation. F.M. Scherer and David Ross concluded their extensive review of the industrial organization literature with the observation that: 'What is needed for rapid technological progress is a subtle blend of competition and monopoly, with more emphasis in general on the former than the latter, and with the role of monopolistic elements diminishing when rich technological opportunities exist.'[67] This being approximately the best that can be said, it is fair to conclude that we do not currently know how to operationalize dynamic efficiency within an antitrust context. Porter, unfortunately, provides very little help in this.

Economist Jerry Ellig says that, although he can see where dynamic analysis can offer insights to antitrust enforcers,

> intellectually, dynamic competition makes antitrust enforcement even more difficult than it already was. Instead of simply defining product markets and hunting for evidence of market power, antitrust officials must assess which firms are capable of innovating in various areas. To avoid artificially restricting the breadth of the innovation market, officials must assess the innovative capabilities of firms that may not even compete with each other in a product market . . . A skeptic would be justified in asking why and how enforcement officials would have the knowledge to make such assessments.[68]

Third, a risk of focusing only on innovation is that it could lead to the absence of competition, at least if the focus is only on achieving innovation in the short term. Schumpeter, for example, extolled monopoly as being a necessary condition for innovation. Under our patent system, we award a 'temporary' monopoly as an incentive to innovate. Although we do not know how much incentive is enough to generate optimal innovation, our copyright protections are subject to political forces that continually extend their duration. The conundrum of intellectual property is that there may be such a thing as too much protection. The problem can be that monopolies gained through innovation, once empowered and in the absence of antitrust constraints, may not roll over to make way for the next innovators. This is what the *Microsoft* case was all about.[69]

**Choosing among the multiple goals of antitrust**
To recapitulate, although Robert Bork teaches that there can only be one goal for antitrust, namely his conception of consumer welfare, there are in fact a number of other goals that have been posited: some are political, some involve the search for static efficiency, and some relate to growth. How is a nation to decide which goals to follow?

There is indeed a yearning to find one goal, the single goal, because then one could design a system of antitrust that would appear to be scientific, objective, safe from the prejudices introduced by such human factors as politics. When multiple goals are acknowledged, logic is likely to suffer. Trade-offs will have to be made. Discretion and hence politics will enter into the process. Compromise is messy. Outcomes are not necessarily pre-dictable, although rules can be invoked to reduce this problem. Nonetheless none of the proffered goals of antitrust, taken alone, withstands criticism or provides a singularly satisfactory standard. Is some sort of multiple-goaled system therefore a necessity?[70]

Porter and others, notably Joseph Brodley, have suggested one approach, which is a hierarchy of goals: dynamic efficiency, productive efficiency and allocative efficiency, in that order of importance. As noted, however, we do not have a way of knowing when or how to mix these various goals. For instance, if the innovation goal were given priority, would strong evidence in favour of a small dynamic gain outweigh weak evidence of a large pro-ductive efficiency gain? Perhaps one could construct a matrix to cover most situations. But how should one compare mathematically calculated evi-dence of a deadweight loss with a prediction that a company will success-fully bring to market a drug that is only now in an R&D phase? When is a bird in the hand worth two in the bush?

An alternative to a hierarchy might be to assign a primary goal which is to be supplemented by other goals. Ellig has suggested that dynamic com-petition analysis might be deemed an 'additional factor' that supplements the primary goal of static efficiency analysis.[71] This could lead to such rules as, e.g., where substantial market power exists but the potential for inno-vation is high, 'there is a strong argument for refraining from antitrust action'.[72] Ellig also sees a trickier decision in those markets where a high degree of market power may be accompanied by a low potential for innov-ation, and notes that, in borderline cases, more complicated trade-offs will be needed. The overall consideration would be how long consumers would be left exposed to monopolistic exploitation.

Similar to an 'additional factor' would be a 'tie-breaker function' for certain clearly articulated goals. Here the additional factor is not merely something to be considered, but is a definitive trump card. This may be a useful rhetorical device, but unless there is a scientific method for first determining a 'tie', invocation of the tie-breaker is ultimately someone's discretionary act.

Thus we have at least three models to consider: a single goal, a hierarchy of goals, and a primary goal supplemented by additional factors that may have specified or unspecified weights. Each has drawbacks. None of the single goals that have been put forward draws universal acceptance. Even most neoclassical economists recognize that innovation needs to be considered in some manner within a solid antitrust analysis. Other types of goals we have examined do not by themselves offer sufficient guidance for policy decisions. A hierarchy of multiple goals offers some prioritization of values and is helpful to that extent. However this approach requires weighing the various goals and assigning rules for when and how they are to be combined. The additional factor approach offers assurance that relevant goals will not be ignored, but, again, it does not tell us how to weigh any additional factors in an analysis. Ellig has given an indication of how researchers might develop rules for adding dynamic considerations to traditional static analyses, but these are still at an early stage of formulation and further elaboration is likely to prove difficult. Moreover there are more 'additional factors', such as various goals like choice and diversity that have been advanced. If we move beyond one-goal antitrust analysis, we still need to determine which goals will have to be considered as legitimate and how the various goals can be operationalized.

At this point, we need to retreat to fundamentals. The first and foremost question is, what economic end should the antitrust system serve? Porter argues that growth of the economy is the proper end, so that all in the society can have more, and therefore antitrust's role should be to contribute to that growth by encouraging innovation. Bork argues that the proper end is allocative efficiency, so that current resources can be maximized for the good of all. It would seem that in many cases there is no conflict between these goals. Static efficiency is a reasonable goal, since in principle nobody favours unnecessary waste, but, as we have seen, efficiency means different things to different people. Growth is also a reasonable goal, since everyone potentially benefits if the pie gets larger. But both efficiency and growth depend for their support on unspoken questions of distribution. Who gains and who loses? Who should gain and who should lose? While economics can help us answer the first, empirical, question, the normative 'should' question is political. Political issues are unavoidable. There is no a priori reason why different political systems should be expected to come to the same answers or why the same political system should not alter its answers over time.

Take this basic question: should the antitrust system favour consumers or producers? An interesting answer was recently recommended by Jonathan Baker, who has the advantage (or curse) of being both an economist and a lawyer.[73] Baker tells 'a story' of a kind of social contract between producers and consumers, two broadly defined coalitions, which could have been worked out through experience in the context of American history. Baker argues the case for a political compromise, in which neither producers nor consumers definitively win out. His compromise is that, when consumer welfare and producer welfare clash, both should get a piece of the action. To give an example, if there is a proposed merger that may have anticompetitive effects but will produce efficiency gains, then the merger would be allowed, provided that *some* of the gains be passed through to consumers – not to the nation in general (which in the first instance would mean the stockholders of the merging companies), but to consumers who purchase the products of the merged firm, receiving a share of the new efficiencies in the form of lower prices. This solution, Baker argues, is roughly the one that exists today in the US, although it is rarely stated explicitly outside of the merger context.[74]

Baker's story is interesting, perhaps compelling. But as he clearly understands, the 'story' is a myth, much like Rousseau's social contract or Rawls' veil of ignorance. It has the value of seeming to provide a solution to the question of what to do about the three surpluses: total surplus, consumer surplus and producer surplus: namely, we should take them all into account. There should be no clear winner. This will disappoint not only advocates of each of the three surpluses, but advocates of a thoroughly objective approach to antitrust. It leaves it to the black box of law enforcement and judicial administration to make in specific cases a judgmental balance.

Helpful as it is in explaining how political issues might be understood to have brought us to a narrowing of the principal economic questions that antitrust must address, this is not a solution to the question of what should be the goal or goals of antitrust. First, it does not attempt to suggest how the trade-off should be made within the black box. What constitutes a fair, appropriate or politically adequate distribution of the gains? Second, it does not deal with the other 'additional factors' such as innovation or the desire for diversity (e.g., choice, variety, freedom) that have so often been voiced. Where were these values when the storied compromise was reached? It is easy enough to imagine a profit-enhancing merger that creates a monopoly, in which the shareholders will absorb half of the cost savings in the form of dividends and consumers will absorb half in the form of reduced prices; but at the same time, it is reasonably predicted that the new monopoly power will be used in ways that will convince investors not to invest in new ideas or companies that will challenge the monopolist. In this, the public should have not only a large interest, but arguably an interest that is weightier than either the shareholders or those who will be consumers.

**Conclusion**
My own approach would be somewhat different. I think that much of the debate described in this chapter conflates primary and secondary goals. I would say that there is only one primary goal of antitrust, namely a market-based economic system in which competition should be the ruling principle so long as it creates a reasonable balance of certain specified outcomes, which constitute the secondary goals: stimulation and opportunity for innovation and growth; efficient production and allocation of resources; competition-determined prices for consumers; a reasonable range of choices for all participants in the market; and a set of guiding rules and practices that provide reasonable predictability for those who have to make decisions within the system. I would admit that sometimes these desired outcomes will clash and that there are no lasting algorithms for setting priorities in such instances. Human judgment (primarily that of law enforcers and courts, egged on by the critiques of learned commentators) will simply have to sort things out on a case-by-case basis, dependent upon the strength of the evidence that happens to be available, and informed by the best economic analyses and legal argumentation of the day. A science? No. More of an art form that goes by the name, common law.

**Notes**
1. Foer is President of the American Antitrust Institute, www.antitrustinstitute.org. He holds a J.D. from the University of Chicago, an M.A. in political science from Washington University and an A.B. from Brandeis University. The author is grateful to Jonathan Baker, Joseph Brodley, John Kirkwood, Robert Lande and Stephen Ross for their comments on an earlier draft.
2. See, e.g., Eisner, Marc Allen (1991), *Antitrust and the Triumph of Economics*, U.N.C. Press; Peritz, Rudolph J.R. (2000), *Competition Policy in America: History, Rhetoric, Law*, Oxford University Press.
3. A famous quote from the time was Senator Sherman's declaration, 'If we will not endure a king as a political power, we should not endure a king over the production, transportation and sale of any of the necessaries of life'. Quoted in Neale, A.D. (1966), *The Antitrust Laws of the USA.*, Cambridge University Press, at 25.
4. See Garvey, George E. and Gerald J. Garvey (1990), *Economic Law and Economic Growth*, Praeger, pp. 4–6.
5. Taylor R.E., 'A talk with antitrust chief William Baxter', *Wall St. J.*, Mar. 4, 1982, at 28, col. 3.
6. Stiglitz, Joseph E. (2002), *Globalization and Its Discontents*, W.W. Norton.

7. The consumer welfare goal (1) gives fair warning, (2) places intensely political and legislative decisions in Congress instead of the courts, (3) maintains the integrity of the legislative process, (4) requires real rather than unreal economic distinctions, and (5) avoids arbitrary or anticonsumer rules. Bork (1978), *The Antitrust Paradox*, Basic Books, pp. 81–9.

8. Ibid., 81.

9. Ibid., 90.

10. Professor Lande says, 'Bork used "consumer welfare" as an Orwellian term of art that has little or nothing to do with the welfare of true consumers', Lande, Robert H. (1988), 'The rise and (coming) fall of efficiency as the ruler of antitrust', *The Antitrust Bulletin*, **33**, at 429 and 436. Also see footnote 11 of John B. Kirkwood's article (2004), 'Consumers, economics, and antitrust' in Kirkwood, John B. (ed.), *Antitrust Law and Economics, Res. J.L.& Econ.*, **21**, 1, in which Kirkwood debates with himself but concludes that it is fair to call Bork 'sly' when he calls the traditional measure of economic efficiency 'consumer welfare'.

11. Timothy Muris, later the Chairman of the FTC under George W. Bush, argued that such a merger should be approved. See Muris (1980), 'The efficiency defense under section 7 of the Clayton Act', *Case W. Res. L. Rev*, **30**, 381, 393–402. This was refuted in Lande, Robert H. (1982), 'Wealth transfers as the original and primary concern of antitrust: the efficiency interpretation challenged', *Hastings L.J.*, **34**, 65. Also see Fisher, Alan A., Frederick I. Johnson and Robert H. Lande (1988), 'Price effects of horizontal mergers', *Cal. L. Rev*. **77**, 777.

12. Posner, Richard A. (2001), *Antitrust Law*, 2nd edn, University of Chicago Press, at ix.

13. Posner's second edition (but not the first edition) notes that game theory models have refined oligopoly theory in recent years, but 'the models do not yet yield implications that differ from those of non-game-theoretic approaches . . . Long before game theory was a part of most economists' tool kits, they were well aware of the strategic character of competition in markets that had only a few sellers' (ibid., at 59–60).

14. Hull, Gary (ed.) (2005), *The Abolition of Antitrust*, Transaction Publishers, at ix. This book presents essays from the 'objectivist' perspective and is replete with quotes from Ayn Rand and sentences like this one: 'The antitrust laws of the United States are an obscene violation of individual rights that have thrown American business into a no-man's land of non-objective law' (John Ridpath, at 17.).

15. Quoted in Ridpath, John, *The Philosophic Origins of Antitrust*, in Gary Hull (ed.) (2005), at 25.

16. Ibid.

17. See the Cato *Handbook for Congress*, available at http://www.cato.org/pubs/handbook/hb105–39.html.

18. Generally, see McChesney, Fred S. and William F. Shughart (1995), *The Causes and Consequences of Antitrust, The Public-Choice Perspective*, Univ. of Chicago Press. Compare, Hovenkamp, H. (1990), 'Legislation, well-being, and public choice', *U. Chi. L. Rev.*, **57**, 63. For a critique of an extreme application of public choice analysis to antitrust, see Foer, Albert A. (2001), 'The politics of antitrust in the United States: public choice and public choices', *U. Pitt. L. Rev.*, **62**, 475.

19. See Walters, Stephen J.K. (1993), *Enterprise Government, and the Public*, McGraw-Hill, ch. 4.

20. White, Lawrence J. (2003), 'Microeconomics and antitrust in MBA programs: what's thought, what's taught', *N.Y.L.S.L. Rev.*, **47**, 87.

21. See the articles in the first three parts of 47 *N.Y.L.S.L.Rev.* (2003). It appears that most business students are exposed to marketing and strategic management courses, but relatively few take industrial organization economics, even though it is offered.

22. Hawker, Norman (2003), 'Antitrust insights from strategic management', *N.Y.L.S.L.Rev.*, **47**, 67, at 73.

23. Bork, above, note 7, 119.

24. Hawker, above, note 22, at 74–5.

25. Ibid. at 75–8.

26. Ibid. at 78–9. For a trenchant analysis of markets applying behaviouralist insights, see Kay, John (2004), *Culture and Prosperity*, Harper Business. An application of behavioural insights to a specific antitrust issue, market entry, can be found in Tor, Avishalom (2002), 'The fable of entry: bounded rationality and the efficacy of competition', *Mich. L. Rev.*, **101**, 482.
27. Hawker, above, note 22, at 80.
28. Porter, Michael E. (1980), *Competitive Strategy*, at 3.
29. Ibid., at 7.
30. Bolton, Patrick, Joseph F. Brodley and Michael H. Riordan. (2000), 'Predatory pricing: strategic theory and legal policy', *Geo. L.J.*, **88**, 2239, at 2242.
31. Compare Brodley, Joseph (1987), 'The economic goals of antitrust: efficiency, consumer welfare and technological progress', *N.Y.U. L. Rev.*, **62**, 1020, in which it is urged that the economic goals of antitrust are innovation, productive efficiency, and allocative efficiency, in that order. Brodley argues that antitrust has a preferred mechanism to achieve its economic goals: competitive process. Moreover the economic goals of antitrust, properly defined, can be connected with political and social goals, which Brodley calls the animating spirit of antitrust.
32. Porter, Michael E. (2004b), in Charles D. Weller (ed.), *Unique Value*, manuscript from 2004, at 158.
33. This is not to suggest that current antitrust policy ignores the importance of innovation and productivity. Chicagoists would argue that their focus on output increases subsumes dynamic considerations. In fact, the attention of enforcers, courts and commentators given to innovation has increased considerably in the past 15 years. In the Chicago theology, however, the emphasis is clearly on static efficiencies. Innovation fits in awkwardly at best.
34. See, e.g., Porter, Michael E. (1990), *The Competitive Advantage of Nations*, Free Press.
35. Gilpin, Robert (2001), *Global Political Economy*, Princeton Univ. Press.
36. Gilpin writes, 'Economics and political economy differ significantly in their view of the market in economic affairs and of the relationship of the market to other aspects of society. Whereas neoclassical economists believe that the market is autonomous, self-regulating, and governed by its own laws, almost all political economists assume that markets are embedded in larger sociopolitical structures that determine to a considerable extent the role and functioning of markets in social and political affairs and that the social, political, and cultural environment significantly influences the purpose of economic activities and determines the boundaries within which markets necessarily must function'. (At 74–5.)
37. Kay, John (2004), *Culture and Prosperity*, Harper Business, at 18.
38. A classic in this field is Klein, Burton (1977), *Dynamic Economics*, Harvard Univ. Press.
39. See www.antitrustinstitute.org.
40. An example of a populist approach to antitrust is reflected in the *Antitrust Law and Economics Review*, available at http://www.metrolink.net/~cmueller/default.html? Approaches that I would designate as populist tend to be more explicit in their political intent than purely economic approaches, although I argue that economic approaches also contain a political programme.
41. In an e-mail to the author, Ross usefully distinguishes between Jeffersonian antitrust (protecting small business for its own sake in spite of efficiency costs) and Jacksonian antitrust (giving equally efficient competitors a level chance but not permitting less efficient small firms to remain in business for Jeffersonian reasons). See: Ross, Stephen F. (2000), 'Network economic effects and the limits of GTE Sylvania's efficiency analysis, University of Illinois College of Law, Law and Economics Working Papers Series, Working Paper No. 00–13', September 2000, available at http://papers.ssrn.com/pape.tar?abstract.id., later published in *Antitrust L.J.*, **68**, 945. This Jacksonian goal was not included as among the top three non-economic goals enunciated by Pitofsky, Robert (1979) in 'The political content of antitrust', *U. Pa. L. Rev.*, **127**, 1051 (identifying as political goals of antitrust the inhibition of antidemocratic political pressure caused by excessive economic concentration; maximization of individual and business discretion;

and avoidance of concentrations of power that inevitably lead to increased government intervention in the economy).

42. See Foer, Albert A. (1996), 'American idealism: level playing fields', *Bus. & Soc. Rev.*, **96**, 27.
43. See Leary, Thomas B. (2000), 'Freedom as the core value of antitrust in the new millennium', *Antitrust L. J.*, **68**, 545.
44. See Lande, Robert H. (2001), 'Consumer choice as the ultimate goal of antitrust', *U. Pitt. L. Rev.*, **62**. Also see Leary, Thomas B. (2001), 'The significance of variety in antitrust analysis', *Antitrust L. J.*, **67**, 1007. ('If it is true that matters other than price are of prime importance to consumers, in ever-growing sectors of the economy, an intelligent antitrust policy should respond accordingly'1021.)
45. *Brown Shoe Co.* v. *US*, 370 U.S. 294 (1962).
46. I thank Robert Lande for making this point, which is supported by numerous quotes from the legislative debates. See Lande, Robert H. (1982), 'Wealth transfers as the original and primary concern of antitrust: the efficiency interpretation challenged', *Hastings L.J.*, **34**, 65.
47. The familiar model for this is drawn, e.g., in Bork, Robert, *The Antitrust Paradox*, ch. 5, comparing (a) the amount above costs that consumers would be willing to pay for the lost output (dead-weight loss) to (b) the gain to all consumers of cost reductions resulting from a merger (cost savings). Bork says, 'This diagram can be used to illustrate all antitrust problems, since it shows the relationship of the only two factors involved, allocative inefficiency and productive efficiency. The existence of these two elements and their respective amounts are the real issues in every properly decided antitrust case' (108).
48. *US* v. *National Society of Professional Engineers*, 435 U.S. 679 (1978). Another example is the Ivy League financing case in which nine schools were charged by the Antitrust Division with conspiring to restrain price competition for students receiving financial aid. The defence was that such an agreement was necessary in order to achieve the social objective of increasing the scholarship money available for needy students. The fact that Congress killed the case raises the whole issue of the political dimension of antitrust. See, e.g., Bamberger, Gustavo, E. and Dennis W. Carlton (1993), 'Antitrust and higher education: MIT Financial Aid', 4th edn, in John E. Kwoka Jr and Lawrence J. White, 188–210.
49. Bork, *The Antitrust Paradox*, ch. 4. Bork says that productive efficiency should be understood as 'offering anything . . . that consumers are willing to pay for. The relative efficiency of firms is therefore measured by their relative success in the market' (105). Much of the Chicago logic follows from this. Any (legal) activity that increases profitability is necessarily efficient. Rational profit maximizers therefore seek to become more efficient; hence the voluntary decisions of business leaders must be seen as efficiency-seeking. Since efficiency is what is best for society, government should keep its hands off.
50. See Lande, Robert H. (1982), 'Wealth transfers as the original and primary concern of antitrust: the efficiency interpretation challenged', *Hastings L.J.*, **34**, 65. The battle as to whether consumer welfare should mean consumer surplus or total welfare, often captured as a dispute between Robert Lande and Robert Bork, is described in Kirkwood, John B. (2004), 'Consumers, economics, and antitrust' in John B. Kirkwood (ed.), *Antitrust Law and Economics, Res. J.L.& Econ.*, **21**, 1. Kirkwood says that Lande is winning in the courts but Bork is winning among economists. Compare *Reiter* v. *Sonotone*, 442 U.S. 330, 343 (1979) (stating that the legislative record 'suggest[s] that Congress designed the Sherman Act as a "consumer welfare prescription"') with *Atlantic Richfield Co.* v. *USA Petroleum Co.*, 495 U.S. 328,360 (1990) ('The Court, in its haste to excuse illegal behavior in the name of efficiency, has cast aside a century of understanding that our antitrust laws are designed to safeguard more than efficiency and consumer welfare')(footnotes omitted) (Stevens J, dissenting).
51. The differences between total welfare and consumer surplus approaches to a merger are starkly presented by the Canadian case of *Superior Propane*. If the facts were found correctly, this was a merger that would harm consumers in the relevant market by raising prices, but would benefit consumers elsewhere in the economy (e.g., stockholders of the

590 *Handbook of research in trans-Atlantic antitrust*

merging companies) by saving resources. The outcome was to permit the merger. A legislative effort to overcome the decision failed. This case represents the rare instance in which a merger was approved by antitrust authorities on the basis of an efficiencies defence. Compare the discussions by Facey, Brian A., Danny H. Assaf and Russell Cohen (Fall 2003), 'The Canadian Competition Tribunal gets it right', and Fisher, Alan A., Robert H. Lande, and Stephen F. Ross (Fall 2003), 'The Canadian Competition Tribunal gets it wrong', in *Antitrust Magazine*. Also see Ross, Stephen F. (2003), 'The political economy of the efficiency defence', **21**, *Canadian Competition Record*, 89, and Zerbe Jr., Richard O. and Suny Knott (2004), 'An economic justification for a price standard in merger policy: the merger of Superior Propane and ICG Propane', in John B., Kirkwood (ed.), *Antitrust Law and Economics, Research in Law and Economics Volume, 21*, Elsevier. An excellent review of issues relating to the role of efficiencies in competition policy may be found in Canadian Competition Bureau, Consultation Paper, Consultations on the Treatment of Efficiencies under the Competition Act (Sept. 24, 2004), available at http://strategis.ic.gc.ca/epic/internet/inch-bc.nsf/en/ct02951e.html.

52. See Klein, Burton (1977), *Dynamic Economics*, Harvard U. Press. Bork considered 'progressiveness' to be a component of consumer welfare, and not a separate goal. Bork, above, n 47, at 132. It is not clear how the short-term static efficiency upon which Bork's system rests is intended to be reconciled with long-term dynamic efficiency. For example, a monopolist may provide the utmost in static efficiency, while at the same time blocking or channelling innovation to serve its own interests in preserving the monopoly status. Interestingly (and to his credit), Bork sided with the opponents of Microsoft during the landmark computer litigation.

53. Porter, Michael (2004), *Competition and Antitrust: A Productivity-Based Approach* in Charles E. Weller (ed.), *Unique Value: Competition Based on Innovation Creating Unique Value*, Manuscript from 2004. This is a later version of a paper that appears in ABA, Report of the Task Force on Fundamental Theory (July 2001).

54. Ibid., at 165 (italics are Porter's).

55. Ibid.

56. Ibid., 167.

57. These are set forth in Porter's major books, *Competitive Strategy: Techniques for Analyzing Industries and Competitors* (1980) and *The Competitive Advantage of Nations* (1990).

58. See above n 53, *Unique Value*, 173–4.

59. For a look at some of the more scandalous tidbits in US antitrust history, see Charles R. Geisst (2000), *Monopolies in America*, Oxford.

60. But see Chace, James (2002), *1912*, Simon & Schuster, the one campaign when antitrust policy was a major issue in an unusual presidential election.

61. See n 43, above.

62. Lasswell, Harold (1958), *Politics: Who Gets What When How?*, World Publishing.

63. Posner argues '[T]hat economic theory provides a solid basis for the belief that monopoly pricing, which results when firms create an artificial scarcity of their product and thereby drive price above its level under competition, is presumptively inefficient in the sense most commonly used by economists in discussing issues of monopoly and competition (the Kaldor–Hicks, or potential Pareto, sense of efficiency)'. Posner, Richard A. (2001), *Antitrust Law*, Univ. of Chicago Press, at 2. See Viscusi, W. Kip., John W. Vernon and Joseph E. Harrington Jr (1995), *Economics of Regulation and Antitrust*, 2nd edn, MIT Press, p. 74 (problem with Pareto criterion is that 'in most cases in the real world, at least some people will be harmed'). For a discussion of the failure of Kaldor–Hicks to capture significant aspects of social utility, see Hovenkamp, H. (1990), 'Legislation, well-being, and public choice', *U. Chi. L. Rev.*, **57**, 63.

64. Of course every model is a simplification of reality, which means that certain factors, deemed insufficiently relevant, will be excluded from the model. In antitrust, there is also a weighty argument about how already-complex cases can be tried if virtually everything that might be relevant is considered fair game in the litigation. Nonetheless, it seems strained to justify a merger as efficient when major elements of cost are disregarded.

65. Ellig, Jerry (ed.) (2001), *Dynamic Competition Policy and Public Policy: Technology, Innovation, and Antitrust Issues*, Cambridge Univ. Press, concluding chapter.
66. Burton Klein wrote, 'Economists have long assumed that the only kind of efficiency is static efficiency. But Schumpeter not only recognized that an economic system can be characterized by a higher or a lower degree of dynamic efficiency, but acknowledged that it cannot achieve a high degree of static and dynamic efficiency simultaneously'. *Dynamic Economics*, p. 35, quoting Schumpeter, Joseph A. (1942), *Capitalism, Socialism, and Democracy*, Harper & Brothers, at 83. Also see Baumol, William J. (2002), *The Free-Market Innovation Machine: Analyzing the Growth Miracle of Capitalism*, Princeton Univ. Press ('*[I]nnovation has replaced price* as the name of the game in a number of important industries.' at 4).
67. Scherer, F.M. and David Ross (1990), *Industrial Market Structure and Economic Performance*, 3rd edn, Houghton Mifflin, p. 660. Also see Landes, William M. and Richard A. Posner (2003), *The Economic Structure of Intellectual Property Law*, Harvard Univ. Press, p. 385. ('[A]fter many years of study, it remains completely uncertain in both theoretical and empirical analysis whether concentration promotes, reduces, or does not affect innovation. So effect on innovation is probably something that should be ignored in the administration of merger law.')
68. Ellig, above, note 65, 265–7.
69. For a useful perspective on the Microsoft litigation, see Abramson, Bruce (2005), *Digital Phoenix*, MIT Press.
70. Shenefield and Stelzer seem to have reached a conclusion similar to mine: Shenefield, John H. and Irwin M. Stelzer (2001), *The Antitrust Laws, A Primer*. ('Courts and prosecutors will surely focus most intensively on the economic goal, but the philosophical and historical underpinnings of the antitrust laws demand that they be sensitive to the noneconomic goals as well.')
71. Ellig, above, n 65 at 264.
72. Ibid., at 265.
73. Baker, Jonathan B., 'Competition as a political bargain', forthcoming in the *Antitrust L.J.*, available as an AAI Working Paper at http://www.antitrustinstitute.org/recent2/382.pdf.
74. In many areas of antitrust enforcement (e.g., cartels), differences between consumer welfare and producer welfare are not important. Baker identifies four settings in which application of the two standards can lead to different conclusions: an agreement among rivals leading to more efficiency and also higher prices; exclusionary conduct that can harm rivals and lead to lower prices; agreement among consumers to use monopsony power to reduce prices in an input market; and price discrimination that can raise aggregate welfare while reducing consumer surplus (ibid., at 45–7). Also see Brodley, Joseph (1996), 'Proof of efficiencies in mergers and joint Ventures', *Antitrust L.J.*, **64**, 576 (all savings do not have to be passed on to consumers, but they should get some benefit).

## References

Abramson, Bruce (2005), *Digital Phoenix*, MIT Press.
Baker, Jonathan B., 'Competition as a political bargain', forthcoming in the *Antitrust L.J.*, available as an American Antitrust Institute Working Paper at: http://www.antitrustinstitute.org/recent2/382.pdf.
Bamberger, Gustavo, E., and Dennis W. Carlton (1993), 'Antitrust and higher education: MIT financial aid', 4th edn, in John E. Kwoka Jr and Lawrence J. White, *The Antitrust Revolution*, Oxford 4th edn.
Baumol, William J. (2002), *The Free-Market Innovation Machine: Analyzing the Growth Miracle of Capitalism*, Princeton University Press.
Bolton, Patrick, Joseph F. Brodley, and Michael H. Riordan (2000), 'Predatory pricing: strategic theory and legal policy', *Geo. L. J.*, **88**, 2239.
Bork, Robert (1978), *The Antitrust Paradox*, Basic Books.

Brodley, Joseph (1987), 'The economic goals of antitrust: efficiency, consumer welfare and technological progress', *N.Y.U. L. Rev.*, **62**, 1020.
Brodley, Joseph (1996), 'Proof of efficiencies in mergers and joint ventures', *Antitrust L.J.*, **64**, 576.
Chace, James (2002), *1912*, Simon & Schuster.
Eisner, Marc Allen (1991), *Antitrust and the Triumph of Economics*, U.N.C. Press.
Ellig, Jerry (ed.) (2001), *Dynamic Competition Policy and Public Policy: Technology, Innovation, and Antitrust Issues*, Cambridge University Press.
Facey, Brian A., Danny H. Assaf and Russell Cohen (Fall 2003), 'The Canadian Competition Tribunal gets it right'.
Fisher, Alan A., Frederick I. Johnson and Robert H. Lande (1988), 'Price effects of horizontal mergers', *Cal. L. Rev.*, **77**, 777.
Fisher, Alan A., Robert H. Lande and Stephen F. Ross (Fall 2003), 'The Canadian Competition Tribunal gets it wrong', in *Antitrust Magazine*.
Foer, Albert A. (1996), 'American idealism: level playing fields', *Bus. & Soc. Rev.*, **96**, 27.
Foer, Albert A. (2001), 'The politics of antitrust in the United States: public choice and public choices', *U. Pitt. L. Rev.*, **62**, 475.
Garvey, George E. and Gerald J. Garvey (1990), *Economic Law and Economic Growth*, Praeger.
Geisst, Charles R. (2000), *Monopolies in America*, Oxford.
Gilpin, Robert (2001), *Global Political Economy*, Princeton University Press.
Hawker, Norman (2003), 'Antitrust insights from strategic management', *N.Y.L.S.L.Rev.*, **47**, 67.
Hovenkamp, H. (1990), 'Legislation, well-being, and public choice', *U. Chi. L. Rev.*, **57**, 63.
Hull, Gary (ed.) (2005), *The Abolition of Antitrust*, Transaction Publishers.
Kay, John (2004), *Culture and Prosperity*, Harper Business.
Kirkwood, John B. (2004), 'Consumers, economics, and antitrust', in John B. Kirkwood (ed.), *Antitrust Law and Economics, Res. J.L.& Econ.*, **21**, 1.
Klein, Burton (1977), *Dynamic Economics*, Harvard University Press.
Lande, Robert H. (1982), 'Wealth transfers as the original and primary concern of antitrust: the efficiency interpretation challenged', *Hastings L.J.*, **34**, 65.
Lande, Robert H. (1988), 'The rise and (coming) fall of efficiency as the ruler of antitrust', *The Antitrust Bulletin*, **33**.
Lande, Robert H. (2001), 'Consumer choice as the ultimate goal of antitrust', *U. Pitt. L.Rev.*, **62**.
Landes, William M. and Richard A. Posner (2003), *The Economic Structure of Intellectual Property Law*, Harvard University Press.
Lasswell, Harold (1958), *Politics: Who Gets What When How?*, World Publishing.
Leary, Thomas B. (2000), 'Freedom as the core value of antitrust in the new millennium', *Antitrust L.J.*, **68**, 545.
Leary, Thomas B. (2001), 'The significance of variety in antitrust analysis', *Antitrust L.J.*, **67**, 1007.
McChesney, Fred S. and William F. Shughart (1995), *The Causes and Consequences of Antitrust, The Public-Choice Perspective*, University of Chicago Press.
Muris, T. (1980), 'The efficiency defense under section 7 of the Clayton Act', *Case W. Res. L. Rev*, **30**, 381.
Neale, A.D. (1966), *The Antitrust Laws of the USA*, Cambridge University Press.
Peritz, Rudolph J.R. (2000), *Competition Policy in America: History, Rhetoric, Law*, Oxford University Press.
Pitofsky, Robert (1979), 'The political content of antitrust', *U. Pa. L. Rev.*, **127**, 1051.
Porter, Michael E. (1980), *Competitive Strategy*, New York: Free Press.
Porter, Michael E. (1990), *The Competitive Advantage of Nations*, Free Press.
Porter, Michael (2004a), *Competition and Antitrust: A Productivity-Based Approach*, in Charles E. Weller (ed.), *Unique Value: Competition Based on Innovation Creating Unique Value*, manuscript from 2004.
Porter, Michael E. (2004b), in Charles D., Weller (ed.), *Unique Value*, manuscript from 2004.
Posner, Richard A. (2001), *Antitrust Law*, University of Chicago Press.

Ross, Stephen F. (2000), 'Network economic effects and the limits of GTE Sylvania's efficiency analysis', University of Illinois College of Law, Law and Economics Working Papers Series, Working Paper No. 00-13, September 2000, available online at http://papers.ssrn.com/pape.tar?abstract.id.
Ross, Stephen F. (2003), 'The political economy of the efficiency defence', *Canadian Competition Record*, **21**, 89.
Scherer, F.M. and David Ross (1990), *Industrial Market Structure and Economic Performance*, 3rd edn, Houghton Mifflin.
Schumpeter, Joseph A. (1942), *Capitalism, Socialism, and Democracy*, Harper & Brothers.
Shenefield, John H. and Irwin M. Stelzer (2001), *The Antitrust Laws, A Primer*, The AEI Press.
Stiglitz, Joseph E. (2002), *Globalization and Its Discontents*, W.W. Norton.
Taylor, R.E. (1982), 'A talk with antitrust chief William Baxter', *Wall St. J.*, 4 March.
Tor, Avishalom (2002), 'The fable of entry: bounded rationality and the efficacy of competition', *Mich. L. Rev.*, **101**, 482.
Viscusi, W. Kip., John W. Vernon and Joseph E. Harrington Jr (1995), *Economics of Regulation and Antitrust*, 2nd edn, MIT Press, p. 74.
Walters, Stephen J.K. (1993), *Enterprise Government, and the Public*, McGraw-Hill.
White, Lawrence J. (2003), 'Microeconomics and antitrust in MBA programs: what's thought, what's taught', *N.Y.L.S.L. Rev.*, **47**, 87.
Zerbe Jr., Richard O. and Sunny Knott (2004), 'An economic justification for a price standard in merger policy: the merger of Superior Propane and ICG Propane', in John B., Kirkwood (ed.), *Antitrust Law and Economics, Research in Law and Economics, Volume 21*, Elsevier.

*Cases*
*Brown Shoe Co. v. US*, 370 U.S. 294 (1962).
*US v. National Society of Professional Engineers*, 435 U.S. 679 (1978).
*Atlantic Richfield Co. v. USA Petroleum Co.*, 495 U.S. 328 (1990).

# 22 Competition enforcement and consumers
*Juan Antonio Rivière y Martí*[1]

## Competition policy for the benefit of consumers
Competition Commissioner Mario Monti stated from the beginning of his mandate that he was giving a central importance to consumers. He said that competition authorities have a role to play in taking account of input from consumers. He brought a clear message: 'The Commission is committed to a proactive, modern and effective competition policy. Not only will this ensure that the market functions in such a way as to maximise benefits for consumers, but it also gives consumers an unparalleled opportunity to participate in the fight against violations of the competition rules.'[2]

The European Commission develops actions for civil society, bringing community policies to European citizens. It means facilitating knowledge and participation of citizens and its organizations in preparation of community rules, so they may encourage its initiatives. 'The Commission has a long tradition of consulting interested parties from outside when formulating its policies. It incorporates external consultation into the development of almost all its policy areas.'[3]

However not all the issues are considered at a community level; for example, the Commission Directorate-General for health and consumer protection depends on the enforcement of national legislations and plays a coordination and initiative role.

> Consumer policy is central to the EU objective of continuously improving the quality of life of all EU citizens. The aim of promoting the interests, health and safety of consumers in the EU is enshrined in Articles 153 and 95 of the Treaty establishing the European Community. Consumer policy involves: a) developing legislative and other actions; b) integrating consumer concerns in all EU policies; c) complementing Member States' consumer policy; d) empowering consumers by actively supporting EU consumer organisations and their involvement in policy making. Consumer policy initiatives and development depend on relevant and reliable information. Policy makers need to understand what matters most to consumers with supporting evidence. The Commission consults widely with interested stakeholders.[4]

The European Commission has the initiative capacity to promote directives of harmonization to all the Member States. Currently a directive to regulate the unfair commercial practices that harm consumers with a view to introducing national legislation in all Member States.

In 2002 Member States urged the Commission to integrate in all their policies the protection of consumers in accordance with Article 153 of the EC Treaty:

> 1. – In order to promote the interests of consumers and to ensure a high level of consumer protection, the Community shall contribute to protecting the health, safety and economic interests of consumers, as well as to promoting their right to information, education and to organise themselves in order to safeguard their interests. 2. – Consumer protection requirements shall be taken into account in defining and implementing other community policies and activities.

Many competition policies around the world declare that their activities are dedicated to ensuring market efficiency for the benefit of consumers. Competition policies followed by the European Commission and the EU Member States have a direct impact on the daily life of its citizens. Ensuring that companies compete favours innovation, reduces costs and prices, and improves quality and supply of goods and services. This benefits consumers since it allows them to exercise their buying power and choices. Competition is made in an open market where interaction is permanent between suppliers acting according to the demand of customers or end consumers. The dynamics of competition is determined by changes and balances in market structure; for this reason it is important to have strong buying power from the demand side.[5]

**From a general framework of good intentions to practice**
This aim to benefit the consumer must be taken into account in our daily action to obtain specific results. The European Commission put into force in May 2004 its competition policy reform. The antitrust reform from Regulation 1/2003[6] has established decentralization and permits the implementation of Article 81 EC by national competition authorities of Member States as well as by the national courts who can decide on compensation for damages incurred as the result of competition infringements.[7]

The Commission is giving consumers and its organizations the opportunity to take part in the fight against competition infringements through presentation of complaints that lead to opening proceedings. Consumers can also provide market information to the Commission when they face anticompetitive effects.

> The Commission wishes to encourage citizens and undertakings to inform it about suspected infringements of the competition rules. There are two different ways to take action; one is by lodging a complaint pursuant to Article 7(2) of Regulation 1/2003. Complaints of this type must fulfil certain legal requirements. In particular, to be admissible, a complaint shall provide the information required by Form 'C'. Exhaustive information on the handling of complaints by

the Commission under Articles 81 and 82 of the EC Treaty can be found in the Commission Notice.[8] Complaint Form "C" explains how to make a complaint regarding antitrust matters and what data you have to provide.[9] The other action possible is providing market information. It does not have to comply with the requirements for complaints pursuant to Article 7(2) of Regulation 1/2003. The Commission has created a mailbox that can be used by citizens and undertakings and their associations who wish to inform the Commission about suspected infringements of Articles 81 and 82. Such information can be the starting point for an investigation by the Commission.[10]

In the case of mergers it has been indicated also through the Notice on horizontal mergers that consumers, when they demonstrate a legitimate interest, can take part in the examination process and in any case can present observations on the effects of the operation.[11]

Furthermore, in the Directorate-General for Competition, a permanent dialogue has been established with consumers and their organizations through the 'Consumer Liaison Officer' who was appointed on the initiative of Commissioner Mario Monti in December 2003. The post had already been announced one year before when adopting the package of competition reform measures. The function will ensure a permanent dialogue with consumers, whose welfare is the primary concern of competition policy, but whose voice is not sufficiently heard when handling individual cases or discussing policy issues. Another objective is to increase consumer awareness about the general benefits of competition policy for civil society. Like the Chief Economist, the Consumer Liaison Officer's role is not confined to the merger control area, but also concerns the antitrust field – cartels and abuses of dominant positions – as well as other competition cases and policies on liberalized network industries or control of State aid. The creation of the post is also designed to intensify contacts between the Directorate-General for Competition and other Commission Directorates-General, most notably with the Health and Consumers Protection DG.

Tasks of the Consumer Liaison Officer will include (a) acting as primary contact point for consumer organizations, but also for individual consumers, by establishing more regular and intensified contacts with consumer organizations. Consumer organizations, as well as individual consumers, will be able to contact the Consumer Liaison Officer directly on competition-related issues: the following website provides a form: http:// europa.eu.int/comm/competition/forms/consumer_complaint_form. html; (b) alerting consumer groups to competition cases when their input might be useful, and advising them on the way they can provide input and express their views; and (c) contacts with National Competition Authorities regarding consumer protection matters.

**Information about consumer needs and competition problems**
In the European Commission, consumer protection policy is the responsibility of the Directorate-General for Health and Consumers Protection (DGSANCO) with which the Directorate-General for Competition cooperates. Dialogue of DGSANCO with the consumer associations is institutionalized in the newly created 'European Consumers Consultative Group'. The ECCG could play a coordinating role for general issues.

Concerning competition policy the link with consumers and their European or national associations is made through the Consumer Liaison Officer and the different Directorates and Units within the Directorate-General for Competition. This activity began in January 2004 and it allows us to receive information to which we respond through each department responsible for an economic sector or activity. Meetings are held with the European Consumers Organization (BEUC).[12] In these meetings we identify those issues of greatest interest and concern to European consumers regarding which Competition policy could contribute in finding solutions. That is how we try to integrate consumer's information in future competition policy implementation. There is always room for more issues that may be examined by national consumer protection or competition authorities.

The guidance to obtain consumers' benefits is reflected in our daily examination of cases in the Directorate-General for Competition. To implement that work, the Consumer Liaison Officer and each Unit of the Directorate-General meets to ensure coherence in all actions, to exchange experiences and have discussions with consumer associations. For each case under examination, the impact on the consumer is taken into account and any benefits are evaluated using a 'Consumer Impact Form', completed by the civil servant responsible for the case. Furthermore the anti-competitive effects against consumer welfare that are identified during examination of operations will be closely controlled by the team of the Chief Economist.

**Identifying the problems of competition that affect the consumer citizen**
In the Directorate-General of Competition there are five Directorates that represent economic sectors' activities.[13] Within the nine Directorates there are Units responsible for each activity or service where competition problems are identified and market structures and companies' behaviour followed. Information is obtained by launching market studies. When collecting information a consultation process is open to professional associations and consumers.

Consumer goods and service activities are close to consumers. Network industries of liberalized public services focus on consumer interest and how the change from public to private ownership could bring them benefits.[14] Special attention is given to sectors such as air transport, telecommunications, electricity and gas that have required a long process of liberalization and, in some cases, are not yet finished. Critics appear when sector Regulators have not foreseen changes in market structures of certain services in view of increasing demand that has brought insufficient investment in infrastructures, losing quality or continuity of service. There are new initiatives of liberalization for other activities such as post or rail transport. In other sectors such as financial services or the liberal professions, there are also new policy initiatives from the Commission to bring greater transparency and competition. There is improvement in automobile distribution following the modified Regulation in favour of greater competition in the market. These are important activities that we have identified jointly with consumer associations, and their market performance will be followed. This approach is complementary to the evaluation of consumer impact during an individual event or case.

Among different problems faced by consumers we can mention some examples: (a) in the automobile industry, there are still difficulties in purchasing an automobile because of obstacles to parallel imports from another distributor not located in the same country as the customer; (b) in electricity, the consumer will have difficulties in perceiving the benefit of having several electricity suppliers and, with the new invoice structure where electricity transport costs and taxes are specified, the incentive to obtain a lower price from the electricity generator supplier is not yet clear; (c) in telecommunications, the diversity of tariffs and interconnections must be studied by consumers in order to choose the best price, but this is not an easy exercise. There are, however, other non-regulated prices as ones of the SMS that a recent survey of the French consumer association[15] has shown a reduced cost, a high price and a large benefit for the company. In another case, the speed of transmission for an ADSL connection, a survey of the Italian consumer association[16] has demonstrated that the access speed is below what was advertised; and (d) with the entry of the Euro the French consumer association is studying the costs of bank current accounts for consumers.

With the identification of various consumer problems the efficient market performance becomes a priority that could prevent more problems. The list of cases to be analysed may be extensive; it implies determining priorities of action to provide solutions to those of greatest impact on consumers. Certain cases may be better solved at national or local level by the national authorities. For this reason institutional coordination between Community and national authorities is essential.

**Coordinating institutional relations at national, regional and international level**

With market globalization the competition and consumer protection authorities have widened their coordination activity at an international level. The European Union has, from 1 May 2004, a coordination network for antitrust matters (ECN – European Competition Network) that facilitates the coordination of all the competition authorities of the Union. Among ECN members there are some authorities that are also responsible for consumer protection, for example in Poland, France and the United Kingdom. In the United Kingdom, the OFT (Office of Fair Trading) is making a positive contribution. Training and guidance have increased, combining market research, implementation of regulations and direct communication with consumers to be more effective. This has led to a new concept of 'super complaints' to promote participation. When taking action we consider coordination thanks to the complementarities that exist between competition and consumer protection authorities.[17]

Outside Europe, coordination of the two disciplines can also be observed in the United States with the Federal Trade Commission, in Canada, in Costa Rica within Coprocom, in Panama within Clicac, in Peru with Indecopi or in Australia within the Commission of Competition and the Consumer. In the same way the OECD is working on complementarities in a joint committee for competition and consumer protection to identify a working programme.

Concerning consumer associations, it is necessary to mention the activities of Consumers International,[18] which has published, for example, a 'Consumer guide to competition' that helps to understand the interaction between both disciplines and the International Network of Control and Protection of the Consumers (ICPEN) that is very active and supportive.[19]

Lately the ICN (International Competition Network), after discussing advocacy at the Mérida meeting in 2003 and at the Seoul meeting in 2004, has decided that a subgroup will take over the 'relations with the consumers' and establish rapport during the conference, in Bonn in 2005. The group examined how competition authorities manage to communicate with consumers and their organizations, open participation to consumers during proceedings and see how demand customers are performing in the market. At the international level, considerable interest is shown in the interaction between competition enforcement and consumer protection.

**Conclusions**

Market suppliers have to consider that those developments linking competition policy and consumer protection will lead to increased participation of consumers and consumer organizations in favour of efficient market competition.

Companies will give more attention throughout to consumer compliance programmes, and better service to customers in order to avoid problems later. New adversarial proceedings will increase in the European Union, so that consumers and consumer organizations will be able to demand compensation for damages caused by competition infringements and gain protection of their rights. It is also hoped that consumer protection will be strengthened in government policies, not creating artificial obstacles that reduce market efficiencies.

**Notes**

1.   Adviser, Consumer Liaison Officer, Directorate General for Competition, European Commission, Brussels. The opinions given in the document are personal and do not represent the official view of the European Commission. The author can be reached at juan.riviere@ec.europa.eu.
2.   Speech at Competition Day in Dublin 29 April 2004.
3.   http://europa.eu.int/comm/civil_society/index.htm.
4.   http://europa.eu.int/comm/consumers/overview/index_en.htm.
5.   In a recent article, 'Beware of buyer power', Robert H. Lande considers the treatment it needs (*Legal Times*, 12 July 2004; also available at www.antitrustinstitute.org).
6.   *Official Journal*, n° L1, 4 January 2003.
7.   http://europa.eu.int/comm/competition/antitrust/others/private_enforcement/index_en. html.
8.   http://europa.eu.int/eur-lex/pri/en/oj/dat/2004/c_101/c_10120040427en00650077.pdf.
9.   It can also be found as an annex to Commission Regulation (EC) No 773/2004 of 7 April 2004 relating to the conduct of proceedings by the Commission pursuant to Articles 81 and 82 of the EC Treaty *Official Journal*, L 123, 27 April 2004, 18–24.
10.   Market Information and Complaints: http://europa.eu.int/comm/competition/antitrust/ others/.
11.   http://europa.eu.int/eur-lex/pri/en/oj/dat/2004/c_031/c_03120040205en00050018.pdf. Point 79: 'The relevant benchmark in assessing efficiency claims is that consumers will not be worse off as result of the merger. For that purpose, efficiencies should be substantial and timely, and should, in principle, benefit consumers in those relevant markets where it is otherwise likely that competition concerns would occur.'
12.   http://www.beuc.org. 'BEUC: the European Consumers' Organisation, is the Brussels-based federation of 36 independent national consumer organizations from the EU, accession and EEA countries. Our job is to try to influence, in the consumer interest, the development of EU policy and to promote and defend the interests of all European consumers.' BEUC is demanding the following: 'Access of all consumers to essential services of a reasonable quality at an affordable price shall be guaranteed. Consumers' expectations in that regard not only encompass physical and geographical access at an affordable price, but also choice, transparency and full information, quality, safety, security, and reliability, fairness, independent regulation, representation and active participation, redress.'
13.   http://europa.eu.int/comm/dgs/competition/directory/organi_en.pdf.
14.   See 'Horizontal evaluation of the performance of network industries providing services of general economic interest – 2004 report – Commission Staff Working Paper', SEC(2004) 886 presented to the EU Council of Ministers on 28 June 2004.

15. Union Fédérale des Consommateurs – Que Choisir?
16. Altroconsumo.
17. At the end of 2003, a joint meeting between national consumer protection and competition authorities with the Commission agreed that in the EU it is important to improve coordination between consumer policy and competition policy in order to increase the efficiency of both policies. Advocacy, the treatment of complaints and market analysis and surveillance are fields where such coordination could appear to be most fruitful. There are large complementarities as to the objectives of both policies, namely the promotion of consumer welfare. A precise institutional structure of how both policies are set and enforced is not really decisive to achieve the highly desirable result of synergies between both policies. Those synergies could be stimulated by an enhanced exchange of information between both competition and consumer policy setters and enforcers and, in the case of the newly liberalized sectors, with the regulatory bodies. Consumer organizations can play an important role in identifying sectors of concern, which could in turn lead to market enquiries.
18. See the following websites: http://www.consumersinternational.org/homepage.asp and http://www.consumidoresint.cl/biblioteca/todos.asp. 'Consumers International (CI) supports links and represents consumer groups and agencies all over the world. It has a membership of over 250 organizations in 115 countries. It strives to promote a fairer society through defending the rights of all consumers, especially the poor, marginalized and disadvantaged, by (a) supporting and strengthening member organizations and the consumer movement in general and (b) campaigning at the international level for policies which respect consumer concerns. Consumers International was founded in 1960 as the International Organisation of Consumers Unions (IOCU) by a group of national consumer organizations.'
19. The International Consumer Protection and Enforcement Network (ICPEN), formerly known as the International Marketing Supervision Network (IMSN), is a membership organization consisting of the trade practices law enforcement authorities of more than two dozen countries, most of which are members of the Organisation for Economic Co-operation and Development (OECD). The mandate of the Network is to share information about cross-border commercial activities that may affect consumer interests, and to encourage international cooperation among law enforcement agencies.

# References

*Article*
Lande, Robert, H. (2004), 'Beware of buyer power', *Legal Times*, 12 July.

*Websites*
http://www.antitrustinstitute.org.
http://www.beuc.org.
http://www.consumersinternational.org/homepage.asp.
http://www.consumidoresint.cl/biblioteca/todos.asp.
http://europa.eu.int/comm/civil_society/index.htm.
http://europa.eu.int/comm/competition/antitrust/others/private_enforcement/index_en.html.
http://europa.eu.int/comm/consumers/overview/index_en.htm.
http://europa.eu.int/comm/dgs/competition/directory/organi_en.pdf.
http://europa.eu.int/eur-lex/pri/en/oj/dat/2004/c_101/c_10120040427en00650077.pdf.

**Annex**
http://europa.eu.int/comm/competition/publications/competition_policy_
and_the_citizen/consumer_liaison/. Contact the Consumer Liaison Office
at http://europa.eu.int/comm/ competition/forms/consumer_complaint_
form.html.

Information on competition problems affecting consumers to be sent
to the Consumer Liaison Office. The Consumer Liaison Office in the
Directorate General for Competition is responsible for receiving information and requests concerning competition problems faced by end consumers
and customers. A team of Consumer Liaison Correspondents responsible
for each economic sector, directed by the Consumer Liaison Officer, will
give advice to consumers within a month of any query and if the Directorate
General for Competition is not the correct department shall transfer the
information to other Directorates General in the European Commission
or to a National Authority dealing with Competition and Consumer
Protection.

Juan Antonio Rivière y Martí is the Consumer Liaison Officer within the
Commission's Competition Directorate General; this post was established
in December 2003 in order to ensure a permanent dialogue with European
consumers, whose welfare is the primary concern of competition policy, but
whose voice is not sufficiently heard when handling individual cases or discussing policy issues. His role concerns the antitrust field (cartels and
abuses of dominant positions) merger control and other competition cases
and policies.

His tasks include the following:

- Acting as primary contact point for consumer organizations, but also
  for individual consumers, by establishing more regular and intensified contacts with consumer organizations.
- Alerting consumer groups to competition cases when their input
  might be useful, and advising them on the way they can provide input
  and express their views.
- Contacts with National Competition Authorities regarding consumer protection matters.
- Intensifying contacts between the competition and other
  Directorates-General, most notably with the Health and Consumers
  Protection Directorate-General.

*Information on competition problems affecting consumers to be sent to the
Consumer Liaison Office:*
*Please complete all the compulsory fields. These are marked thus (#). No
files or documents can be attached to this form. If you do require to*

*make attachments please send them by separate mail to the address at the foot of this page, together with a printed copy of the form or use <u>the attached file</u>.*

Your personal details

First Name: (#) [          ]   Last name:(#) [          ]

Address line 1: (#) [          ]   Address line 2: [          ]

Town/City: (#) [          ]

Postcode: (#) [          ]   Country:(#) [          ]

Telephone: [          ]   Mobile telephone: [          ]

E-mail address: [          ]   Fax: [          ]

1. Against which undertaking or group do you wish to inform? #

[                    ]

2. To what economic sector is your information related? Please choose one: #

[ 1.1 - Energy ▾ ]

If 'Other', please specify: [                    ]

3. What is the matter about which you inform? When did it come to your attention? #

[                    ]

4. What result do you hope to achieve? #

5. Have you already contacted the Directorate General for Competition or other National Competition Authorities or National Regulators in order to obtain assistance? #

○ Yes ○ No (If yes, please specify)

6. Do you agree that your complaint or information may be passed on to another national competition authority, if we are not entitled to deal with it? #

○ Yes ○ No

*Important*                                                                 *Note:*

*E-mail messages sent from this site are not encrypted and thus cannot be considered fully secure.*

The Consumer Liaison Officer – DG Competition European Commission, B-1049 Brussels, Belgium.

For more information:

Juan Antonio Rivière Martí,
Adviser and Consumer Liaison Officer,
Directorate General for Competition DGCOMP J-70 0/171,
European Commission,
B-1049 Brussels,
Belgium.

Tel: +322.295.1146; Fax: +322.296.9803
E-mail: juan.riviere@cec.eu.int.

# 23 The distributional consequences of antitrust

*Okeoghene Odudu*[1]

The purpose of this contribution is to set out a framework in which it can be seen that decisions to apply (or not to apply) antitrust to a particular practice have consequences for the distribution of wealth across society. Depending on whether or not the antitrust rules apply to certain practices in a market economy, wealth is either transferred from one group to another, or remains with one group instead of being transferred to another. Applying antitrust to a particular practice has distributional consequences; by the same token, not applying antitrust to a particular practice also has distributional consequences.[2] The underlying question is the extent to which this transfer, or non-transfer, of wealth from one group to another is relevant in antitrust.

## 1 Antitrust as concerned with allocative inefficiency

The seemingly ubiquitous justification for antitrust laws is that they exist to remedy certain problems of allocative inefficiency. Competitive markets enable society to have more and society is better off when more is had.[3] Whilst society is better off with more, if industry output is reduced, the producers can demand a higher price for each unit. Although producers sell fewer goods if they demand a higher price, it is profitable to sell fewer goods if the increased price more than compensates for lost sales.[4] This contrived scarcity of output is problematic, as demand from consumers willing to pay more than the cost of production, but less than the price actually charged, goes unsatisfied.[5] This unsatisfied demand is termed 'deadweight loss'; it is allocatively inefficient not to supply what consumers demand if that demand can be satisfied at a price that covers the cost of production and a reasonable return on capital.[6] This problem is illustrated in Figure 23.1.[7]

The downward sloping curve represents market demand. The demand curve slopes downwards because the cheaper the price the greater the number of consumers willing and able to buy the goods. $P_c$ and $Q_c$ show the price and output before any anticompetitive agreements or practices take place. $P_c$ also shows the marginal cost of production. Marginal cost is the cost of producing one additional unit of the good and (because it enables the firm to add to profit) a firm will continue producing until the marginal

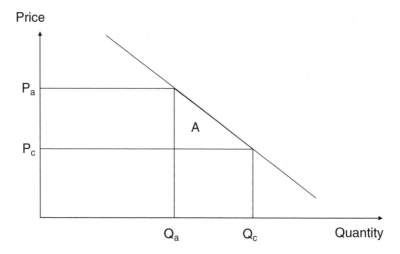

*Figure 23.1   The allocative inefficiency problem*

cost is equal to the sale price; this price includes normal profit. Anticompetitive conduct results in a price increase from $P_c$ to $P_a$ and a fall in output from $Q_c$ to $Q_a$, with the negative consequence, deadweight loss (area A).

## 2   Antitrust as concerned with wealth distribution
Allocative inefficiency is not the only consequence of the contrived scarcity of output. There is also a distributional consequence. The contrived scarcity of output ($Q_c$ to $Q_a$) and the consequent price increase ($P_c$ to $P_a$) extracts more of what those who can still afford the goods and services are willing to pay.[8] This is illustrated in Figure 23.2, area C.

Lande has sought to show that it is this extra payment by consumers to producers (area C), rather than allocative inefficiency (area A), that is the central antitrust concern.[9] What is argued is that antitrust can be seen as endowing consumers with a 'property right or entitlement to purchase competitively priced goods and . . . higher than competitive prices constitute unfair takings or extractions of consumers' property'.[10] Enforcing antitrust not only prevents allocative inefficiency, but also prevents a transfer of wealth from producers to consumers.[11]

It is accepted that '[d]istributive and efficiency goals often work in perfect harmony'.[12] For the most part, area C and area A arise simultaneously, so it has been suggested that whether area A or area C is the central concern is merely a debate about shapes.[13] It needs to be shown that a focus on distribution makes a difference. It can be argued that a focus on distributional

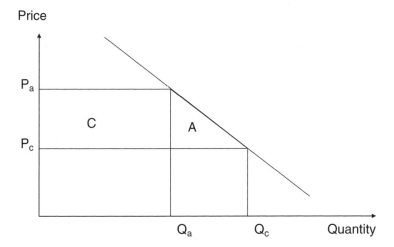

*Figure 23.2    The distributional concern*

issues enables recognition of a dialogue that occurs at various stages in antitrust over which group is entitled to the wealth represented by area C, and in which circumstances. The dialogue occurs when determining the scope of antitrust, in defining and characterizing a substantive infringement and in the determination of whether an antitrust infringement can be justified or excused.

*Scope of antitrust*
Distribution can be considered in determining the scope of the antitrust rules. As noted by Goyder and Neale, '[t]he Sherman Act is all embracing in its terms, so that any exception must be specified in legislation. This . . . means that a majority in Congress has to be persuaded before any part of the economy can be insulated from these laws'.[14] Groups and activities can be favoured by putting them beyond the scope of the antitrust rules; the favoured group are able to require consumers of their goods and services to pay more. Part of the rationale behind leaving some actors or some activity beyond the scope of antitrust is that this preserves or enables a desirable redistribution from a less favoured to a more favoured group, by requiring the less favoured group to pay more.[15] Those lying beyond the scope of antitrust are given a right to the wealth represented by area C. This can be seen in the collective bargaining exception to antitrust in both the US and the EC.

Conceptually, workers organizing themselves together in a union to bargain for better pay and conditions form a cartel, competition is eliminated amongst the members, and those who seek the services of unionized workers are forced to pay more for them.[16] The use of union power to drive up wages may increase the cost to the consumer in the same way that a firm with market power may increase prices to the consumer.[17] Thus antitrust could be and has been applied to such activity.[18] This would reflect the view that area C is wealth that belongs to consumers. However, in *United States* v. *Hutcheson*, the Supreme Court ruled that, read together, sections 6 and 20 of the Clayton Act, and section 4 of the Norris–LaGuardia Act immunize collective bargaining and ancillary activities of trade unions against the reach of US antitrust.[19] In *Albany*, the Court of Justice and Advocate General Jacobs held that the EC antitrust rules do not apply to collective bargaining and ancillary activities of trade unions.[20]

Labour can be seen as a group favoured as against employers, and antitrust immunity enables a redistribution of wealth from producers to their employees. The labour exemption is just one example of antitrust immunity that allows redistribution from a favoured to an unfavoured group.[21] In EC antitrust, it seems to be a more general principle that antitrust does not apply when there is redistribution towards a favoured group.[22] EC antitrust rules apply, and only apply, to economic activity. The Court of Justice has ruled that the pursuit of an 'exclusively social objective' is *not* economic activity.[23] In *Poucet and Pistre*, the Court established that activity is not economic when it 'entails the redistribution of income between those who are better off and those who, in view of their resources . . . would be deprived'.[24] When activity is sufficiently redistributive in a desirable manner, EC antitrust does not apply.

The reduced scope of antitrust in relation to collective bargaining may be warranted because 'collective bargaining still serves important values which cannot easily be served in other ways'.[25] However it should be clear that the legislature and the courts, in determining the scope of the antitrust provisions, are determining which group is entitled to the wealth represented by area C. A decision that certain actors or certain activities are not subject to antitrust has distributional consequences, since it implicitly or explicitly confirms that the distribution that occurs absent antitrust is preferred to the redistribution which antitrust would enforce.[26] Immunities for labour, agriculture, and insurance mean that in relation to these goods and services the legislature or the courts have determined that producers of these goods and services are entitled to the wealth transferred as a result of what would, absent immunity, be seen as anticompetitive conduct.

*The substance of antitrust*

Entitlement to the wealth represented by area C may form part of the substantive antitrust enquiry: an infringement of the antitrust rules may be said to occur if there is a wealth transfer from a group entitled to the wealth to a group not considered entitled. If antitrust were thought to exist to protect consumers, a substantive infringement of the antitrust rules would occur each time there is a transfer of wealth from consumers to producers. In EC law, Article 82(a) EC prohibits 'directly or indirectly imposing unfair purchase or selling prices or other unfair trading conditions'. This prohibition has been held to include the levying of excessive prices.[27] In *Morton Salt*, the Supreme Court of the United States ruled that competition is harmed when parties have to pay 'substantially more for their goods' and that an antitrust prohibition against second-line and third-line price discrimination protects parties from being charged an excessive price.[28]

Prohibitions against excessive pricing suggest a consumer entitlement to the wealth. However, in both EC and US law, the extent to which it is possible to show that a purchaser is paying an excessive price, and the ability to distort the law to protect competitors rather than the competitive outcome, means that such cases 'do not bulk particularly large in the literature'.[29] It is thus difficult to see the substantive law as preventing wealth transfers from consumers to producers; distribution does not seem to be the primary concern of the substantive law.

*Justifications for antitrust infringements*
Whilst the substantive law may not be centrally concerned with preventing wealth transfers from consumers to producers, it may be that antitrust violations are actually excused or justified to *legitimate* a transfer of wealth from consumers to producers. In deciding whether to excuse or justify a substantive infringement, what the parties infringing the substantive antitrust rules are proposing to do with the wealth may form part of the consideration. A choice is then made as to whether consumers should pay more to fund a worthy goal. If conduct falls within the scope of the antitrust rules, is prohibited by the substantive law and is not excused or justified, the consumer has a right to recover the wealth transfer or is protected from the transfer.[30] If a justification or excuse is accepted, the consumer is forced to make the wealth transfer, since antitrust affords no protection: a positive decision legitimizes the wealth transfer and extinguishes the right to recover. Rather than a consumer entitlement to area C, a more general rule would operate, under which parties infringing the substantive antitrust rules may be exonerated if the practice has distributional consequences that are deemed desirable.

In the US, the strict legal position appears to be that it is not possible to excuse or justify a substantive infringement of the competition rules because of the distributional consequences that result. This is the implication of the ruling in *National Society of Professional Engineers* v. *United States* that:

the purpose of the analysis is to form a judgment about the competitive signifi-cance of the restraint; it is not to decide whether a policy favoring competition is in the public interest . . . Subject to exceptions defined by statute, that policy decision has been made by the Congress.[31]

However examples can be found of distributional issues being taken into account. In 1991, the US Department of Justice investigated 23 top-tier US universities.[32] The universities (including eight Ivy League schools) adopted a common policy on how to award financial aid. It was agreed that no student would be awarded more aid than was justified by financial need (determined by a common formula).[33] By ensuring that aid was granted only to the extent that a student was needy, the aid resources would be awarded to a greater number of needy students. The adoption of a common formula was seen as horizontal price fixing in relation to the discount that students would be offered, and thus constituted an infringe-ment of the substantive antitrust rules.[34] In *United States* v. *Brown University*, the Court of Appeals in the third circuit considered social welfare justifications as relevant, accepting that 'MIT could fill its entire entering class with students 'able to pay the full tuition' but instead 'utilizes a need-blind admissions system under which all admission decisions are based entirely on merit without consideration of an applicant's ability to pay tuition. Because financial status is irrelevant, very intelligent but needy students are preferred over less accomplished but more affluent ones'.[35] The needy students were funded from the MIT endowment and it is sug-gested that this redistribution and its consequences might justify the antitrust infringement.[36] Since clearly influential, the question remaining concerns the weight to be attached to the desirable distributional conse-quences that ensue from an antitrust infringement in order for the infringe-ment to be excused.[37]

In EC law, the Treaty allows an antitrust infringement to be justified or excused when there are countervailing gains, and invites a consideration of what are relevant gains and to whom they ought to accrue.[38] Innovation and productive efficiencies are recognized in Article 81(3) as goals that justify or excuse an infringement of the substantive antitrust rules.[39] Society advances not simply by having more and thus cheaper goods, but by having new and different goods and services and new and different methods of producing those goods and services.[40] Firms create these new and better goods and services, or new and better methods of producing goods and services, through research and development activities.[41] The benefits of productive efficiency and innovation are illustrated in Figure 23.3 and are represented by the marginal cost curve falling from $P_c$ to $C_a$, resulting in gains shown by area B.

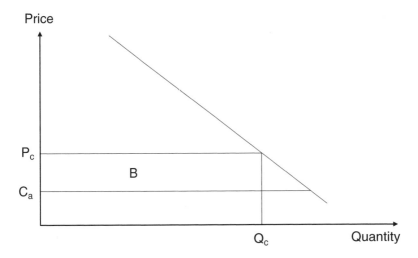

*Figure 23.3   Productive and dynamic efficiencies*

Since society advances by having new and different goods and services and new and different methods of producing those goods and services, antitrust must identify conduct that stifles productive efficiency and innovation.[42] The quantity and quality of current resources devoted to research and development depends on how profitable the future innovation will be for the undertaking; the ability profitably to contrive scarcity of output affects the profitability of innovation.[43] There is a view that an ability profitably to contrive scarcity of output is essential to innovation and cost reduction since, in order to fund the creation of innovation or productive efficiencies (area B) or incentivize firms to innovate or to become productively efficient, a price increase from $P_c$ to $P_a$ is required.[44] This is illustrated in Figure 23.4.

As an example, the Commission accepted that a restriction of competition between the members of the European Committee of Domestic Equipment Manufacturers (CECED) was acceptable in order to develop and promote more environmentally friendly machines. Consumers were required to pay more for their lower energy machines, in part because '[r]educed electricity consumption indirectly leads to reduced pollution from electricity generation' and that 'lower electricity consumption will indirectly help the Union achieve its environmental objectives'.[45] In *Ford/Volkswagen* the Commission justified or excused redistribution from consumers to producers in order to achieve 'extremely positive effects on the infrastructure and employment in one of the poorest regions in the Community'.[46] The antitrust violation appears to be justified or excused,

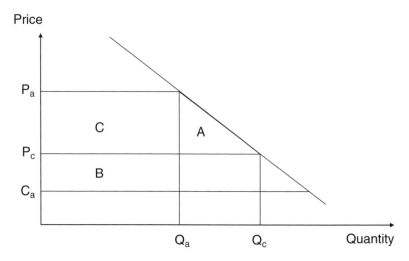

*Figure 23.4   Funding research and development through wealth distribution*

and the wealth transfer sanctioned, because the restrictive conduct 'is esti-mated to lead, inter alia, to the creation of about 5000 jobs and indirectly create up to another 10 000 jobs, as well as attracting other investment in the supply industry'.[47] The justifications for the price increase and conse-quent transfer of wealth from consumers to producers (area C) in order to fund or incentivize productive and dynamic efficiency (area B) is stated by Adams as follows: 'only bigness can provide the sizable funds necessary for technological experimentation and innovation' and '[o]nly monopoly earn-ings can provide the bait that lures the capital onto untried trails'.[48] A wealth transfer from consumers to producers is permitted, either to fund or to reward innovation, since this makes society better off. An unhappy con-sequence of the transfer is allocative inefficiency (area A). Consumers are asked to forgo current consumption (area A) in order to enable access to funds (area C) to invest or incentivize investments resulting in technological progress (area B), which creates more to allocate in the future.[49]

The allocative efficiency loss is not the concern of this contribution.[50] Instead the concern is the extent to which it matters that the gains (area B) are funded by a transfer of resources from consumers to producers (area C). It may be thought that, if the wealth of society as a whole increases, it does not matter that consumer fund advances, the benefits of which (initially at least) accrue to producers, as long as producers are *able* to compensate those that lose and still be better off themselves.[51] The irrelevance of distri-bution does not sit comfortably with the idea that consumers have a prop-erty right in the wealth represented by area C. Since it is consumers that invest in the creation of productive efficiencies and innovation, it may be that they are entitled to some return on their investment.[52] It may be politically desirable to institute a direct system of compensation, redistributing the gains through the tax system, which is an accountable and effective way to achieve distributional aims.[53] Or the compensation might be indirect, trickling back to the consumer in the form of lower long-term prices or increased profits of firms in which the consumer holds shares.[54]

What should be clear is that in deciding whether to excuse or justify a substantive infringement, a choice is being made as to whether consumers should pay more to fund a worthy goal. While the criteria by which it is determined that a substantive infringement can be justified or excused remains unclear, it is clear that rather than a consumer entitlement to area C, the wealth represented by area C may be allocated to any party that uses the wealth for a purpose deemed desirable.

*Conclusion*

When and how antitrust applies has distributional consequences. It has been suggested that the extent to which distributive considerations influence antitrust decisions can be minimized by preventing those influenced by short-term political considerations taking part in the substantive determination or providing substantive rules that expressly prohibit distribution from being considered.[55] However, distributional consequences are rarely if ever considered as part of the substantive assessment. Distribution has the potential to weigh more in the decision to excuse or justify an infringement. Claims are made that the distribution required by antitrust will have disastrous consequences in one dimension or another and, at times, in both US and EC antitrust, such claims have been compelling. Distributional consequences are more clearly considered and more clearly emerge when determining the scope of the antitrust rules. Entities and activities can be favoured by putting them beyond the scope of antitrust, which enables a transfer of wealth from the group denied antitrust protection to the favoured entities. This method is particularly prevalent. Since the scope of antitrust is a political question, taken by those with political constituencies and inherently concerned with who gets what from the market and the state, distributive considerations can never be removed from antitrust. It is thus important to recognize that they exist.

**Notes**

1. Herchel Smith Lecturer and Fellow in Law, Emmanuel College, Cambridge; Deputy Director, Centre for European Legal Studies, Faculty of Law, University of Cambridge.
2. Hovenkamp (1982). Dibadj (2004: 802–10, 814–17) argues that antitrust is simply a form of regulation and that regulation is inherently concerned with distributional goals. The question of whether distribution is a reason for intervention is separate from the question of whether distributional issues arise. It seems that those arguing that distribution

is not a concern argue that it is not a reason for intervention (Castañeda 1998: 46; Wolf 1998: 131–2). However, there is recognition that distributional consequences arise (Castañeda 1998: 49; Fels and Edwards 1998: 58, 63; Schaub 1998: 120–23).

3. The idea that economic growth increases living standards is challenged by Helleiner (1951), Weisskopf (1965), Galbraith (2004: 26–8, 73–5) and Hamilton (2004).
4. Lerner (1934: 157).
5. Bator (1957), Blair and Kaserman (1985: 3–22), Carlton and Perloff (2000: 69–74), Hausman and McPherson (1996: 27–30, 41–5), Motta (2004: 39–89), Scherer and Ross (1990: 15–55).
6. Begg et al. (1997: 138–40), Blair and Kaserman (1985: 25–37), Bork (1993: 90–115), Clarkson and Miller (1982: 107–27), Dalton and Levin (1973), Lerner (1934: 157–65), Lipsey et al. (1993: 286–92), and Posner (1976: 8–10).
7. Williamson (1968a) and Bork (1993: 108).
8. Lande (1982: 74–5) and Collins (1984: 502–3, 508–15).
9. Lande (1982: 93–6, 112–14, 135–6) and Lande (1989: 632, 636–7). Compare with Collins (1999), Feldman (1971: 516–17), Hovenkamp (1982: 16–27) and Markovits (1975: 986–7).
10. Lande (1989: 632). Also Lande (1982: 76–7, 93–6) and Feldman (1971: 516–17).
11. Elzinga (1977: 1194–6). Dibadj (2004: 818–19) suggests that antitrust takes distribution into account by ensuring that the consumer is able to purchase as if a monopolist.
12. Lande (1982: 142).
13. Calvani (1989), contested in Lande (1989: 641 note 40).
14. Neale and Goyder (1980: 6). Compare Letwin (1981: 95–9), Goyder (1993: 4) and Van den Bergh and Camesasca (2001: 161). The UK Competition Act 1998, para. 7 of Schedule 3, confers power on the Secretary of State to exempt certain actors and activities from UK competition law.
15. Compare with Case 1006/2/1/01, *Bettercare Group Limited* v. *the Director General of Fair Trading*, [2002] CAT 7, para. 60, on why some groups are favoured in preference to others (Stigler 1971).
16. (Boarman 1963; Cox 1955; Posner 1986: 299–305). Compare with Case C-67/96, *Albany International BV* v. *Stichting Bedrijfspensioenfonds Textielindustrie*, [1999] ECR I-5751, AG Opinion para. 210–12.
17. Kaysen and Turner (1959: 209).
18. *United States* v. *Debs* 64 Fed 724 (1894) and (Letwin 1981: 123–8, 155–61).
19. *United States* v. *Hutcheson* 312 US 219, 229–232 (1941). The Norris–LaGuardia Act is also known as the Federal Anti-Injunction Act. The precise scope of the antitrust immunity is still subject to debate: *Connell Construction Co* v. *Plumbers Local* 100 421 US 616 (1975) and *Brown* v. *Pro Football* 518 US 231 (1996).
20. Case C-67/96 *Albany International BV* v. *Stichting Bedrijfspensioenfonds Textielindustrie*, [1999] ECR I-5751, paras 46–60, AG Opinion at para. 131–94, 209–17 (Boni and Manzini 2001). As Jones and Sufrin (2004: 120) point out, the employee/employer relationship is only indirectly considered.
21. Another is the reduced intervention of antitrust in the agricultural sector: Neale and Goyder (1980: 7) and Article 36 EC.
22. Compare Prosser (2005: 17–38).
23. Joined Cases C-264/01, C-306/01, C-354/01 and C-355/01 *AOK Bundesverband* v. *Ichthyol-Gesellschaft Cordes*, [2003] ECR I 2493, para. 47.
24. Joined Case C-159/91 and C-160/91 *Christian Poucet* v. *Assurances Générales de France (AGF) and Caisse Mutuelle Régionale Du Languedoc-Roussillon (Camulrac) and Daniel Pistre* v. *Caisse Autonome Nationale de Compensation de L'Assurance Vieillesse des Artisans (Cancava)*, [1993] ECR I-637, para. 10, also AG Opinion paras 9–11. On solidarity: Case C-70/95 *Sodemare SA* v. *Regione Lombardia*, [1997] ECR I-3395, AG Opinion para. 29 Menendez (2003), (Winterstein 1999: 327–31), (Louri 2002: 169–72) and (Spaventa 2004: 275, 284–5). That redistribution is the essence of what is meant by solidarity, which is distinguished from economic activity, is emphasized in Case C-70/95 *Sodemare SA* v. *Regione Lombardia*, [1997] ECR I-3395, para. 29, Joined Cases C-264/01, C-306/01, C-354/01 and C-355/01 *AOK Bundesverband* v. *Ichthyol-Gesellschaft*

Cordes, [2003] ECR I 2493, AG Opinion para. 32, Case C-218/00 *Cisal di Battistello Venanzio & Co.* v. *Istituto Nazionale per L'assicurazione Contro Gli Infortuni Sul Lavoro (Inail)*, [2002] ECR I-691, AG Opinion paras 56, 59–60, Case 1006/2/1/01 *Bettercare Group Limited* v. *the Director General of Fair Trading* [2002] CAT 7, para. 51, 239–40, and Joint Selling of the Commercial Rights of the UEFA Champions League [2003] OJ L 291/25, paras 164–7. It is accepted by Boni and Manzini (2001: 240–41), Hatzopoulos (2002: 684, 711–12), and Van den Bergh and Camesasca (2000: 492, 505).

25. Kaysen and Turner (1959: 209).
26. This explanation is described as 'implausible, but conceivable' in Posner and Easterbrook (1981: 1038).
27. Case 27/76 *United Brands* v. *Commission*, [1978] ECR 207, para. 250 (Peter M Roth QC 2001: paras 9-073–9-075; Whish 2003: 690–93). Compare Case 30/87 *Bodson* v. *Pompes Funèbres des Régions Libérées SA* [1988] ECR 2479, paras 30–31.
28. *Federal Trade Commission* v. *Morton Salt Co* 334 US 37, 46 (1948) on section 2(a) of the Clayton Act, as amended by the Robinson-Patman Act. See Neale and Goyder (1980: 215–20), Sullivan and Hovenkamp (2003: 933–50) and Gellhorn et al. (2004: 505–25, particularly 517–20).
29. Neale and Goyder (1980: 215). Also Bork (1993: 382–401), Kaysen and Turner (1959: 239–240), Whish (2003: 688–90).
30. Reich (2005), Komninos (2002).
31. *National Society of Professional Engineers* v. *United States* 435 US 679, 692 (1978). Also (American Bar Association (Antitrust Section) and Hartley (chairman) 1999: 116–19). Pitofsky (1995) notes that this is perhaps an overly strong statement that does not reflect the true position.
32. An account and analysis is given in Salop and White (1991) and Carlton et al. (1995).
33. *United States* v. *Brown University* 5 F 3d 658, 662 (1993).
34. *United States* v. *Brown University* 5 F 3d 658, 664–8, also footnote 9 (1993).
35. *United States* v. *Brown University* 5 F 3d 658, 661–2 (1993).
36. *United States* v. *Brown University* 5 F 3d 658, 674–8 (1993).
37. (American Bar Association (Antitrust Section) and Hartley (chairman) 1999: 162–3) suggests the weight is minimal. Compare Areeda (1986: 579–80).
38. It is not only Article 81(3) EC, but also Articles 16, 86(2) EC, and objective justification under Article 82 EC that are important in this regard. Under Article 81(3) EC a simple net gain is insufficient; consumers receive a fair share of the benefit identified: distribution is a concern: Cases 56 and 58–64 *Établissements Consten Sàrl and Grundig-Verkaufs-GmbH* v. *Commission* [1966] ECR 299, 348, Guidelines on the Application of Article 81(3) of the Treaty [2004] OJ C 101/97, paras 43, 85, (Collins 1984: 502; Manzini 2002; Whish 2001: 125; Van den Bergh and Camesasca 2001: 252).
39. Guidelines on the Application of Article 81(3) of the Treaty [2004] OJ C 101/97.
40. Schumpeter (1975: 83); Kendrick (1977: 1).
41. Kendrick (1977: 67–9), Romer (1986: 1007), Jones (1998: 84, 89–90), Carlton and Perloff (2000: 506), Aghion and Howitt (1992: 324).
42. Compare Porter (2001: 932); Stelzer (2002).
43. Viscusi et al. (2000: 93), Economist (2002), Cornish (1996: 13–14, 30), Bainbridge (1999: 322), Dutton (1984: 3, 17–23).
44. Scherer (1987: 1010–18; 1992).
45. CECED, [2000] OJ L187/47, para. 48, also para. 51 and Commission Press Release IP/01/1659, 26 November 2001. The Commission rejects the idea that the non-economic environmental benefits were considered. Instead the economic savings from the reduced need to clean up the environment and lower running costs for consumers were considered: CECED, [2000] OJ L187/47, paras 11–12, 52, 56 (Monti 2002: 1073–7; Gyselen 2002: 185–6; Wesseling 2001: 370–71).
46. *Ford/Volkswagen* OJ 1993 L20/14, para. 23.
47. *Ford/Volkswagen* OJ 1993 L20/14, para. 36. In Case T-17/1993 *Matra Hachette SA* v. *Commission* [1994] ECR II 595, 106–111, the Court deny that these non-efficiency characteristics were used to justify or excuse the anticompetitive restraint.

48.   Adams (1953: 477, 478). Also Bork (1993: 134–5), Economist (2001; 2000c: 130), Nelson and Winter (1982: 115–16, 130) and Stelzer (2002: 27–8). Qualified by Carlton and Perloff (2000: 533), Faull and Nikpay (1999: para. 1.122–1.123), Fels and Edwards (1998: 59–63), Rapp (1995: 28–30), Scherer (1992: 1421, 1425–30), Van den Bergh and Camesasca (2001: 36–37), Viscusi et al. (2000: 93–4), Williamson (1968a: 29–31; 1969b: 115–16). Mario Monti, then Commissioner for Competition, is reported as being sceptical of this argument (Economist 2000a).
49.   Romer (1986: 1015, 1019), Nelson and Winter (1982: 114, 116), Aghion and Howitt (1992: 331), Carlton and Perloff (2000: 505), Williamson (1969b: 105–6; 1977: 712), Hildebrand (2002: 8).
50.   Although see the following the trade-off between allocative efficiency loss and productive and dynamic efficiency gain: Docket A-533-00 *Canada (Commissioner of Competition)* v. *Superior Propane Inc., and ICG Propane Inc.* [2001] Carswell National 702, paras 22–37, Guidelines on the Application of Article 81(3) of the Treaty, [2004] OJ C 101/97, para. 85, Guidelines on the Assessment of Horizontal Mergers under the Council Regulation on the Control of Concentrations between Undertakings, [2004] OJ C31/5, para. 8 (Amato 1997: 2–3; Arthur 1994: 15–19; Bork 1993: 20–21, 90–106, 111; DePrano and Nudent 1969; Hildebrand 1998: 144; Hovenkamp 1982; Hylton 2003: 311–17, 330–32; Kaplow and Shavell 2002; Korah 2000: 11–12, 35; Panel Discussion 1998: 482; Peritz 1989; Polinsky 1989: 7; Posner 1976: 18–22; Stelzer 2002; Van den Bergh and Camesasca 2001: 253–4; Williamson 1968a: 21–3, 27–9; 1968b: 1372–3; 1969a; 1977: 711), *contra* Ahdar (2002: 345–7) and Hughes (1994: 280–81).
51.   Hausman and McPherson (1996: 93–9), Polinsky (1989: 7–10), Posner (1981: 91) and Jacobs (1995: 230).
52.   Harberger (1971: 785–7) actually claim that, though distributional consequences matter, they are either too complex for economics to consider, or involve more issues than economists are competent to consider through economics alone.
53.   Kaldor (1939: 550), Bork (1965: 839), Kaplow and Shavell (2002), Polinsky (1989: 119–30), *contra* Feldman (1971), Collins (1984: 512–15) and Markovits (1975: 988–9). On distortions caused by redistribution see Harberger (1978), Layard (1980), Squire (1980), Harberger (1980).
54.   Faull and Nikpay (1999: para. 2.154–2.156), Van den Bergh and Camesasca (2001: 208), Jones and Sufrin (2001: 196), Stelzer (2002: 27), Morris (2002: 17).
55.   Morris (2002: 15–18), Yarrow (2002: 2–3), Schaub (1998: 125–6).

## References

Adams, Walter (1953), 'Competition, monopoly and countervailing power', *Quart J Econ*, **67**, 469–92.
Aghion, Philippe and Peter Howitt (1992), 'A model of growth through creative destruction', *Econometrica*, **60**, 323–51.
Ahdar, Rex (2002), 'Consumers, redistribution of income and the purpose of competition law', *ECLR*, **23**, 341–53.
Amato, Guiliano (1997), *Antitrust and the Bounds of Power: The Dilemma of Liberal Democracy in the History of the Market*, Oxford: Hart.
American Bar Association (Antitrust Section) and James E. Hartley (chairman) (1999), *Monograph No. 23: The Rule of Reason*, Chicago: ABA Section of Antitrust Law.
Areeda, Phillip (1986), 'The rule of reason – a catechism on competition', *Antitrust LJ*, **55**, 571–89.
Arthur, Thomas C. (1994), 'The costly quest for perfect competition: Kodak and nonstructural market power', *NYU L Rev*, **69**, 1–76.
Bainbridge, David (1999), *Intellectual Property*, 4th edn, London: Pitman.
Bator, Francis M. (1957), 'The simple analytics of welfare maximization', *Amer Econ Rev*, **47**, 22–59.
Begg, David, Stanley Fischer and Rudiger Dornbusch (1997), *Economics*, 5th edn, Maidenhead: McGraw-Hill.

Blair, Roger D. and David L. Kaserman (1985), *Antitrust Economics*, Homewood, Illinois: Richard D. Irwin.

Boarman, Patrick M. (1963), *Union Monopolies and Antitrust Restraints*, Washington, DC: Labor Policy Association.

Boni, Stefano and Pietro Manzini (2001), 'National social legislation and EC antitrust law', *W Comp*, **24**, 239–56.

Bork, R.H. (1965), 'The rule of reason and the per se concept: price fixing and market division, I', *Yale LJ*, **74**, 775–847.

Bork, Robert H. (1993), *The Antitrust Paradox: A Policy at War with Itself*, New York: Free Press.

Calvani, Terry (1989), 'Rectangles & triangles: a response to Mr Lande', *Antitrust LJ*, **58**, 657–9.

Carlton, Dennis W. and Jeffrey M. Perloff (2000), *Modern Industrial Organization*, 3rd edn, Harlow: Addison-Wesley.

Carlton, Dennis W. Gustavo E. Bamberger and Roy J. Epstein (1995), 'Antitrust and higher education: was there a conspiracy to restrict financial aid', *RAND J Econ*, **26**, 131–47.

Castañeda, Gabriel (1998), 'Competition policy objectives', in Claus Dieter Ehlermann and Laraine L. Laudati (eds), *European Competition Law Annual 1997: The Objectives of Competition Policy*, Oxford: Hart, pp. 41–52.

Chamberlin, Edward H. (1948), 'Proportionality, divisibility and economies of scale', *Quart J Econ*, **62**, 229–62.

Clarkson, Kenneth W. and Roger LeRoy Miller (1982), *Industrial Organization: Theory, Evidence, and Public Policy*, New York: McGraw-Hill.

Collins, Wayne D. (1984), 'Efficiency and equity in vertical competition law: balancing the tensions in the EEC and the United States', in Barry E. Hawk (ed.), *Annual Proceedings of the Fordham Corporate Law Institute: International Antitrust Law & Policy 1983*, New York: Transnational Juris, pp. 501–27.

Collins, Wayne D. (1999), 'California Dental Association and the future of the rule of reason analysis', *Antitrust*, **14**, 54–62.

Cornish, W.R. (1996), *Intellectual Property*, 3rd edn, London: Sweet & Maxwell.

Cox, Archibald (1955), 'Labour and the Antitrust Laws – a preliminary analysis', *U Pa L Rev*, **104**, 252–84.

Dalton, James A. and Stanford L. Levin (1973), 'Allocative and distributive effects of monopoly', in James A. Dalton and Stanford L. Levin (eds), *The Antitrust Dilemma*, Lexington, Massachusetts: Lexington Books.

DePrano, Michael E. and Jeffrey B. Nudent (1969), 'Economies as an antitrust defense', *Amer Econ Rev*, **59**, 947–53.

Dibadj, Reza (2004), 'Saving Antitrust', *University of Colorado Law Review*, **75**, 745–862.

Diwan, Romesh K. (1966), 'Alternative specifications of economies of scale', *Economica*, **33**, 442–53.

Dobson, Paul W. and Michael Waterson (1996), *Vertical Restraints and Competition Policy*, London: Office of Fair Trading.

Dutton, Harold Irvin (1984), *The Patent System and Inventive Activity During the Industrial Revolution 1750–1852*, Manchester: Manchester University Press.

Economist (2000a), 'Spaghetti Monti', 7 October, *Economist*, 129.

Economist (2000b), 'Bill Rockefeller?', 29 April, *Economist*, 16.

Economist (2000c), 'The New Enforcers', 7 October, *Economist*, 125–30.

Economist (2001), 'Copyrights and Wrongs', 28 April, *Economist*, 82–3.

Economist (2002), 'The growth machine', 18 May, *Economist*, 74.

Elzinga, Kenneth G. (1977), 'The goals of antitrust: other than competition and efficiency, what else counts?', *U Pa L Rev*, **125**, 1191–213.

Faull, Jonathan and Ali Nikpay (eds)(1999), *Faull & Nikpay: The EC Law of Competition*, Oxford: Oxford University Press.

Feldman, Paul (1971), 'Efficiency, distribution, and the role of government in a market economy', *J Polit Economy*, **79**, 508–26.

Fels, Allan and Geoff Edwards (1998), 'Competition policy objectices', in Claus Dieter Ehlermann and Laraine L. Laudati (eds), *European Competition Law Annual 1997: The Objectives of Competition Policy*, Oxford: Hart, pp. 53–65.
Frantz, Roger S. (1988), *X-Efficiency: Theory, Evidence and Applications*, Boston: Kluwer.
Frantz, Roger (1992), 'X-efficiency and allocative efficiency: what have we learned?', *Amer Econ Rev*, **82**, 434–8.
Galbraith, John Kenneth (2004), *The Economics of Innocent Fraud: Truth for Our Time*, London: Penguin.
Gellhorn, Ernest, William E. Kovacic and Stephen Calkins (2004), *Antitrust Law and Economics in a Nutshell*, 5th edn, St. Paul, MN: West.
Goyder, Dan (1993), 'User-friendly competition law', in Piet Jan Slot and Alison McDonnell (eds), *Procedure and Enforcement in EC and US Competition Law*, London: Sweet & Maxwell, pp. 1–5.
Gyselen, Luc (2002), 'The substantive legality test under Article 81(3) EC Treaty – revisited in light of the Commission's modernization initiative' in Armin von Bogdandy, Petros C. Mavroidis and Yves Mény (eds), *European Integration and International Co-Ordination: Studies in Transnational Economic Law in Honour of Claus-Dieter Ehlermann*, The Hague: Kluwer Law International, pp. 181–97.
Hamilton, Clive (2004), *Growth Fetish*, London: Pluto.
Harberger, Arnold C. (1971), 'Three basic postulates for applied welfare economics: an interpretive essay', *J Econ Lit*, **9**, 785–97.
Harberger, Arnold C. (1978), 'On the use of distributional weights in social cost–benefit analysis', *J Polit Economy*, **86**, S87–S120.
Harberger, Arnold C. (1980), 'Reply to Layard and Squire', *J Polit Economy*, **88**, 1050–52.
Hatzopoulos, Vassilis G. (2002), 'Killing national health and insurance systems but healing patients? The European market for health care services after the judgments of the ECJ in Vanbraekel and Peerbooms', *CML Rev*, **39**, 683–729.
Hausman, Daniel M. and Michael S. McPherson (1996), *Economic Analysis and Moral Philosophy*, Cambridge: Cambridge University Press.
Helleiner, Karl F. (1951), 'Moral conditions of economic growth', *Journal of Economic History*, **11**, 97–116.
Hicks, J.R. (1935), 'Annual survey of economic theory: the theory of monopoly', *Econometrica*, **3**, 1–20.
Hildebrand, Doris (1998), *The Role of Economic Analysis in the EC Competition Rules*, The Hague: Kluwer Law International.
Hildebrand, Doris (2002), 'The European school in EC competition law', *W Comp*, **25**, 3–23.
Hovenkamp, Herbert (1982), 'Distributive justice and the antitrust laws', *Geo Wash L Rev*, **51**, 1–31.
Hughes, Edwin J. (1994), 'The left side of antitrust: what fairness means and why it matters', *Marq L Rev*, **77**, 265–306.
Hunter, Alex (1958), 'Notes on countervailing power', *Econ J*, **68**, 89–103.
Hylton, Keith N. (2003), *Antitrust Law: Economic Theory and Common Law Evolution*, Cambridge: Cambridge University Press.
Jacobs, Michael S. (1995), 'An essay on the normative foundations of antitrust economics', *NC L Rev*, **74**, 219–66.
Jones, Alison and Brenda Sufrin (2001), *EC Competition Law: Text, Cases, and Materials*, Oxford: Oxford University Press.
Jones, Alison and Brenda Sufrin (2004), *EC Competition Law: Text, Cases, and Materials*, 2nd edn, Oxford: Oxford University Press.
Jones, Charles I. (1998), *Introduction to Economic Growth*, London: W.W. Norton.
Kaldor, Nicholas (1939), 'Welfare propositions of economics and interpersonal comparisons of utility', *Econ J*, **49**, 549–52.
Kaplow, Louis and Steven Shavell (2002), *Fairness Versus Welfare*, London: Harvard University Press.
Kaysen, Carl and Donald F. Turner (1959), *Antitrust Policy: An Economic and Legal Analysis*, Cambridge, Mass.: Harvard University Press.

Kendrick, John W. (1977), *Understanding Productivity: An Introduction to the Dynamics of Productivity Change*, Baltimore: Johns Hopkins University Press.

Komninos, Assimakis P. (2002), 'New prospects for private enforcement of EC competition law: Courage v. Crehan and the community right to damages', *CML Rev*, **39**, 447–87.

Korah, Valentine (2000), *An Introductory Guide to EC Competition Law and Practice*, 7th edn, Oxford: Hart.

Lande, Robert H. (1982), 'Wealth transfers as the original and primary concern of antitrust: the efficiency interpretation challenged', *Hastings LJ*, **65**, 65–151.

Lande, Robert H. (1989), 'Chicago's false foundation: wealth transfers (not just efficiency) should guide antitrust', *Antitrust LJ*, **58**, 631–44.

Layard, Richard (1980), 'On the use of distributional weights in social cost–benefit analysis', *J Polit Economy*, **88**, 1041–7.

Leibenstein, Harvey (1966), 'Allocative efficiency vs "X-efficiency"', *Amer Econ Rev*, **56**, 392–415.

Leibenstein, Harvey (1988), 'Foreword', in Roger S. Frantz (ed.), *X-Efficiency: Theory, Evidence and Applications*, Boston: Kluwer.

Lerner, A.P. (1934), 'The concept of monopoly and the measurement of monopoly power', *Rev Econ Stud*, **1**, 157–75.

Letwin, William (1981), *Law and Economic Policy in America: The Evolution of the Sherman Antitrust Act*, Phoenix edn, Chicago: University of Chicago Press.

Lipsey, Richard G., Paul N. Courant, Douglas D. Purvis and Peter O. Steiner (1993), *Economics*, 10th edn, New York: HarperCollins College Publishers.

Louri, Victoria (2002), ' "Undertaking" as a jurisdictional element for the application of EC competition rules', *LIEI*, **29**, 143–76.

Manzini, Pietro (2002), 'The European rule of reason–crossing the sea of doubt', *ECLR*, **23**, 392–9.

Markovits, Richard S. (1975), 'A basic structure from microeconomic policy analysis in our worse-than-second-best world: a proposal and related critique of the Chicago approach to the study of law and economics', *Wis L Rev*, 950–1080.

Menendez, Augustin Jose (2003), 'The sinews of peace: rights to solidarity in the Charter of Fundamental Rights of the European Union', *Ratio Juris*, **16**, 374–98.

Monti, Giorgio (2002), 'Article 81 EC and public policy', *CML Rev*, **39**, 1057–99.

Morris, Derek (2002), 'The Enterprise Act: aspects of the new regime', *Economic Affairs*, **22**, 15–24.

Motta, Massimo (2004), *Competition Policy: Theory and Practice*, Cambridge: Cambridge University Press.

Neale, A.D. and D.G. Goyder (1980), *The Antitrust Laws of the United States of America: A Study of Competition Enforced by Law*, 3rd edn, Cambridge: Cambridge University Press.

Nelson, Richard R. and Sidney G. Winter (1982), 'The Schumpeterian tradeoff revisited', *Amer Econ Rev*, **72**, 114–32.

Panel Discussion (1998), 'Future Competition Law', in Claus Dieter Ehlermann and Laraine L. Laudati (eds), *European Competition Law Annual 1997: The Objectives of Competition Policy*, Oxford: Hart Publishing, pp. 459–92.

Panzar, John C. and Robert D. Willig (1981), 'Economies of scope', *Amer Econ Rev*, **71**, 268–72.

Peritz, Rudolph J. (1989), 'The "rule of reason" in antitrust law: property logic in restraint of competition', *Hastings LJ*, **40**, 285–342.

Peter M. Roth (ed.) (2001), *Bellamy & Child: European Community Law of Competition*, 5th edn, London: Sweet & Maxwell.

Pitofsky, Robert (1995), 'Antitrust modified: education, defense, and other worthy enterprises', *Antitrust*, **9**, 23–5.

Polinsky, A. Mitchell (1989), *An Introduction to Law and Economics*, 2nd edn, Boston: Little, Brown.

Porter, Michael E. (2001), 'Competition and antitrust: toward a productivity-based approach to evaluating mergers and joint ventures', *Antitrust Bull*, **46**, 919–57.

Posner, Richard A. (1976), *Antitrust Law: An Economic Perspective*, Chicago: University of Chicago Press.
Posner, Richard A. (1981), *The Economics of Justice*, Cambridge, Mass.: Harvard University Press.
Posner, Richard A. (1986), *Economic Analysis of Law*, 3rd edn, Boston: Little, Brown.
Posner, Richard A. and Frank H. Easterbrook (1981), *Antitrust: Cases, Economic Notes, and Other Materials*, 2nd edn, St. Paul, Minn.: West.
Prosser, Tony (2005), *The Limits of Competition Law: Markets and Public Services*, Oxford: Oxford University Press.
Rapp, Richard T. (1995), 'The misapplication of the innovation market approach to merger analysis', *Antitrust LJ*, **64**, 19–47.
Reich, Norbert (2005), 'The "courage" doctrine encouraging or discouraging compensation for antitrust injuries?', *CML Rev*, **42**, 35–66.
Romer, Paul M. (1986), 'Increasing returns and long-run growth', *J Polit Economy*, **94**, 1002–37.
Salop, Steven C. and Lawrence J. White (1991), 'Policy watch: antitrust goes to college', *J Econ Perspect*, **5**, 193–202.
Schaub, Alexander (1998), 'Competition policy objectives', in Claus Dieter Ehlermann and Laraine L. Laudati (eds), *European Competition Law Annual 1997: The Objectives of Competition Policy*, Oxford: Hart, pp. 119–28.
Scherer, F.M. (1987), 'Antitrust, efficiency, and progress', *NYU L Rev*, **62**, 998–1019.
Scherer, F.M. (1992), 'Schumpeter and plausible capitalism', *J Econ Lit*, **30**, 1416–33.
Scherer, F.M. and David Ross (1990), *Industrial Market Structure and Economic Performance*, 3rd edn, Houghton Mifflin.
Schumpeter, Joseph A. (1975), *Capitalism, Socialism and Democracy*, 1st Harper Colophon edn, with a new introduction by Tom Bottomore, New York: Harper & Row.
Silberston, Aubrey (1972), 'Economies of scale in theory and practice', *Econ J*, **82**, 369–91.
Spaventa, Eleanor (2004), 'Public services and European law: looking for boundaries', in John Bell and Alan Dashwood (eds), *Cambridge Yearbook of European Legal Studies 2003*, Oxford: Hart, pp. 271–91.
Squire, Lyn (1980), 'On the use of distributional weights in social cost–benefit analysis', *J Polit Economy*, **88**, 1048–9.
Stelzer, Irwin M. (2002), 'Innovation, price competition and the "Tilt" of competition policy', *Economic Affairs*, **22**, 25–31.
Stigler, George J. (1971), 'The theory of economic regulation', **2**, *The Bell Journal of Economics and Management Science*, 3–21.
Stigler, George J. (1976), 'The xistence of X-efficiency', *Amer Econ Rev*, **66**, 213–16.
Sullivan, E. Thomas and Herbert Hovenkamp (2003), *Antitrust Law, Policy and Procedure: Cases, Materials, Problems*, 5th edn, Charlottesville, Va.: LexisNexis.
Van den Bergh, Roger J. and Peter D. Camesasca (2000), 'Irreconcilable principles? The Court of Justice exempts collective labour agreements from the wrath of antitrust', *ELRev*, **25**, 492–508.
Van den Bergh, Roger J. and Peter D. Camesasca (2001), *European Competition Law and Economics: A Comparative Perspective*, Antwerp: Intersentia.
Vickers, John (1995), 'Concepts of competition', *Oxford Econ Pap*, **47**, 1–23.
Viscusi, W. Kip, John M. Vernon, and Joseph E. Harrington Jr. (2000), *Economics of Regulation and Antitrust*, 3rd edn, Cambridge, Mass.: MIT Press.
Weisskopf, Walter A. (1965), 'Economic growth versus existential balance', *Ethics*, **75**, 77–86.
Wesseling, Rein (2001), 'The draft-regulation modernising the competition rules: the commission is married to one idea', *ELRev*, **26**, 357–78.
Whish, Richard (2001), *Competition Law*, 4th edn, London: Butterworths.
Whish, Richard (2003), *Competition Law*, 5th edn, London: Butterworths.
Williamson, Oliver E. (1968a), 'Economies as an antitrust defense: the welfare tradeoffs', *Amer Econ Rev*, **58**, 18–36.
Williamson, Oliver E. (1968b), 'Economies as an antitrust defense: correction and reply', *Amer Econ Rev*, **58**, 1372–6.

Williamson, Oliver E. (1969a), 'Economies as an antitrust defense: reply', *Amer Econ Rev*, **59**, 954–9.
Williamson, Oliver E. (1969b), 'Allocative efficiency and the limits of antitrust', *Amer Econ Rev*, **59**, 105–18.
Williamson, Oliver E. (1977), 'Economies as an antitrust defense revisited', *U Pa L Rev*, **125**, 699–735.
Winterstein, Alexander (1999), 'Nailing the jellyfish: social security and competition law', *ECLR*, **20**, 324–33.
Wolf, Dieter (1998), 'Competition policy objectives', in Claus Dieter Ehlermann and Laraine L. Laudati (eds), *European Competition Law Annual 1997: The Objectives of Competition Policy*, Oxford: Hart, pp. 129–32.
Yarrow, George (2002), 'Competition policy: its purposes and scope', *Economic Affairs*, **22**, 2–4.

### Cases

*Albany International BV* v. *Stichting Bedrijfspensioenfonds Textielindustrie*, [1999] ECR I-5751.
*AOK Bundesverband* v. *Ichthyol-Gesellschaft Cordes*, [2003] ECR I 2493*Brown* v. *Pro Football* 518 US 231 (1996).
*Bettercare Group Limited* v. *the Director General of Fair Trading*, [2002] CAT 7.
*Bodson* v. *Pompes Funèbres des Régions Libérées SA*, [1988] ECR 2479.
*Canada (Commissioner of Competition)* v. *Superior Propane Inc. and ICG Propane Inc.*, [2001] Carswell National 702.
*Christian Poucet* v. *Assurances Générales de France (AGF) and Caisse Mutuelle Régionale Du Languedoc-Roussillon (Camulrac) and Daniel Pistre* v. *Caisse Autonome Nationale de Compensation de L' Assurance Vieillesse des Artisans (Cancava)*, [1993] ECR I-637.
*Connell Construction Co* v. *Plumbers Local* 100 421 US 616 (1975).
*Établissements Consten Sàrl and Grundig-Verkaufs-GmbH* v. *Commission*, [1966] ECR 299.
*Federal Trade Commission* v. *Morton Salt Co*, [1948] 334 US 37.
*Ford/Volkswagen* OJ 1993 L 20/14.
*National Society of Professional Engineers* v. *United States*, [1978] 435 US 679.
*Sodemare SA* v. *Regione Lombardia*, [1997] ECR I-3395.
*United Brands* v. *Commission*, [1978] ECR 207.
*United States* v. *Brown University*, [1993] 5 F 3d 658.
*United States* v. *Debs* 64 Fed 724 (1894).
*United States* v. *Hutcheson*, [1941] 312 US 219.

# 24 Merger control and cross-border transactions: a pragmatic view on cooperation, convergence and what is in between
*Ariel Ezrachi*[1]

## Introduction
Cross-border merger control has traditionally been a difficult subject for multilateral cooperation, let alone harmonization. The multitude of interests at stake and the heterogeneous multilateral environment mean that attempts to reduce inefficiencies stemming from multijurisdictional merger review face resistance at various levels. This chapter examines the domestic nature of merger control and how it affects the feasibility and effectiveness of cooperation and convergence in merger regulation. It explores the role of bilateral and multilateral initiatives in merger control and identifies their limits. In doing so, the discussion echoes the challenges for undertakings and agencies operating in the current suboptimal environment of multiple enforcers and the difficulty of resolving present inefficiencies.

## When national (merger control) meets international (business)
The friction generated by the misfit between national merger control and cross-border economic activity has long been recognized. Although globalization processes have strongly influenced national economies and brought them closer to interdependence, the impact of globalization did not lead to similar results in merger review.

This tension is mostly felt at two levels. At the agencies' level it may result in 'system friction'.[2] As each competition agency conducts its independent analysis the simultaneous application of numerous domestic merger regimes to a single transaction may lead to conflicting decisions and remedies. This is even more pronounced when competition agencies apply different laws, different economic models or involve domestic 'industrial' considerations in the decision. In these cases, even when the transaction has similar effects in all jurisdictions, the agencies may reach inconsistent decisions.

At the undertakings' level, the multitude of merger regimes appraising the same transaction generate costs and uncertainty. The proliferation of merger regimes operating worldwide is a welcome product of states' understanding the significance of monitoring transactions, yet it has resulted in marked overregulation and led to a reduction in legal and business certainty. Undertakings are required to identify the relevant jurisdictions and engage in multiple filings and are subject to an array of different regulations. It has become routine for the merging parties of large transactions to submit numerous notifications and to go through multiple investigation procedures, losing predictability that is so valuable to all commercial transactions.[3] In practice the most rigorous jurisdiction which reviews the transaction determines, de facto, the level of burden on the undertakings.[4] When the nexus between the transaction's effect and the reviewing jurisdiction is limited, the unnecessary overscrutiny results in significant inefficiencies.[5]

Faced with these suboptimal effects and in the wake of increased merger activity, the international community sprang into action, attempting to resolve the friction or at least relax it.[6] Yet the heterogeneous nature of the multilateral arena characterized by distinct economic, social and legal policy differences made some initiatives in merger control difficult to advance. Two complementary and interdependent variables should be observed when discussing these initiatives. First, the legal nature of the provisions should be noted. Agreements may include binding provisions or provide voluntary guidelines and they may involve detailed regulation or reflect a minimal approach focusing only on core principles. Second, the scope of membership should be considered. The number of states subscribing to an agreement or joining an initiative is central to its success and its impact on the global arena.

In the domestically oriented area of merger control these two variables tend to cancel each other out. The multitude of incentives and domestic considerations make it difficult to advance an inclusive system with detailed binding provisions. In most cases, owing to negotiation difficulties, an increase in the number of participants dilutes the substance of the agreement. Consequently a move from a multilateral arrangement to a focused multilateral, regional or bilateral agreement may facilitate finding common ground and achieving a binding understanding. Yet these efforts may have a limited impact at the wider multilateral level. Additionally they may lead to fragmentation or result in incompatibility between the regional efforts and wider multilateral agreements.[7]

Several factors may contribute to the difficulty of negotiating a wide membership agreement on multijurisdictional merger review. Naturally, different states may have different views on the role and purpose of competition law and the type of regulation it necessitates. This is especially noticeable when considering the different approaches of developing and developed countries in negotiating such agreements.[8]

Other factors may be traced to domestic considerations which may affect the willingness of states to cooperate. Sovereignty and control over the domestic market are two of the most prominent considerations in this respect. In essence, states are less likely to favour an agreement which would undermine their ability to freely determine the outcome of the merger assessment or to advance domestic non-competition, industrial considerations in their appraisal. Non-competition considerations may include industrial factors used to protect the national market from foreign transactions or strengthen it by not prohibiting an otherwise anticompetitive domestic transaction. They may include a wish to create a 'national champion' or protect domestic industry. They may promote the creation of new local employment opportunities, or they may be aimed at increasing domestic welfare. In the multilateral scene these tend to reduce transparency and legal certainty and increase the likelihood of friction, yet national jurisdictions may refuse to wave the power to consider domestic elements and may therefore oppose joining a framework that would deprive them of such flexibility.

The 'balance of powers' between states may also play a role in their approach toward negotiation. For example, extraterritorial policies may affect the willingness of jurisdictions to join a multilateral effort.[9] States that operate a successful extraterritorial regime may not be inclined to join a wide multilateral agreement on merger control and would arguably favour a more selective form of agreement. These jurisdictions may be able to protect their domestic market through unilateral action without the concessions associated with cooperative agreement with a wide membership. Extraterritoriality may provide them with a protective tool to block remote transactions that affect their local market. The costs of such extraterritoriality are mainly felt by foreign undertakings that are subject to additional notifications and associated costs. This burden may not generate much concern for the appraising jurisdiction as it may be less troubled about costs applied to foreign firms.

Linked to this is the use of extraterritoriality as a vehicle to transfer wealth from consumers and undertakings in one jurisdiction to another.[10] Competition restraints often transfer wealth from consumers to undertakings while reducing economic efficiency. When embedded in a multilateral scene, restraints frequently transfer wealth from consumers in one country to owners and producers in another.[11] While a given jurisdiction may strive to protect its local market from a negative transfer of wealth, the other jurisdiction receiving the positive transfer of wealth caused by the anticompetitive behaviour of local corporations may be reluctant to act against such behaviour. Subsequently nations may lack the incentive to regulate activities which create externalities felt elsewhere. For the same reason, they may disfavour a wide multilateral agreement that would deprive them of these benefits through unilateral action.[12]

Overall this multitude of interests leads to conflicting views on the necessity of agreement. Similarly it results in different views on whether such agreement should aim at full harmonization, convergence or more limited coordination and cooperation. This friction has meant that the binding multilateral level, despite theoretically being the most adequate to advance initiatives on merger control,[13] is at present too fragmented to provide relief. Several failed attempts of the international community to advance binding agreements on competition law reflect this situation. From the Havana Charter,[14] to the Munich group initiative[15] and to attempts in negotiations at the World Trade Organization,[16] the international community was unable to reach meaningful binding agreements on competition law and policy. Merger control, being more domestically oriented and complex, has traditionally been left out of these binding attempts.[17] Indeed the sensitivity of merger control, its direct influence on market structure, economic state and consumer welfare make it an unlikely candidate for a binding multilateral agreement.[18]

The heterogeneous environment of multilateral merger control dictates a balance point that differs from an optimal wide membership binding arrangement. Similarly it implies that proposals for a supranational merger agency or a multilateral code are not viable. Difficulty in negotiating a binding framework on merger control shifts the emphasis to two complementary dimensions. At the wide multilateral level, non-binding, voluntary arrangements were found to provide a useful vehicle to advance cooperation and convergence in merger control. At the bilateral and regional levels, selective binding bilateral or focused multilateral agreements between states which share commonality of interests provided useful platforms for high-volume cooperation. Although in theory both are inferior to a binding multilateral agreement, these currently provide the main vehicles to advance convergence and cooperation in merger control.

Looking back at the two interdependent variables, of the legal nature of the agreement's provisions and the agreement's membership, it is easy to see the strengths and weaknesses of each of these approaches. The binding bilateral agreement, although likely to facilitate high-quality cooperation, extends only to two jurisdictions. On the other hand, the multilateral non-binding framework, although including numerous participants, involves voluntary provisions and may fail to result in wide compliance. In what follows, we assess the contribution of these two vehicles to the global environment of merger control.

**Non-binding multilateral initiatives**
The complexity of achieving a multilateral harmonized system for merger control serves as the fuel for the adoption of non-binding recommendations. The striking benefit of voluntary frameworks is their inclusiveness. 'Soft law' initiatives enable more jurisdictions to take part in the development and consideration of guidelines without undermining their sovereignty. Voluntary initiatives bypass the difficulties associated with binding frameworks and allow jurisdictions to reflect jointly on the law and procedure surrounding merger control and their impact at the national and multilateral level.

On the other hand, the limits of voluntary frameworks lie in the difficulty of transforming general non-binding guidelines into actions. At the implementation stage, voluntary frameworks may face resistance similar to that of binding frameworks. Selective implementation echoes the difficulties in achieving meaningful agreement at the multilateral level. The roots of this selectiveness may vary. Some states may disagree with the legal merit of the provisions. Others may not see the merit in converging toward the agreed benchmark. This may be the case when, for example, the proposed guidelines override domestic interests or undermine the sovereignty of the state. On a practical level, difficulties in implementation may also hinder compliance. In general, recommendations which may be adopted within the existing legal framework may be easier to implement than more fundamental changes which affect the domestic regulation. In this respect it is worth noting that procedural differences which may seem easy to assimilate may in fact reflect different administrative or judicial regimes and may be difficult to bridge over. [19]

With this theoretical background in mind it is interesting to review the recent non-binding multilateral initiatives. Three forums in particular have dominated the multilateral scene, advancing non-binding guidelines and frameworks in competition law. These are the United Nations Conference on Trade and Development (UNCTAD), the Organisation for Economic Cooperation and Development (OECD) and the International Competition Network (ICN). In the area of cross-border merger control, most noticeable are efforts undertaken by the OECD and ICN.[20]

Since its inception in 2001, the ICN has provided a significant contribution in the area of cross-border merger control. The network and its activities emerged out of an understanding that competition authorities and specialists working together could best promote effective competition in a global environment.[21] Members of the ICN are national and multilateral competition agencies that are joined by representatives from the private sector.[22] The composition of the ICN, the work at the agencies' level and the voluntary nature of the recommendations relax some of the difficulties associated with binding multilateral agreements and allow a wide membership on a professional, rather than a political basis. Additionally the flexibility of the network and its focus on working groups permits 'frequent, informal and low cost interaction which can produce concrete results far more quickly than the periodic formal meetings that have characterised the work of more traditional international organizations in the past'.[23]

In the area of merger control the ICN merger working group has engaged in extensive work aimed at promoting guidelines on best practices in the design and operation of merger review. These initiatives are aimed, among others, at facilitating procedural and substantive convergence between jurisdictions and reducing costs and inefficiencies stemming from multijurisdictional merger reviews. The working group, through various subgroups, has developed a range of guidelines and recommended practices. These include, amongst others, Guiding Principles and Recommended Practices for Merger Notification and Review Procedures, Recommended Practices for Merger Notification and Review Processes, Recommended Practices on Remedies and Competition Agency Powers, and discussion papers on Waivers of Confidentiality and Merger Notification Filing Fees.

The work of the ICN led to consensus that arguably would not have been achieved through a binding framework. The contribution of these studies and recommendations is noticeable; the discussion which accompanies them stimulates interaction between different jurisdictions and improves understanding between agencies. Similarly the common voluntary guidelines have significance in the long run as they provide a norm-generating vehicle and a valuable benchmark which agencies can relate to and gradually assimilate into their national regimes.[24] These developments are significant at both the substantive and the procedural levels as they reduce likelihood for conflicting decisions and remedies and contribute to reducing costs and inefficiencies stemming from multijurisdictional merger reviews and notifications.[25]

Beyond the benefit which stems from the interaction between competition agencies, the question of compliance with recommended guidelines is a key to the success of the ICN's activities. A report on the Implementation of the ICN Recommended Practices for Merger Notification and Review Processes was presented at the Fourth Annual ICN Conference which took place in June 2005 (ICN Report).[26] The ICN Report, based on interviews with officials and members of the private sector in 27 jurisdictions reviewed the implementation of guidelines by members and set out recommendations to facilitate compliance. The study highlighted the contribution of the guidelines as a benchmark for competition agencies and a catalyst for change.[27] It additionally underlined the role of all stakeholders, including the agencies, the practitioners and academics in promoting implementation and building consensus. Implementation may be selective and at times difficult, yet the ICN supported by the OECD and other stakeholders, has placed emphasis on devoting resources to promoting successful compliance. Reportedly a large number of ICN members appear to be taking steps to implement the recommended practices for merger notification and review processes: 'As of April 2005, 46% of ICN member jurisdictions with merger laws have made or have proposed changes that bring their merger regimes into closer conformity with the Recommended Practices; an additional 8% are planning to make such changes'.[28]

Evaluating implementation may not always be easy and perceived compliance rates may differ between the private sector and competition agencies.[29] Similarly compliance by some regimes may be the result of their being successful in promoting their domestic regime as the agreed benchmark rather than a willingness on their behalf to conform to agreed principles. Still the encouraging report from the ICN highlights willingness to move toward common principles. Illustrative in this respect are comments made by the Chairman of the Australian Competition and Consumer Commission, Graeme Samuel. Announcing changes to the Australian Competition and Consumer Commission's informal merger clearance guidelines, the Chairman stressed that the new guidelines are underpinned by the ICN Recommended Practices and Guiding Principles for Merger Reviews: 'we acknowledge our own practices must measure up to the world's best practice, as spelled out in the ICN recommendations. To that end we are in the process of developing additional guidelines that address the ICN recommendations'.[30]

The work of the ICN adds to existing activities of the Organisation for Economic Cooperation and Development which has been promoting nonbinding recommendations in the area of competition policy for many years.[31] Through its Committee on Competition Law and Policy, the OECD has pursued international cooperation and convergence since the 1960s.[32] In addition, since 1991, the OECD Global Forum on Competition has provided an inclusive venue for wide membership discussion and further increased the OECD's contribution in fostering convergence in both developed and developing countries.[33]

In the area of merger control the OECD has engaged in developing voluntary tools and recommendations. In 1999, the OECD released a Report on Notification of Transnational Mergers, which included a nonbinding common filing form to assist in notifying transnational mergers.[34] The report partially implemented recommendations of the Whish and Wood study published by the OECD in 1994. This study examined merger control procedures and provided several recommendations to facilitate multijurisdictional merger review. Among them were the utilization of a common filing form with common information requirements and the convergence of time periods for appraisal of transactions.[35] In 2005, the OECD issued a set of Recommendations on Merger Review.[36] The recommendations included reference to the work conducted by the ICN and are in conformity with its Recommended Practices for Merger Notification and Review Processes. In addition to the work on merger notification and review, the OECD fostered debate on a range of subjects, including portfolio effects in conglomerate mergers,[37] merger remedies,[38] media mergers,[39] and merger review in emerging high innovation markets.[40]

Beyond the contribution of the debate within the OECD to stimulating discussion and cross-fertilization and the benefits stemming from the OECD peer review process,[41] work of the OECD in the area of merger control was reported to contribute to the initiating and shaping of merger reform efforts in Brazil, Canada, Mexico and Poland.[42] Additionally, work conducted at the OECD helped the development of the ICN Recommended Practices for Merger Notification and Review Processes.[43]

Without underestimating the significant contribution of the ICN and OECD activities to fostering convergence of thought and analysis and providing a valuable forum for interaction between different jurisdictions, it is worth noting again that the success of each voluntary initiative depends on a critical mass of members endorsing it. The encouraging ICN report signals a positive development. Nonetheless it only heralds the beginning of a process. The substance of the recommendations adopted, the number of states endorsing them, and the real level of compliance will determine the future impact of these voluntary initiatives.

### Bilateral cooperation in a multilateral setting

Moving from the wide multilateral level to more focused arrangements, it is interesting to consider the contribution of binding bilateral agreements to multijurisdictional merger review.

From a multilateral perspective, bilateral agreements may be regarded as inferior to multilateral frameworks. The focus on a limited number of jurisdictions, although valuable, provides limited relief to cross-border inefficiencies stemming from the multitude of enforcers. However it is precisely the limited membership to the agreement which enables states to reach detailed agreement on competition law and merger control. Countries with similar economic strength and trade patterns, which share similar legal systems and maintain reciprocal trading, will arguably share incentives for cooperation. When the intensity of trade with a potential partner justifies it, bilateral agreements provide a valuable platform for detailed cooperation.[44]

Although in principle the contribution of a bilateral agreement, even a very successful one, in the multilateral scene is limited, some bilateral agreements may generate value beyond their realm. This will be the case when the agreement links two powerful mature regimes which are backed by extraterritorial policies. The unequal distribution of merger transactions and commercial activity across the globe also increases the dominance of some merger regimes. Noticeable are the three economic powers, the United States, the EU and Japan, often referred to as the Triad.[45] For example, of the world's largest 500 multilateral enterprises, more than 80 per cent are based within the Triad.[46] These largest 500 multilateral enterprises account for 90 per cent of the world's foreign direct investments and carry out half of all trade, often in the form of inter-company sales between subsidiaries.[47]

The central position of the United States and the European Union, both in commercial terms and in the application of their competition laws, naturally focuses attention on the cooperation between these two leading jurisdictions and its effects.[48] Virtually any sizeable transaction involving international businesses these days is likely to be subject to review under both the US and EU merger regimes.

The EU/US cooperation in merger control has been remarkable in its effect on cross-border transactions scrutinized by both jurisdictions and has often been referred to by officials from both sides of the Atlantic as a notable success.[49] On a case-by-case level, the close cooperation yields significant efficiencies. It facilitates exchange of information between agencies,[50] coordination of requests for information[51] and coordination of action. The agencies routinely notify each other of current investigations, exchange views on the relevant markets and the impact the transaction may generate and coordinate remedies when appropriate.[52] The close cooperation between the agencies also led to remarkable convergence of thought and analysis and resulted in a high degree of consistency and increased legal certainty for the undertakings involved.[53] The increased convergence between the jurisdictions was also reflected in the reform of the European merger regime which took place in 2004.[54] For example, the substantive test in the revised European Merger Regulation was reworded and extended beyond the concept of 'dominance'.[55] This change narrowed the gap which existed between the US's 'substantial lessening of competition' test[56] and the previous European 'dominance' test and brought the substantive tests in both regimes closer together. Also noteworthy are the Horizontal Merger Guidelines issued by the European Commission as part of the merger reform. The Guidelines too reflect marked convergence in analysis between the two jurisdictions.[57] Additionally the reform of the European merger regime introduced changes to the triggering event for which notification is sought and to the time limits for investigation. These changes introduced greater flexibility to the European procedure and potentially facilitate parallel simultaneous investigation by both US and EU authorities.[58]

As part of their mutual efforts to facilitate coordination, the US Federal Trade Commission, the US Department of Justice and the European Commission issued best practice guidelines on cooperation in merger review.[59] The guidelines outline the methods used by the agencies to facilitate coordination. They are 'intended to promote fully-informed decision-making on the part of both sides' authorities, to minimize the risk of divergent outcomes on both sides of the Atlantic, to facilitate coherence and compatibility in remedies, to enhance the efficiency of their respective investigations, to reduce burdens on merging parties and third parties and to increase the overall transparency of the merger review processes'.[60]

Thanks to the central position held by the EU and US in economic and legal terms, the bilateral cooperation between the two jurisdictions, and the convergence it fostered, generate marked efficiencies in cross-border merger control. Arguably these efficiencies are not restricted to the bilateral level. First, they potentially affect jurisdictions which modelled their laws on either the EU or US regimes.[61] Second, these processes, which bring the EU and US regimes closer together, potentially facilitate negotiations at the multilateral level, in which both jurisdictions set the tone and pace.

Beyond the EU/US relationship, the existence of various bilateral agreements on competition law creates a 'web of agreements'. Such web, although far from a multilateral initiative, facilitates cooperation, discussion and information exchange on a bilateral level, and thus has an overall positive effect on the wider multilateral level.[62]

In order to complete the picture on the contribution of bilateral agreements to the wider multilateral scene, the inherent limits of bilateral cooperation should be noted. First, as mentioned above, the contribution of bilateral agreements is limited as it does not resolve inefficiencies stemming from multiple enforcers in the area of merger control.[63]

Second, some bilateral or regional efforts risk being suboptimal from a global perspective if they promote principles that are potentially incompatible with multilateral agreement or complicate the adoption of multilateral principles in the future.[64] Similarly they may result in externalities or a protectionist approach aimed toward those who do not take part in the agreement.[65]

Third, bilateral agreements coordinate the work of two domestic agencies but do not substitute the independent analysis or harmonize their laws or their appraisal process. Focusing back on the EU/US bilateral agreement, although the cooperation contributes significantly to coordinating the investigation and reducing the risk of divergent decisions, it cannot completely eradicate conflicts and inconsistencies. As parties retain independent analysis and decision making, and as they focus on different markets, conflicts, although relatively infrequent, may be inevitable. A few examples from the successful EU/US cooperation may best exemplify this point.

The General Electric/Honeywell transaction which was reviewed by both EU and US competition agencies is very illustrative in this sense. While closely coordinating their actions, each of the jurisdictions held an independent review and relied on different economic theories in its decision making or at least on different interpretations of theory put into practice.[66] The different approach taken in each of the jurisdictions led to conflicting decisions. The transaction was cleared by the US Department of Justice subject to minimal disposals, but was later blocked by the European Commission which found it to severely reduce competition in the aerospace industry. Commenting on the European Commission *GE/Honeywell* decision, Charles A. James, then Assistant Attorney General for Antitrust, US DOJ, issued a statement backing the DOJ decision and stating that clear and longstanding US antitrust policy holds that the antitrust laws protect competition, not competitors, thus stressing that the EU's more intervention-minded decision reflects a significant point of divergence.[67] The case, although unique in its circumstances, reflects the potential limits of cooperation.[68]

Arguably bilateral cooperation may also fail to eliminate possible divergence flowing from differences in domestic perspectives. Even when the same markets are being reviewed, domestic considerations may find their way into the assessment and lead each jurisdiction to pull in a different direction. Linked to this may be the political debate which at times surrounds high-profile transactions. The Boeing/McDonnell Douglas transaction provides an example of such domestic political intervention.[69] The merger, which sparked much attention and criticism, was actually handled by the US and EU in close cooperation, yet it was accompanied by noticeable political pressure and aggressive lobbying.[70] In the end the transaction was cleared by both the European Commission and the US Federal Trade Commission, but this shows how in an arguably domestic-oriented assessment of a high-profile transaction pure competition analysis may become entwined with political debate despite the existence of close cooperation.[71]

In *Boeing/McDonnell Douglas* both jurisdictions assessed the same global market. Absent domestic considerations or divergence in policies or assessment, such circumstances would in most cases increase the probability of comparable decisions. At the risk of stating the obvious, this will not be the case when the transaction generates different effects on different regional or domestic markets. Dissimilar market realities are likely to trigger different competition concerns and result in different decisions and remedies. In such cases, cooperation between agencies may ease the burdens associated with information requirements and coordination of appraisal, but may not prevent different rulings which stem from different market realities.[72]

Reflecting back on the role of bilateral cooperation in the wider global environment of merger control, it is evident that these agreements, although highly beneficial at the bilateral level, serve only partially to reduce multilateral inefficiencies.[73]

On the positive side, bilateral agreements proximate the work of different jurisdictions, facilitate investigation and information gathering and relax some of the inconsistencies in analysis and procedure. With respect to the unique EU/US cooperation, the benefits of the agreement are noticeable thanks to the high level of commerce and domination of the merger regimes. Additionally processes of convergence between the two jurisdictions have a positive impact on the wider multilateral scene.

On the downside, when faced with significant overlap across multiple jurisdictions, the limitations of bilateral cooperation are clear as such cooperation does not prevent the multiple notifications, the duplicative proceedings and externalities between different jurisdictions.[74] From a multilateral perspective, one may regard bilateral agreements as a supporting vehicle which fosters selective cooperation and convergence between leading agencies, but such vehicle only partially relaxes the inefficiencies present at the multilateral level both for undertakings and for agencies.

**Conclusion**

The domestic nature of merger assessment undermines comprehensive attempts to resolve the friction associated with multijurisdictional merger review. It additionally highlights the inherent limits of cooperation and convergence through bilateral agreements and multilateral voluntary frameworks. These, even when successful, can relax, but not eradicate, the burden felt at undertakings' and agencies' levels.

Looking ahead, voluntary frameworks, although suboptimal, provide the international community with the greatest promise for advancing convergence in the area of multijurisdictional merger control. The current agenda predominantly focuses on non-contentious elements which stand a good chance of being endorsed by a large number of jurisdictions. By its nature, this process is slow and limited and all involved should set their expectations accordingly.

Likely catalysts to these processes are developments at the EU and US fronts. The unique position held by the two jurisdictions, the level of trade between them and their dominant merger regimes enable their bilateral relations to affect nations beyond their direct parties. Increased convergence and agreement between the two would arguably facilitate further dialogue at the multilateral level.

In the meantime the existing costs and uncertainties stemming from multijurisdictional merger review remain. Some of these costs and uncertainties may be unavoidable even with further progress in this field as they are inherent to conducting business in the multijurisdictional realm. Others reflect distinct and avoidable inefficiencies and provide a worthy goal for further convergence.[75]

## Notes

1. Slaughter and May Lecturer in Competition Law, The University of Oxford. Director, Oxford Centre for Competition Law & Policy.
2. On system friction see R. Howse and M.J. Trebilcock (1999), *The Regulation of International Trade*, London: Routledge, p. 467.
3. For example, the Exxon/Mobile transaction was reportedly subjected to merger review requirements in roughly 40 jurisdictions. The Alcan/Pechiney/Algroup transaction triggered 16 merger notifications. Similarly, the Gillette/Wilkinson merger needed to be approved in 14 jurisdictions. These multiple procedures are carried out in different languages and involve notification filing fees and legal and consultancy fees. They involve different procedure and substantive law, different notification requirements and different levels of information.
4. Waller, S.W. (2000), 'Bringing globalism home: lessons from antitrust and beyond', *Loyola University Chicago Law Journal*, **32**, 113, 134.
5. See DOJ International Competition Policy Advisory Committee to the Attorney General and Assistant Attorney General for Antitrust (2000), *Final Report* (ICPAC Report). The ICPAC report referred to most transaction costs imposed by merger regimes as legitimate costs of doing business. However the report highlighted the need to focus on 'unnecessary and burdensome costs that have little or no relationship to antitrust enforcement goals'. See ICPAC Report, above, ch. 3, p. 5.
6. It should be noted that competition law is only one of a range of regulations applicable to cross-border transactions and thus not the sole cause of the dissonance accompanying mergers and acquisitions in a global environment.
7. Sampson, G.P. (1996), 'Compatibility of regional and multilateral trading agreements: reforming the WTO process', *American Economic Review*, pp. 88, 89; Krugman, P. (1991), 'Is bilateralism bad?', in E. Helpman and A. Razin (eds), *International Trade and Trade Policy*, Cambridge, Mass: MIT Press, pp. 9–24; Barrier, M.W. (2000), 'Regionalization: the choice of a new millennium', *Currents: International Trade Law Journal*, 25.
8. See, generally, WTO Working Group on the Interaction between Trade and Competition Policy (2004), WT/WGTCP/W/246; UNCTAD Annual Report 2004 (2005); also see generally Berg, W. and H. Bielesz (2003), 'The WTO and competition: options and perspectives', *Int. T.L.R.*, **9**(4), 94–100.
9. See, generally, Guzman, A.T. (2004), 'The case for international antitrust', in R.A. Epstain and M.S. Greve (eds), *Competition Laws in Conflict, Antitrust Jurisdiction in the Global Economy*, Washington DC: AEI press, p. 99; Guzman, A.T. (2001), 'Antitrust and international regulatory federalism', *New York University Law Review*, **76**, 1148; Guzman, A.T. (2002), 'Choice of law: new foundations', *Geo. L.J.*, **90**, 883.
10. Ezrachi, A. (2002), 'Globalization of merger control: a look at bilateral cooperation through the GE/Honeywell case', *Fla. J. Int'l L.*, **14**, 397.
11. Gerber, D.J. (1999–2000), 'The US–European conflict over the globalization of antitrust law: a legal experience perspective', *New England Law Review*, **34**, 124, 125–6; Guzman, (2004), n 9 above.

12. In the absence of other potential benefits achieved through the proposed framework, it may choose to oppose it. See generally Ezrachi, A. (2004), 'The role of voluntary frameworks in multinational cooperation over merger control', *Geo. Wash. Int'l L. Rev.*, **36**, 433.

13. For a proposal to create a limited international merger control regime in the context of the WTO, see Fiebig, A. (2000), 'A role for the WTO in international merger control', *Nw. J. Int'l L. & Bus.*, **20**, 233.

14. See Ingham, B. (1998), *From ITO to WTO: Trade and Protection in a Changing World*; Moore, L. (1985), *The Growth and Structure of International Trade Since The Second World War*, 42–50; Wilcox, C. (1949), *A Charter for World Trade*, New York: Macmillan Co. pp. 103–13,153–60.

15. The Munich Draft International Antitrust Code; reprinted (1993) in *Antitrust & Trade Regulation Report* 65, No. 1628; Trebilcock, M.J. and R. Howse (1999), *The Regulation of International Trade*, London: Routledge, p. 472.

16. Drexl, J. (2004), 'International competition policy after Cancun: placing a Singapore issue on the WTO development agenda', *W. Comp.*, **27**(3), 419–57; WTO Working Group on the Interaction between Trade and Competition Policy, n. 7, above.

17. Referring to the role of the WTO in advancing agreement on multijurisdictional merger control, Frederic Jenny, chairman of the WTO Working Group, commented that a solution was unlikely to come from a global one-stop-shop run by the WTO. The role of the WTO in this context would be limited to overseeing consistency between regimes and ensuring that merger control was not used for political ends; see Pesola, M. (2001), 'Merger control: the search for harmonisation', *Global Competition Review*, pp. 20, 21, reporting from the IBC conference on International Merger Control, February.

18. On the different approaches toward bilateral and multilateral cooperation, see Wood, D.P. (1999), 'Is cooperation possible?', *New England Law Review*, **34**, 103; Wood, D.P. (1995), 'The internationalization of antitrust law: options for the future', *DePaul L. Rev*, **44**; Waller, S.W. (1996–7), 'National laws and international markets: strategies of co-operation and harmonization in the enforcement of competition law', *Cardozo Law Review*, **18**, 1111; Jean–François Pont, deputy Director-General, DG IV, European Commission, 'International co-operation between competition authorities' (Speech, 26.9.1995) Conference 'Competition Policy in Transition Economies', Moscow.

19. Pitofsky, R. (2000), 'EU and US approaches to international mergers – view from the US Federal Trade Commission', in IBA (eds), *EC Merger Control: Ten Years On*, London: IBA, p. 47.

20. In the area of cross-border mergers and acquisitions, work conducted by UNCTAD has been limited to studies on foreign direct investments, the stimulation of discussion and the creation of a Database on Cross-Border Mergers and Acquisitions. Note, however, UNCTAD's Model Law on Competition (2004) (Doc.TD/B/RBP/CONF.5/7/Rev.2) which deals in Chapter VI with 'Notification, investigation and prohibition of mergers affecting concentrated markets'. Also note generally extensive work conducted by UNCTAD on other areas of competition policy: The Set of Multilaterally Agreed Equitable Principles and Rules for the Control of Restrictive Business Practices (5 December 1980) (Doc.TD/RBP/Conf.10/Rev.1), UNCTAD Annual Report 2004 (2005).

21. Support for the creation of this independent framework was found in the ICPAC Report, the EC Merger Control 10th Anniversary Conference, and the 2000 Fordham Corporate Law Institute 27th Annual Conference on International Antitrust Law and Policy. See ICPAC (n. 5 above); Klein, J. (2000), 'Time for a global competition initiative?' in IBA (eds), *EC Merger Control: Ten Years On*, London: IBA, pp. 59, 60–64; Melamed, A.D. (2001), 'Promoting sound antitrust enforcement in the global economy', *Fordham Corporate Law Institute*, 1; Monti, M. (2001), 'European competition for the 21st century', *Fordham Corporate Law Institute*, 257, 264–6.

22. ICPAC (n 5 above).

23. Kolasky, W.J. 'The international competition network guiding principles for merger review' (20 September 2002), presented at the International Bar Association Sixth Annual Competition Conference, Italy.

24. This process of convergence is particularly significant for new or young merger regimes that can assimilate and bring closer their emerging regulation to the multi-lateral agreed benchmark. The effect of voluntary provisions on domestic jurisdictions may be linked to the maturity of the regime. Developing countries and economies in transition, once committed to adopting competition legislation, may find it easier to adopt competition laws that are consistent with multilateral guidelines, as they would be filling a relative void. Jurisdictions with a mature merger regime may find it more difficult to introduce far-reaching changes that may conflict with existing regulation and policy.
25. On the positive effect these guidelines may generate if implemented, see (May 2005) *Global Competition Review*, p. 24.
26. Available online at http://www.internationalcompetitionnetwork.org/bonn/Mergers_ WG/SG1Notification_Procedures/Implementation.pdf.
27. See also presentations at the implementation session, Fourth Annual ICN Conference: Maria Coppola, US Federal Trade Commission; Ron Stern, General Electric, Washington D.C.: available online: http://www.internationalcompetitionnetwork.org/.
28. See *ICN Report*, above, p. 4. The report highlights developments achieved worldwide by various agencies including the Mexican Federal Competition Commission, the Australian Competition and Consumer Commission, The US Department of Justice and the European Commission.
29. Evenett, S.J. (2005), '"Soft law" and international economic regulation: the case of mergers and acquisitions' (Paper, 4 February).
30. For the full text of the speech online, see the following website: http://www.accc.gov.au/content/index.phtml/itemId/510720/fromItemId/8973. Also see comment on the announcement in Maria Coppola's presentation at the implementation session, Fourth Annual ICN Conference, n. 27 above.
31. See, for example, the *Revised Recommendation of the Council Concerning Co-operation Between Member Countries on Anticompetitive Practices Affecting International Trade* (C(95)130/FINAL) and the Recommendation on Co-operation Against Hard-Core Cartels (1998).
32. See, generally, Winslow, T. (2001), 'The OECD's global forum on competition and other activities', **16**, Fall, *Antitrust*, 38.
33. Established in 2001, the forum set out to stimulate policy dialogue beyond the OECD membership. The Fifth Global Forum on Competition meeting took place in February 2005 and was attended by approximately 80 delegations, representing 70 countries and economies, international and regional organizations, the business and labour communi-ties, consumer groups, civil society organizations and the donor community. See the opening remarks of Richard Hecklinger, OECD Deputy Secretary General, available online: http://www.oecd.org/dataoecd/3/15/34461680.pdf.
34. OECD Committee on Competition Law and Policy (1999), *Report on Notification of Transnational Mergers*, DAFFE/CLP(99)2/FINAL.
35. Whish, R. and D. Wood (1994), *Merger Cases in the Real World – A Study of Merger Control Procedures*, OECD Competition Policy Workshop, Paris.
36. OECD Recommendation of the Council on Merger Review (23 March 2005) C(2005)34.
37. OECD Best Practice Roundtable on portfolio effects in conglomerate mergers (January 2002) DAFFE/COMP(2002)5.
38. OECD Best Practice Roundtable on Merger Remedies (Dec. 2004) DAF/COMP(2004)21.
39. OECD Best Practice Roundtable on Media Mergers (September 2003) DAFFE/COMP(2003)16.
40. OECD Best Practice Roundtable on Merger review in emerging high innovation markets (January 2003) DAFFE/COMP(2002)20.
41. Peer review constitutes a unique OECD activity which involves the monitoring of indiv-idual members' policies, laws regulations and institutions. The process aims to improve policy making and compliance with agreed principles.
42. See *ICN Report*, n 28 above, p. 5.
43. Ibid., pp. 5, 6.

44. See illustrating comment from the European Commission Competition Directorate: 'While we have considered going further and concluding further bilateral agreements, we are not inclined to do so where it would be a waste of scarce resources, particularly for countries with whom we would only cooperate concerning one or two cases a year' (Pons, J.F., 'International Cooperation Between Competition Authorities', Speech, Competition Policy in Transition Economies, Moscow, 26 September 1995).

45. See, generally, Narula, R. and A. Zanfei (2003), 'Globalisation of innovation: the role of multinational enterprises', *DRUID Working Paper*, No 03-15; Rugman, A.M. (8 January 2001), 'The illusion of the global company', *Financial Times – Mastering Management*, 8; Fontagne, L., T. Mayer and S. Zignago (2004), 'Trade in the Triad: how easy is the access to large markets?', Discussion Paper No. 4442, Centre For Economic Policy Research.

46. 176 of the companies are located in the US, 161 in the EU, 81 in Japan. From the other 82, 13 are located in Canada, 11 in North Korea, 11 in Switzerland and 16 in China; *The Fortune Global Five Hundred* (25 July 2005).

47. Rugman, A.M. n 45 above.

48. Agreement between the Government of the United States of America and the Commission of the European Committees Regarding the Application of their Competition Laws (23 September 1991) [1995] OJ L95/47. By a joint decision of the Council and the Commission on 10 April 1995, the agreement was approved and declared applicable. See [1995] OJ L95/45; also note the positive comity agreement (1998) which is not applicable to merger transactions.

49. Monti, M. (2001), 'European Competition Policy for the 21st Century', *Fordham Corporate Law Institute*, 257; Pitofsky, R. (2000), 'EU and US approaches to international mergers – view from the US Federal Trade Commission', in IBA (eds), *EC Merger Control: Ten Years On*, London: IBA, 47, 48. Also see, generally, Parisi, J.J., US Federal Trade Commission Counsel for European Affairs, 'Recent developments in EC competition law and policy', remarks before the American Bar Association Washington DC (March 2003).

50. *MCIWorldcom/Sprint* (Case IV/M.1741) [2000] Initiation of Proceedings OJ C143; see also action brought by WorldCom against the Commission before the CFI, Case T-310/2000 *WorldCom* v. *Commission*, [2000] OJ C355/35. For the US perspective see *US v. WorldCom, Inc. & Sprint Corp.* (D.D.C., June 26, 2000); DOJ Antitrust Division, 'Justice department sues to block WorldCom's acquisition of Sprint', news release, 27 June 2000.

51. See, for example, *WorldCom/MCI* (Case IV/M.1069) [1999] OJ L116. Also see DOJ Antitrust Division, 'Justice department clears WorldCom/MCI merger after MCI agrees to sell its Internet business', news release, 15 July 1998.

52. See, for example, *GE/Instrumentarium, DSM/Roche, Bayer/Aventis, Solvay/Ausimont, Hewlett-Packard/Compaq, Carnival/P&O Princess Cruise*. See J.J. Parisi, n. 49 above, 35–42.

53. See, for example, work conducted by the joint EU/US working group on merger remedies, procedures and the analysis of conglomerate mergers. Also note work carried out by the working group on the treatment of intellectual property issues in competition cases. See Tritell, R.W. (2005), 'International antitrust convergence: a positive view', 19 Sum, *Antitrust*, 25.

54. Council Regulation (EC) No. 139/2004 of 20 January 2004 on the control of concentrations between undertakings (the EC Merger Regulation) OJ (2004) L 24/1; See also Green Paper on the review of Council Regulation (EEC) No 4064/89 COM (2001) 745/6 final [11 December 2001].

55. Article 2, EC Merger Regulation. The new substantive test reads: 'A concentration which would significantly impede effective competition, in the common market or in a substantial part of it, in particular by the creation or strengthening of a dominant position, shall be declared incompatible with the common market.'

56. Sec. 7A of the Clayton Act (as amended 02/01/2001) 15 USC, Ch. 1, Sec. 18a.

57. See 'Guidelines on the assessment of horizontal mergers under the Council Regulation on the control of concentrations between undertakings' *Official Journal*, C31,

05.02.2004, pp. 5–18; US DOJ & FTC (1992, revised 1997), *Horizontal Merger Guidelines*. Also note the treatment of efficiencies under the revised ECMR; see Recital 29 and the Guidelines on the assessment of horizontal mergers under the Council Regulation on the control of concentrations between undertakings.

58.  Articles 4, 6, 10, EC Merger Regulation.
59.  US–EU Merger Working Group, Best Practices on Cooperation in Merger Investigations, at www.usdoj.gov/atr/public/international/docs/200405.htm.
60.  Ibid.
61.  See for example the contribution of US bilateral technical assistance programme. See submission to the OECD, 'The United States experience in competition law technical assistance: a ten-year perspective' (2002) CCNM/GF/COMP/WD(2002)20; also see ICN Report p. 6 (n 28 above).
62.  See, for example, the wide range of bilateral agreements signed by both the European Union and the United States, the European Commission website: http://europa.eu. int/comm/competition/international/bilateral/bilateral.html. See also the US Department of Justice website: http://www.usdoj.gov/atr/public/international/int_ arrangements.htm.
63.  Note that bilateral cooperation does not infer harmonization of procedure and law. Subsequently differences in procedure, rights of third parties, timetables as well as in the substantive analysis remain.
64.  Sampson, G.P. (1996), 'Compatibility of regional and multilateral trading agreements: Reforming the WTO process', *American Economic Review*, 88, 89.
65.  Krugman, P. (1991), 'Is bilateralism bad?', in E. Helpman and A. Razin (eds), *International Trade and Trade Policy*, Cambridge, Mass: MIT Press, pp. 9–24.
66.  *General Electric/Honeywell* (Case IV/M.2220) [1997] Prior notification OJ C46; DOJ News Releases (2 May 2001); on the transaction see, generally, Kolasky, W.J. (2002), 'GE/Honeywell: continuing the Transatlantic Dialogue', *University of Pennsylvania Journal of International Economic Law*, 23, 513; Schnell, D.K. (2004), 'All bundled up: bringing the failed GH/Honeywell merger in from the cold', *Cornell Int'l L.J.*, 217.
67.  Statement by Charles A. James, Assistant Attorney General for Antitrust on the EU's decision regarding the GE/Honeywell acquisition: www.usdoj.gov/atr (18 January 2001); the *GE/Honeywell* decision has created a rift between the competition agencies as the EU regarded the public DOJ reaction and criticism as inappropriate. In addition the EU disapproved of the US vocal criticism that was heard in the OECD as part of the discussion on the portfolio effect doctrine. See Spiegel, P. 'US calls for more antitrust agreement with Europe', *Financial Times*, 26 October 2001, 11; also see B. Wootliff, 'Bush under fire over GE', *Daily Telegraph*, 9 June 2001.
68.  In the context of EU–US cooperation the case should be viewed as a unique transaction that triggered an uncommon difference in competition analyses rather than a transaction which reflects the majority of decisions.
69.  The case involved two international corporations located within the US and active in the market for large commercial jet aircrafts. The FTC cleared the transaction. On the other hand, the Commission raised concerns about the effect of the proposed merger. Following a high-profile investigation and increasing tension between the EU and US, the Commission cleared the transaction subject to conditions. See *Boeing/McDonnell Douglas* (Case IV/M.877), [1997] OJ L/336; see also opinion of the Advisory Committee on the case: [1997] OJ C 372; for the US decision, see *In re The Boeing Company/ McDonnell Douglas Corp.*, FTC File No. 971-0051 (1 July 1997) reported in 5 Trade Reg. Rpt. (CCH) ¶24, 295.
70.  Editorial 'Brussels v. Boeing', *The Economist*, 19 July 1997; editorial, 'Peace in our time: Boeing v. Airbus', *The Economist*, 26 July 1997.
71.  On the substantive differences in analysis, see remarks by Muris, T.J., 'Merger enforcement in a world of multiple arbiters', before the Brookings Institution Roundtable on Trade and Investment Policy (December 2001) Washington, DC.
72.  See for example, the *Air Liquide/BOC* transaction (Case IV/M.1630), [1999] Prior notification OJ C 239; FTC file not published; also see *Glaxo Wellcome/SmithKline Beecham* (Case IV/M.1846), [2000]; FTC File No. C-3990; *Ciba-Geigy/Sandoz* transaction (Case

IV/M.737)[1997] OJ L 201; *In re Ciba-Geigy Ltd.*, FTC File No. 961-0055 (8 April 1997) reported in 5 Trade Reg. Rpt. (CCH) ¶24,182; *UPM-Kymmene/Morgan Adhesives* (Case IV/M.2867). Prior notification OJ C 229., *US* v. *UPM-Kymmene Oyj*, (25 July 2003) reported in (2003-2) Trade Cas. (CCH) ¶74, 101.

73. At the bilateral level, these agreements provide the most adequate platform for detailed case-by-case cooperation.

74. Externalities may still occur under a bilateral agreement when a cooperative decision made by two jurisdictions has a negative effect on third countries. The two cooperating jurisdictions are likely to focus on the decision's effect within their markets and ignore negative spillovers on other nations.

75. For example convergence in the areas mentioned in the ICN Recommended Practices for Merger Notification Procedure, focusing on procedural and jurisdictional issues surrounding merger notifications.

## References

Barrier, M.W. (2000), 'Regionalization: the choice of a new millennium', *Currents: International Trade Law Journal*, 25.

Berg, W. and H. Bielesz (2003), 'The WTO and competition: options and perspectives', *Int. T.L.R.*, 9(4), 94–100.

Drexl, J. (2004), 'International competition policy after Cancun: placing a Singapore issue on the WTO development agenda', *W. Comp.*, 27(3), 419–57.

Ezrachi, A. (2002), 'Globalization of merger control: a look at bilateral cooperation through the GE/Honeywell case', *Fla. J. Int'l L.*, 14, 397.

Ezrachi, A. (2004), 'The role of voluntary frameworks in multinational cooperation over merger control', *Geo. Wash. Int'l L. Rev.*, 36, 433.

Evenett, S.J. (2005), ' "Soft Law" and international economic regulation: the case of mergers and acquisitions' (paper, 4 February).

Fiebig, A. (2000), 'A role for the WTO in international merger control', *Nw. J. Int'l L. & Bus.*, 20, 233.

Fontagne, L., T. Mayer and S. Zignago (2004), 'Trade in the triad: how easy is the access to large markets?', Discussion Paper No. 4442, Centre For Economic Policy Research.

Gerber, D.J. (1999–2000), 'The US–European conflict over the globalization of antitrust law: a legal experience perspective', *New England Law Review*, 34, 124.

Guzman, A.T. (2001), 'Antitrust and international regulatory federalism', *New York University Law Review*.

Guzman, A.T. (2002), 'Choice of law: new foundations', 90, *Geo. L.J.*, 883.

Guzman, A.T. (2004), 'The case for international antitrust', in R.A. Epstain and M.S. Greve (eds), *Competition Laws in Conflict, Antitrust Jurisdiction in the Global Economy*, Washington DC: AEI Press, p. 99.

Howse, R. and M.J. Trebilcock (1999), *The Regulation of International Trade*, 2nd edn, London: Routledge.

Ingham, B. (1998), *From ITO to WTO: Trade and Protection in a Changing World*.

International Competition Policy Advisory Committee (ICPAC) to the Attorney General and Assistant Attorney General for Antitrust (2000), *Final Report* (ICPAC Report).

Klein, J. (2000), 'Time for a global competition initiative?', in IBA (eds), *EC Merger Control: Ten Years On*, London: IBA, p. 59.

Kolasky, W.J., (20 September 2002), 'The international competition network guiding principles for merger review', presented at the International Bar Association Sixth Annual Competition Conference, Italy.

Kolasky, W.J. (2002), 'GE/Honeywell: continuing the transatlantic dialogue', *University of Pennsylvania Journal of International Economic Law*, 23.

Krugman, P. (1991), 'Is bilateralism bad?', in E. Helpman and A. Razin (eds), *International Trade and Trade Policy*, Cambridge, Mass: MIT Press.

Melamed, A.D. (2001), 'Promoting sound antitrust enforcement in the global economy', *Fordham Corporate Law Institute*, 1.

Monti, M. (2001), 'European competition for the 21st century', *Fordham Corporate Law Institute*, 257.
Moore, L. (1985), *The Growth and Structure of International Trade Since the Second World War*.
Muris, T.J. (December 2001), 'Merger enforcement in a world of multiple arbiters', before the Brookings Institution Roundtable on Trade and Investment Policy, Washington, DC.
Narula, R. and A. Zanfei (2003), 'Globalisation of innovation: the role of multinational enterprises', *DRUID Working Paper*, No 03-15.
Parisi, J.J., US Federal Trade Commission Counsel for European Affairs (2003), 'Recent developments in EC competition law and policy', remarks before American Bar Association, Washington, DC.
Pesola, M. (2001), 'Merger control: the search for harmonisation', Global Competition Review.
Pitofsky, R. (2000), 'EU and US approaches to international mergers – view from the US Federal Trade Commission', in IBA (eds), *EC Merger Control: Ten Years On*, London: IBA, p. 47.
Rugman, A.M. (8 January 2001), 'The illusion of the global company', *Financial Times – Mastering Management*, 8.
Sampson, G.P. (1996), 'Compatibility of regional and multilateral trading agreements: reforming the WTO process', *American Economic Review*, 88.
Schnell, D.K. (2004), 'All bundled up: bringing the failed GH/Honeywell merger in from the cold', *Cornell Int'l L.J.*, 217.
Spiegel, P. (26 October 2001), 'US calls for more antitrust agreement with Europe', *Financial Times*.
Tritell, R.W. (2005), 'International antitrust convergence: a positive view', 19, Sum, *Antitrust*, 25.
Waller, S.W. (1996), 'National laws and international markets: strategies of co-operation and harmonization in the enforcement of competition law', *Cardozo Law Review*, 18.
Waller, S.W. (2000), 'Bringing globalism home: lessons from antitrust and beyond', *Loyola University Chicago Law Journal*.
Whish, R. and D. Wood (1994), *Merger Cases in the Real World – A Study of Merger Control Procedures*, OECD Competition Policy Workshop, Paris.
Wilcox, C. (1949), *A Charter for World Trade*, New York: Macmillan Co.
Winslow, T. (2001), 'The OECD's global forum on competition and other activities', 16, Fall, *Antitrust*, 38.
Wood, D.P. (1995) 'The internalization of antitrust law: options for the future', *DePaul L. Rev*, 44.
Wood, D.P. (1999), 'Is co-operation possible?', *New England Law Review*, 34.
Wootliff, B. (9 June 2001), 'Bush under Fire over GE', *Daily Telegraph*.

## Cases

*Air Liquide/BOC* transaction (Case IV/M.1630), [1999] Prior notification OJ C 239.
*Boeing/McDonnell Douglas* (Case IV/M.877), [1997] OJ L/336.
*Ciba-Geigy/Sandoz* transaction (Case IV/M.737), [1997] OJ L201.
*General Electric/Honeywell* (Case IV/M.2220), [2001] OJ C1746.
*Glaxo Wellcome/SmithKline Beecham* (Case IV/M.1846), [2000].
*In re Ciba-Geigy Ltd.*, FTC File No. 961-0055 (April 8, 1997) reported in 5 Trade Reg. Rpt. (CCH) ¶ 24,182.
*MCIWorldcom/Sprint* (Case IV/M.1741), [2000] Initiation of Proceedings OJ C143.
*UPM-Kymmene/Morgan Adhesives* (Case IV/M.2867), [2002] Prior notification OJ C229.
*US v. UPM-Kymmene Oyj*, (July 25, 2003) reported in (2003-2) Trade Cas. (CCH) ¶ 74,101.
*WorldCom/MCI* (Case IV/M.1069), [1999] OJ L116.

# 25 Bilateral enforcement cooperation agreements
*Anestis Papadopoulos*[1]

## Common characteristics of enforcement cooperation agreements

*Enforcement cooperation as a substitute/alternative to harmonization of competition laws*

Bilateral (and tripartite) enforcement cooperation agreements do not harmonize the competition laws of the contracting parties. These agreements provide for mechanisms of enforcement cooperation. In the field of competition law enforcement cooperation has been used as an alternative/substitute for harmonization of national competition laws. Since no agreement on a multilateral code on restrictive business practices could be achieved in the twentieth century, countries with active international trade (through multinational firms) and a developed competition law had to cooperate on enforcement of their competition laws in order to face the consequences of restrictive business practices with an international effect. Thus, as early as the late 1950s, when a conflict arose between the governments of Canada and the United States on a case relating to a US investigation of a patent pool among Canadian radio and television makers designed to exclude US manufactured products from the Canadian market, the governments of US and Canada realized that they had to proceed into negotiations in order to coordinate their enforcement activities and avoid conflicts like this. The outcome of this conflict and the subsequent negotiations was the Fulton–Rodgers understanding of 1959,[2] with which the two governments agreed to construct a channel of communication regarding antitrust matters, through notification and consultation.[3]

Furthermore, in 1967, the OECD adopted its first recommendation[4] encouraging its member countries to cooperate in enforcement on antitrust issues. This first recommendation has been modified several times, first in 1973,[5] and then again in 1979,[6] 1986[7] and, lastly, in 1995.[8] Taking as a model the most recent one (recommendation of 1995), member countries are encouraged:

1. to notify other members when the latter's 'important interests' are affected by an investigation or enforcement action;[9]
2. to coordinate parallel investigations where appropriate and practicable;[10]

3. to disclose information concerning an investigation or proceeding which is being conducted in one member country but that may affect important interests of another member country, in order to permit the member country whose interests are affected to comment and consult with the proceeding member;[11]

4. to exchange information which is related to anticompetitive practices in international trade (with the reservation of the rules concerning confidentiality and unless such a disclosure of information would be contrary to significant national interests of a country);[12] and

5. to ask the competition authorities of another member country to take action if it considers that one or more undertakings situated in that country are or have been engaged in anticompetitive practices that are substantially and adversely affecting its interests.[13] Moreover, in the preamble,[14] the member countries are required to take into consideration the principle of international comity ('traditional' or 'negative' comity).

As can be seen, the provisions of the OECD recommendation are relatively vague, and the content of the agreements following the OECD recommendations has been expanded; however the basic structure of all these agreements follows to a greater or lesser extent the OECD recommendation. The recommendation is entirely voluntary; nevertheless it is still an important step since the OECD is the first institution that encouraged its member states to be involved in mechanisms of cooperation on competition enforcement and consequently create a framework of cooperation.[15]

*Basic structure of the agreements*
As is obvious from the table in Annex 1, enforcement cooperation agreements in the field of competition law follow the basic structure of the OECD recommendations. Nonetheless the level of cooperation provided varies. For instance the Brazil–Russia agreement is modest, providing for a general undertaking by the parties to cooperate and consult each other on cases of mutual interest. On the other hand, the US–Australia agreement and the Denmark–Iceland–Norway tripartite agreement are the first to provide for exchange of confidential information and are the first legally binding enforcement cooperation agreements (agreements of the second generation). All the other agreements include limitations on the ability of the competition agencies to share confidential information (the so-called 'confidentiality clause' and the limitation by the existing laws, both discussed below). Almost all of these agreements provide for a basic procedure of cooperation, that is to say notification of cases of mutual interest, exchange of information, cooperation and coordination of enforcement

activities, and negative comity. These mechanisms are analysed below, in the second section of this chapter.

*Bilateralism as a strategy of strong states*
It also becomes obvious from Annex 1 that enforcement cooperation has taken the form of bilateral (and only lately tripartite) agreements. But why bilaterals and not, for example, multilateral or plurilateral enforcement cooperation agreements? This question has to be answered especially in view of the fact that enforcement cooperation agreements have to a great extent been framed in accordance with the OECD recommendation, which itself does not speak about bilateral cooperation.

A number of scholars and politicians attribute bilateralism in the field of competition enforcement cooperation to the US policy on international competition law in the post-World War II period. The US historically resisted participation in international institutional arrangements; they were perceived as jeopardizing its political autonomy,[16] illustrated in the process of internationalization of competition law. Throughout the development of the idea of a multilateral agreement on competition, the US has consistently been the most prominent opponent.[17] Instead, US officials have advocated application of US competition law as the most appropriate way to address problems created by restrictive business practices with an international effect,[18] even in cases where US laws have to be applied in an extraterritorial manner. As Fox has pointed out, '[the US] . . . have the tools of unilateralism, they fear the compromises of bargaining, and they adjure the "relinquishment" of sovereignty'.[19] The analysis below of the US extraterritoriality emphasizes this argument.

Furthermore US officials have used bilateral agreements as a complementary strategy to unilateralism. As Braithwaite and Drahos claim, in international trade generally, the most fundamental US strategy is to act tough on bilateral negotiations to set frameworks for subsequent multilateral negotiation.[20] This trend is observed not only in the field of competition law, where the US is the country with the biggest number of bilateral enforcement cooperation agreements, but also in the area of intellectual property law, where it finally led to the adoption of TRIPs.[21]

Waller further argues that cooperation on enforcement agreements is currently in vogue because it increases national power (Waller, 1997: 378).[22] It is definitely easier for politically and economically strong states to cope with negotiations and cooperation on a bilateral rather than on a multilateral basis. With the absence of a judicial body to decide on cases where a conflict arises it is very much the political and economic power of the contracting parties that will decide the outcome of the conflict. Officials and academics of smaller countries have often expressed this concern. For instance, a Swiss official has stated that the possible conclusion of a multilateral competition agreement would be the best solution with respect to the problems stemming from restrictive business practices conducted by multinational enterprises, since, 'parties with relatively little bargaining power will be able to join forces with similar countries to safeguard their interests, leading to a more balanced agreement'.[23]

All these arguments about bilateralism and the increase of national power are also reflected lately by the EU international trade policy. Having concluded enforcement cooperation agreements only with the US, Canada and Japan, the EU has not been as active as the US in the adoption of this particular legal tool. Nonetheless it has been the most prominent user of bilateral Preferential Trade Agreements, which include competition provisions and actually oblige its co-signing states to adopt legislation similar to the EU.[24]

*Enforcement cooperation where there are trade flows*
Another observation to be made regarding enforcement cooperation agreements is that all these agreements have been concluded between countries with significant trade flows. This justifies to an extent the fact that most of these agreements have been concluded among industrialized countries (such as the EU, the US, Canada, Japan and Australia). Nonetheless the fact that in the last five years or so a number of less developed countries have been involved in bilateral enforcement agreements should not be overlooked; further, considerable trade flows between the contracting parties is one of the main incentives for the conclusion of most of these agreements. For example, Papua-New Guinea has signed an agreement with Australia, and this is justified by the fact that Australia is the country with which Papua New Guinea has the most developed trade relations. Statistically, in the year 2000, Australia was the destination of 29.1 per cent of Papua New Guinea exports and 21.2 per cent of Papua New Guinea's imports came from Australia. Moreover, according to the Australian Competition and Consumer Commission, the agreement is a way to achieve greater access to Papua New Guinea's market for Australian exporters through proper utilization of competition law in this market.[25] It is logical to assume that 'proper utilization of competition law' aims at the creation of an environment of safe investment for Australian firms.

*Enforcement cooperation agreements in the form of soft law*
'Soft law' has been used as an alternative to hard law in the legalization of international relations. Hard law refers to legally binding obligations that are precise (or can be made precise through adjudication or the issuance of detailed regulations) and that delegate authority for interpreting and

implementing the law.[26] Accordingly soft law is chosen once legal arrangements are weakened along one or more of the dimensions of obligations, precision and delegation. Put differently, soft law stands between hard law and purely political arrangements where legalization is largely absent,[27] and includes elements from both these situations (that is, it includes legal provisions – an element of hard law – but these provisions are not legally enforceable: an element of purely political arrangements).

This indistinctness between law and policy has led some international lawyers to condemn soft law as vague and inadequate to regulate international economic relations. Weil, for instance, has argued that the increasing use of soft law can destabilize the whole international normative system into an instrument inadequate to serve its purpose.[28] In fact these arguments to an extent can be applied in the case of this first generation of bilateral and tripartite competition enforcement cooperation agreements. The lack of legally binding obligations, along with the confidentiality clause, give in reality absolute discretion to the contracting parties to overlook the agreements in cases where they consider that their important interests would be impeded if they had to follow the provisions of these agreements. The EU/US conflict over the *Boeing/MDD* and *GE/Honeywell* cases, discussed below, illustrates this inadequacy of soft law to provide radical solutions in some cases.

So what exactly are the factors that have led to the choice of soft law instead of hard law in the process of legalization of international economic relations? Soft law bilateral agreements have been used not only in the field of competition law but also in other areas of international law, such as taxation, investment and securities.[29] The reason for this choice, as a number of scholars have pointed out, is that soft law can overcome deadlocks in the relation of states that result from economic or political differences among them, when efforts at firmer solutions have been unsuccessful.[30] This general assumption can be applied in the process of internationalization of competition law where the lack of success in concluding a multilateral agreement has obviously led countries to opt for alternative solutions such as bilateral (and in fact voluntary) enforcement cooperation agreements. This form of cooperation is definitely more flexible than traditional international agreements with binding provisions and, as Chinkin puts it, 'thanks to soft law we still have people channeling efforts toward law and toward trying to achieve objectives through legal mechanism, rather than going ahead and doing it in other fashions'.[31]

Furthermore, it has also been pointed out that a substantial amount of soft law can be attributed to differences in the economic structures and economic interests of different states.[32] This argument is also relevant in the case of competition law, which may include different aims depending on the interests of different countries. It is recognized that competition law has been and is being used as an instrument to achieve policy objectives other than the maximization of competition welfare in the technical sense (that is, achievement of the most efficient allocation of resources and reduction of cost as far as possible).[33] This fact is also illustrated in bilateral enforcement cooperation agreements. For instance the Canada–Australia–New Zealand[34] and the US–Canada[35] agreements include provisions for deceptive marketing practices and thus also incorporate consumer protection law.[36]

### The content of the agreements
*First agreements of this generation: reactive, rather than proactive*
A first observation to be made is that the basic characteristic of the early agreements of the first generation is that their objective was to resolve conflicts that had already occurred and were relevant to the extraterritorial application of the US antitrust rules, rather than to avoid future conflicts. Thus the agreements were reactive rather than proactive. For example, exchange of information is dealt with in much more detail in the US–Australia agreement and in the US–Canada Memorandum of Understanding,[37] owing to the fact that they were concluded after the confrontation in the Uranium case. During the 1970s, in the *Uranium Cartel* case, a US court held that it was justified in exercising jurisdiction against nine non-US uranium producers.[38] This decision created very serious friction and led a number of countries to adopt blocking statutes and/or claw back statutes. The former prevent or limit the ability of the United States to obtain information located in countries with such statutes. The latter allow citizens to seek compensatory damages paid to plaintiffs that have prevailed in US litigation.[39] This confrontation was the reason for the adoption of the bilateral enforcement cooperation agreements between the United States of America and Australia in 1982, and Canada in 1985, respectively.

*The agreement between the US and the EU*
The first pro-active agreement is the agreement concluded between the European Union and the US.[40] This particular agreement is arguably the most important, considering the impact of such agreements as it relates to the two major 'players' in international trade, with mature competition systems and, most importantly, it has been tested for more than ten years and to a great extent is the only agreement that can give us practical examples of situations where this kind of agreement has proved effective or ineffective. Hence, in examining the content and impact of the first generation of bilateral enforcement cooperation agreements, we will concentrate mainly on the agreement between the US and the EU.

*Negative comity (avoidance of conflicts)*

The principle of comity, or otherwise negative comity – the term 'negative' has been given in order to distinguish it from positive comity – developed in the Netherlands in the last quarter of the seventeenth century,[41] and was especially influenced by the work of Ulrich Huber, who based his analysis on three axioms: (i) that each state had sovereignty in its territory (that is, the laws of its states bind all its subjects in the boundaries of this state but not beyond); (ii) that every person who is found within the state is considered as a subject of this state irrespective of whether he/she resides there permanently or temporarily; and (iii) that states' rulers should ensure (through the concept of comity) that the laws of other states be enforced within its boundaries in order to maintain validity and impartiality to other states' laws and citizens. According to Huber, comity was based on the existence of a *jus gentium* and thus nations were legally obliged to apply comity. In contrast other theorists claimed that comity was a matter of discretion for each sovereign state.[42]

This latter argument has prevailed in international law literature. Even though the notion of comity is not entirely clear in the public international law literature,[43] comity (as it is meant in general terms) is a situation where extraterritorial determinations are often grounded in considerations of politeness or respect; it is 'a willingness to grant a privilege, not as a matter of right, but out of deference and good will',[44] in order to avoid conflicts relating to jurisdiction. Specifically with reference to competition law the principle of comity encourages the parties to take into account, during the enforcement of their competition laws, the important interests of the other party so as to avoid the creation of conflicts during their enforcement activity. In considering the other party's important interests the enforcing party applies the comity clause within the framework of its laws and to the extent compatible with its own important interests.[45]

Negative comity has been included in the OECD recommendations (as described above), and has also formed part of almost every bilateral enforcement agreement. In the EU/US agreement the provision for comity is laid down in Article VI; it is based on three principles. First, it is recognized that important interests of a party would normally be reflected in laws, decisions or statements of policy by its competent authorities. A second principle is the recognition that as a general matter the potential for adverse impact on one party's important interests arising from enforcement activity by the other party is less at the investigative stage and greater at the stage at which conduct is prohibited or penalized, or at which other forms of remedial orders are imposed. The third principle (and actually the novelty introduced in this agreement) is a list of six situations where the important interests of a party may be affected. These include (a) the relative significance to the anticompetitive activities involved of conduct within the enforcing party's territory as compared to conduct within the other party's territory; (b) the presence or absence of a purpose on the part of those engaged in the anticompetitive activities to affect consumers, suppliers or competitors within the enforcing party's territory; (c) the relative significance of the effects of the anticompetitive activities on the enforcing party's interests as compared to the effects on the other party's interests; (d) the existence or absence of reasonable expectations that would be furthered or defeated by the enforcement activities; (e) the degree of conflict or consistency between the enforcement activities and the other party's laws or articulated economic policies; and (f) the extent to which enforcement activities of the other party with respect to the same persons, including judgments or undertakings resulting from such activities, may be affected.

As is obvious, the wording of the comity-related provision of the agreement is quite detailed. This reflects the intention of the contracting parties to limit the possibilities of jurisdictional conflicts. Having said that, the following analysis shows that in both the US and the EU extraterritorial application of competition law is the guiding principle, and comity has been seen as a principle to be applied in exceptional occasions.

In the last 60 years the US courts have consistently applied US antitrust rules in an extraterritorial manner.[46] Nonetheless the extent to which comity considerations may be taken into account in competition cases varies, depending on the particular case under examination.

In the 1945 *Alcoa* case[47] the 'effects doctrine' was first introduced. According to this doctrine, the US courts have the competence to apply US antitrust law to conduct that has occurred wholly or partly in a foreign state, but that is intended to affect the United States and has in fact such an effect. In its 1976 *Timberlane* decision,[48] the Ninth Circuit mitigated the effects test by taking into account a consideration of comity for foreign defendants, creating thus a rule of reason comity analysis, which was codified in the Foreign Trade Antitrust Improvements Act of 1982 (FTAIA).[49] Here it is provided that the challenged conduct must have a 'direct, substantial and reasonably foreseeable effect' on US commerce or on the trade of a US citizen/company engaged in export commerce. The aim of the FTAIA was to provide clear guidance with regard to the extraterritorial application of US competition rules; nonetheless it is broadly acknowledged that it has failed to do so.[50]

In the 1993 *Hartford* decision,[51] the Supreme Court held, in justifying the extraterritorial application of the Sherman Act, that, in terms of comity, the exercising of US jurisdiction would be limited to exceptional occasions and only if there were a 'true conflict'. This statement was confirmed by the Supreme Court in the *Nippon Paper* case, where it held that comity is 'more an aspiration' than an established rule, confirming in the process that the growth of comity in competition matters was stunted by *Hartford Fire*.[52]

Lately, the Supreme Court once more examined the effects test in its *Empagran* decision,[53] where it held that foreign purchasers of vitamins based outside the US did not have the right to bring a claim for treble damages in a US Court for conduct that had taken place solely outside the US market. On remand from the Supreme Court,[54] the Court of Appeals held that, in order to obtain relief, plaintiffs must show that there is a 'direct causal relationship' between the injuries they have suffered and the effect that the anticompetitive practices have on the US market. The Court found that the plaintiffs could not show such 'proximate causation' and thus they did not have the right to claim treble damages. It becomes obvious that the US courts' understanding of comity is not a consistent one. Nevertheless it is rather obvious that comity considerations apply rarely in the US jurisprudence.

Similarly, as far as the European Union is concerned, there has been in the last 20 years or so a continuous effort from the European Commission to establish the effects doctrine in Europe. In the *Wood Pulp* case,[55] the Commission found that 36 out of 42 suppliers of wood pulp were violating European Competition law (Art.81(1)). Of these 42 undertakings, 40 were not resident within the European Union. On appeal, the European Court of Justice (ECJ) ruled that an agreement concluded by undertakings that are not within the borders of the European Union would be an infringement of European competition law, if the agreement is 'implemented' within the EU.[56] In taking this decision, the ECJ refrained from relying on the effects doctrine despite the fact that the Commission argued for the effect test. Instead, it used the implementation doctrine, according to which EU competition law can be applied when a mere sale within the Community occurs. Thus the validity of the application of the effects doctrine in competition cases in Europe is still not clear.[57]

However this is not the case in mergers. In the *Gencor*[58] case, the Commission blocked a merger that was cleared by the South African competition authorities, despite the fact that both the companies involved in the merger were registered in South Africa. Judging on the case, the Court of First Instance declared that 'the application of the [Merger] Regulation is justified under public international law when it is foreseeable that a proposed concentration will have an immediate and substantial effect in the Community'.[59] Furthermore, commenting on this case, former Commissioner Mario Monti[60] expressed his opinion as follows:

> I am confident, however, that this uncertainty is now behind us: the European Court of First Instance . . . clearly states that the Community's exercise of

jurisdiction over a merger taking place wholly outside of the Community is compatible with the principles of public international law, where the merger produces direct substantial and foreseeable effects within the EU.

These facts show that, despite the inclusion of comity provision in the agreement, the main aim of competition officials in the EU is to establish the effects test (and the unilateral application of EU competition law) rather than take into account comity considerations. On the other hand, it has been observed that very little room for comity considerations has been left in the US and, up to the present moment, comity itself has not had any substantial impact on competition cases. Hence we can observe that at least in the case of the EU/US cooperation on competition the principle of comity has had a minimal effect.

*Procedures of positive cooperation that bilateral and tripartite agreements provide for*
Apart from the provision for avoidance of conflicts, the first generation of enforcement cooperation agreements also provide for a mechanism of positive cooperation. This mechanism includes notification, exchange of information between officials, cooperation and coordination of enforcement activities, consultations and, finally, positive comity.

*(a) Notification, cooperation and coordination*    There is a provision for notification (i.e. the exchange of basic information) in every competition enforcement cooperation agreement that has been concluded so far. Notification is in fact the mechanism which triggers the process of cooperation between competition agencies. The basic content of a notification provision is that the parties have to notify one another whenever their competition authorities become aware that their enforcement activities *may affect important interests of the other party*. This provision has been included in cooperation agreements since the first agreement between the United States and Germany (1976). In the first agreements there are no indications of when the important interests of a contracting party may be affected. Hence the test looks very general and it is actually left to the absolute discretion of the parties when to notify the other contracting party.

However this changed with the conclusion of the US–EU agreement of 1991 (as revised), which was the first to specify particular situations where the important interests of 'the other party' may be affected.[61] These include cases that are relevant to enforcement activities of the other party; involve anticompetitive activities other than mergers and acquisitions in which are carried out in significant part in the other party's territory; involve mergers or acquisitions in which one or more parties to the transaction, or a company controlling one or more of the parties of the transactions, is a company incorporated or organized under the laws of the other party or its states; the anticompetitive practice involves conduct that is encouraged or approved by the other party; or involves remedies that would require or prohibit conduct in the other party's territory.

This list includes almost any possible enforcement activity which could have an effect on the other party's important interests and, according to the European Commission, the mechanism of notification is the clearest obligation stemming from the agreement.[62] The notification of the case to the other party should contain adequate information so that the other party's competition authority will be able to evaluate any effects on its interests. Moreover the notification should be made to the other party far enough in advance to enable the other party's views to be taken into account before a final decision is adopted.[63] Hence, for example in a merger case where the European Commission decides to scrutinize the transaction and, according to the above-mentioned provisions, its involvement in the case may affect important interests of the US, it must inform either the US Department of Justice or the US Fair Trade Commission (depending on the case) as soon as it initiates proceedings.[64]

Furthermore, with regard to coordination, the agreement stipulates in Article IV that, where contracting parties have an interest in pursuing enforcement activities with regard to related situations, they agree that it is in their mutual interest to coordinate their enforcement activities. When considering if such coordination should be developed the parties shall take into account a number of factors.[65]

*(b) Exchange of information – meetings between officials* Exchange of information is the cornerstone of international cooperation and the main aim of these agreements. It is in fact *the* factor on which the effectiveness of these agreements depends. The exchange of information (according to the way that these agreements have been framed) has a dual function. Firstly, and most importantly, it offers the chance to cooperating competition authorities to inform each other on cases of mutual interest. Notification, enforcement cooperation and coordination, consultation and positive comity are in one way or another based on exchange of information. However the ability of competition authorities to exchange information is subject to the limitations imposed by the existing laws of the parties and the confidentiality clause, discussed below.

Secondly, exchange of information can also be a process through which officials from different competition authorities can exchange their opinions on economic and political issues that are related to competition law enforcement, thus creating a culture of international competition law.

Perhaps the most important element of these agreements is that they provide for a mechanism through which officials of different national authorities are able to come into contact and share their views on issues of mutual interest. It is interesting to note that lately (after the conclusion of the US/EU agreement) almost all of these agreements include a provision for meetings of officials, either on an annual, semi-annual or periodic basis. The provisions for exchange of information on technical issues, meetings between competition officials and the provisions for technical assistance are evidence of this. All these three mechanisms are part of a process through which officials from different competition authorities can exchange their opinions on economic and political issues that are related to competition law enforcement, thus creating a culture of international competition law. It has to be stressed here again that competition law is a relatively recent legal instrument, especially for countries which have only recently embarked on the process of creating an environment for competition in their internal markets; the existence of these agreements and the exchange of opinions and experience between officials regarding competition law and policy is definitely a positive process towards the creation of a sound and effective framework for competition law.

International relations and politics literature give two alternative explanations of this phenomenon of internationalization of competition law through the exchange of views between officials. First it is related to the literature that discusses *elite learning* and according to which decision makers incorporate new values and interests due to the regular contact with decision makers from other countries.[66] Another alternative explanation for this process is that given by the supporters of institutional isomorphism, who claim that diffusion of interests, values and norms occurs through the *homogenization* of institutional structures.[67]

The result of this process is the creation of what political scientists call a policy, or government network. According to legal and political scholars, transgovernmentalism, which is the outcome of the creation of these networks, is a new vision of global governance. The idea of transgovernmentalism starts from the assumption that the primary state actors in the international realm are no longer foreign ministers or head of states, but the same government institutions that dominate domestic policies, that is, administrative agencies, courts and legislators.[68] It then moves on to the conclusion that through different mechanisms of cooperation (among which are included bilateral enforcement cooperation agreements and memoranda of understandings) these groups of officials and domestic institutions are in fact the most important actors in the governance of global economy. Hence, according to this theory, global governance is horizontal rather than vertical, decentralized rather than centralized, and composed of national government officials rather than a supranational bureaucracy.[69]

Bilateral enforcement cooperation agreements create mechanisms for diffusion of information about technical aspects of competition law and different state interests. The outcome of the creation of this web is twofold. First, competition officials of one country will become familiar with the concerns of competition officials from another country regarding the function of competition policy and the enforcement of competition law. Second, and with reference to the policy network idea, this web reinforces the role of competition officials in international governance.

Regarding specifically the EU/US agreement, this exchange of information through meetings of competition officials happens through administrative Arrangements of Attendance, which include reciprocal attendance at a certain stage of individual cases involving the implementation of their respective competition rules.

*(c) Positive comity*   Positive comity could be characterized as the most revolutionary form of cooperation that some of these agreements provide for, even though as a practice it is not a new one. This mechanism of cooperation has been included in the US–Germany Friendship, Commerce and Navigation Treaty of 1954[70] and subsequently in a number of bilateral Treaties between the US and Greece, Denmark, Japan, Italy and France.[71] It had been used between the US and Japan as a mechanism of cooperation in the past, even before its inclusion in bilateral enforcement cooperation agreements.[72] Despite the fact that it has been included in the OECD recommendations on cooperation since the amendment of 1973, positive comity has not yet been defined in a multilateral context.[73]

Nonetheless, since it was first included in the agreement between the US and the EU, the provision for positive comity has been almost identical in every other agreement of this kind. According to the standard provision in bilateral agreements where positive comity is included, when a contracting party (Party A) believes that its important interests are affected by an anticompetitive practice that has been put into effect within the territories of the other contracting party (Party B) and for which Party A does not have the competence to initiate enforcement proceedings, then Party A is able to request party B to take action for this anticompetitive practice, on behalf of Party A. Thus, rather than avoiding conflicts, positive comity requires the parties to conduct acts of positive cooperation.

*The US/EU Agreement on Positive Comity of 1998*
The agreement between the United States of America and the EU on positive comity expands the notion of positive comity even further than the first

agreement between EU and US.[74] It states that the competition authorities of a requesting party may petition the competition authorities of a requested party to investigate and, if warranted, to remedy anticompetitive activities in accordance with the requested party's competition laws. Such a request may be made even if the activities do not violate the requesting party's competition laws, and regardless of whether the competition authorities of the requesting party have commenced or contemplate taking enforcement activities under their own competition laws.

It also provides for suspension of enforcement activities by the requesting party aimed at anticompetitive activities in the other party's territory (that is, the extraterritorial application of its competition law) in favour of a positive comity referral to the other party in two kinds of cases: (i) where the foreign anticompetitive activities do not directly harm the requesting party's consumers (for example, a cartel on one side that limits exports from the other); and (ii) where the foreign anticompetitive activities occur principally in, and are directed principally towards, the other party's territory, but incidentally harm the requesting party's consumers.

Nevertheless it excludes mergers[75] from its application (even though transnational mergers are the most frequent object for cooperation) because of different deadlines that the EU and the US laws contain for the adoption of decisions.[76] It was also due to the fact that, under the EC Merger Regulation, the Commission has no discretionary power to examine mergers; in effect, it can only review mergers that have a 'community dimension'. Hence, in the case of a request by the US to the Commission to review a merger, the European Commission would not have the competence to review the merger if it does not have a Community dimension.[77] That said, and given this limitation of the agreement, the parties set up a working group on mergers in 2002, which issued best practices on cooperation in merger investigations later that year.[78]

*Positive comity: an assessment*
There are a number of factors that determine whether positive comity can apply upon a request of a contracting party. Firstly, the anticompetitive conduct has to be prohibited not only by the competition law of the requesting party, but also by the competition law of the requested party. An example would be that an export activity permitted under the laws of the requested party is not covered by the positive comity mechanism even if it adversely affects an important interest of the other party. Another example would be different theoretical approaches regarding the same practice. For instance, US antitrust law prohibits an arrangement when it lessens competition substantially, whereas in the European Union a vertical restraint is prohibited when one or more competitors are restricted from entering the

market.[79] On the other hand the Japanese practice of 'Keiretsu', a practice in Japanese markets (involving long-term closely interconnected relationships among Japanese companies through formal and/or informal relations), (Helou, 1991) which actually prevents foreign investors from entering the Japanese market[80] and which traditionally has not been punished by the Japanese competition authorities, reveals that, even in the case where competition authorities are dealing with the same practices, it is not obvious that they will come up with similar decisions.

Secondly, and given the voluntary nature of these 'soft agreements', the application of positive comity as a tool for cooperation depends to a great extent upon the good will of the parties. It also requires great transparency during the enforcement procedures. It has been pointed out above, during the discussion on negative comity, that, where important political and economic interests are involved, it would be an illusion to expect such good will in order to provide radical solutions based on the positive comity provisions. In 1992, Atwood[81] predicted:

> We are dealing here not just with the laws of competition but also with the laws of human nature. . . . We should not expect the principle of positive comity . . . to impact dramatically on the proposition that laws are written and enforced to protect national interests.

Atwood's assumption seems to have been proved correct. Thirteen years after the conclusion of the US/EU agreement, the mechanism of cooperation provided by positive comity has been used only a few times, and only once officially.[82] Informally, positive comity is – at least publicly – known to have been used on three occasions. The first involved a referral by the US Federal Trade Commission to the Italian competition authority regarding anticompetitive practices by Italian ham exporters, which were harming US consumers with supracompetitive prices.[83] The second case involved a complaint by Marathon Oil to the European Commission in relation to anticompetitive practices conducted by European firms and which had great negative effects on the US-based company.[84] Finally the most publicized informal referral based on the procedure that positive comity calls for involved A.C. Nielsen, a company involved in the international market of retail tracking services (gathering of information regarding prices, sales and relevant data sold by manufacturers and retailers in the form of market reports). Following complaints by IRI, a rival firm, both the European Commission and the US Department of Justice initiated investigations with respect to Nielsen's tying practices in countries where the company was in a dominant position, in order to achieve the conclusion of deals in countries where the company faced substantial competition. The US Department of Justice allowed the European Commission to lead the enforcement activities since most of the alleged conduct occurred in Europe. The outcome of this cooperation was an undertaking by A.C. Nielsen to change its practices, which satisfied both the European Commission and the US Department of Justice.[85]

Furthermore the only formal positive comity referral was made in the *Sabre/Amadeus* case, where the US authorities asked the European Commission to investigate specific allegations of discrimination in relation to a computerized system (Amadeus) set up by the airlines Lufthansa, Air France and Iberia. The Commission investigated the case in cooperation with the US Department of Justice, and the outcome was the Commission's decision to open a procedure against Air France for possible abuse of their dominant position.[86] The investigation was finally closed following a private settlement agreement between Sabre and Air France.[87]

More than ten years after the conclusion of the US/EU agreement these are the only occasions where positive comity was used as a cooperative mechanism. Since then it has been included in every agreement in which the United States and the EU have been contracting parties; however it has failed to justify the enthusiasm that it generated in (mainly) US competition officials when it was first introduced. Evidently the International Competition Policy Advisory Comity[88] admitted that 'after nine years and the experience derived from both formal and informal applications, the public officials appear to have tempered their enthusiasm'.

*Limitations of bilateral enforcement cooperation agreements*
As mentioned above, all the previously discussed mechanisms for cooperation are weakened by the fact that most of these agreements are soft law instruments (that is, they do not create legally binding obligations for the contracting parties).[89] The agreements of this generation are not treaties. According to the European Commission they are 'administrative arrangements'; similarly the US authorities regard the agreements as 'executive agreements'.[90] Therefore the provisions of these agreements do not override the existing laws of the parties, and this has become a standard provision in every agreement of the first generation.

*(a) The confidentiality clause*   The lack of legally binding obligations is reflected in the provision relating to the so-called 'confidentiality clause' contained in these agreements. Exchange of confidential information is one of the most sensitive issues relating to enforcement cooperation in the field of competition law. This is due to the fact that there are two groups of opposing interests underlying the exchange of confidential information. On the one hand, there is the interest of the competition authorities to

receive as much information as possible regarding a practice under scrutiny. On the other hand, there are important corporate interests that need to be taken into account. First, the information exchanged and which relates to business goals and marketing strategy of the firms will not be made known to the competitors of the firm. Second, the information exchanged by the agencies in relation to a case will only be used for the particular reason that it is given to the other authority. This point is particularly sensitive in relation to cases where information could be used in cases related to the criminal liability of the firm's board.[91]

According to the 'confidentiality' provision, the parties can refuse disclosure of any information if the law of the party that possesses the information prohibits it or if this would be incompatible with the possessing party's important interests.[92] Put differently, and given the extent of discretion that the confidentiality clause leaves to the parties, in the case of these agreements it is more a matter of policy than a matter of law which finally determines the outcome of cooperation between competition authorities. Or, as Wood has pointed out, it is confirmation that nations believe that sovereignty privileges are much more important than any added benefits for competition law enforcement; it also demonstrates that international companies 'are content to live in a world in which enforcement agencies must operate with one hand tied behind their back'.[93]

With respect to the EU, a distinction is made between confidential agency information and confidential business information. The former relates to information gathered in the context of an investigation by the Commission, such as the identity of the undertakings being investigated and procedural aspects of the investigation. Such information may be given by the Commission to the US authorities, without the prior consent of the parties affected. Instead, the latter relates to business or trade secrets obtained as a result of the investigation. The Commission needs the consent of the affected parties in order to disclose such information to the US Authorities.[94]

Respectively, provisions that are included in the Antitrust Civil Process Act (ACPA), the Federal Trade Commission Act (FTCA) and the Clayton Act restrict the US authorities from sharing confidential information. ACPA states that no documentary material, answers to interrogatories or oral testimony shall be made available for examination without permission by the person who produced that material.[95] A similar provision can be found in the Clayton Act[96] and the FTCA,[97] which in addition extends the protection of confidentiality by stating that the FTC does not have the authority to make public any confidential financial information or trade secret, except that which the Commission may dispose to any law enforcement agencies, and can only be used for official law enforcement purposes.[98]

When these restrictions due to confidentiality apply, the competition authorities of the contracting parties can share information only if they can receive a waiver of confidentiality from the party that is involved in the practice under examination. As is the case, these kinds of waivers mostly occur in merger cases where the companies involved usually allow the sharing of confidential information in order to get a quick clearance for their proposed merger, especially if the competition agencies challenge the merger (owing to lack of sufficient information), and if the case goes to court the companies are likely to abandon the transaction, rather than to litigate the case. It should be remembered in this context that the decision of the courts usually takes up to two years or more.[99] Another incentive for parties to mergers to forgo confidentiality is probably in order to have symmetrical remedies imposed by the antitrust authorities. Hence it is not a surprise that up to now in almost all instances where there has been successful cooperation between competition authorities it involves merger cases. According to US and EU officials, some notable examples regarding the EU/US cooperation include the merger cases *WorldCom/MCI*,[100] *Guinness/Grand Metropolitan*, *Dresser/Halliburton*,[101] *Exxon/Mobile* and *Alcoa/Reynolds*.[102]

On the other hand enforcement cooperation has not proved effective in cases of abuse of dominant position and particularly in relation to cartels. Simply put, parties involved in such practices are not eager to allow competition authorities of different countries to exchange information which, without a waiver of confidentiality from the parties involved, would be impossible to share. The experience of EU/US cooperation reveals that in only one case relating to abuse of a dominant position did a company offer a waiver of confidentiality, and this case was before the European Council approved the agreement. In the 1994 *Microsoft* case, the US Department of Justice and the European Commission cooperated closely in their investigations of Microsoft's activities after the consent of Microsoft to the exchange of confidential information, which otherwise would not be possible to share.[103] The case was finally settled with a trilateral negotiation between the two enforcement authorities together and Microsoft, and was undoubtedly an impetus for the final approval of the agreement.[104]

In the same period there is not even one (publicly known) waiver of confidentiality with respect to a cartel case. It has been suggested by competition officials that the effectiveness of cooperation in cartel cases depends greatly upon the ability of the agencies involved to share confidential information.[105] Thus the view has been expressed that deeper cooperation is needed in cartel cases; currently EU and US officials are exploring the possibility of signing a second-generation agreement which would allow for exchange of confidential information.[106]

*(b) The inability of the first generation of agreements to address some important cases*   Having discussed the mechanisms of cooperation and their impact, we can now return to the issue mentioned in the beginning of this section, that is, the inability of the agreements of this generation (i.e. soft law agreements) to deal with cases when important interests of both contracting parties are affected. The conflict that arose between the US and the EU competition authorities, mainly on the *Boeing/MDD* and *GE/Honeywell* cases, illustrates this argument.

The *Boeing/MDD* case related to the attempt by two American companies (Boeing and McDonnell Douglas) to merge in December of 1996. This merger would have created the largest aerospace company in the world.[107] The US Federal Trade Commission cleared the merger without conditions on 1 July 1997.[108] However this was not the case with the European Commission. Basing its jurisdiction on the financial thresholds of the 'Community dimension' clause of the Merger Regulation, according to which no physical presence in the EC is required,[109] it made clear that it would block the merger. At this point, the American government intervened and threatened the EU that, if the Commission blocked the merger, the US would wage a commercial war against the EC by going to the WTO or by imposing trade sanctions.[110] Following this development, and subject to some commitments that Boeing offered, the Commission decided to clear the merger on 30 July 1997.[111]

The *GE/Honeywell* case concerned the merger between GE (the leading aircraft engine maker) and Honeywell (the leading avionics/non-avionics manufacturer). The merger would have created or strengthened a dominant position in different relevant markets where the two companies were involved. Despite the fact that during the merger review the US and EU agencies cooperated very closely, they did not manage to come up with the same decision. Even though the Antitrust Division of the US Department of Justice reached an agreement with GE and Honeywell regarding the Division's antitrust concerns related to the proposed merger,[112] the European Commission blocked the merger on 3 July 2001,[113] causing profound reactions from the other side of the Atlantic.[114] The divergence with respect to this specific case is related to the correctness of the 'portfolio effect theory', a variety of different means by which a merger may allegedly create or strengthen a dominant position in non-overlap markets.[115] However this incident, like the *Boeing/MDD* case, highlights the fact that in sensitive cases like this one, enforcement cooperation agreements of a voluntary nature are inadequate to provide for radical cooperative mechanisms and solutions.

These conflicts made it clear that, in cases like *Boeing/MDD* and *GE/Honeywell*, where both regulators claim jurisdiction,[116] and very crucial policy issues are involved (namely, in both cases, economic and employment policy in the very sensitive field of the aviation sector), bilateral competition agreements, at least in the form that they are concluded at present, seem to be incapable of offering viable solutions. Given the fast moving globalization of the markets on the one hand and the attempts of states to create national champions in order to participate with good 'players' in the world markets on the other, it is not difficult to predict that such conflicts may occur in the future.

In fact divergences have lately arisen to a lesser extent both on substantive and procedural issues. As to the former (substance), the Commission's recent decision to impose a fine of about €497 million on Microsoft and to oblige the company to disclose a particular source code and supply a version of its Windows operating system without the company's Media Player obviously disappointed US officials,[117] especially in view of the fact that in the USA Microsoft reached a settlement with the US Department of Justice more than two years before the Commission issued its decision. As to the latter (procedure), Commission officials have expressed their concern with regard to the possibility that statements of cartel whistle-blowers may become available through US discovery rules to US plaintiffs seeking recovery of treble damages.[118]

In sum, since contracting parties to these enforcement cooperation agreements are not bound by the provisions of these agreements, and furthermore these agreements do not provide for a mechanism for resolving conflicts, such as provisions for the specification of the competent court or the dispute settlement body in the case where a conflict arises, it is very much an issue of the political power of the contracting parties that will determine the outcome of such a conflict.

This would not cause any major impact in cases where a conflict arises between two equally politically and economically strong states, but it would definitely have a major impact in cases where one of the states involved in the conflict would be much stronger than the other. For instance, if we assume that such a conflict occurred between the US and Brazil, it would be quite safe to presume that the Brazilian authorities would have been quite vulnerable to the threat of economic measures that the US could impose. We return here again to the point that was made at the beginning of this chapter, that bilateralism, and also, as has been shown here, soft law, increase national power. Or as an author from a developing country has put it, bilateral agreements, at least in the form of soft law, cannot overcome the test of hegemony and ethnocentricism.[119]

## Competition enforcement agreements that expressly allow for exchange of confidential information

*The US–Australia agreement on mutual antitrust enforcement assistance: a new step regarding bilateral competition agreements*

The US adopted in 1994 the International Antitrust Enforcement Assistance Act (IAEAA)[120] to overcome constraints on the exchange of confidential information; however constraints were not completely overcome. Owing to business interests pressures,[121] the materials obtained during the Hart–Scott–Rodino pre-merger notifications are protected by the IAEAA and cannot be shared with other competition authorities.[122] Following the adoption of the IAEAA, the US entered in 1999 into a mutual antitrust enforcement agreement with Australia, which had legislation in place which was similar to the IAEAA,[123] paving the way for the second generation of agreements (agreements making it possible to share confidential information and use compulsory process on behalf of the other party). The US/Australia agreement is not an executive agreement of a voluntary nature but a binding treaty. According to Article II.G this agreement complements the 1982 US/Australia Agreement on Enforcement Cooperation and thus the combination of these agreements makes the US/Australia cooperation on antitrust enforcement the most sophisticated of all, at least in terms of the capability to exchange official documents.[124]

The parties have agreed to cooperate on a reciprocal basis in providing or obtaining evidence[125] related to enforcement of the other state's competition law. They also agree to disclose, provide, exchange or discuss antitrust evidence.[126] Moreover the agreement provides that following a request, the type of which is described in great detail in Article III of the agreement, a party may obtain antitrust evidence from the other party. This evidence may include taking the testimony or statements from persons; obtaining documents, or other forms of documentary evidence; locating or identifying persons or things; executing searches and seizures; and disclosing, providing, exchanging or discussing such evidence).

The information exchanged according to the provision of this agreement can be used solely for enforcing antitrust laws.[127] There is however a place in this agreement for refusal to share information. Article IV of the agreement provides that a party may deny assistance in the case where such assistance would not be permitted by the law of the requested party (which shows that there are still laws that do not permit the sharing of information) or when information sharing would be against the requested party's public interest. However there is a provision that the party which refuses to provide the requested information must offer an explanation for the basis of denial.

*Norway/Iceland/Denmark*

Similarly the Denmark–Norway–Iceland 2001 agreement provides for exchange of confidential information. All these three countries have adopted legislation which allow the exchange of such information.[128] The agreement follows the usual procedure of notification in cases where 'one Authority becomes aware of the fact that its enforcement measures could have a bearing on significant competitive interests that come under the competence of another Authority'.[129] Article IV of this agreement provides that the parties agree that it is in their common interest to exchange confidential information, subject to a duty of confidentiality by the authorities which receive the information, and a commitment that they will use the confidential information only for the purposes stipulated in the agreement. The mechanism for cooperation in this process of sharing confidential information is not described in detail as it is in the US/Australia agreement of 1999. Nevertheless it is quite promising that a second agreement has been concluded in such a short period of time.

It should be stressed that these agreements are definitely a positive step for enforcement cooperation since they provide for clear legal obligations for the parties and they also provide competition agencies with the capability to exchange important information regarding enforcement against anticompetitive practices. Nonetheless, given the fact that reciprocal commitment from the contracting parties is needed in order for an agreement like this to be concluded, at the present time we cannot be overoptimistic about the conclusion of many more agreements like the one between the US and Australia, since there are very few countries with legislation similar to the IAEAA. Burnside and Botteman argue that in fact the US has been unsuccessful in its attempts to promote the adoption of agreements of this kind.[130] That said, current negotiations on a possible agreement of this sort between the US and the EU[131] are an indication that more agreements like the US/Australia agreement may be concluded in the near future.

Moreover, and even though these agreements contain provisions that oblige the parties to exchange confidential information, the US/Australia agreement contains exceptions to this obligation for reasons related to *public policy*. This may give a lot of room to the contracting parties to avoid exchange of confidential information in some cases, especially under the pressure that competition officials of the contracting parties may face from business organizations. Even though these agreements include provisions which confirm that the information exchanged will be used only in relation to competition law, business organizations, such as the International Chamber of Commerce and the Union of Industrial and Employers' Confederation of Europe (UNICE), have already expressed their concern about the US/Australia agreement, especially about the fact that the shared information could be used for reasons other than competition, for example to impose criminal liability on the parties involved in the practice under scrutiny or to access the business strategy plans of the enterprises involved.[132]

Finally it has to be pointed out that neither of the competition agencies involved in the implementation of these agreements (such as the US Department of Justice and the Federal Trade Commission and the Australian Competition and Consumer Commission) has issued any documents on the implementation of the agreements of the second generation. Hence we cannot make safe conclusions yet on their impact on international enforcement cooperation.

**Conclusions**

The theme of this chapter is that enforcement cooperation agreements have proved to be effective in relation to a number of problems concerning restrictive business practices with an international impact; however they also have limitations.

Their most positive effect is that they create the mechanism through which officials of different national authorities are able to come into contact and have the opportunity to share their views on issues of mutual interest. The provisions for meetings between competition officials and the provisions for technical assistance are evidence of this. Given that competition law, having only recently been adopted by most countries, is a relatively new legal tool, the frequent communication among competition authorities is definitely beneficial in terms of the creation of a competition culture around the world.

In addition, facts mostly from the application of the US/EU agreement reveal that on the whole the agreement has offered useful mechanisms for cooperation in a number of cases, particularly relating to mergers, where the consent of the parties to give a waiver of confidentiality is quite common. The increase in the number of notifications also shows that the everyday cooperation among competition officials is becoming stronger.

However, as mentioned above, it is indisputable that enforcement agreements have certain limitations. First, most of these agreements include a 'confidentiality clause' making them impractical in cartel cases and cases regarding abuse of dominant position. The two agreements between the US and Australia and the tripartite agreement between Denmark, Iceland

and Norway, are undoubtedly very positive steps, since they provide the agencies of the contracting parties with the opportunity to exchange confidential information. Nevertheless, at the moment, we cannot evaluate the effect of these agreements, given that there are no available data as to their application.

Second, even in merger cases – where the cooperation has been proved effective – the US/EU agreement failed to provide the authorities with adequate legal tools in cases like *Boeing/MDD* and *GE/Honeywell* where very sensitive interests of the contracting parties were affected. This is a reflection of the voluntary nature of the agreements of the first generation.

Third, bilateral and tripartite agreements are by definition insufficient to face situations where interests of more than two or three nations are affected. A very illustrative example is that of the multiple notifications in the case of multijurisdictional mergers. For instance, the *Exxon/Mobil* transaction was notified in 20 jurisdictions.[133] Obviously bilateral or tripartite agreements could not provide for any adequate mechanisms of cooperation in such cases. The only possibility for resolving problems like this, based on provisions of bilateral or tripartite agreements, would be in the case where all the nations with a competition regime have concluded this kind of agreement. Apparently that would be extremely complicated, given that, if we take into account only the OECD countries, we would need 435 bilateral agreements in order to face the problems of international competition enforcement effectively.

All these considerations stress the fact that, even though useful, enforcement cooperation agreements in the field of competition law are by no means adequate in themselves to provide for radical solutions with respect to the problems caused by restrictive business practices with an international effect. It is also noteworthy that two of the most recent enforcement agreements that have been concluded are tripartite and this illustrates the need for expansion of the number of contracting parties. The substantial work that has been carried out by the International Competition Network[134] further highlights the fact that, even in the field of voluntary enforcement cooperation, international problems need international solutions. Even US officials who, as has been illustrated above, have been traditionally opposed to a possible international harmonization of competition law and have accepted that bilateral cooperation will be adequate to solve problems relating to restrictive business practices with an international effect seem to have changed their opinion. Characteristically, Charles James[135] admitted:

> there have been days when we thought (or hoped) that such (bilateral) cooperation itself would eventually minimize or resolve even the most serious areas of antitrust divergence. More recently, however, we have come to understand that

cooperation alone will not resolve some significant areas of divergence among antitrust regimes that must be addressed if we are to maintain the integrity of antitrust on a global stage.

As Gerber[136] has very convincingly assessed, 'only when international obligations created an explicit alignment of the interests of the decision-makers did convergence achieve notable success'. Bilateral enforcement cooperation agreements, even though useful, are definitely inadequate to achieve this goal by themselves.

## Notes

1. Researcher at the London School of Economics (Law Department). Dikigoros, Athens Bar Association, LL.B. (Athens), LL.M. (Manchester). I am grateful to Imelda Maher, Giorgio Monti and Deborah Cass for comments on earlier drafts of this chapter. All remaining errors and omissions are the author's.
2. Named after the Canadian Minister of Justice and the US Attorney General at that time: Finckenstein, Konrad von (2001), 'International antitrust cooperation: bilateralism or multilateralism?', Vancouver, 31 May 2001.
3. Stark, Charles (2000), 'Improving bilateral antitrust cooperation', Washington, D.C., 23 June 2000, at p. 2, available at http://www.usdoj.gov/atr/public/speeches/5075.htm (last visited on 20/8/2005).
4. Recommendation of the Council concerning cooperation between member countries on restrictive business practices affecting international trade of 5 October 1967 [C(567)53(Final)].
5. Recommendation of the Council of 3rd July 1973 [C (73) 99 (Final)].
6. Recommendation of the Council of 25th September 1979 [C (79) 154 (Final)].
7. Recommendation of the Council of 21st May of 1986[C (86) 44 (Final)].
8. Recommendation of the Council of 27th and 28th July of 1995 [C (95) 130 (Final)].
9. Ibid. in Article I.A.1.
10. Ibid. in Article I.A.2.
11. Ibid. in Article I.B.4.(a).
12. Ibid. in Article I.A.3.
13. Ibid. in Article I.B.5.(a) in conjunction with Article I.B.5.(c). The provision relating to positive comity was added to the recommendation in the amendment of 1973.
14. Ibid. in recital 7.
15. Monti, Mario (2000), 'Cooperation between competition authorities – a vision for the future', the Japan Foundation Conference, Washington DC, 23 June 2000, available at http://europa.eu.int/rapid/start/cgi/guesten.ksh?p_action.gettxt=gt&doc=SPEECH/00/234/0/RAPID&lg=EN (last visited on 20/8/2005).
16. Abbott, Kenneth, Robert Keohane, Andrew Moravcsik, Anne Marie Slaughter and Duncan Snidal (2000), 'The concept of legalisation', *International Organisation*, **54**(3), 401–19, at 401.
17. See Wood, Diane P. (1995), 'The internationalisation of antitrust law: options for the future', *De Paul Law Review*, **44**, 1289; and Klein, Joel I. (1996), 'A note of caution with respect to a WTO agenda on competition policy', available at http://www.usdoj.gov/atr/public/speeches/0998.htm (last visited on 20/8/2005). See also the communication of the US, WT/WGTCP/W/116 (25 May 1999).
18. Ibid. See Communication of the US, WT/WGTCP/W/116 (26 May 1999).
19. Fox, Eleanor (1997), 'Toward world antitrust and market access', *American Journal of International Law*, **91**(1), 1, at 12.
20. Braithwaite, John and Peter Drahos (2000), *Global Business Regulation*, Cambridge: Cambridge University Press, at 198.
21. Ibid.

22. Waller, S.W. (1997), 'Internationalisation of antitrust enforcement', *Boston University Law Review*, **77**, 343, at 378.
23. Zach, R. (1998), 'International cooperation between antitrust enforcement agencies: a view from a small country', in Hans Ulrich (ed.), *Comparative Competition Law: Approaching an International System of Antitrust Law*, Baden-Baden: Nomos Verlagsgesellschaft, at 261.
24. See Holmes, Peter, Henrike Müller, Anestis Papadopoulos and Anna Sydorak (2005), 'The legal framework of bilateral relations in the field of competition law and policy: a taxonomic approach', paper presented at the Competition Policy Foundations For Trade Reform, Regulatory Reform and Sustainable Development Mid-term Meeting in Brussels, 26 April 2005.
25. See Australian Competition and Consumer Commission (ACCC) website: http://www.accc.gov.au/international/international.htm.
26. Abbott et al. (2000), n 16.
27. Abott, Kenneth W. and Duncan Snidal (2000), 'Hard and soft law in international governance', *International Organisation*, **54**(3), 421, at 422.
28. Weil, Prosper (1983), 'Towards relative normativity in international law?', *American Journal of International Law*, **77**, 413, at 423.
29. See Slaughter, Anne-Marie (2000), 'Governing the global economy through government networks', in Michael Byers (ed.), *The Role of Law in International Politics: Essays in International Relations and International Law*, Oxford University Press, pp. 177–206.
30. Reismann, M.W. (1991), 'A hard look at soft law', Panel Report, *American Society of International Law*, **82**, 371, at 427.
31. Quoted in Reismann (1991), n 30, at 377.
32. Ibid. at 375.
33. For instance one of the aims of competition policy in the EU is the integration of the internal market.
34. See Canada–Australia–New Zealand Agreement, Art. I 2.
35. See US/Canada Agreement, Art. VII.
36. According to Canadian officials the main aim of these provisions is to solve problems relating to deceptive telemarketing, that is, person-to-person telephone calls used to make false or misleading representations in promoting the supply of a product or business interest. See Murphy, Gavin (2001), 'Canada, Australia and New Zealand competition authorities sign cooperation arrangement', *European Competition Law Review*, **22**(8), 322–4, at 322.
37. Ham, Allard D. (1993), 'International cooperation in the anti-trust field and in particular the agreement between the United States of America and the Commission of the European Communities', *Common Market Law Review*, **30**, 571–97, at 576.
38. Walker, William K. (1992), 'Extraterritorial application of US antitrust laws: the effect of the European Community–United States Agreement', *Harvard International Law Journal*, **33**, 583–91, at 586.
39. Pitofsky, Robert (1999), 'Competition policy in a global economy – today and tomorrow', *Journal of International Economic Law*, **2**(3), 403–11, at 408.
40. The Agreement finally entered into force in 1995 as a result of an action brought by the Government of France against the Commission, successfully challenging the competence of the European Commission to conclude this kind of agreement. See Riley, Alan (1995), 'The jellyfish nailed? The announcement of the EC/US Competition Co-operation Agreement', *European Competition Law Review*, **3**, 185. The problem was finally solved with the approval of the agreement by the European Council.
41. Yntema, H. (1966), 'The comity doctrine', *Michigan Law Review*, **65**(1), 9–32.
42. Ibid. at 26.
43. Joel Paul gives 16 alternative meanings of the principle, found in various scientific articles that deal with comity: Paul, Joel R. (1991), 'Comity in international law', *Harvard International Law Journal*, **32**(1), 2–71, at 3–4.
44. Himelfarb, Allison J. (1996), 'The international language of convergence: reviving the antitrust dialogue between The United States of America and the European Union with

a uniform understanding of extraterritoriality', *University of Pennsylvania Journal of International Economic Law*, **17**(3), 909–55, at 914.

45. Ehlermann, Claus-Dieter (1994), 'The international dimension of competition policy', *Fordham International Law Journal*, **17**, 833–45, at 836.

46. See Barnet, Susan E. (2004), 'Conflicts of jurisdiction and international comity in extraterritorial antitrust', *Emory International Law Review*, **18**, 555–643.

47. *United States* v. *Aluminum Co. of America* 148 F.2d 416 (2d Cir. 1945).

48. *Timberlane Lumber Co.* v. *Bank of America*, 549F.2d 597 (9th Cir. 1976).

49. See 15 U.S.C s.6a (1994).

50. Springman, Christopher (2005), 'Fix prices globally, get sued locally? US jurisdiction over international cartels', Forthcoming, *University of Chicago Law Review*, available at http://cyberlaw.stanford.edu/blogs/sprigman/archives/chicago2.pdf (last visited on 20/8/2005), at 7–9.

51. *Hartford Fire Ins. Co.* v. *California*, 509 US 764 (1993).

52. See *United States of America* v. *Nippon Paper Industries Co. LTD et al.*, 109 F.3 d, p. 9.

53. *Hoffmann La Roche* v. *Empagran, SA* 124 2359 (2004). See Reinker Kenneth S. (2004), 'Case Comment: *Roche* v. *Empagran*', *Harvard Journal of Law and Public Policy*, **28**, 297–306.

54. In particular the Supreme Court remanded to the Court of Appeals to assess the applicants' argument that 'because vitamins are fungible and readily transportable, without an adverse domestic effect (i.e. higher prices in the United States), the sellers could not have maintained their international price fixing arrangement and respondents would not have suffered their foreign injury'. See *Empagram SA* v. *F Hoffmann La Roche, LTD. ET AL*, Opinion of Court of Appeals, No 01-7115c (2005).

55. Joined cases C-89, 104, 114, 116, 117 and 125–129/85 *Ahlstrom and Others* v. *E.C. Commission (Re Wood Pulp Cartel)* [1998] E.C.R. 5193, [1988] 4 C.M.L.R. 901.

56. The decision reads: 'an infringement of Article 85 . . . [is] made up of two elements, the formation of the agreement, decision or concerted practice, and the implementation thereof'. See [1988] 4 C.M.L.R., para. 16.

57. Banks, J.D. (1998), 'The development of the concept of extraterritoriality under European merger law and its effectiveness under the merger regulation following the *Boeing/McDonnell Douglas* Decision 1997', *European Competition Law Review*, **19**(5), 306–11, at 308.

58. *Gencor Ltd* v. *Commission* Case T-102/96, 4 CMLR, 971, [1999].

59. Ibid. at para. 90.

60. Monti, Mario (2000), 'Cooperation between competition authorities – a vision for the future', The Japan Foundation Conference, Washington DC, 23 June 2000, available at http://europa.eu.int/rapid/start/cgi/guesten.ksh?p_action.gettxt=gt&doc=SPEECH/00/234|0|RAPID&lg=EN (last visited on 20/8/2005).

61. See EU/US Agreement, Art. II.

62. EU Commission (1998), 'EU Commission report to the Council and the European Parliament on the Application of the Agreement between the European Communities and the Government of the United States of America regarding the application of their competition laws, 1 January to 31 December 1997', Brussels, 11 May 1998, at 3.

63. See EU/US Agreement, Art. II.3 (a)(iii) and II.3 (b)(iii).

64. Successive notifications may occur in the same case. For example, in a merger case the Commission may notify at the outset of the case; then, when appropriate, when the Commission decides to initiate proceedings; and, eventually, 'far enough in advance . . . to enable the other Party's views to be taken into account', before a final decision is adopted: EU Commission (1998), n 62, above, at 3.

65. For instance, in the EU/US agreement, these factors include the relative ability of the parties' competition authorities to obtain the information necessary to conduct enforcement activity, or the effect of such coordination on each party's ability to achieve its objectives.

66. See Kurzer, Paulette (2001), *Markets and Moral Regulation: Cultural Change in the European Union*, Cambridge University Press.

67.  See Meyer, John W., John Boli, George M. Thomas and Francisco O. Ramirez (1997), 'World society and the nation state', *American Journal of Sociology*, **103**(1), 144–81.
68.  Slaughter (2000), above, note 29, at 178–9.
69.  Ibid. at 193.
70.  Markert, Kurt E. (1968), 'Recent developments in international antitrust cooperation', *Antitrust Bulletin*, **13**, 355, at 359.
71.  See Organisation for Economic Co-operation and Development (1999), OECD, CLP Report on Positive Comity, DAFFE/CLP (99), (14 June 1999).
72.  Iyori, Hiroshi (1998), 'Japanese cooperation in international antitrust law enforcement', in Hans Ulrich (ed.), *Comparative Competition Law: Approaching an International System of Antitrust Law*, Baden-Baden: Nomos Verlagsgesellschaft, at 261.
73.  Grewlich, Alexandre S. (2001), 'Globalisation and conflict in competition law: elements and possible solutions', *World Competition*, **24**(3), 367–404, at 385.
74.  A similar agreement was signed between the US and Canada in 2004.
75.  EU–US Agreement on Positive Comity, Article II (4).
76.  Parisi, John J. (1999), 'Enforcement co-operation among antitrust authorities', *European Competition Law Review*, **20**(3), 133–42, at 136.
77.  Griffin, Joseph P. (1998), 'Antitrust aspects of cross-border mergers and acquisitions', *European Competition Law Review*, **19**(1), 12–20, at 17.
78.  EU Commission (2003), 'Report from the Commission to the Council and the European Parliament on the application of the agreements between the European Communities and the Government of the United States of America and the Government of Canada regarding the application of their competition laws, 1 January 2002 to 31 December 2002', available online at the following website: http://europa.eu.int/comm/competition/international/bilateral/canada/2002_report_en.pdf (last visited on 20/8/2005), at 4.
79.  See Philip Marsden (2000), 'the divide on verticals', in Simon J. Evennett, Alexander Lehman and Benn Steil (eds), *Antitrust Goes Global*, Washington D.C.: Brooking Institution Press.
80.  'Keiretsu' was the practice that urged the American Company Kodak to go to the WTO dispute settlement against the Japanese company Fuji. Case: Japan – measures affecting consumer photographic film and paper, WT/DS44/R; see Mark Furse (1999), 'Competition law and the WTO Report: "Japan–Measures Affecting Consumer Photographic Film and Paper"', *European Competition Law Review*, **20**(1), 9–13.
81.  Atwood, James R. (1992), 'Positive comity: is it a positive step?', in Barry Hawk (ed.) 1992 *Annual Proceedings of the Fordham Corporate Law Institute International Antitrust Law and Policy Conference*, New York: Fordham Corporate Law Institute, pp. 79–89, at p.86.
82.  See EU Commission (1999), 'EU Commission report to the Council and the European Parliament on the application of the agreement between the European Communities and the Government of the United States of America regarding the application of their competition laws, Brussels, 2 April 1999', available at http://europa.eu.int/comm/competition/international/bilateral/usa/1998_comm_report_app_comp_law_en.pdf (last visited on 20/8/2005).
83.  Janow, Merit E. (2000), 'Transatlantic cooperation on competition Policy', in Simon J. Evennett, Alexander Lehman and Benn Steil (eds), *Antitrust Goes Global*, Washington D.C.: Brooking Institution Press, pp. 29–56, at 38.
84.  Ibid.
85.  Rill, James F. and Christine C. Wilson (2000), 'The A.C. Nielsen case' in Simon J. Evennett, Alexander Lehman and Benn Steil (eds), *Antitrust Goes Global*, Washington D.C.: Brooking Institution Press, pp. 222–4, at 193.
86.  See European Commission Press Release IP/99/171 (15 March 1999).
87.  See European Commission Press Release IP/00/835 (25 July 2000).
88.  International Competition Policy Advisory Comity (2000), *ICPAC Final report to the attorney general and the assistant attorney general for Antitrust*, available at http://www.usdoj.gov/atr/icpac/finalreport.htm (last visited on 20/8/2005), at 325.
89.  Furthermore they include a provision according to which contracting parties have the discretion to terminate the application of these agreements at any time (this provision

for discretional termination of the agreements is included even in the two agreements that are not administrative arrangements but treaties).

90. The reason for this is that, under the American laws, in order to be a treaty, an international agreement has to get approval by the Senate, and for the EU the lack of competence of the Commission to sign Treaties on behalf of the EU as a whole.

91. See International Chamber Commerce (1999), *ICC recommendations to the International Competition Policy Advisory Committee (ICPAC) on exchange of confidential information between competition authorities in the merger context*, Commission on Law and Practices relating to Competition, 21 May 1999; and International Chamber of Commerce (1996), *ICC Statement on International Cooperation between Antitrust Authorities*, 28 March 1996, Doc. 225/450 Rev.3.

92. See for instance EU–US agreement (Art. VIII); the EU/Canada agreement (Art X); US/Canada agreement (Art X); and the US/Japan agreement (Art IX(5)).

93. Wood, Diane P. (1999) 'Is cooperation possible?', *New England Law Review*, **34**(1), 103–12, at 110.

94. Kiriazis, Georgios (2001), 'Jurisdiction and cooperation issues in the investigation of international cartels', available online at the following website: http://europa.eu.int/comm/competition/speeches/text/sp 2001_010_en.pdf (last visited on 20/8/2005), at 10–14.

95. 15 U.S.C. s.1313 (c)(3).

96. 15 U.S.C. ss.7 A (h), 18 (a).

97. 15 U.S.C. s.57-2 (b).

98. 15 U.S.C s.46 (f).

99. See Monti, Mario (2001b), 'The future for competition policy in the European Union', Merchant Taylor Hall, London, 9 July 2001, available at the following website: http://www.europa.eu.int/rapid/start/cgi/guesten.ksh_p?action.gettxt=gt&doc=SPEECH/01/340|0|RAPID&lg=EN (last visited on 20/8/2005).

100. See 'Department of Justice Clears WorldCom/MCI Merger after MCI agrees to sell its Internet Business', US Department of Justice Press Release 15 July 1998; thanks to the consent of the companies involved, the competition agencies could exchange confidential information.

101. See Commission Press Release, IP/98/643, 08/07/1998.

102. See Monti, Mario (2000), 'Cooperation between competition authorities – a vision for the future', The Japan Foundation Conference, Washington DC, 23 June, available at http://europa.eu.int/rapid/start/cgi/guesten.ksh?p_action.gettxt=gt&doc=SPEECH/00/234|0|RAPID&lg=EN (last visited on 20/8/2005).

103. Microsoft agreed to negotiate identical consent decrees with the Commission and the DoJ in order to resolve the allegations of anticompetitive practices, by Novell, Microsoft's main competitor in the software application market. See Himelfarb, Allison J. (1996), 'The international language of convergence: reviving the antitrust dialogue between The United States of America and the European Union with a uniform understanding of extraterritoriality', *University of Pennsylvania Journal of International Economic Law*, **17**(3), 909–55, at 910–11.

104. See Microsoft case settlement, European Commission Press Release, IP/94/543.

105. Kiriazis, *supra*, n. 94, at 1.

106. Kroes, Neelie (2005), 'The first hundred days', available at http://europa.eu.int/rapid/pressReleasesAction.do?reference=SPEECH/05/205&format=HTML&aged=0&language=EN&guiLanguage=en, at 5.

107. For an analysis of the facts of the case, see Boeder T.L. and G.J. Dorman (2000), 'The Boeing/Mc Donnell Douglas merger: the economics, antitrust law and politics of the aerospace industry', *Antitrust Bulletin*, **1**(XLV), 119–52.

108. See 'Letter to Marc G. Schildkraut, Esquire and Benjamin S. Sharp, Esquire regarding the proposed acquisition of McDonnell Douglas Corporation by The Boeing Company', available at the FTC website: http://www.ftc.gov/os/caselist/9710051.htm.

109. Griffin, Joseph P. (1994), 'EC and US extraterritoriality: activism and cooperation', *Fordham International Law Journal*, **17**, 353–77, at 360.

110. Kaczorowska, Alina (2000), 'International competition law in the context of global capitalism', *European Competition Law Review*, **21**(2), 117–27, at 217.
111. Commission Decision of 30 July 1997, Case No. IV/M.877, [1997], OJ L336/16.
112. See US DoJ press release of 2 May 2001, 'Justice Department requires divestitures in merger between General Electric and Honeywell'.
113. See European Commission press release of 3 July 2001, 'The Commission prohibits GE's acquisition on Honeywell', IP/01/939.
114. See US DoJ press release of 3 July 2001, 'Statement by Assistant Attorney General Charles A. James on the EU's decision regarding the GE/Honeywell acquisition'.
115. See Giotakos, Dimitri, Lurent Petit, Gaelle Garnier and Peter De Luyck (2001), 'General Electric Honeywell – an insight into the Commission's investigation and decision', *Competition Policy Newsletter*, **3**, 5–13; and Patterson, Donna E. and Carl Shapiro (2001), 'Trans-Atlantic divergence in GE/Honeywell, causes and lessons', available at http://faculty.haas.berkeley.edu/shapiro/divergence.pdf (last visited on 20/8/2005).
116. It should be noted that the decision of EU to take jurisdiction was actually disputed by some commentators. For instance see Barvaso, Antonio F. (1998), '*Boeing/McDonnell Douglas*: did the Commission fly too high?', *European Competition Law Review*, **19**(4), 243–8. However, see also Van Miert, Karel (1997), 'International cooperation in the field of competition: a view from the EC', in Barry Hawk (ed.) (1997), *Fordham Corporate Law Institute International Antitrust Law and Policy Conference*, New York: Fordham Corporate Law Institute, 13, at 18, where the former Commissioner claimed that in *Nippon Paper* in terms of jurisdiction the US authorities went beyond what the Commission did in *Boeing/MDD*.
117. See US DoJ press release, 2 November 2001, 'Department of Justice and Microsoft Corporation reach effective settlement on antitrust lawsuit'. See also Burnside, Alec and Helen Crossley (2005), 'Cooperation in competition: a new era', *European Law Review*, **30**(2), 234–60, at 254–5.
118. Nordlander, Christina (2004), 'Discovering Discovery: US Discovery of EC Leniency Statements', *European Competition Law Review*, **25**(10), 646–59.
119. De Noronha Goyos, D. (1997), 'The globalisation of competition law: a Latin American perspective', *International Trade Law Review*, **3**(1), 20, at 21.
120. International Antitrust Enforcement Assistance Act of 1994, 15 U.S.C. ss.6201–6212.
121. These were related to the fact that such materials include highly-sensitive information regarding business strategies of US firms: Freeman, Laurie N. (1995), 'US–Canadian information sharing and the International Antitrust Enforcement Assistant Act of 1994', *Georgetown Law Journal*, **84**, 339, at 358–9.
122. See U.S.C. 6204 (1).
123. Mutual Assistance in Business Regulation Act 1992 and the Mutual Assistance in Criminal Matters Act 1987.
124. It has to be noted that exchange of confidential information is also provided by Mutual Legal Antitrust Treaties in Criminal Matters (MLATs). The US is the most prominent user of such agreements, as it is a party to 50 of them. These agreements cover practices that constitute violation of criminal law and thus are useful in cases where both contracting parties have criminalized their competition rules. Such examples of relevance to competition law MLATs are the US–Canada and US–UK agreements (Holmes et al., 2005). That said, Zanettin argues that the US–Italy and the US–Spain MLATs may be used on competition cases, since they do not make dual criminality a prerequisite for assistance: Zanettin, Bruno (2002), *Cooperation Between Antitrust Agencies at the International Level*, Oxford: Hart Publishing, at 149.
125. See US/Australia Mutual Antitrust Enforcement Treaty, Art 1, A.
126. Ibid. Art II 1.
127. Art. VII. 1 – with the exception of information that has become publicly known: Art VII.D; and of the existence of a written consent by the party which provided the information: Art. VII. C).
128. See Consolidate Danish Competition Act No 687 of 12 July 2000, Section 18a; see Norwegian Competition Act (Act No 65 of 11 June 1993 ) sections 1–8, as amended by

Act No. 35 of 5 May 2000; see Icelandic Competition Act (Act No. 8 of 5 February 1993), Chapter XII, section 50a , as amended by Act No. 107 of 2000.
129. See agreement between Denmark, Iceland and Norway on cooperation in competition cases, Art. II, para. 1.
130. Burnside, Alec and Yves Botteman (2004), 'Networking amongst competition agencies', *International Trade Law & Regulation*, **10**(1), 1–10, at 3.
131. Kroes, *supra*, n. 106, at 5.
132. Parisi, John J. (1999), 'Enforcement co-operation among antitrust authorities', *European Competition Law Review*, **20**(3), 133–42, at 139.
133. Griffin, Joseph P. (1999), 'What business people want from a world antitrust code', *New England Law Review*, **34**(1), 39–45, at 39.
134. Bode, Marianna and Oliver Budzinski (2005), 'Competing toward international antitrust: the WTO vs. the ICN', Marburg Papers on Economics, 03/2005, 1–33, at 13–15.
135. James, Charles (2001), 'International antitrust in the Bush Administration', Canadian Bar association on Competition Law, Ottawa, Canada, 21 September, available at www.usdoj.gov/atr/public/speeches/9100.pdf (last visited on 20/8/2005).
136. Gerber, David J. (1999), 'The US–European conflict over the globalisation of antitrust law: a legal experience perspective', *New England Law Review*, **34**(1), 123–43, at 133.

## References

Abott, Kenneth W. and Duncan Snidal (2000), 'Hard and soft law in international governance', *International Organisation*, **54**(3), 421–46.
Abbott, Kenneth, Robert Keohane, Andrew Moravcsik, Anne Marie Slaughter and Duncan Snidal (2000), 'The concept of legalisation', *International Organisation*, **54**(3), 401–19.
Atwood, James R. (1992), 'Positive comity: is it a positive step?', in Barry Hawk (ed.), 1992 *Annual Proceedings of the Fordham Corporate Law Institute International Antitrust Law and Policy Conference*, New York: Fordham Corporate Law Institute, pp. 79–89.
Banks, J.D. (1998), 'The development of the concept of extraterritoriality under European merger law and its effectiveness under the merger regulation following the *Boeing/McDonnell Douglas* decision, 1997', *European Competition Law Review*, **19**(5), 306–11.
Barnet, Susan E. (2004), 'Conflicts of jurisdiction and international comity in extraterritorial antitrust', *Emory International Law Review*, **18**, 555–643.
Barvaso, Antonio F. (1998), '*Boeing/McDonnell Douglas*: did the Commission fly too high?', *European Competition Law Review*, **19**(4), 243–8.
Bode, Marianna and Oliver Budzinski (2005), 'Competing toward international antitrust: the WTO vs. the ICN', Marburg Papers on Economics, 03/2005, 1–33.
Boeder T.L. and G.J. Dorman (2000), 'The Boeing/McDonnell Douglas merger: the economics, antitrust law and politics of the aerospace industry', *Antitrust Bulletin*, 1(XLV), 119–52.
Braithwaite, John and Peter Drahos (2000), *Global Business Regulation*, Cambridge: Cambridge University Press.
Burnside, Alec and Yves Botteman (2004), 'Networking amongst competition agencies', *International Trade Law & Regulation*, **10**(1), 1–10.
Burnside, Alec and Helen Crossley (2005), 'Cooperation in competition: a new era', *European Law Review*, **30**(2), 234–60.
De Noronha Goyos, D. (1997), 'The globalisation of competition law: a Latin American perspective', *International Trade Law Review*, **3**(1), 20.
Ehlermann, Claus-Dieter (1994), 'The international dimension of competition policy', *Fordham International Law Journal*, **17**, 833–45.
EU Commission (1998), 'EU Commission report to the Council and the European Parliament on the Application of the Agreement between the European Communities and the Government of the United States of America regarding the application of their competition laws, 1 January to 31 December 1997', Brussels, 11 May.
EU Commission (1999), 'EU Commission report to the Council and the European Parliament on the application of the agreement between the European Communities and the

Government of the United States of America regarding the application of their competition laws, Brussels, 2 April 1999', available online at the following website: http://europa. eu.int/comm/competition/international/bilateral/usa/1998_comm_report_app_comp_law_ en.pdf (last visited on 20/8/2005).

EU Commission (2002), 'EU Commission Report from the Commission to the Council and the European Parliament on the application of the agreements between the European Communities and the Government of the United States of America and the Government of Canada regarding the application of their competition laws, 1 January 2000 to 31 December 2000', Brussels, 29 January 2002, COM (2002) 45 final.

EU Commission (2003), 'Report from the Commission to the Council and the European Parliament on the application of the agreements between the European Communities and the Government of the United States of America and the Government of Canada regarding the application of their competition laws, 1 January 2002 to 31 December 2002', available online at the following website http://europa.eu.int/comm/competition/international/ bilateral/canada/2002_report_en.pdf (last visited on 20/8/2005).

Finckenstein, Konrad von (2001), 'International antitrust cooperation: bilateralism or multi-lateralism?', Vancouver, 31 May.

Fox, Eleanor (1997), 'Toward world antitrust and market access', *American Journal of International Law*, **91**(1), 1–25.

Freeman, Laurie N. (1995), 'US–Canadian information sharing and the International Antitrust Enforcement Assistant Act of 1994', *Georgetown Law Journal*, **84**, 339.

Furse, Mark (1999), 'Competition law and the WTO Report: "Japan – measures affecting consumer photographic film and paper"' *European Competition Law Review*, **20**(1), 9–13.

Gerber, David J. (1999), 'The US–European conflict over the globalisation of antitrust law: a legal experience perspective', *New England Law Review*, **34**(1), 123–43.

Giotakos, Dimitri, Lurent Petit, Gaelle Garnier and Peter De Luyck (2001), 'General Electric Honeywell – an insight into the Commission's investigation and decision', *Competition Policy Newsletter*, **3**, 5–13.

Goldman, Calvin S. and Joel T. Kissack (1994), 'Current issues in cross–border criminal investigations: a Canadian perspective', in Barry Hawk (ed.) 1994 *Fordham Corporate Law Institute International Antitrust Law and Policy Conference*, New York: Fordham Corporate Law Institute, p. 37.

Grewlich, Alexandre S. (2001), 'Globalisation and conflict in competition law: elements and possible solutions', *World Competition*, **24**(3), 367–404.

Griffin, Joseph P. (1993), 'EC/US Antitrust Cooperation Agreement: impact on transnational business', *Law and Policy in International Business*, **24**, 1051–65.

Griffin, Joseph P. (1994), 'EC and US extraterritoriality: activism and cooperation', *Fordham International Law Journal*, **17**, 353–77.

Griffin, Joseph P. (1998), 'Antitrust aspects of cross-border mergers and acquisitions', *European Competition Law Review*, **19**(1), 12–20.

Griffin, Joseph P. (1999), 'What business people want from a world antitrust code', *New England Law Review*, **34**(1), 39–45.

Ham, Allard D. (1993), 'International cooperation in the anti-trust field and in particular the agreement between the United States of America and the Commission of the European Communities', *Common Market Law Review*, **30**, 571–97.

Helou, Angelina (1991), 'The nature and competitiveness of Japan's keiretsu', *Journal of World Trade*, **25**(3), 99–131.

Himelfarb, Allison J. (1996), 'The international language of convergence: reviving the antitrust dialogue between The United States of America and the European Union with a uniform understanding of extraterritoriality', *University of Pennsylvania Journal of International Economic Law*, **17**(3), 909–55.

Holmes, Peter, Henrike Müller, Anestis Papadopoulos and Anna Sydorak (2005), 'The legal framework of bilateral relations in the field of competition law and policy: a taxonomic approach', paper presented at the Competition Policy Foundation for Trade Reform, Regulatory Reform and Sustainable Development Mid-term Meeting in Brussels, 26 April.

International Chamber of Commerce (1996), *ICC Statement on International Cooperation between Antitrust Authorities*, 28 March 1996, Doc. 225/450 Rev.3.

International Chamber of Commerce (1999), *ICC recommendations to the International Competition Policy Advisory Committee (ICPAC) on exchange of confidential information between competition authorities in the merger context*, Commission on Law and Practices relating to Competition, 21 May.

International Competition Policy Advisory Comity (2000), *ICPAC final report to the Attorney general and the assistant attorney general for Antitrust*, available online at http://www.usdoj.gov/atr/icpac/finalreport.htm (last visited on 20/8/2005).

Iyori, Hiroshi (1997), 'Japanese cooperation in international antitrust law enforcement', in Hans Ulrich (ed.), *Comparative Competition Law: Approaching an International System of Antitrust Law*, Baden-Baden: Nomos Verlagsgesellschaft.

James, Charles (2001), 'International antitrust in the Bush Administration', Canadian Bar association on Competition Law, Ottawa, Canada, 21 September 2001, available at www.usdoj.gov/atr/public/speeches/9100.pdf (last visited on 20/8/2005).

Janow, Merit E. (2000), 'Transatlantic cooperation on competition policy', in Simon J. Evennett, Alexander Lehman and Benn Steil (eds), *Antitrust Goes Global*, Washington D.C.: Brooking Institution Press, pp. 29–56.

Kaczorowska, Alina (2000), 'International competition law in the context of global capitalism', *European Competition Law Review*, **21**(2), 117–27.

Kiriazis, Georgios (2001), 'Jurisdiction and cooperation issues in the investigation of international cartels': http://europa.eu.int/comm/competition/speeches/text/sp 2001_010_en.pdf (last visited on 20/8/2005).

Klein, Joel I. (1996), 'A note of caution with respect to a WTO agenda on competition policy', available at http://www.usdoj.gov/atr/public/speeches/0998.htm (last visited on 20/8/2005).

Klein, Joel I. (1997), 'Anticipating the millennium: international antitrust enforcement at the end of the twentieth century', available at the following website: http://www.usdoj.gov/atr/public/speeches/1233.htm (last visited on 20/8/2005).

Kroes, Neelie (2005), 'The first hundred days', available at http://europa.eu.int/rapid/pressReleasesAction.do?reference=SPEECH/05/205&format=HTML&aged=0&language=EN&guiLanguage=en.

Kurzer, Paulette (2001), *Markets and Moral Regulation: Cultural Change in the European Union*, Cambridge University Press.

Markert, Kurt E. (1968), 'Recent developments in international antitrust co-operation', *Antitrust Bulletin*, **13**, 355.

Marsden, Philip, 'The divide on verticals', in Simon J. Evennett, Alexander Lehman and Benn Steil (eds), *Antitrust Goes Global*, Washington D.C.: Brooking Institution Press.

Meyer, John W., John Boli, George M. Thomas and Francisco O. Ramirez (1997), 'World society and the nation state', *American Journal of Sociology*, **103**(1), 144–81.

Monti, Mario (2000), 'Cooperation between competition authorities – a vision for the future', the Japan Foundation Conference, Washington, DC, 23 June, available at the following website: http://europa.eu.int/rapid/start/cgi/guesten.ksh?p_action.gettxt=gt&doc=SPEECH/00/234|0|RAPID&lg=EN (last visited on 20/8/2005).

Monti, Mario (2001a), 'International cooperation and technical assistance: a view from the EU', UNCTAD 3rd IGE 3rd session, Geneva, 4 July, available at http://europa.eu.int/rapid/start/cgi/guesten.ksh?p_action.gettxt=gt&doc=SPEECH/01/328|0|RAPID&lg=EN (last visited on 20/5/2005).

Monti, Mario (2001b), 'The future for competition policy in the European Union', Merchant Taylor Hall, London, 9 July, available at the following website: http://www.europa.eu.int/rapid/start/cgi/guesten.ksh_p?action.gettxt=gt&doc=SPEECH/01/340|0|RAPID&lg=EN (last visited on 20/8/2005).

Murphy, Gavin (2001), 'Canada, Australia and New Zealand competition authorities sign cooperation arrangement', *European Competition Law Review*, **22**(8), 322–4.

Nordlander, Christina (2004), 'Discovering discovery: US discovery of EC leniency statements', *European Competition Law Review*, **25**(10), 646–59.

Organisation for Economic Co-operation and Development (1999), OECD, CLP Report on Positive Comity, DAFFE/CLP (99), (14 June).

Palim, Mark R.A. (1998), 'The worldwide growth of competition law: an empirical analysis', *Antitrust Bulletin*, **XLIII**(1) ,105–45.

Parisi, John J. (1999), 'Enforcement co-operation among antitrust authorities', *European Competition Law Review*, **20**(3), 133–42.

Patterson, Donna E. and Carl Shapiro (2001), 'Trans-Atlantic divergence in GE/Honeywell, causes and lessons', available at http://faculty.haas.berkeley.edu/shapiro/divergence.pdf (last visited on 20/8/2005).

Paul, Joel R. (1991), 'Comity in international law', *Harvard International Law Journal*, **32**(1), 2–71.

Pitofsky, Robert (1999), 'Competition policy in a global economy – today and tomorrow', *Journal of International Economic Law*, **2**(3), 403–11.

Powell, Walter W. (1991), 'Expanding the scope of institutional analysis', in Walter W. Powell and Paul J. DiMaggio (eds), *The New Institutionalism*, University of Chicago Press, pp. 183–204.

Reinker, Kenneth S. (2004), 'Case comment: *Roche vs. Empagran*', *Harvard Journal of Law and Public Policy*, **28**, 297–306.

Reismann, M.W. (1991), 'A hard look at soft law', Panel report, *American Society of International Law*, **82**, 371.

Riley, Alan (1995), 'The jellyfish nailed? The announcement of the EC/US competition co-operation agreement', *European Competition Law Review*, **3**, 185.

Rill, James F. and Christine C. Wilson (2000), 'The A.C. Nielsen case', in Simon J. Evennett, Alexander Lehman and Benn Steil (eds), *Antitrust Goes Global*, Washington D.C.: Brooking Institution Press, pp. 222–4.

Schaub, Alexander (1998), 'International co-operation in antitrust matters: making the point in the wake of the Boeing/MDD proceedings', *Competition Policy Newsletter*, **1**, 2–5.

Slaughter, Anne-Marie (2000), 'Governing the global economy through government networks', in Michael Byers (ed.), *The Role of Law in International Politics: Essays in International Relations and International Law*, Oxford University Press, pp. 1077–206.

Springman, Christopher (2005), 'Fix prices globally, get sued locally? US jurisdiction over international cartels', forthcoming, *University of Chicago Law Review*, available at http://cyberlaw.stanford.edu/blogs/sprigman/archives/chicago2.pdf (last visited on 20/8/2005).

Stark, Charles (2000), 'Improving bilateral antitrust cooperation', Washington, D.C., June 23, at p. 2, available at http://www.usdoj.gov/atr/public/speeches/5075.htm (last visited on 20/8/2005).

Van Miert, Karel (1997), 'International cooperation in the field of competition: a view from the EC', in Barry Hawk (ed.) 1997 *Fordham Corporate Law Institute International Antitrust Law and Policy Conference*, New York: Fordham Corporate Law Institute, p. 13.

Walker, William K. (1992), 'Extraterritorial application of US antitrust laws: the effect of the European Community–United States Agreement', *Harvard International Law Journal*, **33**, 583–91.

Waller, S.W. (1997), 'Internationalisation of antitrust enforcement', *Boston University Law Review*, **77**, 343–95.

Weil, Prosper (1983), 'Towards relative normativity in international law?', *American Journal of International Law*, **77**, 413–42.

Whish, Richard (2003), *Competition Law*, 5th edn, Oxford: Butterworths.

Wood, Diane P. (1995), 'The internationalisation of antitrust law: options for the future', *De Paul Law Review*, **44**, 1289.

Wood, Diane P. (1999), 'Is cooperation possible?', *New England Law Review*, **34**(1), 103–12.

Yntema, H. (1966), 'The comity doctrine', *Michigan Law Review*, **65**(1), 9–32.

Zach, R. (1998), 'International cooperation between antitrust enforcement agencies: a view from a small country', in Hans Ulrich (ed.), *Comparative Competition Law: Approaching an International System of Antitrust Law*, Baden-Baden: Nomos Verlagsgesellschaft.

Zanettin, Bruno (2002), *Cooperation Between Antitrust Agencies at the International Level*, Oxford: Hart Publishing.

Cases

*Ahlstrom and Others* v. *E.C. Commission (Re Wood Pulp Cartel)* [1998] E.C.R. 5193, [1988] 4
    C.M.L.R. 901.
*Gencor Ltd* v. *Commission* Case T-102/96, 4 CMLR, 971, [1999].
*Hartford Fire Ins. Co.* v. *California*, 509 US 764 (1993).
*Hoffmann La Roche* v. *Empagran, SA* 124 2359 (2004).
*Timberlane Lumber Co.* v. *Bank of America*, 549F.2d 597 (9th Cir. 1976).
*United States* v. *Aluminum Co. of America* 148 F.2d 416 (2d Cir. 1945).
*United States of America* v. *Nippon Paper Industries Co. Ltd et al.*, 109 F.3 d 9 (1997).

## Annex 1   Table of bilateral enforcement cooperation agreements

| Agreement | Notification | Exchange of information | Enforcement cooperation | Coordination |
|---|---|---|---|---|
| US–Germany (1976) | √ | √ | √ | |
| US–Australia(1982) | √ | √ | √ | |
| EU–US (1991) | √ | √ | √ | |
| US–Canada (1995) | √ | √ | √ | √ |
| Australia–Taipei (1996) | √ | √ | √ | √ |
| New Zealand–Taipei (1996) | √ | √ | √ | √ |
| EU–US on pos. com. (1998) | | | √ | |
| US–Australia (1999) | | √ | √ | |
| EU–Canada (1999) | √ | √ | √ | √ |
| US–Japan (1999) | √ | √ | √ | √ |
| US–Brazil (1999) | √ | √ | √ | √ |
| Australia–Papua New Guinea (1999) | √ | √ | √ | √ |
| US–Israel (1999) | √ | √ | √ | √ |
| US–Mexico (2000) | √ | √ | √ | √ |
| Canada–Australia– New Zealand (2000) | √ | √ | | |
| Canada–Chile (2001) | √ | √ | √ | √ |
| Russia–Brazil (2001) | | | √ | |
| Canada–Mexico (2001) | √ | √ | √ | √ |
| Denmark–Iceland Norway (2001) | √ | √ | | |
| Australia–Fiji MOU (2002) | | √ | √ | √ |
| Australia–Korea (Sept 2002) | √ | √ | √ | √ |
| Canada–UK (2003) | √ | √ | √ | √ |
| EU–Japan (2003) | √ | √ | √ | √ |
| US–Canada pos. com. (2004) | | | √ | |

*Notes:*
1. *US–Germany (1976)* Agreement Between the Government of the United States of America and the Government of the Federal Republic of Germany Relating to Mutual Cooperation Regarding Restrictive Business Practices.
2. *US–Australia (1982)* Agreement between the Government of the United States of America and the Government of Australia relating to Cooperation on Antitrust Matters.
3. *EU–US (1991)* Agreement between the Government of The United States of America and the Commission of the European Communities Regarding the Application of their Competition Laws.

| Consultations | Meetings between officials | Technical assistance | Comity | Positive comity | Predominance of existing laws of the parties | Right to share confidential information |
|---|---|---|---|---|---|---|
| √ | | | √ | | √ | |
| √ | | | √ | | √ | |
| √ | √ | | √ | √ | √ | |
| √ | √ | √ | √ | | √ | |
| | | √ | √ | | √ | |
| | | | | √ | √ | |
| | | | | | √ | √ |
| √ | √ | | √ | √ | √ | |
| √ | √ | | √ | √ | √ | |
| √ | √ | √ | √ | √ | √ | |
| √ | | | √ | | √ | |
| √ | √ | | √ | √ | √ | |
| √ | √ | √ | √ | √ | √ | |
| √ | √ | | √ | | √ | |
| √ | √ | | √ | √ | √ | |
| | | | | | | √ |
| | √ | √ | √ | | √ | |
| √ | √ | √ | √ | | √ | |
| √ | √ | | √ | √ | √ | |
| | | | | √ | √ | |

4. *US–Canada (1995)* Agreement between the Government of Canada and the Government of the United Mexican States regarding the Application of their Competition Laws.
5. *Australia–Taipei (1996)* Cooperation and Coordination arrangement between the Taipei Economic and Cultural Office and the Australian Commerce and Industry Office regarding the Application of Competition and Fair Trading Laws.
6. *New Zealand–Taipei (1996)* Co-operation and Co-ordination arrangement between the Taipei economic and cultural office and the New Zealand Commerce and Industry Office regarding the Application of the Competition and Fair Trading Laws.

*Notes:*   (continued)
  7. *EU–US on pos. com. (1998)* Agreement between the Government of the United States of America and the European Communities on the Application of Positive Comity Principles on the Enforcement of their Competition Laws.
  8. *Australia–Papua New Guinea (1999)* Co-operation and Co-ordination Agreement between the Australian Competition and Consumer Commission and Papua New Guinea Consumer Affairs Council.
  9. *US–Australia (1999)* Agreement between the Government of the United States of America and the Government of Australia on Mutual Antitrust Enforcement Assistance.
 10. *US–Brazil (1999)* Agreement between the Government of the United States of America and the Government of the Federative Republic of Brazil regarding Cooperation between their Competition Authorities in the Enforcement of their Competition Laws.
 11. *US–Israel (1999)* Agreement between the Government of the United States of America and the Government of the State of Israel on the Application of their Competition Laws.
 12. *US–Japan (1999)* Agreement between the Government of the United States of America and the Government of Japan concerning Cooperation on Anticompetitive Activities.
 13. *EU–Canada (1999)* Agreement between the European Communities and the Government of Canada regarding the application of their competition laws.
 14. *US–Mexico (2000)* Agreement between the Government of the United States of America and the Government of the United Mexican States Regarding the Application of their Competition Laws.
 15. *Canada–Australia–New Zealand (2000)* Cooperation arrangement between the Commissioner for competition (Canada), the Australian Competition and Consumer Commission and the New Zealand Commerce Commission Regarding the Application of their Competition and Consumer Laws.
 16. *Canada–Chile (2001)* Memorandum of Understanding between the Commissioner of Competition (Canada) and the Fiscal Nacional Economico (Chile) Regarding the Application of their Competition Laws.
 17. *Canada–Mexico (2001)* Agreement between the Government of Canada and the Government of the United Mexican States Regarding the Application of their Competition Laws.
 18. *Russia–Brazil (2001)* Agreement on cooperation in the sphere of competition policy between the Government of the Federative Republic of Brazil and the Government of the Russian Federation.
 19. *Denmark–Iceland–Norway (2001)* Agreement between Denmark, Iceland and Norway on Co-operation in Competition Cases.
 20. *Australia–Fiji MOU (2002)* Memorandum of Understanding between the Commerce Commission of the Fiji Islands and the Australian Competition and Consumer Commission.
 21. *Australia–Korea (2002)* Cooperation Arrangement between the Australian Competition and Consumer Commission and the Fair Trade Commission of the Republic of Korea Regarding the Application of their Competition and Consumer Protection Laws.
 22. *Canada–UK (2003)* Cooperation arrangement between the Commissioner of Competition (Canada) and her Majesty's Secretary of State for Trade and Industry and the Office of Fair Trading in the United Kingdom Regarding the Application of their Competition and Consumer Laws.
 23. *EU–Japan (2003)* Agreement between the Government of Japan and the European Community concerning Cooperation on Anticompetitive Activities.
 24. *US–Canada pos. com. (2004)* Agreement between the Government of the United States of America and the Government of Canada on the Application of Positive Comity Principles to the Enforcement of their Competition Laws.

# 26 An antitrust analysis of the World Trade Organization's decision in the US–Mexico arbitration on telecommunications services
*J. Gregory Sidak[1] and Hal J. Singer[2]*

## Introduction

On 2 April 2004, the World Trade Organization (WTO) assumed a new role as a highly specialized, global regulator of domestic telecommunications policy. In response to a complaint filed by the United States against the Republic of Mexico, the WTO's Dispute Settlement Body in April 2002 established an arbitration panel in accordance with Article 6 of the Understanding on Rules and Procedures Governing the Settlement of Disputes. The United States alleged that Mexico had violated its commitments under section 5 of the Annex on Telecommunications to the General Agreement on Trade in Services (GATS) by failing to ensure that Teléfonos de México, S.A. de C.V. (Telmex), the largest Mexican supplier of basic telecommunications services, (1) provide interconnection to US telecommunications carriers at 'cost-oriented' rates, (2) refrain from anticompetitive practices,[3] and (3) provide US telecommunications carriers with 'reasonable and non-discriminatory' access to public telecommunications networks and services as mandated by the GATS Annex on Telecommunications.

In its April 2004 decision, the WTO arbitration panel found that Mexico had not met its GATS commitments with respect to supply of telecommunications services on a 'facilities basis' – that is, services supplied over the service provider's own infrastructure, rather than over leased capacity on someone else's infrastructure.[4] As a result, Mexico became obliged to change its domestic telecommunications regulations or face trade sanctions. The panel report in the US–Mexico decision is the first WTO arbitration to deal solely with trade in services under GATS and the first specifically to address telecommunications services.

On one level, the decision illustrates the potential for the WTO to compel changes in any area of domestic law that corresponds to one of the topics within GATS. It is conceivable that, having established the precedent of intervening in the domestic regulatory policy of one of its signatory nations, the WTO one day will direct this new form of überregulation on an American regulatory institution with oversight of domestic firms that provide at least one service to foreign customers. On another level, the US–Mexico decision provides an additional example of the US Government's recurrent use of trade agreements and institutions to impose specific American regulatory principles on the domestic telecommunications policies of other nations. As we will explain in greater detail below, that exportation of US telecommunications regulation encompasses detailed methodologies used to calculate the costs and permissible prices of regulated carriers. Despite having been exported to other nations, those US policies remain highly controversial within US telecommunications law.[5]

This chapter presents an economic analysis of the US complaint against Mexico. Section 1 summarizes the US and EC approaches to state action under antitrust law and their converging definitions of the relevant market. This background provides context for further criticism of the WTO panel's analysis and highlights critical differences in approaches to regulation that could ultimately result in future WTO proceedings. Section 2 summarizes the lengthy decision of the WTO arbitration panel. The panel accepted most of the arguments and reasoning contained in the US complaint. Therefore our criticisms of the US Government's complaint in most cases apply with equal force to the WTO decision.

Section 3 shows that the US Government conflated *international* settlement rates and *domestic* interconnection pricing. In both the United States and Mexico, international settlement rates have been set by a different pricing methodology from the one used for domestic interconnection. Contrary to the unstated premise of the US Government's complaint, direct comparisons of the two rates are not valid. The complaint of the US Government raised economic policy questions that are not within the scope of the WTO agreement. These policy questions are properly addressed by the domestic authorities in Mexico. For example, the recovery of Telmex's total costs through allowed rates is properly within the discretion and expertise of the Mexican telecommunications regulator, the Comisión Federal de Telecomunicaciones (Cofetel).

At the time that the United States filed its complaint, Mexico's international settlement rates were reasonable and were rationally based on the costs of building and operating the public switched telecommunications network in Mexico. The US Government mischaracterized several of the relevant cost principles. First, the US Government's estimate of the costs of terminating a call in Mexico ignored non-traffic-sensitive costs that Telmex cannot recoup through other charges. Second, international settlement rates vary by region to reflect the legitimate differences in costs that Telmex incurs in providing network access. Third, the US Government incorrectly relied on long-run average incremental cost (LRAIC) as the price that a competitive market would establish. Moreover the US Government's complaint did not recognize that the price of *northbound* long-distance services in Mexico depends primarily on the cross-subsidization policy chosen by the Mexican Government. This policy is also within Cofetel's discretion, and the US Government did not allege that this cross-subsidization was anticompetitive.

Section 4 shows that the WTO panel failed to recognize that the complaint of the US Government collapses if Telmex lacks market power in point-to-point international telecommunications services between the United States and Mexico. It is unlikely that Telmex had such market power in 2002. Point-to-point international telecommunications services – not the termination of long-distance calls onto Telmex's wire line network – constitute the relevant product market. For several reasons, Telmex lacks market power in the relevant product and geographic markets. First, Telmex's share of point-to-point international telecommunications services varies by geographic market within Mexico and is declining rapidly. Second, the demand for southbound calls into Mexico is price-elastic, which implies that US consumers would quickly substitute away from southbound calls terminated onto Telmex's network in response to a price increase for southbound calls. Third, the supply of termination access by rival networks in Mexico is price-elastic, which implies that producers would quickly increase their capacity in response to an increase in the price of termination by Telmex. Fourth, Telmex does not enjoy a significant advantage over its rivals with respect to cost structure, size or resources.

Even if one were to assume counterfactually that Telmex has market power in the *relevant* product and geographic market, Cofetel could regulate an exercise of market power in international settlement rates. Further, even if one were to assume counterfactually (as the WTO panel incorrectly found) that the proper market definition is the termination of southbound calls, Telmex would still lack market power for at least five reasons. First, the market power of US long-distance carriers is a countervailing force that constrains Telmex's ability to charge excessive international settlement rates. Second, illegal bypass forces Telmex to negotiate lower international settlement rates. Third, Telmex is already substantially below the benchmark international settlement rate established by the Federal Communications Commission to protect US long-distance carriers. Fourth, because the marginal cost (as opposed to the long-run average variable cost) of completing such calls is low, the critical share of marginal customers needed to render an exercise of market power by Telmex unprofitable would be small. Fifth, packet-switched networks are nearly a perfect substitute for Telmex's circuit-switched networks and will grow in competitive significance.

We conclude that the WTO decision on the US–Mexico arbitration reveals a startlingly low level of economic sophistication in its analysis of inescapably economic questions. The panel's decision runs to 227 pages with 1052 footnotes, yet it does not cite – much less rely upon – any scholarly work on telecommunications regulation, industrial organization, antitrust policy, international trade or any other branch of economics. Instead the panel's reasoning is overwhelmingly lexical, interpreting critical terms such as cost and market power by resorting to dictionaries and canons of construction rather than microeconomics. The method is reminiscent of how American courts approached antitrust cases in the first half of the twentieth century. Given the high level of economic sophistication that is now standard in competition law and sector-specific regulation throughout the world, the WTO has made an unimpressive start in implementing the GATS arbitration process.

### Section 1   Comparison of US and EC antitrust law

In this section, we summarize the US and EC approaches to state action under antitrust law and their converging definitions of the relevant market. This background provides context for criticism of the WTO panel's analysis and highlights critical differences in approaches to regulation that could ultimately result in future WTO proceedings.

*Antitrust scrutiny of state conduct*

There is no international consensus on whether individual state actions are subject to antitrust scrutiny. Before the WTO's recent venture into competitive analysis, this question was most often addressed in federal systems in which subordinate levels of government implemented legislation that ran counter to federal antitrust law. For example, in the United States, state actions are not subject to scrutiny under federal antitrust law because of the strong US support for federalism and state sovereignty.[6] By contrast, the EC has taken a different position in its pursuit of a common competitive market. The EC applies its competition policy to the public sector and, more specifically, to the legislative acts of its member nations.[7] Further insight into both the US and EC approach to regulated conduct and state action may foreshadow the shape of future 'competition' conflicts before the WTO.

*(a) The US approach to state conduct*   Despite the US arguments in its WTO claim against Mexico, it is well established in the United States that, under the 'state action doctrine', antitrust law does not apply to states when acting as sovereigns.[8] The Supreme Court based its decision on the principles of federalism and state sovereignty.

We find nothing in the language of the Sherman Act or in its history which suggests that its purpose was to restrain a state or its officers or agents from activities directed by its legislature. In a dual system of government in which, under the Constitution, the states are sovereign, save only as Congress may constitutionally subtract from their authority, an unexpressed purpose to nullify a state's control over its officers and agents is not lightly to be attributed to Congress.[9]

Although the Supreme Court held that state actions were protected from antitrust scrutiny, governmental actions of political subdivisions do not enjoy similar blanket protection.[10] These political subdivisions (that is, municipal governments) are only protected from antitrust scrutiny when acting pursuant to a 'clearly expressed state policy'.[11] State legislatures do not have explicitly to authorize political subdivisions to abrogate federal antitrust laws. Instead it is sufficient that 'anticompetitive effects logically would result from th[e] broad authority to regulate' granted by the state legislature.[12] The test for state action protection for political subdivisions is thus whether the suppression of competition is the foreseeable result of a clearly articulated state policy.[13]

*(b) The EC approach to state conduct*   In contrast to the US state action immunity articulated in *Parker* v. *Brown*, European competition law is applied to the actions of the public sector.[14] To promote the common market, the EC has determined that national legislation that infringes on EC competition law is invalid and must be disavowed by its member nations.

Where undertakings engage in conduct contrary to Article 81(1) EC and where that conduct is required or facilitated by national legislation which legitimizes or reinforces the effects of the conduct, specifically with regard to price-fixing or market-sharing arrangements, a national competition authority, one of whose responsibilities is to ensure that Article 81 EC is observed:

– has a duty to disapply the national legislation;
– may not impose penalties in respect of past conduct on the undertakings concerned when the conduct was required by the national legislation;
– may impose penalties on the undertakings concerned in respect of conduct subsequent to the decision to disapply the national legislation, once the decision has become definitive in their regard;
– may impose penalties on the undertakings concerned in respect of past conduct where the conduct was merely facilitated or promoted by the national legislation, whilst taking due account of the specific features of the legislative framework in which the undertakings acted.[15]

The interplay of the EC's competition regulations (Articles 81 and 82) with Article 10 of the European Commission, which makes explicit a duty for

Member States to cooperate, 'require[s] the Member States not to introduce or maintain in force measures, even of a legislative or regulatory nature, which may render ineffective the competition rules applicable to the undertakings'.[16]

This extension of competition policy to state actions might reflect the larger governmental role in the European economy, 'thereby necessitating the application of competition policy in this area to ensure not only the protection of competition values, but also the even more important community trade protecting functions of EU competition law'.[17] It is also possible that the application of competition law to state actions might demonstrate 'the relative weakness of the European Union's commitment to subsidiarity, as compared to the US commitment to federalism'.[18]

### Approaches to market definition

Section 5 will demonstrate that the WTO's flawed determination of the relevant market was an example of its startling low level of economic sophistication in its analysis of manifestly economic questions. Although the EC approach to market definition was previously difficult to predict and utilize, there has been a recent convergence in market definitions between the US and EC approaches based on product substitutability. The WTO, in its future competitive analyses, would be well-advised to utilize the sophisticated economic analyses that both the United States and EC use in their competition inquiries.

*(a) The US approach to market definition*   In the United States, 'product and geographic market definitions are determined by interchangeability/substitutability, as reflected in the hypothetical monopolist paradigm'.[19] A regulator must thus determine whether consumers are willing to switch from one product to another in the face of a price increase. If two products are in the same market, the corresponding high elasticity of demand should result in substitution away from the higher-priced good after a price increase.

The US Horizontal Merger Guidelines more specifically define the relevant product market as 'the smallest set of products for which a hypothetical monopolist could profitably raise price a significant amount (typically 5 per cent) above the competitive level for a sustained period of time'.[20] A potential market definition is therefore too narrow if 'in the face of a 5 per cent price increase, the number of customers who switch to products outside the "market" is sufficiently large to make the price increase unprofitable'.[21]

The Supreme Court has defined other characteristics to aid in the determination of the relevant product market:

> They include such concerns as industry or customer recognition of a group of products as being economically distinct; the peculiar characteristics and uses of

a particular product or group of products; unique production facilities, including the extent to which a facility can be switched from the production of one product to that of another (termed 'cross-elasticity of supply'); distinct customers and specialized vendors; and distinct prices and price sensitivity between particular products.[22]

Submarkets may also have to be taken into consideration when defining the relevant product market. The Supreme Court noted:

> The outer boundaries of a product market are determined by the reasonable interchangeability of use or the cross-elasticity of demand between the product itself and substitutes for it. However, well-defined submarkets may exist which, in themselves, constitute product markets for antitrust purposes. The boundaries of such a submarket may be determined by examining such practical indicia as industry or public recognition of the submarket as a separate economic entity, the product's peculiar characteristics and uses, unique production facilities, distinct customers, distinct prices, sensitivity to price changes, and specialized vendors.[23]

In summary, the Supreme Court provides a very precise approach to market definition.

*(b) The EC approach to market definition*   The EC's approach to market definition has evolved into an approach that closely mirrors the US approach. Before 1997, the Commission's approach to market definition appeared to have 'little apparent analysis or reasoning'.[24] In 1997, the Commission published a Market Definition Notice that gave the public more guidance in market determination.[25] This Notice on market definition 'is based on the notion that the exercise of market power can be constrained by demand substitutability, by supply substitutability and by potential competition'.[26]

There are numerous factors that influence the EC market definition, including the characteristics of the product, the use of the product, the cross-elasticities of supply and demand, government regulations, and the market structure of supply and demand.[27] Thus, as some commentators have noted,[28] the US Horizontal Merger Guidelines and European Market Definition Notice appear to represent a convergence on the issue of market definition. The EC does have unique aspects, however, that make its market determinations more difficult than those in the United States. For example, 'national borders, cultural/linguistic differences, regulatory barriers, and national preferences' all complicate determination of the relevant geographic market.[29]

### Section 2   The US–Mexico arbitration decision
Having established the appropriate framework in which to analyse matters of competition policy, we now turn to the approach embraced by the WTO.

The United States alleged that Mexico violated its commitments under the GATS by failing to ensure that Telmex provided interconnection to US telecommunications suppliers at 'cost-oriented' rates and refrained from engaging in anticompetitive practices. The United States also alleged that Mexico neglected to provide US telecommunications suppliers with 'reasonable and non-discriminatory' access to public telecommunications networks and services as mandated by the GATS Annex on Telecommunications. The panel found that, with respect to supply of services on a 'facilities basis', Mexico had not met its GATS commitments.

*The Mexican regulatory regime*
Before 1997, Telmex supplied Mexico's long-distance and international telecommunications services on a monopoly basis. Thereafter Mexico has allowed multiple Mexican carriers to provide cross-border telecommunications services over Mexican networks. At the time of the arbitration, 27 carriers provided long-distance services in Mexico, of which 11 were 'international gateway operators', which are long-distance service licensees authorized by Cofetel to operate a switching exchange as an international gateway. Telmex remains the country's largest supplier of basic telecommunications services, including international outbound traffic.

Cofetel regulates agreements for interconnection of public telecommunications networks with foreign networks through its International Long-Distance Rules (ILD Rules).[30] The ILD Rules required, among other things, that all international gateway operators apply the same 'uniform settlement rate' to each international long-distance call, regardless of which operator directs the call.[31] The Mexican operator with the greatest market share of outgoing long-distance calls for each country was given the power to negotiate unilaterally the settlement rate with that country.[32] Furthermore the ILD Rules' 'proportionate return' provision mandated that incoming calls from a foreign country be distributed among Mexican operators in proportion to each operator's share of outgoing calls to that country.[33]

*The United States' contentions*
As part of the GATS negotiations in 1996 and 1997, almost all of the signatory countries committed themselves to abide by a set of procompetitive regulatory principles concerning their telecommunications industries. These principles are embodied in the WTO's Reference Paper, to which the United States and Mexico both subscribed.[34] Section 2 of the Reference Paper, labelled 'Interconnection', requires that interconnection with a 'major supplier' of public telecommunications transport networks or services be ensured 'in a timely fashion, on terms, conditions and cost-oriented rates

that are transparent . . . [and] reasonable'.[35] Section 1 of the Reference Paper obliges the Mexican Government to take appropriate measures to prevent a major supplier from engaging in anticompetitive practices. The last treaty provision relevant to the US complaint, section 5 of the GATS Annex, commits Mexico to ensuring that international basic telecommunications service suppliers are accorded access to public and private leased telecommunications transfer networks on 'reasonable and non-discriminatory terms and conditions'.[36]

The United States alleged that Mexico had violated all three sections by failing to regulate Telmex adequately. First, Mexico allegedly breached its obligations under section 2 of the Reference Paper by allowing Telmex to charge interconnection rates that substantially exceeded costs. Second, the US claimed that Mexico violated section 1 not only by failing to prevent Telmex from engaging in anticompetitive practices, including horizontal price-fixing and market-sharing agreements, but also by *requiring* Telmex to do so by granting it the sole power to fix international settlement rates and restrict supply of basic telecommunication services. Third, by allegedly failing to ensure that United States basic telecommunications suppliers were granted access to Mexican telecommunications networks, both public and private leased, on reasonable and non-discriminatory terms, Mexico allegedly contravened its obligations under section 5 of the GATS Annex.

*The panel's findings*
Addressing each of the three GATS provisions individually, the WTO panel concluded that, with regard to the supply of services on a facilities basis, Mexico violated its commitments under sections 2.2 (b) and 1.1 of the Reference Paper and sections 5(a) and 5(b) of the Annex on Telecommunications.[37]

*Mexico's commitments under section 2 of the Reference Paper*   The panel first examined whether section 2 of the Reference Paper applied at all to the telecommunications services at issue. It determined that the US public voice telephony, circuit-switched transmission and facsimile services constituted the 'cross-border' supply of the services and therefore fell within the meaning of GATS Article I: 2(a). (These services can be provided on either a 'facilities basis' or a 'non-facilities basis' by a 'commercial agency' operating over leased facilities.) Furthermore, pursuant to Mexico's schedule of commitments, Mexico undertook a full-national-treatment commitment for the cross-border supply of the services at issue, and full-market-access commitment for the supply of services at issue on a facilities basis, but not on a non-facilities basis. After concluding that section 2 applied to all cross-border services at issue except for those on a non-facilities basis, the panel addressed whether or not Mexico had fulfilled its commitment to provide such services under section 2.2(b). If Telmex constituted a 'major supplier', then Mexico was obliged to ensure that Telmex provided interconnection on 'terms, conditions and *cost-oriented* rates that are transparent, reasonable, having regard to economic feasibility and sufficiently unbundled'.[38]

WAS TELMEX A 'MAJOR SUPPLIER'?    The panel first examined the definition of 'major supplier' listed in the Reference Paper and concluded that Telmex satisfied its meaning: 'A major supplier is a supplier which has the ability to materially affect the terms of participation (having regard to price and supply) in the relevant market for basic telecommunications services . . . '[39] The panel then determined the 'relevant market' to be the *termination* of the services at issue supplied cross-border, not *point-to-point* international telecommunications services. It wrote: 'We find no evidence that a domestic telecommunications service is substitutable for an international one, and that an outgoing call is considered substitutable for an incoming one . . . Even if the price difference between domestic and international interconnection would change, such a price change would not make these differences substitutable in the eyes of a consumer.'[40]

Following the Reference Paper's language, the panel then addressed Telmex's 'ability to materially affect the terms of participation (having regard to price and supply)'. The panel noted that Telmex was legally required by ILD Rule 13 to negotiate settlement rates for the entire Mexican market for termination of the services at issue: 'The long-distance service licensee having the greatest percentage of outgoing long-distance market share for the six months prior to negotiations with a given country shall be the licensee that is authorized to negotiate settlement rates with the operators of said country.'[41] On the basis of that rule, the panel found that Telmex had enough market power to 'materially affect the terms of participation'.[42] In short, Telmex was a 'major supplier' as defined in the Reference Paper.

WERE TELMEX'S INTERCONNECTION RATES 'COST-ORIENTED'? The panel then addressed whether Telmex's interconnection rates were 'cost-oriented', which the panel construed to mean 'brought into a defined relation to known costs or cost principles'.[43] Citing the US Government's written submission, the panel ruled that Mexican law *requires* the use of long-run average-incremental cost (LRAIC) as a basis for such analysis.[44] The panel concluded that the term 'cost-oriented' means 'the costs incurred in supplying the service, and that the use of long term incremental cost methodologies, such as those required in Mexican law, is consistent with its meaning'.[45]

In deciding whether Mexico had ensured that Telmex was interconnecting US suppliers of the services at issue at cost-oriented rates, the panel considered different types of evidence that the United States offered. Basing its analysis on measures such as existing 'grey market' prices and the aggregate cost of relevant network components used to interconnect US suppliers, the panel concluded that the interconnection rates charged by Telmex to United States suppliers were not 'cost-oriented'.[46]

In addition to these considerations, the panel examined ILD Rules 16 and 17, which allow international gateway operators to negotiate financial compensation agreements among themselves instead of having to transfer calls physically when the operators do not receive traffic at their gateways in the proportion of their outgoing calls.[47] Because they suggested the existence of a surplus beyond the costs of receiving calls, the financial compensation agreements in place as part of the 'proportionate allocation' rules also contributed to the panel's decision.[48]

Having determined that Telmex was a 'major supplier' whose interconnection was not implemented at 'cost-oriented rates', the panel concluded that Mexico had failed to meet its commitments under section 2.2(b) of the Reference Paper.

*Mexico's commitments under section 1 of the Reference Paper*   Next the panel addressed Mexico's commitments under section 1.1 of the Reference Paper, which states that 'appropriate measures shall be maintained for the purpose of preventing suppliers who, alone or together, are a major supplier from engaging in or continuing anticompetitive practices'.[49] The panel referred to the definition of 'anticompetitive practices' set forth in the Reference Paper, which states that such practices include, among other things, 'engaging in anticompetitive cross-subsidization'.[50] The panel concluded that, because the list was not exhaustive, the term also includes horizontal price-fixing and market-sharing agreements by suppliers.[51]

To determine the status of Mexico's practices within this meaning, the panel examined the ILD Rules. First, the panel noted that the ILD Rules (1) require all international gateway operators in Mexico to apply a 'uniform settlement rate' to all incoming and outgoing traffic, and (2) grant the operator with the greatest share of outgoing calls to a particular country the sole power to negotiate settlement rates with that country.[52] The panel believed that the effect of this process was that 'Telmex must negotiate a settlement rate for incoming calls with suppliers in the other markets wishing to supply the Mexican market and apply . . . that single rate to interconnection for incoming traffic from the United States.'[53] The panel agreed with the United States that this practice constituted anticompetitive horizontal price fixing in violation of section 1.1: 'The removal of price competition by the Mexican authorities, combined with the setting of the uniform price by the major supplier, has effects tantamount to those of a price-fixing cartel.'[54]

Second, the decision addressed the ILD Rules' 'proportionate return' system which requires international gateway operators (1) to distribute among themselves incoming calls from a country in proportion to the outgoing calls that the operator sends to that country, and (2) to negotiate financial compensation agreements among themselves that replicate proportionality if calls are not distributed accordingly. The panel found that this provision also violated section 1.1 because it limited rivalry and competition among competing suppliers and was therefore anticompetitive: 'The allocation of market share between Mexican suppliers imposed by the Mexican authorities, combined with the authorization of Mexican operators to negotiate financial compensation between them instead of physically transferring surplus traffic, has effects tantamount to those in market sharing arrangements between suppliers'.[55]

Furthermore the panel found, by requiring these anticompetitive practices by law, that Mexico had failed to maintain 'appropriate measures' to prevent such anticompetitive practices. Consequently, because Mexico neglected to undertake 'appropriate measures' to prevent Telmex, a 'major supplier', from engaging in anticompetitive practices, Mexico was found to have violated its section 1.1 obligations.

*Mexico's Commitments under section 5 of the GATS Annex on Telecommunications*   Section 5(a) of the GATS Annex on Telecommunications requires Mexico to ensure that 'any service supplier of any other Member is accorded access to and use of public telecommunications transport networks and services on reasonable and non-discriminatory terms and conditions'.[56] The panel found that the Annex applies on a facilities basis to *basic telecommunications* commitments scheduled by Mexico, as it would be unreasonable to suppose otherwise. The panel qualified this determination, however, by finding that Mexico's Schedule of Specific Commitments and routing requirement failed to grant market access for the cross-border supply of services on a non-facilities basis – services provided over capacity leased by the service supplier.

In determining whether Telmex had provided leased access to networks and services to US suppliers on 'reasonable and non-discriminatory terms and conditions', the panel first examined the rates that Telmex charged. Based on the previous determination that the uniform rates charged to interconnect US suppliers exceeded cost-oriented rates by a substantial margin and precluded price competition, the panel concluded that such rates were inconsistent with the provision of access to and use of public telecommunications transfer networks and services 'on reasonable . . . terms'.[57]

Consequently, with respect to ensuring access on a facilities basis to US suppliers, the panel found that Mexico failed to abide by its commitments under section 5(a) of the GATS Annex on Telecommunications. The panel also held that Mexico failed to meet its section 5(b) obligations by neglecting to ensure that, commercially, present US suppliers had access to and use of private leased circuits and interconnection.

*Summary*
In considering each of the three GATS issues presented by the United States, the WTO panel ruled against Mexico. It concluded that Mexico failed to ensure that Telmex, a 'major supplier' as defined in the Reference Paper, was providing service at 'cost-oriented' rates and avoiding anticompetitive practices such as horizontal price fixing and market sharing. The panel determined that Mexico's failure in these respects violated its obligations under sections 2.2 and 1.1 of the Reference Paper. Furthermore, because the panel found that Telmex did not provide the cross-border services at issue on 'reasonable and non-discriminatory' terms to US suppliers, the panel concluded that Mexico also violated sections 5(a) and 5(b) of the GATS Annex on Telecommunications.

**Section 3  What explains Mexico's international settlement rates?**
One week after the US Government filed its brief with the WTO attacking Mexico's international settlement rates, the Federal Communications Commission (FCC) stated that '[t]he current international settlement rate system was developed as part of a tradition in which international telecommunications services were supplied through a bilateral correspondent relationship between national monopoly carriers'.[58] According to the FCC, the approach of the United States to international settlement rates dates from 'the 1930s and has its genesis in the principles of antitrust law'.[59] Unlike the elaborate provisions contained in the Telecommunications Act of 1996 for the setting of interconnection prices through hundreds of arbitration proceedings run by the state public utilities commissions throughout the United States, the FCC explained that '[h]istorically, the market for international services has been characterized by the model of national monopoly carriers corresponding with one another'.[60] In what follows, we critique the economic reasoning that underlies the US complaint and explain why reductions in the international settlement rate are not producing lower international long-distance prices for US consumers.

The US complaint contained serious economic flaws, which were not detected by the WTO. For example, the US Government's estimate of the costs of terminating a call in Mexico ignored non-traffic-sensitive costs that Telmex cannot recoup through other charges. It also failed to account for regional variation in costs that Telmex incurs in providing network access, and incorrectly relied on long-run average incremental cost as the price that a competitive market would establish. In this section, we address those and other errors in the US Government's arguments to the WTO.

*Non-traffic-sensitive costs that Telmex cannot recoup through other charges*
The Mexican Government has a social policy of universal access, geographically averaged prices, and minimum service-quality standards for telecommunications services. That policy implies for Telmex a particular capacity requirement for its network, as well as an 'obligation to serve' all customers as the 'carrier of last resort'.[61] Unlike its competitors, who bear no such obligation, Telmex may not raise prices (or offer particular customers inferior service quality) to ration limited capacity on its network when faced with excess demand. Nor may Telmex limit its output by restraining the capacity of its network. The universal service mandate compels Telmex to supply a level of network capacity that at least equals (*and most likely exceeds*) the level of network capacity that would be supplied by firms in a perfectly competitive market.[62] Telmex must therefore build its network with 'reserve' or 'standby' capacity that will accommodate peak demand.

To provide customers with the *option* of calling someone on any given day at any given telephone number in Mexico, Telmex must incur certain costs, known in American telecommunications jargon as 'non-traffic-sensitive (NTS) costs', that do not vary with the quantity of calls (minutes of use) that Telmex ultimately carries that day. In 2001, the European Commission embraced this proposition that, in a regulated network industry, capacity costs are not attributable to a specific service, but rather constitute common fixed costs of the network as a whole.[63]

Telmex is implicitly required to offer consumers two valuable services simultaneously: network *access* and network *usage* vary. Consumers outside Mexico benefit from these service offerings. Even if a caller in the United States makes no calls to Mexico on a given day, he will nonetheless have enjoyed the *option* to do so.[64] Long-run average incremental cost by definition does not include such common or sunk costs. Therefore an interconnection settlement rate set equal to LRAIC would be insufficient to recover the total costs that an incumbent network operator legitimately incurs to discharge its obligation to serve the public.

Telmex's investment in network infrastructure necessary to perform its obligation to serve in Mexico has the incidental effect (the *network effect*) of ensuring callers in the United States the option to use Telmex's network whenever they wish. The obligation to serve includes an obligation to provide network access to three groups of cities and regions at three different, geographically averaged prices. The option value of network access is a clear benefit to consumers, and thus its costs deserve to be recovered. As a matter of social policy, the Mexican Government decided to use the international settlement rate as a means to recover the non-traffic-sensitive network costs. Nothing in the WTO agreement on basic telecommunications services or in the Reference Paper remotely suggests that signatories surrender their discretion to permit carriers the opportunity to recover non-traffic-sensitive costs through the international settlement rate.

*Regional variation in costs that Telmex incurs in providing network access*
Mexico has three tiers of international settlement rates that vary by city or larger geographic area. The international settlement rate for smaller cities and remote regions is higher than for Mexico City, Guadalajara and Monterrey. Because there are economies of scale and density in telecommunications networks, this differential pricing reflects the greater cost that Telmex incurs in providing network access to smaller cities and remote regions. In addition, the differential pricing reflects the greater value (the network effect) that is enjoyed by callers to Mexico as Telmex extends the public switched telephone network to provide access to a larger share of the population. Service to these smaller cities and outlying areas is at the heart of Mexico's national policy to provide universal service. Currently, however, there is no universal service fund (USF) in Mexico. The only source of funding for achieving universal service is the revenue earned by Telmex, which alone bears an obligation to serve and the duty to serve as the carrier-of-last-resort.

*Would a competitive market set price equal to long-run average incremental cost?*
In its endorsement of LRAIC as the best measure of an operator's cost, the US Government failed to mention that the WTO telecommunications agreement never endorsed LRAIC.[65] Nor did the US Government mention that the definition of cost can reasonably rest on other economic principles. In a multi-product firm, which by definition has some economies of scope, price must deviate from LRAIC. Otherwise the firm would not be able to meet its revenue requirement and new capital investment would not occur. The US Government's vision of cost-based pricing would not allow Telmex an opportunity to recover its total operating costs plus a non-monopolistic return on its invested capital in the network.

The US Government mischaracterized Mexican telecommunications law as requiring international settlement rates to be based on LRAIC. The

United States made the following claim concerning domestic interconnection rates in Mexico:

> Mexican law requires interconnection rates to reflect 'long run average incremental costs', in line with the general principle that interconnection rates must relate to the cost of providing that service. Reflecting its domestic requirements, Mexico explained to the WTO Negotiating Group on Telecommunications in February 1995 that interconnection charges must be determined on the basis of the true costs of the service provider. ... Since that time, the Mexican Government has underscored on several occasions that Mexico requires interconnection rates to be based in cost, reflecting the cost an efficient enterprise would incur in providing interconnection.[66]

Although it claimed that Article 63 of Mexico's 1995 Federal Law explicitly 'requires' that domestic interconnection rates reflect LRAIC, the US Government's own citation demonstrated that such a requirement is neither explicit nor implied. The law states that the Secretary is 'authorized' to apply domestic interconnection rates on a carrier with significant market power that allow recovery '*at least*, of the long run average incremental cost'.[67] Next, the US Government asserted that domestic interconnection rates 'are meant to allow the supplier to recover long term total incremental costs *as well as imputable common costs*'.[68] Neither passage supports the US Government's economic misconception that domestic interconnection rates in Mexico *must* be set according to LRAIC. Indeed the cited materials do just the opposite.

The US Government also cited the Vienna Convention in support of its LRAIC approach:

> In sum, there appears to be consensus among many WTO Members – including Mexico – that interconnection rates should be based on the cost of providing interconnection. In other words, it appears that WTO Members intended to give the term 'cost-oriented' and '*basadas en costos*' this 'special meaning'. Therefore, in accordance with generally accepted principles of treaty interpretation reflected in Article 31(4) of the Vienna Convention, the Panel should interpret the term *basadas en costos* on this basis.[69]

This passage is another misstatement of then-current economic policy. The US Government asserted that other WTO members consider 'cost-based' to mean based on LRAIC, and included the United States and Mexico in this list, even though the United States has retreated from this position and Mexico specifically enumerates other factors that should be considered in setting domestic interconnection rates.

In short, the US Government failed to prove that domestic interconnection rates in Mexico are set at LRAIC. Consequently, even if one were to assume counterfactually that international settlement rates and domestic interconnection rates are set in the same manner, it still would not follow that the charge for terminating a call from the United States to Mexico should be set at LRAIC.[70]

*The cross-subsidization policy chosen by the Mexican Government*
Prices on international calls to the United States from Mexico are used to subsidize the cost of supplying local telephone service in Mexico. The price of local telephone service, which is approximately US $14 per month, is capped below the LRAIC providing such service. The first 100 local calls are included in the monthly rate. Local calls thereafter are charged on an incremental (per call) basis. There is no per-minute charge for local calls. A 'subscriber' who pays nothing to Telmex still maintains the ability to receive unlimited incoming calls. In this respect, Telmex subsidizes access to the network through the pricing of other services. This cross-subsidization policy of the Mexican Government accepts the tradeoff between faster network deployment and increased long-distance calling.

In addition to this cross-subsidy policy, other domestic regulatory factors may keep long-distance prices artificially high in Mexico. A wireless carrier must contract with an affiliate to offer international long-distance service. That arrangement creates a classic 'double marginalization' problem. The long-distance price faced by wireless customers is marked up twice, once by the affiliated long-distance provider and a second time by the wireless provider. Economists have recognized the price-decreasing effect of this double marginalization for decades.[71]

In seeking Mexico's rapid elimination of its cross-subsidy policy, the US Government ignores its own lengthy transition to cost-based pricing. Before the introduction of competition in most countries, telecommunications prices typically embodied large cross-subsidies that reflect public policy preferences.[72] In particular, access to the network for residential customers has generally been priced below cost. The preponderance of network costs have been recovered through high usage rates for domestic and international long-distance calling. As noted earlier, the economic rationale for these regulatory policies was to promote universal service – and thereby to harness the positive network externalities, or 'bandwagon effects', from increasing the reach of the telecommunications network.[73] Mexico is no different from the United States in this respect. As late as 1999, the FCC delayed implementation of full-rate rebalancing in the CALLS proposal.[74] Fifteen years after the AT&T divestiture, the FCC was still concerned about too rapid a transition to cost-oriented rates.

In Mexico, regulators have yet to adopt explicit mark-ups above cost-oriented domestic interconnection rates. Mexico still does not have a universal service funding mechanism. Such measures, if adopted, would ease Mexico's transition to a fully rebalanced rate structure. Without such measures, however, Mexico would be called upon to complete in a few years what the United States has failed to complete in nearly 19 years. The US Government can insist, upon threat of trade sanctions, that Mexico make this transition immediately, but truculence carries no assurance that it will accomplish what US policy makers have been unable to do at home.

### Section 4    Did Telmex have market power in point-to-point international telecommunications services between the United States and Mexico?

On economic grounds, the US Government's and the WTO's market definition – the termination of international circuit-switched calls from the United States into Mexico – was incorrectly narrow in scope. The proper market definition is point-to-point long-distance services between the United States and Mexico. But even if it uses the US Government's incorrect market definition, it is still doubtful that Telmex had market power.

*Point-to-point international telecommunications services as the relevant product market*

The US Government's allegation that Telmex possessed and exercised market power could not be evaluated without identifying the proper definition of both product and geographic markets. The key to the proper market definition is to recognize that a southbound call is a substitute for a northbound call.

*(a) The relevant product and geographic marke*    Under the 1992 *Merger Guidelines*, used by the Antitrust Division of the US Department of Justice (as well as FCC) to define product markets, a set of services represents a distinct product market if a hypothetical unregulated monopoly provider of those services could profitably sustain a nontransitory, nontrivial price increase – that is, if the unregulated monopolist's profits after the price increase would exceed its profits before the price increase.[75] If the price increase would cause enough buyers to shift their purchases to an alternative product to render the increase unprofitable, that alternative product should be considered to be part of the relevant product market.

A closed user group (CUG) is generally defined as a group where the members are as concerned about the price of receiving a call as about the price of making a call, such as where a group of friends and family located in both the United States and Mexico have an interest in keeping call costs down in general. These CUGs exist both in the private context, where a group of friends and family does not want to impose high costs on other members, and in the business context, where a firm has a substantial interest in minimizing rates paid by calling parties who are clients or potential sources of business.

The consequence of CUGs is that international callers will consider the prices of *incoming* calls when choosing whether to make or receive calls. Because a Telmex customer in Mexico can receive calls for nothing, international calls made from the United States to Mexico act as a constraint on Telmex's negotiation of the international settlement rate and its pricing of the northbound international long-distance service. This form of substitution within a CUG is well recognized in both the economic literature and in regulatory practice.[76] A consumer in Mexico can swap receiving an inbound international call for making an outbound international call, provided that he has an economical way to indicate his desire to have a telephone conversation with a party in the United States. (This alternative is contingent on the consent of the receiving party in the United States, because the receiving party has to pay the charge for the call under this alternative.) Reversing a call from Mexico to the United States will result in the Mexican carrier losing the revenue for the outgoing call, but gaining the international settlement rate. Even if a Mexican consumer elects to call an individual in the United States and arrange to have that individual call him back, the pricing of calls from the United States to Mexico will discipline Telmex's ability to raise its price.

In particular, a Mexican consumer will request a callback from the United States if the savings from the callback (equal to the per-minute difference between the northbound and southbound long-distance rates, multiplied by the duration of the call) exceeds the cost of alerting the party in the United States of the Mexican consumer's interest to engage in conversation. Consequently, for closed user groups making calls of sufficient duration for the per-minute cost savings to exceed the alert cost, southbound calls carried by AT&T, Sprint, and WorldCom are perfect substitutes for northbound calls carried by Telmex.

The substitutability of southbound calls for northbound calls has been demonstrated by the rising trend in the length of northbound calls versus southbound calls as the price of northbound calls has fallen relative to the price of southbound calls, as demonstrated in Figure 26.1.

As the Figure 26.1 shows, the average duration of a southbound call from the United States to Mexico fell from 7.7 minutes to 6.7 minutes between 1999 and 2000.[77] At the same time, the average duration of a northbound call from Mexico to the United States rose from 4.1 minutes to 6.1 minutes.[78] Thus, in one year, the ratio of the northbound to southbound call durations rose from 0.53 to 0.91, which is near parity.

The relevant geographic market is point-to-point. At its most fundamental level, a long-distance connection involves a customer making a connection from one specific location to another specific location.[79] As the FCC has observed, customers do not view long-distance calls originating

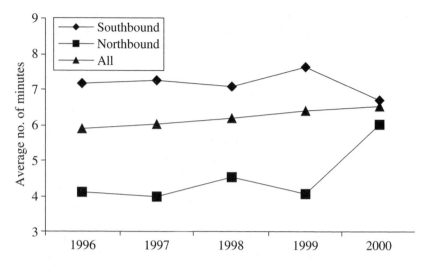

*Source:*  Common Carrier Bureau, FCC, International Telecommunications Data
(1996–2000).

*Figure 26.1    Markup earned by US long-distance carriers providing
international service to Mexico*

in different locations as being close substitutes for one another.[80] In this
respect, the relevant geographic market for international long-distance services between the United States and Mexico is all possible routes that
permit a connection from one particular location in the United States
(Mexico) to another location in Mexico (the United States): that is, a point-
to-point market.[81] It is not necessary to consider refile and reorganization
because there is no third country through which calls on the United
States–Mexico routes could be completed more cheaply.

*(b)  Telmex's incentive to eliminate double marginalization on southbound
calls, and the resulting incentive to lower its price of northbound calls*
Because of the double marginalization effect described earlier, Telmex has
a strong incentive to moderate its prices on the northbound calls to the
United States. The reasoning is as follows. The lower the price that Telmex
charges for a northbound call to the United States, the more that call
becomes a substitute in a closed user group for a southbound call from the
United States to Mexico. Every southbound call is terminated by Telmex
(unless it is illegally terminated through bypass). In other words, termination by Telmex in Mexico is a complementary input to the carriage of a
call by a US long-distance carrier across the border.

As noted earlier, however, the southbound route is imperfectly competitive, if not tacitly or explicitly collusive. Consequently the big three US long-distance carriers have an incentive to set a retail margin in addition to the margin inherent in the international settlement rate that Mexico and the United States have negotiated. Telmex, however, has the incentive to force the US long-distance carriers to reduce their retail prices on the southbound route so that consumers in the United States demand more minutes of use, which Telmex will then terminate at the international settlement rate. The means by which Telmex attempts to increase the derived demand for termination in Mexico is to make the retail rate for northbound calls to the United States more price-competitive with the retail rate that the US long-distance companies charge for southbound calls to Mexico.[82]

### Did Telmex possess market power in the relevant product and geographic markets?

It is doubtful that Telmex had the ability to raise the international settlement rate for the termination of long-distance calls that originate in the United States because it lacked market power in the relevant product market consisting of point-to-point combinations for international calls between the United States and Mexico. The international settlement rate, of course, has fallen steadily and substantially. So, in this context, market power may be considered the refusal to *drop* price in the face of competition and falling input prices.

### (a) Did Telmex have market power in the market for northbound point-to-point telecommunications services?

Although a large market share does not necessarily indicate market power, a low market share usually indicates a lack of market power. Usually a firm with a low market share cannot raise the price of a product by restricting its output.[83] American courts almost never conclude that a firm possesses market power if its market share is less than 50 per cent.[84]

Although Telmex's overall share of the international telecommunications services market exceeded 60 per cent at the time of the WTO case, the swift *decline* in Telmex's share since 1997 implies that Telmex lacked market power. Figure 26.2 shows the rate of decline in Telmex's share from January 1997 to January 2002.

As Figure 26.2 shows, Telmex's share of revenue from outbound international long-distance service decreased from 98.3 per cent in January 1997 to 64.6 per cent in January 2002. As a benchmark for comparison, when the FCC declared in 1995 that AT&T was non-dominant in 'interstate, domestic, interexchange telecommunications services' in the United States, AT&T's market share was estimated to be 60 per cent.[85] By that time, 11

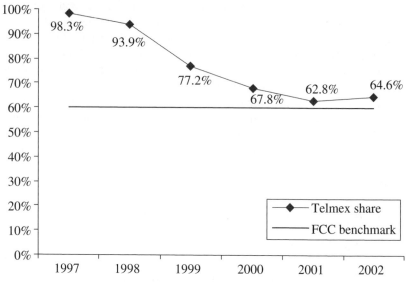

*Source:*   Cofetel.

*Figure 26.2    Telmex's share of international long-distance revenue,
January 1997–January 2002*

years had passed since the US Government's breakup of the Bell System. Likewise, in 1996, AT&T's overall share of the international long-distance services market was estimated to be about 60 per cent when the FCC declared AT&T to be non-dominant in those services.[86] On outbound routes to a number of countries, AT&T's market share was significantly higher. AT&T's average market share (weighted by revenues) on routes to 76 select countries was 74 per cent, and the carrier faced no competition whatsoever on routes to four countries.[87]

*(b)  The demand for southbound calls into Mexico is price elastic: Telmex could not have exercised market power*   The US Government asserted that Telmex had market power in the termination of long-distance calls that originate in the United States because US demand for southbound calls is not sensitive to changes in prices.[88] The available evidence on the relationship between the volume of US southbound traffic and southbound long-distance prices (as opposed to international settlement rates) appears to contradict that assertion. Table 26.1 shows the degree to which demand for southbound traffic has changed in response to changes in the price of southbound calls from 1996 to 2000.

*Table 26.1   Own-price elasticity of demand for southbound calls into Mexico, 1996–2000*

| Year | Number of minutes (thousands) | Percentage increase in number of minutes (A) | Long-distance price ($ per minute) | Percentage decrease in long-distance prices (B) | Own-price elasticity of demand (A/B) |
|---|---|---|---|---|---|
| 1996 | 2 380 007 | | 0.827 | | |
| 1997 | 2 786 488 | 17.0 | 0.732 | −11.5 | −1.48 |
| 1998 | 3 020 570 | 8.4 | 0.641 | −12.4 | −0.68 |
| 1999 | 4 053 381 | 34.2 | 0.525 | −18.1 | −1.89 |
| 2000 | 6 801 152 | 67.8 | 0.462 | −12.0 | −5.65 |
| Average | | | | | −2.42 |

*Note:*   Prices are in constant 2001 US dollars.

*Source:*   FCC, 1996 Section 43.61 International Telecommunications Data, Table A.1 (Jan. 1998); 1997 International Telecommunications Data, Table A.1 (Jan. 1999); FCC, 1998 Section 43.61 International Telecommunications Data, Table A.1 (Jan. 2000); 1999 International Telecommunications Data, Table A.1 (Dec. 2000); 2000 International Telecommunications Data, Table A.1 (Jan. 2001).

As Table 26.1 shows, assuming that a price decrease is the only factor that influences the demand for southbound service, the average own-price elasticity of demand from 1997 to 2000 was 2.42 in absolute terms, which is considered highly elastic.[89] If half of the growth in southbound traffic were attributable to other factors (such as growth in income or growth in population), the elasticity estimate would be 1.21 in absolute terms. Even this own-price elasticity of demand (in excess of one in absolute terms) implies that Telmex could not raise termination rates (an input to the end-user's price of service) excessively without losing a substantial amount of southbound calls.

To generate a smaller estimate of the own-price elasticity of demand to support its case, the US Government relied on a specious economic methodology. It related the change in southbound traffic to the change in *international settlement rates*.

During the longer period from 1998 to 2001, when the settlement rate between the US and Mexico fell from 37 cents to 15.5 cents per minute, a decrease of 58.1 per cent, overall incoming minutes received by Mexican carriers increased by 71 per cent. Adjusting this volume increase for the increase in volume of minutes that likely would have taken place over this period in any case, owing due to extraneous economic factors, based on evidence of the annual growth in US–Mexico traffic of 8.4 per cent from 1997 to 1998 when there was no decrease in the settlement rate, the total price-related change in volume over this period can be estimated at 46.5 per cent, yielding an elasticity of 0.8.[90]

The US Government attributed 100 per cent of the growth in southbound traffic in 1998 to non-price-related factors because the international settlement rate did not change that year. Although the international settlement rate did not change, the price paid by consumers in the United States certainly did change: Table 26.1 shows that southbound long-distance prices decreased by 12.4 per cent in 1998. If the US Government had attributed a lower (and more reasonable) percentage of the growth in southbound traffic to non-price-related factors, then it would have derived a much higher estimate of the own-price elasticity of demand for southbound traffic. Because of this error in analysis, the US Government's estimate of the own-price elasticity of demand on the southbound route was false.

*(c) Supply of northbound international telecommunications services by rival networks is also price elastic: Telmex could not have imposed excessive access charges*    The price elasticity of supply for northbound international calls is an important determinant of whether Telmex has the ability to exercise market power in the relevant product and geographic markets. The FCC assesses supply elasticity based on two main factors: (1) the capacity of existing competitors to expand supply and (2) low entry barriers for new suppliers.[91] The FCC's telecommunications regulations obviously do not bind Mexico. But, even if one adopts the approach used in the United States to measuring supply elasticity with respect to telecommunications carriers, one must conclude that the supply of northbound international telecommunications services is price-elastic.

Telmex's competitors could absorb immediately, and without additional investment, significant numbers of Telmex's long-distance customers. As Table 26.2 shows, there are numerous providers of competitive long-distance services throughout Telmex's region of coverage. In 2002, over 98 per cent of consumers in Telmex regions lived in cities or towns with at least one alternative long-distance carrier. Over 75 per cent of consumers in Telmex regions lived in cities or towns served by five or more long-distance competitors.

As the table shows, the presence of so many facilities-based long-distance competitors, and the ability of those competitors to interconnect to Telmex's network, indicate that they could absorb most of Telmex's current long-distance subscribers without additional dedicated or shared (downstream) investment.

*Table 26.2    Competing long-distance carriers in Telmex regions, 2002*

| Number of facilities-based competitors | Cities served by $X$ competitors | Population living in areas served by $X$ competitors (in thousands) | Percentage of customers with access to at least $X$ competitors |
|---|---|---|---|
| 9 | 2 | 9997 | 24.4 |
| 8 | 4 | 4404 | 35.2 |
| 7 | 10 | 5167 | 47.9 |
| 6 | 17 | 6331 | 63.4 |
| 5 | 20 | 5597 | 77.1 |
| 4 | 16 | 2522 | 83.2 |
| 3 | 17 | 1405 | 86.7 |
| 2 | 36 | 1632 | 90.7 |
| 1 | 47 | 2999 | 98.0 |
| 0 | 29 | 805 | 100.0 |

*Note:*   Population data were not available for five of the cities served by one competitor and seven of the cities served only by Telmex. The total population for the end two rows is obtained by applying the average population of cities for which population data were available in each of these two rows to the cities for which data were unavailable. The resulting population likely overstates the true amount somewhat because it is probable that population data were unavailable because the cities were especially small.

*Source:*   Telmex: Subdirección de Atención a Operadores (on file with authors); *Mexico 2002: Cities and Places*, The World Gazetteer, available at http://www.world-gazetteer.com/fr/fr_mx.htm.

Of course, the WTO did not need to rely on cost estimates to be able to conclude that upstart long-distance providers could readily thwart Telmex's exercise of market power. The rapid rate at which these long-distance providers entered the market and gained market share speaks for itself. Between January 1997 and January 2002, the long-distance market share of Telmex fell by 40 percentage points.[92] Beyond the importance of their then-current market share, however, was the fact that these competitors stood ready to provide service to Telmex's customers in nearly every region of Mexico, should Telmex attempt to exercise market power.

*(d) Telmex did not enjoy any significant advantage with respect to cost structure, size, or resources*    The US Government argued that Telmex had substantial advantages over its competitors with respect to international services.

Telmex has consistently retained most of the market for international services originating within Mexico as a result of various competitive advantages, including its vertical integration with its ubiquitous and irreplaceable local network and inter-city facilities to parts of Mexico without equal access, its ability to discriminate against competitors in providing leased lines and interconnection within Mexico, and its control of the largest share of the capacity available to provide international services of any Mexican carrier. Telmex's market power generally, and specifically in international services, is also evidenced by its ability to set prices to consumers for origination of international traffic well above what other Mexican carriers charge or what US carriers charge for identical traffic in the opposite direction, by the relative inelasticity of demand for both originating and terminating international services in Mexico, and by Telmex's consistently high profitability.[93]

This argument misrepresented a number of key facts and was not persuasive on economic grounds. For example, the US Government implied that Telmex set prices for outbound international calls that were 'well above what other Mexican carriers charge', despite the fact that many of Telmex's competitors had complained that Telmex's international long-distance prices are *too low*.

Each factor cited by the US Government as 'evidence' that Telmex enjoyed 'various competitive advantages' over rivals was either irrelevant or misleading. First, the United States attempted to posit Telmex's vertical integration as a competitive advantage, but ignored the fact that the Mexican affiliates of the US long-distance carriers are also vertically integrated.[94] Second, the United States cited Telmex's 'ubiquitous and irreplaceable local network' as a competitive advantage yet failed to mention that, for 92.5 per cent of Telmex's lines, customers could pre-subscribe to the service of a competing long-distance carrier. Third, the United States pointed to Telmex's 'inter-city facilities to parts of Mexico without equal access', but did not explain that these 'parts' comprised only 7.5 per cent of Telmex's lines. Fourth, the United States claimed that Telmex had the ability to 'discriminate against competitors in providing leased lines and interconnection within Mexico', even though there was no evidence that Telmex had such an ability. Fifth, the United States asserted that Telmex's control of the largest share of the international service capacity in Mexico was a competitive advantage. This 'advantage' was largely irrelevant, however, because there is substantial excess capacity for international services within Mexico and between Mexico and other countries. For example, AT&T controlled fewer ports than Telmex and transported twice as much outgoing cross-border traffic as did Telmex.

Finally, the very phenomenon to which the United States claimed Telmex's purported competitive advantages contributed was itself nonexistent. Although the US Government claimed that Telmex had 'consistently retained most of the market for international services originating within Mexico', Telmex's share of international long-distance revenues had *not* been consistent at all. Indeed, as Figure 26.2 demonstrates, Telmex had lost over a third of the market for international long distance between January 1997 and January 2002.

*Even if the market definition had been the termination of southbound calls, Telmex lacked market power*

The US Government did not undertake standard antitrust analysis of the relevant product market. Instead it defined the relevant product market as '*termination* of voice telephony, facsimile and circuit-switched data transmission services supplied on a cross-border basis from the US into Mexico'.[95] The US Government used the following reasoning to reach this narrow market definition:

> The Mexican competition authority, the Comisión Federal de Competencia ('CFC'), determined in 1998 and reaffirmed in 2001 that international long distance service is a relevant market for which there are 'no close substitutes', and that such service is distinct from domestic local, access, long distance or carrier toll services. This determination was made for the purpose of identifying the broad categories of service in which Telmex would be subject to regulation as a dominant carrier. Accordingly, the CFC's category of international services included several types of switched and non-switched telecommunications services, among which, significantly, were international port services for switching and routing of both originating and terminating international traffic. The CFC's analysis clearly applied to termination of cross-border traffic, as the CFC recognized that the international ports 'permit the accounting of international traffic and compliance with the proportional return scheme set forth in the regulations', that is, Mexico's requirements for termination of international traffic, as discussed below. The CFC also recognized that each international route between Mexico and another country, such as the US, 'constitutes a geographic market'.[96]

This reasoning is unsound on economic grounds and does not support the conclusion that Telmex could exercise market power. Also the US Government did not provide a compelling justification for the exclusion of packet-switched telecommunications services from the relevant product market. Packet-switched telecommunications services are an effective substitute for services that use Mexico's circuit-switched network. Furthermore the importance of packet-switched telecommunications will only increase as data communications services become more popular.

*(a) The critical share of marginal customers needed to render an exercise of market power by Telmex unprofitable would be small*   Telmex was the sole carrier authorized to negotiate with the US carriers over the international

settlement rate for all telecommunications traffic from the United States that was legally terminated in Mexico. However Telmex had no ability to negotiate over the rate of traffic that US carriers terminated illegally in Mexico by bypassing interconnection with an authorized gateway at the Mexican border. For example, the US carrier could simply use a short microwave link to send a call across the border to an unauthorized gateway, which would then make the call appear to originate in Mexico. To the extent that this simple bypass occurred, it strengthened the negotiating position of the US long-distance carriers relative to their counterparts in Mexico, and it prevented Telmex from setting an international settlement rate that approached a monopoly price.

It is likely that termination of southbound calls from the United States onto wireless networks and onto rival wire line networks through bypass constrained the pricing of terminating access onto Telmex's wire line network. From an antitrust perspective, the relevant question should have been: could a hypothetical, unregulated monopoly supplier of the service in question (terminating access onto Telmex's wire line network, in this case) profitably sustain a 5 per cent price increase for a substantial time period, usually assumed to be two years? To answer this standard question in antitrust cases, one conducts 'critical share' analysis.

If Telmex were to raise its prices for terminating access of southbound calls, some US carriers would switch away from terminating their calls onto Telmex's wire line network (through illegally bypassing the authorized points of international connection, for example). Define the original price for terminating a call onto Telmex's wire line network as $P_0$, and the associated derived demand for terminating access onto Telmex's wire line network (measured in minutes) as $Q_0$. When the price of terminating access increases to $P_1$, the number of minutes demanded falls to $Q_1$. Let $c$ denote Telmex's marginal cost of providing terminating access. The decrease in the volume of calls due to the price increase is the difference between $Q_0$ and $Q_1$, which are the 'marginal' minutes. The remaining minutes, $Q_1$, are the 'inframarginal' minutes.

Telmex would raise its price for termination onto its wire line network by 5 per cent if the profits after the price increase would exceed the profits before the price increase. The profitability of a 5 per cent price increase depends on the firm's own-price elasticity of demand. That comparison of profits can be expressed algebraically as

$$(1.05\,P_0 - c)\,Q_1 > (P_0 - c)\,Q_0. \tag{26.1}$$

The (own-price) elasticity of derived demand for termination onto Telmex's wire line network, $\varepsilon$, is the percentage decrease in terminating minutes for every 1 per cent increase in Telmex's price for terminating access. A constant elasticity demand curve implies

$$Q_1/Q_0 = (P_1/P_0)^\varepsilon. \tag{26.2}$$

Substituting this definition of elasticity into equation 26.2 and cancelling terms yields

$$(1.05\, P_0 - c)\, (P_1/P_0)^\varepsilon > (P_0 - c). \tag{26.3}$$

Dividing both sides by the new margin per minute and taking logarithms yields

$$\varepsilon \log[1.05] > \log[P_0 - c] - \log[1.05\, P_0 - c]. \tag{26.4}$$

Equation 26.4 can be used to determine whether Telmex could raise the price of terminating access and increase its profits. In other words, equation 26.4 indicates the own-price elasticity of demand for Telmex (as a firm) that would be necessary to defeat a 5 per cent price increase.

Consider a critical-share analysis of traffic patterns in Zone 2 Mexican cities (approximately 200 medium-sized cities). A similar analysis could be performed for Zone 1 and Zone 3 cities. Using an initial terminating price of 8.5 cents per minute and a marginal cost of 3 cents per minute,[97] the critical level of elasticity for the price increase to be profitable is −1.5. If the own-price elasticity of demand for terminating access onto Telmex's wire line network is less than −1.5 (that is, if the own-price elasticity is greater than 1.5 in absolute terms), then Telmex could *not* profitably raise the price of termination.

As explained earlier, the (market) own-price elasticity of demand for southbound services was between −1.2 and −2.4. Using Marshall's Laws of Derived Demand, one can estimate that the elasticity of demand for terminating access onto Telmex's wire line network (the only input in the production of the final service to US consumers) is also between −1.2 and −2.4. In particular, when an input represents 100 per cent of the cost of supplying the final service, which is the case for terminating access and southbound long-distance service, the own-price elasticity of demand for the input equals the own-price elasticity of demand for the final service.[98] Hence, under conservative estimations of the elasticity of demand for terminating access onto Telmex's wire line network during the relevant time period, Telmex could not have raised its prices for terminating access and thereby increase its profits. That is, Telmex lacked market power.

Another way to consider critical share is in terms of the critical level of lost output. Using equation 26.2 and the above estimate of the own-price elasticity of derived demand for termination, if Telmex were to lose 7.2 per cent of its terminating minutes from US carriers, Telmex would not be willing to raise its price by 5 per cent. Telmex estimated that, in 2001, black market calls displaced up to 18 per cent of its international revenue.[99] Because 18 per cent of southbound traffic represents more than the critical share of 7.2 per cent, Telmex could not have increased its profit by raising the price of terminating access. That is, during the relevant time period, Telmex lacked market power in the termination of southbound traffic.

*(b) Countervailing market power of US long-distance carriers in the bilateral negotiation of international settlement rates*    The US Government argued that Telmex had been able to extract supracompetitive profits from the international settlement rates as a result of its superior negotiating position. Although Telmex was the sole negotiator on behalf of all Mexican firms, it could not impose supracompetitive rates on US carriers because those carriers had substantial market power over the southbound US–Mexico route. The market for calls from the United States into Mexico was highly concentrated. As Table 26.2 shows, the Herfindahl–Hirschman Index (HHI)[100] of market concentration between 1994 and 2000 was quite high (above 4000 every year) and, in 2000, the index increased by more than 2000 to 6215.

If Telmex had been negotiating international settlement rates with a number of small US carriers, the US Government's contention might have been plausible, but it was not plausible that Telmex held a vastly superior position in negotiations over the international settlement rate. In 1999 and 2000, more than 90 per cent of the market for southbound calls into Mexico was controlled by two US carriers that had identical negotiation objectives vis-à-vis Telmex.

*(c) Telmex offered termination access at a price substantially below the benchmark settlement rate*    Mexico's international settlement rates in 2002 were among the lowest 20 per cent of all published settlement rates for the 32 countries in Mexico's teledensity group.[101] Teledensity is a measure of the number of telephone lines per 100 inhabitants. Mexico's teledensity group included the 32 countries that had between ten and 20 telephone lines per 100 inhabitants. Based on these data, Mexico's 2002 international settlement rates complied with the target international settlement rates set forward by the International Telecommunications Union (ITU).[102] Telmex's international settlement rate was significantly below the benchmark settlement rate that the FCC established to protect US long-distance

carriers (a maximum of 11.75 cents in zone 3 cities versus the FCC benchmark rate of 19.0 cents).[103] Indeed the difference between the actual settlement rate and the FCC benchmark rate demonstrates the countervailing market power of the US carriers in the rate-setting process.

*(d) The absence of international simple resale did not give Telmex market power in the termination of southbound calls*   The WTO panel rejected the argument that Mexico's policies toward non-facilities-based service providers violated that nation's various treaty commitments. The US Government had argued that the ILD Rules 'prohibit alternative arrangements for the delivery and termination of international calls in Mexico, such as those available in many other countries for the origination and termination of international traffic over international private lines – also known as "international simple resale" or "ISR" services'.[104] Contrary to that assertion, Telmex could not have exercised market power in the termination of southbound calls even if the Mexican Government continued its policy of not mandating the unbundling of Telmex's long-distance capacity. There is not now, and there was not at the time of the WTO case, any barrier to entry into facilities-based provision of southbound long-distance service in Mexico. Indeed, at the time of the WTO case, the Mexican affiliates of AT&T and WorldCom – Alestra and Avantel – *already* operated their own fibre-optic long-distance facilities, on which American carriers could lease capacity to transport their southbound calls from the United States. In other words, whether facilities-based entry was possible was not a hypothetical question. *It had already happened.* Any supposed barriers to facilities-based entry were not so high that they could not be surmounted. The mandatory, rate-regulated ISR that the US Government asked the WTO to impose would have added nothing to the competitiveness of the market for international calling between Mexico and the United States, given that US carriers already had alternative facilities with ample capacity available to them at competitive prices. Posing the question in these terms highlights the difference between the welfare of consumers and the welfare of competitors.[105]

So why did the US Government seek mandatory ISR? The most plausible economic answer is that mandatory ISR would enlarge the already high margins that US long-distance carriers reaped on the southbound route. The regulated price for mandatory ISR could never exceed the arm's-length market price for such capacity. That was certainly the American experience from the hundreds of arbitrations by which state public utilities commissions in 1996 and 1997 set wholesale discounts that incumbent local exchange carriers were required to offer to their competitors pursuant to the Telecommunications Act of 1996.[106] As the principal beneficiaries,

AT&T, WorldCom, and Sprint were sophisticated participants in those hundreds of rate proceedings. That American experience suggested that strategic use of the WTO complaint process could override the Mexican regulatory process and produce a lower price for resale than the market price. A form of regulatory arbitrage would result. An American carrier would divert traffic from its affiliated carrier in Mexico if the transfer price that the two carriers had struck by arm's-length agreement exceeded the below-market price that the WTO compelled Telmex (through the Mexican government) to offer as a result of the imposition of mandatory ISR.

In light of the widening margins that US long-distance carriers have earned on the southbound route, it could not even be said that the regulatory arbitrage resulting from mandatory, rate-regulated ISR would have subsidized US consumers calling Mexico. Rather US carriers would have captured for themselves the lion's share of the difference between the market price and the regulated price for international wholesale capacity on Telmex's network. Nothing in the 1997 WTO agreement or the 1996 Reference Paper remotely suggested that one signatory nation must compel its incumbent carrier to subsidize the operations of equally experienced carriers from another signatory nation. The US Government evidently thought otherwise.

**Conclusion**

The WTO embraced most of the US Government's policy preferences. It is unlikely that consumers in the United States and Mexico are any better off than if Cofetel had been permitted to oversee Mexico's domestic regulatory reform. As the international settlement rate is lowered to LRAIC, Telmex will have less incentive at the margin to invest to upgrade and maintain its networks. To restore that incentive, Telmex will have to generate an offsetting amount of incremental net revenue from its other services in Mexico. Doing so will have the marginal effect of slowing growth in demand for those services. Perhaps the US Government believes that American consumers benefit when Mexican consumers lose. That reasoning would be fallacious, however, because it ignores the network effects in telecommunications. US consumers benefit from a more ubiquitous network in Mexico. Consequently the US Government's success at the WTO will hurt its own consumers, contrary to stated American policy. The sole beneficiaries of the US policy appear to be US long-distance carriers, which in all likelihood will widen their margins on calls from the United States to Mexico.

Mandatory international simple resale would have undermined Cofetel's efforts to spur facilities-based competition. A US carrier that wants to establish a connection between the United States and Mexico has the choice of building its own facility in Mexico (through its Mexican affiliate) or interconnecting, either through paying access charges to a Mexican carrier or leasing a line from a Mexican carrier. Non-facilities-based competition has been a failure in the United States, largely because carriers that rely too heavily on an incumbent's facilities are incapable of offering distinct or innovative services, and can therefore only compete on price. The sole bright spot in the WTO decision was its rejection of mandatory ISR.

The policies advocated by the US Government before the WTO advanced the private interests of AT&T, Sprint and WorldCom while depriving US consumers of a more ubiquitous telecommunications network in North America. Those policies successfully overturned the informed judgments of an independent regulatory authority in Mexico that, consistent with principles of the WTO agreement and its associated Reference Paper, had based its decisions on expertise and detailed knowledge concerning the industry that it regulates.

## Notes

1. Visiting Professor of Law, Georgetown University Law Center.
2. President, Criterion Economics, L.L.C., Washington, D.C. Criterion Economics advised the Republic of Mexico on economic matters concerning the arbitration discussed in this chapter. The views expressed here are solely those of the authors and not those of the Republic of Mexico, nor are they the views of the Georgetown University Law Center, which does not take institutional positions on specific executive, legislative, judicial, or regulatory matters. Copyright 2005 by J. Gregory Sidak and Hal J. Singer. All rights reserved.
3. United States Government, Mexico – Measures Affecting Telecommunications Services, First Written Submission, Dkt. No. WT/DS204, at 9 ¶ 36, 79 ¶ 207 (filed World Trade Org., 3 October 2002) [hereinafter US Government Written Submission].
4. WTO Dispute Panel Report, Mexico – Measures Affecting Telecommunications Services, Dkt. No. WT/DS204/R (World Trade Org., 2 April 2004) [hereinafter WTO Dispute Panel Report].
5. See Rohlfs, Jeffrey H. and J. Gregory Sidak (2002), 'Exporting telecommunications regulation: the US–Japan negotiations on interconnection pricing', *HARV. INT'L L.J.*, **43**, 317, at 319. The conclusive evidence of the controversy surrounding US unbundling policy is that the FCC's rules on what parts of the local network must be unbundled have been struck down by the Supreme Court or D.C. Circuit three times. See *United States Telecom Ass'n* v. *FCC*, 359 F.3d 554 (D.C. Cir. 2004).
6. See, e.g., *Parker* v. *Brown*, 317 US 341, 350-52 (1941).
7. See, e.g., Case C-198/01, *Consorzi Industrie Fiammiferi (CIF)* v. *Autorita Garante Della Concorrenz E Del Mercato*, 2003 E.C.R. I-8055.
8. See *Parker*, 317 US at 350-52.
9. Ibid., at 350–51.
10. *City of Columbia* v. *Omni Outdoor Advertising*, 499 US 365, 370 (1991).
11. *Town of Hallie* v. *City of Eau Claire*, 471 US 34, 40 (1985).
12. Ibid., at 41; see also *New Motor Vehicle Board* v. *Orrin W. Fox. Co.*, 439 US 96, 109 (1978) (holding that, although there was no express intent to displace antitrust law, statute authorized regulatory structure that 'displace[d] unfettered business freedom').
13. *Town of Hallie*, 471 US at 42, 46.
14. See, e.g., Case C-198/01, *Consorzi Industrie Fiammiferi (CIF)* v. *Autorita Garante Della Concorrenz E Del Mercato*, 2003 E.C.R. I-8055.

15. Ibid. ('Judgment of the Court'); see also Case 267/86, *Van Eycke* v. *ASPA*, 1988 E.C.R. 4769, ¶ 16; Case C-185/91, *Bundesanstalt für den Güterfernverkehr* v. *Gebrüder Reiff*, 1993 E.C.R. I-5801, ¶ 14; C-153/93, *Bundesrepublik Deutschland/Delta Schiffahrts-und Speditionsgesellschaft*, 1994 E.C.R. I-2517, ¶ 14.
16. Case C-198/01, *Consorzi Industrie Fiammiferi (CIF)* v. *Autorita Garante Della Concorrenz E Del Mercato*, 2003 E.C.R. I-8055, ¶ 45.
17. Perez, Antonia (2002), 'International antitrust at the crossroads: the end of antitrust history or the clash of competition policy civilizations?', *LAW & POL'Y INT'L BUS.*, 33, 527, at 548–9; see also Lande, Robert H. (2000), 'Professor Waller's Un-American Approach to Antitrust', *LOY. U. CHI. L.J.*, 32, 137, at 139–42.
18. Ibid., at 549.
19. Facey, Brian A. and Dany. H. Assaf (2002), 'Monopolization and abuse of dominance in Canada, the United States, and the European Union: a survey', ANTITRUST L.J., 70, 513, at 532.
20. Hausman, Jerry A., Gregory K. Leonard and Christopher A. Vellturo (1996), 'Market definition under price discrimination', *ANTITRUST L.J.*, 64, 367, at 368 (citing US Department of Justice and Federal Trade Commission Horizontal Merger Guidelines §§ 1.12, 1.22 (1992)).
21. Ibid.
22. Holmes, William C. (2004), *Antitrust Law Handbook* §3:4 (citing *Brown Shoe Co.* v. *United States*, 370 US 294 (1962)).
23. *Brown Shoe Co.*, 370 US at 325.
24. Facey and Assaf, above, note 19, at 533 (citing Per Jebsen and Robert Stevens (1996), 'Assumptions, goals and dominant undertakings: the regulation of competition under Article 86 of the European Union', *ANTITRUST L.J.*, 64, 443, at 471).
25. European Commission (1997), *Notice on the Definition of the Relevant Market for the Purpose of Community Competition Law*, 1997 O.J. (C 372) 5 [hereinafter Commission Market Definition Notice].
26. Facey and Assaf, above, note 19, at 533.
27. Ibid.
28. See, e.g., Connolly, William P. (2001), 'Lessons to be learned: the conflict in international antitrust law contrasted with progress in international financial law', *FORDHAM J. CORP. & FIN. L.*, 6, 207, at 246, note 138.
29. Facey and Assaf, above, note 19, at 533–4.
30. *Reglas para Prestar el Servicio de Larga Distancia Internacional que deberán aplicar los Concesionarios de Redes Públicas de Telecomunicaciones Autorizados para Prestar este Servicio*, D.O., 11 December 1996 [hereinafter ILD Rules].
31. ILD Rules 2:XII(a), 2:XII(b), 10, cited in WTO Dispute Panel Report, above, note 4, at 4.
32. ILD Rule 13, cited in WTO Dispute Panel Report, above, note 4, at 4.
33. ILD Rules 2:XII, 10, 13, 16, 17 and 19, cited in WTO Dispute Panel Report, above, note 4, at 4.
34. World Trade Organization, Negotiating Group on Basic Telecommunications, Reference Paper §2.2(b) (24 April 1996) [hereinafter Reference Paper], cited in WTO Dispute Panel Report, above, note 4, at 144. For an analysis of the Reference Paper and its relationship to the WTO agreement on basic telecommunications services, see Sidak, J. Gregory (1997), *Foreign Investment in American Telecommunications*, University of Chicago Press, pp. 367–94. For a critique of the vagueness of the Reference Paper, see Barfield, Claude E. (2001), *Free Trade, Sovereignty, Democracy: The Future of the World Trade Organization*, AEI Press, pp. 56–8.
35. Reference Paper, above, note 34, at § 2.2(b), cited in WTO Dispute Panel Report, above, note 4, at 144.
36. World Trade Organization, GATS Annex on Telecommunications §5(a), available at http://www.wto.org/english/docs_e/legal_e/26-gats.pdf [hereinafter GATS Annex].
37. WTO Dispute Panel Report, above, note 4, at 225.
38. See Reference Paper, above, note 34, §2.2(b) (emphasis added).

39. Ibid. (definitions), cited in WTO Dispute Panel Report, above, note 4, at 174.
40. WTO Dispute Panel Report, above, note 4, at 176.
41. ILD Rule 13, cited in WTO Dispute Panel Report, above, note 4, at 4.
42. WTO Dispute Panel Report, above, note 4, at 176.
43. Ibid., at 179.
44. Ibid., at 177.
45. Ibid., at 181.
46. Ibid., at 189.
47. ILD Rules 16, 17, cited in WTO Dispute Panel Report, above, note 4, at 187–8.
48. WTO Dispute Panel Report, above, note 4, at 188.
49. Reference Paper, above, note 34, §1.1, cited in WTO Dispute Panel Report at 191.
50. Reference Paper, above, note 34, §1.2, cited in WTO Dispute Panel Report at 193.
51. WTO Dispute Panel Report, above, note 1, at 193.
52. Ibid., at 196–8.
53. Ibid., at 198.
54. Ibid., at 199.
55. Ibid.
56. GATS Annex, above, note 36, §5(a).
57. WTO Dispute Panel Report, above, note 4, at 200–216.
58. *International Settlements Policy Reform, International Settlement Rates, Notice of Proposed Rulemaking*, IB Dkt. Nos. 02–324, 96–261¶ 1 note 2 (released Oct. 11, 2002) (emphasis added) [hereinafter *International Settlements Policy NPRM*].
59. Ibid., at ¶ 2.
60. Ibid.
61. See, e.g., Sidak, J. Gregory and Daniel F. Spulber (1997a), *Deregulatory Takings and the Regulatory Contract: The Competitive Transformation of Network Industries in the United States*, Cambridge University Press, pp. 119–29 (discussing obligation to serve and carrier of last resort).
62. Ibid., at 513 ('Mandating that the incumbent [local exchange carrier] alone act as the carrier of last resort forces the firm to hold capacity in reserve to meet demand at peak load').
63. Case COMP/35.141, Deutsche Post AG, 2001 O.J. (L 125) 27 at ¶ 9 (citing Baumol, William J. and J. Gregory Sidak (1994), *Toward Competition in Local Telephony*, MIT Press, p. 108).
64. 'There are costs associated with providing both connections and standby capacity to supply the option to achieve a connection. The costs of standby capacity are capital costs of network capacity that are similar to the merchant's cost of holding inventory to provide "immediacy" to customers' (Sidak, J. Gregory and Daniel F. Spulber (1998), 'Cyberjam: the law and economics of Internet congestion of the telephone network', *Harv. J.L. & Pub. Pol'y*, **21**, 337, at 362). See also Baumol, William J. and J. Gregory Sidak (2002), 'The pig in the python: is lumpy capacity investment used and useful?', *Energy L.J.*, **23**, 383.
65. See Reference Paper, above, note 34, at §2.2(b). The Reference Paper states: 'Interconnection to be ensured . . . in a timely fashion, on terms, conditions (including technical standards and specifications) and *cost-oriented rates* that are transparent, reasonable, having regard to economic feasibility, and sufficiently unbundled so that the supplier need not pay for network components or facilities that it does not require for the service to be provided'. Ibid., emphasis added.
66. US Government Written Submission, above, note 3, at ¶ 110.
67. 1995 Federal Law on Telecommunications, Art. 63.
68. US Government Written Submission, above, note 3, at ¶ 110 (emphasis added).
69. Ibid., at ¶ 113.
70. Humpty Dumpty said, 'When I use a word, it means just what I choose it to mean – neither more nor less' (Lewis Carroll (1871), *Through the Looking Glass (& What Alice Found There)* ch. 6). The United States has similarly taken the position in international negotiations on telecommunications services that LRAIC means whatever the US Trade Representative chooses it to mean. See Rohlfs and Sidak (2002), 5.

71. See Spengler, Joseph (1950), 'Vertical integration and antitrust policy', *J. POL. ECON.*, **58**, 347, at 351–2. For a contemporary exposition, see Carlton, Dennis W. and Jeffrey M. Perloff (2000), *Modern Industrial Organization*, Addison-Wesley, pp. 398–401; Tirole, Jean (1988), *The Theory of Industrial Organization*, MIT Press, p.174. Double marginalization occurs when two companies have a vertical supplier–customer relationship. The upstream company sets its price, and thus its margin between price and marginal cost, to maximize its own profits. The downstream company likewise sets its price and margin to maximize its profit, treating what it pays the upstream company as a cost. If the upstream company begins to offer the downstream product also, it will generally set the final price of the downstream product to maximize its profits jointly from both the upstream and downstream products. The company offering the combined product will often find that it can increase its profits by lowering the price of the final product below the price that would be set in the previous situation. The company offering the combined product will take into account how a lower price on the final product will increase the sale of and profits from the upstream product, while a company offering only the final product will not. Although the analysis of double marginalization originally was derived for the case of monopoly, it also applies to imperfect competition, which characterizes telecommunications markets because of the large fixed and common costs. The leading American antitrust treatise, for example, observes that '[t]he double marginalization model appears to make robust predictions that vertical integration results in increased output and lower prices any time the affected markets are something less than perfectly competitive'. See Areeda, Phillip E. and Herbert Hovenkamp (2002), *Antitrust Law*, ¶ 758b at 30.
72. See, e.g., Crandall, Robert W. and Leonard Waverman (2000), 'Who pays for universal service? When telephone subsidies become Transparent', **166**, Brookings Institution, discussing regulatory requirements to price local exchange service below cost.
73. See, e.g., Rohlfs, Jeffrey H. (2001), *Bandwagon Effects in High-Technology Industries*, MIT Press, pp. 177–9.
74. See *Access Charge Reform; Price Cap Performance Review for Local Exchange Carriers; Low-Volume Long Distance Users; Federal-State Joint Board On Universal Service, Sixth Report and Order*, CC Dkt. Nos. 96-262, 94-1, 99-249, 96-45, 15 F.C.C.R. 12,962 (2000).
75. *1992 Department of Justice and Federal Trade Commission Horizontal Merger Guidelines*, at 20,572 §1.0 (defining the relevant product market as 'a product or group of products such that a hypothetical profit maximizing firm that was the only present and future seller of those products ("monopolist") likely would impose at least a "small but significant and nontransitory" increase in price').
76. See, e.g., Hausman, Jerry (2002), 'Mobile telephone', in Martin E. Cave, Sumit K. Majumdar and Ingo Vogelsang (eds), *Handbook of Telecommunications Economics*, (vol. 1) North-Holland, p. 563, at 566.
77. *FCC 1999 International Data*, at Table A.1; *Common Carrier Bureau, FCC, 2000 International Telecommunications Data*, Table A.1 (Dec. 2001) [hereinafter FCC 2000 *International Data*].
78. *FCC 1999 International Data*, at Table A.1; *FCC 2000 International Data*, above, note 77, at Table A.1.
79. See *Regulatory Treatment of LEC Provision of Interexchange Services Originating in the LEC's Local Exchange Area and Policy and Rules Concerning the Interstate, Interexchange Marketplace*, CC Dkt. No. 96-149, 12 F.C.C.R. 15,756, 15,792-93 ¶ 64 (1997) [hereinafter *BOC Classification Order*].
80. Ibid.
81. Ibid.
82. Telmex's incentive to eliminate double-marginalization on the southbound route finds a close analogy in the economic analysis of American telecommunications regulation. Under current regulatory policies in the United States, access and long-distance services are both sold at prices exceeding marginal (incremental) cost, so as to cover the large fixed costs of local and long-distance networks. Consequently, the academic literature in the United States recognizes that a Bell operating company (BOC) has a greater incen-

tive to charge lower long-distance prices in the United States than does an American interexchange carrier (IXC) because the BOC's pricing decisions consider the additional margin earned on access service when long-distance sales are expanded by lower prices. Furthermore, when the BOC lowers the long-distance price, the IXCs will lower their prices, which will increase the number of long-distance minutes demanded and consequently the number of access minutes demanded from the BOCs. See Sappington, David E.M. and Dennis L. Weisman (1996), *Designing Incentive Regulation for the Telecommunications Industry*, MIT Press and AEI Press, pp. 258–61, 267–71. See also Sibley, David S. and Dennis L. Weisman (1998), 'The competitive incentives of vertically integrated local exchange carriers: an economic and policy analysis', *J. POL'Y ANALYSIS AND MGMT.*, **17**, 74; Weisman, Dennis L. (1995), 'Regulation and the vertically integrated firm: the case of RBOC entry into InterLATA long distance', *J. REG. ECON.*, **8**, 249.

83. See, e.g., *BOC Classification Order*, above, note 79, at 15,802–03 ¶ 83 (the ability to raise prices by restricting one's own output 'usually requires a large market share'.); also, at 96 ('the fact that each BOC interLATA affiliate initially will have zero market share in the provision of in-region, interstate, domestic, interLATA services suggests that the affiliate will not initially be able to raise price by restricting its output').

84. See 1 *ABA Antitrust Section, Antitrust Law Developments*, (4th edn, 1997) 213–14 (summarizing case law); see also *United States* v. *Aluminum Co. of America*, 148 F.2d 416, 424 (2d Cir. 1945) ('it is doubtful whether a 60 percent market share would constitute a monopoly, and certainly 33 percent is not'); Landes, William M. and Richard A. Posner (1981), 'Market power in antitrust cases', *HARV. L. REV.*, **94**, 937, at 938 (1981) (surveying case law).

85. Motion of AT&T Corp. to be Reclassified as a Non-Dominant Carrier, 11 F.C.C.R. 3305 ¶ 62 and note 173 (1995).

86. Motion of AT&T Corp. to be Declared Non-Dominant for International Service, 11 F.C.C.R. 17,963, 17,978 ¶ 40 (1996).

87. Ibid.

88. US Government Written Submission, above, note 3, App. A at 5 ¶ 5 ('Available evidence suggests that demand for additional minutes to Mexico from the US in response to settlement reductions has also been somewhat inelastic').

89. See, e.g., Kreps, David M. (1990), *A Course in Microeconomic Theory*, Princeton University Press, p. 300.

90. US Government Written Submission, above, note 3, App. A at 5 ¶ 6 (citations omitted).

91. Motion of AT&T Corp. to be Reclassified as a Non-Dominant Carrier, 11 F.C.C.R. 3271, 3303 (1995) (the greater the capacity of existing competitors to expand supply and the lower the barriers to entry, the more elastic the supply can be judged to be).

92. Cofetel, Communications Sector Program 2001–6, available online at http://www.cft.gob.mx/html/presidencia/communicationsectorprogram.pdf, at 3–4. Cofetel notes, by way of comparison, that it took eight years for international long-distance competitors in the United States to achieve the same market share that competitors in Mexico achieved in only five years. (Ibid., at 4.)

93. US Government Written Submission, above, note 3, at ¶ 98.

94. Indeed, at the time that the US Government filed its complaint with the WTO, AT&T and WorldCom were investors in two of Telmex's principal competitors. Although WorldCom subsequently declared bankruptcy after committing the largest fraud ever witnessed in the telecommunications industry, over the relevant time period it and AT&T did not lack resources or expertise relative to Telmex. See generally Sidak, J. Gregory, (2003), 'The failure of good intentions: the WorldCom fraud and the collapse of American telecommunications after deregulation', *YALE J. REG.*, **20**, 207.

95. US Government Written Submission, above, note 3, at ¶ 81 (emphasis added).

96. Ibid., at ¶ 75, quoting Comisión Federal de Competencia, Teléfonos de Mexico, Declaratoria de poder sustancial en diversos mercados relacionados con la telefonía (Statement of substantial power in different telephone markets), File No. AD-41–97, at 18–19 (24–6 in Spanish original) (21 May 2001).

97. US Government Written Submission, above, note 3, at 38.
98. For a discussion of Marshall's rules of derived demand, see Layard, P.R.G. and A.A. Walters (1978), *Microeconomic Theory*, McGraw-Hill, at p. 260.
99. *Telmex, 2001 Annual Report*, Exhibit US-2, at 11, available at http://telmex.com/inter-nos/inversionistas/finanzas/pdf/Annual101.pdf.
100. The HHI is the sum of the squares of the individual market shares of all market participants. The higher the HHI, the greater the market concentration. See, e.g., Carlton and Perloff (2000), at p. 247. By way of comparison for the HHI numbers for southbound international calls, the Merger Guidelines consider a post-merger HHI above 1800 to be highly concentrated. Horizontal Merger Guidelines, above, note 1, at §1.51c (rev. 8 April 1997).
101. *International Telecommunication Union, World Telecommunication Development Report 2002: Reinventing Telecoms* (2002).
102. Ibid.
103. 'International Settlements Policy and US-International Accounting Rates', available at http://ftp.fcc.gov/ib/pd/pf/account.html. For a complete description of Telmex's interconnection rates provided to US suppliers, see WorldCom Petition for Waiver of the International Settlements Policy, filed with the FCC on 21 March 2002, FCC File No. ISP-WAV-20020322-00012, Ex. US-29.
104. US Government Written Submission, above, note 3, at ¶ 6.
105. See Hausman, Jerry A. and J. Gregory Sidak (1999), 'A consumer-welfare approach to the mandatory unbundling of telecommunications networks', *YALE L.J.*, **109**, 417.
106. See Sidak, J. Gregory and Daniel F. Spulber (1997b), 'The tragedy of the telecommons: government pricing of unbundled network elements under the Telecommunications Act of 1996', *COLUM. L. REV.*, **97**, 1081, at 1082–3.

# References

Areeda, Phillip E. and Herbert Hovenkamp (2002), *Antitrust Law*.
Barfield, Claude E. (2001), *Free Trade, Sovereignty, Democracy: The Future of the World Trade Organization*, AEI Press.
Baumol, William J. and J. Gregory Sidak (1994), *Toward Competition in Local Telephony*, MIT Press.
Baumol, William J. and Gregory J. Sidak (2002), 'The pig in the python: is lumpy capacity investment used and useful?', *ENERGY L.J.*, **23**, 383.
Carlton, Dennis W. and Jeffrey M. Perloff (2000), *Modern Industrial Organization*, Addison-Wesley.
Connolly, William P. (2001), 'Lessons to be learned: the conflict in international antitrust law contrasted with progress in international financial law', *FORDHAM J. CORP. & FIN. L.*, **6**, 207.
Crandall, Robert W. and Leonard Waverman (2000), 'Who pays for universal service? When telephone subsidies become transparent', **166**, Brookings Institution.
Facey, Brian A. and Dany H. Assaf (2002), 'Monopolization and abuse of dominance in Canada, the United States, and the European Union: a survey', *ANTITRUST L.J.*, **70**, 513.
Hausman, Jerry (2002), 'Mobile telephone', in Martin E. Cave, Sumit K. Majumdar and Ingo Vogelsang (eds), *Handbook of Telecommunications Economics*, vol. 1, North-Holland, p. 563.
Hausman, Jerry A. and J. Gregory Sidak (1999), 'A consumer-welfare approach to the mandatory unbundling of telecommunications networks', *YALE L.J.*, **109**, 417.
Hausman, Jerry A., Gregory K. Leonard and Christopher A. Vellturo (1996), 'Market definition under price discrimination', *ANTITRUST L.J.*, **64**, 367.
Jebsen, Per and Robert Stevens (1996), 'Assumptions, goals and dominant undertakings: the regulation of competition under Article 86 of the European Union', *ANTITRUST L.J.*, **64**, 443.
Kreps, David M. (1990), *A Course in Microeconomic Theory*, Princeton University Press.
Lande, Robert H. (2000), 'Professor Waller's un-American approach to antitrust', *LOY. U. CHI. L.J.*, **32**, 137.

Landes, William M. and Richard A. Posner (1981), 'Market power in antitrust cases', *HARV. L. REV.*, 94, 937.
Layard, P.R.G. and A.A. Walters (1978), *Microeconomic Theory*, McGraw-Hill.
Perez, Antonia, 'International antitrust at the crossroads: the end of antitrust history or the clash of competition policy civilizations?', *LAW & POL'Y INT'L BUS.*, 33, 527.
Rohlfs, Jeffrey H. (2001), *Bandwagon Effects in High-Technology Industries*, MIT Press.
Rohlfs, Jeffrey H. and J. Gregory Sidak (2002), 'Exporting telecommunications regulation: the US–Japan negotiations on interconnection pricing', *HARV. INT'L L.J.*, 43, 317.
Sappington, David E.M. and Dennis L. Weisman (1996), *Designing Incentive Regulation for the Telecommunications Industry*, MIT Press & AEI Press.
Sibley, David S. and Dennis L. Weisman (1998), 'The competitive incentives of vertically integrated local exchange carriers: an economic and policy analysis', *J. POL'Y ANALYSIS & MGMT.*, 17, 74.
Sidak, J. Gregory (1997), *Foreign Investment in American Telecommunications*, University of Chicago Press.
Sidak, J. Gregory (2003), 'The failure of good intentions: the WorldCom fraud and the collapse of American telecommunications after deregulation', *YALE J. REG.*, 20, 207.
Sidak, J. Gregory and Daniel F. Spulber (1997a), *Deregulatory Takings and the Regulatory Contract: The Competitive Transformation of Network Industries in the United States*, Cambridge University Press.
Sidak, J. Gregory and Daniel F. Spulber (1997b), 'The tragedy of the telecommons: government pricing of unbundled network elements under the Telecommunications Act of 1996', *COLUM. L. REV.*, 97, 1081, at 1082–3.
Sidak, J. Gregory and Daniel F. Spulber (1998), 'Cyberjam: The law and economics of Internet congestion of the telephone network', *HARV. J.L. & PUB. POL'Y.*, 21, 337.
Spengler, Joseph (1950), 'Vertical integration and antitrust policy', *J. POL. ECON.*, 58, 347, at 351–2.
Tirole, Jean (1988), *The Theory of Industrial Organization*, MIT Press.
Weisman, Dennis L. (1995), 'Regulation and the vertically integrated firm: the case of RBOC entry into InterLATA long distance', *J. REG. ECON.*, 8, 249.

*Cases*
*Bundesanstalt für den Güterfernverkehr* v. *Gebrüder Reiff*, 1993 E.C.R. I-5801.
*Bundesrepublik Deutschland/Delta Schiffahrts-und Speditionsgesellschaft*, 1994 E.C.R. I-2517.
*City of Columbia* v. *Omni Outdoor Advertising*, [1991] 499 US 365.
*Consorzi Industrie Fiammiferi (CIF)* v. *Autorita Garante Della Concorrenz E Del Mercato*, 2003 E.C.R. I-8055.
*Parker* v. *Brown*, 317 US 341 (1943).
*Town of Hallie* v. *City of Eau Claire*, 471 US 34 [1995].
*Van Eycke* v. *ASPA*, 1988 E.C.R. 4769 [1999].

# 27 Mexico's competition law: North American origins, European practice

*Adriaan ten Kate and Gunnar Niels*[1]

## Introduction

When it came into force in 1993, many hailed Mexico's Federal Law on Economic Competition (FLEC) as a state-of-the-art piece of competition legislation, one that might well serve as an example for other developing countries. We consider that the law still deserves this credit today, at least as far as its treatment of anticompetitive practices is concerned. In this chapter we discuss the economic criteria for the assessment of anticompetitive practices under the FLEC, and how they have been applied by the Federal Competition Commission (FCC). We do not discuss the rules on merger control or the legal and institutional framing of the law (indeed, with respect to the latter, the FLEC has probably been somewhat less successful).

The first half of this chapter explains the merits of the way the FLEC treats anticompetitive practices. These lie in particular in the explicit distinction that is drawn between hardcore cartel practices which are per se prohibited, and other horizontal, vertical and unilateral practices which are considered under a rule of reason. The text of the law closely reflects the antitrust *case law* of the US at the time: it does not copy the, now arguably somewhat out-of-date, *wordings* of the Sherman Act or EC Treaty, which is what many other new competition regimes tend to do. The FLEC also has some firm roots in current economic thinking.

In the second half of this chapter we examine the difficulties the FCC has encountered when implementing the outspoken economic approach that the framers of the law had in mind. While North American in origin, Mexican competition law enforcement today seems to have more in common with the European approach towards abuse of dominance, with an emphasis on the *form* of practices engaged in by firms with market power, rather than the effect of these practices on competition. Such an approach to competition law enforcement runs the risk of becoming overly interventionist. In Europe there is now a heated debate on reforming the approach to abuse of dominance. The Mexican experience can be of relevance to this debate.

**The rules on anticompetitive practices**

The FLEC makes a distinction between 'absolute' and 'relative' monopolistic practices. Absolute practices are hardcore cartel agreements between competitors on price, output, market division and bid rigging, and are prohibited per se (Article 9). Relative practices cover various forms of both vertical restraints and unilateral conduct – including exclusive dealing, resale price maintenance (RPM), tying and refusal to deal – and are assessed under a rule of reason based on a 'substantial market power' threshold (Article 10).

By way of comparison, the US Sherman Act divides restrictive conduct into agreements between two or more economic agents (section 1) and unilateral conduct, called monopolization (section II). This is similar to the EC Treaty, which addresses restrictive agreements in Article 81 and abuse of dominance in Article 82. It is only through subsequent (and in the EU quite recent) case law that agreements in these jurisdictions are further split up into horizontal and vertical agreements. The former are prohibited per se; the latter are assessed under a rule of reason together with monopolization cases. The distinction between absolute and relative monopolistic practices of the Mexican law ignores the distinction between agreements and unilateral conduct of the Sherman Act but follows the divide between per se and rule of reason developed under US case law. See Figure 27.1.

The Mexican approach has some significant advantages. The outright prohibition of all restrictive agreements in the original wording of both the Sherman Act and the EC Treaty has arguably caused significant confusion on both sides of the Atlantic. It took the US courts a few decades after 1890 to establish that some restrictive agreements may have benign effects as well, in particular if they are vertical in nature. EC competition law only really made the horizontal–vertical distinction in the late 1990s. Mexico's FLEC calls things by their name. In contrast, other new competition

| | Horizontal agreements | Vertical agreements | Unilateral conduct |
|---|---|---|---|
| US-Sherman Act | section I | | section II |
| Assessment | per se | rule of reason | |
| Mexico-FLEC | absolute | relative | |

*Figure 27.1   US–Mexico comparison*

regimes, including the EU Member States and, recently, Singapore, have copied the wording of the EC Treaty, and may therefore have to go through some period of confusion on how to treat agreements.

Another advantage of the FLEC is that it establishes one and the same rule of reason test for vertical agreements and unilateral conduct. From an economic perspective this makes sense. The main concern with vertical agreements is their potential exclusionary effect on competitors and hence competition, and the way to assess these effects differs little from the assessment of unilateral exclusionary conduct. Substantial market power is a necessary condition in both cases (in contrast, in EC law the threshold for 'appreciability' under Article 81 is much lower than the threshold for 'dominance' under Article 82).[2]

The Mexican rule of reason means that, for relative monopolistic conduct to be illegal, the responsible economic agent must have substantial market power, and there must be an *undue* displacement or exclusion of competitors from the market, either in effect or intentionally. The latter requirement introduces the possibility to take account of the procompetitive effects of the practice under investigation. In particular the word 'undue' recognizes the fact that it is the very purpose of sound competition to displace competitors from the market and that it cannot be the intention of the law to discourage competition on the merits, even in cases where the firm in question has market power. Such an effects-based approach has clearly been on the mind of those who framed Mexico's competition law in the early 1990s. In an accompanying paper they underscored the potentially procompetitive nature of apparently anticompetitive behaviour, giving a variety of specific examples.[3] They also stressed the importance of a balancing of procompetitive and anticompetitive effects on a case-by-case basis.

As noted above, an explicit list of relative monopolistic practices is provided in Article 10 of the FLEC. Among the vertical agreements considered there, exclusive dealing, exclusive territories and RPM are mentioned explicitly. The treatment of RPM under a rule of reason is exceptional – in most competition regimes, even that in the US, RPM is outlawed per se – and arguably more in line with economic theory.[4] In addition, Article 10 lists as forms of unilateral conduct only tying and bundling, and refusals to deal. Interestingly it does not mention predatory pricing. In line with US thinking at the time, the framers of the law did this intentionally as they considered prohibiting predatory pricing to be controversial.[5]

There is however a separate catch-all provision in Article 10 for 'any conduct that unduly harms competition'. This provision has commonly been interpreted as covering practices such as predatory pricing, cross-subsidy, price discrimination and raising rivals' costs. In fact, in the

Regulations to the FLEC, which were issued early in 1998, the catch-all provision was spelled out further so as to include precisely the four above-mentioned types of behaviour.[6]

Another striking feature of the FLEC, and one that is also in line with US antitrust, is that it does not prohibit *exploitative* abuses of dominance. Having market power and its exploitation are perfectly legal; only *exclusionary* abuse is prohibited. This is the more surprising because the FLEC came to replace another law which granted extensive powers to the Executive to control the prices of a vast basket of products.[7] In fact, in the mid-1980s, more than half of Mexico's aggregate value of production of goods had been under some form of price control by the Ministry of Trade and Industry, a proportion which was reduced significantly during the late 1980s with the structural adjustment programmes adopted during that period.

The decision to abstain from prohibiting exploitative abuses of dominant positions seems to have been taken deliberately, in recognition of the fact that market power may not only reflect a lack of competition today but could have been obtained as a result of fierce competition in the past.[8] Apart from that, it was considered that competition authorities should not be turned into price regulators.

Thus Mexican competition law enforcement started off with a typically effects-based approach, i.e. an approach based on the economic analysis of the effects of the conduct. This does not imply a mandate to quantify strictly the procompetitive and anticompetitive effects of the investigated practices according to some welfare standard, which would be virtually impossible, but it recognizes that vertical restraints and unilateral conduct may have significant beneficial effects which must be taken into account on a case-by-case basis.

### The chewing gum predation saga

A full assessment of how anticompetitive practices have been analysed by the FCC in its first 12 years is beyond the scope of this chapter. We confine ourselves to a brief description of two noteworthy cases. The first concerns a predatory pricing complaint by the chewing gum manufacturer Canel's against a rival, Adams.[9] The second case, discussed in the next section, refers to PCTV, a joint venture of regional cable distributors for the acquisition and resale of TV programs, which discriminated against, or refused to deal with, outsiders.

In June 1994, exactly one year after the creation of the FCC, Canel's filed a complaint against Adams for predatory pricing in the chewing gum market. Canel's is a fully Mexican-owned firm whose main product is chewing gum; Adams was a subsidiary of the multinational drugs and confectionery manufacturer Warner Lambert Company, producing chewing gum as part of a wider basket of candies and confectionery for the Mexican market. The main product of Canel's (Canels 4's) had traditionally been sold through the so-called 'informal' channels, such as street vendors and small shops, but was gradually penetrating the 'formal' part of the market (supermarkets) where the presence of Adams' star performer, Chiclets 4's, was much stronger in spite of its higher prices.

Back in 1985, Adams had launched a fighting brand named Clarks, which was almost indistinguishable from Canels 4's and selling at a price significantly lower than that of its branded product, Chiclets 4's. After a dispute on intellectual property rights, Adams changed the presentation of Clarks slightly, but continued selling at the low price. At that time there was no competition law, but price interventions by the state were still pervasive, so that Canel's asked the Ministry of Trade and Industry for mediation. Several settlements were reached through commitments by Adams to charge certain minimum prices, but all these settlements were breached after some time through aggressive marketing strategies with deep discounts and similar incentives.

A year after the enactment of the FLEC, Canel's turned to the FCC, accusing Adams of predatory pricing by selling Clarks systematically below costs in order to drive Canel's from the market, or at least to prevent it from penetrating the formal segment of the market further. For the FCC it was the first case of this type and in the absence of precedents it established a number of criteria to assess such cases. Some of them had to do with the cost concept and with the way in which indirect costs should be allocated among products in the case of multi-product firms; others addressed the likelihood of success of exclusion. Apart from that, the mandatory substantial market power test of Article 10 was applied.

The relevant market was defined as that of chewing gum. Candies and other confectionery were not considered close enough substitutes to exercise any pricing discipline over chewing gum. Somewhat more surprisingly, the formal and informal distribution channels were included in the same relevant market, in spite of the fact that prices in the formal segment were more than double the prices in the informal segment. This decision was justified with arguments of supply-side substitution: since Chiclets 4's was virtually the same product as Clarks, the production capacity of the former could readily be switched to produce the latter. The market was considered national, mainly because at that time import tariffs from the US were still considerable.[10]

A finding of market power for Adams was established considering (i) its high market share (above 60 per cent), (ii) the fact that it was able to raise its prices unilaterally without its competitors being able to counteract this behaviour, as evidenced by the fact that it could maintain the price of Chiclets 4's significantly above that of Clarks and Canels 4's without losing market share, and (iii) high entry barriers, mainly consisting of the strength of Adams' brand.

Regarding costs, the FCC established that, for there to be predation, price must be below average *total* cost for an extended period of time. Below-cost pricing for introductory purposes or temporary promotion campaigns would not fall into this category. With respect to product cost it was held that indirect costs should preferably (that is, unless there are specific reasons not so do so) be allocated according to cost of sales, not to sales values, as Adams had done in its own accounting exercise. This was because taking sales value as a basis for cost division would allocate a much higher proportion of indirect costs to the more expensive product, Chiclets, and so disguise possible losses incurred on Clarks. Regarding the likelihood of successful exclusion, the FCC held that predatory conduct must induce losses to the victim, otherwise the exclusionary intent would not be credible.

Applying these criteria the FCC resolved the case in February 1996 by declaring no violation of the law, mainly because Canel's had not been able to demonstrate that it had suffered losses during the period Adams had been selling below cost. It warned Adams, however, that, if the presumption of predatory pricing should continue, it might initiate an ex-officio investigation any time in the future. In spite of this favourable decision, Adams filed an appeal before the FCC protesting against the warning ('why are you warning me if I did nothing wrong?') and against some aspects of the criteria for cost accounting. In the final decision the FCC maintained its position with some minor adjustments in the phrasing of its warning and of the criteria for cost accounting.

Canel's was unpleasantly surprised with this outcome. In particular, the fact that it should have demonstrated losses was difficult to understand, where it was precisely the below-cost pricing by *Adams* that it had attacked as a violation of the law. Moreover Canel's itself also had a considerable market share. In the informal segment of the market where the alleged predatory pricing occurred it was in fact the larger player of the two. Thus a showing of losses incurred by Canel's might even be interpreted as an admission by the plaintiff of being equally guilty of predatory pricing as the defendant. Perhaps the decision would have raised less confusion if the FCC had linked the likelihood of success of the exclusionary conduct more directly with an analysis of the evolution of market shares, which could have been performed in a straightforward way without the need of cost-accounting exercises.

However, a few months later (in April 1996), the FCC started an ex-officio investigation in light of the apparent persistence of aggressive pricing strategies by Adams, which at that time had become part of Grupo Warner Lambert México (GWLM). The results of the new investigation were quite similar to those of the previous one but Canel's, now convinced of the need to show losses, demonstrated that it had suffered such losses by moving the period of investigation a couple of years ahead. In November 1997, the FCC resolved the case by declaring the existence of price predation in violation of the FLEC, ordering GWLM to abstain from such conduct in the future and imposing a fine. Once more, GWLM appealed before the FCC but the arguments were rejected and in May 1998 the FCC confirmed its previous decision without any modifications.

The way in which the FCC handled this case was heavily criticized both inside and outside Mexico. Within Mexico there were the usual skirmishes about whether the relevant market was defined properly[11] and whether GWLM had market power. However, the defendant's arguments that the market should be wider were weakened by the fact that it had hardly protested against the market delineation of the original investigation. Regarding market power, GWLM's market share in the chewing gum market was held to be approximately 70 per cent in terms of sales values, but would have been significantly lower (probably just above 50 per cent) when measured in terms of volumes, because in the formal segment of the market, where GWLM was the dominant player, prices were almost three times those of the informal segment.[12] In this respect, a market share of just above 50% would probably be considered low in monopolization cases in the US but sufficient in abuse-of-dominance cases in the EU. The credibility of Canel's cause was further weakened by a, rather badly timed, interview with the company's CEO in a business magazine in which he bragged about the success and expansionary ambitions of his company.[13]

From outside Mexico the decision was criticized for three reasons. In the first place, the FCC was, somewhat unfairly, perceived as protecting national companies against foreign competition.[14] In the second place, it was considered that the average total cost criterion adopted by the FCC was too severe and not in accordance with international practice which relies more on average variable cost. The third objection had to do with the absence of a recoupment test. For predatory pricing to be successful it is not only necessary that competitors be effectively driven out of the market (or disciplined): there must also be recoupment of predatory losses. If recoupment is not possible, there is no harm to competition even if competitors are expelled from the market. Since *Brooke Group*,[15] the recoupment test has become widely accepted as a criterion for the assessment of predatory pricing cases in the US and some other countries, though not in the EU.[16] Since then the OECD has recommended Mexican competition law enforcers on several occasions to introduce such a test.[17]

Already during the course of the ex-officio investigation, GWLM had filed a constitutional appeal (amparo) before the Judicial System, seeking protection against the vagueness of the phrasing of the Article 10 catch-all provision and similar concepts of the law, such as 'relevant market' and 'substantial market power'. According to GWLM, this would leave defendants in a position of great legal uncertainty, particularly in view of the allegedly arbitrary way in which the FCC had established its own criteria to define these concepts in the case at issue.

After the final decision of the ex-officio investigation, issued in May 1998, GWLM filed another amparo alleging that the FCC had transgressed principles of due process, among others. What followed was a skirmish among all participants in the procedure – defendant, plaintiff and the FCC – and the Judicial System, in which both amparos went all the way up to the Supreme Court and the FCC ultimately had to reinstate the investigation procedure in 2002, arriving at essentially the same outcome as in 1998. In the end, in March 2004, the Supreme Court held that the concepts of relevant market and market power were sufficiently specified in the FLEC so as not to give rise to legal uncertainty, as had been claimed by GWLM. However, it did decide in favour of protecting GWLM against the vagueness of the catch-all provision. It therefore annulled the FCC's finding of an anticompetitive practice.

This Supreme Court decision has effectively declared the catch-all provision of Article 10 unconstitutional and has left the FCC unarmed in its struggle against predatory and discriminatory conduct by dominant firms. Given the discussion in the previous section, this is rather ironic. The FLEC is one of the most explicit competition laws when it comes to defining anticompetitive practices – at least much more explicit than both the Sherman Act and the EC Treaty – and predatory pricing had been left out on purpose. Currently proposals are under way to amend the FLEC in such a way as to incorporate the descriptions of predatory and discriminatory pricing, cross-subsidy and raising rivals' costs, which are now in the Regulations of the FLEC, into the text of the law itself. The fate of these proposals remains uncertain at this stage, however.[18]

### Investigation into the sale of TV programmes

In August 1999, Telecable de Oriente and a number of other regional cable TV operators filed a complaint against Productora y Comercializadora de Televisión (PCTV) for relative monopolistic practices in violation of the FLEC.[19] The alleged offences were refusals to deal, price discrimination and exclusivity in the sales of bundled TV programmes. The FCC admitted the complaint and started an investigation.

PCTV is a joint venture of regional cable operators, founded before the enactment of the FLEC, with the aim of enhancing their bargaining power

vis-à-vis programme producers in order to obtain TV programs and channels on conditions more favorable than would be possible through individual negotiations. PCTV also bundles those channels, and adds some value
by incorporating mostly local advertising before reselling them to its
members and other interested parties.

PCTV's members are regional cable operators who are not directly competing with each other because at the time PCTV was founded there was
only one concession per region. The picture changed with the issuing of a
new Code of Regulations for Telecommunications which allowed for so-
called 'second concessions'.[20] The plaintiffs were holders of such second
concessions. They had a double second-mover disadvantage: one due to the
economies of scale involved in building the cable network infrastructure
and the other arising from programme acquisition where they lacked the
critical mass necessary to obtain favourable conditions. Little wonder they
tried to acquire content from PCTV on the same terms as granted to the
members. Less wonder that PCTV's shareholders did not want to share free
of charge the benefits of their past efforts with what they saw as unwelcome
competitors. After the adoption of the Code of Regulations, PCTV
changed its statute and rules of operations so as to exclude second concessionaries from membership and charge them prices for content that were
higher than the prices charged to members.

In the course of the investigation horizontal market segmentation was
added to the list of alleged monopolistic practices. Some of the plaintiffs
had argued that the members of the Board of Directors of PCTV, who
themselves were holders of concessions in different regions, had implicitly
agreed not to invade each other's territories and to defend their territories
against entry of newcomers with the aforementioned change of the statute.
Horizontal market segmentation is an absolute monopolistic practice
described in Article 9 of the FLEC, which is forbidden per se.

In the first round of the investigation the relevant market was defined as
that of distribution and commercialization of content for cable TV at the
national level. PCTV was held to have substantial market power because its
members served more than 80 per cent of all cable TV subscribers in
Mexico. Moreover it was considered that there was sufficient evidence to
conclude that PCTV and its Board members had committed the alleged
practices. Thus the FCC accused PCTV in October 2002 of all the monopolistic practices that were alleged in the complaints: clauses for exclusive
distribution in Mexico with content producers, refusals to deal with, and
discrimination against, non-members, as well as market segmentation. The
latter accusation was not against PCTV but against its Board members.

In its defence, PCTV argued that the market definition adopted by the
FCC was incorrect; in the first place because PCTV does not participate

in the distribution of TV signals but only in their commercialization; secondly because it is not only cable operators to which it resells content but also to distributors using other technologies such as terrestrial (MMDS) and satellite (DTH) broadcasting; and thirdly because the market should also include the free-to-air channels which are available to everybody but which also must be included in any pay TV package because consumers find it important to have access to them through their subscriptions.

Regarding market power, PCTV argued that (i) the number of sub-scribers among its members was an inadequate base for measuring market shares; (ii) there were other firms commercializing content for pay-TV, offering channels not necessarily the same as PCTV but of the same kind as PCTV's channels and thus competing with PCTV's supply; (iii) individual cable operators could also acquire content directly with program producers because PCTV had no exclusivity but only what was called 'first choice' with some programme producers (that is, programme producers reserved the right to sell directly to operators not served by PCTV); and (iv) there was sufficient room in the market for non-members of PCTV to form their own joint venture for acquiring content.

As regards the relative monopolistic practices (price discrimination and refusals to deal) the defendant asked the FCC to consider the fact that, if second concessionaries were given access on equal terms to programmes and channels offered by PCTV, they would effectively be free-riding on the achievements of a joint venture they did not help to establish in the first place. Moreover, regarding exclusivity, PCTV disclosed its contracts with program producers to the FCC, from which it became clear that it was indeed 'first choice' that prevailed. Exclusivity was only present with some channels with relatively low ratings.

With respect to the absolute monopolistic practice of market segmenta-tion the arguments of the defendants were rather formalistic. In the first place, it was claimed that it was not the members of the Board of Directors but the assembly of shareholders that had the power to change the statute of the association. In the second place, it was argued that neither the members of the Board nor the shareholders were competing amongst each other because they were holding concessions in different regions, so that the fundamental condition for absolute monopolistic practices (that there be an agreement between competitors) was not satisfied.

In its final decision the FCC admitted that the relevant market should be defined as that of commercialization (not distribution) of content to pay-TV operators irrespective of the technology used to transmit the signals to the final consumers. Only the defendant's argument about open channels was not accepted because the FCC considered those channels to be just a supplement to the restricted channels even though they played an important role in consumer choice. Moreover the FCC presented the results of an extensive analysis of substitute channels offered by other firms commercializing TV content, from which it appeared that the choice of cable operators that were not members of PCTV was not as limited as the plaintiffs had claimed. All these elements led to an annulment of its previous finding of market power and the FCC absolved PCTV from the commission of the alleged relative monopolistic practices.

However the FCC did uphold its finding of an absolute monopolistic practice in the form of market segmentation. It argued that, whatever the precise role of the members of the Board or the shareholders, the change of the statute of PCTV had been a vehicle to withhold its members from entering other regions with second concessions for which they would be perfect candidates. The fact that they were not actual competitors did not imply that they were not potential competitors and, in fact, with any geographical market segmentation, potential competitors are no longer actual competitors precisely owing to such an agreement.

PCTV appealed this decision before the FCC and proposed a settlement consisting in a modification of its statute so as to admit new shareholders, subject to an evaluation of its market power in 2005. PCTV argued that the market was changing rapidly and that by that time there would be more competition by second concessions and from MMDS and DTH technologies. This proposal was accepted by the FCC, which settled the conflict for the time being.

**Insight with hindsight**
Some outside observers consider the final decisions in the 'chewing gum war' as the worst antitrust essays written by the FCC since its creation. Whether they are right or wrong is up for discussion, but there is little doubt that the backlash of the case, the recent declaration of unconstitutionality of the catch-all provision of Article 10 owing to its vagueness, is an important setback for competition policy in Mexico. Ironically the phrasing of the catch-all provision ('any act that unduly harms or impedes competition') is hardly vaguer than that of Section I of the Sherman Act ('every contract . . . in restraint of trade') or of Article 81 of the EC Treaty ('agreements . . . which have as their object of effect the prevention, restriction or distortion of competition').

In contrast, the final decision in the case of the cable-TV operators might be seen as one of the better antitrust essays in the history of the FCC. Indeed the decision gives testimony to a careful listening to the arguments of the defendants and of a thorough analysis of all the issues brought up by both plaintiffs and defendants during the procedure.

It should be noticed, however, that in both cases most of the arguments have focused on three elements: first, on whether the investigated conduct matched the description of relative monopolistic practices as provided in Article 10 of the FLEC; second, on the definition of the relevant market; and third, on whether the defendants had substantial power in that market. Little attention has been paid to displacement and exclusion of competitors from the market and even less to whether such displacement was 'undue'. In the chewing gum case the likelihood of displacement of the plaintiff was addressed by considering its current losses, but no attention was given to recoupment. In the PCTV case, the impediments to entry to related markets were only mentioned in relation to absolute monopolistic practices, but not in relation to the relative practices, where they could have played a role. Nor was the issue of the undueness of the possible foreclosure effects commented upon.

One may wonder, for example, what would have happened if the FCC had upheld its initial finding of market power for PCTV. Everything seems to indicate that such a finding would have resulted in an establishment of an infringement of the FLEC. Effects-based questions on whether the shareholders were entitled to appropriate the benefits of their past investments by not sharing them with newcomers and on whether vertical risk sharing implicit in non-linear pricing schemes between PCTV and its clients were sufficient to justify its discriminatory conduct remained largely unanswered.

Altogether, although Mexican competition law was designed in the spirit of an effects-based antitrust regime, at least with respect to the assessment of relative monopolistic practices, the cases discussed in this chapter suggest that its application has mainly focused on the form of the conduct and a market-power test with little attention to the possible economic justifications for the conduct under investigation. As we argue below, this is not so surprising in view of the practical difficulties involved in an evaluation of economic effects in general.

Owing to the movement away from an effects-based approach, Mexico's competition policy has become more interventionist than originally envisaged by the framers of the law. In fact Mexican competition enforcement has come closer to the form-based approach which still prevails in Europe.[21] This is the case not only of unilateral conduct but also of vertical restraints for which a simple finding of market power is often considered sufficient to declare the conduct illegal.

Moreover there are voices advocating reform of the FLEC in such a way as also to prohibit exploitative abuses of market power, and also to introduce the concept of collective dominance, not only in the ambit of merger control but also for the assessment of relative monopolistic conduct.

A proposal to amend the law accordingly is currently under discussion. This would bring Mexico's competition policy even closer to EU practice.

While these developments may be seen as deplorable (at least from our economist's point of view), one should recognize that in most developing countries – and Mexico is no exception – there are forces at work that push competition policy in that direction. What is more, some of these forces are equally present in the more advanced countries, which would provide some food for thought for competition officials in traditional jurisdictions who consider the introduction of more economic elements in the assessment of their cases.

In the first place, newly installed competition agencies in developing countries are usually under great pressure to 'perform'. All too often, to get the legislation through, greater than realistic expectations had to be raised about the benefits competition policies can bring to society. In the popular view, the 'big-is-bad' paradigm is still strong and price increases are unpopular, so the public at large expects the competition authority to remedy such evils. 'How is it possible that our competition agency sits back in its chair, while gas prices go up or Walmart eats up our corner shops one by one?' In such circumstances, temptations to intervene are strong and it is not at all easy for a competition authority to 'keep its head cool' and justify non-intervention on the basis of some economic concepts that are often complicated, counterintuitive and not always well understood by the public.

Secondly, recently installed agencies in developing countries are not only under great pressure to perform; they are also anxious to perform mostly out of a professional vocation to promote competition in an environment where it is most needed. Competition officials in such countries are often little aware of the pitfalls that antitrust enforcement has gone through in the older regimes.

Altogether it is unsurprising that Mexico's FCC has opted for an essentially form-based approach and has gradually become more interventionist, much like European competition enforcement. This in spite of the original intentions to implement an effects-based system. Other competition agencies in developing countries and transition economies may well go down a similar path.

### Notes

1.  Adriaan ten Kate was Head of the Economics Department, Federal Competition Commission, Mexico, from 1995 to 2006. Gunnar Niels is Director at Oxera, UK, having worked at the Federal Competition Commission from 1995 to 1999. The opinions expressed in this chapter are those of the authors alone.
2.  This is not to say that the Mexican FCC was happy with this market power test. To the contrary, the FCC has often struggled to intervene in cases involving vertical restraints or buyer power, precisely because it could not prove the existence of substantial market power. EU competition authorities have greater scope for intervention in these kinds of practices. Whether that is actually a good thing is a separate debate.

3. See Castañeda, Gabriel, Santiago Levy, and Gabriel Martínez y. Gustavo Merino (December 1992), *Antecedentes Económicos para una Ley Federal de Competencia Económica*.
4. See, for example, Marvel, Howard, 'The resale price maintenance controversy: beyond the conventional wisdom', *Antitrust Law Journal*, **63**, 59–92.
5. See Castañeda et al., above, note 3.
6. Now that this chapter goes to print (October 2006) the FLEC has been amended (June 2006) so as to include the four types of conduct in the law itself.
7. Ley sobre Atribuciones del Ejecutivo Federal en Materia Económica, *Diario Oficial de la Federación*, 30 December 1950, and its reforms.
8. See Castañeda et al., above, note 3.
9. Comisión Federal de Competencia, *Informe Annual 1997*, p. 73, and Gaceta de Competencia Económica, *Chicles Canel's/Chicle Adams/Grupo Warner Lambert México*, No. 14, September–December 2002, 289–398.
10. In 1994 these import tariffs were 18 per cent ad-valorem. Under the North American Free Trade Agreement with the US and Canada, which came into force in 1994, all tariffs on imports from those countries are phased out over periods of, at most, 15 years.
11. The FCC's argument that the market was confined to chewing gum because these 'satisfy the need to chew something' did not do much to pre-empt any such skirmishes.
12. Measuring market shares in terms of sales values may be inconsistent with the argument about supply-side substitution used earlier to include formal and informal sales in a single relevant market. If the production capacity of Chiclets 4's can readily be switched to the production of Clarks, it is volumes that matter, not values.
13. Huerta, José Ramón, 'Canel's: Pegó Su Chicle', *Expansión*, No. 718, 18 June, 1997, p. 58.
14. Such accusations from the US will not sound unfamiliar to European competition officials.
15. *Brooke Group Ltd.* v. *Brown & Williamson Tobacco Corp.*, 509 U.S. at 209 (1993).
16. See Niels, Gunnar and Adriaan Ten Kate (2000), 'Predatory pricing standards: is there a growing international consensus?', *Antitrust Bulletin*, **45**, 787–809.
17. See, for example, OECD (1999), *Mexico: The Role of Competition Policy in Regulatory Reform*, p. 27.
18. See note 6.
19. Comisión Federal de Competencia (2003), *Gaceta de Competencia Económica*, No. 15, Enero-Abril 2003, pp. 462–502.
20. See Article 23 of the Reglamento de Telecomunicaciones, issued in October 1990.
21. Both take what could be called a 'form-plus' approach: once dominance or substantial market power is found, it is the form of the practice that matters.

## References

Castañeda, Gabriel, Santiago Levy and Gabriel Martínez y Gustavo Merino (December 1992), *Antecedentes Económicos para una Ley Federal de Competencia Económica*.
Comisión Federal de Competencia (1997), *Informe Annual 1997*.
Comisión Federal de Competencia (2003), *Gaceta de Competencia Económica*, No. 15.
Gaceta de Competencia Económica (September–December 2002), *Chicles Canel's/Chicle Adams/Grupo Warner Lambert México*, No. 14.
Huerta, José Ramón (18 June 1997), 'Canel's: Pegó Su Chicle', *Expansión*, No. 718.
Ley sobre Atribuciones del Ejecutivo Federal en Materia Económica (30 December 1950), *Diario Oficial de la Federación*.
Marvel, Howard (1995), 'The resale price maintenance controversy: beyond the conventional wisdom', *Antitrust Law Journal*, **63**, 59–92.
Niels, Gunnar and Adriaan Ten Kate (2000), 'Predatory pricing standards: is there a growing international consensus?', *Antitrust Bulletin*, **45**, 787–809.
OECD (1999), *Mexico: The Role of Competition Policy in Regulatory Reform*.

*Case*
*Brooke Group Ltd.* v. *Brown & Williamson Tobacco Corp.*, 509 U.S. 209 (1993).

# 28 Competition policies in Latin America, post-Washington Consensus
*Julián Peña*

## Introduction

Although Latin America is a sweeping concept representing very different political, economic, social and cultural realities, it has been possible until recently to draw some common comparisons when analysing its competition policies or, better yet, the role of the state in the markets. However, in the past few years, different approaches have been taken following the perception of the collapse of the guiding consensus on government intervention in the economies for Latin American countries.

The history of competition policy in Latin America may be divided into three periods.[1] A first period could be broadly drawn from the 1920s to the 1980s. Although most Latin American countries have been influenced by free market ideals since their respective independence and some had anti-monopoly legislation in the first decades of the twentieth century, this period can be characterized by very active state intervention in the markets. This intervention was manifested through various anticompetitive mechanisms such as state-owned monopolies, price controls or protectionist measures and inefficient government regulation. This has been the common pattern in almost all of the countries of the region.

Although it is difficult to determine exactly when it began, most Latin American countries adopted a set of competition policies influenced by the Washington-based international financial organizations. This set of market-oriented recommendations, known as the 'Washington Consensus', represented the core policy that most governments implemented in different ways during the 1990s. As a result of some of these policies, which turned many public services over to private hands, the need for new rules was reflected in the number of new competition laws and regulatory norms enacted throughout the region. Some countries adopted new regimes, while others modernized their obsolete legal systems.

Towards the end of the twentieth century, the population's great disappointment with the region's development and wealth distribution was reflected in the results of various presidential elections throughout the region. This sense of failure has been attributed by many politicians to the application of the Washington Consensus policies. This new consensus is

*Table 28.1*    *State intervention in Latin American markets*

| Pre-Washington Consensus | During the Washington Consensus | Post-Washington Consensus |
| --- | --- | --- |
| • Strong government presence in the markets<br>• Price controls<br>• Large government corporations<br>• Local industries with strong government incentives<br>• Low FDI flows<br>• Strong trade barriers | • Weak government presence in the markets<br>• Market-driven prices<br>• Privatization of major government companies<br>• End of some government incentives<br>• Sale of local companies<br>• Important FDI flows<br>• Trade barriers reduced | • Greater government presence in the markets<br>• Greater government pressure on prices<br>• Still fewer large state enterprises<br>• Some large national companies<br>• Low FDI flows<br>• New requirements on foreign investments<br>• New NTB are created |

not based on what should be done but instead on what not, or at least how not to achieve development. Even today, there is a lack of a new positive consensus, and most observers agree that (when reached) it should include social awareness and equity. Some trends can be perceived in different ways and at various levels of intensity. There is some evidence reflecting a tendency towards more state intervention in the markets through different mechanisms. Although some reflect old practices, others try to be innovative. However the current economic scenario makes it very difficult to return to the old interventionism scenario.

This chapter will analyze the evolution of competition policies in Latin America before, during and after the Washington Consensus in order to determine whether a new consensus has been created. The use of the Washington Consensus as a reference is due only to its symbolic value as a milestone during a period marked by a strong influence of the Washington-based international financial organizations in the highly indebted Latin American countries. It is important to point out that these recommended policies have not been fully implemented by any of the region's governments and their impact has varied in each country.

In order to analyze competition policies in Latin America it is necessary not only to consider the treatment of the market failures originating from restrictive business practices, but also to consider government involvement in the markets. These policies too have, historically, followed similar pathways within the region.

**The Washington Consensus**
Towards the end of Latin America's so-called 'lost decade' of the 1980s, the economist John Williamson prepared a 'list of prescriptions that would command general assent in the Washington of George H.W. Bush shortly after Ronald Reagan had left office':[2] these recommendations became known as the Washington Consensus. Although Williamson's original paper was to frame a World Bank conference 'whose ulterior motive was to persuade Washington that Latin America was engaged in serious reform, and not to furnish a policy agenda for Latin America',[3] the term he had coined began to have a life of its own[4] and has been assimilated as a synonym for concepts such as 'neoliberalism' or 'market fundamentalism' according to George Soros.[5]

The Washington Consensus, as described in Williamson's paper,[6] contained a set of ten recommendations for a highly-indebted Latin America based on three main ideas: macroeconomic discipline, a market economy and openness to the world in respect of trade and foreign direct investment.[7] These recommended policies consisted of fiscal discipline; redirection of public expenditure priorities; tax reform through lower marginal rates and a broader tax base; interest rate liberalization; competitive exchange rate; trade liberalization; liberalization of FDI inflows; privatization; deregulation and secure property rights. The first five recommendations are fiscal-oriented measures, but the last five are the free market policies which, according to its author, reflected 'the opinion in Washington of the international financial institutions and the central economic agencies of the US government'.[8] These policies were focused on reducing the role of government through privatizations, deregulation and trade liberalization.

Most of these policies were adopted in different forms by the majority of Latin American nations during the 1990s, and their application and interpretation have been inconsistent. As Moisés Naím stated, 'throughout the decade the core for the Consensus has experienced extraordinary mutations and shrinkage' and 'policy makers in reforming countries saw how the bar defining success kept being raised and how the changes they were expected to make became increasingly complex and, sometimes, politically impossible'.[9]

The Washington Consensus has been mainly criticized for having failed to provide equitable growth in the region, deepening poverty levels and widening the socioeconomic gaps. After the Mexican crisis of 1994, a certain disappointment began to assert itself in the region, reaching its peak with the Argentine crisis of 2001.

**Competition policies before the Washington Consensus**
Most Latin American countries have had free market ideals since their independence in the nineteenth century. However, since the 1920s and until

the 1980s, competition policies had been determined by strong state intervention in the markets, either as a direct participant or as a heavy regulator. Protecting local industries from foreign competition and regulating internal markets were the two pillars of development policies within the Latin American region.

In a landmark case, the Argentine Supreme Court supported a 1922 law trying to freeze housing rents in the name of free competition and against the effects of monopoly and abuse in the commercial and residential rental market, in what could be the emergence of federal interventionist legislation in Argentina.[10]

Most Latin American countries up to the 1990s had similar economic policies that included a strong government presence in the markets through the following:

- Price and exchange controls. The prices were negotiated with the government officials and some sectors had a specific agency that dealt with the prices of their products (e.g. sugar, grains and meat).
- Large government corporations. Most of the public services were provided by state-owned companies.
- Strong government incentives to promote production of certain goods or regions.
- Foreign investment limitations. The foreign investment laws were designed and implemented to restrict the entrance of new competitors in order to protect and strengthen local industries.
- Strong trade barriers. A protectionist import substitution model with high tariff barriers isolated local industries from foreign competition.

As Naím summarized it, 'decades of protectionist, *clientelistic*, anticompetitive behavior, growing out of prevalent State intervention, import substitution, and volatility induced defensive business strategies, created an entrenched web of collusive practices and a broad degree of acceptance of them'.[11]

During this period the region developed obsolete industries with highly indebted governments ending up in what was called the 'lost decade' of the 1980s. This was the scenario that inspired Williamson to prepare the policy recommendations for the region so that it could obtain financial assistance from the Washington-based international financial institutions.

*Competition law enforcement*
Until the 1990s, only a few Latin American countries had competition laws or something similar. The highly punishing goals of those laws (and the

political and economic context in which they have been 'enforced') resulted in an almost irrelevant jurisprudence.

The first competition law in the region was enacted in Argentina in 1923, later amended in 1946. Both laws had a repressive goal (they were even named 'Law of Repression of Monopolies') and, owing to their imprecise wording and lack of political will, they were barely enforced and no important cases were registered. These laws were replaced by a 1980 law that introduced significant changes to the previous regime. It broadened the legal spectrum to behaviour that limits, restricts or distorts competition; adopted the 'rule of reason' system; introduced the abuse of dominant position as anticompetitive conduct; and created the Comisión Nacional de Defensa de la Competencia ('CNDC'). A few other Latin American countries adopted similar laws before the 1990s: Mexico did so in 1934, Chile and Colombia in 1959 (Chile amended hers in 1973) and Brazil in 1962.

As Rowat said, 'In Argentina and particularly Colombia, a combination of vested interests, gaps in the legislative coverage, weak implementation and enforcement capacity drastically undermined the impact of such legislation' while 'only Chile's law, revised in 1973, enjoyed effective enforcement'.[12]

### Competition policies during the Washington Consensus
The Washington Consensus brought about a change in the role of state intervention in Latin American markets. There was a pendulum shift from the traditional interventionism to a period where the state was mostly absent from the markets. This change was implemented without a proper transition period. During the Washington Consensus era most Latin American countries acted as follows:

- deregulated, sometimes overnight, their highly regulated economies and turned to a system of market-driven prices.
- privatized the state-owned companies, mainly in the infrastructure sectors, giving former public monopolies to private ones.
- eliminated some government incentives previously aimed at promoting either production or exports. This was due, mainly, to financial problems.
- experienced the acquisition of many local companies by multinationals as a result of having their economies opened to foreign competition and investment.
- received important foreign direct investment inflows, especially in privatized infrastructure sectors.
- liberalized their foreign trade by reducing barriers, signing trade agreements such as Mercosur in 1991, and relaunching the Andean Community in 1996.

These reforms, though, have not proved to be sufficient to achieve the desired development. As De León concludes:

> one salient common feature that characterizes competition enforcement throughout the region is the conviction that implementing the new pro-market regulatory competition policies requires much more than challenging market concentration or – from the opposite corner – even simply liberalizing trade or supporting privatization processes . . . Effective promotion of competition entails difficult decisions, where the welfare effects of private gains of market liberalization are balanced with necessary questions of social welfare.[13]

*Competition law enforcement*

Different reasons explain the development of competition law enforcement in Latin America during the 1990s. Some attribute it to a need to counterattack the effects of privatizing monopolies and the elimination of sector regulations as a consequence of implementing Washington Consensus policies,[14] while others argue instead that 'competition policy emerged as a reaction against conventional state interventionism and generally, against the culture of mercantilism that has prevailed in the region'.[15]

In fact, both arguments include examples that make them sustainable. In some countries, such as Peru, Mexico and Venezuela, the competition laws were enacted as part of the liberalization process at the beginning of the 1990s.

In Argentina, for instance, it was not until 1996, within the context of the Second State Reform, that the CNDC had been reinforced and thus began to increase its law enforcement significantly. Paradoxically it is also during the second half of the decade that the application of antidumping measures began to show an important increase in Argentina, protecting local competitors from foreign competition. Something similar occurred in Brazil, with the enactment of the 1994 law amendment. In a more reluctant manner, Uruguay did not begin competition law enforcement until 2000, with the introduction of a few articles within its budget law.

Varied reasons have been given to explain the relative development of competition enforcement in the region during the 1990s. The most important ones are that the agencies lacked sufficient economic and human resources, political independence and experience. Another reason was the lack of a 'competition culture' within the society (owing to political and economic history) which was reflected in distrust of the new system.

Bruce Owen also mentions as obstacles to effective competition policy in the region the fact that 'both Latin American courts and Latin American governments have difficulty making credible commitments upon which firms and markets can base a stable set of expectations' and, particularly for the smaller countries, 'the scale of local markets and the geographical extent of antitrust markets are often incongruent with the legal jurisdiction of the agency'.[16] Regardless of why and how the competition policy was implemented, during the 1990s there was a consensus among Latin American governments that it was 'a safeguard of the gains brought about by economic liberalization against business or government distortions on markets'.[17]

*(a) Proliferation of competition laws*    Although some Latin American countries have previously had competition laws, there was a proliferation of such laws during the 1990s.[18] Even those countries with previous legal frameworks introduced changes in their respective laws during that decade (see Table 28.2). One can argue that effective competition enforcement, even in those countries, did not occur in Latin America until the 1990s. As Owen states, 'in Latin America, competition law was established where none had existed previously and, in some countries, even made applicable to sectors where competition had previously been forbidden'.[19]

In those countries with previous competition legislation, the approach of the new laws shifted drastically from a repressive system against monopolies to a broader market-oriented system. Most of the laws have both economic efficiency and consumer protection as their main goals. They also introduced an administrative procedure and did not include criminal sanctions (except in Brazil and Peru). Most legislation penalized the abuse of dominant position (except Chile, Costa Rica and Panama) and included some kind of merger control (except Chile and Costa Rica). Although it is not a clear issue in every case, some legislation has some per se offences (for example, price fixing agreements in Peru, Chile, Costa Rica, Panama, Venezuela, Colombia and Mexico), while most have a *rule of reason* system.[20]

With respect to territorial jurisdiction, some countries have adopted the 'Effects Doctrine'. The extraterritorial enforcement of the competition law is contemplated in the laws of Argentina, Brazil, Chile and Peru. However it has only been applied to oblige foreign-based companies to provide notice of certain transactions in Argentina, prior to the 2001 competition law amendment, and in Brazil as well, before the 2005 change in the threshold interpretation.

The Latin American competition legal framework has been mainly influenced by the European model (for example Argentina, Brazil and Peru), both in substance (for instance, the abuse of dominant positions) and in procedures.[21] However there has been a growing American influence in the economic reasoning, perhaps as a consequence of the continuing movement by the EU towards the US style, as European Competition Commissioner Neelie Kroes recognized in a September 2005 conference at Fordham.

*Table 28.2   Enactment or amendment of competition laws in Latin American countries*

| Pre-Washington Consensus | During the Washington Consensus | Post-Washington Consensus |
|---|---|---|
| Argentina (1923, 1946, 1980) | Andean Community (1991) | Andean Community (2005) |
| Brazil (1962) | Argentina (1999) | Chile (2003) |
| Chile (1959, 1973) | Brazil (1991, 1994) | El Salvador (2005) |
| Colombia (1959) | Chile (1999) | Mexico (2006) |
| Mexico (1934) | Colombia (1992) | |
| | Costa Rica (1994) | |
| | Mercosur (1996) | |
| | Mexico (1992) | |
| | Panama (1996) | |
| | Peru (1991) | |
| | Uruguay (2000) | |
| | Venezuela (1991) | |

*(b) Creation of competition agencies*   During the 1990s, new competition agencies were created or existing ones rebuilt. Some of the Latin American agencies were created as collegiate bodies in the form of Commissions (Argentina, Brazil, Costa Rica, Chile, Mexico, Panama and Peru) while others have a single individual in charge of a Superintendencia, as in the case of Venezuela and Colombia. Some of the jurisdictions have more than one administrative agency intervening in competition law enforcement. Such is the case of Argentina (Secretaría de Coordinación Técnica); Brazil (Secretaria de Acompanhamento Econômico – 'SEAE' – and the Secretaria de Direito Econômico – 'SDE'); Colombia (Delegatura para la Promoción de la Competencia de Colombia); Chile (Fiscalía Nacional Económica – 'FNE'), and Peru (Tribunal de la Competencia de Perú).

Among the agencies created by the new competition laws, some have been assigned only antitrust-related issues (i.e. Venezuela's Superintendencia de Promoción y Protección de la Libre Competencia – ProCompetencia), while others such as Peru's Instituto Nacional de Defensa de la Competencia y de la Propiedad Intelectual (Indecopi) or Panama's Comisión de Libre Competencia y Asuntos del Consumidor ('CLICAC'), were created to deal with broader objectives such as consumer protection, intellectual property and dumping.

In Brazil, the already existing Conselho Administrativo de Defesa Econômica ('CADE') was given autarchic status in 1994, while the

Brazilian Competition Defense System, created de facto by the introduction of the SEAE in the process (along with CADE and the SDE), was finally organized and consolidated.

In 1996, Argentina's CNDC was given greater administrative independence, a larger budget, a new full-time presidency and a highly qualified staff. As a result of these changes, the number of rulings per year grew, the level of those rulings improved, important cases were solved and new studies and guidelines issued. In the 1999 Competition Law, a new independent agency, the Tribunal Nacional de Defensa de la Competencia, was created to replace the CNDC. The idea of the new law was to have an agency completely independent from political influence, thus eliminating any possible government intervention. However this independent agency has not yet been constituted by the Argentine Government.

With respect to its relationship with regulatory agencies, although most legislation excludes regulated sectors from the competition agencies' jurisdiction and some laws give priority to one agency over the other, reality shows it remains a pending issue to be solved. According to José Tavares de Araujo, introducing a clear-cut division of functions between the competition policy authority and the sectorial regulatory agencies represents a major challenge within the region.[22]

In order to combat the lack of a 'competition culture' within the region, one of the main tasks of the competition agencies during the 1990s was to promote competition within their societies as well as within the government. This is why the agencies have devoted an important part of their resources to competition advocacy. The competition agencies received during the 1990s technical cooperation from different international organizations such as UNCTAD, the OECD, the World Bank, the Inter American Development Bank, the Organization of American States and the European Commission.

UNCTAD, for instance, has actively contributed to the development of competition policies in Latin America by training many enforcers through a vast series of conferences, courses and publications, among other activities. Another example is the European Commission's newsletter (Boletín Latinoamericano de Competencia) which has turned into a vehicle for Latin American regulators to share their incipient and unique experiences on the matter.

Other national agencies also cooperated with their Latin American counterparts such as the US Department of Justice and Federal Trade Commission, Spain's Tribunal de Defensa de la Competencia and France's Conseil de la Concurrence, among others. Institutions such as Germany's Center for Economic and Social Development (ZWS) and the Brazilian Institute of Studies on Competition, Consumer Affairs and International

*Table 28.3*   *Merger control regimes in Latin America*

|  | Pre-merger | Post-merger |
|---|---|---|
| Mandatory | Mexico | Argentina |
|  | Colombia | Brazil |
|  | El Salvador |  |
|  | Peru (electricity) |  |
| Voluntary | Argentina |  |
|  | Brazil |  |
|  | Chile (some cases) |  |
|  | Costa Rica |  |
|  | Panama |  |
|  | Venezuela |  |

Trade (IBRAC) also played a key role in the development of competition policies in Latin America during the 1990s.

*(c) Introduction of merger control regimes*   One of the main characteristics of the competition laws enacted worldwide during the 1990s was the introduction of merger control regimes. Latin America was no exception in this field since most of the countries in the region began a merger control regime then.

Some of these systems include all sectors of the economy while others (e.g. Chile and Peru) control only sectorial mergers. Although all the countries that have introduced merger control had a preventive objective, some of the jurisdictions have a pre-merger system while others have a post-merger one.[23] With respect to the notification requirements, in some of the Latin American countries with a merger control system the filing is mandatory, while in others the filing is voluntary (Table 28.3).

As a result of the introduction of merger control in Latin America, the competition agencies were forced to reduce their fight against anticompetitive practices because of the lack of sufficient human resources to allocate to both anticompetitive and merger cases. On the quantitative side, the percentage of transactions prohibited or conditional on divestiture is similar to the statistics reflected in other jurisdictions worldwide. However, on the qualitative side, it has attracted some criticism within the region. In Brazil, for instance, an analysis of the market effects in cases with imposed divestitures have been either negative or neutral.[24]

**Competition policies post-Washington Consensus**
In 1998, disenchantment with the Washington Consensus policies began to materialize. In December 1994, with the onset of the Mexican crisis,

a turning point in the development of policies occurred in the region. Afterwards the economic situation started to erode the political support for the structural reform process. Since then, the people of Venezuela, Chile, Ecuador, Brazil, Argentina, Bolivia, Peru, Panama and Uruguay have elected as their Presidents the candidates who had, at least in their political discourse, an anti-Washington Consensus position. However the way these countries have implemented an alternative model differs significantly from case to case. Although in the rhetoric a common pattern may be found, in reality that uniformity does not exist.

Instead of having a new positive consensus, there is now an agreement on the failure of the Washington Consensus policies as a valid alternative to solve the region's historical development problems. All the countries involved would agree that a fiscal-oriented model without equity and social awareness cannot be a legitimate path towards inserting the region into a globalized world.

As a response to the Washington Consensus model, the governments of Argentina and Brazil signed a declaration called the 'Buenos Aires Consensus' in October 2003. This 22 paragraph declaration is a set of noble principles such as combating poverty, hunger, illiteracy and disease, through sustainable development and the creation of an environment for business and productive investment. However it does not mention how to achieve these goals. This consensus does not include any references with regard to state intervention in the markets, but it recognizes the strategic role that the state should play, thus assuming the commitment to strengthen its institutions, professionalizing the public administration, increasing its efficiency and adopting a more transparent decision-making system.

The reasons for the setback of the Washington Consensus in the region can be found in its origin, its implementation and its results. First, the structural changes suggested in the recipe were not necessarily a 'consensus' but rather a condition the financial institutions imposed upon highly-indebted countries in order to obtain the much-needed cash flows. As Williamson recognized, it was a set of measures needed to convince Washington officials that Latin America was a credible debtor worth investing in. In other words, the need for reforms arose owing to financial needs rather than as a consequence of the recognition that the historical market behaviour needed a change.

Second, the way the different policies were implemented throughout the region varied significantly from country to country. However not one of the Latin American governments fully implemented the Consensus policies. The lack of sufficient transparency (if not corruption), planning and of a necessary transition (as well as a deeply rooted social resistance due to a historical legacy of strong state intervention in the markets and an unstable political and economic scenario) also contributed to an incomplete and flawed implementation of the recommended policies. Some governments also used the rhetoric of the Washington Consensus to pursue very different goals. Finally, the reforms were focused only on macroeconomic policies and completely ignored the need for a change in the microeconomic level as well.

Third, the implementation of the policies contained in the Washington Consensus not only failed to achieve its goal of providing sustained development in the region, but it also brought more poverty and a widening socioeconomic gap. These results, though, cannot be exclusively attributed to the implementation of the Washington Consensus policies.

There are currently at least as many alternative paths as there are countries in the region. The role of state intervention in the markets is a crucial issue that has recently been interpreted in different ways throughout the region. Arguably this is so in Venezuela and in Argentina where there have been greater changes relative to the previous decade. However, even in those countries, the change is not and could not be a full return to the pre-Washington Consensus scenario for a number of diverse reasons.

A common response to the crisis of the Washington Consensus in the region is characterized by a greater presence of the state in the markets. The difference is, however, the degree of this return to state interventionism. Perhaps Venezuela and Argentina are the countries where this trend is more prominent. Either through price controls, the creation of new state-controlled enterprises, changes in the regulatory frameworks, or by revoking concessions, among other practices, the state in these countries has gained a more significant participation than in the past decade. However, since the world has also changed over the last ten years, the traditionally state-owned companies have been privatized, and there is an important need to attract foreign investment, for the threat of returning to the past is almost too terrible to contemplate.

This was envisioned by Brazilian and Uruguayan politicians, for example. Although there was a change of government in 2003 in Brazil, the new President rapidly realized that it was impossible to go back to the pre-Washington Consensus status. This was stated publicly in the June 2002 'Letter to the Brazilians', where the then future President promised a firm pro-export policy and a state that would stimulate production without going back to protectionism or having the state running key businesses. The leaders of the ruling party had taken the Argentine experience as a warning of what could happen if abrupt changes were made in its economic policies. After the March 2005 change of government in Uruguay, the new President rapidly aligned the country's economic policy with the Brazilian model.

Some governments in the region have returned to exerting influence on pricing, though most of them are very concerned not to return to the price control regimes of the past. The Government of Venezuela introduced, in 2003, a price control system for basic items such as food, drugs, construction materials and public services; it also set up an exchange control regime. The measures established maximum prices for certain goods and services in order to stabilize the internal market and to guarantee a certain standard of living for the people of Venezuela.

In Argentina, although the government has stated that it will not return to a price control system, since 2004 it has promoted different price agreements with various sectors, owing to inflationary concerns. These agreements originally had a limited duration but later had been renewed. The government has also started selling bottled gas to establish 'witness prices' in order to lower costs for lower-income groups. In 2005, the President called for a boycott on an oil company that 'unjustifiably' raised its prices. Similarly, in July 2005, the Government of Peru also asked two important oil companies to stop raising their prices, although it rejected the idea of implementing a price control system.[25]

International trade conflicts among Latin American countries have increasingly been solved through government-promoted private sector agreements. In particular, Argentina and Brazil have used this mechanism since the Brazilian crisis of 1999. These agreements have been implemented either directly as a private agreement (e.g., the footwear and paper agreements) or through price and/or quota commitments within antidumping investigations (e.g., steel and poultry). Other non-trade barriers such as non-automatic import licences have been implemented in order to regulate the exchange of certain goods, such as television sets and washing machines in 2004,[26] and footwear and toys in August 2005, among others.[27]

In past years, there has been a return by the state to an active partner as a player in the markets either through expropriation of private companies, a return to state enterprises of formerly privatized companies or by the creation of new state-controlled companies. The Venezuelan Government expropriated two companies: Venezolana de Pulpas y Papel (Venepal) in January 2005 and Constructora Nacional de Válvulas (now Inveval) in April 2005, as well as some assets from the leading Venezuelan food company Polar in September 2005.

Formerly privatized services have returned to state hands. In Uruguay, all of the water services were nationalized after a referendum in 2004. In Argentina, the official postal service was privatized in 1998 and the concession contract with the private operator was breached in 2003. Since then, the government has operated the postal service through a newly created state-owned company (Corasa) and has stated its decision not to call for tenders in the near future. Similarly this process has occurred with a railway company (Ferrocarril San Martín and Belgrano Cargas), a communications satellite company (ArSat) and with the radio wavelength frequency control company. Bolivia naturalized its hydrocarbons in 2006.

New state-owned companies have been created in different countries. In 2003, the Venezuelan Government created a state-owned telecommunication company, Corporación Venezolana de Telecomunicaciones (Covetel), to compete with the two existing companies, CNTV and Telcel. In 2005, the Government of Venezuela also created a series of new companies in the agricultural sector (CVA Cereales, CVA Lácteos, CVA Azúcar, CVA Oleaginosas and Comercializadora de Insumos y Suministros Agropecuarios) with the purpose of securing a sustainable food provision system and to compete against the private industries. The Argentine Government acted similarly by creating an energy company (Energía Argentina S.A. – Enarsa) as well as an airline (Líneas Aéreas Federales S.A. – Lafsa) in order to absorb the employees of two bankrupt, privately owned companies (LAPA and Dinar). Lafsa, though, does not operate any aircraft.

The regulation of public services has also been a post-Washington Consensus concern. Both Brazil and Argentina proposed similar new regulatory regimes that have not yet been approved by their respective legislative bodies. Although the two projects differ in technical aspects, they have in common a greater role of government intervention in public services regulation.

*Competition law enforcement*
The enforcement of the competition laws in Latin America in the post-Washington Consensus era could be characterized by the introduction of non-traditional concepts, a weakening of the institutional framework and, therefore, a more flexible and politically driven enforcement. Compared to the 1990s, currently there is more flexible and politically driven competition law enforcement in most Latin American countries. The greater government presence in the markets has generated a greater politically driven enforcement and, together with the lack of a competition culture, they have been critical factors in the setback of competition policy in the region.

Furthermore, as a consequence of the implementation of the Washington Consensus policies, the competition policies have lost some political support in various countries throughout the region. According to a Peruvian Government's submission to the APEC, competition and market oriented policies in Peru and the Andean Region are facing opposition from the majority of the impoverished population who do not have a clear perception of the benefits of a market economy . . . The increasing opposition has halted any attempt to implement necessary reforms and improve competition environment.[28]

As a result, all this has brought a more flexible enforcement of competition laws to Latin America. An example of this situation can be found in Peru, where a minimum price agreement in the transport sector was approved by the government in August 2003 in order to protect the small companies from 'the savage market forces' of the larger companies. Meanwhile in Mexico, the Comisión Federal de Competencia ('CFC') has suffered a sharp reduction of its enforcement activities and is collecting less than 10 per cent of the levied fines.

The CNDC of Argentina received nearly 500 new antitrust claims in the first five years of the enactment of the new competition law in 1999. However the first of these claims to conclude with the imposition of a sanction was an exclusionary practice case in June 2005. In the meantime, approximately 30 cases have been temporarily solved through preventive measures taken by the Commission. In July 2005, the CNDC announced two very important fines on oxygen and cement companies allegedly involved in cartel practices. The announcement of these two fines (of approximately US$24 million and US$107 million) was made by the Minister of the Economy amidst anti-inflation measures.[29]

A different scenario may be found in Brazil and Chile. In Brazil, the competition policy was reinforced after the 2003 change of government. The Brazilian competition agencies have strengthened their fight against cartels, introducing changes in the legislation such as a leniency programme, and signing a cooperation agreement with the United States. However, although progress has been made, a heavier judicial intervention has overshadowed the agencies' achievements. Chile has reinforced its competition regime by creating an independent court, while having a National Prosecutor with a very proactive role. However significant enforcement results are still pending. The procompetitive reform has been given an important place in the government's 'Pro-Growth Agenda'.[30]

*(a) Introduction of non-traditional concepts in antitrust analysis*   Broad concepts have been introduced and social considerations have been mingled within the technical analyses of both anticompetitive behaviour and merger cases. The introduction of these 'social' considerations has significantly increased the discretionary levels of the competition authorities and, as Alfredo Bullard says, this could be introducing the idea of social convenience in solving the conflicts in a particular way, according to the

*coyuntura* (the socio-political or economic circumstances of a specific moment).[31] This has been reflected in a more flexible position towards certain anticompetitive conduct. Alfredo Bullard claims that the problem for a populist politician who wants to take a hard line against the cartels is that he will see his discretionary powers reduced and this could be politically awkward.

In Peru, for instance, with regard to cartels, the per se rule has been interpreted in such a flexible manner that now a cartel may be legal if the Indecopi finds it 'reasonable', applying a *sui generis* rule of reason system that does not contemplate, for instance, market power elements. Indecopi also proposed a bill to Congress in 2005 introducing greater discretionary powers to the antitrust authorities by bringing in flexible rules allowing the antitrust agency to determine each person's degree of responsibility on a case-by-case basis, taking into consideration the dynamics of the markets and, therefore, generating harmony among the legal order and the dynamics of social life. In another case, the Peruvian agency has obliged an energy company to allow a cable TV operator to use its power supply network because the 'exercise of the private interests of an individual . . . cannot damage the equality among the competitors nor the legitimate interests of the consumers'. In other words, it invoked the antitrust law in order to force a company to do something against its will, regardless of the non-existence of anticompetitive conduct.[32]

The Indecopi has also interpreted traditional antitrust concepts in unconventional ways. In any case, the Tribunal reversed a Comisión's decision by defining a bank branch as an 'essential facility'. Similarly it reversed another Comisión's ruling by interpreting 'excessive pricing' as behaviour banned by the competition law,[33] something similar to what occurred in Mexico in the *Nestlé* case in 2001 and in Chile in at least two cases.

With respect to merger cases in Argentina, the CNDC has approved, with certain caveats, the merger between the two most important local bakeries (Bimbo and Fargo) taking into consideration the effects that a possible bankruptcy of the acquired company could have on unemployment levels through not applying the failing company defence doctrine. In the *Perez Companc Forestal* transaction, the CNDC has included as one of the conditions of its approval that the acquirer maintain the assistance and technological cooperation previously agreed by the acquired company with a local university. In other merger cases, the CNDC has included regulatory conditions, such as was the case of the *Telefónica-Bell South* transaction in which the only condition for approval was a divestiture that the regulatory agency had previously ordered.[34]

A peculiar case was the direct intervention of the President of Argentina in the *Petrobras-Pecom* transaction in 2003. In this case, the President ordered the companies to exclude an energy transmission company (Transener) from the transaction as a condition of antitrust clearance: because of 'strategic interests', the President determined that this sector could not be sold to a Brazilian company and the parties voluntarily agreed to sell Transener.[35]

In Brazil, the Nestlé–Garoto merger was denied by CADE, while the SDE and the SEAE introduced in their analysis the element of a social welfare increase.[36]

*(b) Weakening the institutional framework*    With respect to the institutional framework, there has been a progressive weakening of the agencies in some jurisdictions, either through budget reduction, institutional reforms or by politically driven appointments, forsaking the technical expertise acquired in the past decade.

Different governments have decided to reduce the competition agencies' budgets. The reason behind these cuts may be found in general budget reductions due to public economic and financial crises, political decisions to give a higher priority to other policies or a new hierarchy of the political objectives.

The Peruvian Government, for instance, decided in 2003 to eliminate all public funding to the Indecopi, which now relies fully on the fees collected and the fines it imposes. The Indecopi's independence has also suffered a series of setbacks. It first lost the protection against unjustified removals and afterwards started suffering politically influenced appointments. Furthermore the Indecopi now reports directly to the President of the Council of Ministers, instead of the Minister of Industry.

As a reaction to its economic crisis and fiscal needs, the Argentine government has made a number of cuts in its annual budget, including that of its competition agency. The independent TNDC created by law in 1999 has never been constituted. The TNDC was supposed to replace the CNDC, the current agency that depends both politically and economically on the Ministry of Economy and Production.

Since there was external pressure from international financial organizations to constitute the independent agency, an attempt to diminish the TNDC's independence occurred in 2001 when the Competition Law was regulated. Through a Presidential Decree, the Secretariat of Competition Defense was incorporated as an enforcement authority, with an active role in the procedures. This change was considered unconstitutional by the antitrust community. However, since the TNDC has not yet been constituted, the newly created double agency system was never implemented either. Finally, in August 2005, the Government of Argentina sent a bill to Congress in order to limit the TNDC's independence in merger cases involving 'national interests' or 'high levels' of employment or investment.

In Brazil, although there have been different projects to unite the Brazilian Competition Defense System, there has been a steady increase in the number of agencies responsible for enforcement of the law. To the three agencies contemplated by law, the system has added the General Attorney of CADE as well as the Federal Public Ministry, causing major delays and costs to the process as well as weakening the power of the already divided agencies. Different bills have been proposed and debated with the idea of unifying the system, but no progress has so far been achieved.

Although different countries have bills creating independent agencies (e.g., Ecuador, Paraguay, Peru, Venezuela and Uruguay), the only countries in which this has partially succeeded are Brazil and Chile, where CADE and the Tribunal de Defensa de la Libre Competencia coexist with political authorities such as the SDE and SEAE in Brazil and the FNE in Chile. The idea of a completely independent agency, such as the one contemplated in the Argentine system, will very rarely prevail in the current Latin American context.

*(c) Merger control* Different countries are either re-analysing their respective merger control systems or debating whether to have one. In July 2005, the Uruguayan government submitted a draft Competition Law Bill to Congress which eliminates the chapter on merger control from a previously discussed bill. There were three reasons for the change: (a) the growing criticism to the 'structure–conduct–performance' paradigm; (b) the size of the Uruguayan economy and the fact that its merger control is still at an embryonic stage, and (c) the need to dedicate its limited resources to fighting anticompetitive behaviour. A similar criterion was adopted in Chile by not including merger control in its 2003 law reform.

On the other hand, the Peruvian 2005 draft Competition Law bill, a country with twice as many inhabitants as Uruguay, proposes the introduction of a mandatory merger control regime, while El Salvador, with almost half of Uruguay's population, introduced mandatory pre-merger control in its 2005 law.

The Argentine Government has sent a bill in 2005 to Congress to reform the Competition Law in order to keep certain decisions on 'national interest' merger cases within the sphere of influence of the Ministry of Economy. The current legislation states that all mergers should be analysed by an independent agency, but this agency has not yet been constituted.

Some countries with merger controls have come to realize the need to change their thresholds. Argentina did this in 2001 by eliminating the worldwide threshold as well as introducing a minimum local transaction value. The Brazilian authorities acted similarly in early 2005, by interpreting the Reais 400 millions as a local threshold and not as a worldwide one, as had been done hitherto. These changes have significantly reduced the workload of the antitrust agencies.

With regard to the preference for an ex ante or ex post control, different approaches have been taken as well. Although there are sufficient reasons to maintain that the Argentine merger control regime was conceived as a pre-merger system, the legal interpretation given by the regulation of the law has transformed it into an ex post control. In Brazil, meanwhile, the 1994 law has converted a post-merger control as interpreted by CADE into a pre-merger system, given that the 15-day period is to be counted from the first binding document and not the closing of the transaction. Furthermore the 2005 Brazilian competition bill wants to change the merger control regime into an ex ante system.

*(d) 'Judicialization' of competition enforcement*    A new trend known as the 'judicialization' of competition enforcement is emerging in Latin America, especially in Argentina and Brazil. There are a growing number of cases in which the Courts are not acting as a comptroller of the competition agencies, but instead are sometimes replacing them.

In Argentina, the delay by the Argentine Government in constituting the TNDC has been used as an argument for judges to intervene in merger cases in a first instance. Different federal judges, arguing that the CNDC lacks legitimacy because it should have been replaced by the TNDC, have started to act in two merger cases, one in the retail sector and the other on the cable television market. The CNDC has also been called into question because it lacks a sufficient quorum to act. For almost four years (early 2001 to early 2005) it has worked with an incomplete board arising from one to three vacancies out of a total of five commissioners.

Furthermore, in the AmBev-Quilmes merger transaction, two competitors have constantly battled the CNDC's January 2003 decision to approve the merger under certain conditions and, owing to these judicial interventions, the divestiture process has been suspended until the Supreme Court confirmed the government's resolution in February 2006. There have also been cases in which the competition law was interpreted by labour courts.

In Brazil, it is in the anticompetitive conduct cases that this trend is clearer. Franceschini maintains that the 'judicialization' of Competition Defense in Brazil is an empirical evolutionary process and 'the more attention is given to the Repression Regime, the more the adversely affected private parties will resort to the Courts to question the legality or the merits of CADE's opinion'. He foresees the judiciary taking over the exclusive role of enforcer of the Brazilian Competition Laws, leaving CADE a role as expert dedicated to assisting Judicial Enforcement.[37]

At the moment, private antitrust enforcement has not evolved in Latin America, and it is not likely to evolve significantly in the near future.

*(e) Governments drive new draft competition law bills* Although during the first half of the present decade competition law has not been a priority among many Latin American governments, in recent years the governments of Argentina (2005), Brazil (2005), Chile (2004), El Salvador (2005), Honduras (2005), Mexico (2005), Paraguay (2004), Peru (2005), Venezuela (2004) and Uruguay (2005) have sent to their respective Congresses draft competition law bills.

Some of these bills propose reforms to the existing laws (Argentina, Brazil, Chile, Mexico, Peru, Venezuela and Uruguay) while the rest would be their country's first competition laws (El Salvador, Honduras and Paraguay). The Congresses of Chile and El Salvador have already approved their respective bills while the remaining countries are still in the legislative process.

This new wave of competition laws shows that this instrument still has political and social acceptance in Latin America, although it is not yet a priority among some governments' policies.

*(f) New channels of communication* In the past five years, a growing number of new channels of communication have surged throughout the region on competition-related matters. The Inter-American Development Bank and the OECD have created the 'Latin American Competition Forum'. This forum is held once a year and gathers together the Latin American competition agencies to 'promote dialogue, consensus building and networking between competition policymakers and law enforcers, and the identification and dissemination of best practices in competition law and policy in a collegiate setting'. The Forum has met annually since 2003 and has implemented a 'peer review' system in which the experiences of a particular country are analysed by the rest of the region's agencies.

In 2002, the 'Iberoamerican Competition Forum' (*Foro Iberoamericano de la Competencia*) was launched in Spain. It also gathers together the Latin American Competition agencies annually and has created the Iberoamerican Competition School, to train the agencies' staff members.

Latin American competition professionals launched a discussion group, 'ForoCompetencia', in 2001, for the purposes of analysing different competition and regulation issues from an interdisciplinary perspective. It is also a network of lawyers and economists from the public, private and academic sectors of over 20 different countries in Latin America and Europe, who share their knowledge and experiences. The debates are held through an e-group and the members meet every two years in a debate-oriented Colloquium.

There has also been, in the past few years, a growing number of competition-related institutions in different countries such as Brazil, Peru and Colombia, as well as a stronger media coverage of antitrust issues, especially in Argentina and Brazil.

**Conclusions**
Latin American countries, despite their diversity, have historically followed a similar paradigm with regard to state intervention in the markets. The historic approach of a strong public presence in the market was temporarily replaced by one with a weaker state intervention. This new 'consensus' originated from the international financial organizations known as the Washington Consensus. Now, after the collapse of the Washington Consensus, Latin America is facing a period where there is no common paradigm to follow. However some trends can be perceived, such as a greater social awareness and stronger state intervention in the markets.

In March 2005, the former Uruguayan President Julio Sanguinetti noted that 'in Latin America we are still submerged in a sea of confusion'. Thus it is difficult to predict what the new paradigm on state intervention in Latin American markets will be, or even if there will ever be one, or more.

The current international and regional economic scenarios make it very difficult to return to the pre-Washington Consensus status. The future of competition policy in Latin America is closely linked to the development of the post-Washington Consensus scenario and, especially, to the way each country defines what the role of state intervention in the markets should be.

Although competition enforcement was not a post-Washington Consensus priority at the beginning of the decade, over the past few years many Latin American governments have proposed draft competition bills to their respective Congresses. However most of them have the legislative approval still pending.

This shows that there is some social and political acceptance of the benefits of competition laws in Latin America, but only up to the point where those laws have to be enforced. That is why, although an incipient fight against cartels can be observed in some countries, most of the competition activity in the region is focused on merger control cases. Owing to the lack of a strong competition culture within the region, a great deal of competition advocacy will be necessary for the agencies to obtain the necessary political support to enforce the law, since in Latin America most citizens ignore the benefits arising from the enforcement of competition laws. In this respect, the civil society should play an active role as well, through the universities, the NGOs and the media.

It might be added that, in order for competition enforcement to become a relevant instrument, the agencies should be energized with greater budgets and technical training for their professionals. Cooperation from international organizations is very useful and necessary, but not sufficient. The governments must allocate enough resources for the agencies to be able to investigate properly.

Since the Latin American countries have a cultural, economic and political scenario very different from the one developed countries face when enforcing their laws, there is a need for Latin American competition agencies to find appropriate solutions to their unique problems. The legal framework and jurisprudence of developed countries should only be taken as a reference from which to learn.

The post-Washington Consensus competition policies in Latin America may be characterized by a greater politically driven enforcement through the introduction of non-traditional concepts in antitrust analysis (such as 'national interest', 'strategic interest' or 'social' and 'labour' considerations) and a weakening of the institutional framework. As a result, there is now a more flexible enforcement in most Latin American countries. The use of these broad concepts should be restricted and defined as much as possible in order not to convert competition law enforcement into an unpredictable discretionary instrument. This is a pending issue and directly affects the credibility of the system. If the introduction of non-traditional antitrust concepts persists without specific and clear limits, it could convert these competition policies into a case-by-case system instead of being one based on predictable and reasonable rules.

The judiciary is clearly attaining a growing participation in competition enforcement in the region, not only by questioning the agencies' decisions, but sometimes by even replacing them as enforcers. Most certainly this seems to be a trend that will continue to develop in the future. However it is foreseeable that private antitrust enforcement will not develop significantly in Latin America.

A favourable trend in Latin American competition is the establishment of new channels of formal and informal communication among enforcers. These networks, as well as other international frameworks such as the International Competition Network, UNCTAD and the OECD, are helping to strengthen the links between the region's enforcers. However this is not the case when analysing the relationship of the competition agencies with the regulatory agencies. The lack of sufficient communication and the constant conflicts of power have left many key issues unsolved in the infrastructure sector. Much still has to be done in order to resolve this crucial aspect of competition policies.

In our opinion, the search for a new paradigm on state intervention in the markets will last for an uncertain period, and there is a growing groundswell of protectionism. Within this context, competition law enforcement will continue to develop in Latin America. Much work is still to be done and a strong political commitment needed, but the foundations established over the past decade form a solid basis on which to build. Stronger technical agencies and fewer discretionary powers are key factors for this to happen.

**Notes**

1. See Table 28.1, below.
2. See Williamson, John (2002), 'Did the Washington Consensus fail?', outline of remarks to the Center for Strategic & International Studies.
3. Ibid.
4. See Williamson, John (1999), 'What should the Bank think about the Washington Consensus?', paper prepared as a background to the World Bank's *World Development Report 2000*.
5. Soros, George (1998), *The Crisis of Global Capitalism*, New York: Public Affairs.
6. Williamson, John (1998), 'What Washington means by policy reform', in John Williamson (ed.), *Latin American Adjustment: How Much has Happened?*, Washington DC: Institute for International Economics.
7. Williamson, John (2002), 'Did the Washington Consensus fail?', outline of remarks to the Center for Strategic & International Studies.
8. Williamson, John (1999), 'What should the Bank think about the Washington Consensus', paper prepared as a background to the World Bank's *World Development Report 2000*.
9. Naím, Moisés (1999b), 'Does Latin America need competition policy to compete?' in Moisés Naím and Joseph Tulchin (eds), *Competition Policy, Deregulation, and Modernization in Latin America*, Boulder, Colorado: Lynne Rienner Publishers.
10. Berensztein, Sergio and Horacio Spector (2003), 'Business, government, and law' in Gerardo della Paolera and Alan Taylor (eds), *A New Economic History of Argentina*, Cambridge University Press, p. 341.
11. Naím, Moisés (1999), 'Does Latin America need competition policy to compete?', in Moisés Naím and Joseph Tulchin (eds), *Competition Policy, Deregulation, and Modernization in Latin America*, Boulder, Colorado: Lynne Rienner Publishers, p. 2.
12. Rowat, Malcolm (1995), 'Competition policy in Latin America: legal and institutional issues', Seminar on Good Government and Law, British Council, London, p. 4.
13. De León, Ignacio (2000), 'A market process analysis of Latin American competition policy', UNCTAD regional meeting on Competition Law and Policy. San José, Costa Rica, p. 10.
14. See Coutinho, Luciano (2004), 'Política de concorrência e desenvolvimento', *Valor Econômico*, 2 July; Naím, Moisés (1999b), 'Does Latin America need competition policy to compete?' in Moisés Naím and Joseph Tulchin (eds), *Competition Policy, Deregulation, and Modernization in Latin America*, Boulder, Colorado: Lynne Rienner Publishers; Tineo, Luis (1996), 'Políticas y leyes sobre competencia en América Latina. De regulaciones distributivas a regulaciones eficientes', OECD's EMEF Workshop on Competition Policy and Enforcement, Buenos Aires; Rowat (1995), above, note 12.
15. De León, Ignacio (2001), *Latin American Competition Law and Policy. A Policy in Search of Identity*, London: Kluwer Law International, p. 35.
16. Owen, Bruce (2003), 'Competition policy in Latin America', Stanford Law School John M. Olin Program in Law and Economics, Working Paper 268, 2.
17. De León (2001), above, note 15, p. 25.
18. See Table 28.2.
19. Owen (2003), above, note 16, 4.
20. Tineo (1996), above, note 14.

21. Cabanellas, Guillermo (2005), *Derecho antimonopólico y de defensa de la competencia*, Buenos Aires: Heliasta, p. 127; Coloma, Germán (2003), *Defensa de la competencia. Análisis económico comparado*, Buenos Aires: Ciudad Argentina-UCEMA, p. 27.
22. See Tavares de Araujo, José Jr. (1999), 'Schumpeterian competition and its policy implications: the Latin American case', OAS Trade Unit.
23. See Table 28.3.
24. See Franceschini, José Inácio (2005a), 'Conditions imposed by the CADE to the clearance of mergers: a mistaken paradigm', *Boletín Latinoamericano de Competencia, European Commission*, vol.19.
25. See La Primera (2005), 'Kuczynski: Que Indecopi investigue lo que quiera', Lima, Peru, 15 July.
26. Secretary of Industry and Trade Resolution N° 177/2004.
27. Ministry of Economy and Production Resolutions N° 485/2005 and 486/2005.
28. OECD and InterAmerican Development Bank (2004), *Competition law and policy in Peru. A Peer Review*, Paris.
29. See Clarín (2005a), 'Anuncio de multas y suspensión de exportaciones. Lavagna se reunió con Kirchner: buscan cómo contener precios', 19 July; Clarín (2005b), 'Pelea contra la inflación. Ofensiva de Lavagna. Aplicaron una multa récord a cementeras: $310 millones', 27 July 2005.
30. OECD and InterAmerican Development Bank (2003), *Competition law and policy in Chile. A peer review*, Paris.
31. Bullard González, Alfredo (2005), 'El Regreso del Jedi (O de la discresionalidad en la aplicación de las Normas de Libre Competencia)', Lima, Peru.
32. Ibid.
33. OECD and IADB (2004), above, note 28.
34. Secretary of Technical Coordination Resolution N° 196/2004.
35. Clarín (2003).
36. SEAE (Secretaria de Acompanhamento Econômico) (2002), Parecer Técnico N° 196. Rio de Janeiro, 7 October, at 38.
37. Franceschini, José Inácio (2005b), 'Private competition enforcement: is there room for CADE?', 1st Antitrust Spring Conference, IBA-IBRAC, Rio de Janeiro, 12–13 May.

# References

Berensztein, Sergio and Horacio Spector (2003), 'Business, government, and law', in Gerardo della Paolera and Alan Taylor (eds), *A New Economic History of Argentina*, Cambridge University Press.

Bielsa, Rafael (2004), 'El consumidor anarcocapitalista', *InfoBae*, 16 July.

Bradford, Colin Jr. (2004), 'Más allá del Consenso de Washington. Y ahora qué?', *CSIS Policy Papers on the Americas*, vol. XV. N° 4, Washington.

Bullard González, Alfredo (2005), 'El Regreso del Jedi (O de la discresionalidad en la aplicación de las Normas de Libre Competencia)', Lima, Peru.

Bustillo, Pablo (2003), 'Desarrollo económico: del Consenso al Post-Consenso de Washington y más allá' in *Estudios en homenaje al profesor Francisco Bustelo*, Madrid: Editorial Complutense.

Cabanellas, Guillermo (2005), *Derecho antimonopólico y de defensa de la competencia*, Buenos Aires: Heliasta.

Cardozo, Julio Sergio (2005), 'O avanço do sistema brasileiro de defesa da concurrência', *Valor Econômico*, 17 June.

Castañeda, Jorge (2005), 'Las dos izquierdas latinoamericanas', *La Nación*, 4 January.

Clarín (2003), 'Brasil rechaza el freno a la venta de Transener', 16 April.

Clarín (2005a), 'Anuncio de multas y suspensión de exportaciones. Lavagna se reunió con Kirchner: buscan cómo contener precios', 19 July.

Clarín (2005b), 'Pelea contra la inflación. Ofensiva de Lavagna. Aplicaron una multa récord a cementeras: $310 millones', 27 July.

Coloma, Germán (2003), *Defensa de la competencia. Análisis económico comparado*, Buenos Aires: Ciudad Argentina-UCEMA.

Coutinho, Luciano (2004), 'Política de concorrência e desenvolvimento', *Valor Econômico*, 2 July.

Coutinho, Ruy (2005), 'O CADE e o interesse nacional', *Valor Econômico*, 21 July.

De León, Ignacio (2000), 'A market process analysis of Latin American competition policy', UNCTAD regional meeting on Competition Law and Policy, San José, Costa Rica.

De León, Ignacio (2001), *Latin American Competition Law and Policy. A Policy in Search of Identity*, London: Kluwer Law International.

Espert, José Luis (2003), 'El Consenso de Buenos Aires', Buenos Aires, 7 November.

Fara, Carlos (2005), 'Volvió el Estado', *El Cronista*, 5 April.

Franceschini, José Inácio (2005a), 'Conditions imposed by the CADE to the clearance of mergers: a mistaken paradigm', *Boletín Latinoamericano de Competencia, European Commission*, vol. 19.

Franceschini, José Inácio (2005b), 'Private competition enforcement: is there room for CADE?', 1st Antitrust Spring Conference, IBA-IBRAC, Rio de Janeiro, 12–13 May.

Fuente, Carmen (2001), 'Competition policy in Latin America: implication for infrastructure services', Inter-American Development Bank, Washington.

Gacek, Stanley (2004), 'Brazil and Venezuela: Differing responses to the Washington Consensus', at www.venezuelaanalysis.com.

Gheventer, Alexander (2004), 'A dimensão política da regulação antitruste', *Boletín Latinoamericano de Competencia*, European Comisión, Brussels, vol. 18, p. 24.

Grondona, Mariano (2005), 'Hay en América Latina dos izquierdas', *La Nación*, 13 March.

Gundzik, Jephraim (2005), 'BA deposes Washington Consensus', *Buenos Aires Herald*, 3 August.

Hernández, René and Claudia Schratan (2002), 'Políticas de competencia y de regulación en el Istmo Centroamericano', CEPAL, Unidad de Desarrollo Industrial, Mexico.

InterAmerican Development Bank and OECD (2005a), 'Merger control laws and procedures in Latin America and the Caribbean'.

InterAmerican Development Bank and OECD (2005b), 'Fighting hard core cartels in Latin America and the Caribbean'.

Kuczynski, Pedro-Pablo and John Williamson (ed.) (2003), 'After the Washington Consensus. Restarting growth and reform in Latin America', Institute for International Economics, Washington.

La Primera (2005), 'Kuczynski: Que Indecopi investigue lo que quiera', Lima, Peru, 15 July.

Naím, Moisés (1999a), 'Fads and fashion in economic reforms: Washington Consensus or Washington confusion?', working draft of a paper prepared for the IMF Conference on Second Generation Reforms, Washington.

Naím, Moisés (1999b), 'Does Latin America need competition policy to compete?' in Moisés Naím and Joseph Tulchin (eds), *Competition Policy, Deregulation, and Modernization in Latin America*, Boulder, Colorado: Lynne Rienner Publishers.

OECD and InterAmerican Development Bank (2003), *Competition law and policy in Chile. A peer review*, Paris.

OECD and InterAmerican Development Bank (2004), *Competition law and policy in Peru. A peer review*, Paris.

Oliveira, Gesner and Joao Grandino Rodas (2004), *Direito e economia da concurrencia*, Rio de Janeiro: Renovar.

Oppenheimer, Andrés (2005), 'La ola izquierdista en América Latina', *La Nación*, 8 March.

Ortiz, Guillermo (2003), 'Latin America and the Washington Consensus. Overcoming reform fatigue', *Finance and Development*.

Owen, Bruce (2003), 'Competition policy in Latin America', Stanford Law School John M. Olin Program in Law and Economics, Working Paper 268.

Philip, George (1999), 'Washington Consensus politics in Latin American context: Some lessons from Mexico, Peru and Venezuela'.

Rowat, Malcolm (1995), 'Competition policy in Latin America: legal and institutional issues', Seminar on Good Government and Law, British Council, London.

Sabino, Paulo Ricardo (2005), 'Desafios da defesa da concorrência no Brasil', *Valor Econômico*, 12 July.

Sallum Jr., Brasilio and Eduardo Kugelmas (2003), 'Gobierno de Lula, continuidad, avance o retroceso?' in Alvarez, Chacho (Comp.) et al, *La Argentina de Kirchner y el Brasil de Lula*, Prometeo Libros, Buenos Aires.

Samor, Geraldo (2005), 'Trustbusters take aim in Brazil', *The Wall Street Journal*, 12 July 2005.

Sanguinetti, Julio María (2005), 'Derecha de la izquierda?', *La Nación*. 27 February 2005.

SEAE (Secretaria de Acompanhamento Econômico) (2002), Parecer Técnico N° 196. Rio de Janeiro, 7 October.

Soros, George (1998), *The Crisis of Global Capitalism*, New York: Public Affairs.

Tavares de Araujo, José Jr. (1999), 'Schumpeterian competition and its policy implications: the Latin American case', OAS Trade Unit.

Tineo, Luis (1996), 'Políticas y leyes sobre competencia en América Latina. De regulaciones distributivas a regulaciones eficientes', OECD's EMEF Workshop on Competition Policy and Enforcement, Buenos Aires.

UNCTAD–COMPAL Programme (2005), 'Strengthening institutions and capacities in the area of competition and consumer protection policies in Latin America. Cases of Bolivia, Costa Rica, El Salvador, Honduras, Guatemala, Nicaragua and Peru', Geneva.

Williamson, John (1998), 'What Washington means by policy reform', in John Williamson (ed.), *Latin American Adjustment: How Much has Happened?*, Institute for International Economics.

Williamson, John (1999), 'What should the bank think about the Washington Consensus', paper prepared as a background to the World Bank's *World Development Report 2000*.

Williamson, John (2002), 'Did the Washington Consensus fail?', outline of remarks to the Center for Strategic & International Studies.

# Index

*California Inc.* v. *California State Council of Carpenters* 522
*Associated Press* (1945) (United States) 407
*Astra/Zeneca* (1999) 120–21
*Astral/Télémédia* (2002) 117, 132
AT&T 697, 699, 700, 704, 709, 710, 711
*AT&T/MediaOne* (2000) 126–7
*Atlantic Richfield Co.* v. *USA Petroleum Co.* 522
Atomic Austria GmbH 124
attorney–client privilege 531
Attorneys General 159, 473
   Assistant 20, 74
   behavioural merger remedies 124, 125
   regime dynamics in merger control 74, 90, 93–5
Atwood, J.R. 655
Australia 508, 599, 644, 646
   Competition and Consumer Commission 628, 644, 663
Austria 60–61, 449, 451, 467
automobile industry 598
Avantel 709
aviation security 458
*Avis/Budget Rent–a–Car* (2002) 117

Babine Forest Products Ltd. 49
Bailey, D. 195–234
Baker, D. 472, 484
Baker, D.I. 398–412
*Baker Hughes* (United States) 179
Baker, J. 83, 585
Barrot, Vice–President 459–60
*Barry Wright* v. *ITT Grinnell* 215–16
BASF AG 472
Baxter, W. 568
Bearing Point 21
behavioural merger remedies 108–47
   appropriateness 128–30
   Canada: enforcement agency practice 114
   Canada: leading cases 114–18
   Canada: legal framework 113–14
   divestiture remedies, strengths and weaknesses of 111–13
   enforceability 130–31

Europe: enforcement agency practice 118–20
Europe: leading cases 120–24
Europe: legal framework 118
and non–merger cases 133–4
private benefits and costs 110–11
privatization of enforcement 131–3
privatization of monitoring 131
public interest in effective remedies 109–10
United States: enforcement agency practice 125–6
United States: leading cases 126–8
United States: legal framework 124–5
Belgium 449, 451
Belgrano Cargas 745
Bell System 700
Bertrand model 3, 6–9
Bertrand–Nash equilibrium 3
best-of-breed vendors 25
bilateral cooperation in multilateral setting 629–33
bilateral enforcement cooperation agreements 641–71, 676–8
basic structure of agreements 642–3
between United States and European Union 646
confidentiality clause 656–9
exchange of information – meetings between officials 651–3
first generation agreements, inability of to address important cases 659–61
negative comity (avoidance of conflicts) 647–50
Norway/Iceland/Denmark 662–3
notification, cooperation and coordination 650–51
positive comity 653, 654–6
reactive agreements 646
soft law 644–6
as strategy of strong states 643–4
as substitute/alternative to harmonization of competition laws 641–2
and trade flows 644
United States/Australia agreement on mutual antitrust enforcement assistance 661–2